AF575169

American Paintings

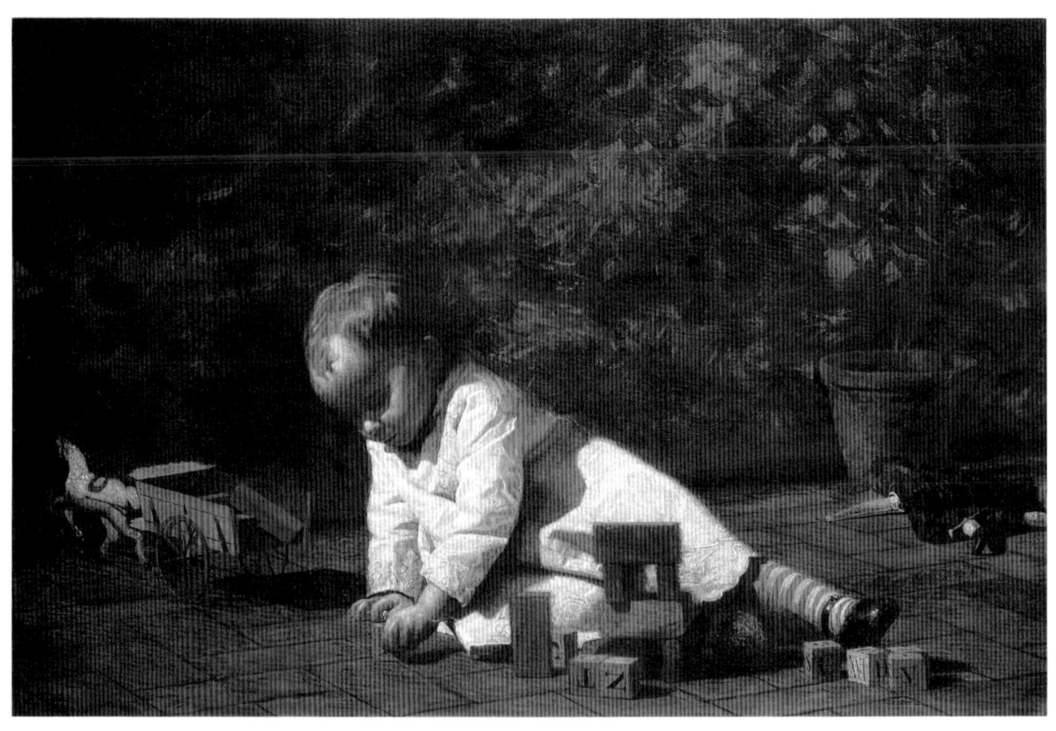

Thomas Eakins, *Baby at Play*, 1876

American Paintings

AN ILLUSTRATED CATALOGUE

National Gallery of Art
Washington 1992

Cover: Rembrandt Peale,
Rubens Peale with a Geranium, 1801

This publication was produced by the Editors Office, National Gallery of Art, Washington. Editor-in-chief, Frances Smyth

Designed by Three Communication Design, Chicago, Illinois

Printed by Meridian Printing, East Greenwich, Rhode Island

The type is Sabon set by Monotype Composition Company, Inc., Baltimore, Maryland

Library of Congress Cataloging-in-Publication Data

National Gallery of Art (U.S.)
American paintings : an illustrated catalogue.
p. cm.
"Third summary catalogue of American paintings in the National Gallery of Art . . . published . . . since 1970"—Pref.
Includes indexes.
ISBN 0-89468-171-0 (hardcover)
1. Painting, American—Catalogs. 2. Painting—Washington (D.C.)—Catalogs. 3. National Gallery of Art (U.S.)—Catalogs. I. Title.
ND205.N29 1992
759.13'074'753—dc20 91-46631 CIP

TABLE OF CONTENTS

FOREWORD

American paintings represent the National Gallery of Art's largest single group of works, numbering almost fourteen hundred. This concentration of American works has evolved steadily since the Gallery opened its doors fifty years ago. Recently our collecting effort in this area has gained momentum, so that more than one quarter of the works listed here were acquired in the last ten years.

Since the opening of the East Building in 1978 and the completion of renovations to the West Building in the early 1980s, more space for the display of American paintings is available now than ever before. Yet, such a large and diverse collection cannot be on view in its entirety in one location; many of the pictures not on view at the Gallery are on loan elsewhere. This summary catalogue thus plays an important role in making illustrations and data for each work easily accessible in one place. The majority of paintings in the Gallery's National Lending Service, which makes works available to institutions throughout America and to our embassies around the world, is American. In addition to the many individual works that have been lent, special touring exhibitions of paintings by Catlin have traveled extensively in this country and in South America, and a choice group of American naive paintings has been shown in Europe.

Among our American paintings, in addition to the many well-known works by familiar masters, several concentrations form collections within the collection. The American naive paintings given over a period of many years by Edgar William and Bernice Chrysler Garbisch, and the comprehensive series by George Catlin donated by Paul Mellon in 1965—each numbering more than three hundred works—were included in our previous summary catalogues. Published for the first time, however, are one hundred and ninety-six paintings by Mark Rothko, all but one given by the Mark Rothko Foundation in 1985 and 1986.

This catalogue also makes available the latest information derived from research for the four-volume systematic catalogue of American paintings now in preparation. A number of paintings that were listed as being by unknown painters in the previous edition of the summary catalogue have now been identified as the work of known painters, and many refinements in dates and titles also have been made. The works by Catlin have been given revised titles based on those used by the artist himself and, for the first time, the entire group has been arranged in three distinct series comprising North American Indian, South American Indian, and the La Salle themes.

Many people on the staff of the National Gallery, working under the direction of Suzannah Fabing, head of the division of research on collections, played important roles in the creation of this summary catalogue. In particular, special thanks are due to Nicolai Cikovsky, Jr., and Jack Cowart, respectively the heads of our American and

Barnett Newman, *Twelfth Station,* 1965

twentieth-century departments, and to their associates David Anfam, Nancy Anderson, Julie Aronson, Sarah Cash, Deborah Chotner, Catherine Craft, Franklin Kelly, Marla Prather, and Jeremy Strick, and former associate Nan Rosenthal. Mary Ellen Fraser organized and compiled the data for the catalogue, assisted by Michael Godfrey who gathered the photographs and did preliminary work, and Robin Dowden who generated information from the Gallery's computerized database. Trudi Olivetti of the library compiled the subject index. Finally, our editors office carried through the painstaking editorial and production process.

In an institution devoted to collecting and exhibiting great works of art from the whole Western tradition, it is appropriate that our nation's art receive thoughtful attention. It is hoped that this new illustrated summary catalogue will prove to be a useful resource for all those interested in our nation's rich artistic heritage.

J. Carter Brown
Director

PREFACE

This is the third summary catalogue of American paintings in the National Gallery of Art that has been published each decade since 1970. It represents nearly half a century of collecting. In that time, through the generosity of dozens of donors and by timely purchases, the number of American paintings has grown from less than a dozen in 1941, when the Gallery opened its doors, to the approximately 1,380 it contained at the end of 1989, on the eve of its fiftieth anniversary. None of the Gallery's other collections of national schools grew so rapidly in quantity or in quality. Today, the National Gallery's holdings of American paintings—supplemented by its holdings of prints, drawings, watercolors, photographs, sculpture, and the Index of American Design—is one of the most distinguished in the country.

This fully illustrated handbook is a guide to the National Gallery's American collections. It is also a valuable resource for the study of American painting from the eighteenth through the twentieth centuries. Scholarly study of the collection has kept pace with its growth, and this catalogue, as did its predecessors, incorporates the findings of continuing curatorial scholarship in changed or refined attributions, titles, and dates.

At no time during this period of tremendous growth did the number of American paintings increase so greatly as it did in the decade of the 1980s when more than 350 objects entered the collection. Much is owed in this respect, of course, to my predecessor John Wilmerding, curator of American art from 1977 to 1983 (when he became the Gallery's deputy director), and to E. A. Carmean, curator of twentieth-century art from 1974 to 1984, and to Jack Cowart, who currently heads the latter department. Especially through the discernment of John Wilmerding, some of the finest objects entered the collection—the exceptional Fitz Hugh Lane, *Lumber Schooners at Evening on Penobscot Bay*, for instance, acquired in 1980 from the Andrew W. Mellon Fund and as a gift of Mr. and Mrs. Francis Hatch, Sr., and Martin Johnson Heade's lovely *Cattleya Orchid and Three Brazilian Hummingbirds*, a 1982 gift of the Morris and Gwendolyn Cafritz Foundation.

In his foreword to the 1980 catalogue John Wilmerding summarized, decade by decade, the Gallery's notable acquisitions preceding that date. The succeeding decade has been so rich in significant acquisitions—close to three times the number of the preceding decade—that it alone deserves a similarly methodical, year by year description.

The decade began with the bequest of 65 American naive paintings, including works by Edward Hicks, Thomas Chambers, and Joseph Whiting Stock, from the collection of Colonel Edgar William and Bernice Chrysler Garbisch. Added to gifts made during the 1950s through the 1970s of 250 paintings, the Garbisch collection is one of the most important collections of naive paintings in this country, and is consistently one of the most popular with the Gallery's viewers. The systematic catalogue of the Garbisch paintings, to be published by the Gallery in 1992, will be a major resource for the future study of American naive art.

As it has been in the past, the American collections were enriched on several occasions in this decade by major gifts from Mr. and Mrs. Paul Mellon: First, in 1981, by Robert Salmon's *The Ship* Favorite *Maneuvering off Greenock*; again in 1983, by a splendid group of five paintings by George Bellows which, when added to another Mellon gift in 1986 and to earlier gifts from the John Hay Whitney and Chester Dale collections, makes the National Gallery preeminent in its holdings of the greatest American realist painter of the first quarter of the twentieth century; and in 1983 also by two Mary Cassatt oils, the delightful *Child in a Straw Hat* and exquisite *Little Girl in a Blue Armchair.* Once again, in 1985 by a varied group that included a beautiful and important Winslow Homer of the late 1870s, *Autumn*, two of Thomas Eakins' studies for his large watercolor *Negro Boy Dancing*, Lyonel Feininger's futurist *The Bicycle Race*, and, a painting equally modern in its terms, Maurice Prendergast's oil *Salem Cove*. And still again, in 1986, perhaps the most ambitious of Bellows' urban subjects, the large *New York* of 1911.

The John Hay Whitney Collection, presented to the National Gallery in 1982 by Mrs. Whitney, included four American paintings of utmost importance: Bellows' *Club Night*, the second of that artist's boxing pictures (the other given earlier by Chester Dale) to enter the collection; Eakins' charming yet profoundly moving *Baby at Play*; James A. M. Whistler's early masterpiece, *Wapping on Thames*, a key addition to the Gallery's superb group of Whistlers; and a major Edward Hopper, *Cape Cod Evening*.

Also in 1982 Mr. and Mrs. William Howard Adams presented the Gallery with our second historically important Andy Warhol painting, *Let Us Now Praise Famous Men (Rauschenberg Family)*, 1963. The Lila Acheson Wallace Fund continued its support of American contemporary art acquisitions by providing funds to purchase Frank Stella's *Jarama II* of 1982 and the next year, Roy Lichtenstein's *Cubist Still Life* of 1974. In 1982 the Collectors Committee donated Frank Stella's Concentric Square painting *Sacramental Mall Proposal #4*, 1978, and the following year, Jackson Pollock's enamel painting *Number 7*, 1951. Formed in the 1970s for a limited term to support commissions of public art for the new East Building from living artists, the Collectors Committee is now a permanent donor of important paintings and sculpture to the department of twentieth-century art. Through the committee's annual contributions the Gallery also acquired important abstract expressionist works by Sam Francis, *White Line*, 1958/1959, in 1985, and Richard Diebenkorn's *Berkeley No. 52*, 1955, in 1986.

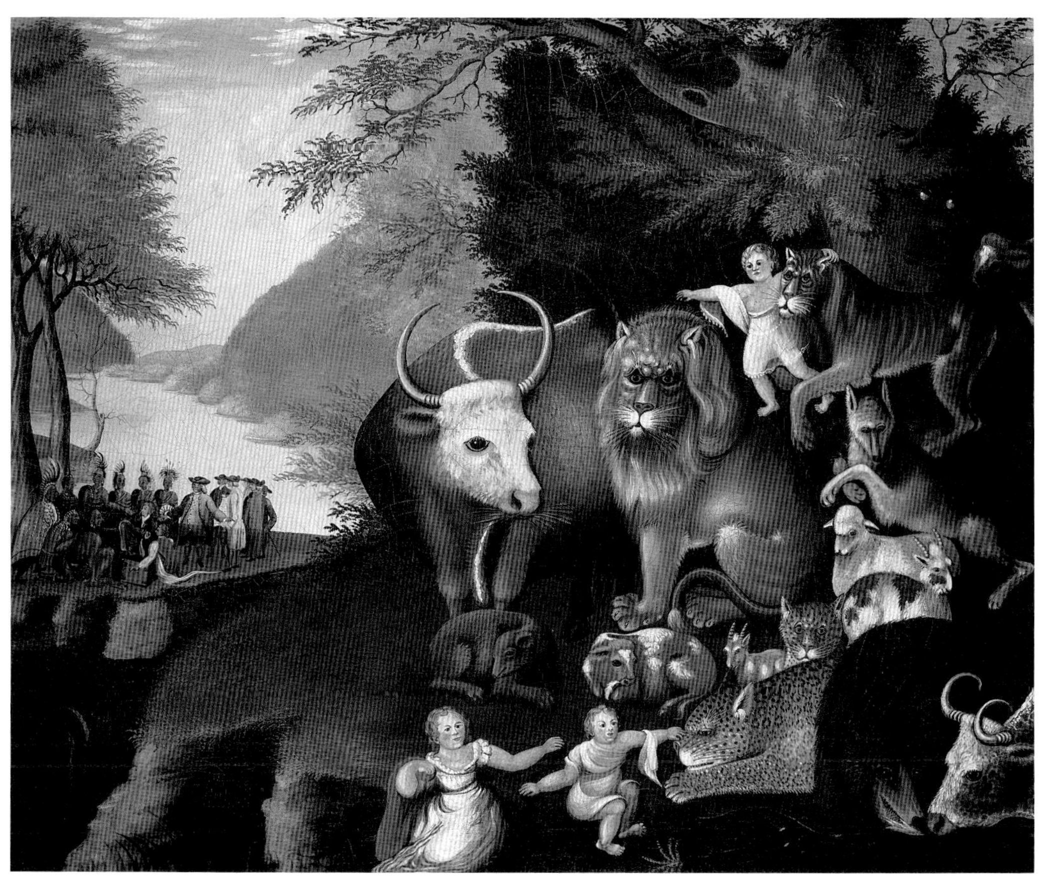

Edward Hicks, *Peaceable Kingdom*, c. 1834

In 1983 the portrait of *Martha Eliza Stevens Edgar Paschall* by an unknown artist, given by Mary Paschall Young Doty and Katharine Campbell Young Keck, became the first non-Garbisch naive painting to enter the collection.

Charles Willson Peale's early full-length portrait of his friend and patron *John Beale Bordley*, a gift of the Barra Foundation, Inc. in 1984, added an impressive example to the gallery's strong holdings of colonial portraiture. In this year, Mr. and Mrs. Joseph Helman presented us with our first painting by Ellsworth Kelly, *White Curve VIII* of 1976. The Lila Acheson Wallace Fund income permitted the Gallery to purchase our first Lee Krasner painting, the monumental *Cobalt Night*, 1962.

In 1985, Rembrandt Peale's tender and iconic portrait of his brother, *Rubens Peale with a Geranium*, was acquired as the first purchase of the new Patrons' Permanent Fund. Earlier the same year John Singleton Copley's *Mrs. Adam Babcock*, the gift of Mrs. Robert Low Bacon, added a particularly fine example to our important group of Copley's American portraits. The Gallery's first Robert Rauschenberg painting, *Doric Circus* of 1979, was acquired through the Lila Acheson Wallace Fund.

Three immensely important gifts of twentieth-century American paintings were made in 1986. Twelve oils by John Marin were given by his son, John Marin, Jr., as part of the John Marin Archive (which included also watercolors, letters, drawings, etchings, and sketchbooks). Our collection of paintings by the abstract expressionist artist Mark Rothko increased by 189 works from all phases of his career, given by the Mark Rothko Foundation (preceded in 1985 by the Foundation's gift of six panels of Rothko's Seagram Building murals). And the fifteen paintings comprising Barnett Newman's impressive Stations of the Cross/Lema Sabachthani series and *Be II* came to the Gallery as part of the Robert and Jane Meyerhoff Collection through the interest of the artist's widow, Mrs. Annalee Newman, who also subsequently donated five additional earlier Newman paintings.

In 1987 another John Marin oil, *Grey Sea*, also the gift of John Marin, Jr., came to the Gallery. That same year the Alfred Stieglitz collection of eight paintings by Georgia O'Keeffe, including her Jack-in-the-Pulpit series, was bequeathed by Miss O'Keeffe. In a more contemporary vein, the Lila Acheson Wallace Fund was used to purchase Chuck Close's large oil, *Fanny/Fingerpainting*, of 1985.

In 1988 the Circle of the National Gallery provided the essential funds to complete the purchase of Ad Reinhardt's *Untitled*, 1947.

Three earlier American paintings came to the Gallery in 1989. A large, newly discovered Biblical painting by Benjamin West, *The Expulsion of Adam and Eve from Paradise*, was purchased by the

Avalon Fund and Patrons' Permanent Fund. Thomas Cole's early *Sunrise in the Catskills* was a gift from Mrs. John D. Rockefeller III in honor of the fiftieth anniversary. William Stanley Haseltine's large Italian landscape, *Natural Arch at Capri*, was purchased by the Patrons' Permanent Fund.

Few collections are as deep or definitive as their curators would ideally like them to be, or as they realistically can be. But during the decade of the 1980s the distance between the ideal and the real, between hope and possibility, narrowed dramatically. Important refinements were made—the early Thomas Cole landscape, the late Benjamin West religious painting. Serious omissions were corrected—the first Fitz Hugh Lane entered the collection, the first Edward Hopper, the first Maurice Prendergast and John Marin oils, and numerous first paintings by other American twentieth-century artists. Existing areas of strength—colonial portraits, naive painting, Bellows, and Whistler—were strengthened further, and majestic new strengths—Marin, Rothko, Newman—were established. When compared to other important public collections of American painting the National Gallery's is still young and in many respects not yet fully formed. In the past decade, however, it has not only grown remarkably in size but has now attained the fullness and authority of maturity.

Nicolai Cikovsky, Jr.
Curator of American and British Paintings

DONORS TO THE AMERICAN COLLECTION

Gordon Abbott
Mrs. George Cotton Smith Adams
Mr. and Mrs. William Howard Adams
Avalon Foundation
Mrs. Robert Low Bacon
Edna L. Barbour
The Barra Foundation, Inc.
Katharine A. Batchelder
John W. Beatty, Jr.
Ferdinand Lammot Belin
Thomas Hart Benton
Constance Cushing Bessey
Horace Binney
Countess Mona Bismarck
Leslie Bokor
Marcella Louis Brenner
Ailsa Mellon Bruce
Charles Terry Butler
Mrs. Mellon Byers
The Morris and Gwendolyn Cafritz Foundation
Mary Endicott Carnegie
Elizabeth O. Carville
Marian Corbett Chamberlain
The Circle of the National Gallery of Art
Stephen C. Clark
The Collectors Committee
Department of Commerce, Maritime Commission
Mrs. Philip Connors
Thomas Jefferson Coolidge IV
Mrs. Edward Corbett
Mrs. W. Murray Crane
Chester Dale
Leslie Dame
Gene Davis
Mr. and Mrs. George W. Davison
Frederic A. Delano
Mrs. Gordon Dexter
Lamar Dodd
Alice Dodge
Mary Paschall Young Doty
Jean McGinley Draper
Mrs. Cooper R. Drewry
Mr. and Mrs. Ernest du Pont, Jr.
Mr. and Mrs. Robert Eichholz
Louise Thoron Endicott
Julia Feininger
Lorser Feitelson
David Edward and Margaret Eustis Finley
John George Fischer
Dr. and Mrs. Robert Fishman
Henry Prather Fletcher
William C. Freeman
Albert M. Friend, Jr.
Edgar William and Bernice Chrysler Garbisch
Edith Stuyvesant Gerry
Mr. and Mrs. Ira Glackens
Olga Roosevelt Graves
E. J. L. Hallstrom
Margaret I. Handy
W. Averell Harriman Foundation
Mrs. Leland Harrison
Jane Haslem Gallery
Mrs. Francis W. Hatch, Sr.
Olivia Stokes Hatch
Enid A. Haupt
Mr. and Mrs. Joseph Helman
John Hill
Mrs. Robert Homann
Katharine Husson Horstick
Ernest Iselin
Billy Morrow Jackson
Patrick T. Jackson
Oscar Doyle Johnson
Katharine Campbell Young Keck
Frances Frieseke Kilmer
Samuel H. Kress Foundation
Brenda Kuhn
Evelyn and Leonard Lauder
The Children of the Rt. Rev. William Lawrence
Sylvia Benson Lawson
H. H. Walker Lewis
Sam A. Lewisohn
Denise Lindner
Louise Alida Livingston
Eleanor Lothrop
Christina Macomb
Nannie R. Macomb
Mr. and Mrs. John Marin, Jr.
Marian B. Maurice
Florence S. McCormick
Ethelyn McKinney
Andrew W. Mellon
The Andrew W. Mellon Educational and Charitable Trust
Paul Mellon
W. L. and May T. Mellon Foundation
Vincent Melzac
Robert and Jane Meyerhoff
Adolph Caspar Miller
Beatrice Monk
Robert Motherwell
Henry A. and Caroline C. Murray
Annalee Newman
Mrs. Robert B. Noyes
Georgia O'Keeffe
Mrs. Seymour Obermer

Violet Organ
Patrons' Permanent Fund
Duncan Phillips
Admiral Neill Phillips
Eugene S. Pleasonton
Helen Haseltine Plowden
Herbert L. Pratt
Curt H. Reisinger
Edith Reynolds
Mr. and Mrs. John Ridgely
Mrs. John D. Rockefeller III
Mrs. Huttleston Rogers
James N. Rosenberg
Lessing J. Rosenwald
The Mark Rothko Foundation
John H. Safer
Morris Schapiro
Mrs. William C. Seitz
Donald D. Shepard
Helen Farr Sloan
Mr. and Mrs. Gerard C. Smith
Robert H. Smith
Julia Marlowe Sothern
Mrs. McFadden Staempfli
James C. Stotlar
Michael Straight
Mrs. Irwin Strasburger
Frederick Sturges, Jr.
Mrs. Augustus Vincent Tack
Horton and Chiyo Telford
Alexander Dallas Thayer
The Honorable and Mrs. Robert H. Thayer
Mrs. Sigourney Thayer
Clarence Van Dyke Tiers
Mrs. Walter Timme
Mr. and Mrs. Burton Tremaine
Allen Tucker Memorial
James Twitty
Gertrude Mauran Vail
Lady Vereker
Maude Monell Vetlesen
Lila Acheson Wallace
Eleanor Ward
Martha E. Warner
Mrs. Sumner Welles
Dr. and Mrs. Robert Wetmore
Mrs. E. Laurence White
Cornelius Vanderbilt Whitney
Trustees of the John Hay Whitney Charitable Trust
The William C. Whitney Foundation
J. H. Whittemore Company
Thomas Whittemore
Joseph E. Widener
Howard Wise
Collection of the Zorach Children

NOTES TO THE READER

Entries are arranged alphabetically by artist, using surnames unless the artist is better known by a sobriquet. Works by the same artist are arranged chronologically by date of execution; works of the same date are arranged alphabetically by title; works of the same date and title are arranged by National Gallery accession numbers. Pendants are grouped together, listing the male first.

Specialized organizations were necessary for sections of the collection. The Thomas Cole paintings in the Voyage of Life series are listed by subject matter. Other sections include the works by Catlin, Newman, and unknown painters. Explanations, which follow, are also listed at the beginning of the sections for these artists:

Catlin's works are listed as follows under three subheadings: "North American Subjects" and "South American Subjects," alphabetically by title; "La Salle Series," in the sequential order in which they were published by the artist. Titles for Catlin's works have been revised to reflect those used by the artist in the 1871 catalogue, *Catalogue Descriptive and Instructive of Catlin's Indian Cartoons.*

Newman's paintings in the Stations of the Cross series are listed in numerical order under the subheading "Stations of the Cross (Lema Sabachthani)."

Works by unknown artists are arranged alphabetically by title at the end of this catalogue under the heading "Anonymous American." Entries of the same title are listed by accession number.

Titles in parentheses have been assigned by the National Gallery. Dimensions are given height before width, in meters followed by inches in parentheses. Paintings are in oil unless otherwise specified. The term "canvas" is used for fabric supports in the absence of fiber analysis.

Inscriptions, unless noted, are from the face of the work. Illegible or missing words or letters are indicated by an ellipsis in brackets, [. . .]; unclear words or letters are placed in brackets. A slash, /, signifies the end of a line.

Dates assigned follow this system:

1775: painted in 1775

1775–1780: begun in 1775, finished in 1780

1775/1780: painted between 1775 and 1780 inclusive

probably 1775: 1775 is likely, but not certain

c. 1775: painted about 1775

c. 1775/1780: painted between approximately 1775 and 1780

active 1775/1780: although life dates are not known, primary sources show the artist working between approximately 1775 and 1780

Attribution Terms

Artist: a named artist

Attributed to: indicates probably by the artist

(?): following an artist's name indicates less conviction than "attributed to"; following a title indicates uncertainty regarding the painting's name

Studio of: produced in the artist's studio

After: a copy of any date

This catalogue reflects the National Gallery's holdings at the end of November 1989.

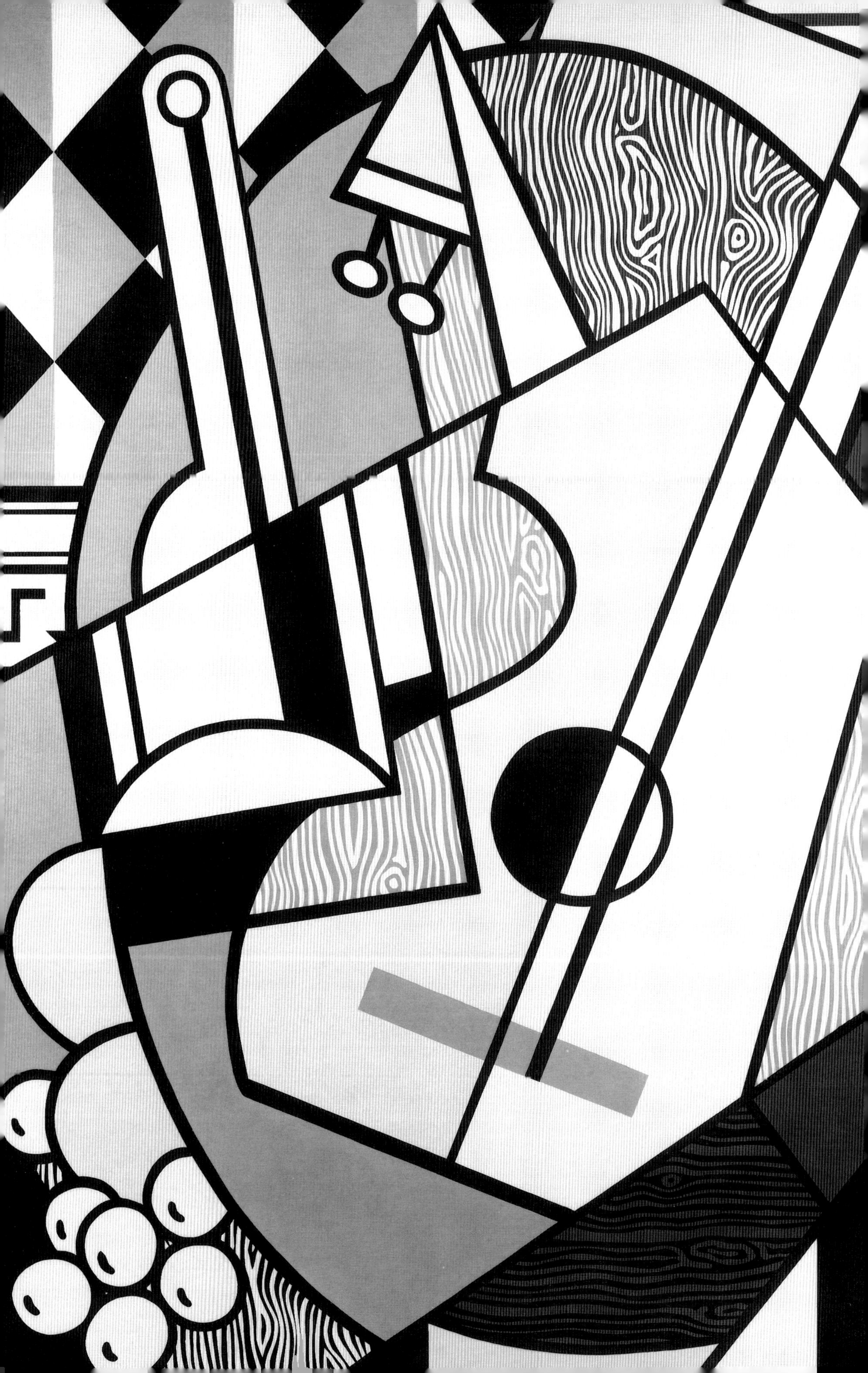

PAINTINGS

Detail: Roy Lichtenstein, *Cubist Still Life*, 1974

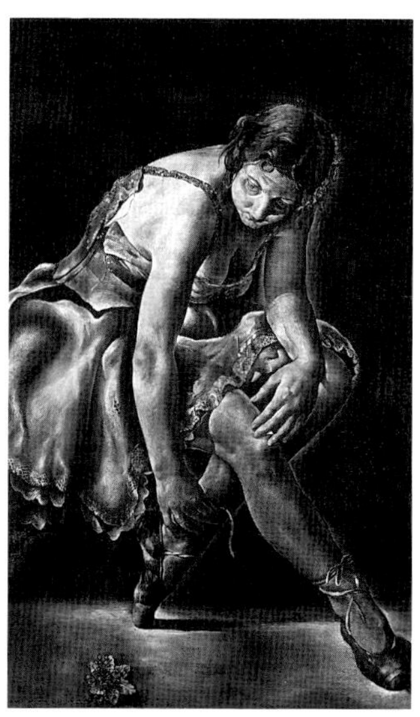

IVAN LE LORRAINE ALBRIGHT
1897–1983

There Were No Flowers Tonight, 1929
Canvas, 1.232 x 0.772 (48½ x 30⅜)
Inscribed at lower left: *IVAN LE LORRAINE ALBRIGHT*
Gift of Robert H. and Clarice Smith
1972.7.1

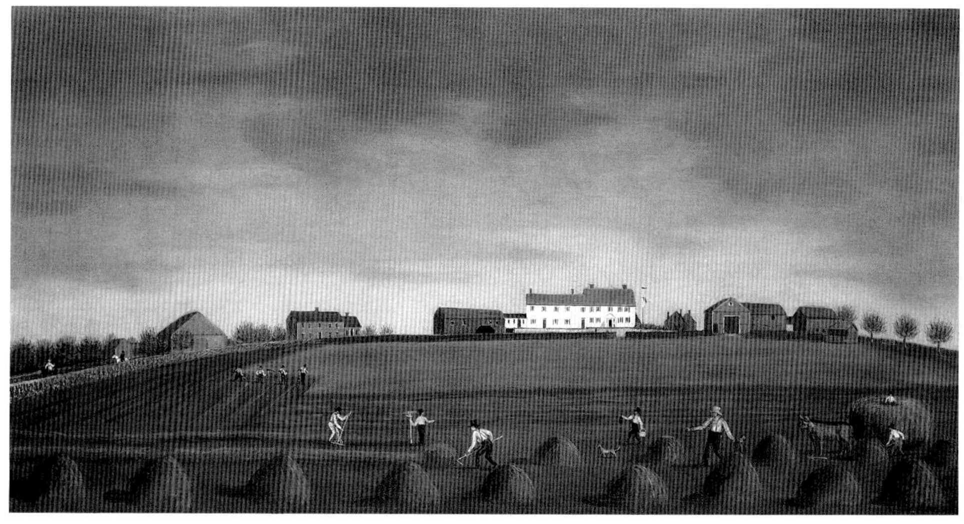

FRANCIS ALEXANDER
1800–1880

Ralph Wheelock's Farm, c. 1822
Canvas, 0.641 x 1.222 (25¼ x 48⅛)
Gift of Edgar William and Bernice Chrysler Garbisch
1965.15.3

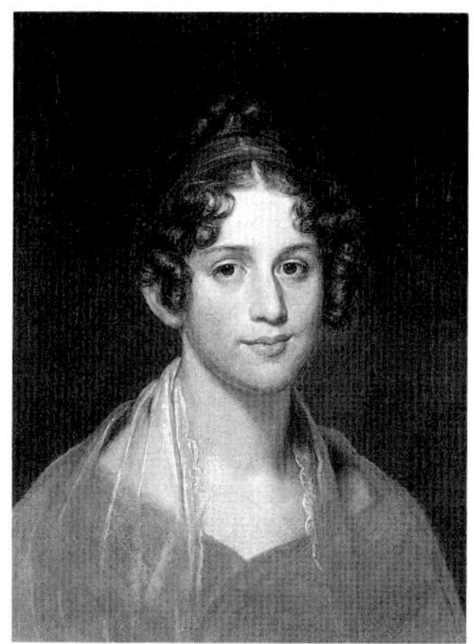

Sarah Blake Sturgis (?), c. 1830
Canvas, 0.613 x 0.460 (24⅛ x 18⅛)
Andrew W. Mellon Collection
1947.17.18

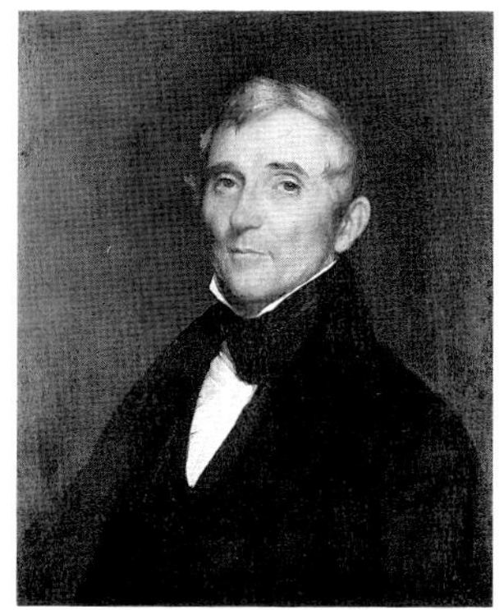

Aaron Baldwin, c. 1835
Wood, 0.645 x 0.545 (25 3/8 x 21 3/8)
Gift of Constance Cushing Bessey
1945.11.1

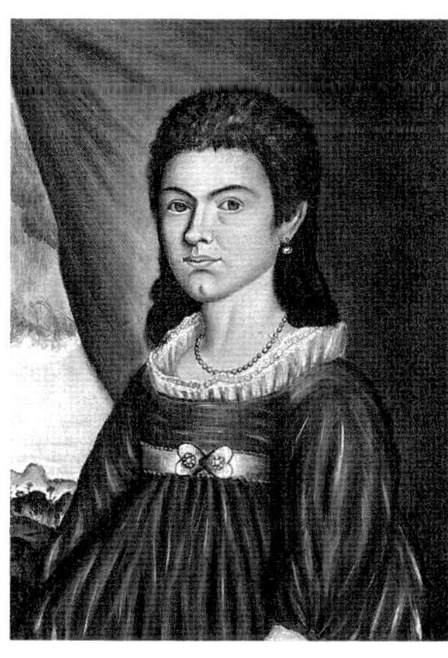

LUTHER ALLEN
1780–1821

Lucia Leonard, 1801
Canvas, 0.610 x 0.457 (24 x 18)
Inscribed at lower right: *L. Allen, Pi/1801*
Gift of Edgar William and Bernice Chrysler Garbisch
1953.5.1

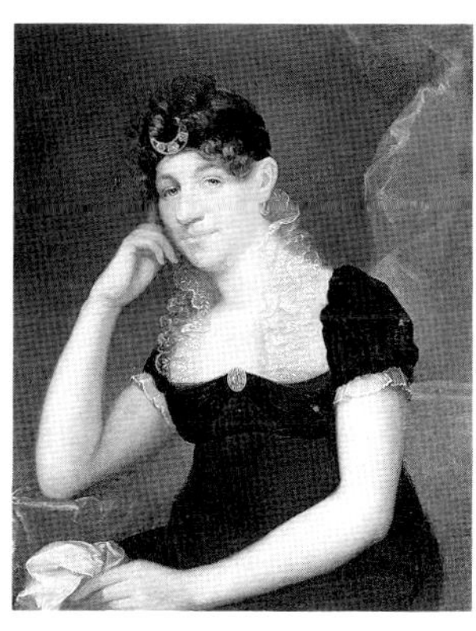

EZRA AMES
1768–1836

Maria Gansevoort Melville, c. 1815
Wood, 0.762 x 0.597 (30 x 23 1/2)
Andrew W. Mellon Collection
1947.17.20

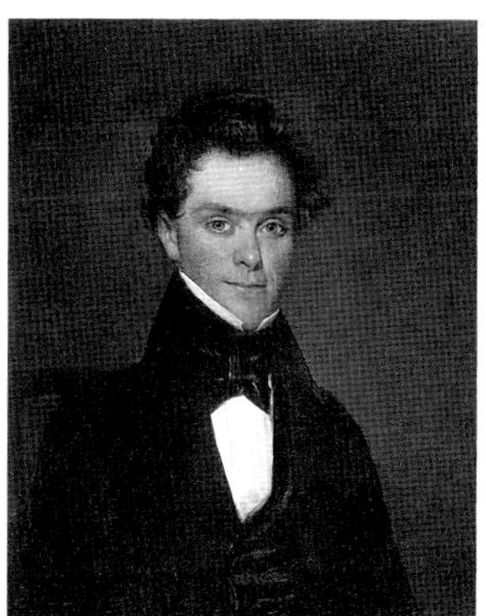

JOSEPH ALEXANDER AMES
1816–1872

George Southward, c. 1835
Wood, 0.762 x 0.619 (30 x 24 3/8)
Andrew W. Mellon Collection
1947.17.21

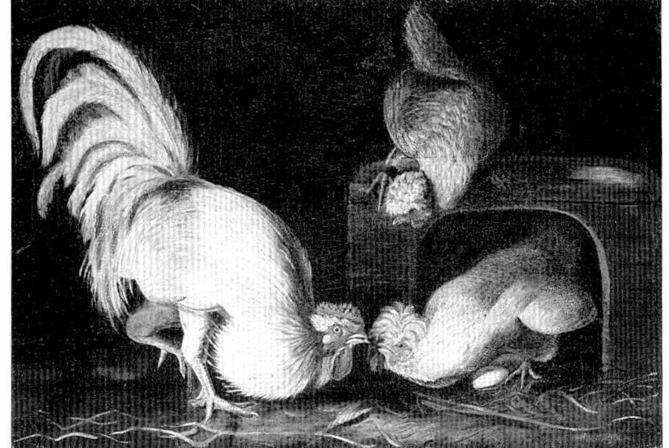

JOHN JAMES AUDUBON
1785–1851

Farmyard Fowls, c. 1827
Canvas, 0.721 x 1.042 (28⅜ x 41)
Inscribed at lower right: *Audubon*
Gift of E.J.L. Hallstrom
1951.9.3

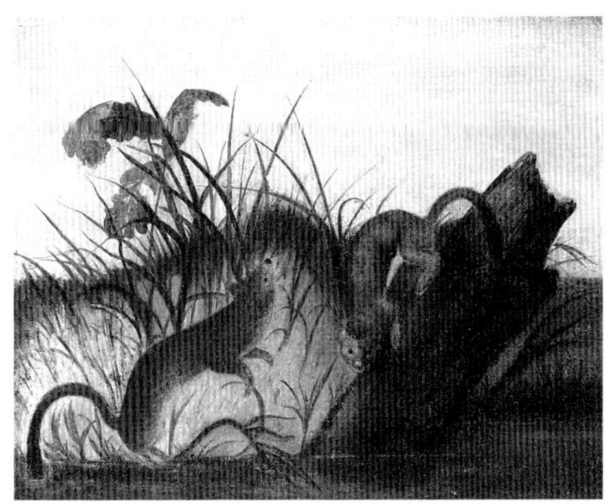

STUDIO OF
JOHN JAMES AUDUBON

Long-tailed Weasel, 1840/1845
Canvas, 0.515 x 0.617 (20¼ x 24¼)
Gift of E.J.L. Hallstrom
1951.9.4

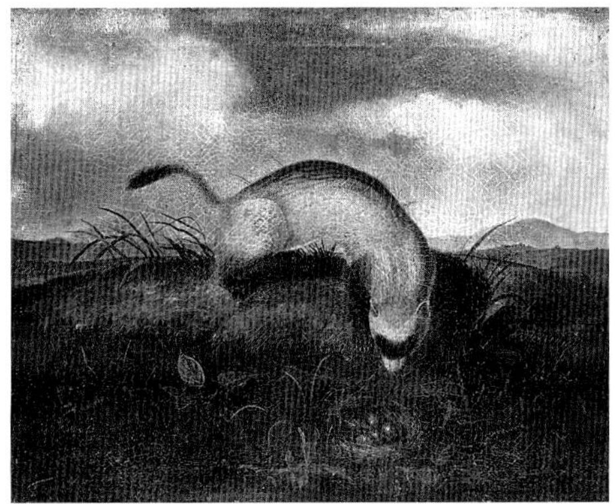

JOHN WOODHOUSE AUDUBON
1812–1862

Black-footed Ferret, 1840/1846
Canvas, 0.559 x 0.689 (22 x 27⅛)
Gift of E.J.L. Hallstrom
1951.9.1

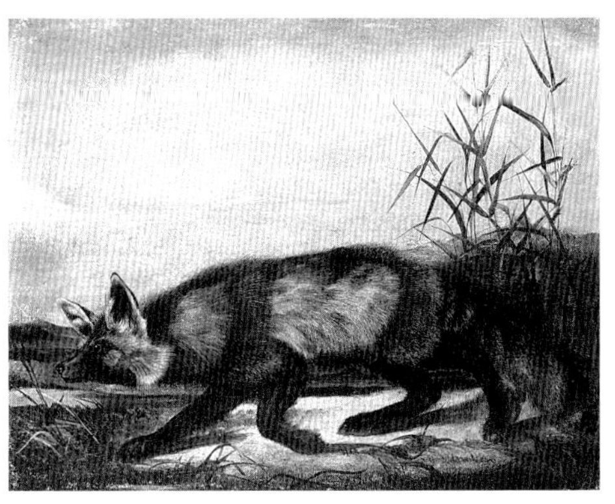

Long-tailed Red Fox, 1848/1854
Canvas, 0.562 x 0.693 (22⅛ x 27¼)
Gift of E.J.L. Hallstrom
1951.9.9

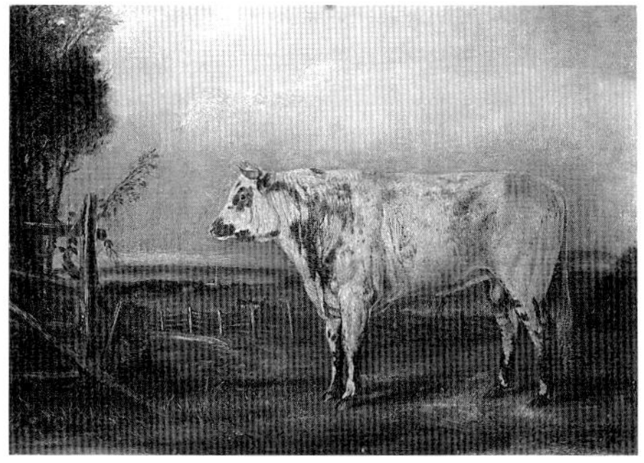

ATTRIBUTED TO
JOHN WOODHOUSE AUDUBON
1812–1862

A Young Bull, c. 1845
Canvas, 0.358 x 0.508 (14⅛ x 20)
Gift of E.J.L. Hallstrom
1951.9.2

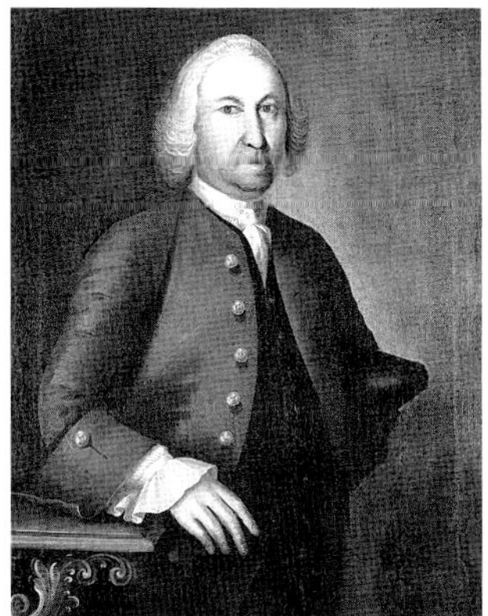

JOSEPH BADGER
1708–1765

Captain Isaac Foster, 1755
Bed ticking, 0.914 x 0.711 (36 x 28)
Inscribed at lower right: *1755*
Gift of Edgar William and Bernice Chrysler Garbisch
1957.11.1

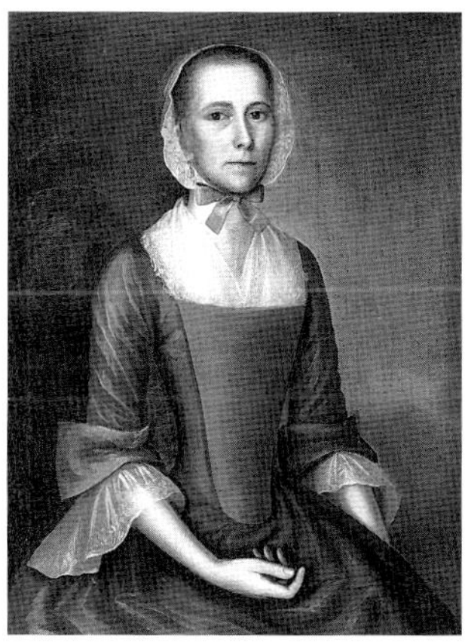

Mrs. Isaac Foster, 1755
Bed ticking, 0.920 x 0.707 (36¼ x 27⅞)
Inscribed at lower right: *1755*
Gift of Edgar William and Bernice Chrysler Garbisch
1957.11.2

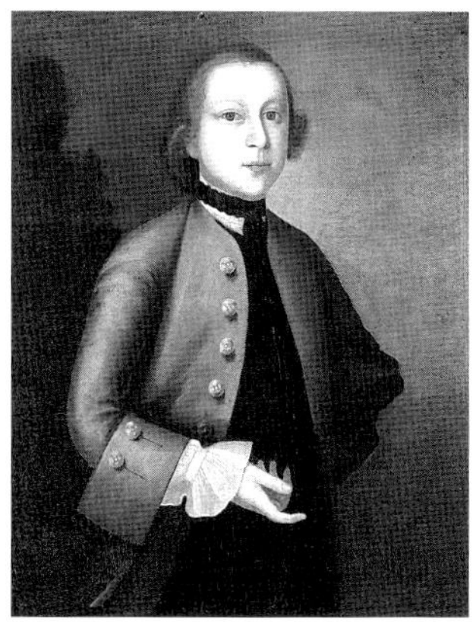

Isaac Foster, Jr., 1755
Canvas, 0.813 x 0.661 (32 x 26)
Inscribed at lower right: *1755*
Gift of Edgar William and Bernice Chrysler Garbisch
1957.11.3

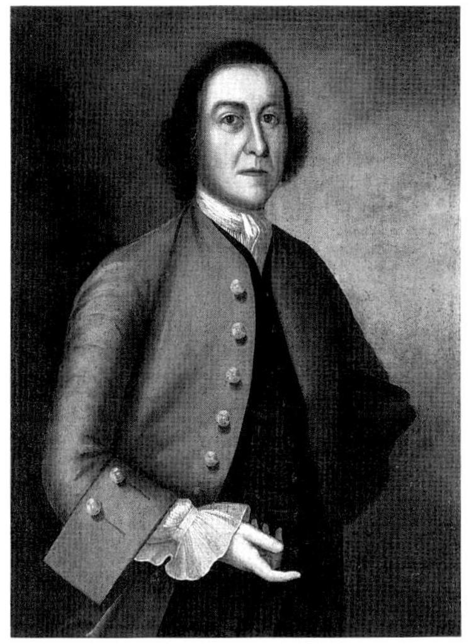

Dr. William Foster, 1755
Canvas, 0.914 x 0.714 (36 x 28 1/8)
Inscribed at lower right: *1755*
Gift of Edgar William and Bernice Chrysler Garbisch
1957.11.4

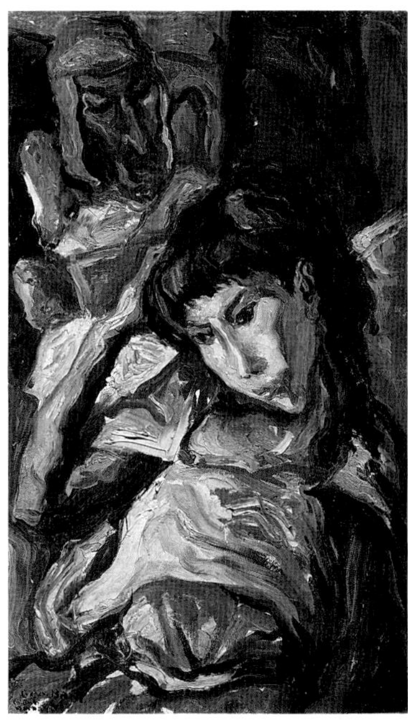

GEORGE BAER
1893–1971

Masouba, 1927
Canvas, 0.552 x 0.331 (21 3/4 x 13)
Inscribed at lower left: *Geo. Baer / Colomb / Bechar 27*
Chester Dale Collection
1964.19.1

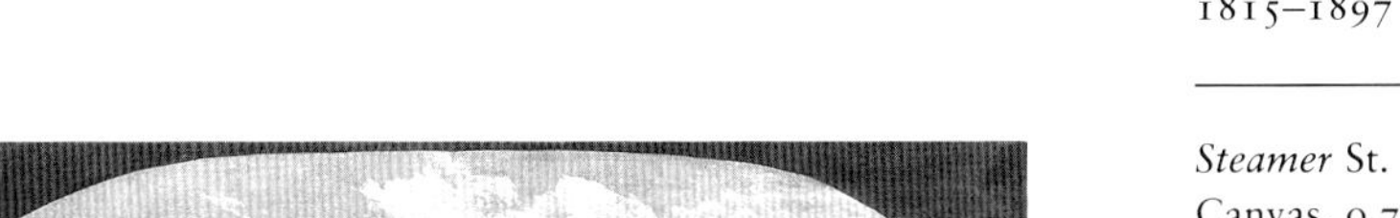

JAMES BARD
1815–1897

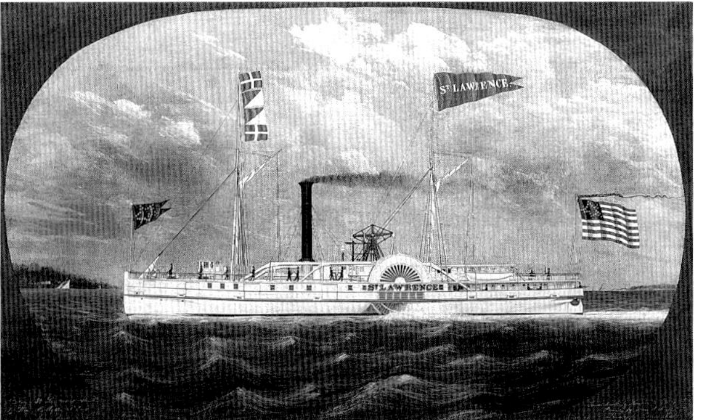

Steamer St. Lawrence, 1850
Canvas, 0.733 x 1.219 (28 7/8 x 48)
Inscribed at lower left: *Steamer St. Lawrence Built / by Wm. Collyer NY. [. . .] / Engine Built by the [Morgan Iro]n Works NY*; at lower right: *Joiner Work by Sampson & Perry. [. . .] / Painting by John A. Bowell NY / Painting [an]d Drawing by James Bard, N.Y. / Decr th 18th, 1850*
Gift of Edgar William and Bernice Chrysler Garbisch
1953.5.2

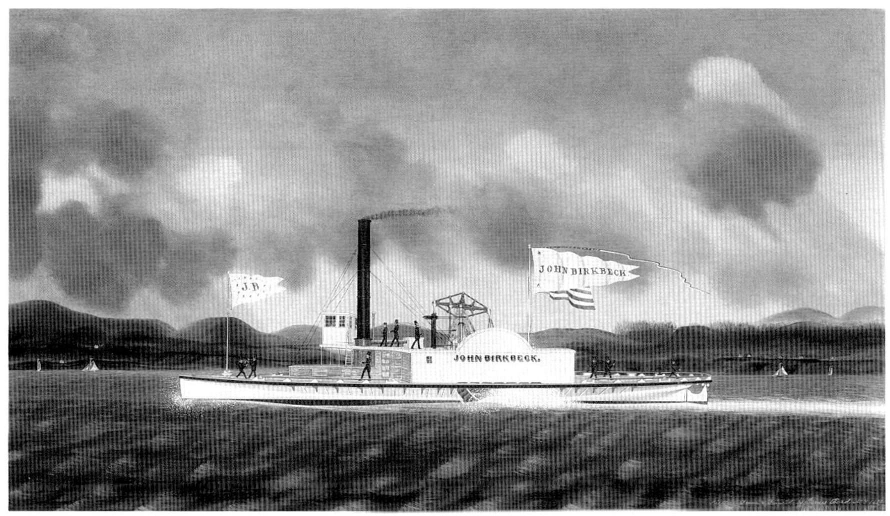

Towboat John Birkbeck, 1854
Canvas, 0.758 x 1.330 (29⅞ x 52⅜)
Inscribed at lower right: *Picture Drawn & Painted by James Bard N.Y. 1854 / 162 Perry Street*
Gift of Edgar William and Bernice Chrysler Garbisch
1971.83.1

LEILA T. BAUMAN
active 1850 or later

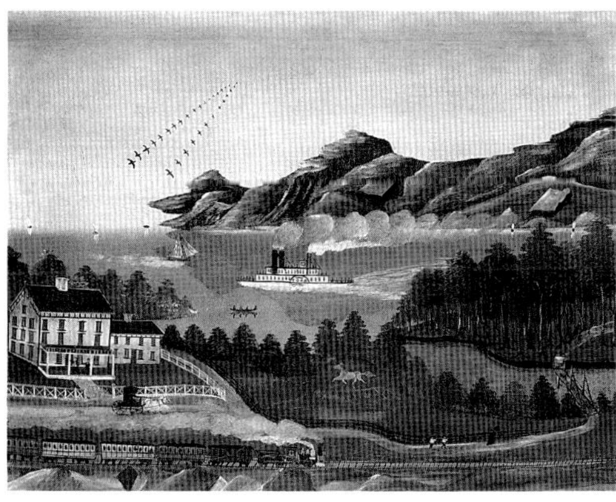

Geese in Flight, 1850 or later
Canvas, 0.516 x 0.668 (20⅜ x 26¼)
Gift of Edgar William and Bernice Chrysler Garbisch
1958.9.1

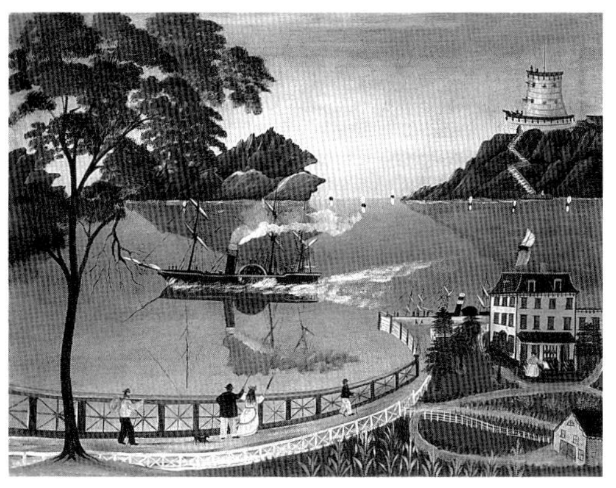

U.S. Mail Boat, 1855 or later
Canvas, 0.514 x 0.673 (20¼ x 26½)
Gift of Edgar William and Bernice Chrysler Garbisch
1958.9.2

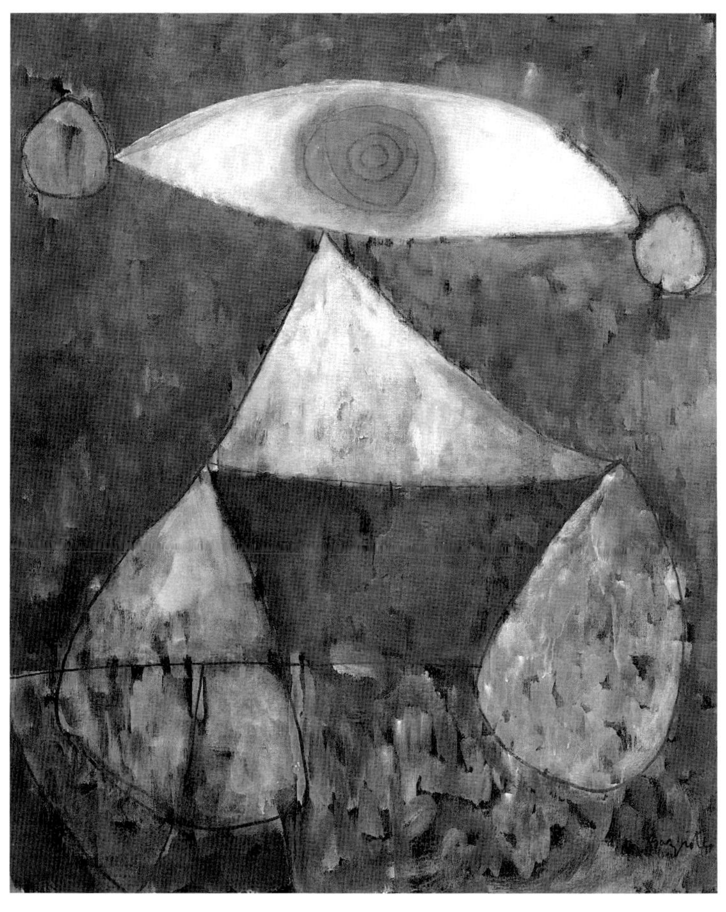

WILLIAM BAZIOTES
1912–1963

Pierrot, 1947
Canvas, 1.070 x 0.915 x 0.015
(42⅛ x 36 x ⅝)
Inscribed at lower right: *Baziotes*; upper left on reverse: *"PIERROT" / W. BAZIOTES / 1947*
Ailsa Mellon Bruce Fund
1984.43.1

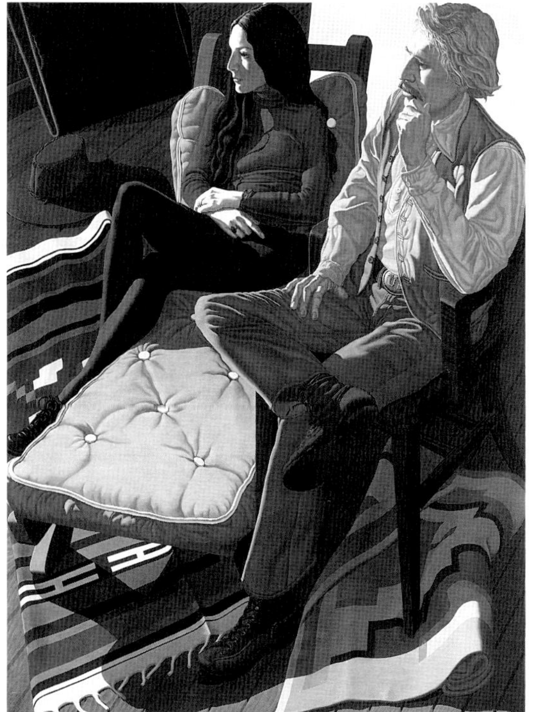

JACK BEAL
born 1931

Portrait of the Doyles, 1970
Canvas, 1.937 x 1.476 (76¼ x 58⅛)
Inscribed at lower right: *Jack Beal*
Gift of Evelyn and Leonard Lauder
1984.86.1

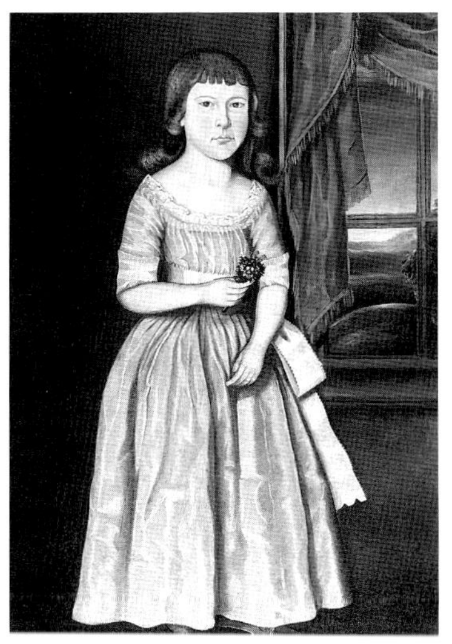

THE BEARDSLEY LIMNER
active 1785/1805

Girl in a Pink Dress, c. 1790
Canvas, 1.018 x 0.721 (40⅛ x 28⅜)
Gift of Edgar William and Bernice Chrysler Garbisch
1953.5.24

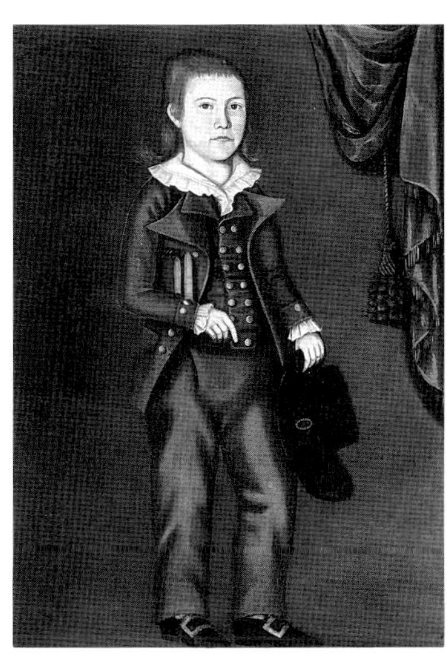

Charles Adams Wheeler, c. 1790
Canvas, 1.074 x 0.771 (42¼ x 30¼)
Gift of Edgar William and Bernice Chrysler Garbisch
1953.5.57

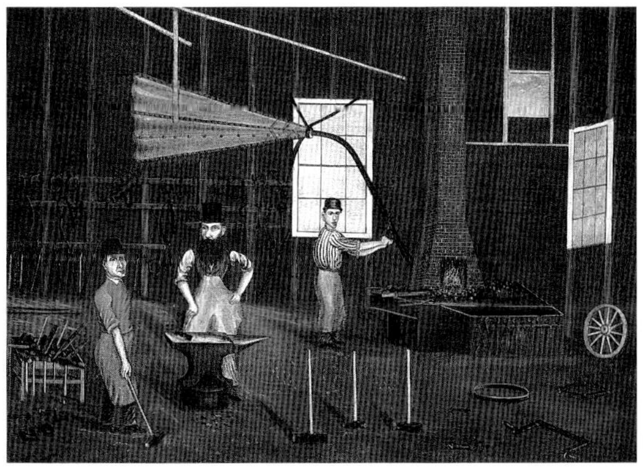

FRANCIS A. BECKETT
c. 1833–living 1884

Blacksmith Shop, c. 1880
Canvas, 0.590 x 0.816 (23¼ x 32⅛)
Inscribed at center left: *F. A Beckett*
Gift of Edgar William and Bernice Chrysler Garbisch
1966.13.4

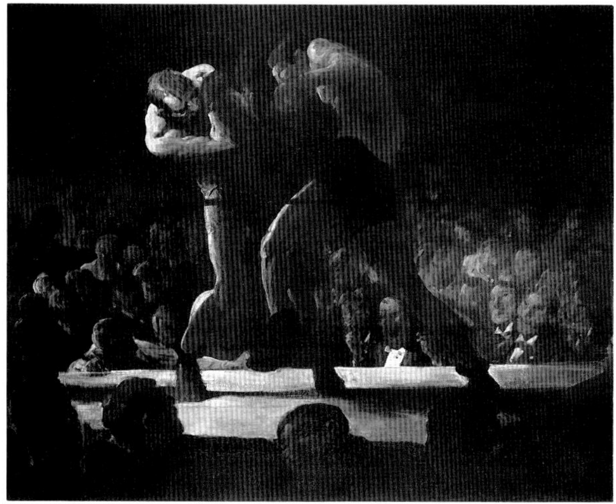

GEORGE BELLOWS
1882–1925

Club Night, 1907
Canvas, 1.092 x 1.350 (43 x 53 1/8)
John Hay Whitney Collection
1982.76.1

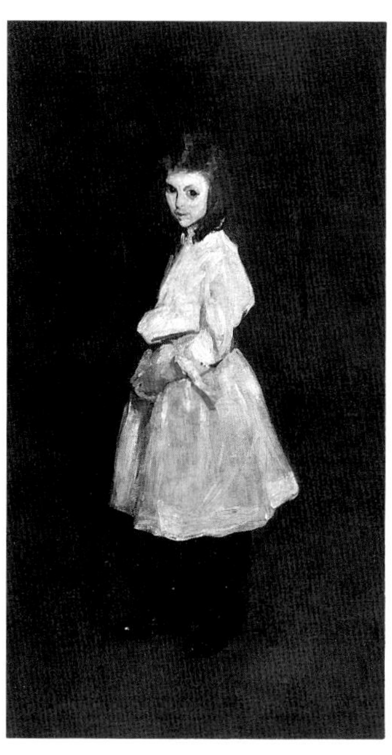

Little Girl in White (Queenie Burnett), 1907
Canvas, 1.580 x 0.870 (62 1/4 x 34 1/4)
Collection of Mr. and Mrs. Paul Mellon
1983.1.2

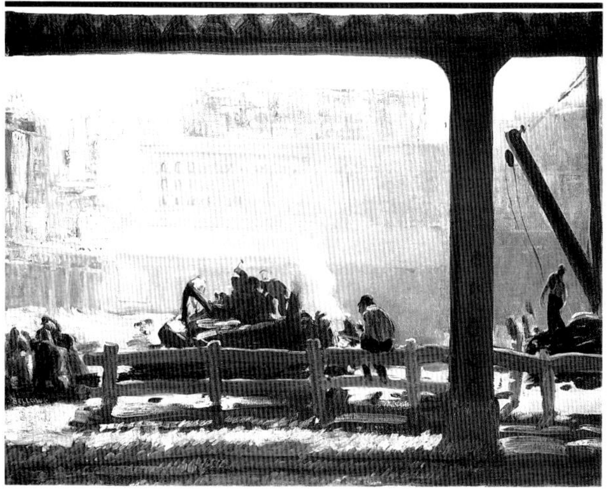

Blue Morning, 1909
Canvas, 0.863 x 1.117 (34 x 44)
Inscribed at lower left: *BELLOWS*
Chester Dale Collection
1963.10.82

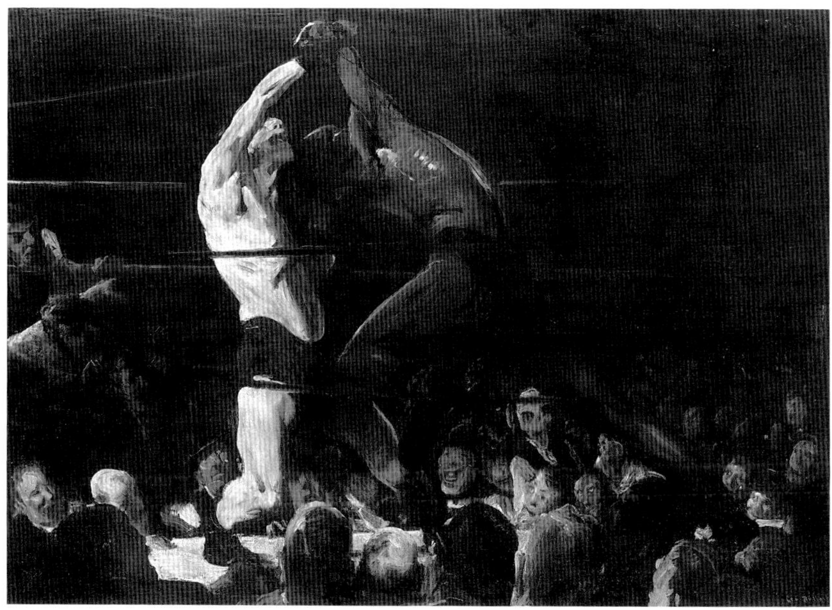

Both Members of This Club, 1909
Canvas, 1.150 x 1.605 (45¼ x 63⅛)
Inscribed at lower right: *Geo Bellows*
Chester Dale Collection
1944.13.1

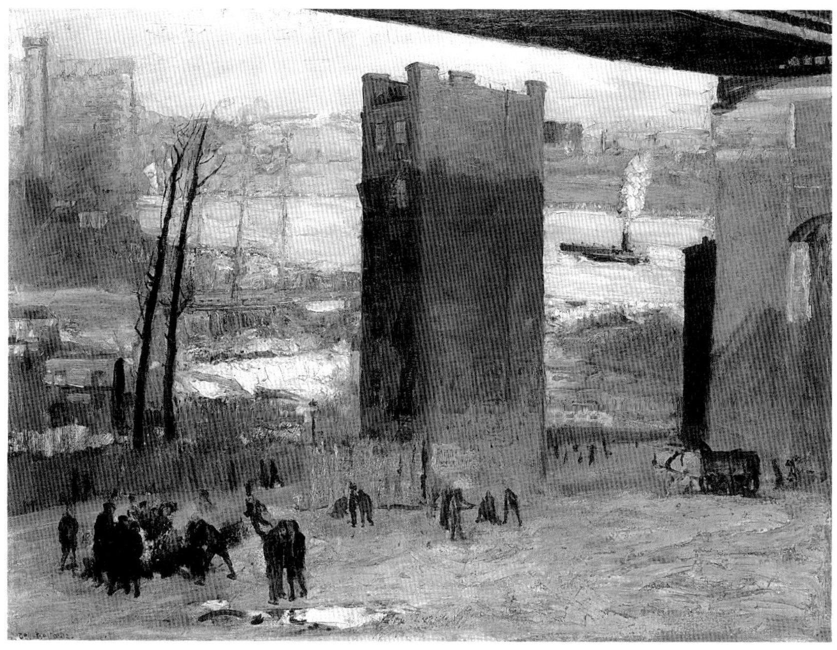

The Lone Tenement, 1909
Canvas, 0.918 x 1.223 (36⅛ x 48⅛)
Inscribed at lower left: *Geo Bellows*
Chester Dale Collection
1963.10.83

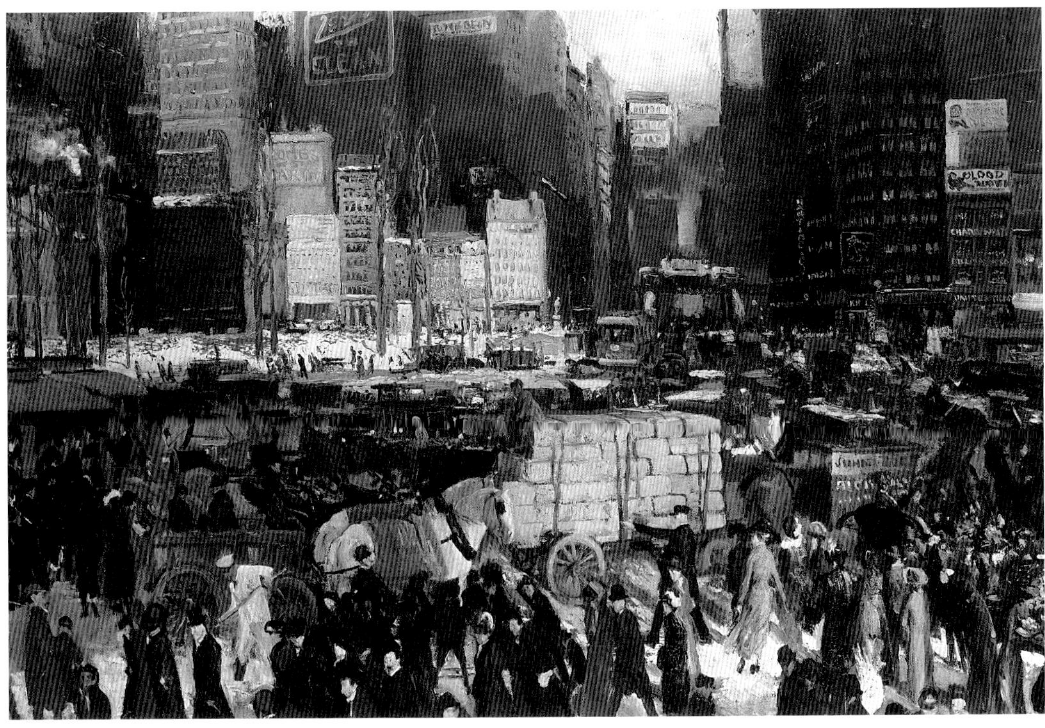

New York, 1911
Canvas, 1.067 x 1.524 (42 x 60)
Inscribed across bottom: *Geo Bellows*;
upper left on reverse: *GEO BELLOWS / 146 E 19 / N.Y.*
Collection of Mr. and Mrs. Paul Mellon
1986.72.1

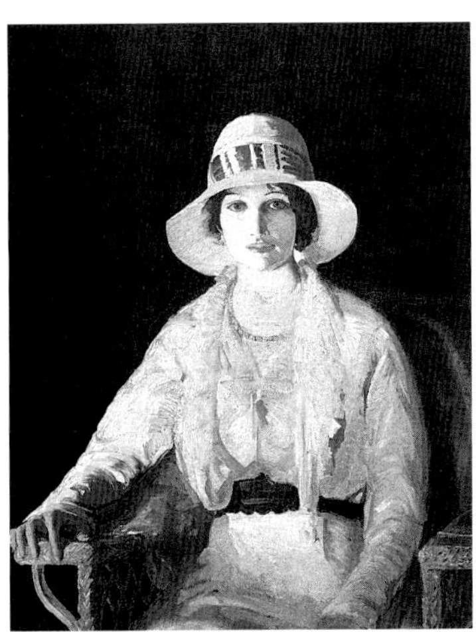

Florence Davey, 1914
Wood, 0.965 x 0.760 (38 x 30)
Inscribed at lower left: *Geo. Bellows*
Gift of Florence S. McCormick
1979.80.1

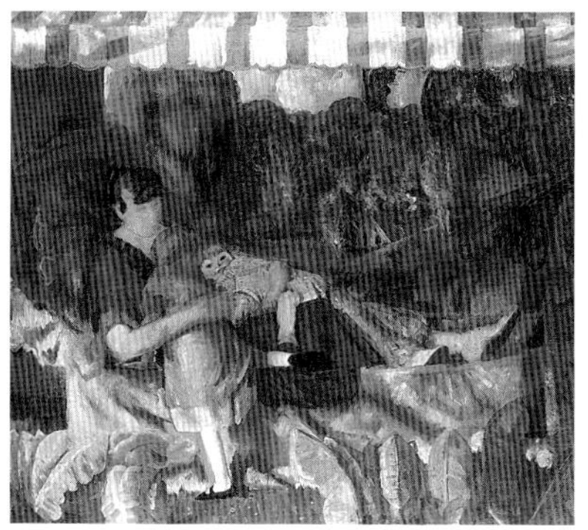

My Family, 1916
Canvas, 1.517 x 1.679 (59¾ x 66⅛)
Collection of Mr. and Mrs. Paul Mellon
1983.1.3

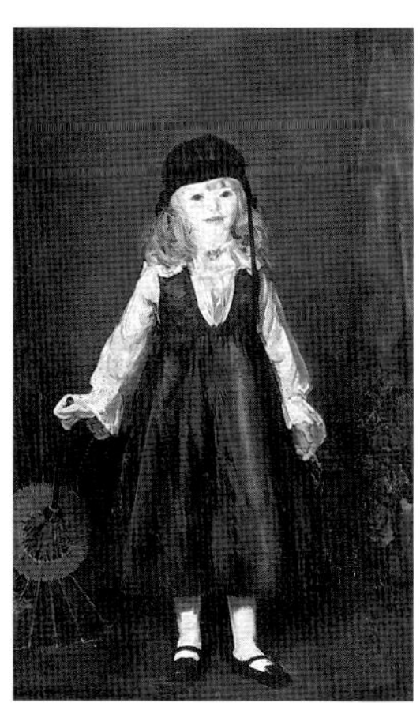

Anne with a Japanese Parasol, 1917
Canvas, 1.501 x 0.917 (59⅛ x 36⅛)
Inscribed at lower right: *Geo Bellows*
Collection of Mr. and Mrs. Paul Mellon
1983.1.1

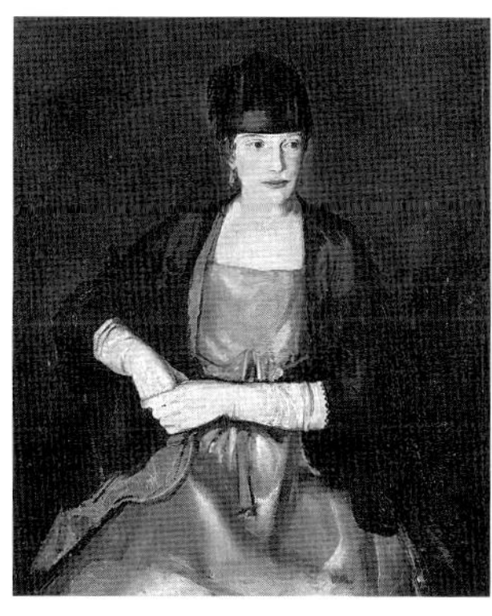

Maud Dale, 1919
Wood, 1.015 x 0.850 (40 x 33½)
Inscribed at lower left: *Geo Bellows.*
Chester Dale Collection
1944.15.1

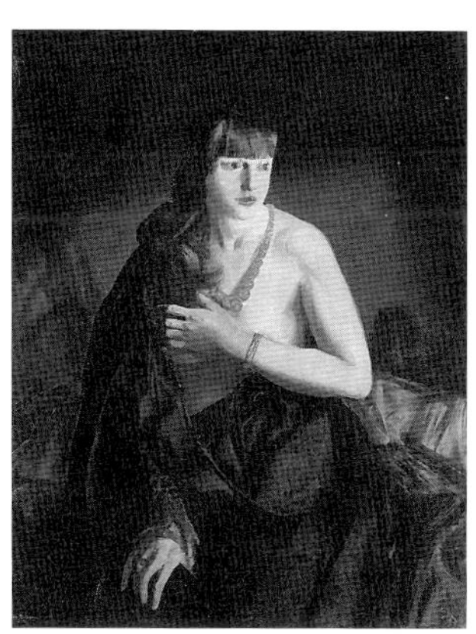

Nude with Red Hair, 1920
Canvas, 1.121 x 0.867 (44⅛ x 34⅛)
Inscribed by Emma S. Bellows, lower left:
Geo. Bellows / E. S. B.
Chester Dale Collection
1963.10.84

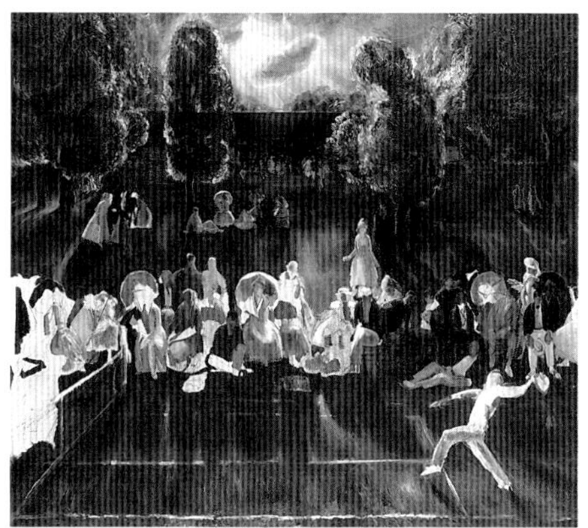

Tennis Tournament, 1920
Canvas, 1.498 x 1.676 (59 x 66)
Collection of Mr. and Mrs. Paul Mellon
1983.1.5

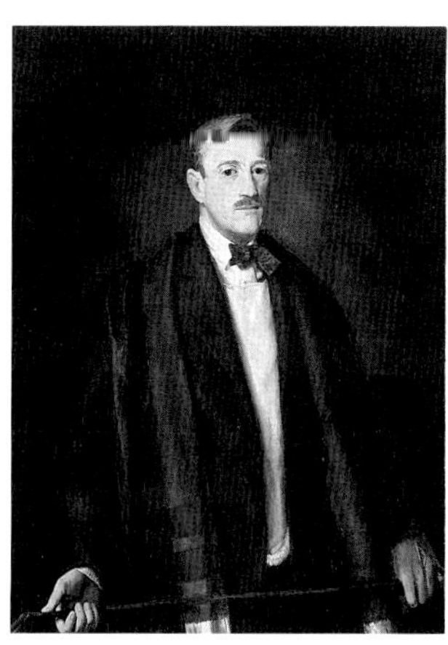

Chester Dale, 1922
Canvas, 1.137 x 0.883 (44¾ x 34¾)
Inscribed at lower right: *Geo Bellows*
Chester Dale Collection
1944.16.1 Special Collection

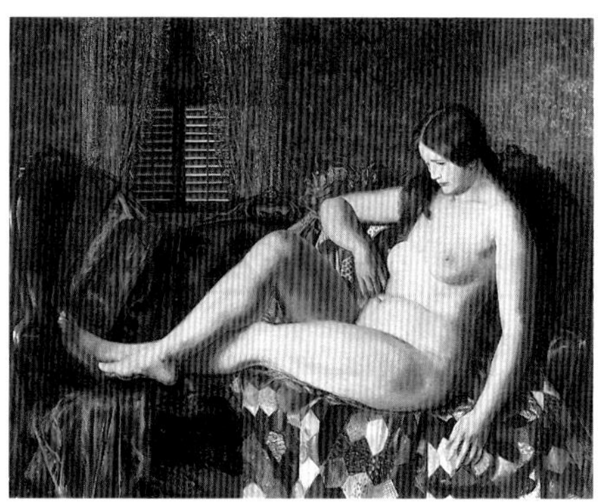

Nude with Hexagonal Quilt, 1924
Canvas, 1.295 x 1.600 (51 x 63)
Inscribed at lower right: *Geo Bellows.*
Collection of Mr. and Mrs. Paul Mellon
1983.1.4

HENRY BENBRIDGE
1743–1812

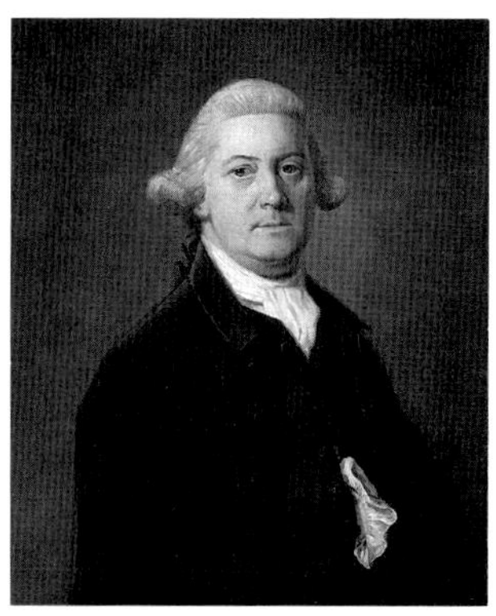

Portrait of a Man, 1771
Canvas, 0.762 x 0.638 (30 x 25⅛)
Inscribed at lower right: *H Benbridge* (HB in ligature) *1771*
Andrew W. Mellon Collection
1947.17.24

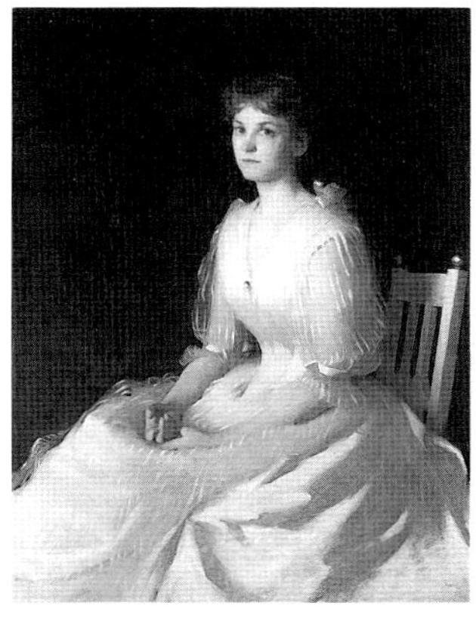

FRANK WESTON BENSON
1862–1951

Portrait in White, 1889
Canvas, 1.222 x 0.970 (48⅛ x 38¼)
Inscribed at upper left:
Frank W. Benson / '89
Gift of Sylvia Benson Lawson
1977.4.1

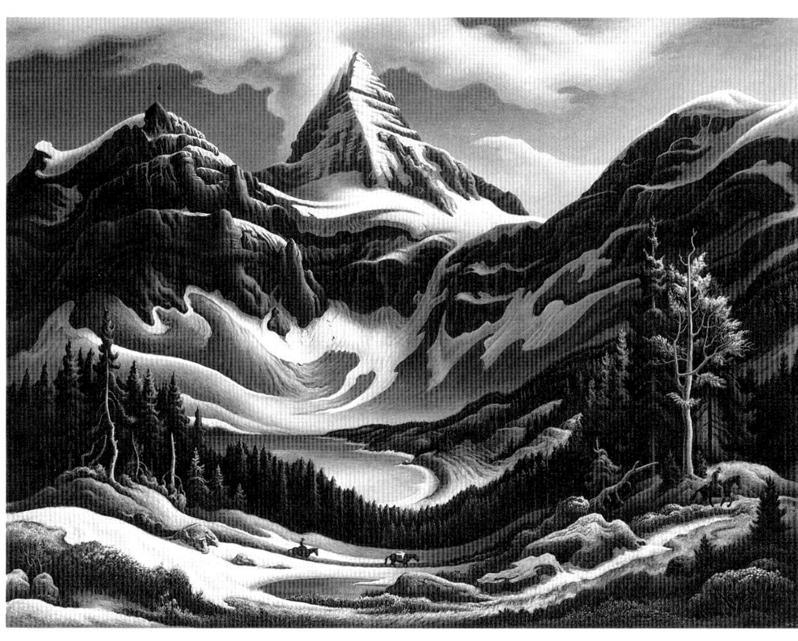

THOMAS HART BENTON
1889–1975

Trail Riders, 1964/1965
Canvas, 1.426 x 1.880 (56⅛ x 74)
Inscribed at lower right: *Benton '64–65*
Gift of the Artist
1975.42.1

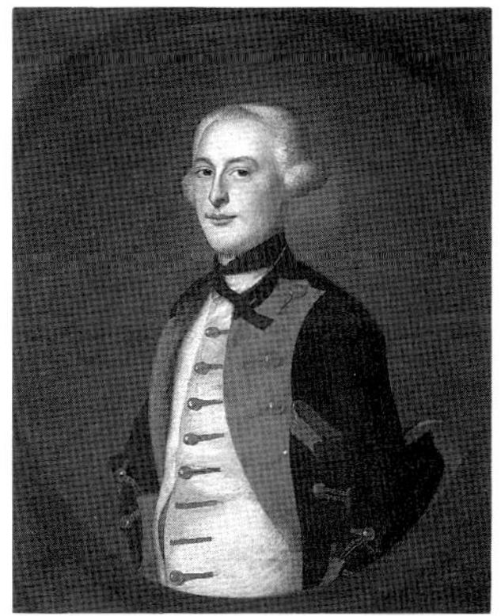

JOSEPH BLACKBURN
active 1752/1778

A Military Officer, 1756
Canvas, 0.775 x 0.636 (30½ x 25⅛)
Inscribed at lower left: *I Blackburn Pinxt 1756*
Andrew W. Mellon Collection
1947.17.25

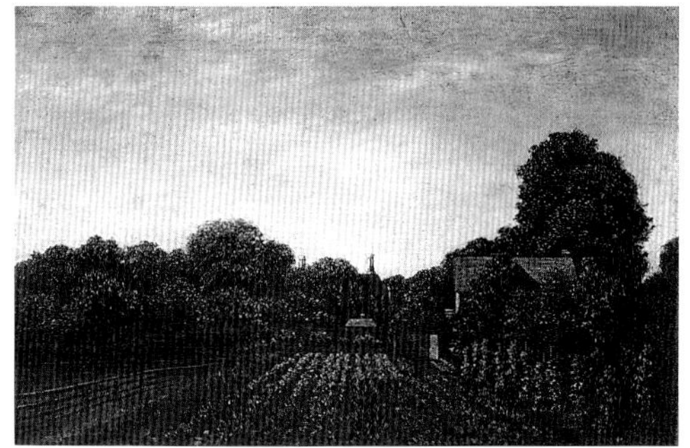

RALPH ALBERT BLAKELOCK
1847–1919

The Artist's Garden, c. 1880
Canvas, 0.407 x 0.610 (16 x 24)
Inscribed at lower right within arrowhead: *R. A. Blakelock*
Chester Dale Collection
1954.4.2

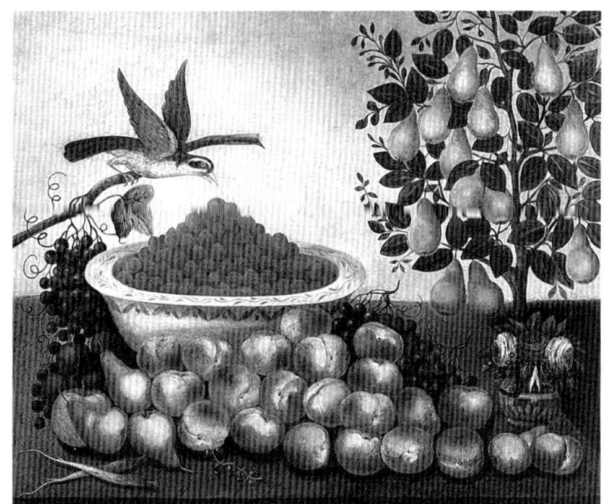

CHARLES V. BOND
c. 1825–1864 or later

Still Life: Fruit, Bird, and Dwarf Pear Tree, 1856
Canvas, 0.635 x 0.765 (25 x 30⅛)
Inscribed on reverse: *C. V. Bond, Chicago 1856*
Gift of Edgar William and Bernice Chrysler Garbisch
1980.62.2

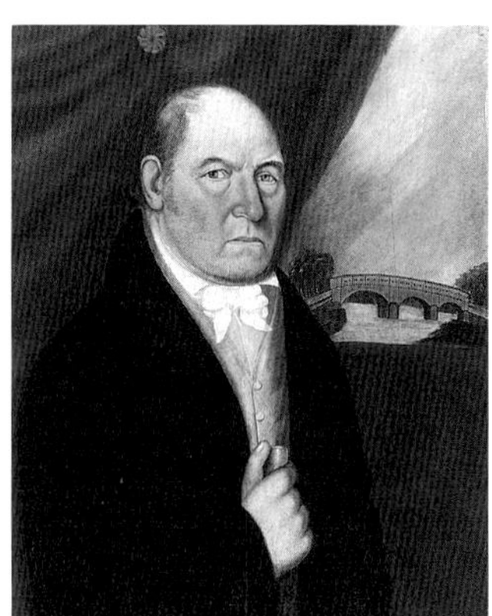

WILLIAM BONNELL
1804–1865

Clement Bonnell, c. 1825
Wood, 0.736 x 0.603 (29 x 23¾)
Gift of Edgar William and Bernice Chrysler Garbisch
1953.5.3

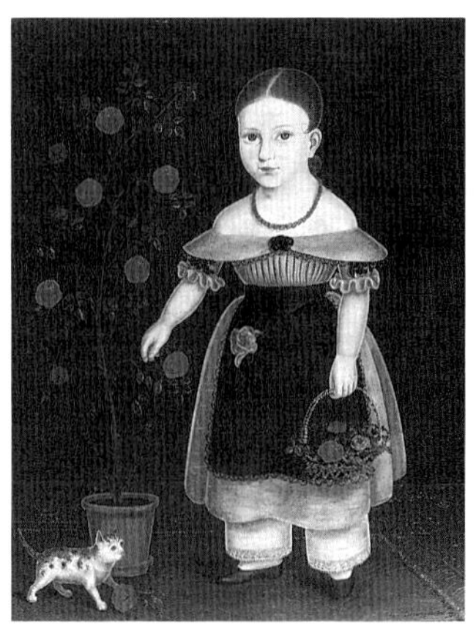

JOHN BRADLEY
active 1831/1847

Little Girl in Lavender, c. 1840
Canvas, 0.857 x 0.694 (33¾ x 27 5/16)
Inscribed at lower right: *by J. Bradley 128 Spring St.*
Gift of Edgar William and Bernice Chrysler Garbisch
1958.9.3

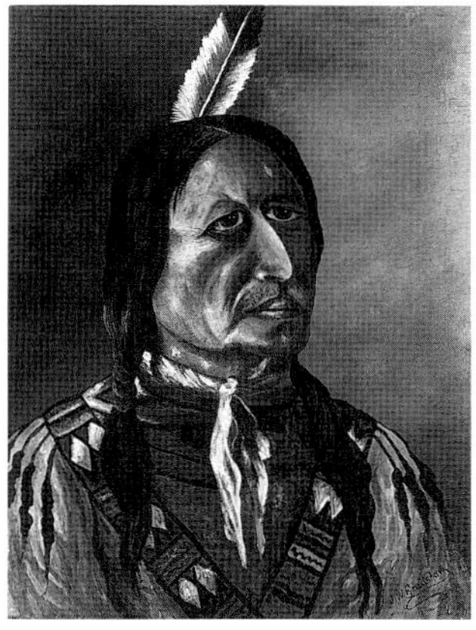

J. W. BRADSHAW
active fourth quarter 19th century

Plains Indian, fourth quarter 19th century
Canvas, 0.510 x 0.408 (20 x 16)
Inscribed at lower right: *J. W. Bradshaw*
Gift of Edgar William and Bernice Chrysler Garbisch
1968.26.1

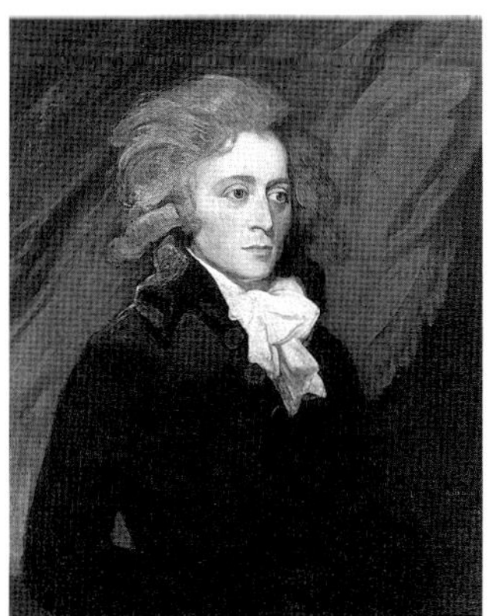

MATHER BROWN
1761–1831

William Vans Murray, 1787
Canvas, 0.762 x 0.637 (30 x 25 1/16)
Inscribed at lower right: *M. Brown. / London / 1787*
Andrew W. Mellon Collection
1940.1.1

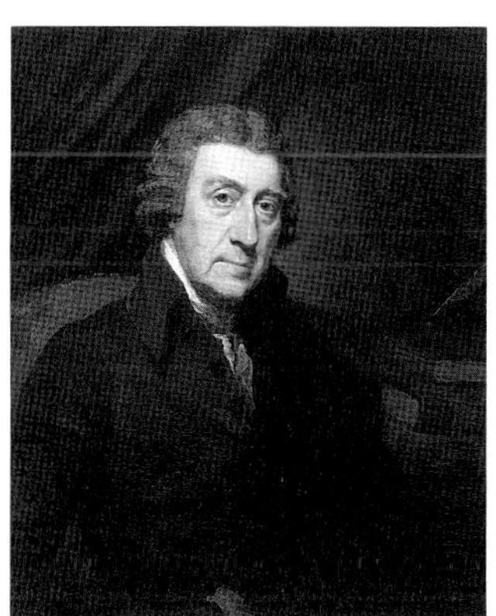

Thomas Dawson, Viscount Cremorne, c. 1788
Canvas, 0.752 x 0.633 (29 5/8 x 24 7/8)
Inscribed at lower right: *M. Brown-*
Andrew W. Mellon Collection
1947.17.28

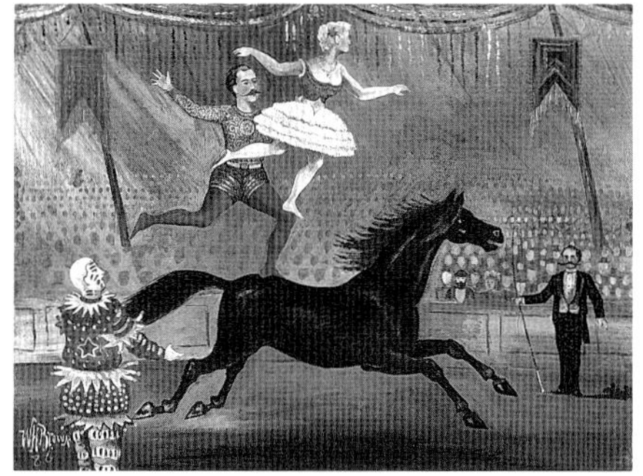

W. H. BROWN
active 1886/1887

Bareback Riders, 1886
Cardboard, 0.470 x 0.622 (18 1/2 x 24 1/2)
Inscribed at lower left: *W. H. Brown / 86*
Gift of Edgar William and Bernice Chrysler Garbisch
1958.9.4

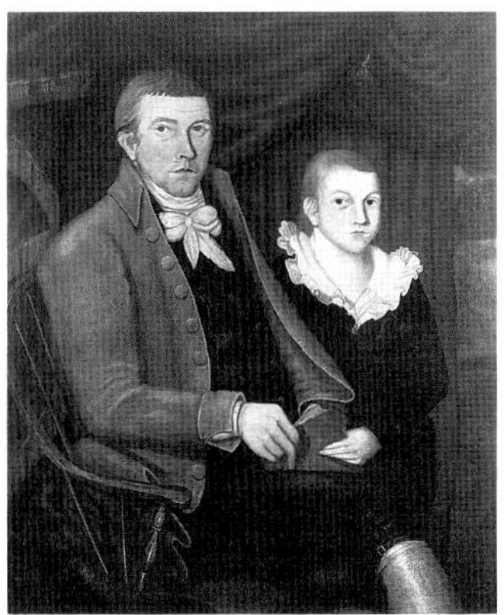

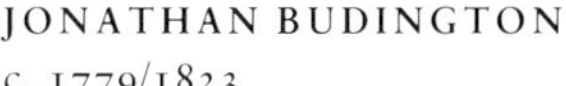

JONATHAN BUDINGTON
c. 1779/1823

Father and Son, 1800
Canvas, 1.041 x 0.898 (41 x 35⅜)
Inscribed at lower left: *J. Budington Pinxt. 1800*
Gift of Edgar William and Bernice Chrysler Garbisch
1956.13.1

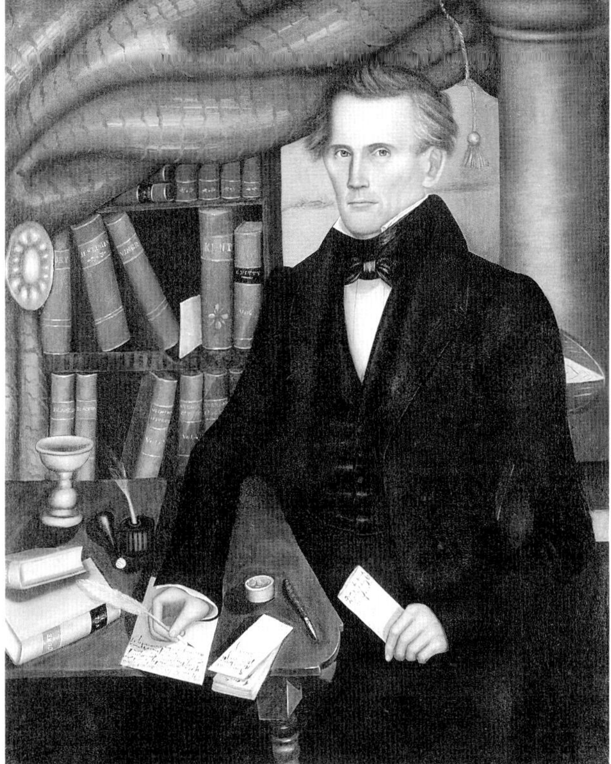

HORACE BUNDY
1814–1883

Vermont Lawyer, 1841
Canvas, 1.118 x 0.903 (44 x 35½)
Inscribed at lower left on letter: *Manchester August 1841. . .*
Gift of Edgar William and Bernice Chrysler Garbisch
1953.5.4

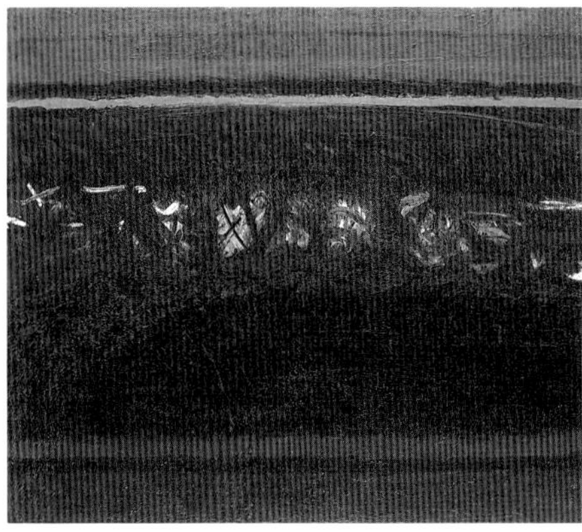

LAWRENCE CALCAGNO
born 1913

San Andreas III, 1963
Canvas, 1.730 x 1.988 (68 x 78¼)
Gift of Mrs. Seymour Obermer
1970.2.2

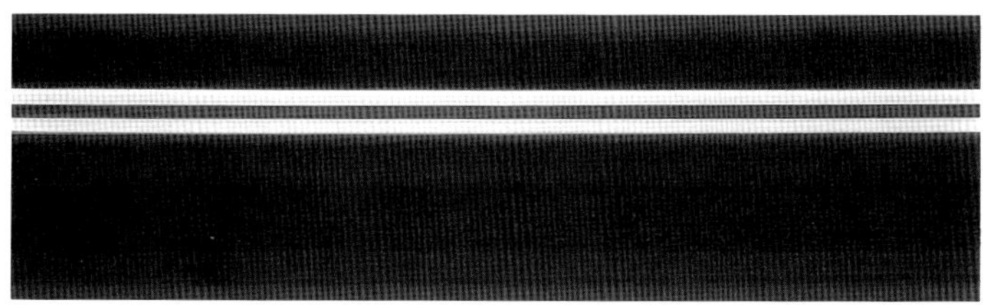

Black Light, 1969
Canvas, 0.814 x 2.744 (32 x 108)
Gift of Mrs. Seymour Obermer
1970.2.1

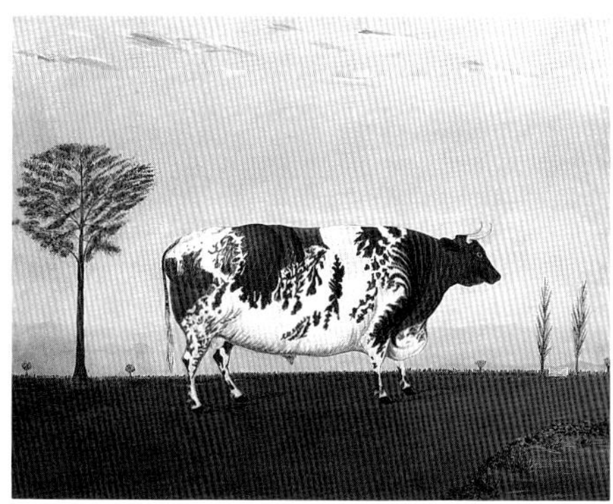

H. CALL
active 1876

Prize Bull, 1876
Canvas, 0.507 x 0.630 ($19^{15}/_{16}$ x $24^{13}/_{16}$)
Inscribed at lower center: *H. CALL / 1876*
Gift of Edgar William and Bernice Chrysler Garbisch
1980.62.3

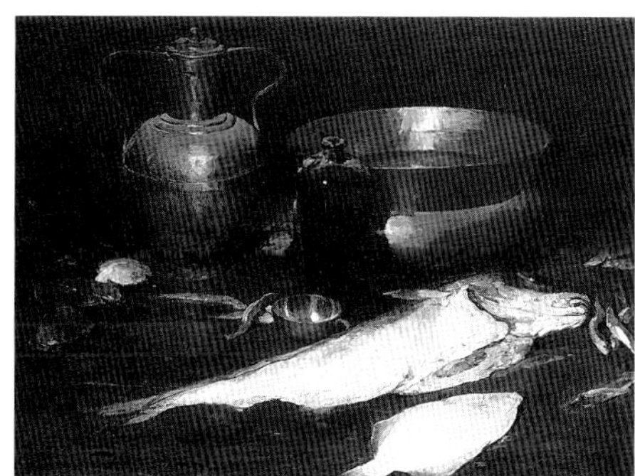

EMIL CARLSEN
1853–1932

Still Life with Fish, 1882
Canvas, 0.752 x 1.010 ($29^{5}/_{8}$ x $39^{3}/_{4}$)
Inscribed at lower left: *Emil. Carlsen. 1882–*
Chester Dale Collection
1963.10.93

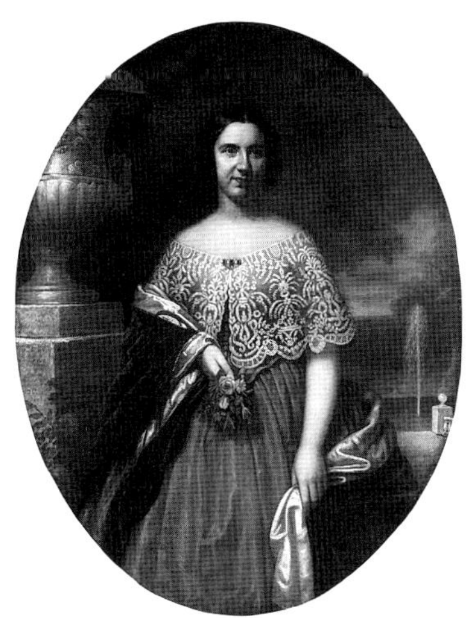

FRANCIS BICKNELL CARPENTER
1830–1900

Mrs. Henry C. Bowen, 1859
Canvas, oval: 1.429 x 1.118 ($56^{1}/_{4}$ x 44)
Inscribed at center left:
F. B. Carpenter / 1859.
Gift of Lady Vereker
1961.10.1

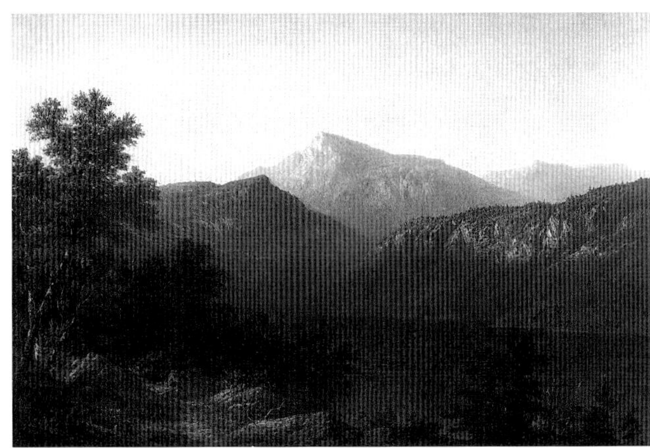

JOHN WILLIAM CASILEAR
1811–1893

View on Lake George, 1857
Canvas, 0.505 x 0.762 (19⅞ x 30)
Inscribed at lower center: *JW.C.* (in monogram) / *57*.
Gift of Frederick Sturges, Jr.
1978.6.1

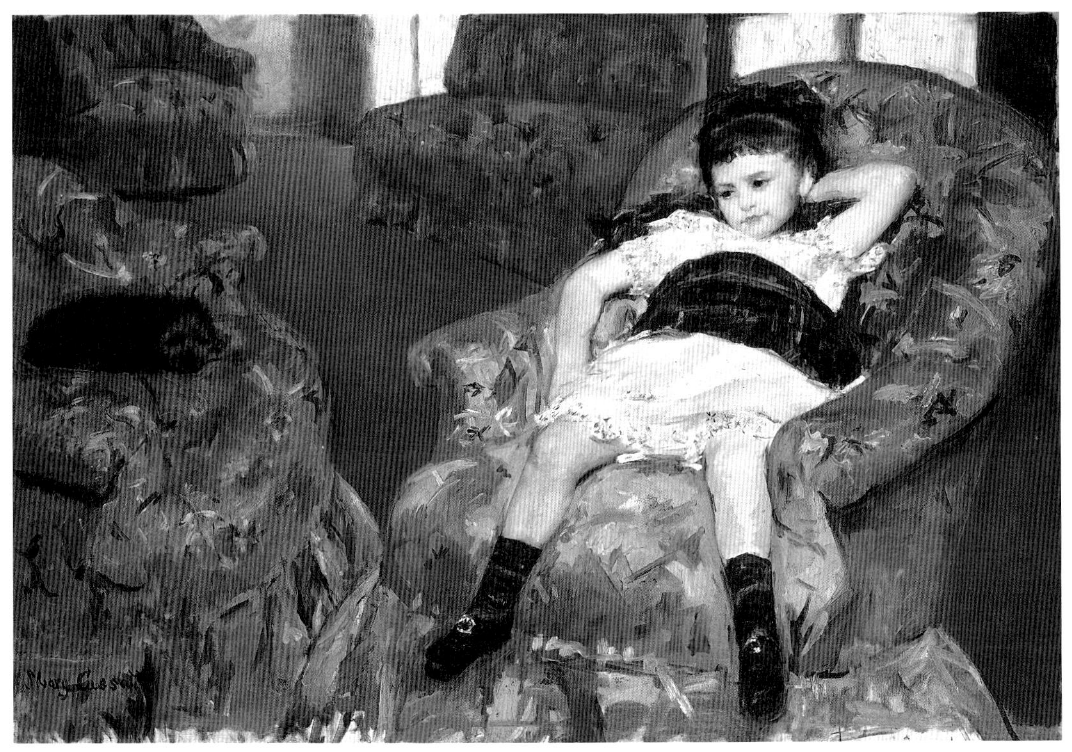

MARY CASSATT
1844–1926

Little Girl in a Blue Armchair, 1878
Canvas, 0.895 x 1.298 (35¼ x 51⅛)
Inscribed at lower left: *Mary Cassatt*
Collection of Mr. and Mrs. Paul Mellon
1983.1.18

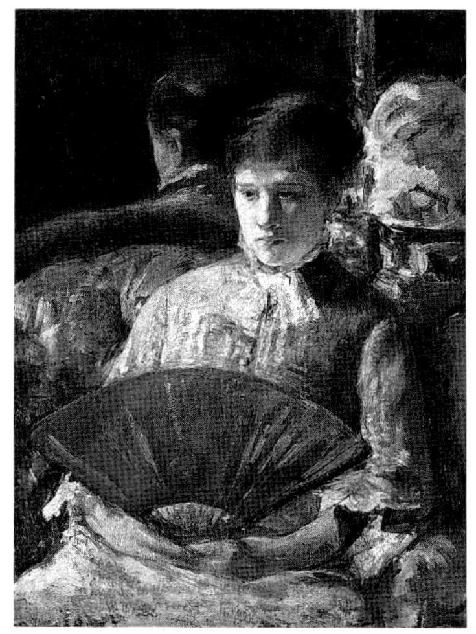

Miss Mary Ellison, c. 1880
Canvas, 0.850 x 0.653 (33½ x 25¾)
Inscribed at center left: *Mary Cassatt*
Chester Dale Collection
1963.10.95

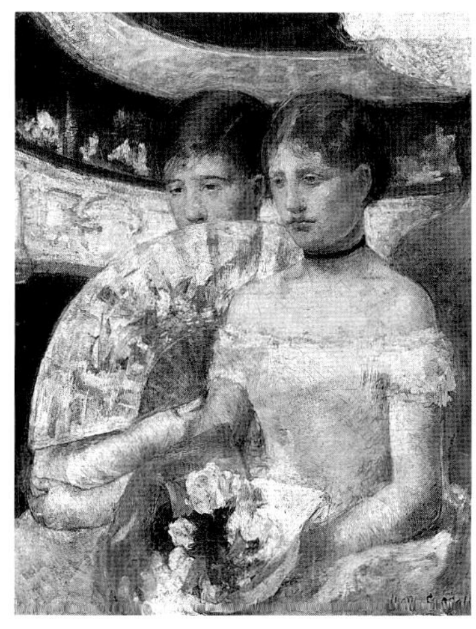

The Loge, 1882
Canvas, 0.798 x 0.638 (31⅜ x 25⅛)
Inscribed at lower right: *Mary Cassatt*
Chester Dale Collection
1963.10.96

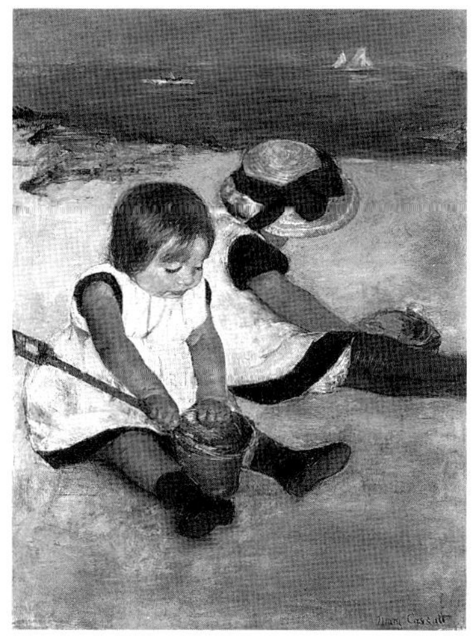

Children Playing on the Beach, 1884
Canvas, 0.974 x 0.742 (38⅜ x 29¼)
Inscribed at lower right: *Mary Cassatt*
Ailsa Mellon Bruce Collection
1970.17.19

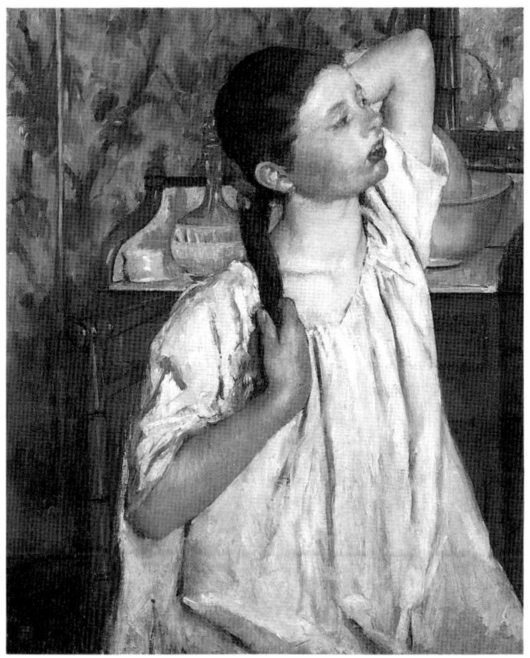

Girl Arranging Her Hair, 1886
Canvas, 0.751 x 0.625 (29 5/8 x 24 5/8)
Chester Dale Collection
1963.10.97

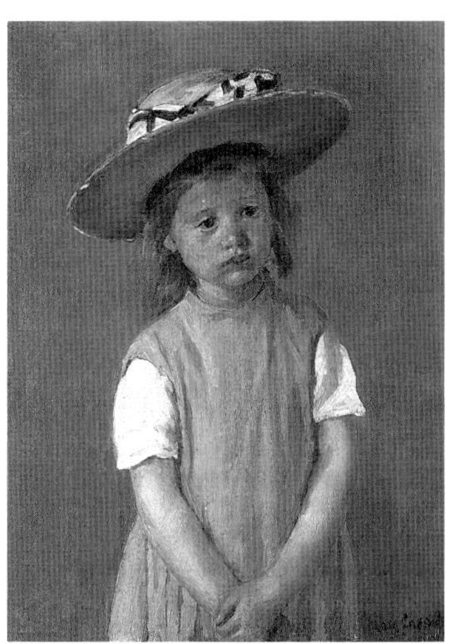

Child in a Straw Hat, c. 1886
Canvas, 0.653 x 0.495 (25 3/4 x 19 1/2)
Inscribed at lower right: *Mary Cassatt*
Collection of Mr. and Mrs. Paul Mellon
1983.1.17

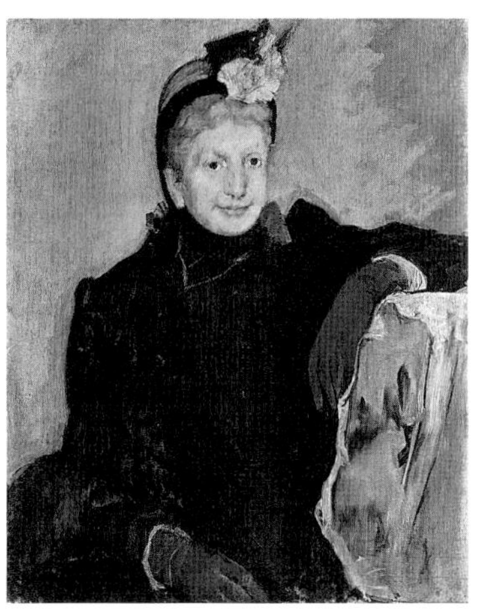

Portrait of an Elderly Lady, c. 1887
Canvas, 0.728 x 0.603 (28 5/8 x 23 3/4)
Chester Dale Collection
1963.10.7

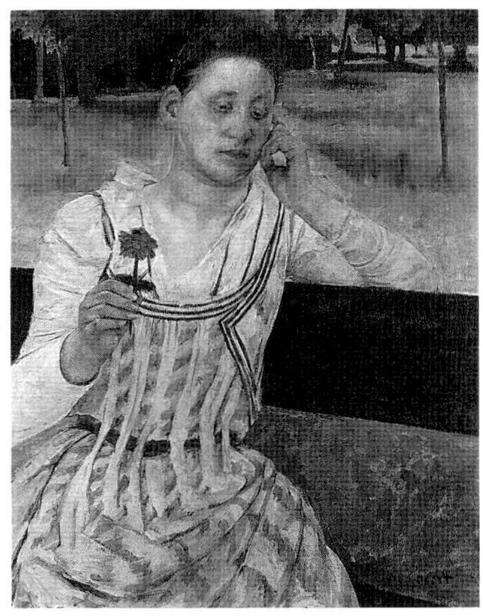

Woman with a Red Zinnia, 1891
Canvas, 0.736 x 0.603 (29 x 23¾)
Inscribed at lower right: *Mary Cassatt*
Chester Dale Collection
1963.10.99

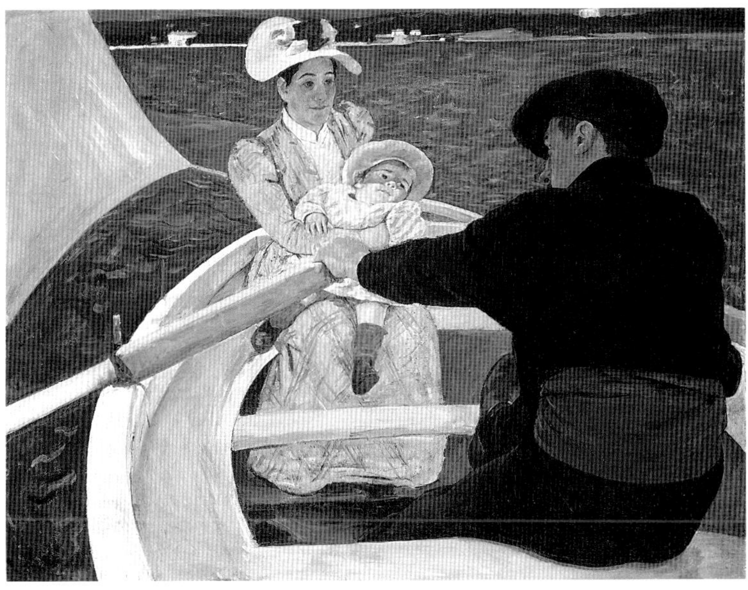

The Boating Party, 1893/1894
Canvas, 0.902 x 1.171 (35½ x 46⅛)
Chester Dale Collection
1963.10.94

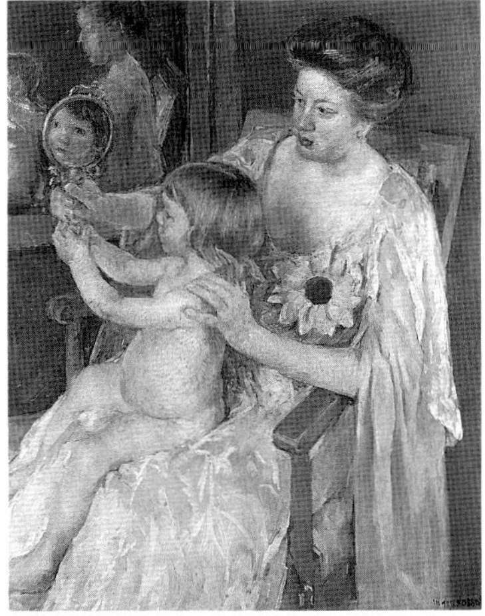

Mother and Child, c. 1905
Canvas, 0.921 x 0.737 (36¼ x 29)
Inscribed at lower right: *Mary Cassatt*
Chester Dale Collection
1963.10.98

GEORGE CATLIN
1796–1872

Works are listed as follows under three subheadings: "North American Subjects" and "South American Subjects," alphabetically by title; "La Salle Series," in the sequential order in which they were published by the artist.

North American Subjects

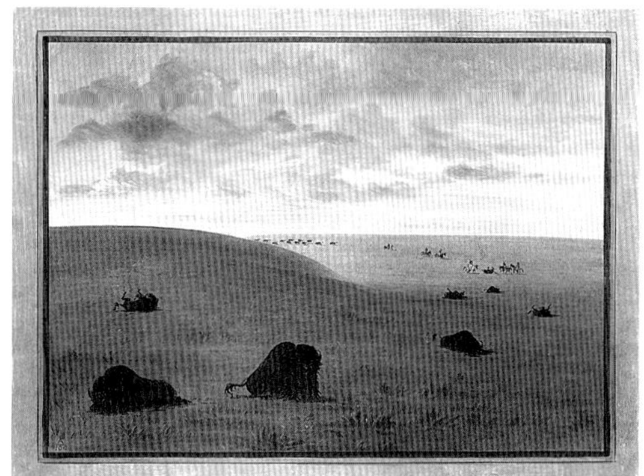

After the Buffalo Chase—Sioux, 1861/1869
Paperboard, 0.476 x 0.638 (18¾ x 25⅛)
Paul Mellon Collection
1965.16.11

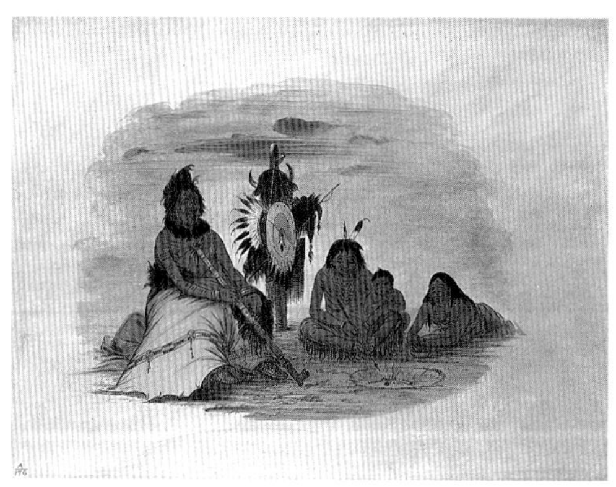

An Aged Minatarree Chief and His Family, 1861/1869
Paperboard, 0.465 x 0.621 (18 5/16 x 24 7/16)
Paul Mellon Collection
1965.16.76

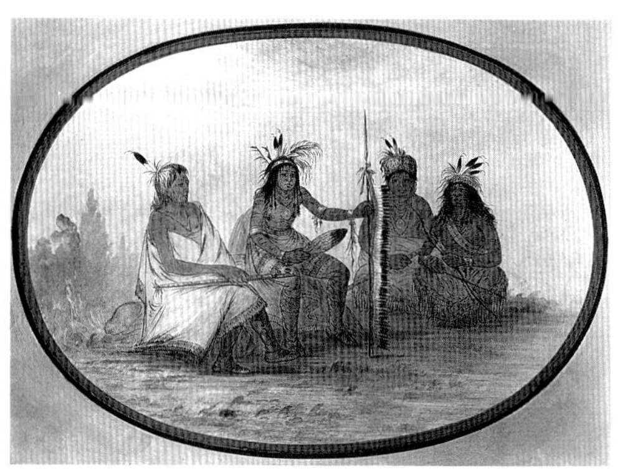

An Aged Ojibbeway Chief and Three Warriors, 1861/1869
Paperboard, 0.474 x 0.630 (18⅝ x 24⅞)
Paul Mellon Collection
1965.16.91

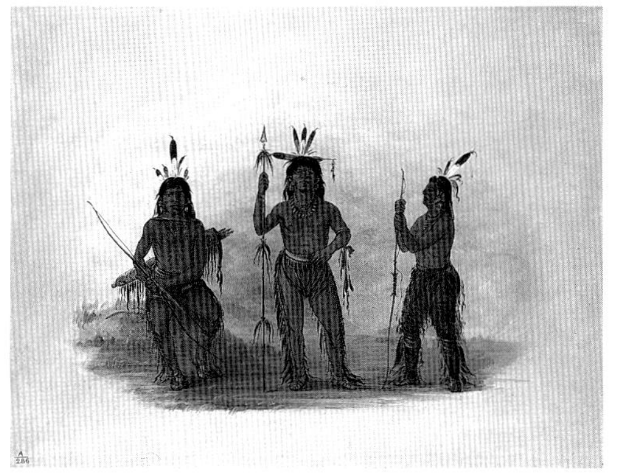

Alaeutian Chief and Two Warriors, 1855/1869
Paperboard, 0.463 x 0.615 (18¼ x 24³⁄₁₆)
Paul Mellon Collection
1965.16.169

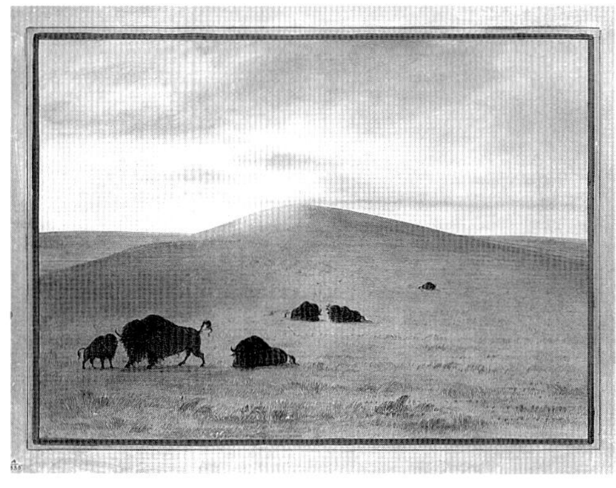

American Pasturage—Prairies of the Platte, 1861/1869
Paperboard, 0.470 x 0.625 (18½ x 24⅝)
Paul Mellon Collection
1965.16.208

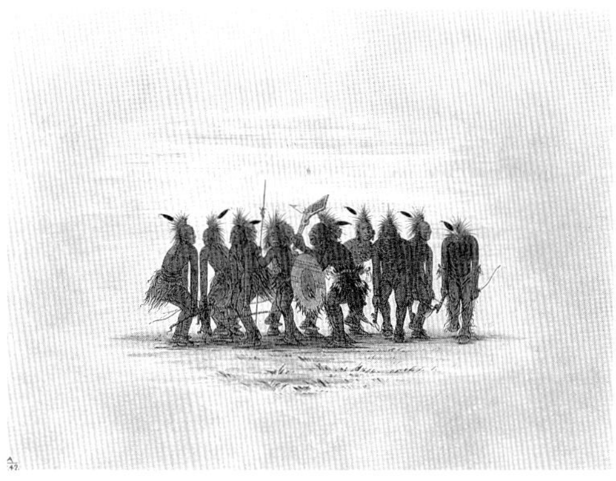

Amusing Dance—Saukie, 1861/1869
Paperboard, 0.455 x 0.617
(17¹⁵⁄₁₆ x 24⁵⁄₁₆)
Paul Mellon Collection
1965.16.130

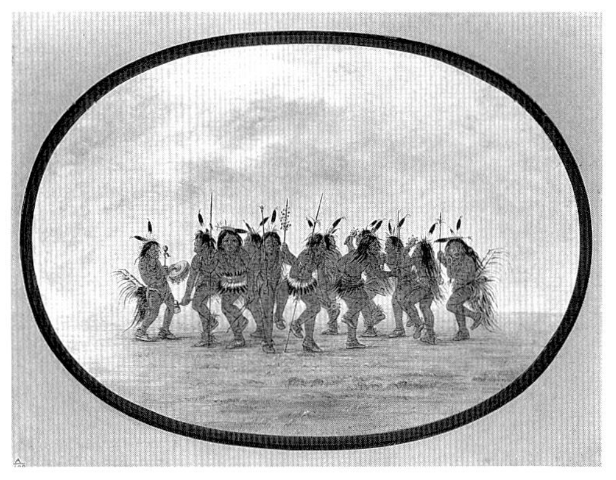

Amusing Dance—Sioux, 1861/1869
Paperboard, 0.467 x 0.617 (18⅜ x 24⁵⁄₁₆)
Paul Mellon Collection
1965.16.17

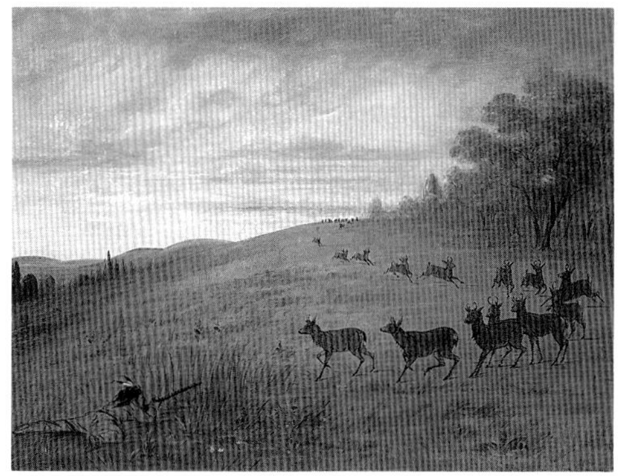

Antelope Shooting—Assinneboine, 1861/1869
Canvas, 0.453 x 0.630 (18 1/8 x 24 7/8)
Paul Mellon Collection
1965.16.35

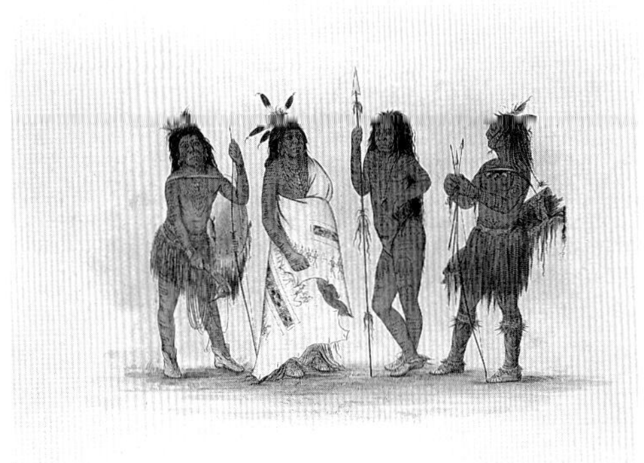

Apachee Chief and Three Warriors, 1855/1869
Paperboard, 0.451 x 0.614 (17 3/4 x 24 3/16)
Inscribed at lower center: *Catlin p.*
Paul Mellon Collection
1965.16.145

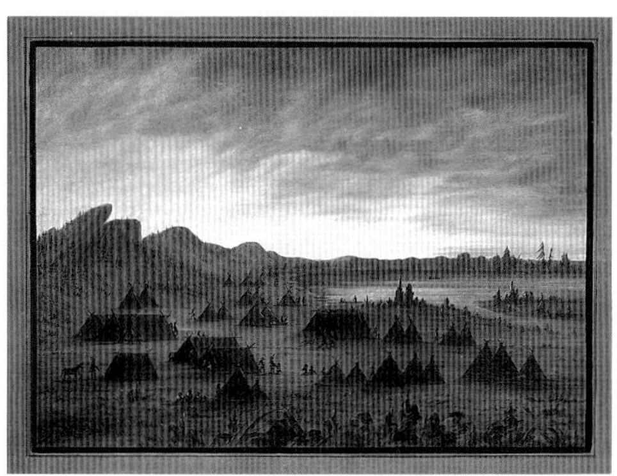

An Apachee Village, 1855/1869
Paperboard, 0.457 x 0.623 (18 x 24 5/8)
Paul Mellon Collection
1965.16.200

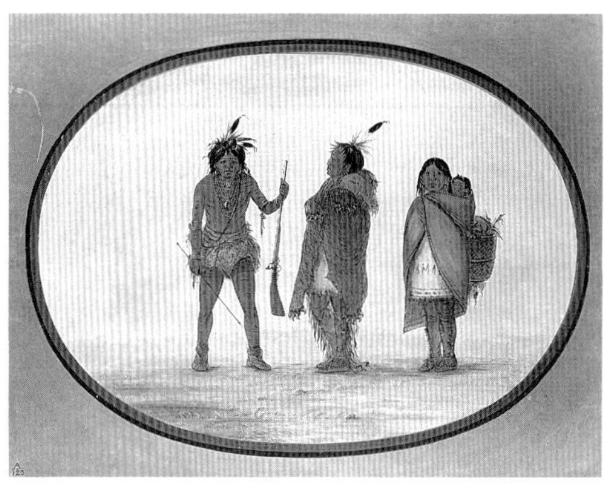

Arapaho Chief, His Wife, and a Warrior, 1861/1869
Paperboard, 0.472 x 0.629 (18 9/16 x 24 3/4)
Paul Mellon Collection
1965.16.30

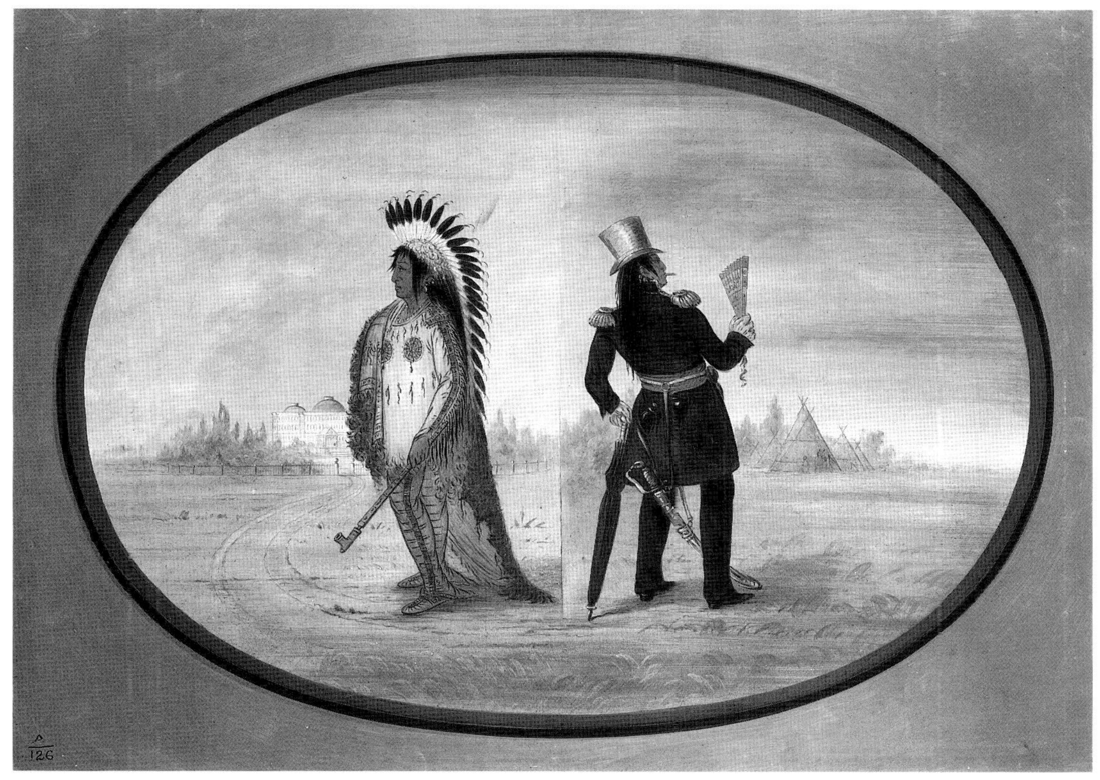

Assinneboine Chief before and after Civilization, 1861/1869
Paperboard, 0.469 x 0.640
(18 7/16 x 25 3/16)
Paul Mellon Collection
1965.16.33

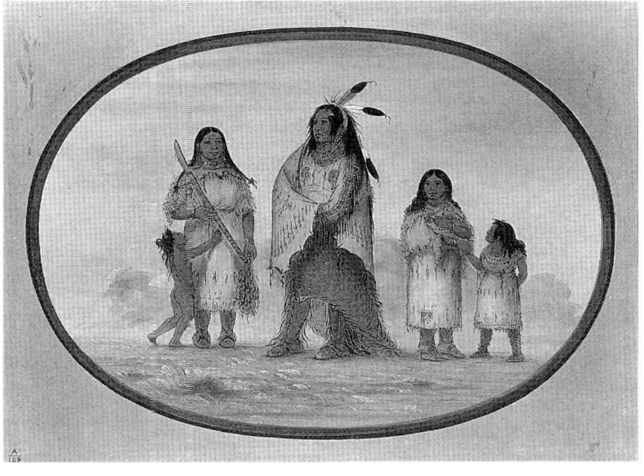

Assinneboine Warrior and His Family, 1861/1869
Paperboard, 0.473 x 0.635 (18 5/8 x 25)
Paul Mellon Collection
1965.16.32

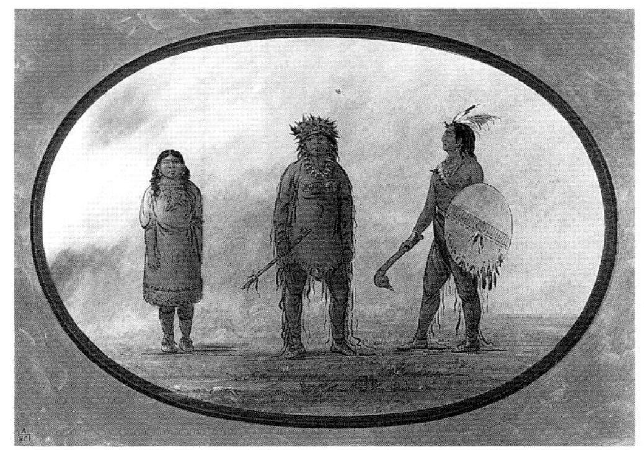

Athapasca Chief, His Wife, and a Warrior, 1855/1869
Paperboard, 0.455 x 0.620 (18 x 24⅝)
Paul Mellon Collection
1965.16.164

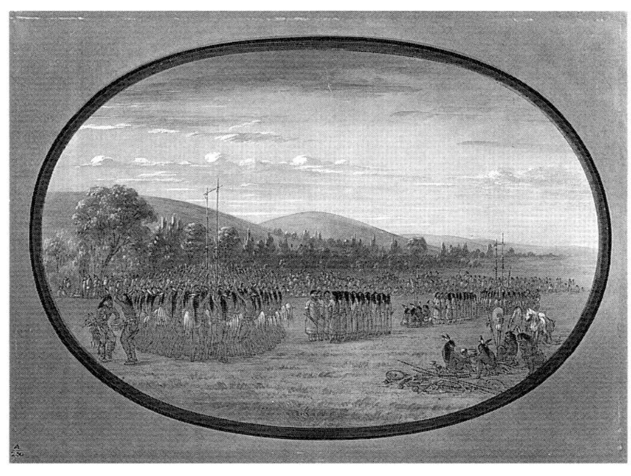

Ball-Play Dance—Choctaw, 1861/1869
Paperboard, 0.473 x 0.635 (18⅝ x 25)
Paul Mellon Collection
1965.16.137

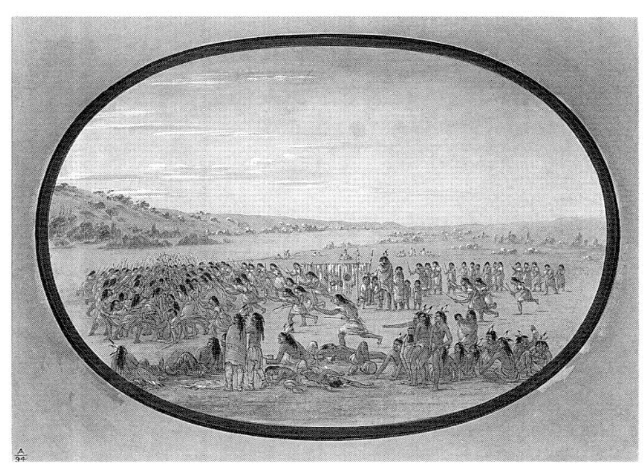

Ball-Play of the Women—Sioux, 1861/1869
Paperboard, 0.468 x 0.635 (18 7/16 x 25)
Paul Mellon Collection
1965.16.7

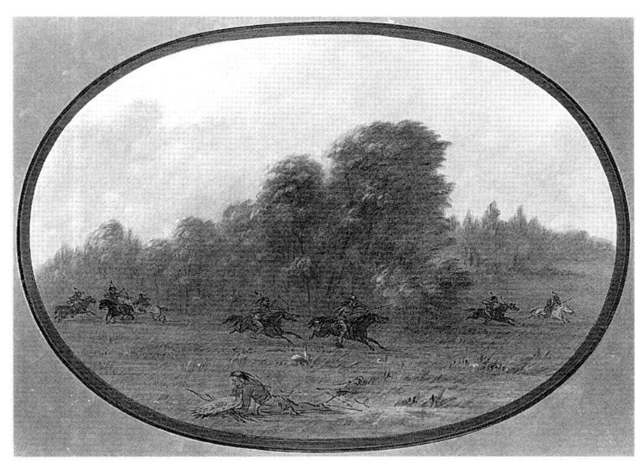

Battle between the Jiccarilla Apachees and Camanchees, 1861/1869
Paperboard, 0.459 x 0.619 (18 1/16 x 24⅜)
Paul Mellon Collection
1965.16.52

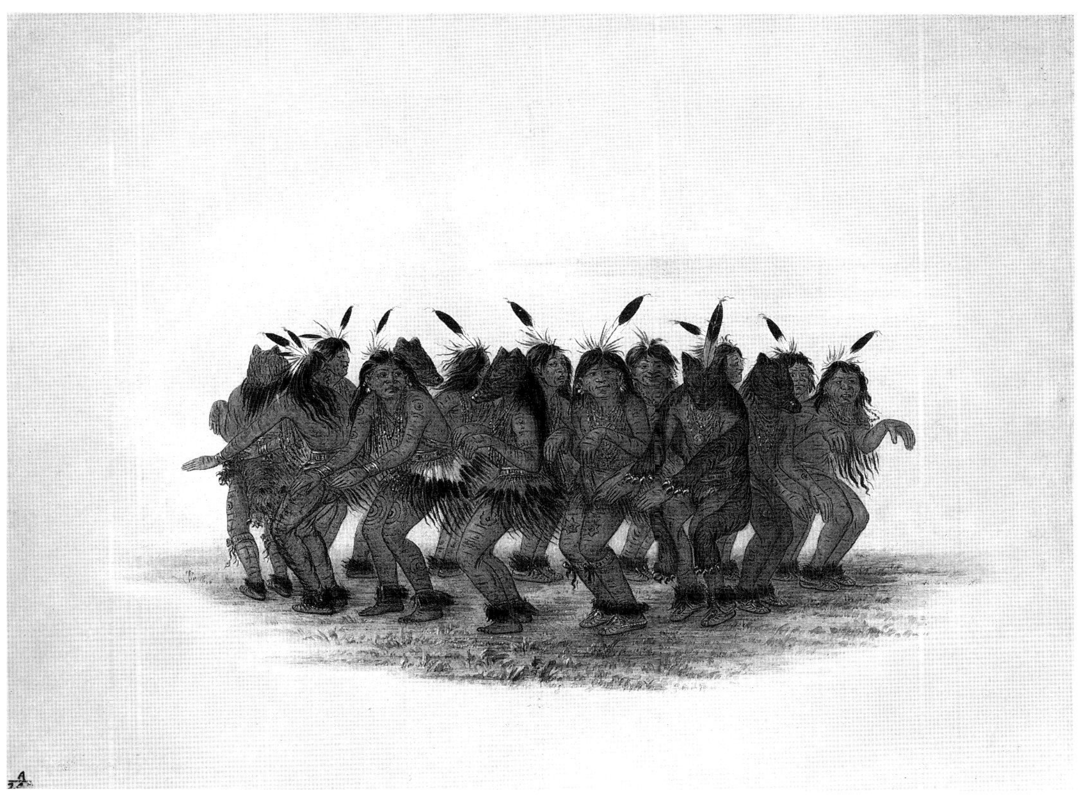

Bear Dance—K'nisteneux, 1861
Paperboard, 0.465 x 0.612 (18¼ x 24)
Inscribed at lower left: *Geo. Catlin 1861*
Paul Mellon Collection
1965.16.134

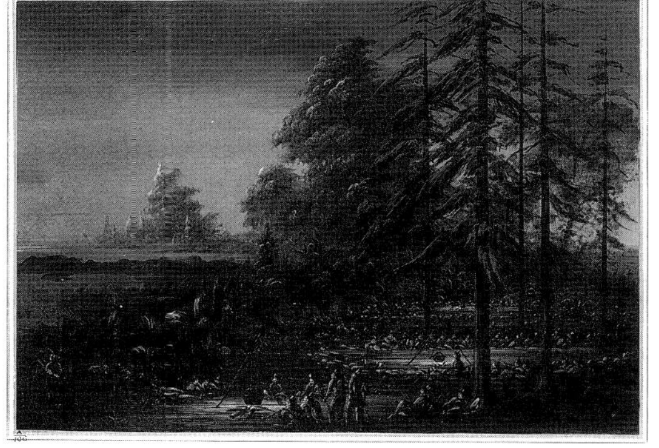

Bivouac of a Sioux War Party, 1861/1869
Paperboard, 0.472 x 0.623 (18⅝ x 24 9/16)
Paul Mellon Collection
1965.16.16

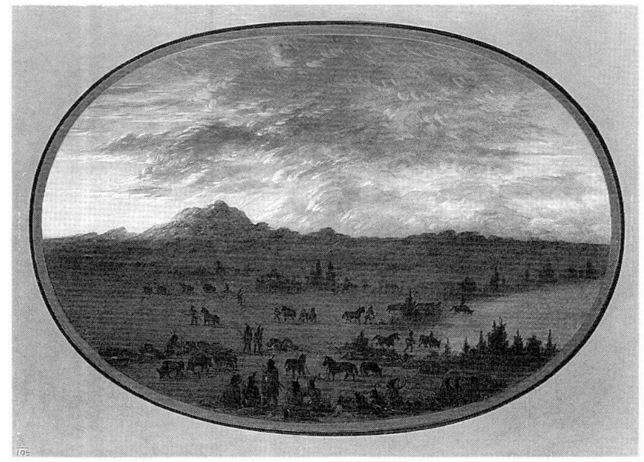

Bivouac of a Sioux War Party at Sunrise, 1861/1869
Paperboard, 0.458 x 0.623 (18 x 24½)
Paul Mellon Collection
1965.16.18

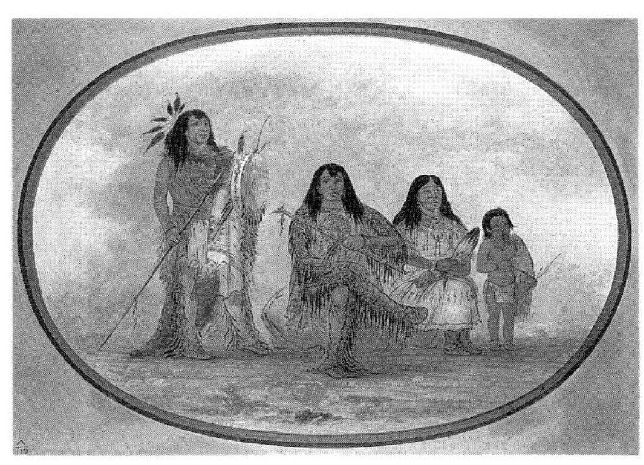

A Blackfoot Chief, His Wife, and a Medicine Man, 1861/1869
Paperboard, 0.461 x 0.617 (18⅛ x 24$^{5}/_{16}$)
Paul Mellon Collection
1965.16.28

Black Hawk and Five Other Saukie Prisoners, 1861/1869
Paperboard, 0.473 x 0.633 (18⅝ x 24$^{15}/_{16}$)
Paul Mellon Collection
1965.16.95

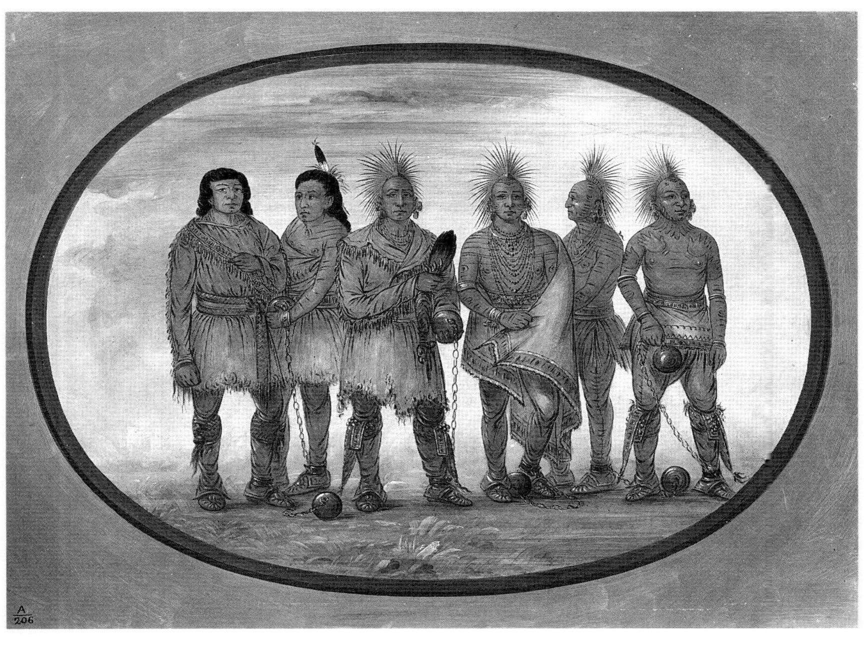

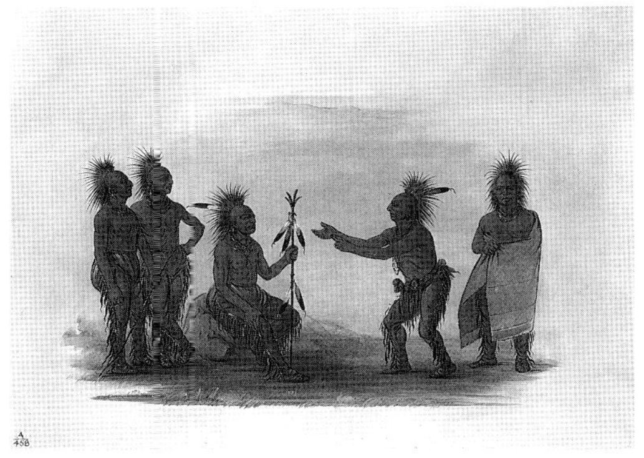

Black Hawk and the Prophet—Saukie, 1861/1869
Paperboard, 0.464 x 0.624 (18¼ x 24⁹⁄₁₆)
Paul Mellon Collection
1965.16.314

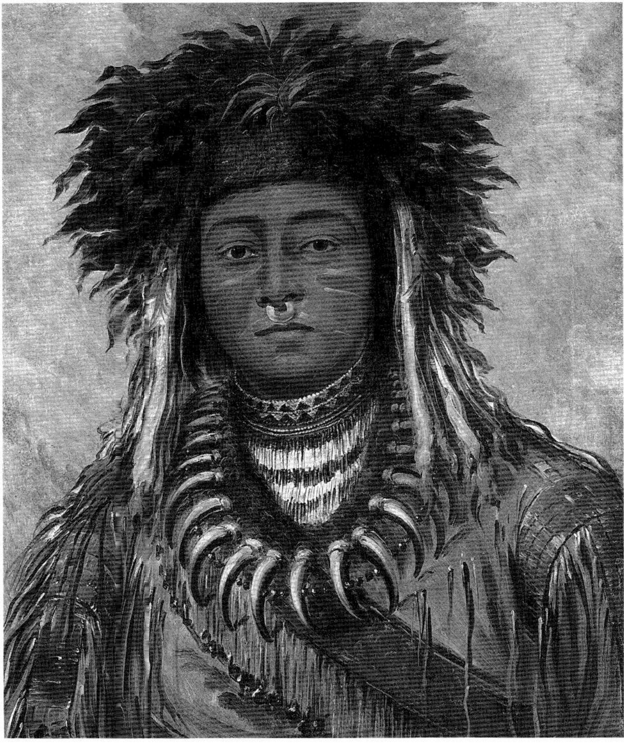

Boy Chief—Ojibbeway, 1843
Canvas, 0.710 x 0.583 (28 x 23)
Paul Mellon Collection
1965.16.349

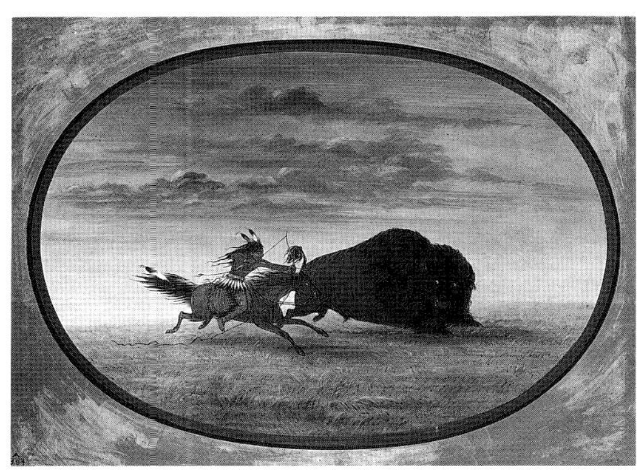

Buffalo Chase, 1861/1869
Paperboard, 0.463 x 0.630 (18¼ x 24⅞)
Paul Mellon Collection
1965.16.175

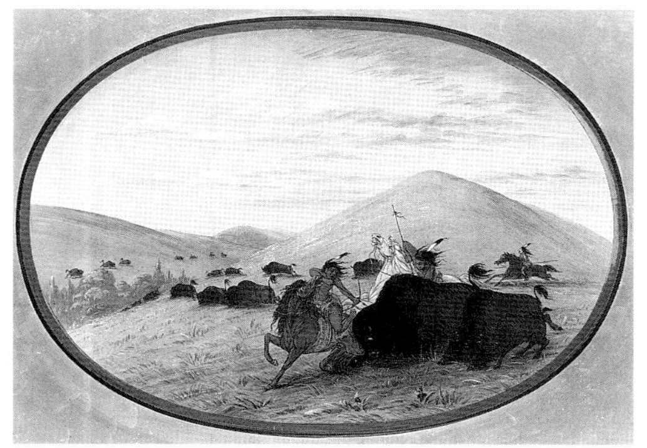

Buffalo Chase—Bulls Protecting the Calves, 1861/1869
Paperboard, 0.470 x 0.636 (18½ x 25¹⁄₁₆)
Paul Mellon Collection
1965.16.179

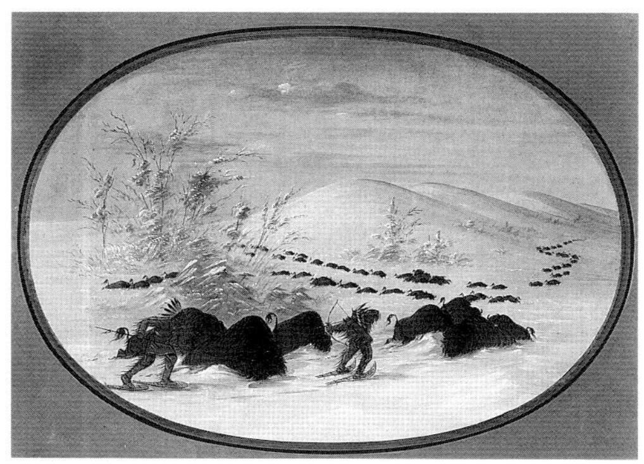

Buffalo Chase in the Snow Drifts—Ojibbeway, 1861/1869
Paperboard, 0.475 x 0.633
(18⅝ x 24¹¹⁄₁₆)
Paul Mellon Collection
1965.16.129

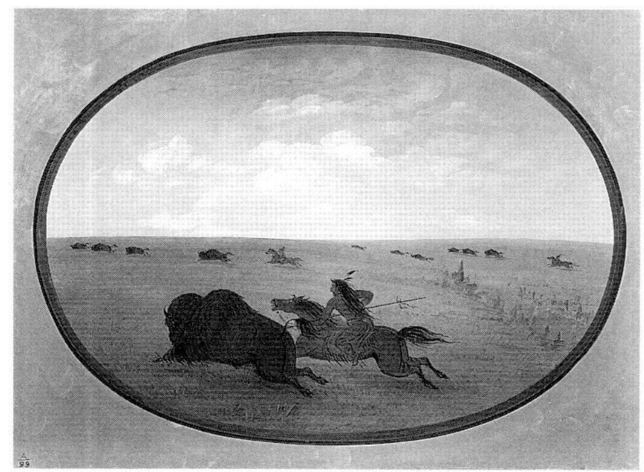

Buffalo Chase, Sioux Indians, Upper Missouri, 1861/1869
Paperboard, 0.469 x 0.625 (18½ x 24⅝)
Paul Mellon Collection
1965.16.10

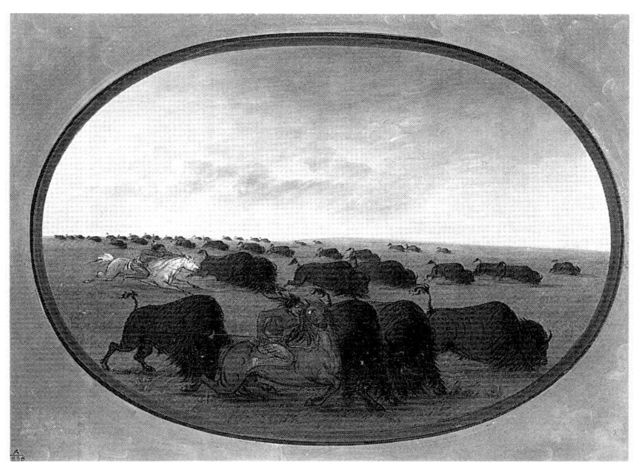

Buffalo Chase, with Accidents, 1861/1869
Paperboard, 0.462 x 0.623 (18¼ x 24⅝)
Paul Mellon Collection
1965.16.176

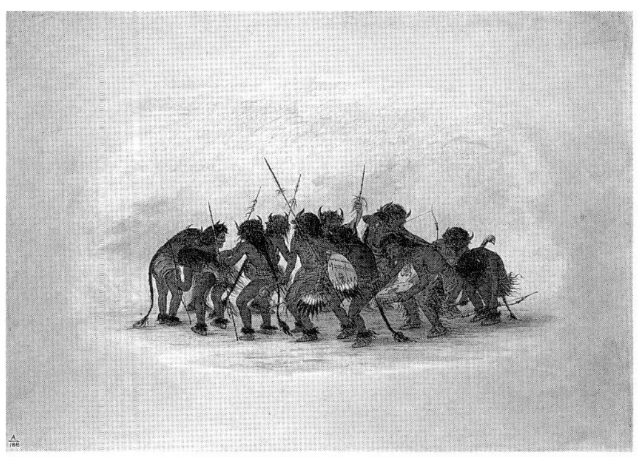

Buffalo Dance—Mandan, 1861
Paperboard, 0.448 x 0.614
(17⅝ x 23$^{15}/_{16}$)
Inscribed at lower center:
Geo. Catlin, 1861.
Paul Mellon Collection
1965.16.82

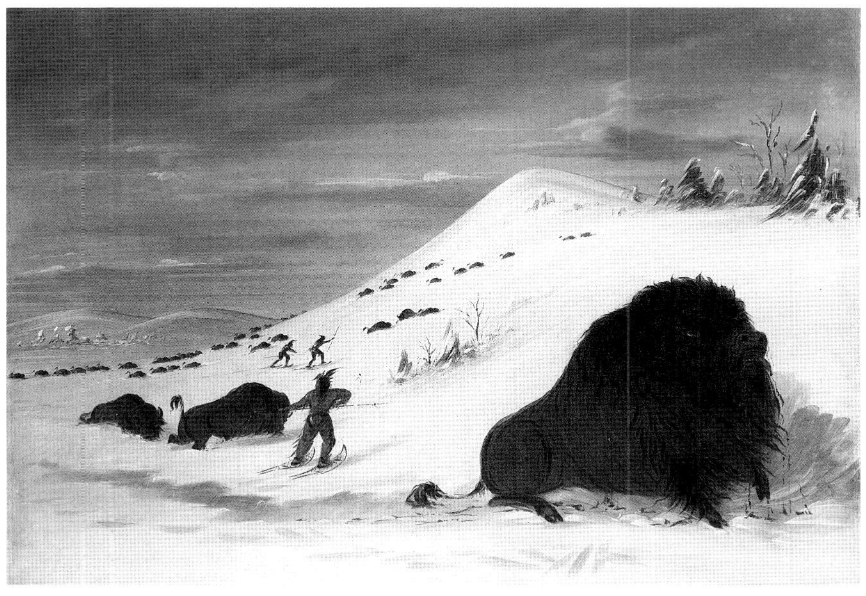

Buffalo Lancing in the Snow Drifts—Sioux, 1861/1869
Canvas, 0.459 x 0.638 (18$^{1}/_{16}$ x 25⅛)
Paul Mellon Collection
1965.16.345

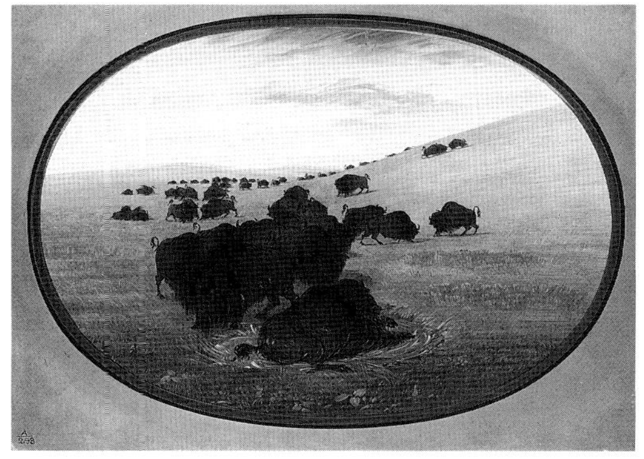

A Buffalo Wallow, 1861/1869
Paperboard, 0.467 x 0.625 (20 x 26¼)
Paul Mellon Collection
1965.16.178

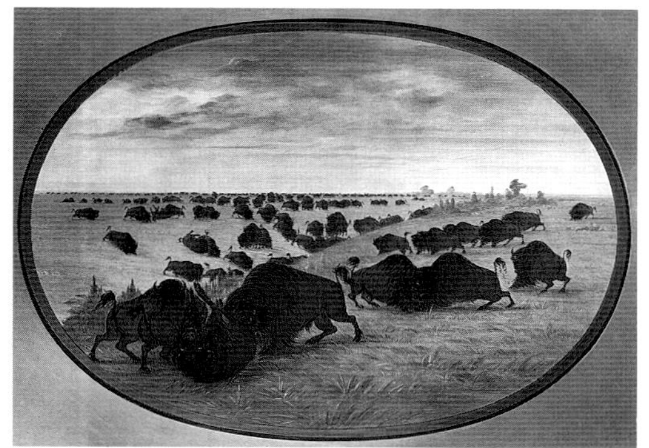

Bulls Fighting, 1861/1869
Paperboard, 0.470 x 0.635 (18½ x 25)
Paul Mellon Collection
1965.16.180

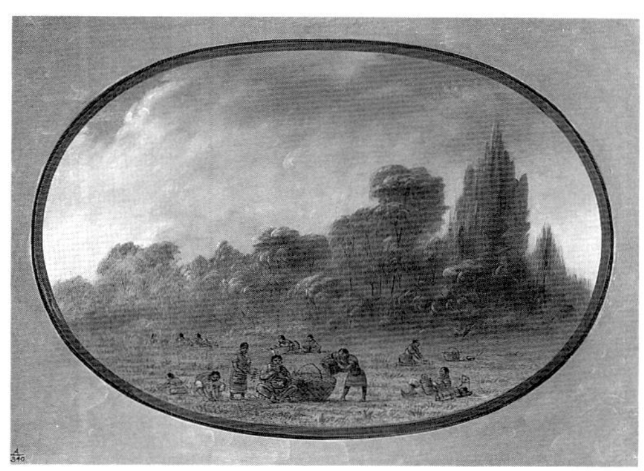

Caddoe Indians Gathering Wild Strawberries, 1861/1869
Paperboard, 0.468 x 0.731 (18 7/16 x 24 7/8)
Paul Mellon Collection
1965.16.211

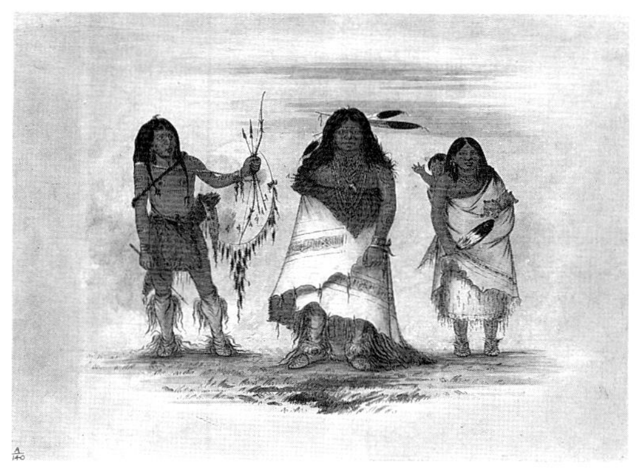

Camanchee Chief, His Wife, and a Warrior, 1861
Paperboard, 0.457 x 0.609 (18 x 24)
Inscribed at lower right: *Geo. Catlin. 1861*
Paul Mellon Collection
1965.16.47

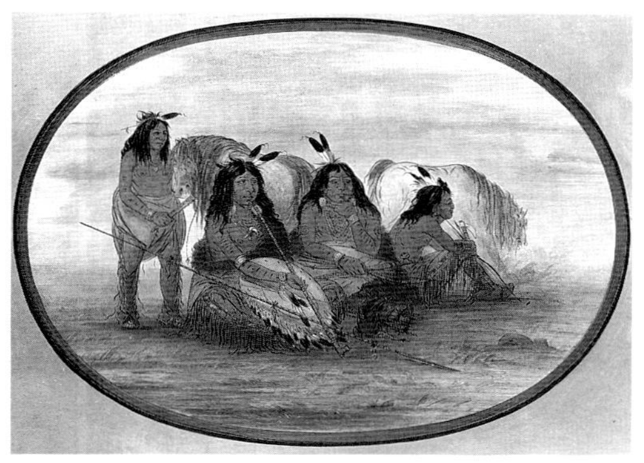

Camanchee Chief with Three Warriors, 1861/1869
Paperboard, 0.474 x 0.638 (18 11/16 x 25 1/8)
Paul Mellon Collection
1965.16.48

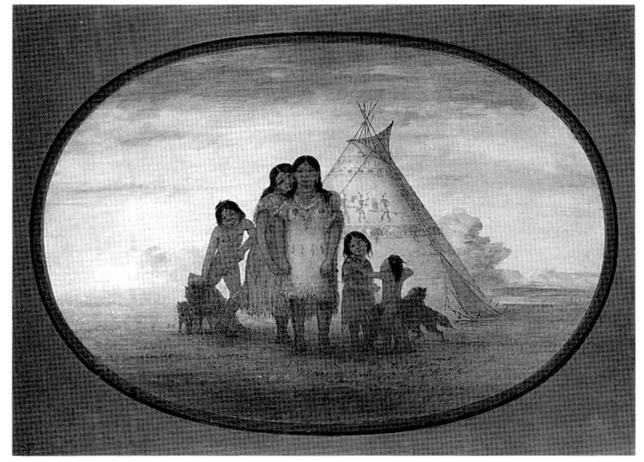

Camanchee Chief's Children and Wigwam, 1861/1869
Paperboard, 0.473 x 0.634 (18⅝ x 24¹⁵⁄₁₆)
Paul Mellon Collection
1965.16.49

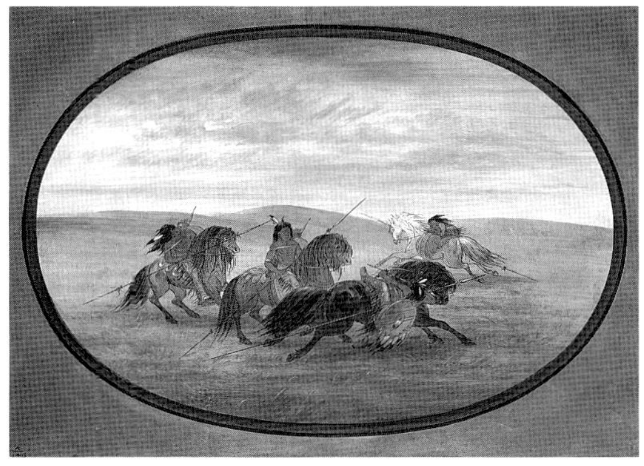

Camanchee Horsemanship, 1861/1869
Paperboard, 0.477 x 0.630 (18¾ x 24¾)
Paul Mellon Collection
1965.16.51

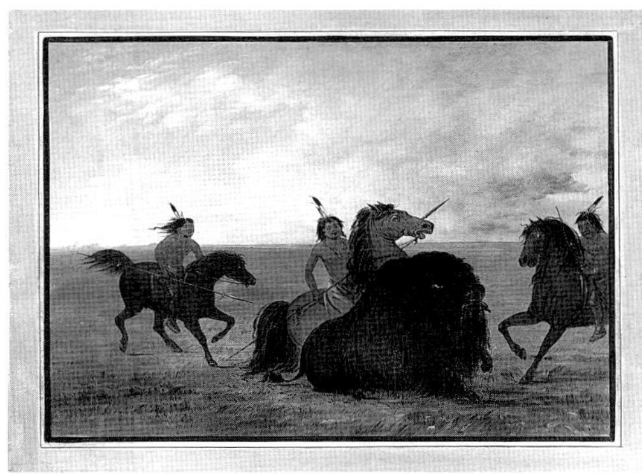

Camanchees Lancing a Buffalo Bull, 1861/1869
Paperboard, 0.465 x 0.617 (18⁵⁄₁₆ x 24⁵⁄₁₆)
Paul Mellon Collection
1965.16.204

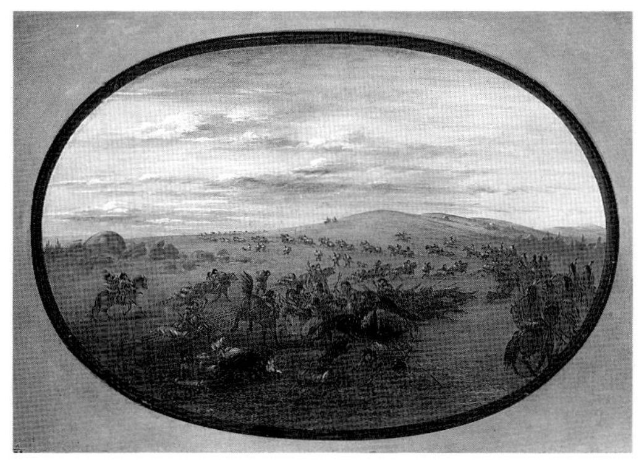

Camanchees Moving, 1861/1869
Paperboard, 0.465 x 0.627 (18⁵⁄₁₆ x 24¾)
Paul Mellon Collection
1965.16.53

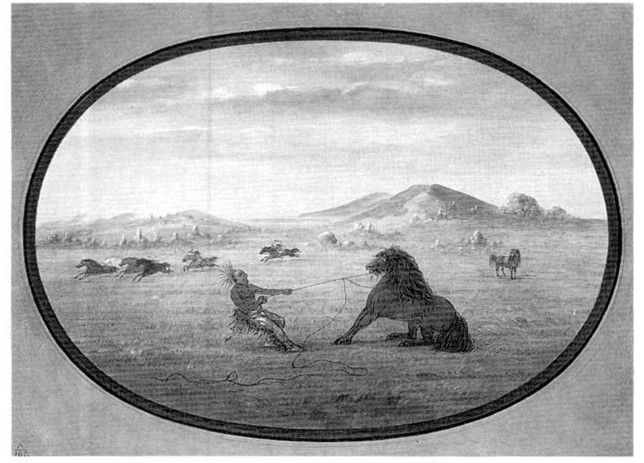

Catching Wild Horses—Pawnee,
1861/1869
Paperboard, 0.466 x 0.621 (18⅜ x 24½)
Paul Mellon Collection
1965.16.66

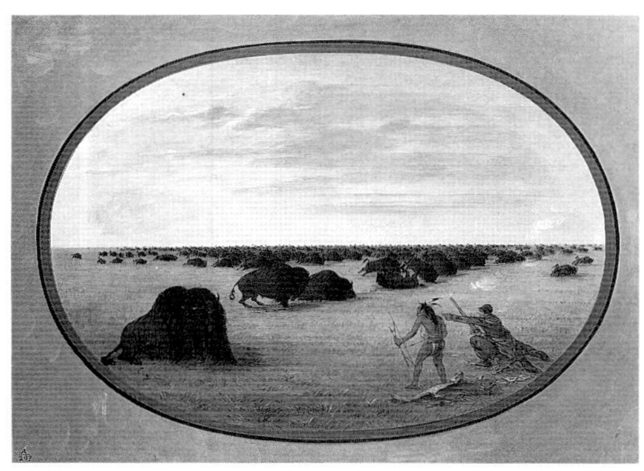

Catlin and Indian Attacking Buffalo,
1861/1869
Paperboard, 0.465 x 0.629
(18 5/16 x 24 13/16)
Paul Mellon Collection
1965.16.177

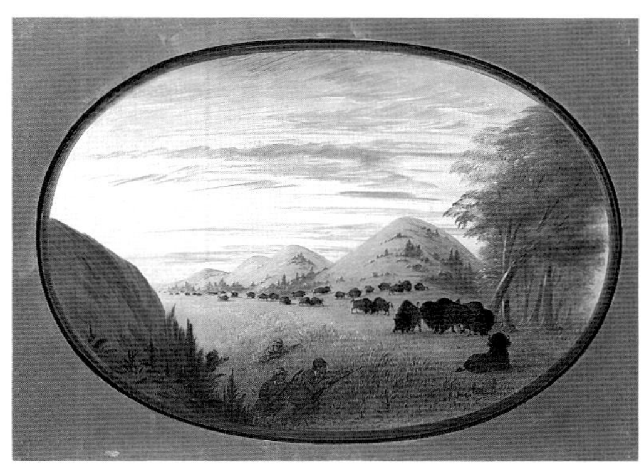

Catlin and Two Companions Shooting Buffalo, 1861/1869
Paperboard, 0.459 x 0.627
(18 1/16 x 24 11/16)
Paul Mellon Collection
1965.16.197

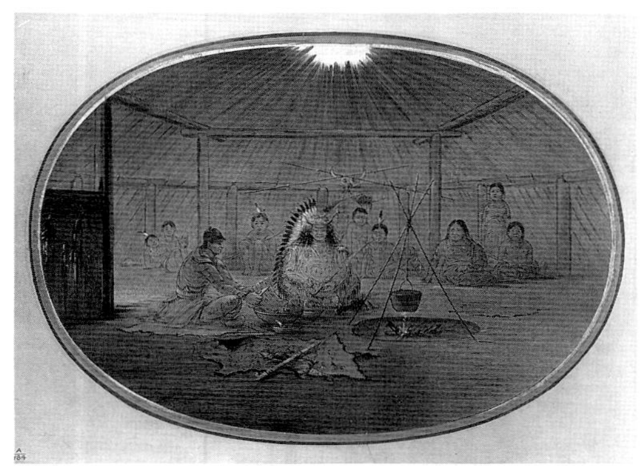

Catlin Feasted by the Mandan Chief,
1861/1869
Paperboard, 0.463 x 0.624 (18¼ x 24 9/16)
Paul Mellon Collection
1965.16.80

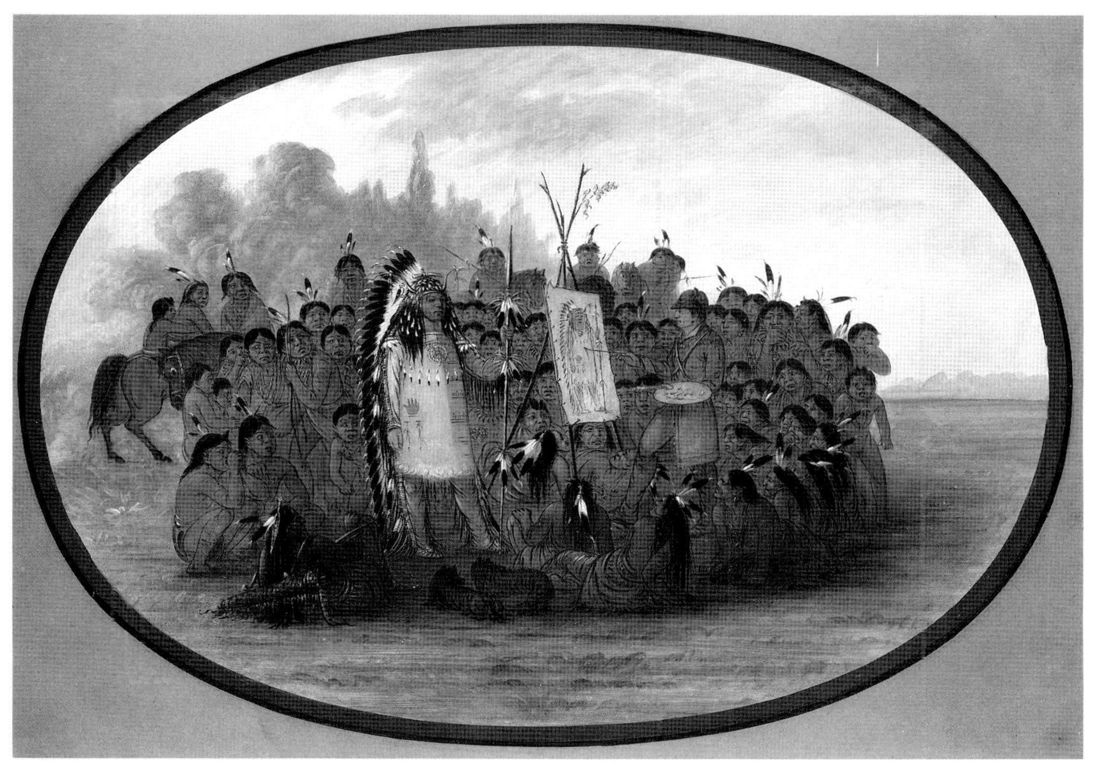

Catlin Painting the Portrait of Mah-to-toh-pa—Mandan, 1861/1869
Paperboard, 0.470 x 0.623 (18½ x 24)
Paul Mellon Collection
1965.16.184

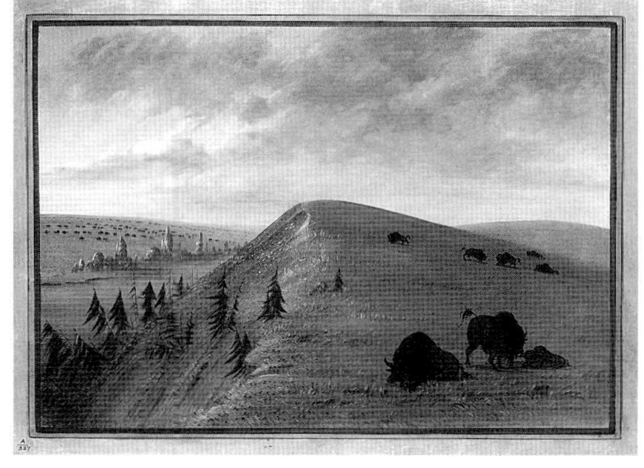

Cedar Bluffs, 1861/1869
Paperboard, 0.466 x 0.618 (18⅜ x 24$\frac{5}{16}$)
Paul Mellon Collection
1965.16.210

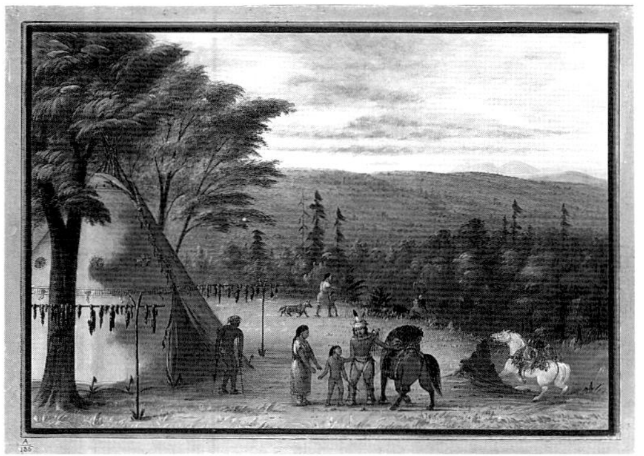

The Cheyenne Brothers Starting on Their Fall Hunt, 1861/1869
Paperboard, c.460 x 0.621 (18 1/8 x 24 7/16)
Paul Mellon Collection
1965.16.42

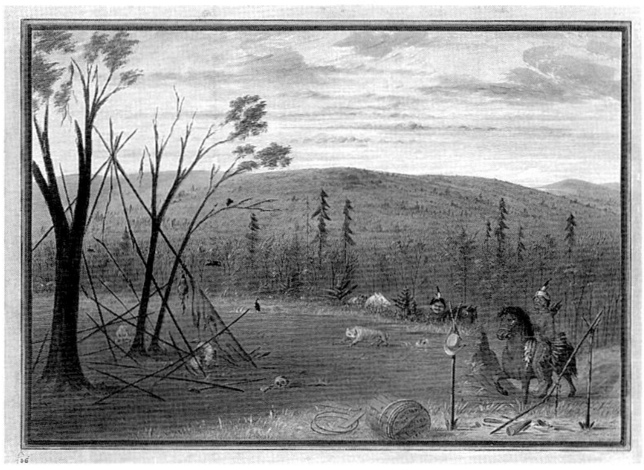

The Cheyenne Brothers Returning from Their Fall Hunt, 1861/1869
Paperboard, c.462 x 0.620 (18 1/4 x 24 5/8)
Paul Mellon Collection
1965.16.43

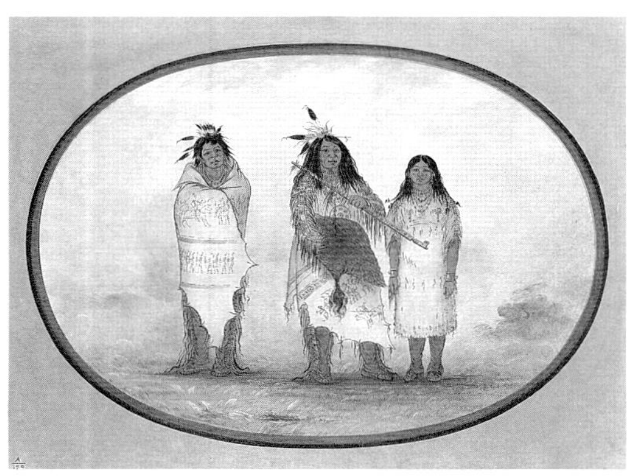

A Cheyenne Chief, His Wife, and a Medicine Man, 1861/1869
Paperboard, c.472 x 0.632 (18 9/16 x 24 7/8)
Paul Mellon Collection
1965.16.36

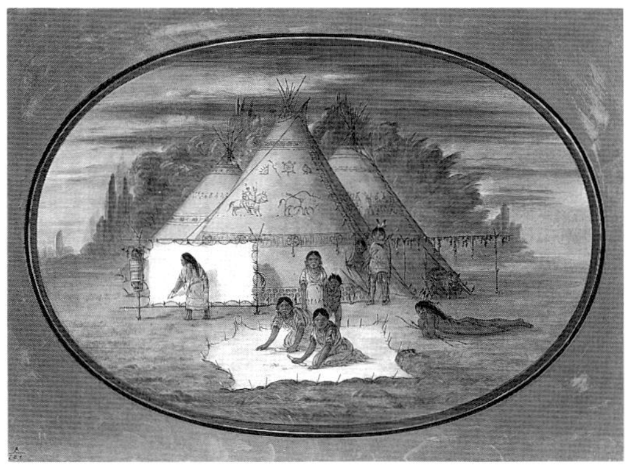

Cheyenne Village, 1861/1869
Paperboard, c.470 x 0.633 (18 1/2 x 24 7/8)
Paul Mellon Collection
1965.16.38

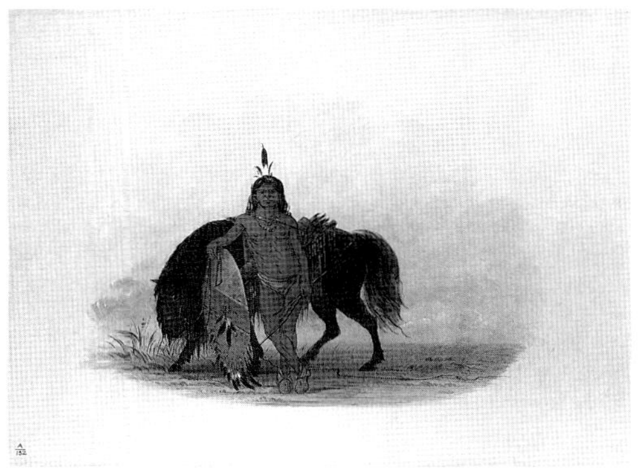

A Cheyenne Warrior Resting His Horse, 1861/1869
Paperboard, 0.467 x 0.613 (18 3/8 x 24 1/8)
Paul Mellon Collection
1965.16.39

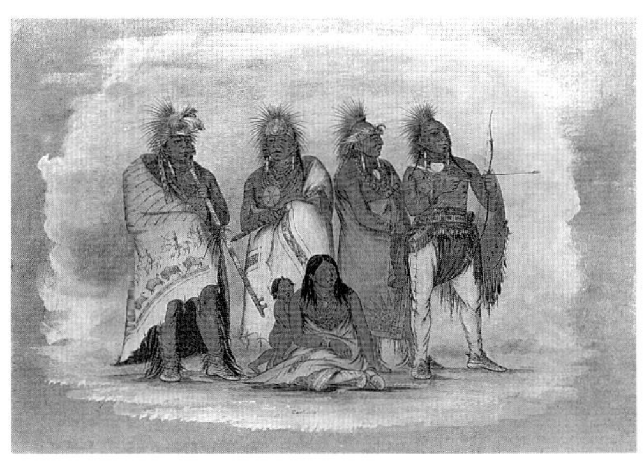

Chief and Members of the Konza Tribe, 1861/1869
Paperboard, 0.446 x 0.603 (17 9/16 x 24 1/8)
Inscribed at lower center: *Catlin p.*
Paul Mellon Collection
1965.16.311

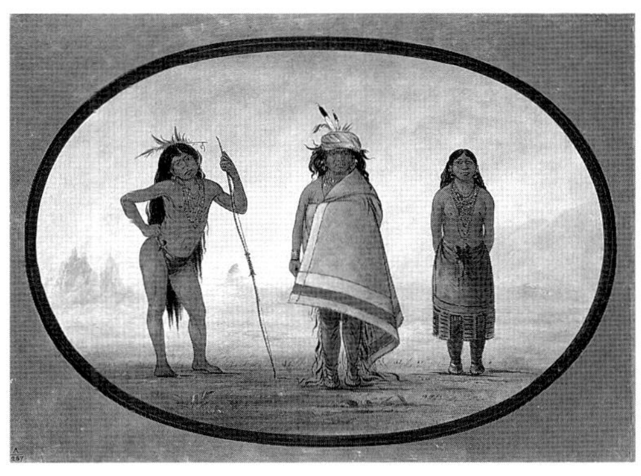

Cochimtee Chief, His Wife, and a Warrior, 1855/1869
Paperboard, 0.458 x 0.613 (18 x 24 1/8)
Paul Mellon Collection
1965.16.170

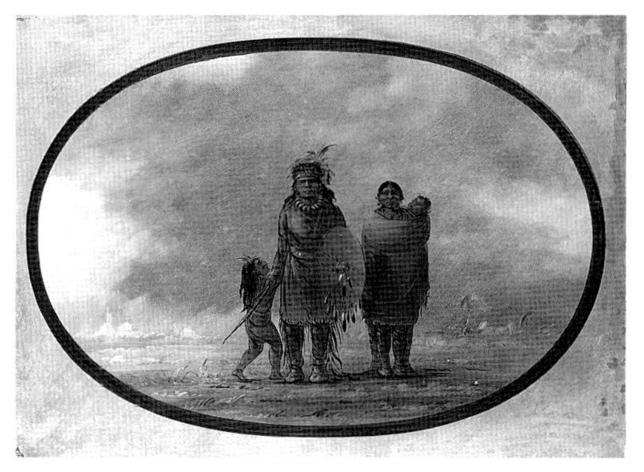

Copper Chief, His Wife, and Children, 1855/1869
Paperboard, 0.466 x 0.619 (18 5/16 x 24 3/8)
Paul Mellon Collection
1965.16.162

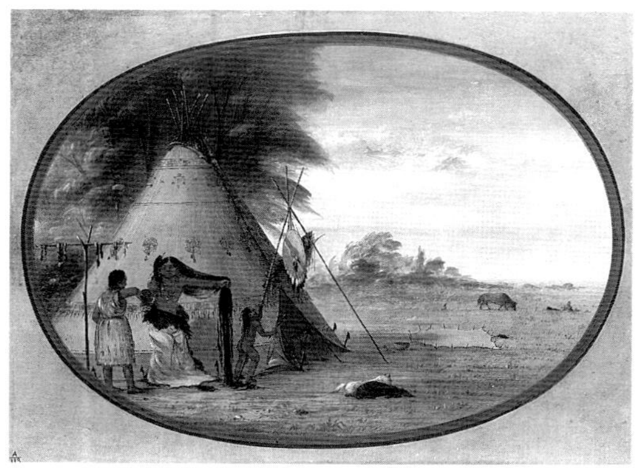

A Crow Chief at His Toilette, 1861/1869
Paperboard, 0.470 x 0.633 (18½ x 24⅞)
Paul Mellon Collection
1965.16.22

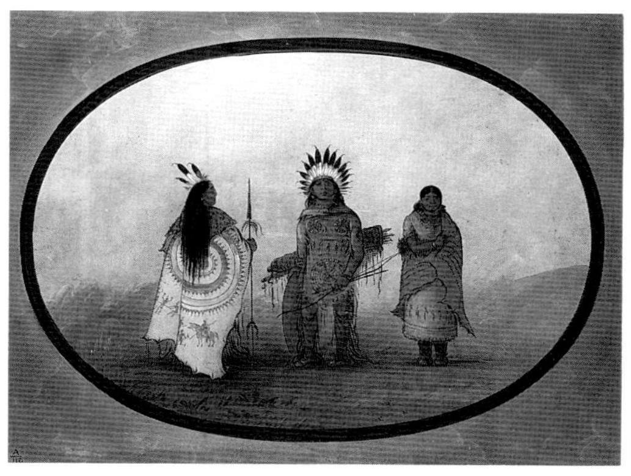

A Crow Chief, a Warrior, and His Wife, 1855/1869
Paperboard, 0.470 x 0.620 (18½ x 24⅜)
Paul Mellon Collection
1965.16.21

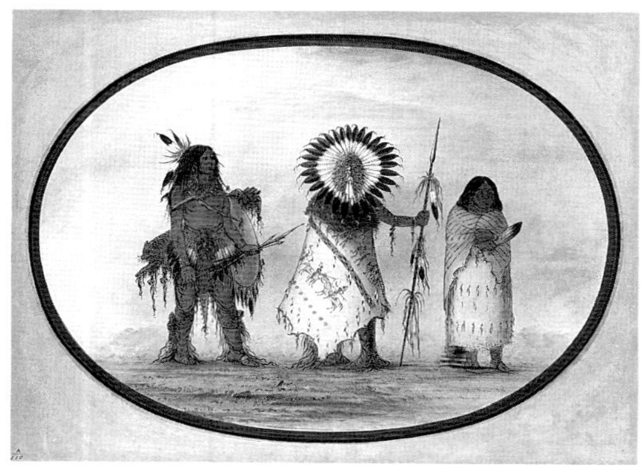

Crow Chief, His Wife, and a Warrior, 1861/1869
Paperboard, 0.463 x 0.621 (18¼ x 24 7/16)
Paul Mellon Collection
1965.16.19

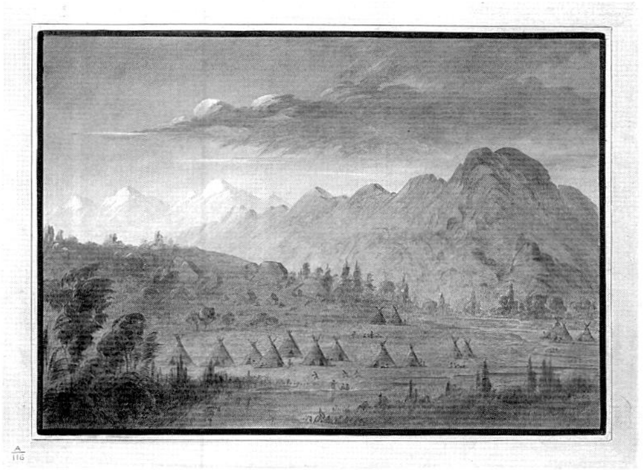

A Crow Village and the Salmon River Mountains, 1855/1869
Paperboard, c.468 x 0.625 (18 7/16 x 24⅝)
Paul Mellon Collection
1965.16.25

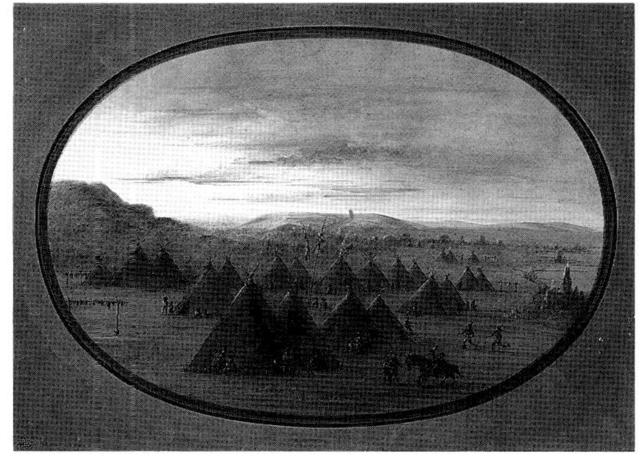

A Crow Village of Skin Tents on the Salmon River, 1855/1869
Paperboard, 0.470 x 0.628 (18½ x 24¾)
Paul Mellon Collection
1965.16.350

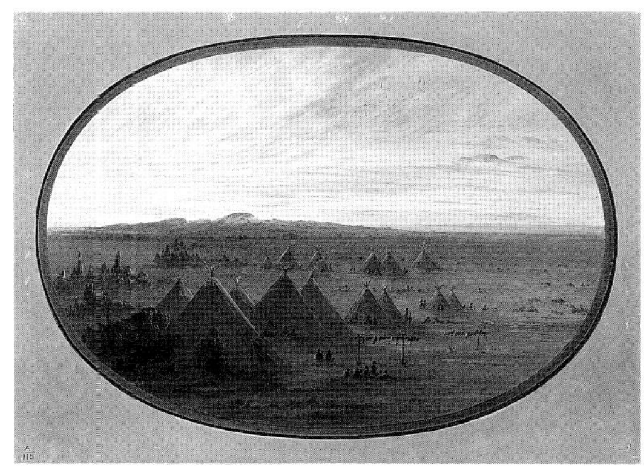

A Crow Village on the Salmon River, 1855/1869
Paperboard, 0.464 x 0.625 (18¼ x 24⅝)
Paul Mellon Collection
1965.16.24

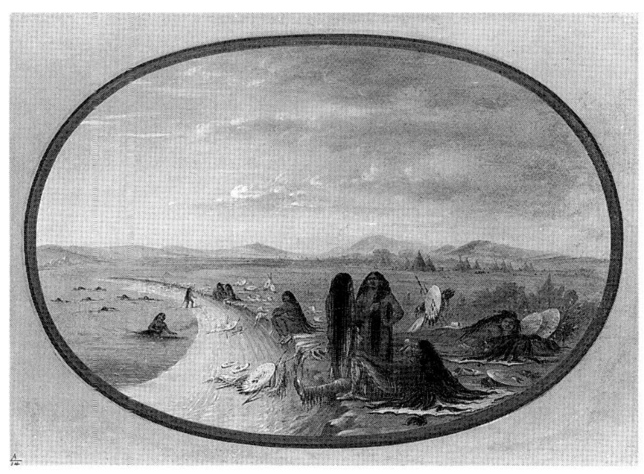

Crow Warriors Bathing, 1861/1869
Paperboard, 0.468 x 0.625 (18⅜ x 24⅝)
Paul Mellon Collection
1965.16.23

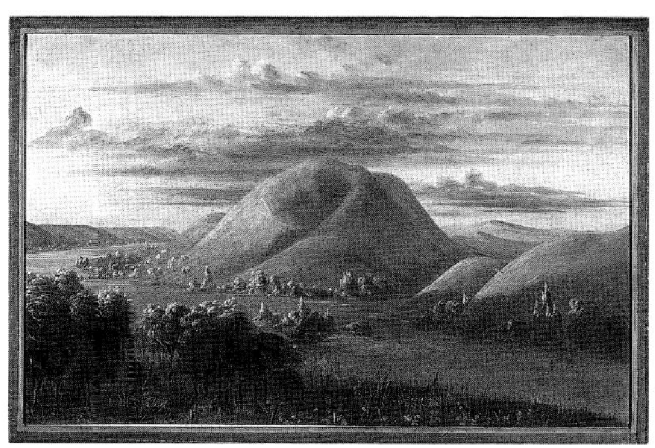

Curious Grassy Bluffs, St. Peter's River, 1861/1869
Canvas, 0.375 x 0.563 (14¾ x 22³⁄₁₆)
Paul Mellon Collection
1965.16.190

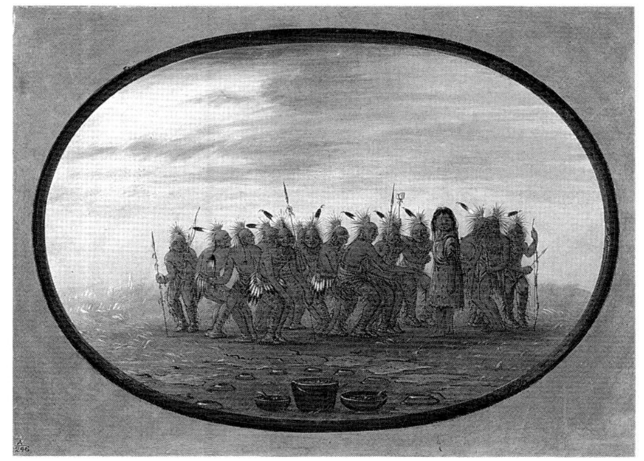

Dance to the Berdache—Saukie,
1861/1869
Paperboard, 0.470 x 0.632 (18½ x 24⅞)
Paul Mellon Collection
1965.16.133

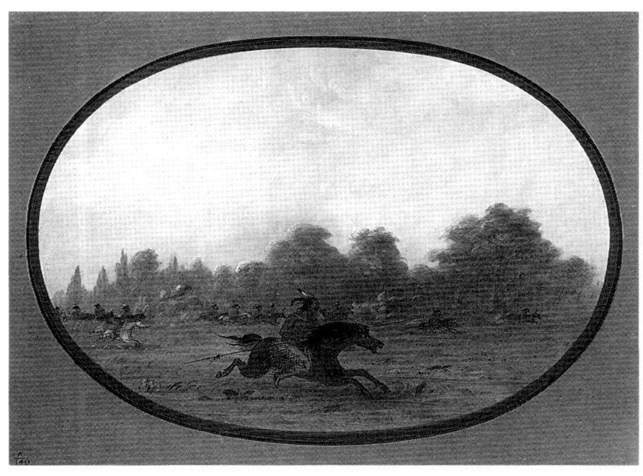

Defile of a Camanchee War Party,
1861/1869
Paperboard, 0.467 x 0.629 (18⅜ x 24¾)
Paul Mellon Collection
1965.16.54

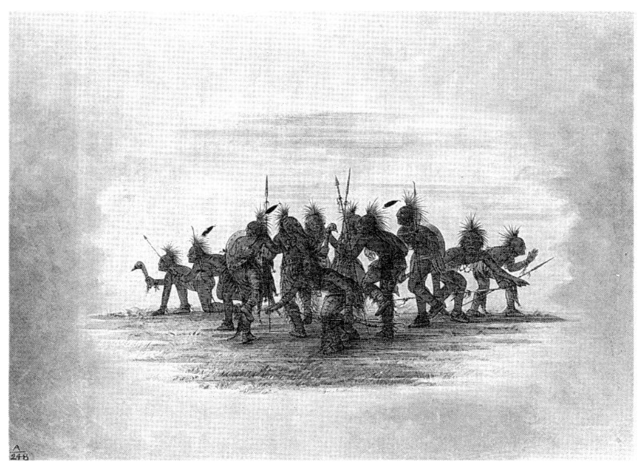

Discovery Dance—Saukie, 1861
Paperboard, c.442 x 0.595 (17 7/16 x 23½)
Inscribed at lower center: *Geo. Catlin. 1861*
Paul Mellon Collection
1965.16.135

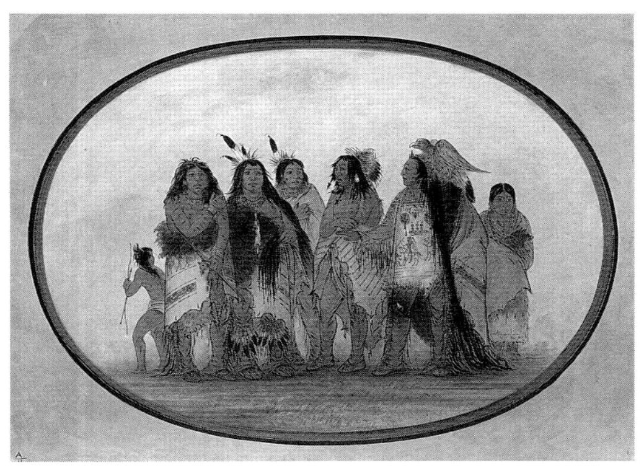

Distinguished Crow Indians, 1861/1869
Paperboard, c.471 x 0.635 (18 9/16 x 25)
Paul Mellon Collection
1965.16.20

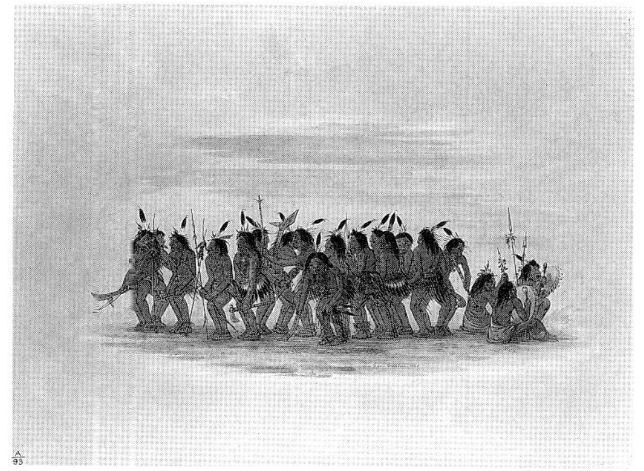

Dog Dance—Sioux, 1861
Paperboard, 0.467 x 0.622 (18⅜ x 24½)
Inscribed at lower center: *Geo. Catlin. 1861*
Paul Mellon Collection
1965.16.6

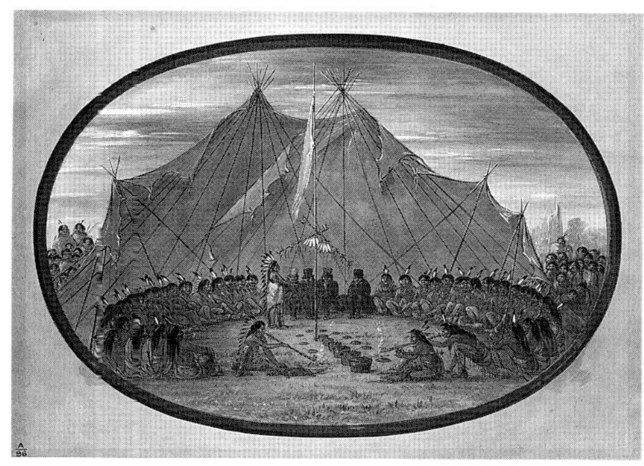

A Dog Feast—Sioux, 1861/1869
Paperboard, 0.473 x 0.638 (18⅝ x 25⅛)
Paul Mellon Collection
1965.16.8

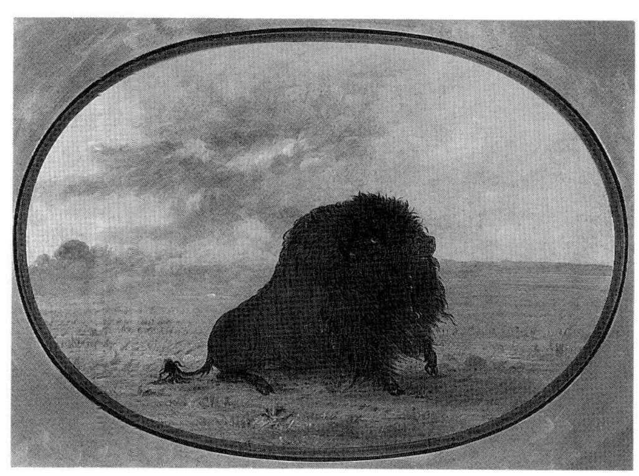

Dying Buffalo Bull, 1861/1869
Paperboard, 0.445 x 0.605 (17½ x 23⅞)
Paul Mellon Collection
1965.16.206

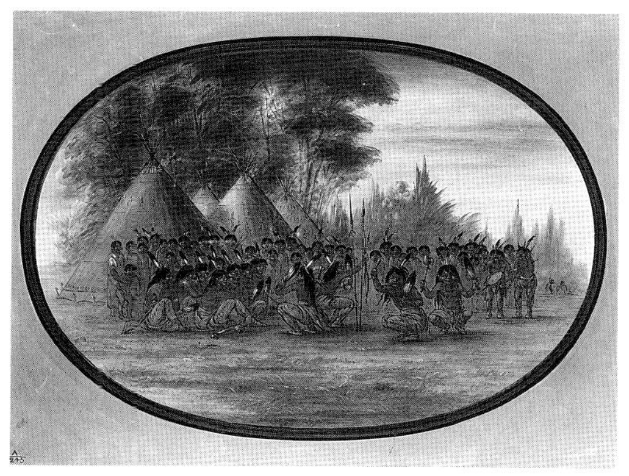

Eagle Dance—Choctaw, 1861/1869
Paperboard, 0.472 x 0.619 (18⅝ x 24⅜)
Paul Mellon Collection
1965.16.132

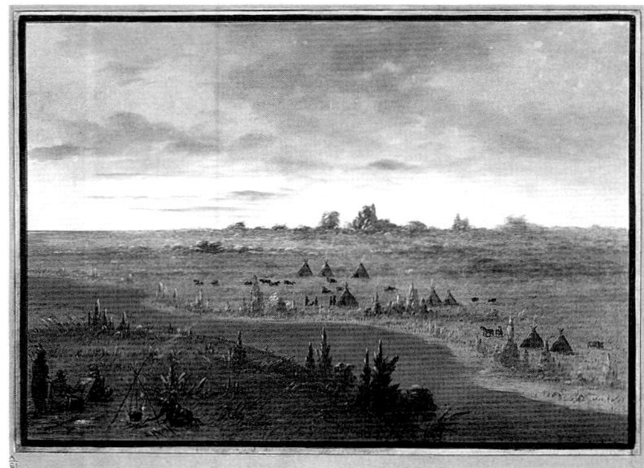

Encampment of Pawnee Indians at Sunset, 1861/1869
Paperboard, c.470 x 0.628 ($18\frac{1}{2}$ x $24\frac{3}{4}$)
Paul Mellon Collection
1965.16.65

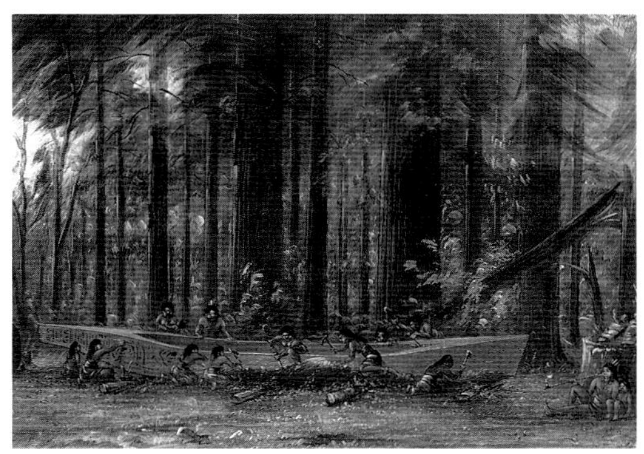

Excavating a Canoe—Nayas Indians, 1855/1869
Paperboard, c.465 x 0.617 ($18\frac{5}{16}$ x $24\frac{5}{16}$)
Paul Mellon Collection
1965.16.215

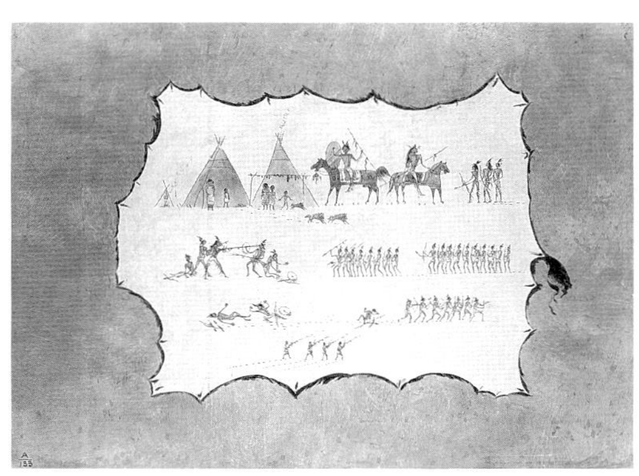

Facsimile of a Cheyenne Robe, 1861/1869
Paperboard, c.459 x 0.617 ($18\frac{1}{16}$ x $24\frac{5}{16}$)
Paul Mellon Collection
1965.16.40

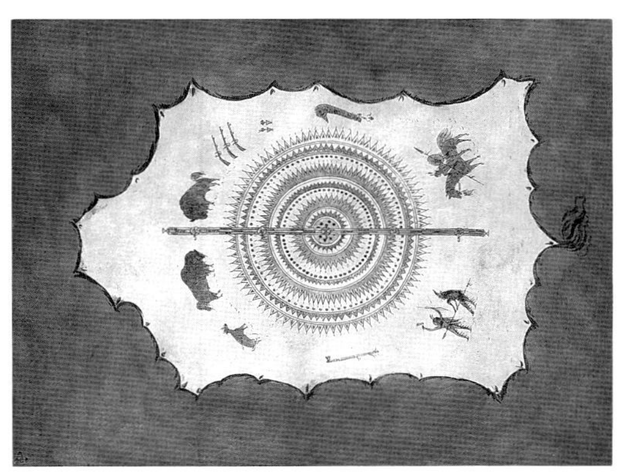

Facsimile of a Mandan Robe, 1861/1869
Paperboard, c.458 x 0.600 (18 x $23\frac{5}{8}$)
Paul Mellon Collection
1965.16.344

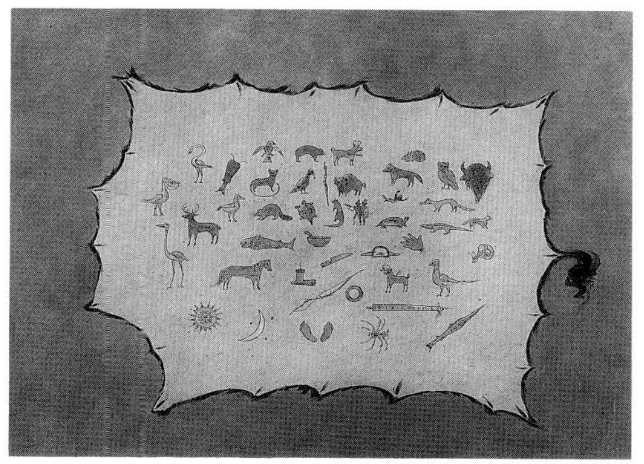

Facsimile of an Ojibbeway Robe, 1861/1869
Paperboard, 0.462 x 0.625 (18½ x 24¾)
Paul Mellon Collection
1965.16.140

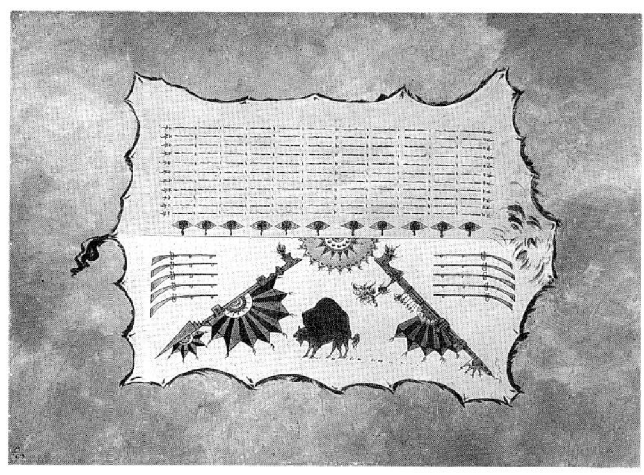

Facsimile of an Omaha Robe, 1861/1869
Paperboard, 0.462 x 0.625 (18½ x 24¾)
Paul Mellon Collection
1965.16.70

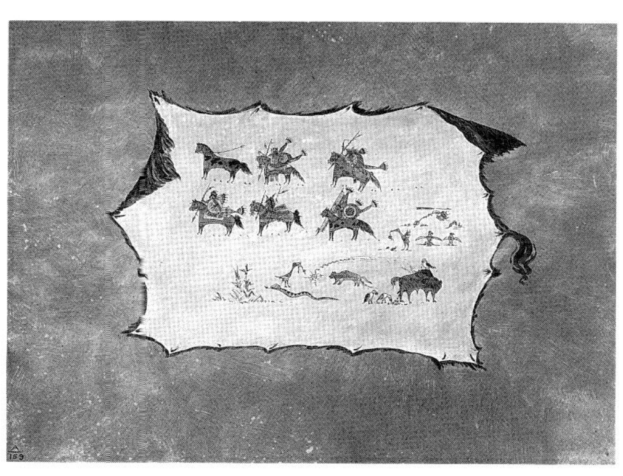

Facsimile of a Pawnee Doctor's Robe, 1861/1869
Paperboard, 0.460 x 0.623 (18⅛ x 24$^{9}/_{16}$)
Paul Mellon Collection
1965.16.63

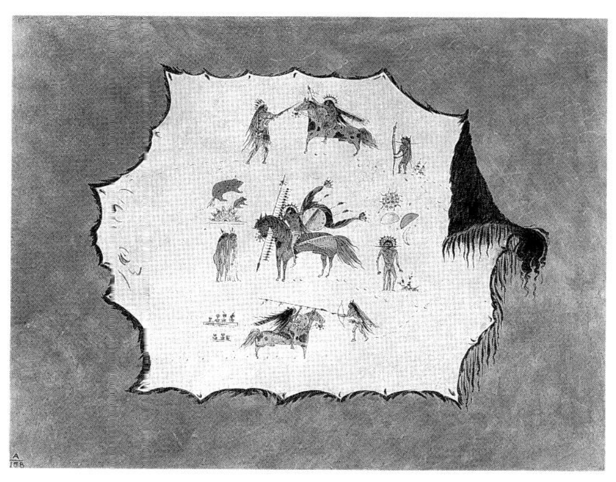

Facsimile of a Pawnee Doctor's Robe with Fantastic Professional Designs, 1861/1869
Paperboard, 0.466 x 0.612 (18⅜ x 24⅛)
Paul Mellon Collection
1965.16.62

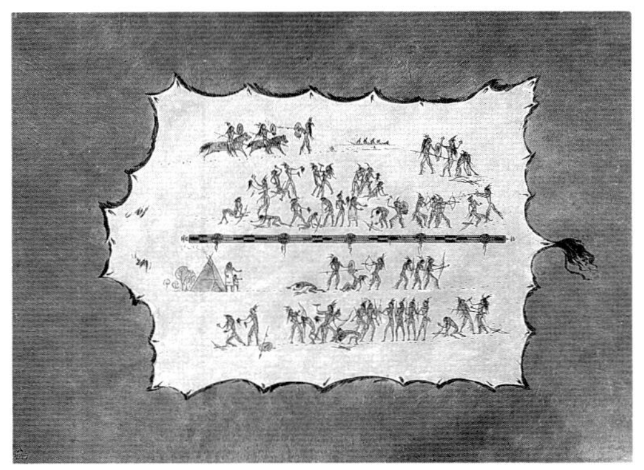

Facsimile of a Sioux Robe, 1861/1869
Paperboard, 0.462 x 0.617
(18 3/16 x 24 5/16)
Paul Mellon Collection
1965.16.16C

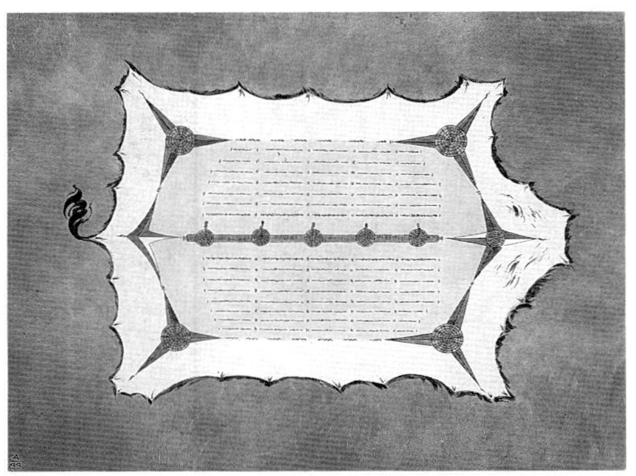

Facsimile of a Sioux Robe with Porcupine Quills, 1861/1869
Paperboard, 0.460 x 0.618 (18 1/8 x 24 5/16)
Paul Mellon Collection
1965.16.9

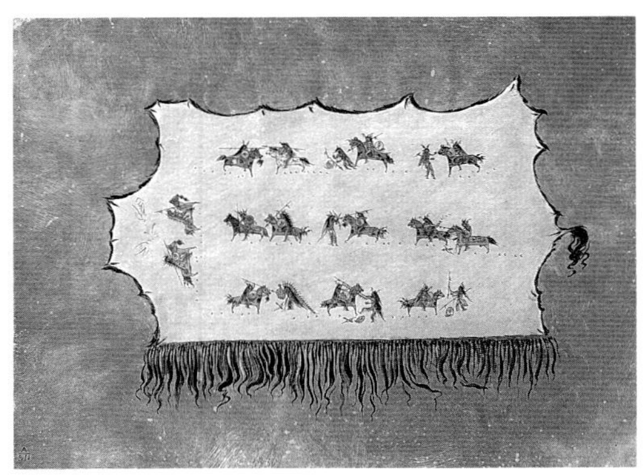

Facsimile of Chief Four Men's Robe—Mandan, 1861/1869
Paperboard, 0.460 x 0.620 (18 x 24 3/8)
Paul Mellon Collection
1965.16.188

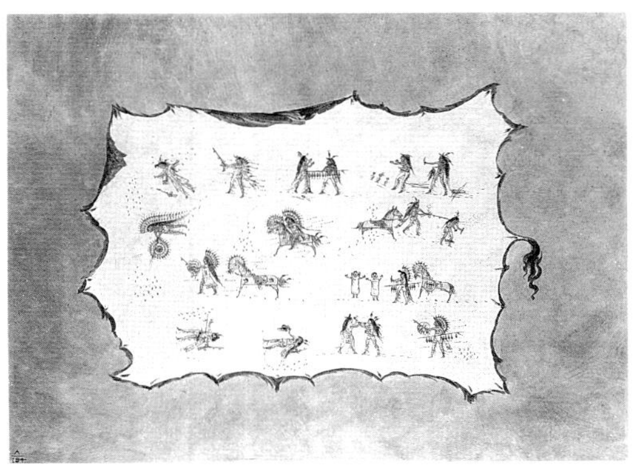

Facsimile of the Robe of Mah-to-toh-pa—Mandan, 1861/1869
Paperboard, 0.454 x 0.614 (17 7/8 x 24 3/16)
Paul Mellon Collection
1965.16.86

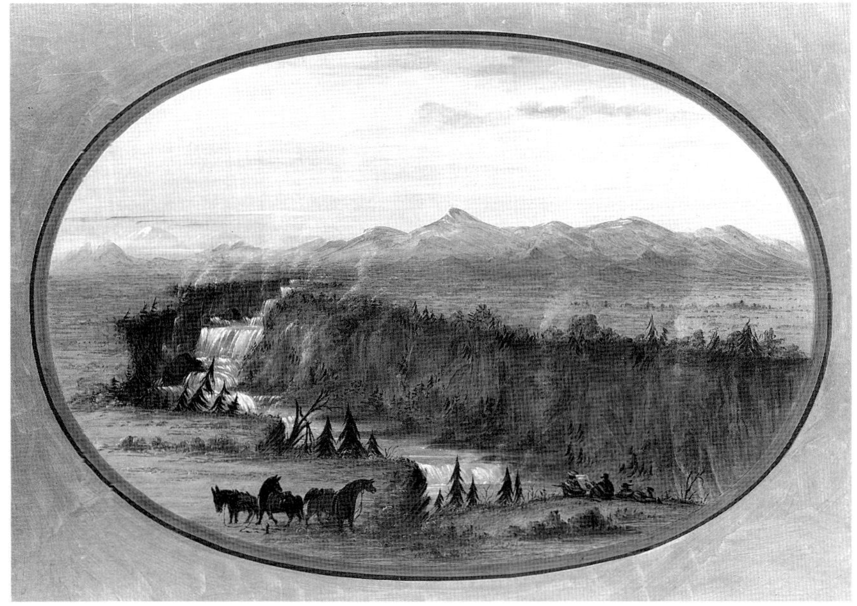

Falls of the Snake River, 1855/1869
Paperboard, 0.465 x 0.622 (18 5/16 x 24 1/2)
Paul Mellon Collection
1965.16.192

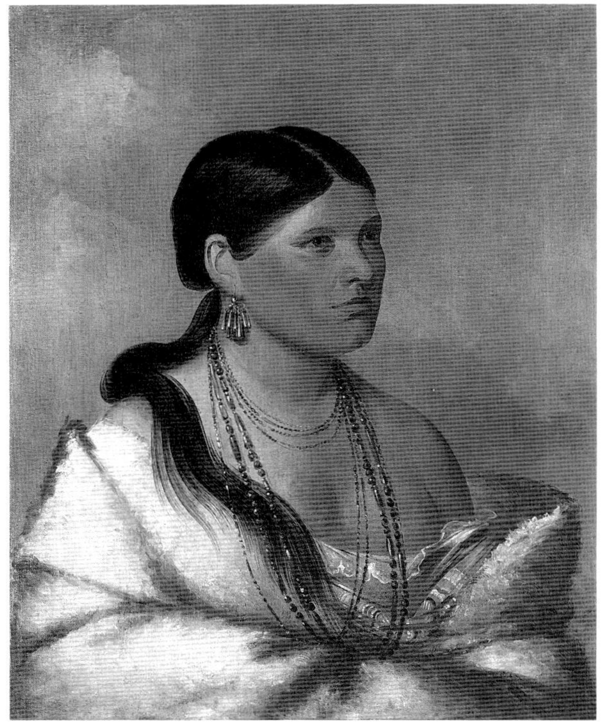

The Female Eagle—Shawano, 1830
Canvas, 0.722 x 0.590 (28 5/16 x 23 1/4)
Paul Mellon Collection
1965.16.348

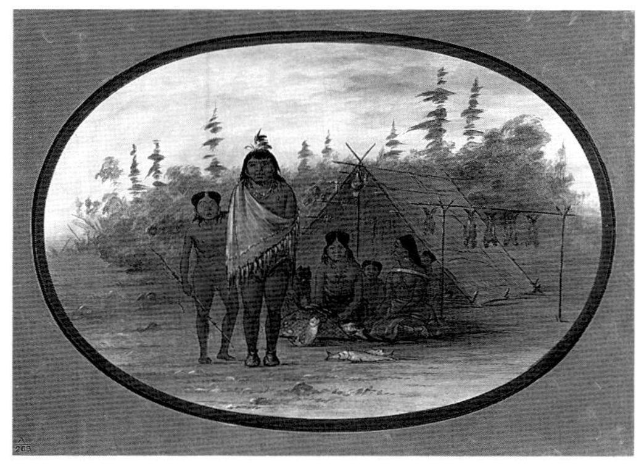

A Flathead Chief with His Family, 1855/1869
Paperboard, 0.463 x 0.625 (18 1/4 x 24 5/8)
Paul Mellon Collection
1965.16.151

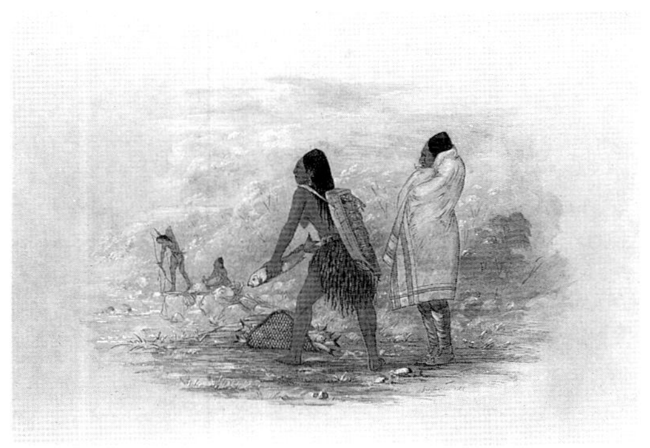

Flathead Indians, 1861
Paperboard, 0.457 x 0.604 (18 x 23 13/16)
Inscribed at lower right: *Geo. Catlin. 1861.*
Paul Mellon Collection
1965.16.149

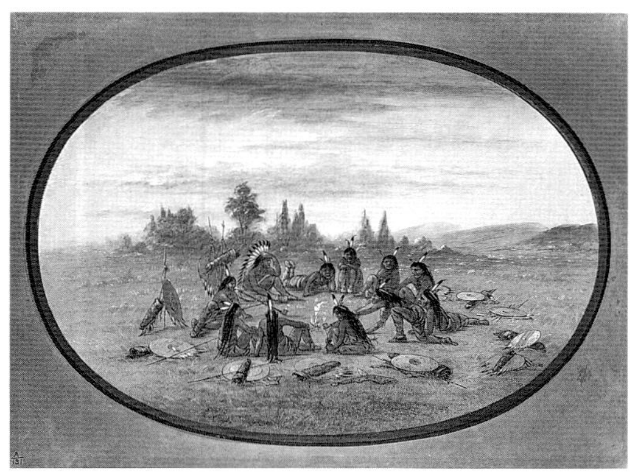

A Foot War Party in Council—Mandan, 1861/1869
Paperboard, 0.469 x 0.626 (18 5/16 x 24 5/8)
Paul Mellon Collection
1965.16.84

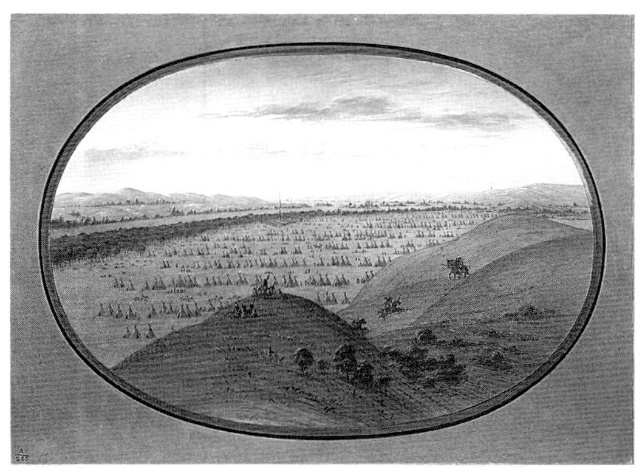

Fort Pierre, 1861/1869
Paperboard, 0.475 x 0.640 (18 11/16 x 25 [illegible]/16)
Paul Mellon Collection
1965.16.139

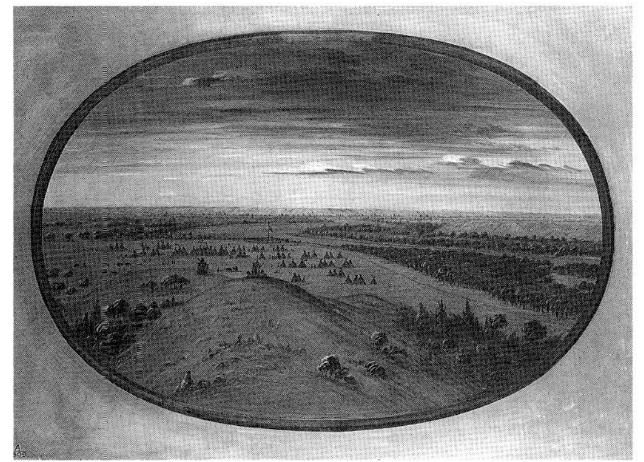

Fort Union, 1861/1869
Paperboard, 0.475 x 0.635 (18 11/16 x 25)
Paul Mellon Collection
1965.16.186

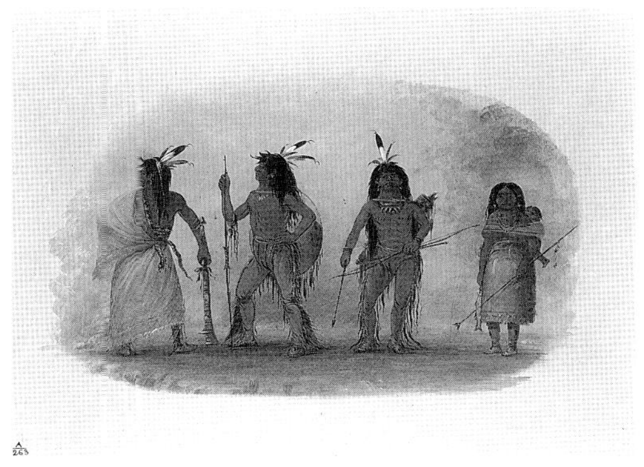

Four Apachee Indians, 1855/1869
Paperboard, 0.472 x 0.626
(18 5/8 x 24 11/16)
Paul Mellon Collection
1965.16.146

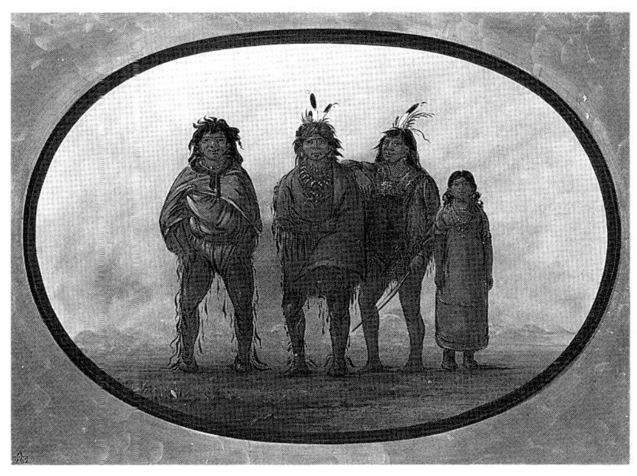

Four Dogrib Indians, 1855/1869
Paperboard, 0.456 x 0.617
(17 15/16 x 24 5/16)
Paul Mellon Collection
1965.16.165

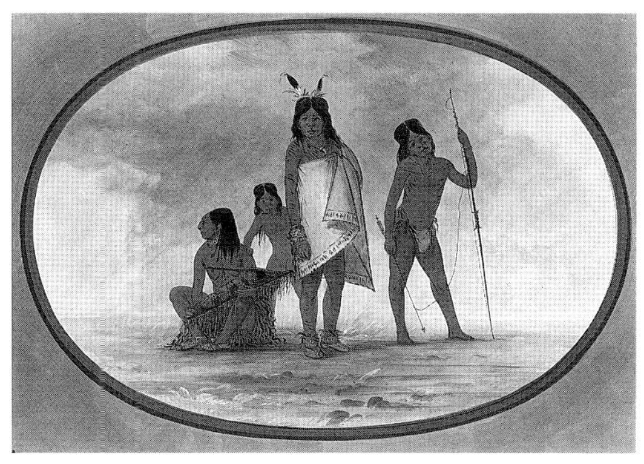

Four Flathead Indians, 1855/1869
Paperboard, 0.470 x 0.628 (18 1/2 x 24 3/4)
Paul Mellon Collection
1965.16.150

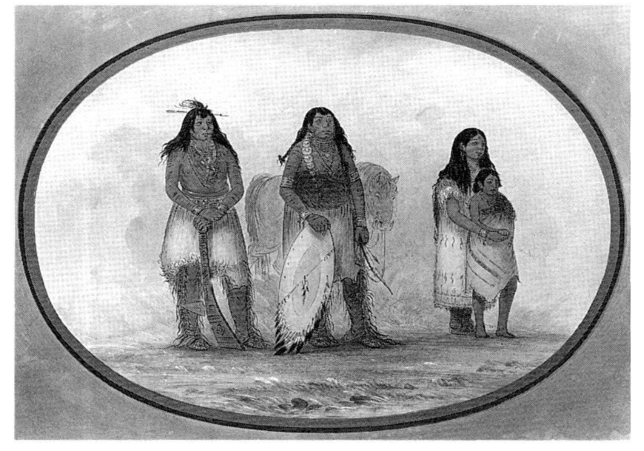

Four Kiowa Indians, 1861/1869
Paperboard, 0.469 x 0.633
(18 7/16 x 24 15/16)
Paul Mellon Collection
1965.16.44

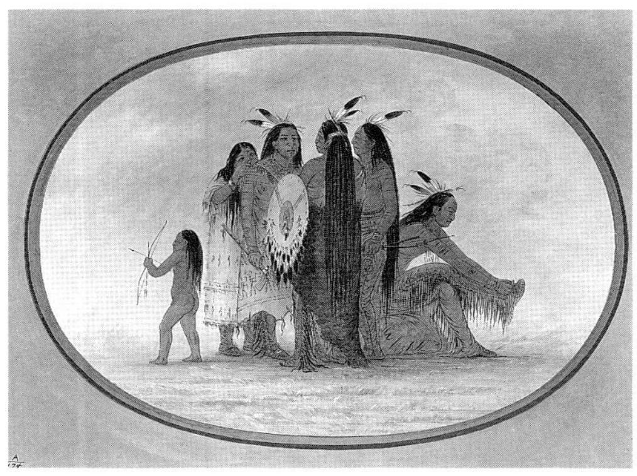

Four Mandan Warriors, a Girl, and a Boy, 1861/1869
Paperboard, 0.472 x 0.630
(18 9/16 x 24 13/16)
Paul Mellon Collection
1965.16.74

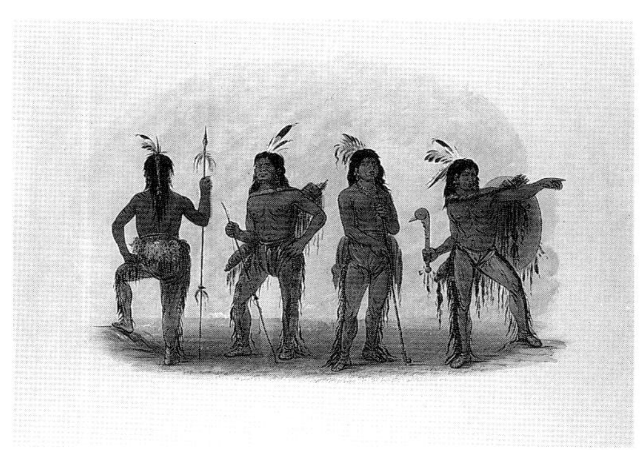

Four Navaho Warriors, 1861/1869
Paperboard, 0.464 x 0.620 (18 1/4 x 27 7/16)
Paul Mellon Collection
1965.16.148

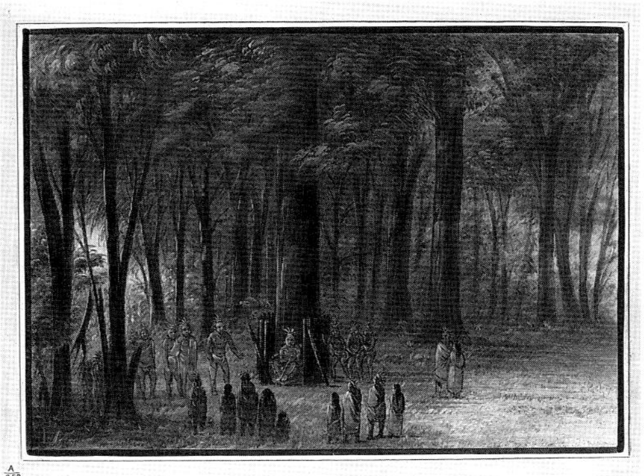

Funeral of Black Hawk—Saukie, 1861/1869
Paperboard, 0.462 x 0.607 (18 3/16 x 23 7/8)
Paul Mellon Collection
1965.16.142

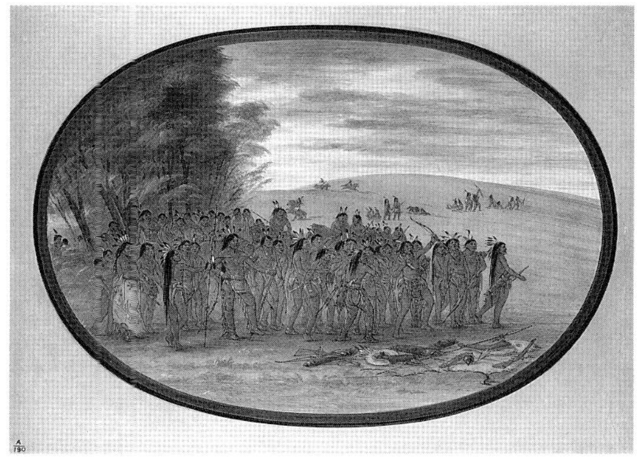

Game of the Arrow—Mandan, 1861/1869
Paperboard, 0.478 x 0.638
(18 13/16 x 24 15/16)
Paul Mellon Collection
1965.16.83

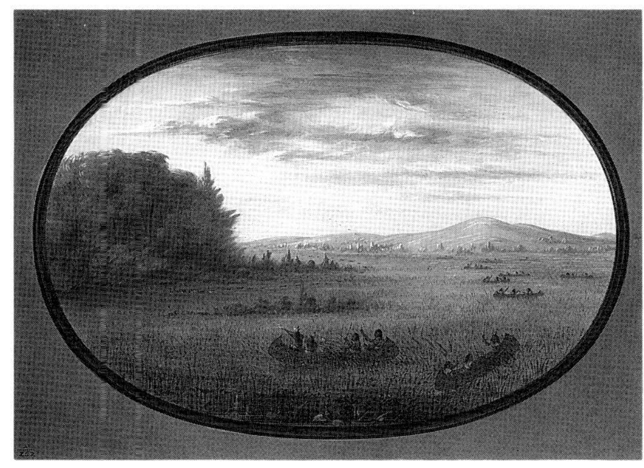

Gathering Wild Rice—Winnebago,
1861/1869
Paperboard, 0.467 x 0.627
(18 3/8 x 24 11/16)
Paul Mellon Collection
1965.16.138

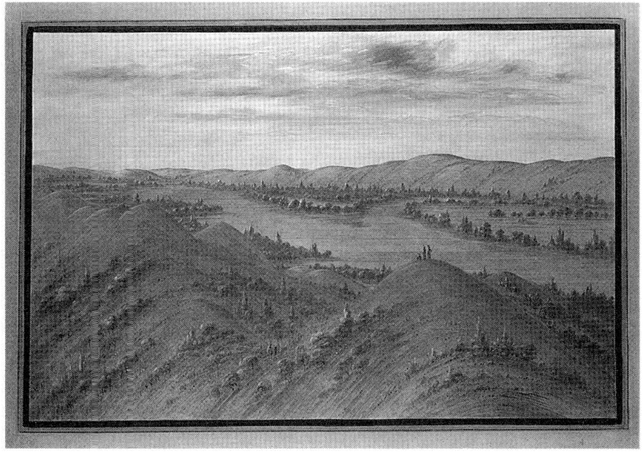

Grassy Bluffs, Upper Missouri, 1861/1869
Paperboard, 0.450 x 0.625 (17 3/4 x 24 3/4)
Paul Mellon Collection
1965.16.193

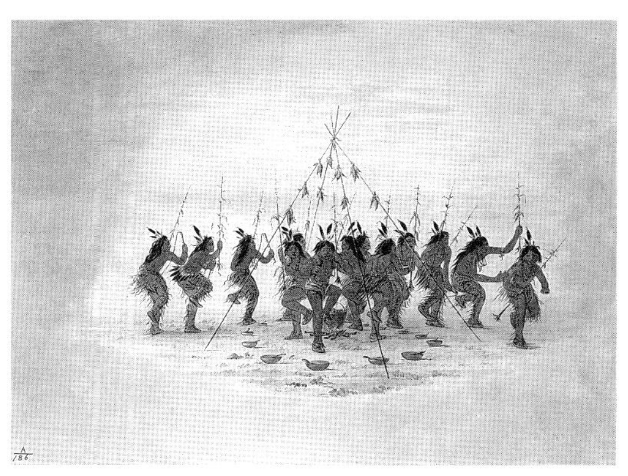

Green Corn Dance—Minatarrees, 1861
Paperboard, 0.452 x 0.600
(17 13/16 x 23 5/8)
Inscribed at lower center:
Geo. Catlin. 1861.
Paul Mellon Collection
1965.16.81

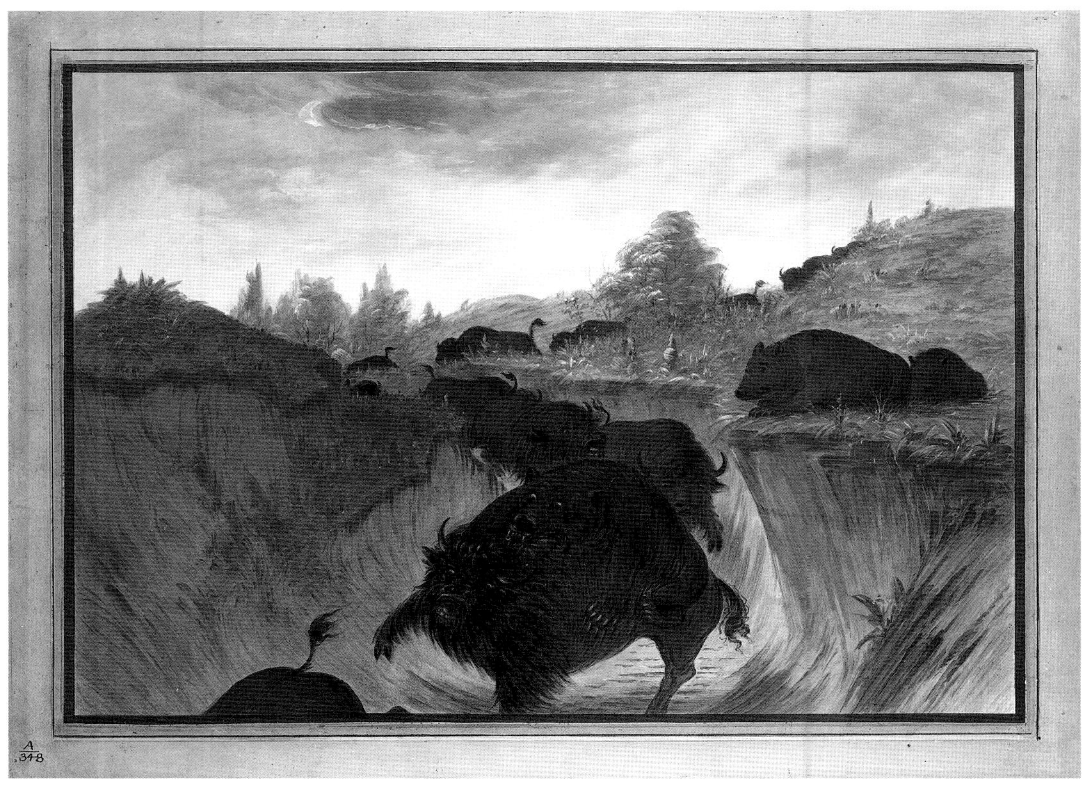

Grizzly Bears Attacking Buffalo, 1861/1869
Paperboard, 0.465 x 0.622 (18 3/8 x 24)
Paul Mellon Collection
1965.16.218

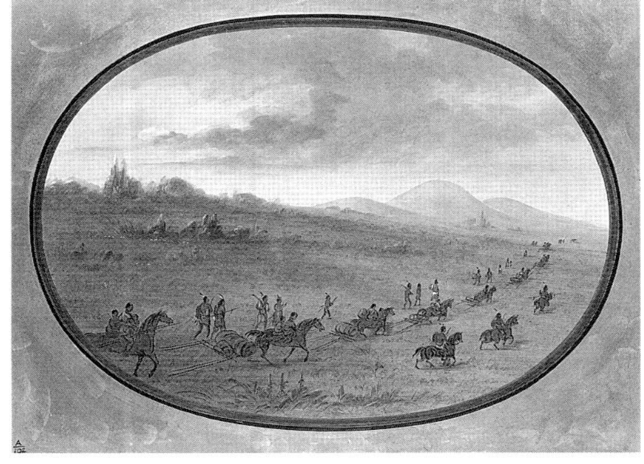

Halsey's Bluff—Sioux Indians on the March, 1861/1869
Paperboard, 0.465 x 0.618 (18 5/16 x 24 5/16)
Paul Mellon Collection
1965.16.13

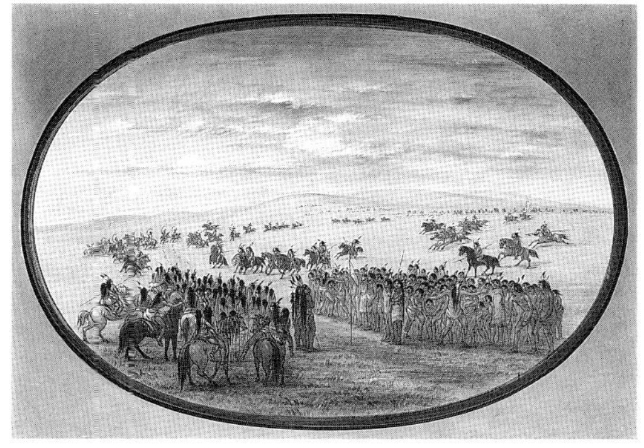

Horse Racing—Minatarrees, 1861/1869
Paperboard, 0.469 x 0.635 (18 7/16 x 25)
Paul Mellon Collection
1965.16.183

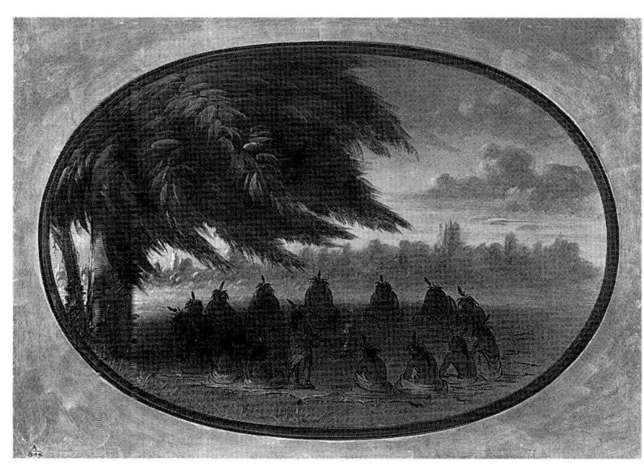

An Indian Council—Sioux, 1861/1869
Paperboard, 0.470 x 0.632 (18 1/2 x 24 7/8)
Paul Mellon Collection
1965.16.217

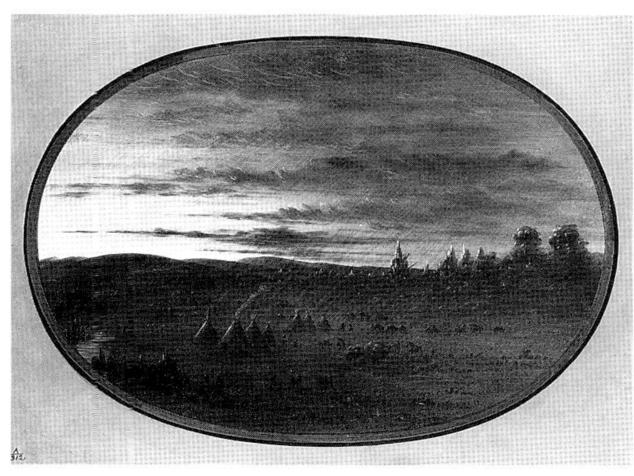

An Indian Encampment at Sunset, 1861/1869
Paperboard, 0.461 x 0.626 (18 1/8 x 24 5/8)
Paul Mellon Collection
1965.16.189

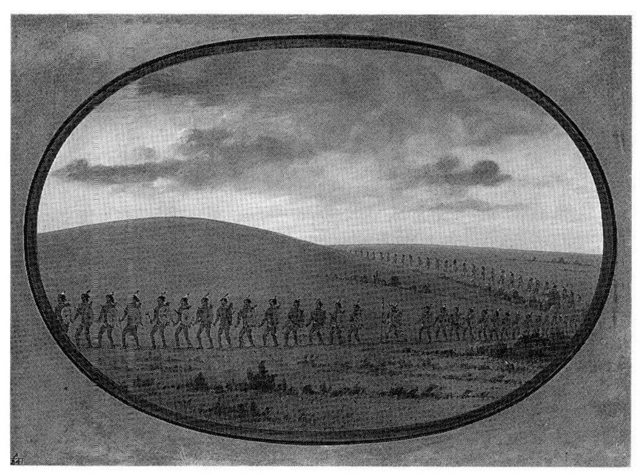

Indian File—Iowa, 1861/1869
Paperboard, 0.467 x 0.618 (18 3/8 x 24 3/8)
Paul Mellon Collection
1965.16.212

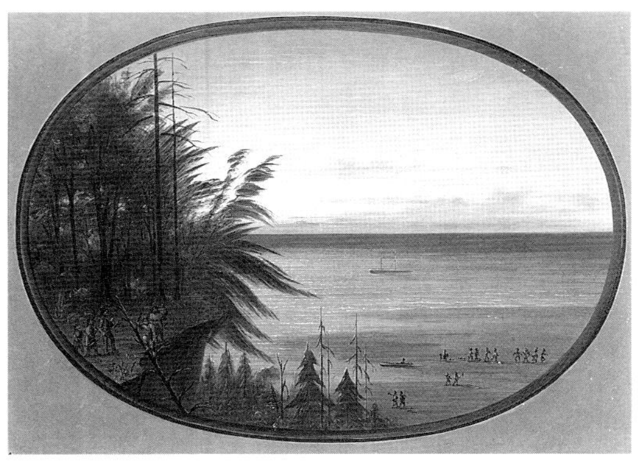

An Indian Ladder—Nayas Indians, 1855/1869
Paperboard, c.463 x 0.625 (18¼ x 24⅝)
Paul Mellon Collection
1965.16.221

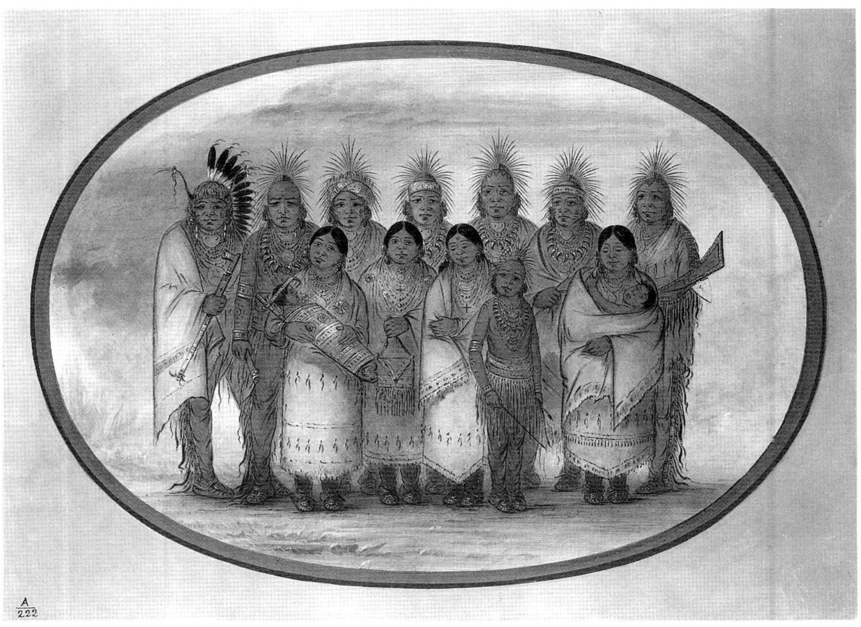

Iowa Indians Who Visited London and Paris, 1861/1869
Paperboard, 0.471 x 0.630 (18½ x 24⅞)
Paul Mellon Collection
1965.16.111

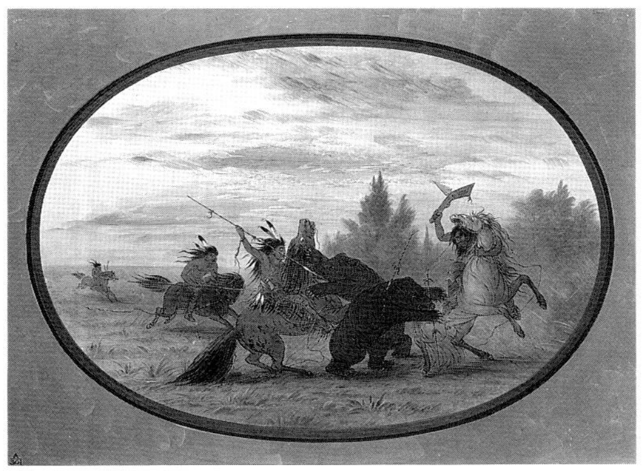

K'nisteneux Indians Attacking Two Grizzly Bears, 1861/1869
Paperboard, 0.473 x 0.635 (18⅝ x 25)
Paul Mellon Collection
1965.16.181

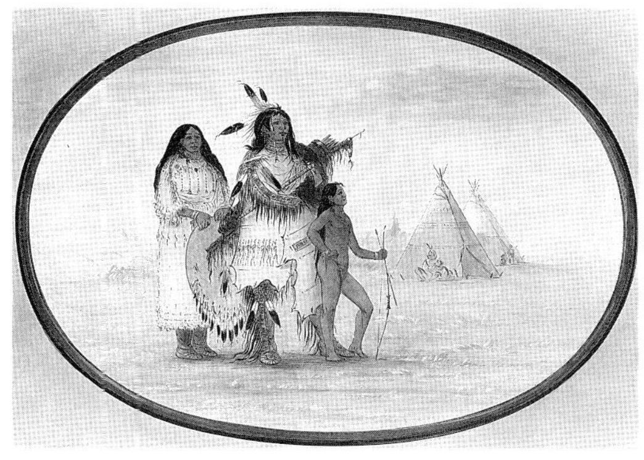

A K'nisteneux Warrior and Family,
1861/1869
Paperboard, 0.470 x 0.638 (18½ x 25⅓)
Paul Mellon Collection
1965.16.124

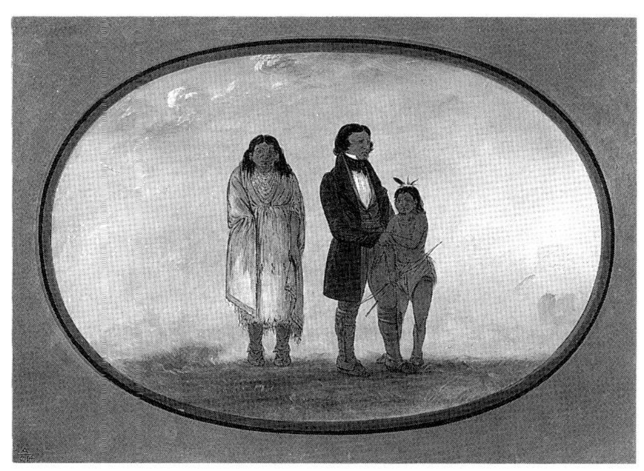

Kaskaskia Chief, His Mother, and Son,
1861/1869
Paperboard, 0.477 x 0.638
(18¹³⁄₁₆ x 25⅛)
Paul Mellon Collection
1965.16.103

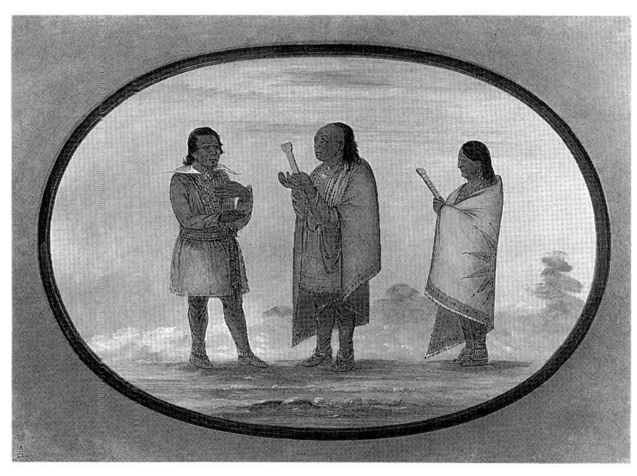

Kickapoo Indians Preaching and Praying,
1861/1869
Paperboard, 0.473 x 0.639 (18⅝ x 25⅛)
Paul Mellon Collection
1965.16.121

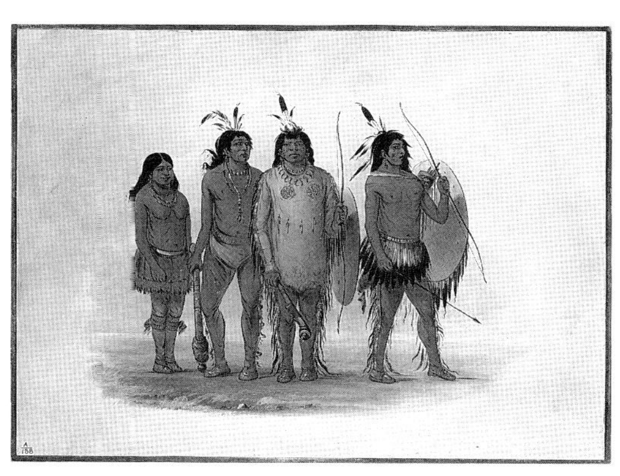

Kiowa Chief, His Wife, and Two Warriors, 1861/1869
Paperboard, 0.456 x 0.605
(17¹⁵⁄₁₆ x 23¹³⁄₁₆)
Paul Mellon Collection
1965.16.45

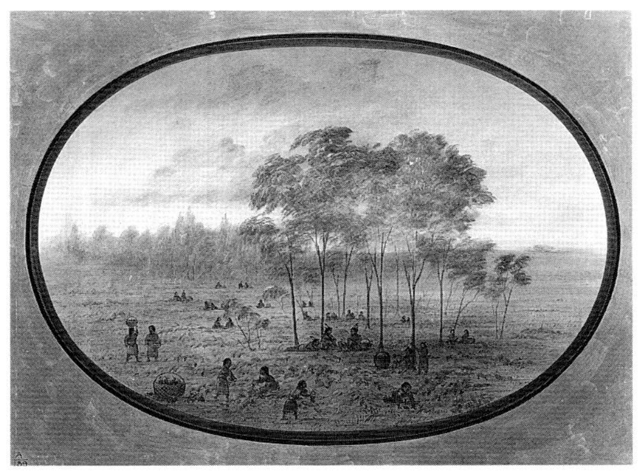

Kiowa Indians Gathering Wild Grapes, 1861/1869
Paperboard, 0.466 x 0.628 (18³⁄₈ x 24¹¹⁄₁₆)
Paul Mellon Collection
1965.16.46

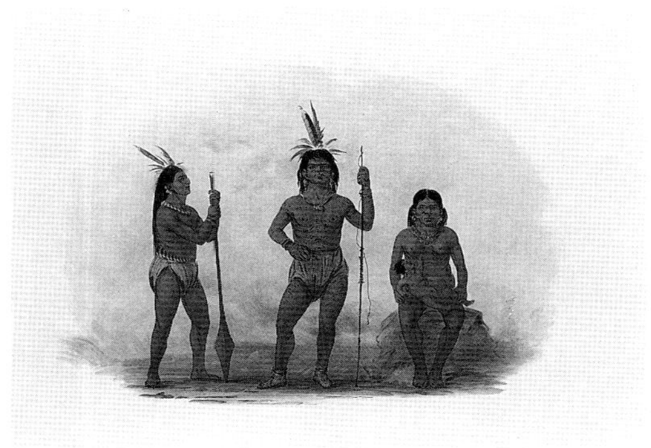

Klahoquaht Chief, His Wife, and Son, 1855/1869
Paperboard, 0.467 x 0.625 (18³⁄₈ x 24⁵⁄₈)
Paul Mellon Collection
1965.16.157

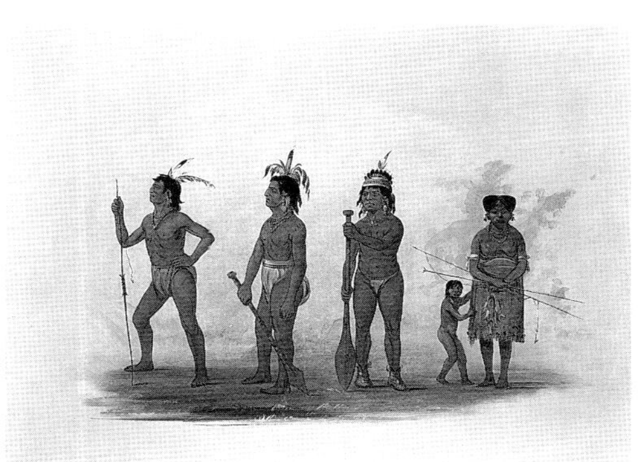

Klatsop Indians, 1855/1869
Paperboard, 0.463 x 0.615 (18¼ x 24³⁄₁₆)
Paul Mellon Collection
1965.16.158

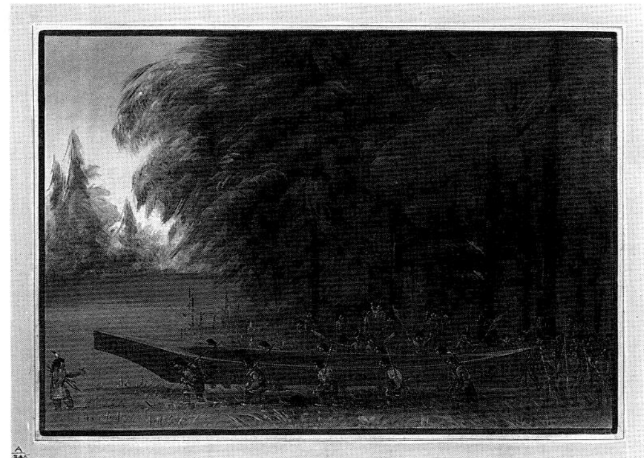

Launching a Canoe—Nayas Indians, 1855/1869
Paperboard, 0.464 x 0.621 (18¼ x 24⁷⁄₁₆)
Paul Mellon Collection
1965.16.216

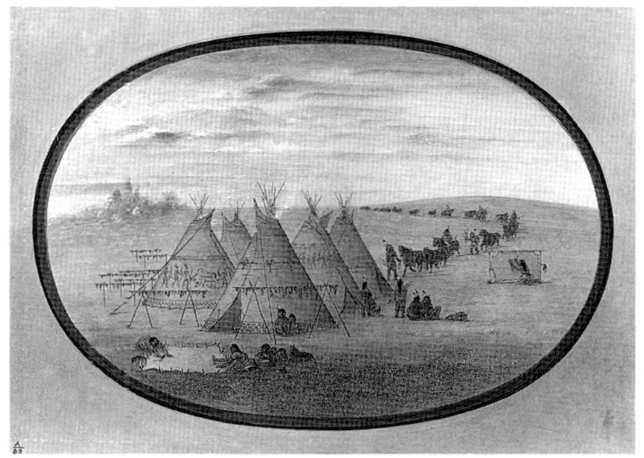

A Little Sioux Village, 1861/1869
Paperboard, 0.476 x 0.638 (18¾ x 25⅛)
Paul Mellon Collection
1965.16.4

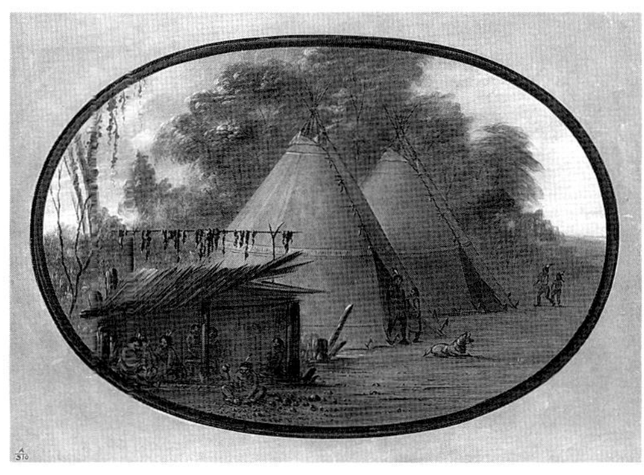

Making Flint Arrowheads—Apachees, 1855/1869
Paperboard, 0.469 x 0.630 (18 7/16 x 24 13/16)
Paul Mellon Collection
1965.16.187

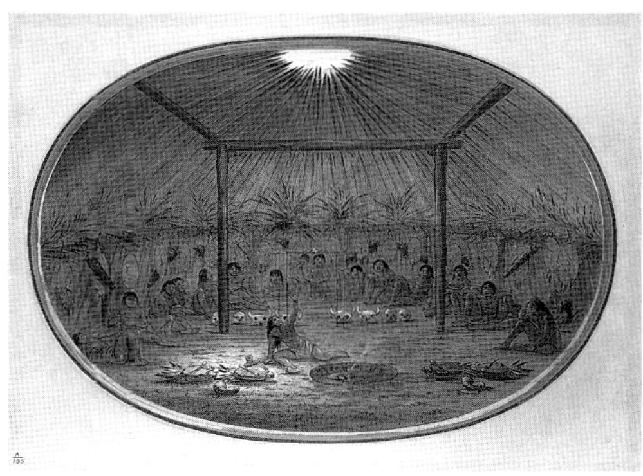

Mandan Ceremony—The Water Sinks Down, 1861/1869
Paperboard, 0.472 x 0.637 (18⅜ x 25⅛)
Paul Mellon Collection
1965.16.87

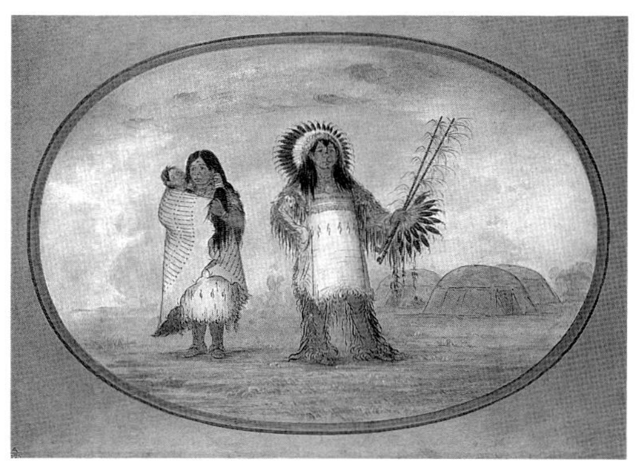

Mandan Civil Chief, His Wife, and Child, 1861/1869
Paperboard, 0.468 x 0.641 (18 7/16 x 25¼)
Paul Mellon Collection
1965.16.75

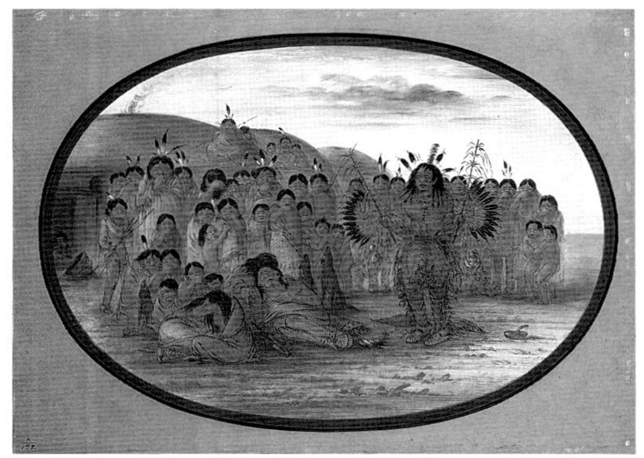

A Mandan Medicine Man, 1861/1869
Paperboard, c.470 x 0.630
(18½ x 24¹³⁄₁₆)
Paul Mellon Collection
1965.16.85

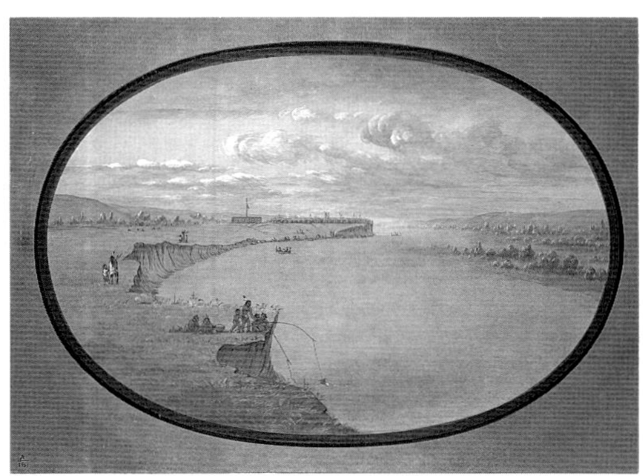

Mandan Village—A Distant View, 1861/1869
Paperboard, c.470 x 0.635 (18½ x 25)
Paul Mellon Collection
1965.16.79

Mandan War Chief with His Favorite Wife, 1861/1869
Paperboard, c.464 x 0.617 (18¼ x 24⁵⁄₁₆)
Inscribed at lower center: *Catlin p.*
Paul Mellon Collection
1965.16.72

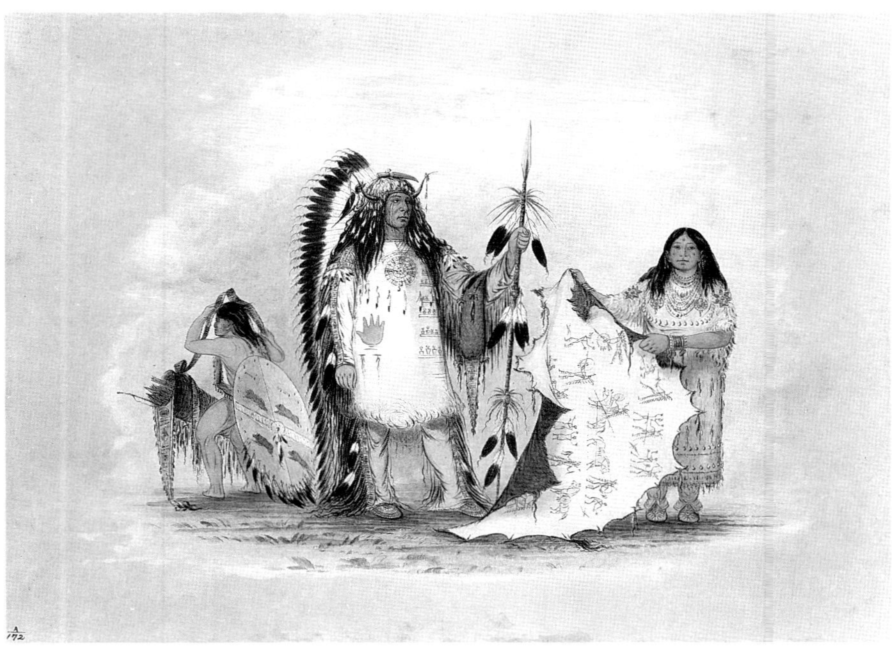

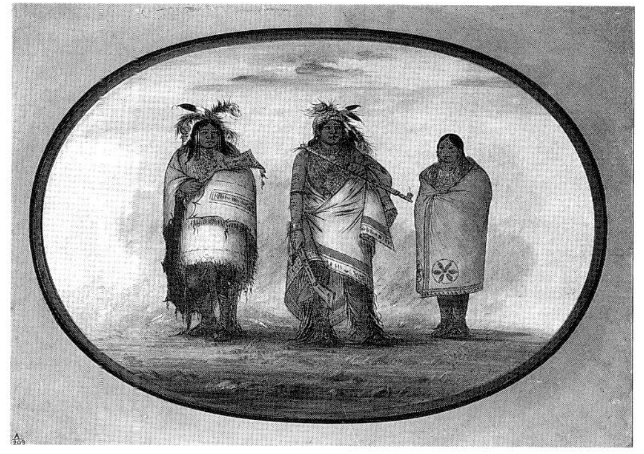

Menomonie Chief, His Wife, and Son, 1861/1869
Paperboard, 0.472 x 0.531 (18 9/16 x 24 13/16)
Paul Mellon Collection
1965.16.98

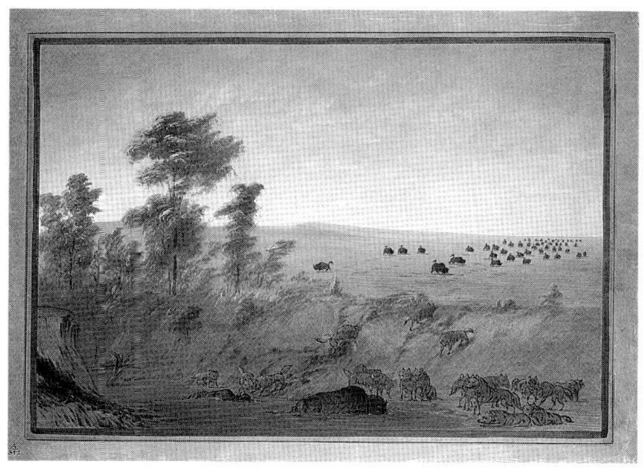

Mired Buffalo and Wolves, 1861/1869
Paperboard, 0.462 x 0.629 (18 1/2 x 24 3/4)
Paul Mellon Collection
1965.16.213

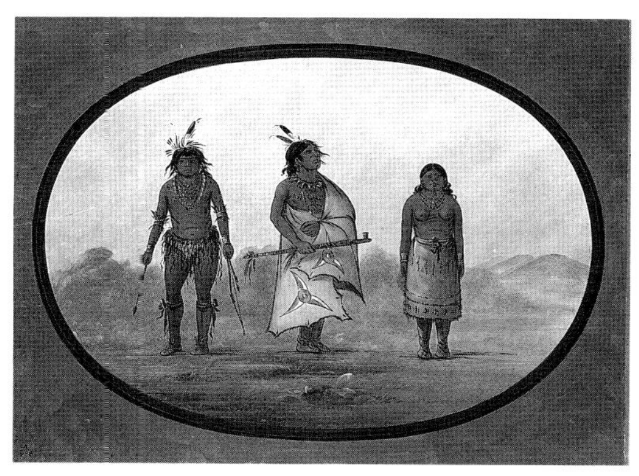

Mohave Chief, a Warrior, and His Wife, 1855/1869
Paperboard, 0.470 x 0.625 (18 1/2 x 24 5/8)
Paul Mellon Collection
1965.16.171

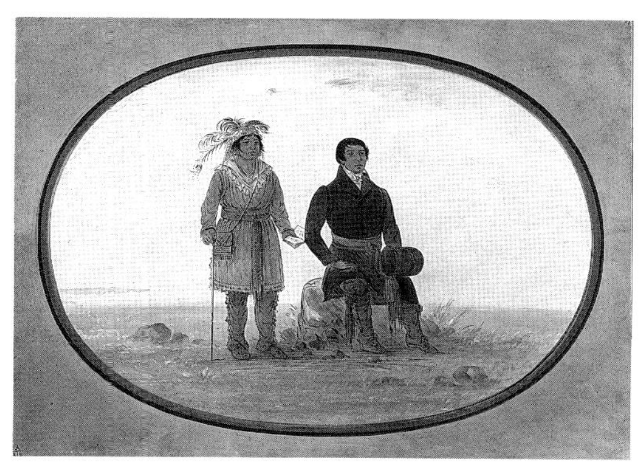

Mohigan Chief and a Missionary, 1861/1869
Paperboard, 0.469 x 0.638 (18 7/16 x 25 1/8)
Paul Mellon Collection
1965.16.108

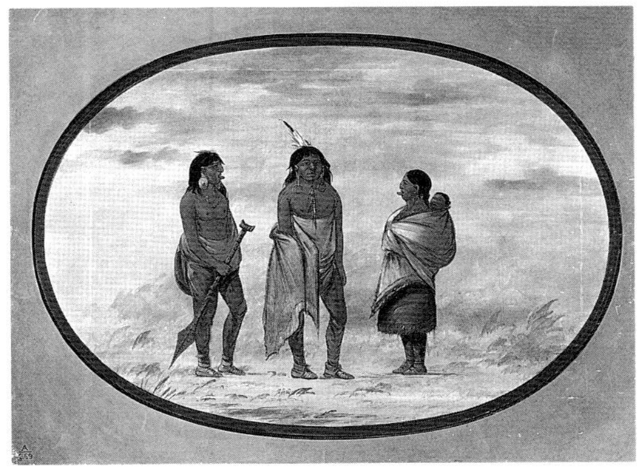

Nayas Indian Chief, His Wife, and a Warrior, 1855/1869
Paperboard, 0.470 x 0.618 ($18\frac{1}{2}$ x $24\frac{5}{16}$)
Paul Mellon Collection
1965.16.152

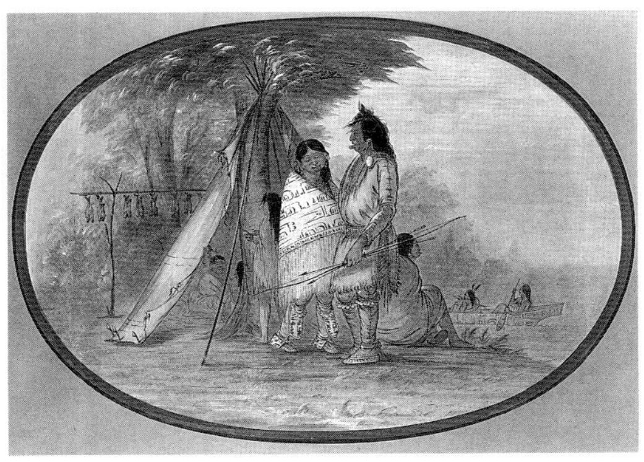

Nayas Indians, 186[2?]
Paperboard, 0.467 x 0.628 ($18\frac{3}{8}$ x $26\frac{3}{8}$)
Inscribed at lower center: *Geo. Catlin 186[2?]*
Paul Mellon Collection
1965.16.153

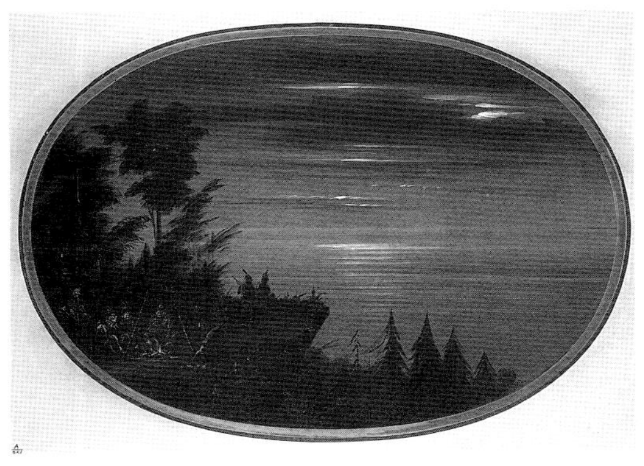

Nayas Village at Night, 1855/1869
Paperboard, 0.446 x 0.616 ($17\frac{1}{2}$ x $24\frac{1}{2}$)
Paul Mellon Collection
1965.16.220

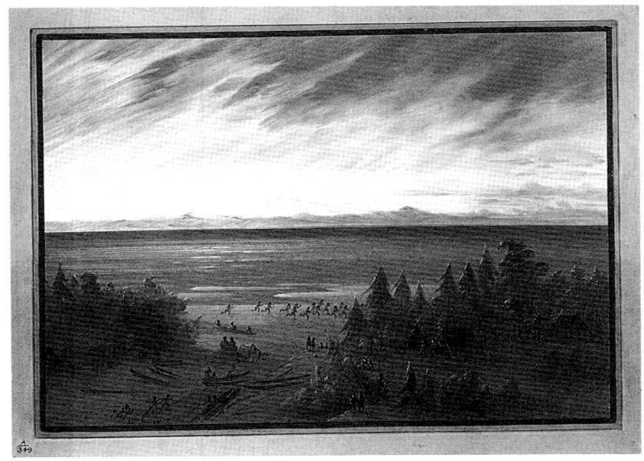

Nayas Village at Sunset, 1855/1869
Paperboard, 0.470 x 0.628 ($18\frac{1}{2}$ x $24\frac{7}{8}$)
Paul Mellon Collection
1965.16.219

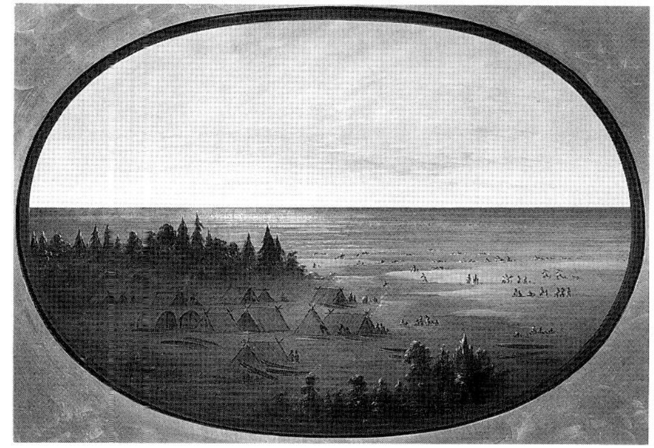

Nayas Village—Indians Bathing,
1855/1869
Paperboard, 0.462 x 0.626 (18 3/16 x 24 5/8)
Paul Mellon Collection
1965.16.198

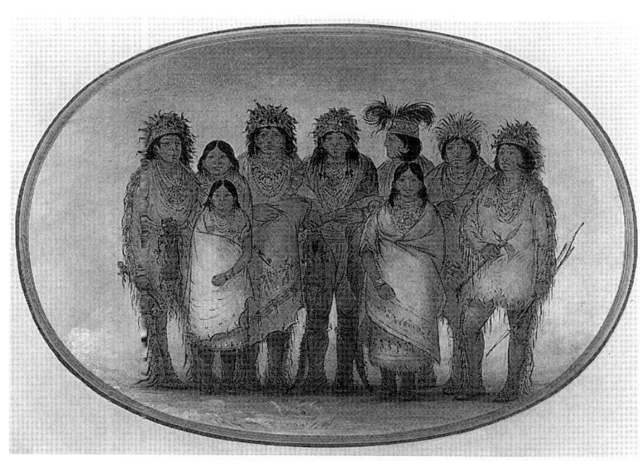

Nine Ojibbeway Indians in London,
1861/1869
Paperboard, 0.466 x 0.624 (18 3/8 x 24 9/16)
Paul Mellon Collection
1965.16.110

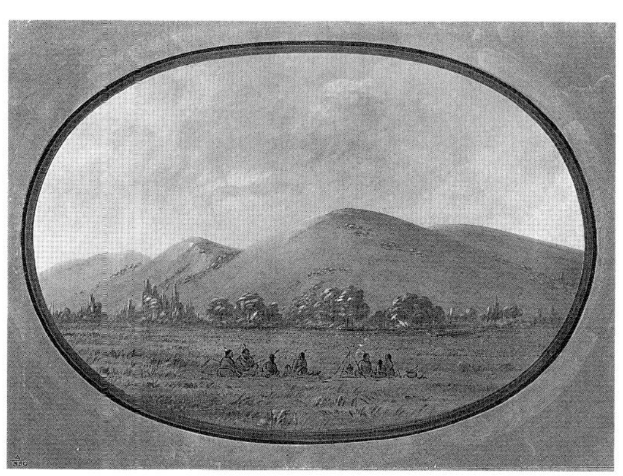

Nishnabotana Bluffs, Upper Missouri,
1861/1869
Paperboard, 0.477 x 0.622 (18 3/4 x 24 1/2)
Paul Mellon Collection
1965.16.203

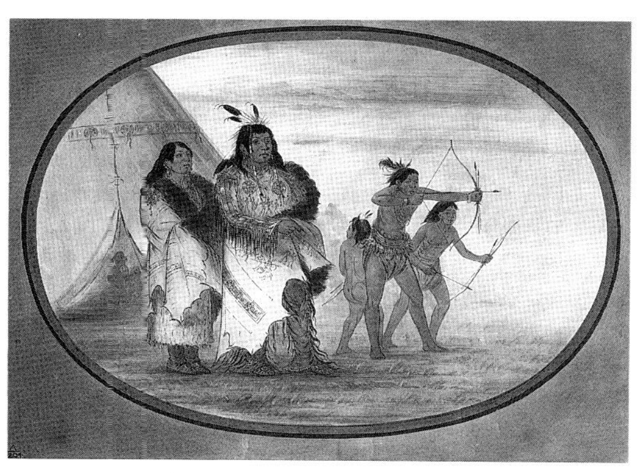

Ojibbeway Indians, 1861/1869
Paperboard, 0.463 x 0.625 (18 1/4 x 24 5/8)
Paul Mellon Collection
1965.16.93

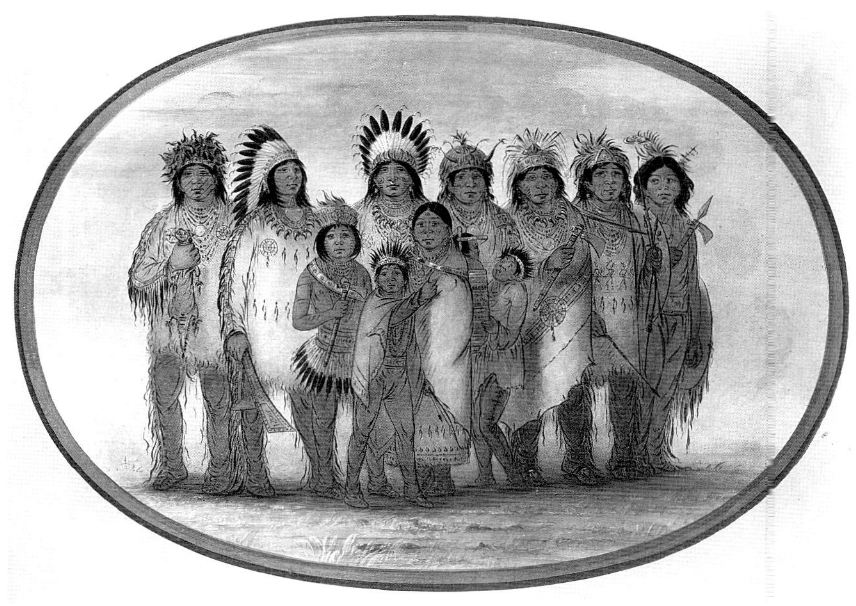

Ojibbeway Indians in Paris, 1861/1869
Paperboard, 0.464 x 0.630 (18⅜ x 24¾)
Paul Mellon Collection
1965.16.112

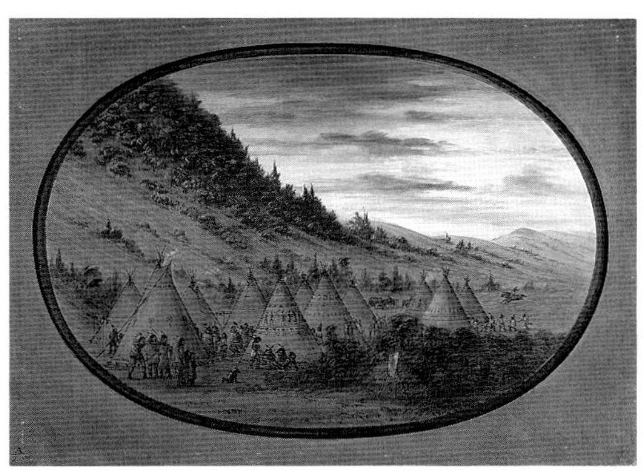

An Ojibbeway Village of Skin Tents, 1861/1869
Paperboard, 0.475 x 0.639
(18^{11}/16 x 25⅛)
Paul Mellon Collection
1965.16.128

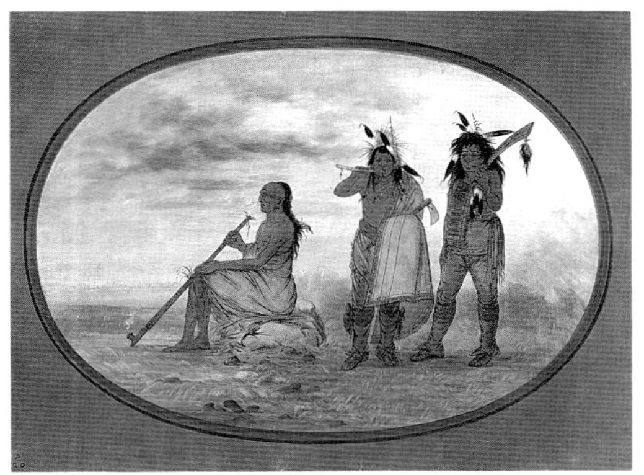

Old Menomonie Chief with Two Young Beaux, 1861 1869
Paperboard, 0.472 x 0.621
(18^{9}/16 x 24^{7}/16)
Paul Mellon Collection
1965.16.99

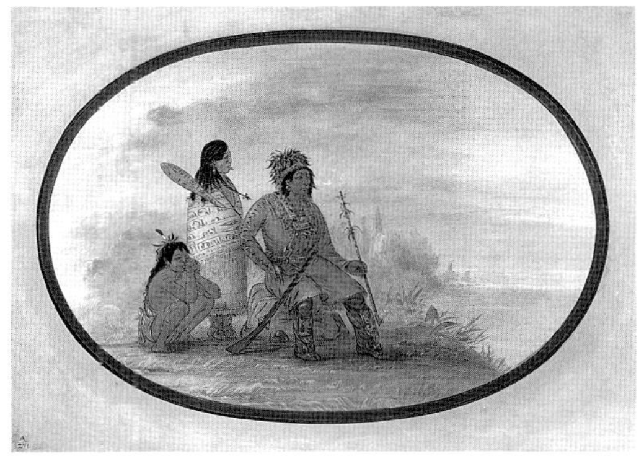

An Old Nayas Indian, His Granddaughter, and a Boy, 1855/1869
Paperboard, 0.475 x 0.640 (18 11/16 x 25 3/16)
Paul Mellon Collection
1965.16.154

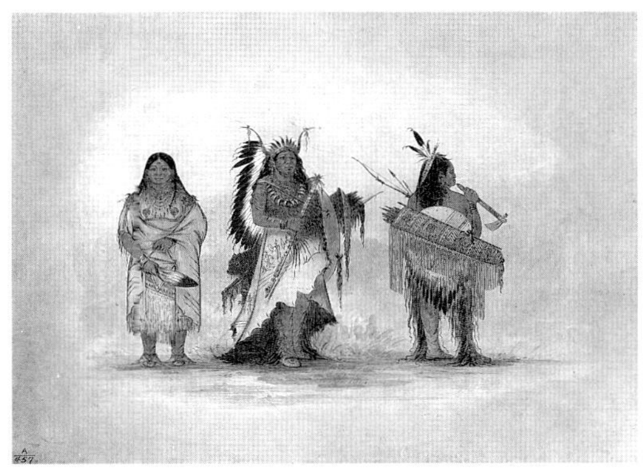

Omaha Chief, His Wife, and a Warrior, 1861
Paperboard, 0.451 x 0.600 (17 3/4 x 23 5/8)
Inscribed at lower center: [Catl]in 1861.
Paul Mellon Collection
1965.16.313

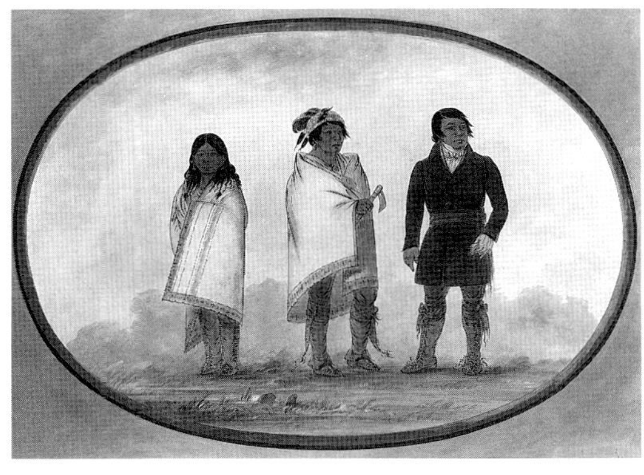

Oneida Chief, His Sister, and a Missionary, 1861/1869
Paperboard, 0.476 x 0.639 (18 3/4 x 25 3/16)
Paul Mellon Collection
1965.16.113

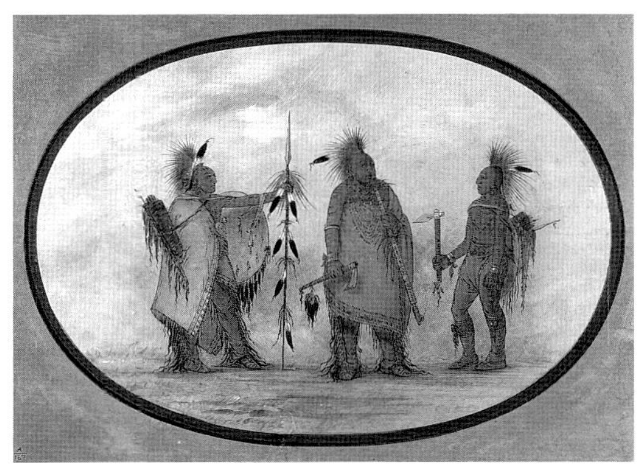

Osage Chief with Two Warriors, 1861/1869
Paperboard, 0.462 x 0.622 (18 3/16 x 24 1/2)
Paul Mellon Collection
1965.16.68

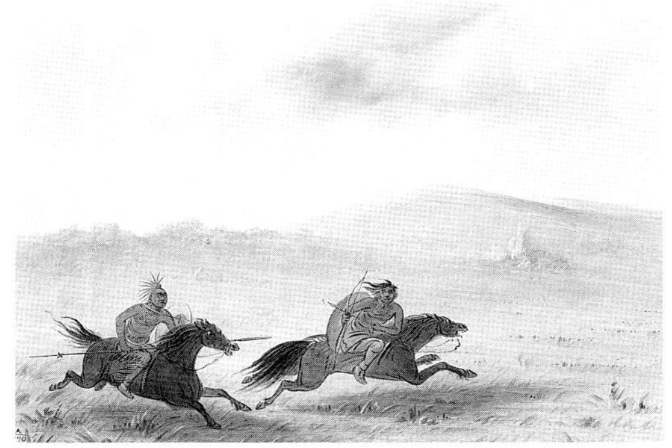

An Osage Indian Pursuing a Camanchee, 1861/1869
Paperboard, 0.463 x 0.628 (18¼ x 24¾)
Paul Mellon Collection
1965.16.71

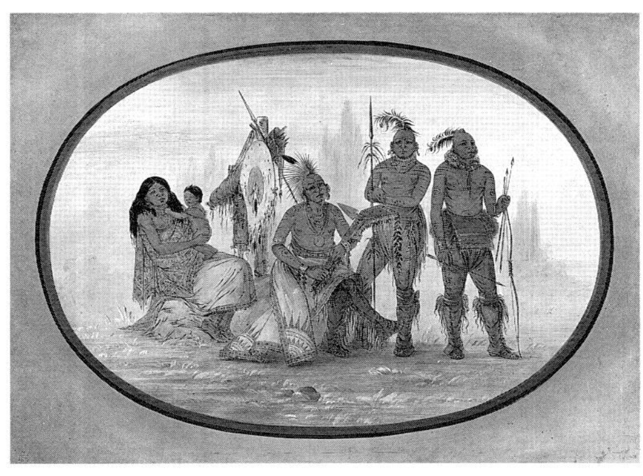

Osage Indians, 1861/1869
Paperboard, 0.476 x 0.640 (18¾ x 25$\frac{3}{16}$)
Paul Mellon Collection
1965.16.69

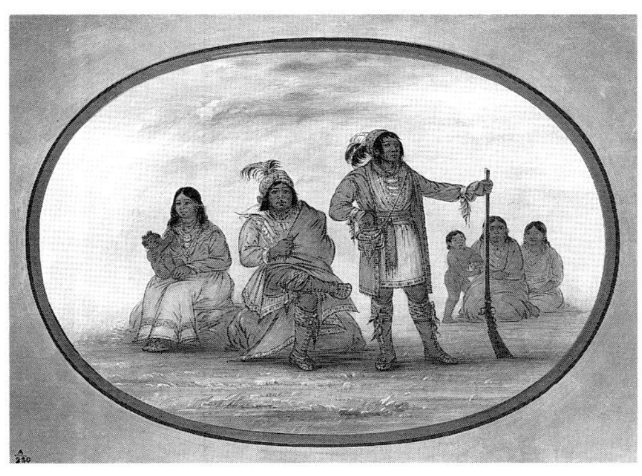

Osceola and Four Seminolee Indians, 1861/1869
Paperboard, 0.465 x 0.628
(21⅞ x 24$\frac{11}{16}$)
Paul Mellon Collection
1965.16.119

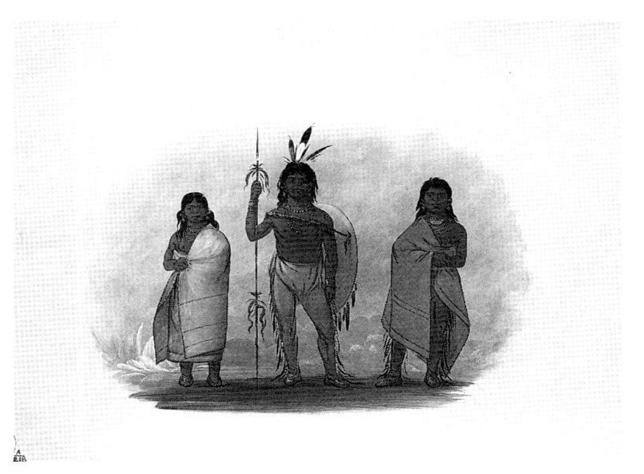

Ottowa Chief, His Wife, and a Warrior, 1861/1869
Paperboard, 0.469 x 0.625 (18$\frac{7}{16}$ x 24⅝)
Paul Mellon Collection
1965.16.107

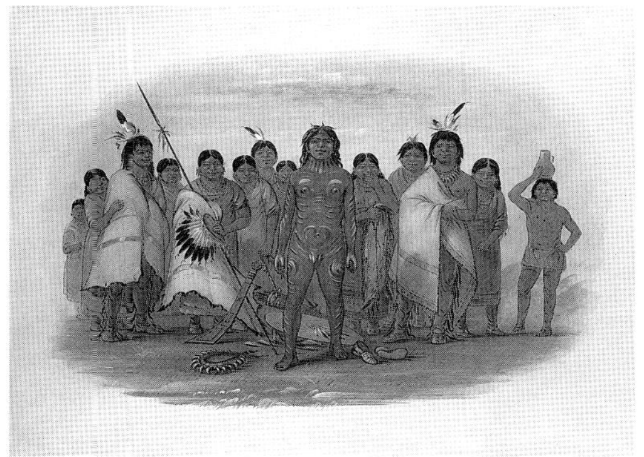

"Paint Me"—Apachee, 1855/1869
Paperboard, 0.466 x 0.622 (18 3/8 x 24 1/2)
Paul Mellon Collection
1965.16.202

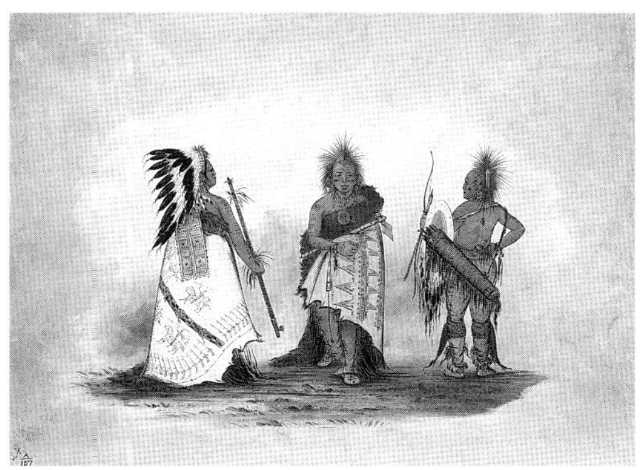

A Pawnee Chief with Two Warriors, 1861/1869
Paperboard, 0.500 x 0.618 (19 3/4 x 24 1/4)
Inscribed at lower center: *Catlin p.*
Paul Mellon Collection
1965.16.61

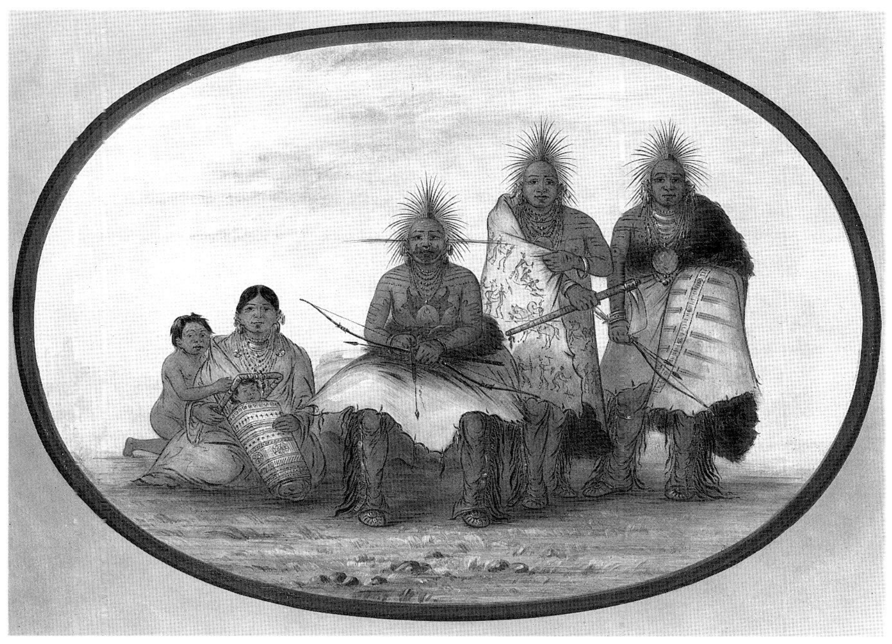

Pawnee Indians, 1861/1869
Paperboard, 0.477 x 0.635 (18 13/16 x 25)
Paul Mellon Collection
1965.16.60

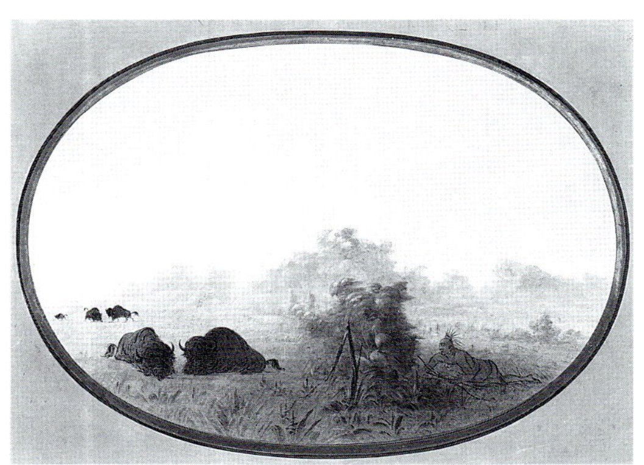

Pawnee Indians Approaching Buffalo, 1861/1869
Paperboard, 0.473 x 0.628 (18⅝ x 24¾)
Paul Mellon Collection
1965.16.64

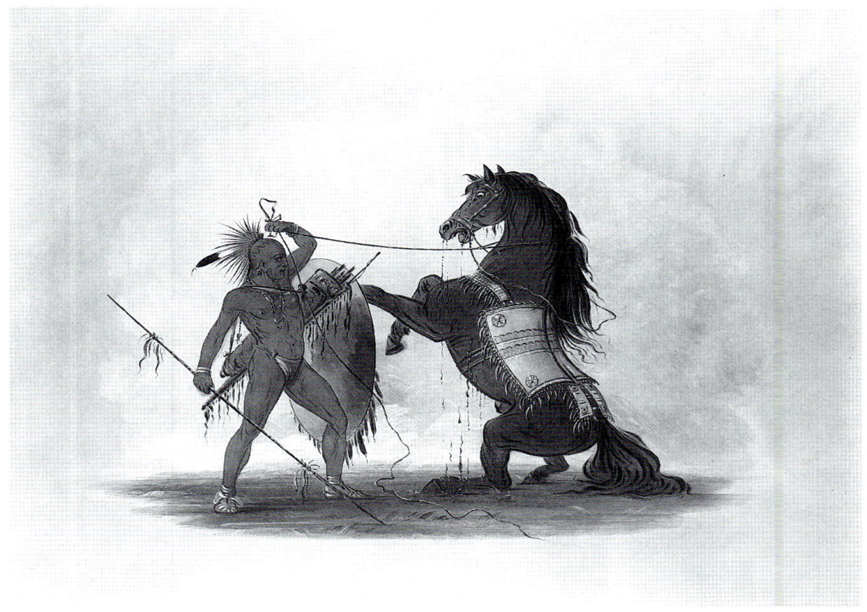

A Pawnee Warrior Sacrificing His Favorite Horse, 1861/1869
Paperboard, 0.473 x 0.620 (18⅝ x 23⅞)
Paul Mellon Collection
1965.16.67

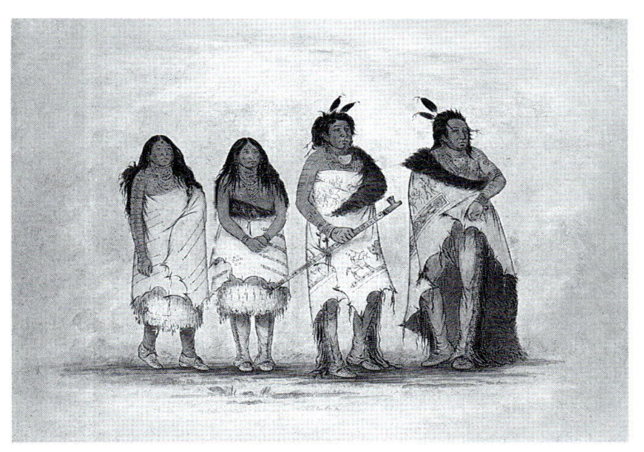

Pawneepict Chief, Two Daughters, and a Warrior, 1861/1869
Paperboard, 0.419 x 0.565 (16½ x 22¼)
Inscribed at lower center: *Catlin p.*
Paul Mellon Collection
1965.16.56

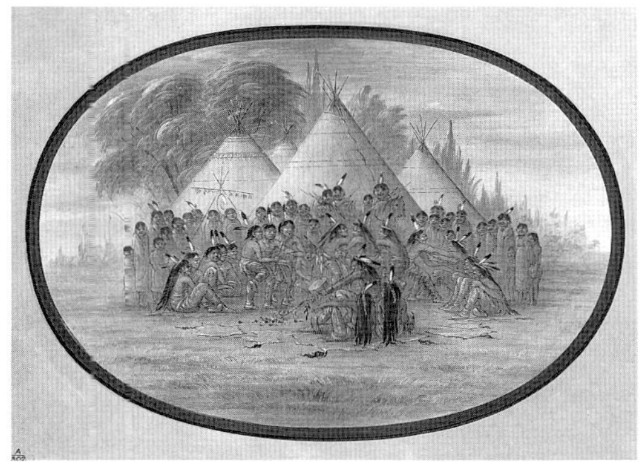

Pipe Dance—Assinneboine, 1861/1869
Paperboard, 0.467 x 0.628 (18⅜ x 24¾)
Paul Mellon Collection
1965.16.182

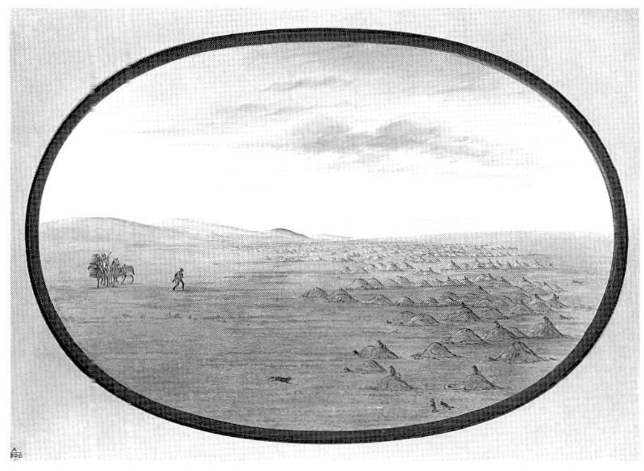

Prairie Dog Village, 1861/1869
Paperboard, 0.469 x 0.634 (18½ x 25)
Paul Mellon Collection
1965.16.185

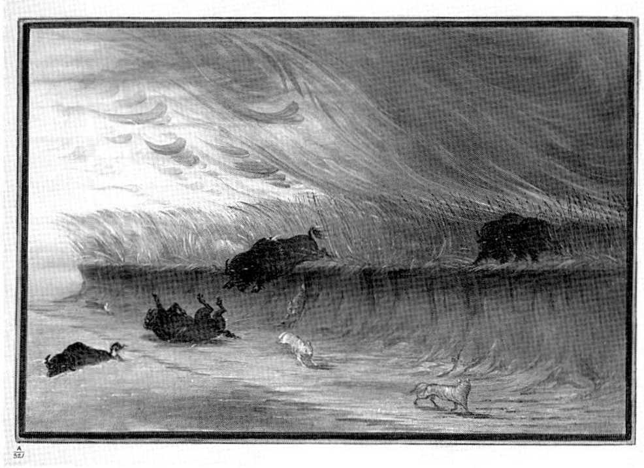

Prairie Meadows Burning, 1861/1869
Paperboard, 0.465 x 0.625 (18⅜ x 24⅝)
Paul Mellon Collection
1965.16.194

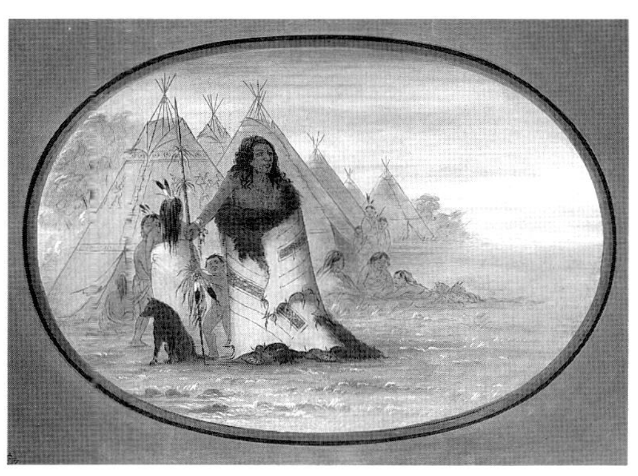

Puncah Chief Surrounded by His Family, 1861/1869
Paperboard, 0.473 x 0.632 (18⅝ x 24⅞)
Paul Mellon Collection
1965.16.106

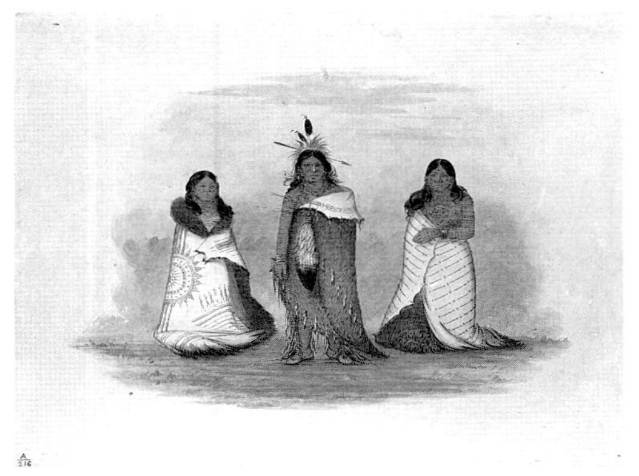

Puncah Indians, 1861
Paperboard, c.472 x 0.623 (18 9/16 x 24 1/2)
Inscribed at lower right: *Geo. Catlin. 1861.*
Paul Mellon Collection
1965.16.105

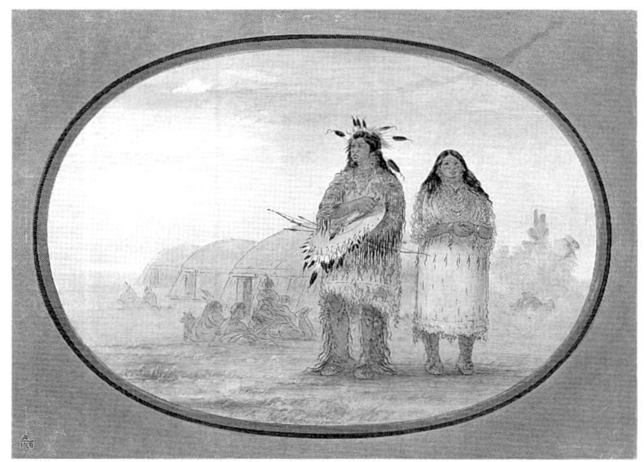

Riccarree Chief and His Wife, 1861/1869
Paperboard, c.470 x 0.635 (18 1/2 x 25)
Paul Mellon Collection
1965.16.78

The Running Fox on a Fine Horse—Saukie, 1861/1869
Paperboard, c.475 x 0.635 (18 3/4 x 25)
Paul Mellon Collection
1965.16.97

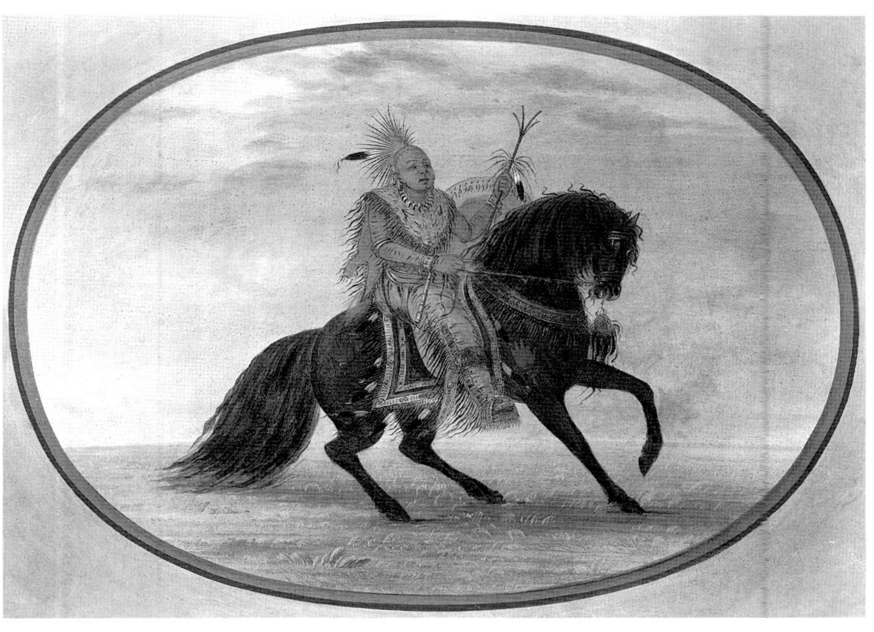

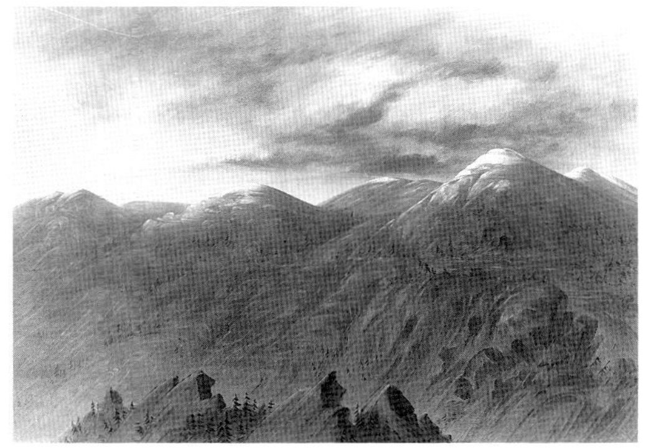

Salmon River Mountains, 1855/1869
Paperboard, 0.475 x 0.621
(18 11/16 x 24 7/16)
Paul Mellon Collection
1965.16.201

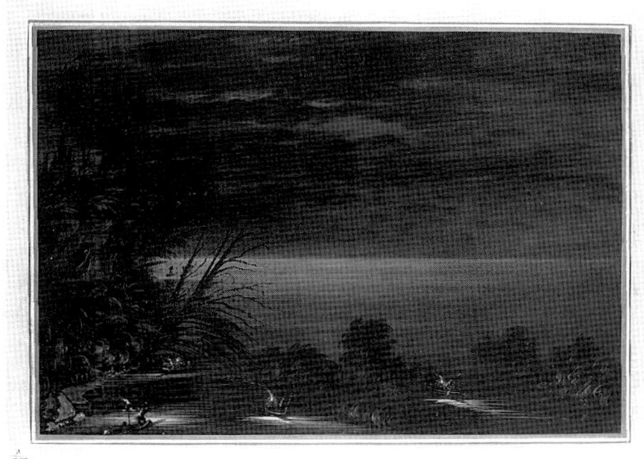

Salmon Spearing—Ottowas, 1861/1869
Paperboard, 0.467 x 0.621 (18 3/4 x 24 1/2)
Paul Mellon Collection
1965.16.141

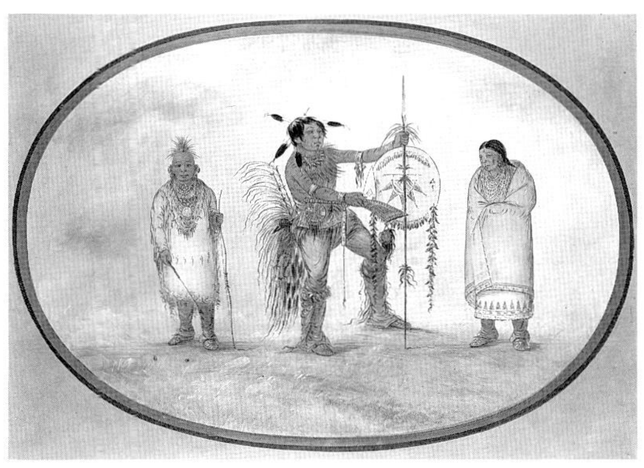

Saukie Warrior, His Wife, and a Boy, 1861/1869
Paperboard, 0.475 x 0.639
(18 11/16 x 25 3/16)
Paul Mellon Collection
1965.16.94

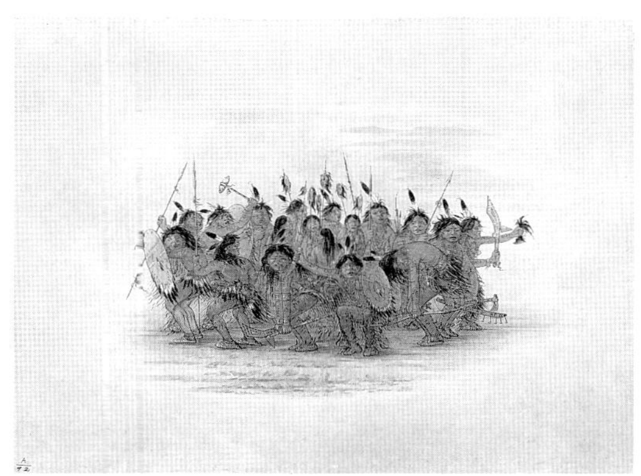

Scalp Dance—Sioux, 1861
Paperboard, 0.463 x 0.621 (18 1/4 x 24 7/16)
Inscribed at lower center: *Geo. Catlin. 1861.*
Paul Mellon Collection
1965.16.5

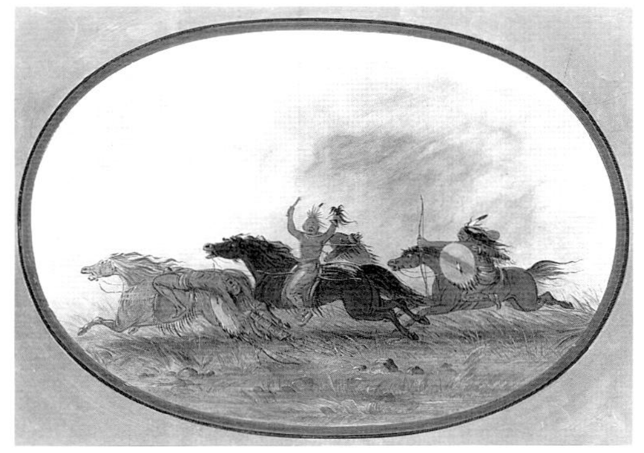

The Scalper Scalped—Pawnees and Cheyennes, 1861/1869
Paperboard, 0.461 x 0.621 (18⅛ x 24$\frac{7}{16}$)
Paul Mellon Collection
1965.16.199

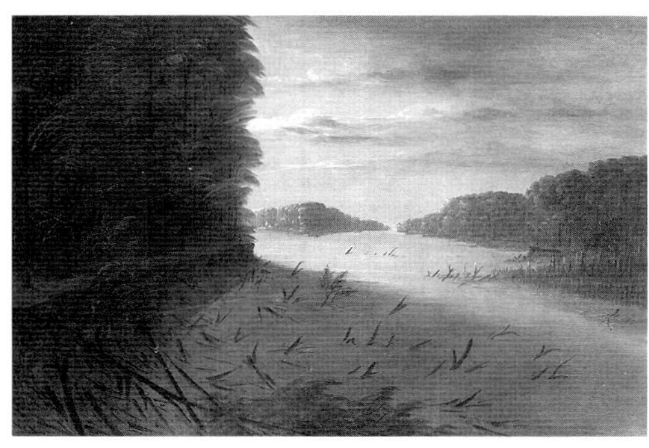

Scene from the Lower Mississippi, 1861/1869
Paperboard, 0.450 x 0.630 (17¾ x 24$\frac{13}{16}$)
Paul Mellon Collection
1965.16.196

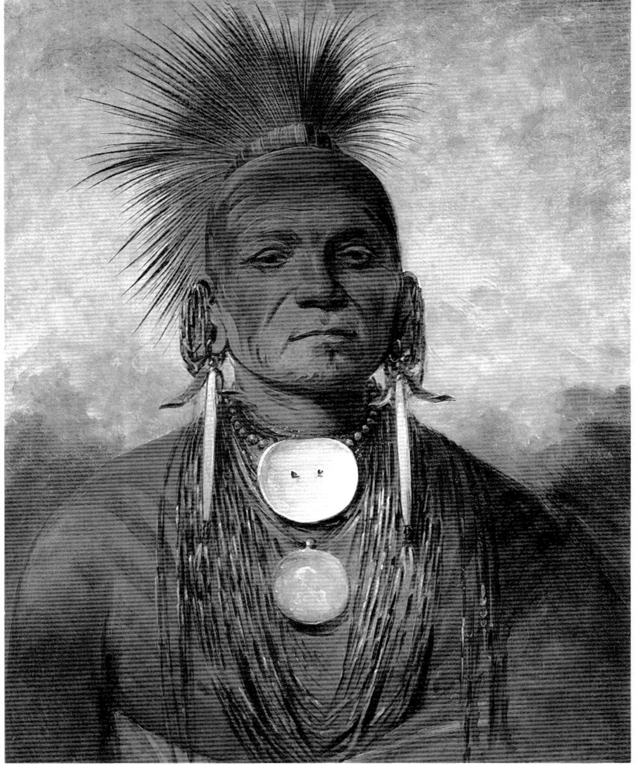

See-non-ty-a, an Iowa Medicine Man, 1844/1845
Canvas, 0.710 x 0.580 (28 x 22⅞)
Paul Mellon Collection
1965.16.346

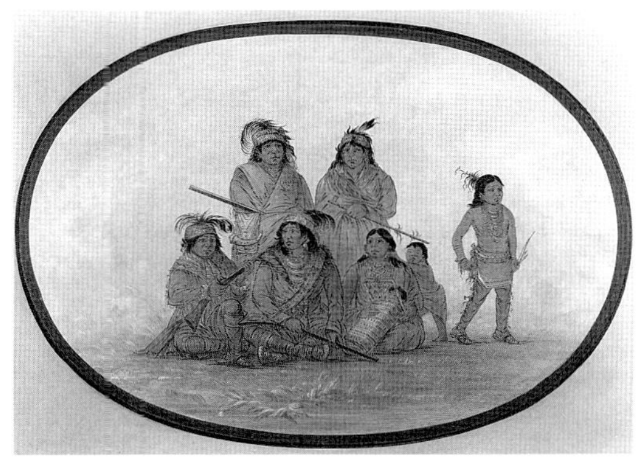

Seminolee Indians, Prisoners at Fort Moultrie, 1861/1869
Paperboard, 0.468 x 0.628 (18 7/16 x 24 3/4)
Paul Mellon Collection
1965.16.118

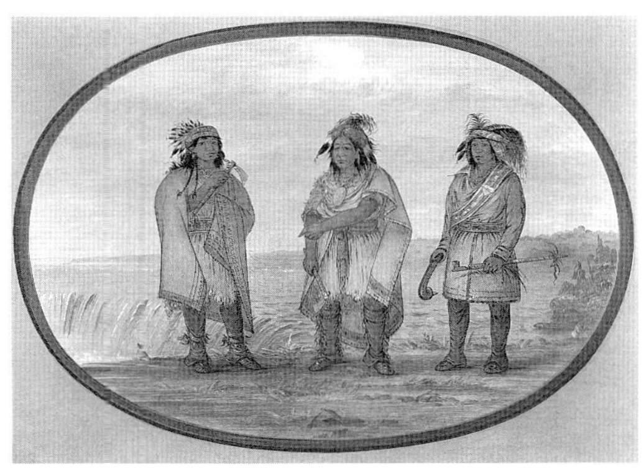

Seneca Chief, Red Jacket, with Two Warriors, 1861/1869
Paperboard, 0.476 x 0.633
(18 3/4 x 24 15/16)
Paul Mellon Collection
1965.16.104

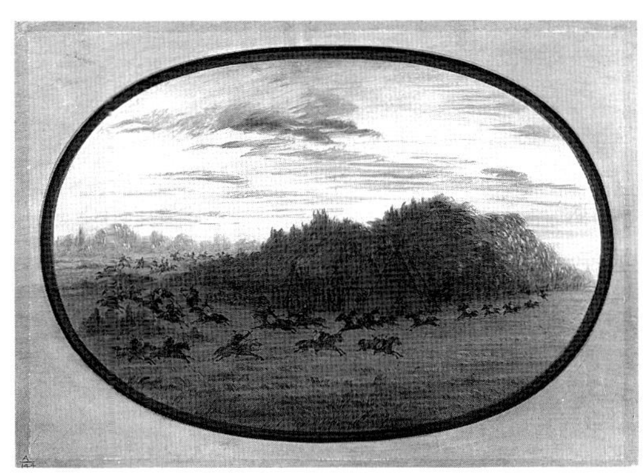

Sham Fight of the Camanchees, 1861/1869
Paperboard, 0.473 x 0.638 (18 5/8 x 25 1/8)
Paul Mellon Collection
1965.16.50

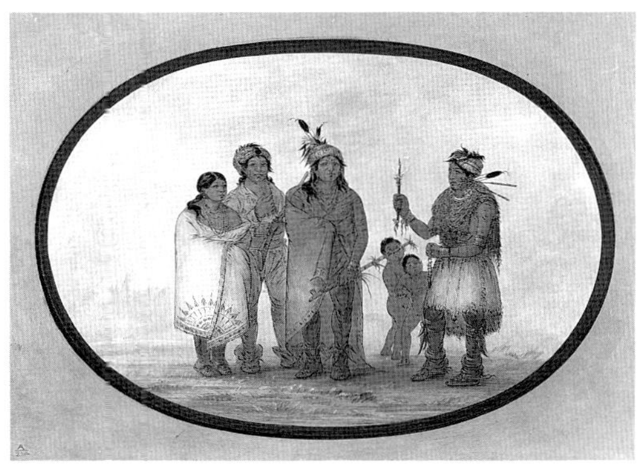

Shawano Indians, 1861/1869
Paperboard, 0.469 x 0.635 (18 1/2 x 25)
Paul Mellon Collection
1965.16.123

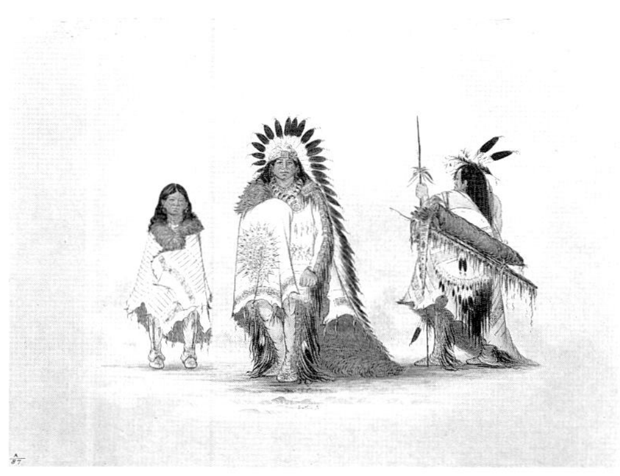

A Sioux Chief, His Daughter, and a Warrior, 1861/1869
Paperboard, 0.461 x 0.618 (18⅛ x 24$^{5}/_{16}$)
Inscribed at lower center: *Catlin p.*
Paul Mellon Collection
1965.16.2

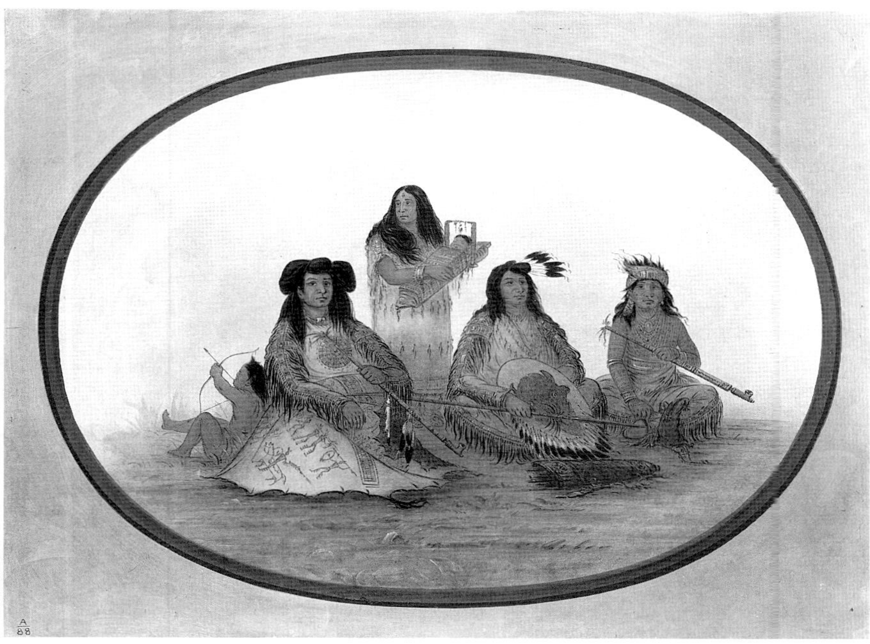

The Sioux Chief with Several Indians, 1861/1869
Paperboard, 0.471 x 0.636
(18$^{9}/_{16}$ x 25$^{1}/_{16}$)
Paul Mellon Collection
1965.16.3

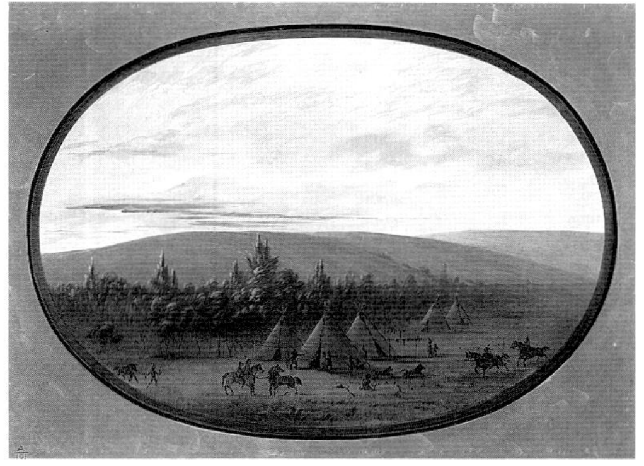

A Sioux Village, 1861/1869
Paperboard, 0.457 x 0.621 (18 x 24$^{7}/_{16}$)
Paul Mellon Collection
1965.16.12

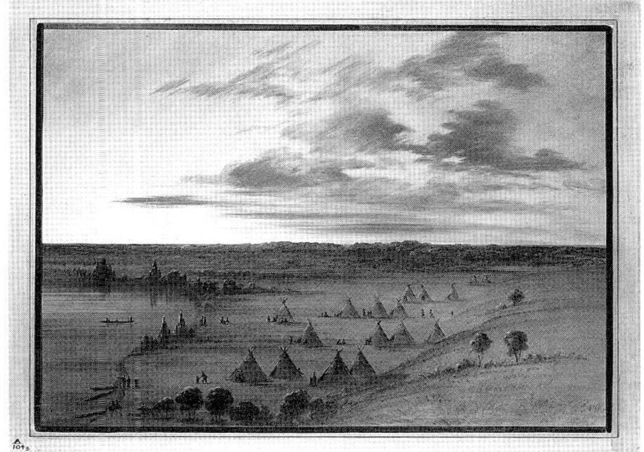

Sioux Village—Lac du Cygne, 1861/1869
Paperboard, 0.469 x 0.615 (18½ x 24³⁄₁₆)
Paul Mellon Collection
1965.16.14

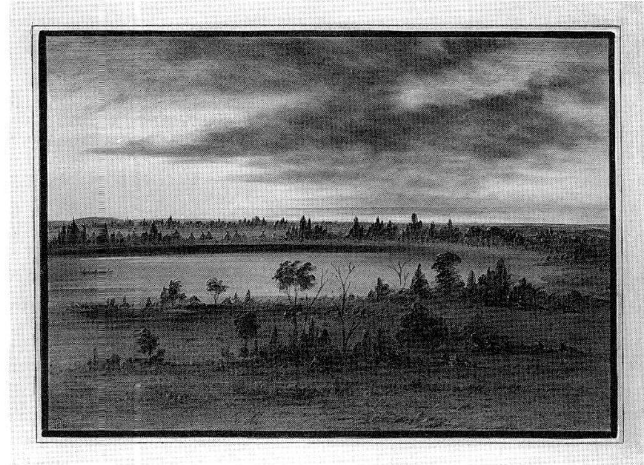

A Sioux War Party, 1861/1869
Paperboard, 0.469 x 0.615 (18½ x 24³⁄₁₆)
Paul Mellon Collection
1965.16.15

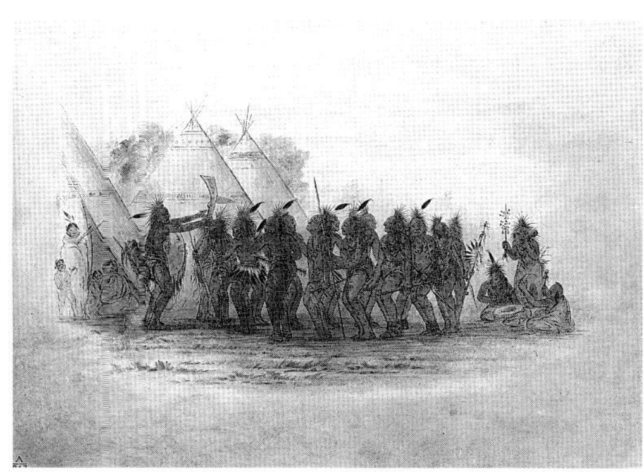

Slaves' Dance—Saukie, 1861
Paperboard, 0.468 x 0.610 (18⁷⁄₁₆ x 24)
Inscribed at lower center: *Geo. Catlin 1861*
Paul Mellon Collection
1965.16.131

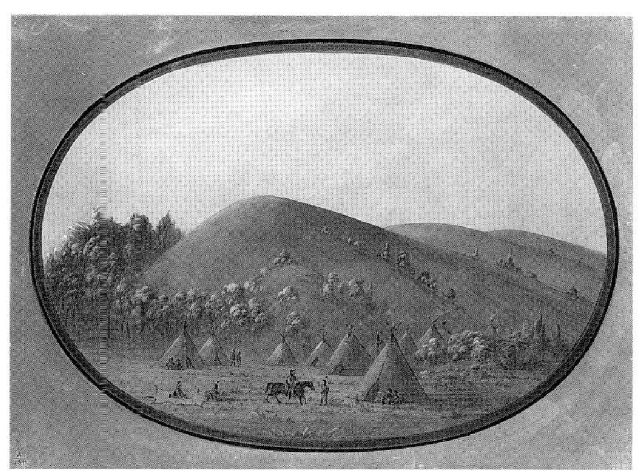

A Small Cheyenne Village, 1861/1869
Paperboard, 0.457 x 0.622 (18 x 24½)
Paul Mellon Collection
1965.16.41

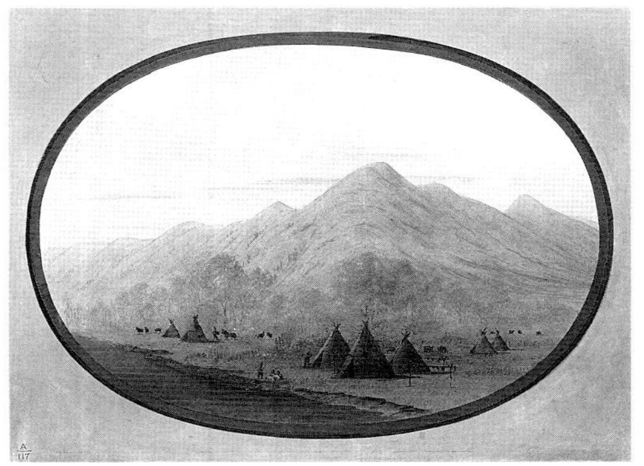

A Small Crow Village, 1855/1869
Paperboard, c.468 x 0.628 (18 7/16 x 24 3/4)
Paul Mellon Collection
1965.16.26

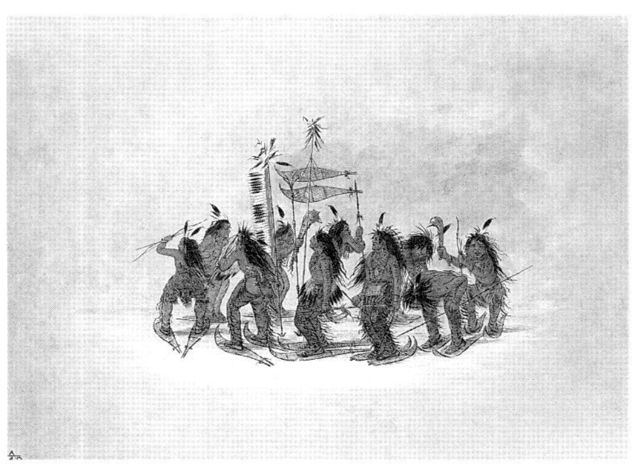

Snow Shoe Dance—Ojibbeway, 1861/1869
Paperboard, c.465 x 0.620 (18 1/4 x 24 1/2)
Paul Mellon Collection
1965.16.136

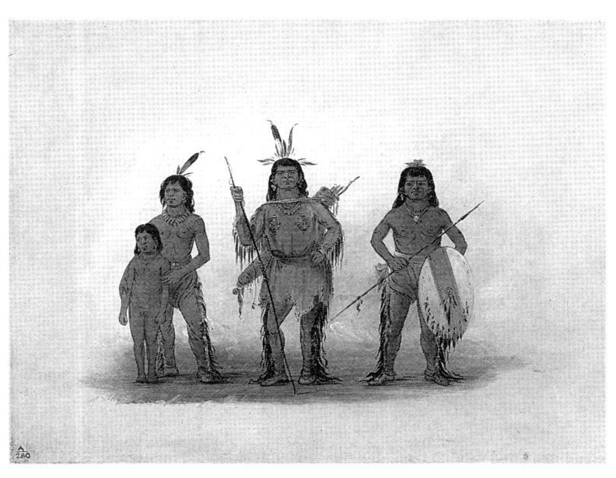

Spokan Chief, Two Warriors, and a Boy, 1855/1869
Paperboard, c.473 x 0.613 (18 5/8 x 24 1/8)
Paul Mellon Collection
1965.16.163

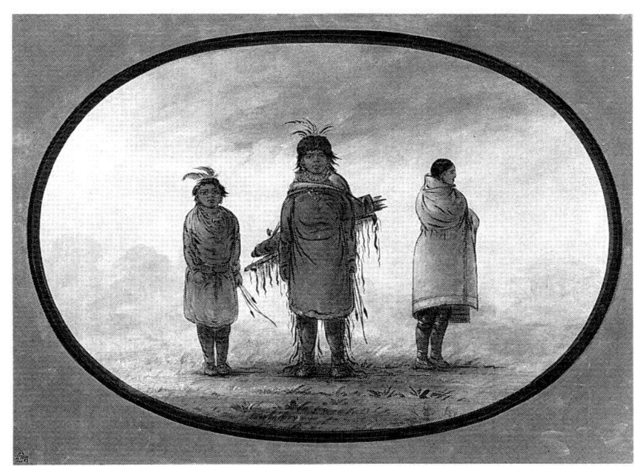

A Stone Warrior, His Wife, and a Boy, 1855/1869
Paperboard, c.457 x 0.618 (18 x 24 5/16)
Paul Mellon Collection
1965.16.161

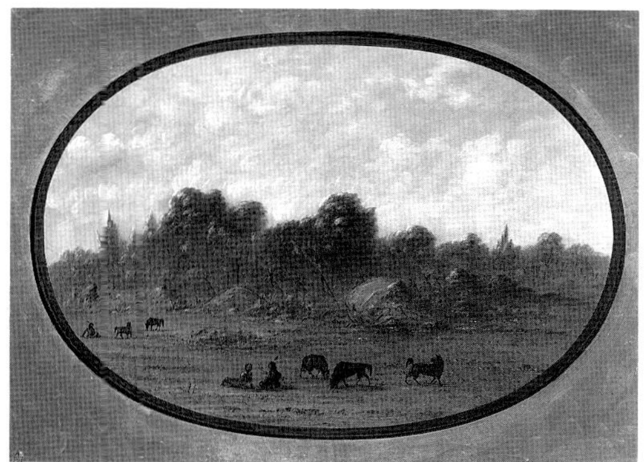

Tawahquena Village, 1861/1869
Paperboard, 0.467 x 0.619
(18 5/16 x 24 5/16)
Paul Mellon Collection
1965.16.55

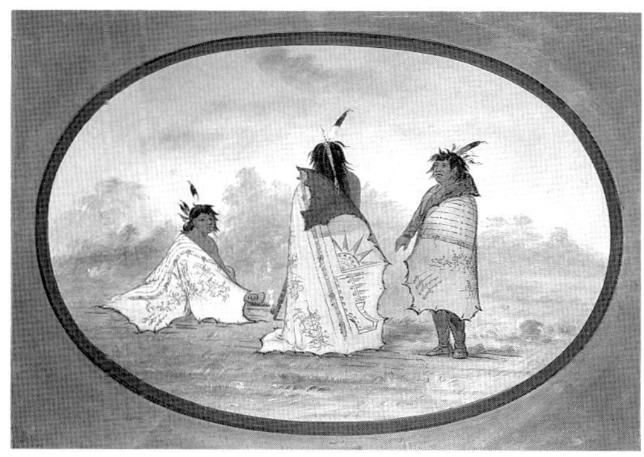

Three Blackfoot Men, 1855/1869
Paperboard, 0.461 x 0.620 (18 1/8 x 24 3/8)
Paul Mellon Collection
1965.16.29

Three Celebrated Ball Players—Choctaw, Sioux, and Ojibbeway, 1861
Paperboard, 0.451 x 0.609 (17 3/4 x 24)
Inscribed at lower right: *Geo. Catlin. 1861.*
Paul Mellon Collection
1965.16.127

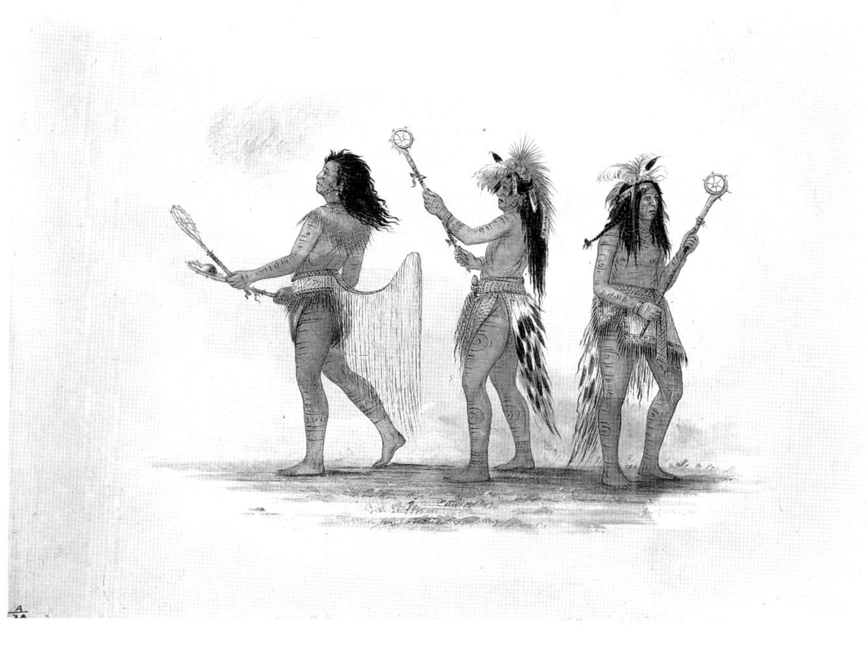

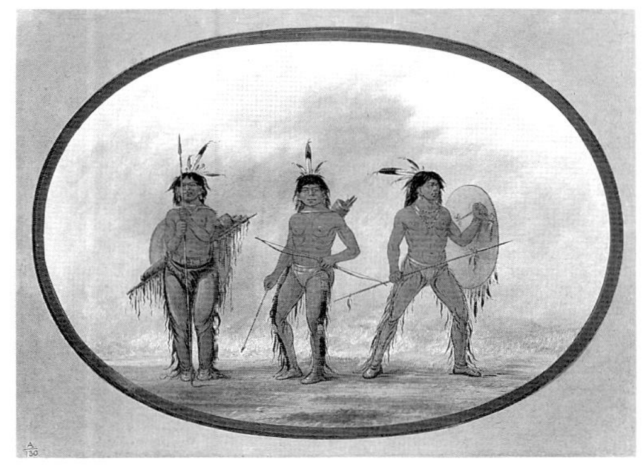

Three Cheyenne Warriors, 1861/1869
Paperboard, c.457 x 0.617 (18 x $24\frac{5}{16}$)
Paul Mellon Collection
1965.16.37

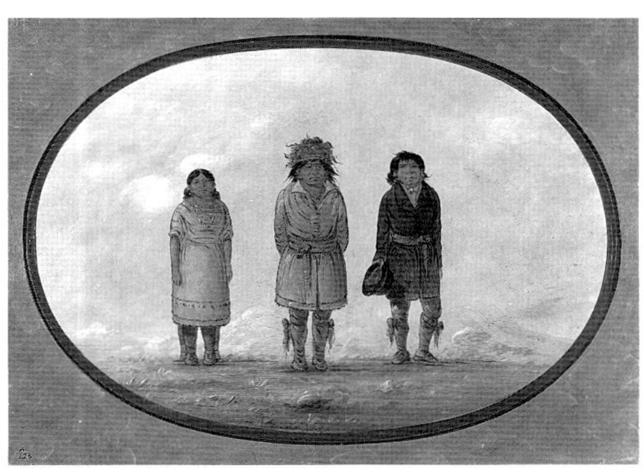

Three Creek Indians, 1861/1869
Paperboard, 0.456 x 0.618
($17\frac{15}{16}$ x $24\frac{5}{16}$)
Paul Mellon Collection
1965.16.115

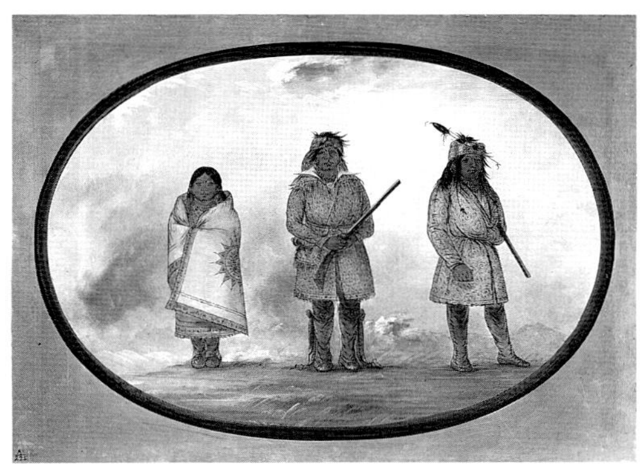

Three Delaware Indians, 1861/1869
Paperboard, 0.470 x 0.631 ($18\frac{1}{2}$ x $24\frac{7}{8}$)
Paul Mellon Collection
1965.16.114

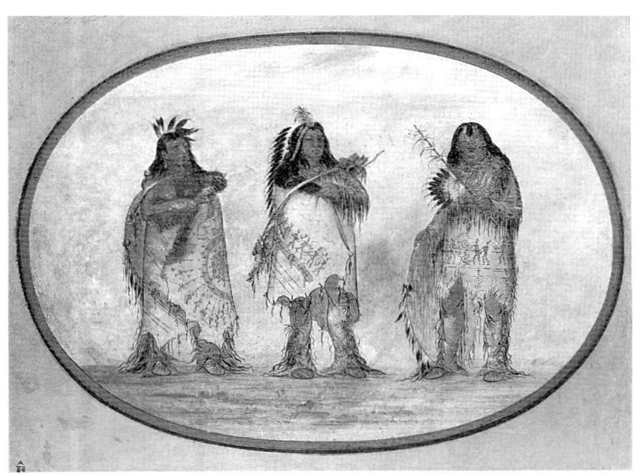

Three Distinguished Warriors of the Sioux Tribe, 1861
Paperboard, 0.465 x 0.611
($18\frac{5}{16}$ x $24\frac{1}{16}$)
Inscribed at lower right: *Geo. Catlin. 1861.*
Paul Mellon Collection
1965.16.1

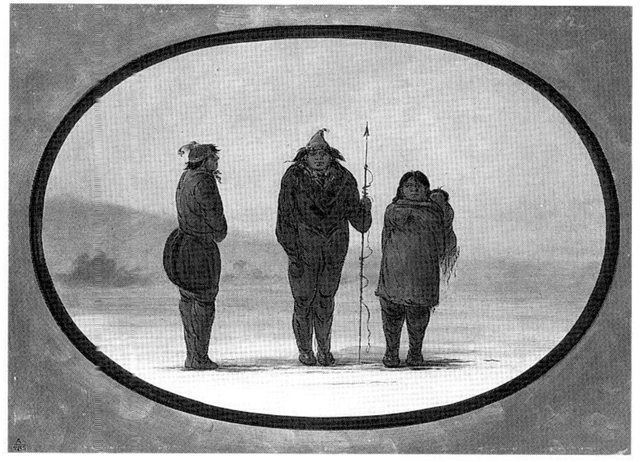

Three Esquimaux, 1855/1869
Paperboard, 0.463 x 0.622 (18¼ x 24½)
Paul Mellon Collection
1965.16.168

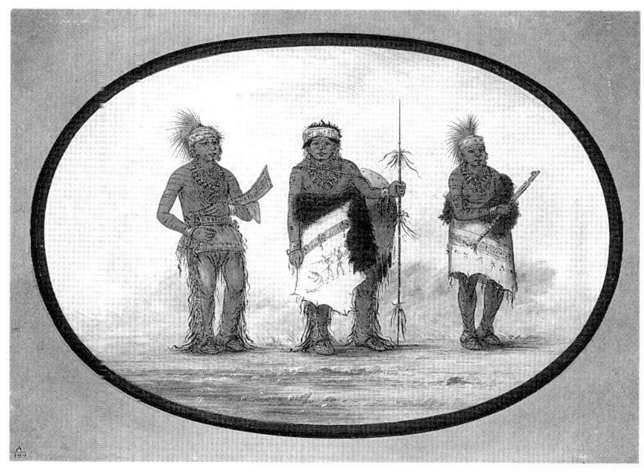

Three Iowa Indians, 1861/1869
Paperboard, 0.468 x 0.632 (18 7/16 x 24⅞)
Paul Mellon Collection
1965.16.88

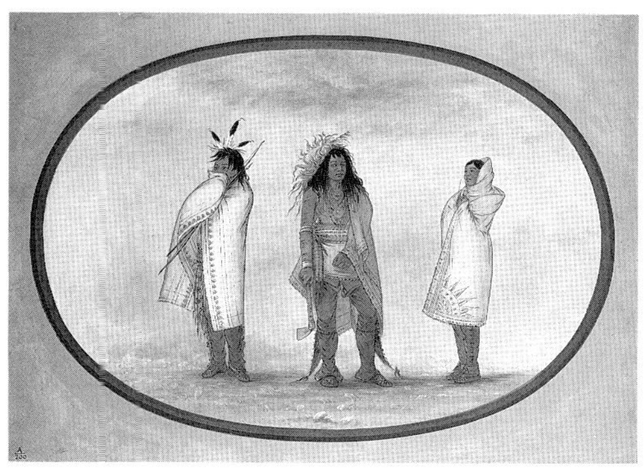

Three Iroquois Indians, 1861/1869
Paperboard, 0.465 x 0.634
(18 5/16 x 24 15/16)
Paul Mellon Collection
1965.16.89

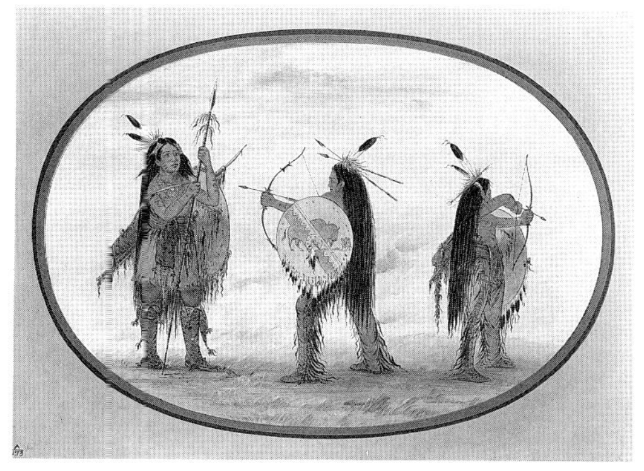

Three Mandan Warriors Armed for War, 1861/1869
Paperboard, 0.473 x 0.629 (18⅝ x 24⅞)
Paul Mellon Collection
1965.16.73

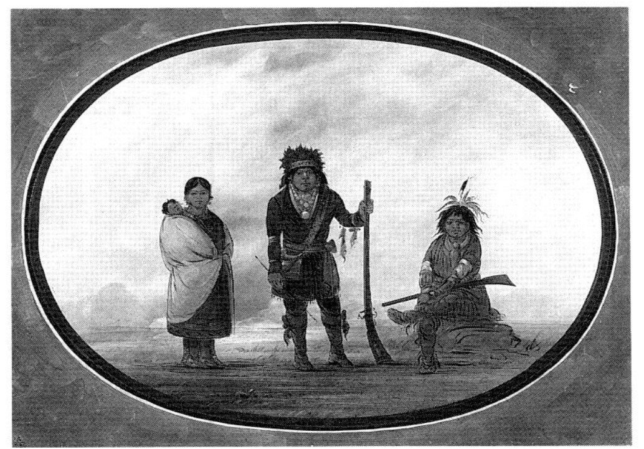

Three Micmac Indians, 1861/1869
Paperboard, c.458 x 0.616 (18 x 24¼)
Paul Mellon Collection
1965.16.125

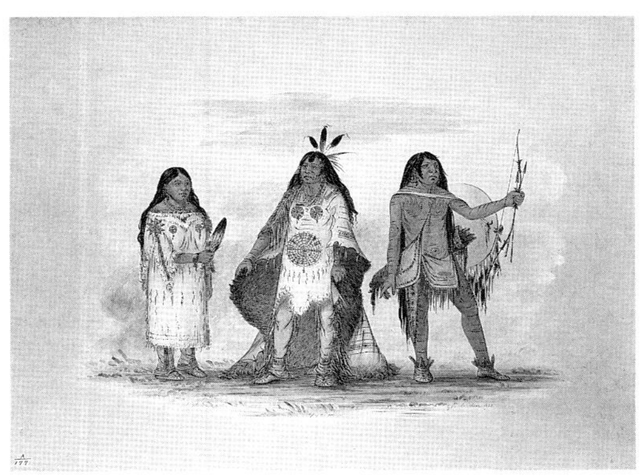

Three Minatarree Indians, 1861
Paperboard, c.455 x 0.603
(17 15/16 x 23¾)
Inscribed at lower right: *Geo. Catlin. 1861.*
Paul Mellon Collection
1965.16.77

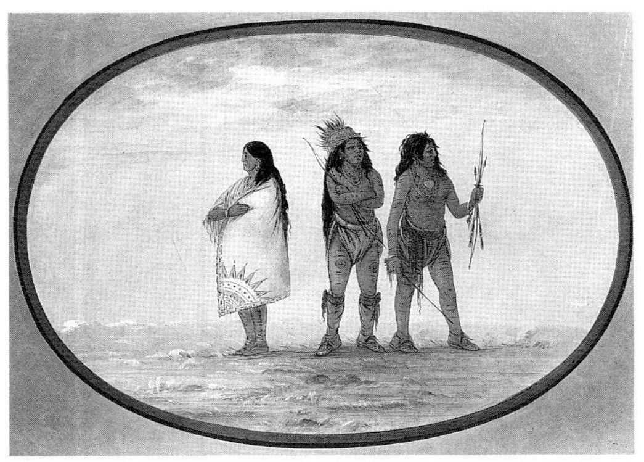

Three Navaho Indians, 1861/1869
Paperboard, c.474 x 0.637
(18 11/16 x 25 1/16)
Paul Mellon Collection
1965.16.144

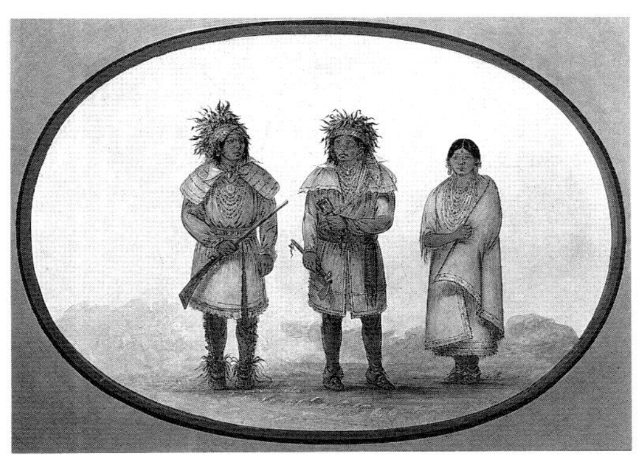

Three Peoria Indians, 1861/1869
Paperboard, c.474 x 0.639
(18 11/16 x 25 3/16)
Paul Mellon Collection
1965.16.109

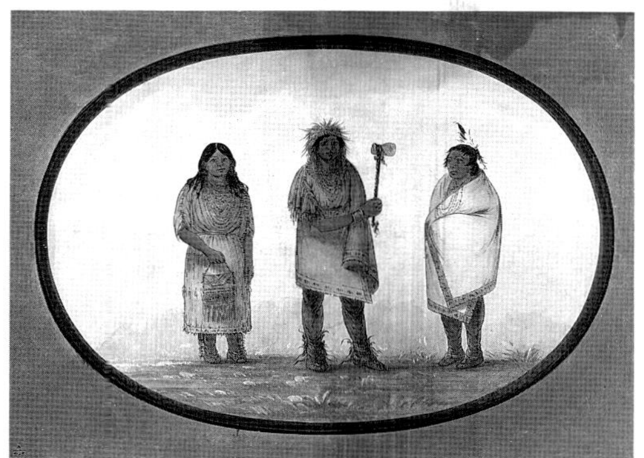

Three Piankeshaw Indians, 1861/1869
Paperboard, 0.474 x 0.639
(18 11/16 x 25 3/16)
Paul Mellon Collection
1965.16.102

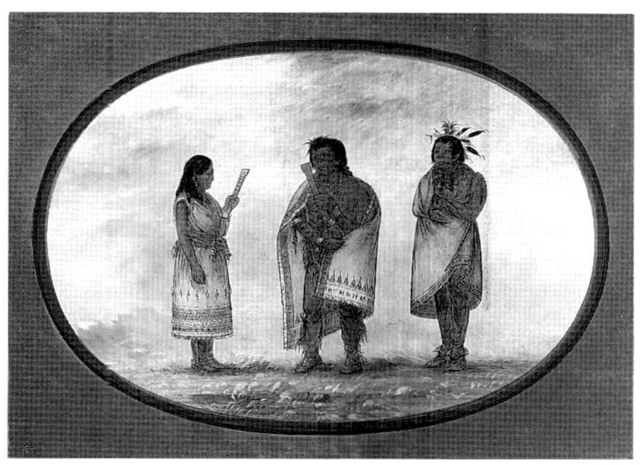

Three Potowotomie Indians, 1861/1869
Paperboard, 0.475 x 0.640
(18 11/16 x 25 3/16)
Paul Mellon Collection
1965.16.122

Three Riccarree Indians, 1861
Paperboard, 0.472 x 0.617
(18 9/16 x 24 5/16)
Inscribed at lower center: *Geo. Catlin / 61.*
Paul Mellon Collection
1965.16.90

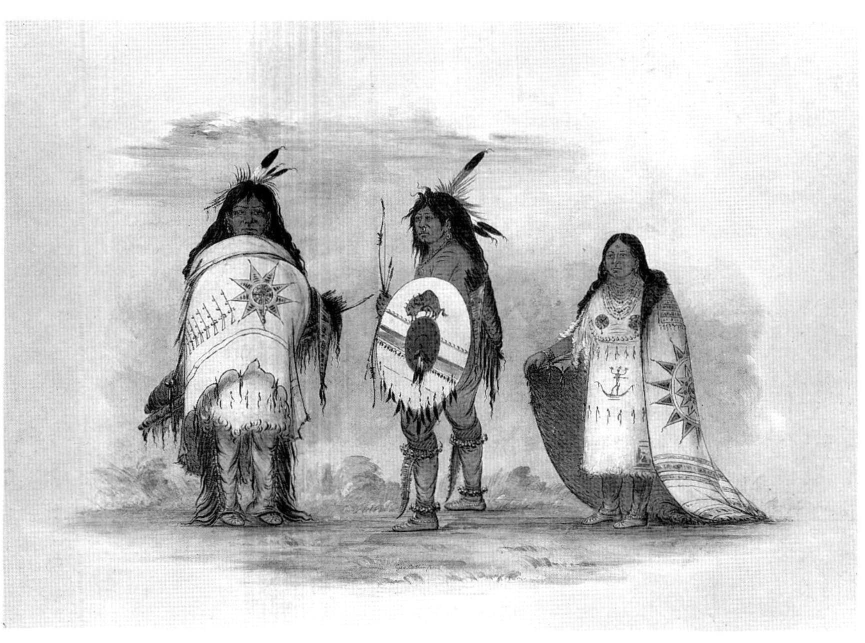

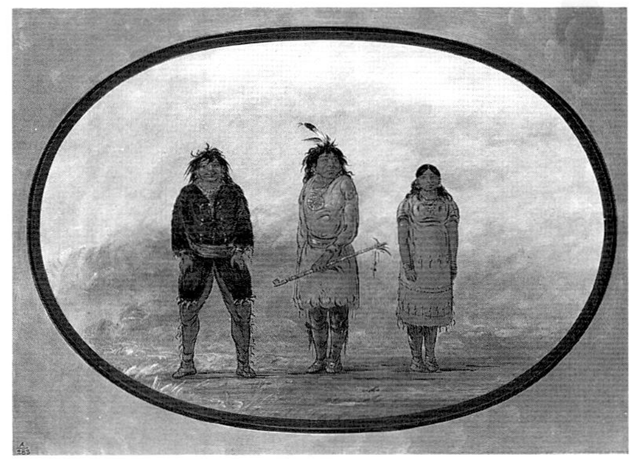

Three Selish Indians, 1855/1869
Paperboard, 0.458 x 0.616 (18 x 24¼)
Paul Mellon Collection
1965.16.166

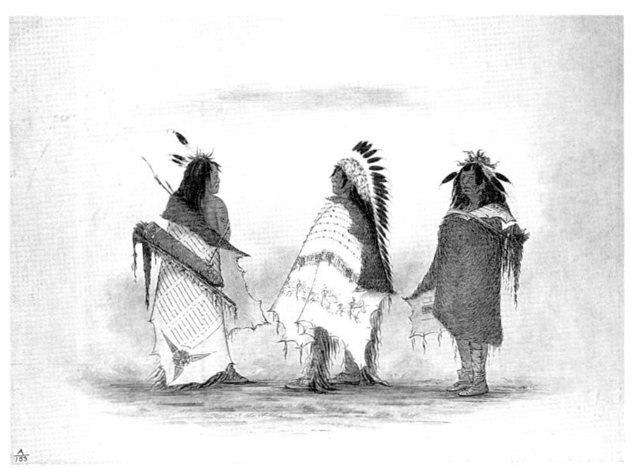

Three Shoshonee Warriors, 1861
Paperboard, 0.456 x 0.604
(17 15/16 x 23¾)
Inscribed at lower right: *G. Catlin / 1861*
Paul Mellon Collection
1965.16.57

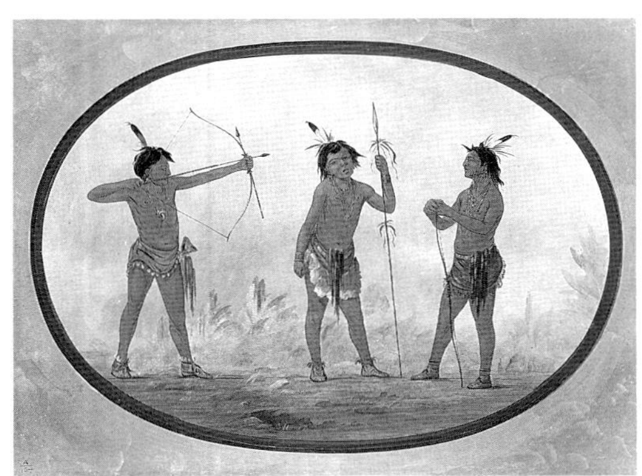

Three Shoshonee Warriors Armed for War, 1861/1869
Paperboard, 0.461 x 0.615 (18⅛ x 24 3/16)
Paul Mellon Collection
1965.16.58

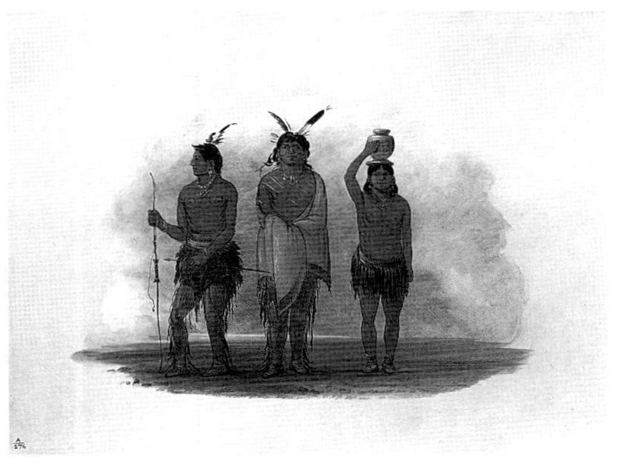

Three Walla Walla Indians, 1855/1869
Paperboard, 0.472 x 0.618 (18½ x 24⅜)
Paul Mellon Collection
1965.16.159

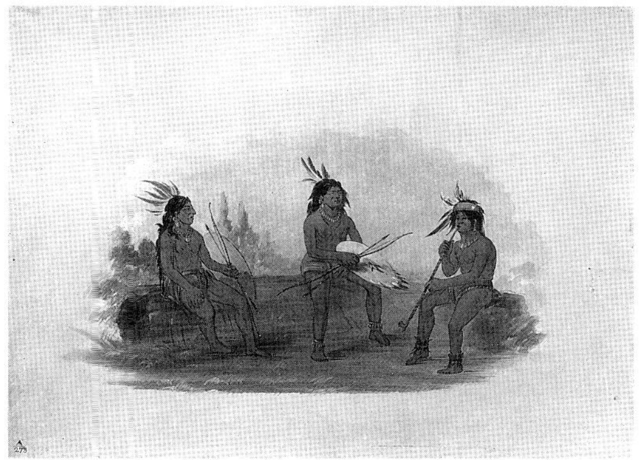

Three Young Chinook Men, 1855/1869
Paperboard, 0.468 x 0.623 (18 7/16 x 24 1/2)
Paul Mellon Collection
1965.16.156

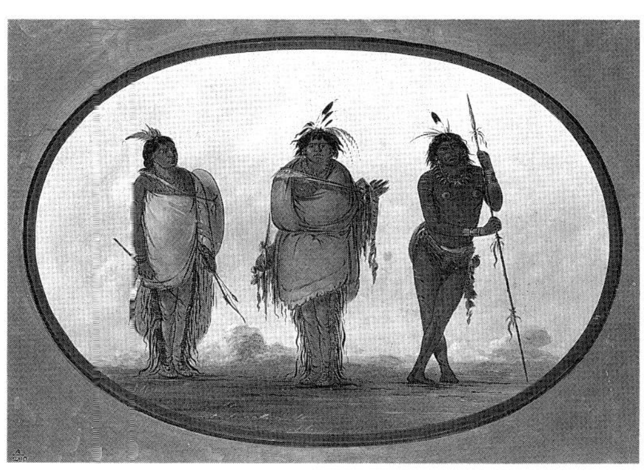

Three Yumaya Indians, 1855/1869
Paperboard, 0.457 x 0.618 (18 x 24 1/4)
Paul Mellon Collection
1965.16.173

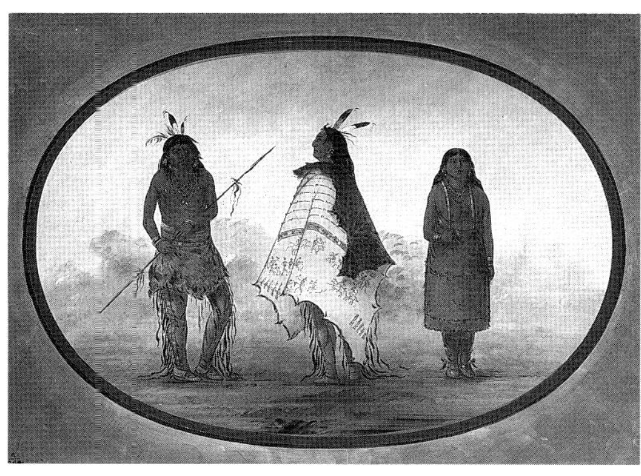

Two Apachee Warriors and a Woman, 1855/1869
Paperboard, 0.467 x 0.622 (18 3/8 x 24 1/2)
Paul Mellon Collection
1965.16.147

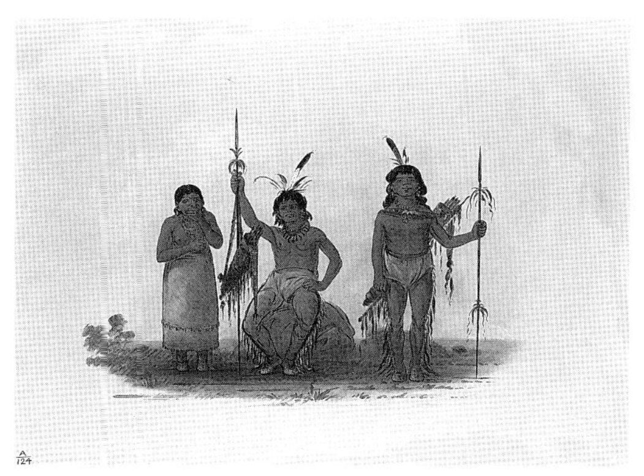

Two Arapaho Warriors and a Woman, 1861/1869
Paperboard, 0.470 x 0.623 (18 1/2 x 24 1/2)
Paul Mellon Collection
1965.16.31

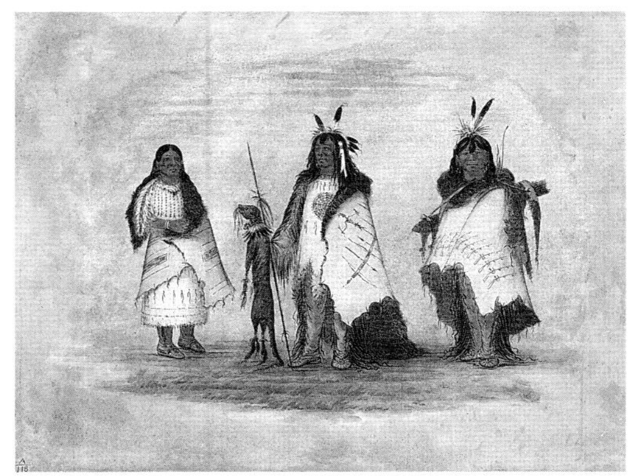

Two Blackfoot Warriors and a Woman, 1861/1869
Paperboard, 0.467 x 0.615 (18⅜ x 24¼)
Paul Mellon Collection
1965.16.27

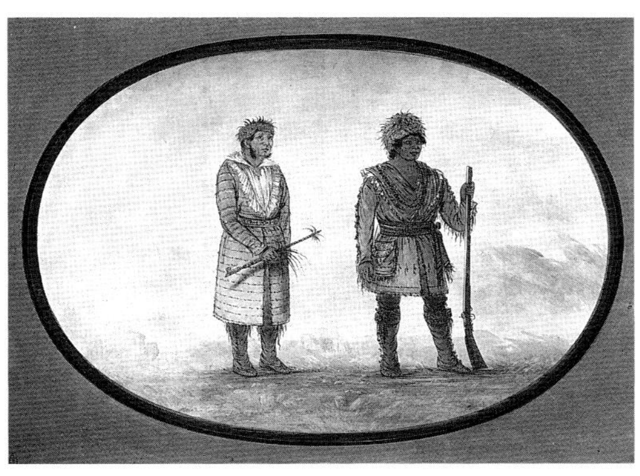

Two Cherokee Chiefs, 1861/1869
Paperboard, 0.462 x 0.629 (18½ x 24¾)
Paul Mellon Collection
1965.16.120

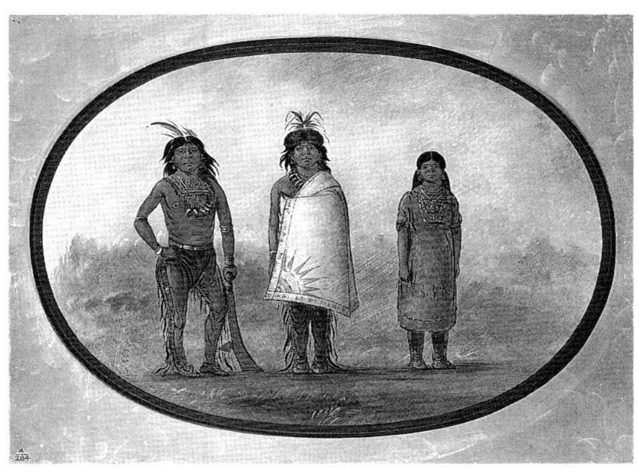

Two Chippewyan Warriors and a Woman, 1855/1869
Paperboard, 0.470 x 0.624 (18½ x 24 9/16)
Paul Mellon Collection
1965.16.167

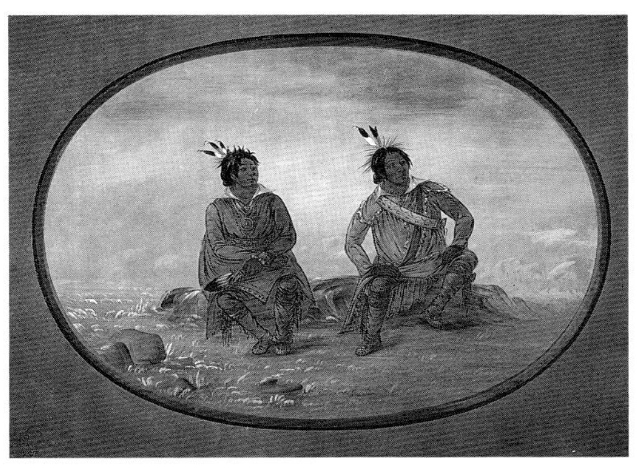

Two Choctaw Indians, 1861/1869
Paperboard, 0.472 x 0.638 (18 9/16 x 25⅛)
Paul Mellon Collection
1965.16.116

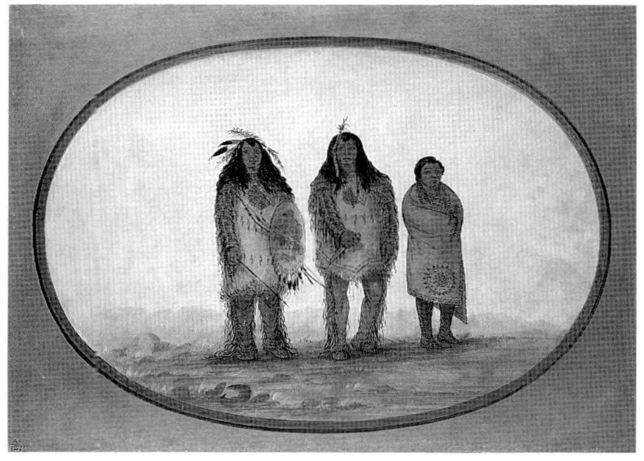

Two Nezperce Warriors and a Boy,
1855/1869
Paperboard, 0.472 x 0.638 ($18\frac{9}{16}$ x $25\frac{1}{8}$)
Paul Mellon Collection
1965.16.34

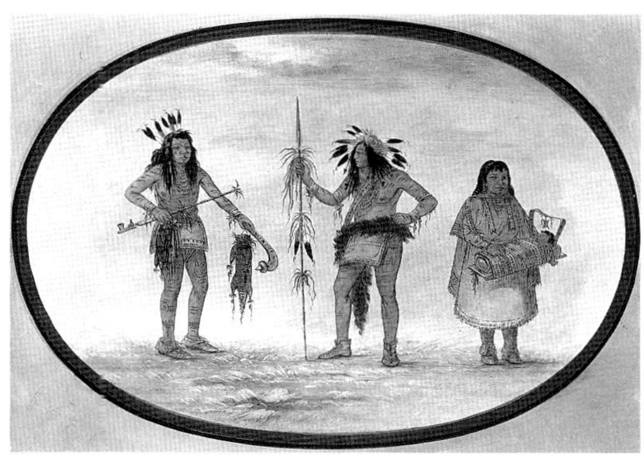

Two Ojibbeway Warriors and a Woman,
1861/1869
Paperboard, 0.468 x 0.628 ($18\frac{3}{8}$ x $24\frac{3}{4}$)
Paul Mellon Collection
1965.16.92

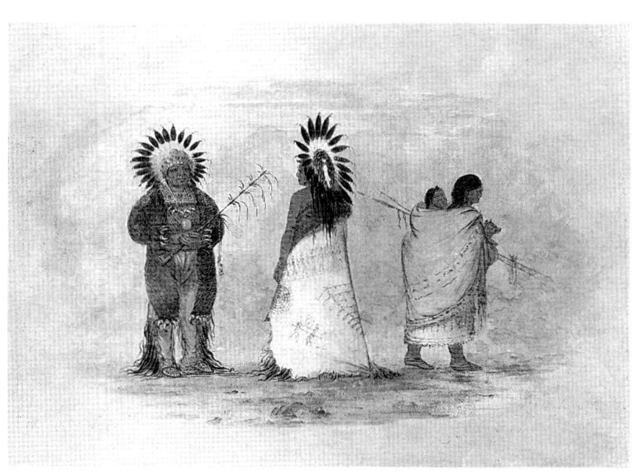

Two Ottoe Chiefs and a Woman,
1861/1869
Paperboard, 0.454 x 0.609
($17\frac{7}{8}$ x $23\frac{15}{16}$)
Paul Mellon Collection
1965.16.100

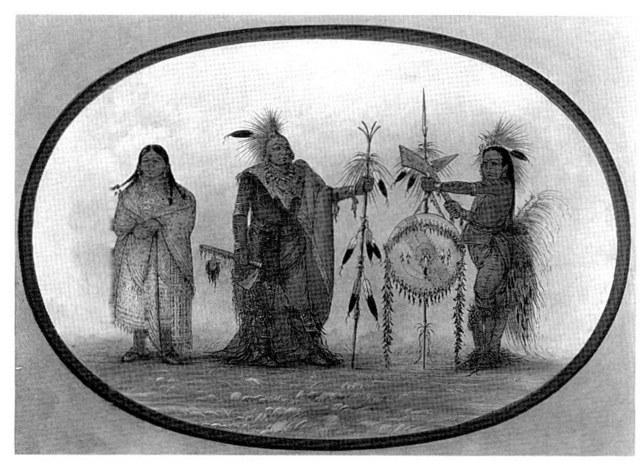

Two Saukie Chiefs and a Woman,
1861/1869
Paperboard, 0.468 x 0.632 ($18\frac{7}{16}$ x $24\frac{7}{8}$)
Paul Mellon Collection
1965.16.96

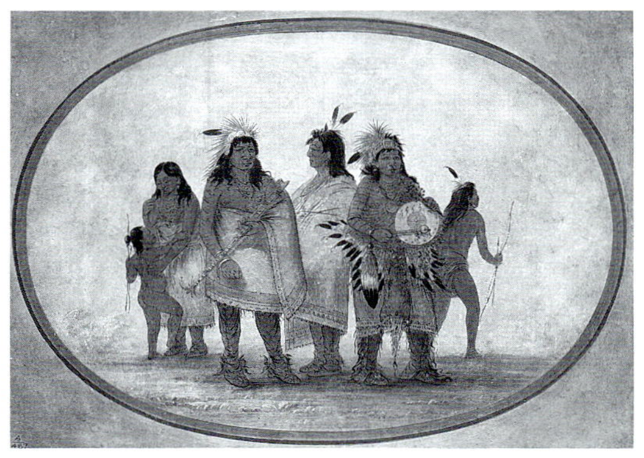

Two Sioux Chiefs, a Medicine Man, and a Woman with a Child, 1861/1869
Paperboard, c.442 x 0.610 (17 3/8 x 24)
Paul Mellon Collection
1965.16.343

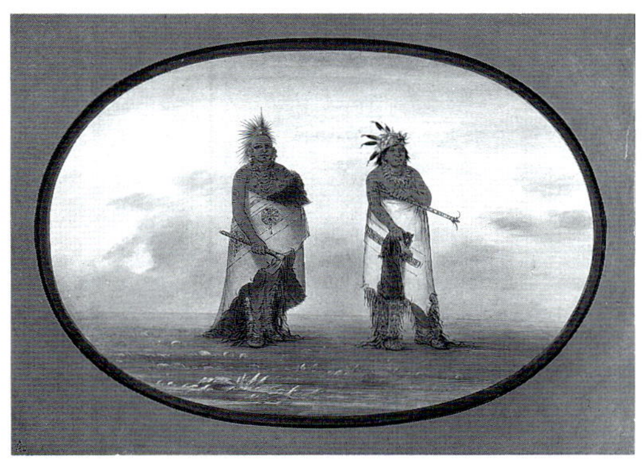

Two Unidentified North American Indians, 1861/1869
Paperboard, c.474 x 0.640 (18 11/16 x 25 3/16)
Paul Mellon Collection
1965.16.59

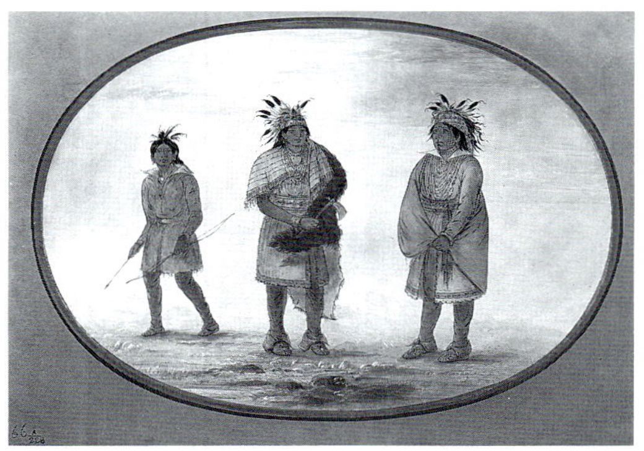

Two Weeah Warriors and a Woman, 1861/1869
Paperboard, 0.475 x 0.638 (18 3/4 x 25 1/8)
Paul Mellon Collection
1965.16.117

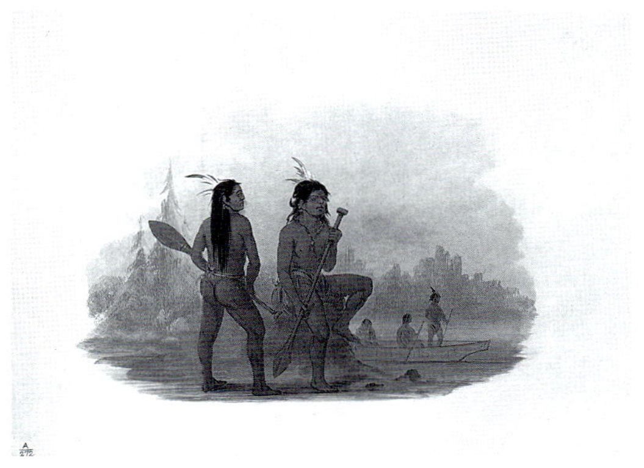

Two Young Hyda Men, 1855/1869
Paperboard, 0.469 x 0.625 (18 7/16 x 24 5/8)
Paul Mellon Collection
1965.16.155

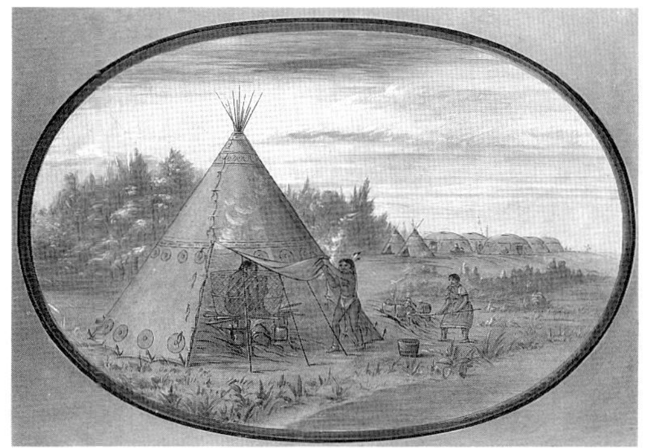

Vapor Bath—Minatarree, 1861/1869
Paperboard, 0.468 x 0.634
(18 7/16 x 24 15/16)
Paul Mellon Collection
1965.16.342

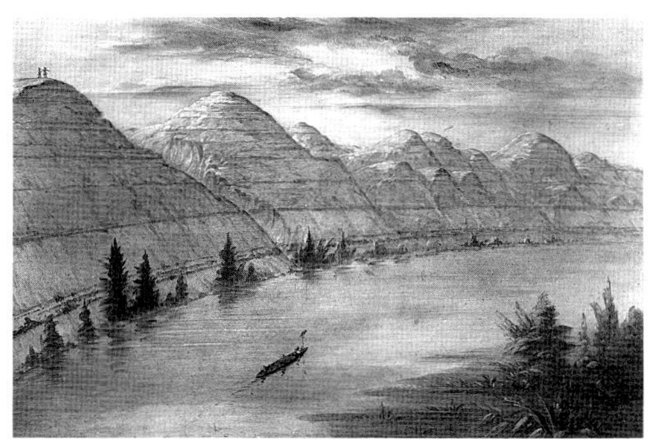

View in the "Grand Detour," Upper Missouri, 1861/1869
Paperboard, 0.461 x 0.622 (18 1/8 x 24 1/2)
Paul Mellon Collection
1965.16.191

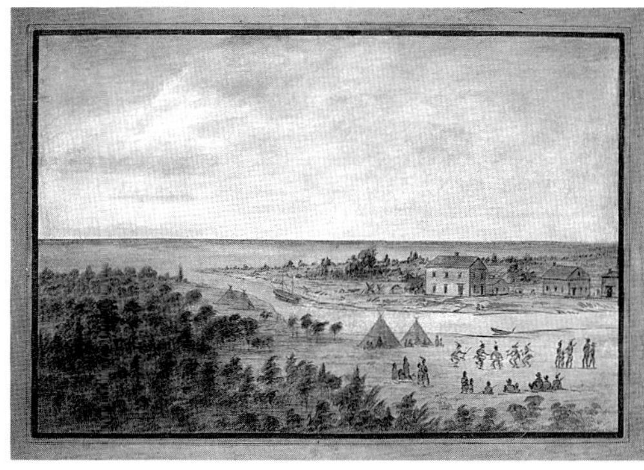

View of Chicago in 1834. 1861/1869
Paperboard, 0.459 x 0.614 (17 7/8 x 24 3/16)
Paul Mellon Collection
1965.16.207

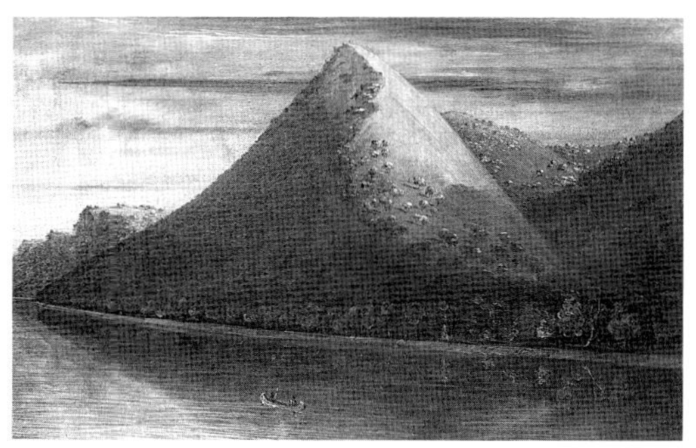

View of "Pike's Tent," 1861/1869
Paperboard, 0.380 x 0.590 (15 x 23 1/4)
Paul Mellon Collection
1965.16.195

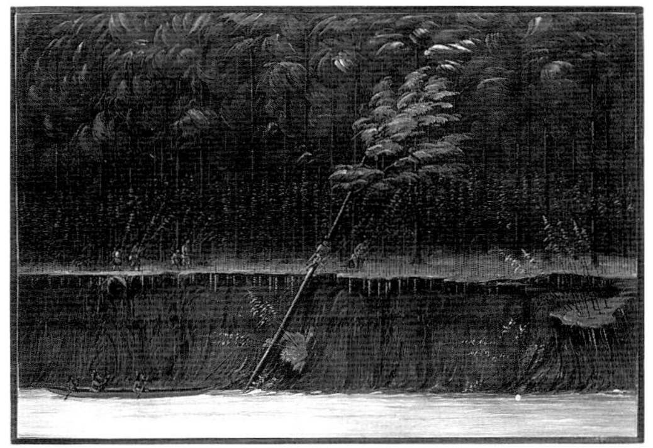

View of the Lower Mississippi, 1861/1869
Paperboard, 0.469 x 0.630
($18\frac{1}{2}$ x $24\frac{13}{16}$)
Paul Mellon Collection
1965.16.209

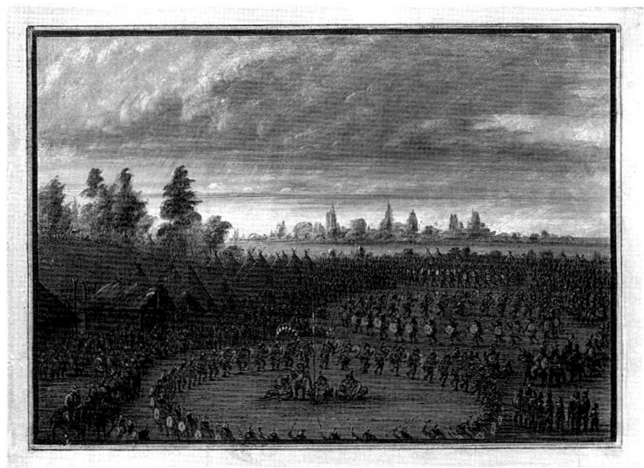

War Dance of the Apachees, 1855/1869
Paperboard, 0.463 x 0.608
($18\frac{3}{16}$ x $23\frac{15}{16}$)
Paul Mellon Collection
1965.16.315

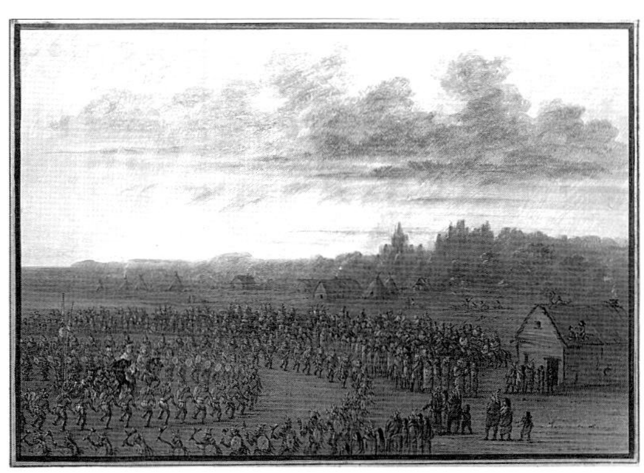

War Dance of the Saukies, 1861/1869
Paperboard, 0.460 x 0.609 ($18\frac{1}{8}$ x 24)
Paul Mellon Collection
1965.16.143

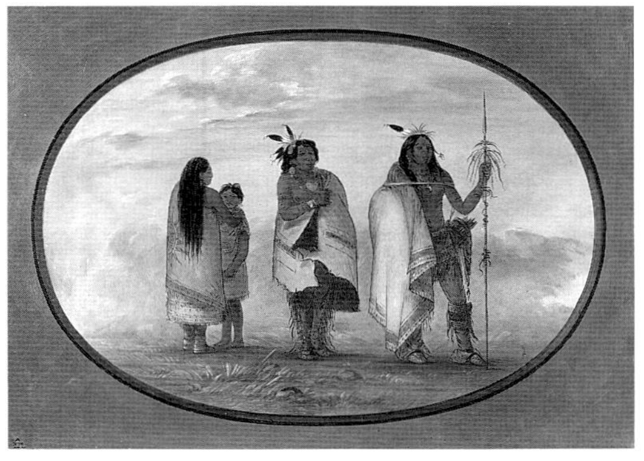

Weeco Chief, His Wife, and a Warrior, 1861/1869
Paperboard, 0.471 x 0.636 ($18\frac{1}{2}$ x $25\frac{1}{16}$)
Paul Mellon Collection
1965.16.101

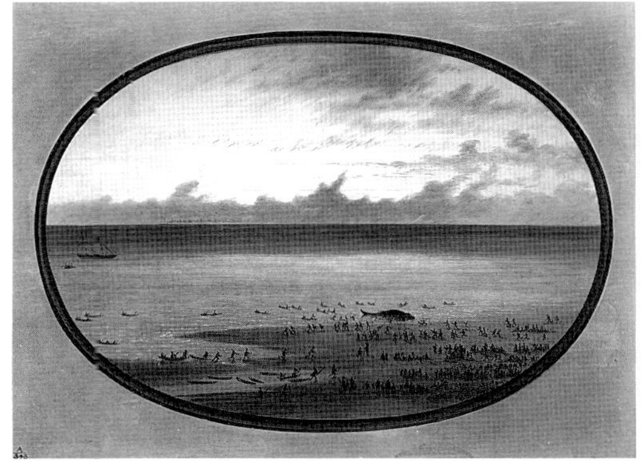

A Whale Ashore—Klahoquat, 1855/1869
Paperboard, 0.480 x 0.641 (18⅞ x 25¼)
Paul Mellon Collection
1965.16.214

The White Cloud, Head Chief of the Iowas, 1844/1845
Canvas, 0.710 x 0.580 (28 x 22⅞)
Paul Mellon Collection
1965.16.347

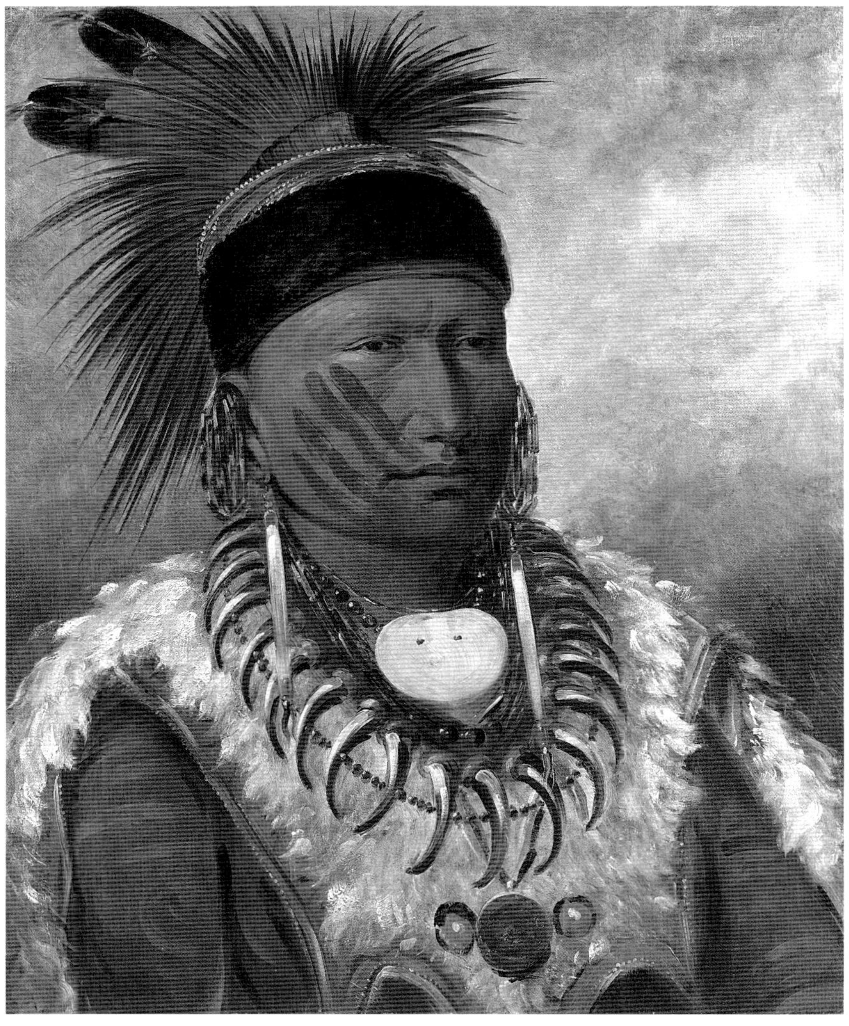

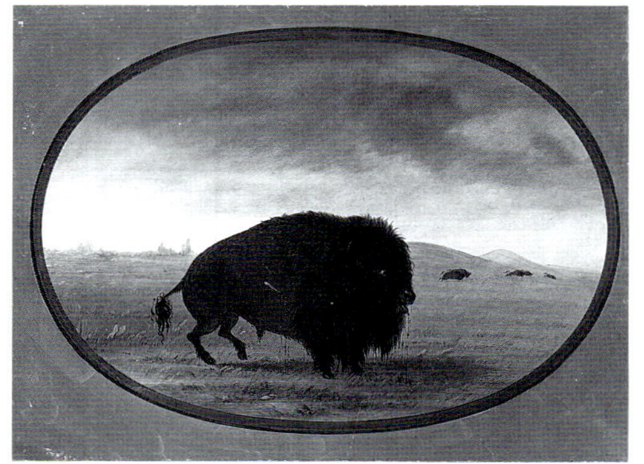

Wounded Buffalo Bull, 1861/1869
Paperboard, 0.468 x 0.625 (18⅜ x 24⅝)
Paul Mellon Collection
1965.16.205

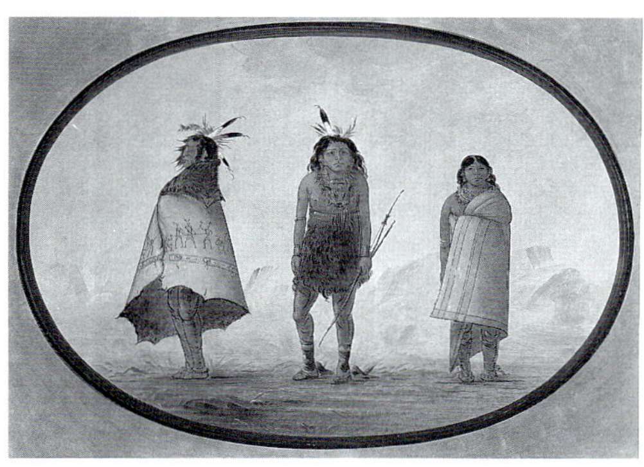

Yntah Medicine Man, a Warrior, and a Woman, 1855/1869
Paperboard, 0.463 x 0.626 (18¼ x 24⅝)
Paul Mellon Collection
1965.16.126

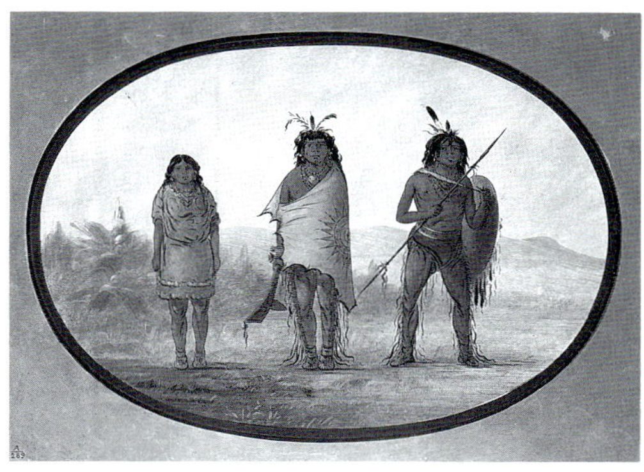

A Yuma Chief, His Daughter, and a Warrior, 1855/1869
Paperboard, c.465 x 0.621 (18¼ x 24½)
Paul Mellon Collection
1965.16.172

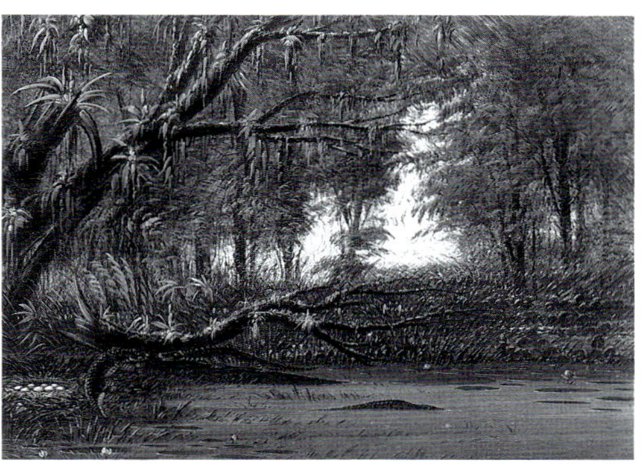

South American Subjects

An Alligator's Nest, 1854/1869
Paperboard, c.463 x 0.612 (18¼ x 24⅛)
Paul Mellon Collection
1965.16.293

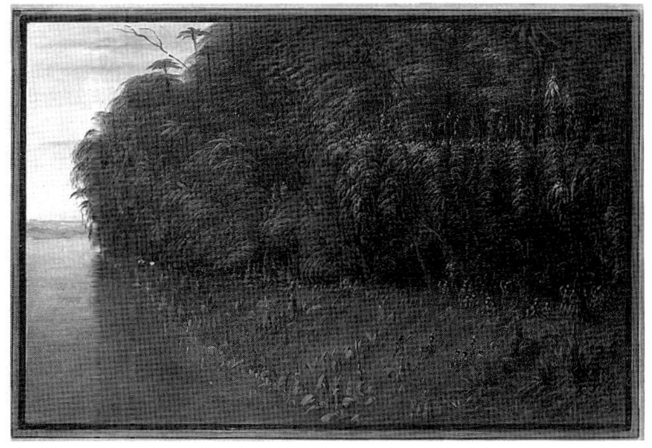

An Amazon Forest—Looking Ashore, 1854/1869
Paperboard, 0.462 x 0.627
(18 3/16 x 24 11/16)
Paul Mellon Collection
1965.16.272

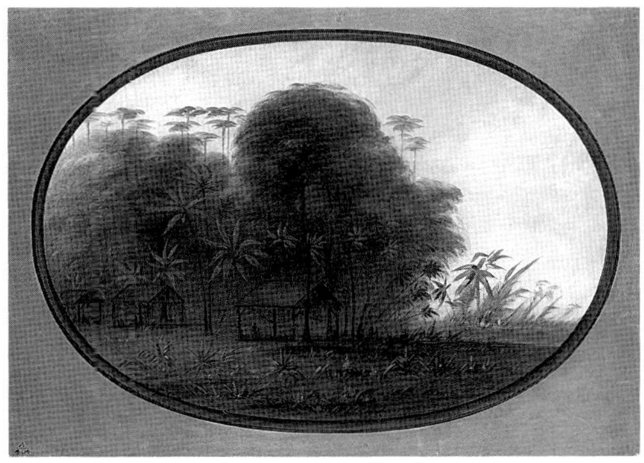

Arowak Village, 1854/1869
Paperboard, 0.467 x 0.624 (18 3/8 x 24 5/8)
Paul Mellon Collection
1965.16.267

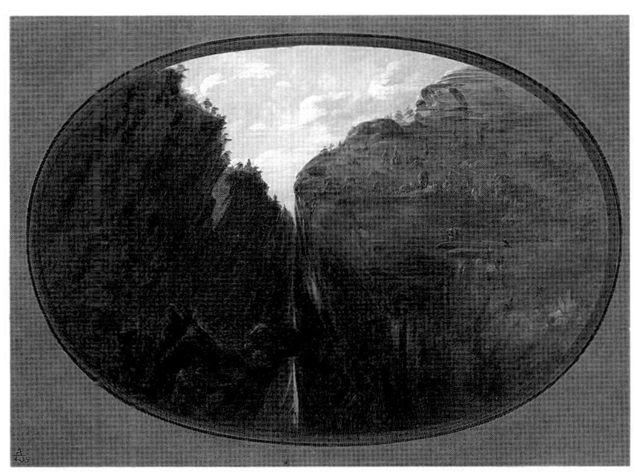

The Beetle Crevice, 1854/1869
Paperboard, 0.459 x 0.623 (18 x 24 1/2)
Paul Mellon Collection
1965.16.268

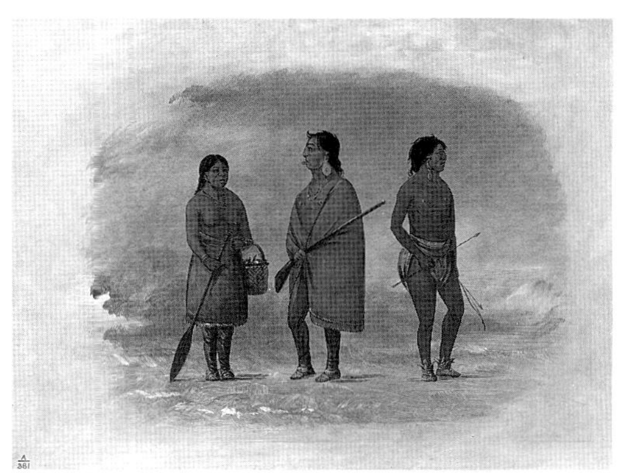

Botocudo Chief, His Wife, and a Young Man, 1854/1869
Paperboard, 0.460 x 0.598 (18 1/4 x 23 1/2)
Paul Mellon Collection
1965.16.249

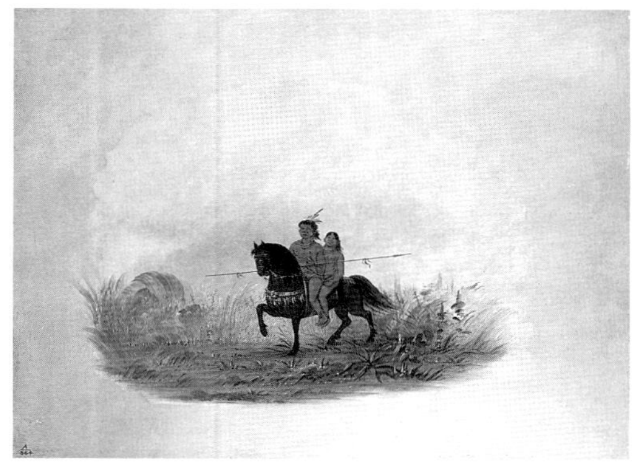

Bride and Groom on Horseback—Connibo, 1854/1869
Paperboard, 0.466 x 0.618 (18⅜ x 24 5/16)
Paul Mellon Collection
1965.16.232

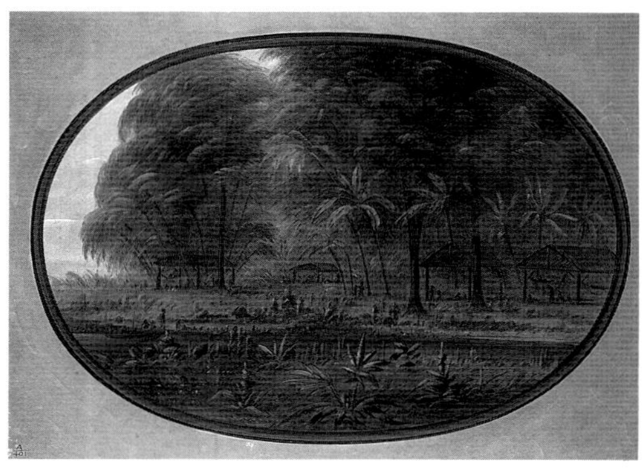

A Caribbe Village in Dutch Guiana, 1854/1869
Paperboard, 0.458 x 0.624 (18 x 24⅝)
Paul Mellon Collection
1965.16.265

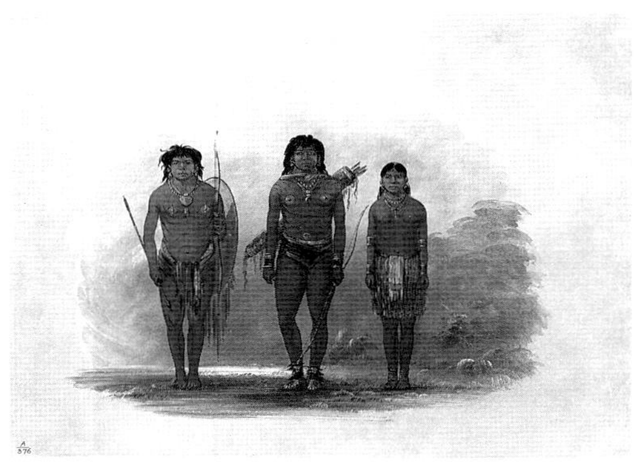

Chaco Chief, His Wife, and a Warrior, 1854/1869
Paperboard, 0.457 x 0.607 (17⅞ x 23 15/16)
Paul Mellon Collection
1965.16.244

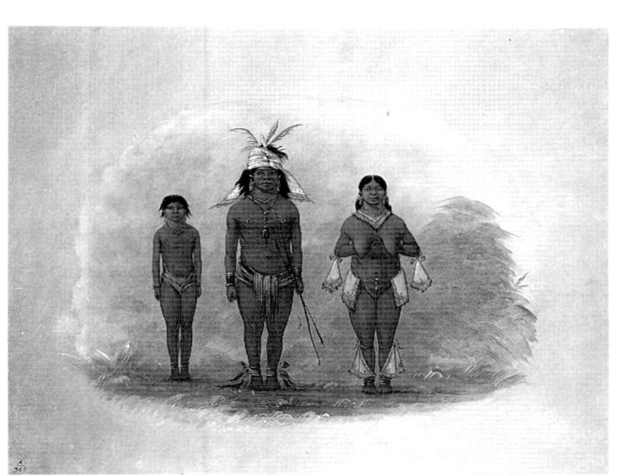

A Chetibo Family, 1854/1869
Paperboard, 0.468 x 0.617 (18⅜ x 24 5/16)
Paul Mellon Collection
1965.16.233

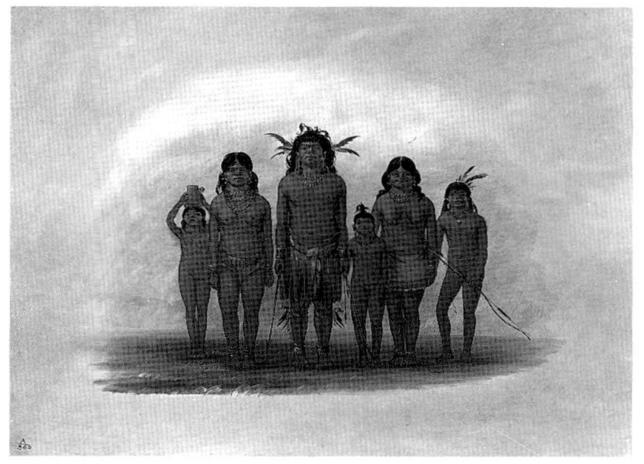

A Connibo Indian Family, 1854/1869
Paperboard, 0.465 x 0.615 (18⅜ x 24⅛)
Paul Mellon Collection
1965.16.231

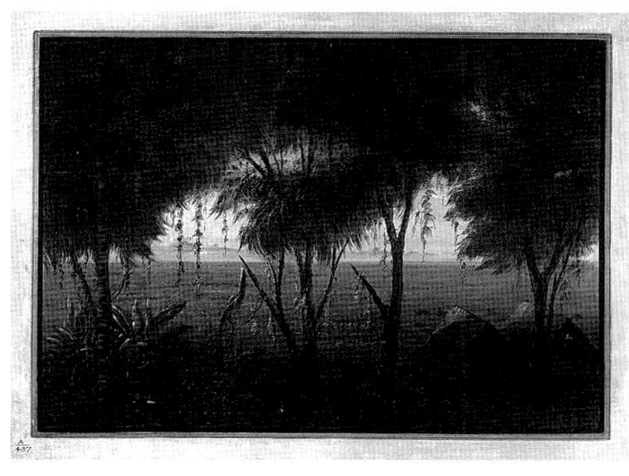

A Connibo Village, 1854/1869
Paperboard, 0.460 x 0.598 (18¼ x 23½)
Paul Mellon Collection
1965.16.295

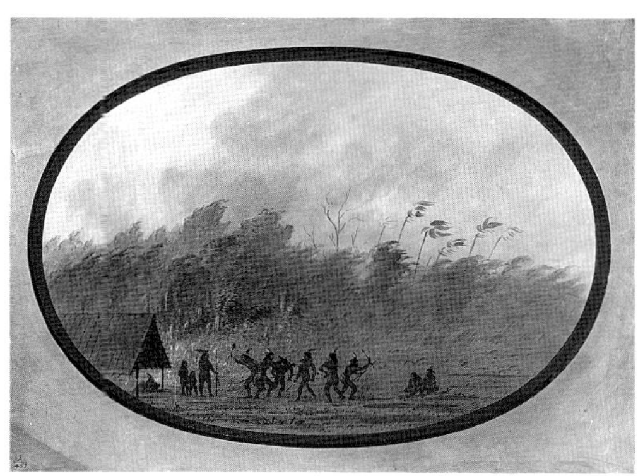

A Connibo Wigwam, 1854/1869
Paperboard, 0.475 x 0.626 (18¾ x 24⅝)
Paul Mellon Collection
1965.16.308

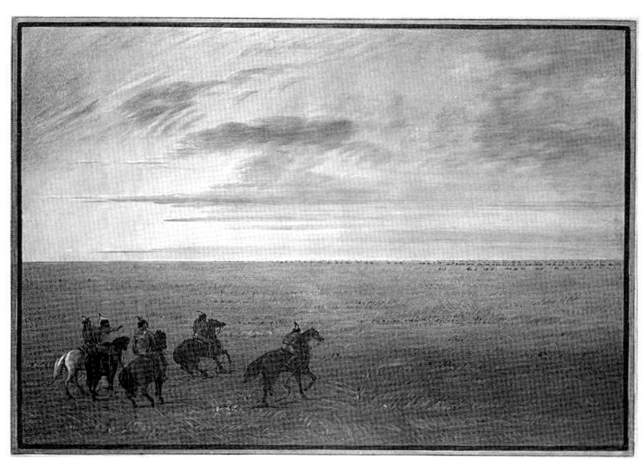

Connibos Starting for Wild Horses, 1854/1869
Paperboard, 0.472 x 0.635 (18⅝ x 25)
Paul Mellon Collection
1965.16.296

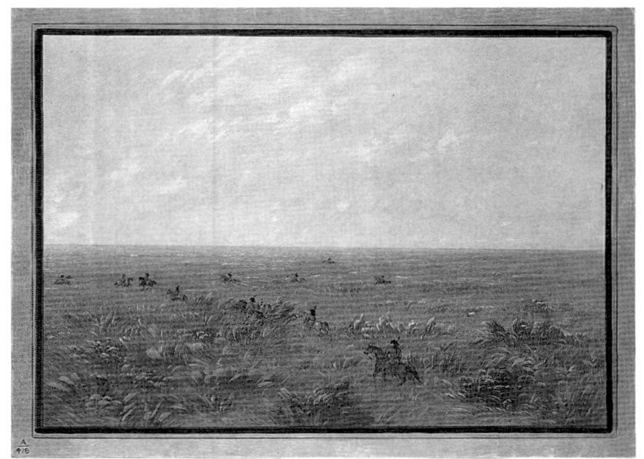

Driving the Pampas for Wild Cattle—Connibo, 1854/1869
Paperboard, c.460 x 0.615 (18¼ x 24⁵⁄₁₆)
Paul Mellon Collection
1965.16.278

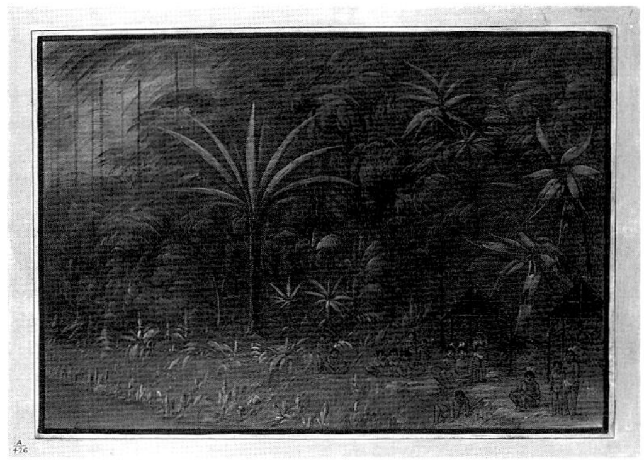

Encampment of Cocomas—Looking Ashore, 1854/1869
Paperboard, c.467 x 0.630 (18⅜ x 24¹³⁄₁₆)
Paul Mellon Collection
1965.16.285

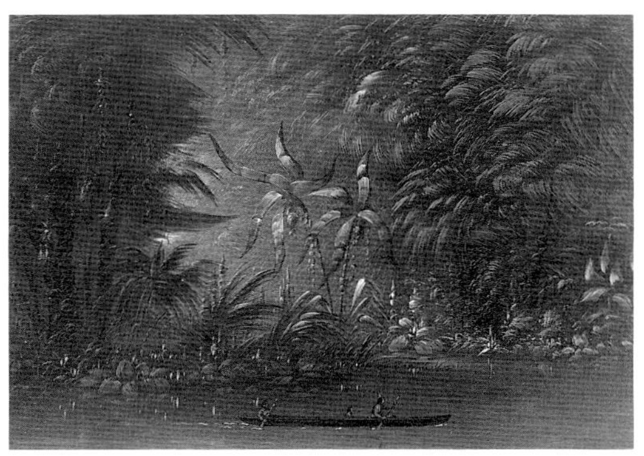

Entrance to a Lagoon, Shore of the Amazon, 1854/1869
Paperboard, 0.482 x 0.633 (19 x 24¹⁵⁄₁₆)
Paul Mellon Collection
1965.16.294

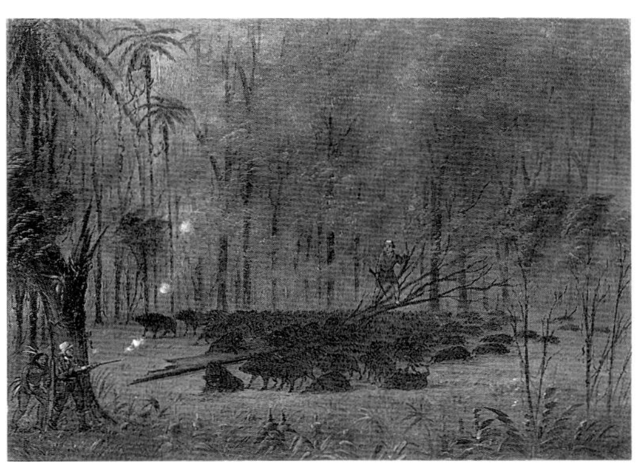

A Fight with Peccaries—Caribbe, 1854/1869
Canvas, 0.452 x 0.610 (17¹³⁄₁₆ x 24¹⁄₁₆)
Paul Mellon Collection
1965.16.260

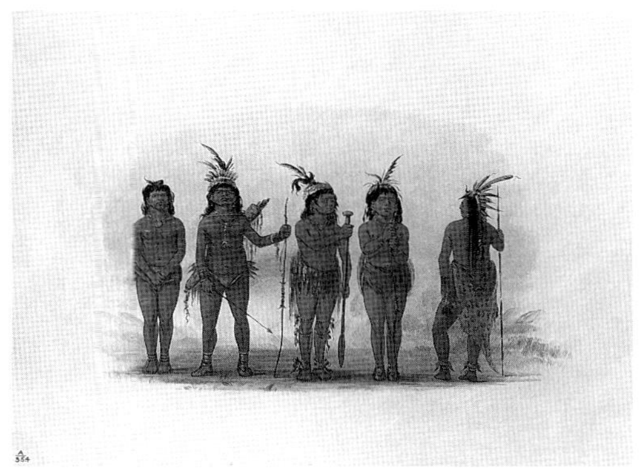

Five Caribbe Indians, 1854/1869
Paperboard, 0.467 x 0.620 (18 3/8 x 24 3/8)
Paul Mellon Collection
1965.16.222

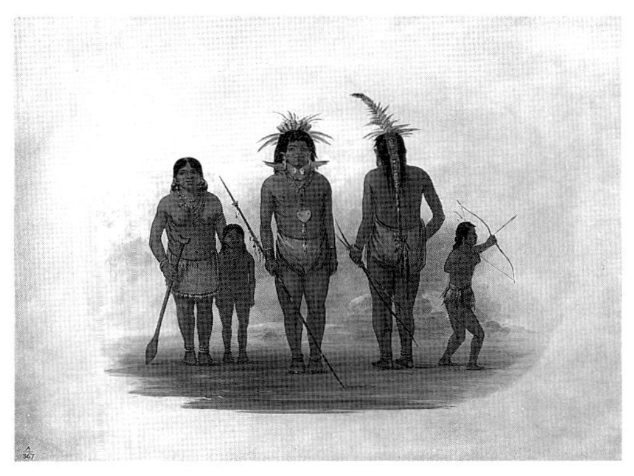

Five Iquito Indians, 1854/1869
Paperboard, 0.465 x 0.625 (18 3/8 x 24 5/8)
Paul Mellon Collection
1965.16.235

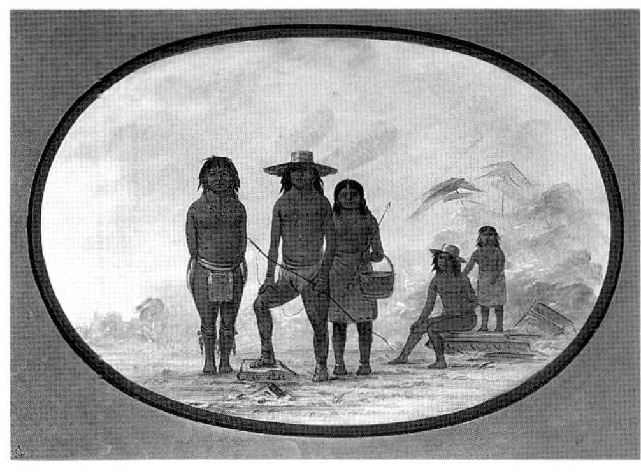

Five Maya Indians, 1855/1869
Paperboard, 0.465 x 0.624
(18 5/16 x 24 9/16)
Paul Mellon Collection
1965.16.174

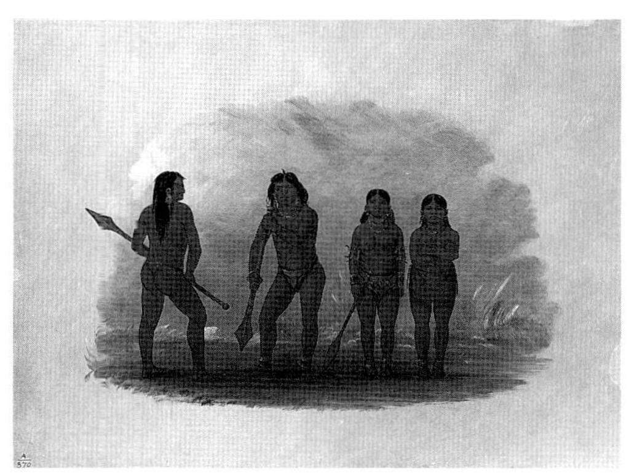

Four Angustura Indians, 1854/1869
Paperboard, 0.465 x 0.622 (18 1/4 x 24 1/2)
Paul Mellon Collection
1965.16.238

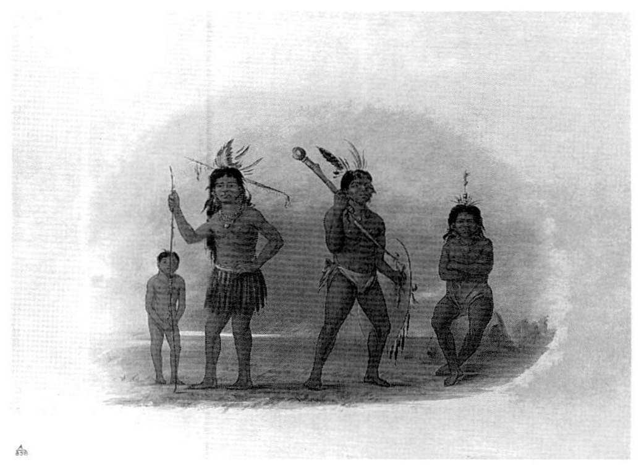

Four Arowak Indians, 1854/1869
Paperboard, c.467 x 0.620 (18 3/8 x 24 3/8)
Paul Mellon Collection
1965.16.226

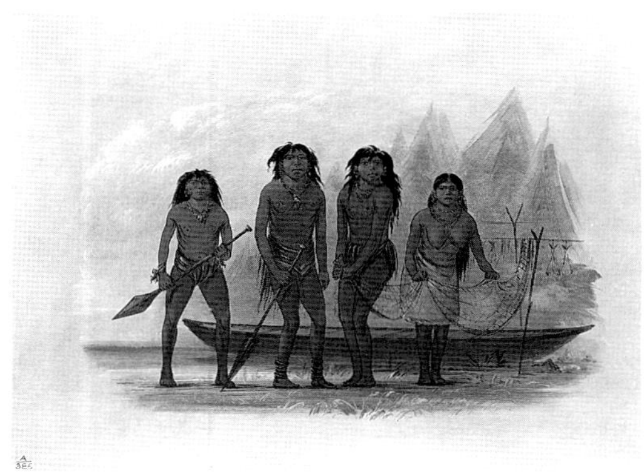

Four Fuegian Indians, 1856/1869
Paperboard, c.452 x 0.604
(17 13/16 x 23 7/8)
Paul Mellon Collection
1965.16.254

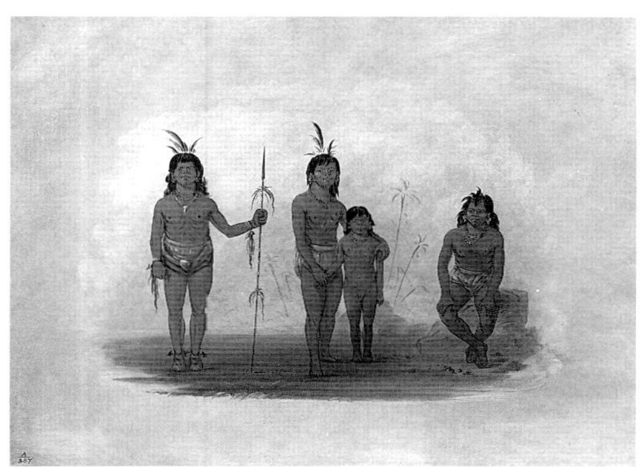

Four Goo-a-give Indians, 1854/1869
Paperboard, c.455 x 0.622 (18 x 24 5/8)
Paul Mellon Collection
1965.16.225

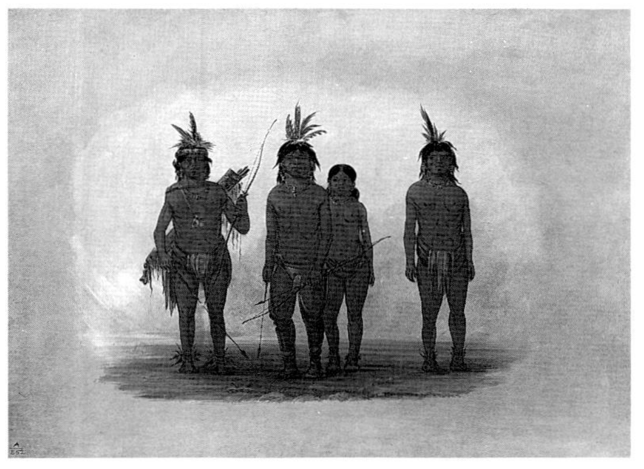

Four Macouchi Indians, 1854/1869
Paperboard, c.464 x 0.621 (18 1/4 x 24 7/16)
Paul Mellon Collection
1965.16.230

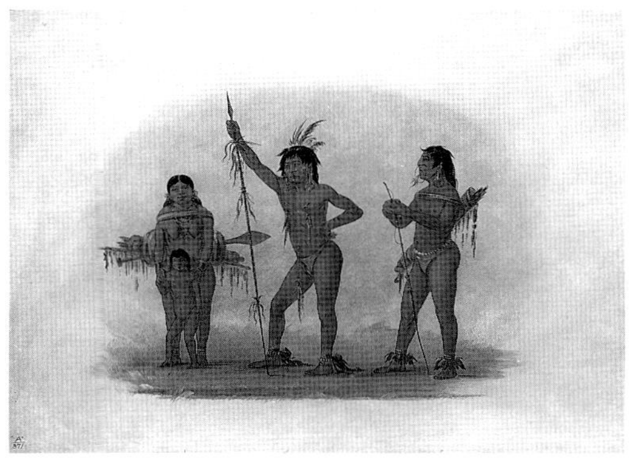

Four Mura Indians, 1854/1869
Paperboard, 0.468 x 0.624 (18⅜ x 24⅝)
Paul Mellon Collection
1965.16.239

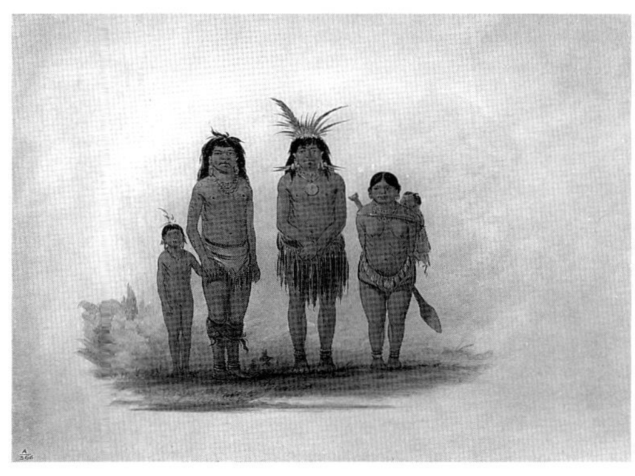

Four Sepibo Indians, 1854/1869
Paperboard, 0.467 x 0.615 (18⅜ x 24¼)
Paul Mellon Collection
1965.16.234

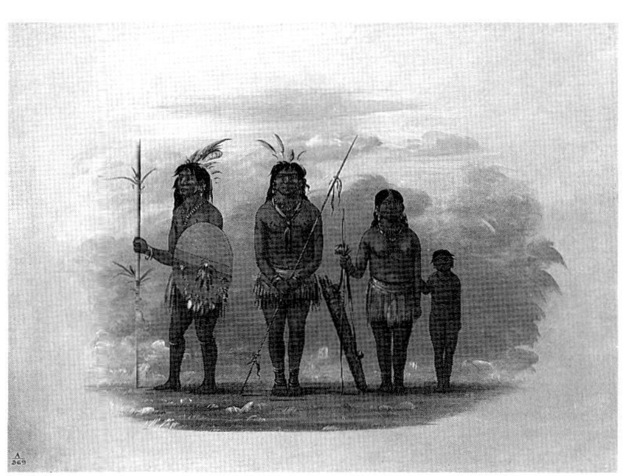

Four Xingu Indians, 1854/1869
Paperboard, 0.458 x 0.605 (18 x 23⅞)
Paul Mellon Collection
1965.16.237

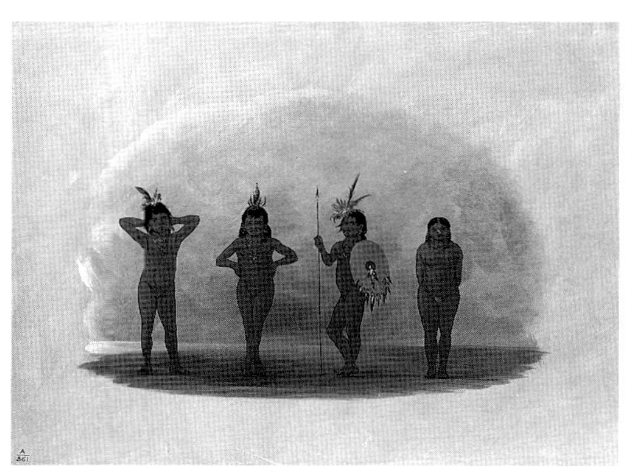

Four Zurumati Children, 1854/1869
Paperboard, 0.463 x 0.622 (18¼ x 24½)
Paul Mellon Collection
1965.16.229

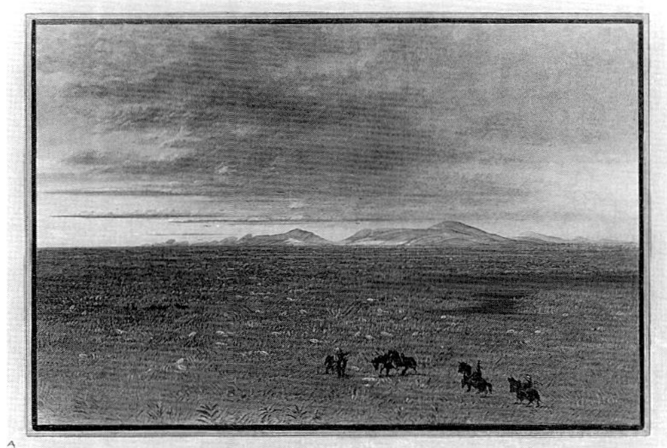

Grand Lavoir Pampa del Sacramento, 1854/1869
Paperboard, 0.438 x 0.612 ($17\frac{1}{4}$ x $24\frac{1}{8}$)
Paul Mellon Collection
1965.16.297

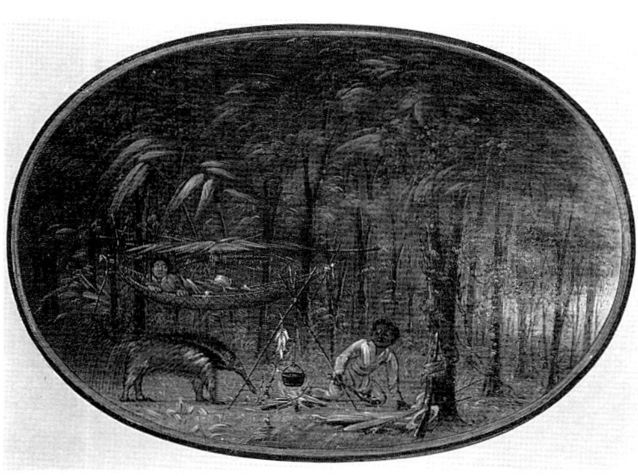

The Great Ant-Eater, 1854/1869
Paperboard, 0.462 x 0.619
($18\frac{3}{16}$ x $24\frac{5}{16}$)
Paul Mellon Collection
1965.16.255

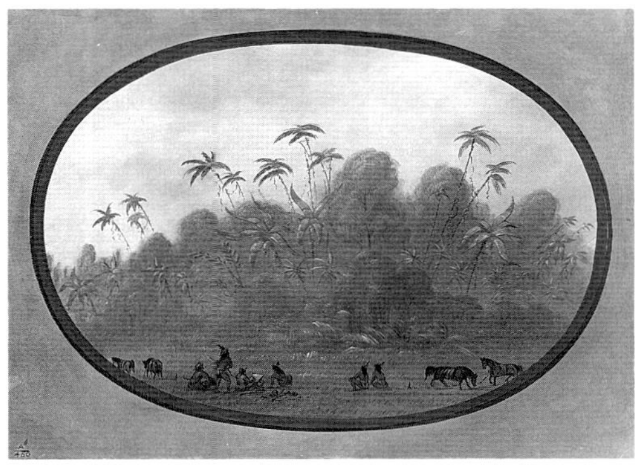

Halting to Make a Sketch, 1854/1869
Paperboard, 0.470 x 0.629 ($18\frac{1}{2}$ x $24\frac{3}{4}$)
Paul Mellon Collection
1965.16.307

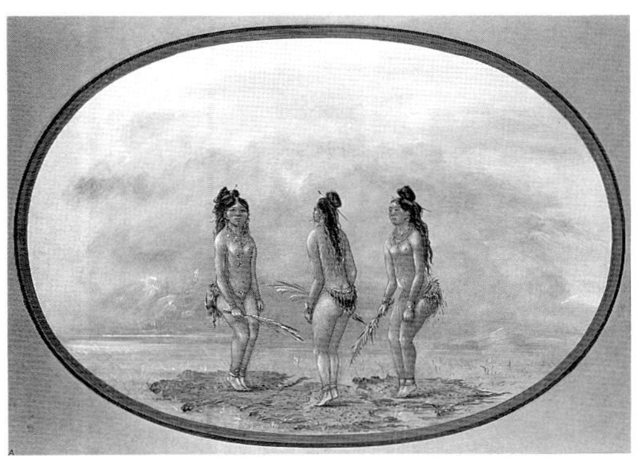

The Handsome Dance—Goo-a-give, 1854/1869
Paperboard, 0.458 x 0.625 (18 x $24\frac{5}{8}$)
Paul Mellon Collection
1965.16.256

Ignis Fatuus, Rio Uruguay, 1854/1869
Paperboard, 0.466 x 0.622 (18⅜ x 24½)
Paul Mellon Collection
1965.16.292

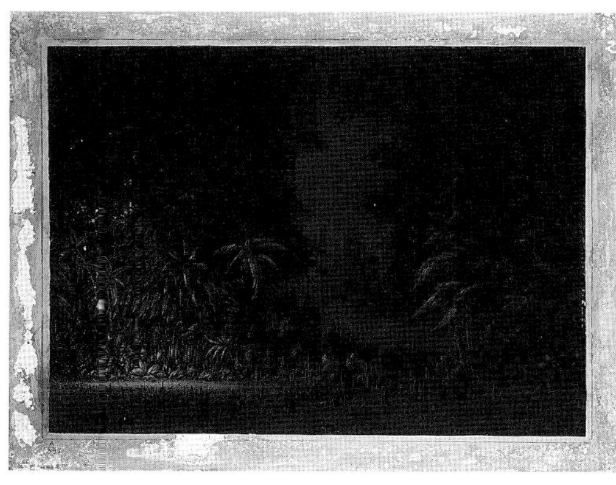

Ignis Fatuus—Zurumati, 1854/1869
Canvas, 0.462 x 0.612 (18³⁄₁₆ x 24⅛)
Paul Mellon Collection
1965.16.261

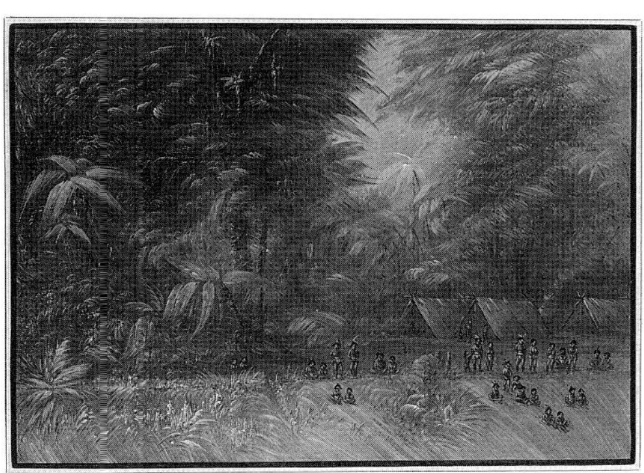

Indian Camp in the Forest, 1854/1869
Paperboard, 0.475 x 0.628 (18⅝ x 24¾)
Paul Mellon Collection
1965.16.289

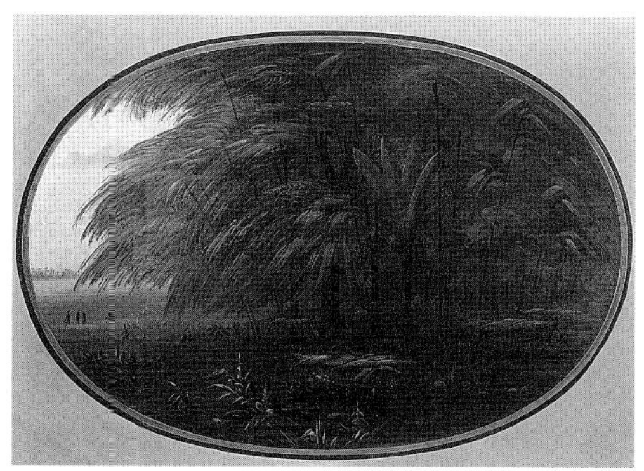

An Indian Village—Shore of the Amazon, 1854/1869
Paperboard, 0.468 x 0.625 (18⅜ x 24⅝)
Paul Mellon Collection
1965.16.270

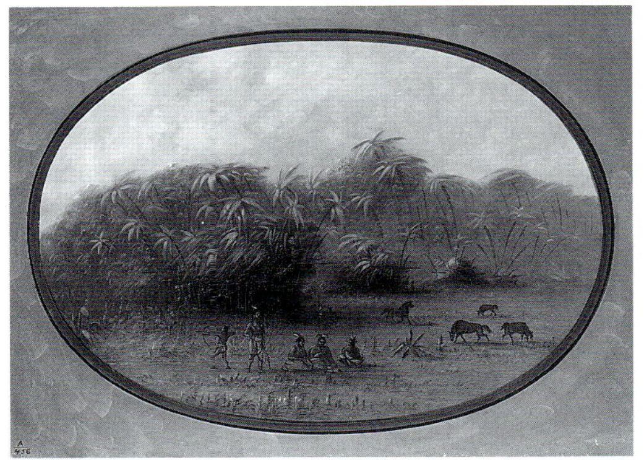

Indians and Horses in a Forest,
1854/1869
Paperboard, 0.468 x 0.623 (18⅜ x 24½)
Paul Mellon Collection
1965.16.312

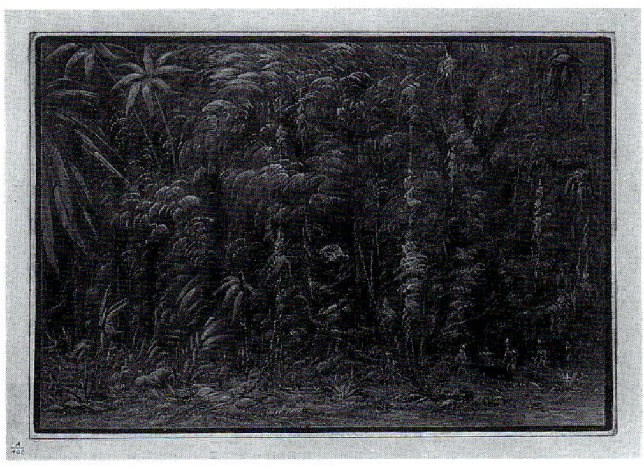

Interior of an Amazon Forest—Zurumati,
1854/1869
Paperboard, 0.467 x 0.633 (18⅜ x 24⅞)
Paul Mellon Collection
1965.16.271

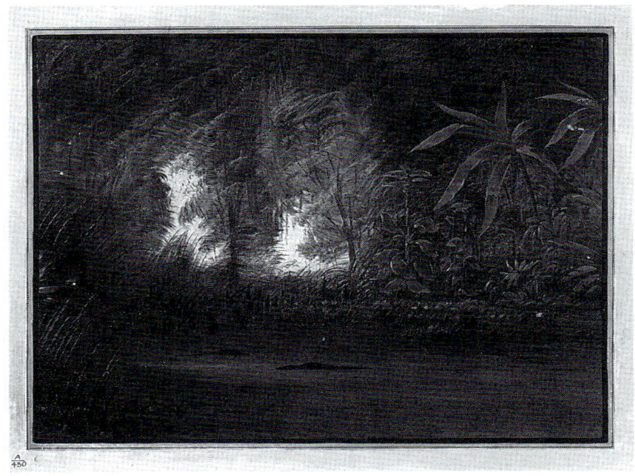

A Lagoon of the Upper Amazon,
1854/1869
Canvas, 0.46[illegible] x 0.601 (18¼ x 23¾)
Paul Mellon Collection
1965.16.288

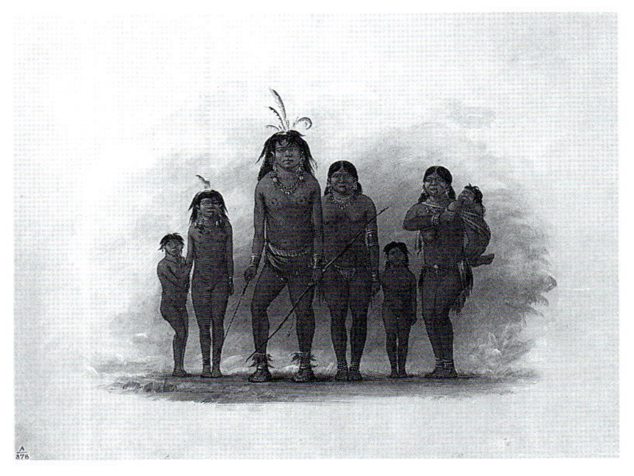

Lengua Chief, His Two Wives, and Four Children, 1854/1869
Paperboard, 0.457 x 0.605 (18 x 23⅞)
Paul Mellon Collection
1965.16.246

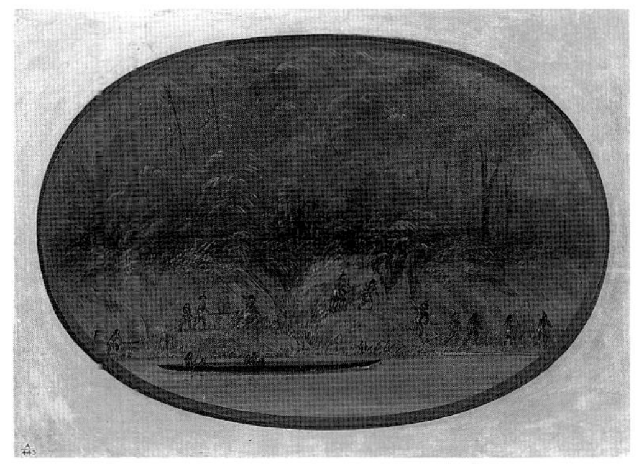

Lengua Indians Ascending the Rapids of the Rio Uruguay, 1854/1869
Paperboard, 0.475 x 0.630 (18 11/16 x 24 13/16)
Paul Mellon Collection
1965.16.300

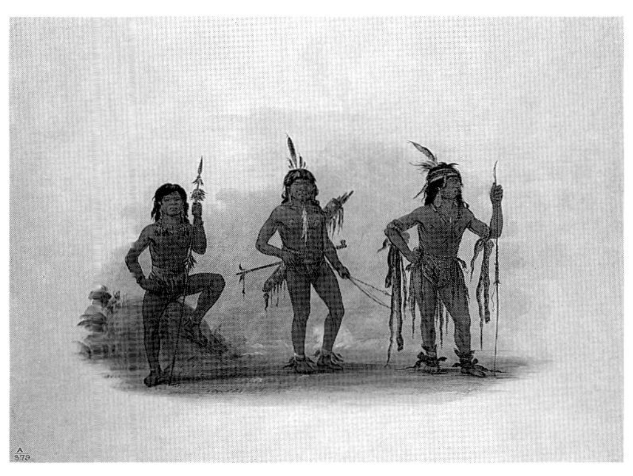

Lengua Medicine Man with Two Warriors, 1854/1869
Paperboard, 0.465 x 0.615 (18 3/8 x 24 1/4)
Paul Mellon Collection
1965.16.247

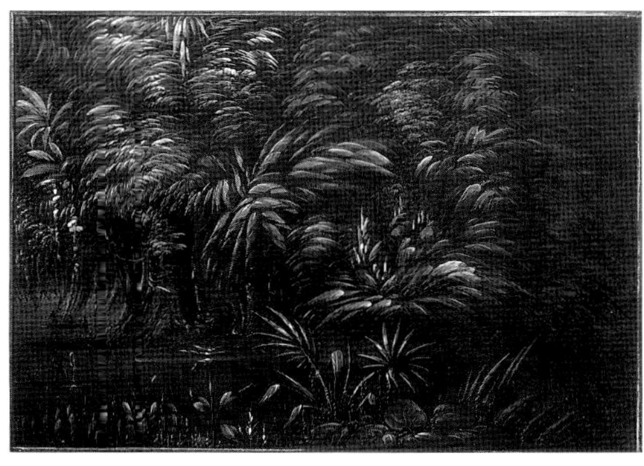

Luxuriant Forest on the Bank of the Amazon, 1854/1869
Paperboard, 0.473 x 0.625 (18 5/8 x 24 5/8)
Paul Mellon Collection
1965.16.264

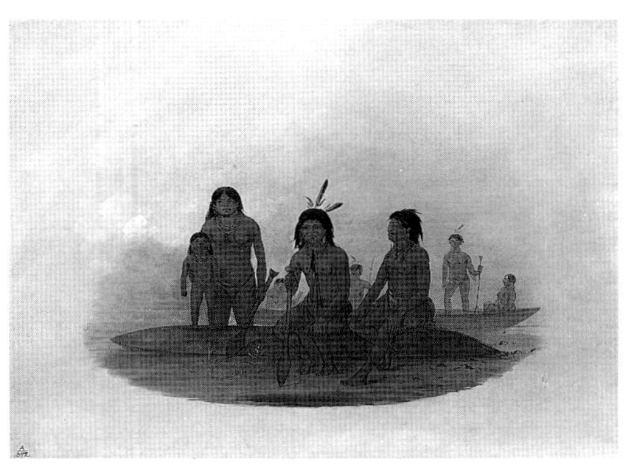

Marahua Indians, 1854/1869
Paperboard, 0.466 x 0.616 (18 1/4 x 24 /4)
Paul Mellon Collection
1965.16.240

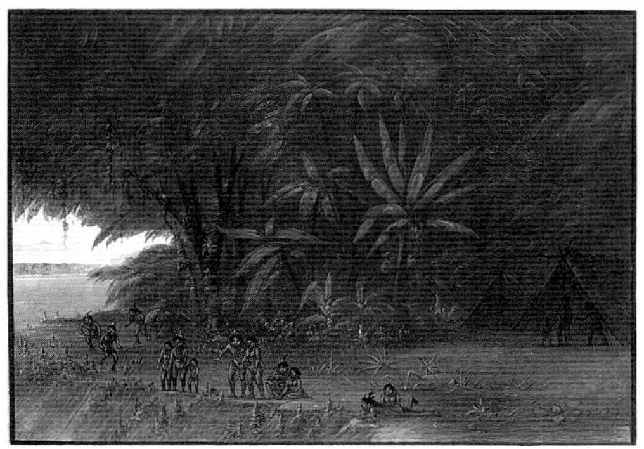

Mauhees Encampment, 1854/1869
Paperboard, 0.475 x 0.629 (18¾ x 24¾)
Paul Mellon Collection
1965.16.287

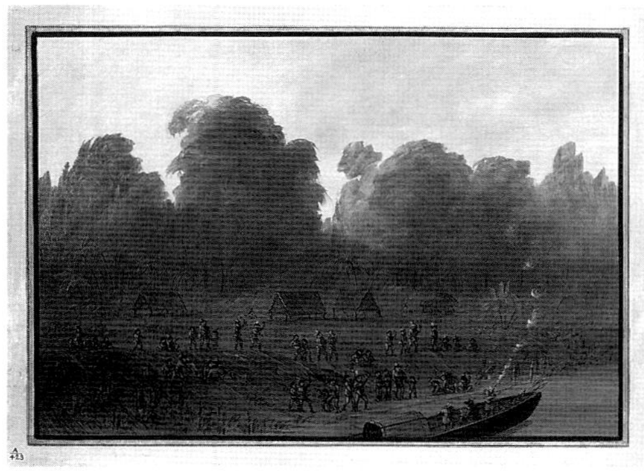

A Mayoruna Village, 1854/1869
Paperboard, 0.480 x 0.642
(18 15/16 x 25¼)
Paul Mellon Collection
1965.16.282

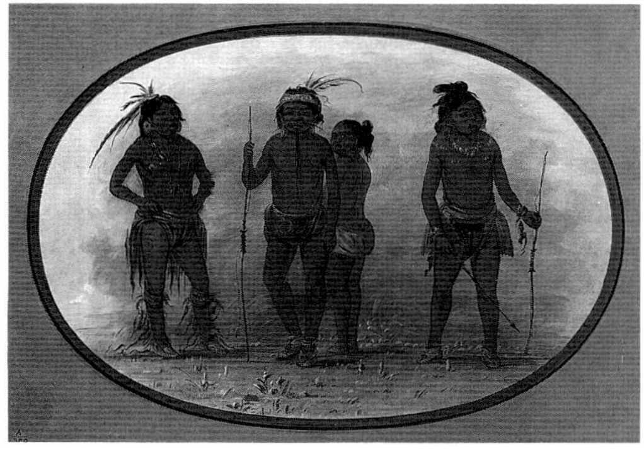

Members of the Botocudo Tribe,
1854/1869
Paperboard, 0.460 x 0.627 (18¼ x 24⅝)
Paul Mellon Collection
1965.16.248

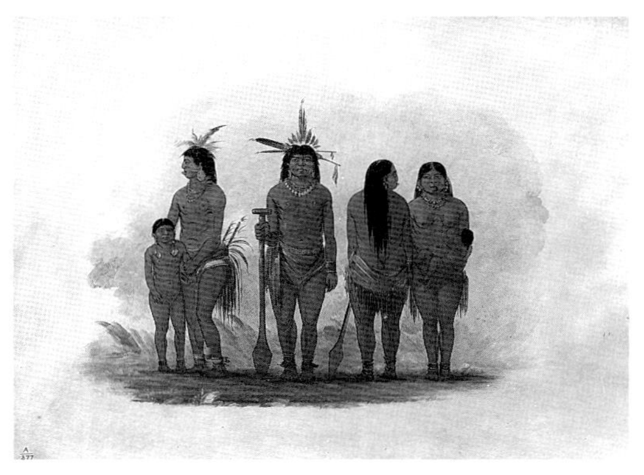

Members of the Payaguas Tribe,
1854/1869
Paperboard, 0.467 x 0.619 (18⅜ x 24 5/16)
Paul Mellon Collection
1965.16.245

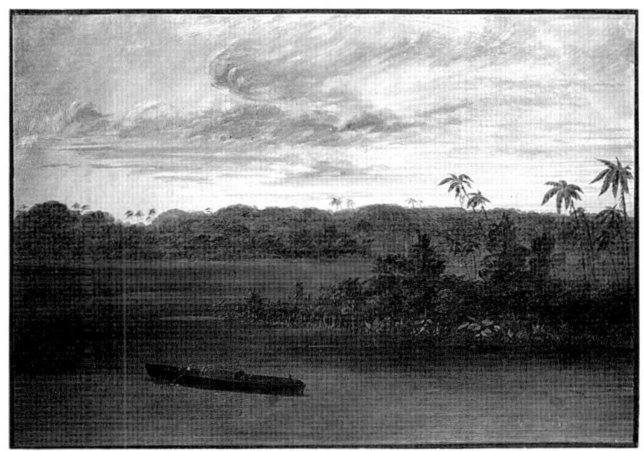

Mouth of the Rio Purus, 1854/1869
Paperboard, 0.470 x 0.627 (18½ x 24⅝)
Paul Mellon Collection
1965.16.306

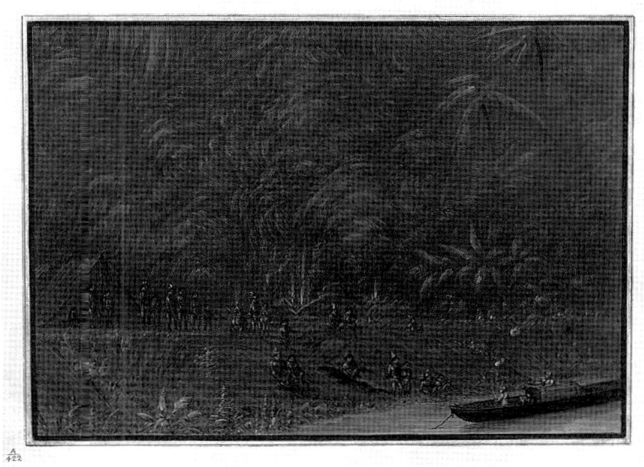

A Mura Encampment—Boat Sketch, 1854/1869
Paperboard, 0.478 x 0.632 (18¹³⁄₁₆ x 24⅞)
Paul Mellon Collection
1965.16.281

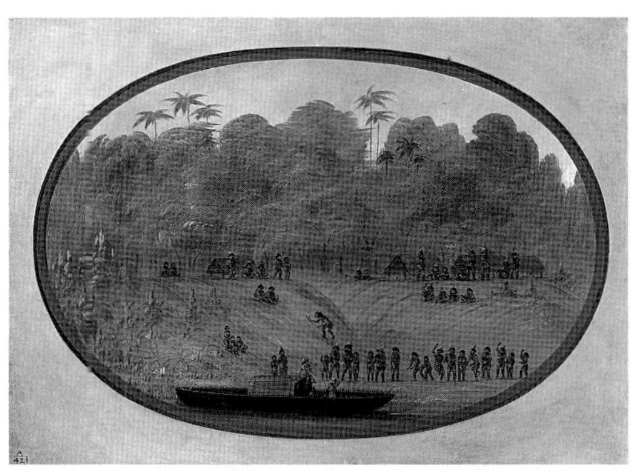

An Omagua Village—Boat Sketch, 1854/1869
Paperboard, 0.475 x 0.629 (18¹¹⁄₁₆ x 24¾)
Paul Mellon Collection
1965.16.280

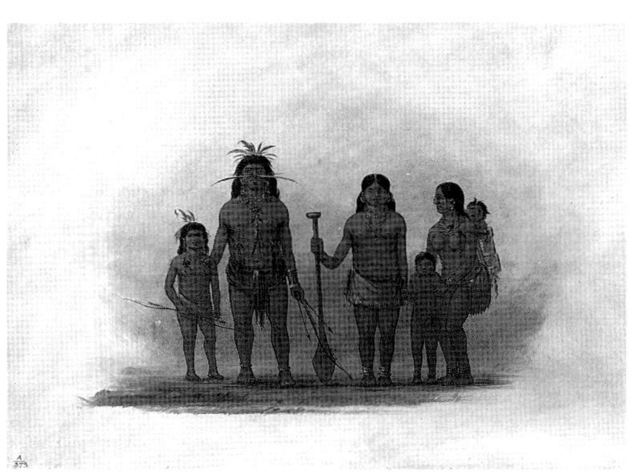

Orejona Chief and Family, 1854/1869
Paperboard, 0.465 x 0.622 (18⁵⁄₁₆ x 24½)
Paul Mellon Collection
1965.16.241

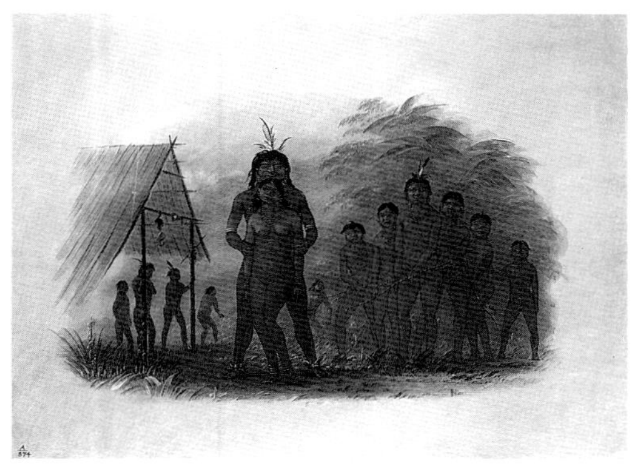

Orejona Indians, 1854/1869
Paperboard, c.461 x 0.608
(18$\frac{1}{8}$ x 23$\frac{15}{16}$)
Paul Mellon Collection
1965.16.242

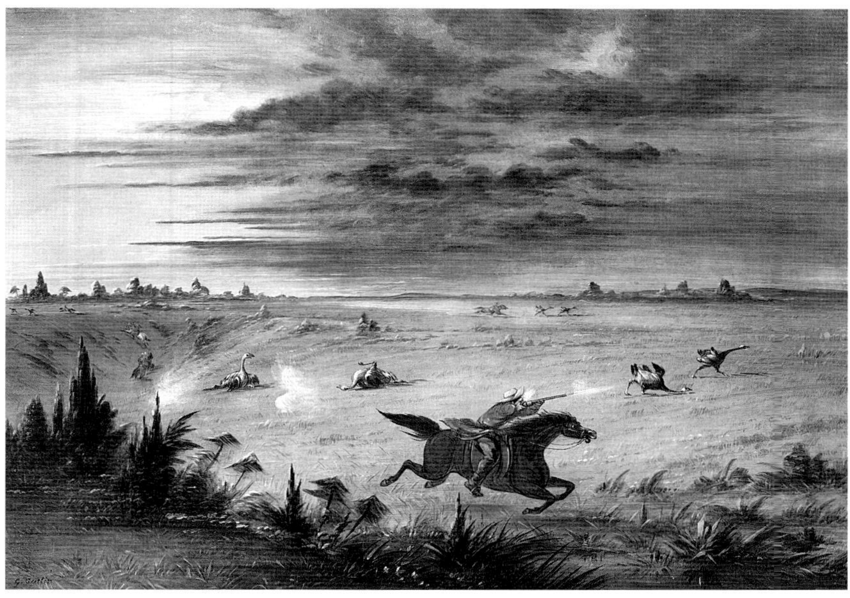

Ostrich Chase, Buenos Aires—Auca, 1854/1869
Paperboard, c.473 x 0.658 (18$\frac{5}{8}$ x 25$\frac{7}{8}$)
Inscribed at lower left: *G. Catlin*
Paul Mellon Collection
1965.16.257

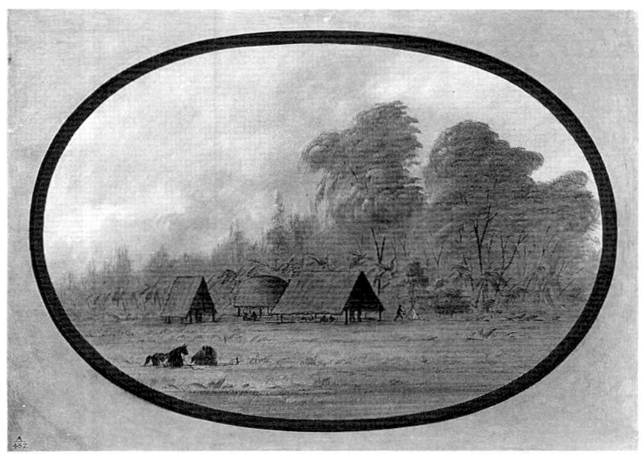

Pacapacurus Village, 1854/1869
Paperboard, c.461 x 0.629 (18$\frac{1}{8}$ x 24$\frac{3}{4}$)
Paul Mellon Collection
1965.16.309

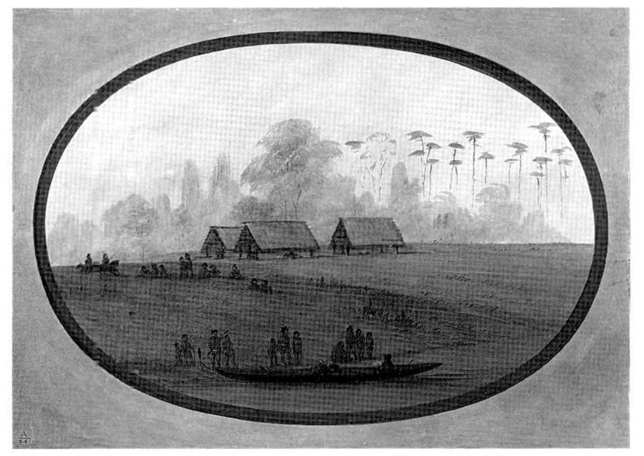

Painting the Lengua Chief, 1854/1869
Paperboard, 0.470 x 0.625 (18½ x 24⅝)
Paul Mellon Collection
1965.16.298

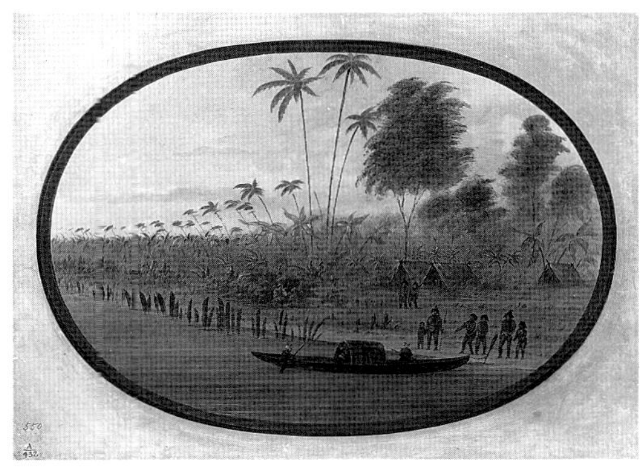

Painting the Tobos Chief, 1854/1869
Paperboard, 0.475 x 0.630 (18¾ x 24¾)
Paul Mellon Collection
1965.16.290

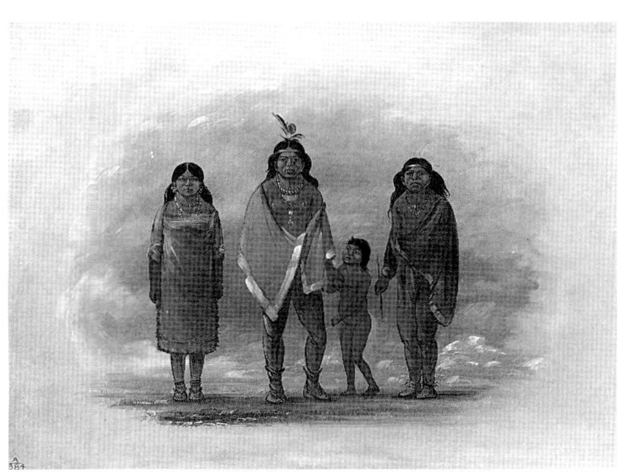

Patagon Chief, His Brother, and Daughter, 1856/1869
Paperboard, 0.458 x 0.605
(18 1/16 x 23 13/16)
Paul Mellon Collection
1965.16.252

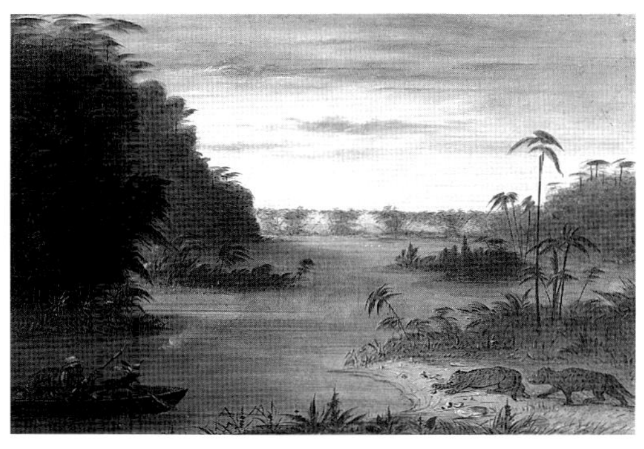

Pont de Palmiers and Tiger Shooting, 1854/1869
Paperboard, 0.452 x 0.637 (17¾ x 25
Paul Mellon Collection
1965.16.258

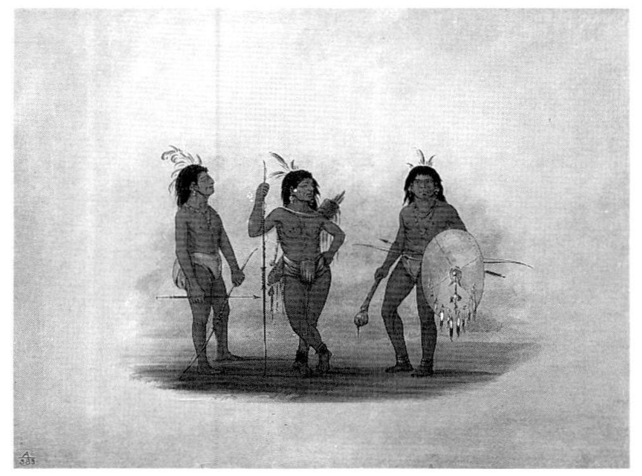

A Puelchee Chief and Two Young Warriors, 1854/1869
Paperboard, c.466 x 0.624 ($18\frac{3}{8}$ x $24\frac{9}{16}$)
Paul Mellon Collection
1965.16.251

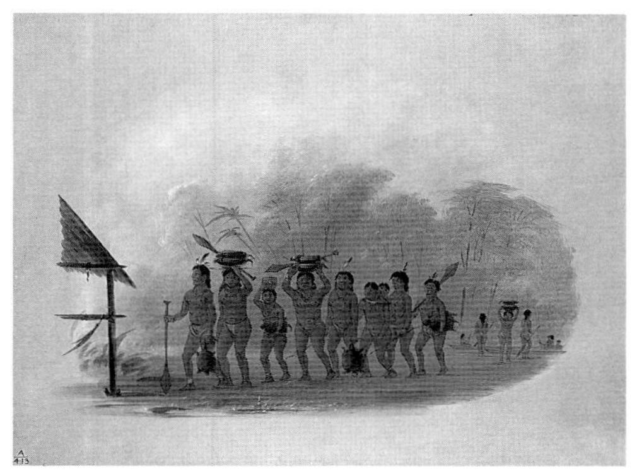

Return from a Turtle Hunt—Connibo, 1854/1869
Paperboard, c.465 x 0.620 ($18\frac{3}{8}$ x $24\frac{1}{2}$)
Paul Mellon Collection
1965.16.275

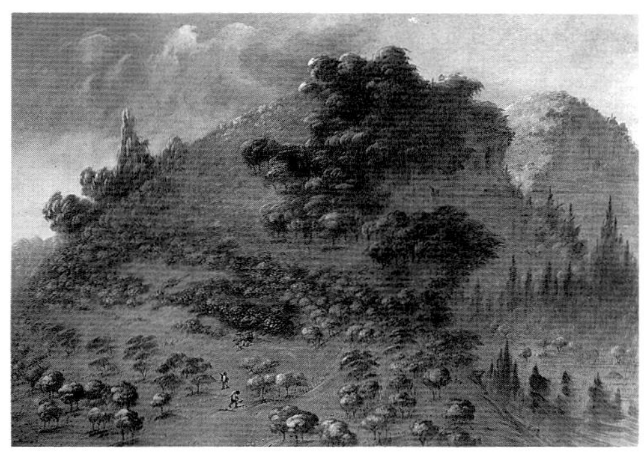

Rhododendron Mountain, 1854/1869
Paperboard, c.463 x 0.620 ($18\frac{1}{4}$ x $24\frac{3}{8}$)
Paul Mellon Collection
1965.16.273

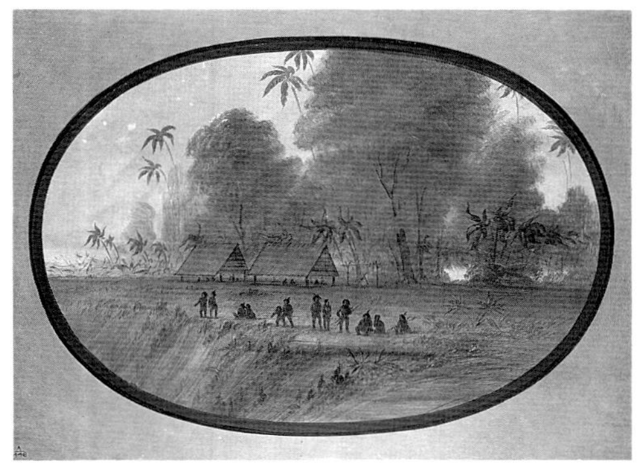

A Sepibo Village, 1854/1869
Paperboard, c.470 x 0.628 ($18\frac{1}{2}$ x $24\frac{3}{4}$)
Paul Mellon Collection
1965.16.305

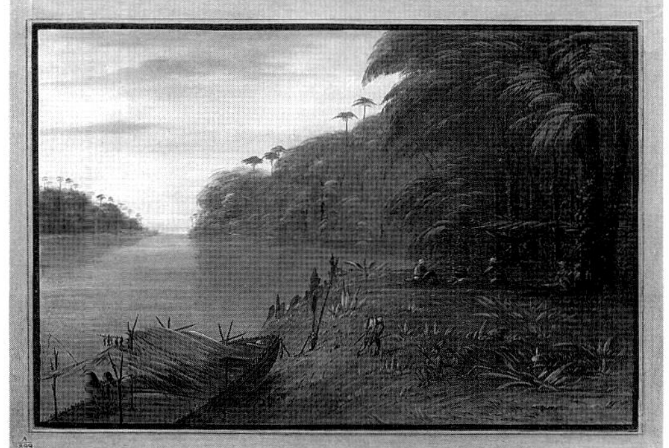

Shore of the Essequibo, 1854/1869
Paperboard, 0.460 x 0.630 (18⅛ x 24¾)
Paul Mellon Collection
1965.16.263

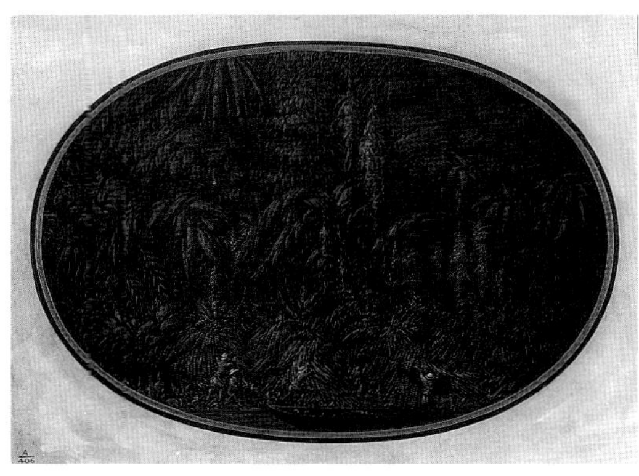

Shore of the Trombetas, 1854/1869
Paperboard, 0.471 x 0.625 (18½ x 24⅝)
Paul Mellon Collection
1965.16.269

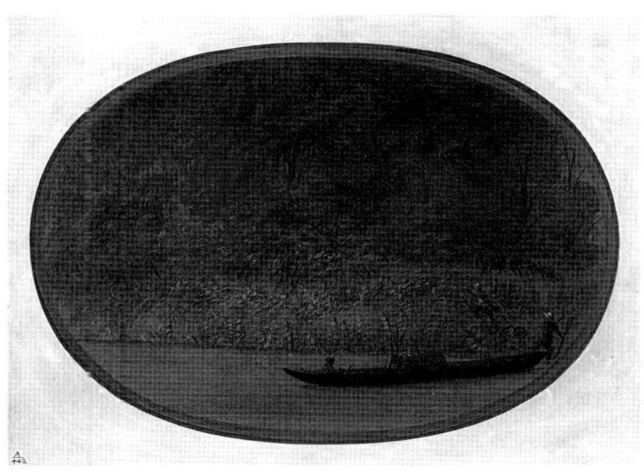

Shore of the Uruguay—Making a Sketch, 1854/1869
Paperboard, 0.474 x 0.633 (18⅝ x 24⅞)
Paul Mellon Collection
1965.16.299

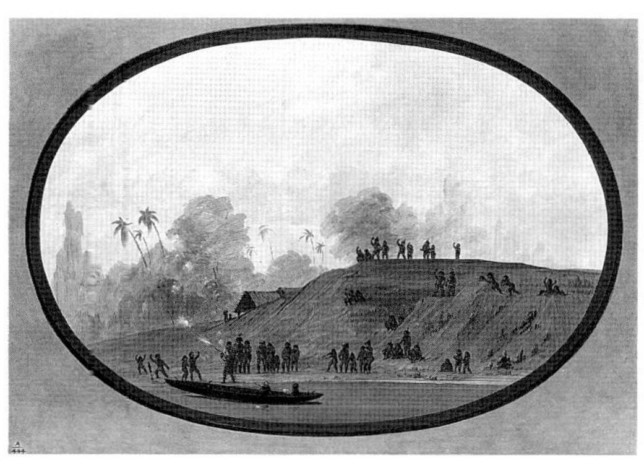

A Small Lengua Village, 1854/1869
Paperboard, 0.467 x 0.623 (18⅜ x 24½)
Paul Mellon Collection
1965.16.301

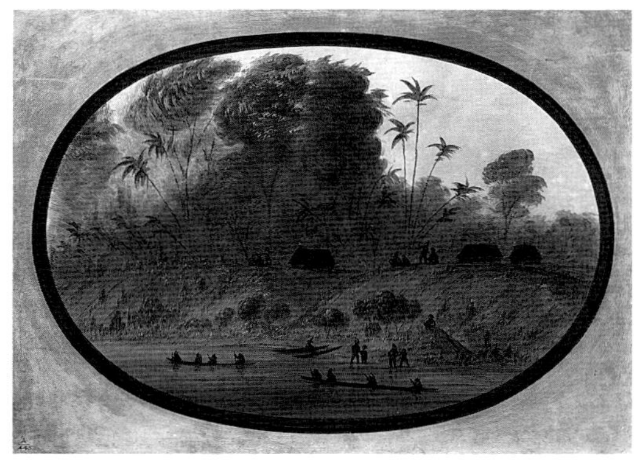

A Small Lengua Village, Uruguay,
1854/1869
Paperboard, 0.465 x 0.626 (18⅜ x 24⅝)
Paul Mellon Collection
1965.16.302

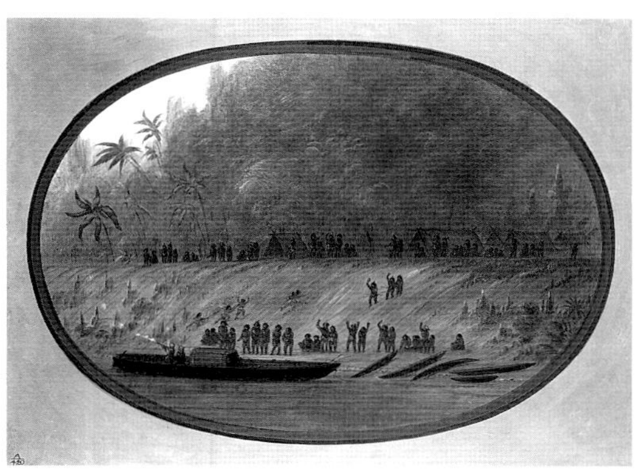

A Small Orejona Village, 1854/1869
Paperboard, 0.465 x 0.625 (18$\frac{5}{16}$ x 24⅝)
Paul Mellon Collection
1965.16.279

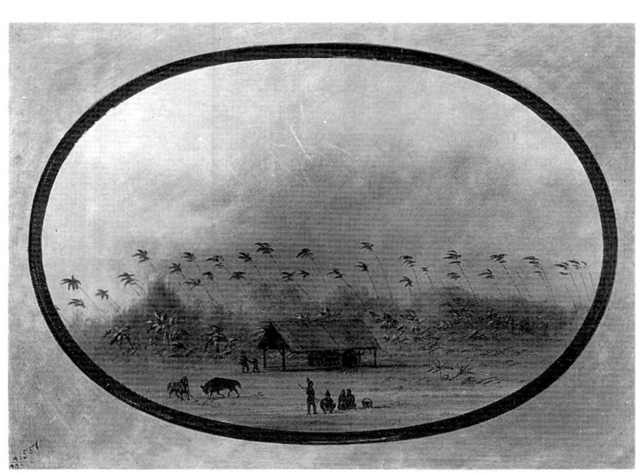

A Small Tobos Village, 1854/1869
Paperboard, 0.465 x 0.626 (18¼ x 24⅝)
Paul Mellon Collection
1965.16.291

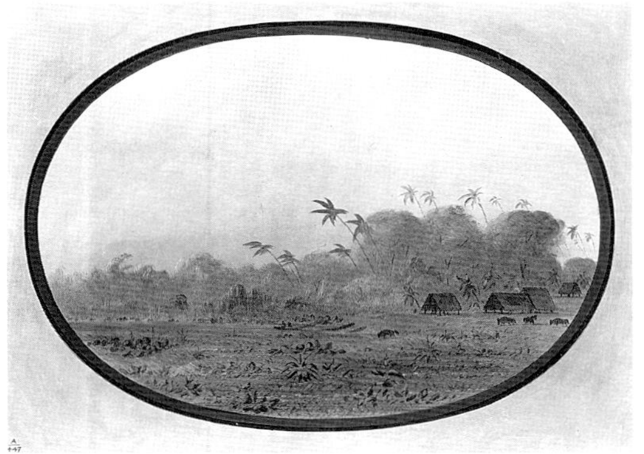

A Small Village of Remos Indians,
1854/1869
Paperboard, 0.472 x 0.630 (18⅝ x 24⅞)
Paul Mellon Collection
1965.16.304

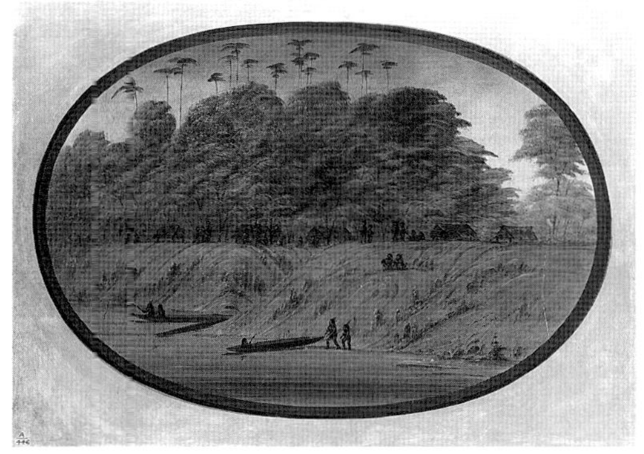

A Small Village—Payaguas Indians, 1854/1869
Paperboard, 0.476 x 0.633 (18¾ x 24⅞)
Paul Mellon Collection
1965.16.303

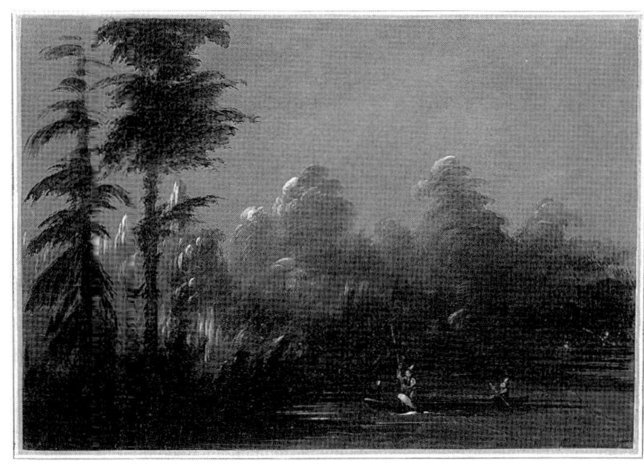

Spearing by Moonlight—Chaco, 1854/1869
Paperboard, 0.470 x 0.620 (18½ x 24⅜)
Paul Mellon Collection
1965.16.277

Spearing by Torchlight, 1854/1869
Paperboard, 0.464 x 0.620 (18¼ x 24⅜)
Paul Mellon Collection
1965.16.310

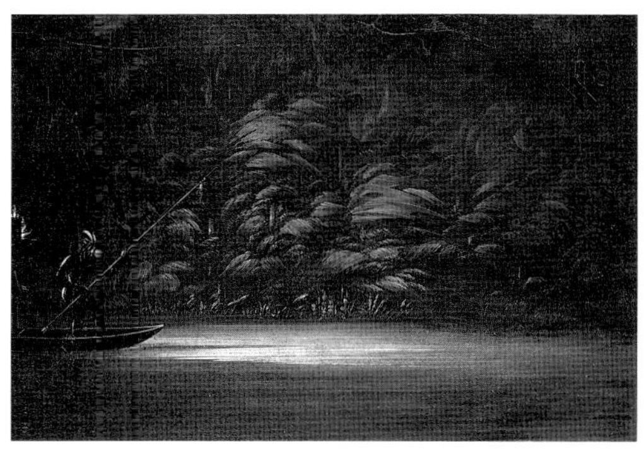

Spearing by Torchlight on the Amazon, 1854/1869
Paperboard, 0.410 x 0.570 (16⅛ x 22⅜)
Paul Mellon Collection
1965.16.351

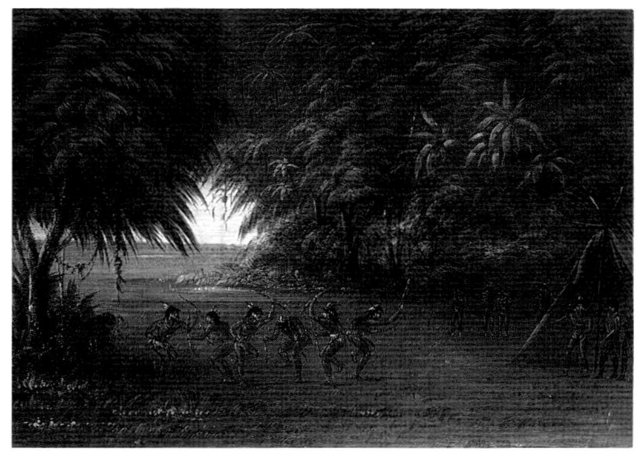

Tapuya Encampment, 1854/1869
Paperboard, c.464 x 0.611 ($18\frac{1}{4}$ x 24)
Paul Mellon Collection
1965.16.286

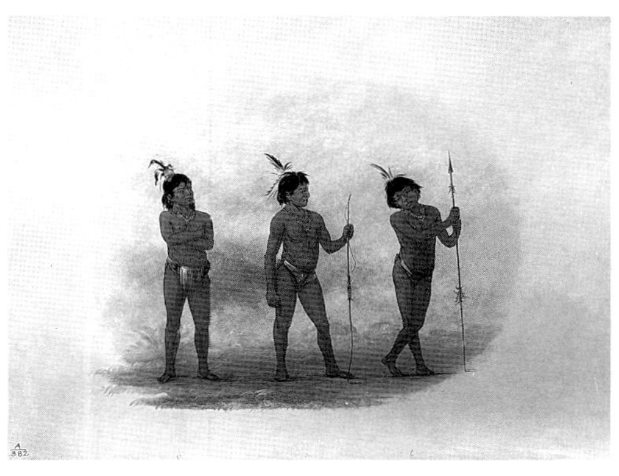

Three Auca Children, 1854/1869
Paperboard, c.464 x 0.620 ($18\frac{3}{8}$ x $24\frac{5}{8}$)
Paul Mellon Collection
1965.16.250

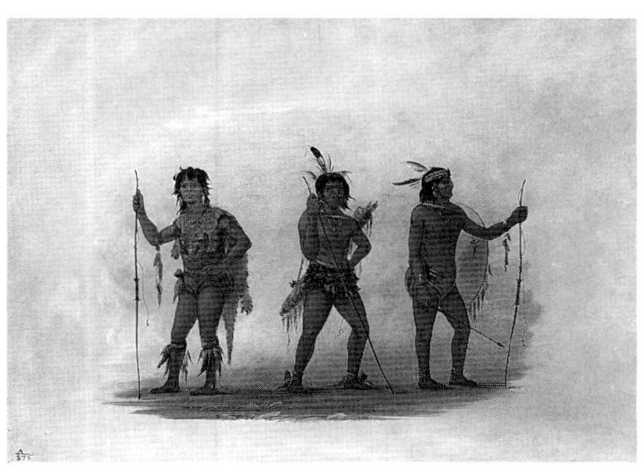

Three Chaymas Men, 1854/1869
Paperboard, c.460 x 0.622 ($18\frac{1}{16}$ x $24\frac{1}{2}$)
Paul Mellon Collection
1965.16.243

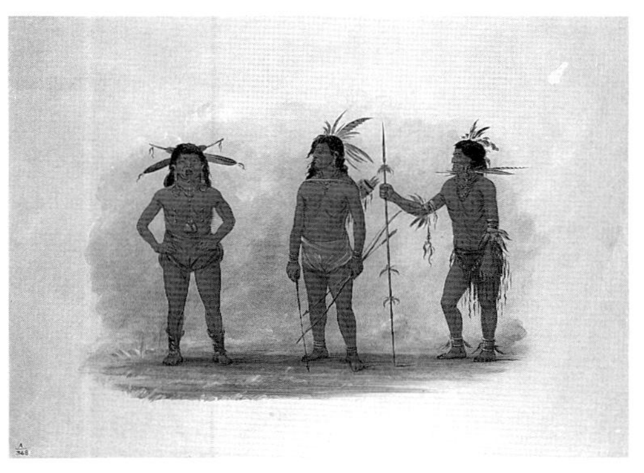

Three Omagua Men, 1854/1869
Paperboard, c.464 x 0.625 ($18\frac{1}{4}$ x $21\frac{5}{8}$)
Paul Mellon Collection
1965.16.236

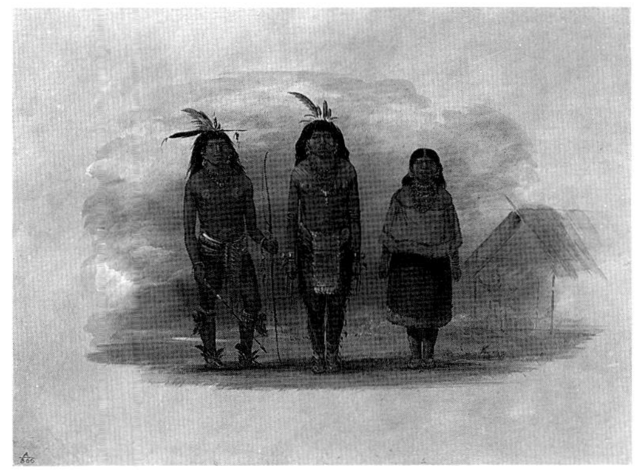

Three Taruma Indians, 1854/1869
Paperboard, 0.460 x 0.597 (18⅛ x 23½)
Paul Mellon Collection
1965.16.224

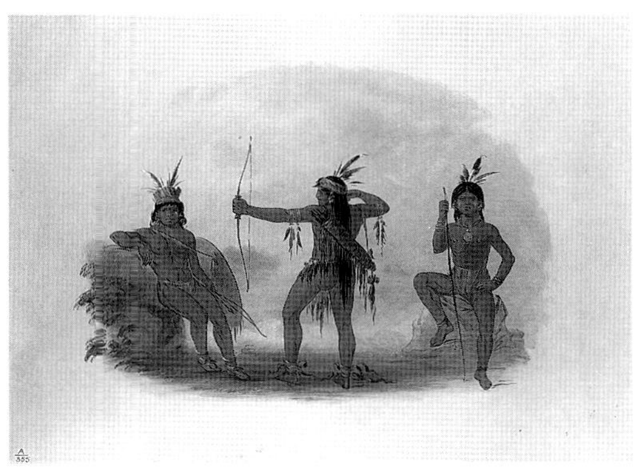

Three Woyaway Indians, 1854/1869
Paperboard, 0.467 x 0.624 (18⅜ x 24$^{9}/_{16}$)
Paul Mellon Collection
1965.16.223

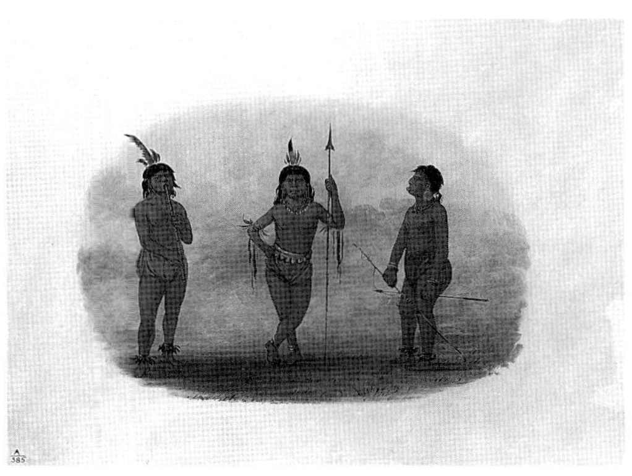

Three Young Tobos Men, 1854/1869
Paperboard, 0.468 x 0.621 (18⅜ x 24½)
Paul Mellon Collection
1965.16.253

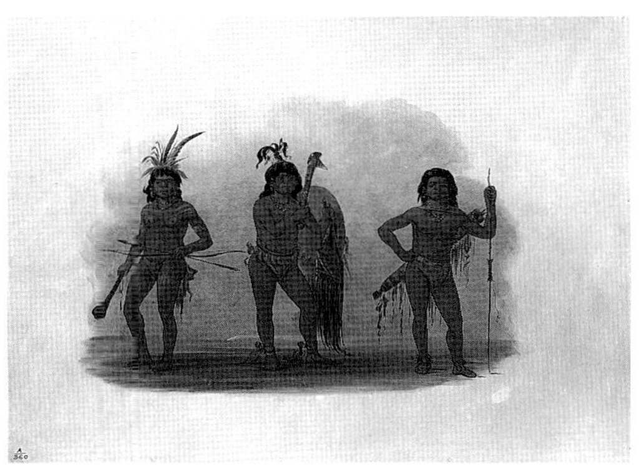

Three Zurumati Indians, 1854/1869
Paperboard, 0.466 x 0.615 (18⅜ x 24¼)
Paul Mellon Collection
1965.16.228

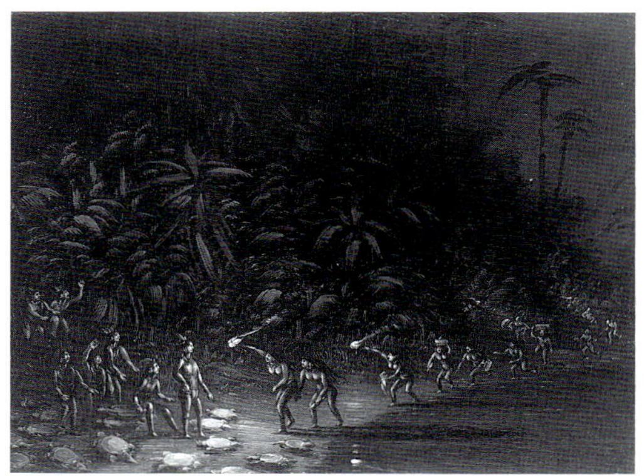

Turtle Hunt, 1854/1869
Canvas, 0.455 x 0.611 (17⅞ x 24)
Paul Mellon Collection
1965.16.259

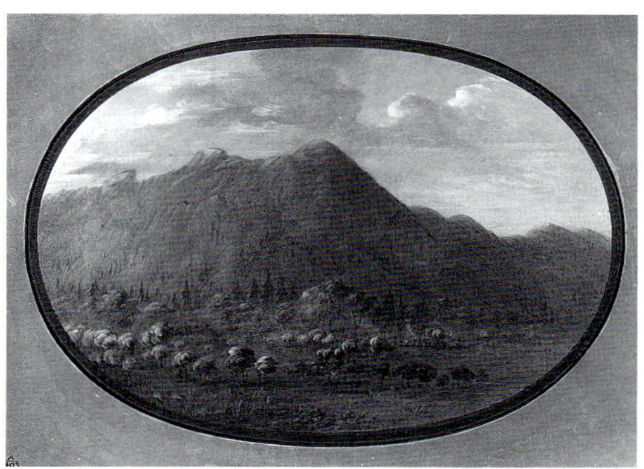

View in the Crystal Mountains, 1854/1869
Paperboard, 0.470 x 0.629 (18½ x 24¾)
Paul Mellon Collection
1965.16.266

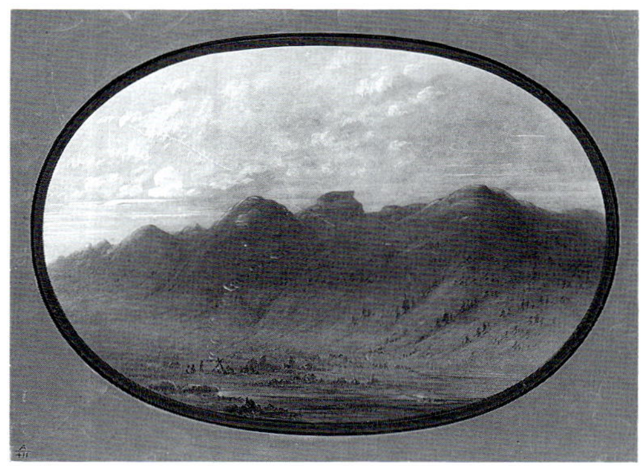

View of the Crystal Mountains, Brazil, 1854/1869
Paperboard, 0.470 x 0.624 (18½ x 24⅝)
Paul Mellon Collection
1965.16.274

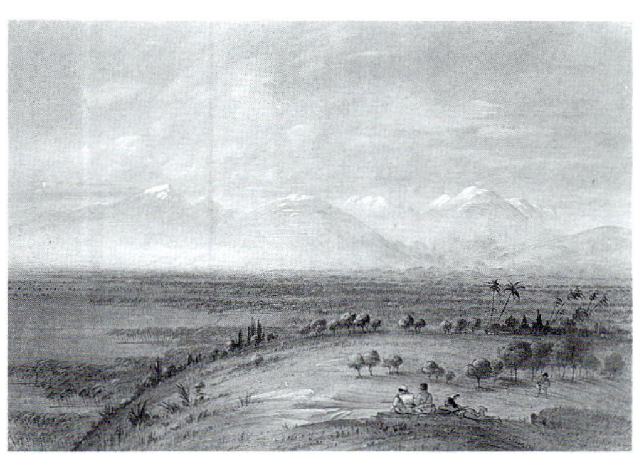

View of the Pampa del Sacramento, 1854/1869
Paperboard, 0.457 x 0.624 (18 x 24⅝)
Paul Mellon Collection
1965.16.262

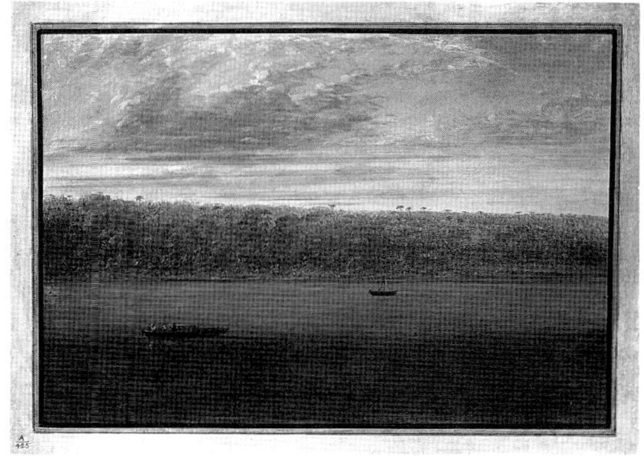

View of the Shore of the Amazon—Boat Sketch, 1854/1869
Paperboard, 0.470 x 0.625 (18½ x 24⅝)
Paul Mellon Collection
1965.16.284

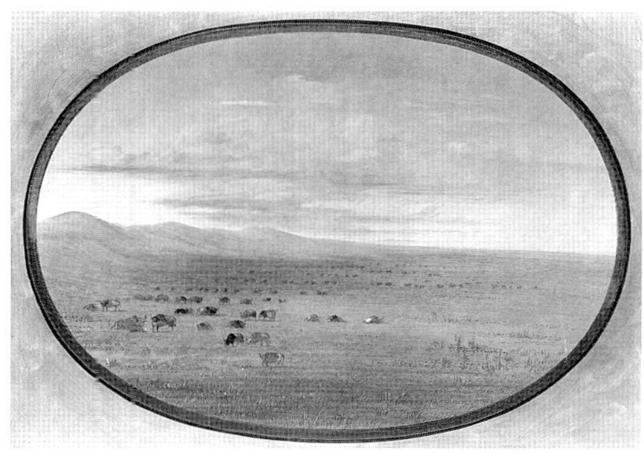

Wild Cattle Grazing on the Pampa del Sacramento, 1854/1869
Paperboard, 0.470 x 0.6[illegible]1 (18½ x 26¼)
Paul Mellon Collection
1965.16.276

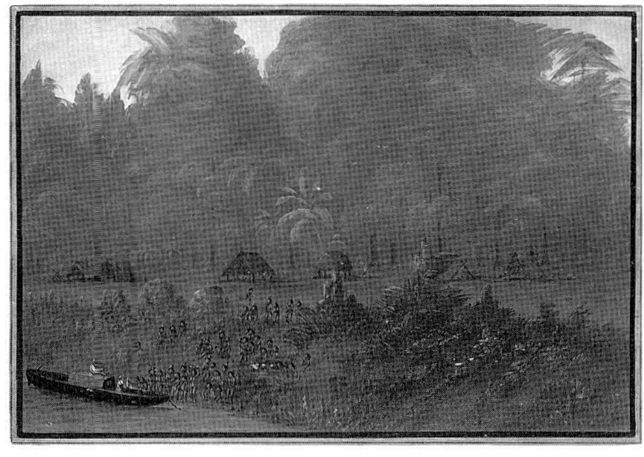

A Yahua Village, 1854/1869
Paperboard, 0.480 x 0.640 (18⅞ x 26½)
Paul Mellon Collection
1965.16.283

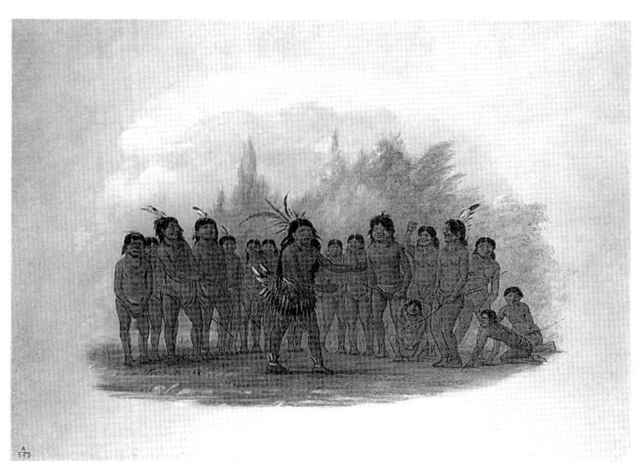

Zurumati Indians, 1854/1869
Paperboard, 0.464 x 0.620 (18¼ x 24 7/16)
Paul Mellon Collection
1965.16.227

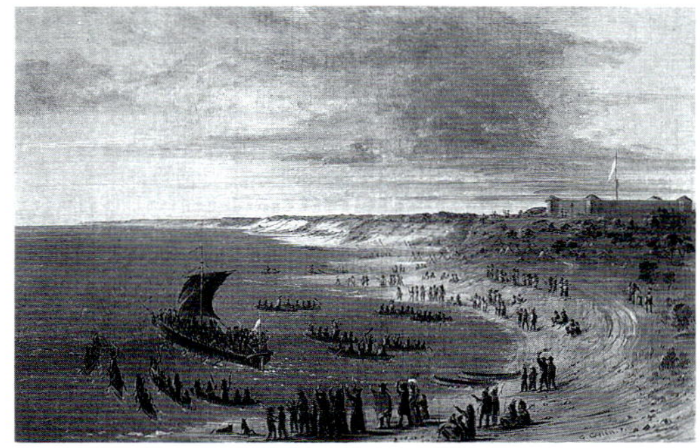

La Salle Series

The Expedition Leaving Fort Frontenac on Lake Ontario. November 18, 1678, 1847/1848
Canvas, 0.378 x 0.510 (14⅞ x 20¹⁄₁₆)
Inscribed at lower right: *G. Catlin. P.*
Paul Mellon Collection
1965.16.316

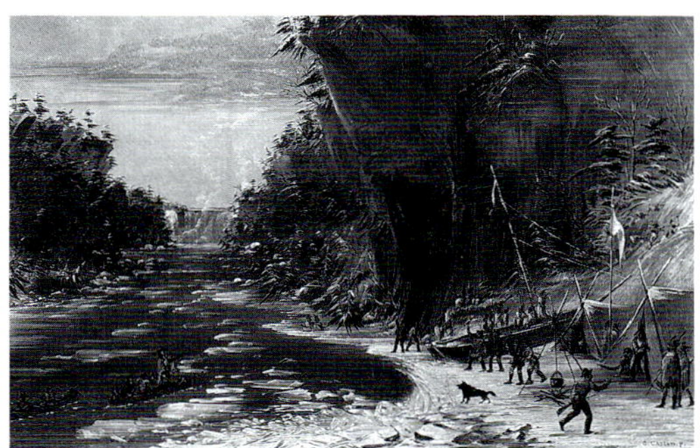

The Expedition Encamped below the Falls of Niagara. January 20, 1679, 1847/1848
Canvas, 0.378 x 0.562 (14⅞ x 22⅛)
Inscribed at lower right: *G. Catlin. p.*
Paul Mellon Collection
1965.16.317

Portage around the Falls of Niagara at Table Rock, 1847/1848
Canvas, 0.378 x 0.562 (14⅞ x 22⅛) sight
Inscribed at lower right: *G. Catlin. p.*
Paul Mellon Collection
1965.16.318

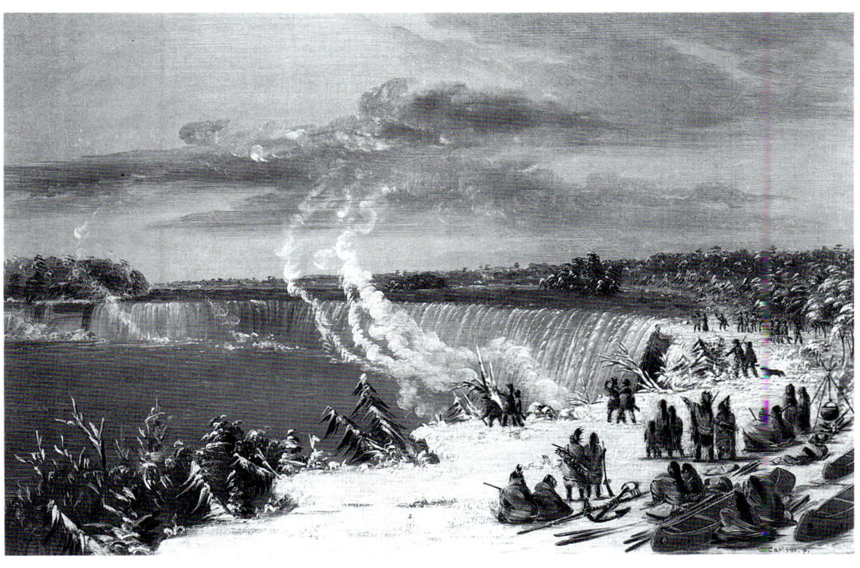

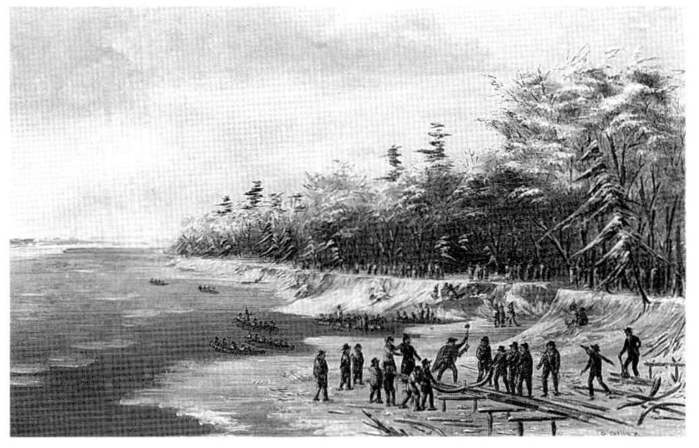

La Salle Driving the First Bolt for the Griffin. *January 26, 1679*. 1847/1848
Canvas, 0.378 x 0.563 (14 7/8 x 22 3/16)
Inscribed at lower right: *G. Catlin. p.*
Paul Mellon Collection
1965.16.319

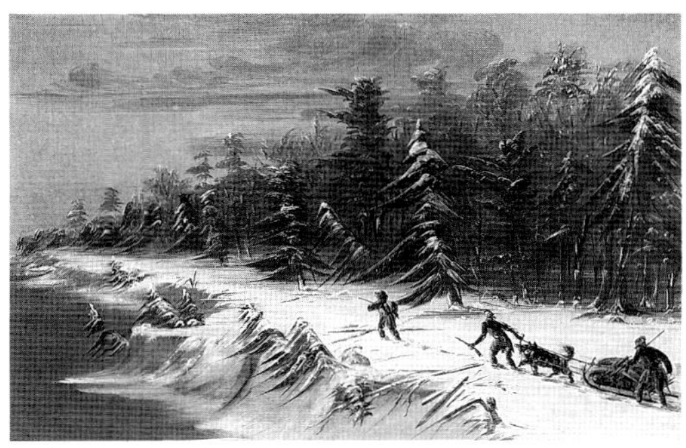

Returning to Fort Frontenac by Sled. February 1679, 1847/1848
Canvas, 0.378 x 0.562 (14 7/8 x 22 1/8) sight
Inscribed at lower left: *G. Catlin P.*
Paul Mellon Collection
1965.16.320

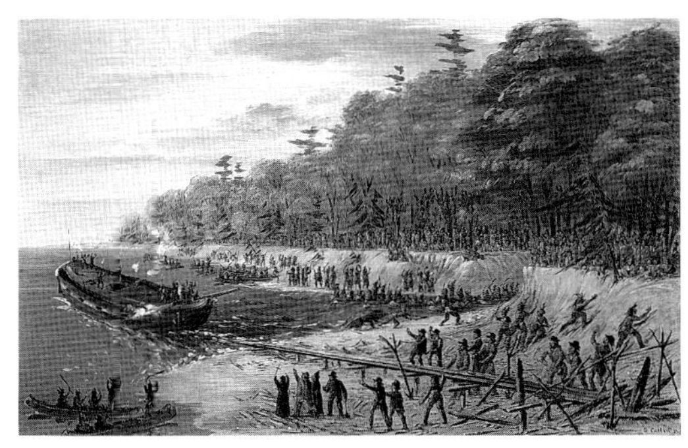

Launching of the Griffin. *July 1679*, 1847/1848
Canvas, 0.378 x 0.562 (14 7/8 x 22 1/8) sight
Inscribed at lower right: *G. Catlin. p.*
Paul Mellon Collection
1965.16.321

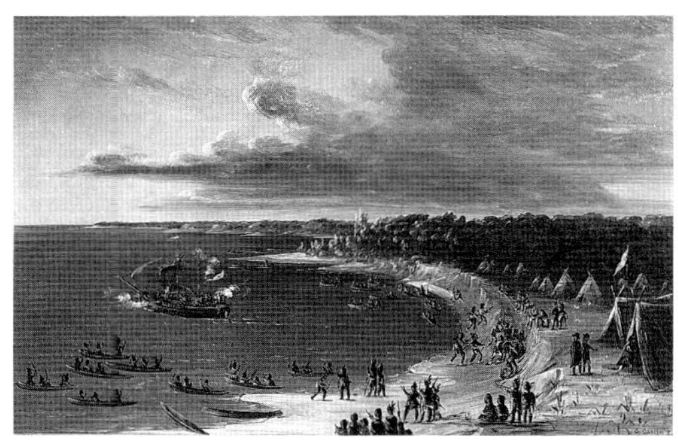

First Sailing of the Griffin *on Lake Erie. August 7, 1679*, 1847/1848
Canvas, 0.378 x 0.565 (14 7/8 x 22 1/4)
Inscribed at lower right: *G. Catlin P.*
Paul Mellon Collection
1965.16.322

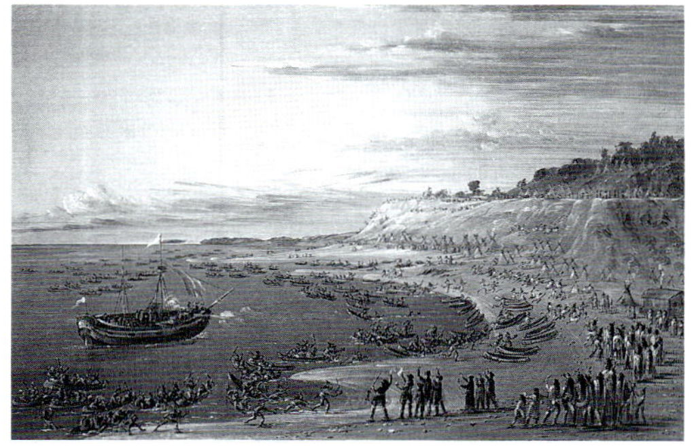

The Griffin Entering the Harbor at MacKinaw. August 27, 1679, 1847/1848
Canvas, 0.380 x 0.562 ($14\frac{15}{16}$ x $22\frac{1}{8}$)
Inscribed at lower right: *G. Catlin P.*
Paul Mellon Collection
1965.16.323

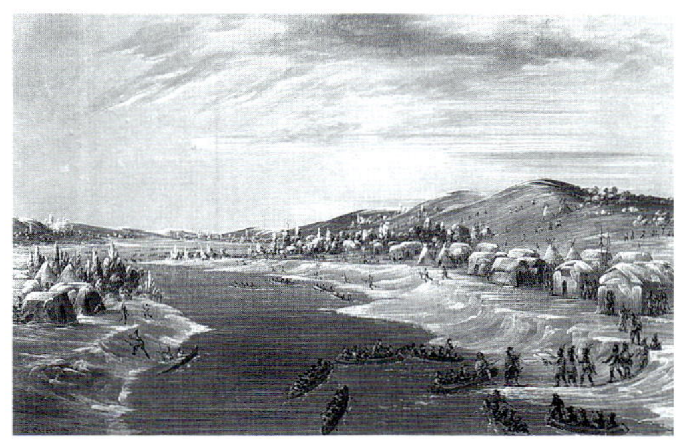

La Salle and Party Arrive at the Village of the Illinois. January 1, 1680, 1847/1848
Canvas, 0.378 x 0.562 ($14\frac{7}{8}$ x $22\frac{1}{8}$)
Inscribed at lower left: *G. Catlin. P.*
Paul Mellon Collection
1965.16.324

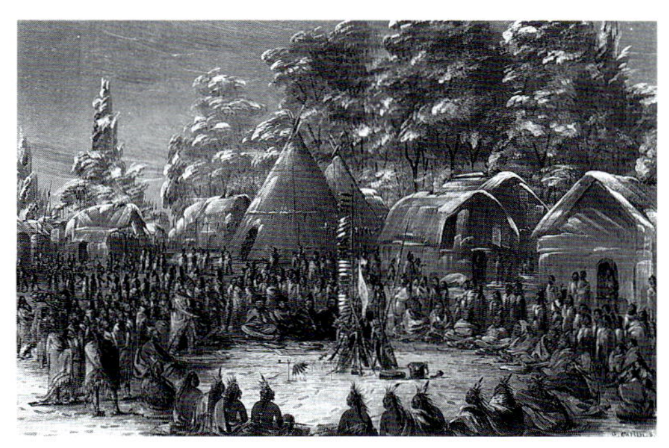

La Salle's Party Feasted in the Illinois Village. January 2, 1680, 1847/1848
Canvas, 0.420 x 0.605 ($16\frac{1}{2}$ x $23\frac{13}{16}$)
Inscribed at lower right: *G. Catlin p.*
Paul Mellon Collection
1965.16.325

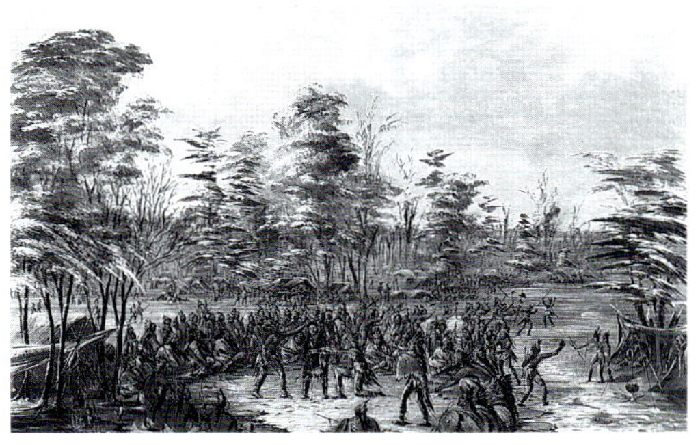

De Tonty Suing for Peace in the Iroquois Village. January 2, 1680, 1847/1848
Canvas, 0.378 x 0.564 ($14\frac{7}{8}$ x $22\frac{1}{4}$)
Inscribed at lower left: *G. Catlin p.*
Paul Mellon Collection
1965.16.326

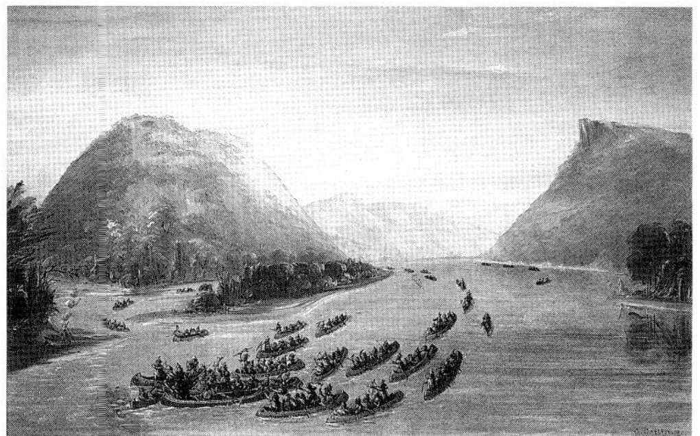

Father Hennepin and Two Companions Made Prisoners by the Sioux. April 1680, 1847/1848
Canvas, 0.420 x 0.605 (16½ x 23¹³⁄₁₆)
Inscribed at lower right: *G. Catlin p.*
Paul Mellon Collection
1965.16.327

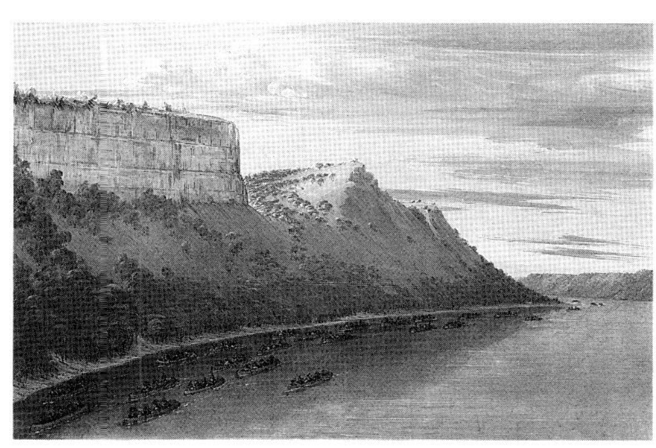

Father Hennepin and Companions Passing Lover's Leap. April 1680, 1847/1848
Canvas, 0.378 x 0.562 (14⅞ x 22⅛)
Inscribed at lower right: *G. Catlin p.*
Paul Mellon Collection
1965.16.328

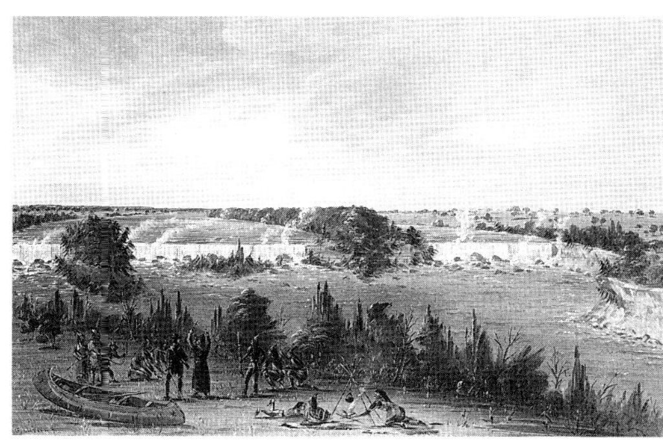

Father Hennepin and Companions at the Falls of St. Anthony. May 1, 1680, 1847/1848
Canvas, 0.378 x 0.564 (14⅞ x 22¼)
Inscribed at lower left: *G. Catlin p.*
Paul Mellon Collection
1965.16.329

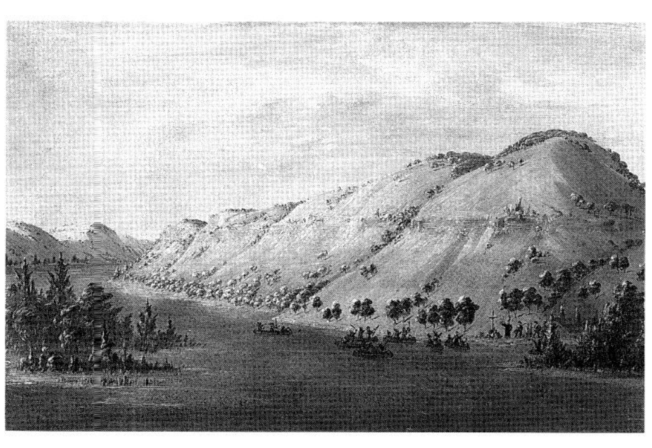

Father Hennepin Leaving the Mississippi to Join La Salle. May 8, 1680, 1847/1848
Canvas, 0.378 x 0.564 (14⅞ x 22¼)
Inscribed at lower right: *G. Catlin p.*
Paul Mellon Collection
1965.16.330

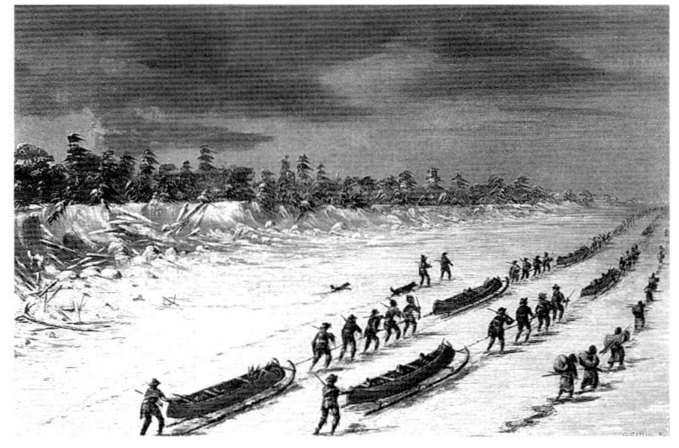

La Salle Crossing Lake Michigan on the Ice. December 8, 1681, 1847/1848
Canvas, 0.373 x 0.564 (14⅞ x 22¼)
Inscribed at lower right: *G. Catlin p.*
Paul Mellon Collection
1965.16.331

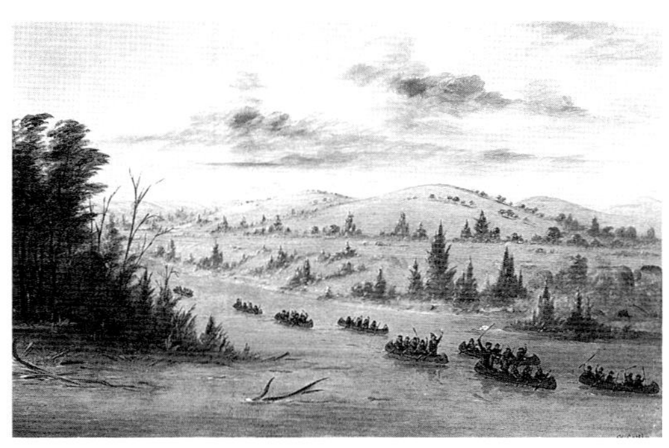

La Salle's Party Entering the Mississippi in Canoes. February 6, 1682, 1847/1848
Canvas, 0.373 x 0.564 (14⅞ x 22¼)
Inscribed at lower right: *G. Catlin*
Paul Mellon Collection
1965.16.332

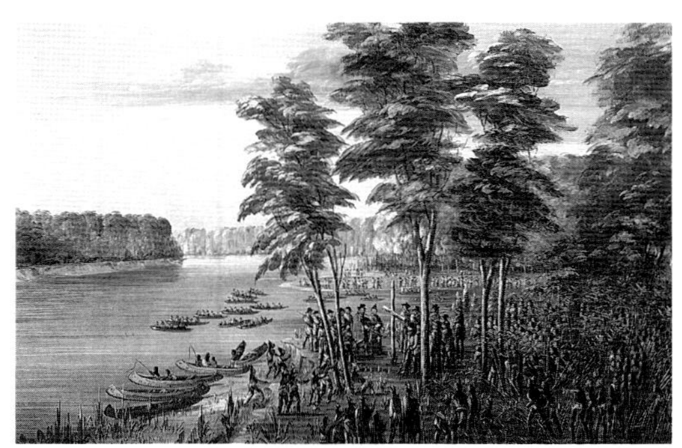

La Salle Taking Possession of the Land at the Mouth of the Arkansas. March 10, 1682, 1847/1848
Canvas, 0.373 x 0.564 (14⅞ x 22¼)
Inscribed at lower left: *G. Catlin p.*
Paul Mellon Collection
1965.16.333

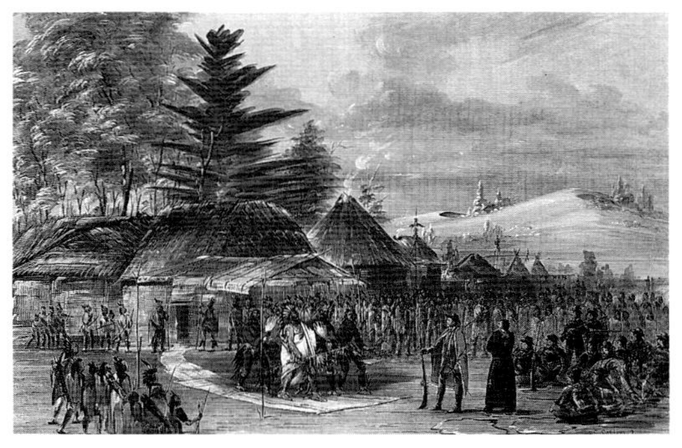

Chief of the Taensa Indians Receiving La Salle. March 20, 1682, 1847/1848
Canvas, 0.420 x 0.603 (16½ x 23¾)
Inscribed at lower right: *G. Catlin. p.*
Paul Mellon Collection
1965.16.334

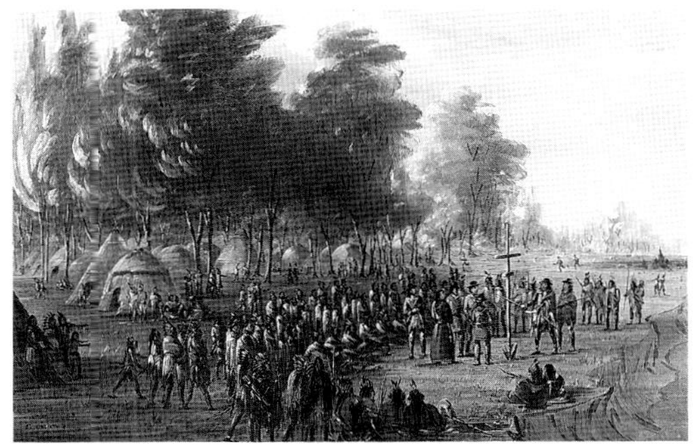

La Salle Erecting a Cross and Taking Possession of the Land. March 25, 1682, 1847/1848
Canvas, 0.374 x 0.567 (14¾ x 22⅜)
Inscribed at lower left: *G. Catlin. p.*
Paul Mellon Collection
1965.16.335

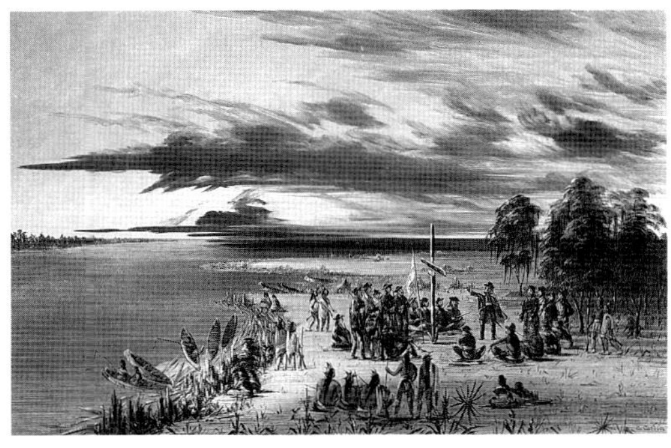

La Salle Claiming Louisiana for France. April 9, 1682, 1847/1848
Canvas, 0.378 x 0.564 (14⅞ x 22¼)
Inscribed at lower right: *G. Catlin P.*
Paul Mellon Collection
1965.16.336

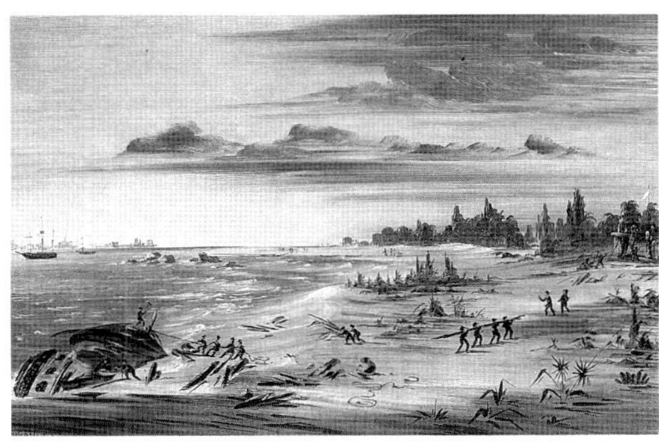

Wreck of the Aimable, *on the Coast of Texas. 1685*, 1847/1848
Canvas, 0.378 x 0.564 (14⅞ x 22¼)
Inscribed at lower left: *G. Catlin. p.*
Paul Mellon Collection
1965.16.337

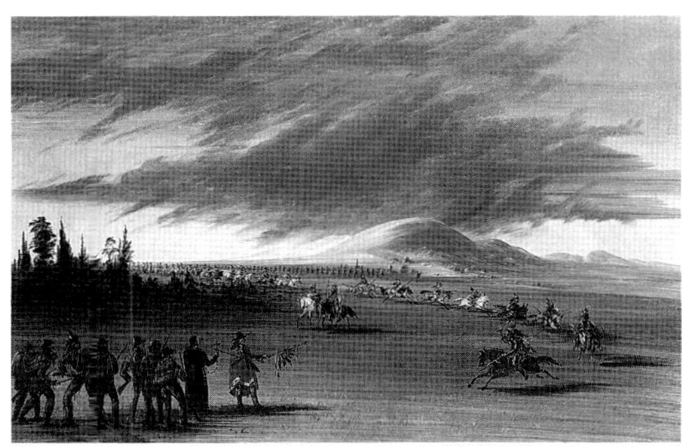

La Salle Meets a War Party of Cenis Indians on a Texas Prairie. April 25, 1686, 1847/1848
Canvas, 0.378 x 0.565 (14⅞ x 22¼)
Inscribed at lower left: *G. Catlin. p.*
Paul Mellon Collection
1965.16.338

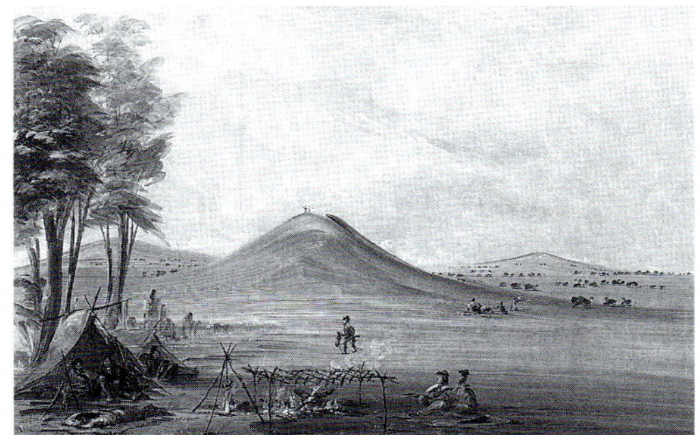

Expedition Encamped on a Texas Prairie. April 1686, 1847/1848
Canvas, 0.378 x 0.564 (14⅞ x 22¼)
Inscribed at lower right: *G. Catlin. p.*
Paul Mellon Collection
1965.16.339

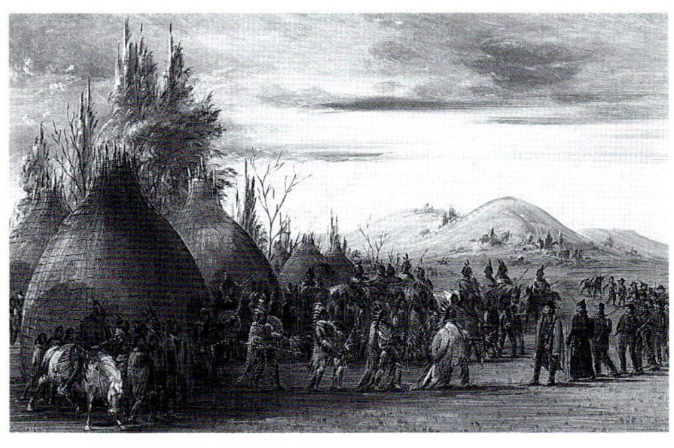

La Salle Received in the Village of the Cenis Indians. May 6, 1686, 1847/1848
Canvas, 0.376 x 0.564 (14¾ x 22¼)
Inscribed at lower left: *G. Catlin p.*
Paul Mellon Collection
1965.16.340

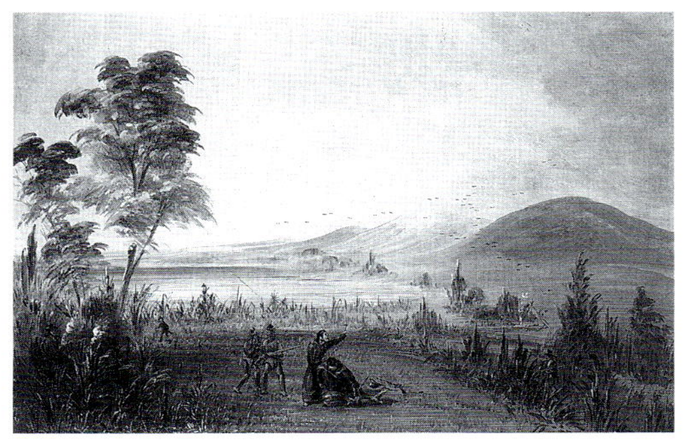

La Salle Assassinated by Duhaut. May 19, 1686, 1847/1848
Canvas, 0.378 x 0.564 (14⅞ x 22¼)
Inscribed at lower right: *G. Catlin p.*
Paul Mellon Collection
1965.16.341

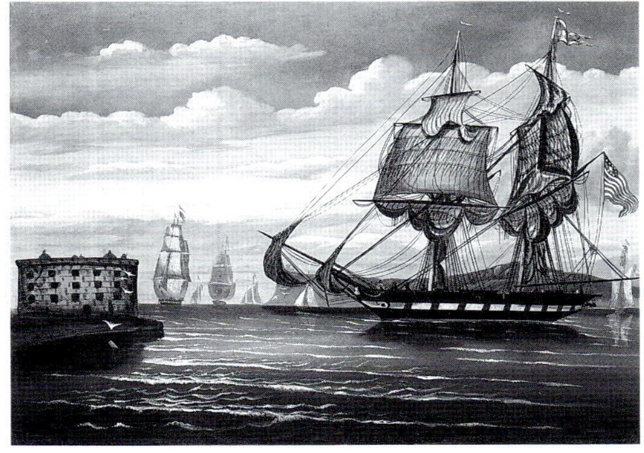

THOMAS CHAMBERS
1808–1866 or after

Bay of New York, Sunset, mid-19th century
Canvas, 0.560 x 0.763 (22 x 30)
Gift of Edgar William and Bernice Chrysler Garbisch
1973.67.1

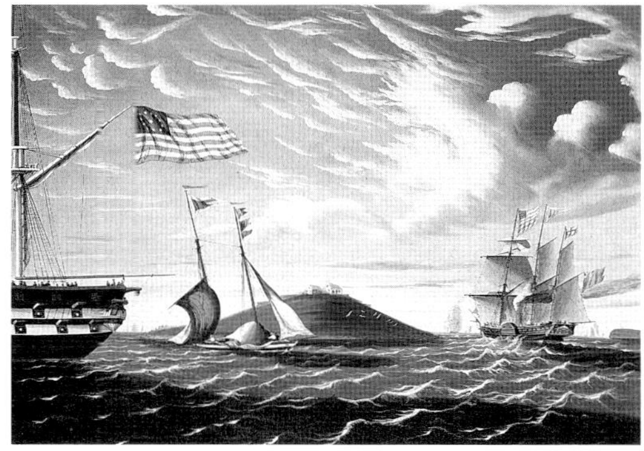

Boston Harbor, mid-19th century
Canvas, 0.558 x 0.765 (22 x 30⅛)
Gift of Edgar William and Bernice Chrysler Garbisch
1980.62.4

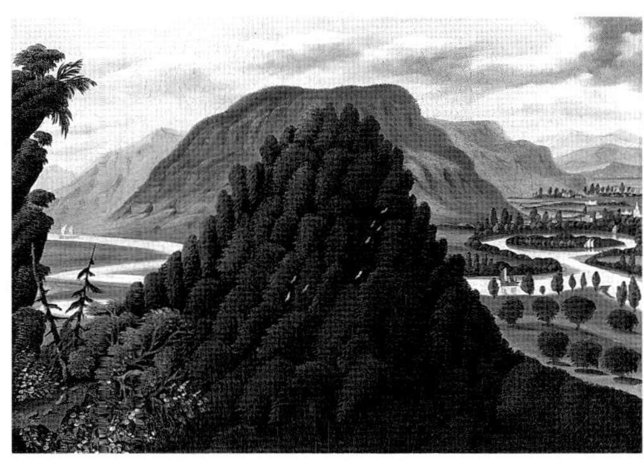

The Connecticut Valley, mid-19th century
Canvas, 0.457 x 0.610 (18 x 24½)
Gift of Edgar William and Bernice Chrysler Garbisch
1956.13.2

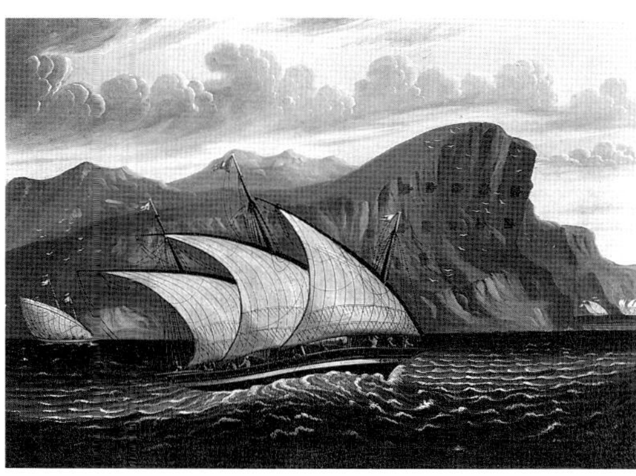

Felucca off Gibraltar, mid-19th century
Canvas, 0.558 x 0.766 (22 x 30¼)
Gift of Edgar William and Bernice Chrysler Garbisch
1968.26.2

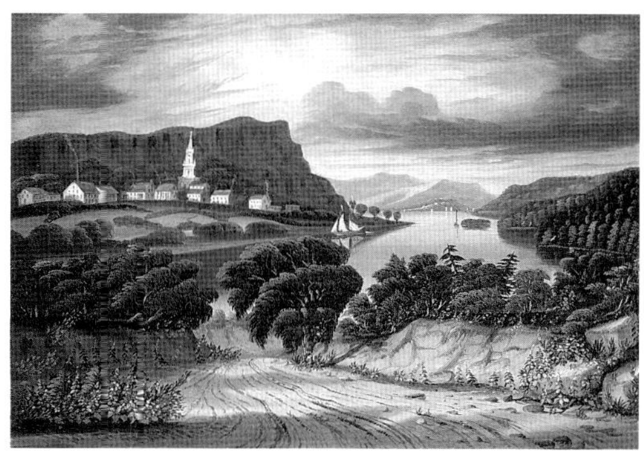

The Hudson Valley, Sunset, mid-19th century
Canvas, 0.562 x 0.761 (22⅛ x 30)
Gift of Edgar William and Bernice Chrysler Garbisch
1966.13.1

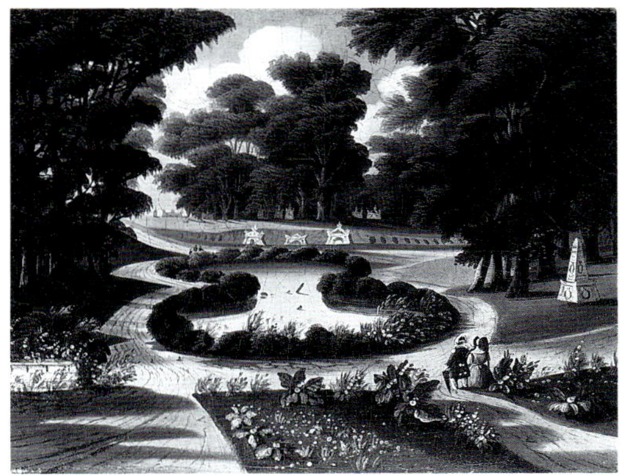

Mount Auburn Cemetery, mid-19th century
Canvas, 0.356 x 0.460 (14 x 18⅛)
Gift of Edgar William and Bernice Chrysler Garbisch
1958.5.1

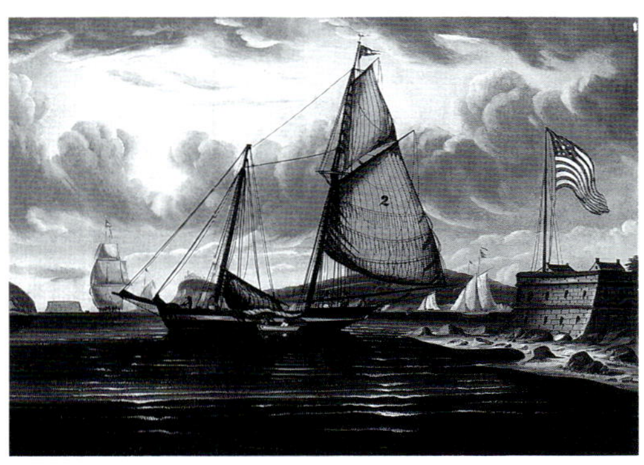

New York Harbor with Pilot Boat George Washington, mid-19th century
Canvas, 0.560 x 0.763 (22 x 30)
Gift of Edgar William and Bernice Chrysler Garbisch
1978.80.1

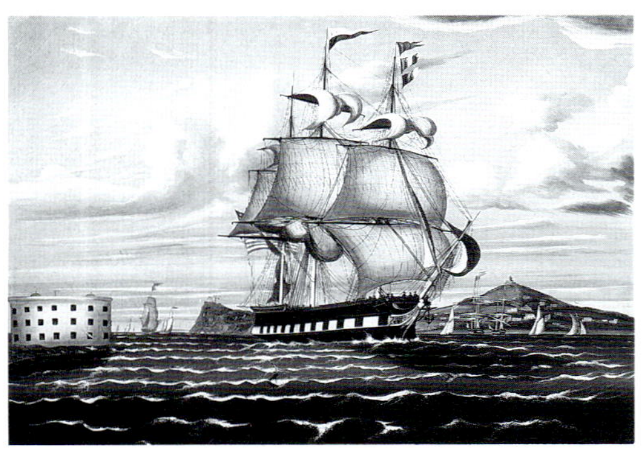

Packet Ship Passing Castle Williams, New York Harbor, mid-19th century
Canvas, 0.565 x 0.761 (22¼ x 30)
Gift of Edgar William and Bernice Chrysler Garbisch
1980.62.5

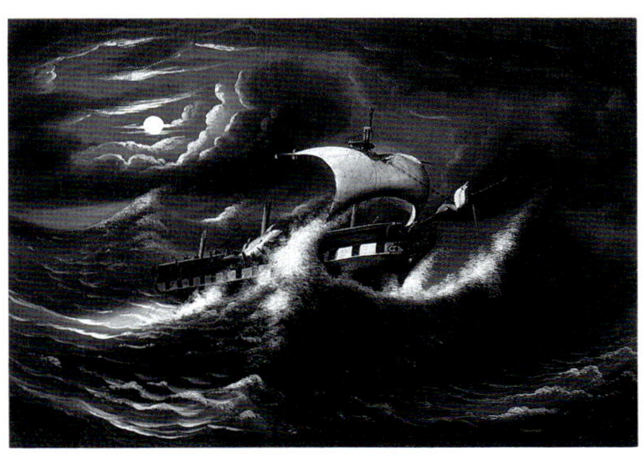

Storm-Tossed Frigate, mid-19th century
Canvas, 0.544 x 0.772 (21⅜ x 30⅜)
Gift of Edgar William and Bernice Chrysler Garbisch
1969.11.1

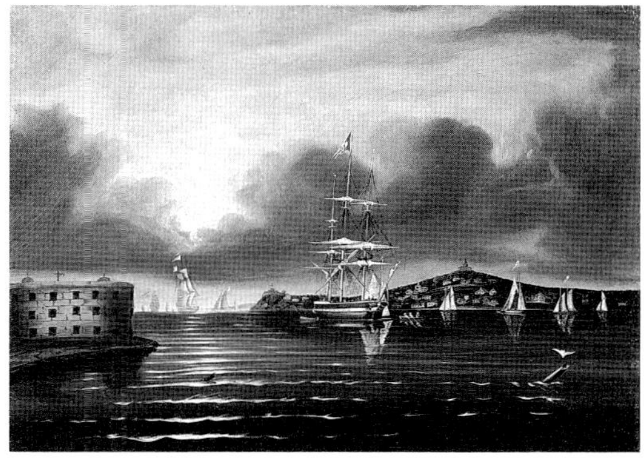

Threatening Sky, Bay of New York, mid-19th century
Canvas, 0.460 x 0.615 (18⅛ x 24¼)
Gift of Edgar William and Bernice Chrysler Garbisch
1973.67.2

JOSEPH GOODHUE CHANDLER
1813–1884

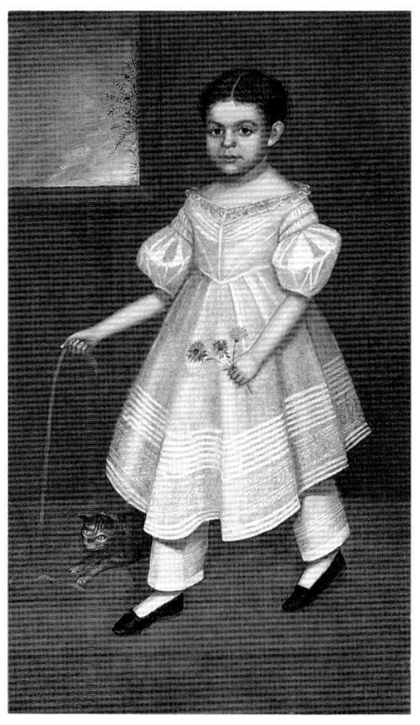

Girl with Kitten, c. 1836/1838
Canvas, 1.220 x 0.706 (48 x 27¾)
Gift of Edgar William and Bernice Chrysler Garbisch
1980.62.42

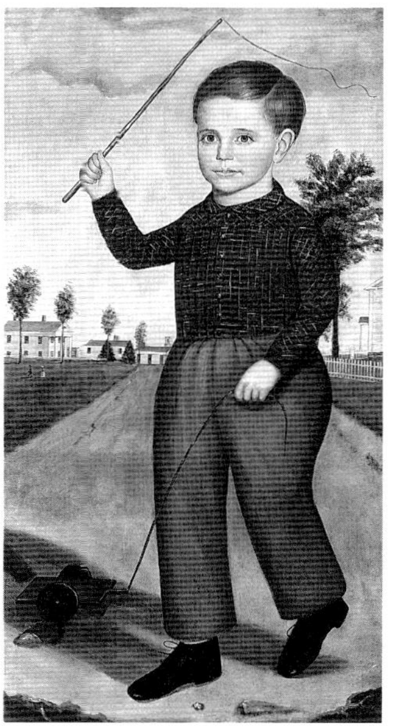

Charles H. Sisson, 1850
Canvas, 1.223 x 0.637 (48⅛ x 25$^{1}/_{16}$)
Gift of Edgar William and Bernice Chrysler Garbisch
1953.5.5

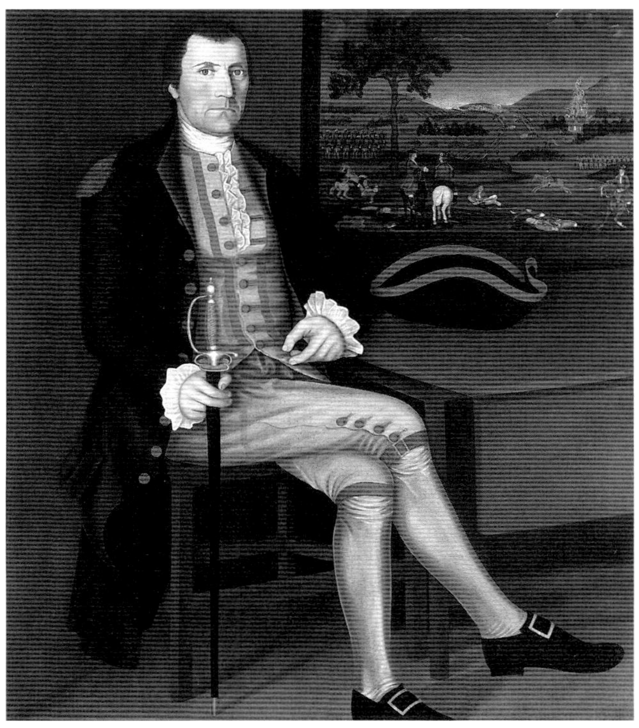

WINTHROP CHANDLER
1747–1790

Captain Samuel Chandler, c. 1780
Canvas, 1.390 x 1.217 (54¾ x 47⅞)
Gift of Edgar William and Bernice Chrysler Garbisch
1964.23.1

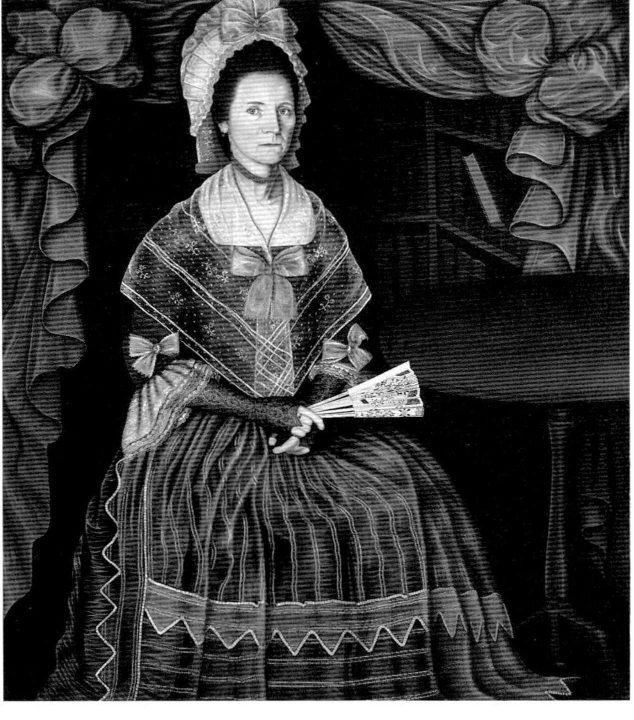

Mrs. Samuel Chandler, c. 1780
Canvas, 1.391 x 1.217 (54¾ x 47⅞)
Gift of Edgar William and Bernice Chrysler Garbisch
1964.23.2

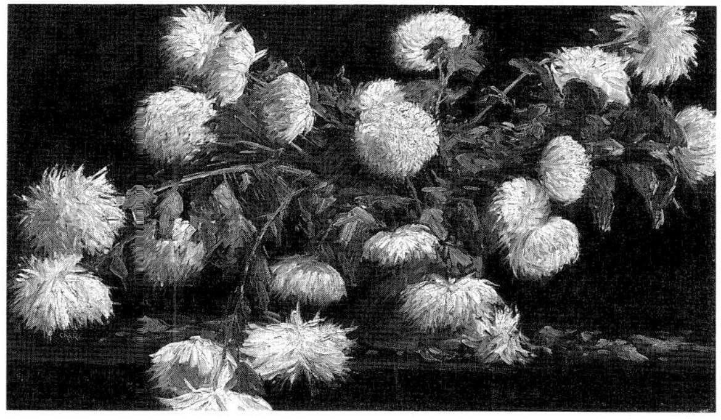

WILLIAM MERRITT CHASE
1849–1916

Chrysanthemums, c. 1878
Canvas, 0.684 x 1.137 (26⅞ x 44¾)
Inscribed at lower left: *Chase.*
Chester Dale Collection
1963.10.106

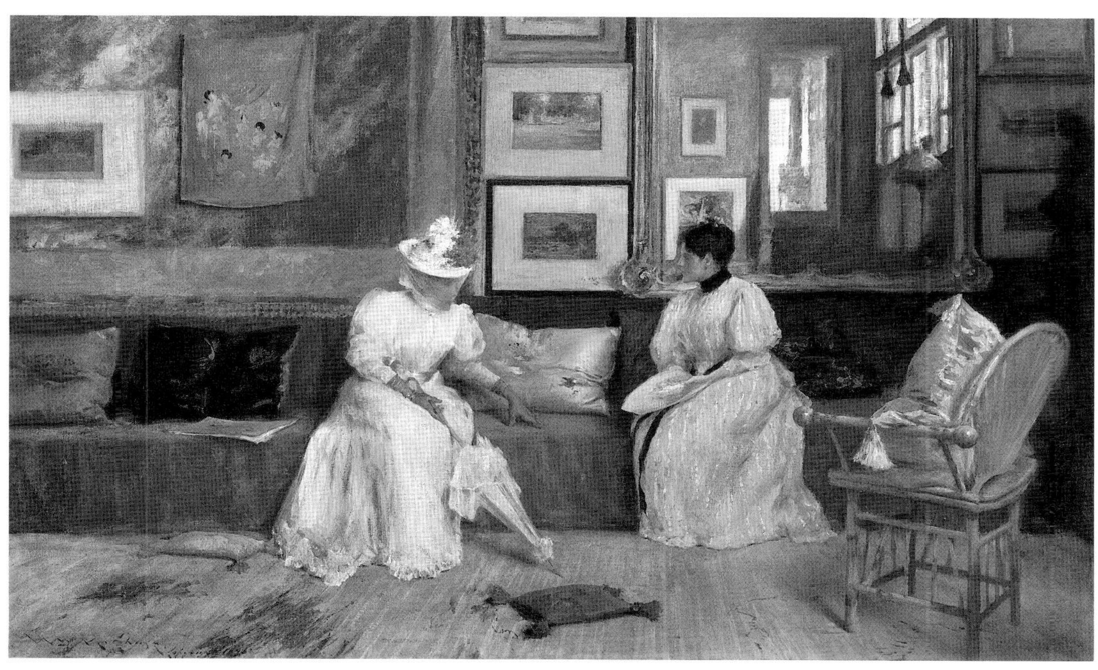

A Friendly Call, 1895
Canvas, 0.765 x 1.225 (30⅛ x 48¼)
Inscribed at lower left: *Wm M. Chase. / Copyright 1895*
Chester Dale Collection
1943.1.2

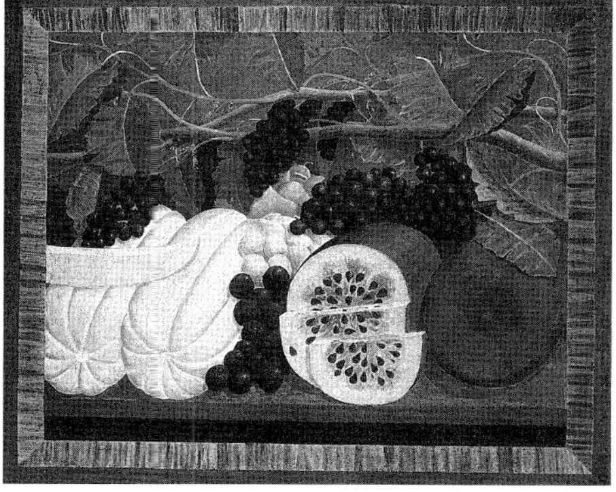

CHIPMAN
active c. 1840/1850

Melons and Grapes, mid-19th century
Canvas, 0.515 x 0.607 (20¼ x 23⅞)
Gift of Edgar William and Bernice Chrysler Garbisch
1957.11.5

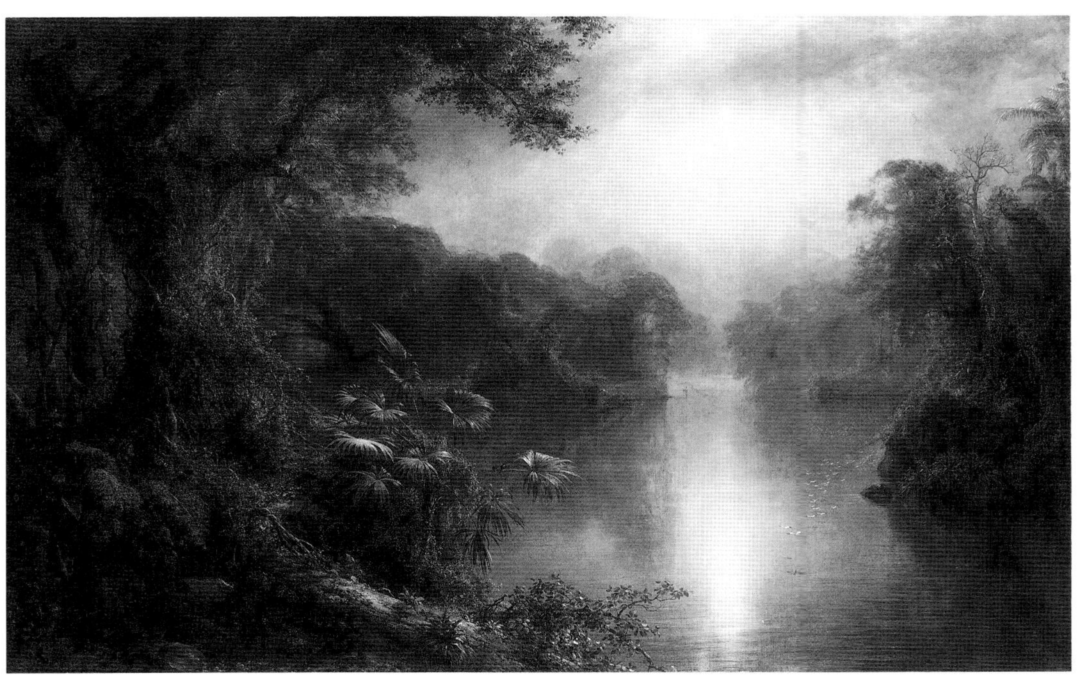

FREDERIC EDWIN CHURCH
1826–1900

Morning in the Tropics, 1877
Canvas, 1.38[illegible] x 2.137 (54⅜ x 84⅛)
Inscribed at lower right:
F. E. CHURCH / 1877
Gift of the Avalon Foundation
1965.14.1

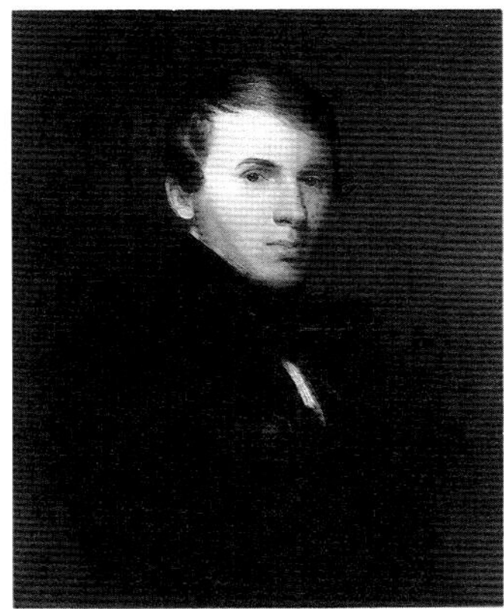

ALVAN CLARK
1804–1887

Barnabus Clark, c. 1838
Canvas, 0.695 x 0.565 (27⅜ x 22¼)
Andrew W. Mellon Collection
1947.17.30

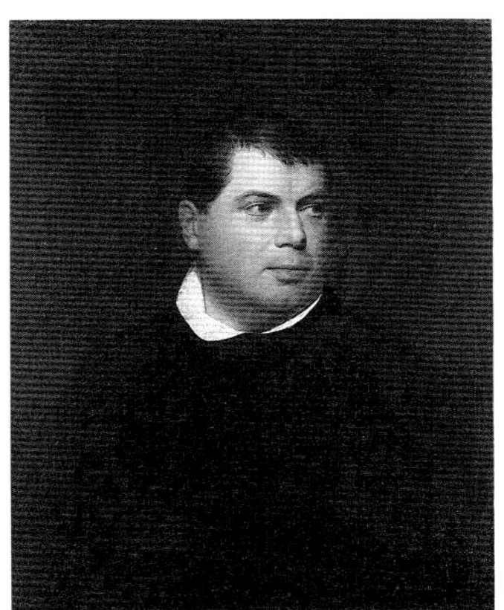

Thomas Whittemore, 1844
Canvas, 0.765 x 0.638 (30⅛ x 25⅛)
Gift of Thomas Whittemore
1950.8.1

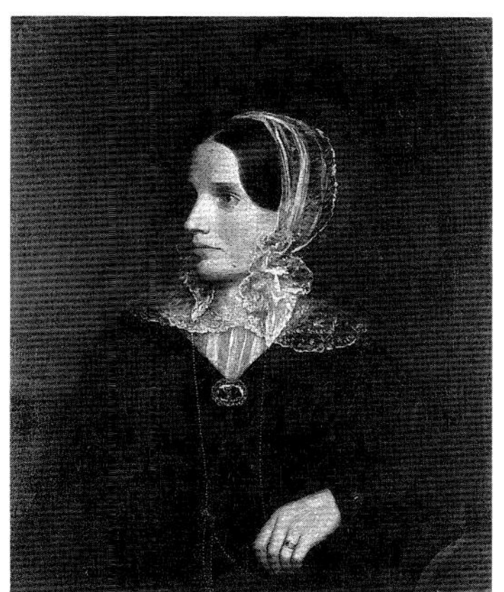

Lovice Corbett Whittemore, 1845
Canvas, 0.762 x 0.635 (30 x 25)
Gift of Thomas Whittemore
1950.8.2

CHUCK CLOSE
born 1940

Fanny/Fingerpainting, 1985
Canvas, 2.591 x 2.134 (102 x 84)
Inscribed at upper left on reverse: *c 1985 / C Close / Fanny-Fingerpainting / oil on gessoed canvas*
Gift of Lila Acheson Wallace
1987.2.1

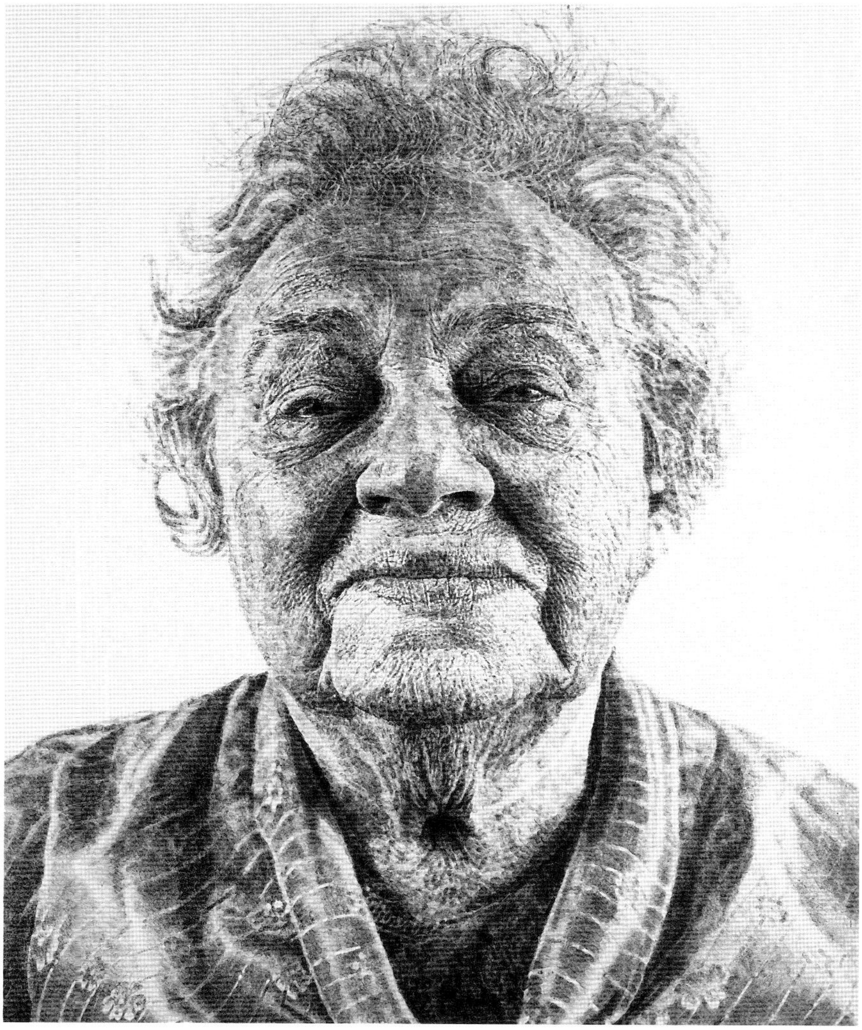

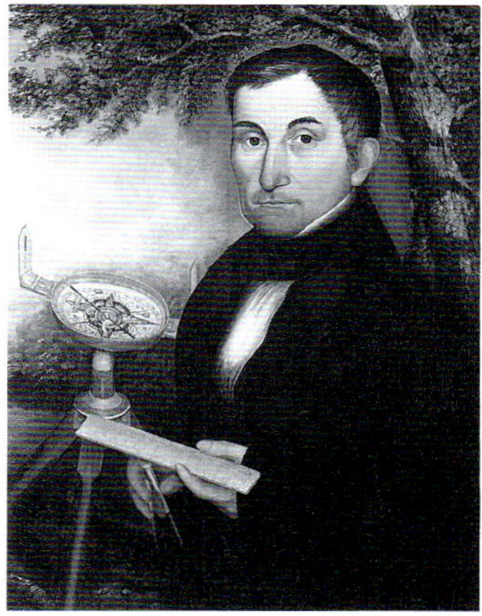

ELIAS V. COE
probably 1794–probably 1843

Henry W. Houston, 1837
Canvas, 0.713 x 0.559 (28⅛ x 22)
Gift of Edgar William and Bernice Chrysler Garbisch
1957.11.6

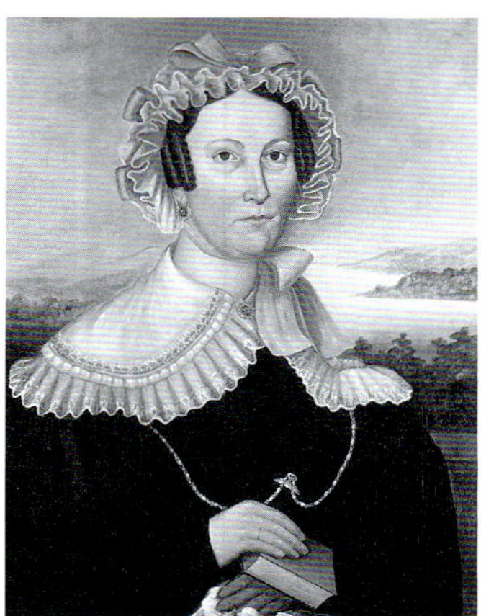

Mrs. Phebe Houston, 1837
Canvas, 0.713 x 0.558 (28 1/16 x 22)
Gift of Edgar William and Bernice Chrysler Garbisch
1953.5.6

THOMAS COLE
1801–1848

Sunrise in the Catskills, 1826
Canvas, 0.648 x 0.901 (25½ x 35½)
Gift of Mrs. John D. Rockefeller 3rd in honor of the Fiftieth Anniversary of the National Gallery of Art
1989.24.1

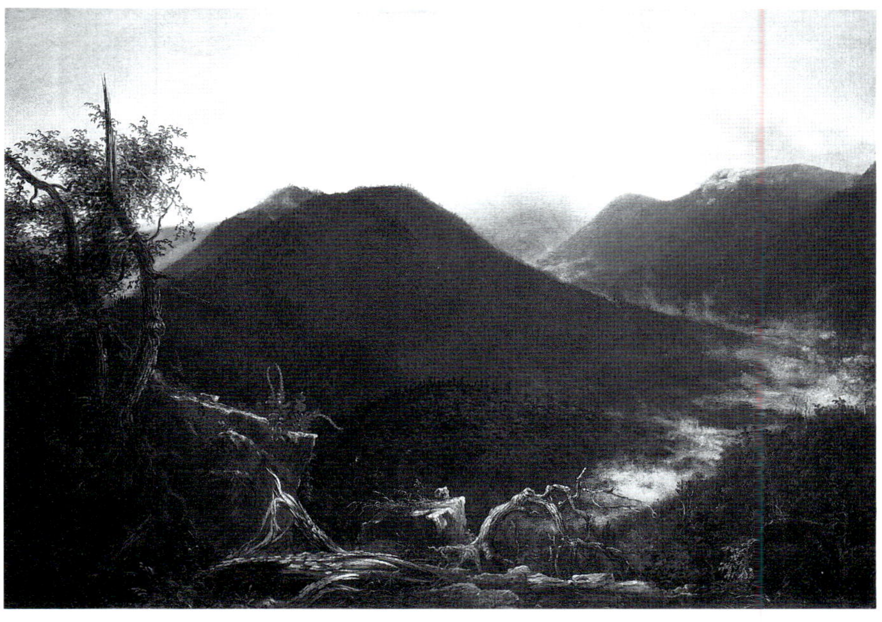

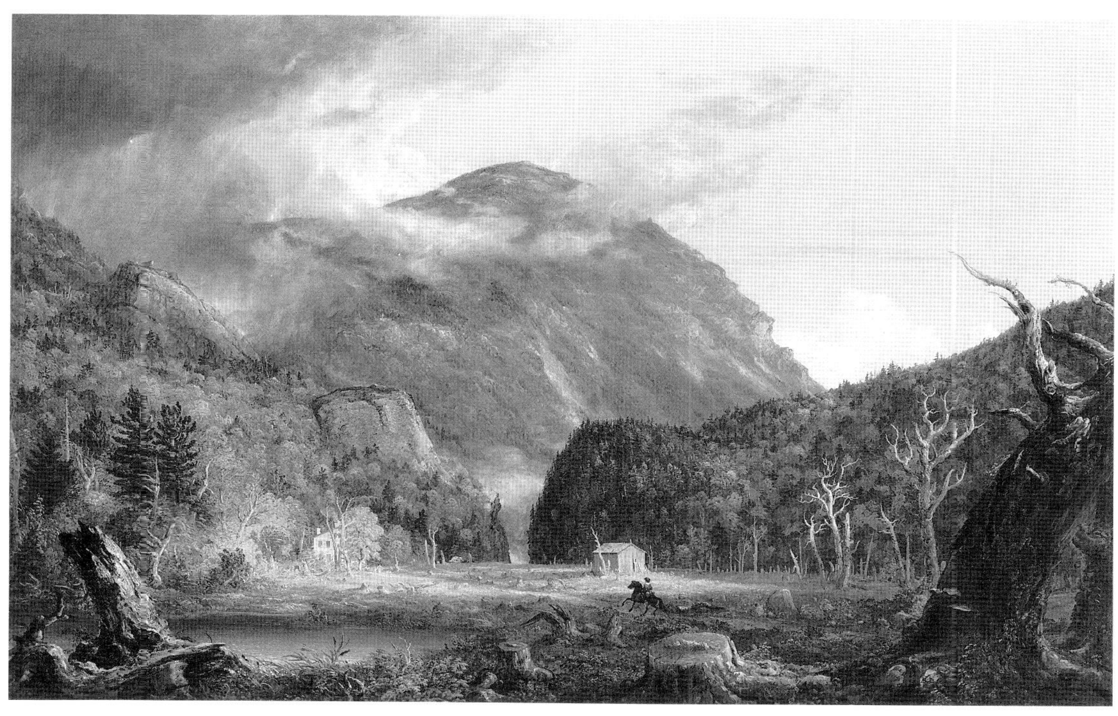

The Notch of the White Mountains (Crawford Notch), 1839
Canvas, 1.016 x 1.560 (40 x 61½)
Inscribed at lower left: *T. Cole. / 1839*
Andrew W. Mellon Fund
1967.8.1

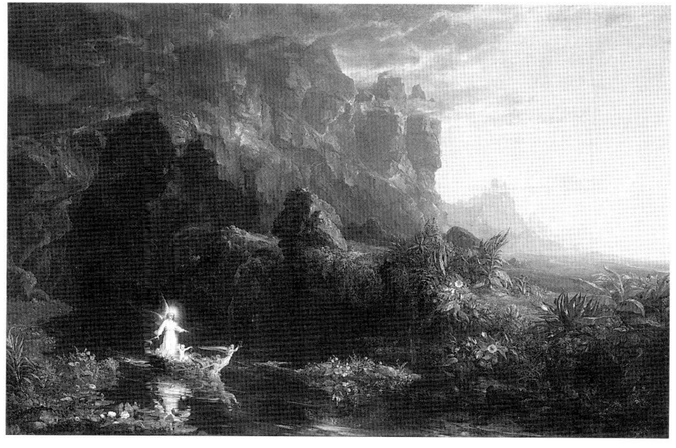

The Voyage of Life: Childhood, 1842
Canvas, 1.343 x 1.977 (52⅞ x 77⅞)
Inscribed at lower left: *1842 / T Cole / Rome*
Ailsa Mellon Bruce Fund
1971.16.1

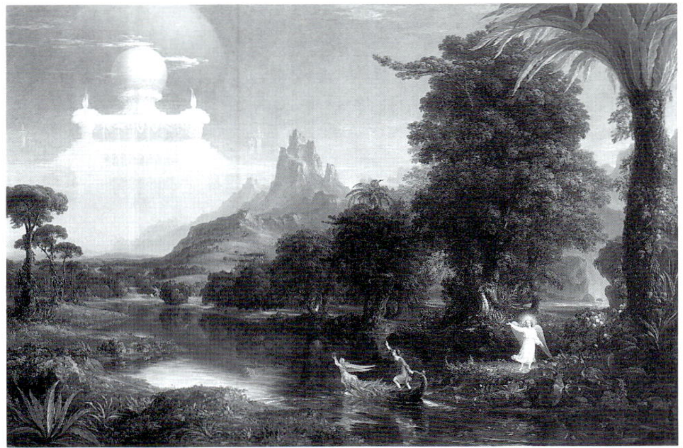

The Voyage of Life: Youth, 1842
Canvas, 1.343 x 1.949 (52⅞ x 76¾)
Inscribed at lower left: *Rome / 1842 / T Cole*
Ailsa Mellon Bruce Fund
1971.16.2

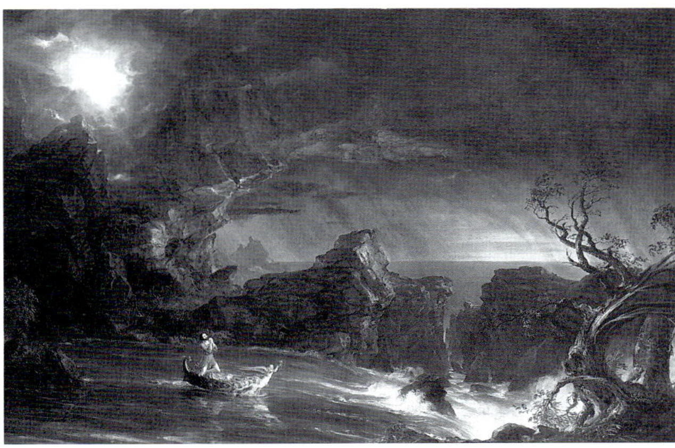

The Voyage of Life: Manhood, 1842
Canvas, 1.343 x 2.026 (52⅞ x 79¾)
Ailsa Mellon Bruce Fund
1971.16.3

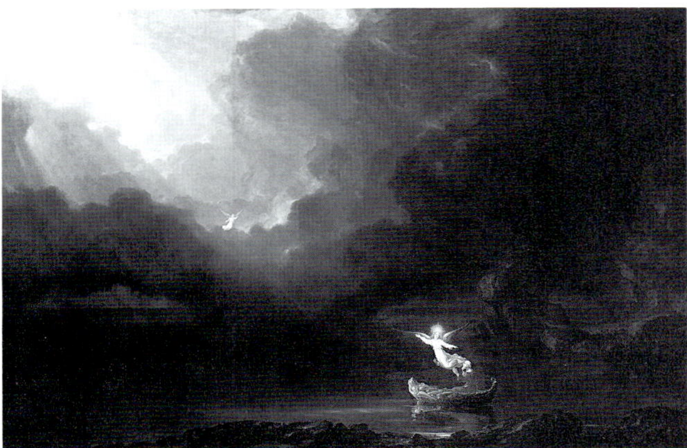

The Voyage of Life: Old Age, 1842
Canvas, 1.333 x 1.962 (52½ x 77¼)
Inscribed at lower center: *T Cole / 1842.*; lower right: *Rome*
Ailsa Mellon Bruce Fund
1971.16.4

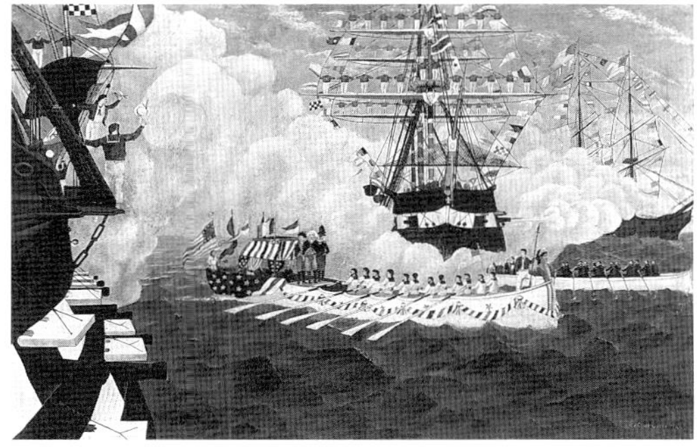

L. M. COOKE
active c. 1875

Salute to General Washington in New York Harbor, 1901
Canvas, 0.686 x 1.019 (27 x 40)
Inscribed at lower right: *L. M. Cooke. 18[. . .]*; lower left: *L. M. C. / [. . .]*
Gift of Edgar William and Bernice Chrysler Garbisch
1953.5.7

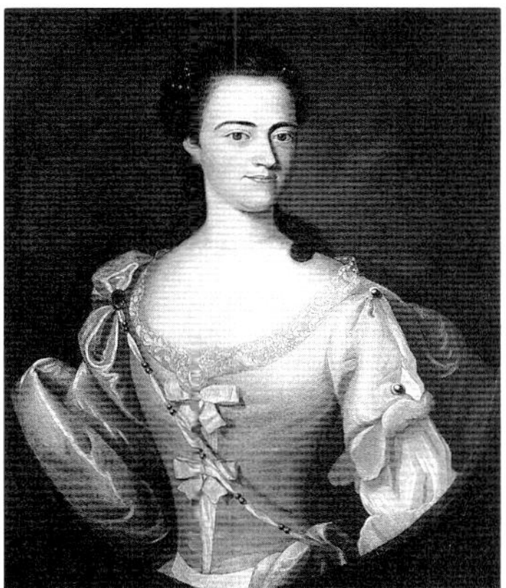

JOHN SINGLETON COPLEY
1738–1815

Jane Browne, 1756
Canvas, 0.756 x 0.626 (29¾ x 24⅝)
Inscribed at lower right: *J. S. Copley. Pinx. 1756*
Andrew W. Mellon Collection
1942.8.2

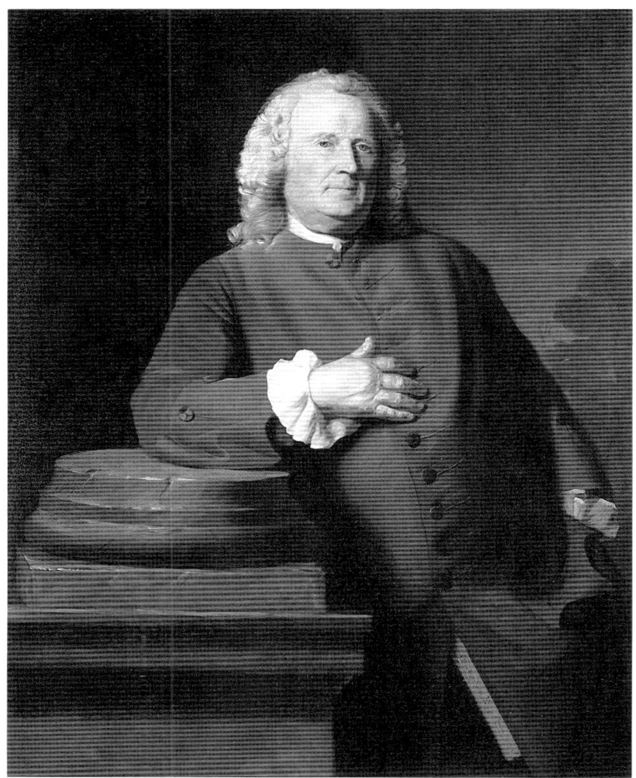

Epes Sargent, c. 1760
Canvas, 1.266 x 1.017 (49⅞ x 40)
Gift of the Avalon Foundation
1959.4.1

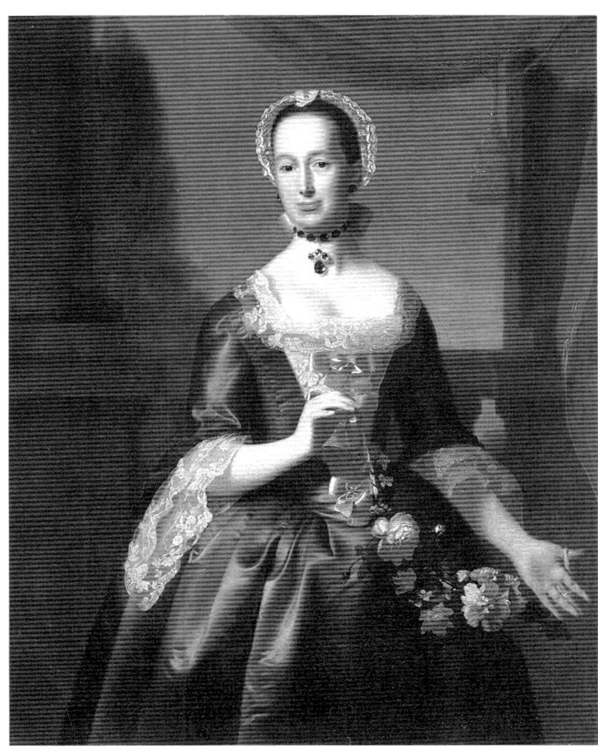

Mrs. Metcalf Bowler, c. 1763
Canvas, 1.270 x 1.020 (50 x 40)
Gift of Louise Alida Livingston
1968.1.1

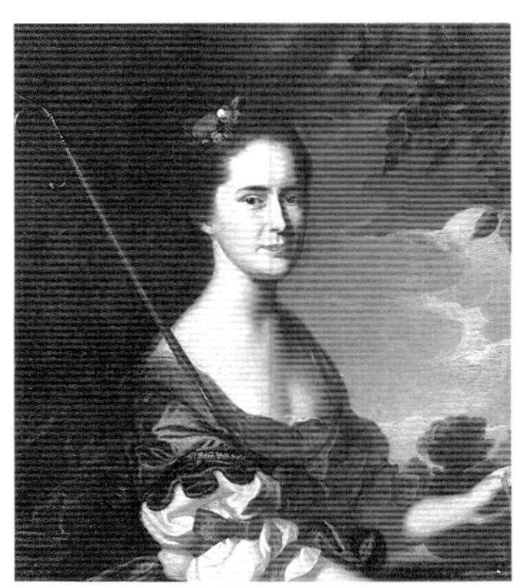

Mrs. Samuel Alleyne Otis (Elizabeth Gray), c. 1764
Canvas, 0.787 x 0.692 (31 x 27¼)
Gift of the Honorable and Mrs. Robert H. Thayer
1980.11.1

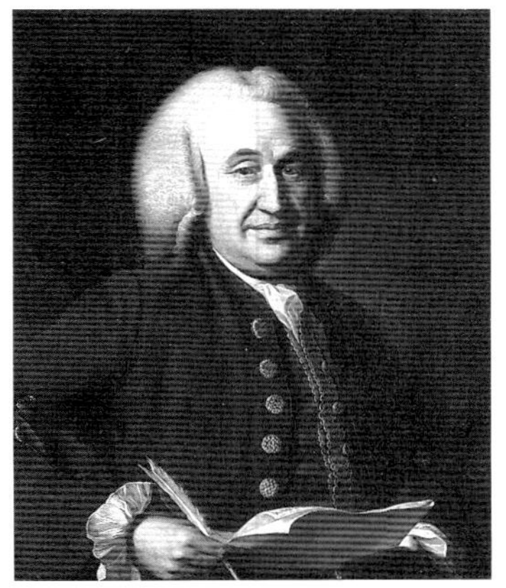

Harrison Gray, c. 1767
Canvas, 0.775 x 0.650 (30½ x 25 9/16)
Gift of the Honorable and Mrs. Robert H. Thayer
1976.25.1

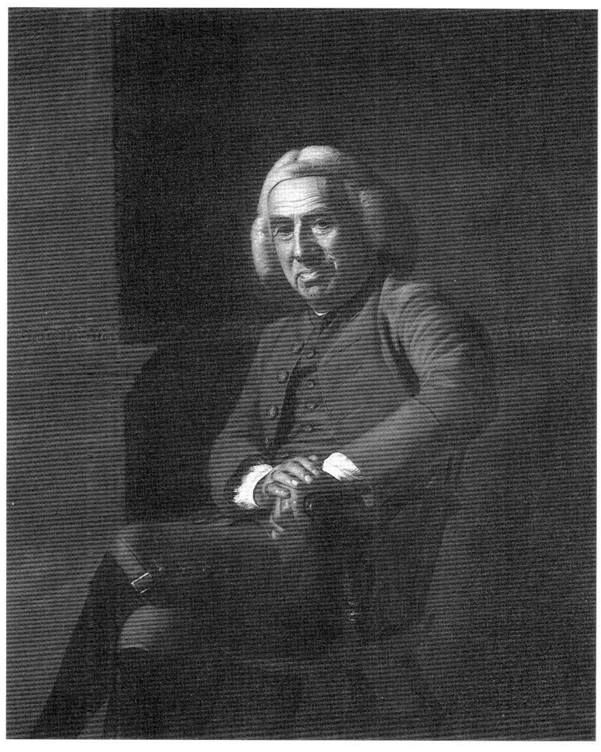

Eleazer Tyng, 1772
Canvas, 1.265 x 1.002 (49¾ x 40⅛)
Inscribed at lower left: *John Singleton Copley / pinx 1772. Boston.-*
Gift of the Avalon Foundation
1965.6.1

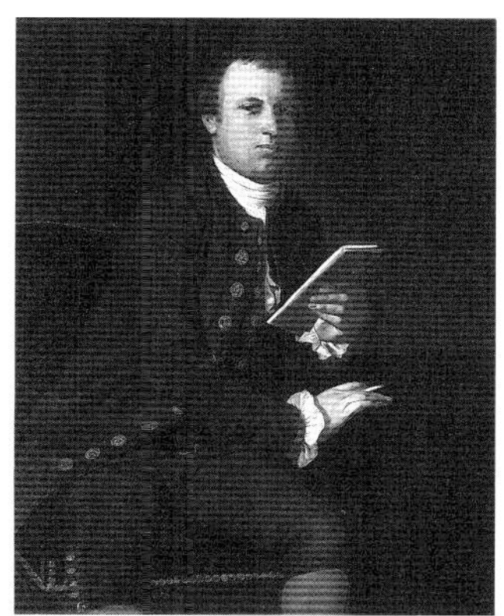

Adam Babcock, c. 1774
Canvas, 1.170 x 0.917 (46$^{1}/_{16}$ x 36⅛)
Gift of Henry A. and Caroline C. Murray
1978.79.1

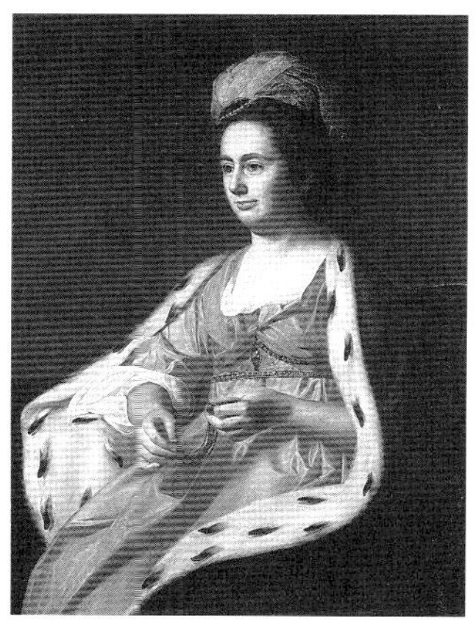

Mrs. Adam Babcock, c. 1774
Canvas, 1.168 x 0.908 (46 x 35¾)
Gift of Mrs. Robert Low Bacon
1985.20.1

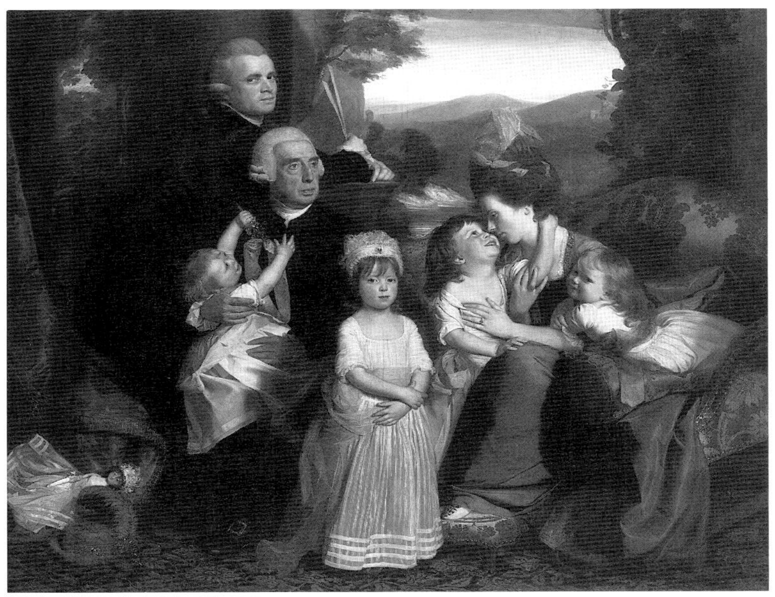

The Copley Family, 1776/1777
Canvas, 1.841 x 2.292 (72½ x 90¼)
Andrew W. Mellon Fund
1961.7.1

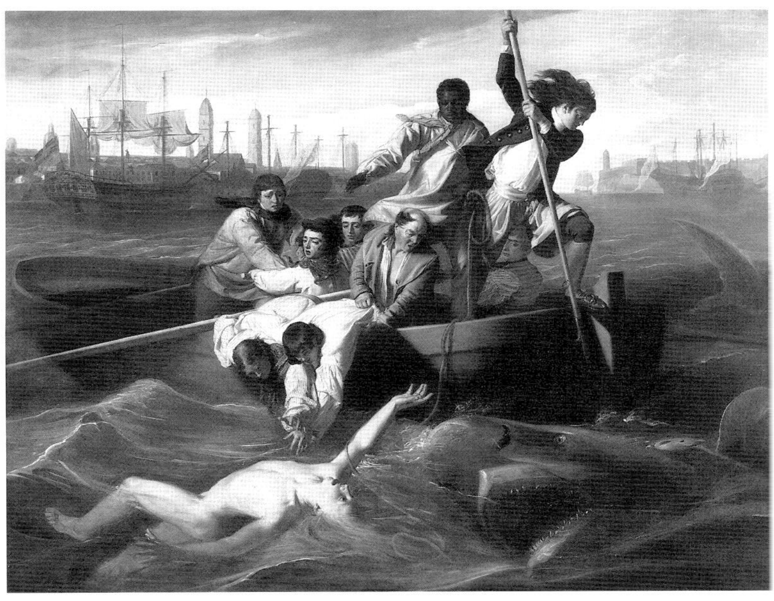

Watson and the Shark, 1778
Canvas, 1.821 x 2.297 (71¾ x 90½)
Inscribed on stern of skiff: *JS Copley. P. 1778-*
Ferdinand Lammot Belin Fund
1963.6.1

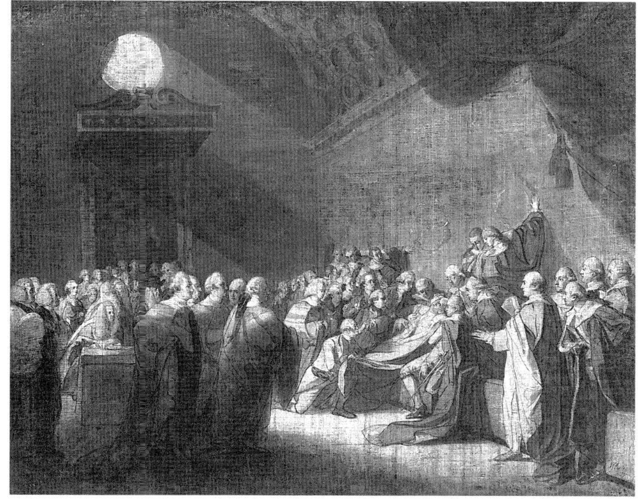

The Death of the Earl of Chatham, 1779
Canvas, 0.527 x 0.643 (20½ x 25¼)
Inscribed at lower right: *J S Copley / 1779*
Gift of Mrs. Gordon Dexter
1947.15.1

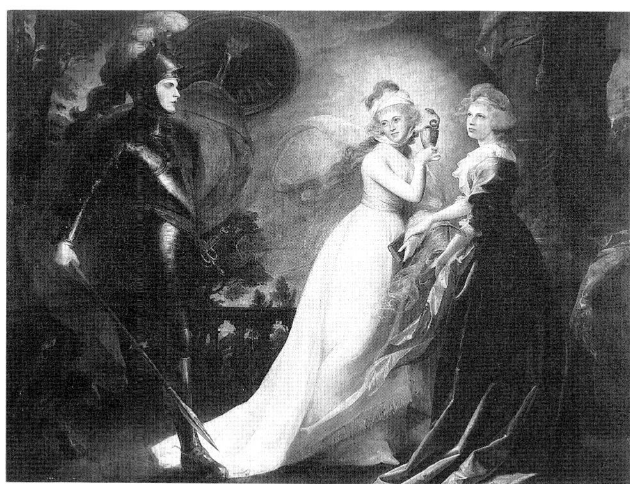

The Red Cross Knight, 1793
Canvas, 2.135 x 2.730 (84 x 107½)
Gift of Mrs. Gordon Dexter
1942.4.2

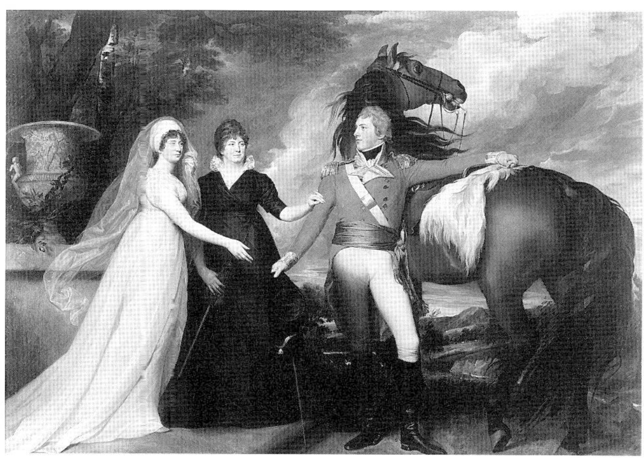

Colonel Fitch and His Sisters, 1800/1801
Canvas, 2.570 x 3.404 (101½ x 134)
Gift of Eleanor Lothrop, Gordon Abbott, and Katharine A. Batchelder
1960.4.1

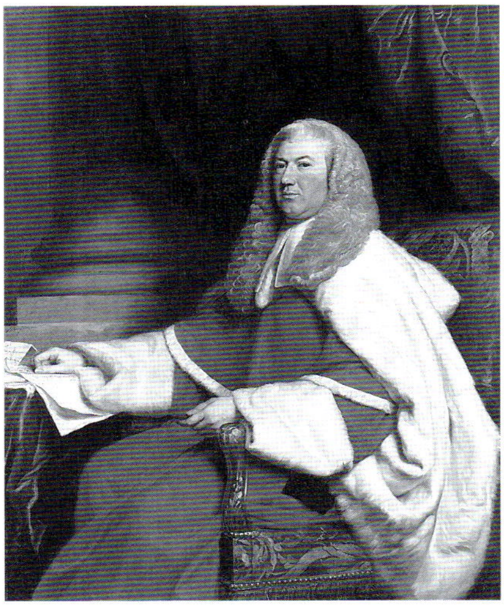

Baron Graham, 1804
Canvas, 1.448 x 1.188 (57 x 46¾)
Inscribed at center left: *J S Copley. R A. pinx*; and on envelope: *Mr:Baron Graham / London*
Gift of Mrs. Gordon Dexter
1942.4.1

EDWARD CORBETT
1919–1971

Washington, D.C. November 1963 III, 1963
Canvas, 1.009 x 0.914 (39¾ x 36)
Gift of Marian Corbett Chamberlain and Mrs. Edward Corbett
1974.14.1

MARY ANN CORSE
born 1945

Untitled, 1971
Canvas, 2.138 x 2.136 (84¼ x 84⅛)
Gift of Mr. and Mrs. Burton Tremaine
1977.75.1

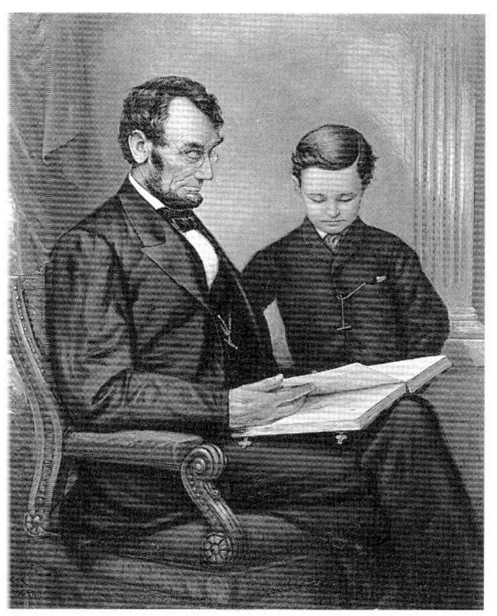

FRANKLIN C. COURTER
1854–1947

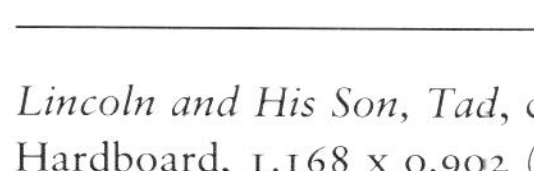

Lincoln and His Son, Tad, c. 1929
Hardboard, 1.168 x 0.902 (46 x 35½)
Andrew W. Mellon Collection
1954.1.2

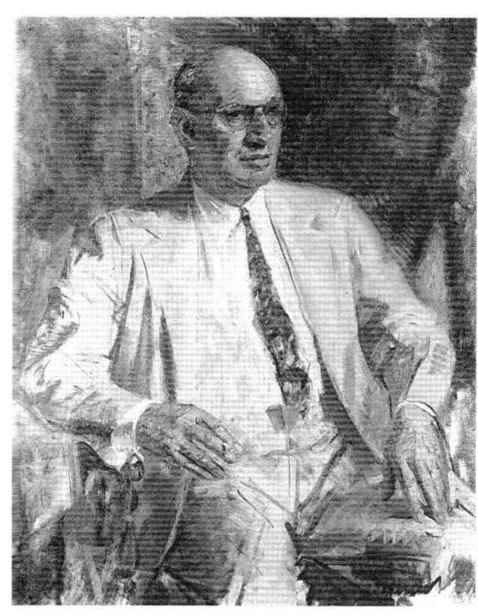

GARDNER COX
born 1906

Lessing J. Rosenwald, 1955
Canvas, 1.146 x 0.886 (45⅛ x 34 13/16)
Inscribed at lower left: *Gardner Cox '55*
Gift of Lessing J. Rosenwald
1955.8.1 Special Collection

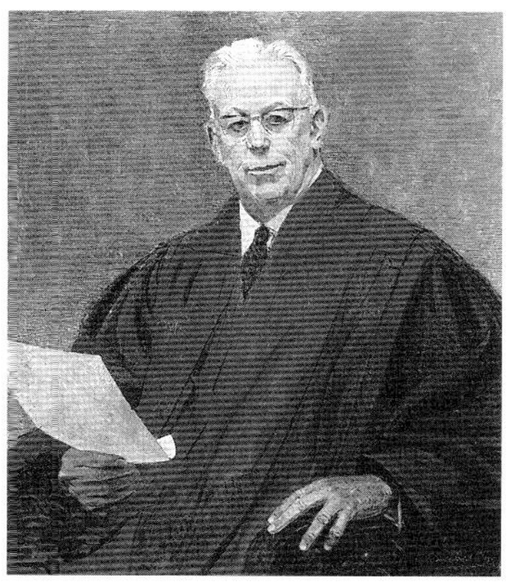

Earl Warren, 1963
Canvas, 1.041 x 0.892 (41 x 35⅛)
Inscribed at lower right: *Gardner Cox / 1963*
Gift of the Avalon Foundation
1962.1.1 Special Collection

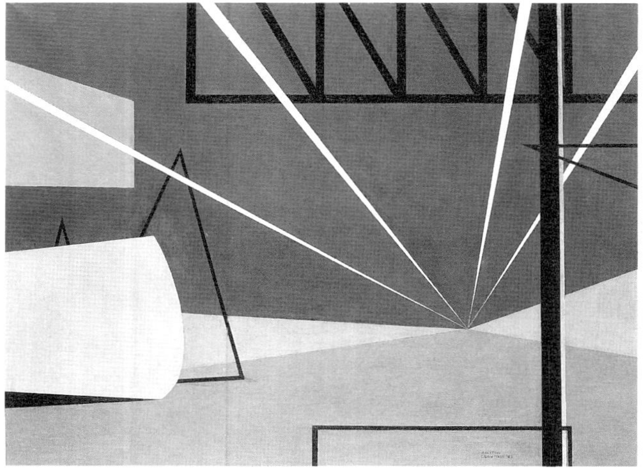

RALSTON CRAWFORD
1906–1978

Lights in an Aircraft Plant, 1945
Canvas, 0.772 x 1.022 (30⅜ x 40¼)
Inscribed at lower right: *RALSTON / CRAWFORD '45*
Gift of Mr. and Mrs. Burton Tremaine
1971.87.1

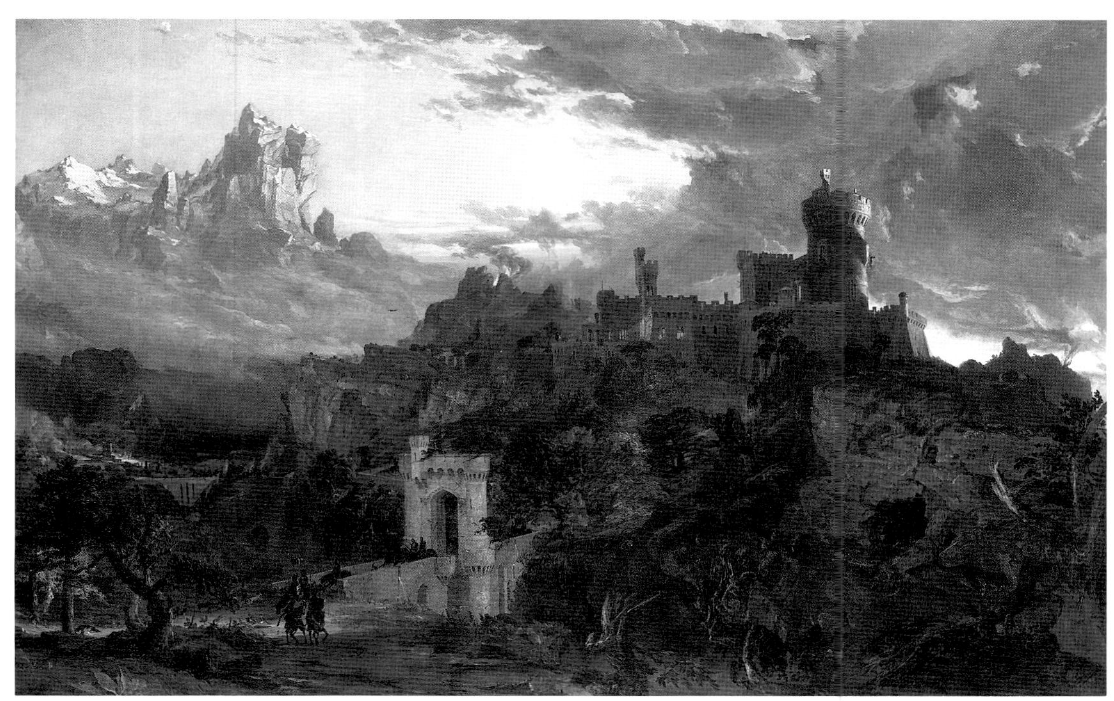

JASPER FRANCIS CROPSEY
1823–1900

The Spirit of War, 1851
Canvas, 1.108 x 1.716 (43⅝ x 67⅝)
Inscribed at lower left on rocks: *1851/ J.F. Cropsey*
Avalon Fund
1978.12.1

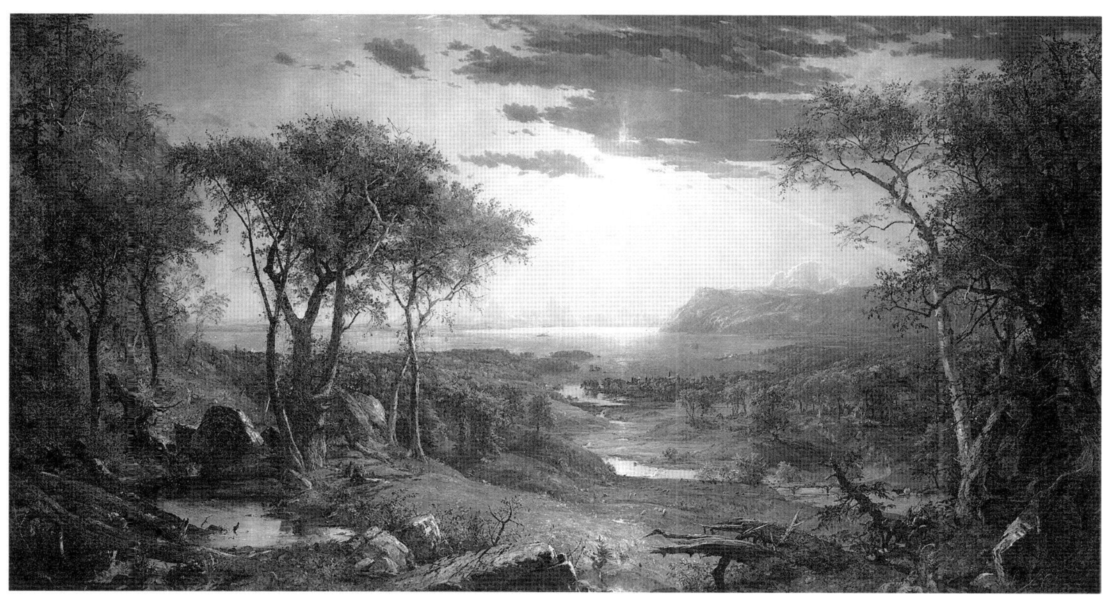

Autumn—On the Hudson River, 1860
Canvas, 1.518 x 2.749 (59¾ x 108¼)
Inscribed at lower center: *Autumn, -on the Hudson River / J. F Cropsey / London 1860*
Gift of the Avalon Foundation
1963.9.1

JOHN STEUART CURRY
1897–1946

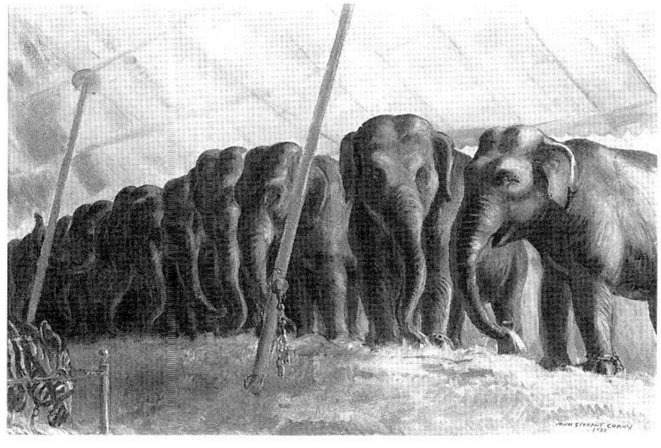

Circus Elephants, 1932
Canvas, 0.640 x 0.918 (25¼ x 36)
Inscribed at lower right: *John Steuart Curry / 1932*
Gift of Admiral Neill Phillips in memory of Grace Hendrick Phillips
1976.50.1

ARTHUR B. DAVIES
1862–1928

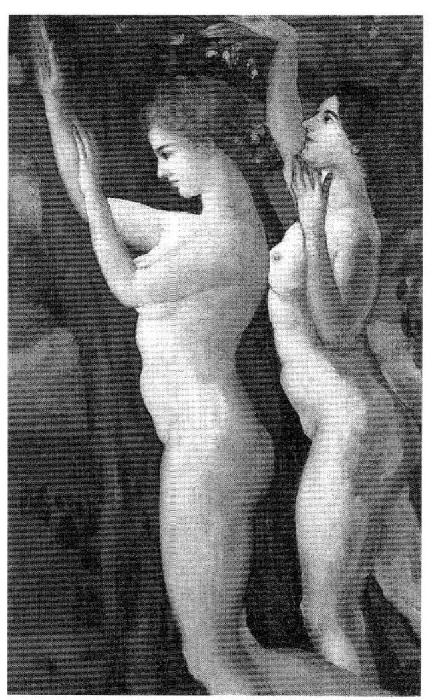

Sweet Tremulous Leaves, 1922/1923
Canvas, 0.772 x 0.464 (30⅜ x 18¼)
Chester Dale Collection
1963.10.119

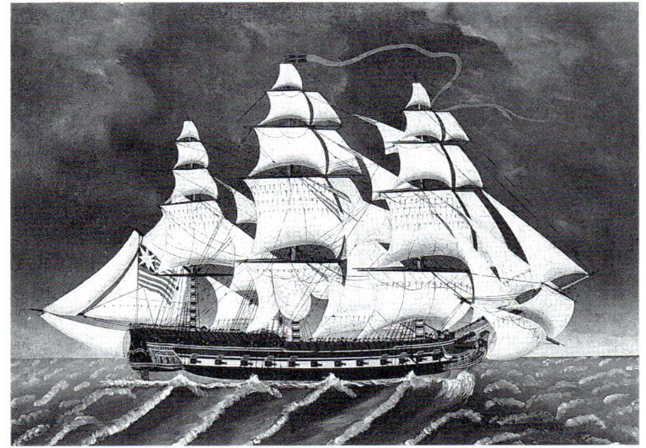

T. DAVIES
active 1827

Ship in Full Sail, 1827
Canvas, 0.680 x 0.923 (26¾ x 36⅝)
Gift of Edgar William and Bernice Chrysler Garbisch
1980.62.1

GENE DAVIS
1920–1985

Satan's Flag, 1970
Canvas, 2.901 x 10.994 (114¼ x 443)
Anonymous Gift
1974.16.1

Narcissus III, 1975
Canvas, 2.441 x 2.899 (96⅛ x 114⅛)
Anonymous Gift
1980.6.1

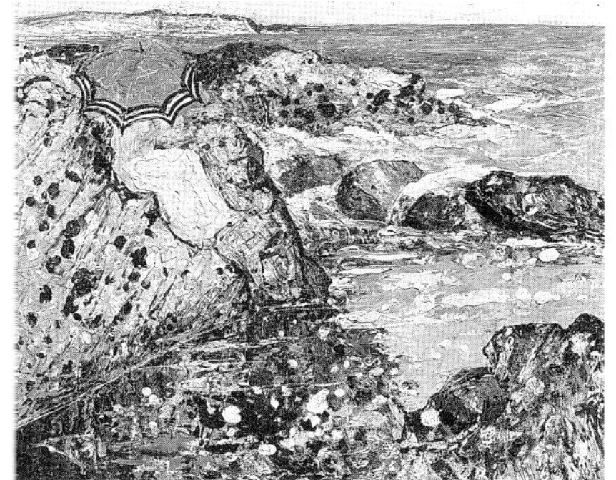

HENRY GOLDEN DEARTH
1864–1918

Flecks of Foam, c. 1911/1912
Wood, 0.453 x 0.550 (17⅞ x 21⅝)
Inscribed at lower right: *Dearth*
Chester Dale Collection
1963.10.120

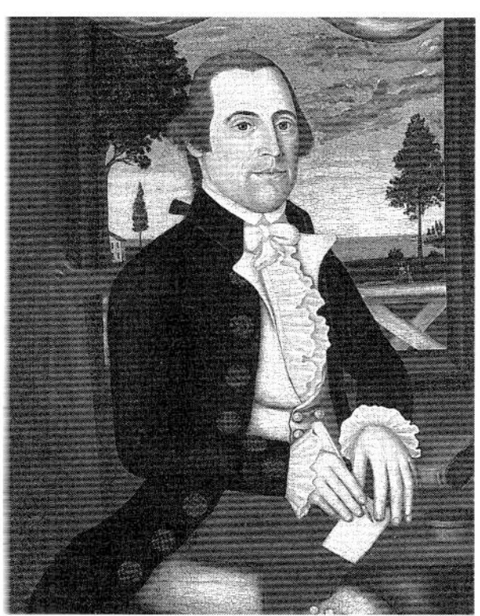

THE DENISON LIMNER
active c. 1790

Captain Elisha Denison, c. 1790
Canvas, 0.863 x 0.689 (34 x 27⅛)
Gift of Edgar William and Bernice Chrysler Garbisch
1980.62.26

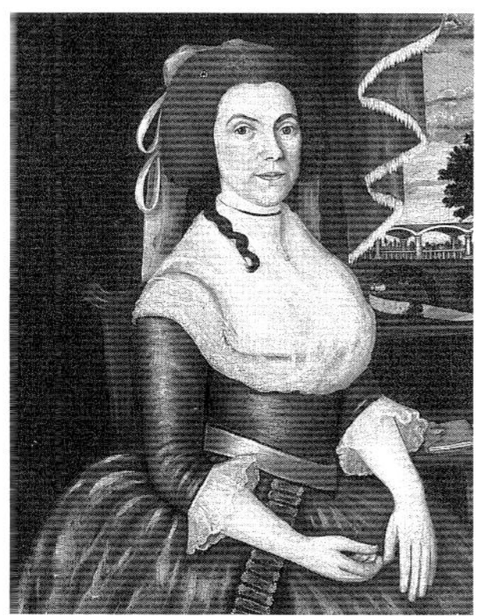

Mrs. Elizabeth Noyes Denison, c. 1790
Canvas, 0.866 x 0.687 (34⅛ x 27¹⁄₁₆)
Gift of Edgar William and Bernice Chrysler Garbisch
1980.62.27

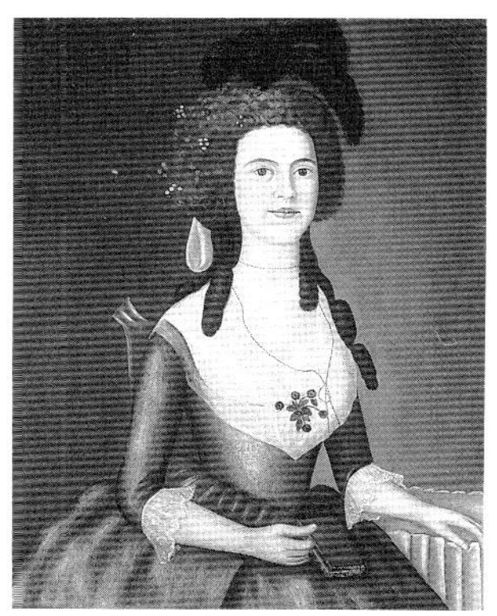

Elizabeth Denison, c. 1790
Canvas, 0.854 x 0.678 (33⅝ x 26⅝)
Gift of Edgar William and Bernice Chrysler Garbisch
1953.5.35

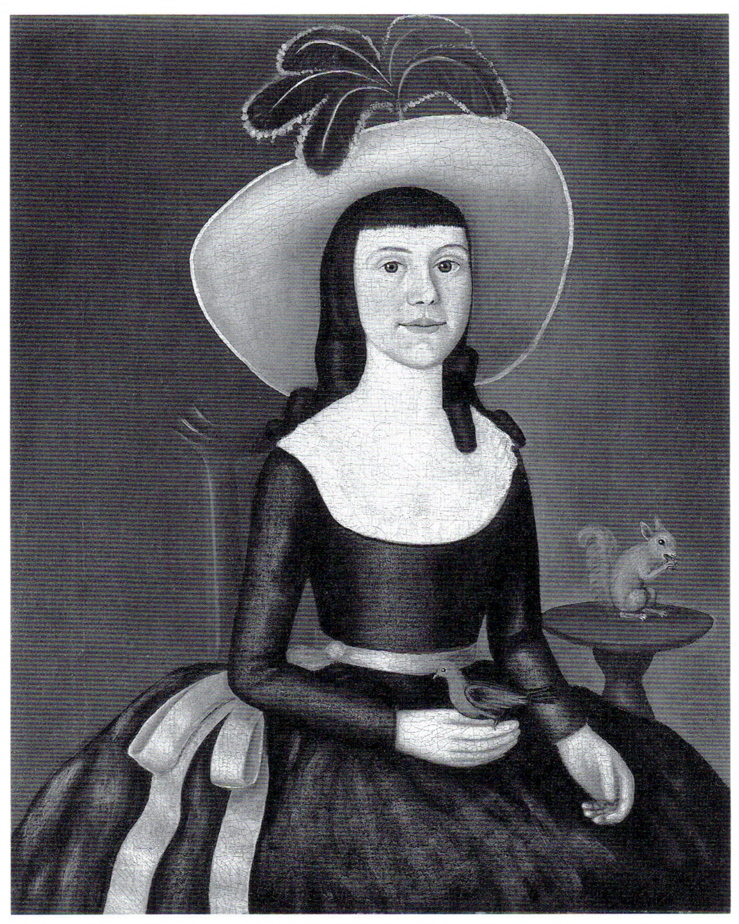

Miss Denison of Stonington, Connecticut (possibly Matilda Denison), c. 1790
Canvas, 0.876 x 0.688 (34½ x 27¹⁄₁₆)
Gift of Edgar William and Bernice Chrysler Garbisch
1980.62.28

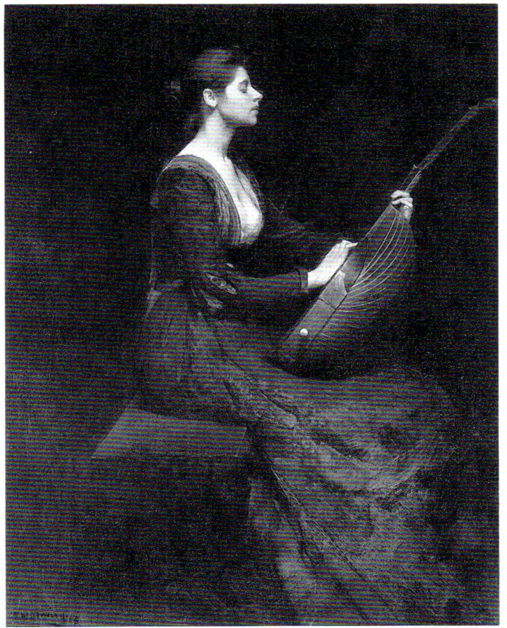

THOMAS WILMER DEWING
1851–1938

Lady with a Lute, 1886
Wood, 0.508 x 0.381 (20 x 15)
Inscribed at lower left: *T W Dewing / 86*
Gift of Dr. and Mrs. Walter Timme
1978.60.1

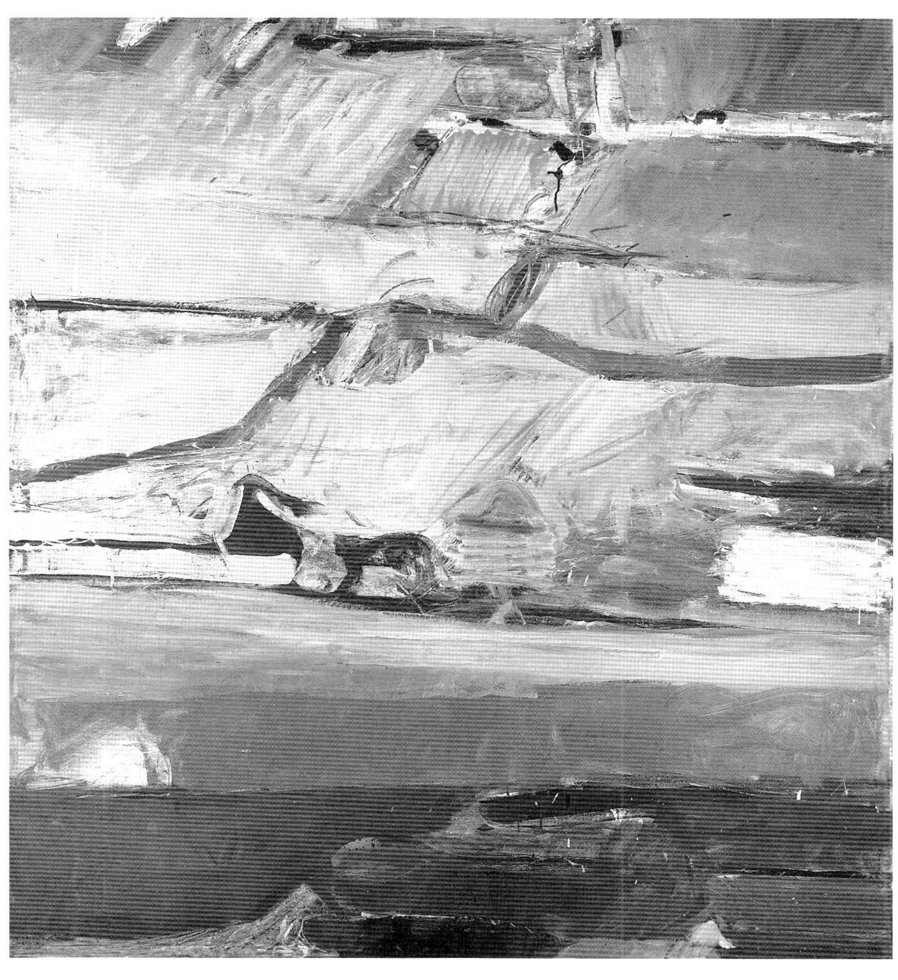

RICHARD DIEBENKORN
born 1922

Berkeley No. 52, 1955
Canvas, 1.489 x 1.368 (58⅝ x 53⅞)
Inscribed at lower left: *RD55*
Gift of the Collectors Committee
1986.68.1

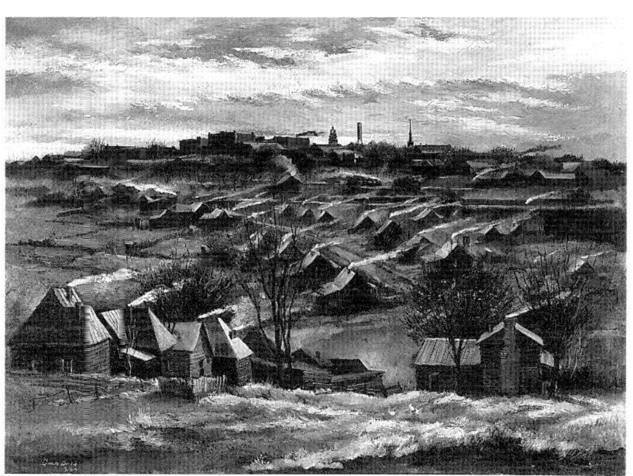

LAMAR DODD
born 1909

Winter Valley, 1944
Canvas, 0.966 x 1.270 (38 x 50)
Inscribed at lower left: *Lamar Dodd / 1944*
Anonymous Gift
1971.3.1

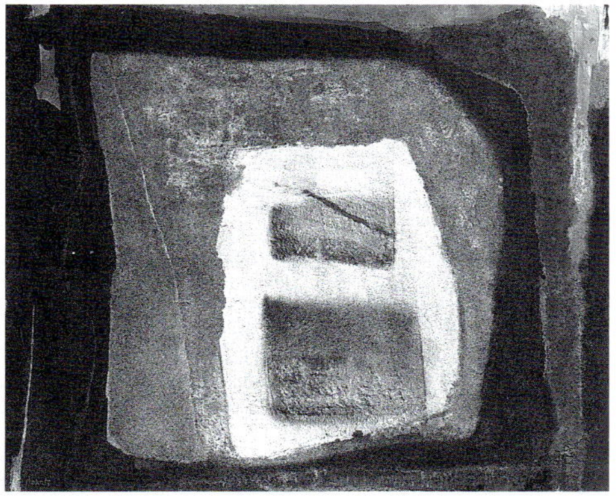

ENRICO DONATI
born 1909

Cat's Eyes, 1960
Canvas, 1.271 x 1.527 (50 x 60⅛)
Inscribed at lower left: *Donati*
Gift of Mrs. McFadden Staempfli
1971.88.2

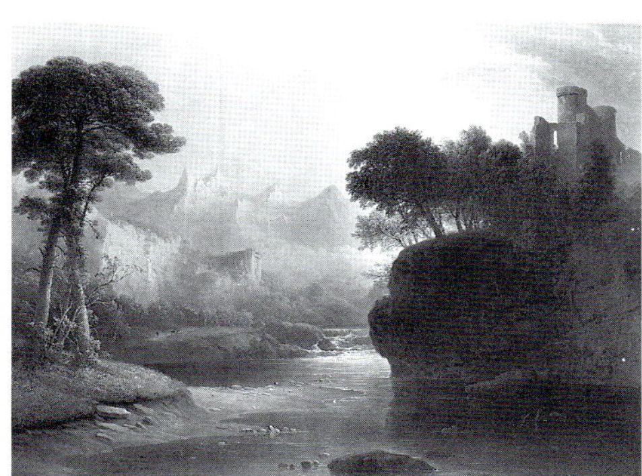

THOMAS DOUGHTY
1793–1856

Fanciful Landscape, 1834
Canvas, 0.765 x 1.015 (30⅛ x 39⅞)
Inscribed at lower right: *T DOUGHTY / BOSTON / 1834*
Gift of the Avalon Foundation
1963.9.2

ARTHUR DOVE
1880–1946

Moth Dance, 1929
Canvas, 0.513 x 0.663 (20³⁄₁₆ x 26⅛)
Inscribed at lower right: *Dove*
Alfred Stieglitz Collection
1949.2.1

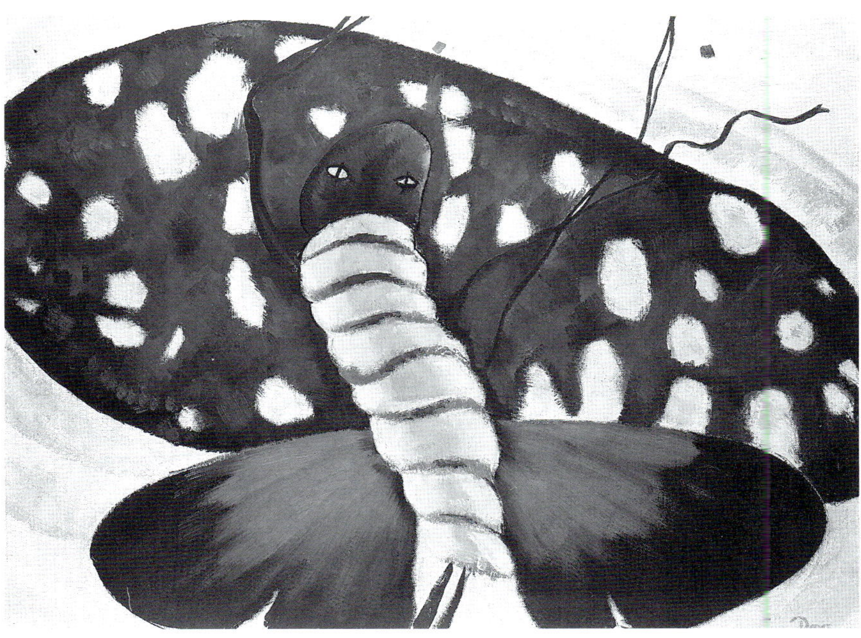

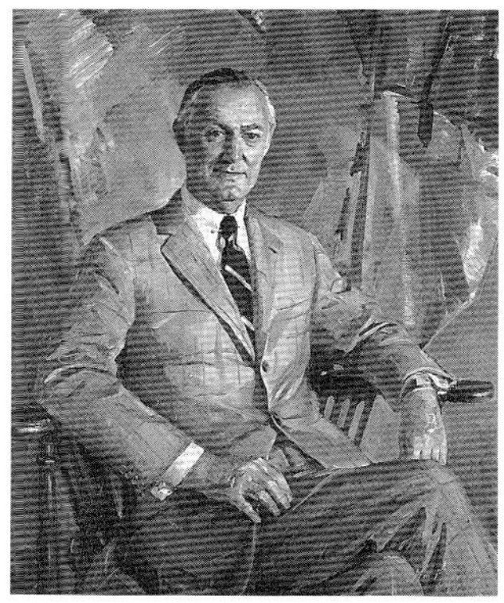

WILLIAM FRANKLIN DRAPER
born 1912

Paul Mellon, 1974
Canvas, 1.225 x 1.019 (48¼ x 40⅛)
Inscribed at lower right: *Wm. F. Draper / '74*
Paul Mellon Collection
1983.75.1 Special Collection

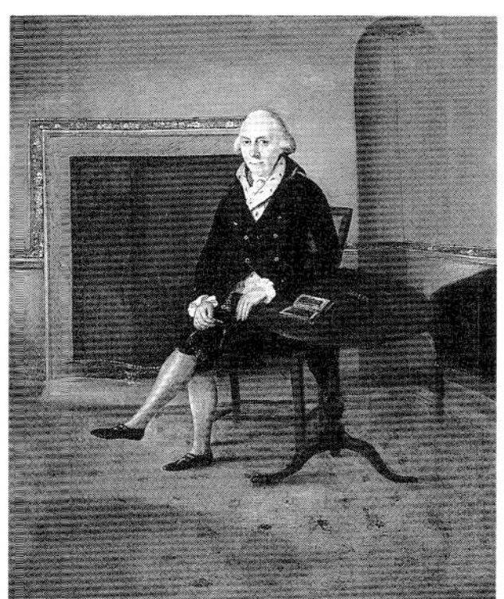

ATTRIBUTED TO
WILLIAM DUNLAP
1766–1839

Samuel Griffin (?), c. 1805
Canvas, 0.754 x 0.633 (29 11/16 x 24 15/16)
Gift of Edgar William and Bernice Chrysler Garbisch
1953.5.80

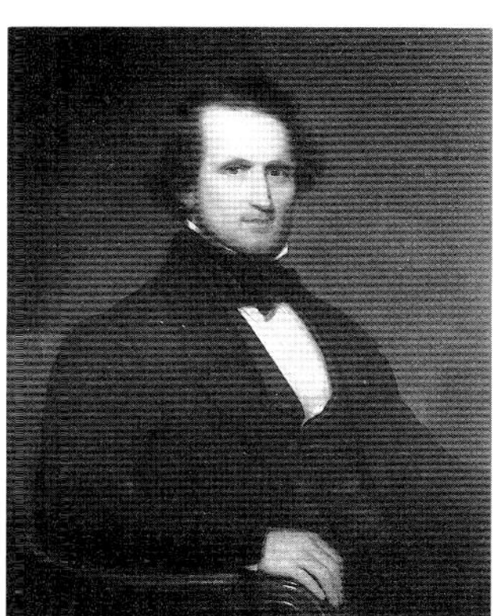

ASHER BROWN DURAND
1796–1886

Portrait of a Man, c. 1840
Canvas, 0.867 x 0.689 (34⅛ x 27⅛)
Andrew W. Mellon Collection
1947.17.37

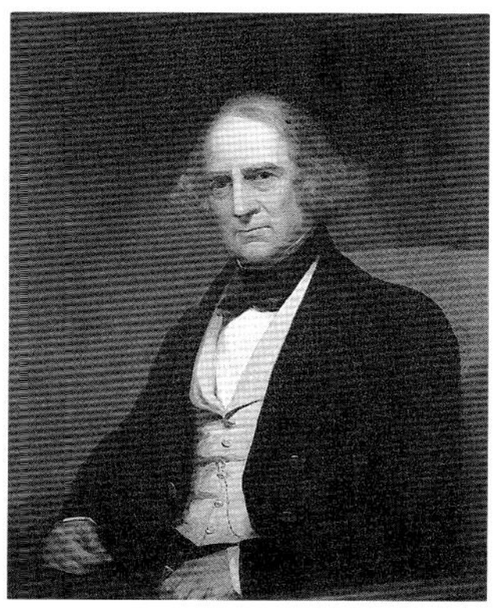

Gouverneur Kemble, 1853
Canvas, 0.870 x 0.683 (34¼ x 26⅞)
Inscribed at lower right: *A.B.D. / 1853*
Andrew W. Mellon Collection
1947.17.2

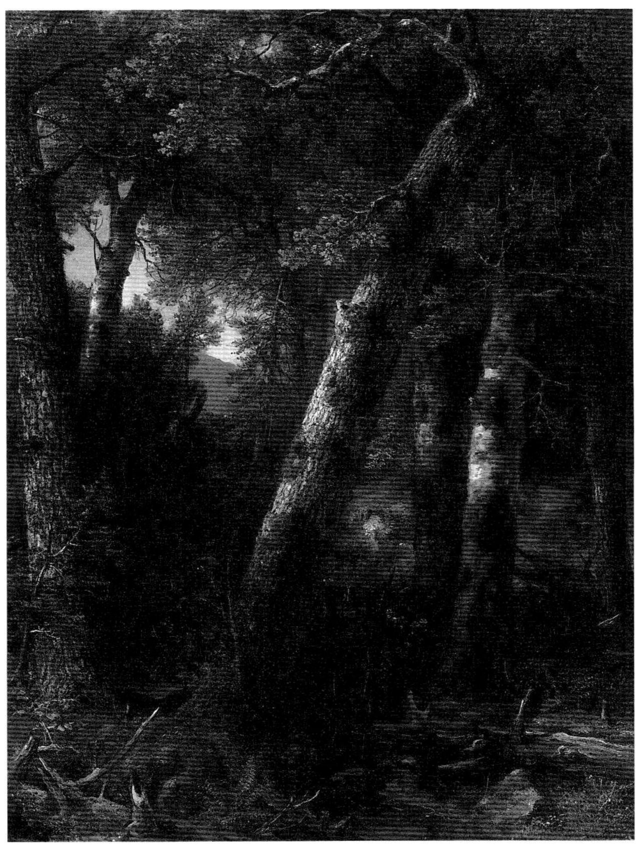

Forest in the Morning Light, c. 1855
Canvas, 0.615 x 0.462 (24 1/4 x 18 1/4)
Inscribed at lower right: *ABD*
Gift of Frederick Sturges, Jr.
1978.6.2

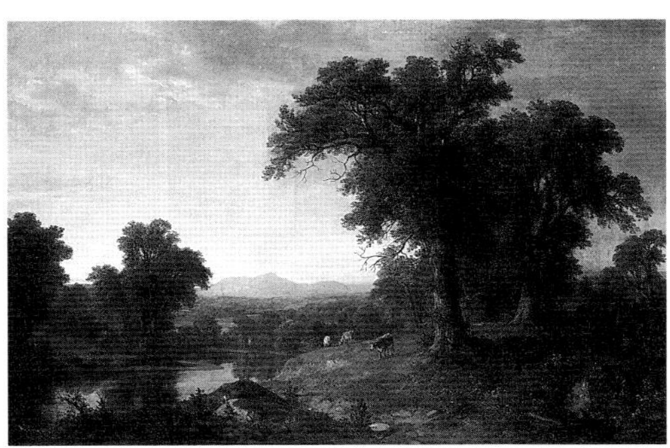

A Pastoral Scene, 1858
Canvas, 0.555 x 0.823 (21 7/8 x 32 3/8)
Inscribed at lower center on rock:
A B Durand / 1858
Gift of Frederick Sturges, Jr.
1978.6.3

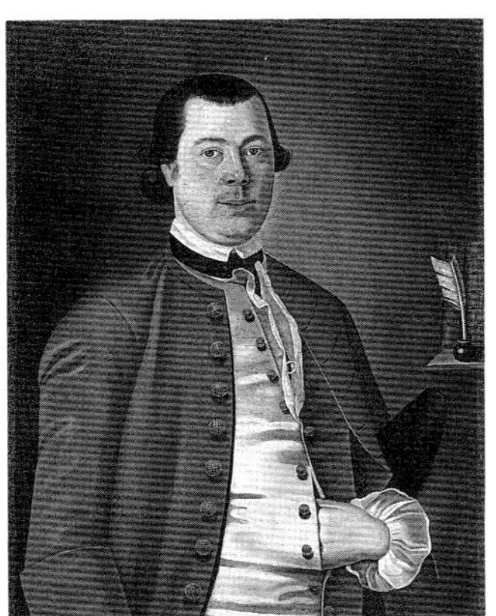

JOHN DURAND
active 1765/1782

John Lothrop, c. 1770
Canvas, 0.908 x 0.706 (35 3/4 x 27 13/16)
Gift of Edgar William and Bernice Chrysler Garbisch
1980.62.70

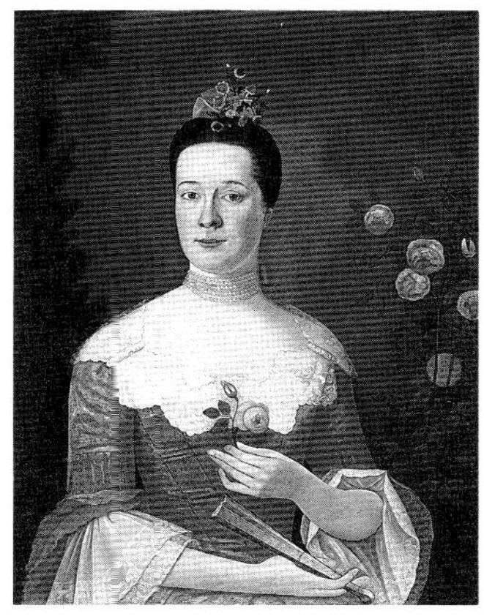

Mrs. John Lothrop, c. 1770
Canvas, 0.909 x 0.708 (35 13/16 x 27 7/8)
Gift of Edgar William and Bernice Chrysler Garbisch
1980.62.6

WILLIAM DUTTERER
born 1943

Equal, No. 2, 1968
Canvas, 2.441 x 1.523 (96 1/8 x 60)
Inscribed at center left on reverse: *Wm. S. Dutterer / Oct. 1968, "Equal"*
Gift of Mr. and Mrs. Burton Tremaine
1977.75.2

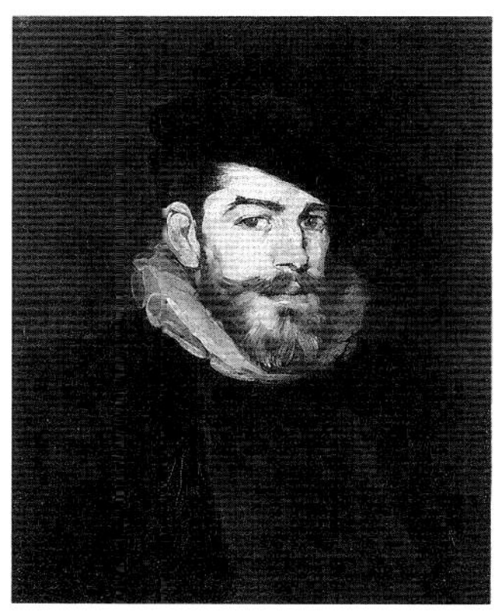

FRANK DUVENECK
1848–1919

Leslie Pease Barnum, 1876
Canvas, 0.560 x 0.460 (22 x 18)
Andrew W. Mellon Collection
1942.8.3

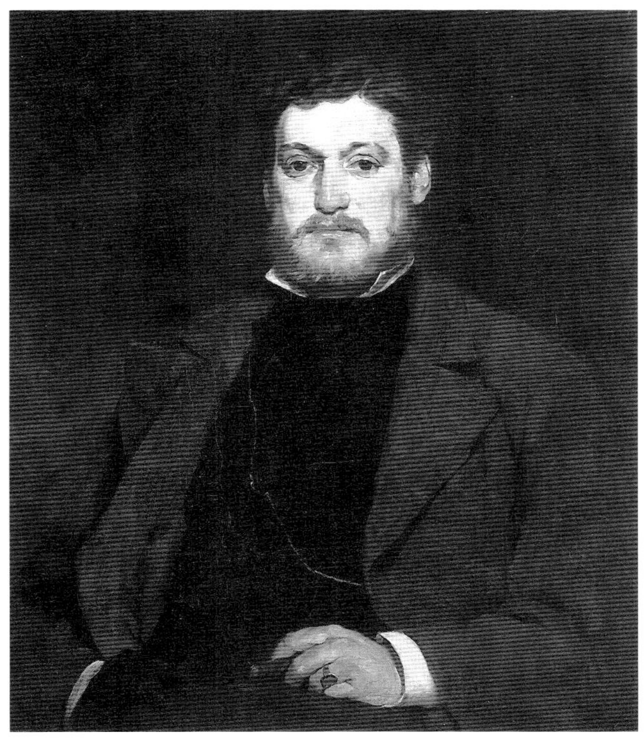

William Gedney Bunce, c. 1878
Canvas, 0.775 x 0.660 (30½ x 26)
Andrew W. Mellon Collection
1942.8.4

ATTRIBUTED TO
GERARDUS DUYCKINCK
1695–1746

Lady Undressing for a Bath, first half
18th century
Canvas, 0.842 x 1.076 (33¼ x 42⅜)
Gift of Edgar William and Bernice
Chrysler Garbisch
1956.13.11

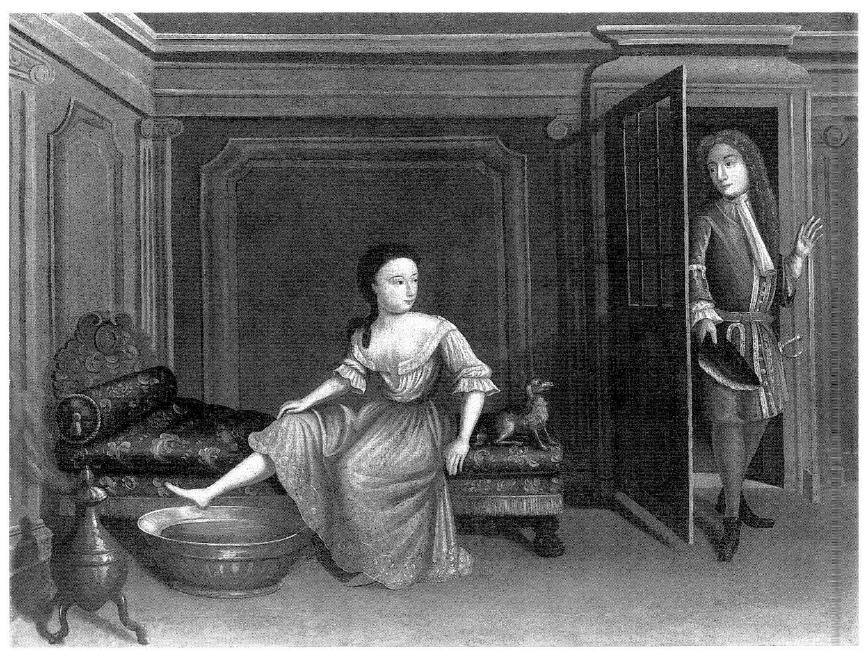

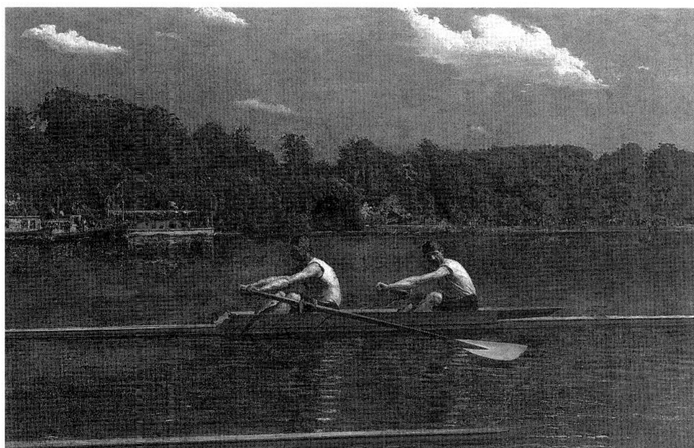

THOMAS EAKINS
1844–1916

The Biglin Brothers Racing, c. 1873
Canvas, 0.612 x 0.916 (24 1/8 x 36 1/8)
Gift of Cornelius Vanderbilt Whitney
1953.7.1

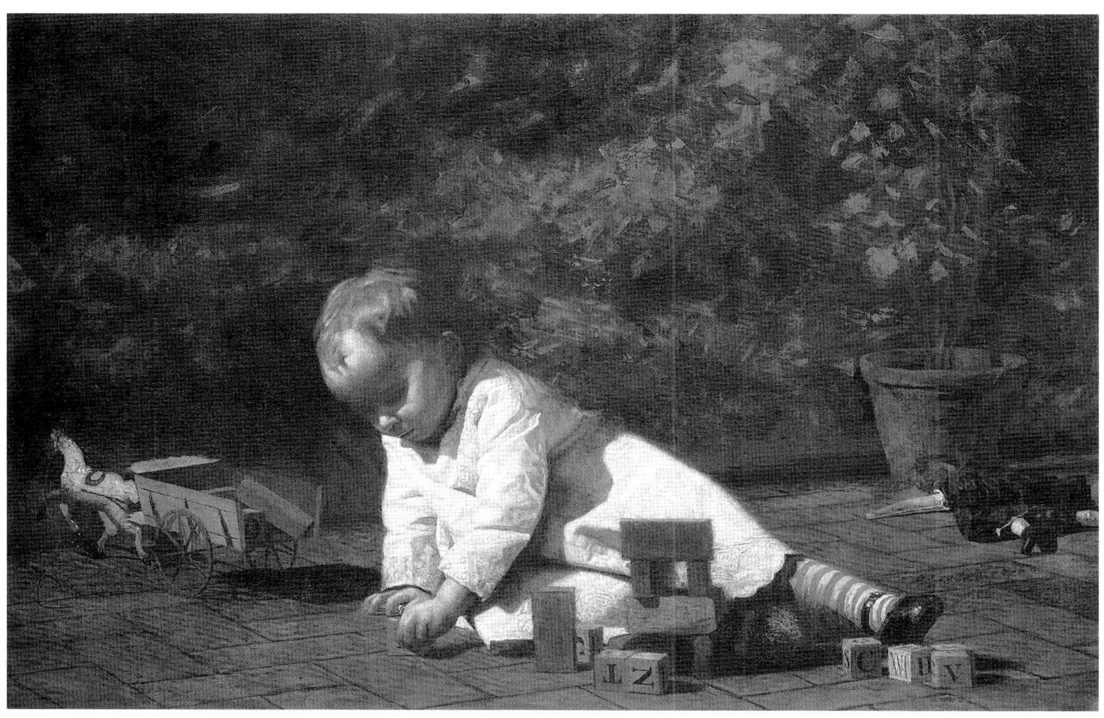

Baby at Play, 1876
Canvas, 0.819 x 1.225 (32 1/4 x 48 1/4)
Inscribed at lower right on brick pavement: *Eakins / 76*
John Hay Whitney Collection
1982.76.5

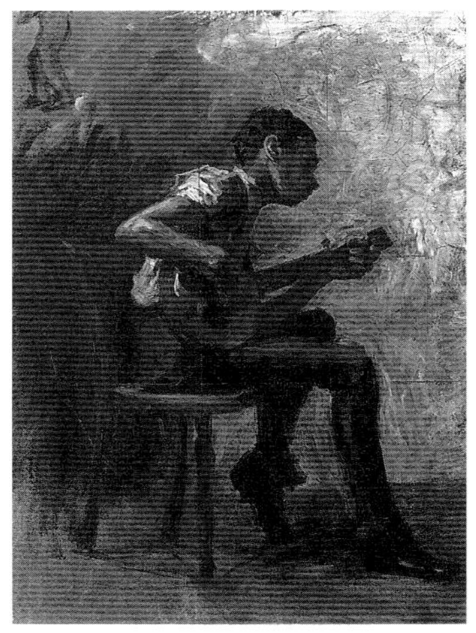

Study for "Negro Boy Dancing": The Banjo Player c. 1878
Canvas mounted on cardboard,
0.508 x 0.387 (20 x 15¼)
Collection of Mr. and Mrs. Paul Mellon
1985.64.16

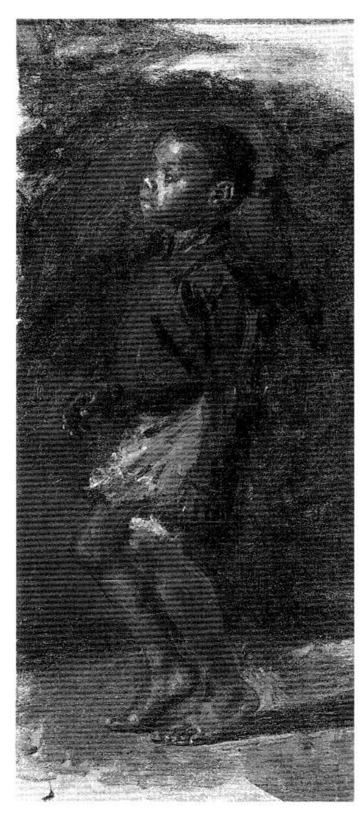

Study for "Negro Boy Dancing": The Boy, c. 1878
Canvas, 0.533 x 0.232 (21 x 9⅛)
Collection of Mr. and Mrs. Paul Mellon
1985.64.15

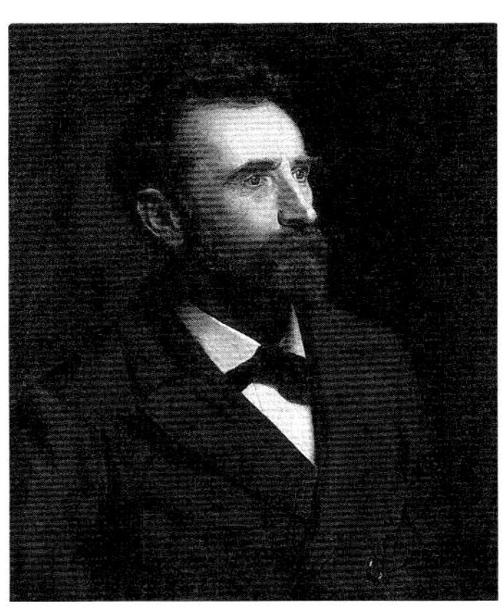

Louis Husson, 1899
Canvas, 0.610 x 0.509 (24 x 20)
Inscribed at upper right: *To his friend / Louis Husson / Thomas Eakins / 1899*;
on reverse: *TO KATY HUSSON / FROM HER FRIEND / THOMAS EAKINS*
Gift of Katharine Husson Horstick
1957.2.1

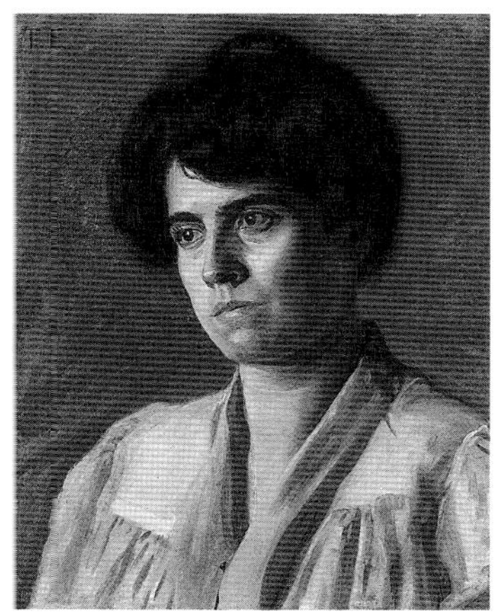

Harriet Husson Carville, 1904
Canvas, 0.512 x 0.405 (20⅛ x 16)
Inscribed at upper left: *T.E.*; at center on reverse: *TO HIS FRIEND / HARRIET CARVILLE / THOMAS EAKINS 1904*
Gift of Elizabeth O. Carville
1976.27.1

Archbishop Diomede Falconio, 1905
Canvas, 1.832 x 1.377 (72⅛ x 54¼)
Gift of Stephen C. Clark
1946.16.1

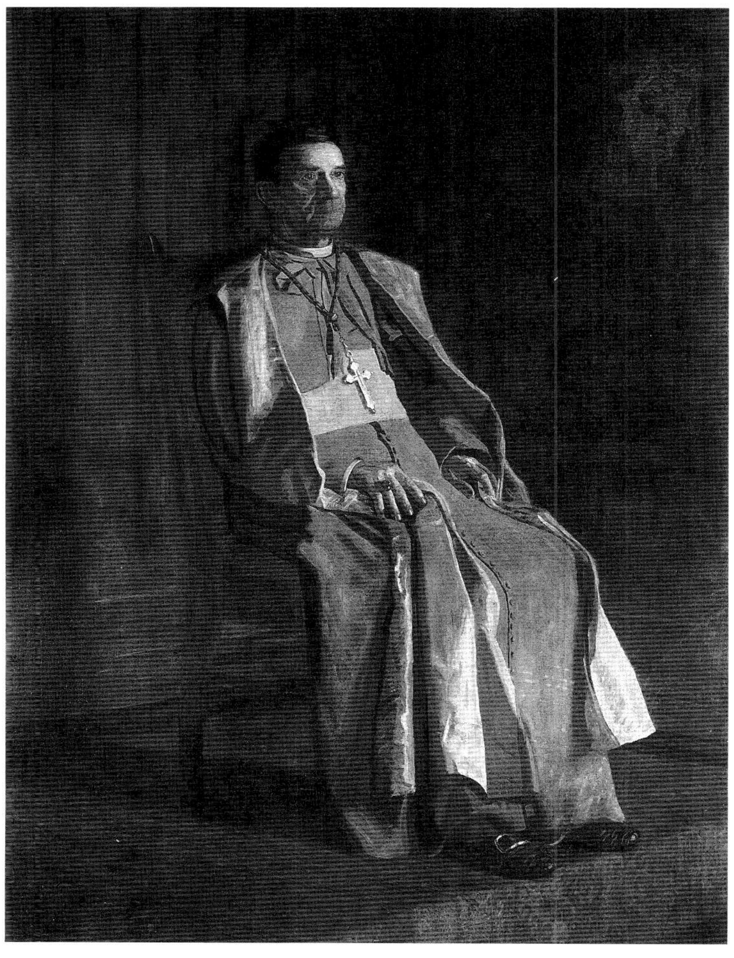

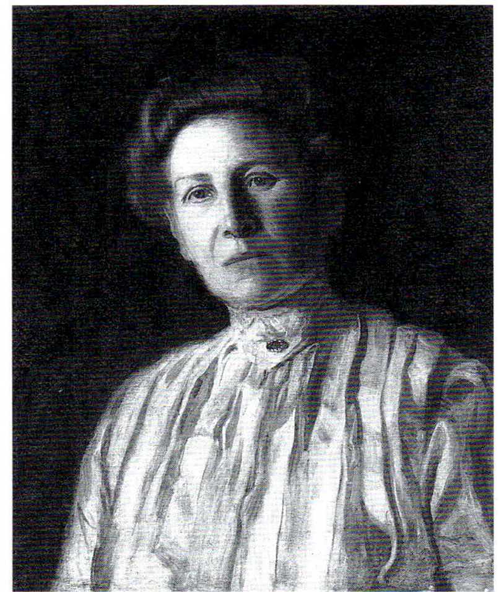

Mrs. Louis Husson, c. 1905
Canvas, 0.611 x 0.509 (24 x 20)
Inscribed at upper right: *T.E.*; at center on reverse: *TO KITTY HUSSON / FROM HER FRIEND / THOMAS EAKINS*
Gift of Katharine Husson Horstick
1957.2.2

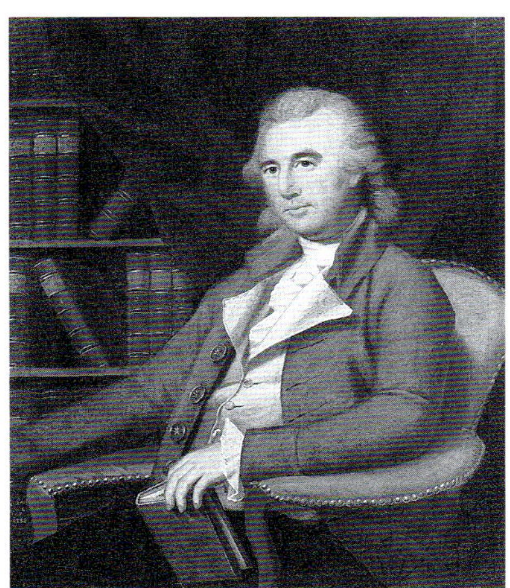

RALPH EARL
1751–1801

Dr. David Rogers, 1788
Canvas, 0.867 x 0.736 (34⅛ x 29)
Inscribed at lower left: *R. Earl / Pinxt 1788*
Gift of Edgar William and Bernice Chrysler Garbisch
1965.15.8

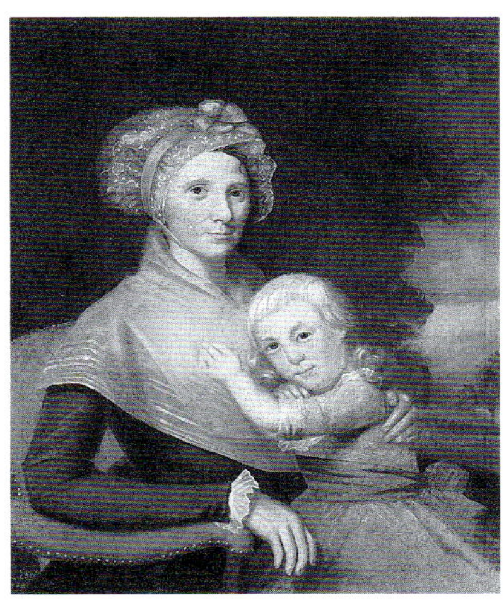

Martha Tennent Rogers and Daughter, 1788
Canvas, 0.867 x 0.735 (34⅛ x 29)
Inscribed at lower left: *R. Earl / 1788*
Gift of Edgar William and Bernice Chrysler Garbisch
1965.15.9

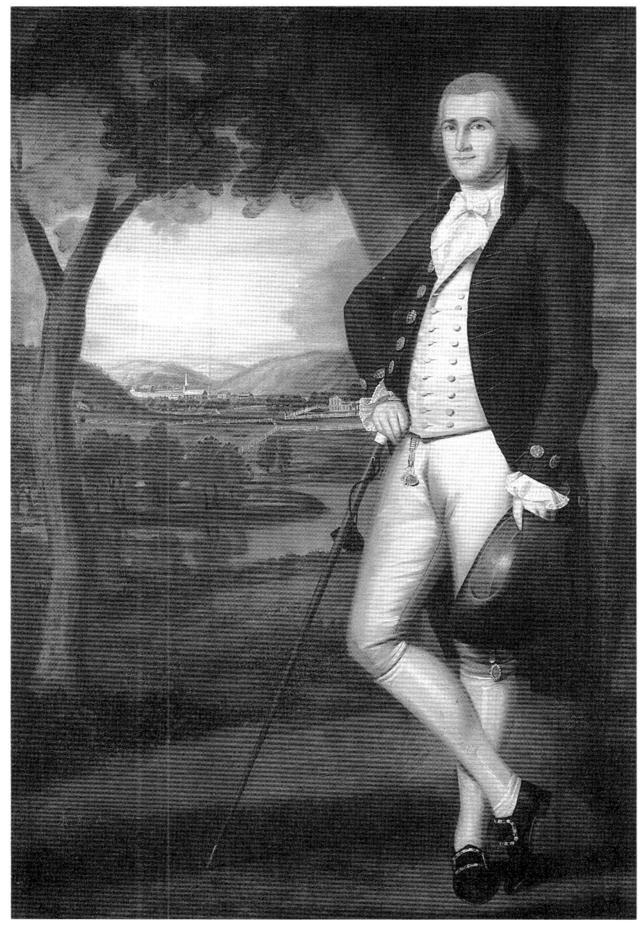

Daniel Boardman, 1789
Canvas, 2.075 x 1.405 (81⅝ x 55¼)
Inscribed at lower left: *R Earl Pinxt 1789*
Gift of Mrs. W. Murray Crane
1948.8.1

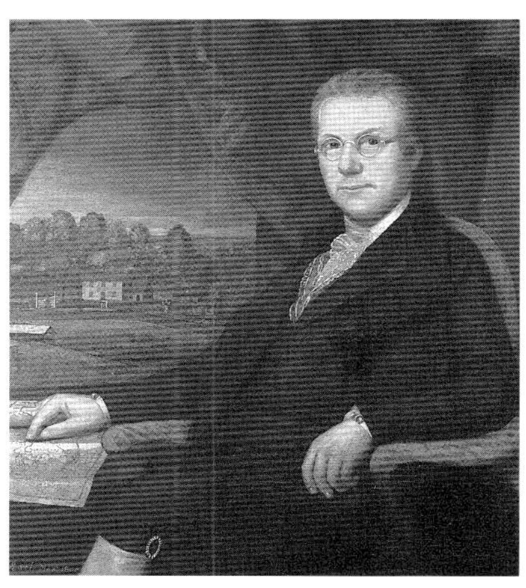

Thomas Earle, c. 1800
Canvas, 0.955 x 0.861 (37⅝ x 33⅞)
Inscribed probably by a later hand, lower left: *R. Earle Pinxt 1800*
Andrew W. Mellon Collection
1947.17.42

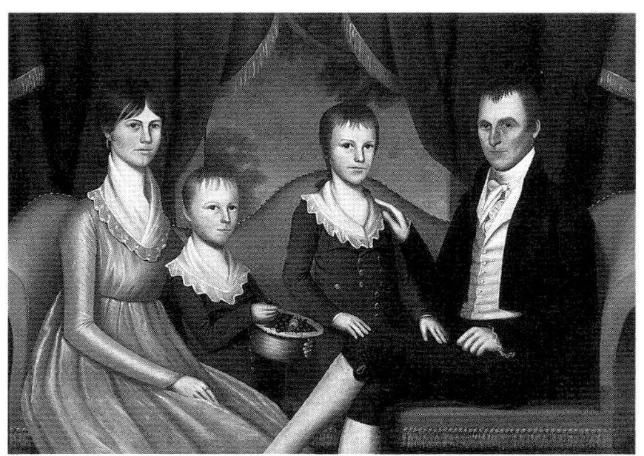

RALPH ELEASER WHITESIDE EARL
1788–1838

Family Portrait, 1804
Canvas, 1.185 x 1.613 (46⅝ x 63½)
Inscribed at lower right: *R. Earl Pinxit 1804*
Gift of Edgar William and Bernice Chrysler Garbisch
1953.5.8

FRANCIS WILLIAM EDMONDS
1806–1863

The Bashful Cousin, c. 1842
Canvas, 0.635 x 0.761 (25 x 30)
Gift of Frederick Sturges, Jr.
1978.6.4

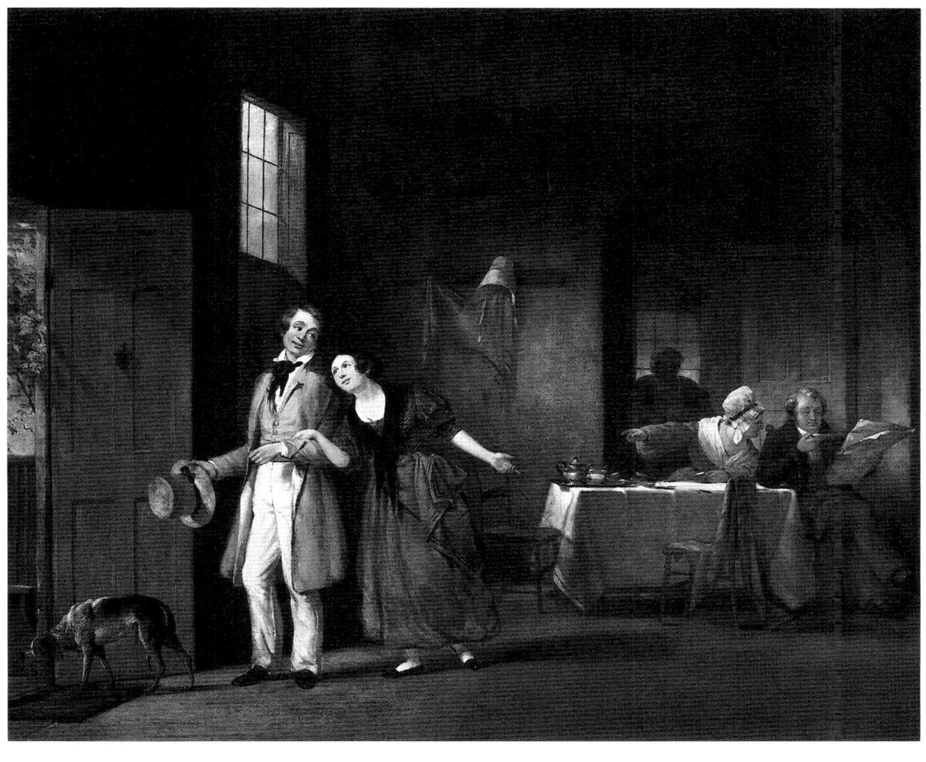

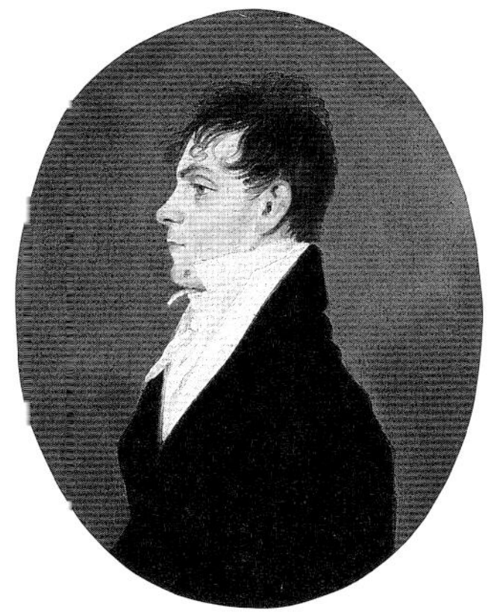

JACOB EICHHOLTZ
1776–1842

Mr. Kline, c. 1808
Wood, 0.227 x 0.176 (8 15/16 x 6 15/16)
Gift of Edgar William and Bernice Chrysler Garbisch
1953.5.11

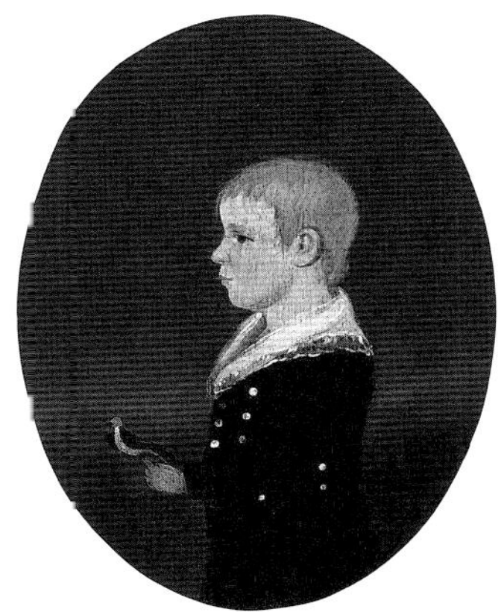

Joseph Leman, c. 1808
Wood, 0.229 x 0.172 (9 x 6 3/4)
Gift of Edgar William and Bernice Chrysler Garbisch
1953.5.13

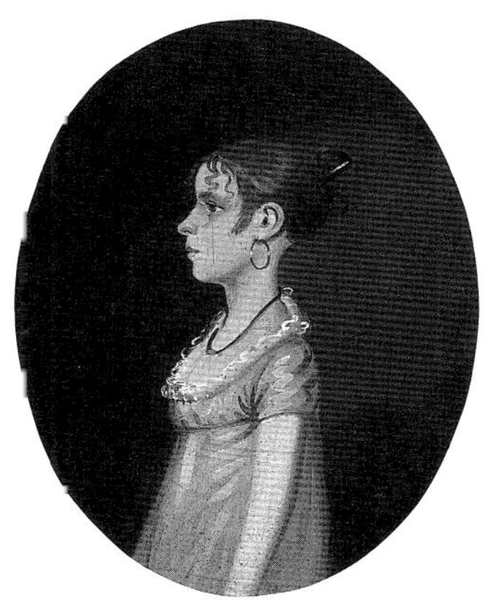

Miss Leman, c. 1808
Wood, 0.210 x 0.170 (8 1/4 x 6 11/16)
Inscribed at lower left under oval mat: *Sept 23 18[. . .]*; lower right: *J E Scrip*
Gift of Edgar William and Bernice Chrysler Garbisch
1953.5.14

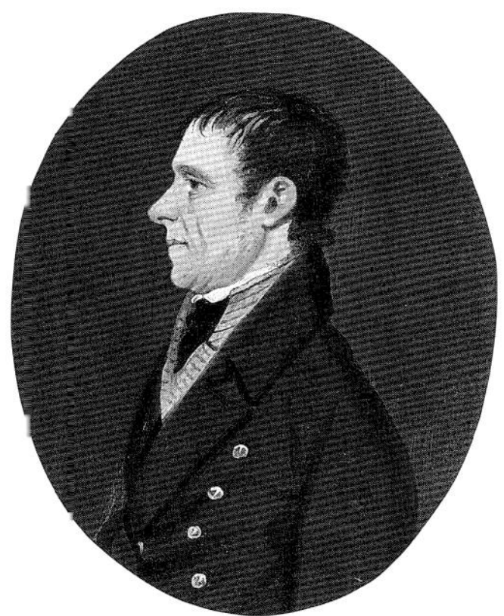

Mr. Leman, c. 1808
Wood, 0.229 x 0.175 (9 x 6 7/8)
Gift of Edgar William and Bernice Chrysler Garbisch
1953.5.12

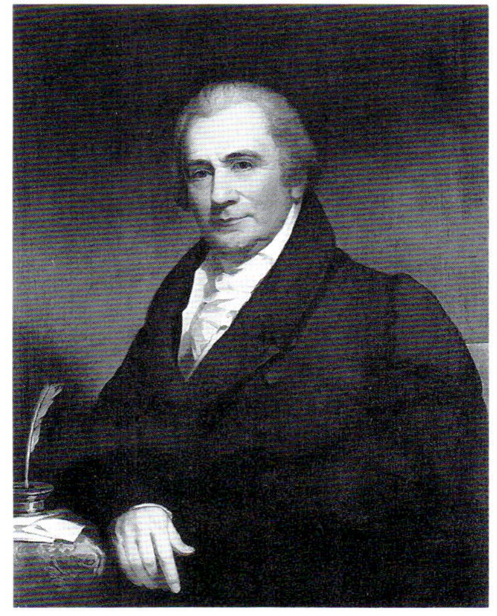

Robert Coleman, c. 1820
Canvas, 0.917 x 0.712 (36⅛ x 28)
Gift of William C. Freeman
1947.9.2

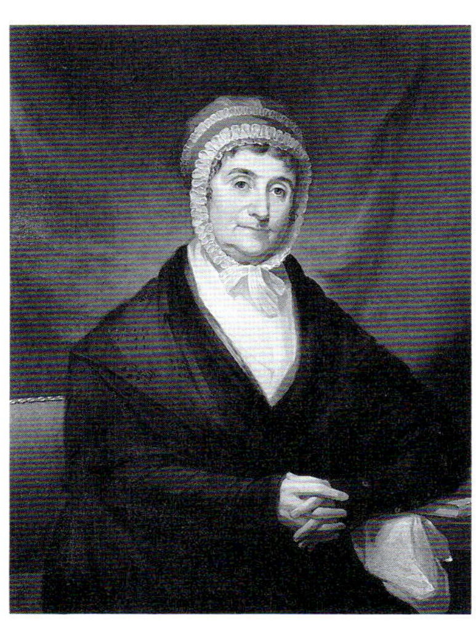

Mrs. Robert Coleman, c. 1820
Canvas, 0.923 x 0.720 (36¼ x 28⅜)
Gift of William C. Freeman
1947.9.1

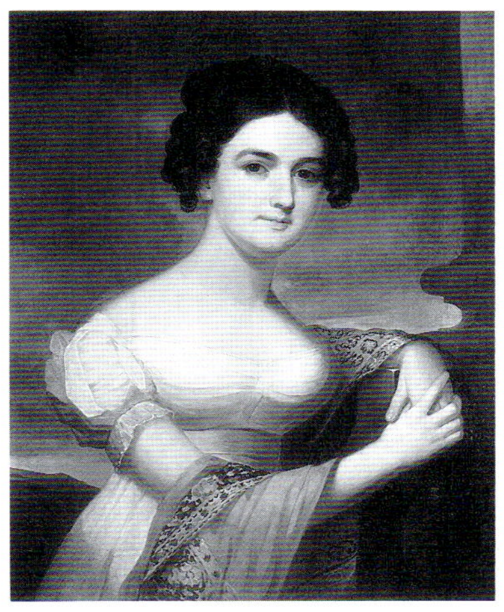

Julianna Hazlehurst, c. 1820
Canvas, 0.753 x 0.632 (29⅝ x 24⅞)
Falsely inscribed, lower right in monogram: *TS*
Andrew W. Mellon Collection
1947.17.110

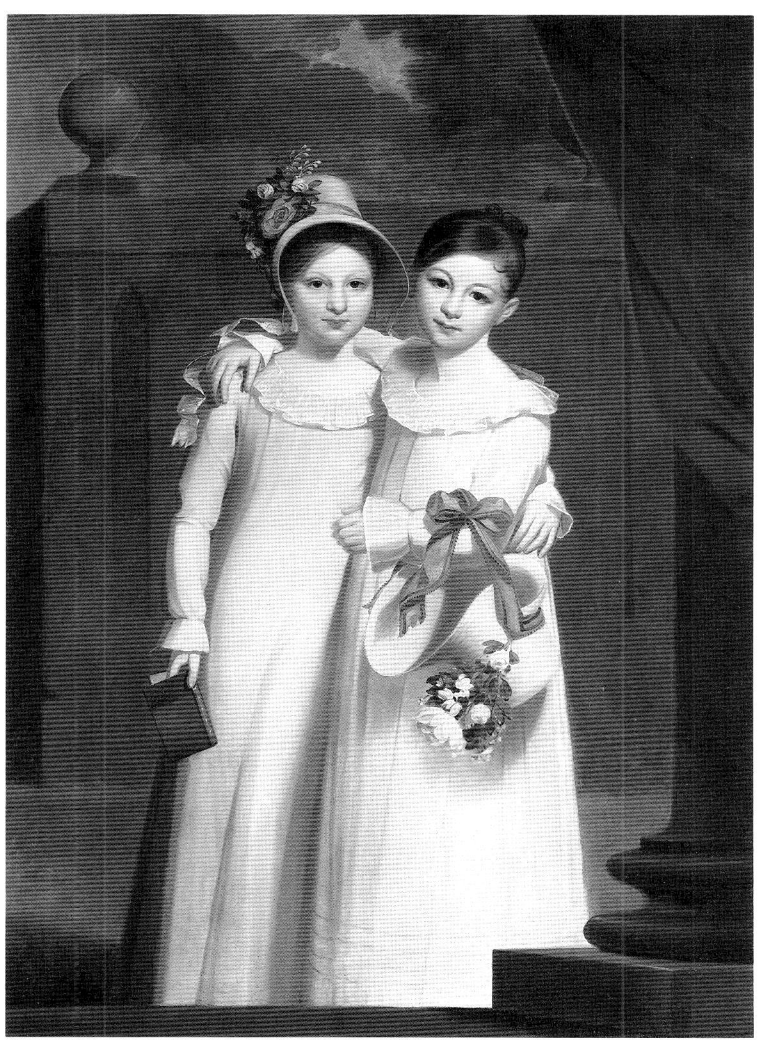

The Ragan Sisters, c. 1820
Canvas, 1.500 x 1.095 (59 x 43)
Gift of Mrs. Cooper R. Drewry
1959.6.1

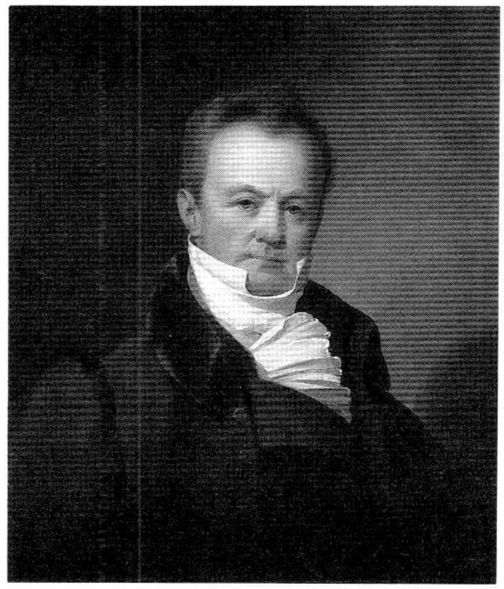

William Clark Frazer, c. 1830
Canvas, 0.762 x 0.635 (30 x 25)
Andrew W. Mellon Collection
1947.17.3

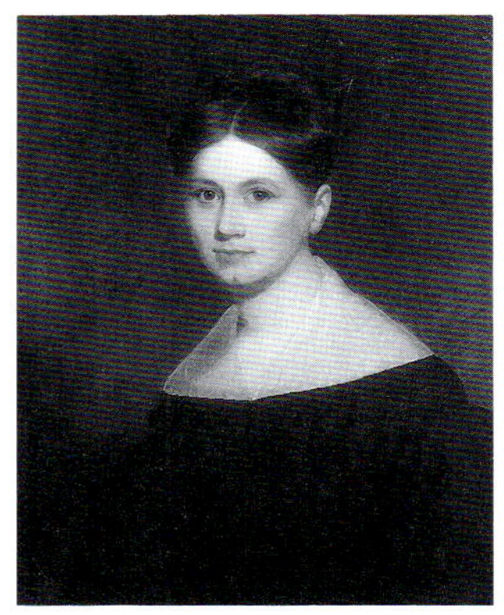

Phoebe Cassidy Freeman, c. 1830
Canvas, 0.699 x 0.565 (27½ x 22¼)
Andrew W. Mellon Collection
1947.17.45

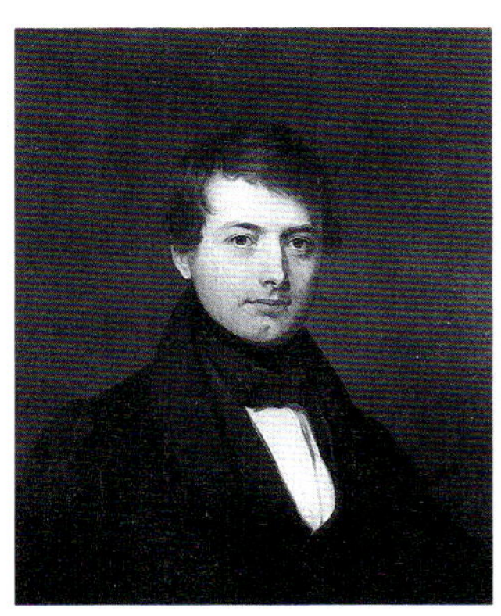

Henry Eichholtz Leman, c. 1835
Canvas, 0.762 x 0.638 (30 x 25⅛)
Andrew W. Mellon Collection
1954.1.5

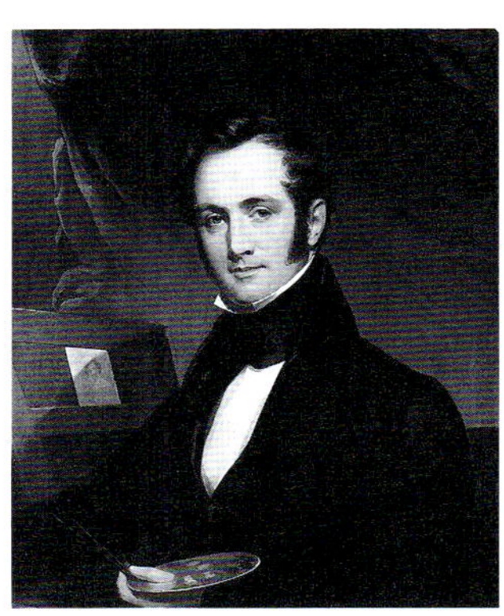

James P. Smith, c. 1835
Canvas, 0.759 x 0.638 (29⅞ x 25⅛)
Andrew W. Mellon Collection
1947.17.4

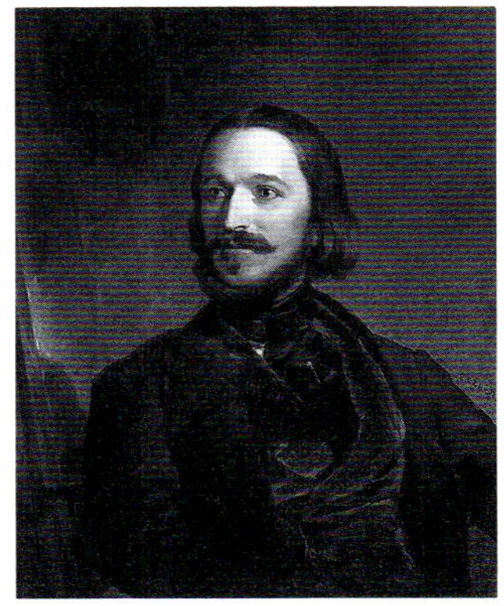

CHARLES LORING ELLIOTT
1812–1868

William Sidney Mount, c. 1850
Canvas, 0.772 x 0.635 (30⅜ x 25)
Inscribed at center right: *C.L. Elliott.*
Andrew W. Mellon Collection
1947.17.6

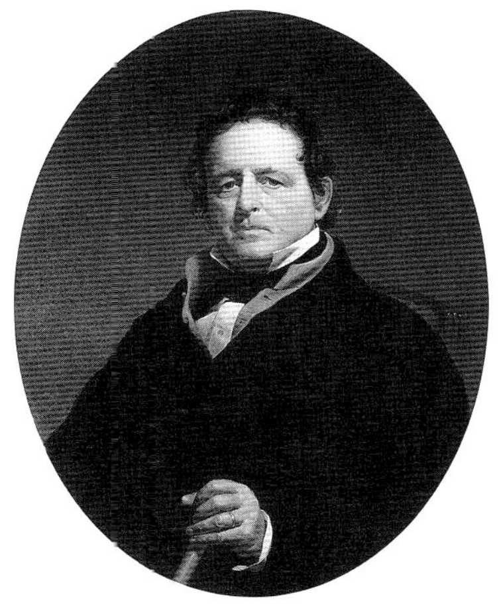

Captain Warren Delano, 1852
Canvas, 0.911 x 0.721 (35⅞ x 28⅜)
Inscribed at center left: *C L.E.*
Gift of Frederic A. Delano
1942.10.1

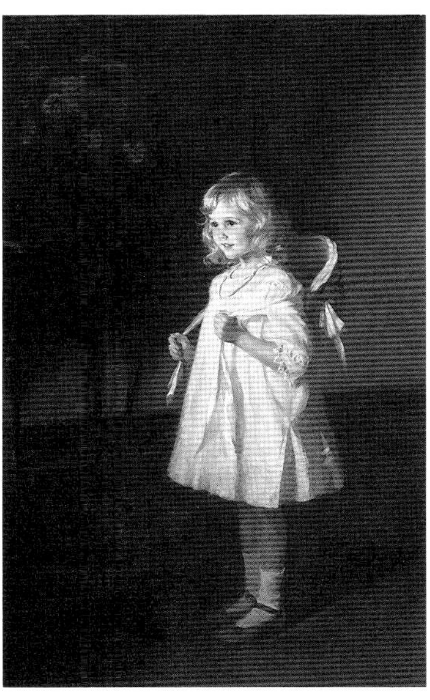

LYDIA FIELD EMMET
1866–1952

Olivia, 1911
Canvas, 1.626 x 1.029 (64 x 40½)
Inscribed at upper right: *Lydia Field Emmet*
Gift of Olivia Stokes Hatch
1983.96.1

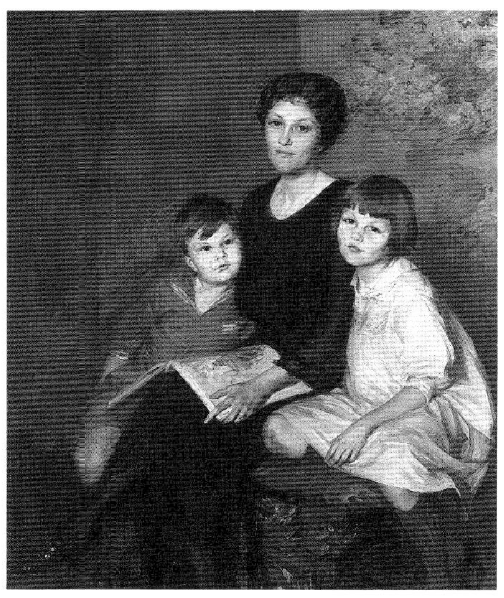

Harriet Lancashire White and Her Children, 1922
Canvas, 1.373 x 1.173 (54 x 46⅛)
Inscribed at upper left: *Lydia Field Emmet*
Gift of Mrs. E. Laurence White
1961.15.1

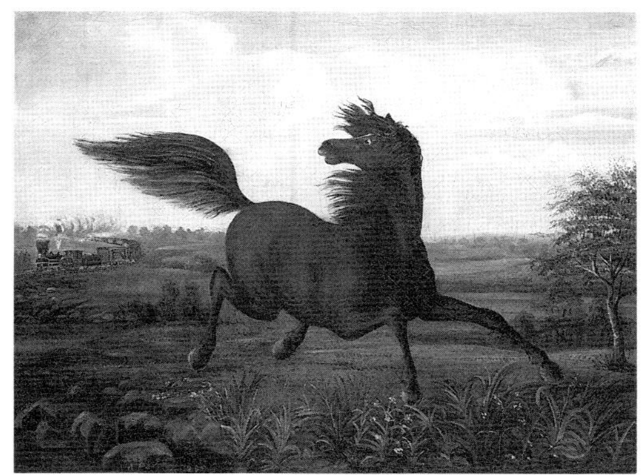

JOSEPH ANDERSON FARIS
1833–1909

The Neigh of an Iron Horse, 1860s
Canvas, 0.350 x 0.454 (13¾ x 17⅞)
Inscribed at lower left: *A Fari[s] 186[. . .]*
Gift of Edgar William and Bernice Chrysler Garbisch
1980.62.69

LYONEL FEININGER
1871–1956

The Bicycle Race, 1912
Canvas, 0.803 x 1.003 (31⅝ x 39½)
Inscribed at lower left: *Feininger / 1912*
Collection of Mr. and Mrs. Paul Mellon
1985.64.17

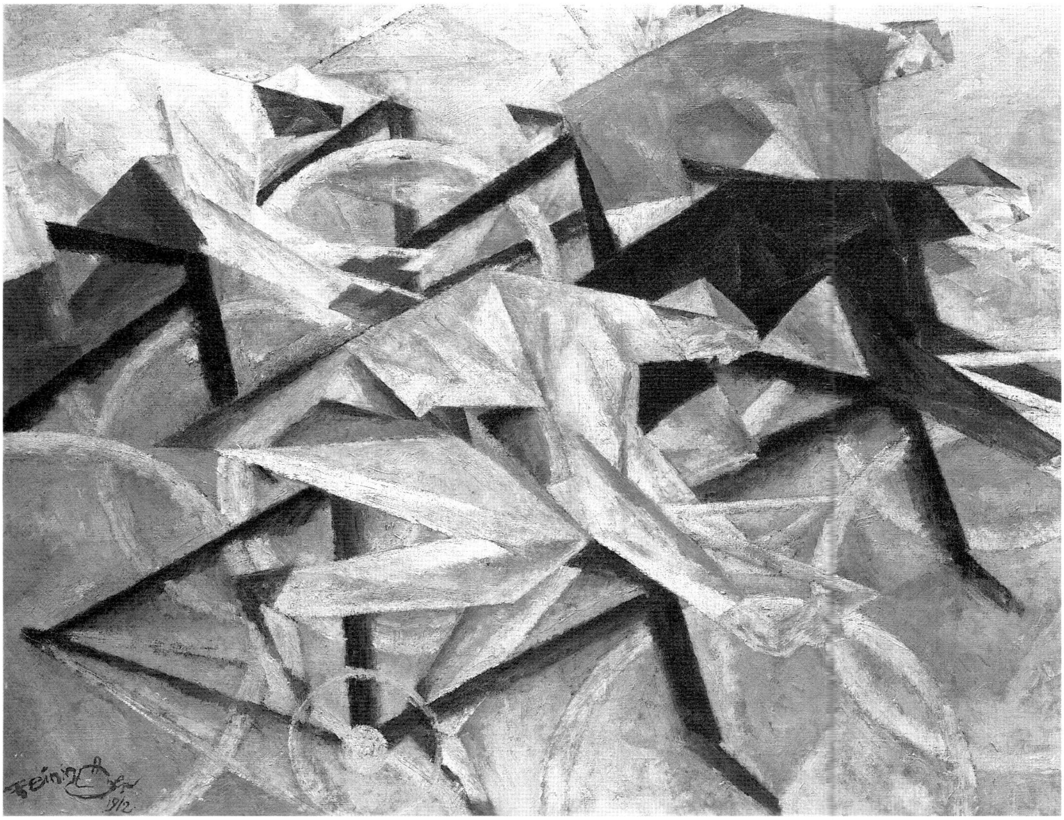

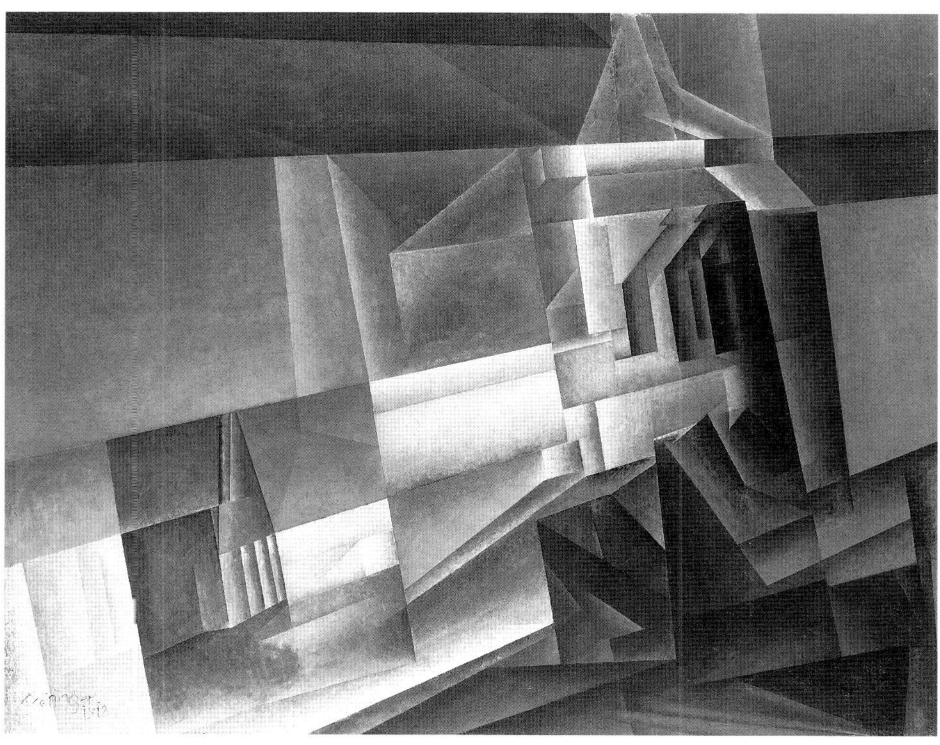

Zirchow VII, 1918
Canvas, 0.807 x 1.006 (31¾ x 39⅝)
Inscribed at lower left: *Feininger / 1918*
Gift of Julia Feininger
1966.3.1

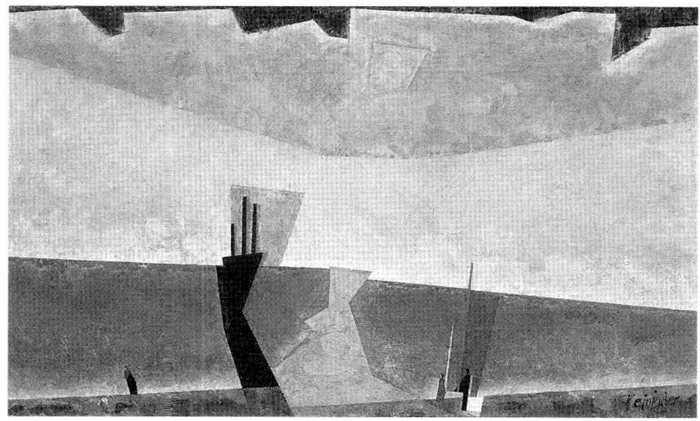

Storm Brewing, 1939
Canvas, 0.485 x 0.775 (19⅛ x 30⅝)
Inscribed at lower right: *Feininger*
Gift of Julia Feininger
1967.12.1

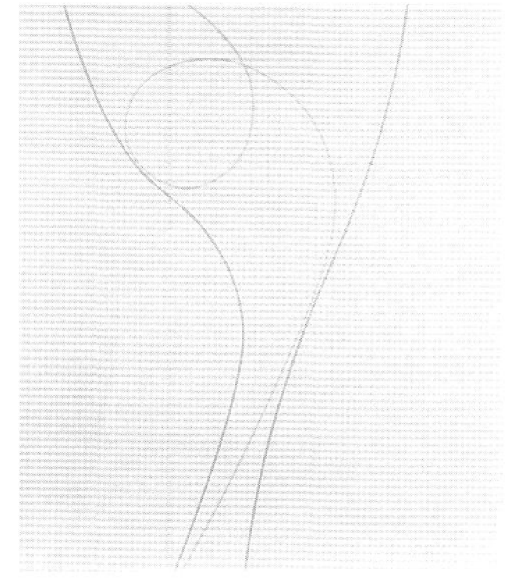

LORSER FEITELSON
1898–1978

Untitled, 1964
Canvas, 1.524 x 1.271 (60 x 50)
Gift of the artist in memory of
William C. Seitz
1975.78.1

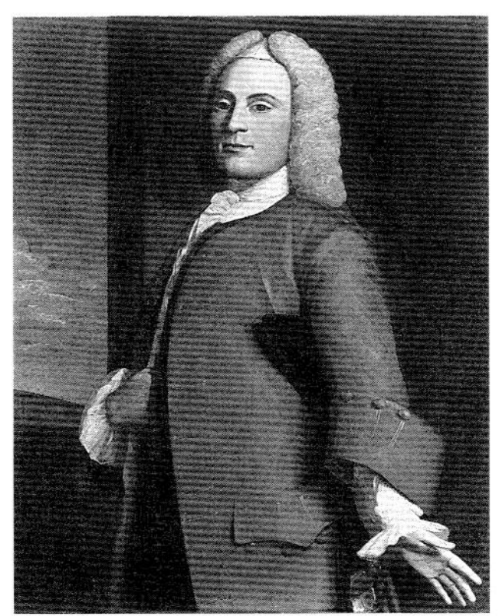

ROBERT FEKE
c. 1707–175[illegible]

Captain Alexander Graydon, c. 1746
Canvas, 1.012 x 0.811 (39⅞ x 31⅞)
Gift of Edgar William and Bernice
Chrysler Garbisch
1966.13.2

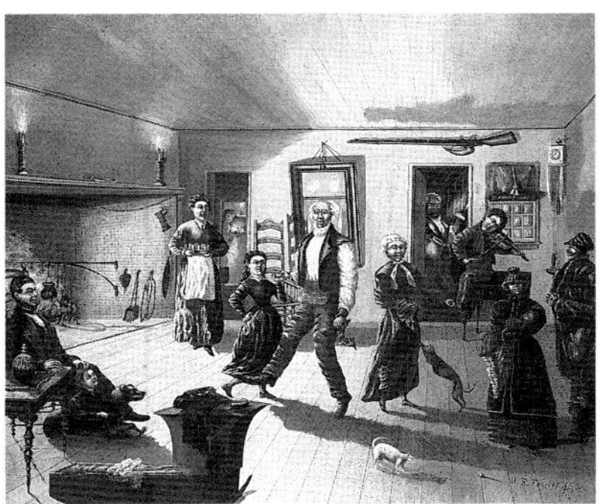

MARTIN EDGAR FERRILL
c. 1837–189[illegible]

Country Dance, 1883
Canvas, 0.622 x 0.720 (24½ x 28¼)
Inscribed at lower right: *M. E. Ferrill / 83.*
Gift of Edgar William and Bernice
Chrysler Garbisch
1971.83.2

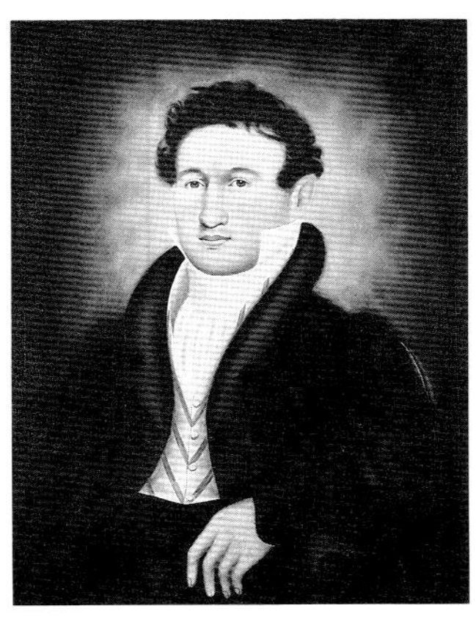

ERASTUS SALISBURY FIELD
1805–1900

Biel Le Doyt, 1827
Canvas, 0.763 x 0.584 (30 x 23)
Gift of Edgar William and Bernice
Chrysler Garbisch
1971.83.3

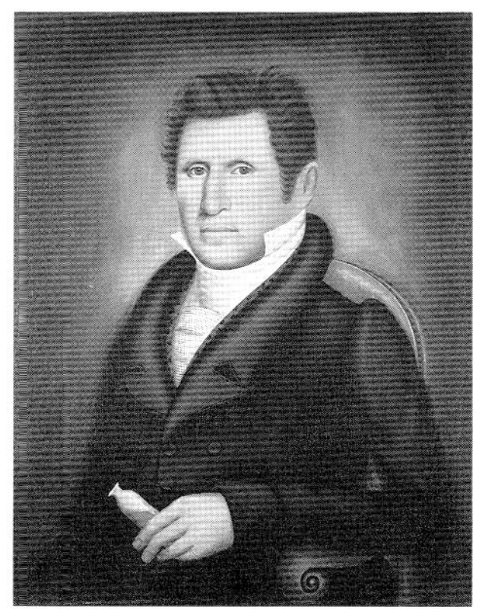

Man with Vial, c. 1827
Canvas, 0.750 x 0.595 (29½ x 23½)
Gift of Edgar William and Bernice Chrysler Garbisch
1955.11.19

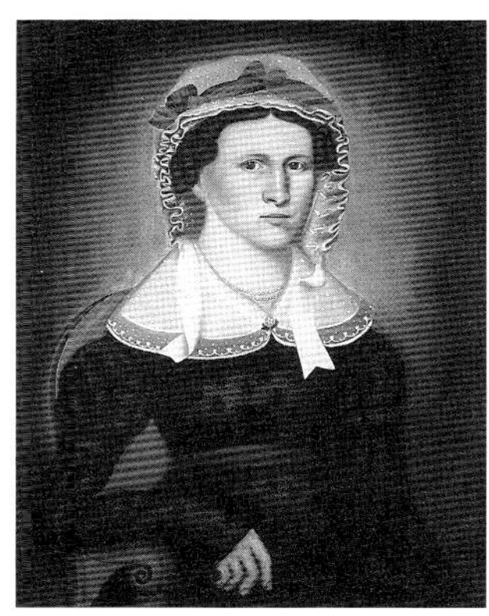

Wife of Man with Vial, c 1827
Canvas, 0.750 x 0.600 (29⅝ x 23⅝)
Gift of Edgar William and Bernice Chrysler Garbisch
1955.11.20

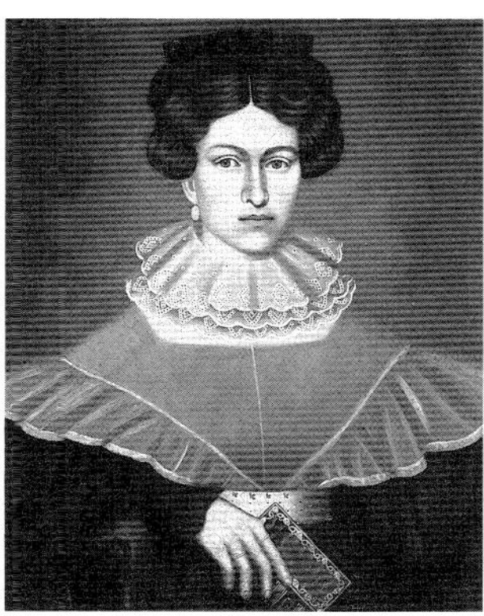

Woman Holding a Book, c. 1835
Canvas, 0.756 x 0.603 (29¾ x 23¾)
Gift of Edgar William and Bernice Chrysler Garbisch
1980.62.7

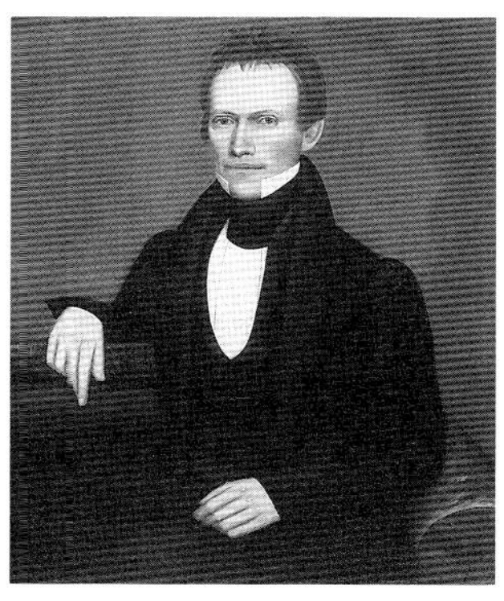

Paul Smith Palmer, 1835/1838
Canvas, 0.864 x 0.734 (34 x 28⅞)
Gift of Edgar William and Bernice Chrysler Garbisch
1971.83.4

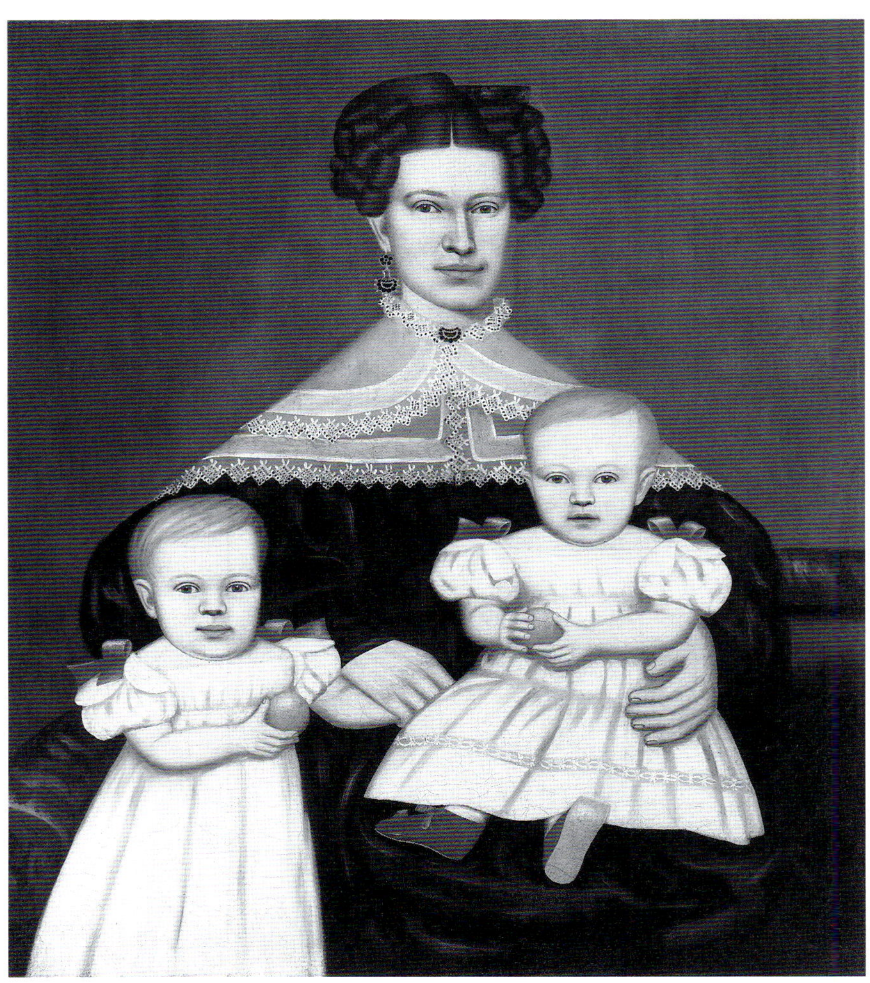

Mrs. Paul Smith Palmer and Her Twins,
1835/1838
Canvas, 0.978 x 0.863 (38½ x 34)
Gift of Edgar William and Bernice
Chrysler Garbisch
1971.83.5

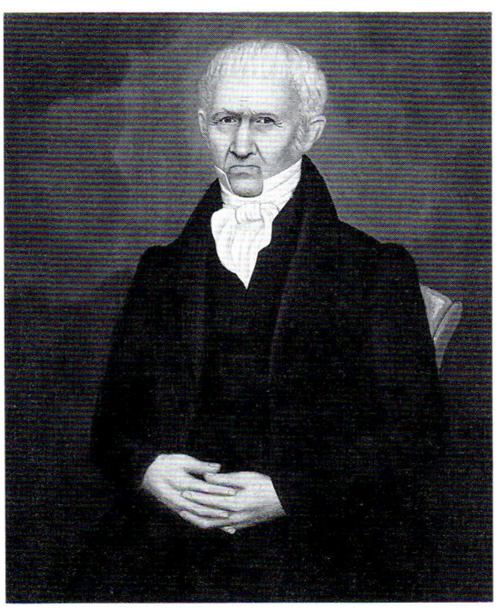

Mr. Pease, c. 1837
Canvas, 0.899 x 0.740 (35⅜ x 29⅛)
Gift of Edgar William and Bernice
Chrysler Garbisch
1965.15.1

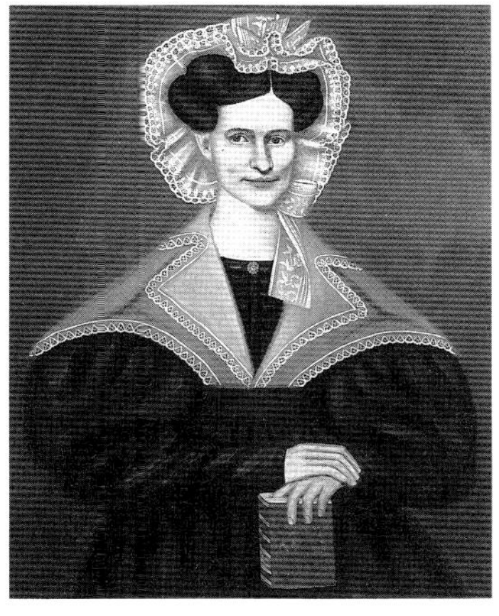

Mrs. Harlow A. Pease, c. 1837
Canvas, 0.896 x 0.740 (35 3/8 x 29 1/8)
Gift of Edgar William and Bernice Chrysler Garbisch
1965.15.2

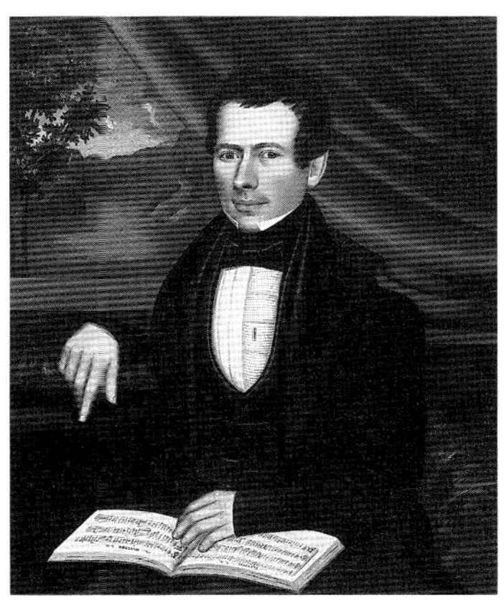

Man with a Tune Book: Mr. Cook (?), c. 1838
Canvas, 0.891 x 0.740 (35 x 29 1/8)
Gift of Edgar William and Bernice Chrysler Garbisch
1978.80.6

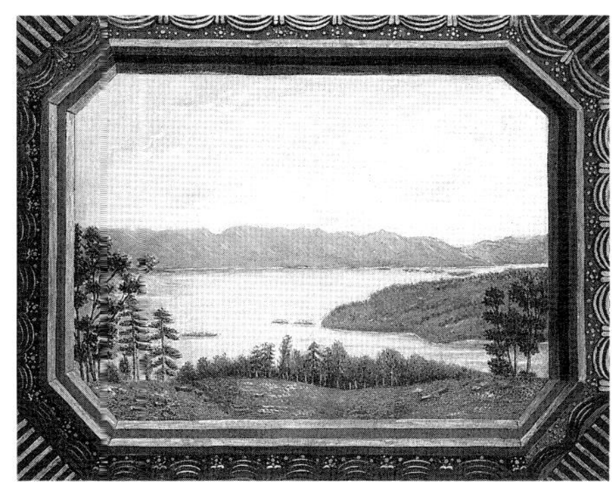

Leverett Pond, c. 1860/1880
Canvas, 0.558 x 0.691 (22 x 27 1/4)
Gift of Edgar William and Bernice Chrysler Garbisch
1978.80.5

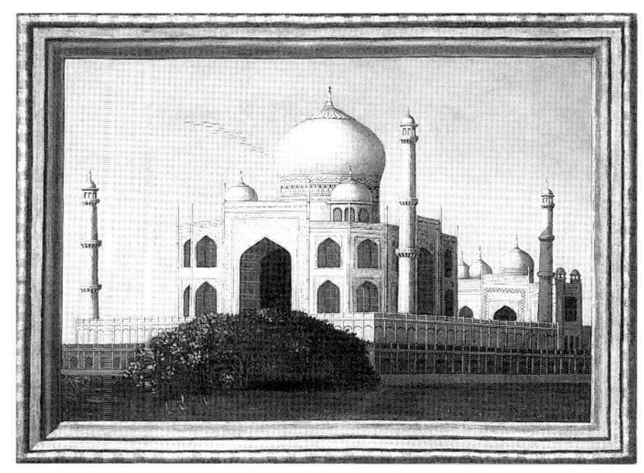

The Taj Mahal, c. 1860/1880
Canvas, 0.887 x 1.167 (34 15/16 x 46)
Gift of Edgar William and Bernice Chrysler Garbisch
1978.80.3

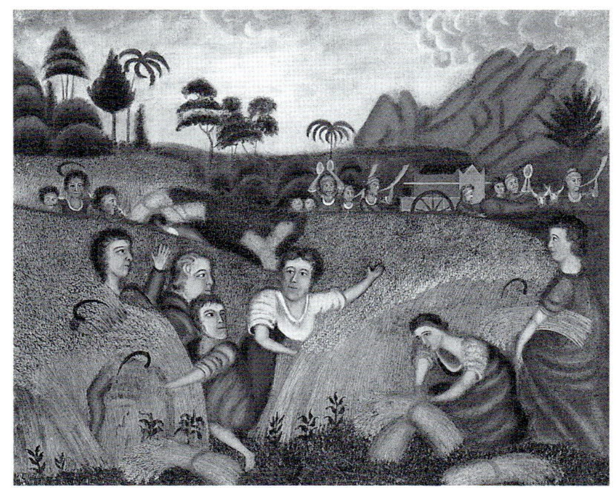

Ark of the Covenant, c. 1865/1880
Canvas, 0.508 x 0.613 (20 x 24⅛)
Gift of Edgar William and Bernice Chrysler Garbisch
1956.13.3

"He Turned Their Waters into Blood," c. 1865/1880
Canvas, 0.768 x 1.030 (30¼ x 40½)
Gift of Edgar William and Bernice Chrysler Garbisch
1964.23.3

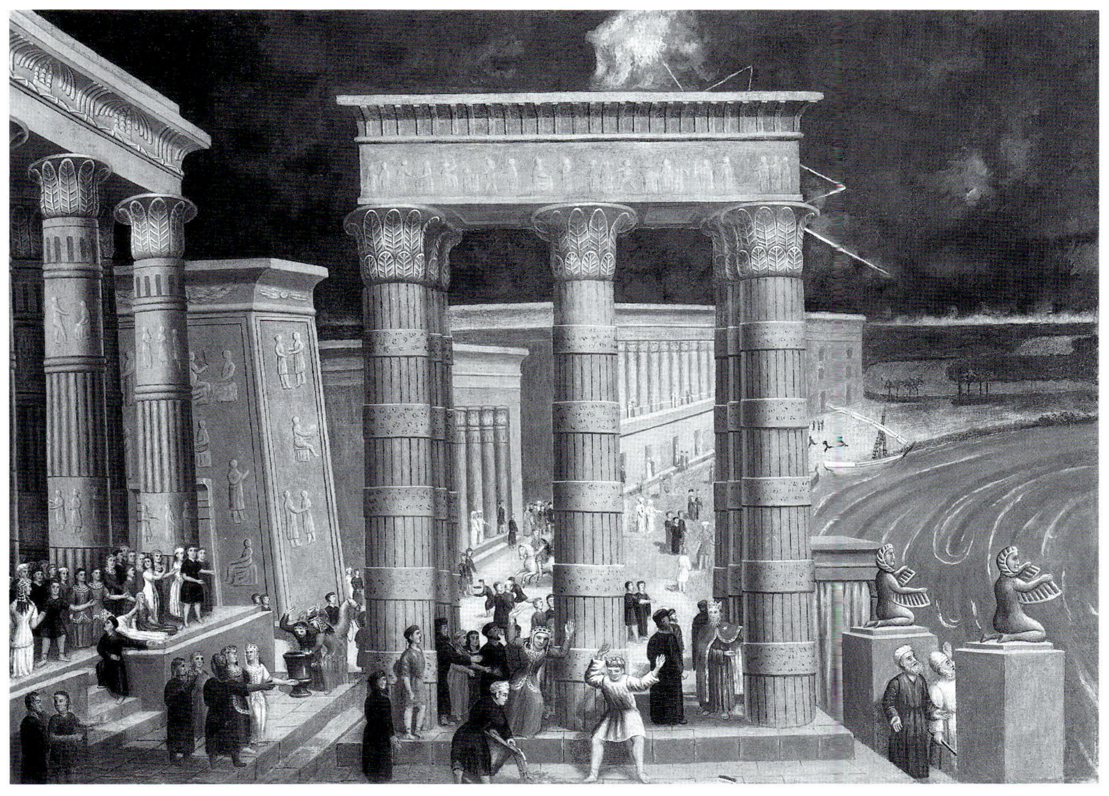

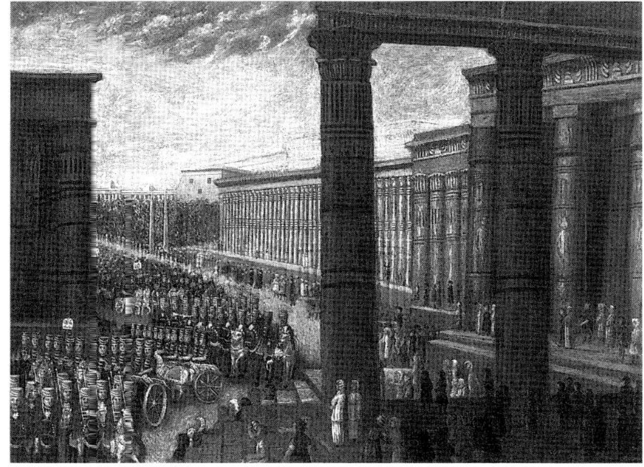

Pharaoh's Army Marching, c. 1865/1880
Canvas, 0.890 x 1.168 (35 x 46)
Gift of Edgar William and Bernice Chrysler Garbisch
1978.80.4

SAM FRANCIS
born 1923

White Line, 1958/1959
Canvas, 2.756 x 1.924 (108½ x 75¾)
Gift of the Collectors Committee
1985.56.1

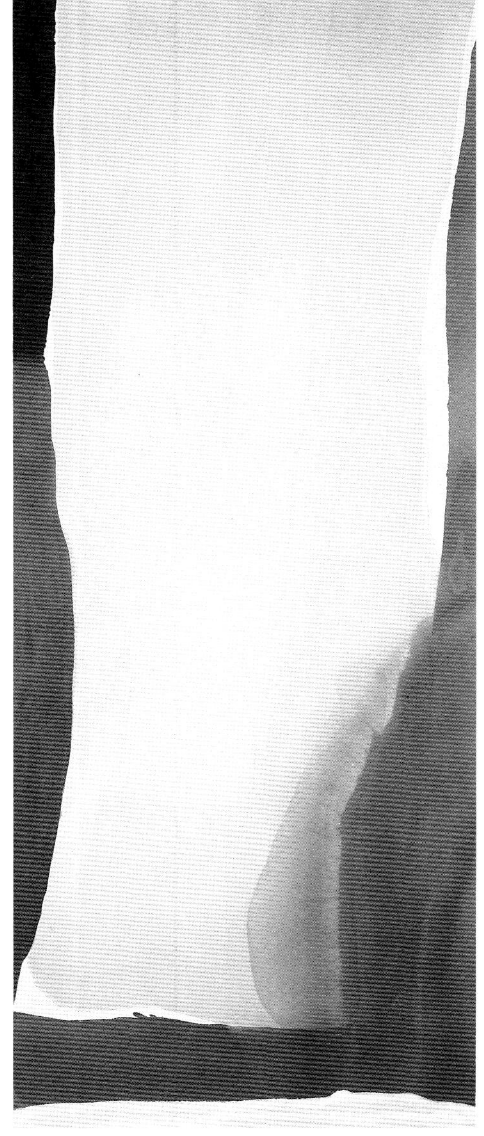

HELEN FRANKENTHALER
born 1928

Wales, 1966
Canvas, 2.87[illegible] x 1.144 (113¼ x 45)
Anonymous Gift
1981.86.1

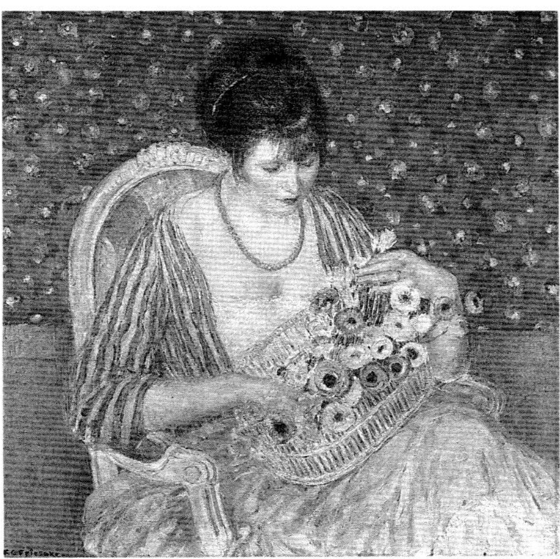

FREDERICK CARL FRIESEKE
1874–1939

The Basket of Flowers, c. 1913/1917
Canvas, 0.81[illegible] x 0.815 (32 x 32⅛)
Inscribed at lower left: *F.C. Frieseke.*
Chester Dale Collection
1963.10.147

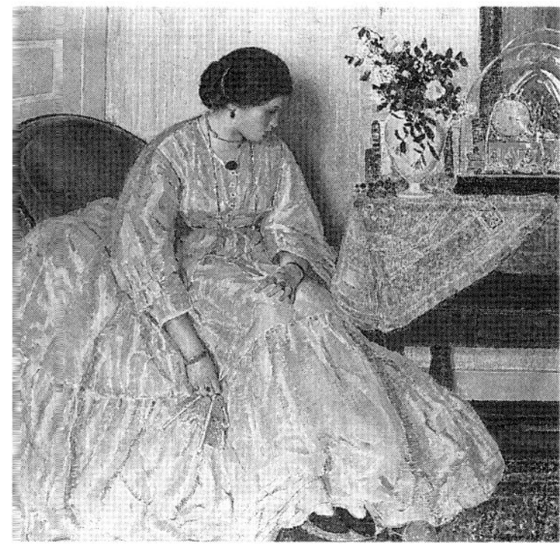

Memories, 1915
Canvas, 1.315 x 1.303 (51¾ x 51¼)
Inscribed at lower right: *F.C. Frieseke. 1915*
Gift of Frances Frieseke Kilmer
1969.5.1

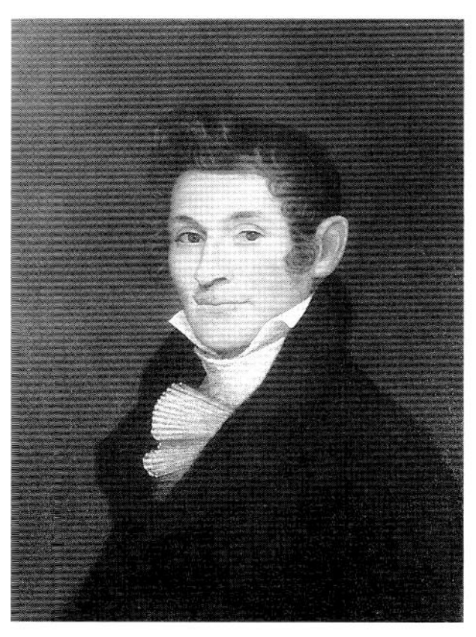

JAMES FROTHINGHAM
1786–1864

Ebenezer Newhall, c. 1810
Canvas, 0.660 x 0.508 (26 x 20)
Andrew W. Mellon Collection
1947.17.50

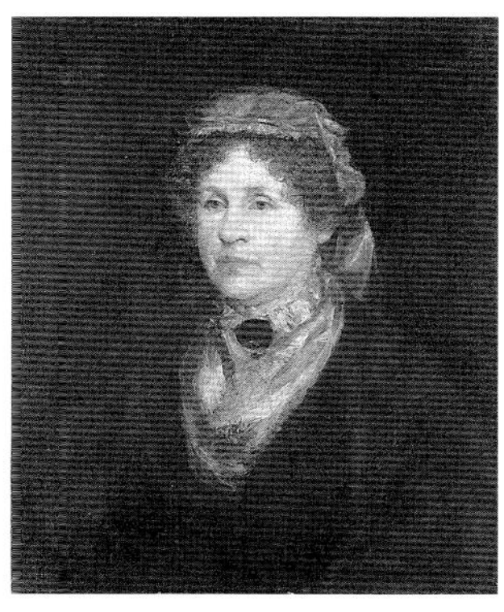

GEORGE FULLER
1822–1884

Mrs. Stephen Higginson, 1876
Canvas, 0.688 x 0.560 (27⅛ x 22)
Gift of Mrs. Augustus Vincent Tack
1953.9.2

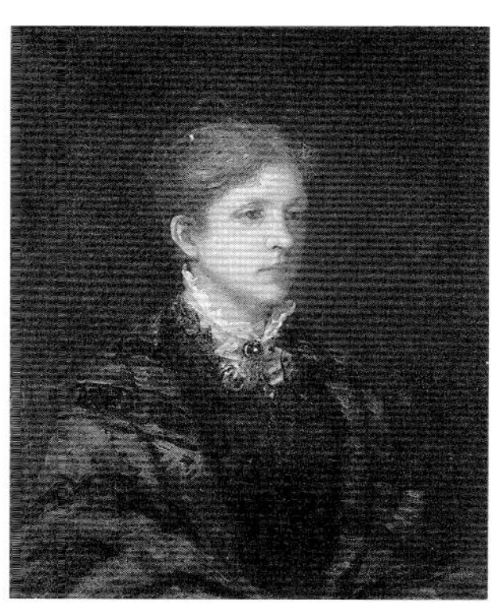

Agnes Gordon Higginson, Wife of George Fuller, c. 1877
Canvas, 0.692 x 0.559 (27¼ x 22)
Given in memory of the sitter's granddaughter, Agnes Gordon Hilton
1948.1.1

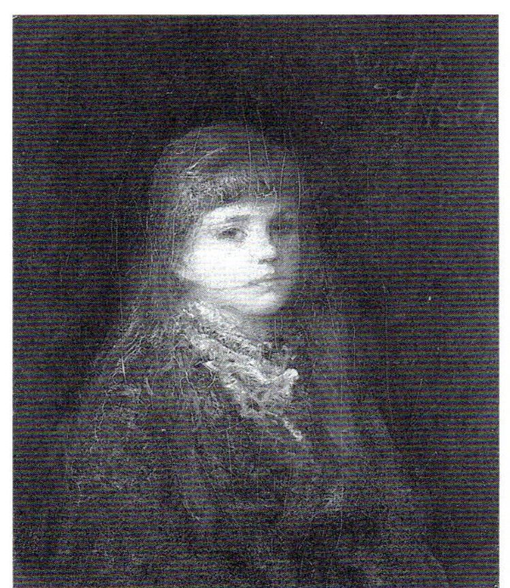

Violet, 1882
Canvas, 0.685 x 0.560 (27 x 22)
Inscribed at upper right: *Violet / Sept. / 1882*
Gift of Mrs. Augustus Vincent Tack
1953.9.1

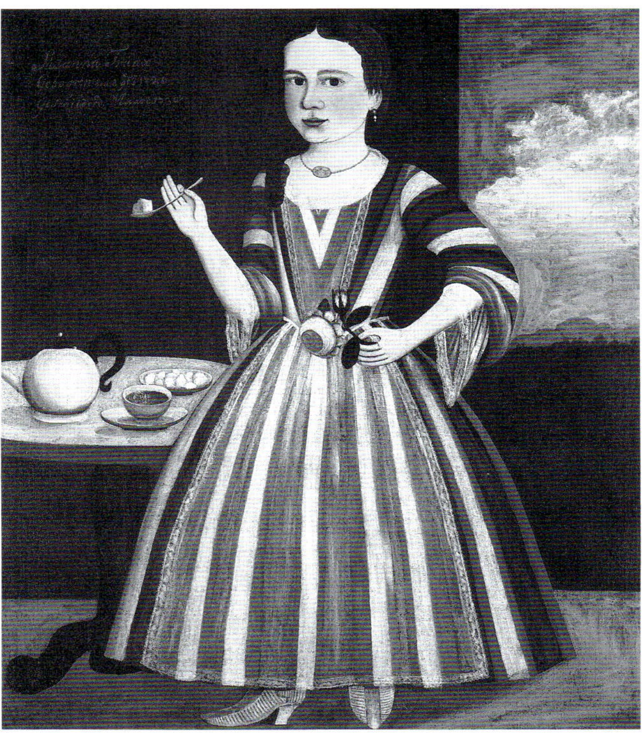

THE GANSEVOORT LIMNER
(possibly **PIETER VANDERLYN**)
active 1730/1745

Susanna Truax, 1730
Bed ticking, 0.958 x 0.836 (37¾ x 32⅞)
Inscribed at upper left: *Susanna Truax / Gebooren den 8* [followed by Latin abbreviation for November]: *1726, / Geschilderd, Maart 1730*
Gift of Edgar William and Bernice Chrysler Garbisch
1980.62.31

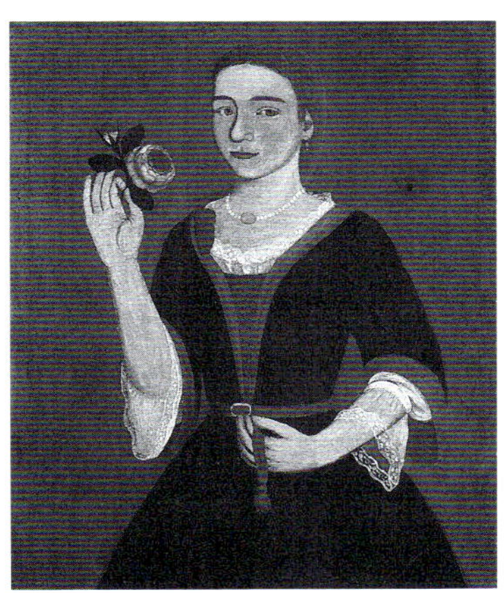

Miss Van Alen, c. 1735
Canvas, 0.791 x 0.664 (31⅛ x 26⅛)
Gift of Edgar William and Bernice Chrysler Garbisch
1956.13.14

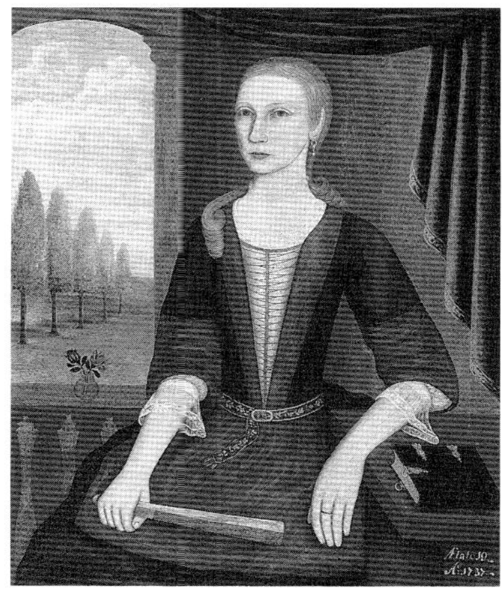

Young Lady with a Fan, 1737
Canvas, 0.965 x 0.809 (38 x $31^{3}/_{4}$)
Inscribed at lower right: *AEtate 19- / Ao 1737-*
Gift of Edgar William and Bernice Chrysler Garbisch
1980.61.5

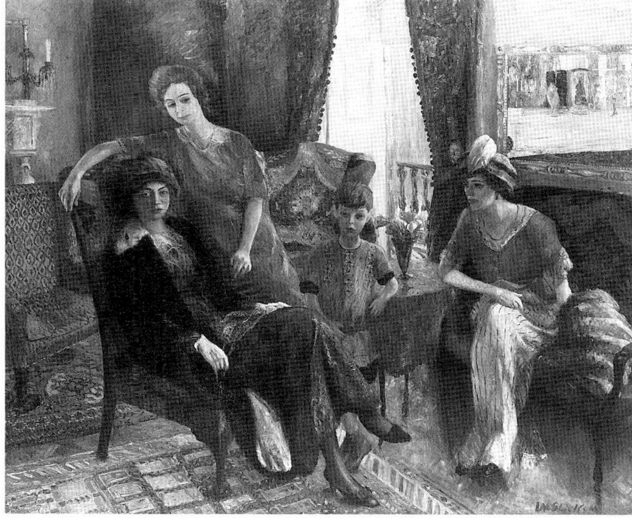

WILLIAM GLACKENS
1870–1938

Family Group, 1910/1911
Canvas, 1.828 x 2.133 (72 x 84)
Inscribed at lower right: *W. Glackens*
Gift of Mr. and Mrs. Ira Glackens
1971.12.1

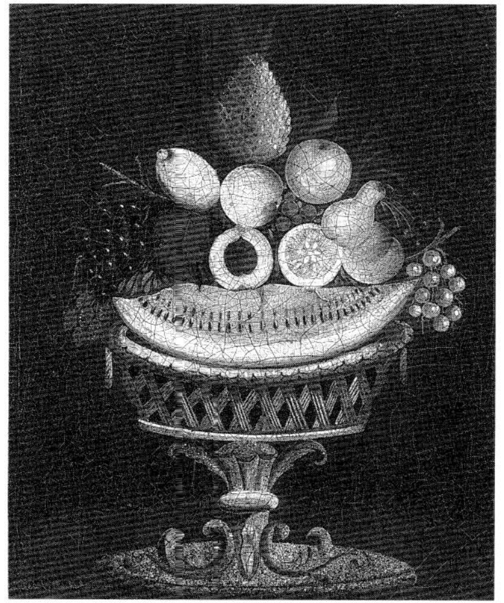

M. A. GOODE
active second half 19th century

Still Life, second half 19th century
Canvas, 0.660 x 0.555 (26 x $21^{7}/_{8}$)
Inscribed at lower left: *Painted by Mrs. M. A. Goode*
Gift of Edgar William and Bernice Chrysler Garbisch
1978.80.7

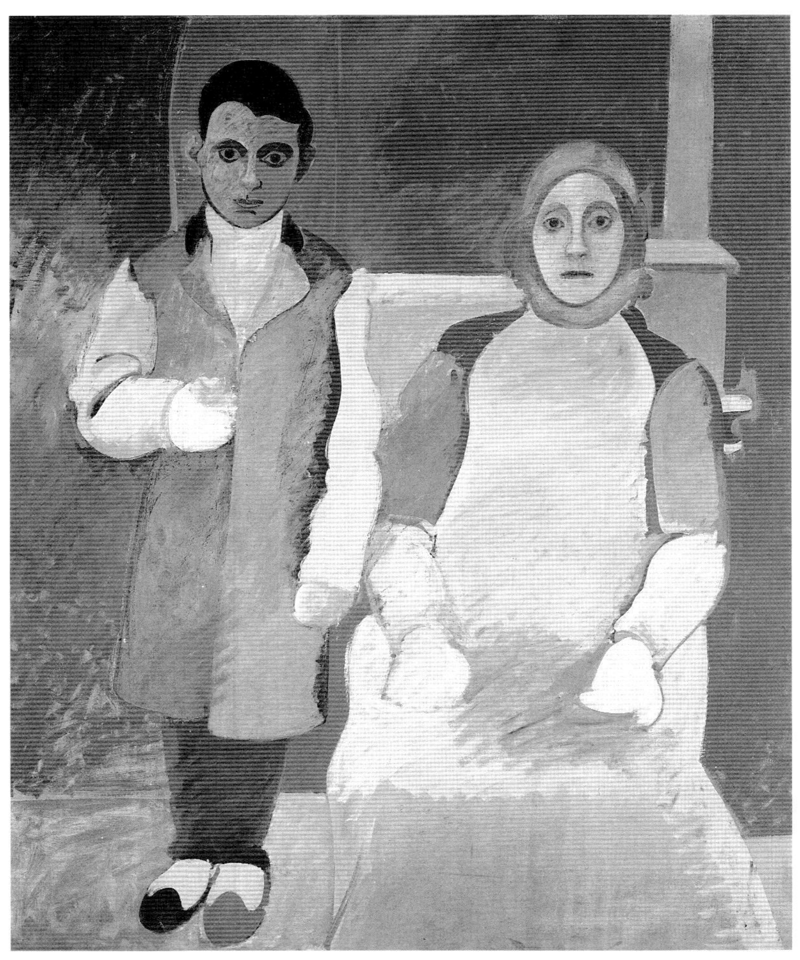

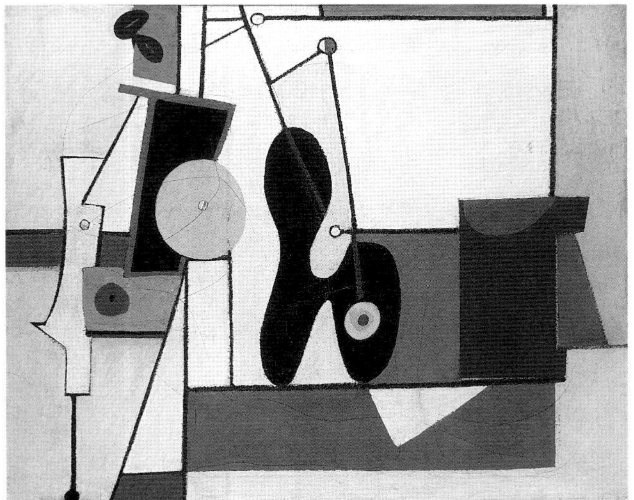

ARSHILE GORKY
1904–1948

The Artist and His Mother, c. 1926/1936
Canvas, 1.524 x 1.270 (60 x 50)
Ailsa Mellon Bruce Fund
1979.13.1

Organization, 1933–1936
Canvas, 1.264 x 1.524 (49¾ x 60)
Ailsa Mellon Bruce Fund
1979.13.3

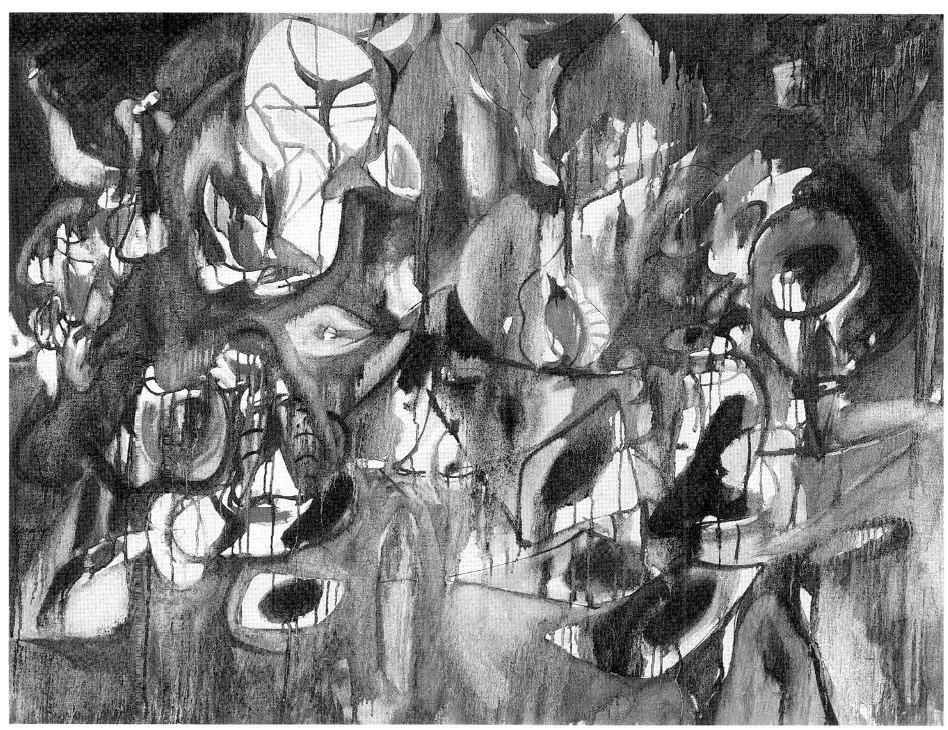

One Year the Milkweed, 1944
Canvas, 0.942 x 1.193 (37 x 47)
Inscribed at lower left: *A Gorky / 44*
Ailsa Mellon Bruce Fund
1979.13.2

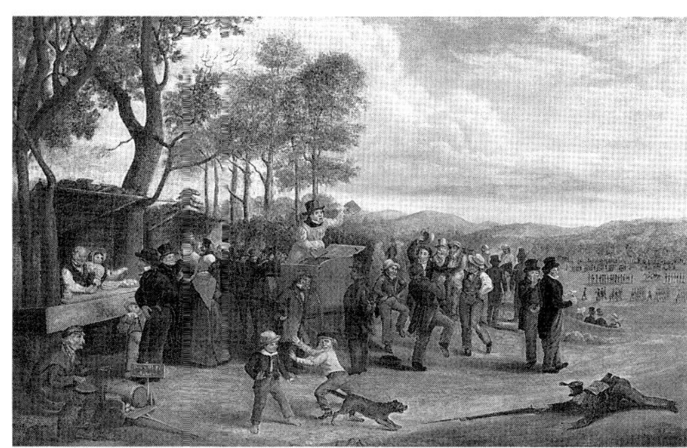

CHARLES HENRY GRANGER
1812–1893

Muster Day, 1843 or after
Canvas, 0.559 x 0.839 (22 x 33)
Gift of Edgar William and Bernice Chrysler Garbisch
1980.62.32

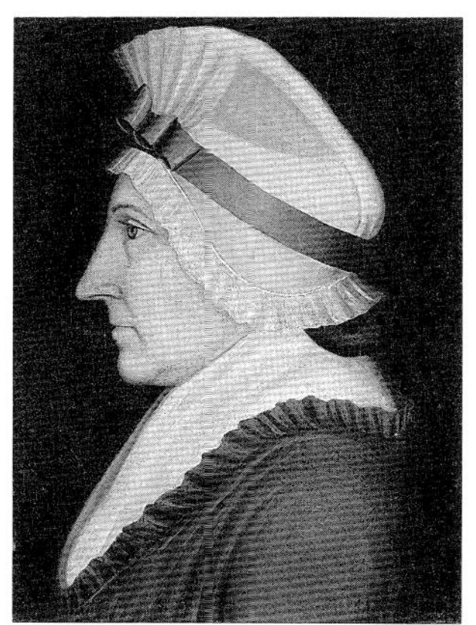

BENJAMIN GREENLEAF
1769–1821

Lady in a White Mob Cap, c. 1805
Canvas, 0.365 x 0.267 (14 3/8 x 10 1/2)
Gift of Edgar William and Bernice Chrysler Garbisch
1959.11.12

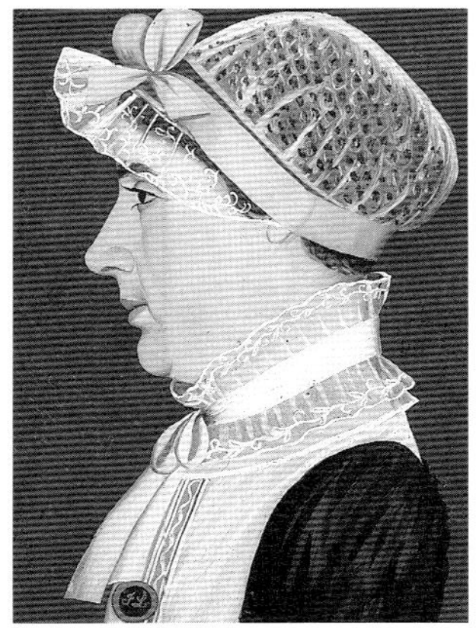

Portrait of J. L., c. 1810/1818
Reverse painting on glass, 0.332 x 0.255 (13 1/8 x 10)
Inscribed at lower left on brooch: *J. L.*
Gift of Edgar William and Bernice Chrysler Garbisch
1953.5.41

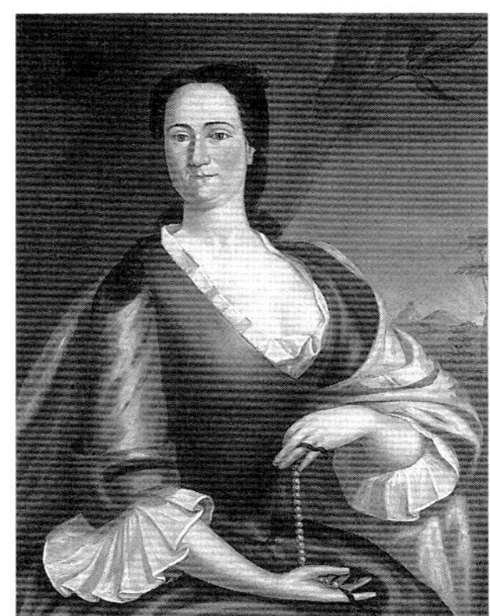

JOHN GREENWOOD
1727–1792

Mrs. Welshman, 1749
Canvas, 0.915 x 0.711 (36 x 28)
Inscribed at center left: *J. Greenwood pinxt. / 1749.*
Gift of Edgar William and Bernice Chrysler Garbisch
1961.4.1

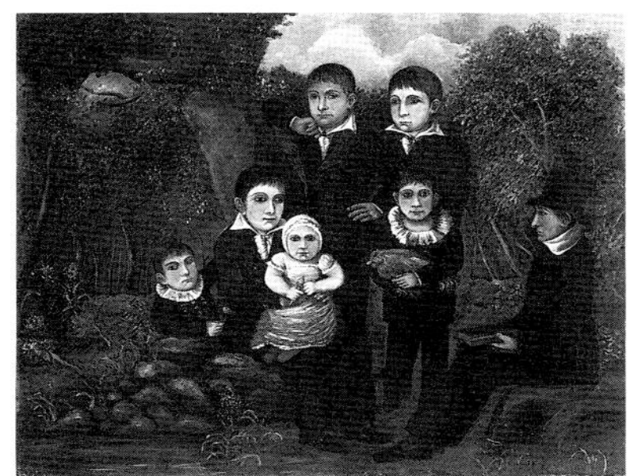

J. H.
active 1822

Abraham Clark and His Children, 1822
Wood, 0.648 x 0.813 (25 1/2 x 32)
Inscribed on reverse: *April / 29.1822 / JH* (in monogram)
Gift of Edgar William and Bernice Chrysler Garbisch
1953.5.40

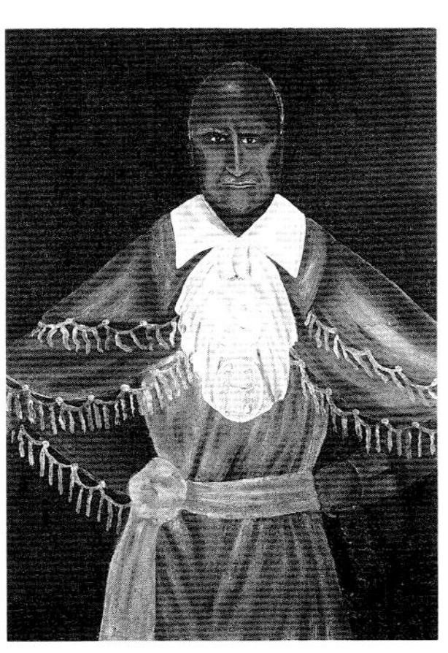

A. HADDOCK
active c. 1828

Red Jacket, 1828 or after
Cardboard, 0.641 x 0.451 (25 1/4 x 17 3/4)
Inscribed at lower left: *A. Haddock.*
Gift of Edgar William and Bernice Chrysler Garbisch
1958.9.5

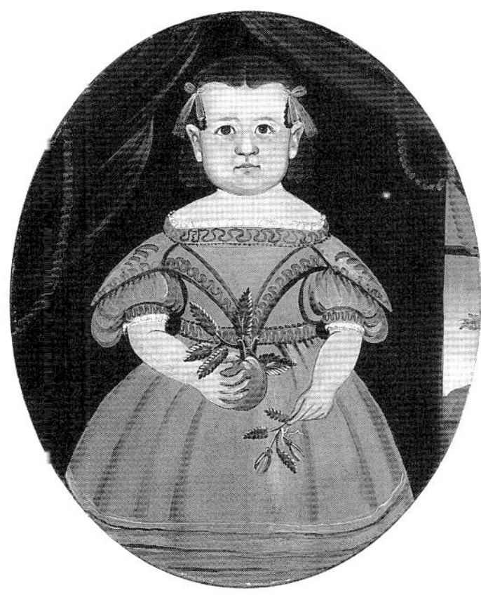

STURTEVANT J. HAMBLIN
active 1837/1856

Little Girl Holding Apple, c. 1840
Canvas, 0.572 x 0.467 (22½ x 18⅜)
Gift of Edgar William and Bernice Chrysler Garbisch
1978.80.10

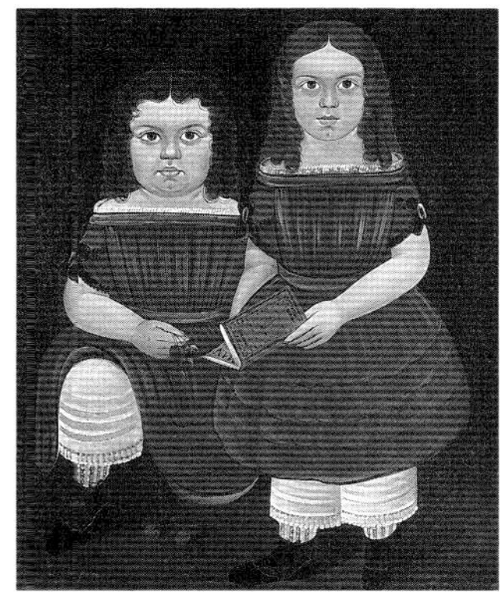

Sisters in Blue, c. 1840
Canvas, 0.683 x 0.560 (26⅞ x 22⅛)
Gift of Edgar William and Bernice Chrysler Garbisch
1978.80.19

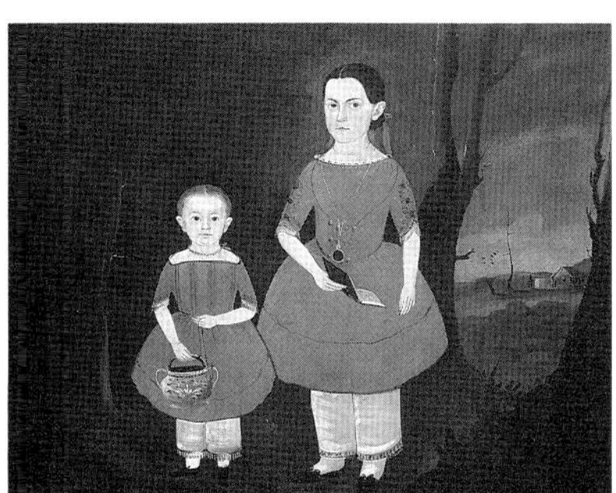

Sisters in Red, c. 1840/1850
Canvas, 0.635 x 0.765 (25 x 30⅛)
Gift of Edgar William and Bernice Chrysler Garbisch
1980.62.19

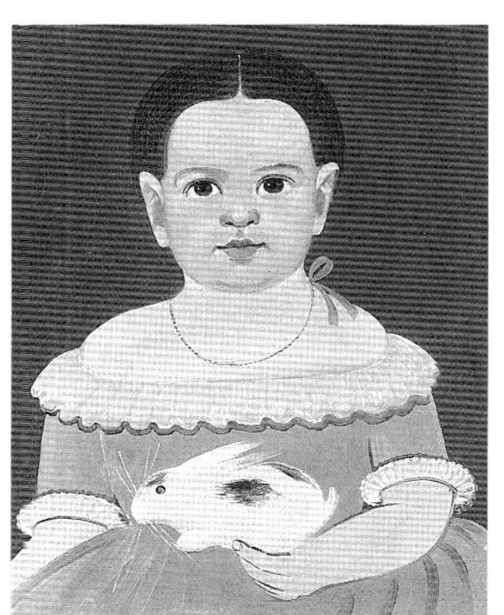

Little Girl with Pet Rabbit, c. 1845
Cardboard, 0.307 x 0.245 (12$\frac{1}{16}$ x 9⅝)
Gift of Edgar William and Bernice Chrysler Garbisch
1953.5.70

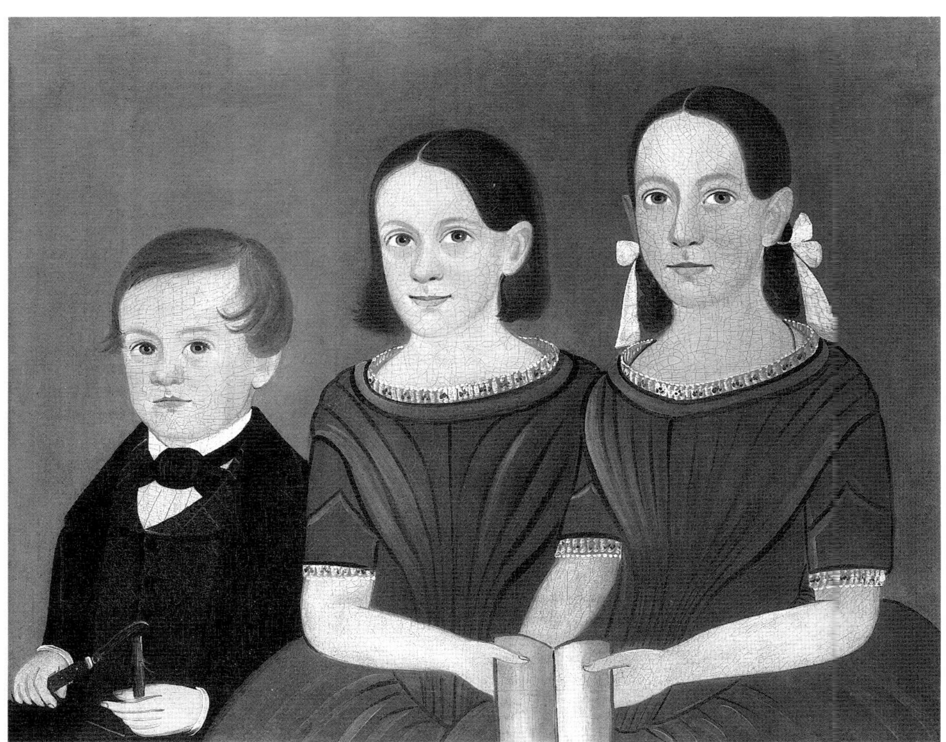

The Younger Generation, c. 1850
Canvas, 0.555 x 0.682 (21⅞ x 26⅞)
Gift of Edgar William and Bernice Chrysler Garbisch
1966.13.5

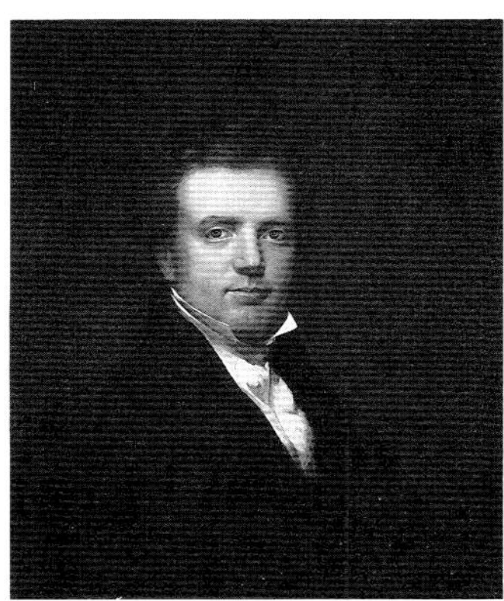

CHESTER HARDING
1792–1866

Self-Portrait, c. 1825
Canvas, 0.762 x 0.635 (30 x 25)
Andrew W. Mellon Collection
1947.17.54

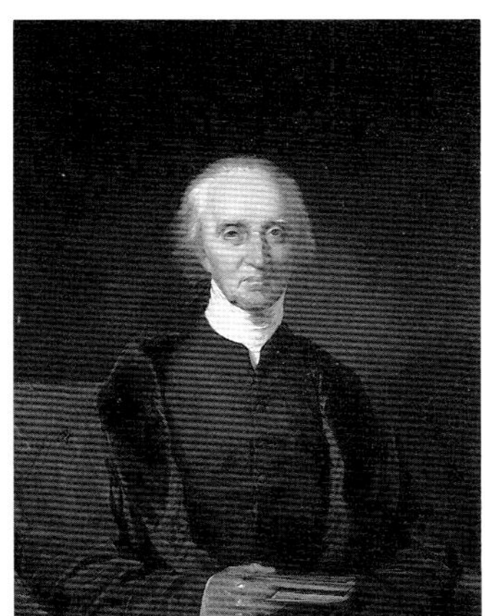

Charles Carroll of Carrollton, c. 1828
Canvas, 0.911 x 0.708 (35⅞ x 27⅞)
Gift of Mr. and Mrs. Alexander Dallas Thayer
1956.15.1

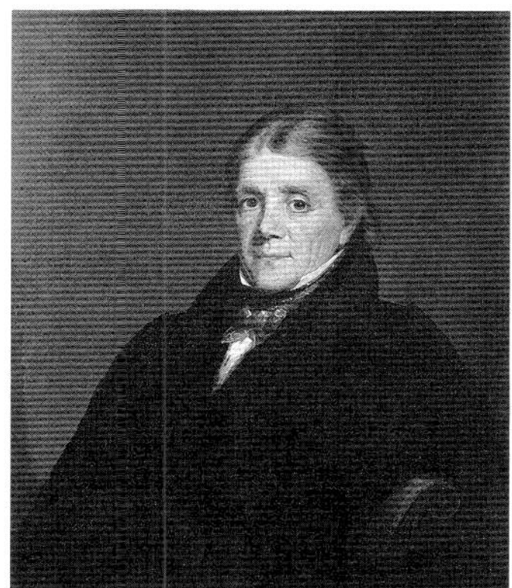

John Randolph, 1829
Canvas, 0.760 x 0.640 (30⅛ x 25)
Andrew W. Mellon Collection
1940.1.7

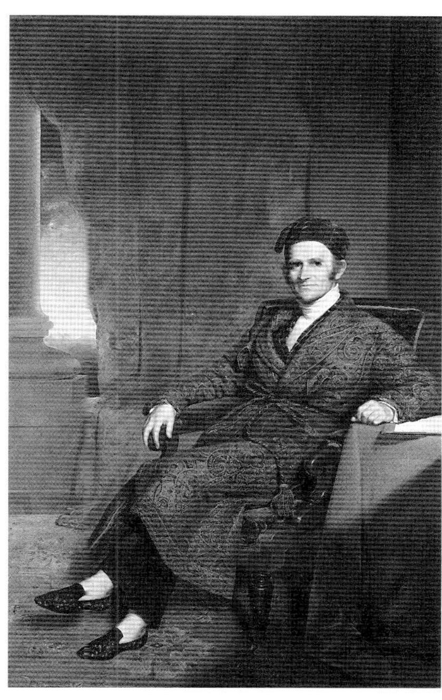

Amos Lawrence, c. 1845
Canvas, 2.150 x 1.360 (84⅝ x 53½)
Given in memory of the Rt. Rev. William Lawrence by his children
1944.1.1

WILLIAM MICHAEL HARNETT
1848–1892

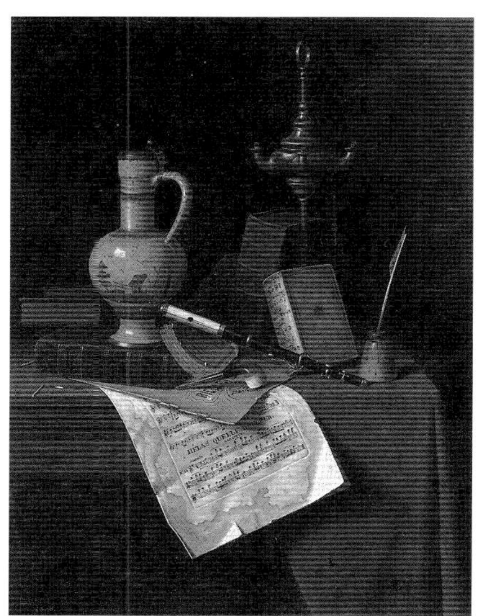

My Gems, 1888
Wood, 0.457 x 0.355 (18 x 14)
Inscribed at lower left: *WMHARNETT.* (M H in monogram) / *1888.*
Gift of the Avalon Foundation
1957.5.1

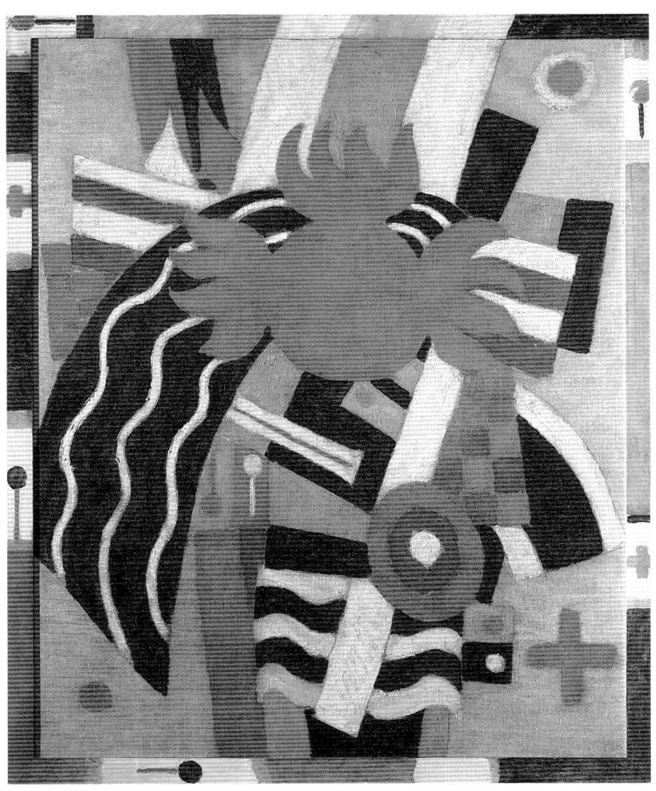

MARSDEN HARTLEY
1877–1943

The Aero, 1914
Canvas, 1.070 x 0.876 (42½ x 34)
Andrew W. Mellon Fund
1970.31.1

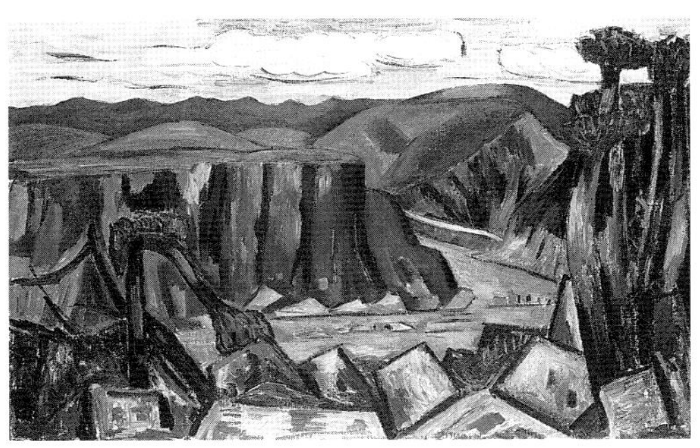

Landscape No. 5, 1922/1923
Canvas, 0.582 x 0.900 (23 x 35½)
Alfred Stieglitz Collection
1949.2.2

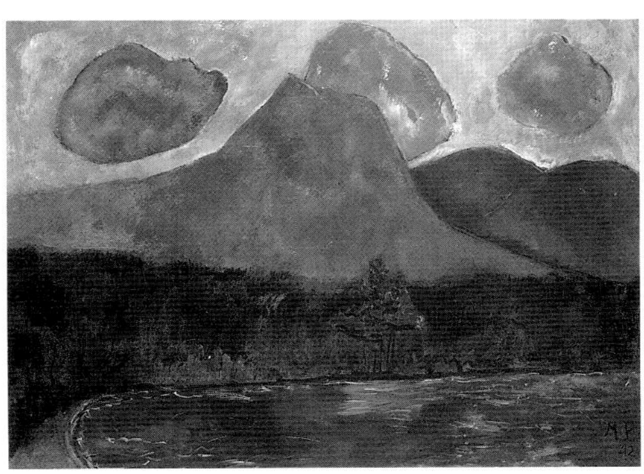

Mount Katahdin, Maine, 1942
Hardboard, 0.760 x 1.020 (30 x 40⅛)
Inscribed at lower right: *M.H.* / 42
Gift of Mrs. Mellon Byers
1970.27.1

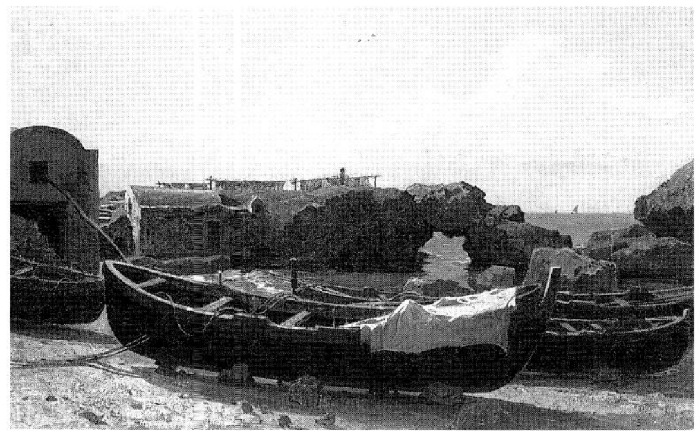

WILLIAM STANLEY HASELTINE
1835–1900

Marina Piccola, Capri, c. 1856 / 1858
Paper on canvas, 0.305 x 0.470 (12 x 18½)
Gift of Helen Haseltine Plowden
1953.10.1

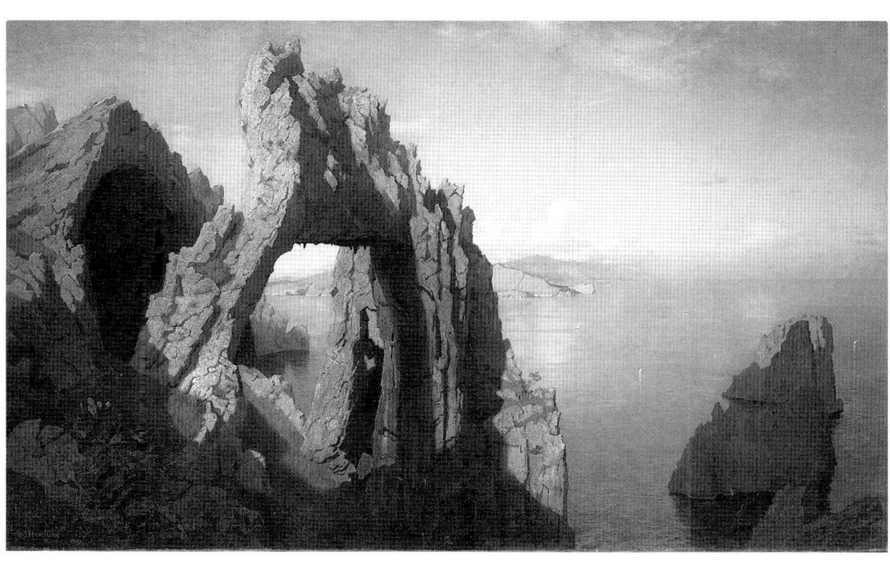

Natural Arch at Capri, 1871
Canvas, 0.864 x 1.397 (34 x 55)
Inscribed at lower left: *WSHaseltine / Rome 1871.*
Gift of General Services, Inc. in honor of the Fiftieth Anniversary of the National Gallery of Art
1989.13.1

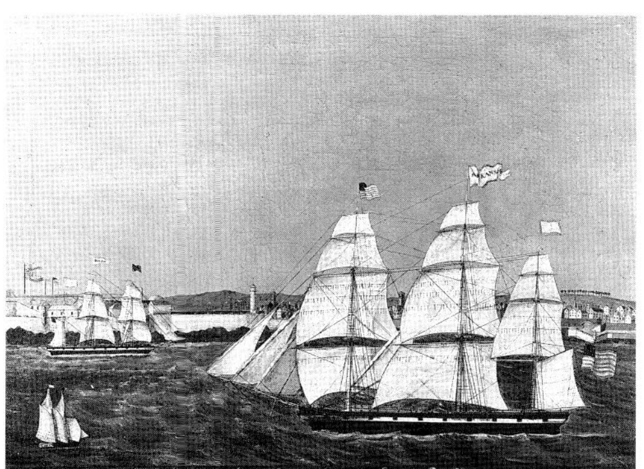

A. HASHAGEN
active 1847

Ship Arkansas *Leaving Havana*, 1847
Canvas, 0.575 x 0.727 (22⅝ x 28⅝)
Inscribed across bottom: *Ship Arkansas Capt Nehemiah Laribee. Left the Port Havana. MAY 1847*; lower right: *A. HASHAGEN.*
Gift of Edgar William and Bernice Chrysler Garbisch
1956.13.4

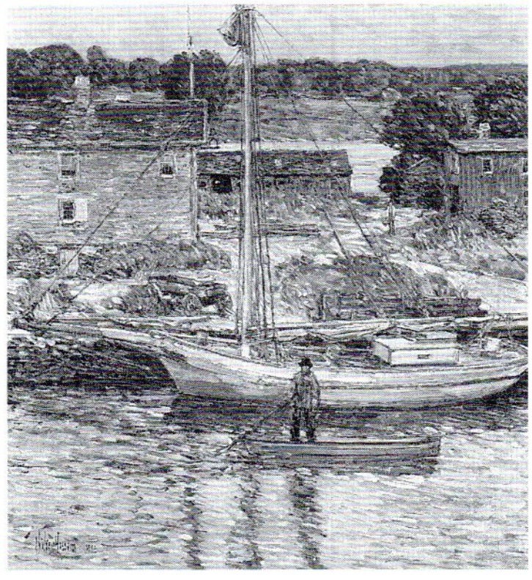

CHILDE HASSAM
1859–1935

Oyster Sloop, Cos Cob, 1902
Canvas, 0.620 x 0.568 (24³⁄₈ x 22³⁄₈)
Inscribed at lower left: *Childe Hassam 1902*
Ailsa Mellon Bruce Collection
1970.17.100

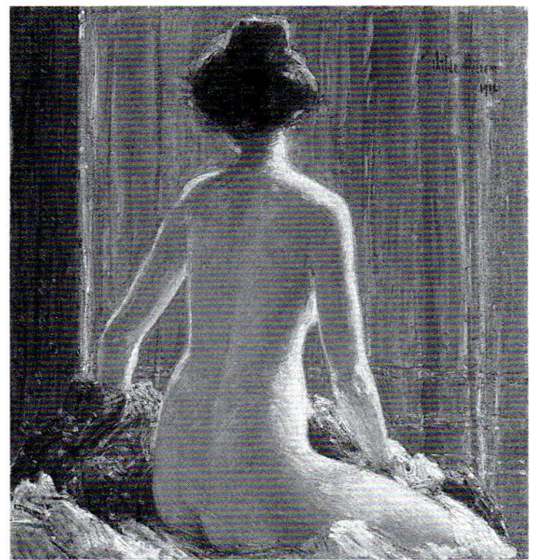

Nude Seated, 1912
Canvas, 0.612 x 0.559 (24¹⁄₈ x 22)
Inscribed at upper right: *Childe Hassam / 1912*
Chester Dale Collection
1963.10.156

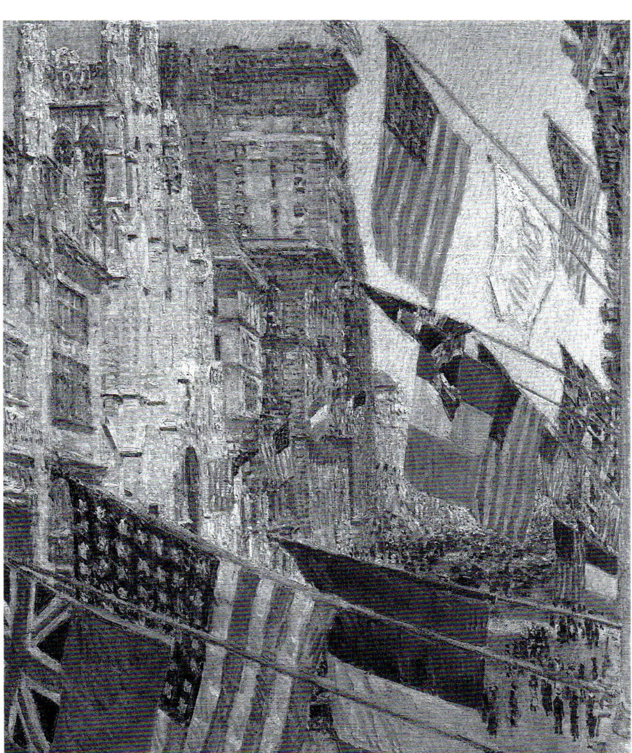

Allies Day, May 1917, 1917
Canvas, 0.933 x 0.770 (36³⁄₄ x 30¹⁄₄)
Inscribed at center left: *Childe Hassam / May 17 1917*
Gift of Ethelyn McKinney in memory of her brother, Glenn Ford McKinney
1943.9.1

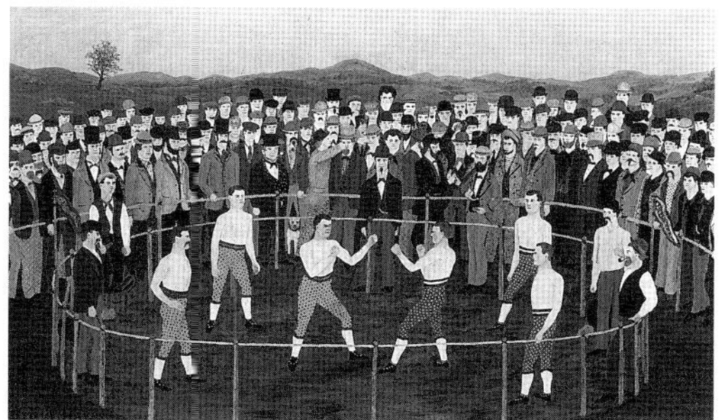

GEORGE A. HAYES
active c. 1870/1885

Bare Knuckles, c. 1870/1885
Paperboard attached to wood panel, 0.305 x 0.485 (12 x 19⅛)
Inscribed at lower left: *GEO. A. HAYES*
Gift of Edgar William and Bernice Chrysler Garbisch
1980.62.9

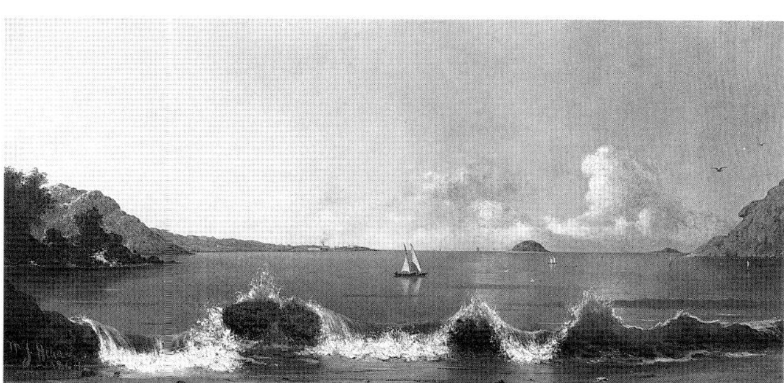

MARTIN JOHNSON HEADE
1819–1904

Rio de Janeiro Bay, 1864
Canvas, 0.455 x 0.911 (17⅞ x 35⅞)
Inscribed at lower left: *M. J. Heade / 1864*
Gift of the Avalon Foundation
1965.2.1

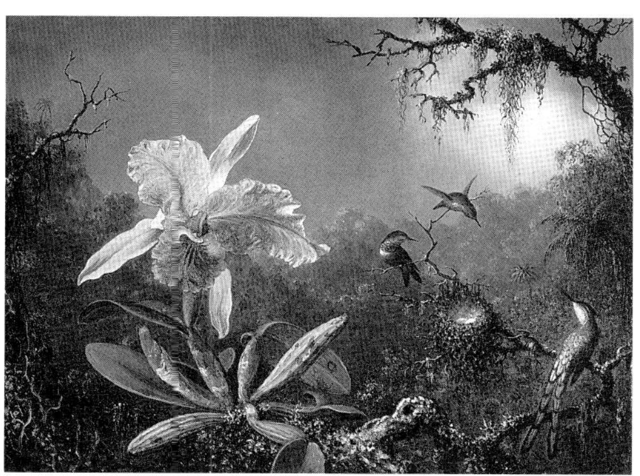

Cattleya Orchid and Three Brazilian Hummingbirds, 1871
Wood, 0.348 x 0.456 (13¾ x 18)
Inscribed at lower right: *M. J. Heade / 1871*
Gift of The Morris and Gwendolyn Cafritz Foundation
1982.73.1

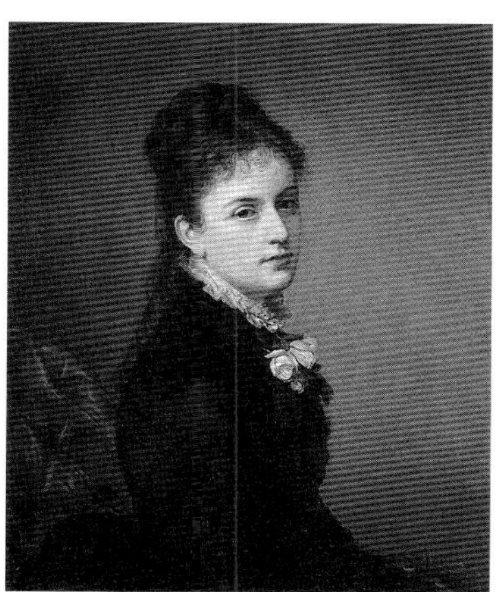

GEORGE PETER ALEXANDER HEALY
1813–1894

Roxanna Atwater Wentworth, 1876
Canvas, 0.768 x 0.635 (30¼ x 25)
Inscribed at center left: *G.P.A. Healy / 1876*
Gift of Lady Vereker
1970.34.1

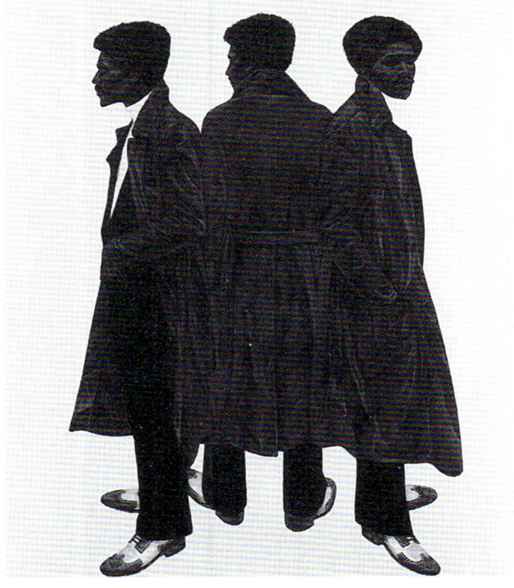

BARKLEY LEONNARD HENDRICKS
born 1945

Sir Charles, Alias Willy Harris, 1972
Canvas, 2.136 x 1.829 (84⅛ x 72)
Inscribed at upper right: *B. Hendricks 72*
William C. Whitney Foundation
1973.19.1

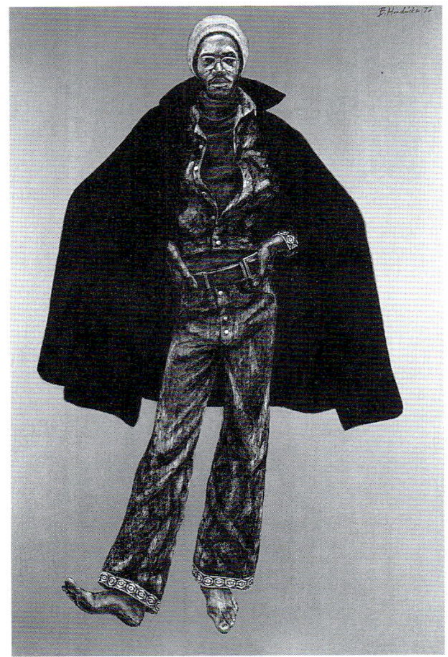

George Jules Taylor, 1972
Canvas, 2.323 x 1.530 (91½ x 60¼)
Inscribed at upper right: *B. Hendricks 72*
William C. Whitney Foundation
1973.19.2

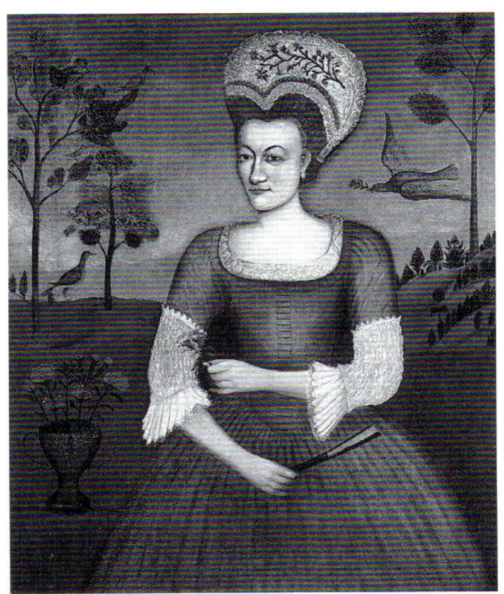

ATTRIBUTED TO DANIEL HENDRICKSON
1723–1788

Catharine Hendrickson, c. 1770
Canvas, 1.170 x 0.962 (46 1/16 x 37⅞)
Gift of Edgar William and Bernice Chrysler Garbisch
1953.5.45

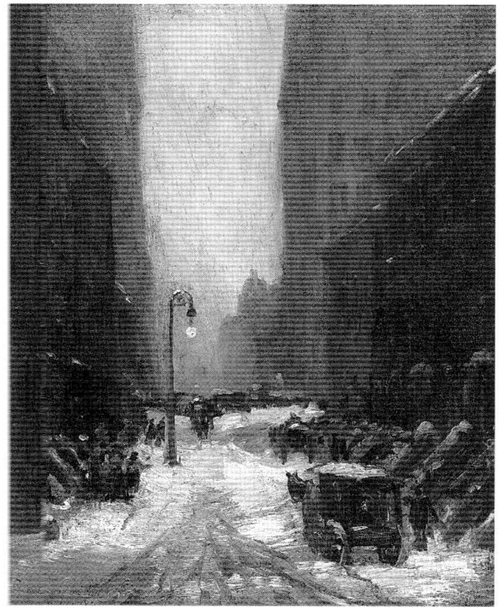

ROBERT HENRI
1865–1929

Snow in New York, 1902
Canvas, 0.813 x 0.655 (32 x 25¾)
Inscribed at lower left: *Robert Henri / Mar 5 1902*
Chester Dale Collection
1954.4.3

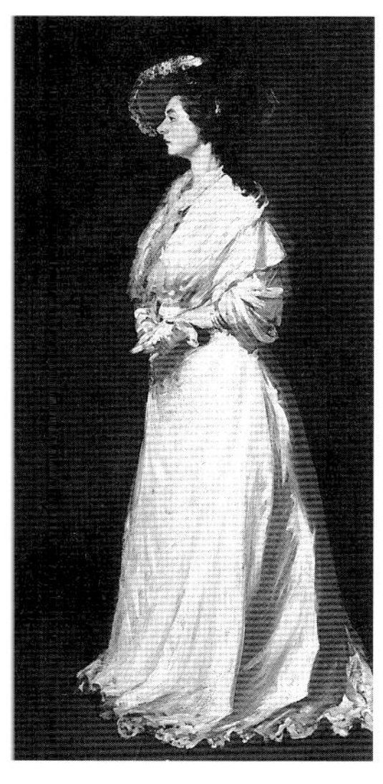

Young Woman in White, 1904
Canvas, 1.988 x 0.968 (78¼ x 38⅛)
Inscribed at lower left: *Robert Henri*
Gift of Violet Organ
1949.9.1

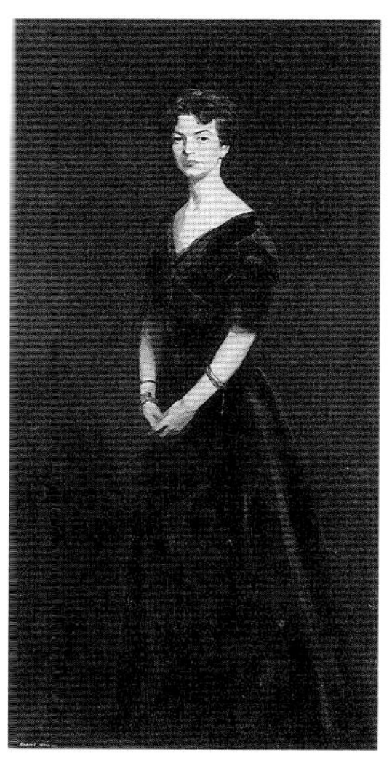

Edith Reynolds, 1908
Canvas, 1.935 x 0.946 (76⅛ x 37¼)
Inscribed at lower left: *Robert Henri*
Gift of Edith Reynolds
1956.7.1

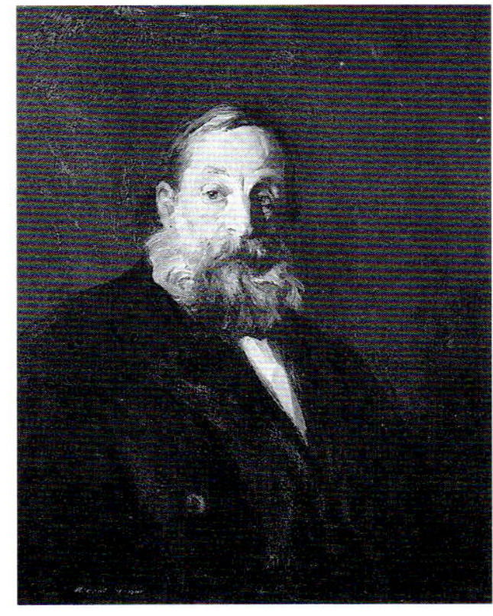

Mr. George Cotton Smith, 1908
Canvas, 0.813 x 0.660 (32 x 26)
Inscribed at lower left: *Robert Henri*; across top on reverse: *Portrait of / Mr. George Cotton Smith / by Robert Henri / at Wilkes Barre. Pa. / Jan 1908 / E 171*
Gift of Mrs. George Cotton Smith Adams in memory of George Cotton Smith Adams
1986.93.1

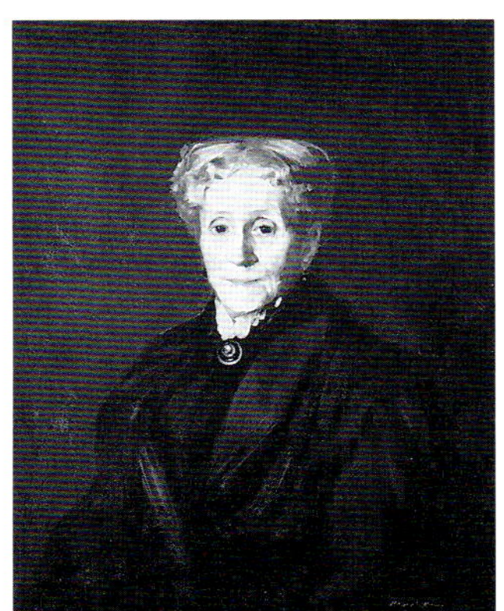

Mrs. George Cotton Smith, 1908
Canvas, 0.813 x 0.660 (32 x 26)
Inscribed at lower right: *Robert Henri*; across top on reverse: *Portrait of / Mrs. George Cotton Smith / by Robert Henri / at Wilkes Barre Pa / Jan 1908 / E 172*
Gift of Mrs. George Cotton Smith Adams in memory of George Cotton Smith Adams
1986.93.2

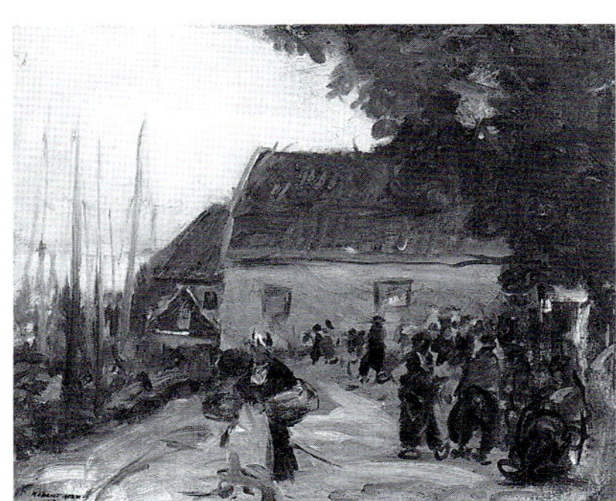

Volendam Street Scene, 1910
Canvas, 0.510 x 0.611 (20⅛ x 24)
Inscribed by Violet Organ, lower left: *ROBERT HENRI / VO*
Gift of Mr. and Mrs. Gerard C. Smith
1973.70.1

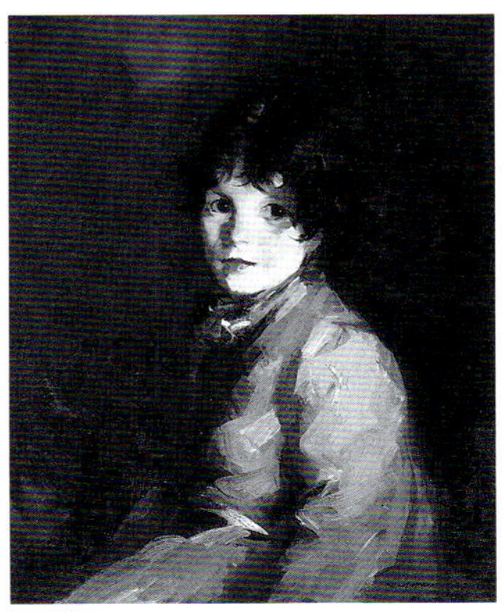

Catharine, 1913
Canvas, 0.610 x 0.511 (24 x 20⅛)
Inscribed at lower right: *Robert Henri*
Given in memory of Mr. and Mrs. William J. Johnson
1948.7.1

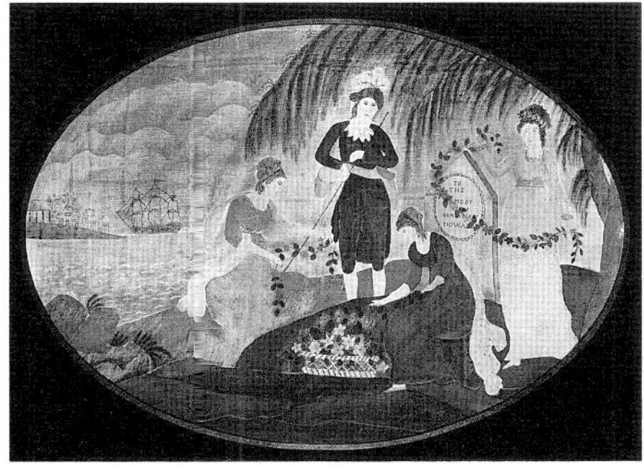

SALOME HENSEL
active 1823

To the Memory of the Benevolent Howard, 1823
Velvet, 0.635 x 0.826 (25 x $32\frac{1}{2}$)
Inscribed at center right on monument: *TO / THE / MEMORY / OF THE / BENEVOLENT / HOWARD*
Gift of Edgar William and Bernice Chrysler Garbisch
1971.83.22

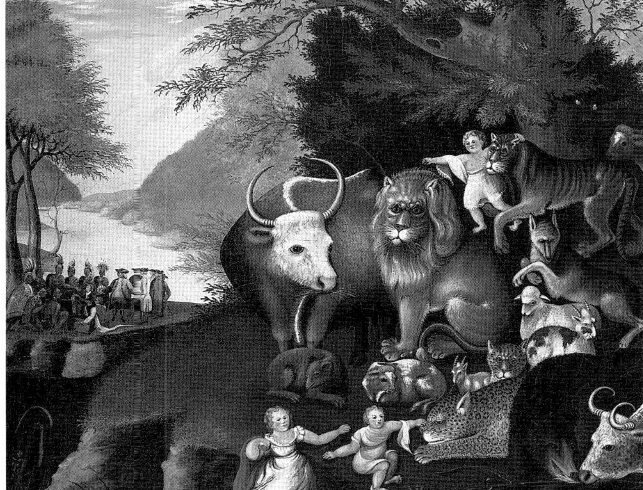

EDWARD HICKS
1780–1849

Peaceable Kingdom, c. 1834
Canvas, 0.745 x 0.901 ($29\frac{3}{8}$ x $35\frac{1}{2}$)
Gift of Edgar William and Bernice Chrysler Garbisch
1980.62.15

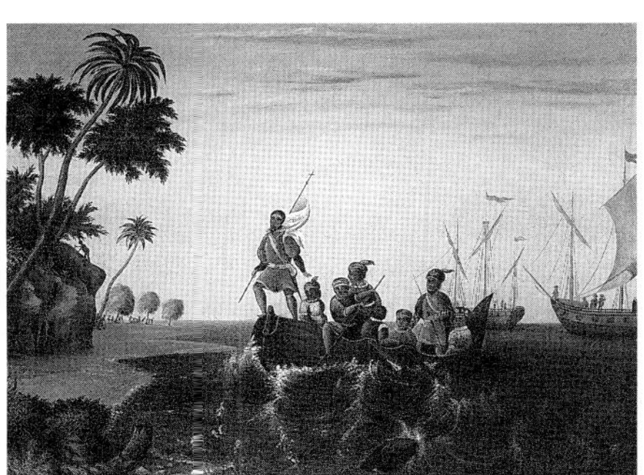

The Landing of Columbus, c. 1837
Canvas, 0.450 x 0.600 ($17\frac{11}{16}$ x $23\frac{11}{16}$)
Inscribed at lower center: *COLUMBUS*
Gift of Edgar William and Bernice Chrysler Garbisch
1980.62.13

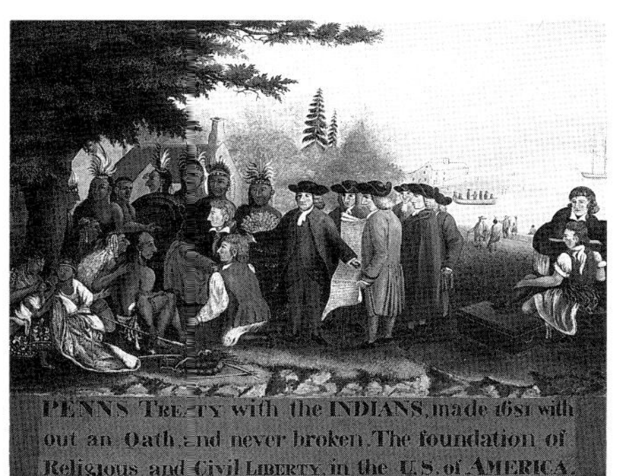

Penn's Treaty with the Indians, c. 1840/1844
Canvas, 0.617 x 0.765 ($24\frac{1}{4}$ x 30)
Inscribed across bottom: *PENNS TREATY with the INDIANS, made 1681 with/out an Oath, and never broken. The foundation of / Religious and Civil LIBERTY, in the U.S. of AMERICA.*
Gift of Edgar William and Bernice Chrysler Garbisch
1980.62.11

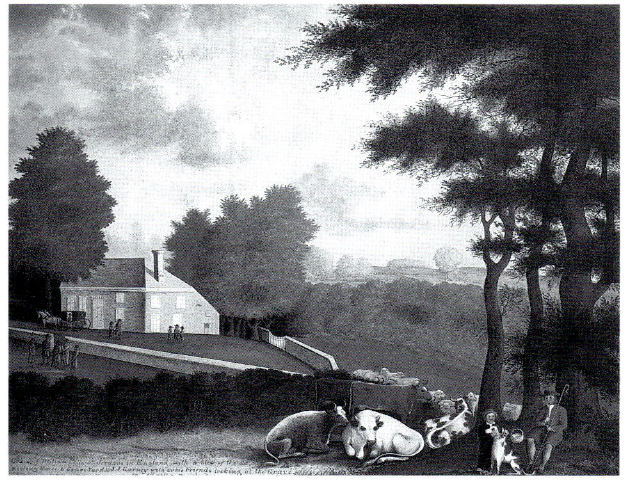

The Grave of William Penn, c. 1847/1848
Canvas, 0.602 x 0.755 (23¾ x 29¹¹⁄₁₆)
Inscribed at lower left and lower center: *Grave of William Penn at Jordans in England with a view of the old / Meeting House & Grave-Yard, & J. J. Gurney with some Friends looking at the Grave.*
Gift of Edgar William and Bernice Chrysler Garbisch
1980.62.12

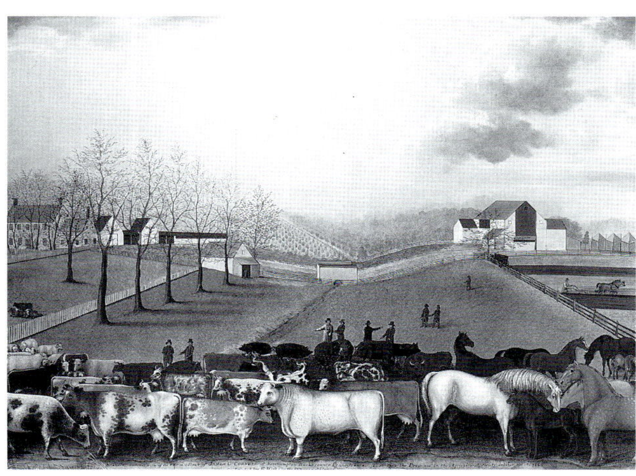

The Cornell Farm, 1848
Canvas, 0.933 x 1.244 (36¾ x 49)
Inscribed across bottom: *An Indian summer view of the Farm & Stock of JAMES C. CORNELL of Northampton Bucks county Pennsylvania. That took the Premium in the Agricultural society, october the 12, 1848 / Painted by E. Hicks in the 69th year of his age.*
Gift of Edgar William and Bernice Chrysler Garbisch
1964.23.4

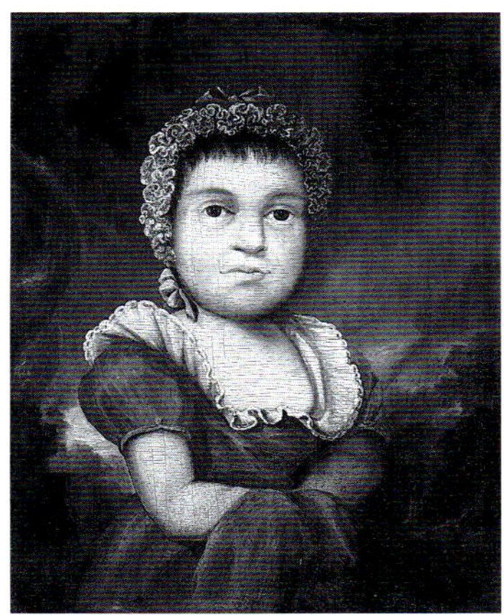

ATTRIBUTED TO EDWARD HICKS
1780–1849

Portrait of a Child, c. 1840
Wood, 0.442 x 0.369 (17⅜ x 14½)
Gift of Edgar William and Bernice Chrysler Garbisch
1980.62.14

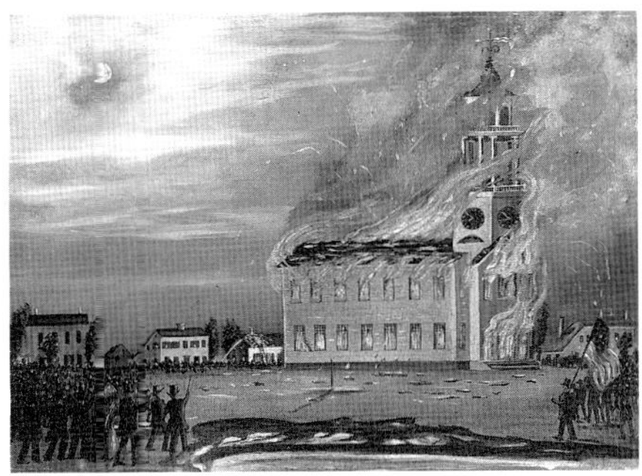

JOHN HILLING
c. 1822–1894

Burning of Old South Church, Bath, Maine, c. 1854
Canvas, 0.465 x 0.618 (18 5/16 x 24 3/8)
Gift of Edgar William and Bernice Chrysler Garbisch
1958.9.7

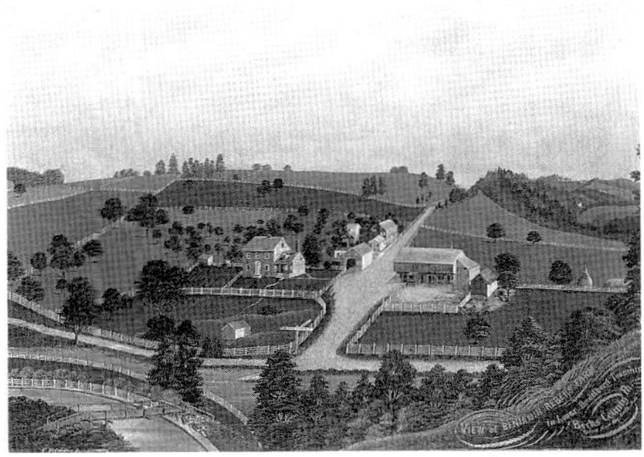

CHARLES C. HOFMANN
1821–1882

View of Benjamin Reber's Farm, 1872
Canvas, 0.640 x 0.885 (25 1/4 x 34 3/4)
Inscribed at lower left: *C. Hofmann Painter 1872*; lower right: *VIEW of BENJAMIN REBER'S FARM, / in Lower-Heidelberg Township, / Berks County Pa. / taken from the North-Side.*
Gift of Edgar William and Bernice Chrysler Garbisch
1955.11.16

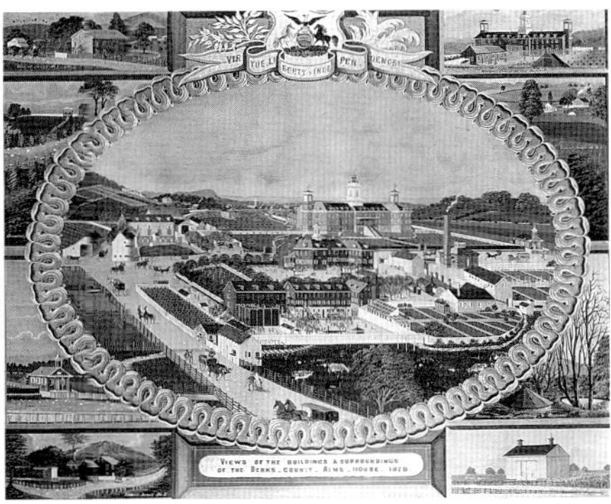

Berks County Almshouse, 1878, 1878
Zinc, 0.825 x 0.996 (32 1/2 x 39 1/4)
Inscribed at upper center: *VIRTUE, LIBERTY & INDEPENDENCE!*; lower center: *VIEWS OF THE BUILDINGS & SURROUNDINGS / OF THE BERKS-COUNTY-ALMS-HOUSE. 1878.*; lower right: *1878-Charles Hofman* [sic], *Painter.*
Gift of Edgar William and Bernice Chrysler Garbisch
1953.5.17

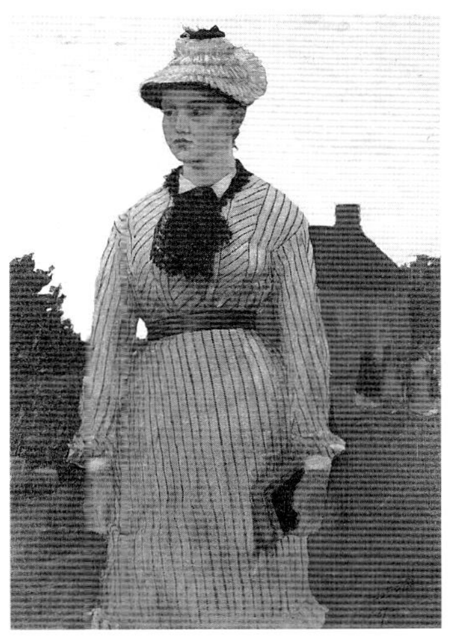

WINSLOW HOMER
1836–1910

The Red School House, 1873
Canvas mounted on board, 0.555 x 0.390 (21 7/8 x 15 3/8)
Inscribed at lower right: *HOMER / 1873*
Collection of Mr. and Mrs. Paul Mellon
1985.64.21

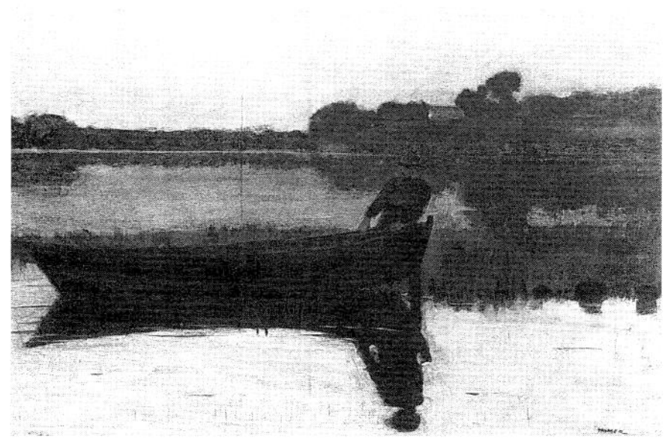

Sunset, c. 1875
Canvas, 0.394 x 0.572 (15 1/2 x 22 1/2)
Inscribed at lower right: *HOMER*
Gift of John W. Beatty, Jr.
1964.4.1

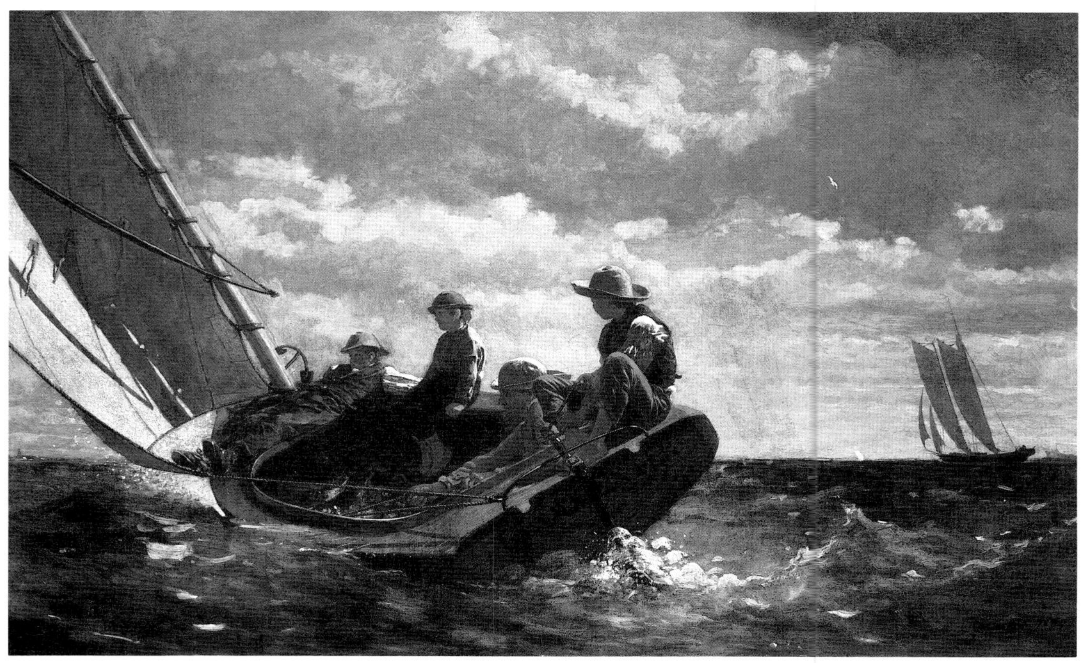

Breezing Up (A Fair Wind), 1876
Canvas, 0.615 x 0.970 (24 1/8 x 38 1/8)
Inscribed at lower right: *HOMER 1876*;
lower left: *HOMER*
Gift of the W. L. and May T. Mellon Foundation
1943.13.1

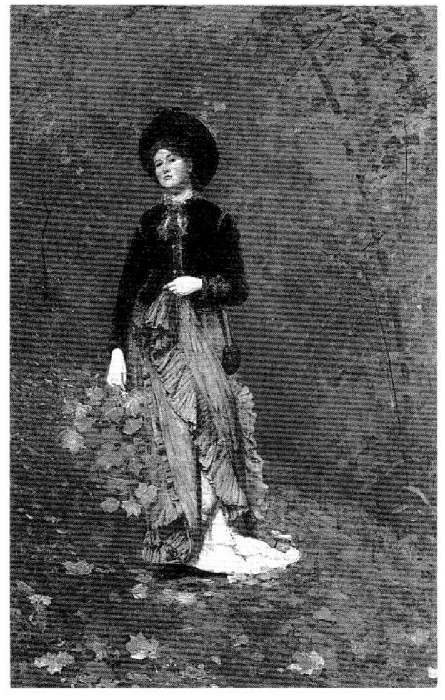

Autumn, 1877
Canvas, 0.971 x 0.589 (38 1/4 x 24 3/16)
Inscribed at lower right: *HOMER '77*
Collection of Mr. and Mrs. Paul Mellon
1985.64.22

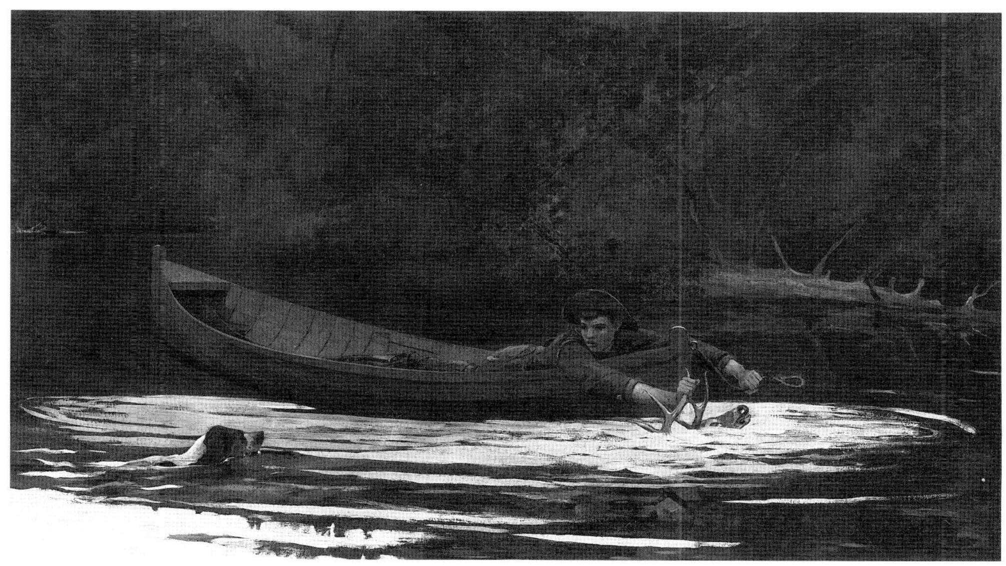

Hound and Hunter, 1892
Canvas, 0.718 x 1.223 (28¼ x 48¼)
Inscribed at lower right: *Winslow Homer 1892*
Gift of Stephen C. Clark
1947.11.1

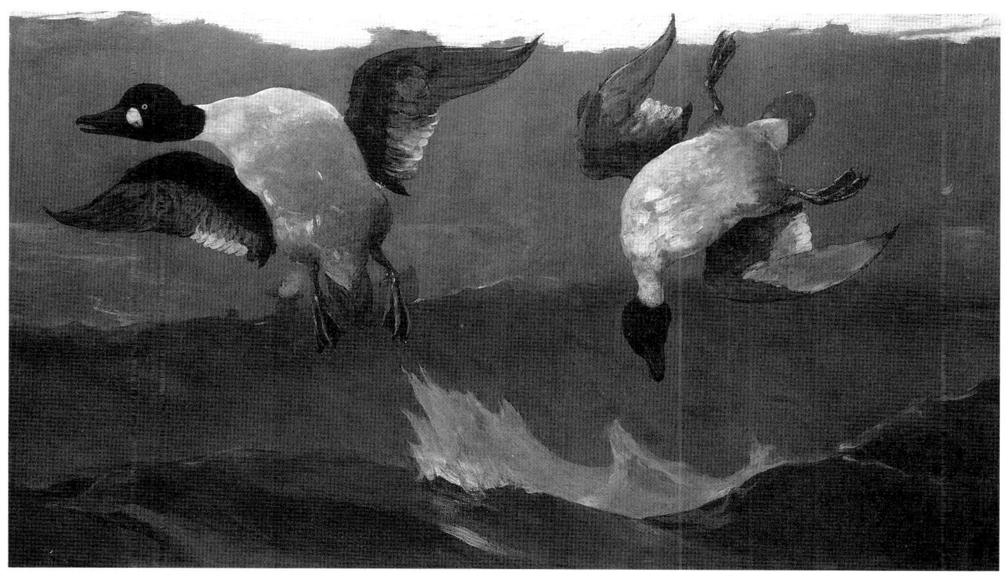

Right and Left, 1909
Canvas, 0.718 x 1.229 (28¼ x 48⅜)
Inscribed at lower right: *HOMER / 1909*
Gift of the Avalon Foundation
1951.8.1

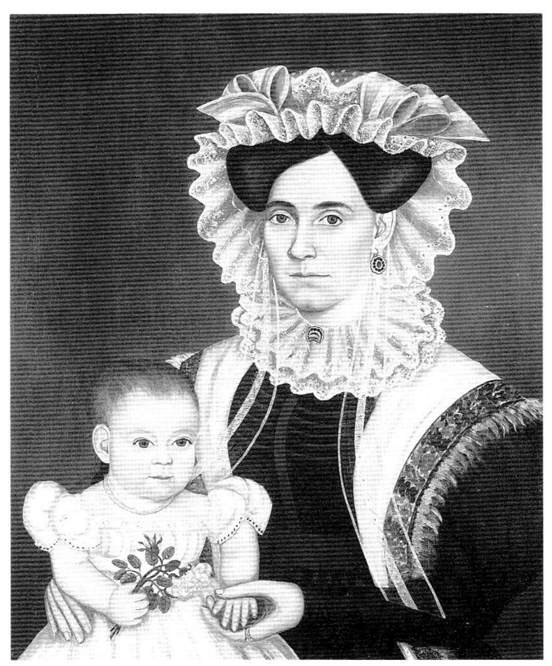

MILTON W HOPKINS
1789–1844

Aphia Salisbury Rich and Baby Edward, c. 1833
Wood, 0.758 x 0.616 (29⅞ x 24¼)
Gift of Edgar William and Bernice Chrysler Garbisch
1958.9.12

EDWARD HOPPER
1882–1967

Cape Cod Evening, 1939
Canvas, 0.768 x 1.022 (30¼ x 40¼)
Inscribed at lower right: *Edward Hopper*
John Hay Whitney Collection
1982.76.6

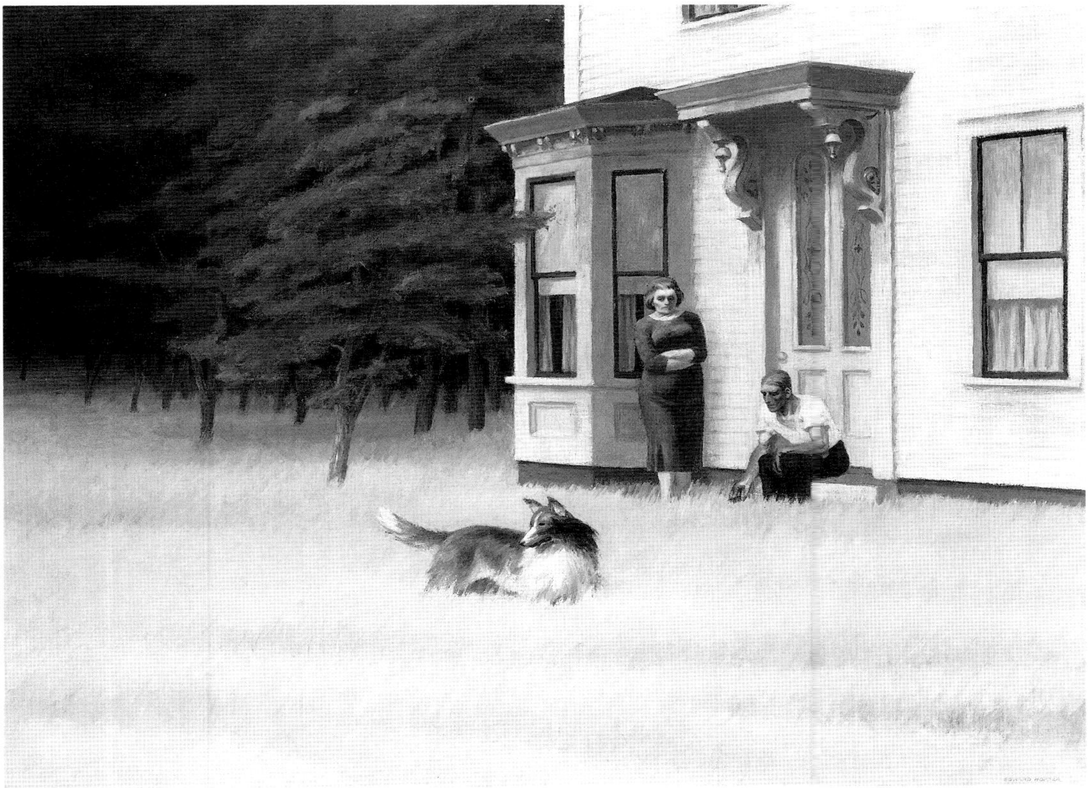

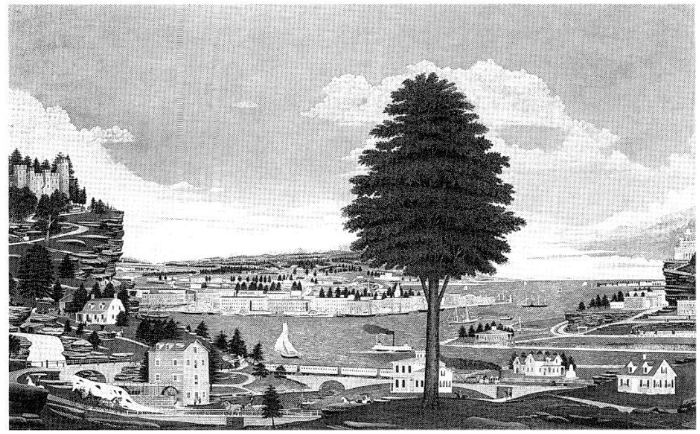

JURGAN FREDERICK HUGE
1809–1878

Composite Harbor Scene with Castle, c. 1875
Canvas, 0.648 x 1.017 (25½ x 40)
Gift of Edgar William and Bernice Chrysler Garbisch
1969.11.2

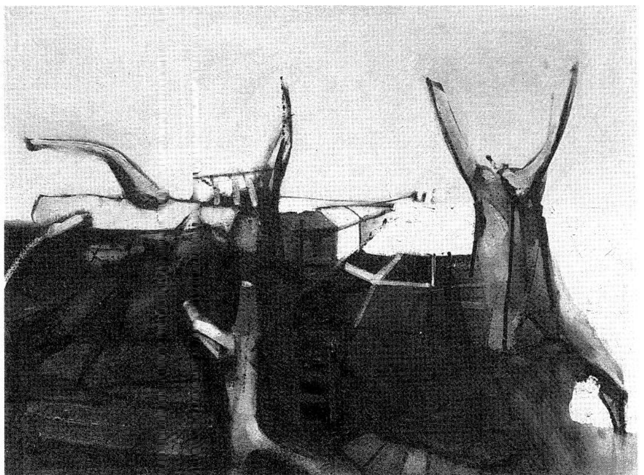

JOHN HULTBERG
born 1922

The Island, 1957
Canvas, 0.635 x 0.816 (25 x 32⅛)
Gift of John George Fischer
1970.28.1

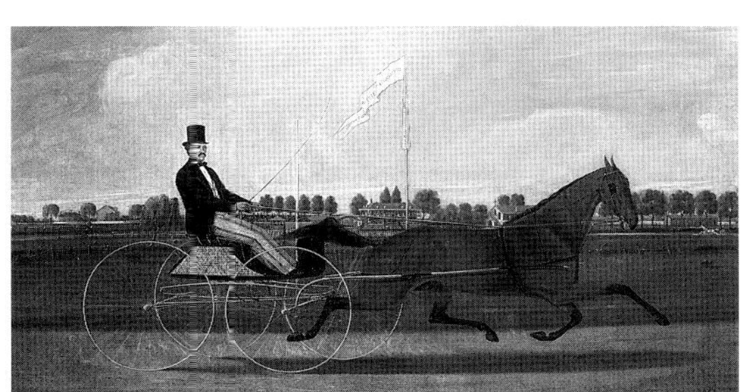

CHARLES S. HUMPHREYS
1818–1880

The Trotter, c. 1860
Canvas, 0.508 x 0.916 (20 x 36¹⁄₁₆)
Inscribed on banner: *POIN[T] BREEZE [PAR]K ASSOCIATION.*
Gift of Edgar William and Bernice Chrysler Garbisch
1953.5.95

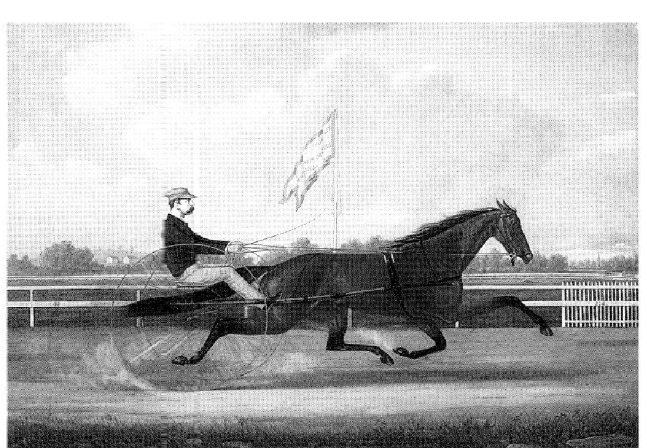

Budd Doble Driving Goldsmith Maid at Belmont Driving Park, 1876
Canvas, 0.660 x 0.916 (26 x 36)
Inscribed at center on flag in reverse: *BELMONT / DRIVING PARK / ASSOCIATION*; center left on lower fence rail: *CSH* (in monogram);
center right on lower fence rail: 214;
lower right on rock: *CHAS. S. HUMPHREYS / Camden, N.J. 1876*
Gift of Edgar William and Bernice Chrysler Garbisch
1971.83.6

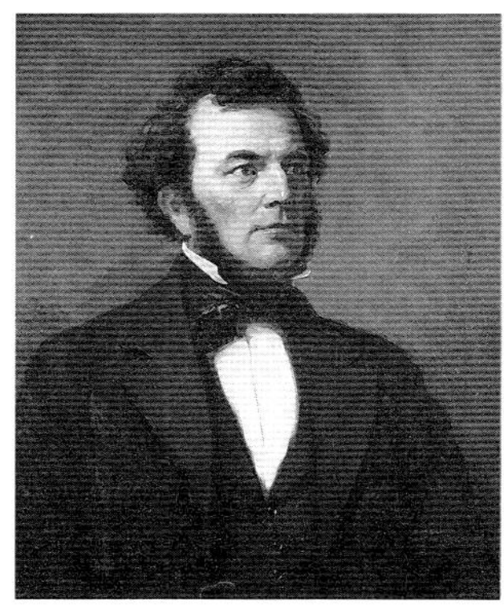

DANIEL HUNTINGTON
1816–1906

Dr. James Hall, 1857
Canvas, 0.76[illegible] x 0.633 ($30\frac{1}{8}$ x $24\frac{7}{8}$)
Andrew W. Mellon Collection
1947.17.56

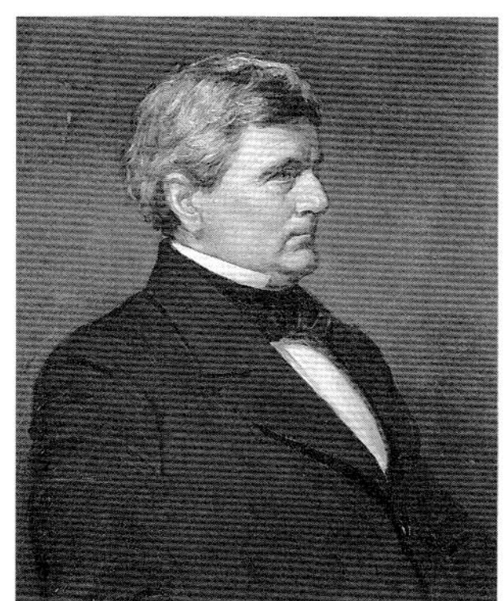

Dr. John Edwards Holbrook, 1857
Canvas, 0.72[illegible] x 0.589 ($28\frac{5}{16}$ x $23\frac{1}{4}$)
Andrew W. Mellon Collection
1947.17.57

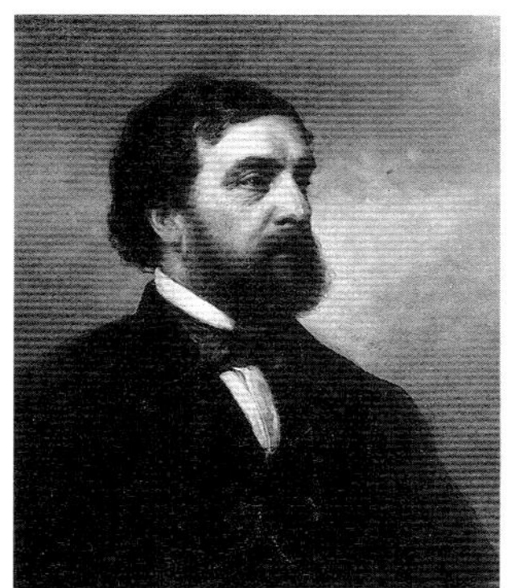

Henry Theodore Tuckerman, 1866
Canvas, 0.68[illegible] x 0.562 ($27\frac{1}{16}$ x $22\frac{3}{16}$)
Inscribed at lower left: *D. Huntington / 1866*
Andrew W. Mellon Collection
1947.17.7

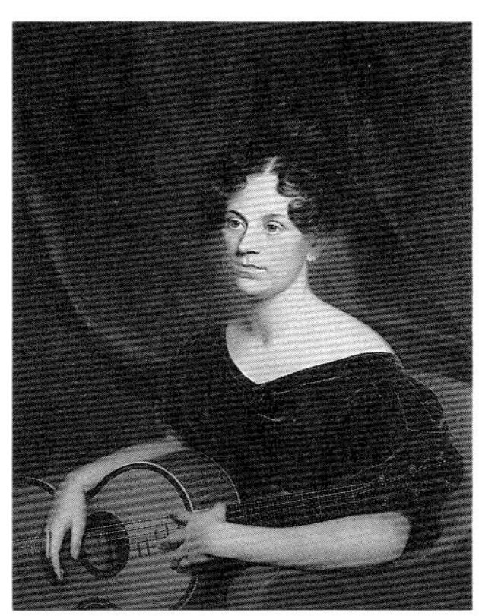

CHARLES CROMWELL INGHAM
1796–1863

Coralie Livingston(?), c. 1833
Canvas, 0.91[illegible] x 0.711 (36 x 28)
Andrew W. Mellon Collection
1947.17.73

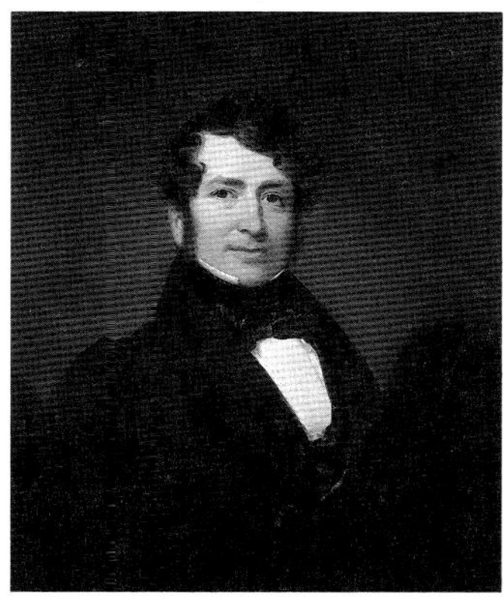

HENRY INMAN
1801–1846

George Pope Morris, c. 1836
Canvas, 0.762 x 0.635 (30 x 25)
Andrew W. Mellon Collection
1947.17.8

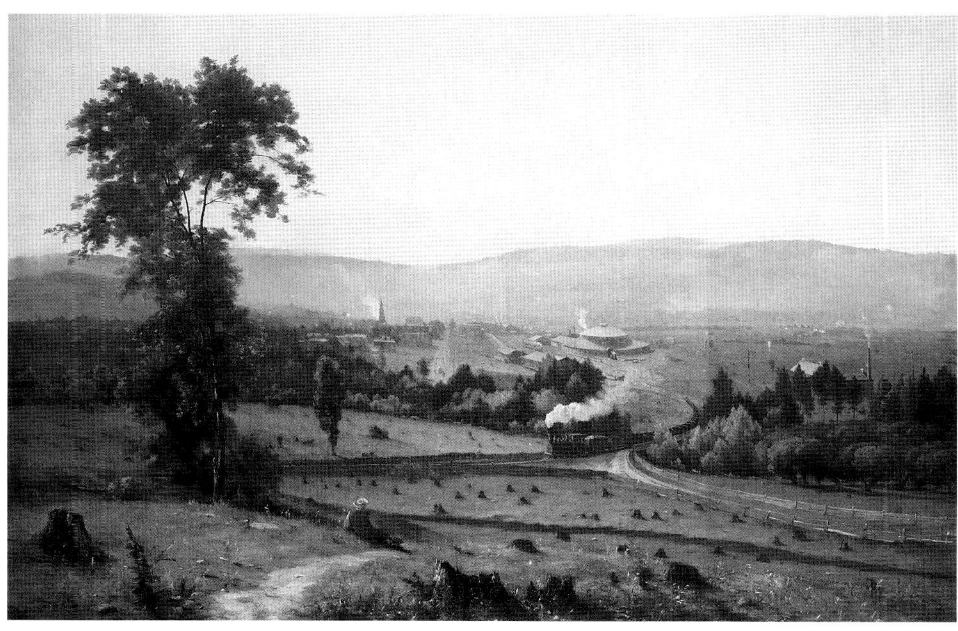

GEORGE INNESS
1825–1894

The Lackawanna Valley, 1855
Canvas, 0.860 x 1.275 (33⅞ x 50¼)
Inscribed at lower left: G. *Inness*
Gift of Mrs. Huttleston Rogers
1945.4.1

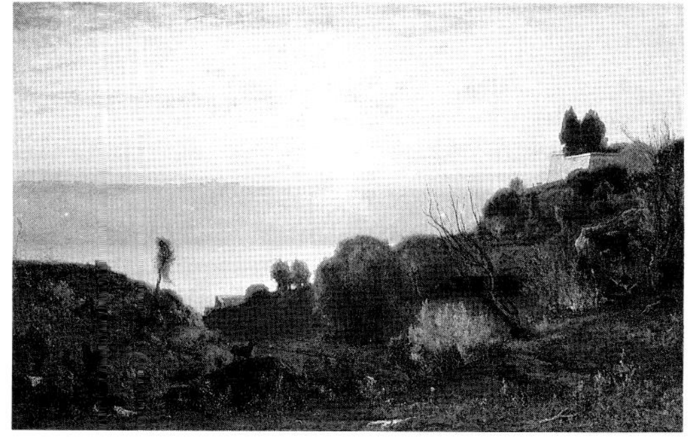

Lake Albano, Sunset, 1872/1874
Canvas, 0.765 x 1.144 (30⅛ x 45)
Inscribed at lower left: G. *Inn[ess] 187[. . .]*
Gift of Alice Dodge in memory of her father, Henry Percival Dodge
1962.2.1

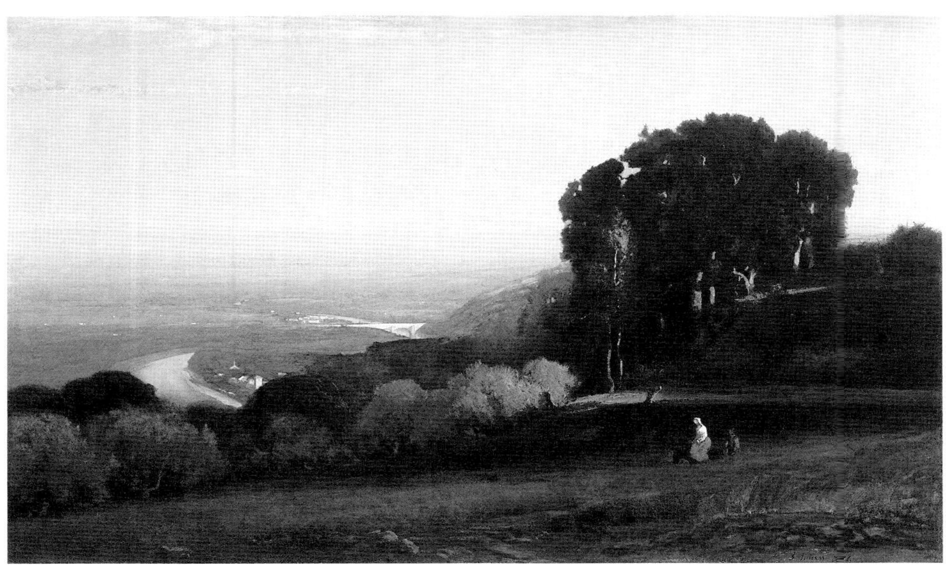

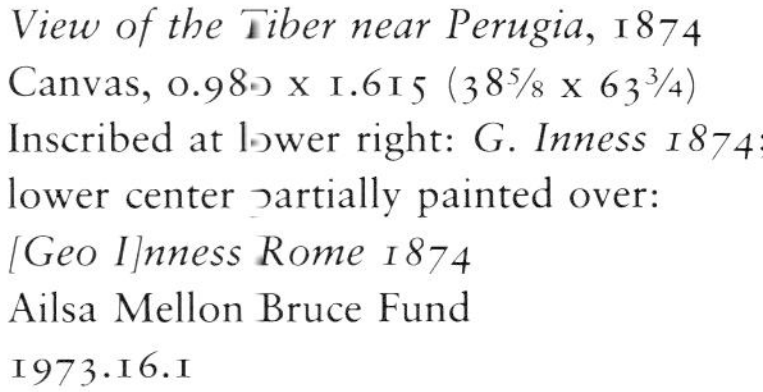

View of the Tiber near Perugia, 1874
Canvas, 0.980 x 1.615 (38⅝ x 63¾)
Inscribed at lower right: *G. Inness 1874*;
lower center partially painted over:
[Geo I]nness Rome 1874
Ailsa Mellon Bruce Fund
1973.16.1

ROBERT IRWIN
born 1928

Untitled, 1967
Canvas, 2.144 x 2.098 (84½ x 82⅝)
Gift of Mr. and Mrs. Burton Tremaine
1977.75.3

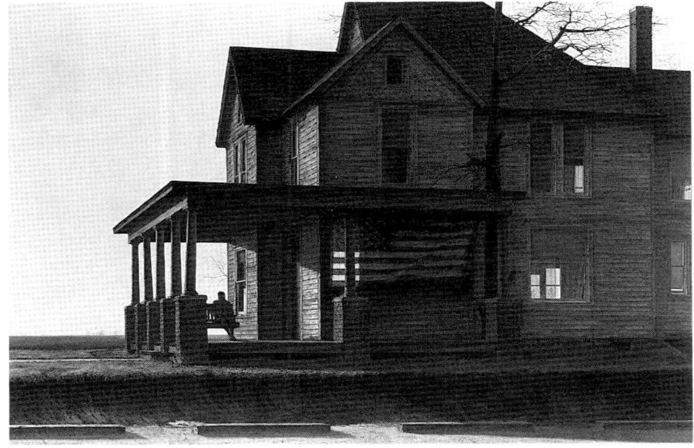

BILLY MORROW JACKSON
born 1926

Eve, 1967
Hardboard, 1.221 x 1.829 (48 x 72)
Gift of the Artist
1970.15.1

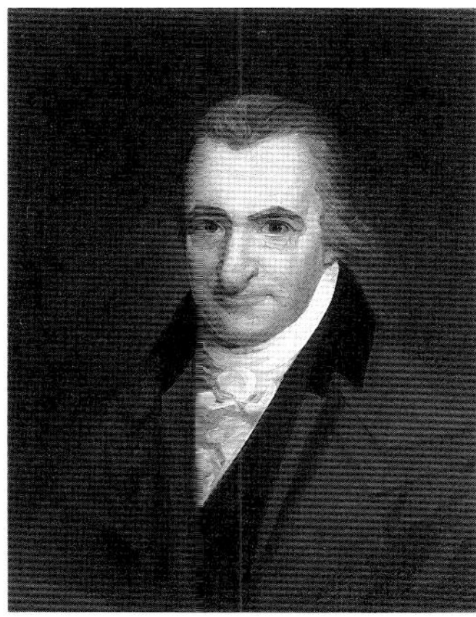

JOHN WESLEY JARVIS
1780–1840

Thomas Paine, c. 1806/1807
Canvas, 0.654 x 0.521 ($25\frac{3}{4}$ x $20\frac{1}{2}$)
Gift of Marian B. Maurice
1950.15.1

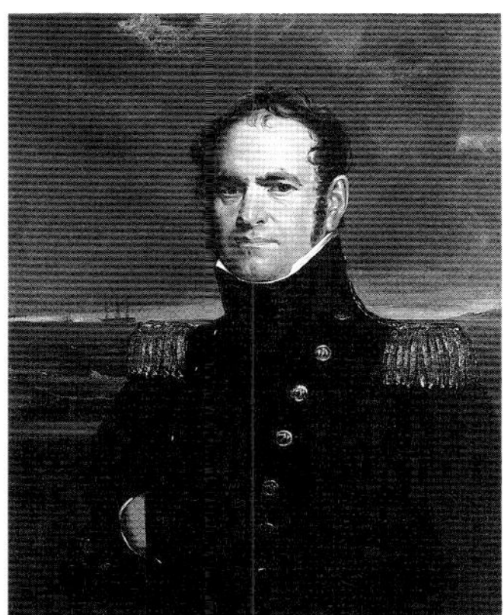

Commodore John Rodgers, c. 1814
Canvas, 0.912 x 0.711 ($35\frac{7}{8}$ x 28)
Gift of Nannie R. and Christina Macomb
1943.14.1

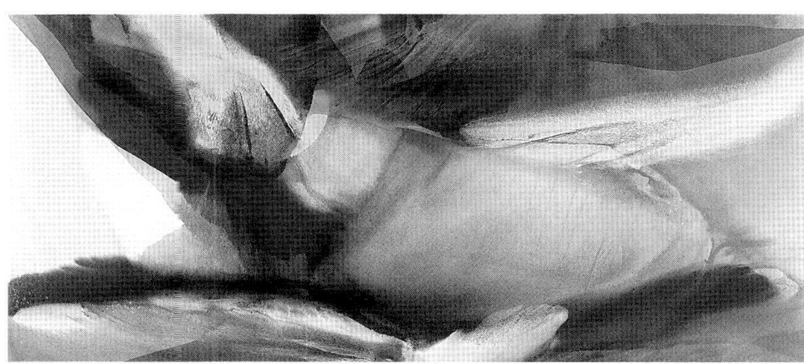

PAUL JENKINS
born 1923

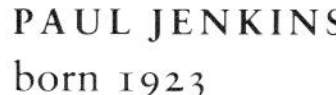

Phenomena Sound of Sundials, 1971
Canvas, 2.139 x 4.570 ($84\frac{1}{4}$ x 180)
Inscribed at lower left: *Paul Jenkins*
Gift of Vincent Melzac
1972.45.1

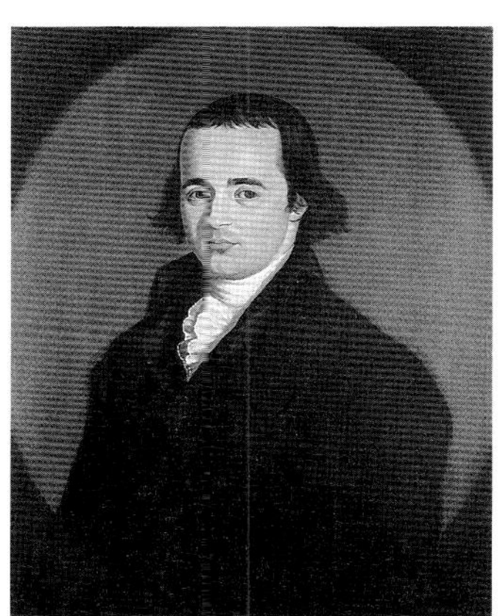

WILLIAM JENNYS
active 1793/1807

Asa Benjamin, 1795
Canvas, 0.762 x 0.635 (30 x 25)
Gift of Edgar William and Bernice Chrysler Garbisch
1953.5.19

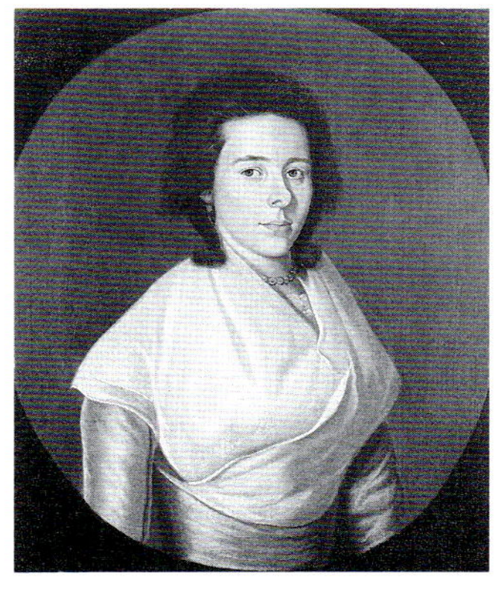

Mrs. Asa Benjamin, 1795
Canvas, 0.756 x 0.635 (29¾ x 25)
Gift of Edgar William and Bernice Chrysler Garbisch
1953.5.20

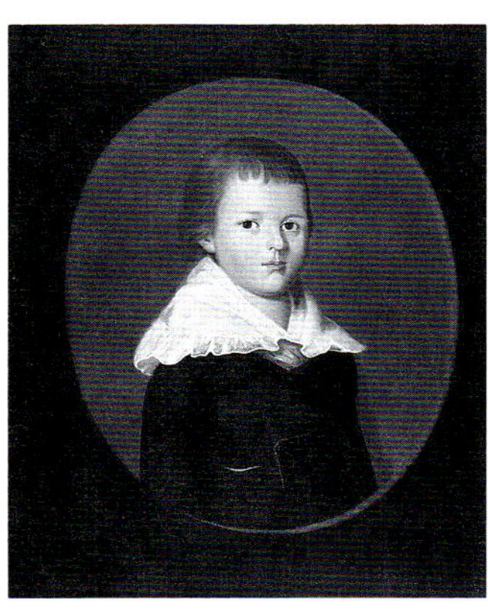

Everard Benjamin, 1795
Canvas, 0.762 x 0.635 (30 x 25)
Gift of Edgar William and Bernice Chrysler Garbisch
1953.5.21

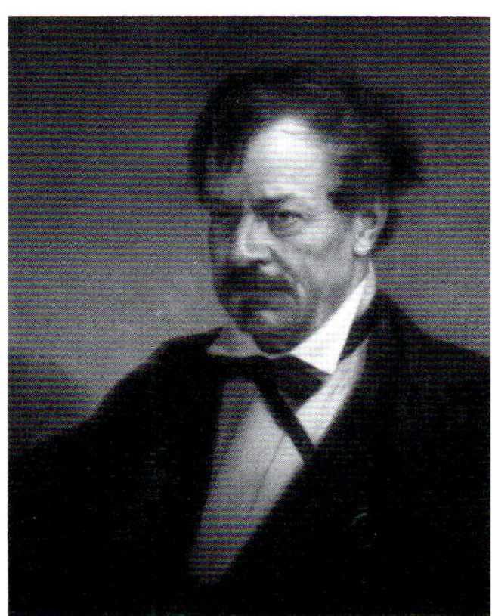

DAVID JOHNSON
1827–1908

Edwin Forrest, 1871
Canvas, 0.613 x 0.511 (24⅛ x 20⅛)
Inscribed at center left: *David Johnson. / 1871.*
Andrew W. Mellon Collection
1947.17.62

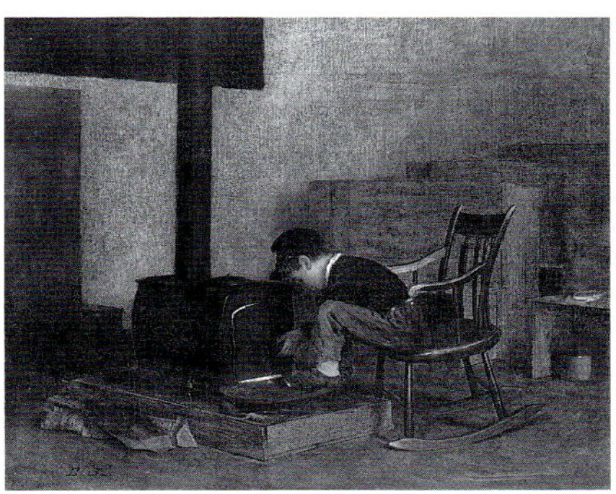

EASTMAN JOHNSON
1824–1906

The Early Scholar, c. 1865
Academy board on canvas, 0.432 x 0.537 (17 x 21⅛)
Inscribed at lower left: *E.J-*
Chester Dale Collection
1963.10.157

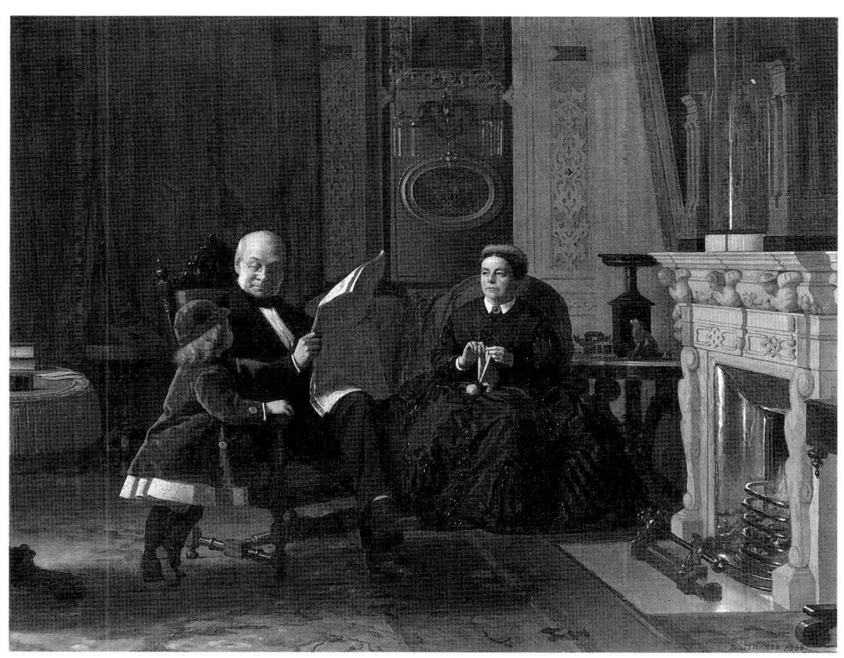

The Brown Family, 1869
Paper mounted on canvas, 0.593 x 0.724 (23⅝ x 28½)
Inscribed at lower right: *E. Johnson / 1869*
Gift of David Edward Finley and Margaret Eustis Finley
1978.72.1

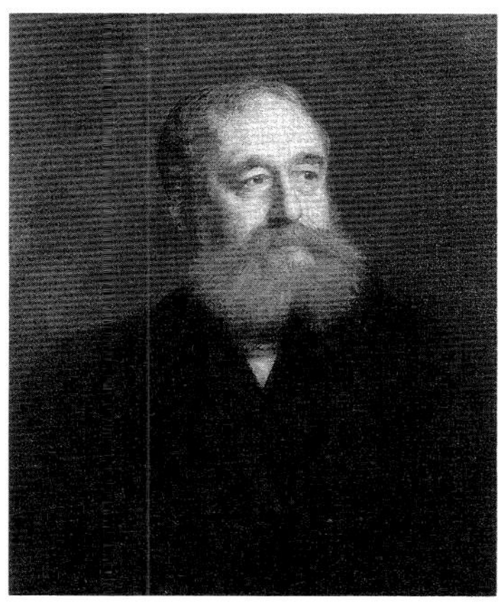

Joseph Wesley Harper, Jr., c. 1885
Canvas, 0.692 x 0.565 (27¼ x 22¼)
Inscribed at lower left: *EJ*
Andrew W. Mellon Collection
1947.17.63

JOSHUA JOHNSON
active 1796/1824

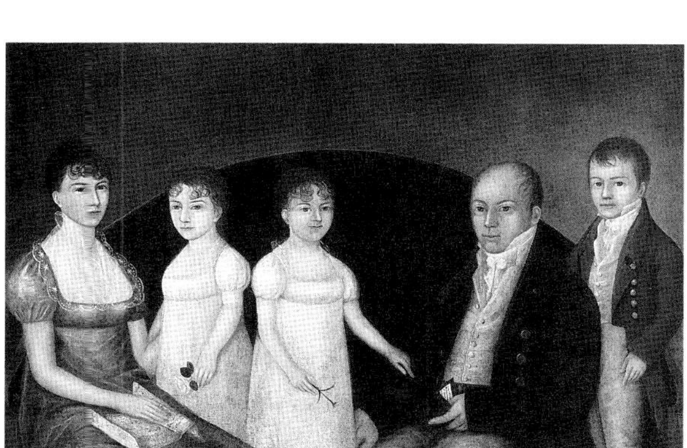

Family Group, c. 1800
Canvas, 0.885 x 1.360 (34⅞ x 53½)
Gift of Edgar William and Bernice Chrysler Garbisch
1980.61.3

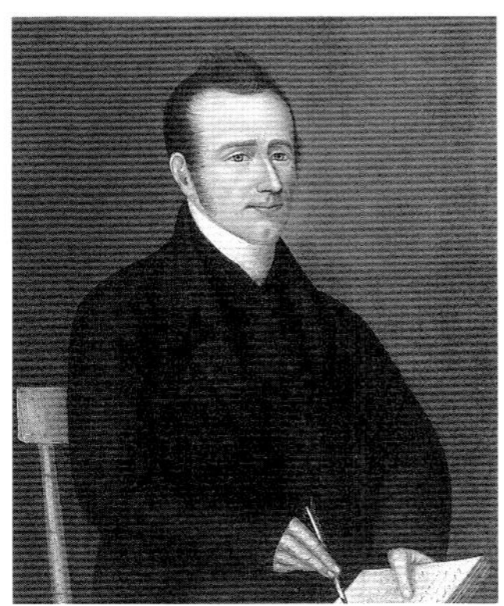

Mr. Baylor, c. 1805
Canvas, 0.610 x 0.500 (24 x 19 13/16)
Gift of Edgar William and Bernice Chrysler Garbisch
1978.80.8

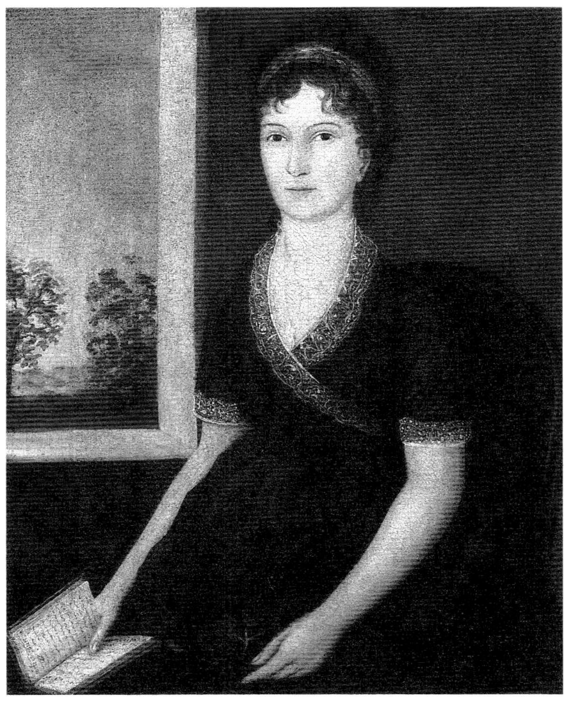

Sarah Ogden Gustin, c. 1805
Canvas, 0.711 x 0.572 (28 x 22½)
Inscribed at lower left on top right hand page of book: *JOSHU[A] JOHNSON*; and below: *J.J.* (in monogram)
Gift of Edgar William and Bernice Chrysler Garbisch
1971.83.7

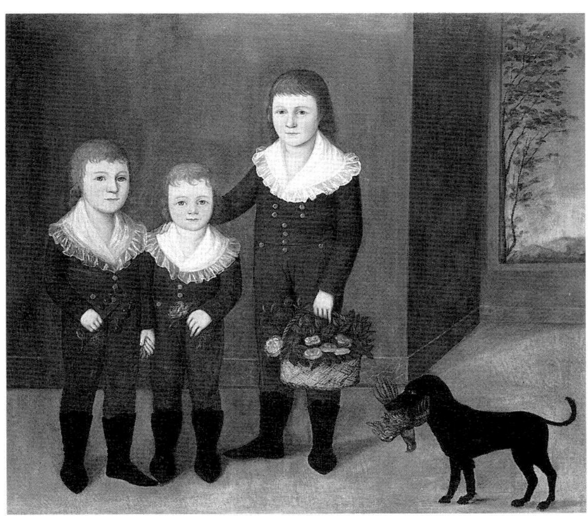

The Westwood Children, c. 1807
Canvas, 1.045 x 1.170 (41⅛ x 46)
Gift of Edgar William and Bernice Chrysler Garbisch
1959.11.1

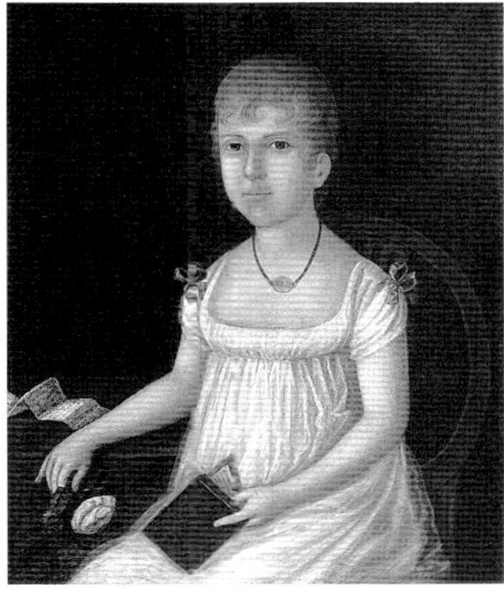

Adelina Morton, c. 1810
Canvas, 0.615 x 0.514 (24 3/8 x 20 1/4)
Gift of Edgar William and Bernice Chrysler Garbisch
1980.61.4

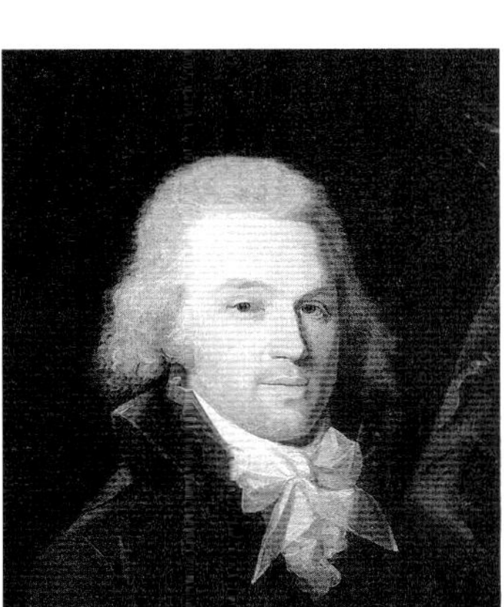

JOHN JOHNSTON
1753–1818

John Peck, c. 1795
Canvas, 0.635 x 0.479 (25 x 18 7/8)
Andrew W. Mellon Collection
1947.17.65

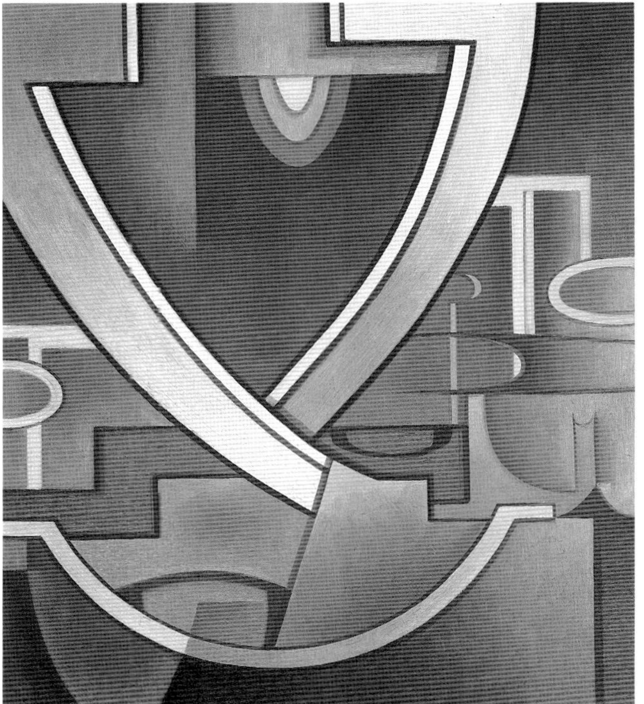

RAYMOND JONSON
1891–1982

Variations on a Rhythm—U, 1933
Canvas, 0.838 x 0.737 (33 x 29)
Inscribed at lower center: 33 / *Jonson*
Gift of Dr. and Mrs. Robert Fishman
1988.72.1

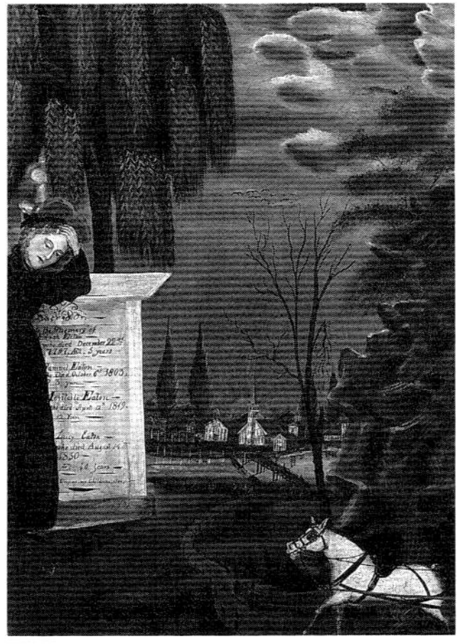

SAMUEL JORDAN
1803/1804–1831 or after

Eaton Family Memorial, 1831
Canvas, 0.55[illegible] x 0.394 (21⅞ x 15½)
Inscribed at center left on base of memorial: *S.J Sc 1831;* center left on memorial: *to the Memory of / Ednah Eaton / who died December 22nd / 1797, AEt, 3 years / Samuel Eaton / [w]ho Died October 6th 1803, / [. . .] years/ [M]ehitable Eaton / [w]ho died April 12, 1819 / 12 Years / Lucy Eaton / who died August 14th / 1830 / AEt 40 years / Sleep on, my Children, sleep / S.J. sc 1831*
Gift of Edgar William and Bernice Chrysler Garbisch
1955.11.9

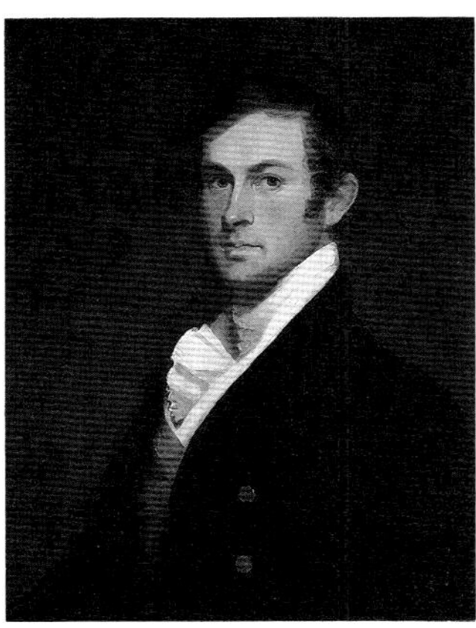

MATTHEW HARRIS JOUETT
1787/1788–1827

Augustus Fielding Hawkins, c. 1820
Wood, 0.690 x 0.535 (27¼ x 21)
Andrew W. Mellon Collection
1942.8.6

ELLSWORTH KELLY
born 1923

White Curve VIII, 1976
Canvas, 2.440 x 1.954 (96$^{1}/_{16}$ x 76$^{15}/_{16}$)
Gift of Mr. and Mrs. Joseph Helman
1984.105.1

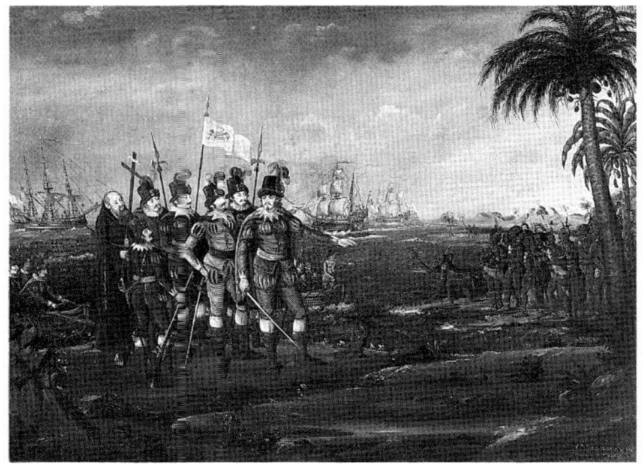

FREDERICK KEMMELMEYER
active 1788/1816

First Landing of Christopher Columbus, 1800/1805
Canvas, 0.701 x 0.926 (27⅝ x 36½)
Inscribed at lower left: *[Kemmelm]eyer Pin[xi]t th[. . .] January 180[. . .]*;
lower right: *First Landing of / CR. COLUMBUS at the / Ifland St. SALVADOR South / AMERICA the 11th Octo[ber]*
Gift of Edgar William and Bernice Chrysler Garbisch
1966.13.3

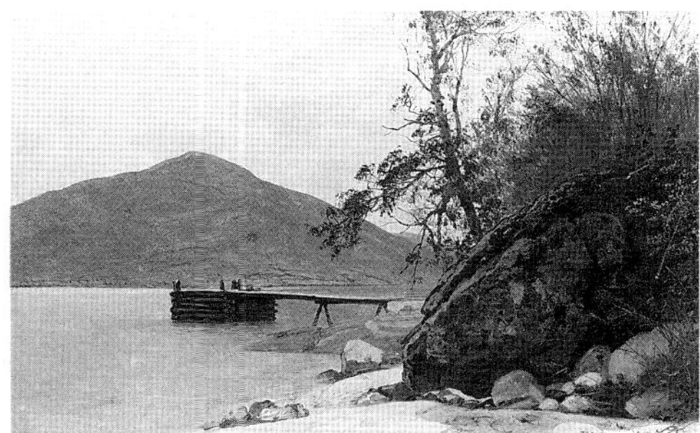

JOHN FREDERICK KENSETT
1816–1872

Landing at Sabbath Day Point, Lake George, c. 1850/1853
Canvas, 0.254 x 0.399 (10 x 15¾)
Inscribed at lower right: *JF.K.* (JF in monogram)
Gift of Mrs. Sigourney Thayer
1968.7.1

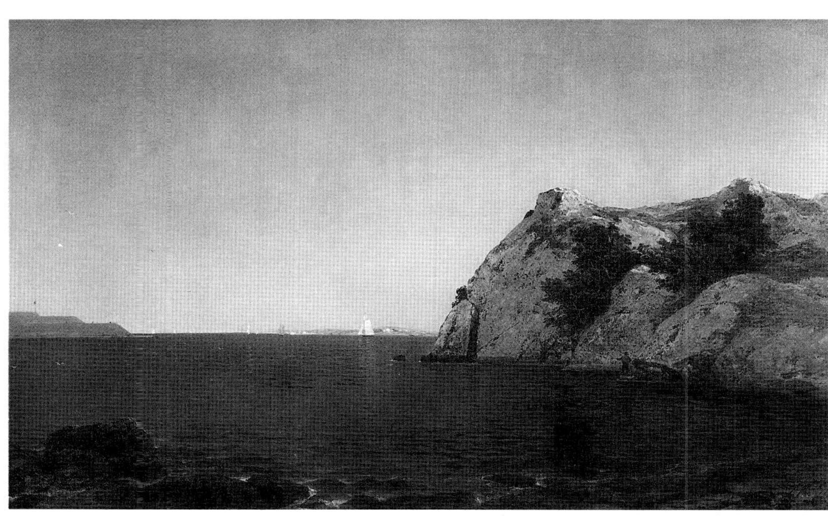

Beacon Rock, Newport Harbor, 1857
Canvas, 0.572 x 0.914 (22½ x 36)
Inscribed at lower right: *JF. K.* (JF in monogram) 57
Gift of Frederick Sturges, Jr.
1953.1.1

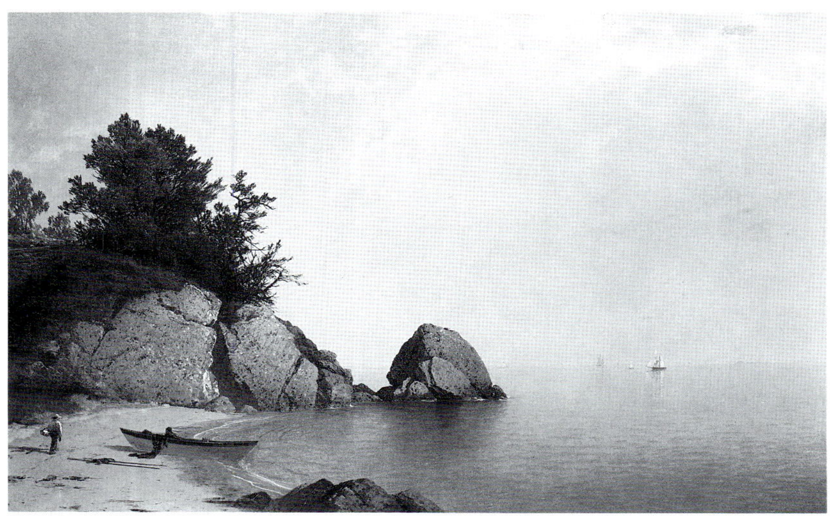

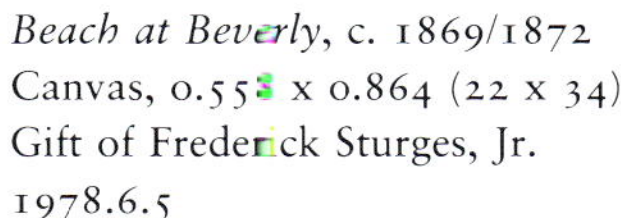

Beach at Beverly, c. 1869/1872
Canvas, 0.558 x 0.864 (22 x 34)
Gift of Frederick Sturges, Jr.
1978.6.5

FRANZ KLINE
1910–1962

Four Square, 1956
Canvas, 1.990 x 1.289 (78⅜ x 50¾)
Gift of Mr. and Mrs. Burton Tremaine
1971.87.12

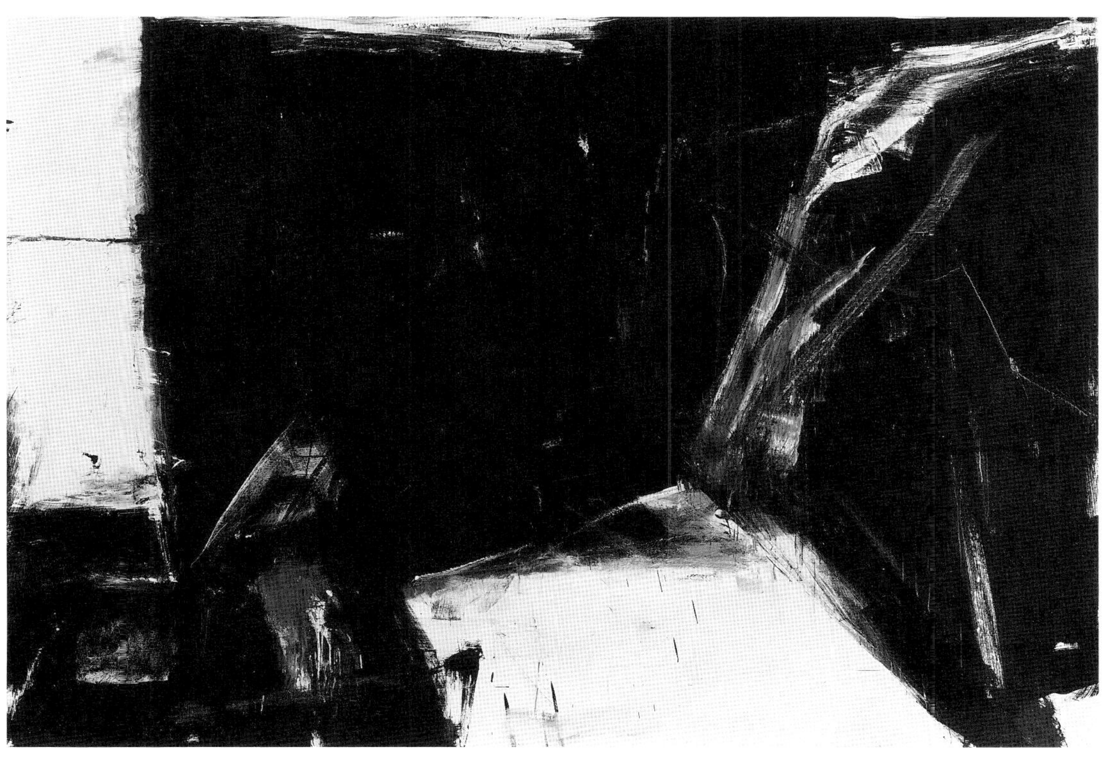

C & O, 1958
Canvas, 1.956 x 2.794 (77 x 110)
Gift of Mr. and Mrs. Burton Tremaine
1971.87.4

KARL KNATHS
1891–1971

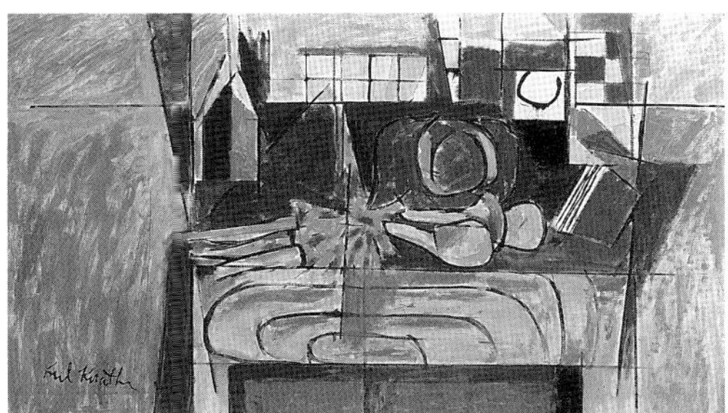

Marble Mantel, 1966
Canvas, 0.762 x 1.277 (30 x 50⅓)
Inscribed at lower left: *Karl Knaths*
Paul Mellon Collection
1984.29.1

BILL KOMODORE
born 1932

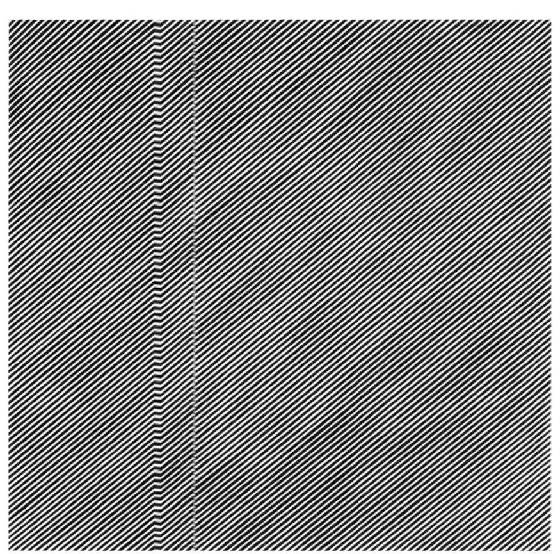

Vermont, 1964
Canvas, 1.599 x 1.594 (63 x 62¾)
Gift of Mr. and Mrs. Burton Tremaine
1971.87.5

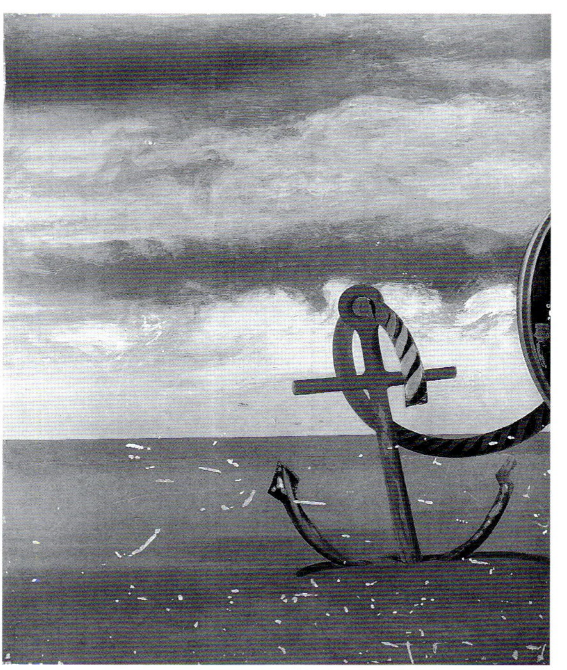

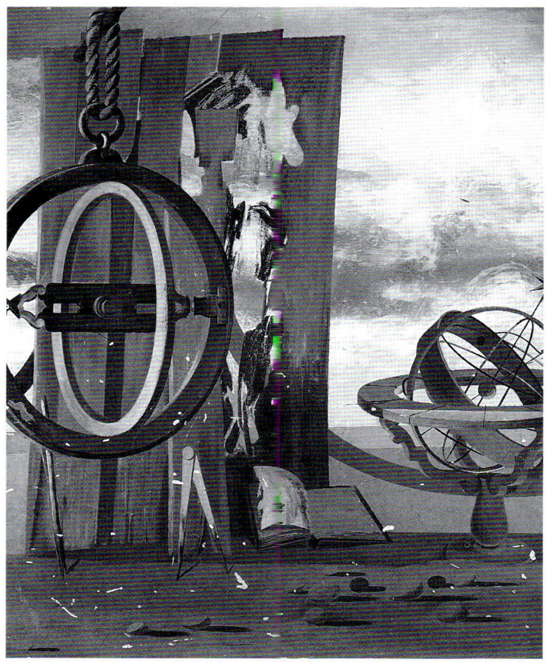

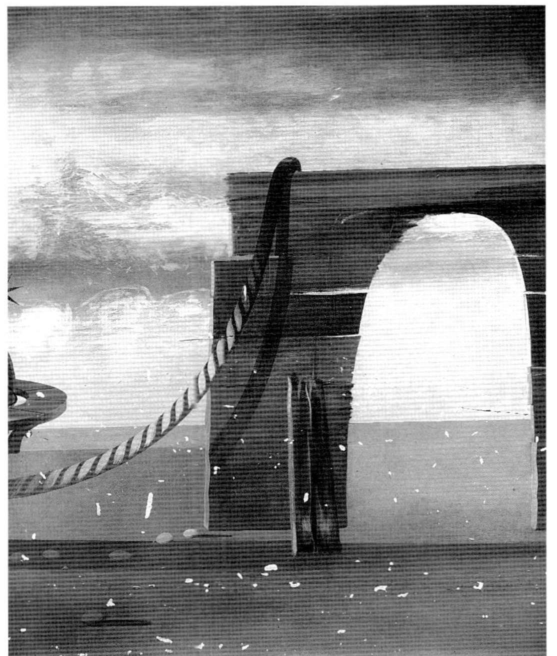

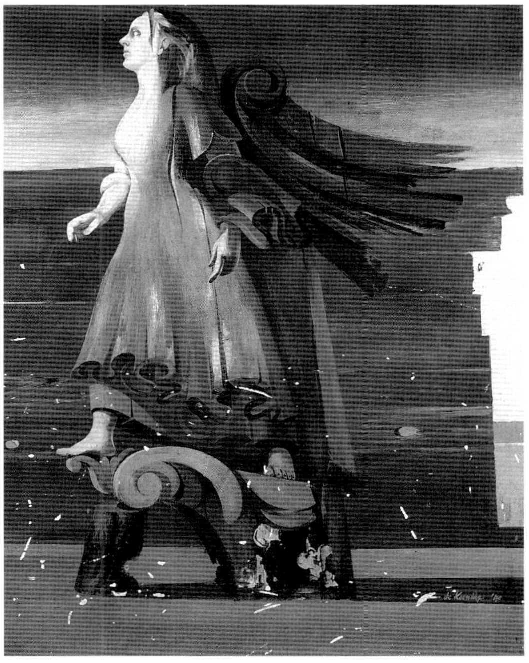

WILLEM DE KOONING
born 1904

Legend and Fact, 1940
Gypsum board, far left panel: 1.524 x 1.219 (60 x 48); middle left panel: 1.507 x 1.219 (59⅟16 x 48); middle right panel: 1.521 x 1.219 (59⅞ x 48); far right panel: 1.529 x 1.179 (60³⁄16 x 46⁵⁄16)
Inscribed at lower right on far right panel: *de Kooning '40*
Transferred from the Department of Commerce, Maritime Commission
1971.52.1a-d

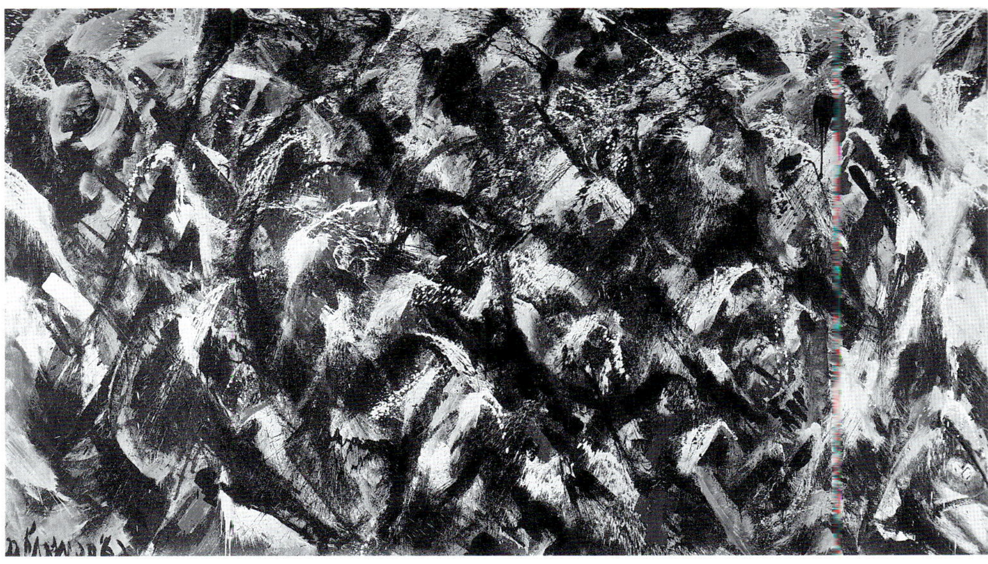

LEE KRASNER
1908–1984

Cobalt Night, 1962
Canvas, 2.375 x 4.099 (93½ x 161⅜)
Inscribed at lower left: *Lee Krasner '62*
Gift of Lila Acheson Wallace
1984.40.1

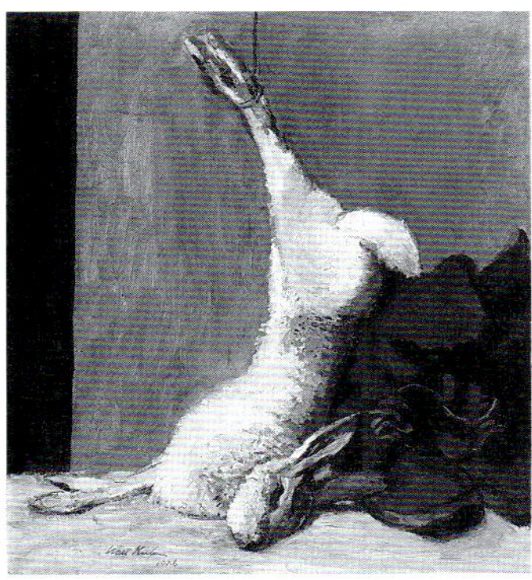

WALT KUHN
1877–1949

Hare and Hunting Boots, 1926
Canvas, 0.736 x 0.685 (29 x 27)
Inscribed at lower left: *Walt Kuhn / 1926*
Gift of the W. Averell Harriman Foundation in memory of Marie N. Harriman
1972.9.15

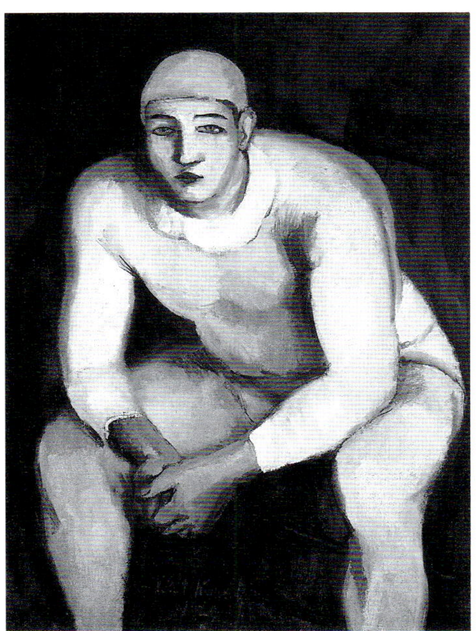

The White Clown, 1929
Canvas, 1.023 x 0.769 (40¼ x 30¼)
Inscribed at lower center: *Walt Kuhn / 1929*
Gift of the W. Averell Harriman Foundation in memory of Marie N. Harriman
1972.9.16

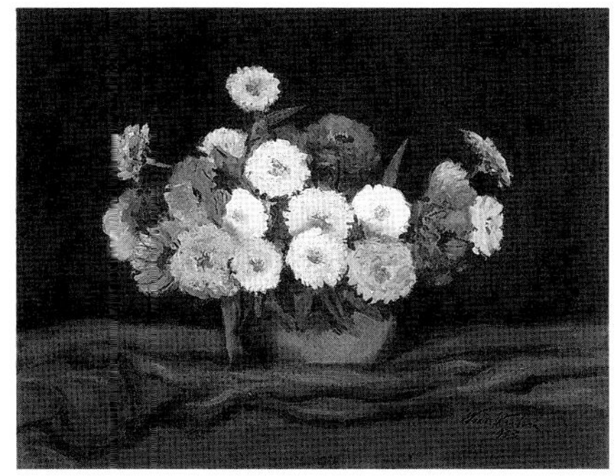

Zinnias, 1933
Canvas, 0.636 x 0.765 (25 x 30⅛)
Inscribed at lower right: *Walt Kuhn / 1933*
Gift of the W. Averell Harriman Foundation in memory of Marie N. Harriman
1972.9.17

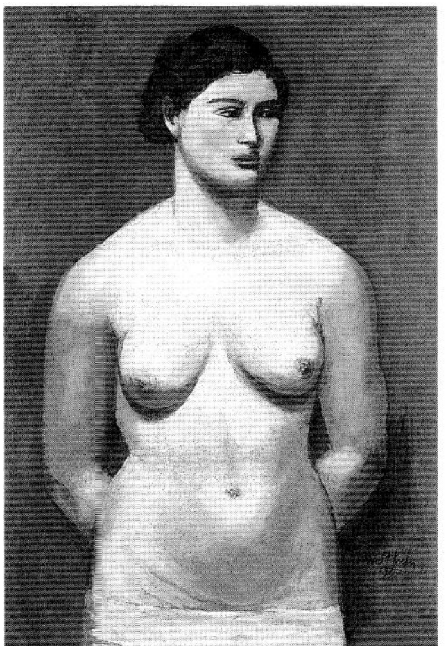

Dryad, 1935
Canvas, 0.864 x 0.586 (34 x 23)
Inscribed at lower right: *Walt Kuhn / 1935*
Gift of the W. Averell Harriman Foundation in memory of Marie N. Harriman
1972.9.13

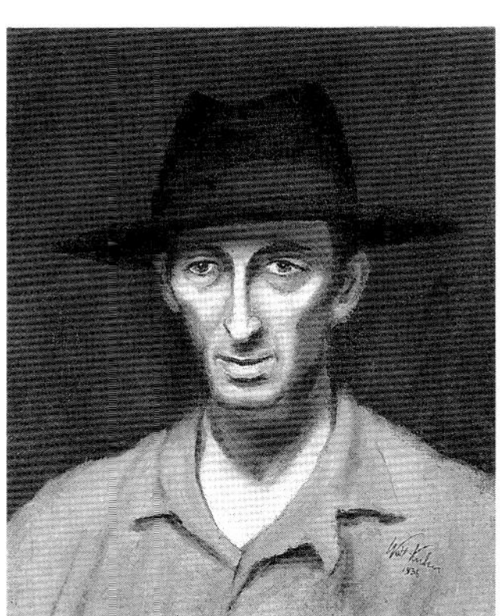

Wisconsin, 1936
Canvas, 0.508 x 0.407 (20 x 16)
Inscribed at lower right: *Walt Kuhn / 1936*
Gift of Brenda Kuhn
1968.25.1

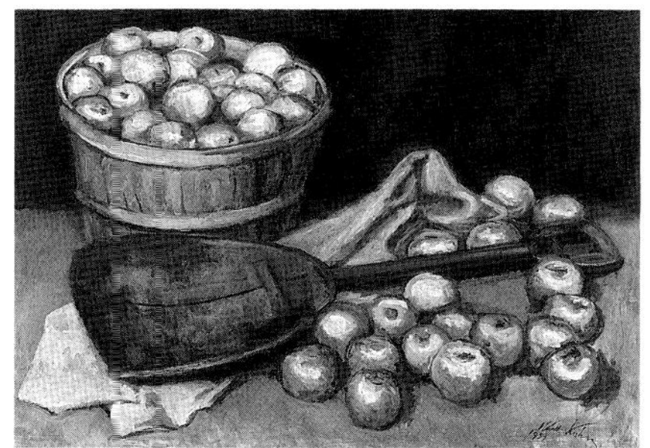

Green Apples and Scoop, 1939
Canvas, 0.770 x 1.023 (30¼ x 40¼)
Inscribed at lower right: *Walt Kuhn / 1939*
Gift of the W. Averell Harriman Foundation in memory of Marie N. Harriman
1972.9.14

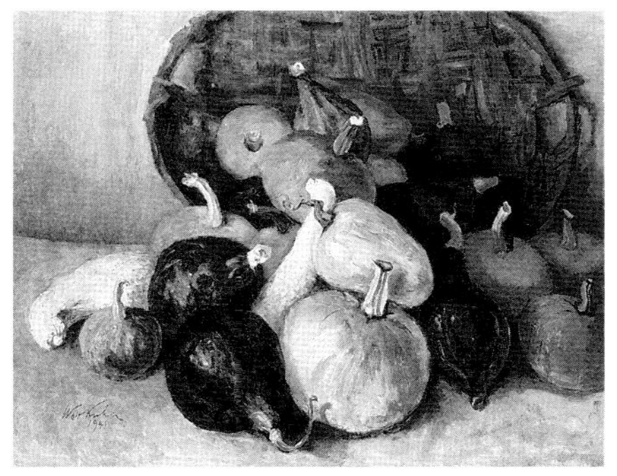

Pumpkins, 1941
Canvas, 1.016 x 1.277 (40 x 50¼)
Inscribed at lower left: *Walt Kuhn / 1941*
Gift of the Avalon Foundation
1968.3.1

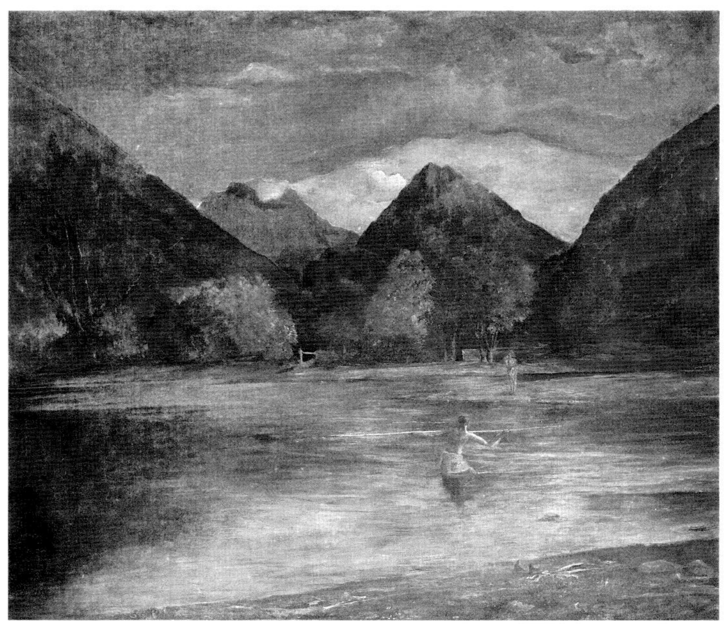

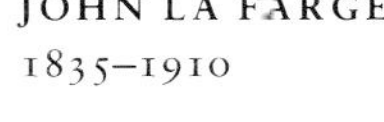

JOHN LA FARGE
1835–1910

The Entrance to the Tautira River, Tahiti
Fisherman Spearing a Fish, c. 1895
Canvas, 1.359 x 1.523 (53½ x 60)
Adolph Caspar Miller Fund
1966.6.1

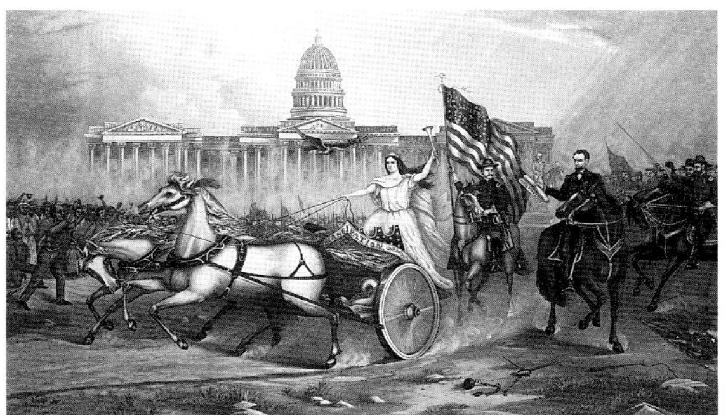

A. A. LAMB
active 1864 or later

Emancipation Proclamation, 1864 or later
Canvas, 0.825 x 1.372 (32⅜ x 54)
Inscribed at lower left on rock: *A. A. Lamb.*
Gift of Edgar William and Bernice Chrysler Garbisch
1955.11.10

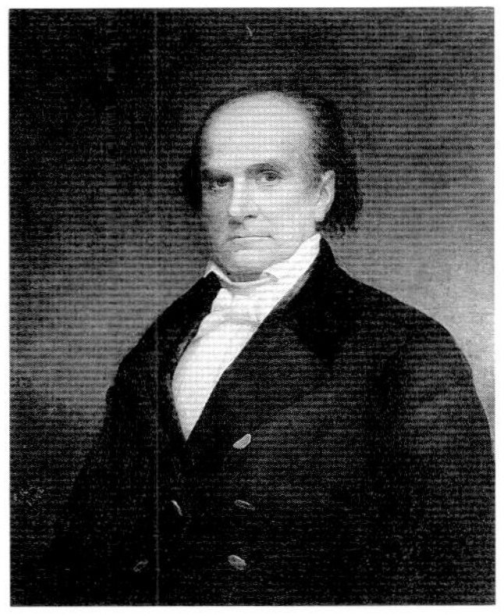

ATTRIBUTED TO
JAMES REID LAMBDIN
1807–1889

Daniel Webster, c. 1850
Canvas, 0.918 x 0.740 (36⅛ x 29⅛)
Inscribed by a later hand, lower left:
JRL / 1848
Andrew W. Mellon Collection
1954.1.1

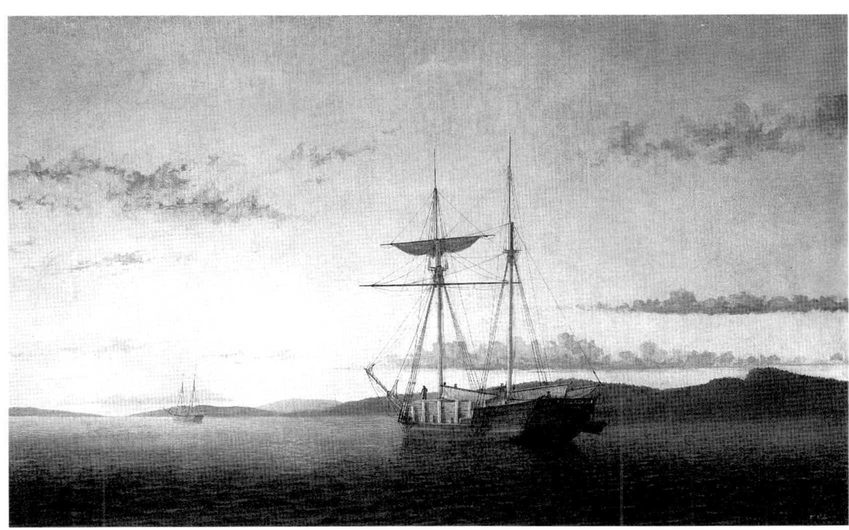

FITZ HUGH LANE
1804–1865

Lumber Schooners at Evening on Penobscot Bay, 1860
Canvas, 0.625 x 0.968 (24⅝ x 38⅛)
Inscribed at lower right: *F. H. Lane / 1860*
Andrew W. Mellon Fund and Gift of Mr. and Mrs. Francis W. Hatch, Sr.
1980.29.1

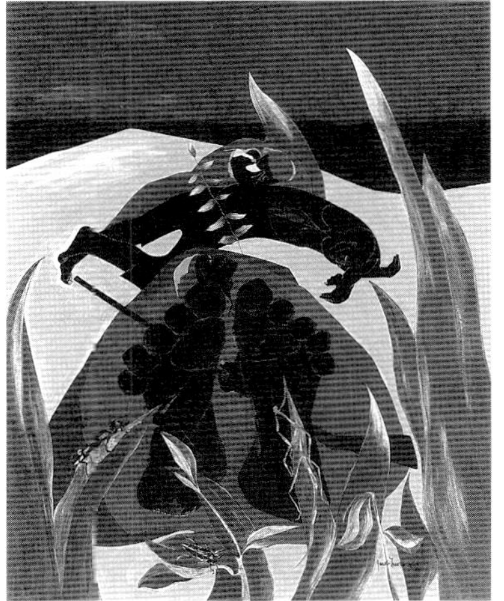

JACOB LAWRENCE
born 1917

Daybreak—A Time to Rest, 1967
Hardboard, 0.762 x 0.610 (30 x 24)
Inscribed at lower right: *Jacob Lawrence 67*
Anonymous Gift
1973.8.1

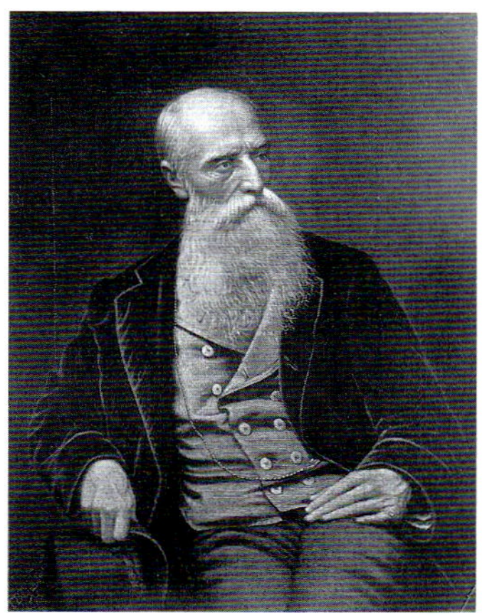

THOMAS BAYLEY LAWSON
1807–1888

William Morris Hunt, 1879
Canvas, 0.460 x 0.359 (18⅛ x 14⅛)
Inscribed at lower left: *T. B. Lawson / 1879*
Andrew W. Mellon Collection
1947.17.68

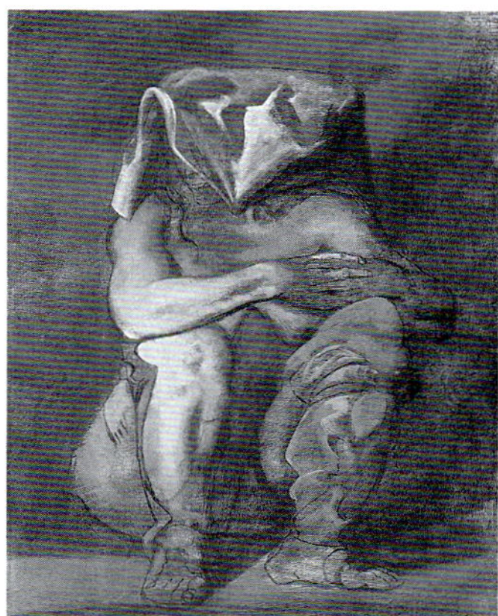

RICO LEBRUN
1900–1964

The Ragged One, 1944
Canvas, 1.172 x 0.918 (46⅛ x 36⅛)
Inscribed at lower right: *Lebrun 1944*
Gift of Michael Straight
1974.87.2

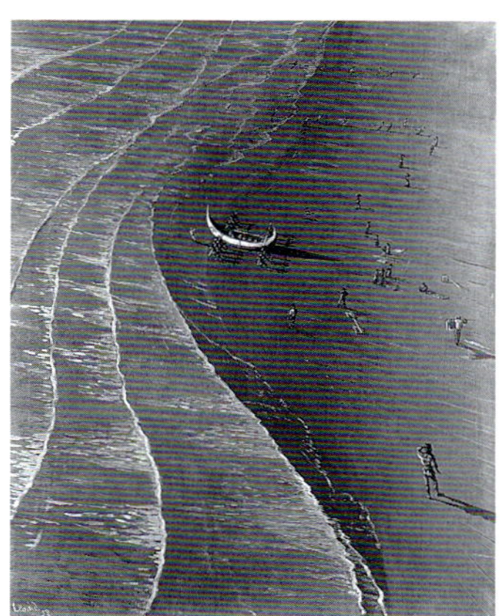

LEONID
1896–1976

Faraduro, Portugal, 1952
Canvas, 1.016 x 0.813 (40 x 32)
Inscribed at lower left: *Leonid. / 52.*
Gift of the Avalon Foundation
1952.12.1

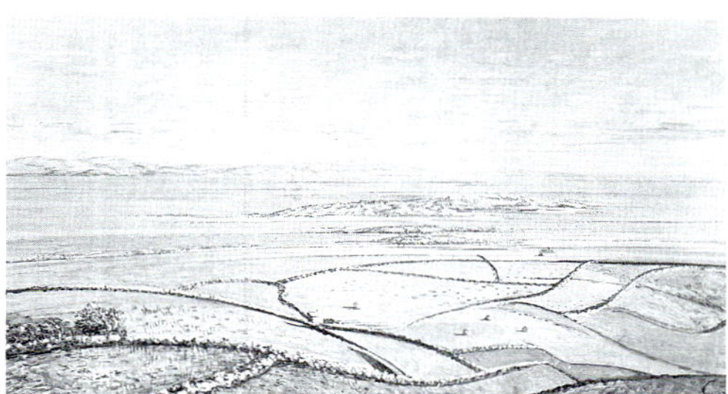

Derrynane Harbor, Ireland, 1961
Canvas, 0.511 x 0.920 (20⅛ x 36¼)
Inscribed at lower right: *L. 61*
Ailsa Mellon Bruce Collection
1970.17.124

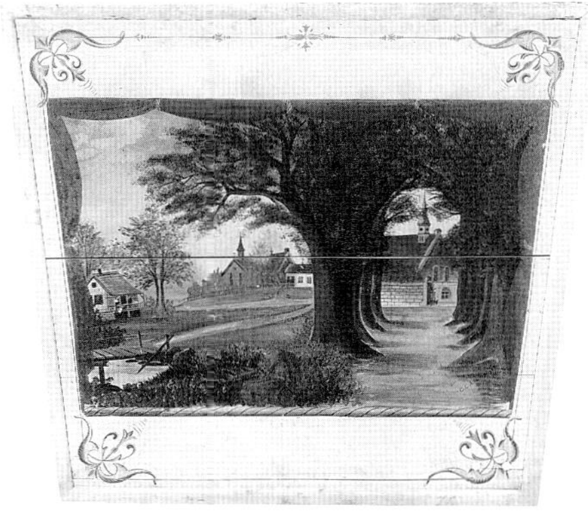

CHARLES C. E. LERMOND
1858–1944

Landscape with Churches, c. 1890/1930
Wood, trapezoidal sleighback; overall height: 0.892 (35½); width at top: 1.019 (40⅛); width at bottom: 0.832 (32⅔)
Inscribed at lower right: *C.C.E. Lermond*
Gift of Edgar William and Bernice Chrysler Garbisch
1953.5.23

ALEXANDER LIBERMAN
born 1912

Omega IV, 1961
Canvas, 1.525 x 0.940 (60 x 37)
Inscribed at upper right on reverse: *A. Liberman 1961*
Gift of Mr. and Mrs. Burton Tremaine
1977.75.4

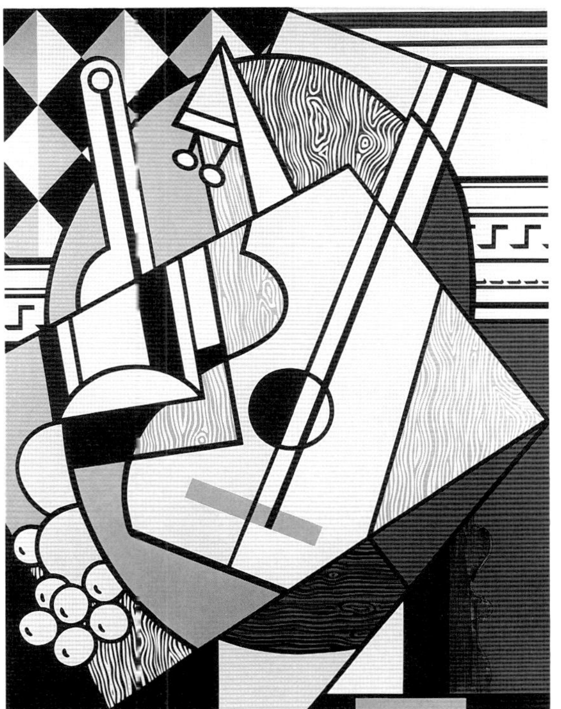

ROY LICHTENSTEIN
born 1923

Cubist Still Life, 1974
Canvas, 2.286 x 1.732 (90 x 68³⁄₁₆)
Gift of Lila Acheson Wallace
1983.50.1

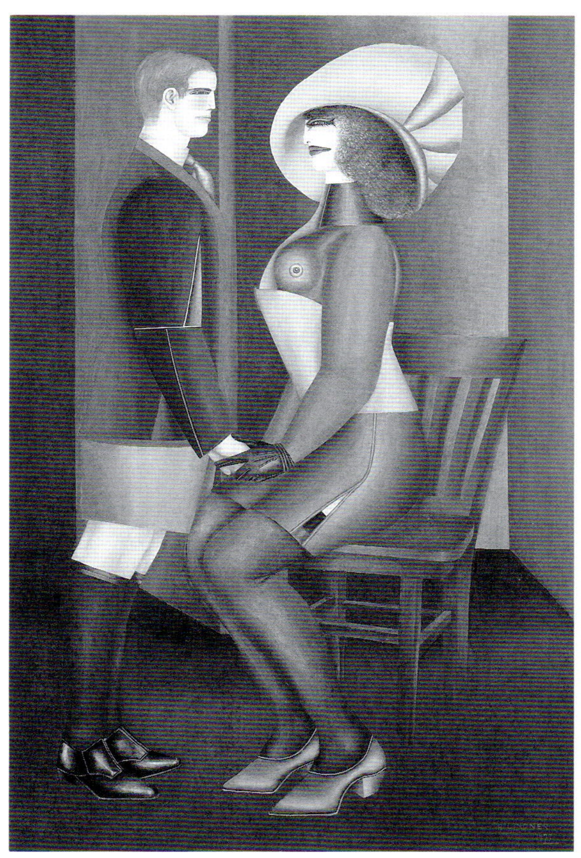

RICHARD LINDNER
1901–1978

Contact, 1977
Canvas, 2.032 x 1.375 (80 x 54⅛)
Inscribed at lower right: *R. LINDNER / 1977*
Gift of Denise Lindner
1986.73.1

MORRIS LOUIS
1912–1962

Beta Kappa, 1961
Canvas, 2.623 x 4.394 (103¼ x 173)
Gift of Marcella Louis Brenner
1970.21.1

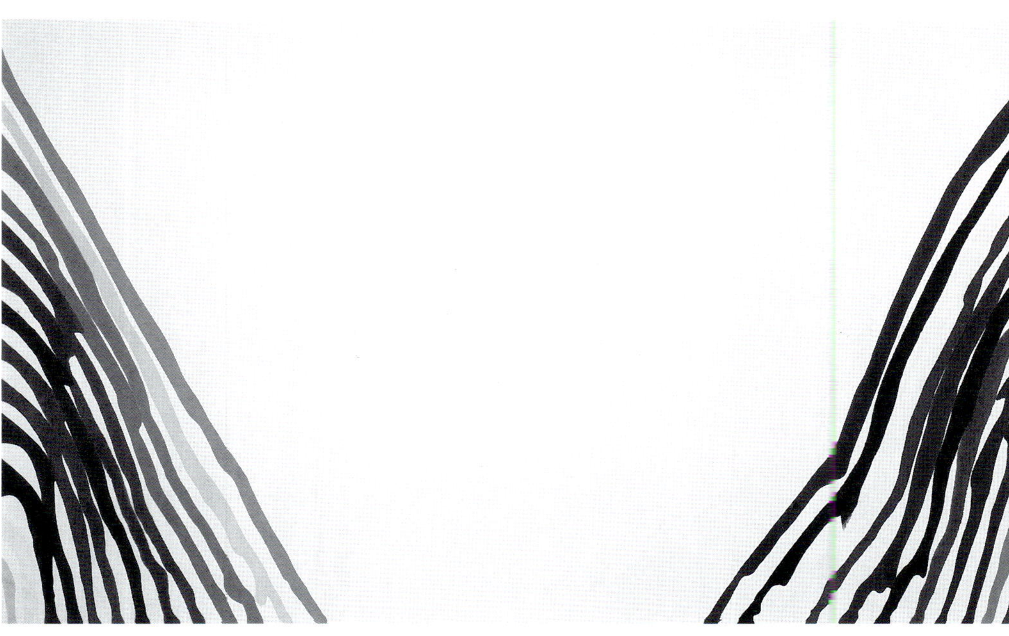

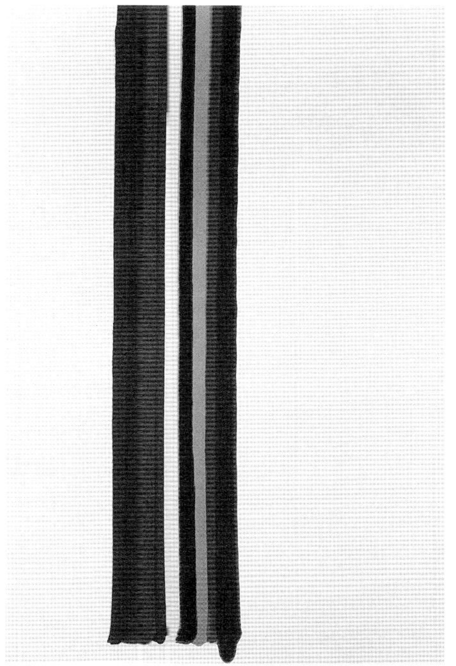

133, 1962
Canvas, 2.107 x 1.372 (83 x 54)
Gift of Mr. and Mrs. Burton Tremaine
1976.64.1

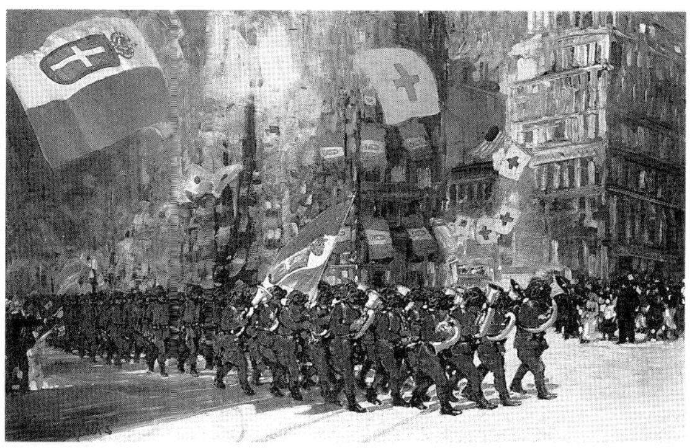

GEORGE BENJAMIN LUKS
1866–1933

The Bersaglieri, 1918
Canvas, 1.019 x 1.515 ($40\frac{1}{8}$ x $59\frac{5}{8}$)
Inscribed at lower left: *George Luks*
Gift of the Avalon Foundation
1950.5.1

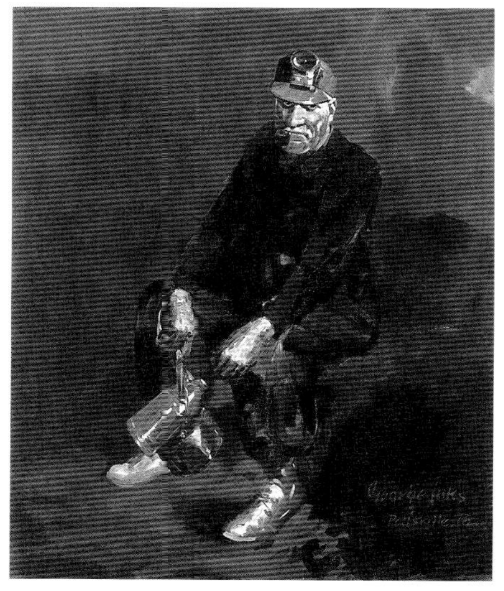

The Miner, 1925
Canvas, 1.531 x 1.280 ($60\frac{1}{4}$ x $50\frac{3}{8}$)
Inscribed at lower right: *George Luks / Pottsville. Pa.*
Chester Dale Collection
1954.2.1

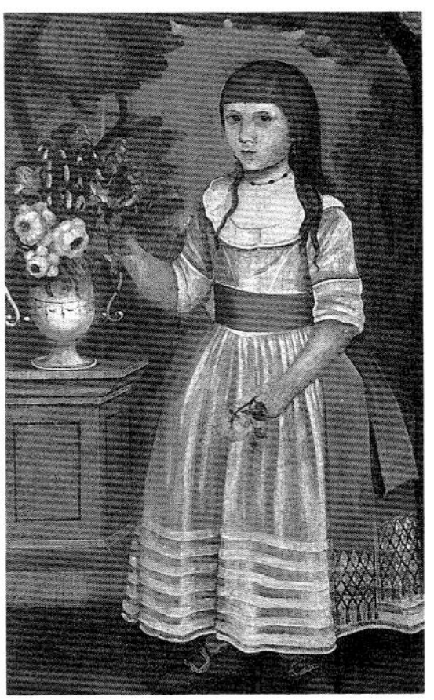

MACKAY
active 1791

Catherine Brewer, 1791
Canvas, 1.155 x 0.702 (45½ x 27⅝)
Inscribed at lower left: *Mackay Pinxt. [1]791*
Gift of Edgar William and Bernice Chrysler Garbisch
1956.13.5

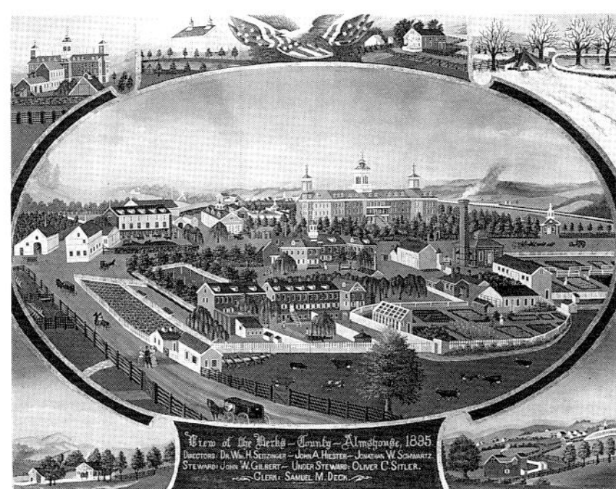

LOUIS MADER
1842–1899 or after

Berks County Almshouse, 1895, 1895
Metal, 0.829 x 1.007 (32⅝ x 39⅝)
Inscribed at lower right: *Louis Mader*; lower center: *View of the Berks-County-Almshouse, 1895. / DIRECTORS DR WM. H. SEITZINGER - JOHN A. HIESTER - JONATHAN W. SCHWARTZ. / STEWARD: JOHN W. GILBERT - UNDER STEWARD: OLIVER C. SITLER. / CLERK: SAMUEL M. DECK*
Gift of Edgar William and Bernice Chrysler Garbisch
1953.5.25

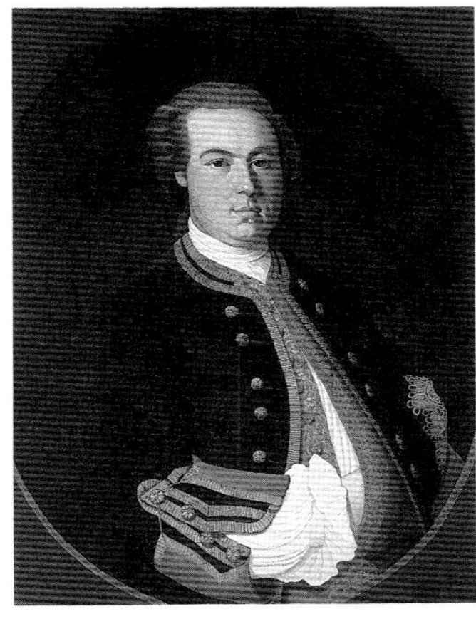

ATTRIBUTED TO
JOHN MARE
probably 1739–c. 1802

Robert Monckton, mid-18th century
Canvas, 0.787 x 0.607 (31 x 23⅞)
Inscribed at lower right: *Jn Mare. / Pinxt: / 1761*
Andrew W. Mellon Collection
1947.17.71

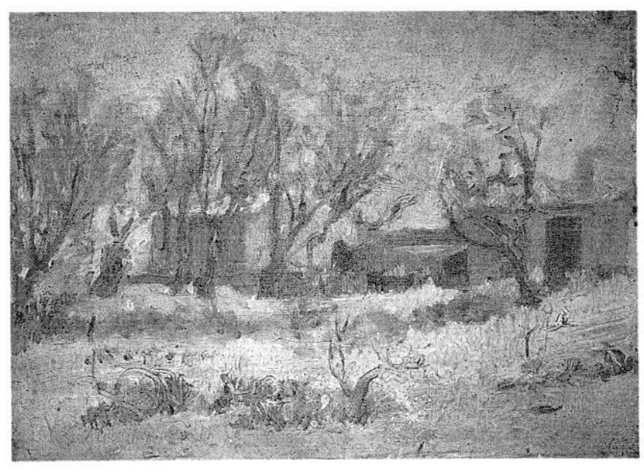

JOHN MARIN
1870–1953

Winter Landscape, c. 1900
Canvas, 0.228 x 0.295 (9 x 11⅝)
Gift of John Marin, Jr.
1986.54.1

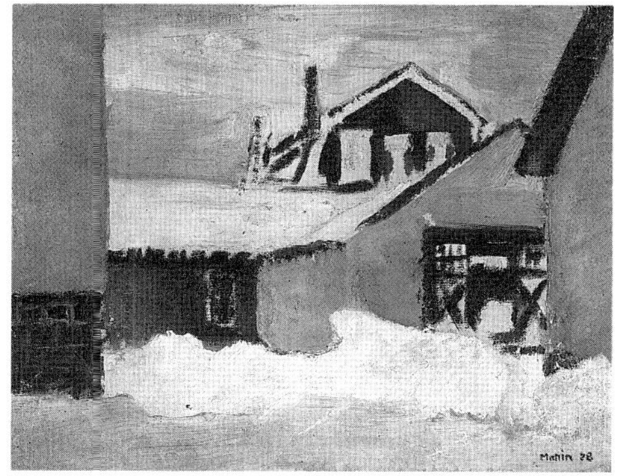

Buildings with Snowbank, Cliffside, New Jersey, 1928
Canvas board, 0.225 x 0.283 ($8\frac{7}{8}$ x $11\frac{1}{8}$)
Inscribed at lower right: *Marin 28*
Gift of John Marin, Jr.
1986.54.2

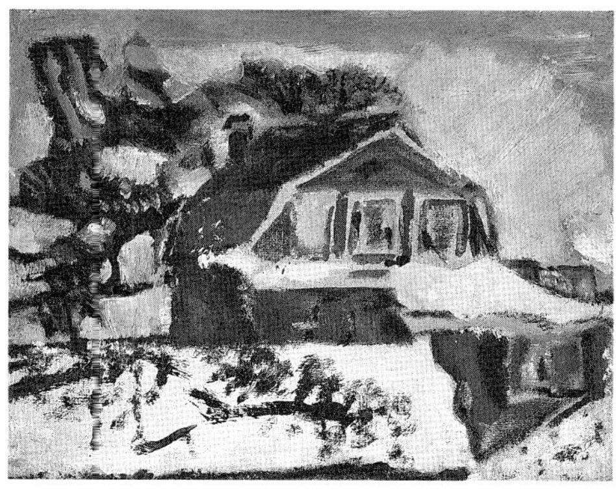

House with Dutch Roof, c. 1928
Canvas board, 0.203 x 0.250 (8 x $9\frac{7}{8}$)
Gift of John Marin, Jr.
1986.54.3

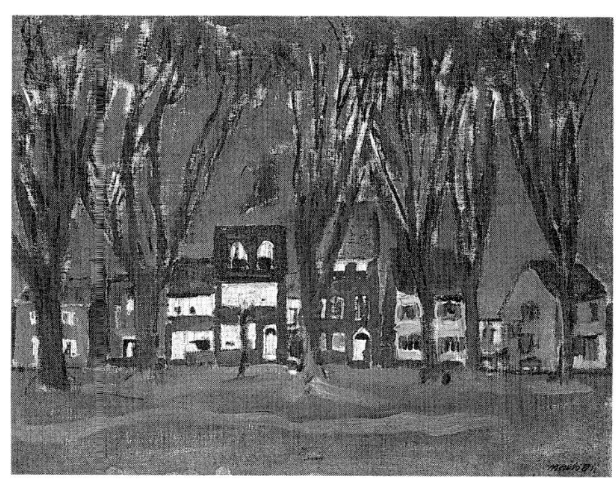

Houses and Trees, 1931
Canvas on cardboard, 0.350 x 0.450 (14 x $17\frac{3}{4}$)
Inscribed at lower right: *Marin 31*
Gift of John Marin, Jr.
1986.54.5

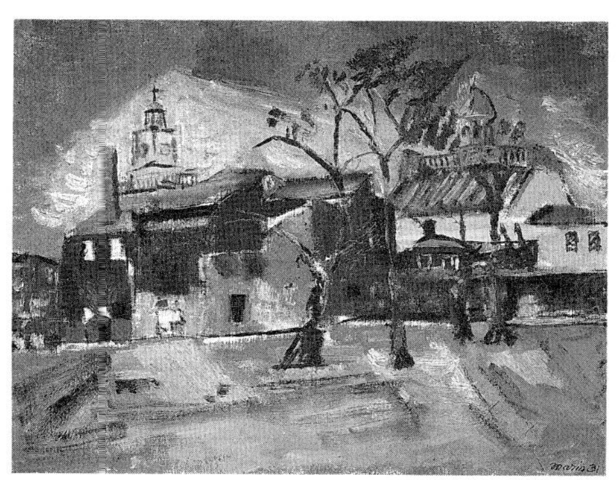

Landscape with Houses and Trees, 1931
Canvas on cardboard, 0.360 x 0.452 ($14\frac{3}{16}$ x $17\frac{13}{16}$)
Inscribed at lower right: *Marin 31*
Gift of John Marin, Jr.
1986.54.4

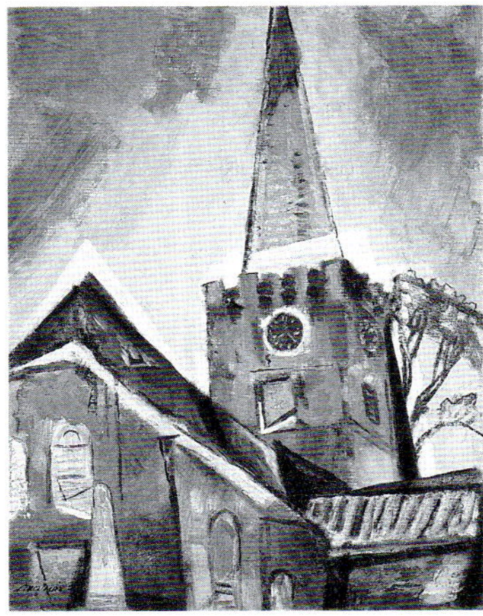

Old Swedish Church, New Castle, Delaware: Close View, 1931
Canvas on cardboard, 0.454 x 0.359 (17⅞ x 14⅛)
Inscribed at lower left: *Marin 31*
Gift of John Marin, Jr.
1986.54.6

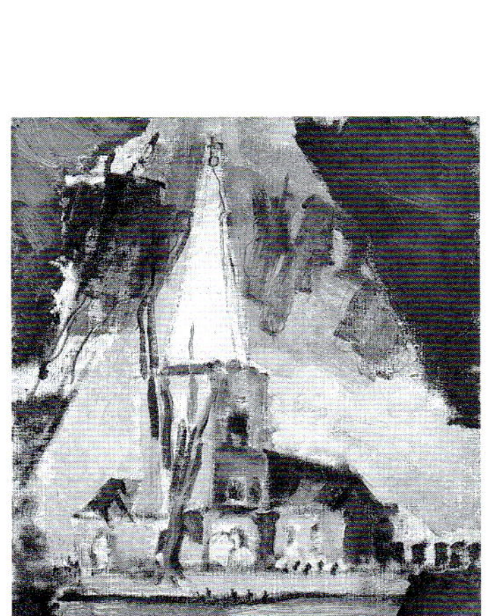

Old Swedish Church, New Castle, Delaware: Distant View, 1931
Canvas on cardboard, 0.451 x 0.355 (17¾ x 14)
Inscribed at lower right: *Marin 31*
Gift of John Marin, Jr.
1986.54.7

Grey Sea, 1938
Canvas, 0.559 x 0.711 (22 x 28)
Inscribed at lower right: *Marin 38*
Gift of Mr. and Mrs. John Marin, Jr.
1987.19.1

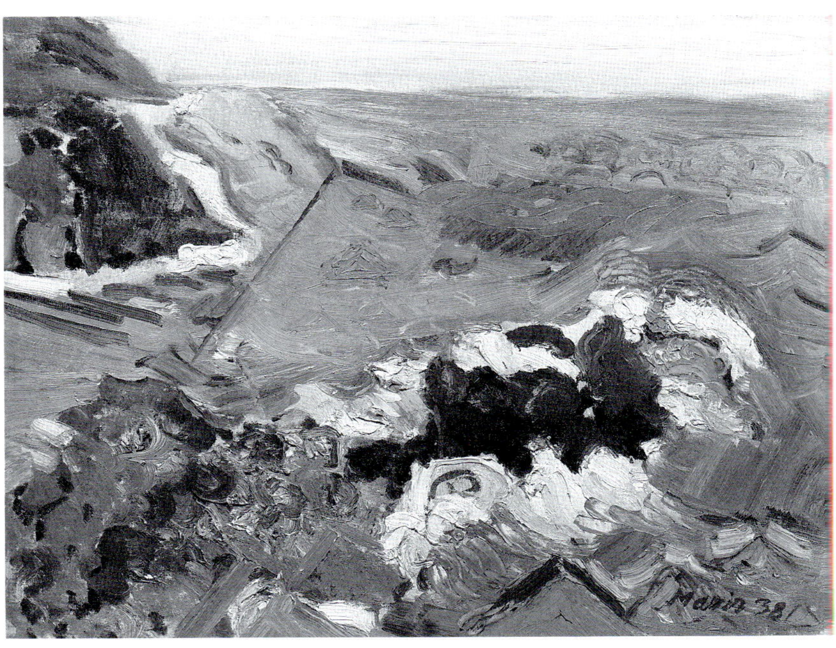

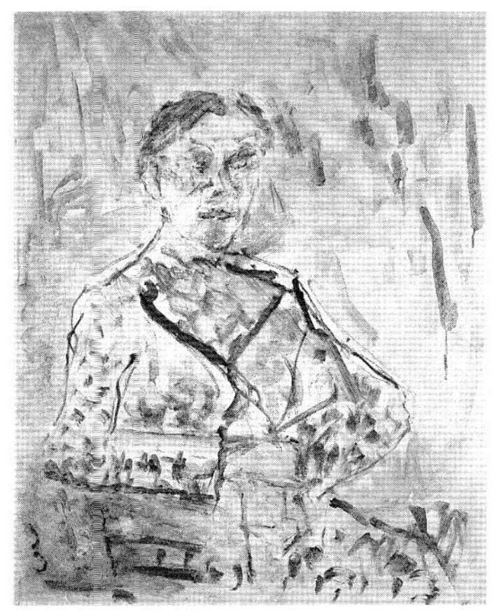

Mrs. John Marin, c. 1944
Canvas, 0.711 x 0.559 (28 x 22)
Gift of John Marin, Jr.
1986.54.8

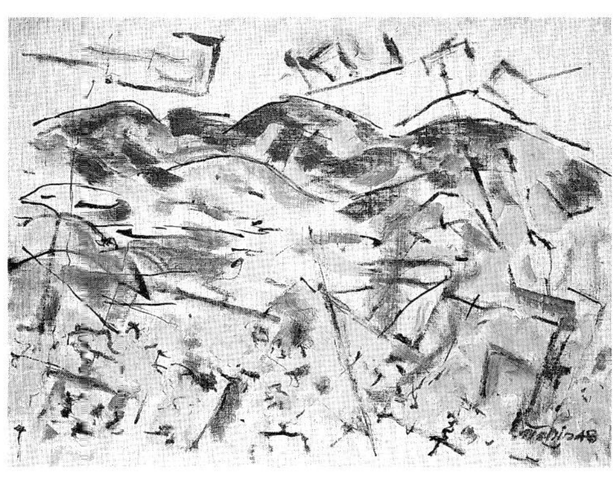

Tunk Mountains, Maine, 1948
Canvas board, 0.354 x 0.457
(13 15/16 x 18)
Inscribed at lower right: *Marin 48*
Gift of John Marin, Jr.
1986.54.9

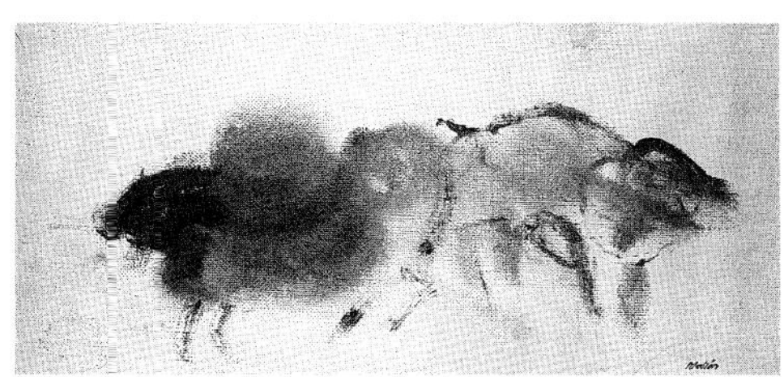

Sketch of Two Bison, c. 1950
Canvas on board, 0.136 x 0.281
(5 3/8 x 11 1/16)
Inscribed at lower right: *Marin*
Gift of John Marin, Jr.
1986.54.10

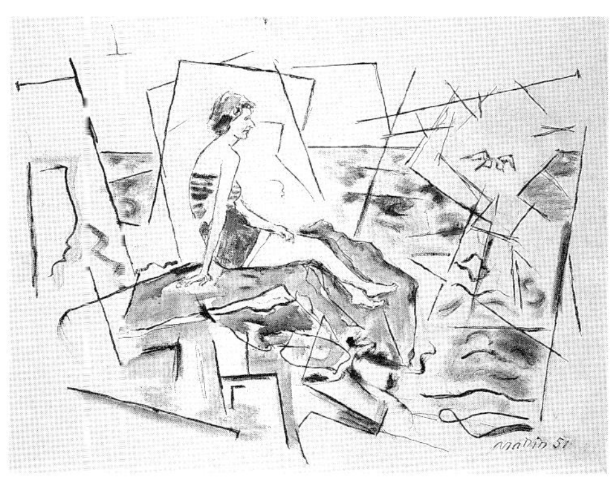

Bather Seated on Rocks, 1951
Canvas, 0.550 x 0.711 (21 7/8 x 28)
Inscribed at lower right: *Marin 51*
Gift of John Marin, Jr.
1986.54.11

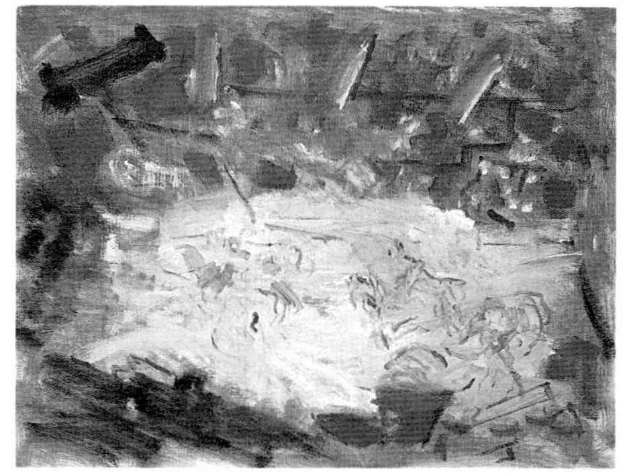

Untitled: Circus, c. 1953
Canvas, 0.559 x 0.711 (22 x 28)
Gift of John Marin, Jr.
1986.54.12

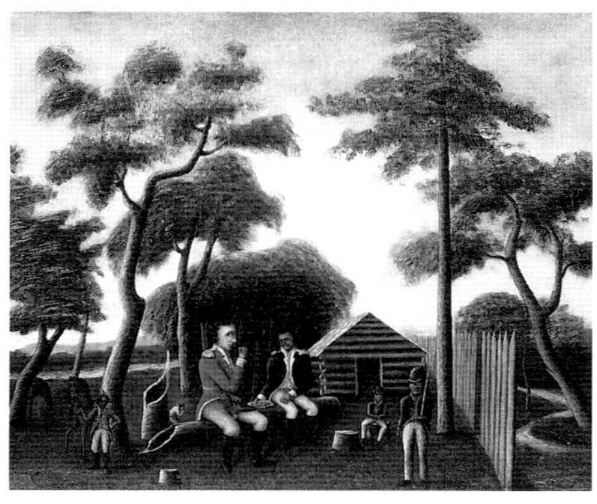

GEORGE WASHINGTON MARK
1795–1879

Marion Feasting the British Officer on Sweet Potatoes, 1848
Canvas, 0.810 x 0.951 ($31\frac{7}{8}$ x $37\frac{3}{8}$)
Gift of Edgar William and Bernice Chrysler Garbisch
1967.20.1

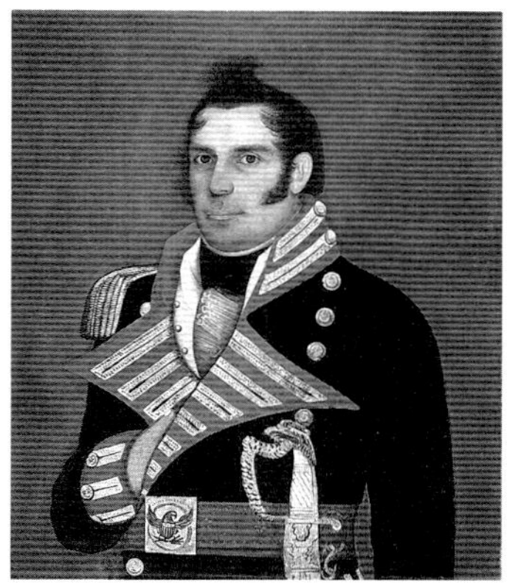

FREDERICK MAYHEW
1785–1854

John Harrisson, c. 1823
Canvas, 0.760 x 0.634 ($29\frac{15}{16}$ x $24\frac{15}{16}$)
Gift of Edgar William and Bernice Chrysler Garbisch
1980.62.16

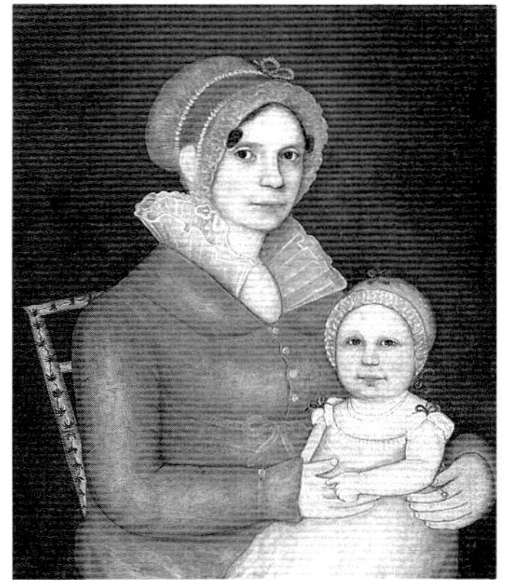

Mrs. John Harrisson and Daughter, c. 1823
Canvas, 0.760 x 0.635 ($29\frac{15}{16}$ x 25)
Gift of Edgar William and Bernice Chrysler Garbisch
1980.62.17

HOWARD MEHRING
1931–1978

Sequence, 1960
Canvas, 2.145 x 2.602 (84½ x 102½)
Gift of Horton and Chiyo Telford in grateful memory of the artist
1978.40.1

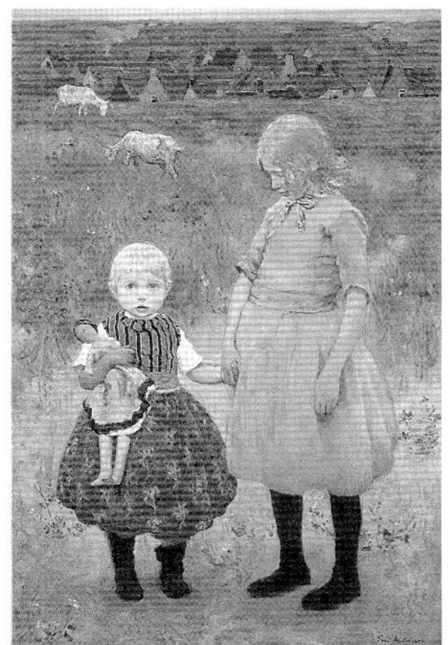

GARI MELCHERS
1860–1932

The Sisters, 1884/1900
Canvas, 1.505 x 1.008 (59¼ x 39⅝)
Inscribed at lower right: *Gari Melchers*
Gift of Curt H. Reisinger
1957.4.2

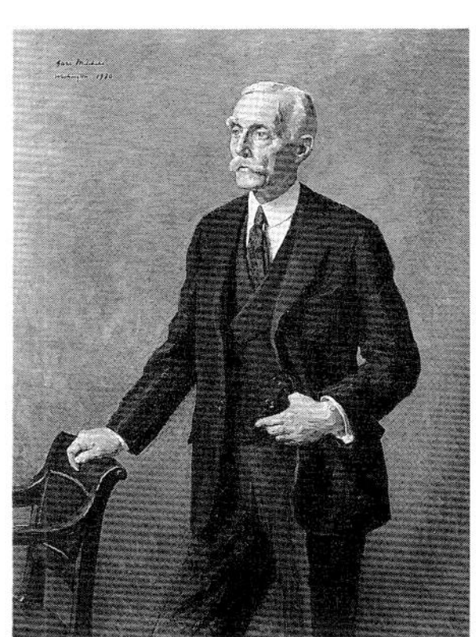

Andrew W. Mellon, 1930
Canvas, 1.403 x 1.045 (55¼ x 41⅛)
Inscribed at upper left: *Gari Melchers./ Washington. 1930*
Gift of Donald D. Shepard
1953.11.1

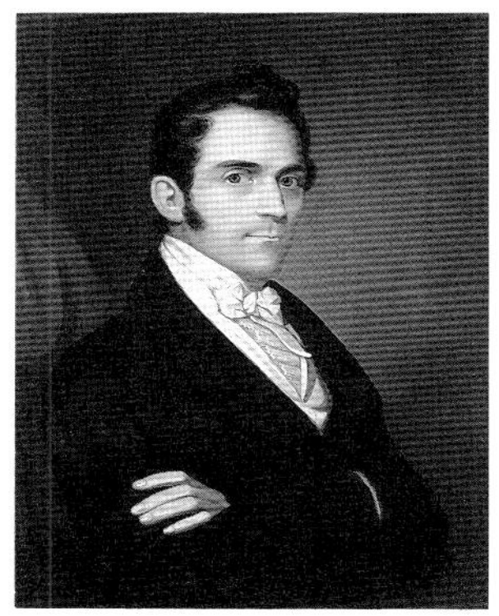

ELIAB METCALF
1785–1834

Self-Portrait, c. 1815
Canvas, 0.686 x 0.543 (27 x 21⅜)
Andrew W. Mellon Collection
1947.17.72

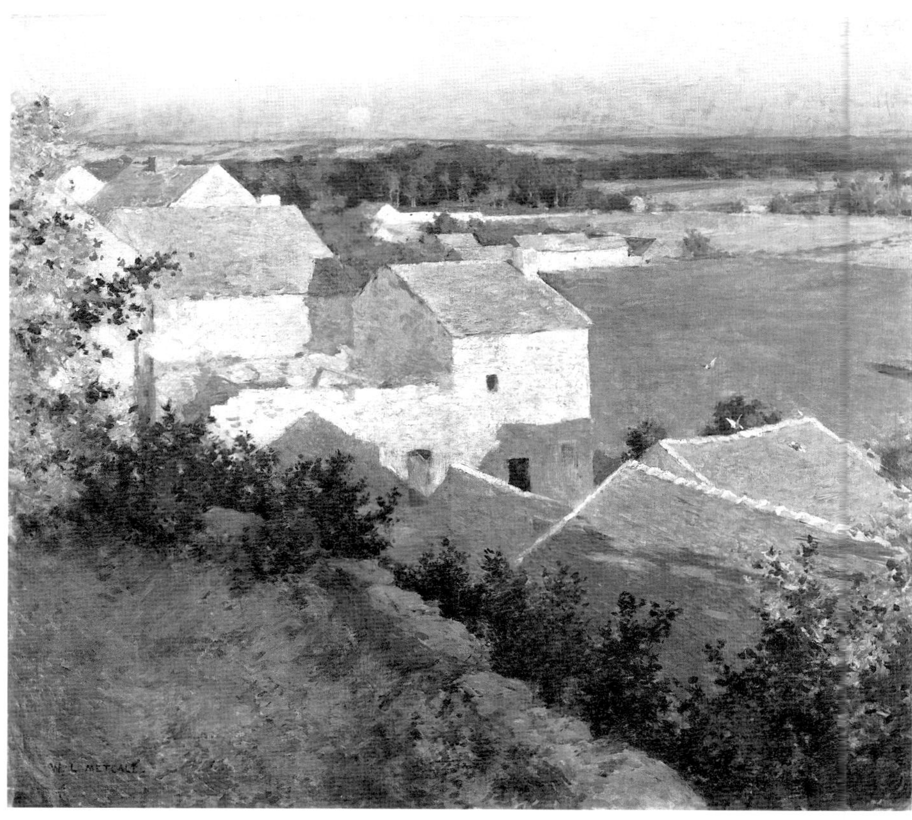

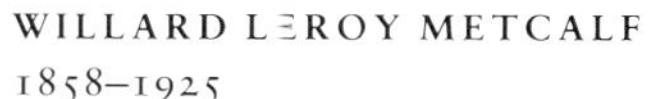

WILLARD LEROY METCALF
1858–1925

Midsummer Twilight, c. 1885/1887
Canvas, 0.818 x 0.904 (32¼ x 35⅝)
Inscribed at lower left: *W. L. METCALF*
Gift of Admiral Neill Phillips in memory of Grace Hendrick Phillips
1976.50.2

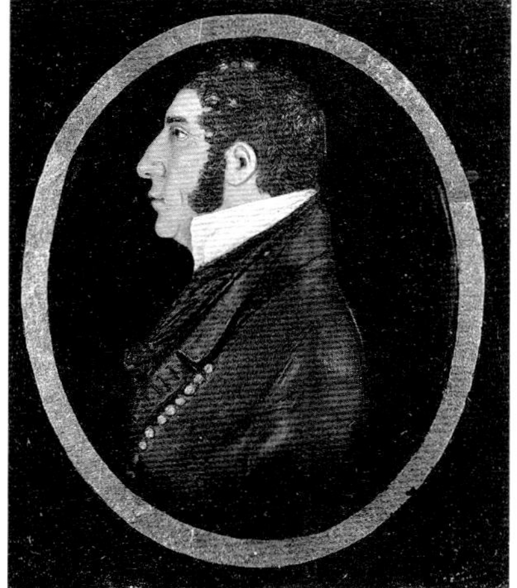

GEORGE M. MILLER
died 1819

William Henry Vining, c. 1810
Painted wax, 0.108 x 0.089 (4¼ x 3½)
Gift of Edgar William and Bernice Chrysler Garbisch
1953.5.106

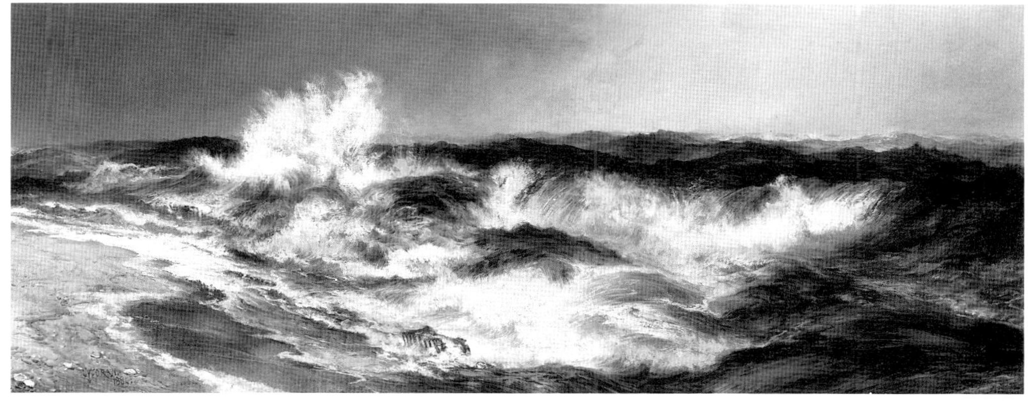

THOMAS MORAN
1837–1926

The Much Resounding Sea, 1884
Canvas, 0.636 x 1.576 (25 x 62)
Inscribed at lower left: *TMORAN.* (TM in monogram) / *1884*.
Gift of the Avalon Foundation
1967.9.1

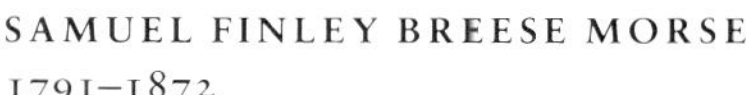

SAMUEL FINLEY BREESE MORSE
1791–1872

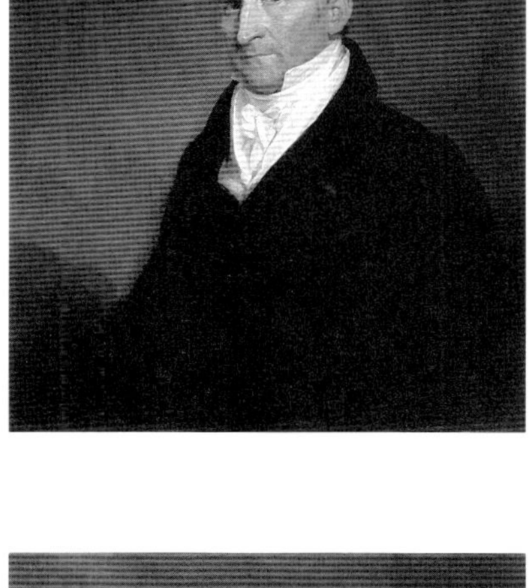

Eliphalet Terry, c. 1824/1825
Canvas, 0.757 x 0.632 ($29\frac{3}{4}$ x $24\frac{7}{8}$)
Gift of Dr. Charles Terry Butler
1981.46.1

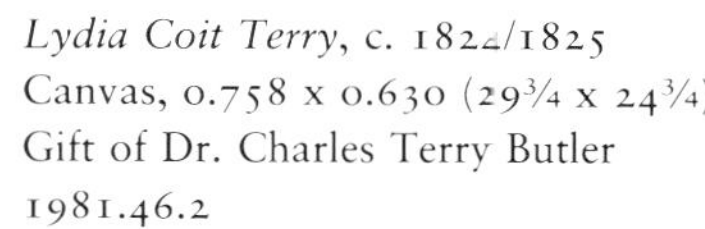

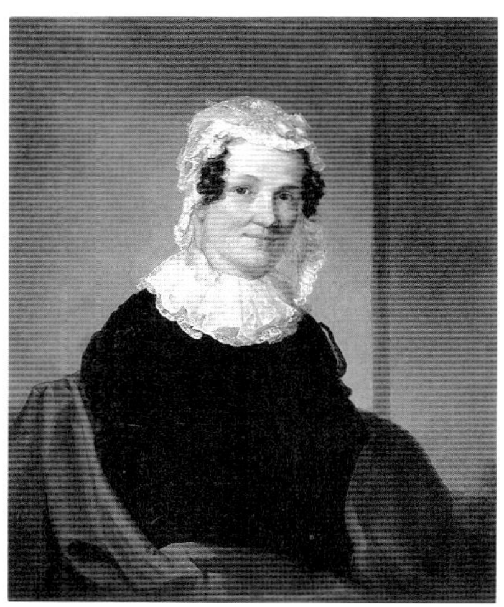

Lydia Coit Terry, c. 1824/1825
Canvas, 0.758 x 0.630 ($29\frac{3}{4}$ x $24\frac{3}{4}$)
Gift of Dr. Charles Terry Butler
1981.46.2

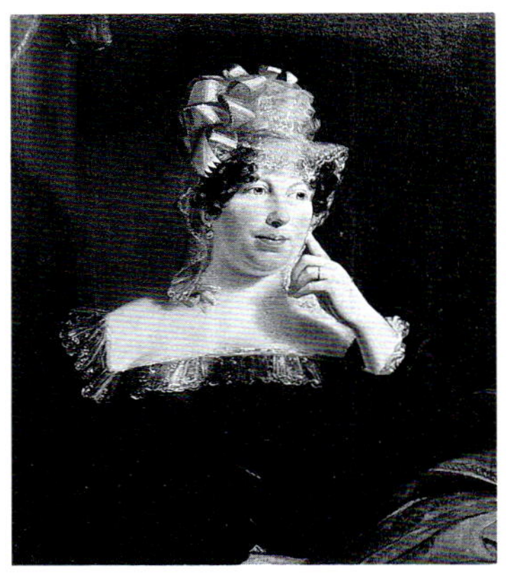

Portrait of a Lady, c. 1825
Canvas, 0.760 x 0.640 (30 x 25¼)
Chester Dale Collection
1943.1.6

ROBERT MOTHERWELL
born 1915

Reconciliation Elegy, 1978
Canvas, 3.048 x 9.242 (120 x 364)
Inscribed at lower right: *R. Motherwell / 1978*
Gift of the Collectors Committee
1978.20.1

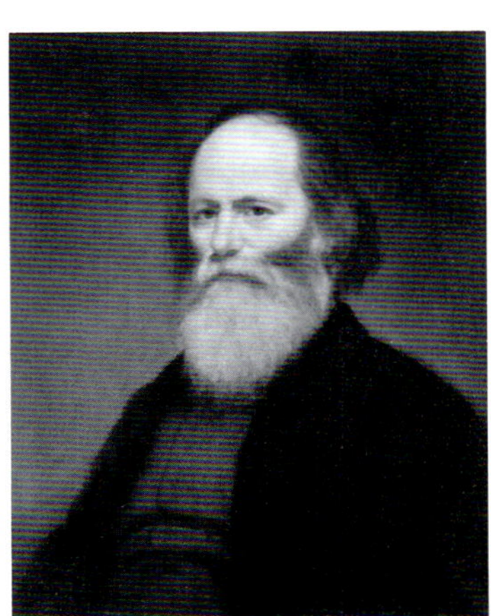

WILLIAM SIDNEY MOUNT
1807–1868

Charles Loring Elliott, c. 1865
Canvas, 0.689 x 0.562 (27⅛ x 22⅛)
Andrew W. Mellon Collection
1947.17.9

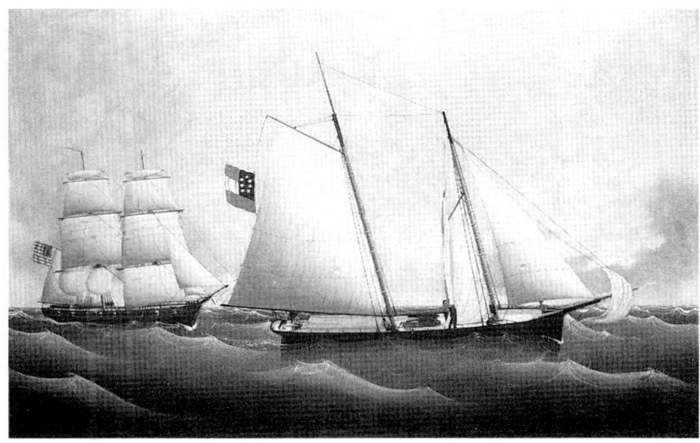

FRITZ MÜLLER
1814–after 1861

Capture of the Savannah *by the* U.S.S. Perry, 1861
Canvas, 0.590 x 0.912 (23¼ x 35⅞)
Inscribed at lower left: *Fr. Muller. 1861.*
Gift of Edgar William and Bernice Chrysler Garbisch
1967.20.2

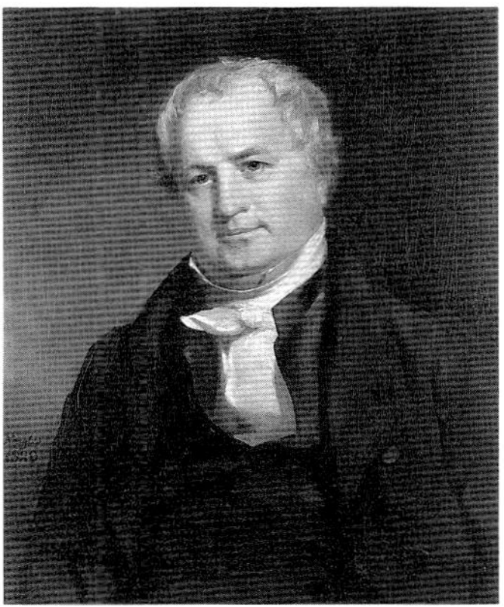

JOHN NEAGLE
1796–1865

Reverend John Albert Ryan, 1829
Canvas, 0.765 x 0.638 (30⅛ x 25⅛)
Inscribed at lower left: *J. Neagle / 1829*
Andrew W. Mellon Collection
1947.17.81

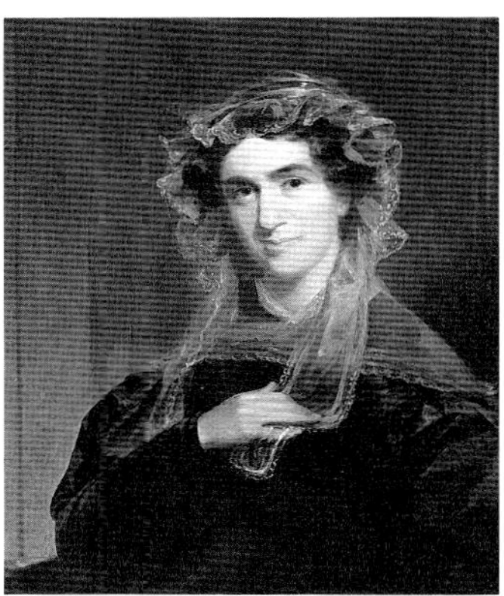

Mrs. John Dickson, c. 1835
Canvas, 0.768 x 0.638 (30¼ x 25⅛)
Andrew W. Mellon Collection
1947.17.77

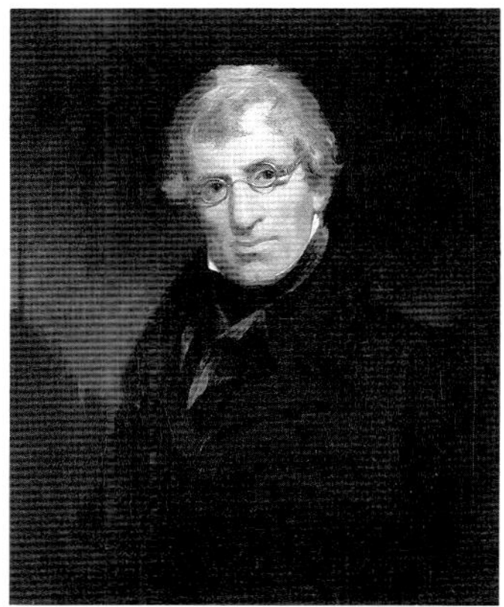

Thomas W. Dyott, c. 1836
Canvas, 0.762 x 0.635 (30 x 25)
Andrew W. Mellon Collection
1947.17.78

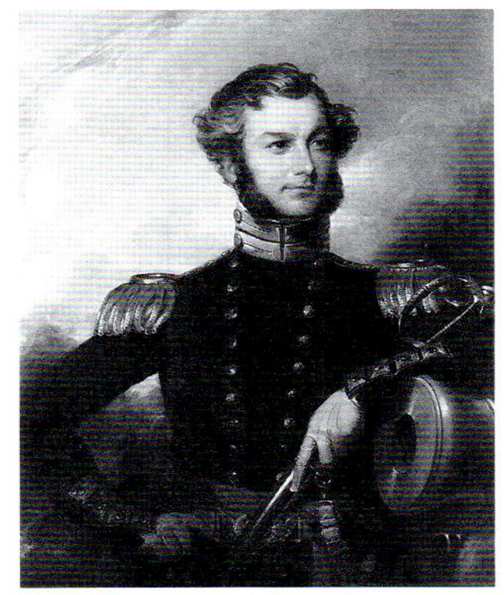

Colonel Augustus James Pleasonton, 1846
Canvas, 0.920 x 0.742 (36¼ x 29⅛)
Gift of Eugene S. Pleasonton
1957.9.1

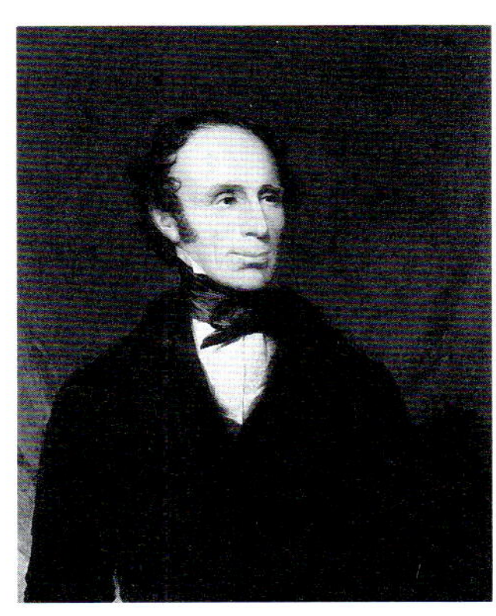

George Dodd, 1852
Canvas, 0.761 x 0.637 (30 x 25⅛)
Gift of Albert M. Friend, Jr.
1957.3.1

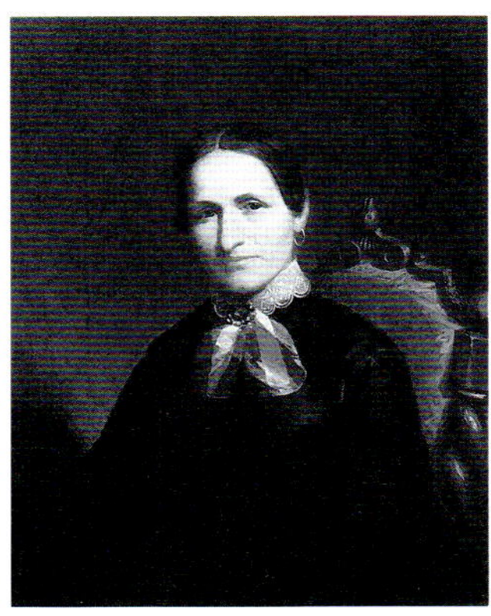

Mrs. George Dodd, 1852
Canvas, 0.762 x 0.631 (30 x 24⅞)
Gift of Albert M. Friend, Jr.
1957.3.2

LOWELL NESBITT

born 1933

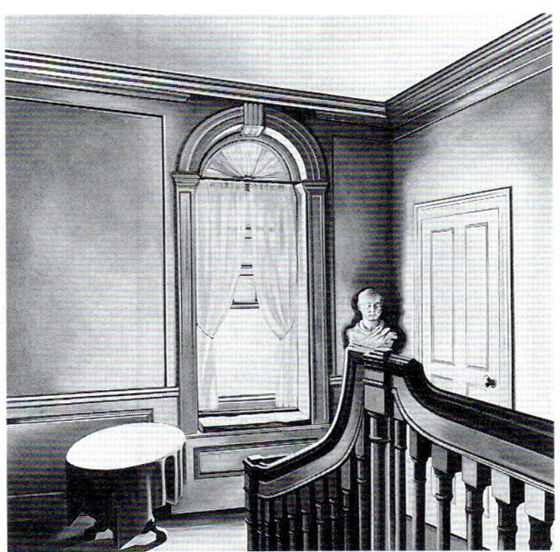

Stairway Landing, 1969
Canvas, 1.962 x 1.955 (77¼ x 77)
Gift of John H. Safer
1970.23.1

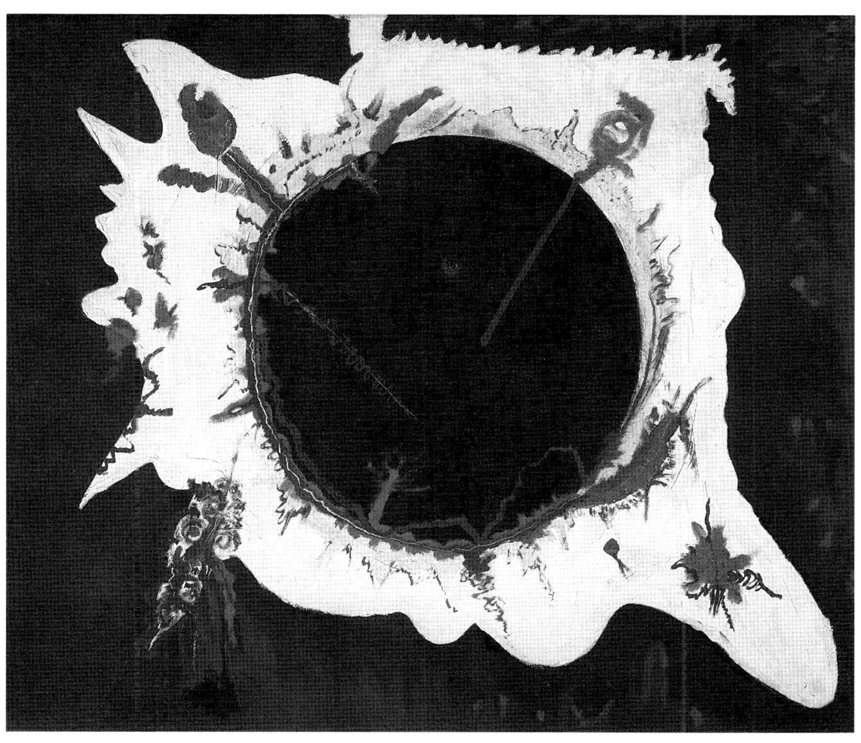

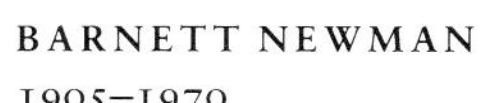

BARNETT NEWMAN
1905–1970

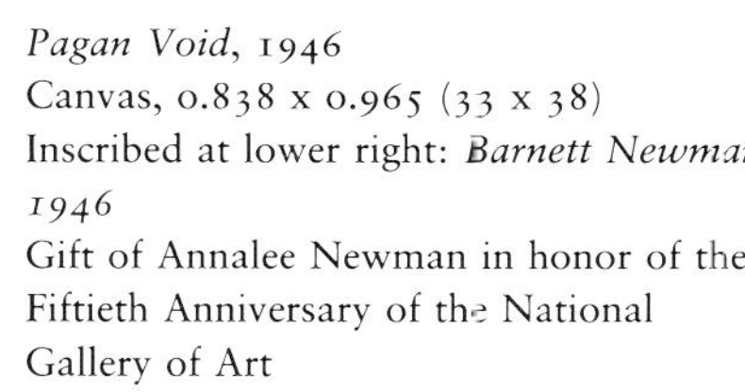

Pagan Void, 1946
Canvas, 0.838 x 0.965 (33 x 38)
Inscribed at lower right: *Barnett Newman 1946*
Gift of Annalee Newman in honor of the Fiftieth Anniversary of the National Gallery of Art
1988.57.1

Dionysius, 1949
Canvas, 1.702 x 1.245 (67 x 49)
Inscribed at lower right: *Barnett Newman 1949*
Gift of Annalee Newman in honor of the Fiftieth Anniversary of the National Gallery of Art
1988.57.2

Yellow Painting, 1949
Canvas, 1.712 x 1.331 (67½ x 52⅜)
Gift of Annalee Newman in honor of the Fiftieth Anniversary of the National Gallery of Art
1988.57.3

The Name II, 1950
Canvas, 2.642 x 2.400 (104 x 94½)
Gift of Annalee Newman in honor of the Fiftieth Anniversary of the National Gallery of Art
1988.57.4

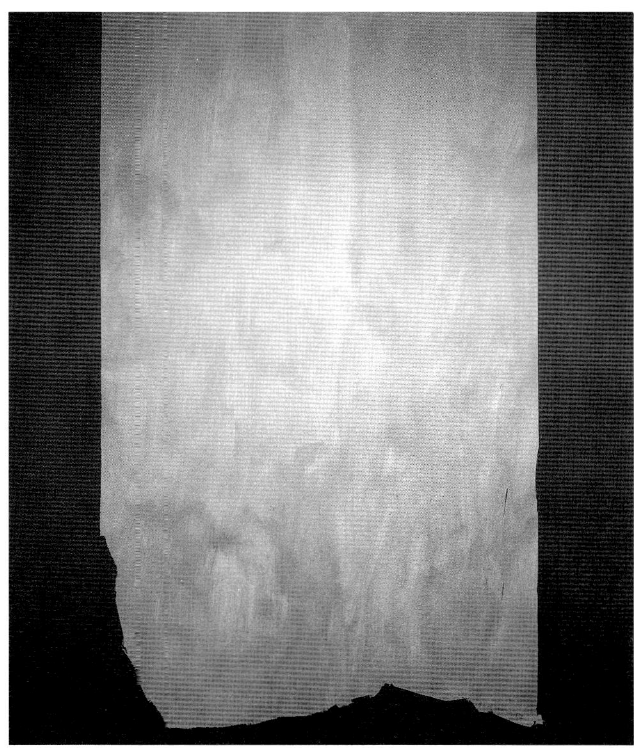

Achilles, 1952
Canvas, 2.416 x 2.010 (95⅛ x 79⅛)
Inscribed at lower right: *Barnett Newman 1952*
Gift of Annalee Newman in honor of the Fiftieth Anniversary of the National Gallery of Art
1988.57.5

Stations of the Cross
(Lema Sabachthani)

Paintings in the Stations of the Cross series are listed in numerical order.

First Station, 1958
Canvas, 1.978 x 1.537 (77⅞ x 60½)
Inscribed at lower right: *Barnett Newman 1958*
Robert and Jane Meyerhoff Collection
1986.65.1

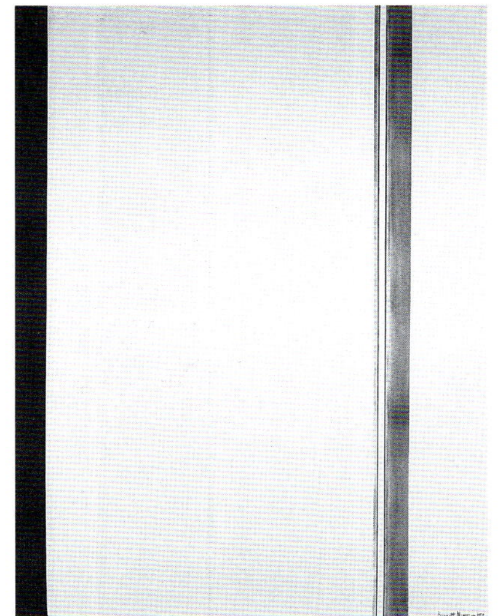

Second Station, 1958
Canvas, 1.984 x 1.532 (78⅛ x 60½)
Inscribed at lower right: *Barnett Newman 1958*
Robert and Jane Meyerhoff Collection
1986.65.2

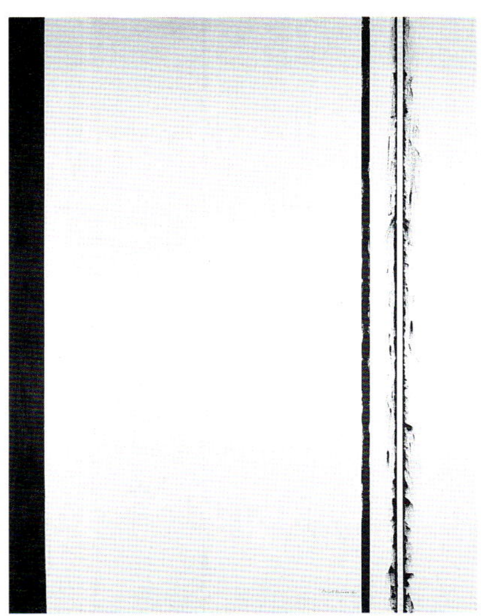

Third Station, 1960
Canvas, 1.984 x 1.521 (78⅛ x 59⅞)
Inscribed at lower right: *Barnett Newman 1960*
Robert and Jane Meyerhoff Collection
1986.65.3

Fourth Station, 1960
Canvas, 1.981 x 1.530 (78 x 60¼)
Inscribed at lower right: *Barnett Newman 1960*
Robert and Jane Meyerhoff Collection
1986.65.4

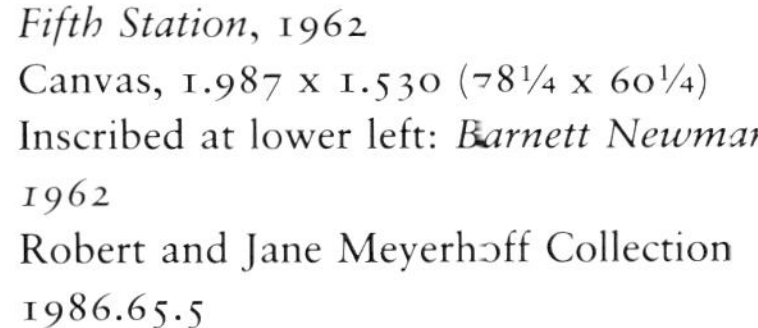

Fifth Station, 1962
Canvas, 1.987 x 1.530 (78¼ x 60¼)
Inscribed at lower left: *Barnett Newman 1962*
Robert and Jane Meyerhoff Collection
1986.65.5

Sixth Station, 1962
Canvas, 1.984 x 1.521 (78⅛ x 59⅞)
Inscribed at lower right: *Barnett Newman 1962*
Robert and Jane Meyerhoff Collection
1986.65.6

Seventh Station, 1964
Canvas, 1.981 x 1.524 (78 x 60)
Inscribed at lower left: *Barnett Newman 1964*
Robert and Jane Meyerhoff Collection
1986.65.7

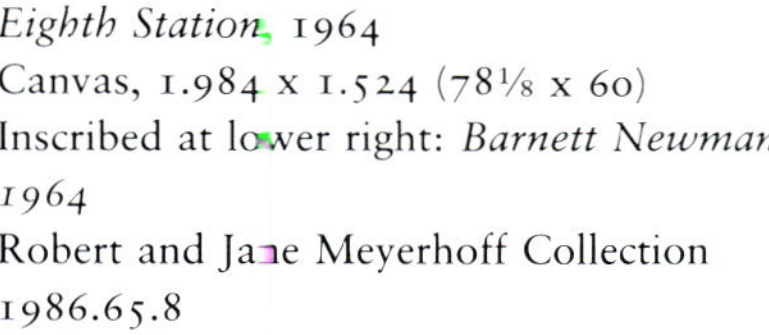

Eighth Station, 1964
Canvas, 1.984 x 1.524 ($78\frac{1}{8}$ x 60)
Inscribed at lower right: *Barnett Newman 1964*
Robert and Jane Meyerhoff Collection
1986.65.8

Ninth Station, 1964
Canvas, 1.981 x 1.527 (78 x $60\frac{1}{8}$)
Inscribed at lower right: *Barnett Newman 1964*
Robert and Jane Meyerhoff Collection
1986.65.9

Tenth Station, 1965
Canvas, 1.981 x 1.525 (78 x $60\frac{1}{16}$)
Inscribed at lower left: *Barnett Newman 1965*
Robert and Jane Meyerhoff Collection
1986.65.10

Eleventh Station, 1965
Canvas, 1.981 x 1.524 (78 x 60)
Inscribed at lower right: *Barnett Newman 1965*
Robert and Jane Meyerhoff Collection
1986.65.11

Twelfth Station, 1965
Canvas, 1.981 x 1.524 (78 x 60)
Inscribed at lower right: *Barnett Newman 1965*
Robert and Jane Meyerhoff Collection
1986.65.12

Thirteenth Station, 1965/1966
Canvas, 1.982 x 1.525 (78 1/16 x 60 1/16)
Inscribed at lower left: *Barnett Newman / 1966*
Robert and Jane Meyerhoff Collection
1986.65.13

Fourteenth Station, 1965/1966
Canvas, 1.981 x 1.522 (78 x 59 15/16)
Inscribed at lower left: *Barnett Newman 1966*
Robert and Jane Meyerhoff Collection
1986.65.14

Be II, 1961/1964
Canvas, 2.045 x 1.835 (80 1/2 x 72 1/4)
Inscribed at lower right: *Barnett Newman '61 + 64*
Robert and Jane Meyerhoff Collection
1986.65.15

KENNETH NOLAND
born 1924

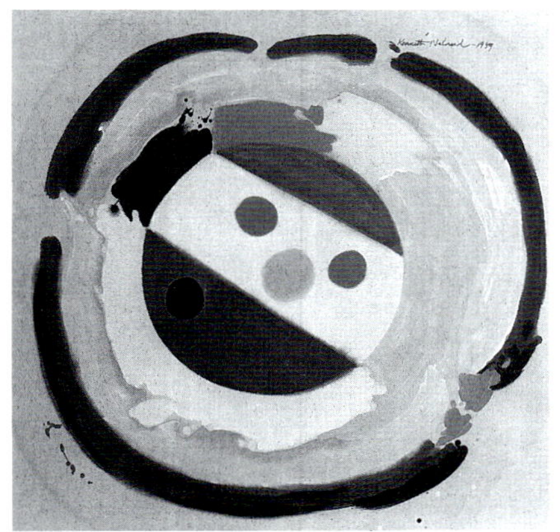

The Clown, 1959
Canvas, 1.172 x 1.169 (46 1/8 x 46)
Inscribed at lower right: *Kenneth Noland / 1959*
Gift of Dr. and Mrs. Robert Wetmore
1975.98.1

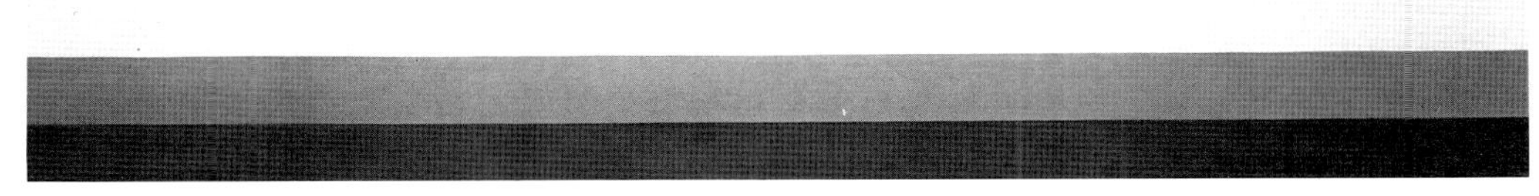

Sound, c. 1966
Canvas, 0.762 x 5.490 (30 x 216¼)
Gift of Mr. and Mrs. Ernest du Pont, Jr.
1980.73.1

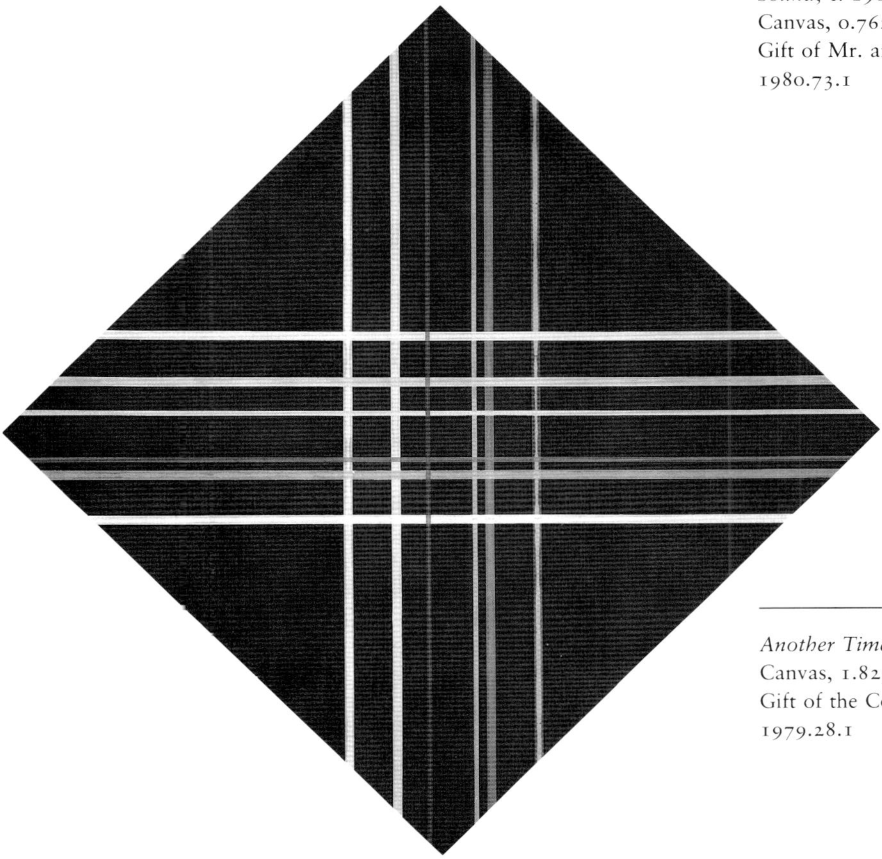

Another Time, 1973
Canvas, 1.829 x 1.829 (72 x 72)
Gift of the Collectors Committee
1979.28.1

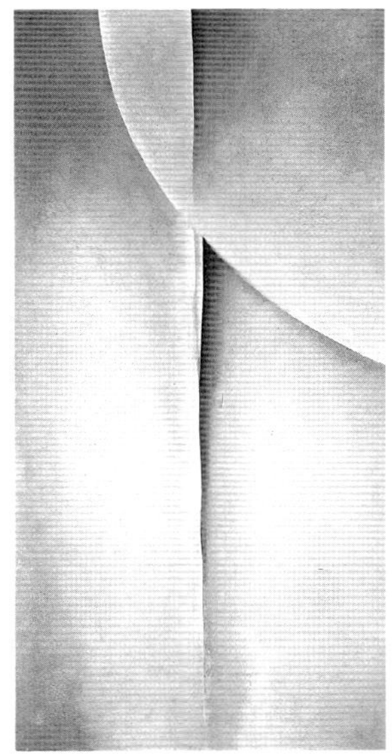

GEORGIA O'KEEFFE
1887–1986

Line and Curve, 1927
Canvas, 0.813 x 0.410 (32 x 16⅛)
Inscribed across top on reverse: *Line and Curve–27 / OK* (OK within five-pointed star)
Alfred Stieglitz Collection, Bequest of Georgia O'Keeffe
1987.58.6

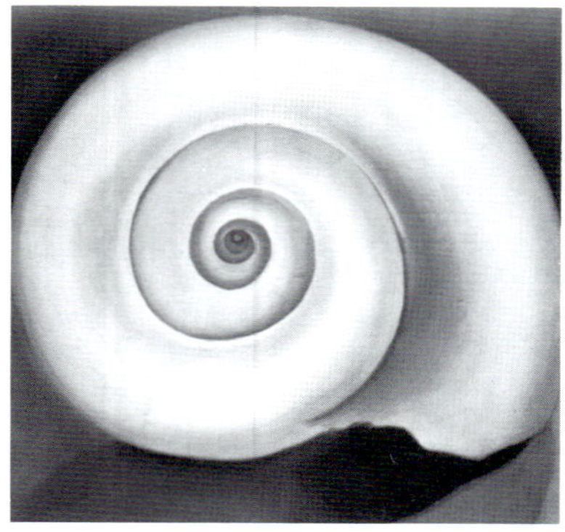

Shell No. 1, 1928
Canvas, 0.178 x 0.178 (7 x 7)
Inscribed across center on reverse: *1928 / Georgia O'Keeffe Coiled / Shell No 1 / Exhibition 1929 / OK* (OK within five-pointed star)
Alfred Stieglitz Collection, Bequest of Georgia O'Keeffe
1987.58.7

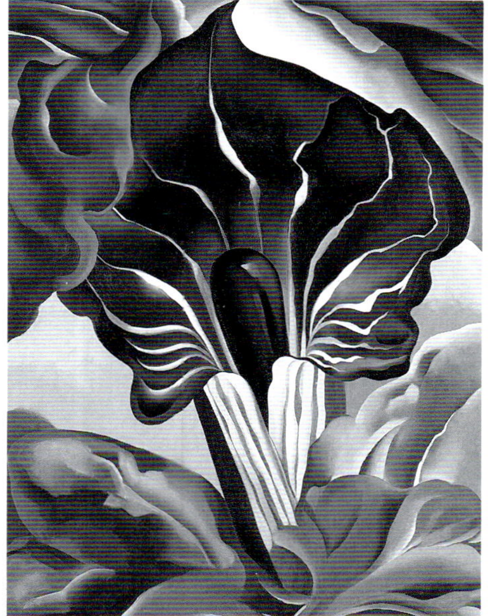

Jack-in-the-Pulpit No. II, 1930
Canvas, 1.016 x 0.762 (40 x 30)
Inscribed at upper left on reverse: *Jack in Pulpit-No 2–30 / OK* (OK within five-pointed star)
Alfred Stieglitz Collection, Bequest of Georgia O'Keeffe
1987.58.1

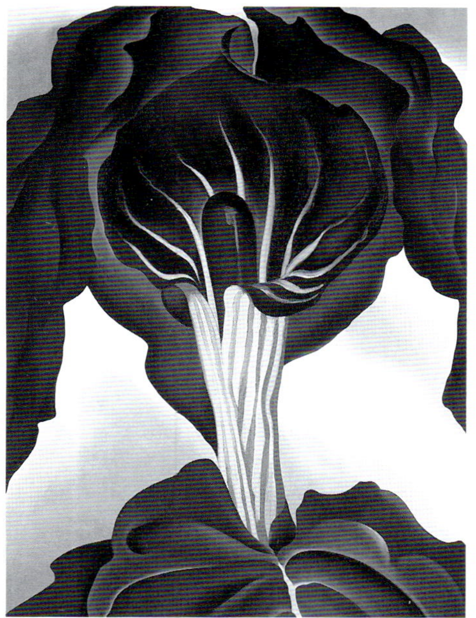

Jack-in-the-Pulpit No. III, 1930
Canvas, 1.016 x 0.762 (40 x 30)
Inscribed at center on reverse within five-pointed star: *OK*
Alfred Stieglitz Collection, Bequest of Georgia O'Keeffe
1987.58.2

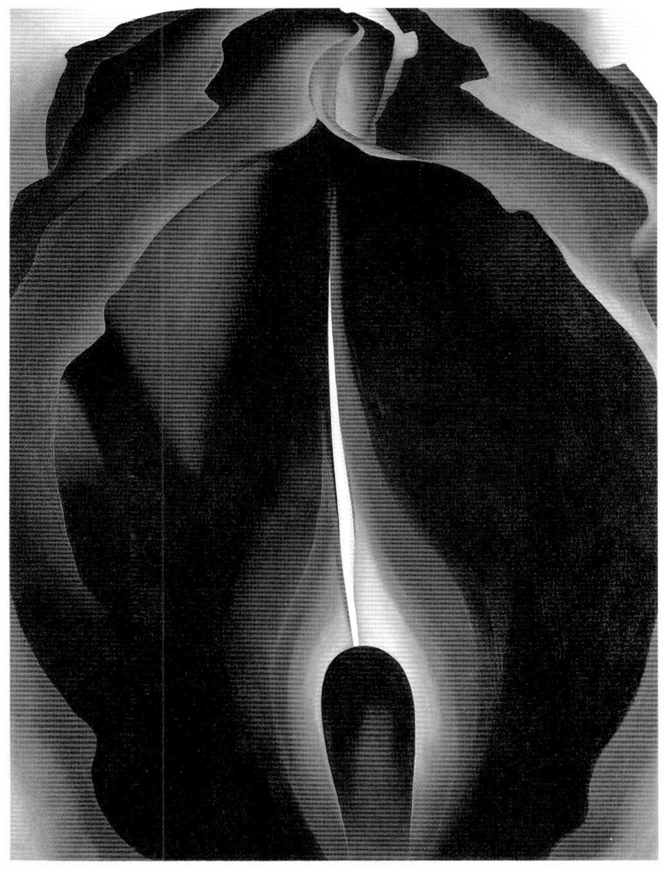

Jack-in-the-Pulpit No. IV, 1930
Canvas, 1.016 x 0.762 (40 x 30)
Inscribed across top of old back board, now taped to bottom half of back: *Jack in Pulpit—30 / OK* (OK within five-pointed star)
Alfred Stieglitz Collection, Bequest of Georgia O'Keeffe
1987.58.3

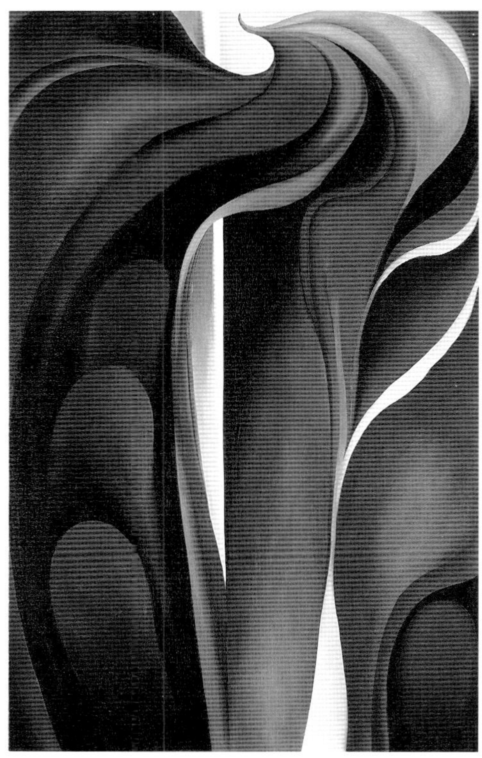

Jack-in-the-Pulpit No. V, 1930
Canvas, 1.219 x 0.762 (48 x 30)
Inscribed across top on reverse: *Jack in the Pulpit Abstraction—1930 / No.5 / OK* (OK within five-pointed star)
Alfred Stieglitz Collection, Bequest of Georgia O'Keeffe
1987.58.4

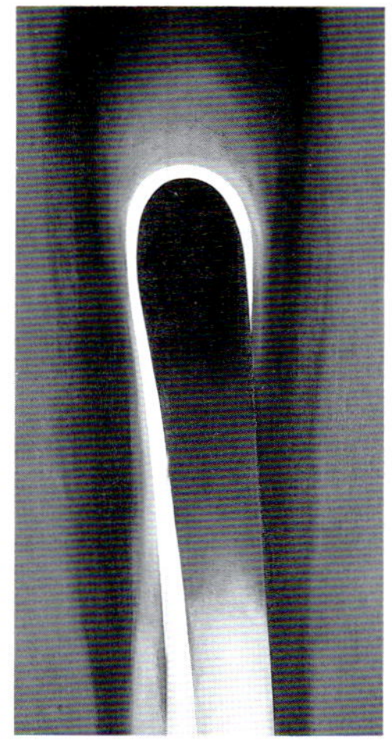

Jack-in-the-Pulpit No. VI, 1930
Canvas, 0.914 x 0.457 (36 x 18)
Inscribed across top on reverse: *Jack in Pulpit–30 / OK* (OK within five-pointed star)
Alfred Stieglitz Collection, Bequest of Georgia O'Keeffe
1987.58.5

Sky Above White Clouds I, 1962
Canvas, 1.524 x 2.032 (60 x 80)
Inscribed at center right on reverse: *Sky With Flat White Cloud / 1961*
Alfred Stieglitz Collection, Bequest of Georgia O'Keeffe
1987.58.8

KENZO OKADA
1902–1982

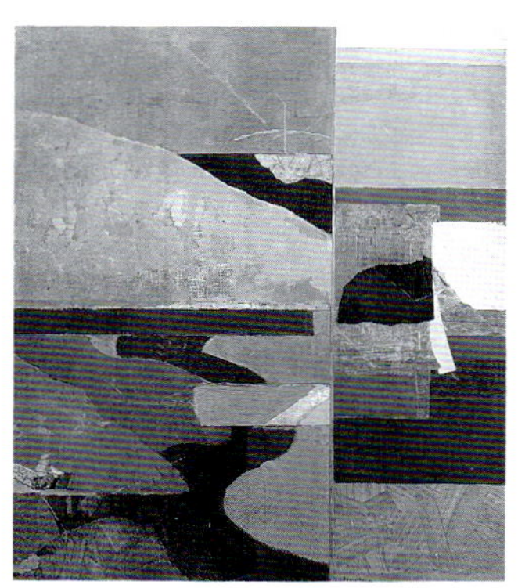

Kasaner, 1963
Canvas, 1.854 x 1.600 (73 x 63)
Inscribed at lower right: *Kenzo Okada*
Collection of Mr. and Mrs. Paul Mellon
1983.1.31

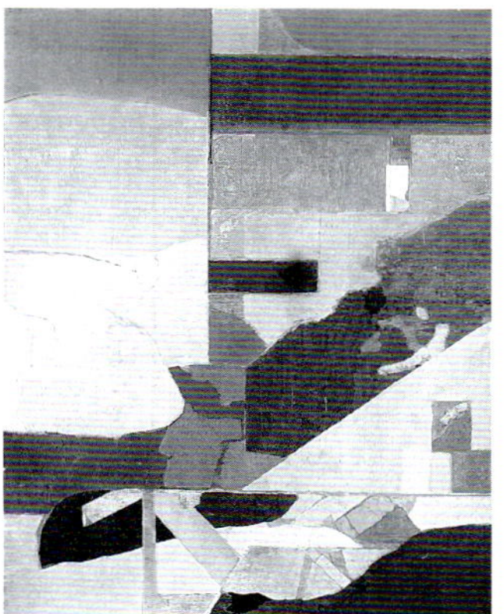

Blue, 1970
Canvas, 2.184 x 1.650 (86 x 65)
Inscribed at lower right: *Kenzo Okada*
Collection of Mr. and Mrs. Paul Mellon
1983.1.30

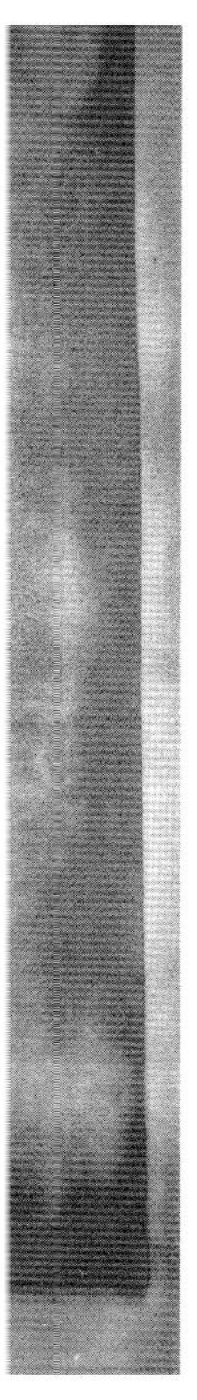

JULES OLITSKI
born 1922

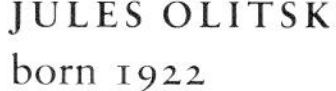

Unlocked, 1966
Canvas, 3.568 x 0.482 (140½ x 19)
Gift of Mr. and Mrs. Robert Eichholz
1978.39.1

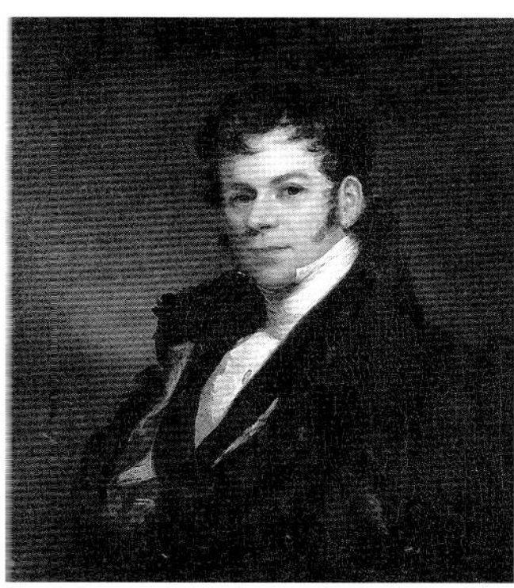

BASS OTIS
1784–1861

John Smith Warner, 1827
Canvas, 0.768 x 0.635 (30¼ x 25)
Gift of Martha E. Warner
1961.8.1

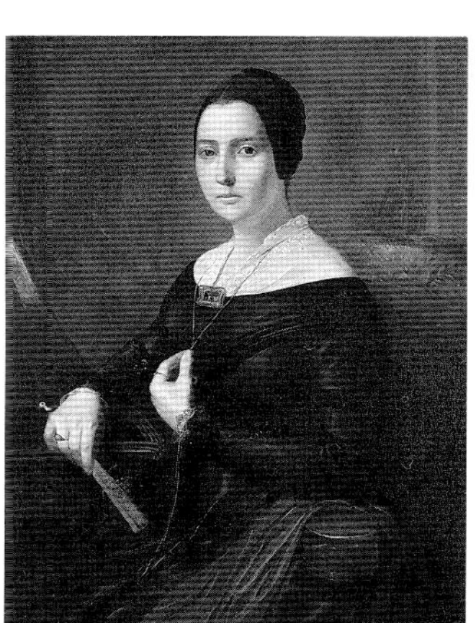

JOHN WESLEY PARADISE
1809–1862

Mrs. Elizabeth Oakes Smith, c. 1845
Canvas, 0.866 x 0.651 (34⅛ x 25⅝)
Inscribed at lower left: *Elizabeth. O. Smith / John. W. Paradis—f.*
Chester Dale Collection
1963.10.188

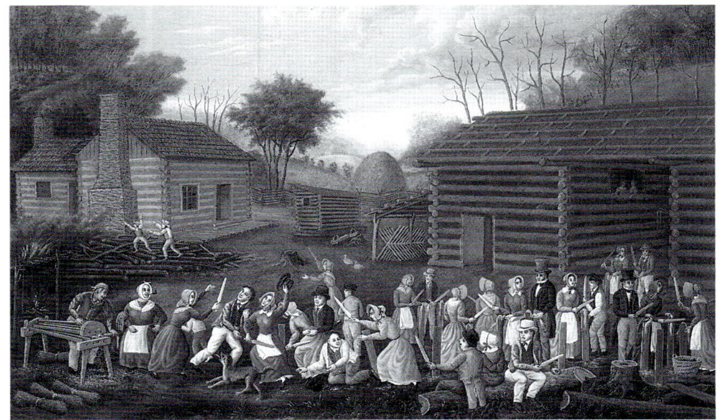

LINTON PARK
1826–1906

Flax Scutching Bee, 1885
Bed ticking, 0.800 x 1.283 (31½ x 50½)
Gift of Edgar William and Bernice Chrysler Garbisch
1953.5.26

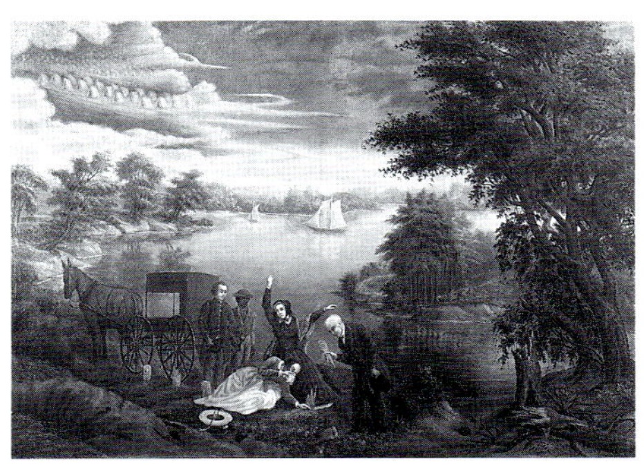

The Burial, c. 1890
Canvas, 0.613 x 0.842 (24⅛ x 33⅛)
Gift of Edgar William and Bernice Chrysler Garbisch
1953.5.27

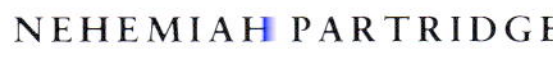

NEHEMIAH PARTRIDGE
(See The Schuyler Limner, *Mr. Van Vechten*, 1947.17.74 and *Mr. Willson*, 1957.11.9)

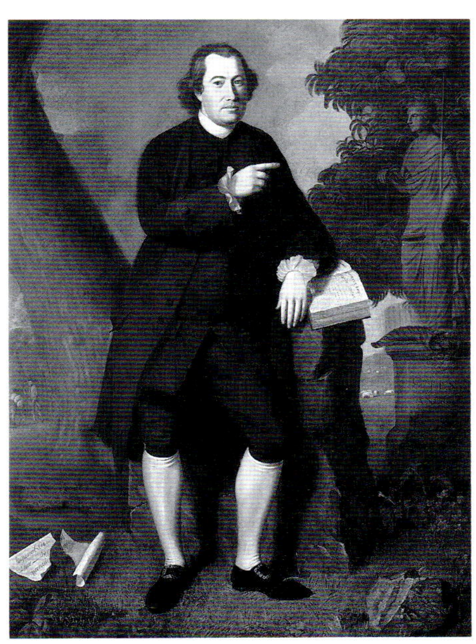

CHARLES WILLSON PEALE
1741–1827

John Beale Bordley, 1770
Canvas, 2.008 x 1.474 (79 1/16 x 58 1/16)
Inscribed at lower right on rock: *[Charles Wilso]n Peale / [Mary]land / [17]70*
Gift of The Barra Foundation, Inc.
1984.2.1

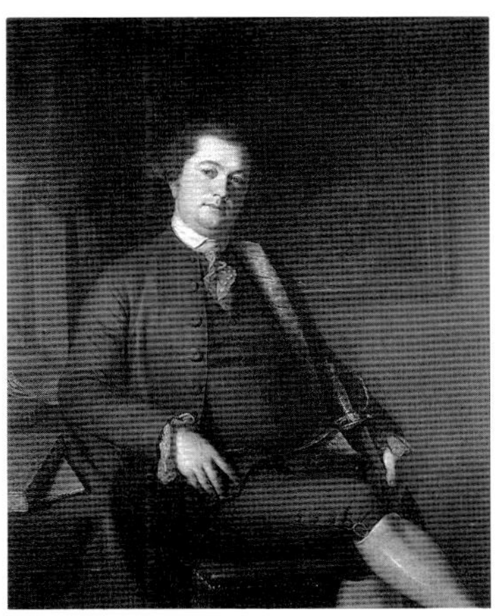

John Philip de Haas, 1772
Canvas, 1.270 x 1.015 (50 x 40)
Inscribed at lower right: C. W. *Peale pinxt 1772*
Andrew W. Mellon Collection
1942.8.9

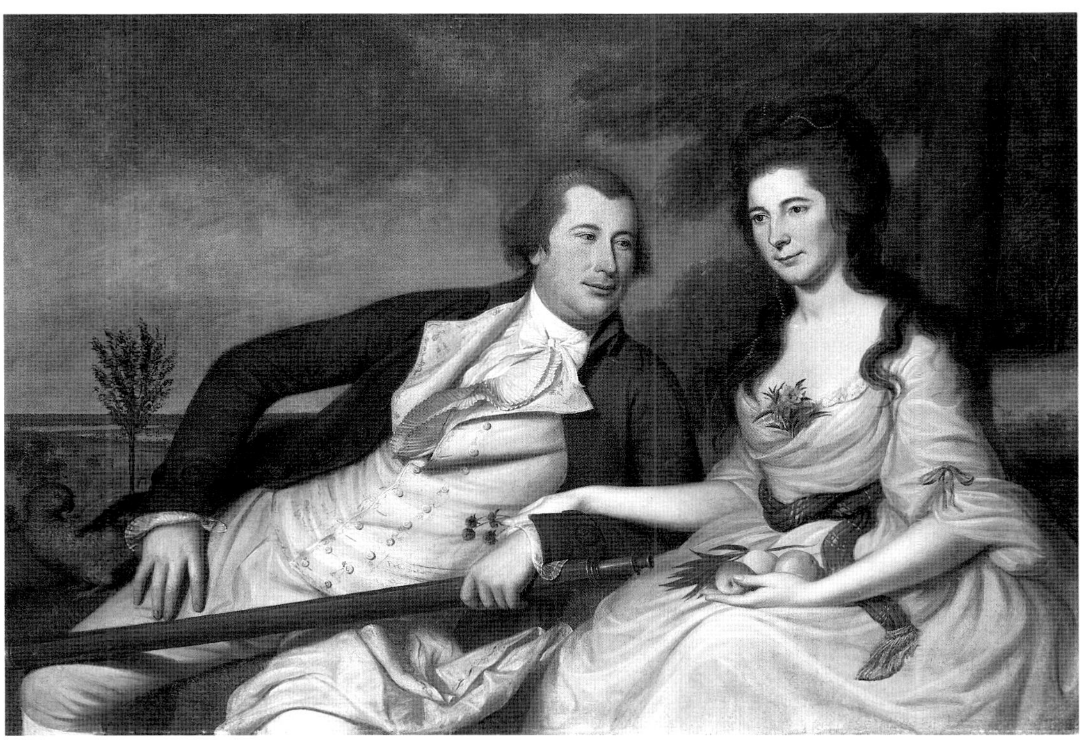

Benjamin and Eleanor Ridgely Laming, 1788
Canvas, 1.060 x 1.525 (42 x 60)
Gift of Morris Schapiro
1966.10.1

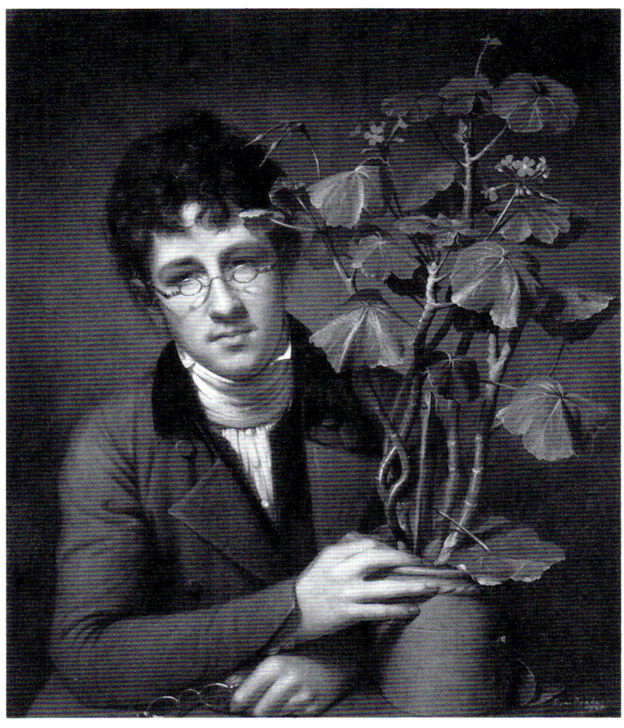

REMBRANDT PEALE
1778–1860

Rubens Peale with a Geranium, 1801
Canvas, 0.714 x 0.610 (28⅛ x 24)
Inscribed at lower right: *Rem Peale / 1801*
Patrons' Permanent Fund
1985.59.1

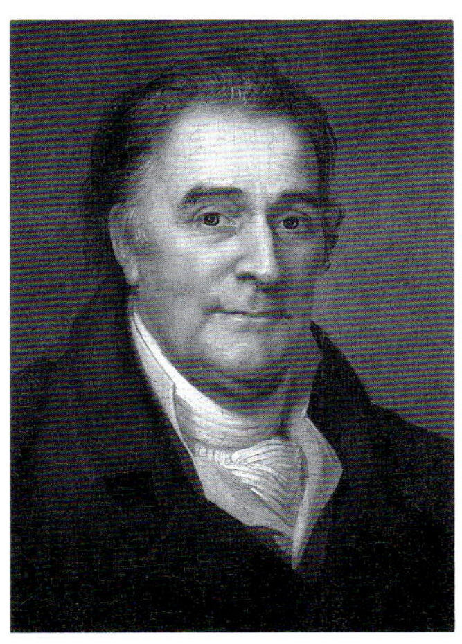

Richardson Stuart, c. 1815
Canvas, 0.524 x 0.372 (20⅝ x 14⅝)
Andrew W. Mellon Collection
1947.17.85

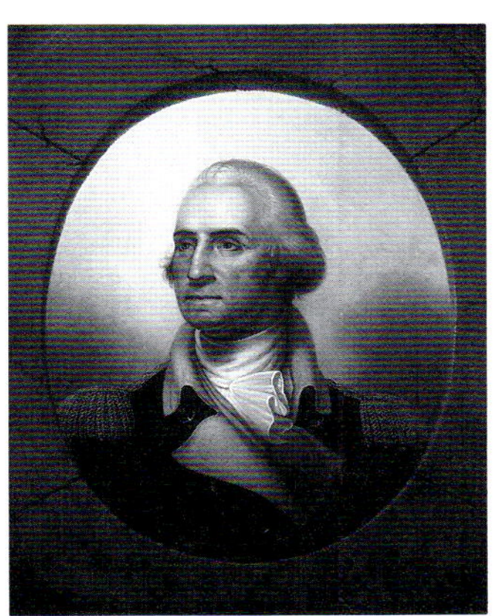

George Washington, c. 1850
Canvas, 0.914 x 0.733 (36 x 28⅞)
Inscribed by a later hand, lower left:
Rembrandt Peal[e]
Gift of Mr. and Mrs. George W. Davison
1942.7.1

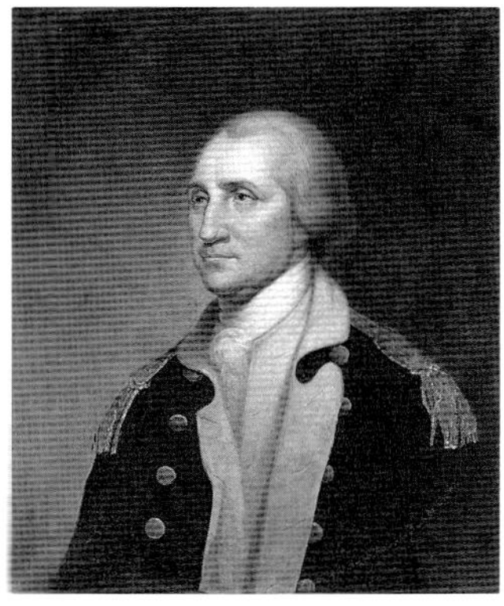

George Washington, c. 1857
Canvas, 0.762 x 0.635 (30 x 25)
Inscribed by a later hand, lower right: *Painted by Rembrandt Peale from Pine's Washington*
Andrew W. Mellon Collection
1947.17.16

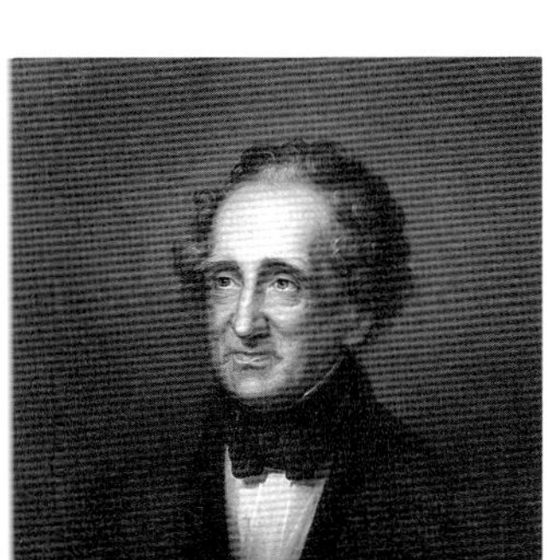

Thomas Sully, 1859
Canvas board, 0.606 x 0.508 (23⅞ x 20)
Inscribed at center right: *R. Peale / 1859*
Gift of Mrs. Leland Harrison
1955.2.1

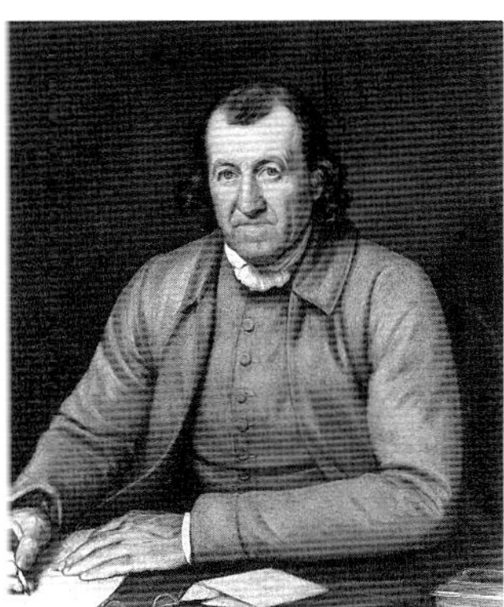

ATTRIBUTED TO REMBRANDT PEALE
1778–1860

Timothy Matlack, c. 1805
Canvas, 0.765 x 0.648 (30⅛ x 25½)
Andrew W. Mellon Collection
1947.17.10

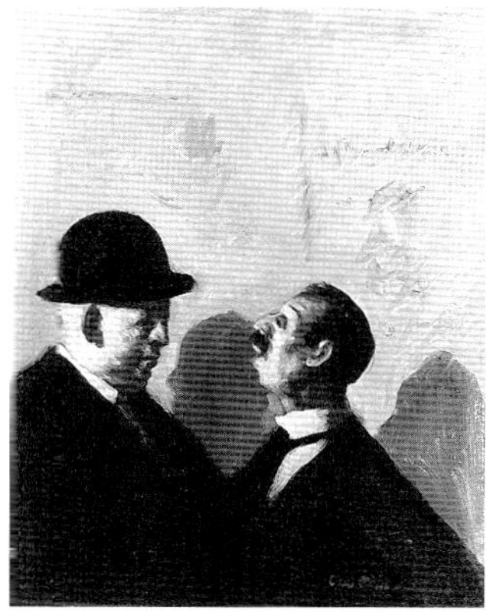

GUY PÈNE DU BOIS
1884–1958

The Politicians, c. 1912
Canvas board, 0.408 x 0.306 (16⅛ x 12⅛)
Inscribed at lower right: *Guy Pène du Bois*
Chester Dale Collection
1963.10.138

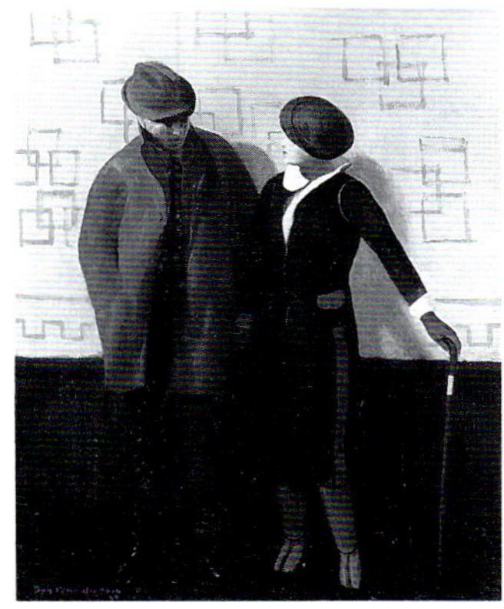

Hallway, Italian Restaurant, 1922
Canvas, 0.638 x 0.512 (25⅛ x 20⅛)
Inscribed at lower left: *Guy Pène du Bois / 22*
Chester Dale Collection
1963.10.137

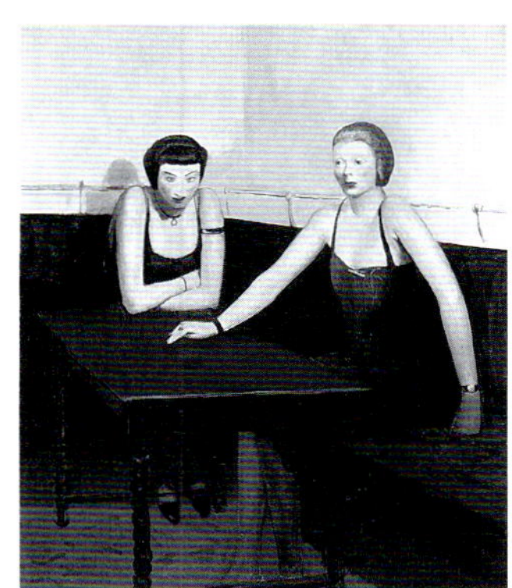

Café du Dôme, 1925/1926
Wood, 0.552 x 0.461 (21¾ x 18¼)
Inscribed at lower left: *Guy Pène du Bois [19]25*; lower right: *Guy Pène du Bois [19]26*
Chester Dale Collection
1963.10.136

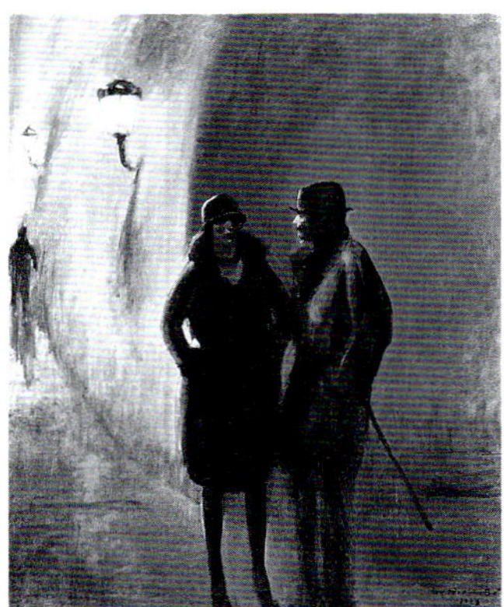

La Rue de la Santé, 1928
Canvas, 0.920 x 0.730 (36¼ x 28¾)
Inscribed at lower right: *Guy Pène du Boi[s] / 192[8?]*
Chester Dale Collection
1963.10.139

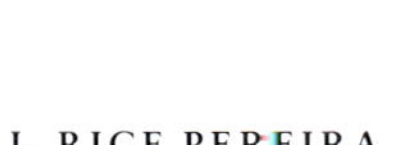

I. RICE PEREIRA
1907–1971

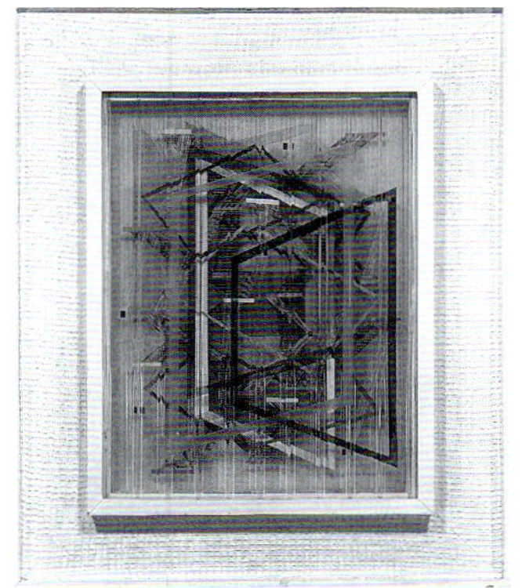

Transfluent Lines, 1946
Corrugated glass and cardboard, 0.609 x 0.456 (24 x 18)
Inscribed at lower right: *I. RICE PEREIRA '46*
Gift of Mr. and Mrs. Burton Tremaine
1973.71.2

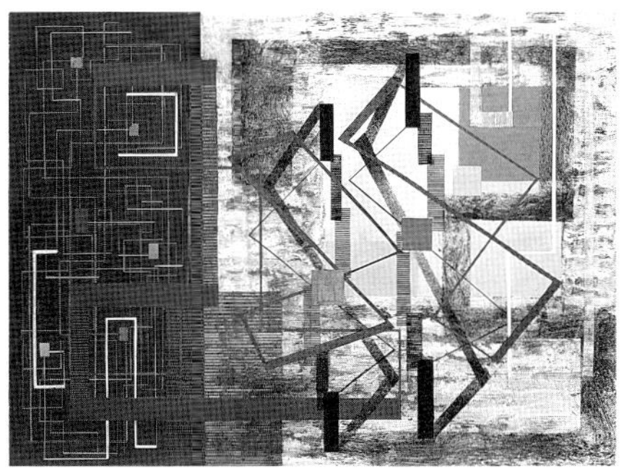

Green Mass, 1950
Canvas, 1.019 x 1.271 ($40\frac{1}{8}$ x 50)
Inscribed at lower right: *I. RICE PEREIRA*
Gift of Leslie Bokor and Leslie Dame
1973.72.1

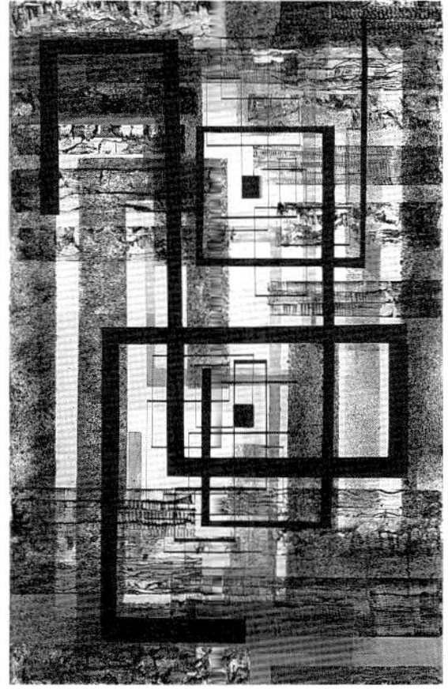

Zenith, 1953
Canvas, 1.264 x 0.764 ($49\frac{3}{4}$ x $30\frac{1}{8}$)
Inscribed at lower right: *I. RICE PEREIRA*
Gift of Leslie Bokor and Leslie Dame
1973.72.2

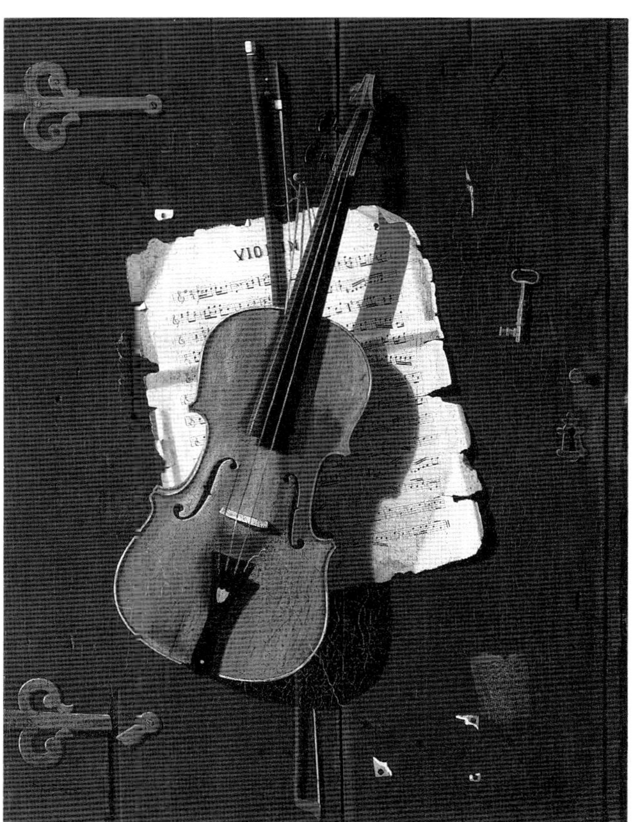

JOHN FREDERICK PETO
1854–1907

The Old Violin, c. 1890
Canvas, 0.772 x 0.581 ($30\frac{3}{8}$ x $22\frac{7}{8}$)
Inscribed at lower left: *John F. PETO*;
upper left in simulated carving: *JFP*
Gift of the Avalon Foundation
1974.19.1

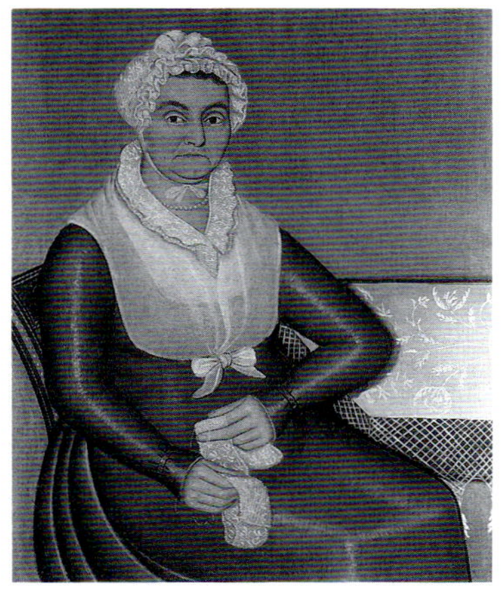

AMMI PHILLIPS
1788–1865

Alsa Slade, 1816
Canvas, 1.020 x 0.833 (40⅛ x 33)
Gift of Edgar William and Bernice Chrysler Garbisch
1953.5.53

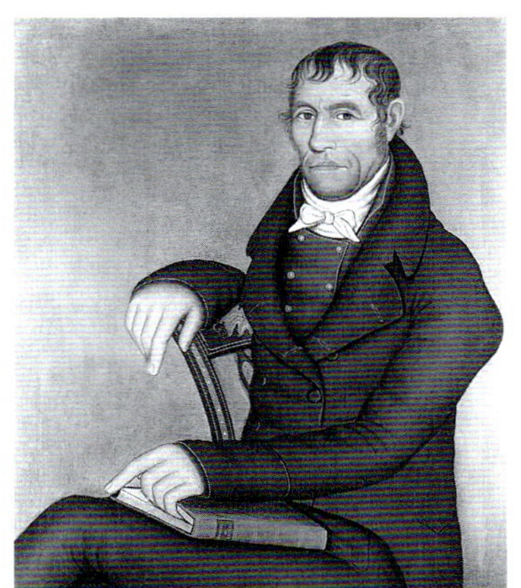

Joseph Slade, 1816
Canvas, 1.020 x 0.840 (40⅛ x 33)
Gift of Edgar William and Bernice Chrysler Garbisch
1953.5.52

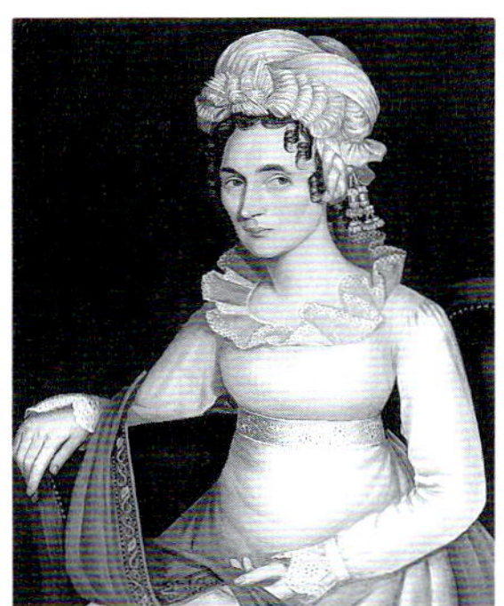

Lady in White, c. 1820
Canvas, 0.820 x 0.660 (32½ x 25 15/16)
Gift of Edgar William and Bernice Chrysler Garbisch
1959.11.9

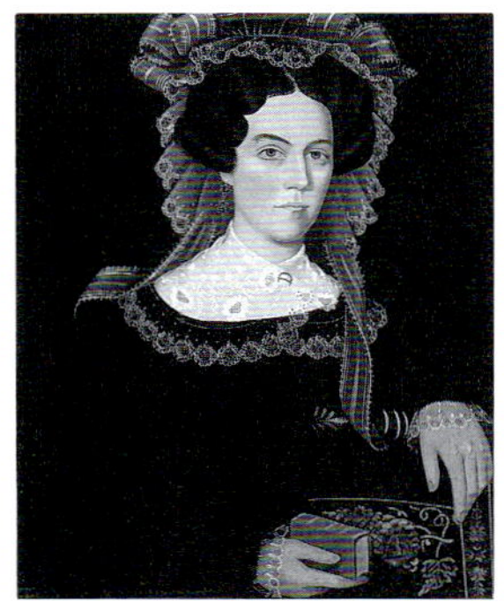

Catherine A. May, c. 1830
Canvas, 0.790 x 0.634 (31⅛ x 25)
Gift of Edgar William and Bernice Chrysler Garbisch
1978.80.16

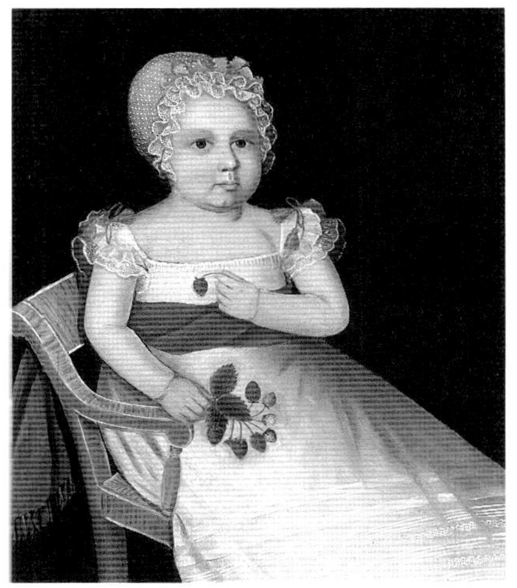

The Strawberry Girl, c. 1830
Canvas, 0.663 x 0.563 (26⅛ x 22⅛)
Gift of Edgar William and Bernice Chrysler Garbisch
1953.5.59

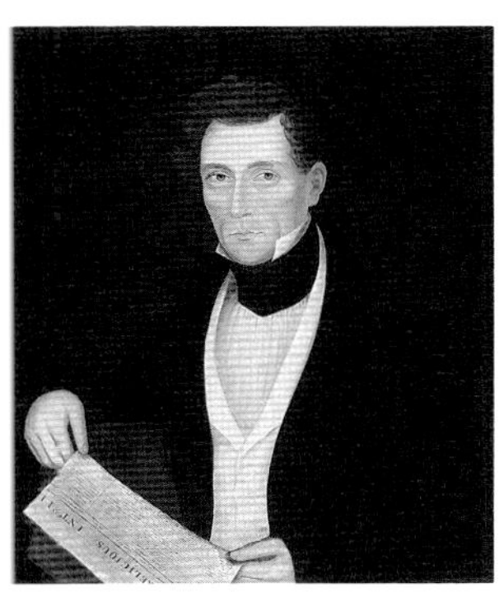

Mr. Day, c. 1835
Canvas, 0.830 x 0.712 (32¾ x 28)
Gift of Edgar William and Bernice Chrysler Garbisch
1953.5.28

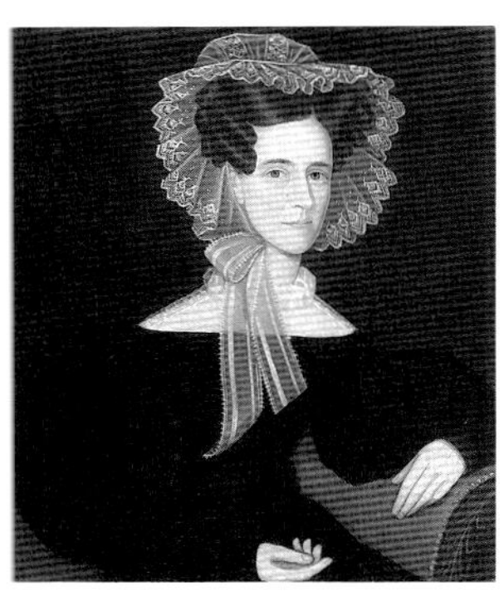

Mrs. Day, c. 1835
Canvas, 0.825 x 0.712 (32½ x 28)
Gift of Edgar William and Bernice Chrysler Garbisch
1953.5.29

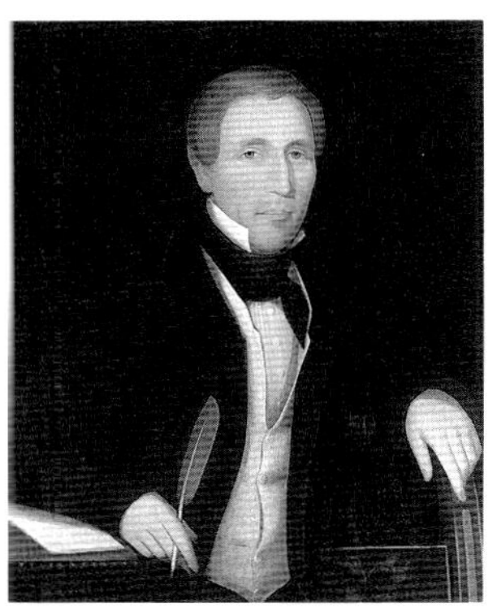

Henry Teller, c. 1835
Canvas, 0.847 x 0.685 (33⅜ x 26$^{15}/_{16}$)
Gift of Edgar William and Bernice Chrysler Garbisch
1953.5.30

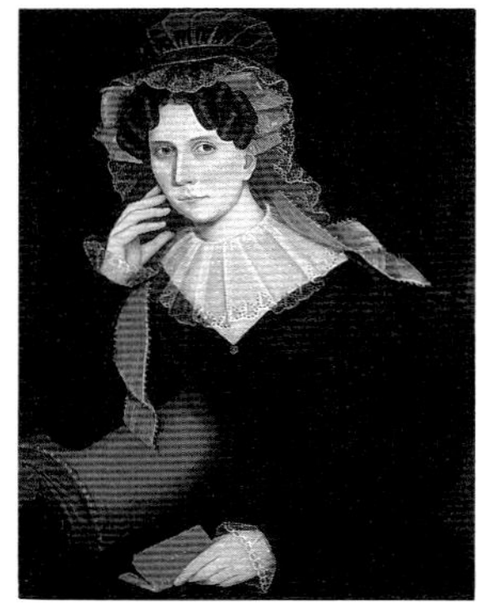

Jane Storm Teller, c. 1835
Canvas, 0.837 x 0.685 (32 15/16 x 26 15/16)
Gift of Edgar William and Bernice Chrysler Garbisch
1953.5.31

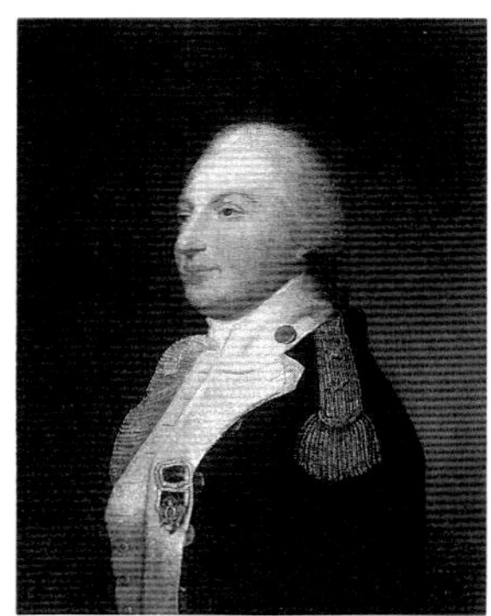

ROBERT EDGE PINE
probably 1730–1788

General William Smallwood, 1788
Canvas, 0.740 x 0.610 (29 1/8 x 24)
Andrew W. Mellon Collection
1947.17.89

Copy after Robert Edge Pine
(See Rembrandt Peale, *George Washington*, 1947.17.16)

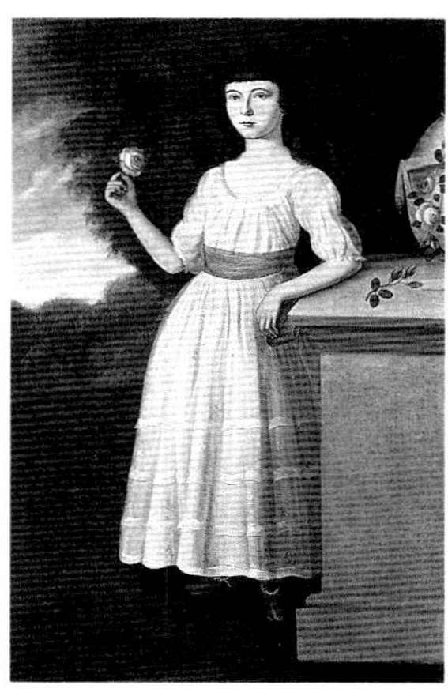

CHARLES PEALE POLK
1767–1822

Anna Maria Cumpston, c. 1790
Canvas, 1.470 x 0.956 (57 7/8 x 37 5/8)
Inscribed at center right: *C. Polk*
Gift of Edgar William and Bernice Chrysler Garbisch
1953.5.32

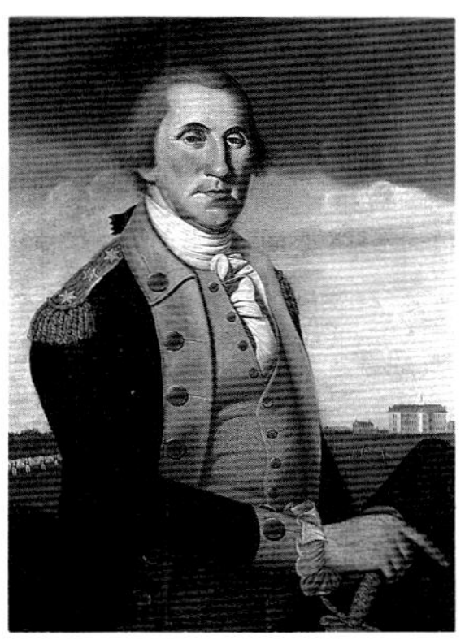

General Washington at Princeton, c. 1790
Canvas, 0.915 x 0.707 (36 x 27 7/8)
Gift of William C. Freeman
1947.13.1

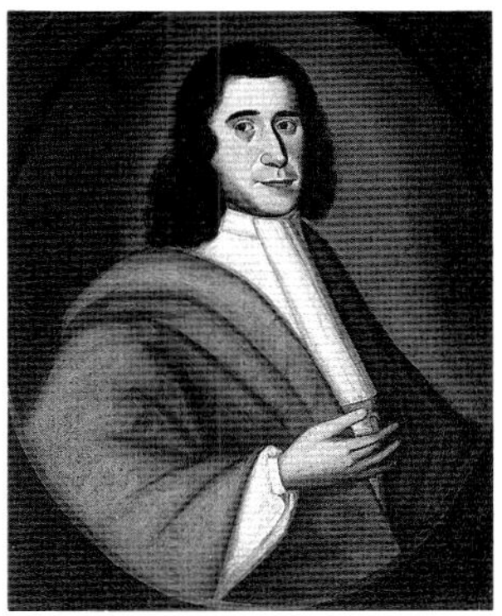

ATTRIBUTED TO THE
POLLARD LIMNER
active c. 1690/1730

William Metcalf (?), c. 1730
Canvas, 0.718 x 0.575 (28¼ x 22 13/16)
Gift of Edgar William and Bernice Chrysler Garbisch
1980.61.1

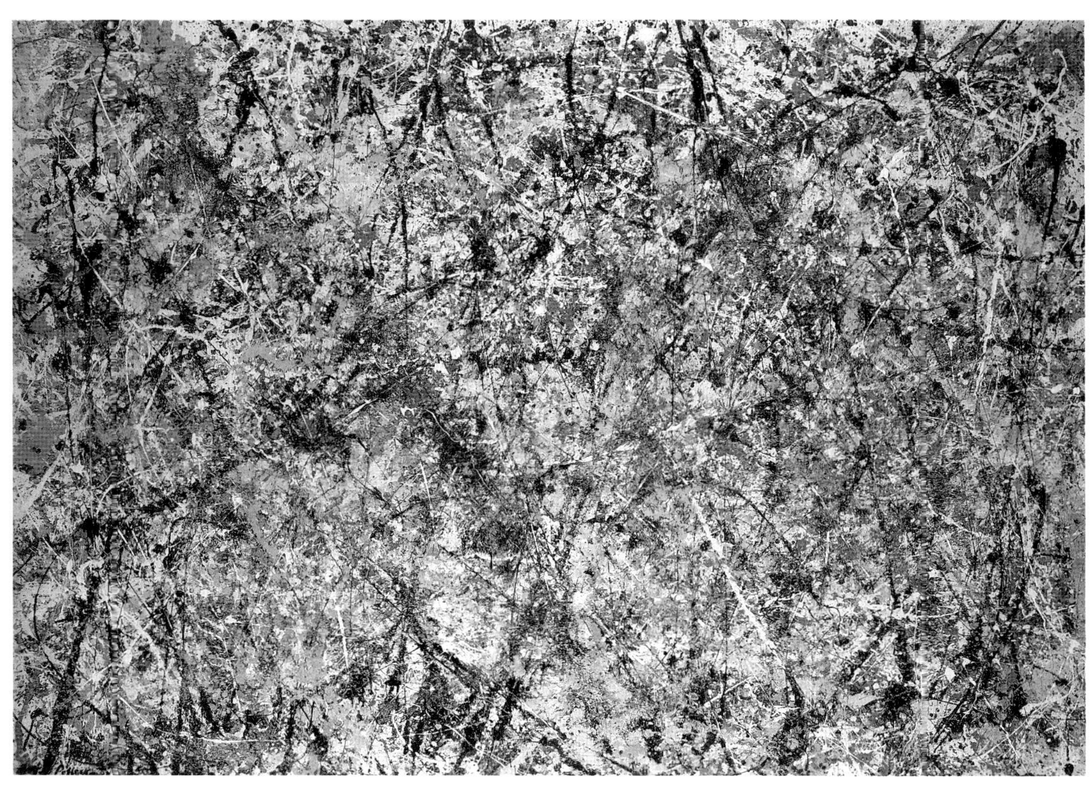

JACKSON POLLOCK
1912–1956

Number 1, 1950 (Lavender Mist), 1950
Canvas, 2.210 x 2.997 (87 x 118)
Two hand prints (Pollock's) at upper right; inscribed at lower left: *Jackson Pollock '50*
Ailsa Mellon Bruce Fund
1976.37.1

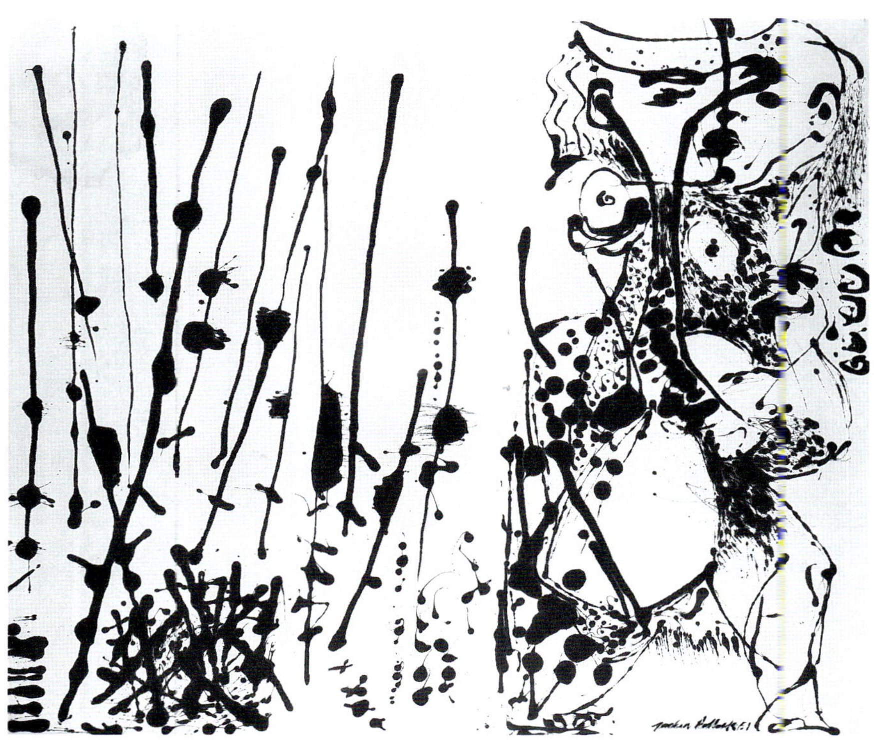

Number 7, 1951, 1951
Canvas, 1.435 x 1.676 (56½ x 66)
Inscribed at lower right: *Jackson Pollock 51*
Gift of the Collectors Committee
1983.77.1

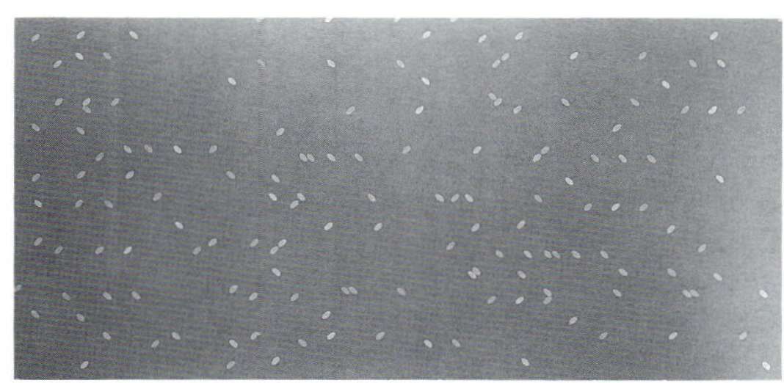

LARRY POONS
born 1937

Tristan da Cunha, 1964
Canvas, 1.831 x 3.662 (72⅛ x 144¼)
Gift of Mr. and Mrs. Burton Tremaine
1977.75.5

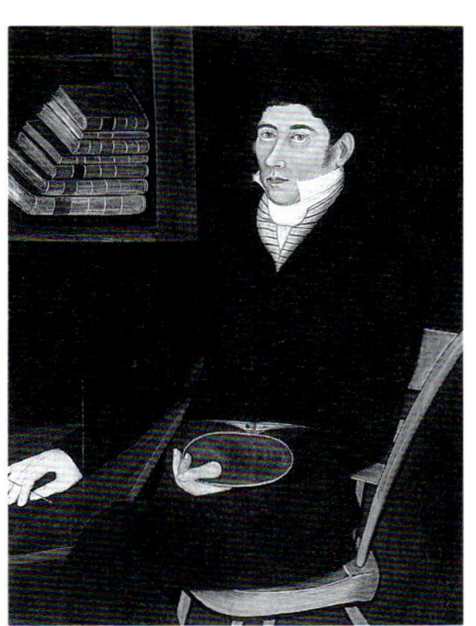

ASAHEL POWERS
1813–1843

William Sheldon (?), c. 1831
Wood, 1.044 x 0.787 (41⅛ x 31)
Gift of Edgar William and Bernice Chrysler Garbisch
1953.5.50

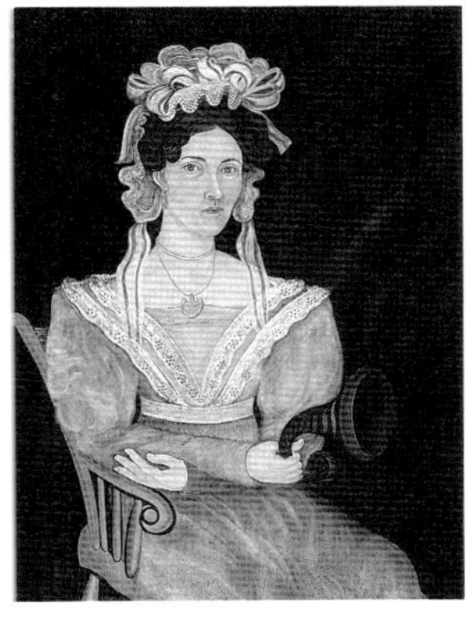

Mrs. William Sheldon (?), c. 1831
Wood, 1.041 x 0.775 (4[illegible] x 30½)
Gift of Edgar William and Bernice Chrysler Garbisch
1953.5.51

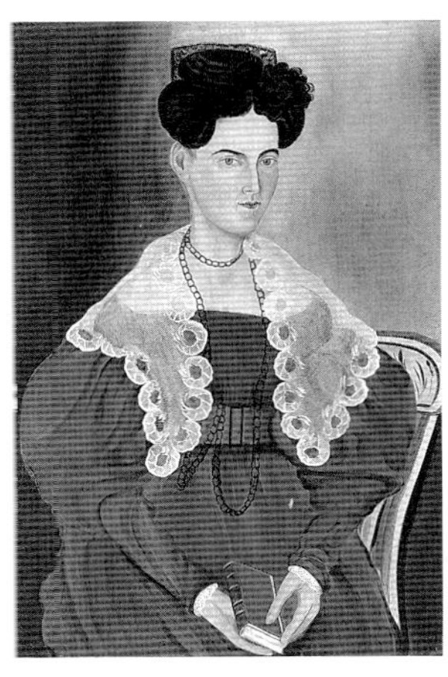

Hannah Fisher Stedman, 1833
Wood, 0.915 x 0.630 (36 x 24¾)
Gift of Edgar William and Bernice Chrysler Garbisch
1953.5.54

MATTHEW PRATT
1734–1805

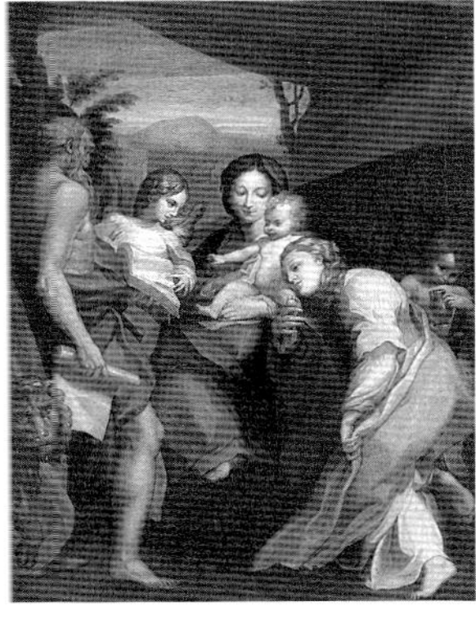

Madonna of Saint Jerome, 1764/1766
Canvas, 0.778 x 0.600 (30⅝ x 23⅝)
Gift of Clarence Van Dyke Tiers
1944.17.1

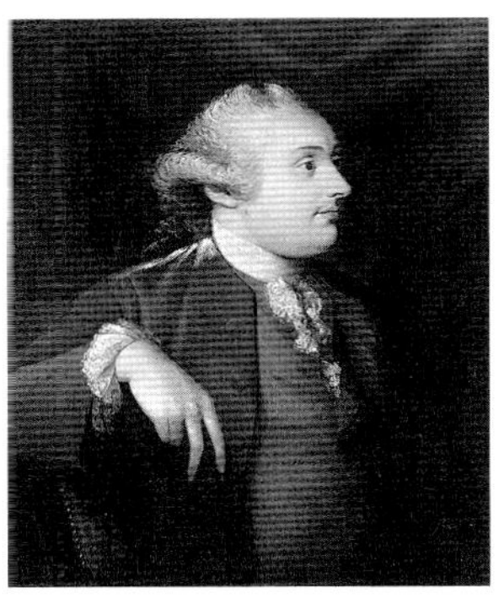

The Duke of Portland, 1774 or after
Canvas, 0.763 x 0.632 (30$^{1}/_{16}$ x 25$^{1}/_{16}$)
Gift of Clarence Van Dyke Tiers
1942.13.2

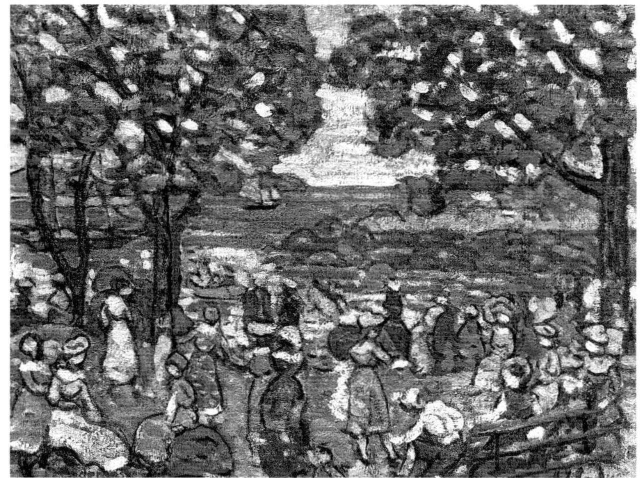

MAURICE BRAZIL PRENDERGAST
1858–1924

Salem Cove, 1916
Canvas, 0.612 x 0.765 (24⅛ x 30⅛)
Inscribed at lower left: *Prendergast*
Collection of Mr. and Mrs. Paul Mellon
1985.64.33

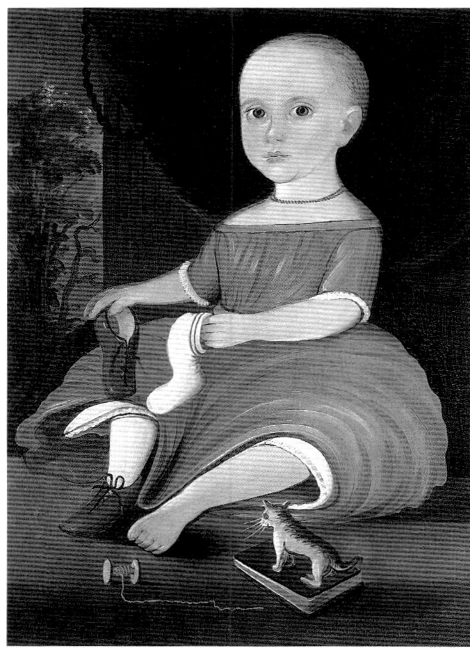

WILLIAM MATTHEW PRIOR
1806–1873

Baby in Blue, c. 1845
Paper attached to panel, 0.603 x 0.432 (23¾ x 17)
Gift of Edgar William and Bernice Chrysler Garbisch
1953.5.58

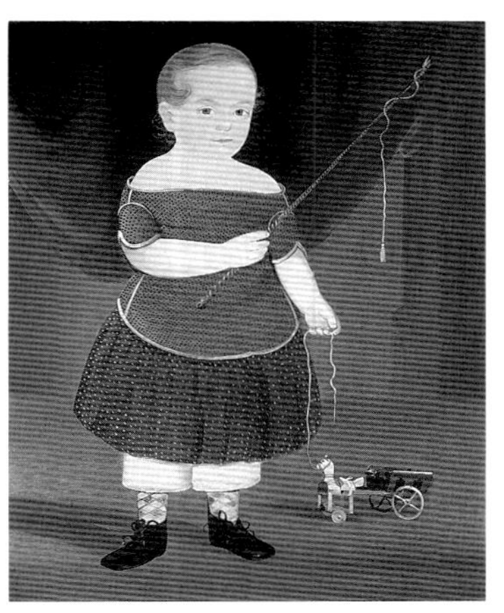

Boy with Toy Horse and Wagon, c. 1845
Canvas, 0.770 x 0.637 (30⅜ x 25)
Gift of Edgar William and Bernice Chrysler Garbisch
1953.5.67

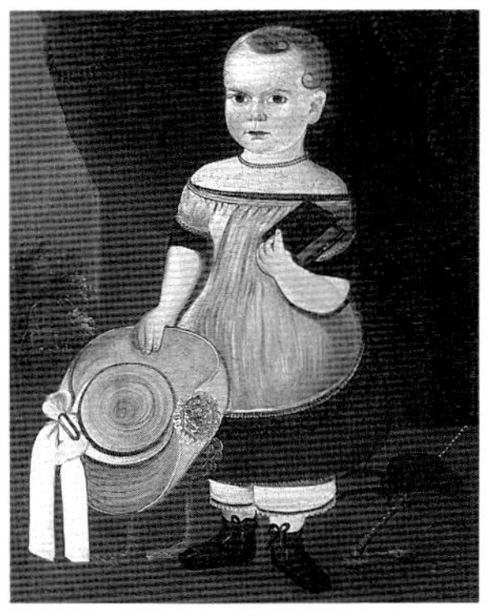

Child with Straw Hat, c. 1846/1873
Canvas, 0.765 x 0.605 (30⅛ x 23$^{13}/_{16}$)
Gift of Edgar William and Bernice
Chrysler Garbisch
1978.80.9

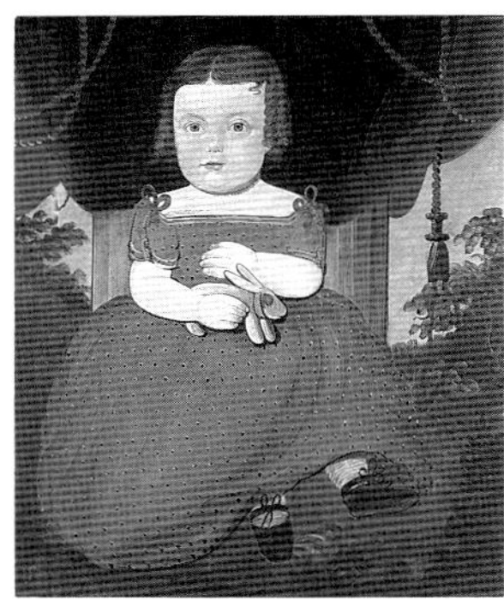

Little Miss Fairfield, 1850
Canvas, 0.610 x 0.509 (24 x 20)
Gift of Edgar William and Bernice
Chrysler Garbisch
1971.83.9

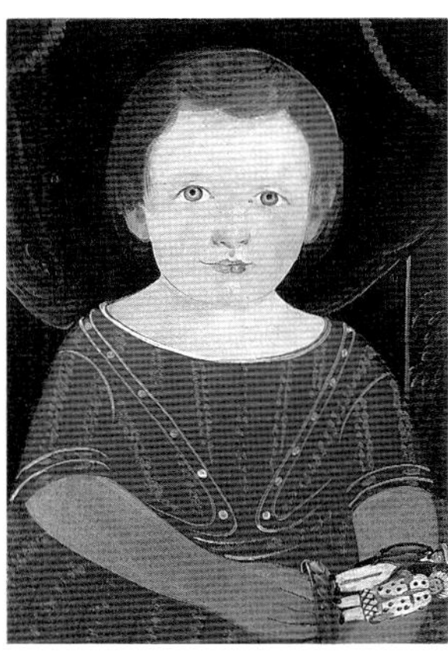

Master Cleeves, c. 1850
Cardboard, 0.413 x 0.303 (16¼ x 11⅞)
Gift of Edgar William and Bernice
Chrysler Garbisch
1953.5.33

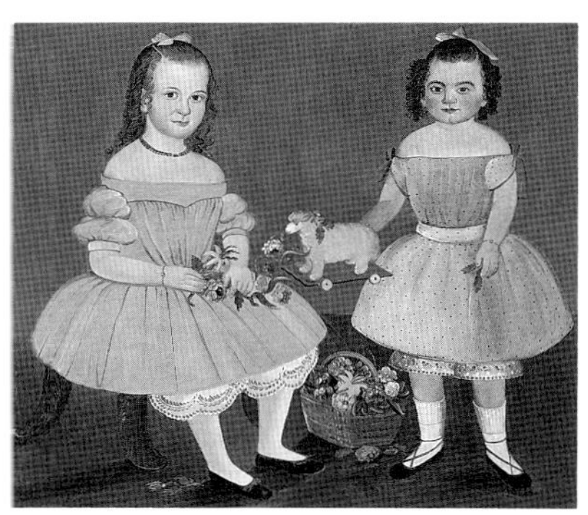

The Burnish Sisters, 1854
Canvas, 0.902 x 1.018 (35½ x 40⅛)
Gift of Edgar William and Bernice
Chrysler Garbisch
1980.62.18

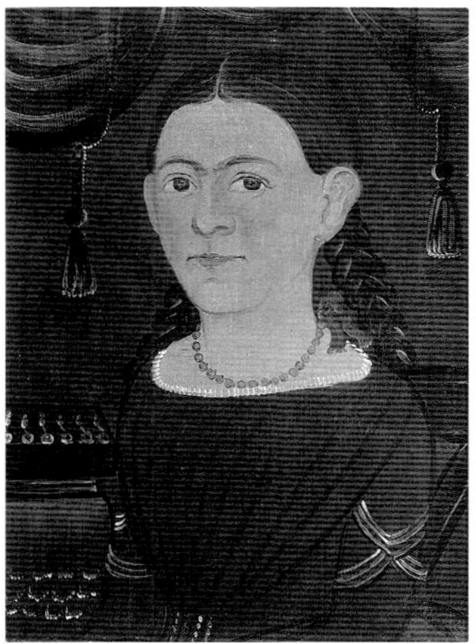

PRIOR-HAMBLIN SCHOOL
active c. 1845

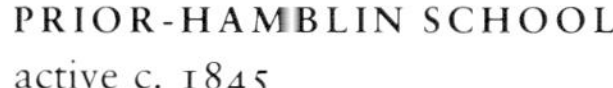

Daughter, c. 1845
Academy board, 0.346 x 0.243
(13 5/8 x 9 9/16)
Gift of Edgar William and Bernice
Chrysler Garbisch
1953.5.43

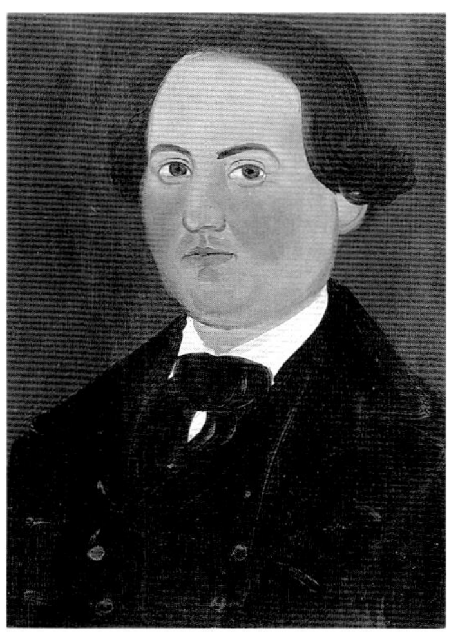

Husband, c. 1845
Cardboard, 0.364 x 0.260 (14 3/8 x 10 1/4)
Gift of Edgar William and Bernice
Chrysler Garbisch
1953.5.42

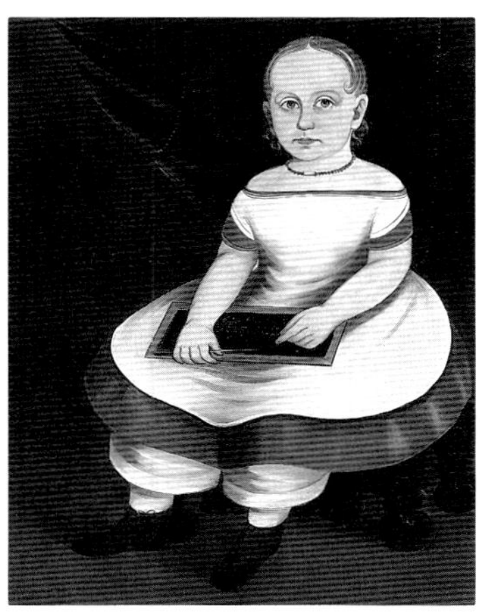

Little Girl with Slate, c. 1845
Canvas, 0.688 x 0.560 (27 1/8 x 22 1/16)
Gift of Edgar William and Bernice
Chrysler Garbisch
1953.5.66

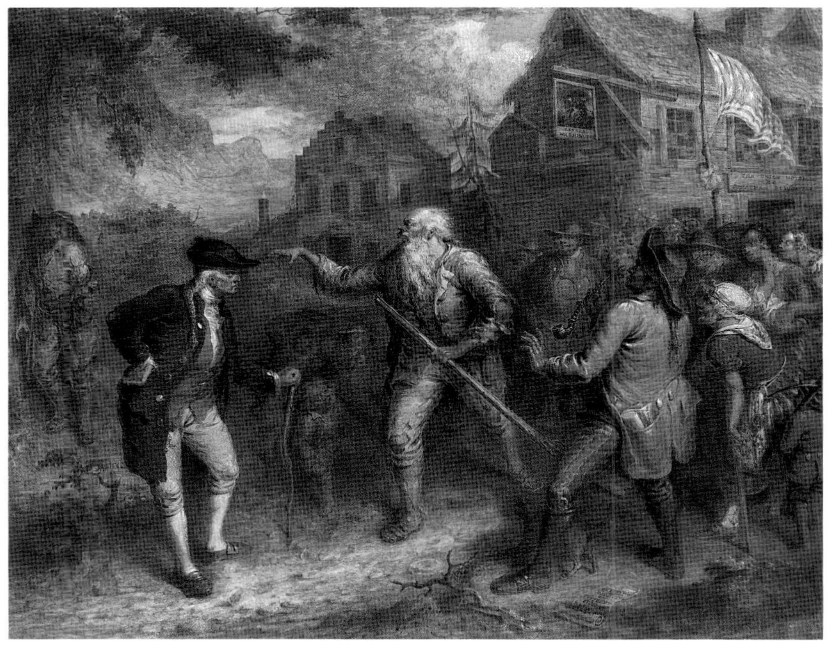

JOHN QUIDOR
1801–1881

The Return of Rip Van Winkle, c. 1849
Canvas, 1.010 x 1.265 (39¾ x 49¾)
Inscribed at lower center on rock:
J. Quidor, / N.Y. / 18[4?]9
Andrew W. Mellon Collection
1942.8.10

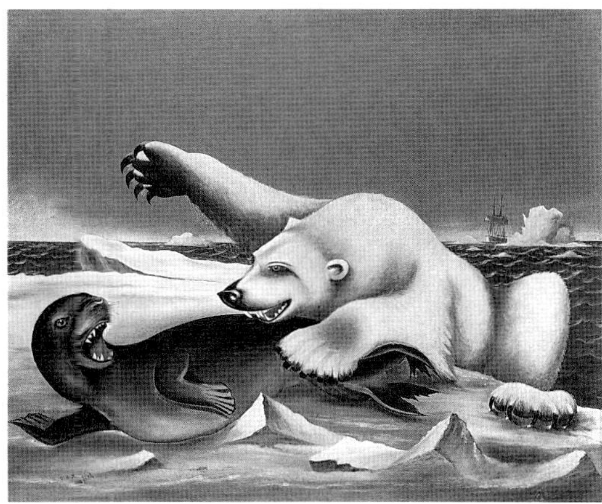

CHARLES S. RALEIGH
1831–1925

Law of the Wild, 1881
Canvas, 0.895 x 1.020 (35¼ x 40⅛)
Inscribed at lower left: *C. S. Raleigh / 1881*
Gift of Edgar William and Bernice Chrysler Garbisch
1971.83.10

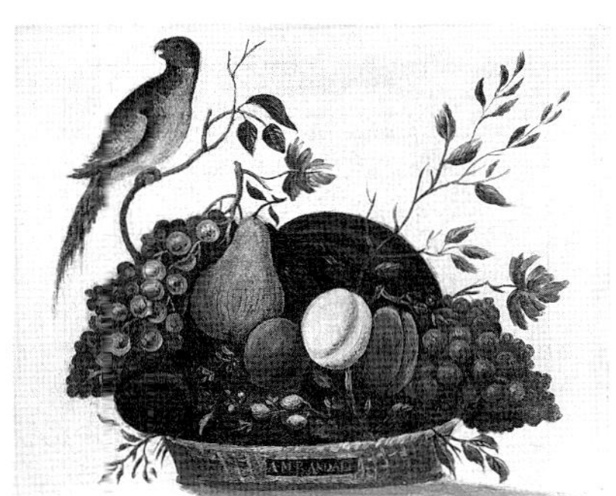

A. M. RANDALL
active 1777

Basket of Fruit with Parrot, 1777
Canvas, 0.434 x 0.508 (17⅛ x 20)
Inscribed at lower center on basket: *A.M. RANDALL / 1777*
Gift of Edgar William and Bernice Chrysler Garbisch
1980.62.20

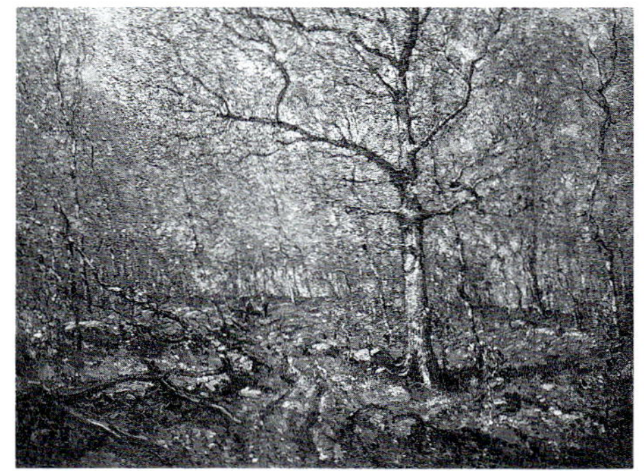

HENRY WARD RANGER
1858–1916

Spring Woods, c. 1910
Canvas, 0.712 x 0.917 (28 x 36⅛)
Inscribed at lower left in rectangle, superimposed on triangle: *RANGER; N A D* (in points of the triangle)
Chester Dale Collection
1963.10.202

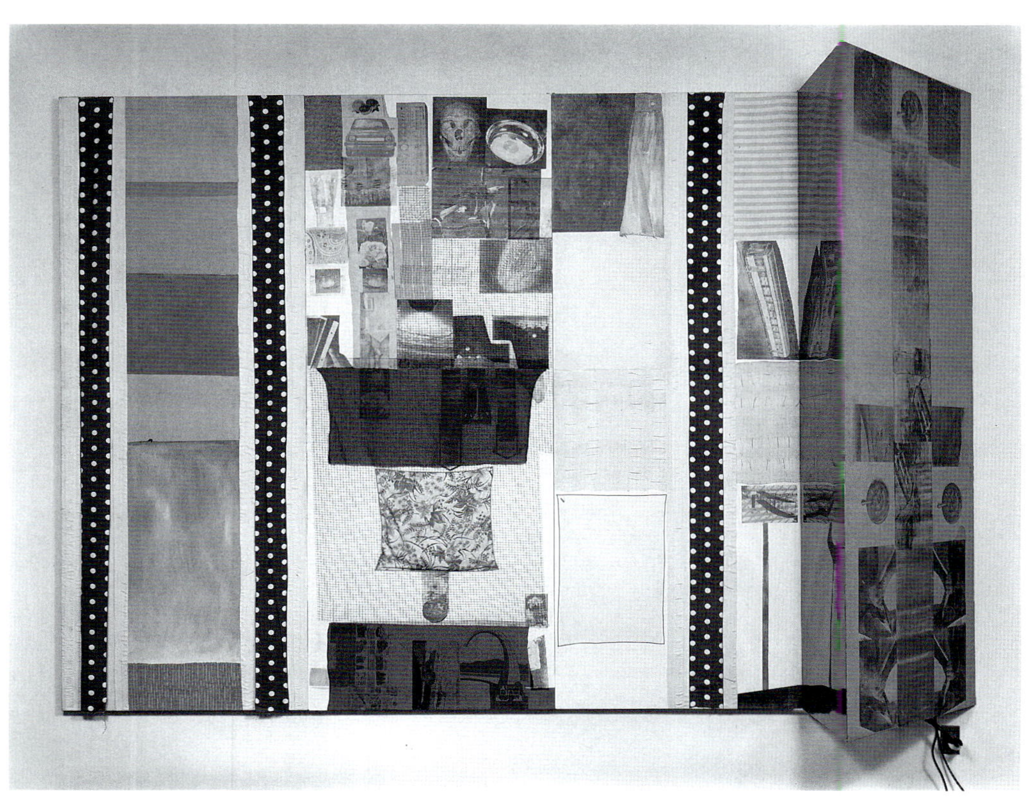

ROBERT RAUSCHENBERG
born 1925

Doric Circus, 1979
Board, 2.438 x 3.467 x 0.660 (96 x 136½ x 26)
Inscribed on reverse of each panel: *RAUSCHENBERG 79*
Gift of Lila Acheson Wallace
1985.28.1

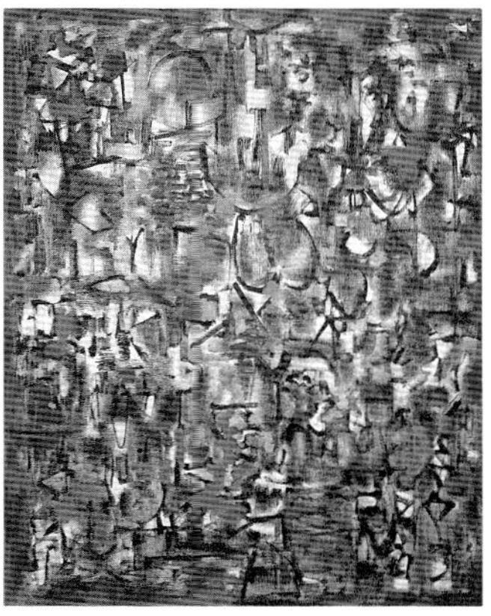

AD REINHARDT
1913–1967

Untitled, 1947
Canvas, 1.016 x 0.813 (40 x 32)
Inscribed at lower right:
REINHARDT '47
Ailsa Mellon Bruce Fund and Gift of The Circle of the National Gallery of Art
1988.60.1

Black Painting No. 34, 1964
Canvas, 1.530 x 1.526 (60¼ x 60⅛)
Gift of Mr. and Mrs. Burton Tremaine
1970.37.1

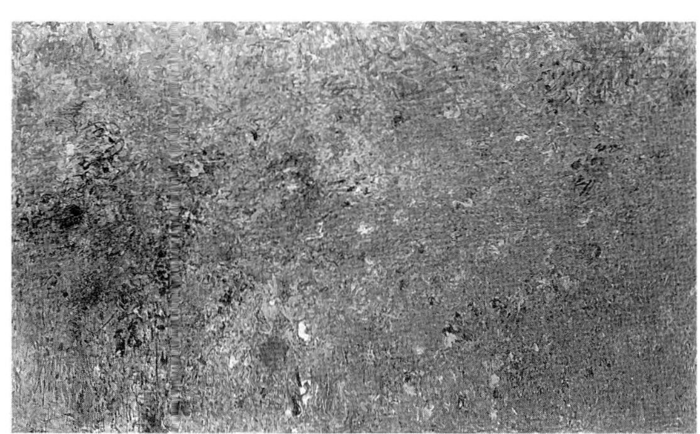

MILTON RESNICK
born 1917

Mound, 1961
Canvas, 2.920 x 4.698 (115 x 185)
Inscribed at lower left: *61 / Resnick*
Gift of Howard Wise
1974.15.1

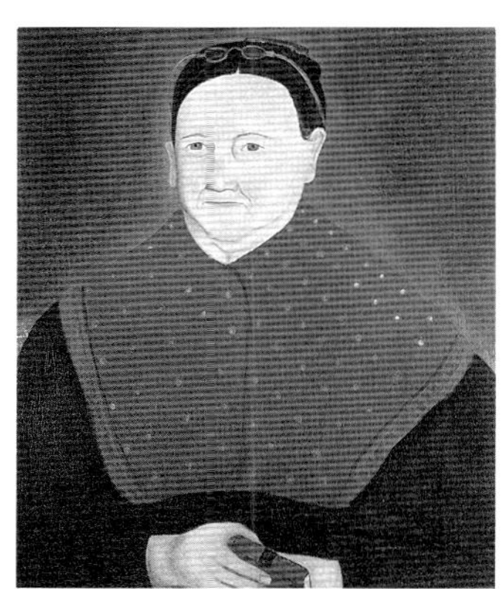

J. C. ROBINSON
active 1848

Portrait of an Old Lady, 1848
Canvas, 0.660 x 0.553 (26 x 21¾)
Inscribed at center left: *B[. . .] / June 4 / 1784*
Gift of Edgar William and Bernice Chrysler Garbisch
1955.11.15

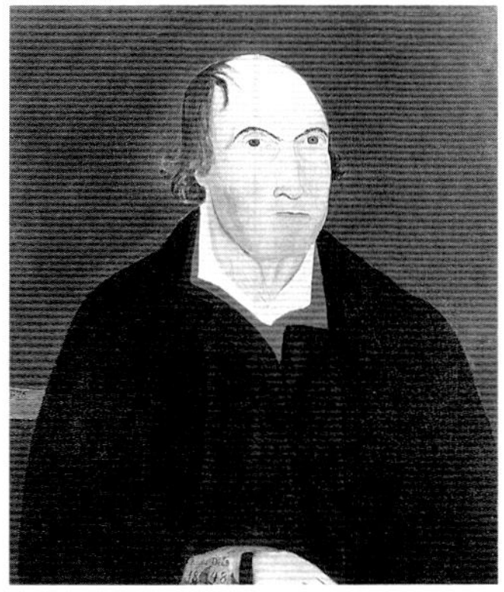

Portrait of an Old Man, 1848
Canvas, 0.660 x 0.554 (26 x 21 13/16)
Inscribed at lower center: *Painted Dec. 9 / 18 48*; center left: *Ag. 76*
Gift of Edgar William and Bernice Chrysler Garbisch
1955.11.14

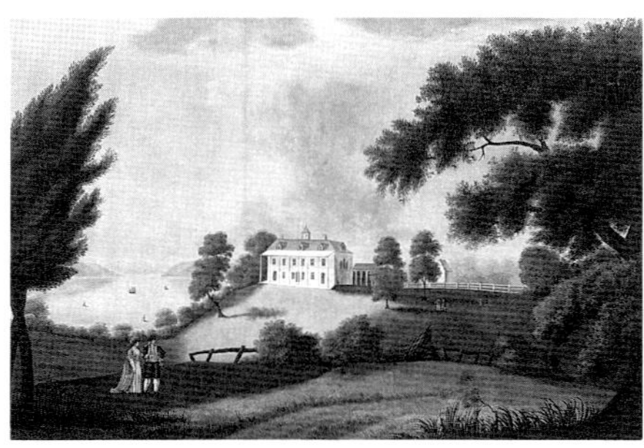

GEORGE ROPES
1788–1819

Mount Vernon, 1806
Canvas, 0.940 x 1.346 (37 x 53)
Inscribed at lower right: *G. Ropes / Salem 1806*
Gift of Edgar William and Bernice Chrysler Garbisch
1956.13.6

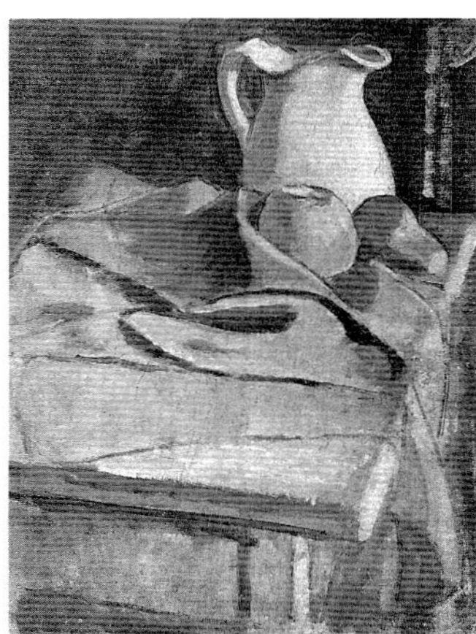

MARK ROTHKO
1903–1970

Untitled (still life with pitcher), c. 1924/1930
Canvas board, 0.403 x 0.302 (15 7/8 x 11 7/8)
Gift of The Mark Rothko Foundation
1986.56.663

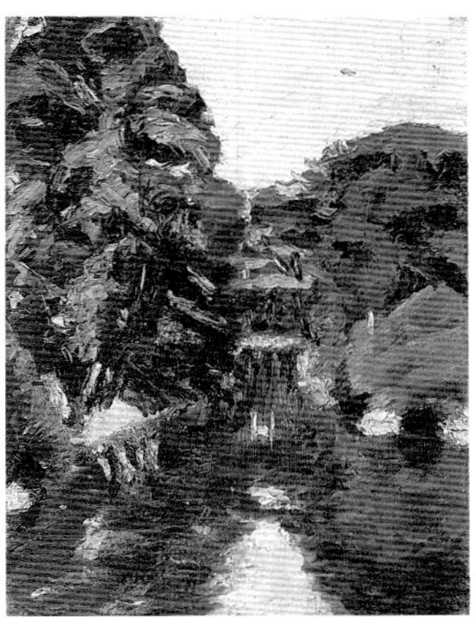

In the Shade, 1925
Canvas board, 0.405 x 0.300 (15 15/16 x 11 13/16)
Inscribed across bottom on reverse: *SKETCH IN THE SHADE JULY 1925*
Gift of The Mark Rothko Foundation
1986.56.650

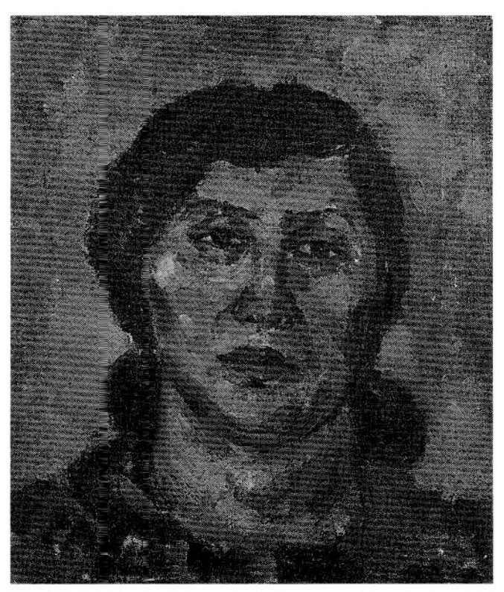

Untitled (female portrait) c. 1925/1933
Canvas, 0.441 x 0.371 (17 3/8 x 14 5/8)
Gift of The Mark Rothko Foundation
1986.56.660

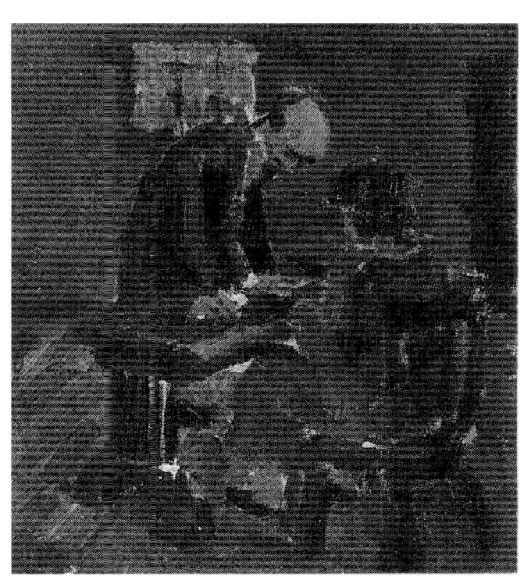

Untitled (man and seated woman),
c. 1925/1933
Canvas, 0.332 x 0.287 (13 1/16 x 11 5/16)
Inscribed at lower right: *M. Rothkowitz*
Gift of The Mark Rothko Foundation
1986.56.652

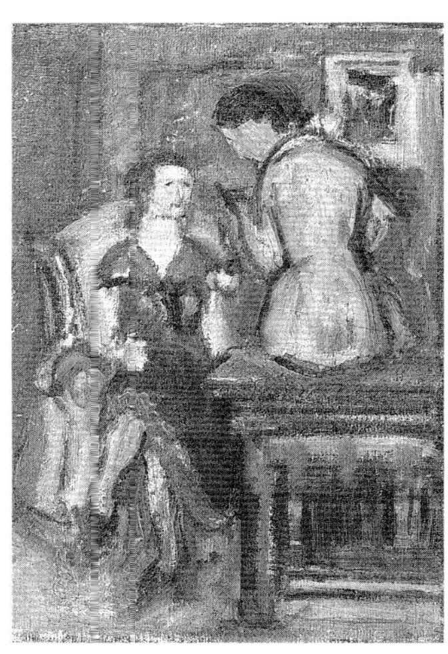

Untitled (two figures), c. 1925/1933
Canvas board, 0.381 x 0.276 (15 x 10 7/8)
Gift of The Mark Rothko Foundation
1986.56.651

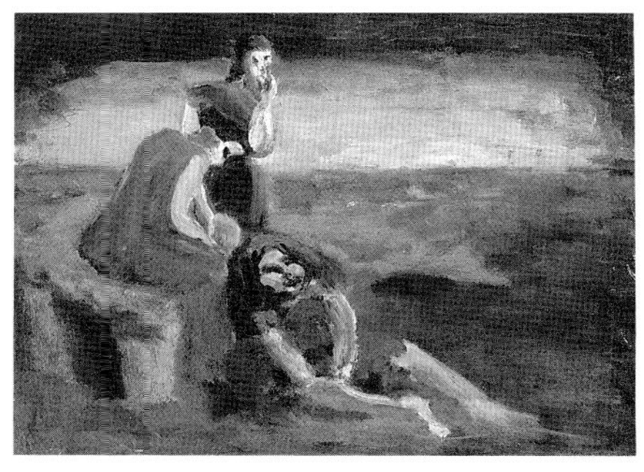

Untitled (three girls in a landscape),
1925/1935
Canvas, 0.610 x 0.813 (24 x 32)
Inscribed at center left on reverse:
Mark Rothko
Gift of The Mark Rothko Foundation
1986.43.41

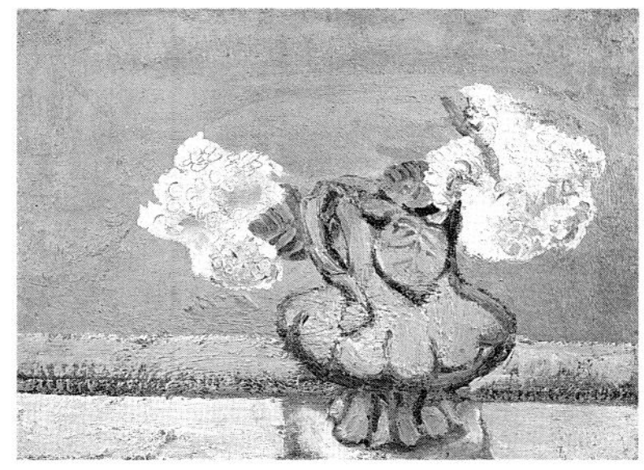

Untitled (vase of flowers) (recto), 1925/1938
Paperboard, 0.317 x 0.419 (12½ x 16½)
Gift of The Mark Rothko Foundation
1986.56.649a

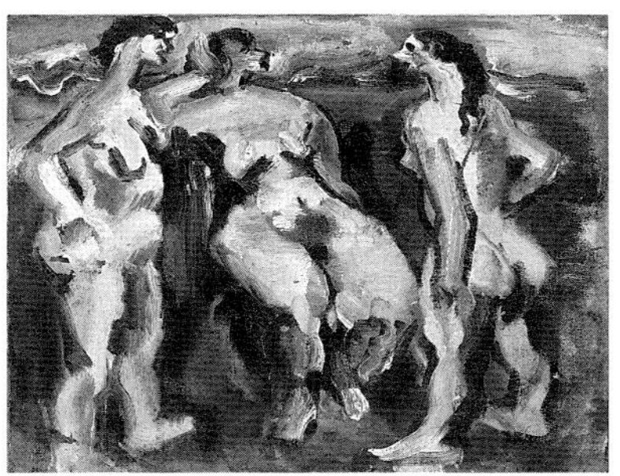

Untitled (three nudes), c. 1926/1935
Black cloth, 0.403 x 0.505 (15¹⁵⁄₁₆ x 19¹⁵⁄₁₆)
Gift of The Mark Rothko Foundation
1986.43.94

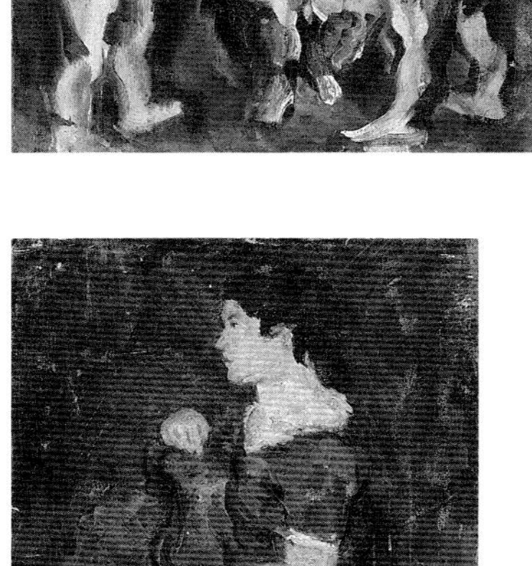

Minna, c. 1930/1933
Canvas, 0.755 x 0.500 (29¾ x 19¹¹⁄₁₆)
Inscribed at lower right: *M. Rothkowitz*; across center on reverse: *MARK ROTHKO/ 1930–1933 / Rothkowitz /*
Gift of the Mark Rothko Foundation
1986.43.99

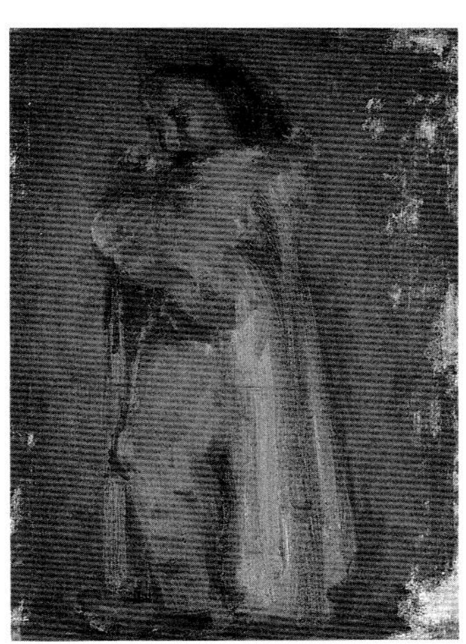

Untitled, c. 1930/1933
Canvas, 0.812 x 0.606 (31⅞ x 23⅞)
Inscribed upper center on reverse: *1930–1933*
Gift of The Mark Rothko Foundation
1986.43.39

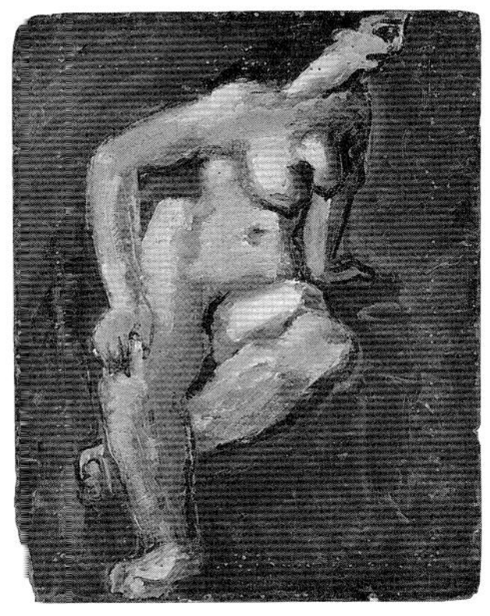

Nude, 1930/1934
Hardboard, 0.916 x 0.713 (36 1/16 x 28 1/16)
Inscribed at lower right: *M.Rothkowitz*;
across center on reverse: *M. Rothkowitz/*
NUDE
Gift of The Mark Rothko Foundation
1986.43.29

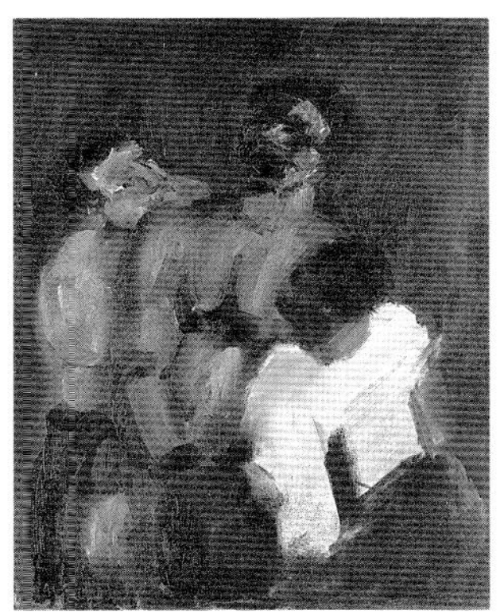

The Pugilist, c. 1930/1934
Canvas, 0.545 x 0.449 (21 7/16 x 17 15/16)
Inscribed at lower left: *M Rothkowitz*;
across center on reverse: *M Rothkowitz*
Gift of The Mark Rothko Foundation
1986.43.93

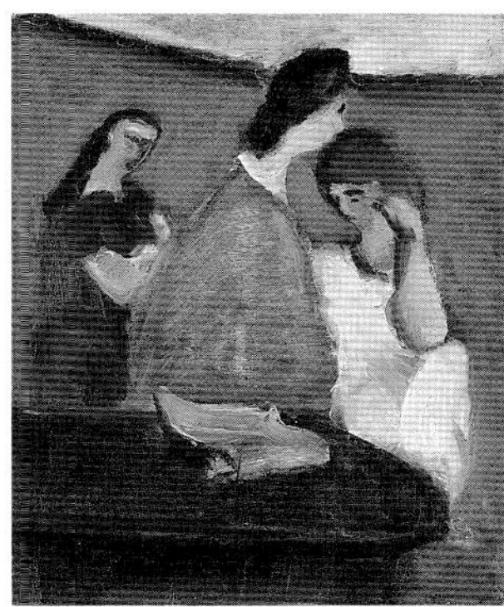

Untitled (three women), c. 1930/1934
Canvas, 0.584 x 0.480 (23 1/8 x 19)
Inscribed at lower center on reverse:
Mark Rothko
Gift of The Mark Rothko Foundation
1986.43.56

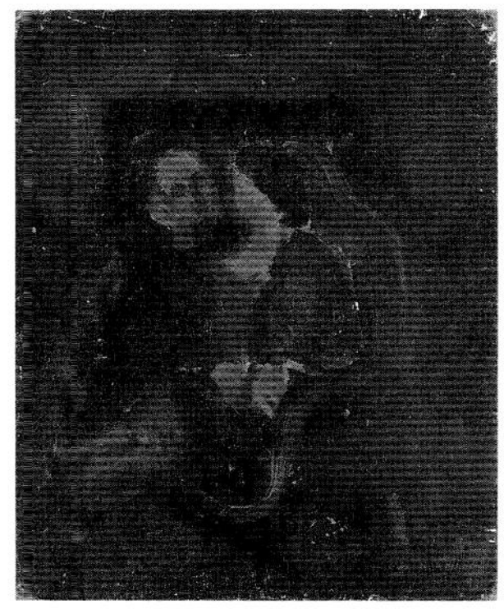

Untitled (two figures on a couch),
c. 1930/1934
Canvas, 0.508 x 0.407 (20 x 16)
Inscribed at lower right: *M.Rothkowitz*;
across center on reverse:
M. ROTHKOWITZ
Gift of The Mark Rothko Foundation
1986.43.25

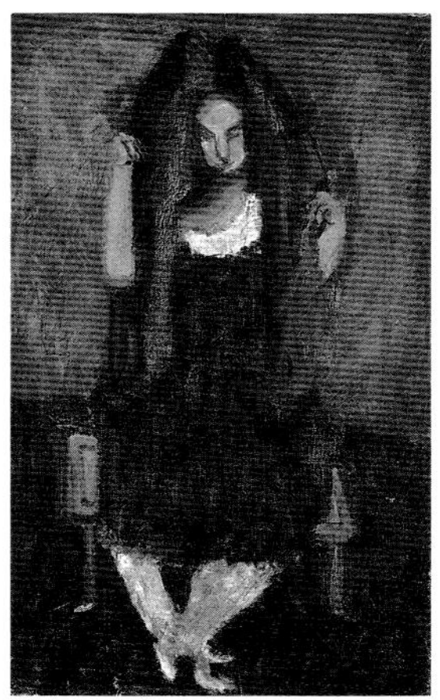

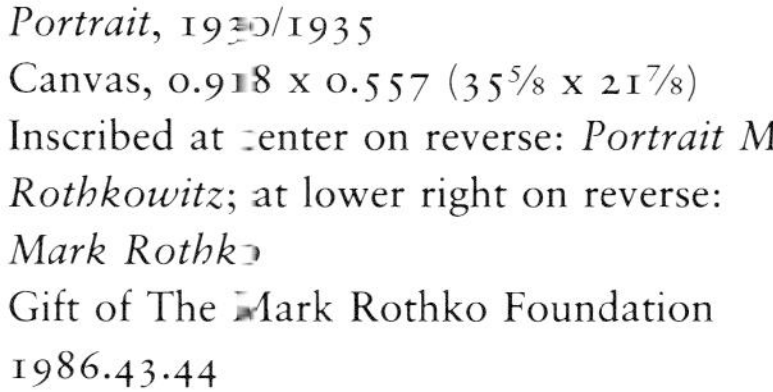

Portrait, 1930/1935
Canvas, 0.908 x 0.557 (35⅝ x 21⅞)
Inscribed at center on reverse: *Portrait M. Rothkowitz*; at lower right on reverse: *Mark Rothko*
Gift of The Mark Rothko Foundation
1986.43.44

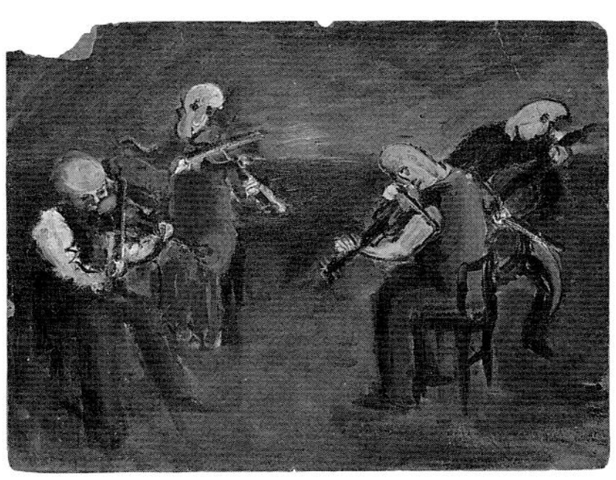

Untitled (string quartet), 1930/1935
Hardboard, 0.710 x 0.917
(27 15/16 x 36 1/16)
Inscribed at upper right: *Mark Rothko*
Gift of The Mark Rothko Foundation
1986.43.30

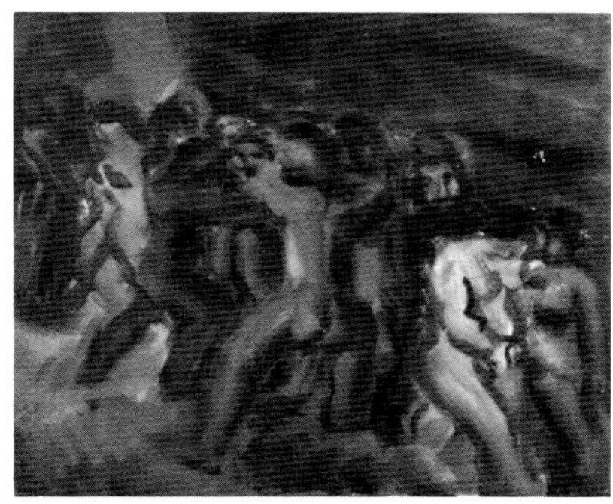

Untitled, c. 1930/1935
Canvas board, 0.360 x 0.422
(14 3/16 x 16⅝)
Gift of The Mark Rothko Foundation
1986.56.661

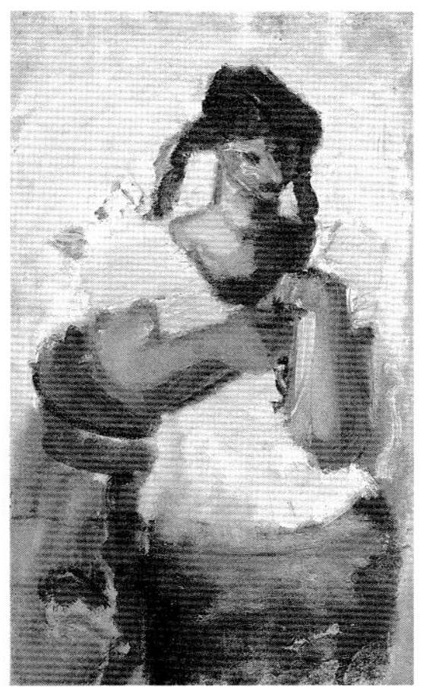

Untitled (girl with pigtails), c. 1930/1935
Canvas, 0.806 x 0.473 (31 11/16 x 18⅝)
Gift of The Mark Rothko Foundation
1986.43.90

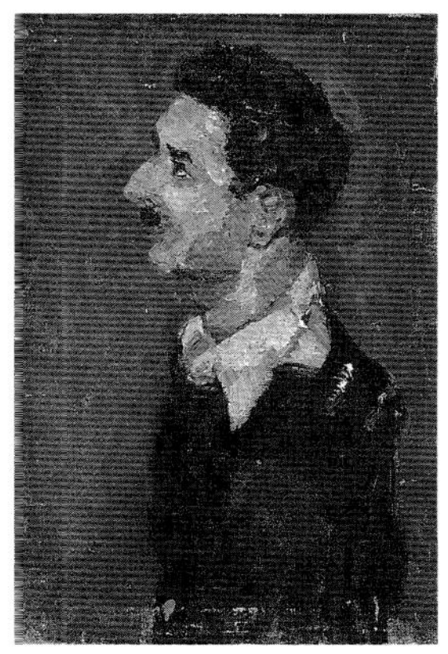

Untitled (male portrait), c. 1930/1935
Canvas, 0.635 x 0.421 (25 x 16 9/16)
Inscribed at lower right on reverse:
Mark Rothko
Gift of The Mark Rothko Foundation
1986.43.91

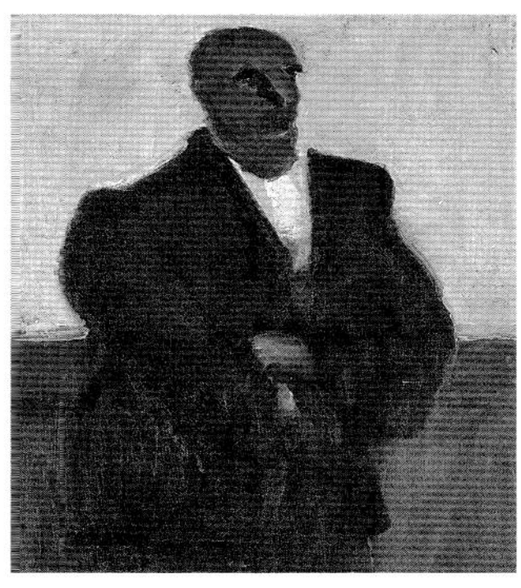

Untitled (man with green face),
c. 1930/1935
Canvas, 0.715 x 0.609 (27 11/16 x 23 11/16)
Gift of The Mark Rothko Foundation
1986.43.100

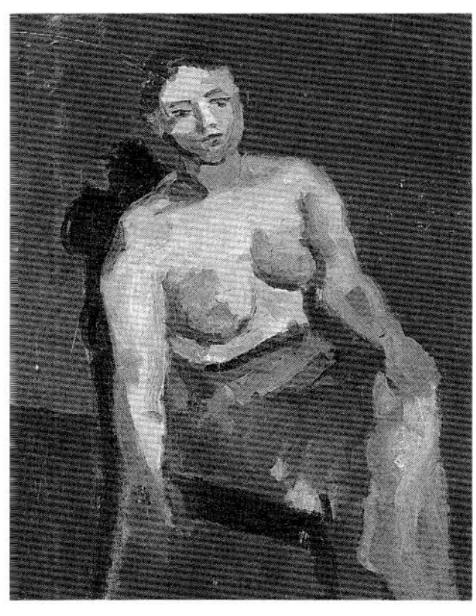

Untitled (seated female nude),
c. 1930/1935
Canvas on board, 0.809 x 0.616
(31 7/8 x 24 1/4)
Gift of The Mark Rothko Foundation
1986.43.27

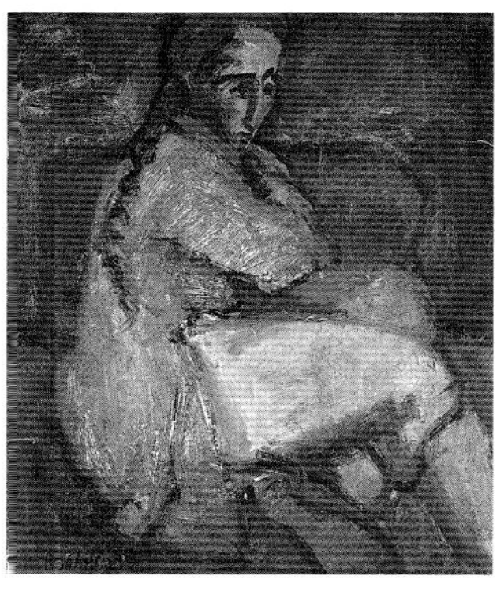

Untitled (seated girl with braids),
c. 1930/1935
Canvas, 0.662 x 0.558 (26 1/16 x 21 15/16)
Inscribed at lower left: *Rothkowitz*; at
upper center on reverse: *Rothkowitz*
Gift of The Mark Rothko Foundation
1986.43.101

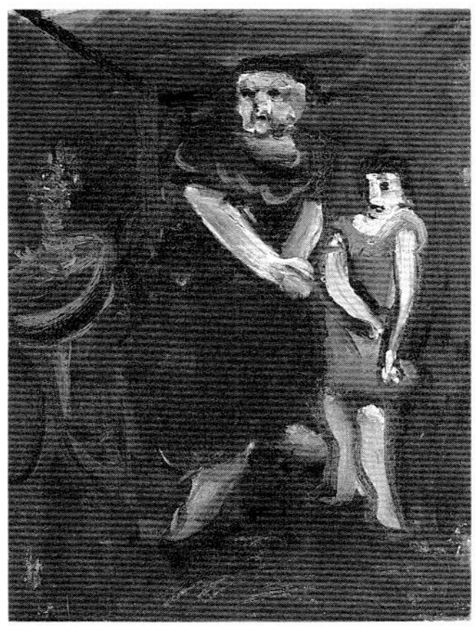

Untitled (woman and child in interior), c. 1930/1935
Canvas, 0.641 x 0.487 (25¼ x 19 3/16)
Inscribed at lower center on reverse: *Mark Rothko*
Gift of The Mark Rothko Foundation
1986.43.95

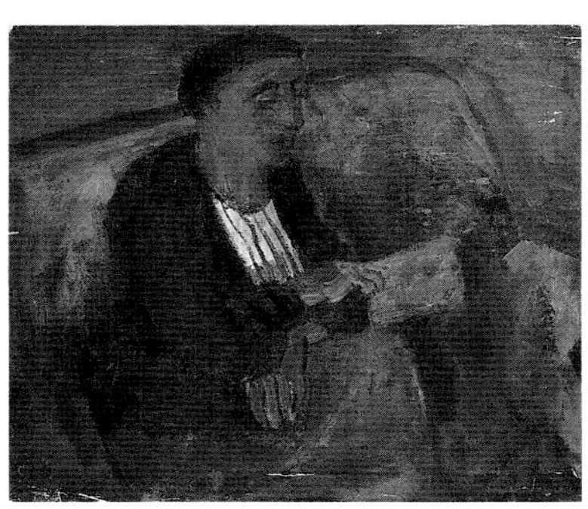

Untitled (woman sitting on a couch), c. 1930/1935
Canvas, 0.607 x 0.712 (23⅞ x 28)
Inscribed at lower right on reverse: *Mark Rothko / Mark Rothko*
Gift of The Mark Rothko Foundation
1986.43.98

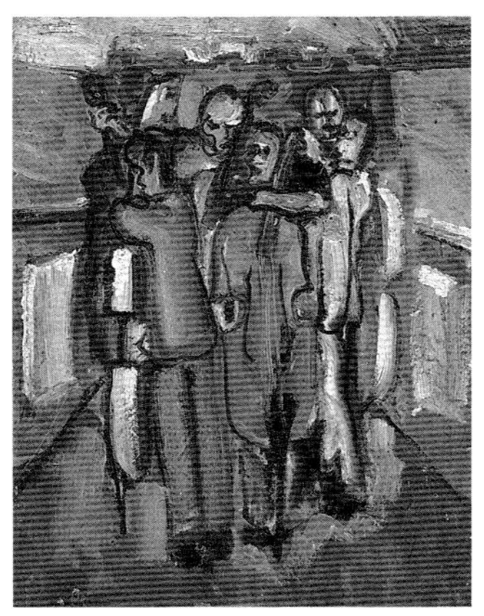

Untitled (musicians), c. 1930/1936
Hardboard, 0.809 x 0.638 (31⅞ x 25⅛)
Gift of The Mark Rothko Foundation
1986.43.121

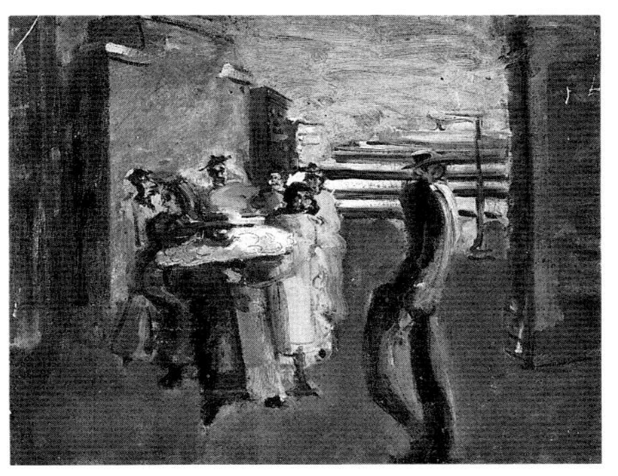

Untitled (street scene), c. 1930/1936
Hardboard, 0.610 x 0.765 (24 x 30⅛)
Gift of The Mark Rothko Foundation
1986.43.122

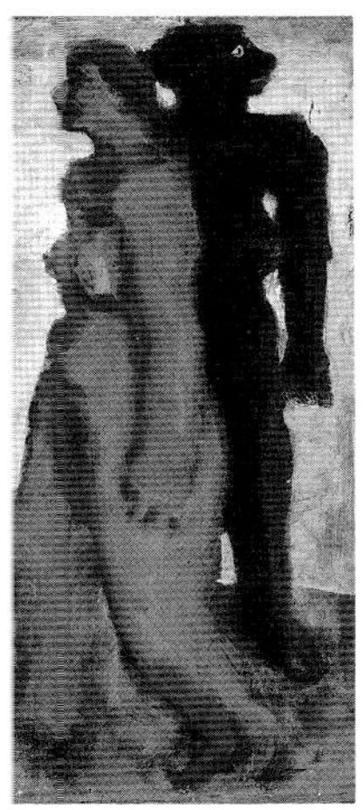

Untitled (two nudes), c. 1930/1936
Canvas, 1.003 x 0.448 (39½ x 17⅝)
Inscribed at lower center on reverse:
Mark Rothko
Gift of The Mark Rothko Foundation
1986.43.40

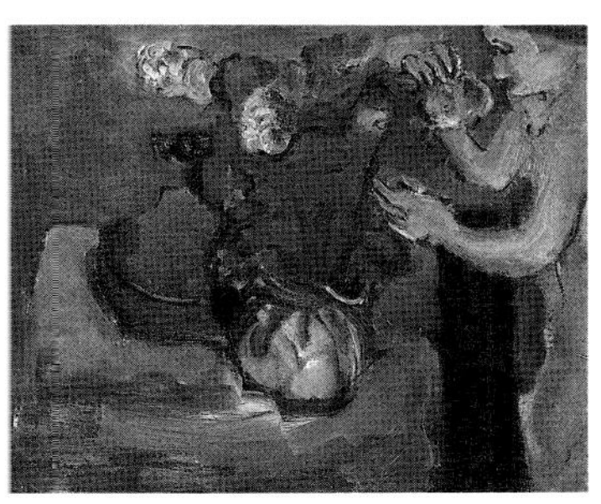

Untitled (woman arranging flowers), c. 1930/1936
Canvas, 0.579 x 0.678 (22¹³⁄₁₆ x 26¾)
Inscribed at center left on reverse:
Mark Rothko
Gift of The Mark Rothko Foundation
1986.43.92

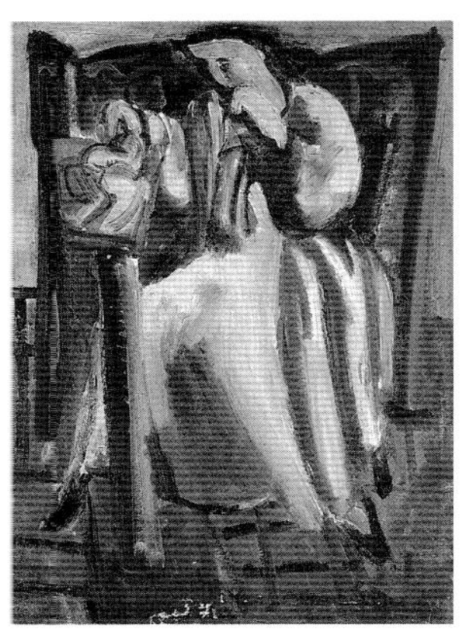

Untitled (sculptress), 1932/1934
Canvas, 0.814 x 0.607 (32 x 23⅞)
Inscribed at lower center on reverse:
MARK ROTHKO
Gift of The Mark Rothko Foundation
1986.43.46

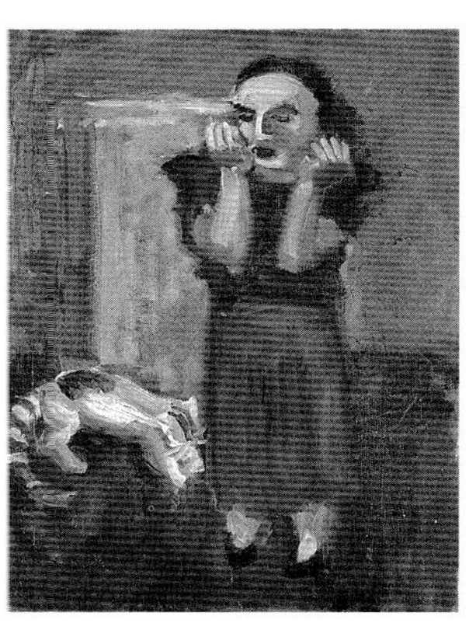

Untitled (woman and cat), 1932/1934
Canvas, 0.806 x 0.610 (31¾ x 24)
Inscribed at lower right: *MRothkowitz*
Gift of The Mark Rothko Foundation
1986.43.47

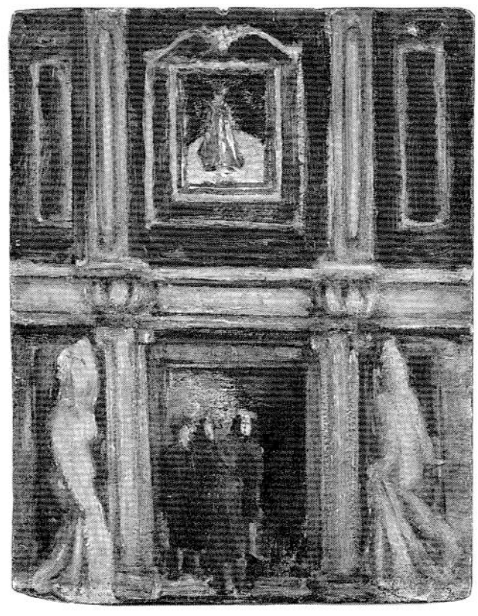

Interior, 1932/1935
Hardboard, 0.607 x 0.465
(23 15/16 x 18 5/16)
Inscribed across center on reverse:
INTERIOR / M.ROTHKO
Gift of The Mark Rothko Foundation
1986.43.26

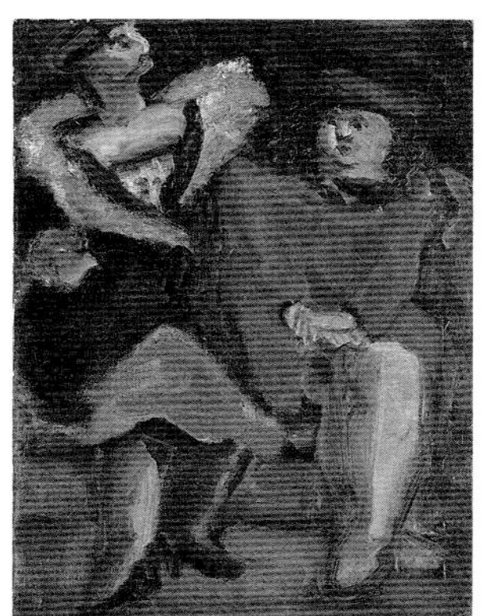

Untitled (two seated women),
c. 1932/1935
Canvas, 0.797 x 0.597 (31 3/8 x 23 1/2)
Inscribed at lower center on reverse:
Mark Rothko
Gift of The Mark Rothko Foundation
1986.43.23

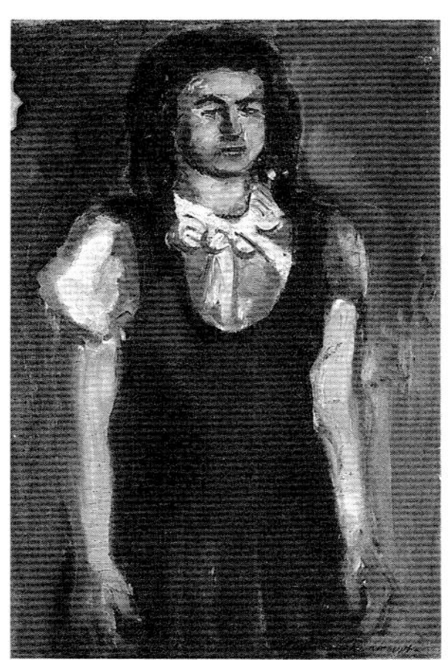

Untitled (portrait of Irene Goldin?),
c. 1933
Canvas, 0.807 x 0.542 (31 13/16 x 21 9/16)
Inscribed at lower right: *MRothkowitz*;
across center on reverse: *M.Rothkowitz /*
MARK ROTHKO
Gift of The Mark Rothko Foundation
1986.43.43

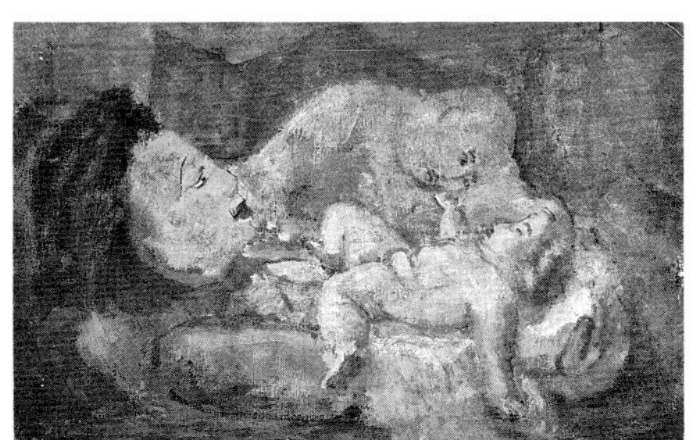

Family, 1933/1936
Canvas, 0.513 x 0.765 (20 3/16 x 30 1/8)
Inscribed at lower left: *Rothkowitz*; across
bottom on reverse: *Rothkowitz Family*
Gift of The Mark Rothko Foundation
1986.43.97

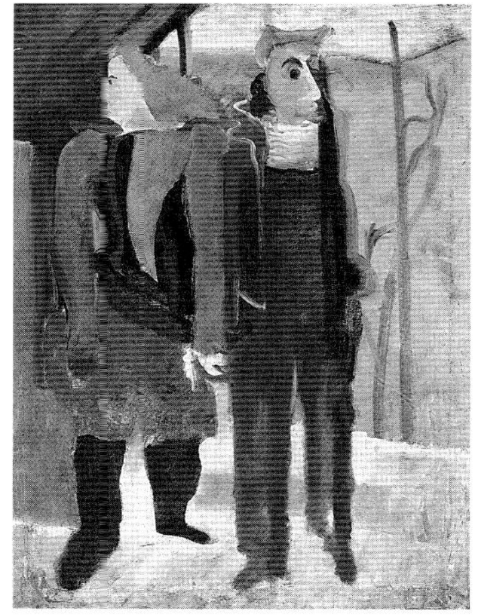

Untitled (man and woman holding hands), c. 1933/1936
Canvas, 0.815 x 0.609 (32⅛ x 24)
Inscribed at lower right: *Rothkowitz*; at lower center on reverse: *Mark Rothko*
Gift of The Mark Rothko Foundation
1986.43.42

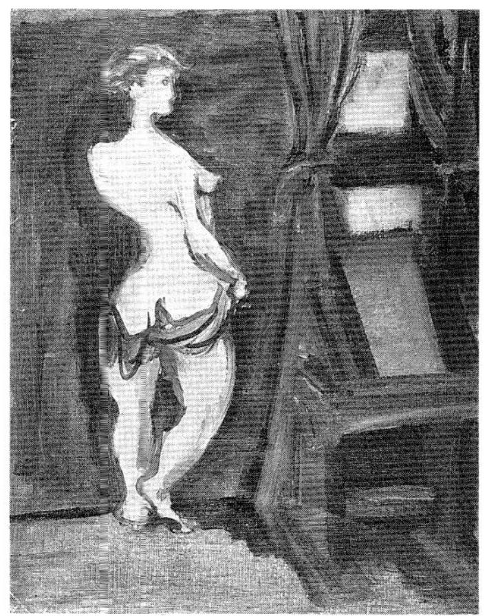

Untitled (nude), c. 1933/1938
Canvas, 0.359 x 0.292 (14⅛ x 11½)
Gift of The Mark Rothko Foundation
1986.56.662

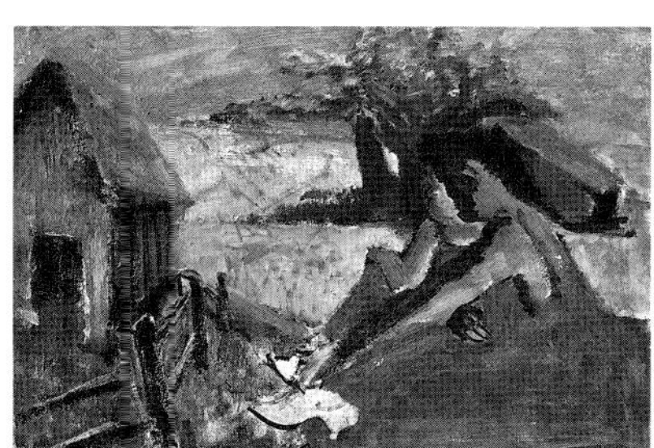

Rural Scene, c. 1934
Canvas, 0.685 x 0.968 (27 x 38⅛)
Inscribed at center left on reverse: *1934 Rural Scene Mark Rothko*
Gift of The Mark Rothko Foundation
1986.43.19

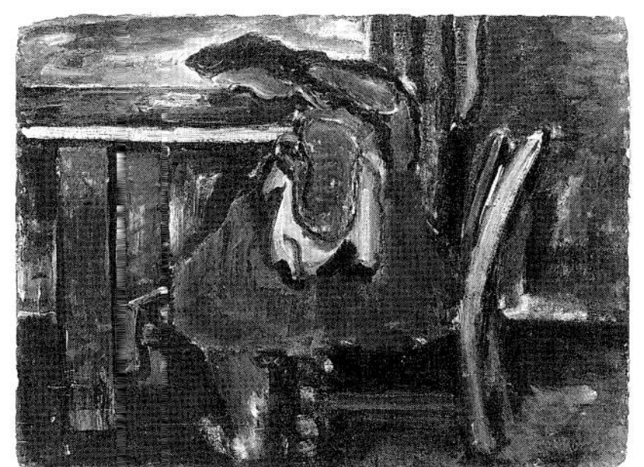

Woman Sewing, c. 1934
Hardboard, 0.711 x 0.915 (28 x 36$^{1}/_{16}$)
Inscribed at lower right: *M.Rothkowitz*; across center on reverse: *Woman Sewing/ M.Rothkowitz*
Gift of The Mark Rothko Foundation
1986.43.28

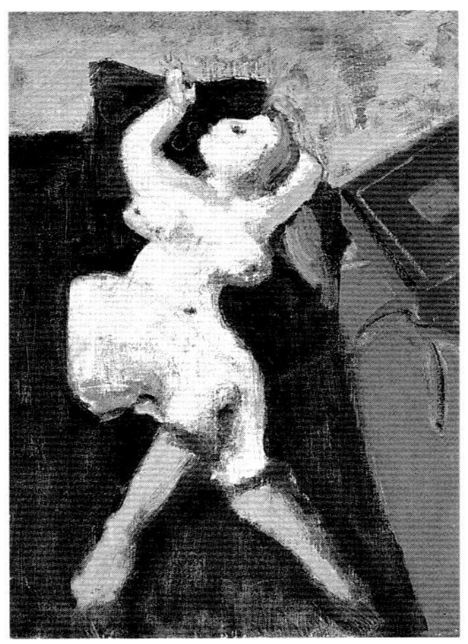

Untitled (reclining nude), c. 1934/1936
Canvas, 0.609 x 0.456 (24 x 18)
Inscribed at lower center on reverse:
Mark Rothko
Gift of The Mark Rothko Foundation
1986.43.50

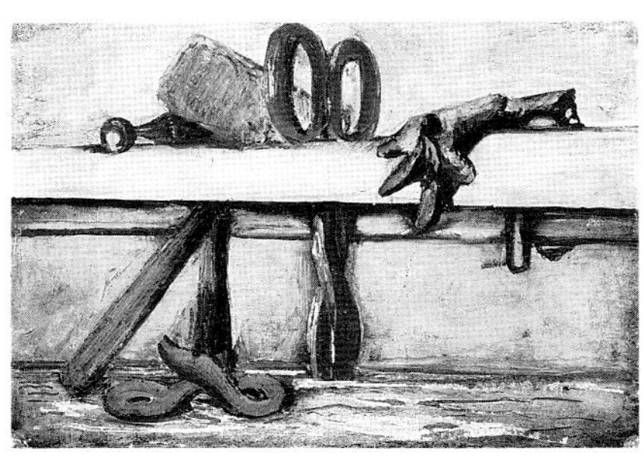

Untitled (still life with scissors),
c. 1934/1936
Paperboard, 0.126 x 0.176 (4 15/16 x 6 15/16)
Gift of The Mark Rothko Foundation
1986.56.655

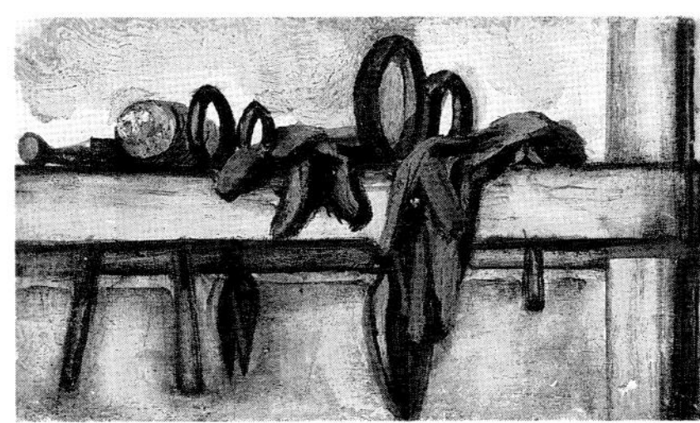

Untitled (still life with scissors),
c. 1934/1936
Paperboard, 0.075 x 0.126 (2 15/16 x 4 15/16)
Gift of The Mark Rothko Foundation
1986.56.659

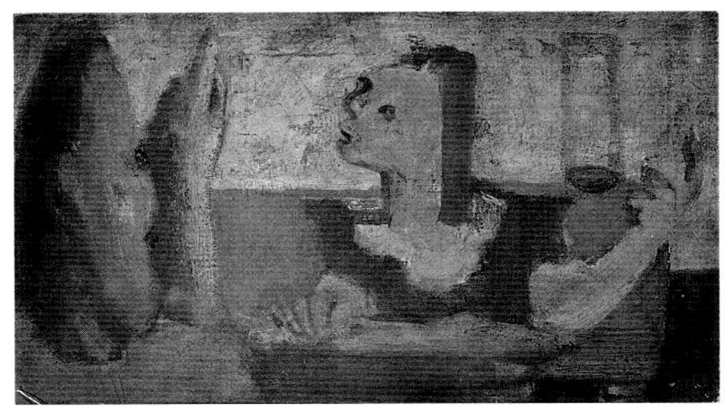

Untitled (woman with sculpture),
c. 1934/1936
Canvas, 0.359 x 0.609 (14 1/8 x 24 1/16)
Inscribed at center on reverse: *Mark Rothko*
Gift of The Mark Rothko Foundation
1986.43.57

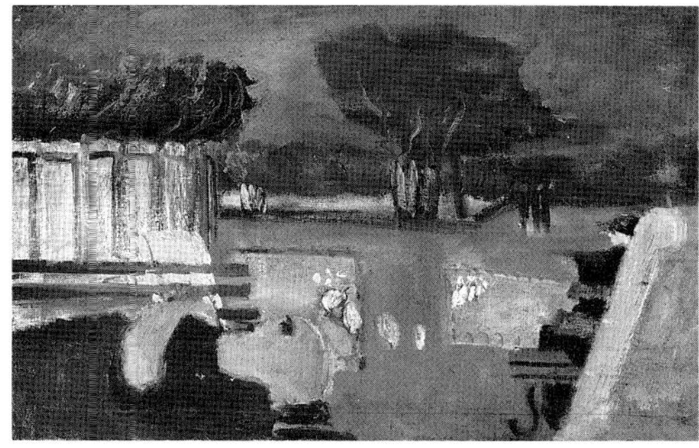

Untitled (man lying on park bench), 1934/1938
Canvas, 0.511 x 0.764 (20⅛ x 30$^{1}/_{16}$)
Inscribed at center on reverse: *Mark Rothko*
Gift of The Mark Rothko Foundation
1986.43.49

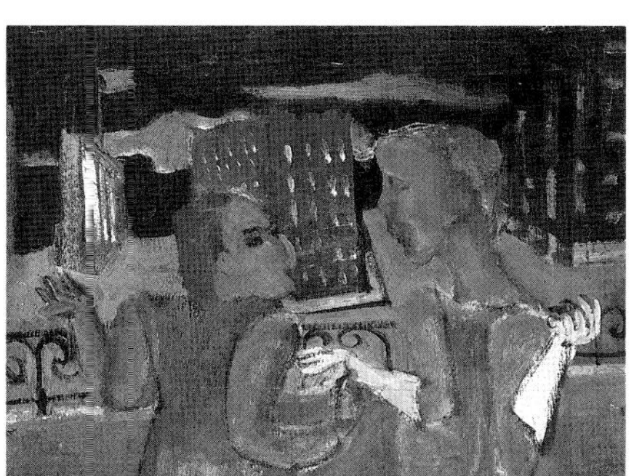

Untitled (two women in front of a cityscape), 1934/1938
Canvas, 0.560 x 0.709 (22 x 27⅞)
Inscribed at center left on reverse: *M. Rothko*
Gift of The Mark Rothko Foundation
1986.43.52

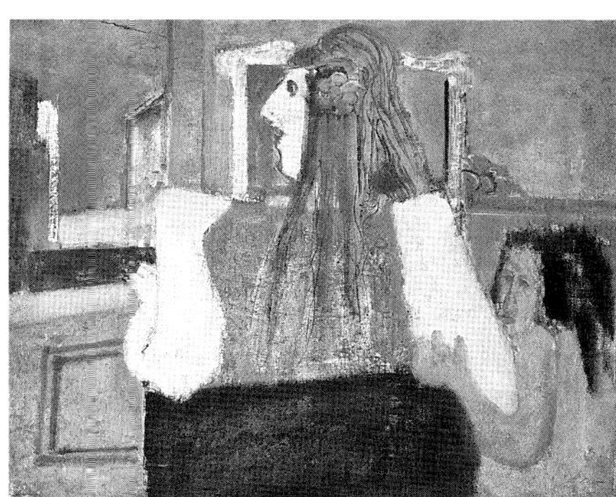

Untitled (woman and girl in an interior), 1934/1938
Canvas, 0.511 x 0.613 (20$^{1}/_{16}$ x 24⅛)
Inscribed at center left on reverse: *Mark Rothko*
Gift of The Mark Rothko Foundation
1986.43.48

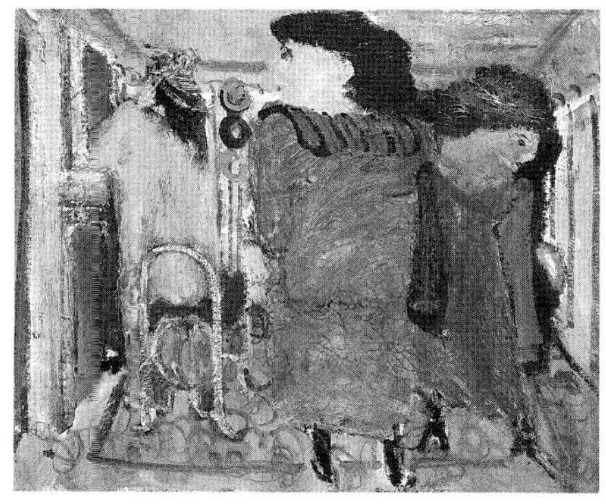

Untitled (women in a hat shop), c. 1934/1938
Canvas, 0.611 x 0.711 (24$^{1}/_{16}$ x 28)
Gift of The Mark Rothko Foundation
1986.43.55

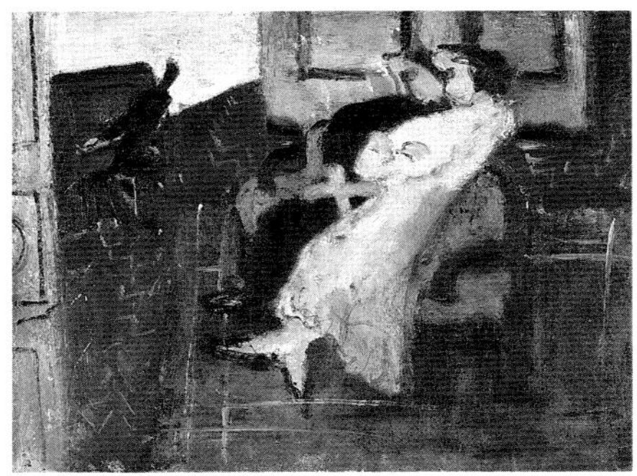

Music, c. 1935
Canvas, 0.485 x 0.632 (18⅛ x 24⅞)
Inscribed across center on reverse: *Music / M Rothkowitz*
Gift of The Mark Rothko Foundation
1986.43.96

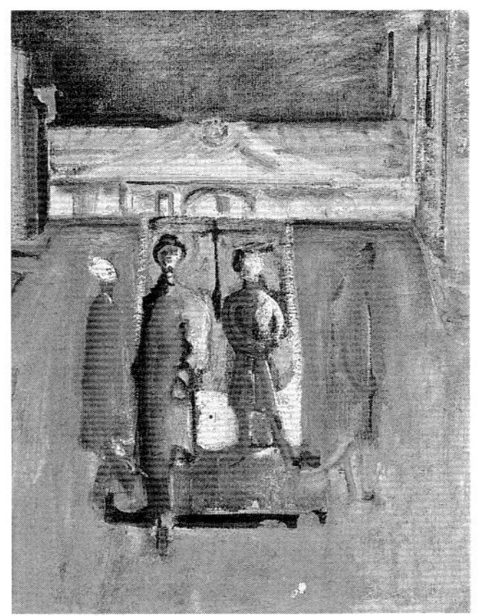

Untitled, 1935/1939
Canvas, 0.611 x 0.459 (24⅙ x 18 1/16)
Inscribed at lower center on reverse: *Mark Rothko*
Gift of The Mark Rothko Foundation
1986.43.112

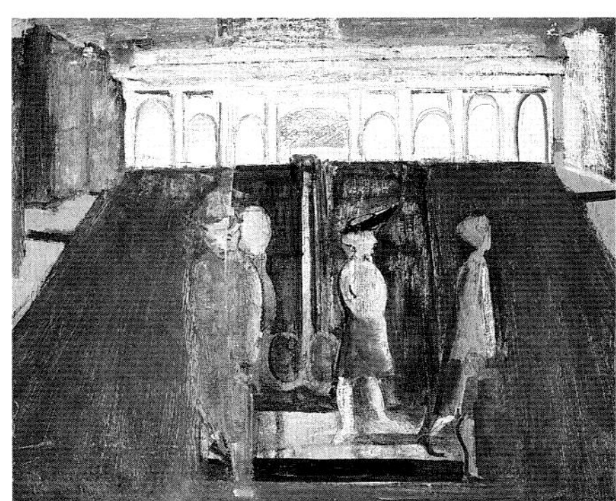

Untitled, 1935/1939
Canvas, 0.558 x 0.663 (21⅞ x 26 1/16)
Inscribed at lower right: *Mark Rothko*
Gift of The Mark Rothko Foundation
1986.43.116

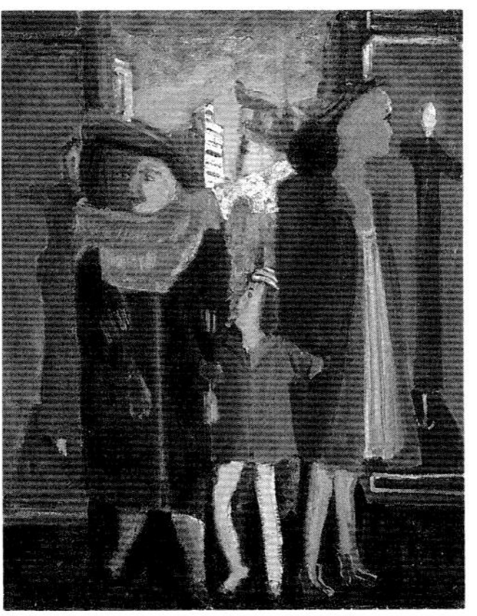

Untitled (figures and mannequins), 1935/1939
Canvas, 0.913 x 0.715 (35 13/16 x 28 3/16)
Inscribed at lower center on reverse: *Mark Rothko*
Gift of The Mark Rothko Foundation
1986.43.24

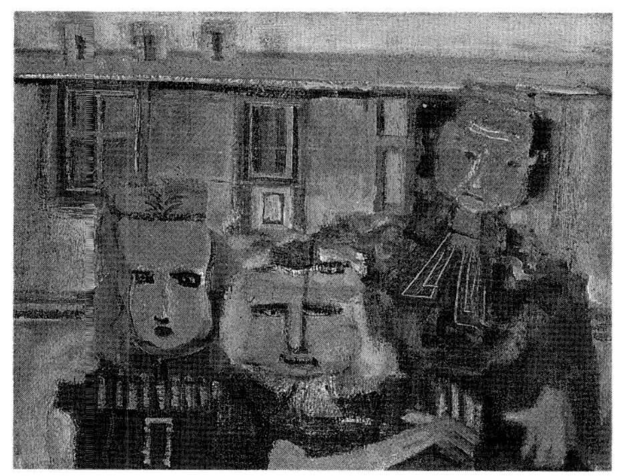

Untitled (three figures), 1935/1939
Canvas, 0.407 x 0.509 (16 1/16 x 20 1/16)
Inscribed at lower right: *Rothkowitz*; at center on reverse: *Rothkowitz*; at lower center on reverse: *MRotoko*
Gift of The Mark Rothko Foundation
1986.43.51

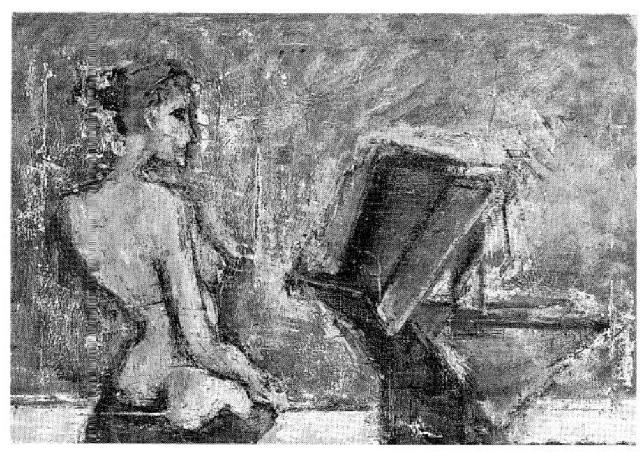

Untitled (nude) (recto), c. 1935/1939
Canvas, 0.512 x 0.715 (20 1/8 x 28 1/8)
Gift of The Mark Rothko Foundation
1986.43.117a

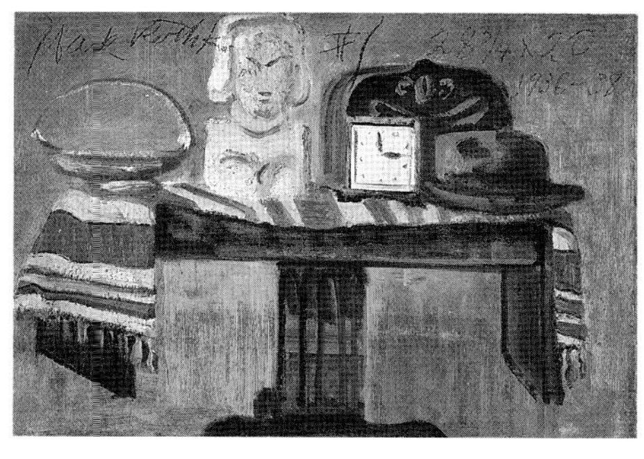

Untitled (still life) (verso), c. 1935/1939
Canvas, 0.512 x 0.715 (20 1/8 x 28 1/8)
Inscribed at top: *Mark Rothko #1 28 3/4 x 20 / 1936–1938*
Gift of The Mark Rothko Foundation
1986.43.117b

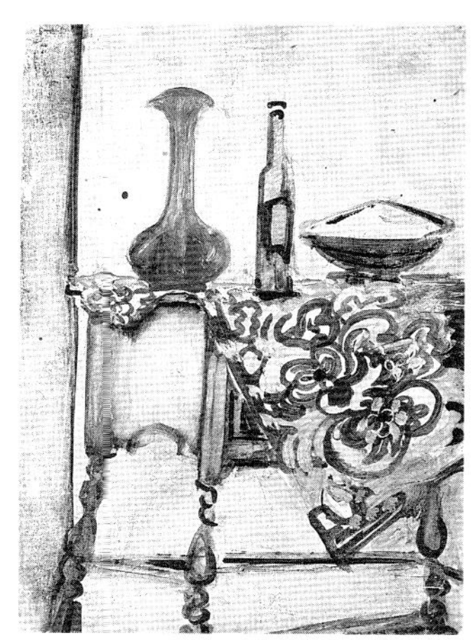

Untitled (still life), c. 1935/1939
Paperboard, 0.176 x 0.126 (6 15/16 x 4 15/16)
Gift of The Mark Rothko Foundation
1986.56.656

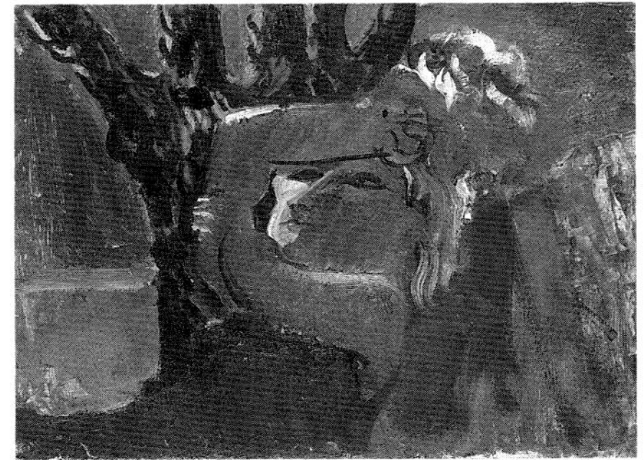

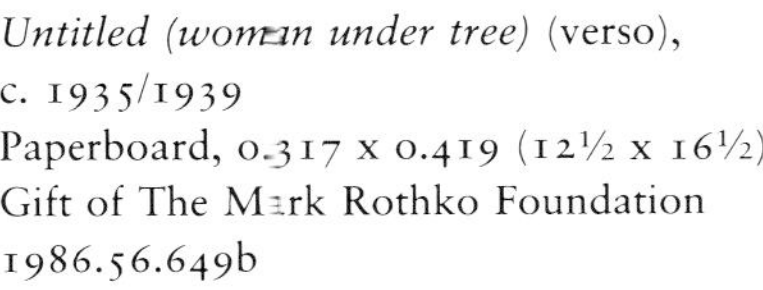

Untitled (woman under tree) (verso), c. 1935/1939
Paperboard, 0.317 x 0.419 (12½ x 16½)
Gift of The Mark Rothko Foundation
1986.56.649b

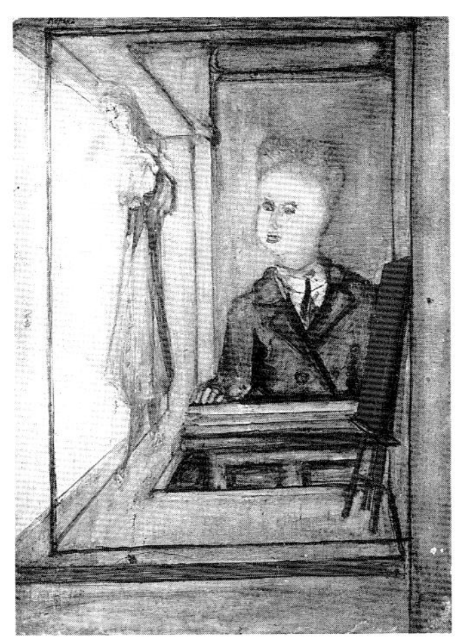

Thru the Window, 1935/1940
Paperboard, 0.251 x 0.175 (9⅞ x 6⅞)
Inscribed at upper left: *Rothko*; lower right on reverse: *Thru the Window*
Gift of The Mark Rothko Foundation
1986.56.653

Untitled (figures around a piano), 1935/1940
Canvas, 0.600 x 0.806 (23⅝ x 31¾)
Inscribed at upper right: *Rothko*; at center on reverse: *M Rothkowitz*; at center left on reverse: *Mark Rothko*
Gift of The Mark Rothko Foundation
1986.43.54

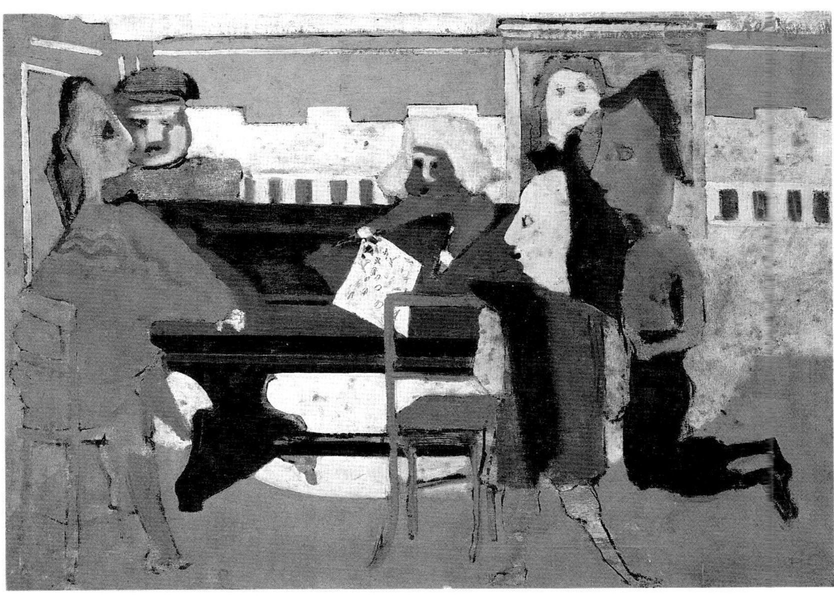

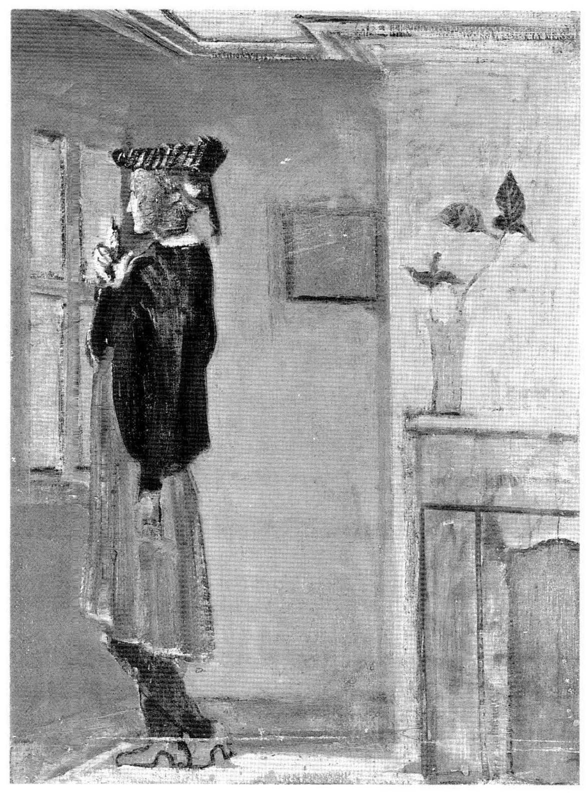

Untitled (woman at window), 1935/1940
Canvas, 0.705 x 0.526 (27¾ x 20$^{11}/_{16}$)
Inscribed across bottom on reverse: *MARK ROTHKO*
Gift of The Mark Rothko Foundation
1986.43.118

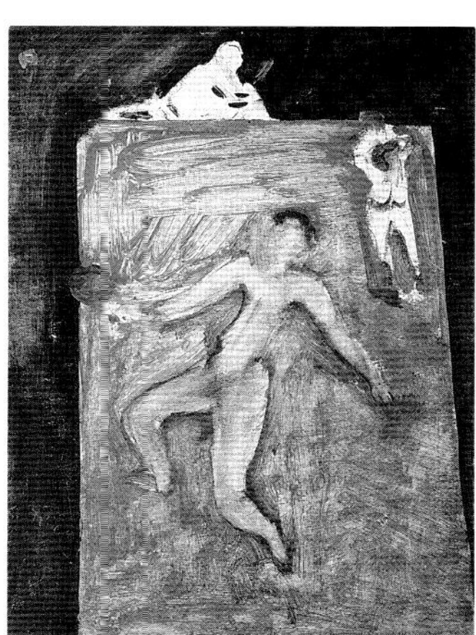

Untitled, c. 1935/1940
Paperboard, 0.302 x 0.227 (11⅞ x 8$^{15}/_{16}$)
Gift of The Mark Rothko Foundation
1986.56.654

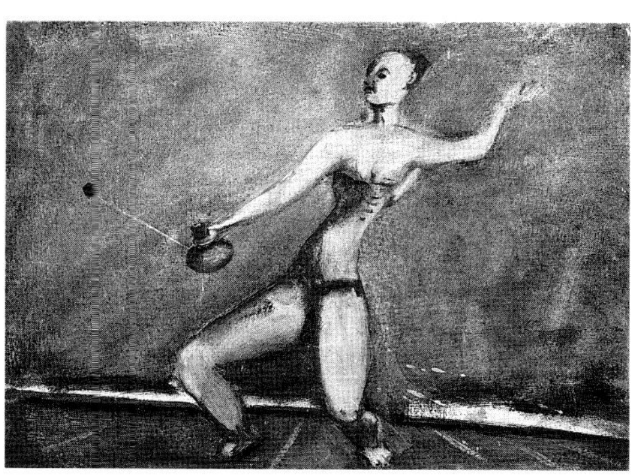

Untitled (man with paddle and ball), c. 1935/1940
Paperboard, 0.227 x 0.302 (8$^{15}/_{16}$ x 11⅞)
Gift of The Mark Rothko Foundation
1986.56.658

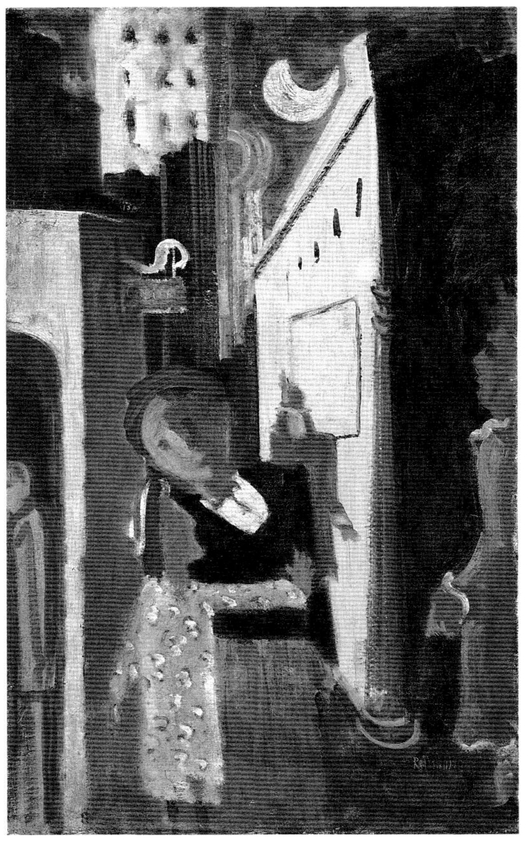

Street Scene, 1936/1938
Canvas, 0.91[illegible] x 0.558 (36 x 22)
Inscribed at lower right: *Rothkowitz*; upper center on reverse: *Street Scene M Rothkowitz*
Gift of The Mark Rothko Foundation
1986.43.45

Subway, 193[illegible]/1939
Canvas, 0.87[illegible] x 1.182 (34 5/16 x 46 1/2)
Inscribed at lower right: *Rothko*; at upper center on reverse: *Mark Rothko*
Gift of The Mark Rothko Foundation
1986.43.130

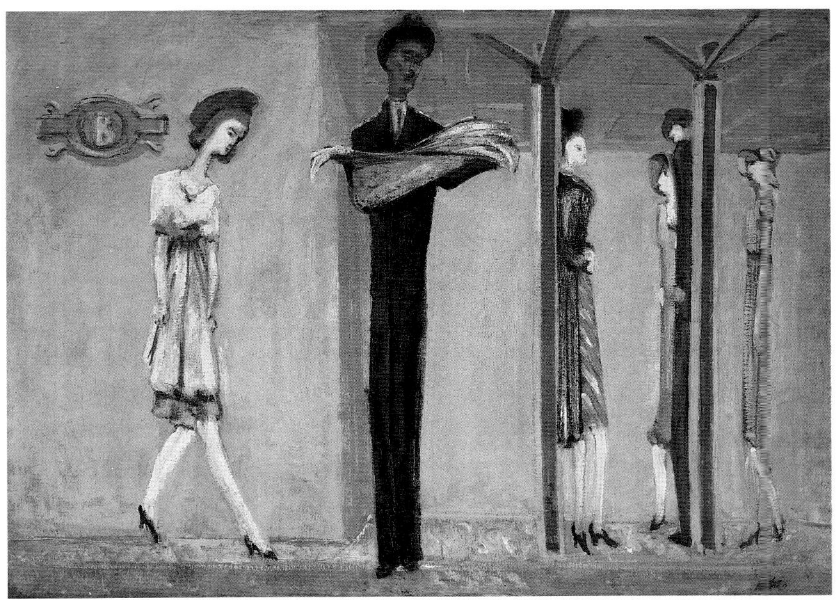

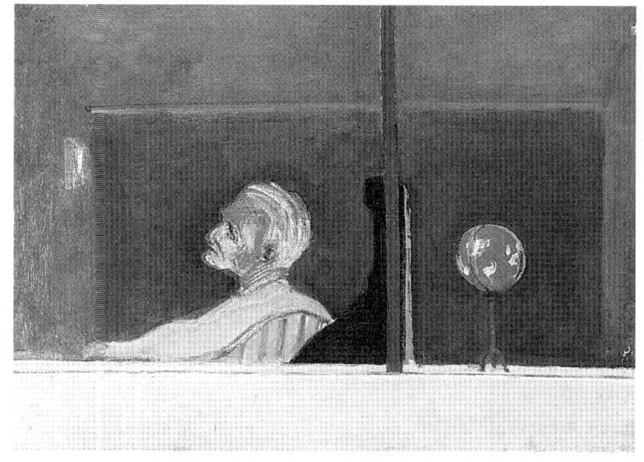

Untitled (man and globe at window), 1936/1939
Canvas, 0.615 x 0.816 (24 3/16 x 32 1/8)
Inscribed at upper left: *Rothko* (signature smudged)
Gift of The Mark Rothko Foundation
1986.43.38

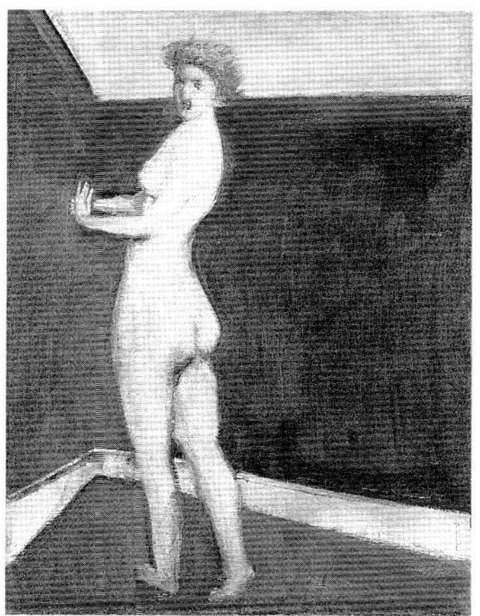

Untitled (nude), 1936/1939
Canvas, 0.607 x 0.461 (23 7/8 x 18 1/8)
Inscribed at lower center on reverse: *Mark Rothko*
Gift of The Mark Rothko Foundation
1986.43.115

Untitled (still life in front of window), 1936/1939
Canvas, 0.714 x 0.918 (28 1/16 x 36 1/8)
Inscribed at lower left: *Rothko*; lower left on reverse: *Mark Rothko*
Gift of The Mark Rothko Foundation
1986.43.37

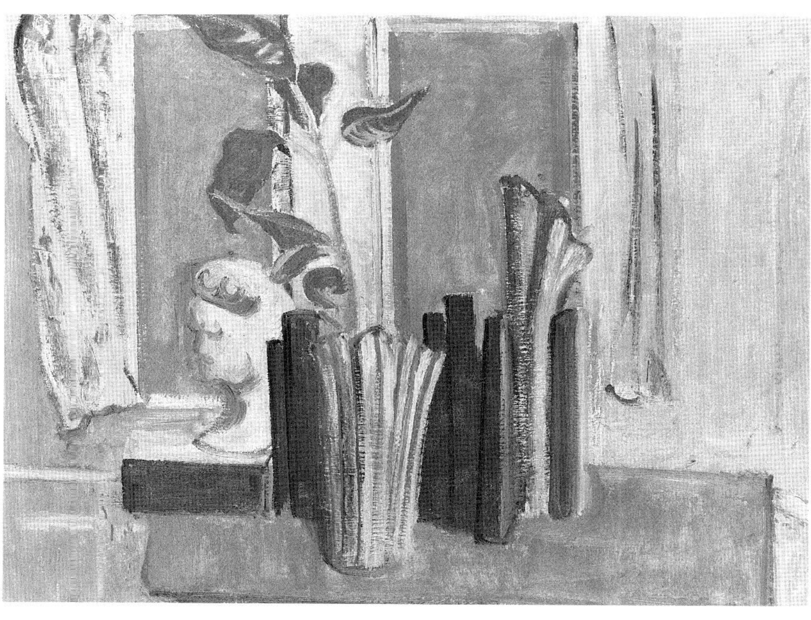

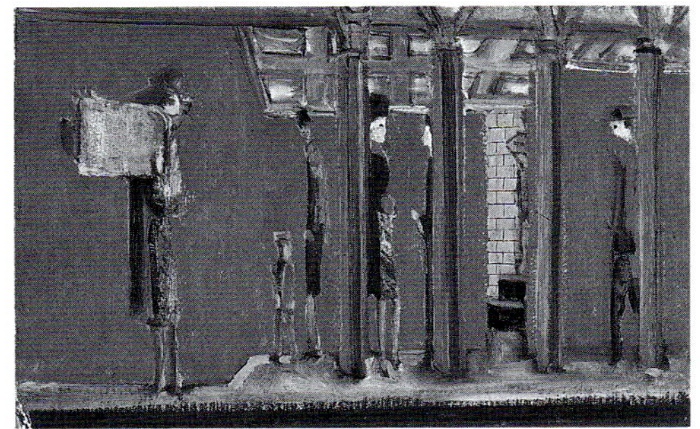

Untitled (subway), 1936/1939
Canvas, 0.509 x 0.762 (20 1/16 x 30 1/8)
Inscribed at center left on reverse: *Mark Rothko*
Gift of The Mark Rothko Foundation
1986.43.113

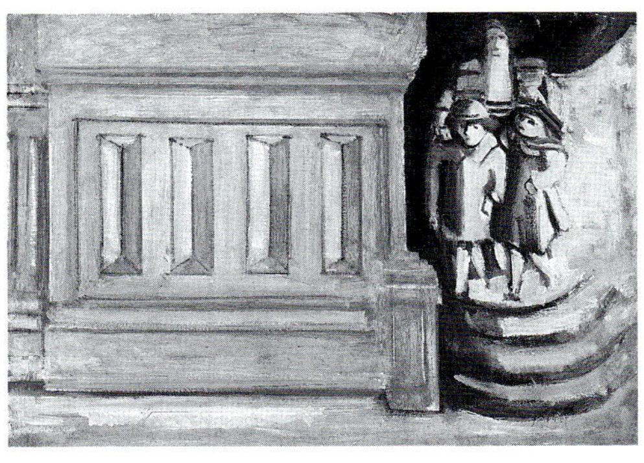

Street Scene XX, c. 1936/1939
Canvas, 0.737 x 1.014 (29 x 40)
Inscribed at lower right on reverse: *Mark Rothko*; at center left on reverse: *1936 Street Scene XX*
Gift of The Mark Rothko Foundation
1986.43.21

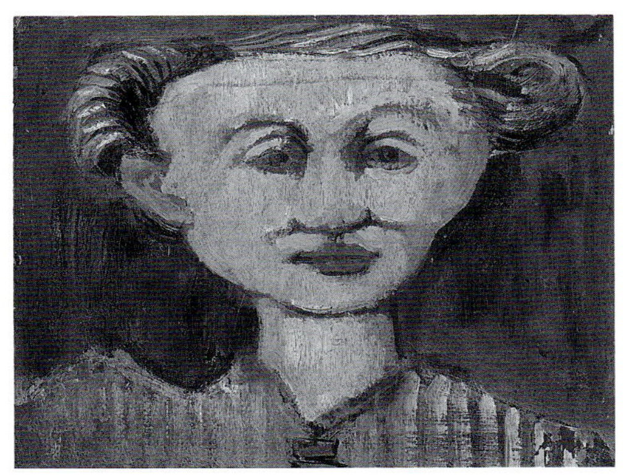

Untitled (head), c. 1936/1939
Canvas, 0.407 x 0.511 (16 x 20 1/8)
Inscribed at center left on reverse: *Mark Rothko*
Gift of The Mark Rothko Foundation
1986.43.110

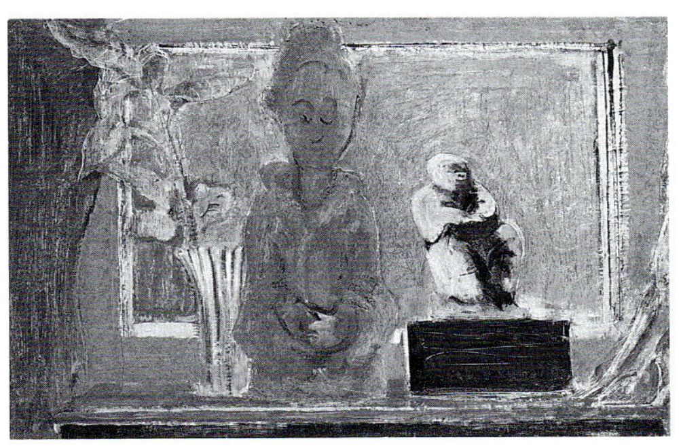

Untitled (still life with vase and two statues), 1936/1940
Canvas, 0.511 x 0.764 (20 1/8 x 30 1/16)
Inscribed at center left on reverse: *Mark Rothko*
Gift of The Mark Rothko Foundation
1986.43.114

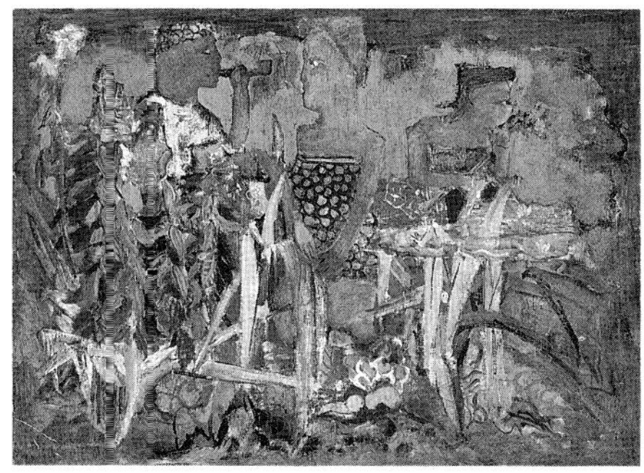

Untitled (three people in a field), 1936/1940
Canvas, 0.720 x 0.918 (28⅜ x 36⅛)
Inscribed at upper right: *Mark Rothko*; at center on reverse: *M. Rothkowitz*; at center left on reverse: *Mark Rothko*
Gift of The Mark Rothko Foundation
1986.43.53

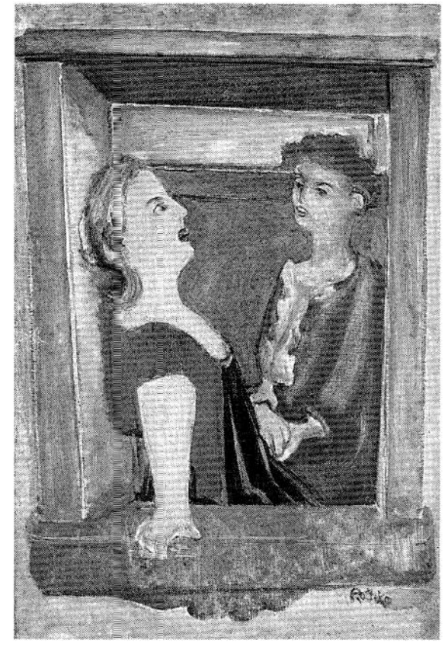

Untitled (two women at the window), 1936/1940
Canvas, 0.914 x 0.610 (36 x 24)
Inscribed at lower right: *M Rothko*
Gift of The Mark Rothko Foundation
1986.37.1

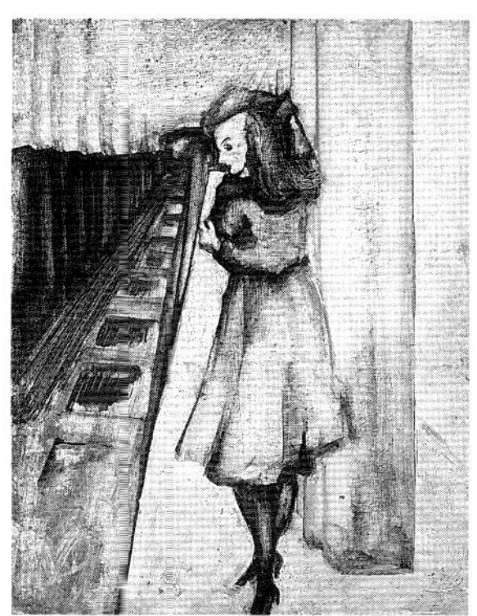

Untitled (woman in subway), 1936/1940
Paperboard, 0.302 x 0.227 (11⅞ x 8¹⁵⁄₁₆)
Gift of The Mark Rothko Foundation
1986.56.657

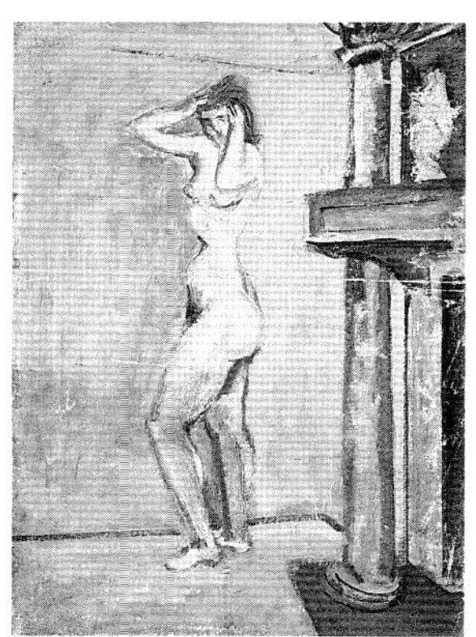

Untitled (nude and mantel), c. 1936/1940
Canvas, 0.715 x 0.511 (28³⁄₁₆ x 20⅛)
Inscribed across bottom on reverse: *MARK ROTHKO*
Gift of The Mark Rothko Foundation
1986.43.111

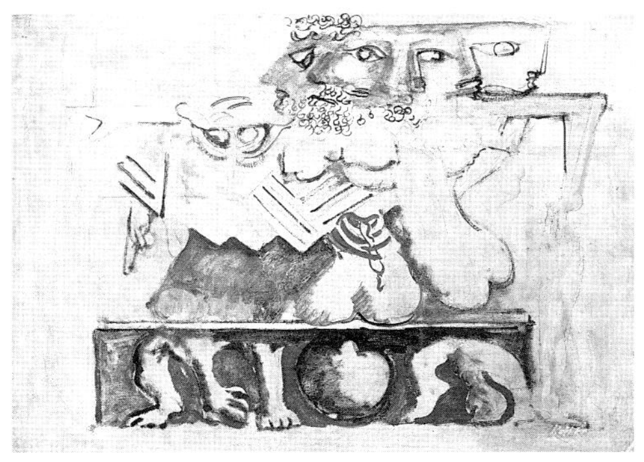

Antigone, c. 1941
Canvas, 0.864 x 1.162 (34 x 45¾)
Inscribed at lower right: *Rothko*; on reverse at upper center: *Mark Rothko*; across stretcher at center top: *Antigone*
Gift of The Mark Rothko Foundation
1986.43.119

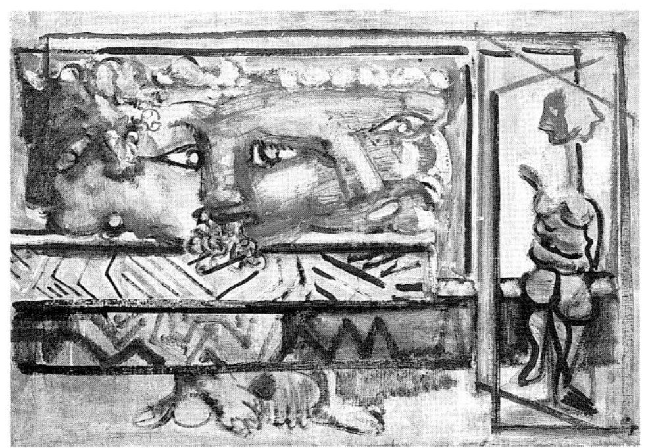

Untitled, c. 1941
Canvas, 0.508 x 0.708 (20 x 27$^{13}/_{16}$)
Inscribed at center left on reverse:
M. Rothko
Gift of The Mark Rothko Foundation
1986.43.32

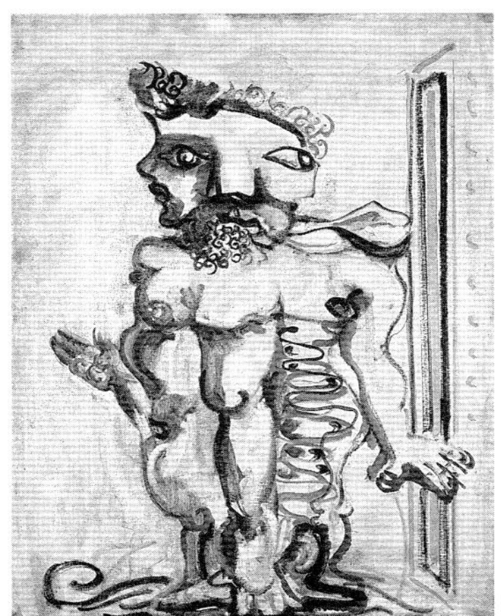

Untitled, c. 1941
Canvas, 0.915 x 0.713 (36$^{1}/_{16}$ x 28$^{1}/_{16}$)
Inscribed at lower center on reverse:
M Rothko
Gift of The Mark Rothko Foundation
1986.43.36

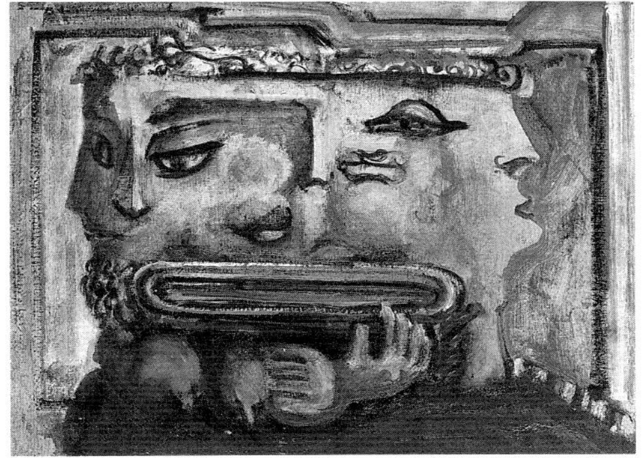

Untitled, c. 1941/1942
Canvas, 0.457 x 0.610 (18 x 24)
Inscribed at lower left on reverse:
M. Rothko
Gift of The Mark Rothko Foundation
1986.43.31

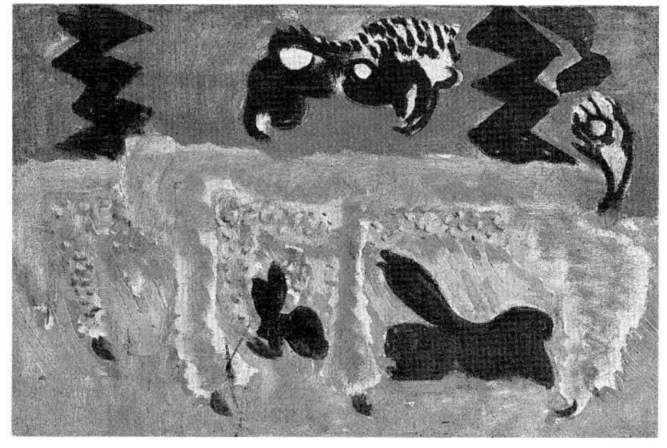

Untitled, 1941/1943
Canvas, 0.324 x 0.474 (12⅞ x 18¾)
Inscribed at lower center on reverse: *Mar Rothko* [sic]
Gift of The Mark Rothko Foundation
1986.43.109

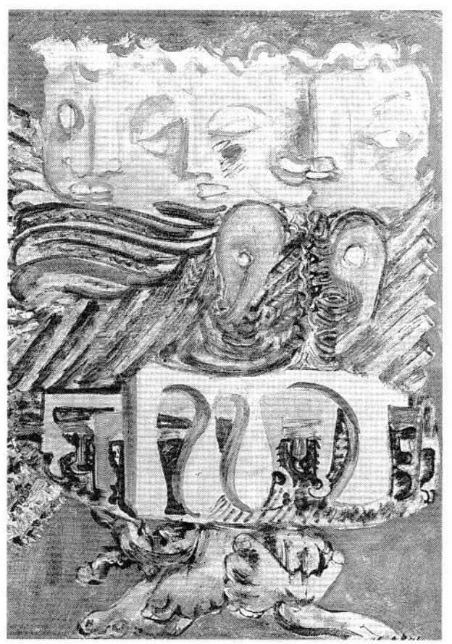

The Omen of the Eagle, 1942
Canvas, 0.654 x 0.451 (25¾ x 17¾)
Inscribed at lower right: *Mark Rothko*; at center left on reverse: *Mark Rothko*
Gift of The Mark Rothko Foundation
1986.43.107

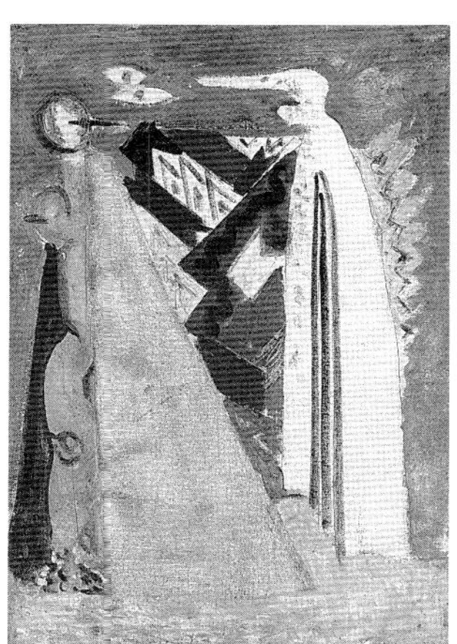

The Omen, c. 1942
Canvas, 0.491 x 0.338 (19$^{5}/_{16}$ x 13$^{1}/_{16}$)
Inscribed at upper center on reverse: *Mark Rothko The Omen*
Gift of The Mark Rothko Foundation
1986.43.128

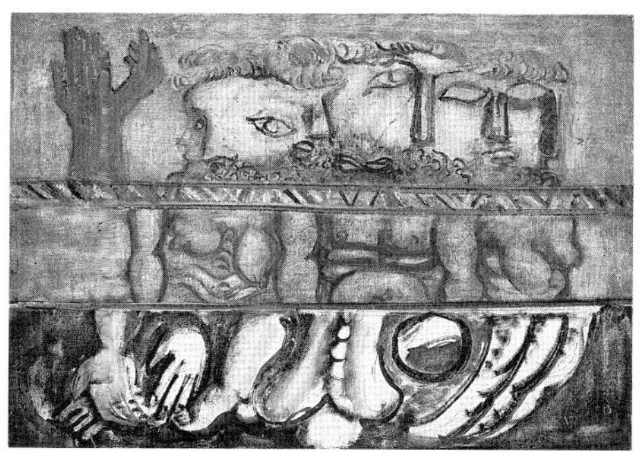

Untitled, c. 1942
Canvas, 0.606 x 0.810 (23⅞ x 31⅞)
Inscribed at lower right: *Rothko*; at lower left on reverse: *M. Rothko*
Gift of The Mark Rothko Foundation
1986.43.33

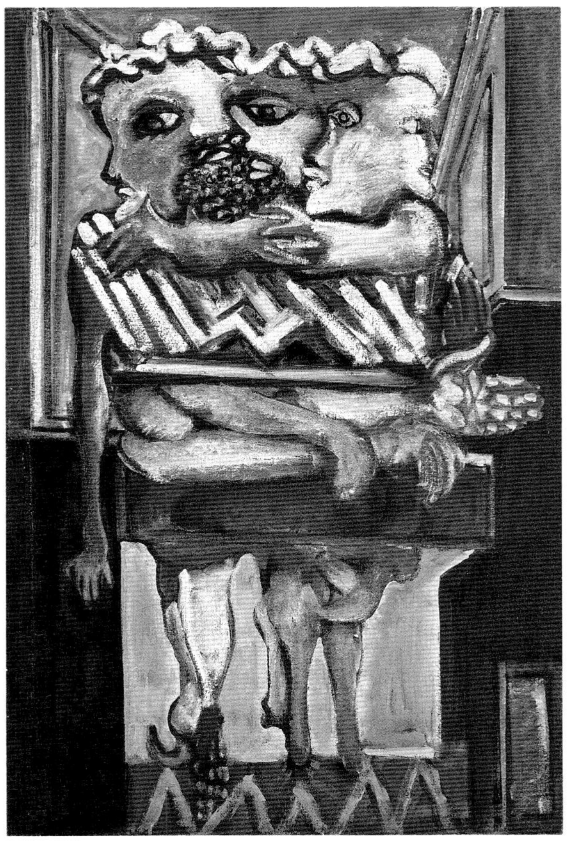

Untitled, c. 1942
Canvas, 0.910 x 0.606 (35 13/16 x 23 7/8)
Inscribed at lower center on reverse: *Mark Rothko*
Gift of The Mark Rothko Foundation
1986.43.35

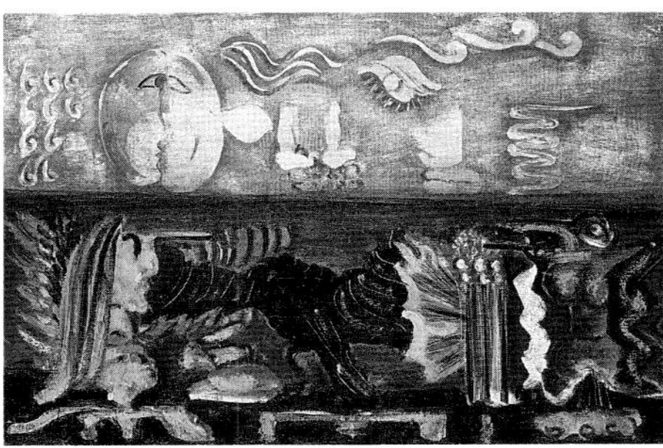

Untitled (The Eagle and the Hare?), c. 1942
Canvas, 0.454 x 0.654 (17 7/8 x 25 3/4)
Inscribed at center left on reverse: *Mark Rothko*
Gift of The Mark Rothko Foundation
1986.43.105

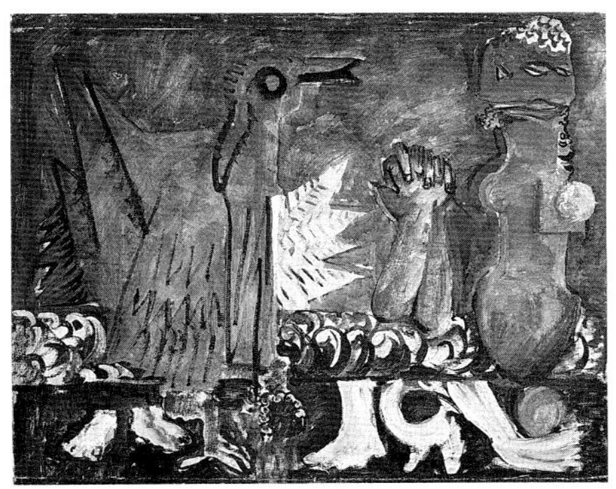

Untitled, 1942/1943
Canvas, 0.759 x 0.918 (29 7/8 x 35 7/8)
Inscribed at center on reverse: *Mark Rothko*
Gift of The Mark Rothko Foundation
1986.43.59

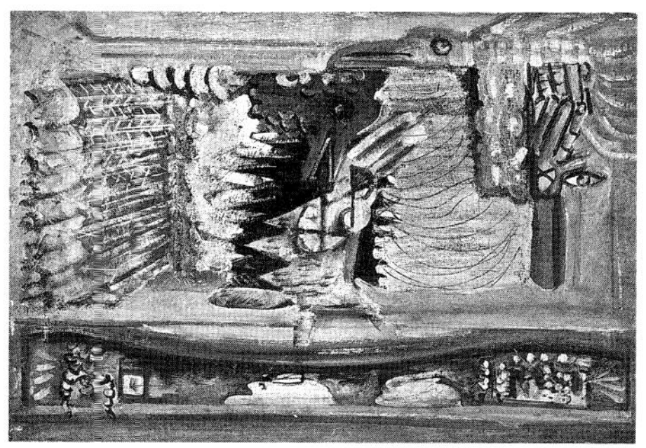

Untitled, 1942/1943
Canvas, 0.511 x 0.713 (20 1/8 x 28 1/16)
Inscribed at center left on reverse: *Mark Rothko*
Gift of The Mark Rothko Foundation
1986.43.104

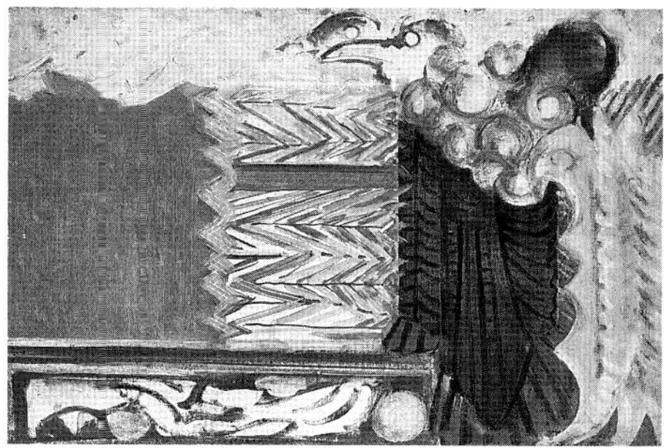

Untitled, 1942/1943
Canvas, 0.453 x 0.655 (17 3/16 x 25 3/4)
Inscribed at center left on reverse: *Mark Rothko*
Gift of The Mark Rothko Foundation
1986.43.106

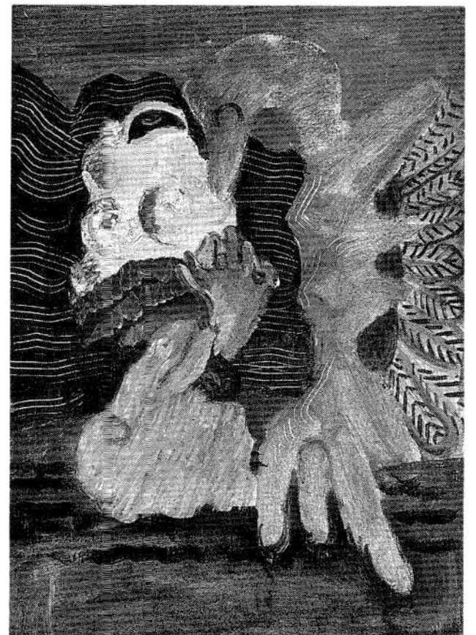

Untitled, 1942/1943
Canvas, 0.479 x 0.332 (18 7/8 x 13 1/16)
Gift of The Mark Rothko Foundation
1986.43.123

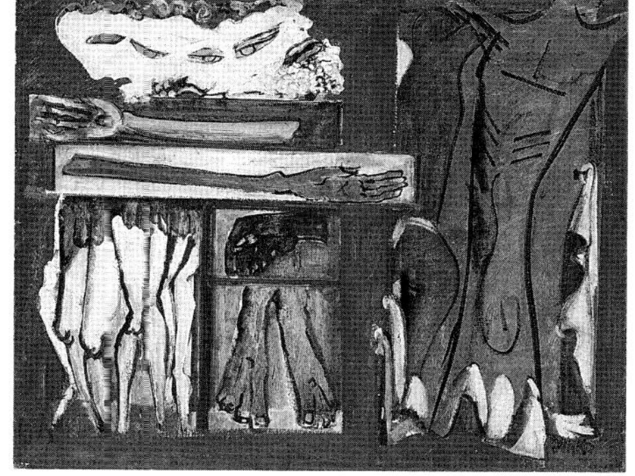

Untitled, c. 1942/1943
Canvas, 0.760 x 0.913 (29 15/16 x 35 15/16)
Inscribed at lower right: *Rothko*; at lower left on reverse: *Mark Rothko*
Gift of The Mark Rothko Foundation
1986.43.34

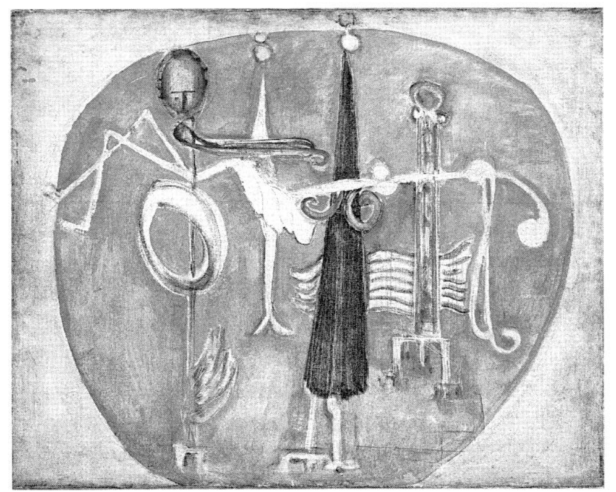

Untitled, 1942/1944
Canvas, 0.756 x 0.910 ($29\frac{3}{4}$ x $35\frac{13}{16}$)
Inscribed at lower center on reverse: *Mark Rothko*
Gift of The Mark Rothko Foundation
1986.43.60

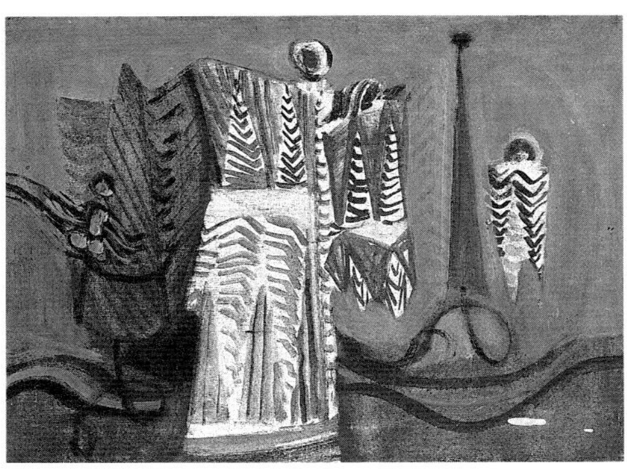

Untitled, c. 1943
Canvas, 0.298 x 0.398 ($11\frac{3}{4}$ x $15\frac{3}{4}$)
Inscribed diagonally from left to top right on reverse: *Mark Rothko*
Gift of The Mark Rothko Foundation
1986.43.124

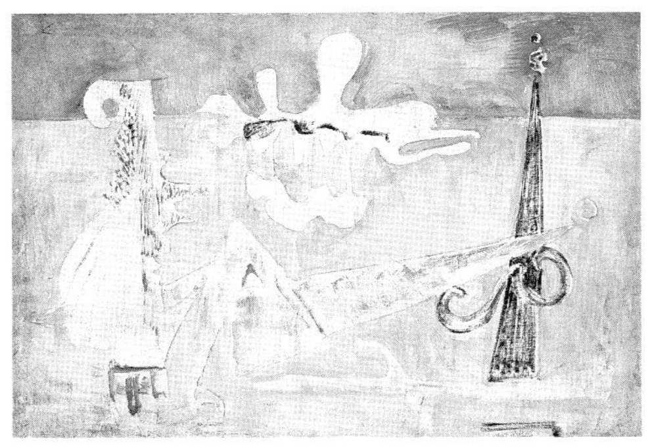

Olympian Play, 1943/1944
Canvas, 0.499 x 0.701 ($19\frac{5}{8}$ x $27\frac{9}{16}$)
Inscribed at lower right: *Mark Rothko*; at upper left on reverse: *Mark Rothko Olympian Play*; center left on reverse: *Mark Rothko*
Gift of The Mark Rothko Foundation
1986.43.72

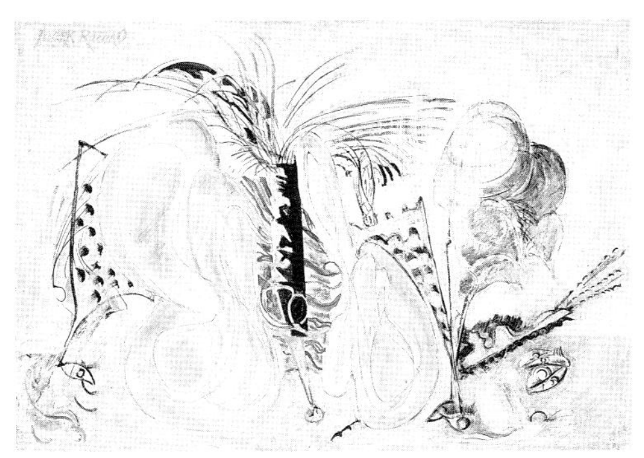

Birth of Cephalopods, 1944
Canvas, 1.006 x 1.365 ($39\frac{5}{8}$ x $53\frac{11}{16}$)
Inscribed at upper left: *MARK ROTHKO*; at upper right on reverse: *Mark Rothko Birth of the Cephalopods 1944*
Gift of The Mark Rothko Foundation
1986.43.22

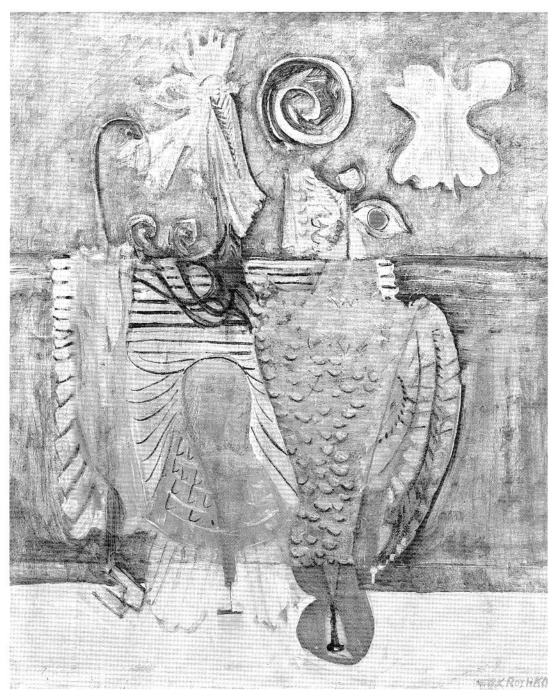

Hierarchical Birds, c. 1944
Canvas, 1.007 x 0.805 (39 5/8 x 31 5/8)
Inscribed at lower right: *MARK ROTHKO*
Gift of The Mark Rothko Foundation
1986.43.20

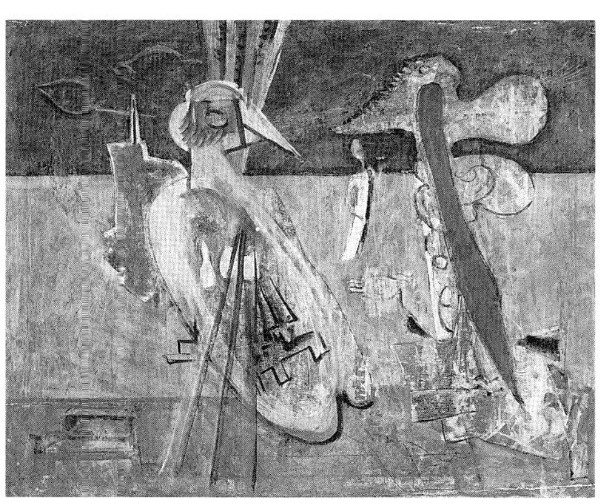

Untitled, c. 1944
Canvas, 0.763 x 0.915 (30 1/8 x 36)
Inscribed at center right on reverse: *Mark Rothko*
Gift of The Mark Rothko Foundation
1986.43.58

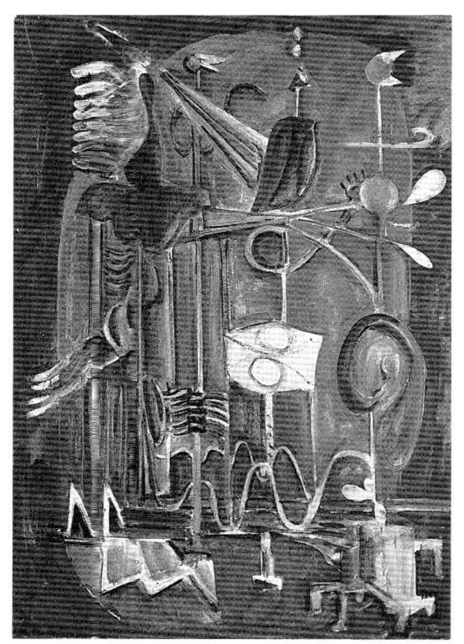

Untitled, 1944/1945
Canvas, 1.000 x 0.698 (39 3/8 x 27 7/16)
Inscribed at center on reverse: *Mark Rothko*
Gift of The Mark Rothko Foundation
1986.43.62

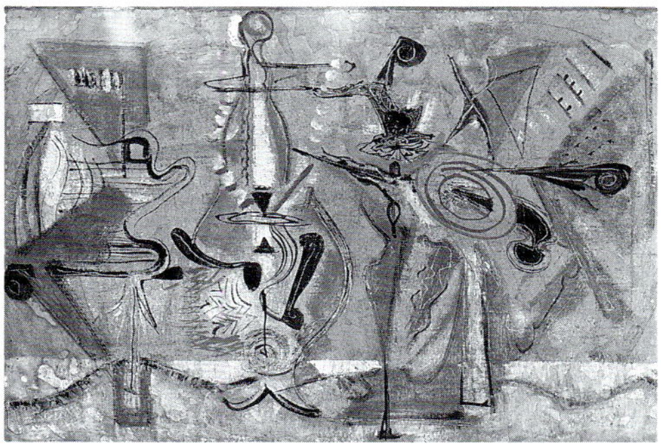

Untitled, 1944/1945
Canvas, 0.328 x 0.480 (12 15/16 x 18 7/8)
Inscribed at center on reverse: *Mark Rothko*
Gift of The Mark Rothko Foundation
1986.43.126

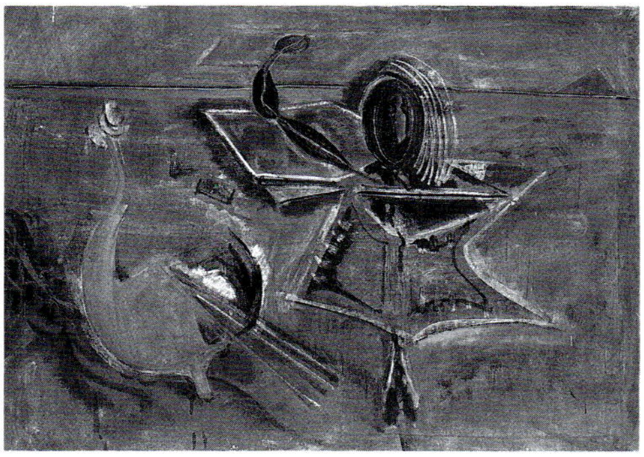

Untitled, 1944/1946
Canvas, 0.702 x 0.961 (27 9/16 x 37 13/16)
Inscribed at upper center on reverse: *Mark Rothko*
Gift of The Mark Rothko Foundation
1986.43.61

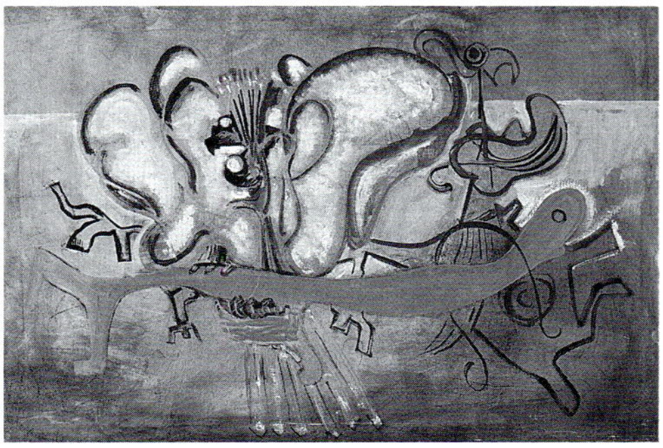

Untitled, 1944/1946
Canvas, 0.692 x 0.991 (27 1/4 x 39)
Inscribed at center left on reverse: *Mark Rothko*
Gift of The Mark Rothko Foundation
1986.43.71

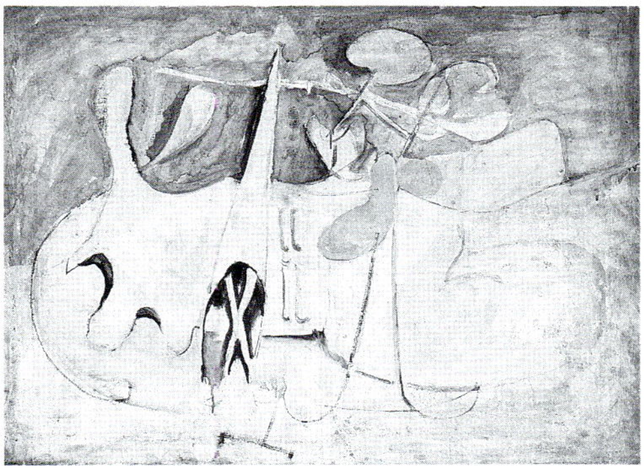

Untitled, 1944/1946
Canvas, 0.611 x 0.801 (24 1/8 x 31 15/16)
Inscribed at center left on reverse: *Mark Rothko*
Gift of The Mark Rothko Foundation
1986.43.73

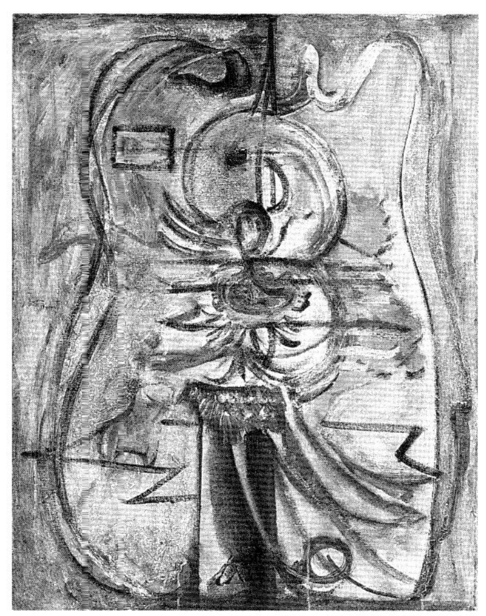

Untitled, 1944/1946
Canvas, 0.650 x 0.499 (25 9/16 x 19 5/8)
Inscribed at upper center on reverse: *Mark Rothko*
Gift of The Mark Rothko Foundation
1986.43.86

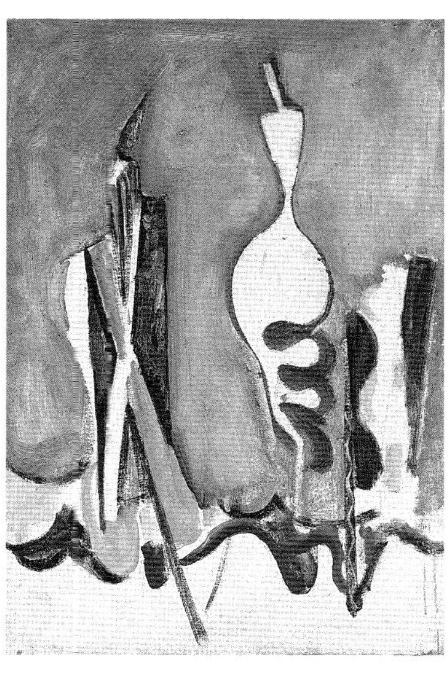

Untitled, 1944/1946
Canvas, 0.476 x 0.326 (18 7/8 x 12 15/16)
Inscribed at center on reverse: *Mark Rothko*
Gift of The Mark Rothko Foundation
1986.43.108

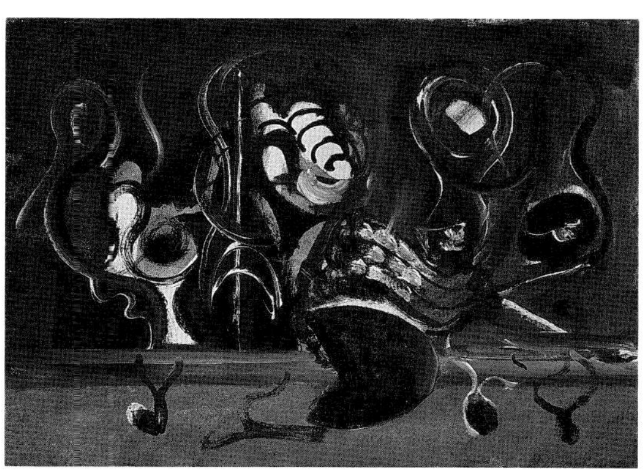

Untitled, 1944/1946
Canvas, 0.295 x 0.399 (11 3/4 x 15 3/4)
Inscribed on reverse: *Mark Rothko*
Gift of The Mark Rothko Foundation
1986.43.125

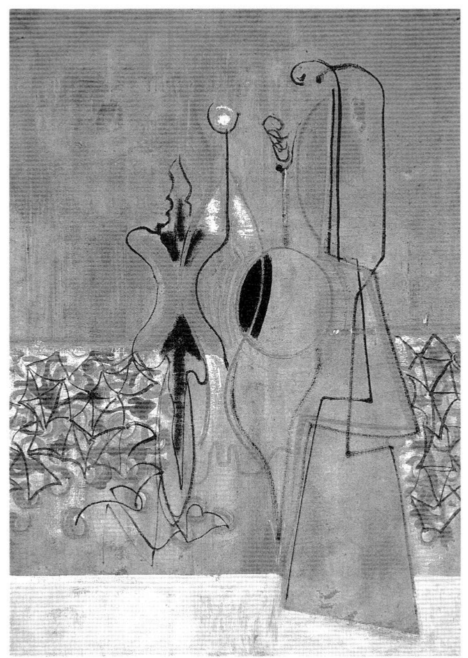

Untitled, c. 1944/1946
Canvas, 1.003 x 0.704 (39 1/2 x 27 11/16)
Inscribed at center right on reverse: *Mark Rothko*
Gift of The Mark Rothko Foundation
1986.43.70

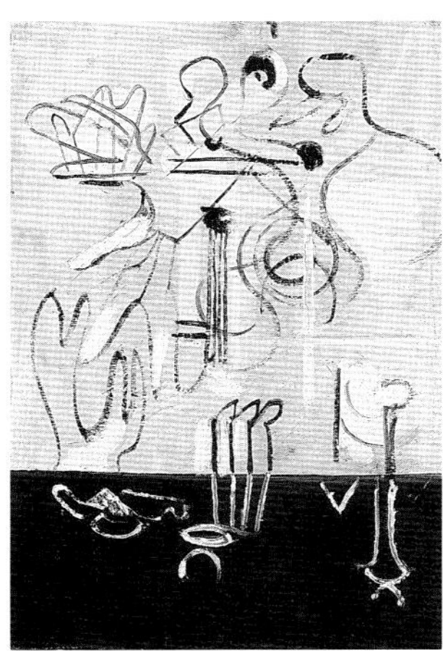

Untitled, c. 1944/1946
Canvas, 0.474 x 0.324 (18 7/8 x 12 13/16)
Inscribed at center on reverse: *Mark Rothko*
Gift of The Mark Rothko Foundation
1986.43.127

Untitled, c. 1944/1946
Canvas, 0.332 x 0.478 (13 1/16 x 18 13/16)
Inscribed at upper center on reverse: *Mark Rothko*
Gift of The Mark Rothko Foundation
1986.43.129

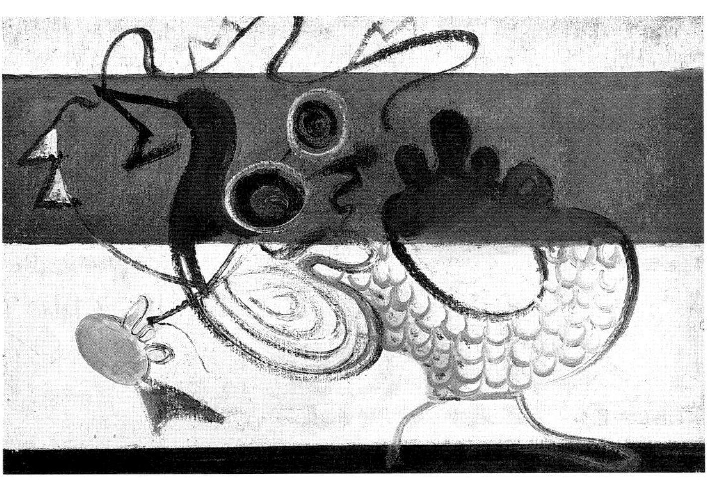

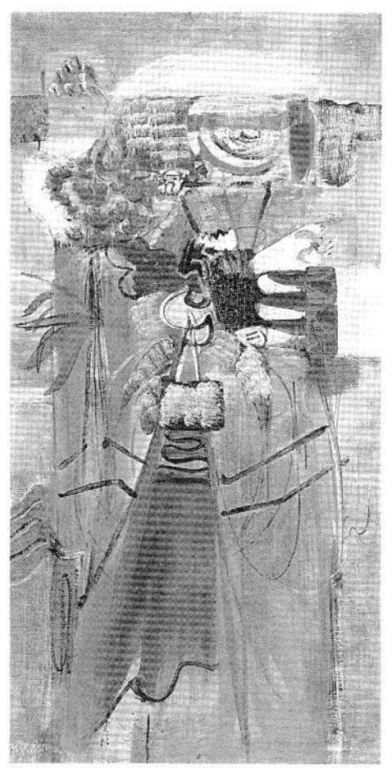

Archaic Phantasy, 1945
Canvas, 1.231 x 0.614 (48 7/16 x 24 1/8)
Inscribed at lower left: *MARK ROTHKO*; across center on reverse: *Mark Rothko Archaic Phantasy 1945*
Gift of The Mark Rothko Foundation
1986.43.11

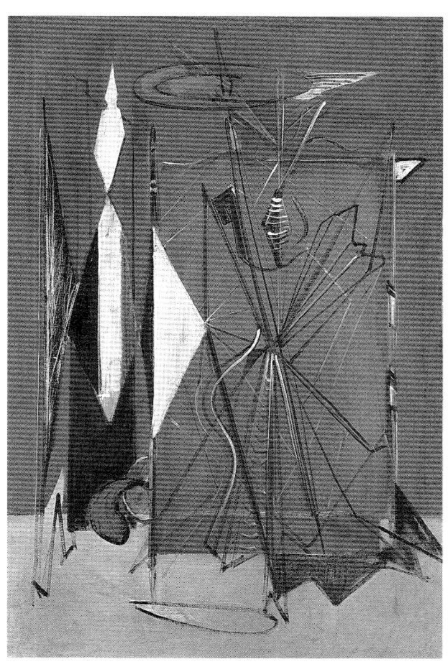

Phalanx of the Mind, 1945
Canvas, 1.379 x 0.908 (54 5/16 x 35 3/4)
Inscribed at lower right: *MARK ROTHKO*
Gift of The Mark Rothko Foundation
1986.43.6

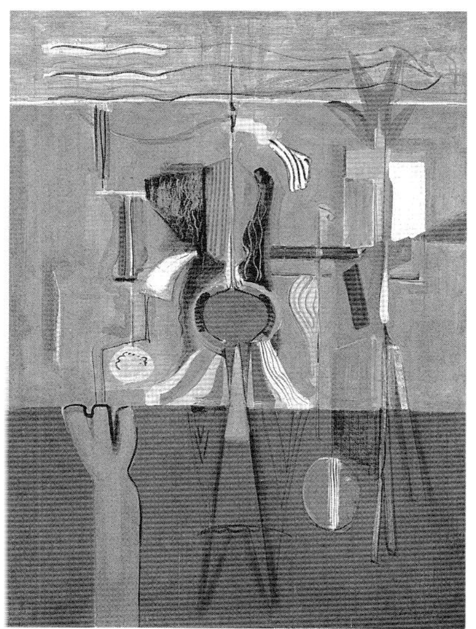

Ceremonial, c. 1945
Canvas, 1.366 x 1.005 (53 13/16 x 39 9/16)
Inscribed at lower right: *MARK ROTHKO*
Gift of The Mark Rothko Foundation
1986.43.7

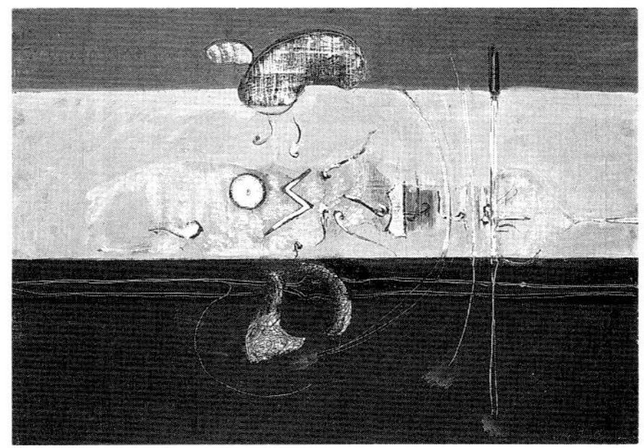

Untitled, c. 1945
Canvas, 0.565 x 0.769 (22¼ x 30⁵⁄₁₆)
Inscribed at lower right: *Mark Rothko*
Gift of The Mark Rothko Foundation
1986.43.88

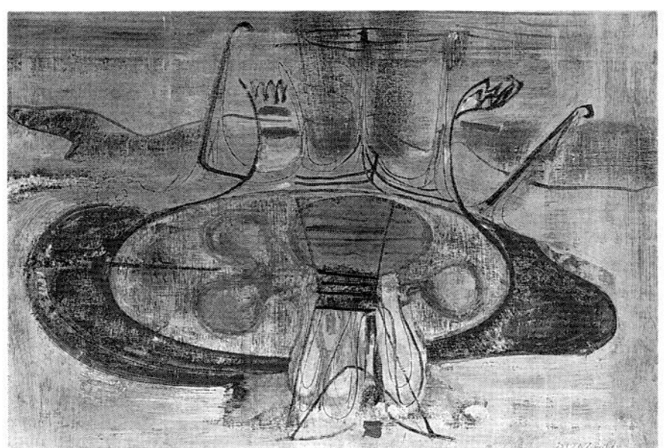

Memory, 1945/1946
Canvas, 0.710 x 0.980 (27¾ x 38¹¹⁄₁₆)
Inscribed at lower right: *MARK ROTHKO*; across center on reverse: *Mark Rothko*; across top on reverse: *Memory*
Gift of The Mark Rothko Foundation
1986.43.65

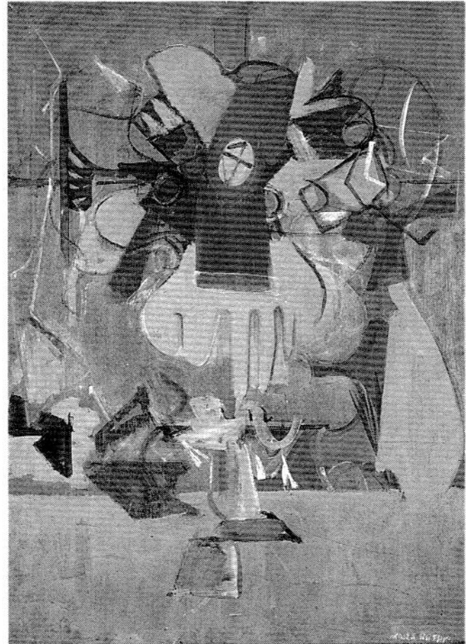

Untitled, 1945/1946
Canvas, 0.997 x 0.698 (39⁵⁄₁₆ x 27½)
Inscribed at lower right: *MARK ROTHKO*; at upper center on reverse: *Mark Rothko*
Gift of The Mark Rothko Foundation
1986.43.63

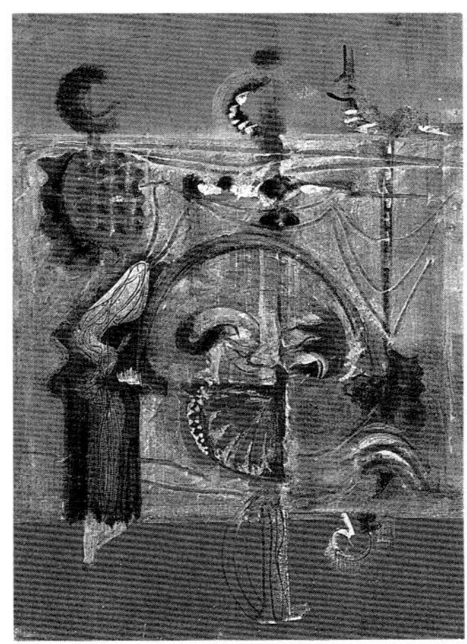

Untitled, 1945/1946
Canvas, 0.697 x 0.491 (27⁷⁄₁₆ x 19⅝)
Inscribed at center on reverse: *Mark Rothko*
Gift of The Mark Rothko Foundation
1986.43.85

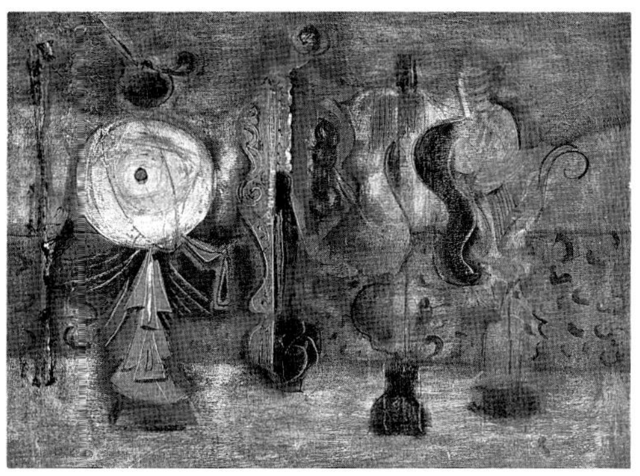

Untitled, 1945/1946
Canvas, 0.486 x 0.638 (19 3/16 x 25 1/8)
Inscribed at center right on reverse: *Mark Rothko*
Gift of The Mark Rothko Foundation
1986.43.87

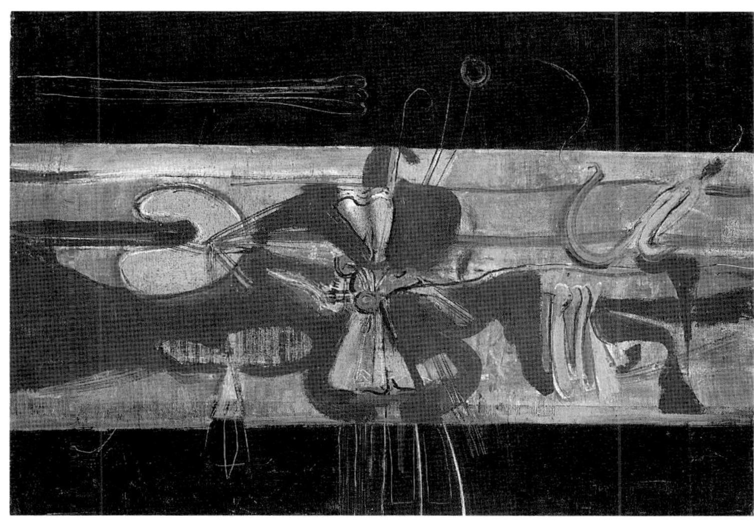

Untitled, 1945/1946
Canvas, 0.564 x 0.765 (22 1/4 x 30 1/8)
Inscribed at center left on reverse: *Mark Rothko*
Gift of The Mark Rothko Foundation
1986.43.89

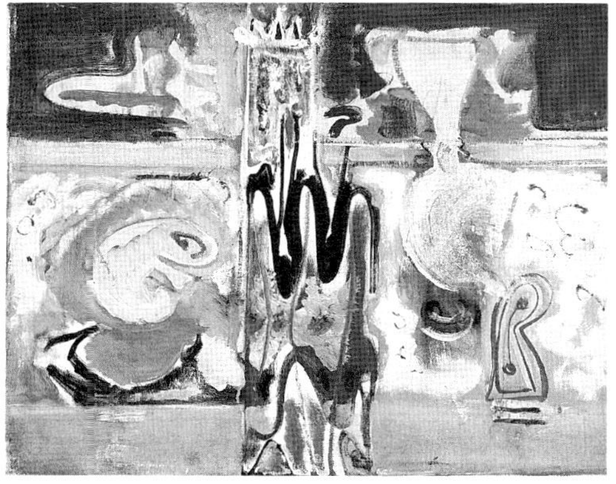

Untitled, 1945/1946
Canvas, 0.538 x 0.655 (21 3/16 x 25 13/16)
Gift of The Mark Rothko Foundation
1986.43.103

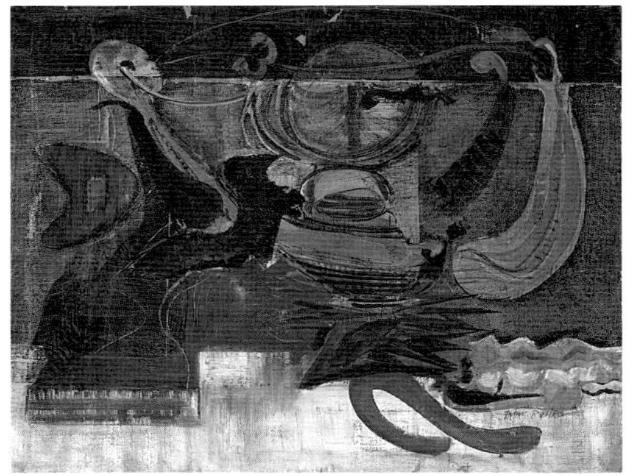

Untitled, c. 1945/1946
Canvas, 0.797 x 1.007 ($31\frac{3}{8}$ x $39\frac{5}{8}$)
Inscribed at lower right: *Mark Rothko*; at lower left on reverse: *Mark Rothko*
Gift of The Mark Rothko Foundation
1986.43.68

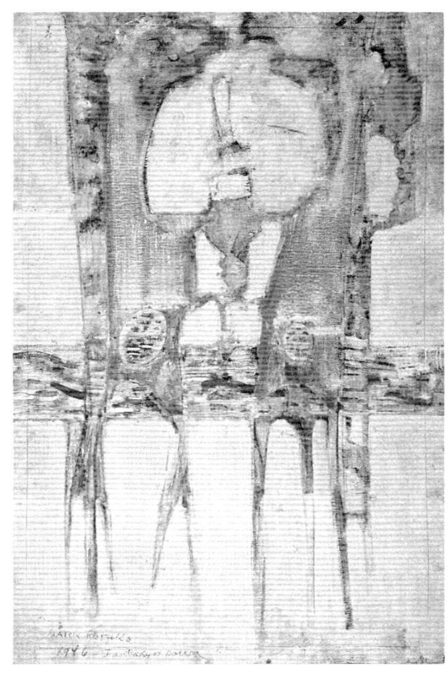

Fantasy at Dawn (recto), 1946
Canvas, 1.385 x 0.901 ($54\frac{1}{2}$ x $35\frac{1}{2}$)
Inscribed at lower left: *MARK ROTHKO / 1946 - Fantasy at Dawn*
Gift of The Mark Rothko Foundation
1986.43.5a

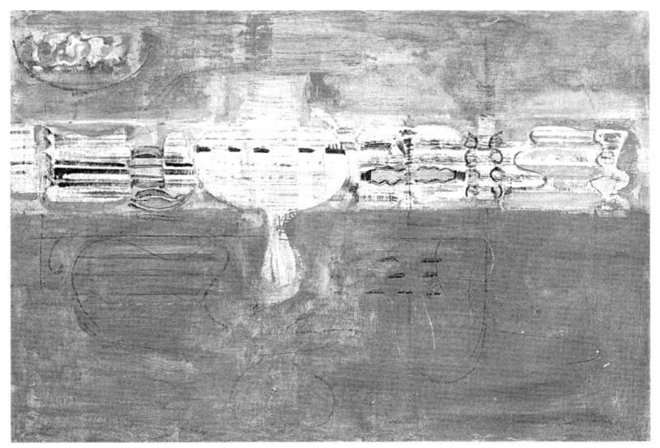

Horizontal Vision, 1946
Canvas, 0.989 x 1.388 ($38\frac{15}{16}$ x $54\frac{5}{8}$)
Inscribed at center on reverse: *Horizontal Vision 1946 Mark Rothko*
Gift of The Mark Rothko Foundation
1986.43.9

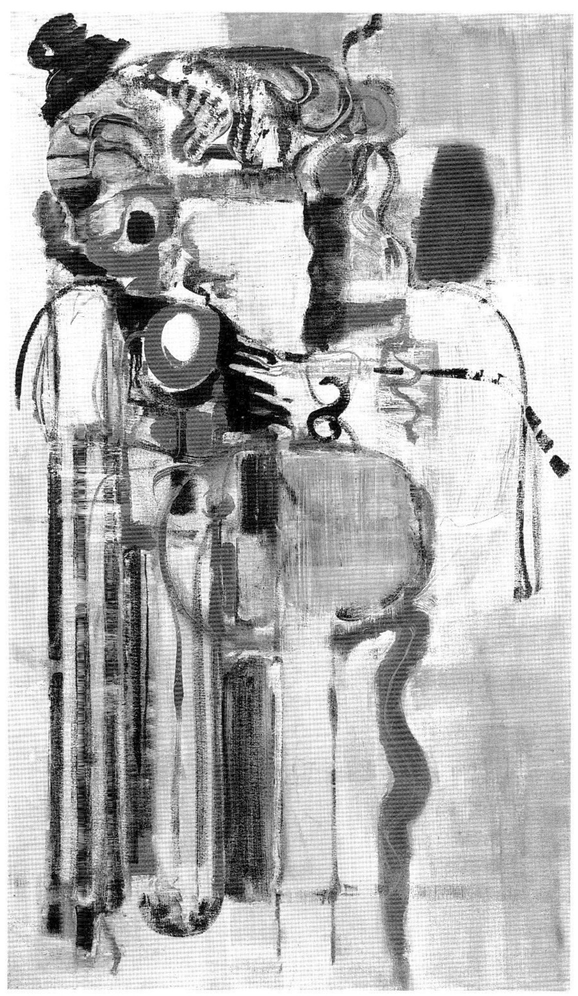

Personage Two, 1946
Canvas, 1.425 x 0.819 (55 1/16 x 32 1/4)
Inscribed at upper center on reverse:
Personage Two Mark Rothko 1946
Gift of The Mark Rothko Foundation
1986.43.12

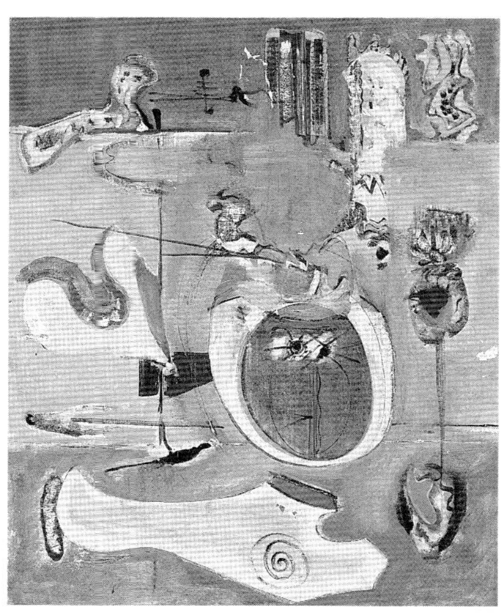

Sea Fantasy, 1946
Canvas, 1.118 x 0.918 (44 x 36 1/8)
Inscribed across top on reverse:
Sea Fantasy / 1946
Gift of The Mark Rothko Foundation
1986.43.8

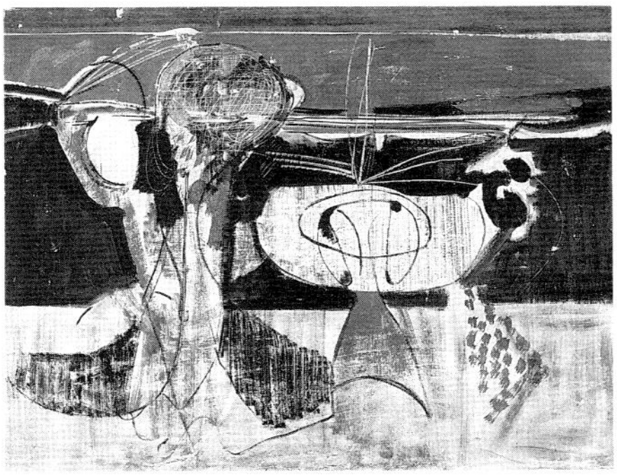

Vision at End of Day, 1946
Canvas, 1.016 x 1.271 (40 x 50)
Inscribed across center on reverse: *Vision at End of Day / 1946 / MARK ROTHKO*
Gift of The Mark Rothko Foundation
1986.43.13

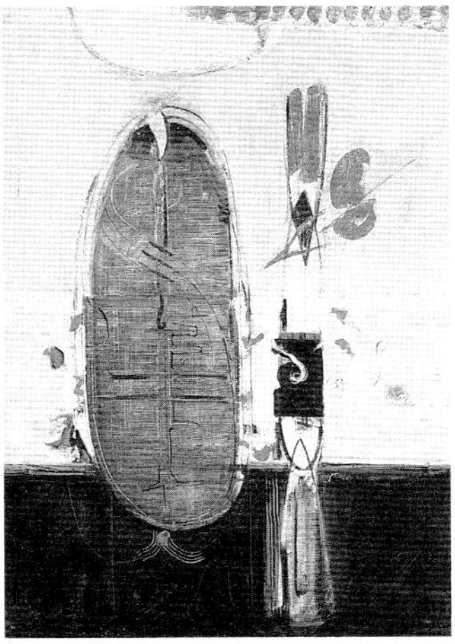

The Source, c. 1946
Canvas, 1.008 x 0.711 ($39\frac{5}{8}$ x $27\frac{15}{16}$)
Inscribed at lower right on reverse: *Mark Rothko*
Gift of The Mark Rothko Foundation
1986.43.69

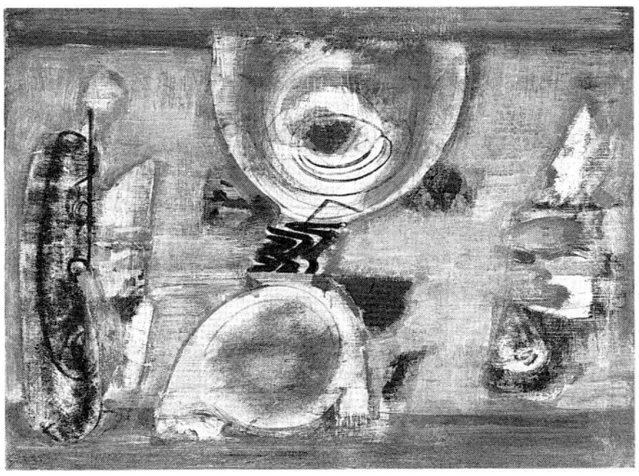

Untitled, c. 1946
Canvas, 0.712 x 0.901 ($28\frac{1}{16}$ x $35\frac{15}{16}$)
Inscribed on reverse: *Mark Rothko*
Gift of The Mark Rothko Foundation
1986.43.80

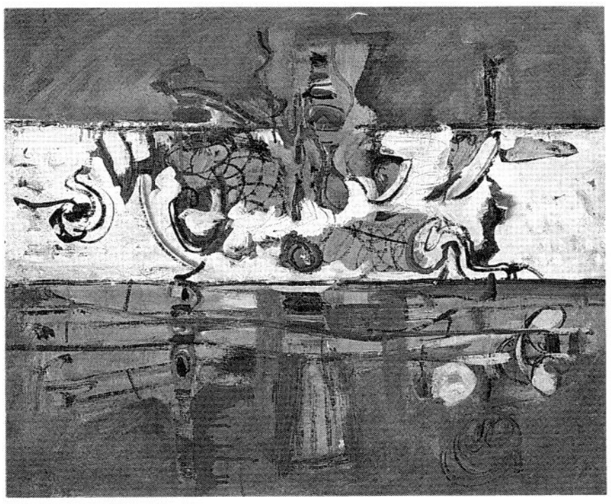

Untitled, c. 1946
Canvas, 0.548 x 0.651 ($21\frac{9}{16}$ x $25\frac{5}{8}$)
Inscribed on reverse: *M. Rothko*
Gift of The Mark Rothko Foundation
1986.43.102

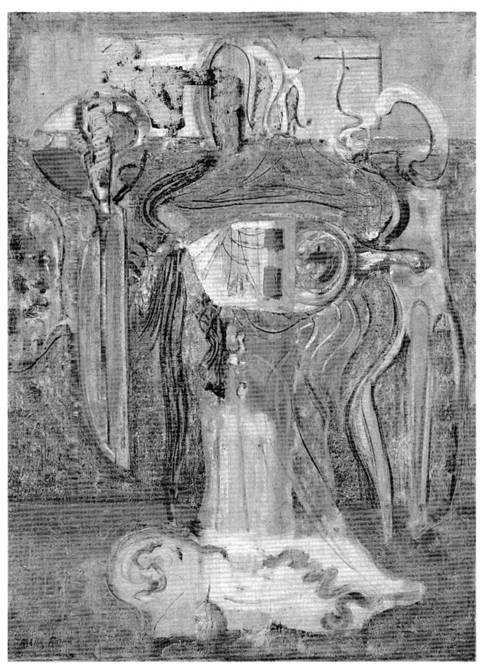

Untitled (sacrificial moment?), c. 1946
Canvas, 0.980 x 0.703 (38½ x 27 11/16)
Inscribed at lower left: *MARK ROTHKO*
Gift of The Mark Rothko Foundation
1986.43.74

Aquatic Drama, 1946/1947
Canvas, 0.922 x 1.225 (36 5/16 x 48 3/16)
Inscribed at upper center on reverse:
Aquatic Drama 1946 Mark Rothko
Gift of The Mark Rothko Foundation
1986.43.10

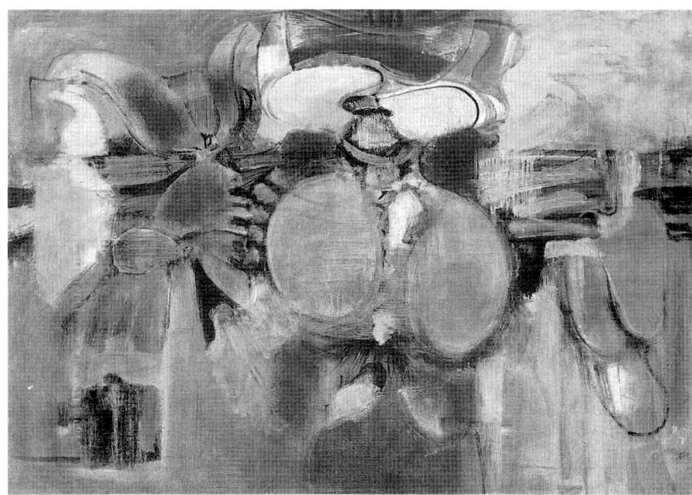

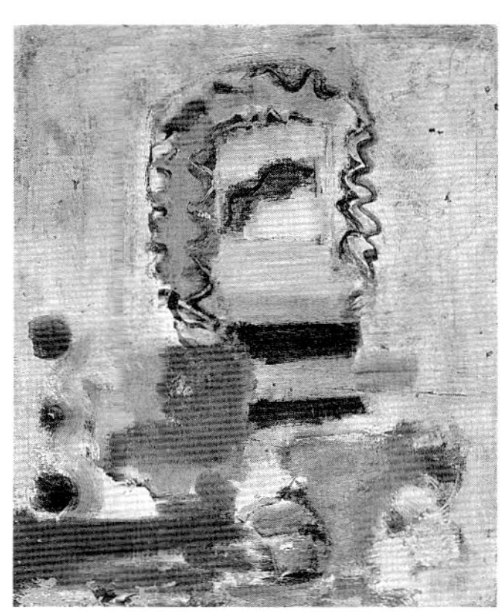

Untitled, c. 1946/1947
Canvas, 0.981 x 0.803 (39 9/16 x 31 5/8)
Inscribed on reverse: *Mark Rothko*
Gift of The Mark Rothko Foundation
1986.43.17

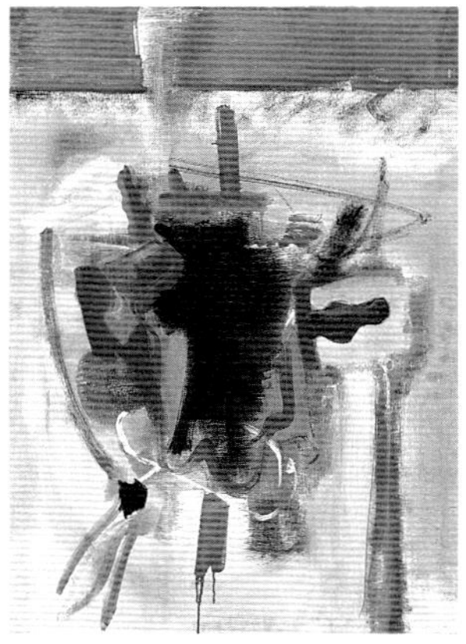

Untitled, c. 1946/1947
Canvas, 0.999 x 0.699 (39 5/16 x 27 1/2)
Inscribed at upper center on reverse: *Mark Rothko*
Gift of The Mark Rothko Foundation
1986.43.64

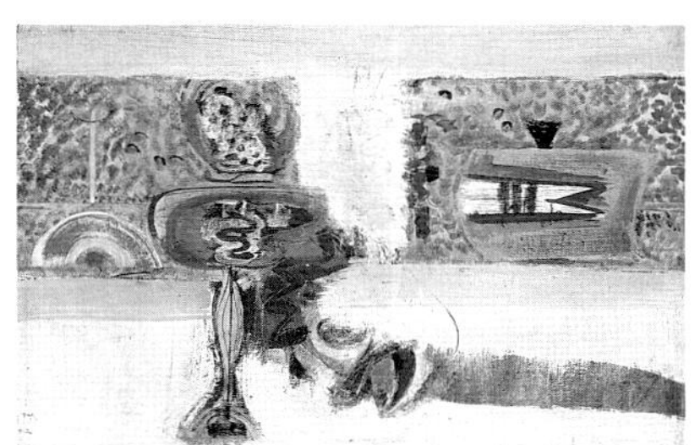

Untitled, c. 1946/1947
Canvas, 0.702 x 0.997 (27 5/8 x 39 1/4)
Inscribed on reverse: *Mark Rothko*
Gift of The Mark Rothko Foundation
1986.43.67

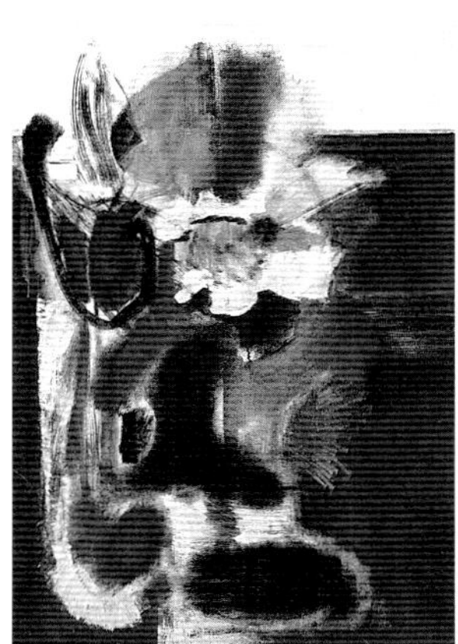

Untitled, 1946/1948
Canvas, 1.000 x 0.700 (39 3/8 x 27 9/16)
Inscribed at upper center on reverse: *Mark Rothko*
Gift of The Mark Rothko Foundation
1986.43.66

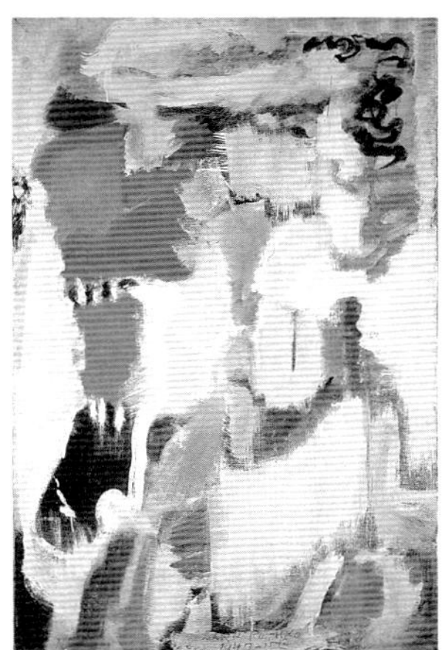

Fantasy at Dawn (verso), 1947
Canvas, 1.385 x 0.901 (54 1/2 x 35 1/2)
Inscribed across bottom: *MARK ROTHKO / 1947–[. . .]B*
Gift of The Mark Rothko Foundation
1986.43.5b

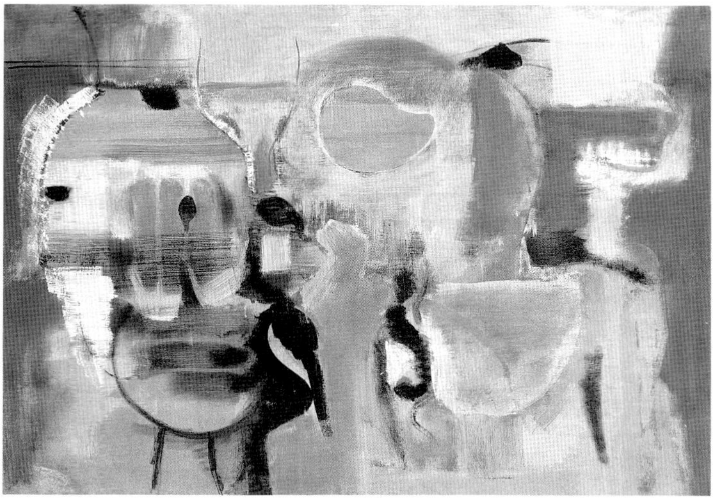

Number 3, 1947
Canvas, 1.008 x 1.383 (39 5/8 x 54 7/16)
Inscribed at upper center on reverse: *Mark Rothko - 1947*
Gift of The Mark Rothko Foundation
1986.43.3

Number 9 or Number 22, 1947
Canvas, 0.976 x 0.995 (38 7/16 x 39 3/16)
Inscribed at upper center on reverse: *#9 Mark Rothko 1947*; sideways at upper center on reverse: *#22*
Gift of The Mark Rothko Foundation
1986.43.2

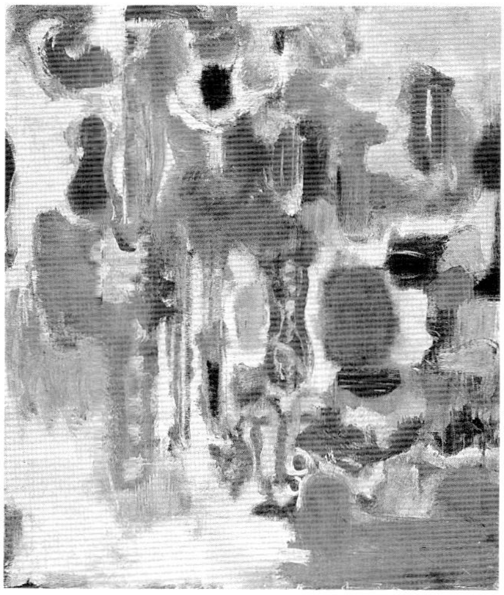

Number 10, 1947
Canvas, 1.164 x 0.962 (45 13/16 x 37 7/8)
Inscribed on reverse: *Mark Rothko #10*
Gift of The Mark Rothko Foundation
1986.43.1

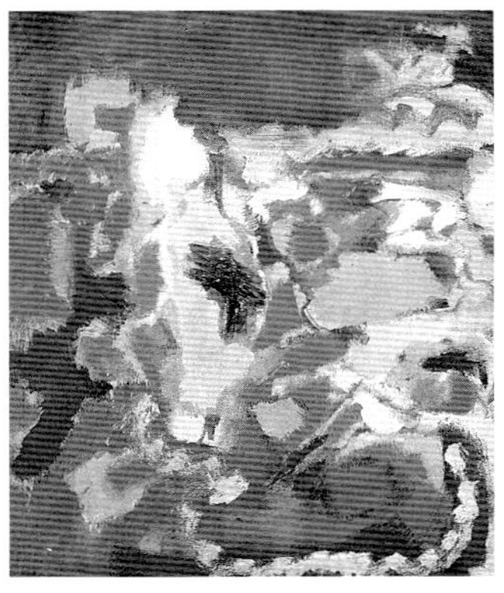

Untitled, 1947
Canvas, 0.983 x 0.838 (38⅞ x 33)
Gift of The Mark Rothko Foundation
1986.43.15

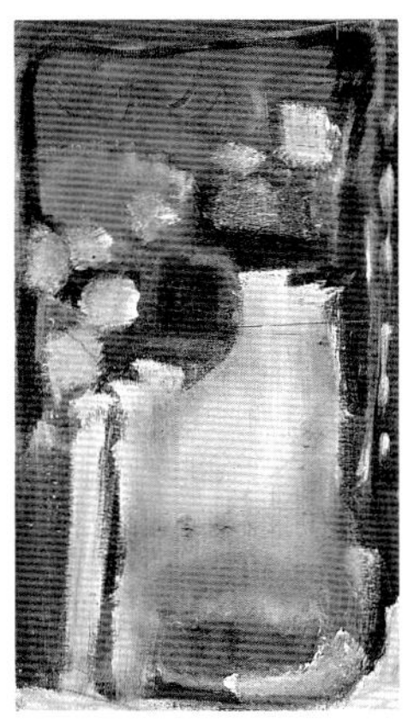

Untitled, 1947
Canvas, 0.962 x 0.530 (37⅞ x 20⅞)
Inscribed on reverse: *Mark Rothko*
Gift of The Mark Rothko Foundation
1986.43.16

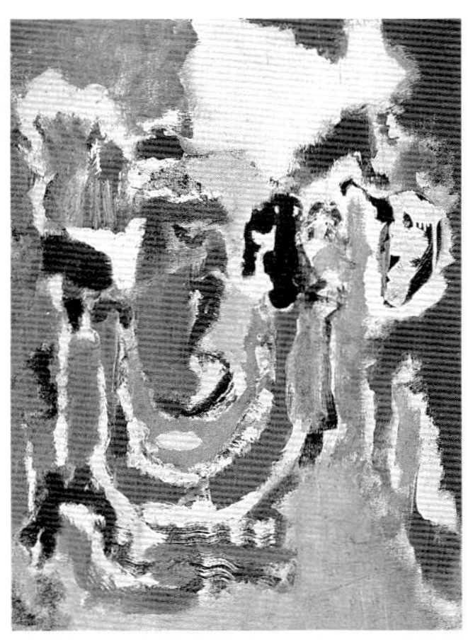

Untitled, 1947
Canvas, 0.984 x 0.708 (38¾ x 27⅞)
Inscribed at upper center on reverse: *Mark Rothko*
Gift of The Mark Rothko Foundation
1986.43.18

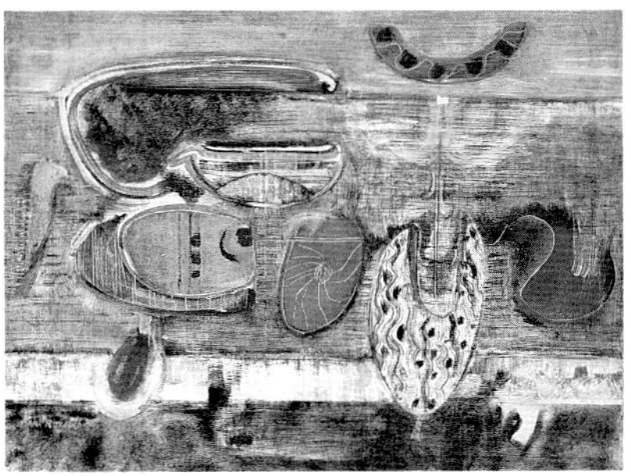

Untitled, c. 1947
Canvas, 0.805 x 1.004 (31¾ x 39¾)
Inscribed at lower left: *MARK ROTHKO*
Gift of The Mark Rothko Foundation
1986.43.75

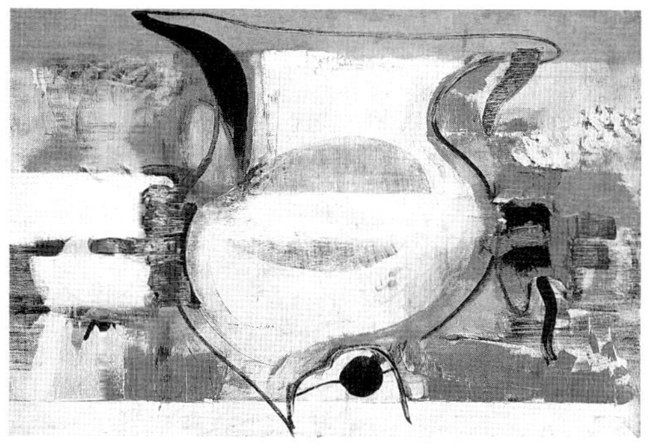

Untitled, c. 1947
Canvas, 0.700 x 0.970 (27 9/16 x 38 1/2)
Inscribed on reverse: *Mark Rothko*
Gift of The Mark Rothko Foundation
1986.43.81

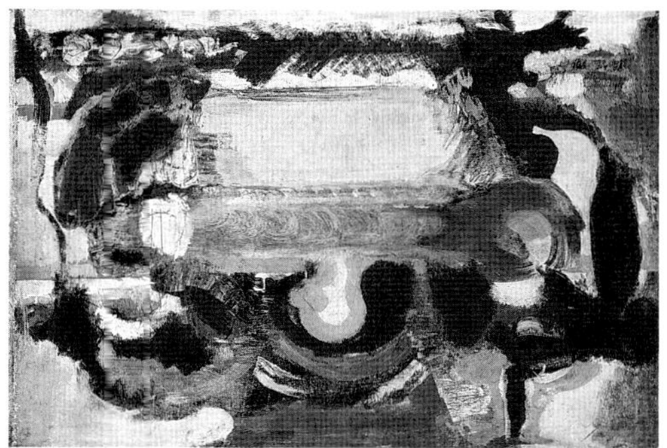

Untitled, c. 1947
Canvas, 0.699 x 0.979 (27 3/4 x 38 7/16)
Inscribed on reverse: *Mark Rothko*
Gift of The Mark Rothko Foundation
1986.43.82

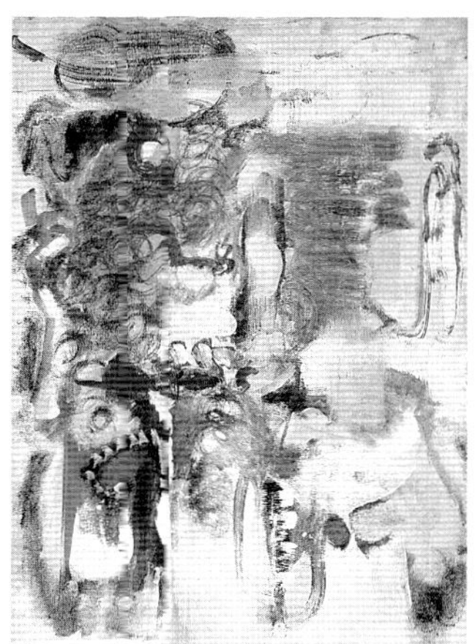

Untitled, c. 1947
Canvas, 0.999 x 0.693 (39 3/8 x 27 7/8)
Gift of The Mark Rothko Foundation
1986.43.83

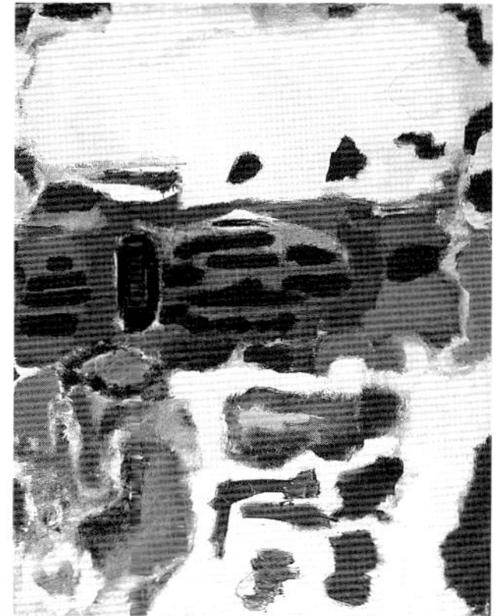

Number 2, 1947/1948
Canvas, 1.454 x 1.124 (57 1/4 x 44 1/4)
Inscribed at upper right and across center on reverse: *Mark Rothko*
Gift of The Mark Rothko Foundation
1986.43.131

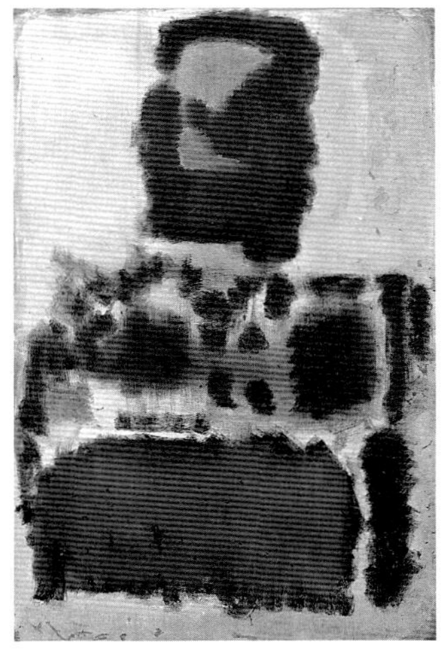

Number 10, 1947 (Number 12, 1948), 1947/1948
Canvas, 1.632 x 1.081 (64 1/16 x 42 9/16)
Inscribed at upper center on reverse: *Mark Rothko 1948*
Gift of The Mark Rothko Foundation
1986.43.136

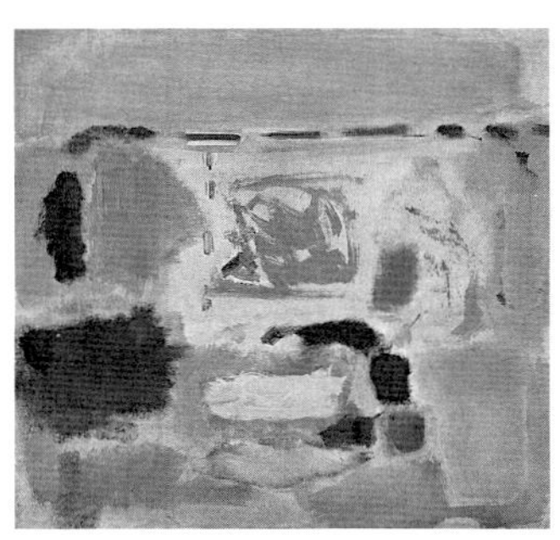

Number 7, c. 1947/1948
Canvas, 1.082 x 1.117 (42 9/16 x 43 15/16)
Inscribed across upper center on reverse: *#7 Mark Rothko 194[. . .]*
Gift of The Mark Rothko Foundation
1986.43.120

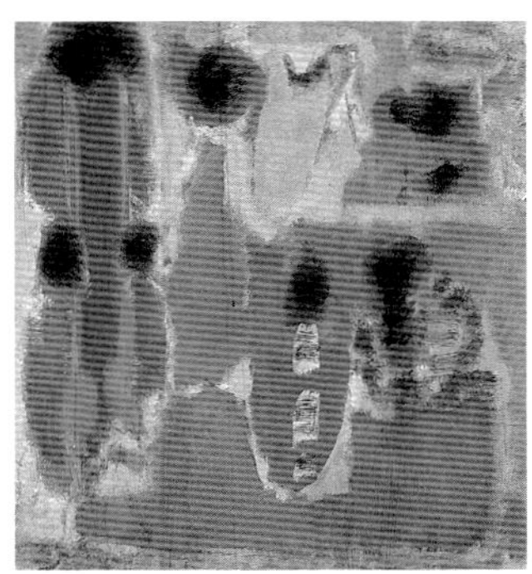

Untitled, c. 1947/1948
Canvas, 0.910 x 0.845 (35 13/16 x 33 1/4)
Inscribed at upper left, reverse: *Mark Rothko*
Gift of The Mark Rothko Foundation
1986.43.14

Untitled, c. 1947/1948
Canvas, 0.702 x 0.546 (27 9/16 x 21 9/16)
Inscribed on reverse: *Mark Rothko*
Gift of The Mark Rothko Foundation
1986.43.84

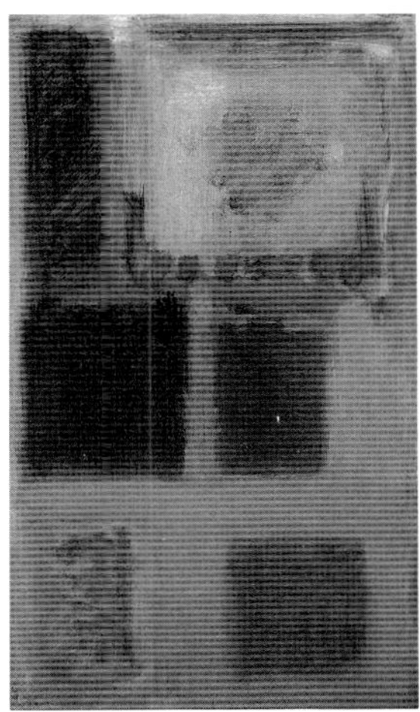

Number 10, 1948
Canvas, 1.410 x 0.814 (55⅞ x 32⅝)
Gift of The Mark Rothko Foundation
1986.43.145

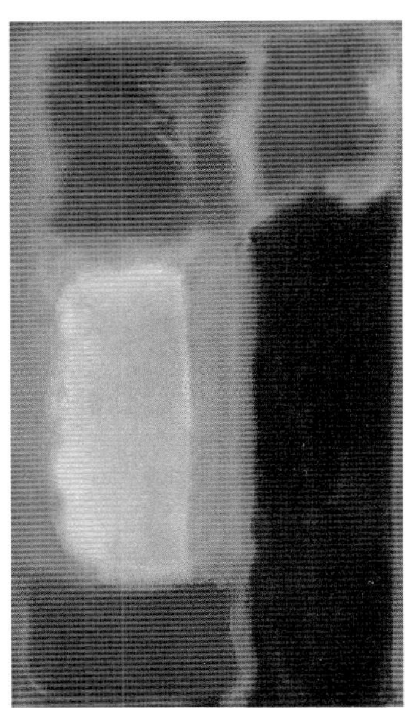

Number 15, 1948
Canvas, 1.318 x 0.740 (51⅞ x 29⅛)
Inscribed at upper right on reverse: *Mark Rothko 1948*
Gift of The Mark Rothko Foundation
1986.43.142

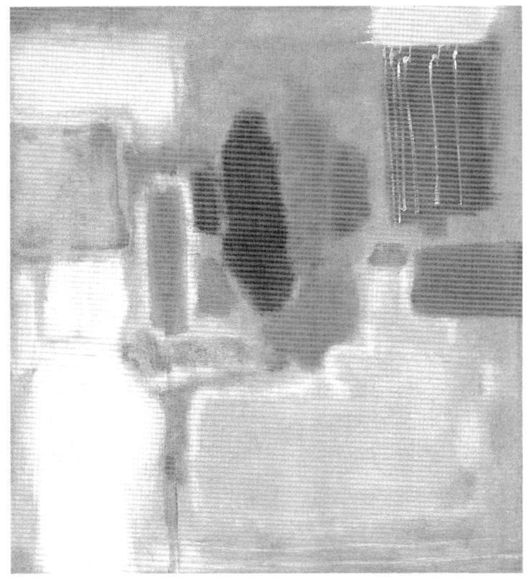

Untitled, 1948
Canvas, 1.347 x 1.184 (53 x 46⅝)
Gift of The Mark Rothko Foundation
1986.43.143

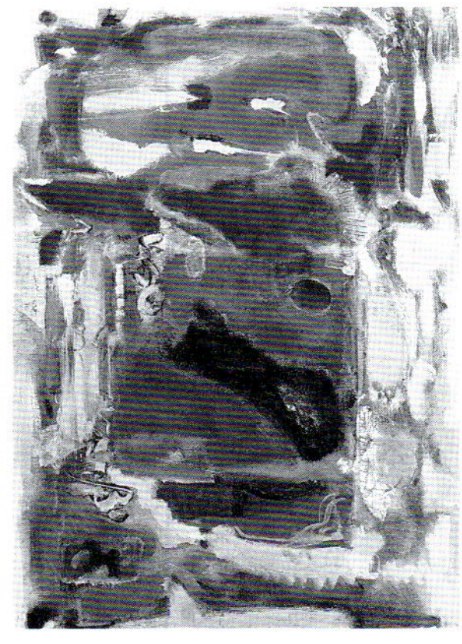

Number 18, c. 1948
Canvas, 1.550 x 1.098 (61 x 43¼)
Inscribed at lower left: *MARK ROTHKO*; at upper right on reverse: *Mark Rothko 1946*
Gift of The Mark Rothko Foundation
1986.43.132

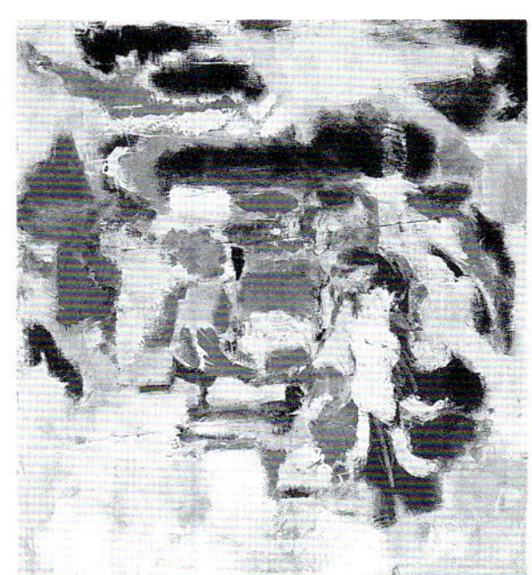

Untitled, c. 1948
Canvas, 1.264 x 1.118 (49¾ x 44)
Inscribed at reverse: *Mark Rothko*
Gift of The Mark Rothko Foundation
1986.43.4

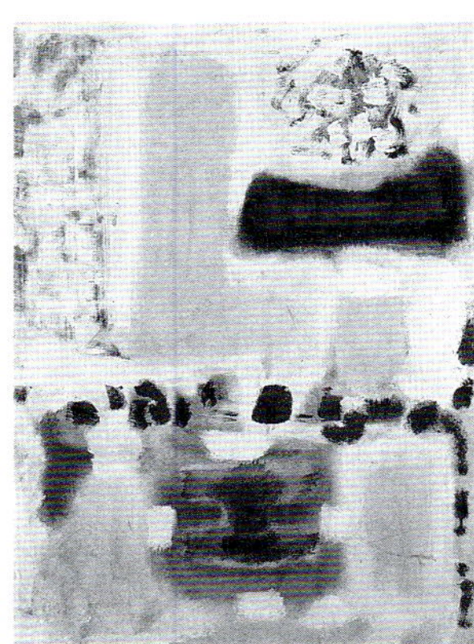

Untitled, c. 1948
Canvas, 0.991 x 0.692 (39 x 27¼)
Inscribed at center left on reverse: *Mark Rothko*
Gift of The Mark Rothko Foundation
1986.43.76

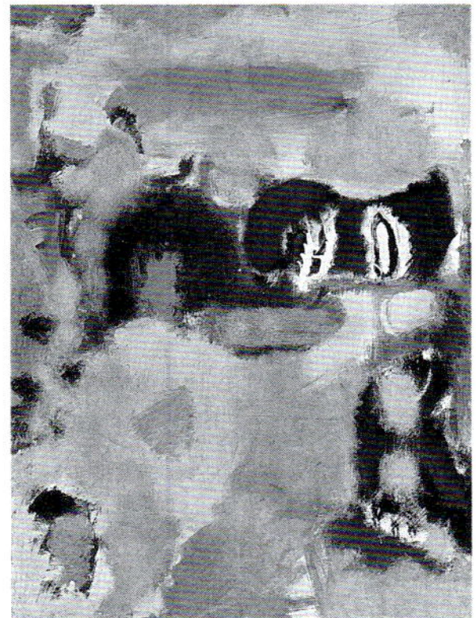

Untitled, c. 1948
Canvas, 0.972 x 0.694 (38¼ x 27 5/16)
Inscribed at upper center on reverse: *Mark Rothko*
Gift of The Mark Rothko Foundation
1986.43.77

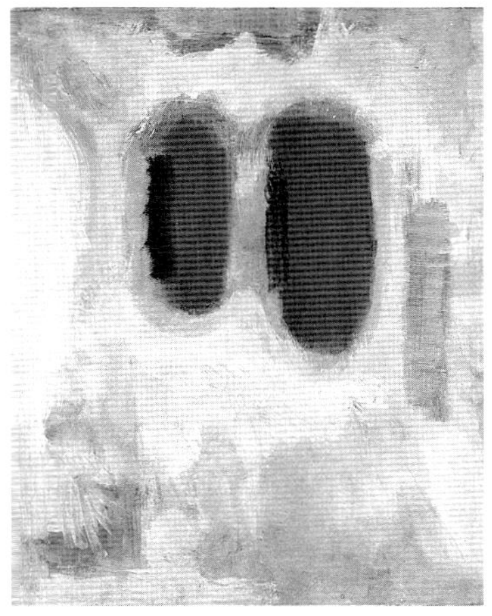

Untitled, c. 1948
Canvas, 0.937 x 0.761 (36⅝ x 29⅞)
Inscribed on reverse: *Mar Rothko* [sic]
Mark Rothko
Gift of The Mark Rothko Foundation
1986.43.78

Untitled, c. 1948
Canvas, 0.975 x 0.673 (38⅜ x 26½)
Inscribed on reverse: *Rotako*
Gift of The Mark Rothko Foundation
1986.43.79

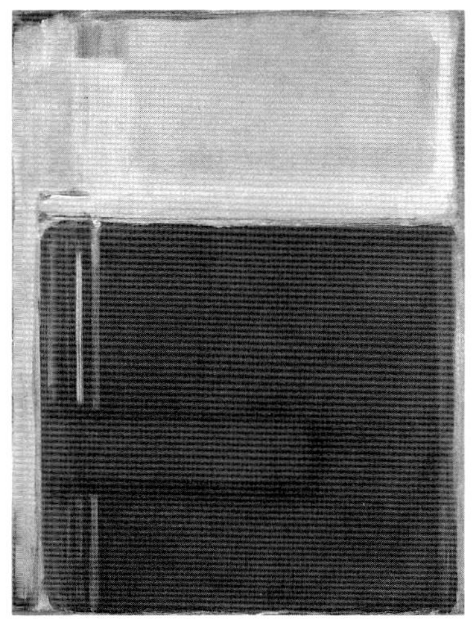

Number 8, 1949
Canvas, 2.282 x 1.674 (89 13/16 x 65⅞)
Inscribed at center on reverse: *Mark Rothko*
Gift of The Mark Rothko Foundation
1986.43.147

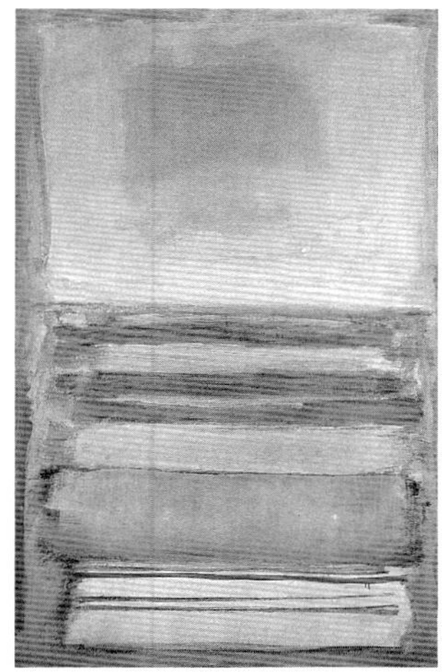

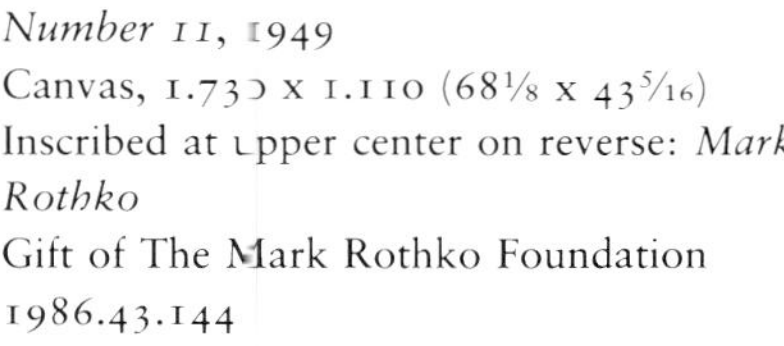

Number 11, 1949
Canvas, 1.730 x 1.110 (68⅛ x 43 5/16)
Inscribed at upper center on reverse: *Mark Rothko*
Gift of The Mark Rothko Foundation
1986.43.144

Untitled, 1949
Canvas, 2.067 x 1.686 (81⅜ x 66⅜)
Gift of The Mark Rothko Foundation
1986.43.138

Untitled, c. 1949
Canvas, 2.289 x 1.120 (90⅛ x 44⅛)
Gift of The Mark Rothko Foundation
1986.43.158

Untitled, 1950
Canvas, 2.115 x 2.356 (83¼ x 92¾)
Inscribed at center left on reverse: *Mark Rothko 1950*
Gift of The Mark Rothko Foundation
1986.43.153

Untitled, c. 1950/1955
Canvas, 1.096 x 1.262 (43⅛ x 49$^{11}/_{16}$)
Gift of The Mark Rothko Foundation
1986.43.159

Untitled, 1951
Canvas, 1.126 x 0.951 (42$^{5}/_{16}$ x 37$^{7}/_{16}$)
Inscribed at center on reverse: *M Rothko 1951*
Gift of The Mark Rothko Foundation
1986.43.157

Untitled, 1952
Canvas, 0.752 x 1.660 (29⅝ x 65⅜)
Gift of The Mark Rothko Foundation
1986.43.161

Untitled, 1953
Canvas, 1.951 x 1.723 (76¹³⁄₁₆ x 67¹³⁄₁₆)
Inscribed at center right on reverse: *Mark Rothko 1953*
Gift of The Mark Rothko Foundation
1986.43.135

Orange and Tan, 1954
Canvas, 2.064 x 1.606 (81¼ x 63¼)
Inscribed at upper right on reverse: *MARK ROTHKO / 1954*
Gift of Enid A. Haupt
1977.47.13

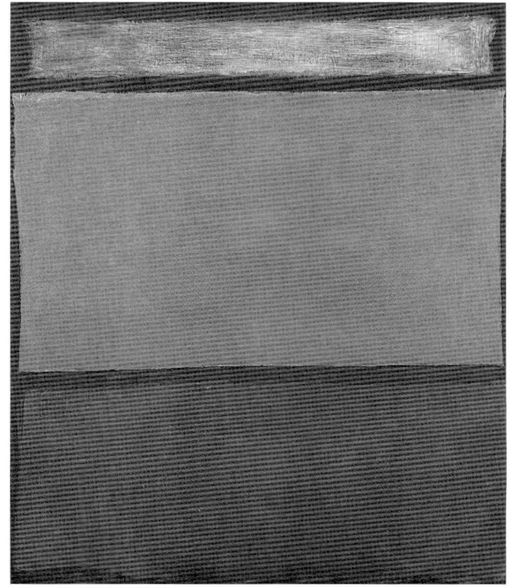

Untitled, 1955
Canvas, 2.042 x 1.717 (80¼ x 68½)
Inscribed at center on reverse: *Mark Rothko 1955*; at lower right on reverse: *Mark Rothko*
Gift of The Mark Rothko Foundation
1986.43.155

Untitled, 1956
Canvas, 2.432 x 2.070 (95¹¹⁄₁₆ x 81½)
Inscribed at center right on reverse: *Mark Rothko 1956*
Gift of The Mark Rothko Foundation
1986.43.148

Untitled, 1956
Canvas, 1.658 x 1.032 (65¼ x 40⅝)
Inscribed at upper center on reverse: *Mark Rothko 1956*
Gift of The Mark Rothko Foundation
1986.43.160

Untitled, 1957
Canvas, 2.475 x 2.078 (97 7/16 x 81 3/4)
Gift of The Mark Rothko Foundation
1986.43.141

Number 11, 1957/1958
Canvas, 2.319 x 1.767 (91 1/2 x 69 1/2)
Inscribed at upper right on reverse: *Mark Rothko*
Gift of The Mark Rothko Foundation
1986.43.154

Untitled, 1958
Canvas, 1.143 x 2.668 (45 x 105 1/16)
Inscribed at upper right on reverse: *Mark Rothko 1958*; at center on reverse: *Mark Rothko 1958*
Gift of The Mark Rothko Foundation
1986.43.146

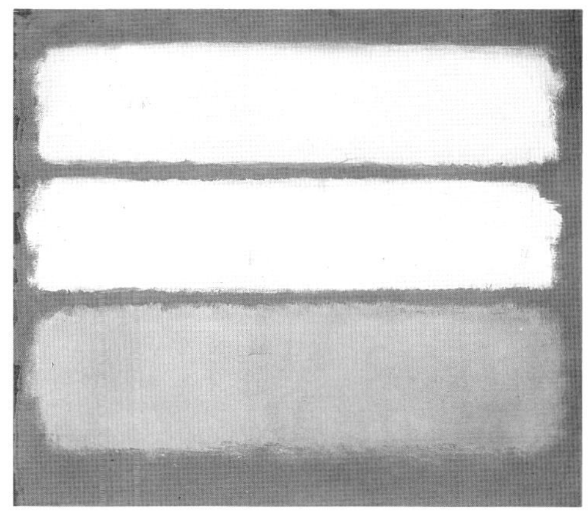

Untitled, 1958
Canvas, 1.426 x 1.578 (56⅛ x 62⅛)
Inscribed at upper left on reverse: *Mark Rothko 1958*
Gift of The Mark Rothko Foundation
1986.43.150

Untitled, 1958
Canvas, 1.678 x 1.052 (66⅙ x 41⅜)
Gift of The Mark Rothko Foundation
1986.43.162

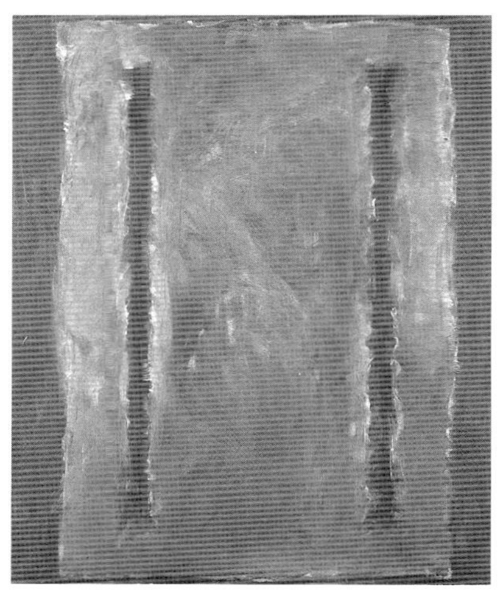

Untitled (Seagram Mural), 1958
Canvas, 1.831 x 1.526 (72⅛ x 60⅛)
Inscribed at upper right on reverse: *MARK ROTHKO / 1958*
Gift of The Mark Rothko Foundation
1985.38.1

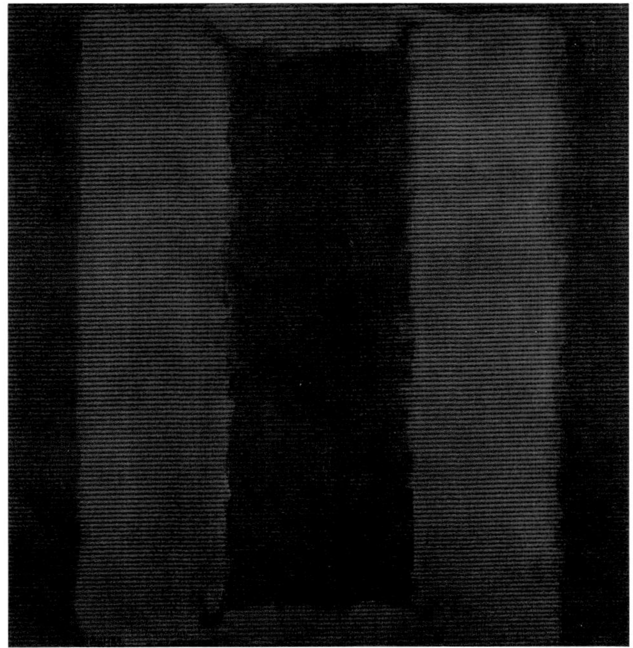

Untitled (Seagram Mural), 1958
Canvas, 2.661 x 2.524 (104 3/4 x 99 3/8)
Inscribed at center right on reverse: *Mark Rothko 1958*
Gift of The Mark Rothko Foundation
1986.43.170

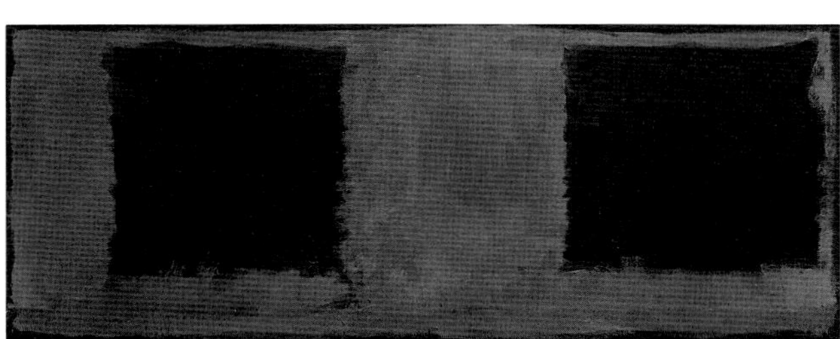

Untitled (Seagram Mural), c. 1958
Canvas, 1.826 x 4.504 (71 7/8 x 177 5/16)
Inscribed at upper left on reverse: *Mark Rothko*
Gift of The Mark Rothko Foundation
1986.43.156

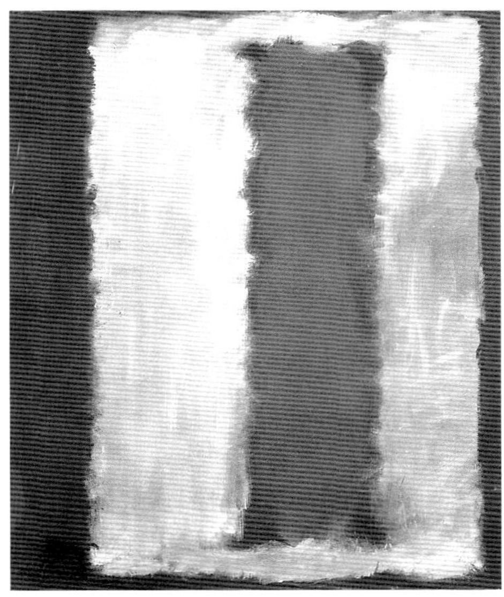

Mural Sketch, 1959
Canvas, 1.828 x 1.526 (72 x 60 1/8)
Inscribed at upper left on reverse: *MARK ROTHKO / 1959*
Gift of The Mark Rothko Foundation
1985.38.2

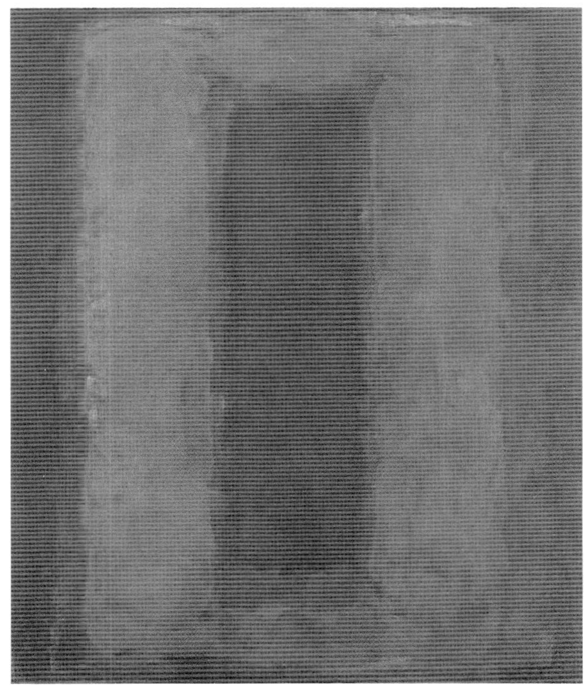

Untitled (Seagram Mural), 1959
Canvas, 1.828 x 1.526 (72 x 60 1/8)
Inscribed at upper left on reverse: *MARK ROTHKO / 1959*
Gift of The Mark Rothko Foundation
1985.38.3

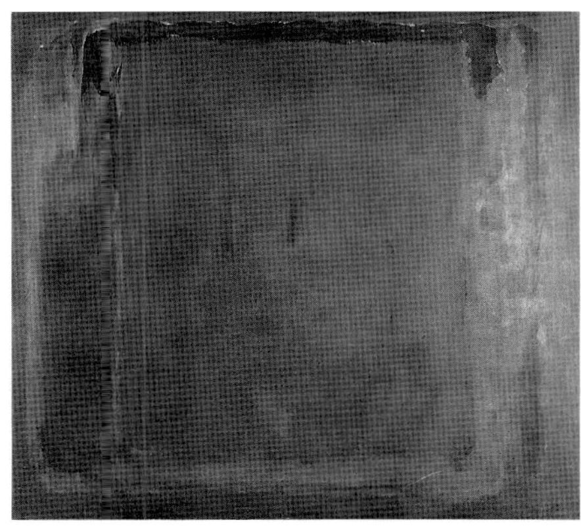

Untitled (Seagram Mural), 1959
Canvas, 2.672 x 2.892 (105 1/4 x 113 7/8)
Gift of The Mark Rothko Foundation
1985.38.4

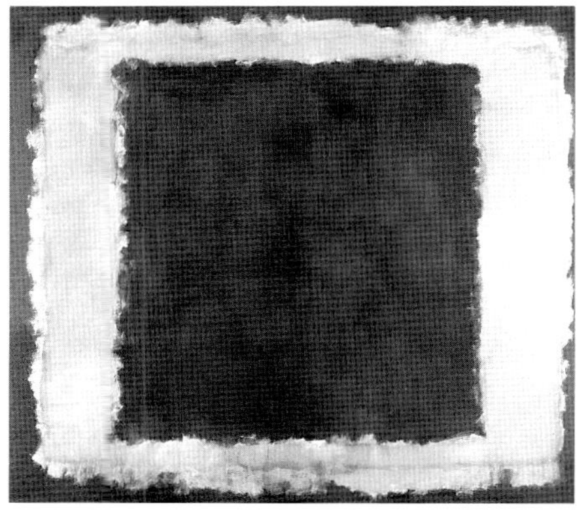

Untitled (Seagram Mural), 1959
Canvas, 2.654 x 2.883 (104 1/2 x 113 1/2)
Inscribed at lower left on reverse: *MARK ROTHKO / 1961*
Gift of The Mark Rothko Foundation
1985.38.5

Untitled (Seagram Mural), 1959
Canvas, 2.654 x 4.572 (104½ x 180)
Inscribed at upper right on reverse: *MARK ROTHKO*
Gift of The Mark Rothko Foundation
1985.38.6

Untitled (Seagram Mural), 1959
Canvas, 2.690 x 4.578 (106 x 180¼)
Inscribed at upper right on reverse: *Mark Rothko*
Gift of The Mark Rothko Foundation
1986.43.167

Untitled, 1961
Canvas, 2.586 x 2.276 (101 13/16 x 89⅝)
Inscribed at center left on reverse: *Mark Rothko 1961*
Gift of The Mark Rothko Foundation
1986.43.151

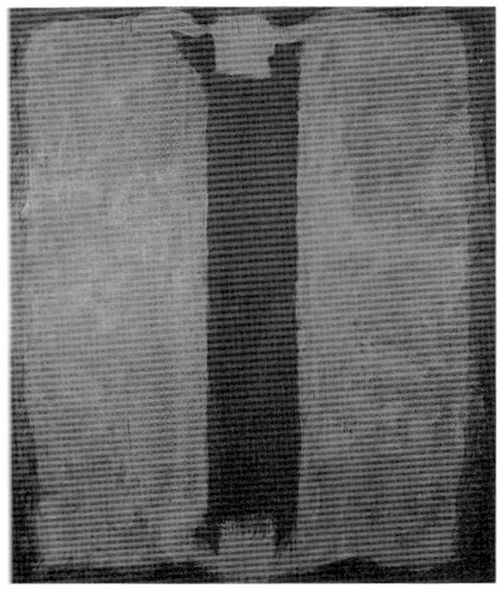

Untitled (Harvard Mural), 1961
Canvas, 2.791 x 2.350 (110½ x 92⅞)
Gift of The Mark Rothko Foundation
1986.43.168

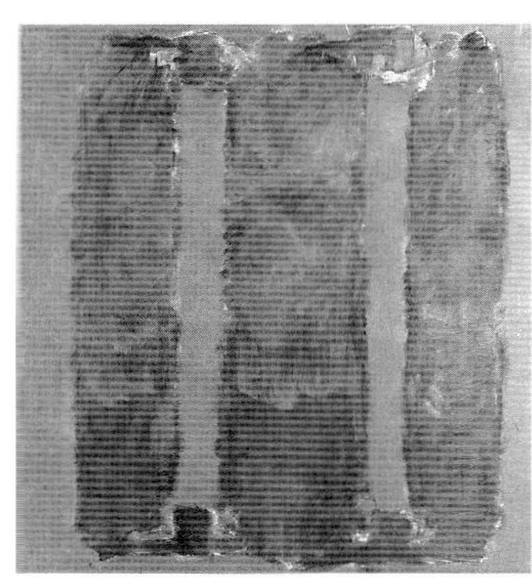

Untitled (Harvard Mural), 1961
Canvas, 2.663 x 2.430 (104$\frac{13}{16}$ x 95$\frac{11}{16}$)
Gift of The Mark Rothko Foundation
1986.43.169

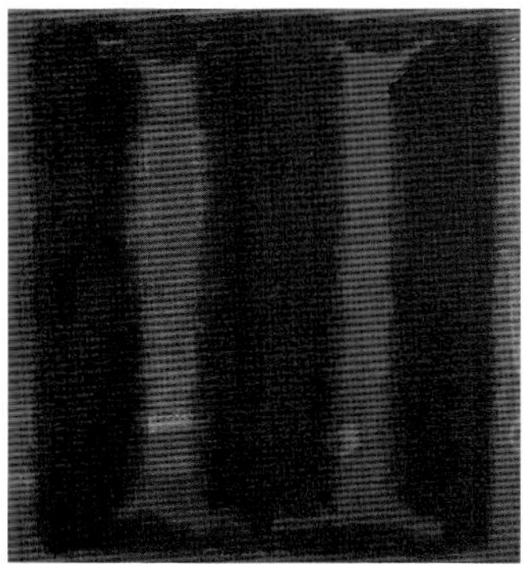

Mural 5K #1, 1962
Canvas, 2.063 x 1.862 (81$\frac{3}{16}$ x 73$\frac{5}{16}$)
Inscribed at upper left on reverse: *Mark Rothko 1959*
Gift of The Mark Rothko Foundation
1986.43.172

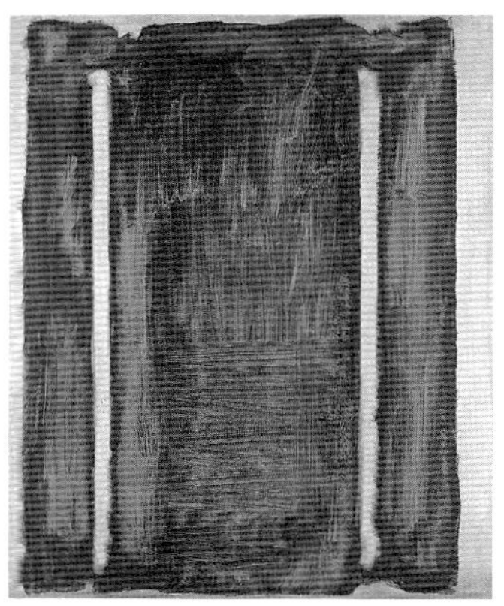

Sketch for Mural H, 1962
Canvas, 1.760 x 1.430 (69¼ x 56$\frac{5}{16}$)
Gift of The Mark Rothko Foundation
1986.43.149

Untitled, 1965
Canvas, 3.415 x 1.832 (134 7/16 x 72 1/8)
Gift of The Mark Rothko Foundation
1986.43.171

Number 5, 1964
Canvas, 2.061 x 1.939 (81 1/8 x 76 5/16)
Inscribed at center left on reverse:
Mark Rothko 1964
Gift of The Mark Rothko Foundation
1986.43.133

Number 7, 1964
Canvas, 2.364 x 1.936 (93 1/8 x 76 1/4)
Inscribed at center right on reverse: *Mark Rothko 1964*
Gift of The Mark Rothko Foundation
1986.43.134

Number 8, 1964
Canvas, 2.673 x 2.038 (105 3/16 x 80 3/16)
Inscribed at center left on reverse: *Mark Rothko 1964*
Gift of The Mark Rothko Foundation
1986.43.139

Untitled, 1964
Canvas, 1.755 x 1.676 (69⅛ x 66)
Inscribed at upper right on reverse: *Mark Rothko 1962*
Gift of The Mark Rothko Foundation
1986.43.137

Untitled, 1964
Canvas, 2.365 x 1.938 (93⅛ x 75$\frac{5}{16}$)
Inscribed at center left on reverse: *Mark Rothko 1960*
Gift of The Mark Rothko Foundation
1986.43.140

Untitled, 1964
Canvas, 2.641 x 2.265 (104 x 89½)
Gift of The Mark Rothko Foundation
1986.43.152

Untitled (black and gray), 1969
Canvas, 1.769 x 1.579 (69⅝ x 62$\frac{3}{16}$)
Inscribed at upper left on reverse: *Mark Rothko 1969*
Gift of The Mark Rothko Foundation
1986.43.163

Untitled (black and gray), 1969
Canvas, 2.295 x 1.759 (90 3/8 x 69 1/4)
Inscribed at center right on reverse: *Mark Rothko 1969*
Gift of The Mark Rothko Foundation
1986.43.164

Untitled (black and gray), 1969
Canvas, 1.378 x 1.735 (54 1/4 x 68 5/16)
Inscribed at upper right on reverse: *Mark Rothko 1969*
Gift of The Mark Rothko Foundation
1986.43.165

Untitled (black and gray), 1969
Canvas, 2.067 x 1.937 (81 3/8 x 76 1/4)
Inscribed at center left on reverse: *Mark Rothko 1969*
Gift of The Mark Rothko Foundation
1986.43.166

Untitled, 1970
Canvas, 1.529 x 1.452 (60¼ x 57⅛)
Gift of The Mark Rothko Foundation
1986.43.173

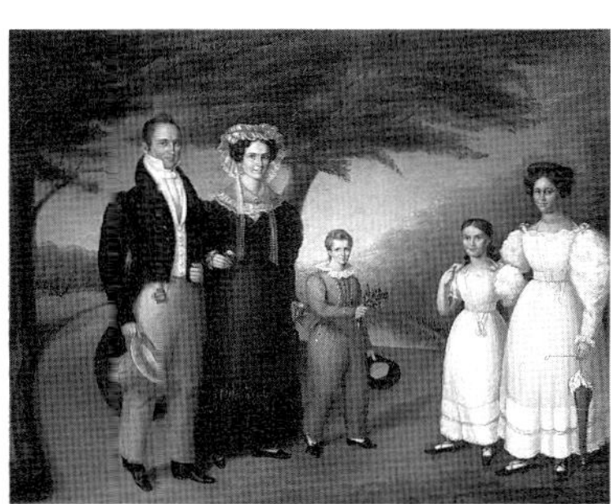

ATTRIBUTED TO
REUBEN ROWLEY
active c. 1825/1836

Dr. John Safford and Family, c. 1830
Canvas, 0.695 x 0.850 (27 7/16 x 33½)
Gift of Edgar William and Bernice Chrysler Garbisch
1980.62.46

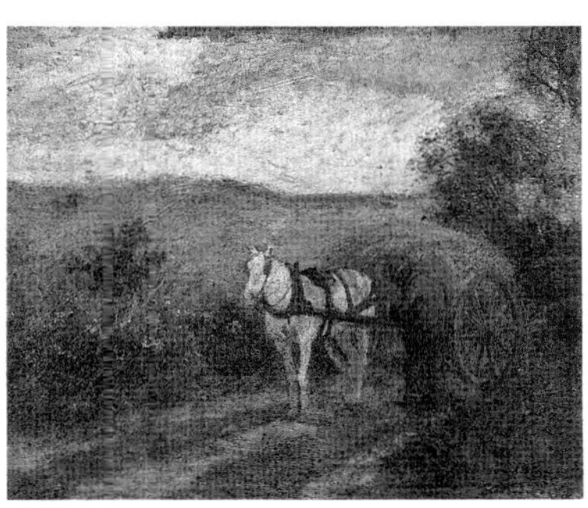

ALBERT PINKHAM RYDER
1847–1917

Mending the Harness, c. 1875
Canvas, 0.484 x 0.572 (19 x 22½)
Inscribed at lower right: *A. P. Ryder*
Gift of Sam A. Lewisohn
1951.5.3

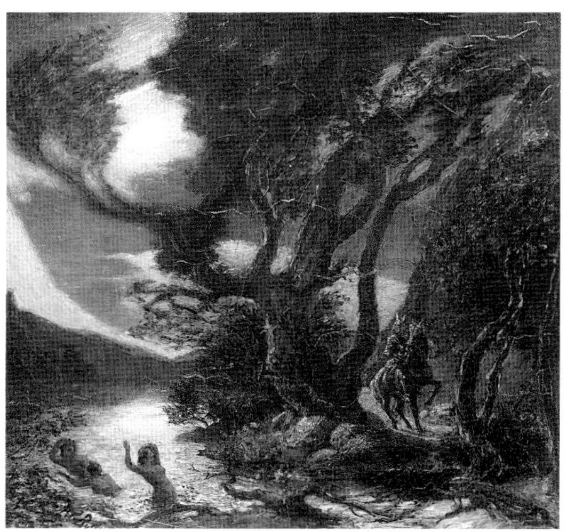

Siegfried and the Rhine Maidens, 1888/1891
Canvas, 0.505 x 0.520 (19⅞ x 20½)
Inscribed at lower left: *A. P Ryder.*
Andrew W. Mellon Collection
1946.1.1

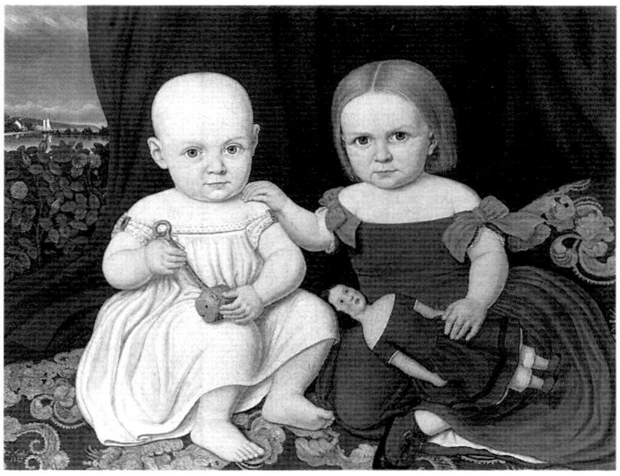

LAMBERT SACHS
1818–1903

The Herbert Children, 1857
Canvas, 0.632 x 0.803 (24⅞ x 31⅝)
Inscribed at lower left: *L. Sachs / 1857*
Gift of Edgar William and Bernice Chrysler Garbisch
1955.11.2

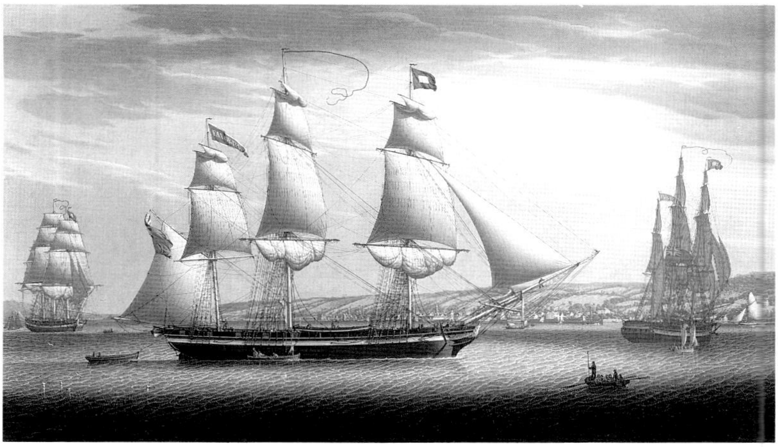

ROBERT SALMON
1775–c. 1845

The Ship Favorite *Maneuvering Off Greenock*, 1819
Canvas, 0.762 x 1.283 (30 x 50½)
Inscribed at lower right: *RS 1819*
Paul Mellon Collection
1981.54.1

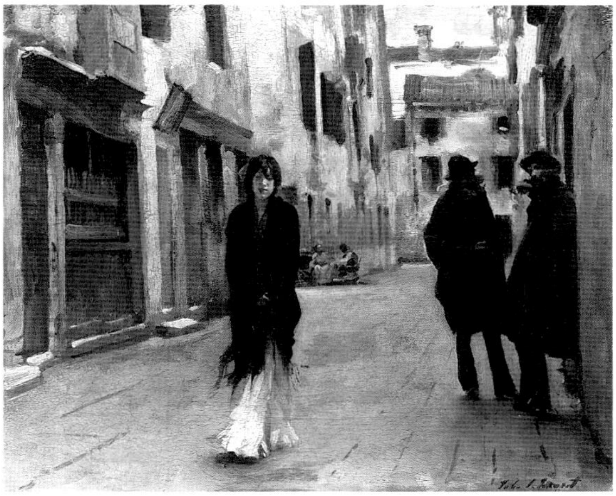

JOHN SINGER SARGENT
1856–1925

Street in Venice, 1882
Wood, 0.451 x 0.539 (17¾ x 21¼)
Inscribed at lower right: *John S. Sargent*
Gift of the Avalon Foundation
1962.4.1

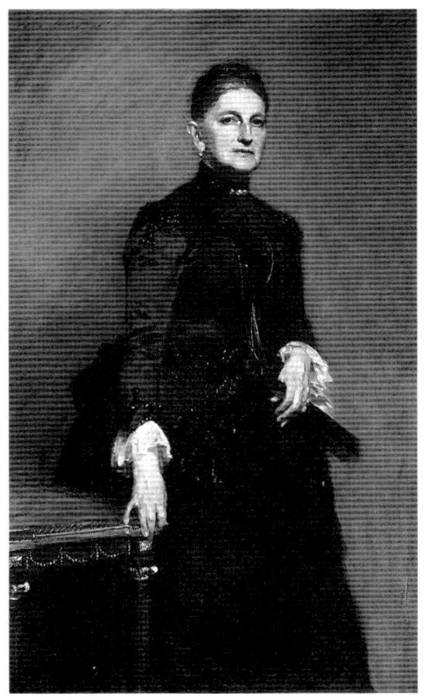

Mrs. Adrian Iselin, 1888
Canvas, 1.537 x 0.930 (60½ x 36⅝)
Inscribed at upper left: *John S. Sargent*; upper right: *1888*
Gift of Ernest Iselin
1964.13.1

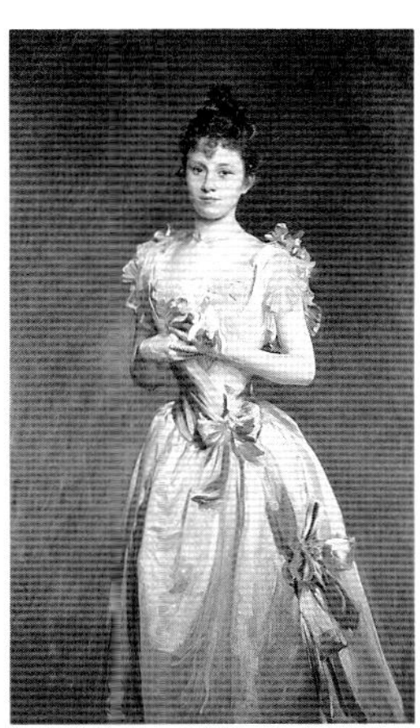

Miss Grace Woodhouse, 1890
Canvas, 1.629 x 0.940 (64⅛ x 37)
Inscribed at upper left: *John S. Sargent*; upper right: *1890*
Gift of Olga Roosevelt Graves
1962.6.1

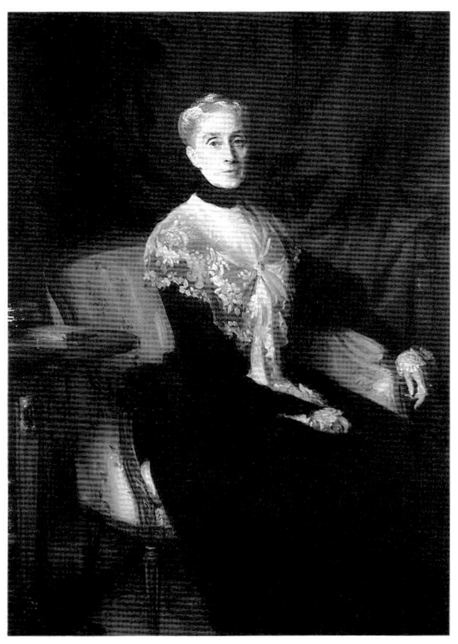

Mrs. William Crowninshield Endicott, 1901
Canvas, 1.632 x 1.146 (64¼ x 45⅛)
Inscribed at upper right: *John S. Sargent 1901*
Gift of Louise Thoron Endicott in memory of Mr. and Mrs. William Crowninshield Endicott
1951.20.1

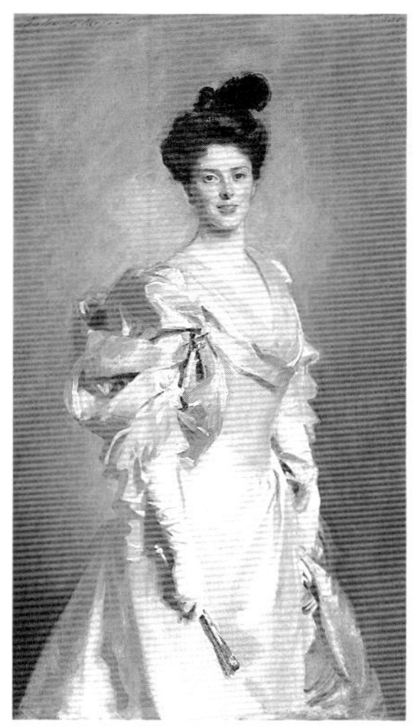

Mrs. Joseph Chamberlain, 1902
Canvas, 1.505 x 0.838 (59¼ x 33)
Inscribed at upper left: *John S. Sargent*;
upper right: *1902*
Gift of the sitter, Mary Endicott
Chamberlain Carnegie
1958.2.1

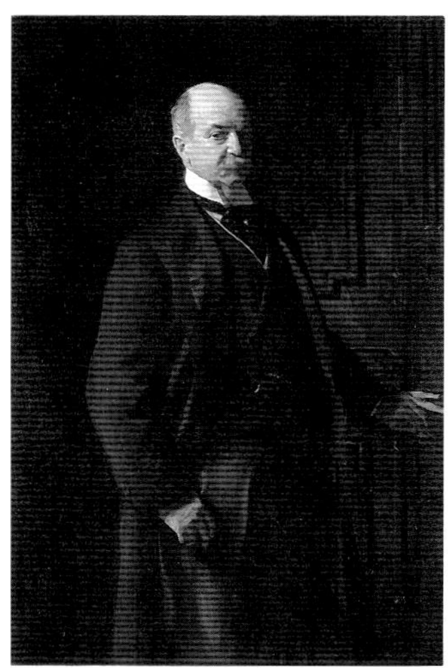

Peter A. B. Widener, 1902
Canvas, 1.489 x 0.984 (58⅝ x 38¾)
Inscribed at upper right: *John S. Sargent*
1902
Widener Collection
1942.9.101 Special Collection

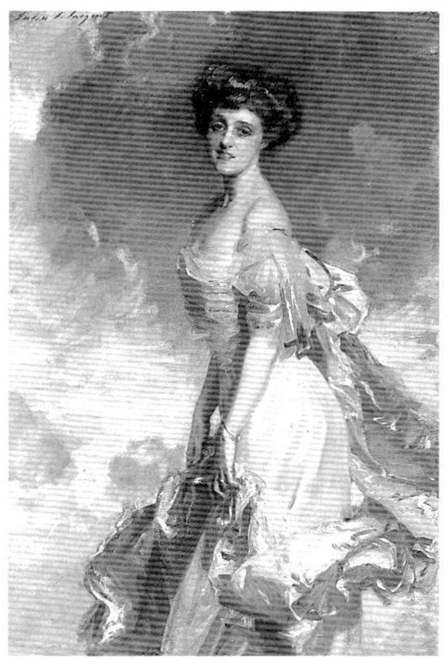

Mathilde Townsend, 1907
Canvas, 1.533 x 1.022 (60⅜ x 40¼)
Inscribed at upper left: *John S. Sargent*;
upper right: *1907*
Gift of the sitter, Mrs. Sumner Welles
1952.3.1

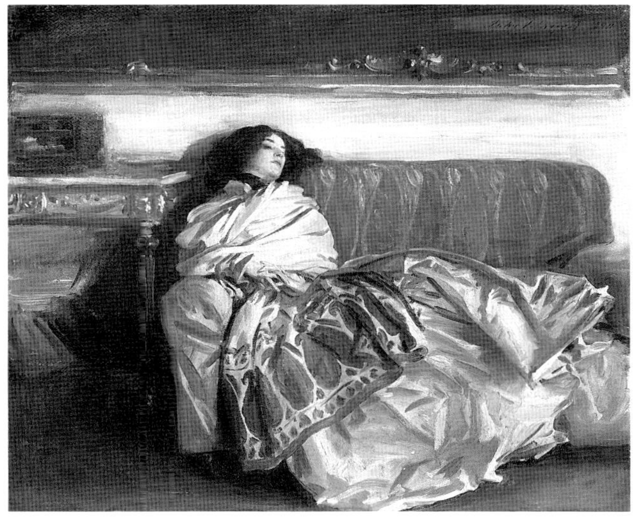

Repose, 1911
Canvas, 0.638 x 0.762 (25⅛ x 30)
Inscribed at upper right: *John S. Sargent 1911*
Gift of Curt H. Reisinger
1948.16.1

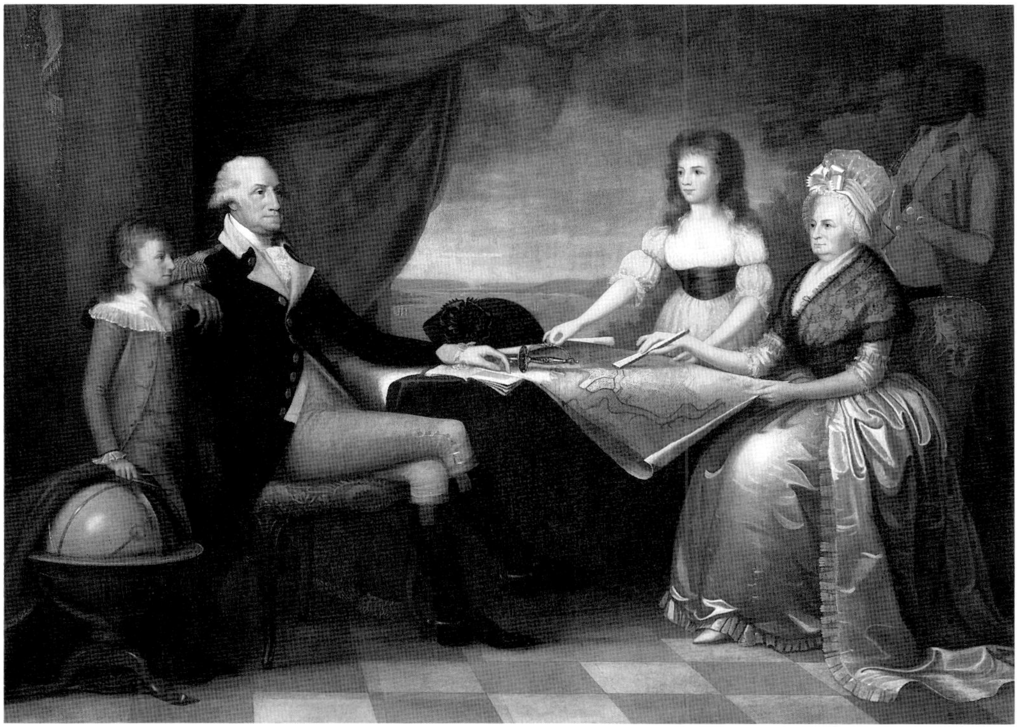

EDWARD SAVAGE
1761–1817

The Washington Family, 1796
Canvas, 2.136 x 2.842 (84⅛ x 111⅞)
Andrew W. Mellon Collection
1940.1.2

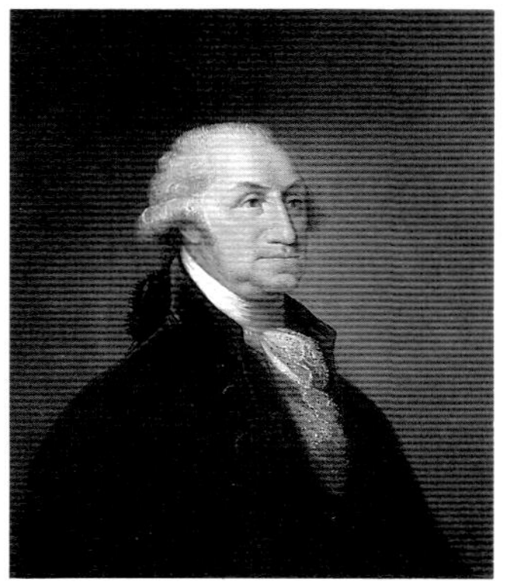

George Washington, c. 1796
Canvas, 0.762 x 0.633 (30 x 24 7/8)
Gift of Henry Prather Fletcher
1960.3.1

THE SCHUYLER LIMNER
(possibly **NEHEMIAH PARTRIDGE**)
active c. 1717/1725

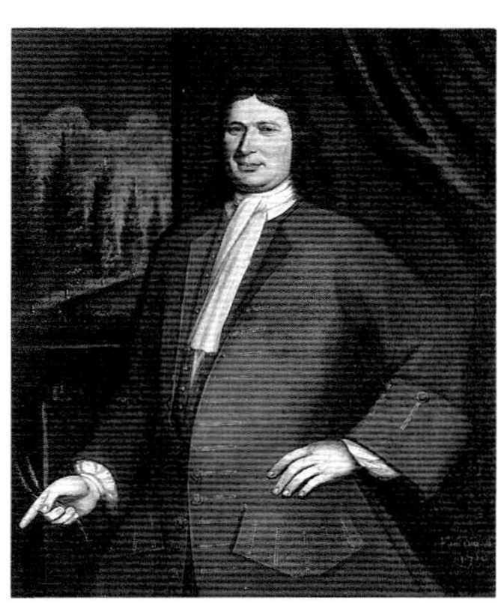

Mr. Van Vechten, 1719
Canvas, 1.159 x 0.965 (45 5/8 x 38)
Inscribed at lower right: *Etas. Sue. 43 / 1719*
Andrew W. Mellon Collection
1947.17.74

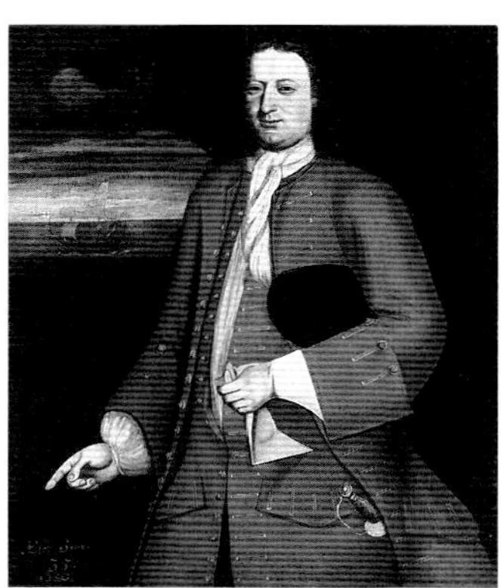

Mr. Willson, 1720
Canvas, 1.063 x 0.916 (42 x 36)
Inscribed at lower left: *AEtas. Suae. / 35. years / 1720*
Gift of Edgar William and Bernice Chrysler Garbisch
1957.11.9

WILLIAM CHAPIN SEITZ
1914–1974

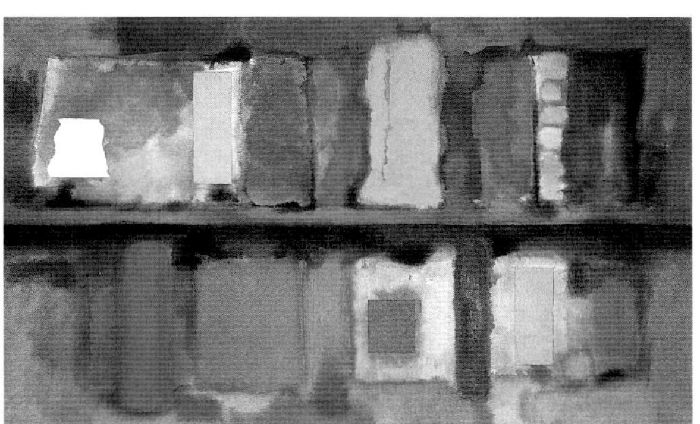

Millstone #1, 1956
Canvas, 0.865 x 1.372 (34 1/8 x 54)
Gift of Mrs. William C. Seitz
1982.33.1

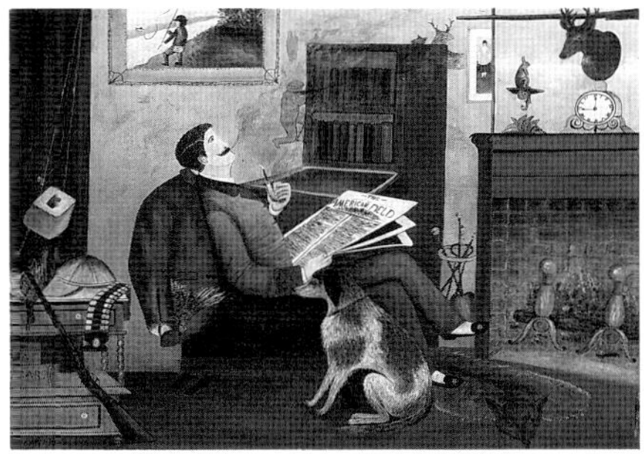

C. F. SENIOR
active 1881 or after

The Sportsman's Dream, 1881 or after
Canvas, 0.562 x 0.766 (22⅛ x 30¼)
Inscribed at lower left: *C. F. Senior*
Gift of Edgar William and Bernice Chrysler Garbisch
1980.62.21

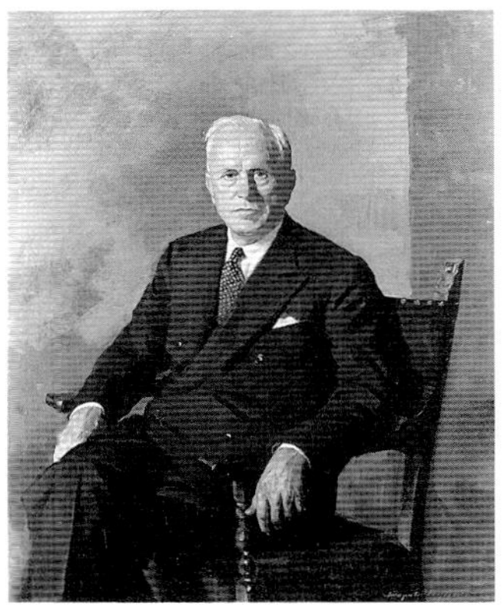

LEOPOLD SEYFFERT
1887–1956

Rush Harrison Kress, 1953
Canvas, 1.270 x 1.022 (50 x 40¼)
Inscribed at lower right: *Leopold Seyffert / 53*
Samuel H. Kress Collection
1961.9.93 Special Collection

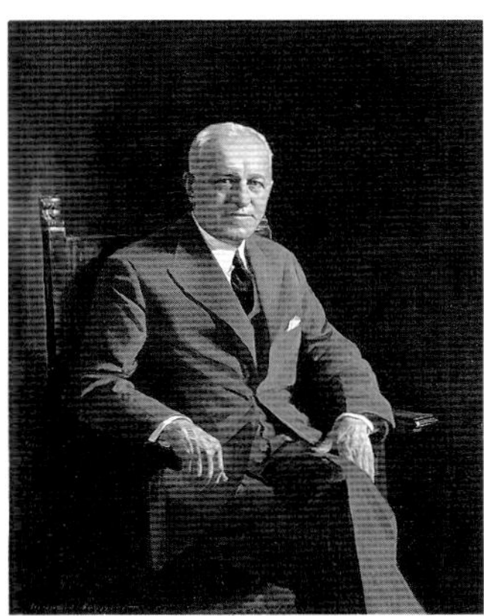

Samuel Henry Kress, 1953
Canvas, 1.273 x 1.022 (50⅛ x 40¼)
Inscribed at lower left: *Leopold Seyffert 53*
Samuel H. Kress Collection
1953.2.3 Special Collection

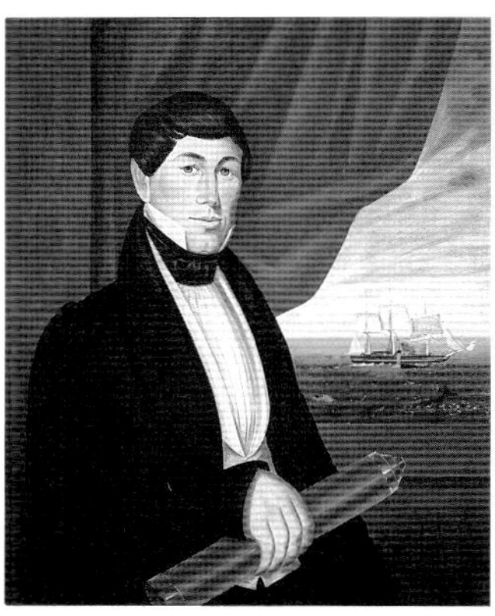

ISAAC SHEFFIELD
1807–1845

Connecticut Sea Captain, 1833
Wood, 0.762 x 0.623 (30 x 24½)
Inscribed on reverse: *I. Sheffield, Pinxt. / April 1833*
Gift of Edgar William and Bernice Chrysler Garbisch
1965.15.4

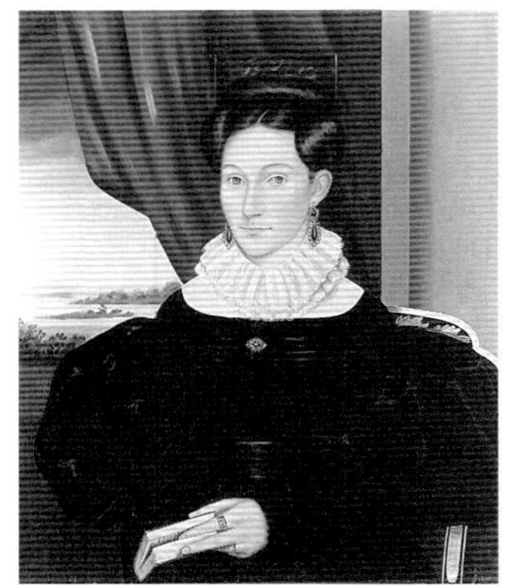

Connecticut Sea Captain's Wife, 1833
Wood, 0.762 x 0.626 (30 x 24⅝)
Gift of Edgar William and Bernice Chrysler Garbisch
1965.15.5

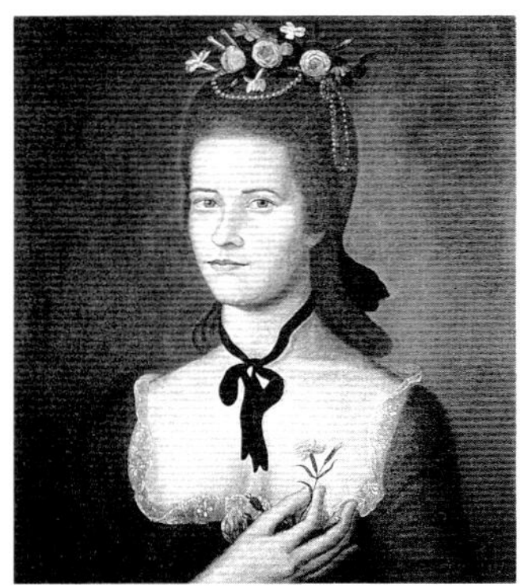

THE SHERMAN LIMNER
active c. 1785/1790

Portrait of a Lady in Red, c. 1785/1790
Canvas, 0.565 x 0.485 (22¼ x 19⅛)
Gift of Edgar William and Bernice Chrysler Garbisch
1980.62.36

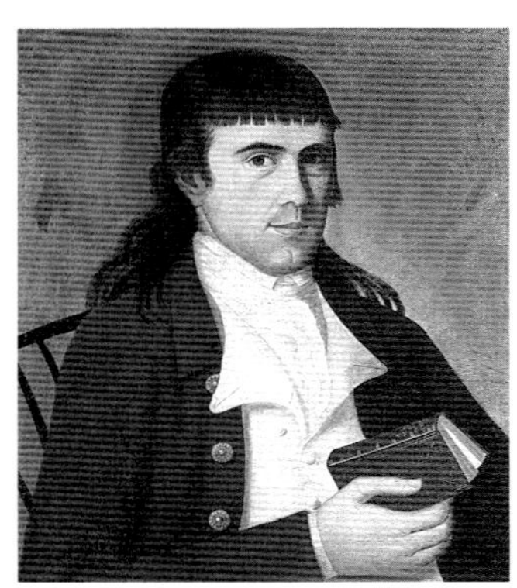

Portrait of a Man in Red, c. 1785/1790
Canvas, 0.572 x 0.496 (22½ x 19½)
Gift of Edgar William and Bernice Chrysler Garbisch
1980.62.35

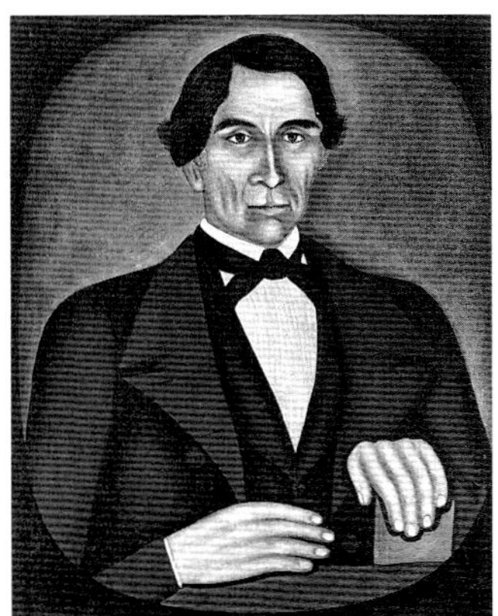

THOMAS SKYNNER
active 1840–1847

Portrait of a Man, c. 1845
Canvas, 0.764 x 0.612 (30⅛ x 24⅛)
Gift of Edgar William and Bernice Chrysler Garbisch
1967.20.4

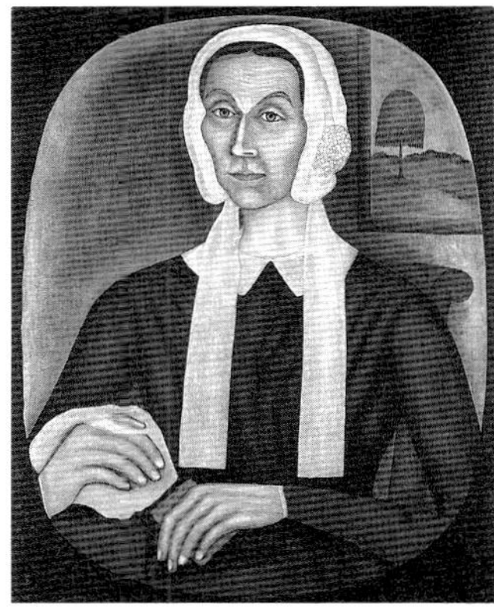

Portrait of a Woman, c. 1845
Canvas, 0.764 x 0.612 (30⅛ x 24⅛)
Gift of Edgar William and Bernice Chrysler Garbisch
1967.20.5

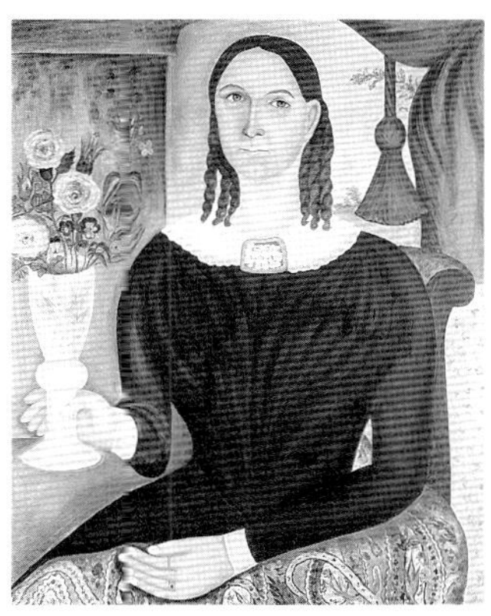

Eliza Welch Stone, c. 1845
Canvas, 0.767 x 0.612 (30³⁄₁₆ x 24⅛)
Gift of Edgar William and Bernice Chrysler Garbisch
1953.5.56

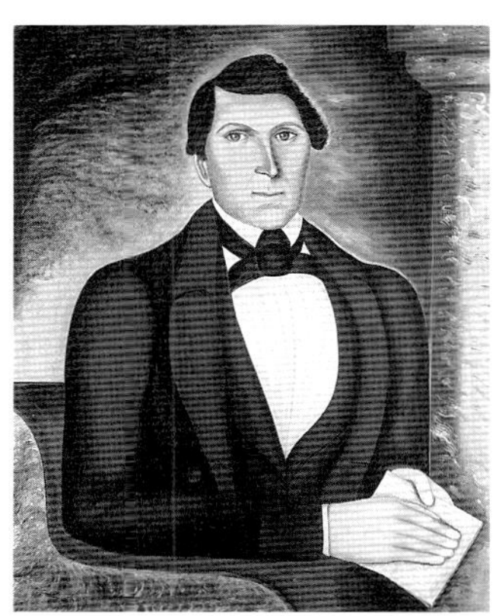

John Stone, c. 1845
Canvas, 0.770 x 0.610 (30¼ x 24¹⁄₁₆)
Gift of Edgar William and Bernice Chrysler Garbisch
1953.5.55

JOHN SLOAN
1871–1951

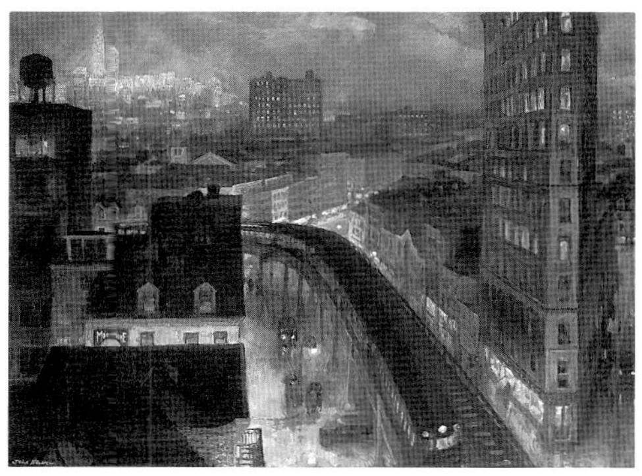

The City from Greenwich Village, 1922
Canvas, 0.660 x 0.857 (26 x 33¾)
Inscribed at lower left: *John Sloan* -
Gift of Helen Farr Sloan
1970.1.1

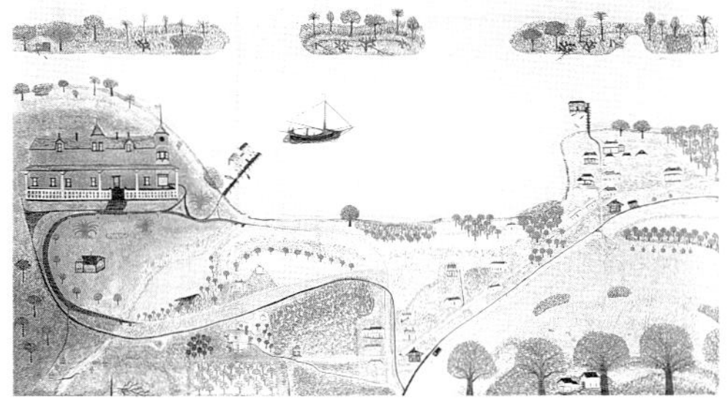

DANA SMITH
1805–1901

Southern Resort Town, c. 1880
Canvas, 0.563 x 0.780 (22⅛ x 30¾)
Gift of Edgar William and Bernice Chrysler Garbisch
1971.83.11

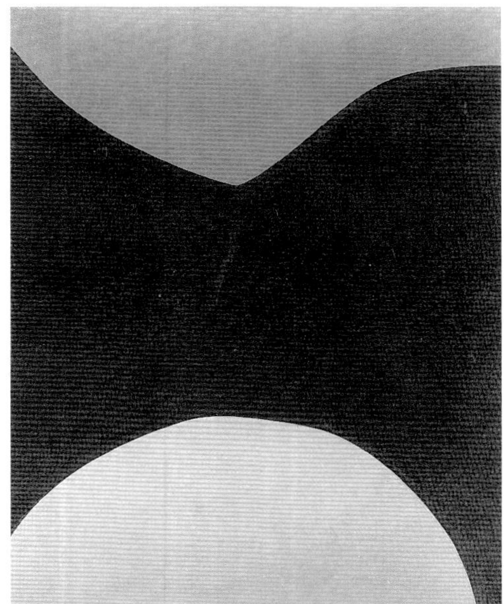

LEON POLK SMITH
born 1906

Stretch of Black III, 1961
Canvas, 0.611 x 0.482 (24 x 19)
Gift of Eleanor Ward
1971.89.1

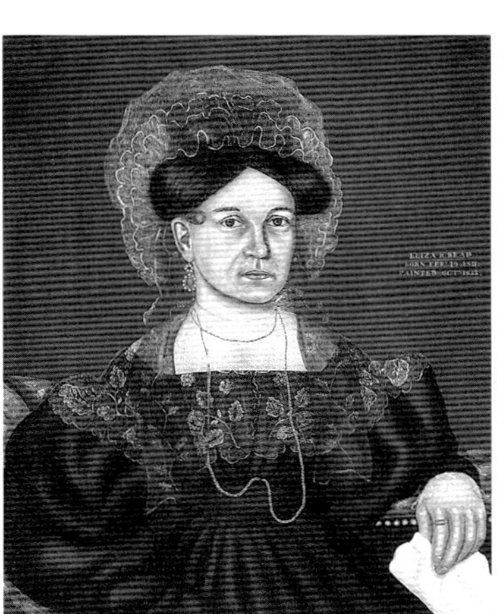

ROYALL BREWSTER SMITH
1801–1855

Eliza R. Read, 1833
Canvas, 0.795 x 0.645 (31¼ x 25⅜)
Inscribed at center right: *ELIZA R. READ / BORN FEBY 19. 1811. / PAINTED OCT' 1833.*
Gift of Edgar William and Bernice Chrysler Garbisch
1978.80.17

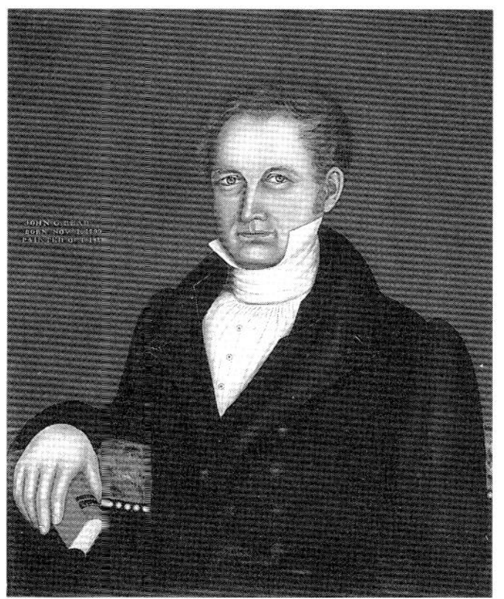

John G. Read, 1833
Canvas, 0.796 x 0.644 ($31\frac{3}{8}$ x $25\frac{3}{8}$)
Inscribed at center left: *JOHN G. READ / BORN NOV' 1. 1799 / PAINTED OCT' 1833*; lower left on book: *USEFUL KNOWLEDGE*
Gift of Edgar William and Bernice Chrysler Garbisch
1978.80.18

TONY SMITH
1912–1980

Untitled, 1962
Canvas, 1.627 x 2.444 (64 x $96\frac{1}{4}$)
Gift of Mr. and Mrs. Burton Tremaine
1975.100.1

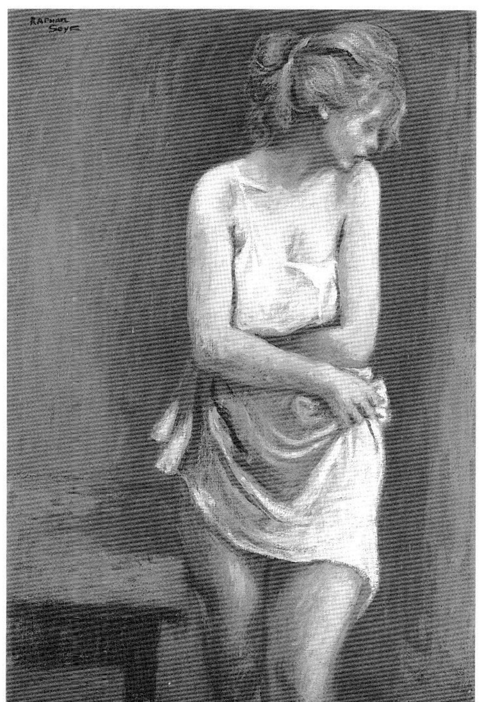

RAPHAEL SOYER
1899–1987

Blond Figure, 1940s
Canvas, 0.813 x 0.533 (32 x 21)
Inscribed at upper left: *RAPHAEL / SOYER*
Gift of James N. Rosenberg
1989.25.1

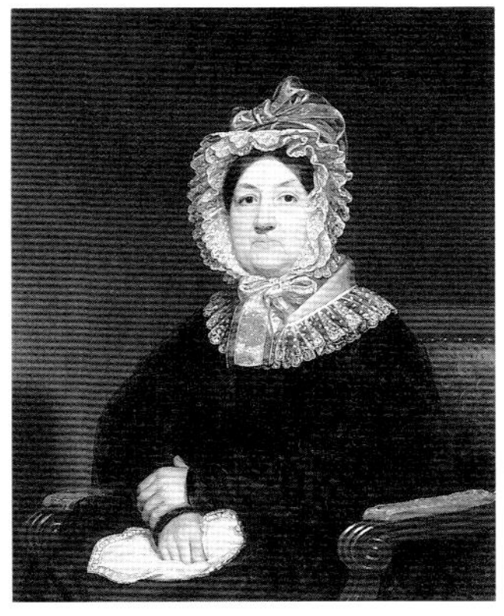

FREDERICK R. SPENCER
1806–1875

Frances Ludlum Morris, 1838
Canvas, 0.911 x 0.743 (35⅞ x 29¼)
Andrew W. Mellon Collection
1947.17.96

JULIAN STANCZAK
born 1928

Shimmer, 1972
Canvas, 1.270 x 1.023 (50 x 40¼)
Gift of the Jane Haslem Gallery
1974.45.1

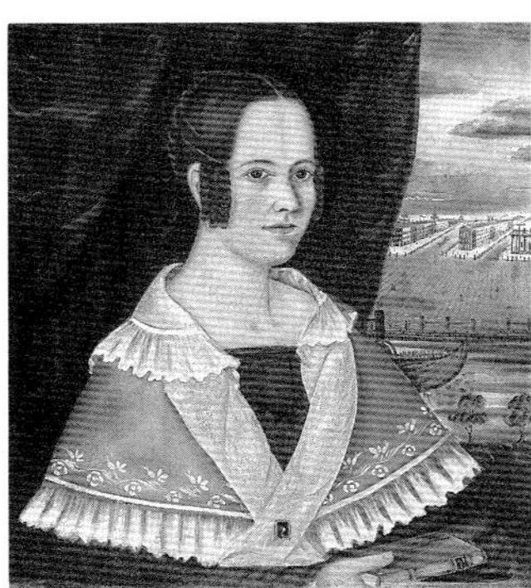

ABRAM ROSS STANLEY
probably 1816–1873/1880

Eliza Wells, 1840
Canvas, 0.641 x 0.596 (25¼ x 23½)
Gift of Edgar William and Bernice Chrysler Garbisch
1955.11.11

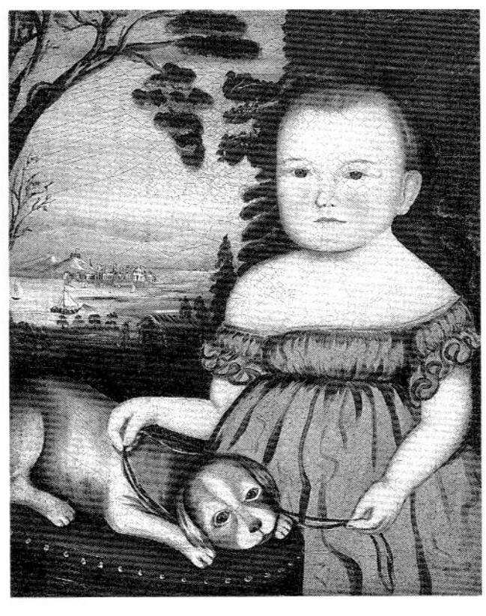

Joshua Lamb, 1842
Canvas, 0.619 x 0.484 (24⅜ x 19)
Gift of Edgar William and Bernice Chrysler Garbisch
1980.62.22

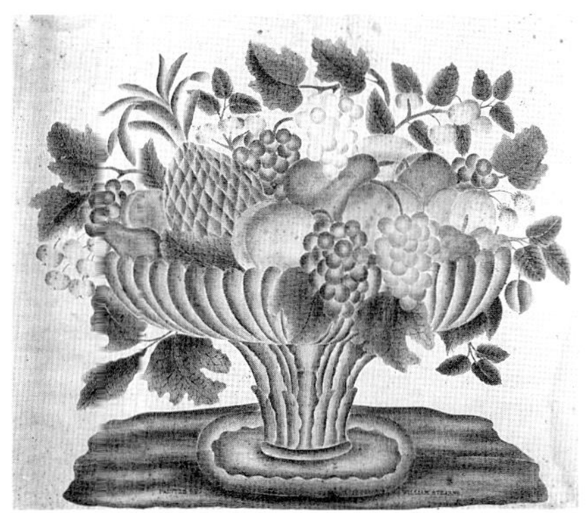

WILLIAM STEARNS
active c. 1840

Bowl of Fruit, c. 1830/1840
Velvet, 0.473 x 0.520 (18⅝ x 20½)
Inscribed lower left center: *PAINTED BY*; lower right center: *WILLIAM STEARNS*
Gift of Edgar William and Bernice Chrysler Garbisch
1953.5.34

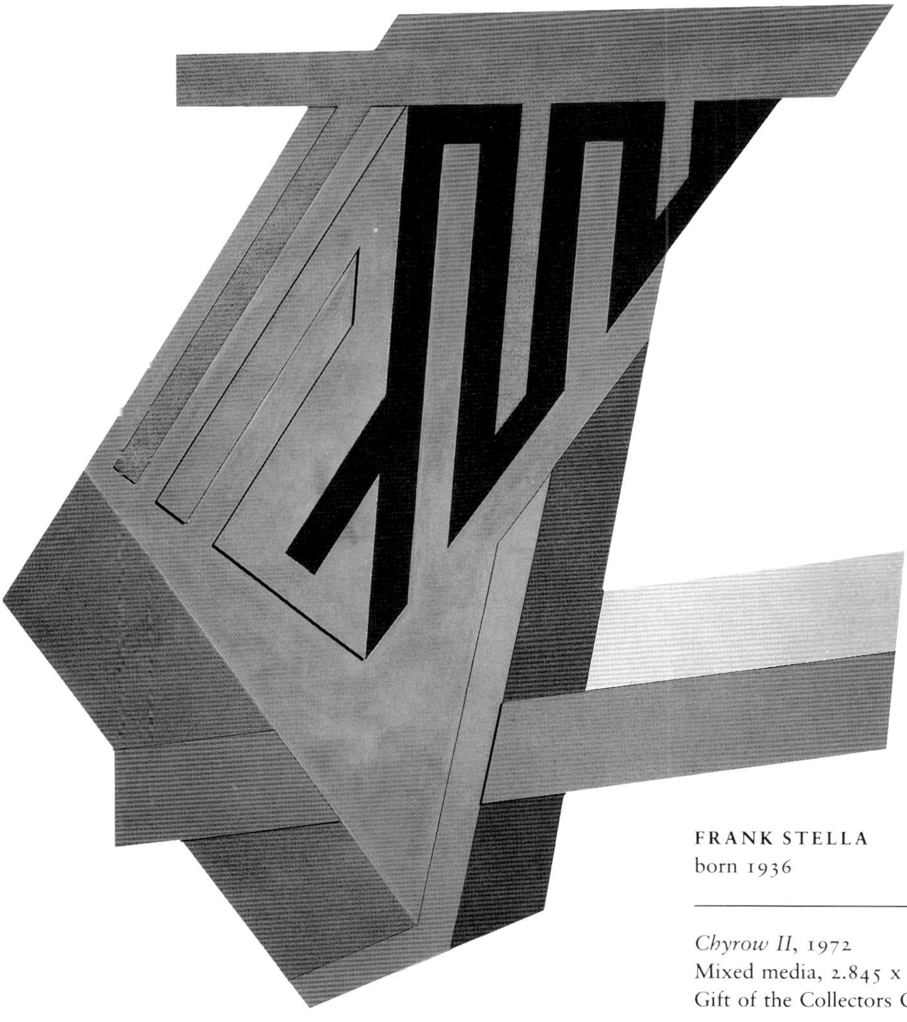

FRANK STELLA
born 1936

Chyrow II, 1972
Mixed media, 2.845 x 2.540 (112 x 100)
Gift of the Collectors Committee
1979.29.1

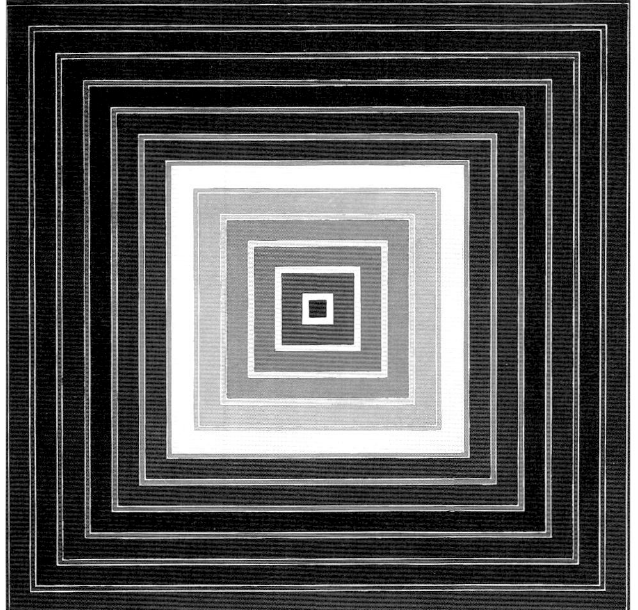

Sacramento Mall Proposal #4, 1978
Canvas, 2.625 x 2.621 (103 3/8 x 103 1/4)
Gift of the Collectors Committee
1982.53.1

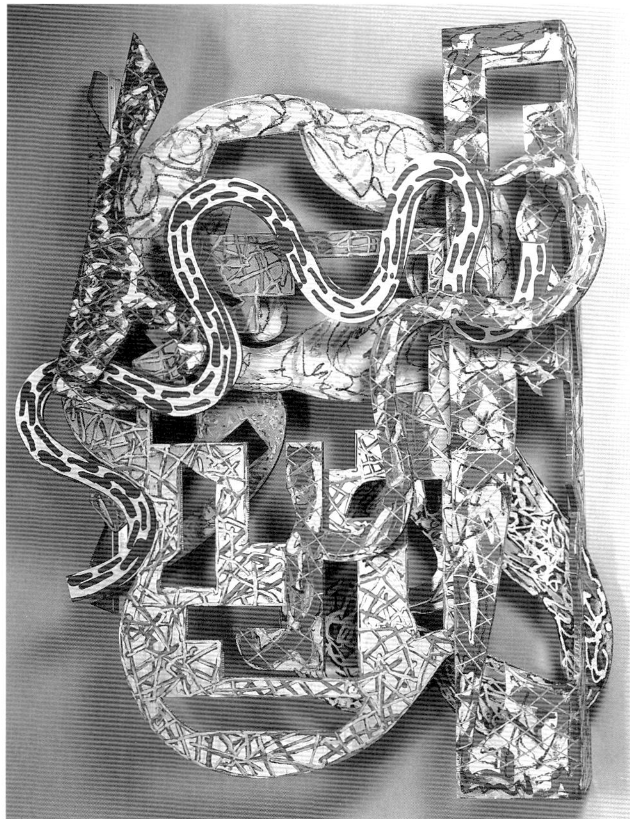

Jarama II, 1982
Etched magnesium, 3.199 x 2.539 x 0.628
(126 x 100 x 24 3/4)
Gift of Lila Acheson Wallace
1982.35.1

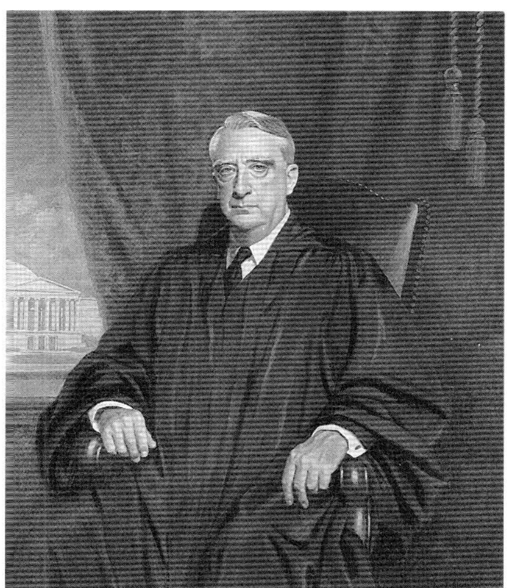

THOMAS E. STEPHENS
1885–1966

Fred M. Vinson, 1950
Canvas, 1.448 x 1.193 (57 x 47)
Inscribed at lower right: *Thos. E. Stephens*
Anonymous Gift
1950.19.1 Special Collection

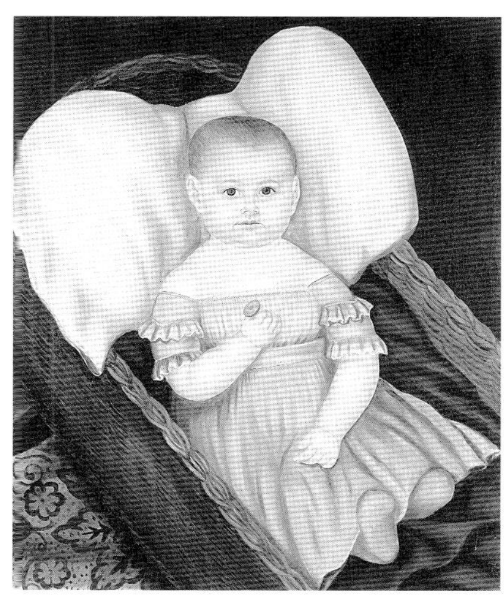

JOSEPH WHITING STOCK
1815–1855

Baby in Wicker Basket, c 1840
Canvas, 0.774 x 0.663 (30½ x 26⅛)
Gift of Edgar William and Bernice Chrysler Garbisch
1980.62.23

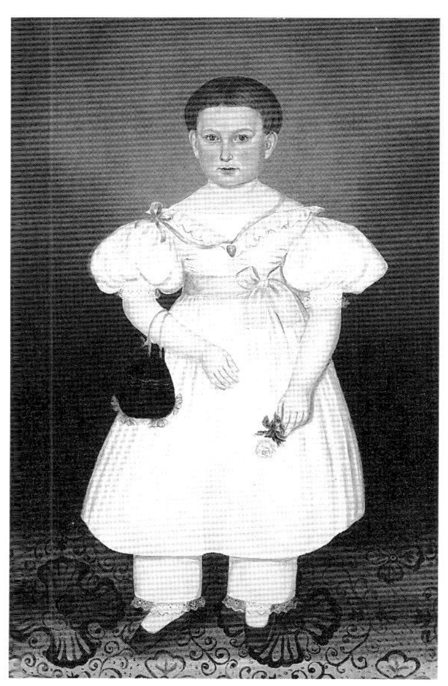

Girl with Reticule and Rose, c. 1840
Canvas, 1.186 x 0.750 (46⅝ x 29½)
Gift of Edgar William and Bernice Chrysler Garbisch
1980.62.8

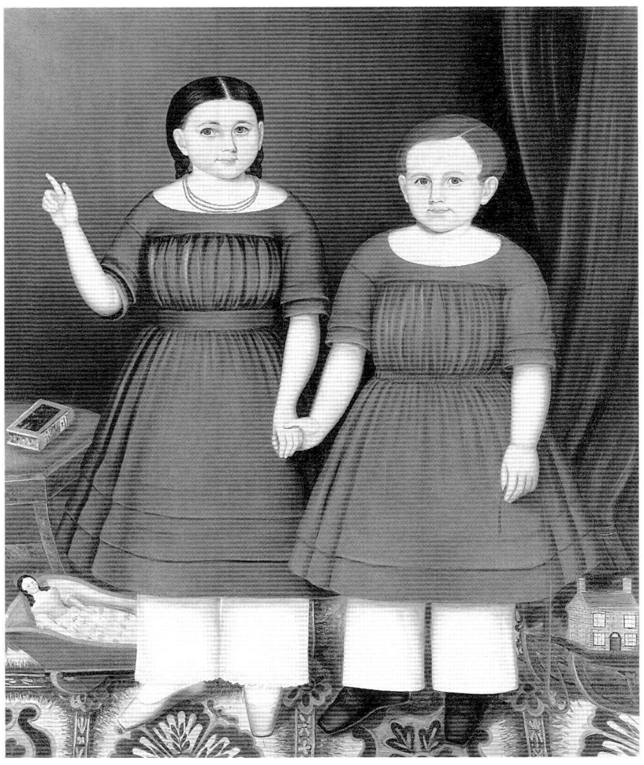

Mary and Francis Wilcox, 1845
Canvas, 1.220 x 1.016 (48 x 40)
Gift of Edgar William and Bernice Chrysler Garbisch
1959.11.2

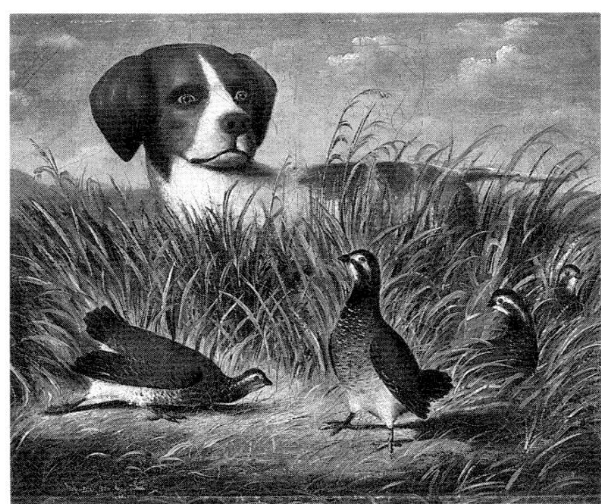

D. G. STOUTER
active 1854 or later

On Point, 1854 or later
Canvas, 0.464 x 0.521 (18 5/16 x 21 5/16)
Inscribed at lower left: *D. G. Stouter, / Artist*
Gift of Edgar William and Bernice Chrysler Garbisch
1980.62.68

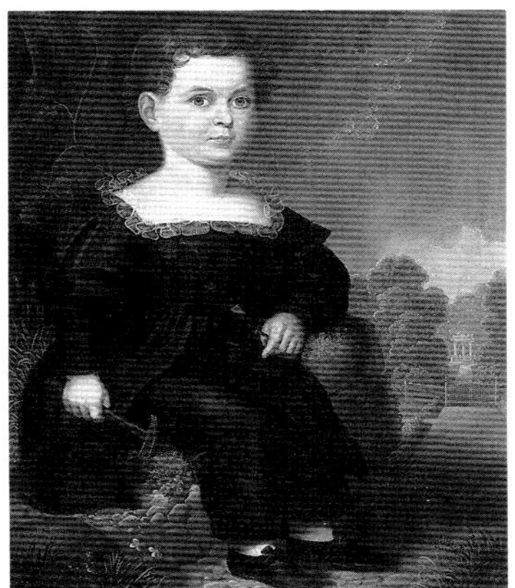

ROBERT STREET
1796–1865

George Washington Deal, 1834
Canvas, 0.762 x 0.635 (30 x 25)
Inscribed at lower left: *BY R. STREET / 1834*
Gift of Edna L. Barbour
1973.3.1

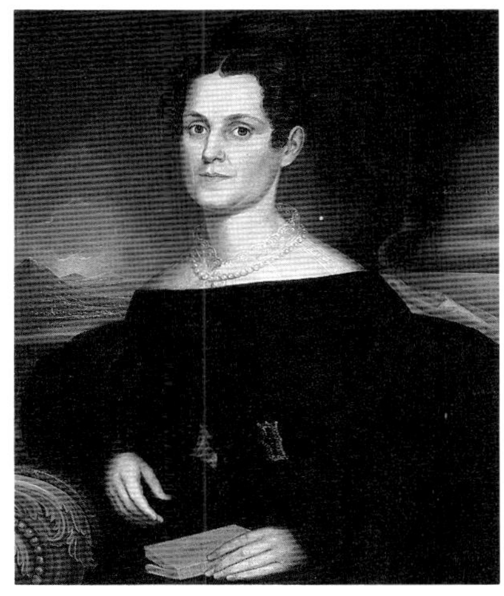

Elizabeth Price Thomas, 1834
Canvas, 0.762 x 0.635 (30 x 25)
Inscribed at upper right on column: *BY R. STREET 1834*
Gift of Edna L. Barbour
1973.3.2

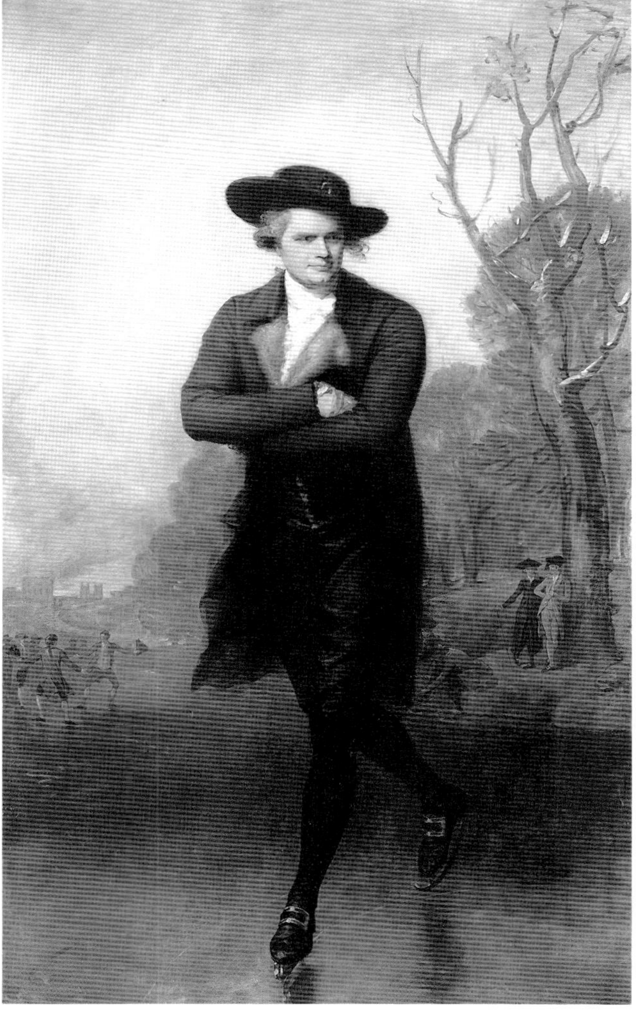

GILBERT STUART
1755–1828

The Skater (Portrait of William Grant), 1782
Canvas, 2.455 x 1.476 (96⅝ x 58⅛)
Andrew W. Mellon Collection
1950.18.1

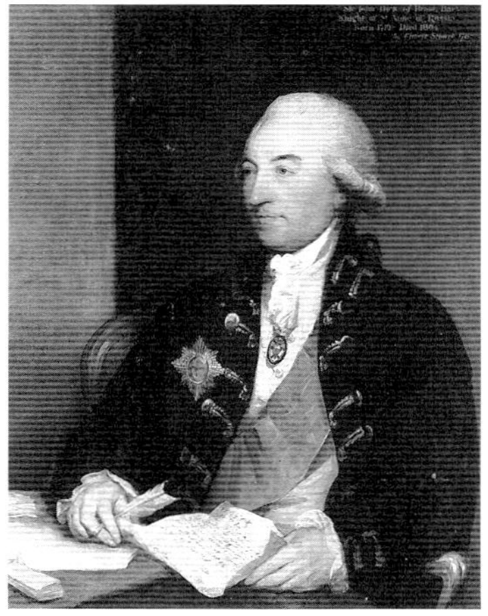

Sir John Dick 1783
Canvas, 0.918 x 0.714 (36 1/8 x 28 1/8)
Inscribed by a later hand, upper right: *Sir John Dick of Braid, Bart / Knight of St Anne of Russia. / Born 1719-Died 1804. / by Gilbert Stuart 1782* [sic]
Andrew W. Mellon Collection
1954.1.10

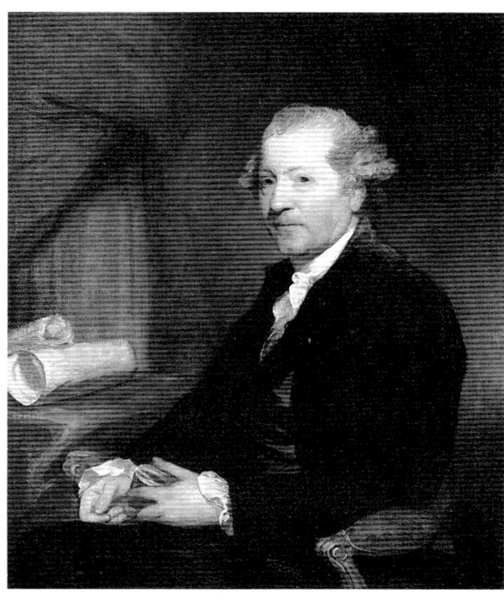

Sir Joshua Reynolds, 1784
Canvas, 0.916 x 0.764 (36 1/16 x 30 1/16)
Andrew W. Mellon Collection
1942.8.21

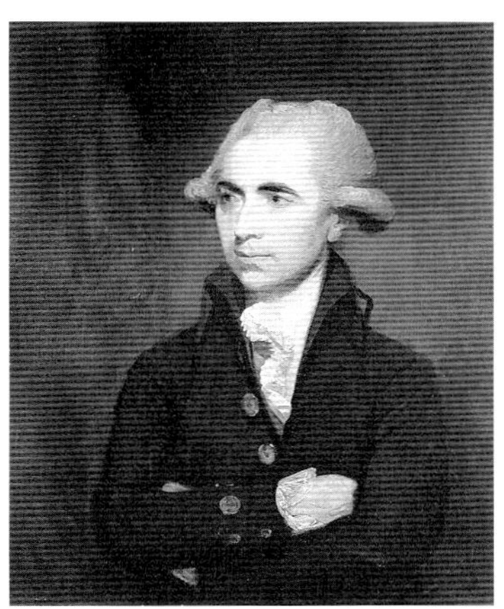

Luke White, c. 1790
Canvas, 0.762 x 0.635 (30 x 25)
Andrew W. Mellon Collection
1942.8.28

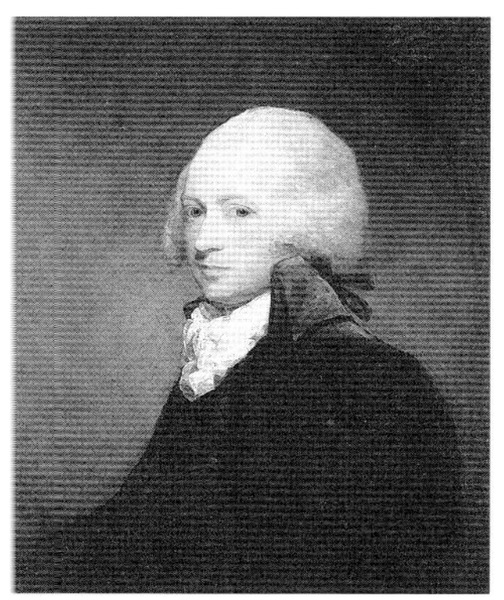

Dr. William Hartigan (?) c. 1793
Canvas, 0.762 x 0.635 (30 x 25)
Andrew W. Mellon Collection
1942.8.16

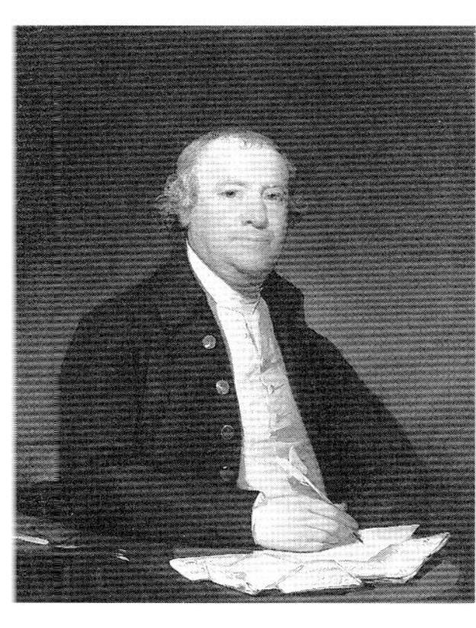

Captain Joseph Anthony, 1793/1794
Canvas, 0.915 x 0.710 (36 x 28)
Andrew W. Mellon Collection
1942.8.11

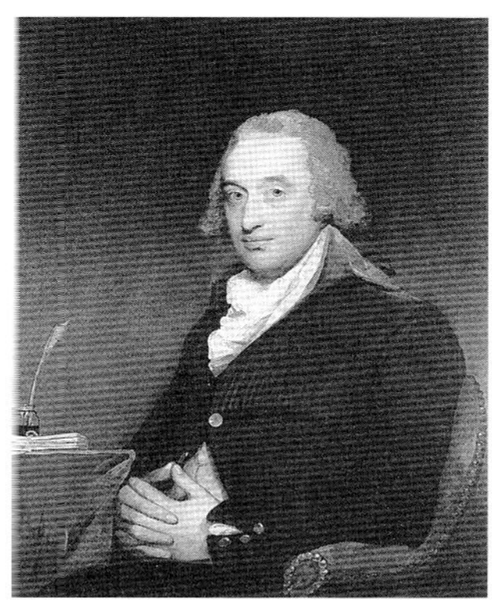

George Pollock, 1793/1794
Canvas, 0.920 x 0.720 (36¼ x 28¼)
Andrew W. Mellon Collection
1942.8.18

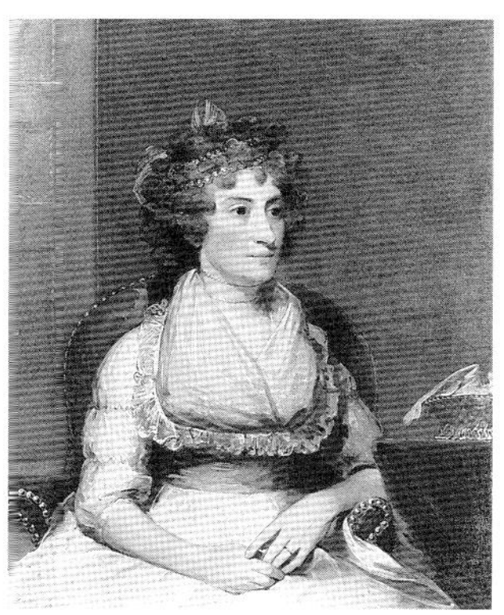

Mrs. George Pollock, 1793/1794
Canvas, 0.915 x 0.720 (36 x 28⅜)
Andrew W. Mellon Collection
1942.8.19

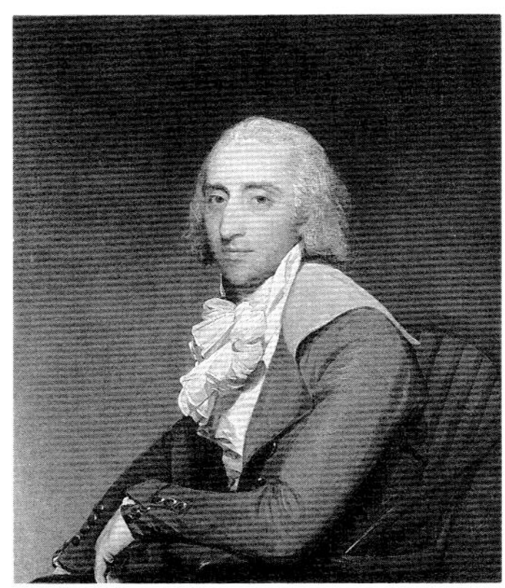

Lawrence Reid Yates, 1793/1794
Canvas, 0.762 x 0.635 (30 x 25)
Andrew W. Mellon Collection
1940.1.5

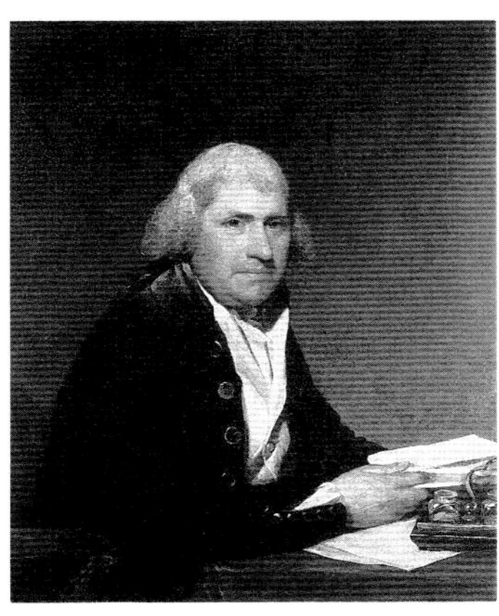

Richard Yates, 1793/1794
Canvas, 0.756 x 0.629 (29¾ x 24⅞)
Andrew W. Mellon Collection
1942.8.29

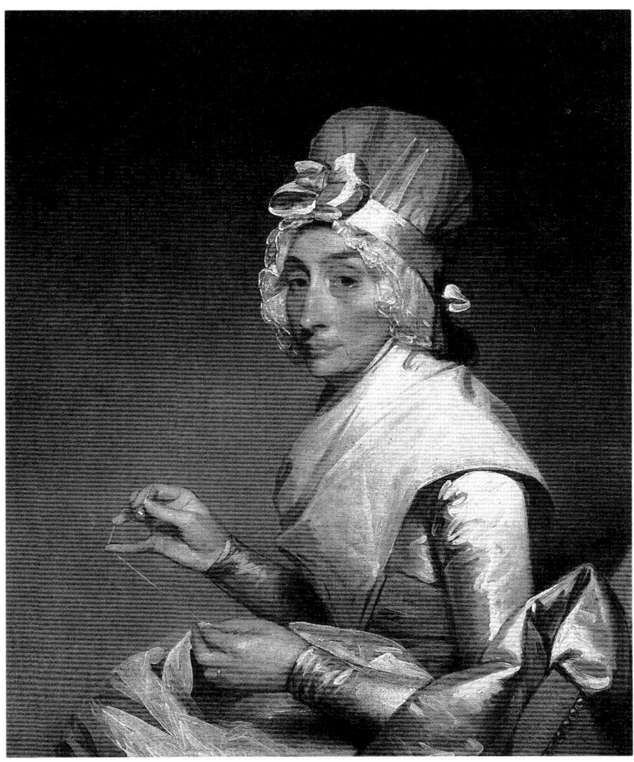

Mrs. Richard Yates, 1793/1794
Canvas, 0.762 x 0.635 (30 x 25)
Andrew W. Mellon Collection
1940.1.4

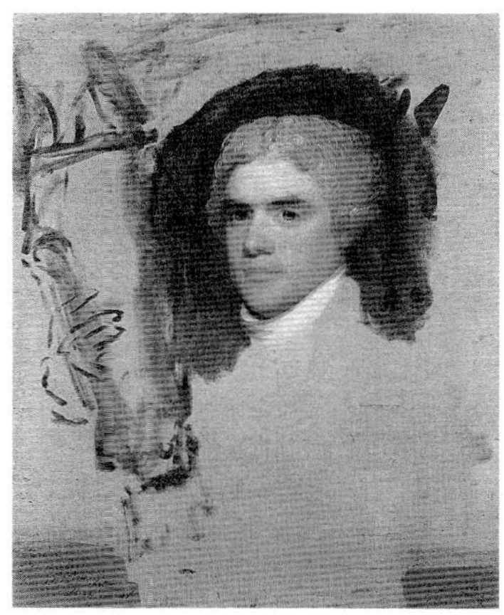

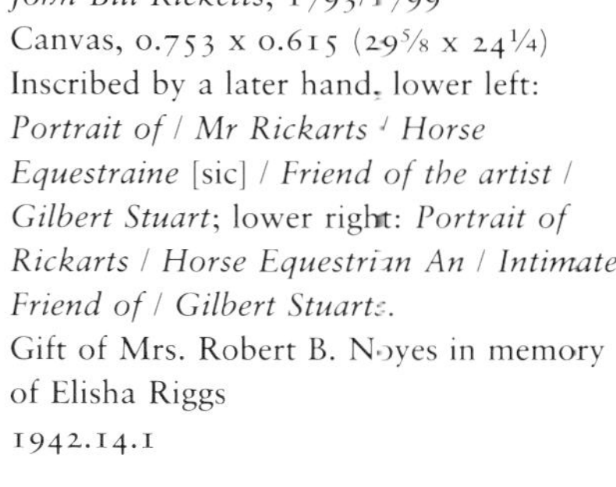

John Bill Ricketts, 1793/1799
Canvas, 0.753 x 0.615 (29⅝ x 24¼)
Inscribed by a later hand, lower left: *Portrait of / Mr Rickarts / Horse Equestraine* [sic] */ Friend of the artist / Gilbert Stuart*; lower right: *Portrait of Rickarts / Horse Equestrian An / Intimate Friend of / Gilbert Stuarts.*
Gift of Mrs. Robert B. Noyes in memory of Elisha Riggs
1942.14.1

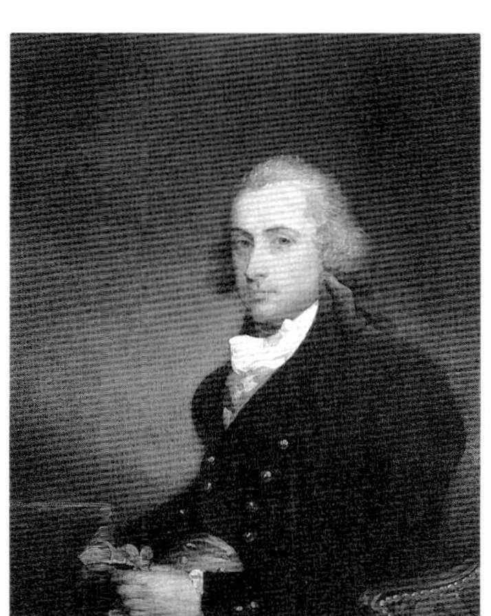

Stephen Van Rensselaer, c. 1794
Canvas, 0.917 x 0.713 (36⅛ x 28⅛)
Andrew W. Mellon Collection
1942.8.20

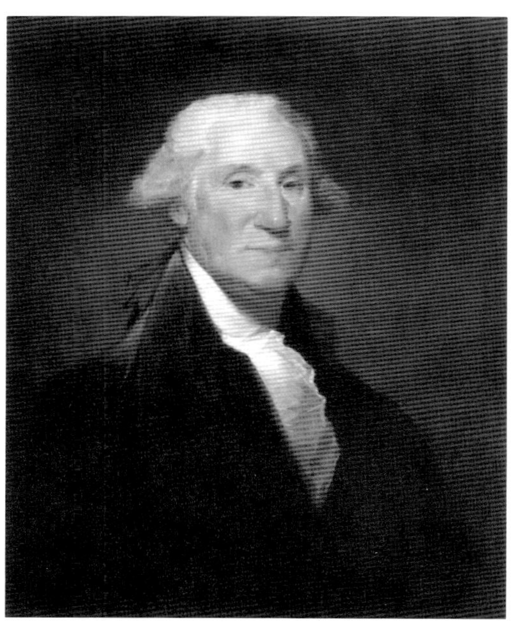

George Washington (Vaughan portrait), 1795
Canvas, 0.735 x 0.605 (29 x 23¾)
Andrew W. Mellon Collection
1942.8.27

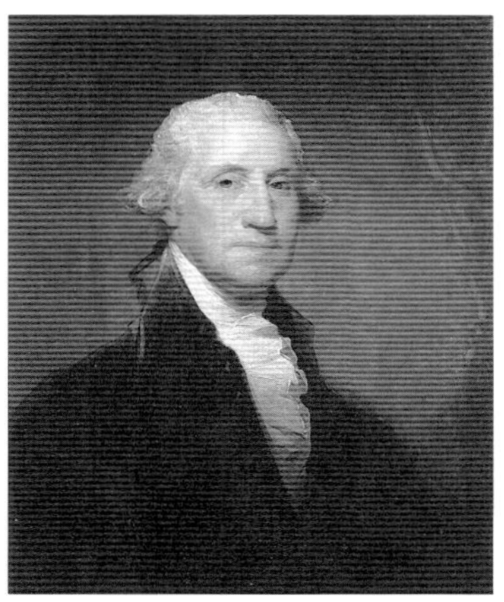

George Washington (Vaughan-Sinclair portrait), 1795/1796
Canvas, 0.733 x 0.611 (29⅛ x 24⅛)
Andrew W. Mellon Collection
1940.1.6

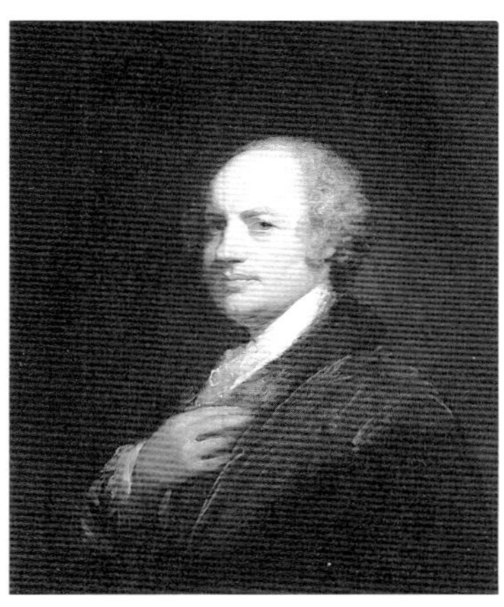

Counsellor John Dunn, c. 1798
Canvas, 0.740 x 0.615 (29¼ x 24¼)
Andrew W. Mellon Collection
1942.8.14

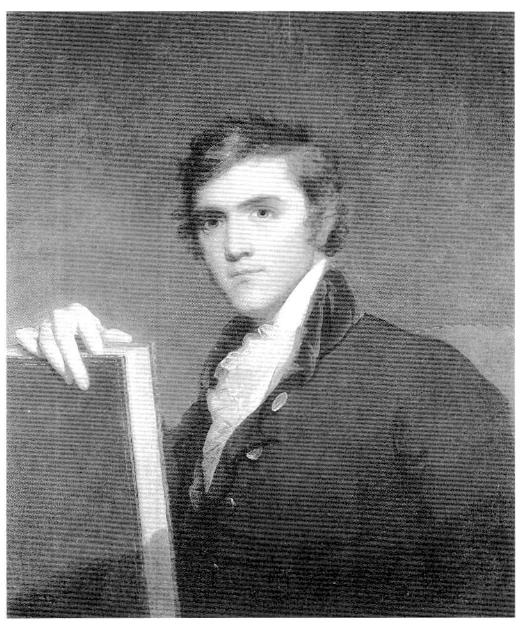

Horace Binney, 1800
Wood, 0.735 x 0.605 (29 x 23¾)
Gift of Horace Binney
1944.3.1

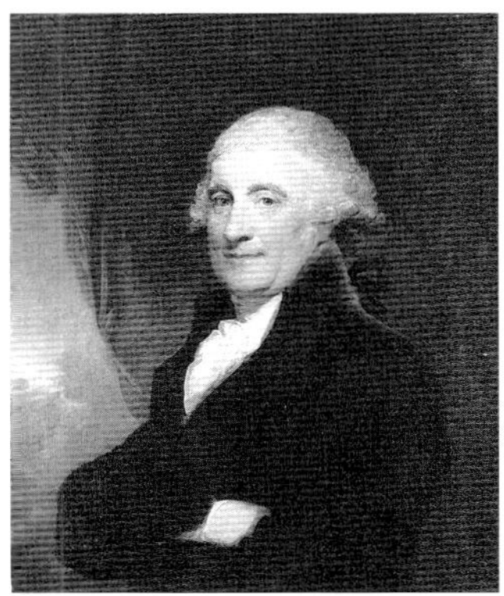

Robert Liston, 1800
Canvas, 0.738 x 0.610 (29 x 24)
Chester Dale Collection
1957.10.1

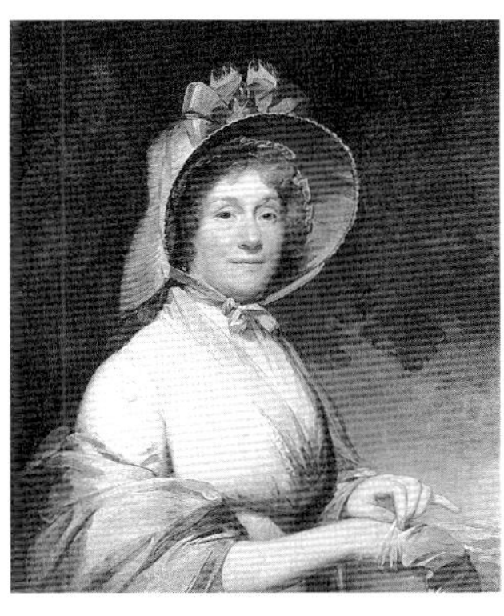

Mrs. Robert Liston, 1800
Canvas, 0.740 x 0.613 (29⅛ x 24⅛)
Chester Dale Collection
1960.12.1

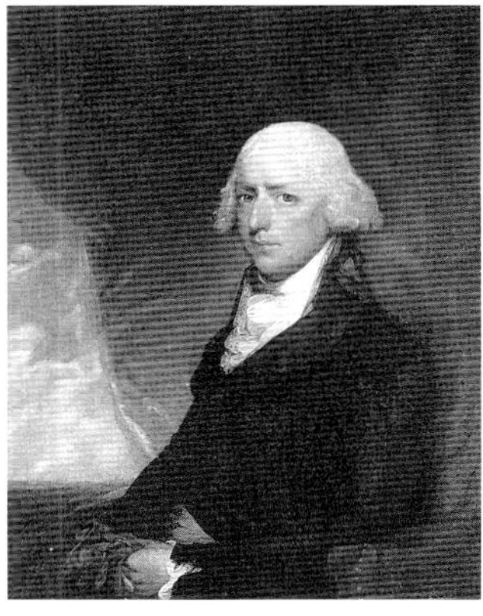

Mr. Ashe, c. 1800
Canvas, 0.915 x 0.704 (36 x 27⅞)
Andrew W. Mellon Collection
1942.8.12

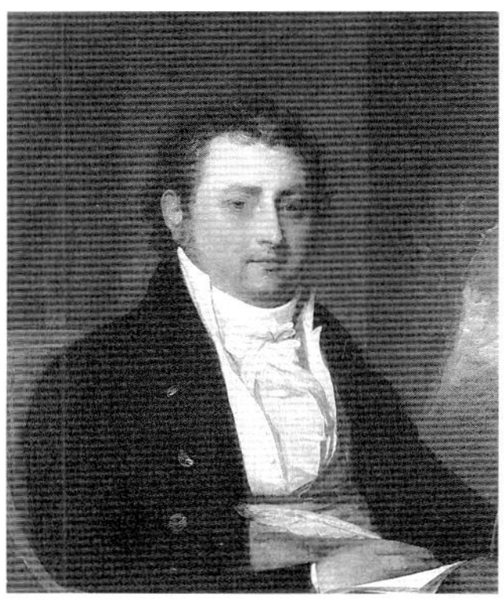

Edward Stow, c. 1803
Wood, 0.740 x 0.600 (29⅛ x 23⅝)
Andrew W. Mellon Collection
1942.8.23

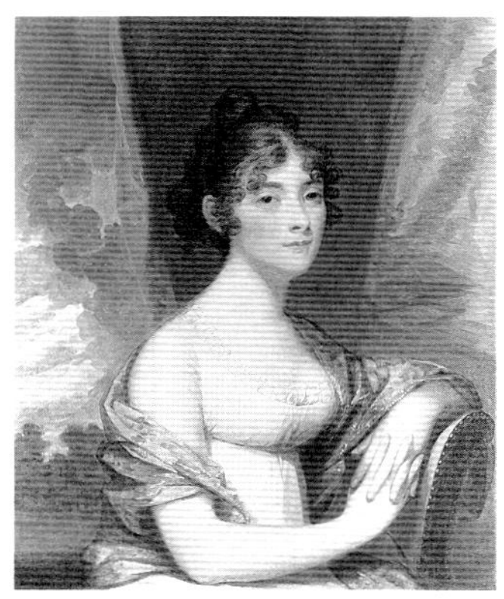

Ann Barry, 1803/1805
Canvas, 0.743 x 0.610 (29¼ x 24)
Gift of Jean McGinley Draper
1954.9.3

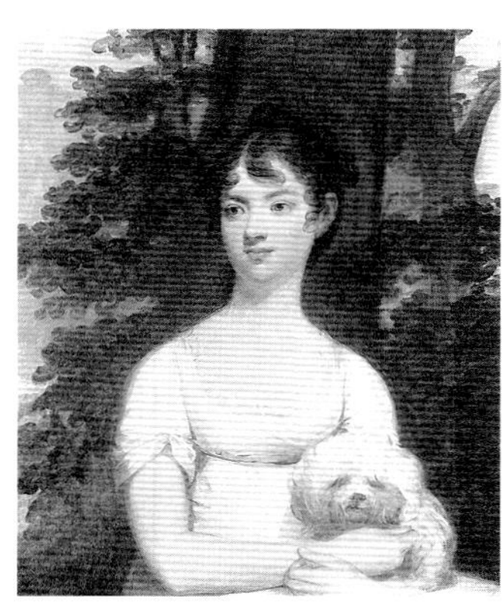

Mary Barry, 1803/1805
Canvas, 0.743 x 0.616 (29¼ x 24¼)
Gift of Jean McGinley Draper
1954.9.4

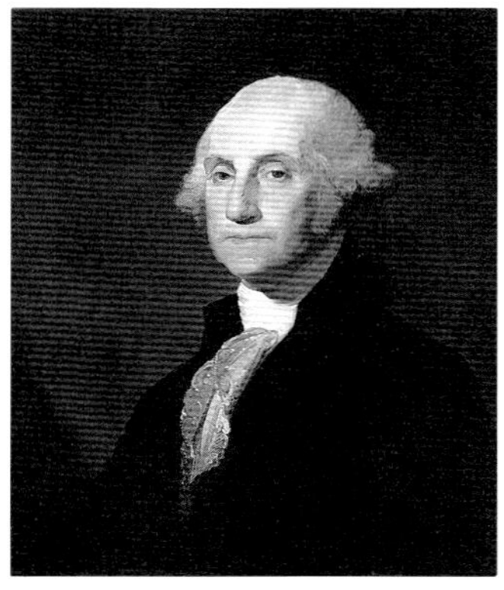

George Washington, c. 1803/1805
Canvas, 0.737 x 0.613 (29 x 24⅛)
Gift of Jean McGinley Draper
1954.9.2

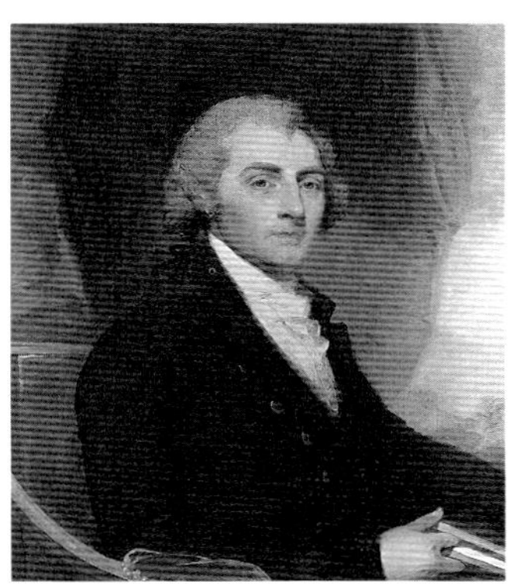

William Thornton, 1804
Canvas, 0.735 x 0.615 (29 x 24⅛)
Andrew W. Mellon Collection
1942.8.25

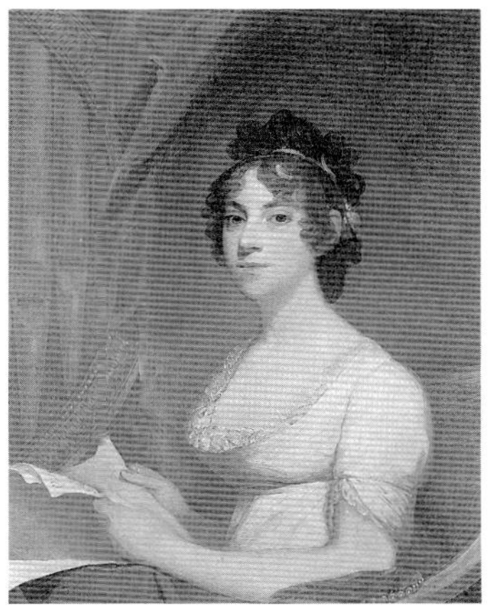

Mrs. William Thornton, 1804
Canvas, 0.730 x 0.610 (28¾ x 24)
Andrew W. Mellon Collection
1942.8.26

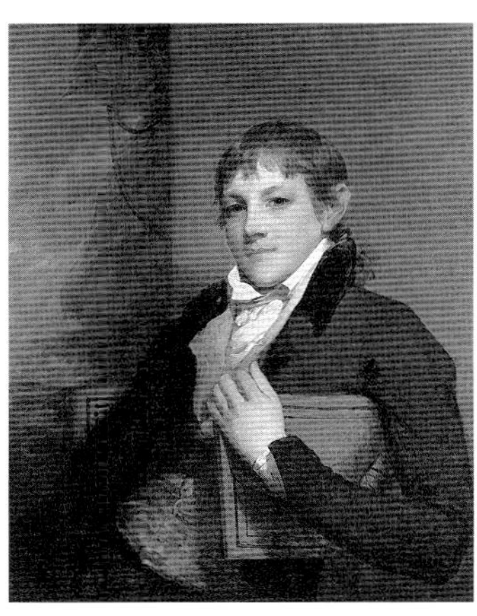

John Randolph, 1805
Canvas, 0.740 x 0.610 (29⅛ x 24⅛)
Andrew W. Mellon Collection
1940.1.9

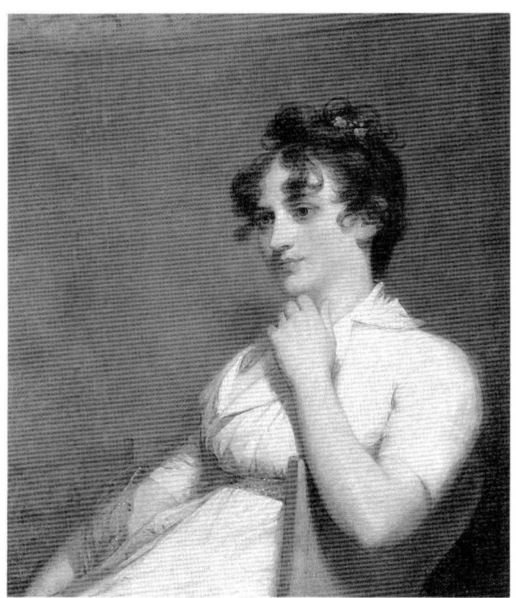

Mrs. Lawrence Lewis, c. 1805
Canvas, 0.737 x 0.616 (29 x 24¼)
Gift of H. H. Walker Lewis in memory of his parents, Mr. and Mrs. Edwin A. S. Lewis
1974.108.1

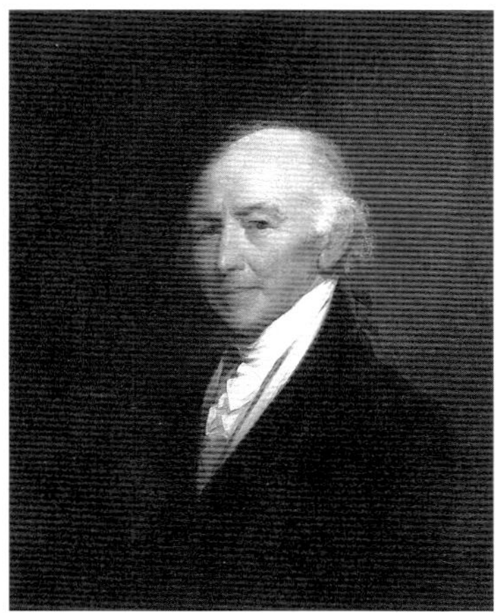

Samuel Alleyne Otis, 1809
Wood, 0.716 x 0.578 (28³⁄₁₆ x 22¾)
Gift of the Honorable and Mrs. Robert H. Thayer
1980.11.2

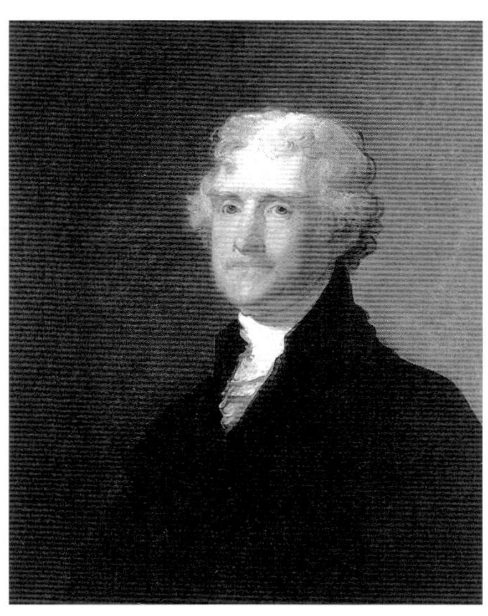

Thomas Jefferson, c. 1810/1815
Wood, 0.660 x 0.545 (26 x 21⁷⁄₁₆)
Gift of Thomas Jefferson Coolidge IV in memory of his great-grandfather, Thomas Jefferson Coolidge, his grandfather, Thomas Jefferson Coolidge II, and his father, Thomas Jefferson Coolidge III
1986.71.1

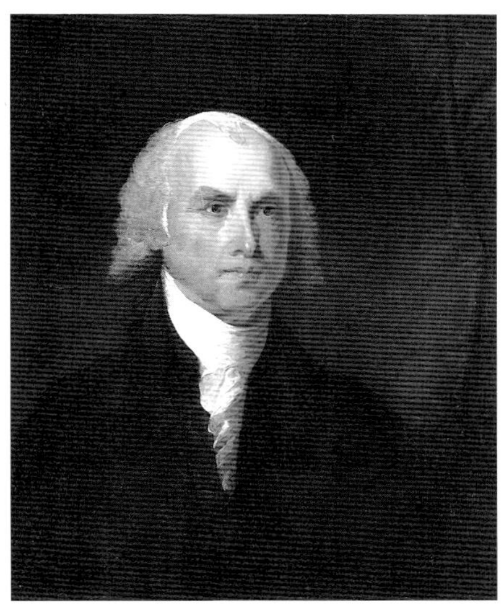

James Madison, c. 1810/1815
Wood, 0.652 x 0.539 (25¹¹⁄₁₆ x 21³⁄₈)
Ailsa Mellon Bruce Fund
1979.4.2

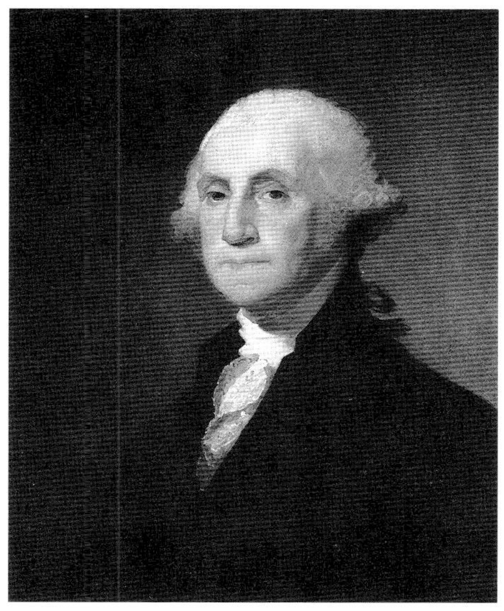

George Washington (Athenaeum portrait), c. 1810/1815
Wood, 0.670 x 0.546 (26⅜ x 21½)
Gift of Thomas Jefferson Coolidge IV in memory of his great-grandfather, Thomas Jefferson Coolidge, his grandfather, Thomas Jefferson Coolidge II, and his father, Thomas Jefferson Coolidge III
1979.5.1

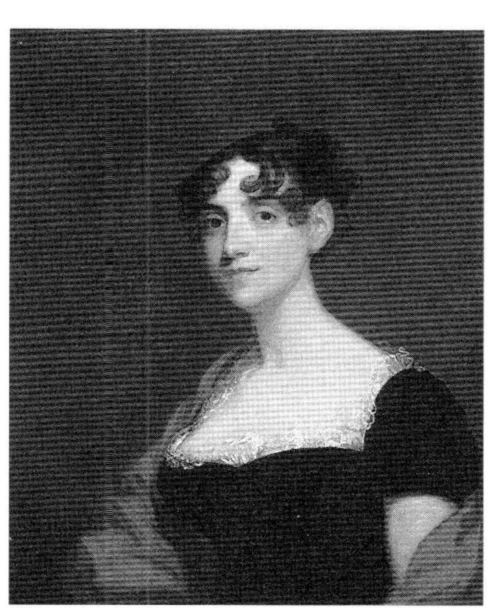

Mrs. William Robinson, c 1812
Wood, 0.720 x 0.580 (28¼ x 22¾)
Andrew W. Mellon Collection
1942.8.22

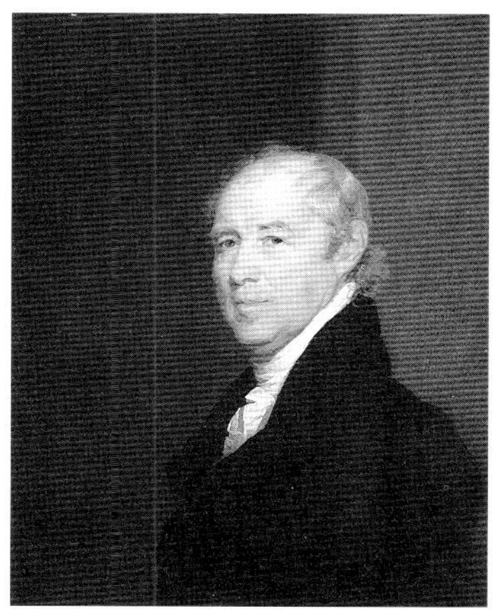

Benjamin Tappan, 1814
Wood, 0.728 x 0.590 (28⅝ x 23¼)
Gift of Lady Vereker
1970.34.2

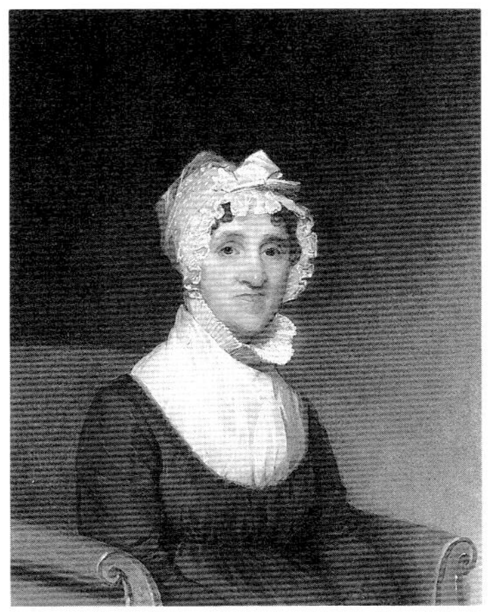

Mrs. Benjamin Tappan, 1814
Wood, 0.725 x 0.584 (28½ x 23)
Gift of Lady Vereker
1970.34.3

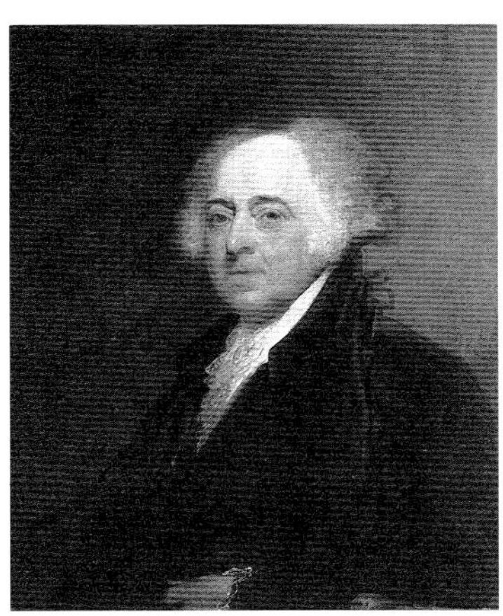

John Adams 1815
Canvas, 0.737 x 0.610 (29 x 24)
Gift of Mrs. Robert Homans
1954.7.1

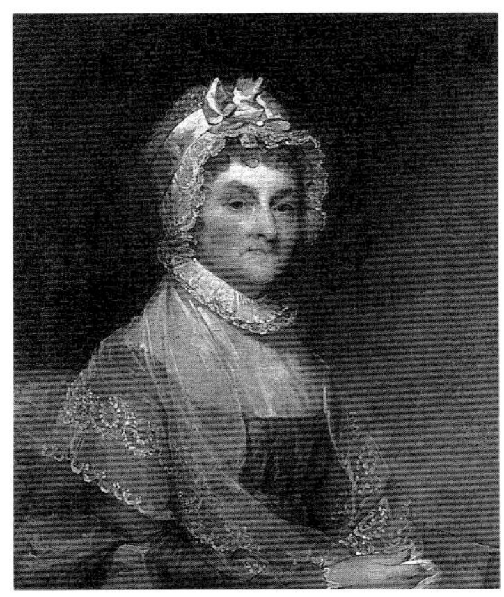

Mrs. John Adams, 1815
Canvas, 0.737 x 0.603 (29 x 23¾)
Gift of Mrs. Robert Homans
1954.7.2

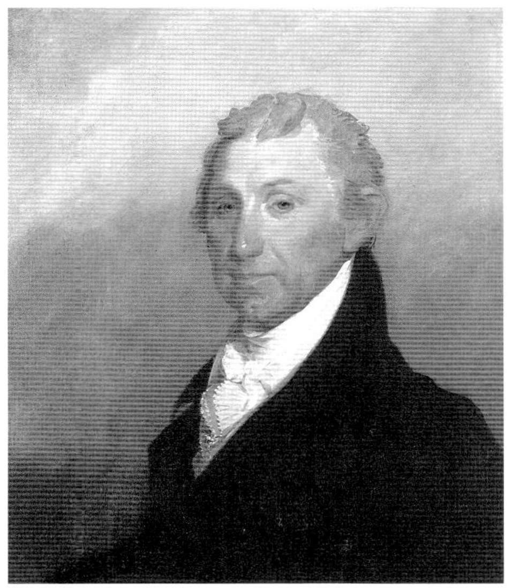

James Monroe, c. 1817
Wood, 0.648 x 0.550 (25½ x 21⅝)
Ailsa Mellon Bruce Fund
1979.4.3

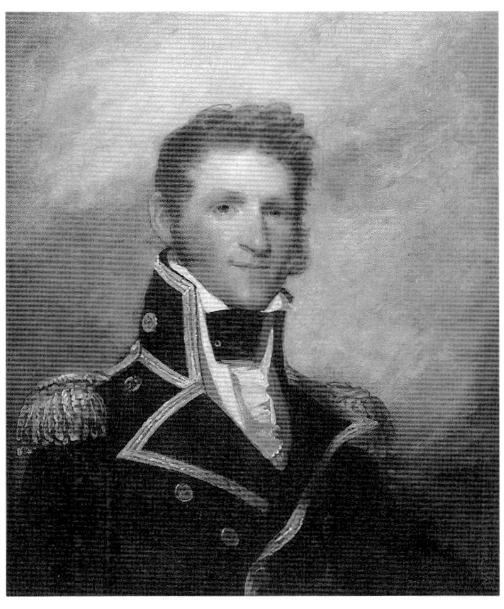

Commodore Thomas Macdonough, c. 1818
Wood, original fabric: 0.725 x 0.571 (28½ x 22½); with additions: 0.725 x 0.585 (28½ x 23)
Andrew W. Mellon Collection
1942.8.17

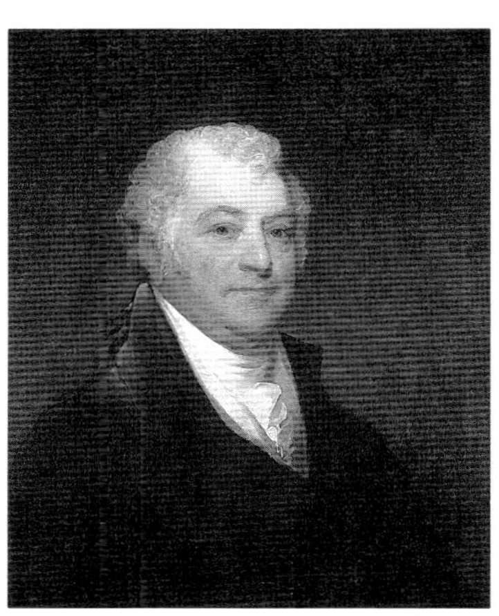

Joseph Coolidge, 1820
Canvas, 0.710 x 0.580 (28⅛ x 22¾)
Andrew W. Mellon Collection
1940.1.3

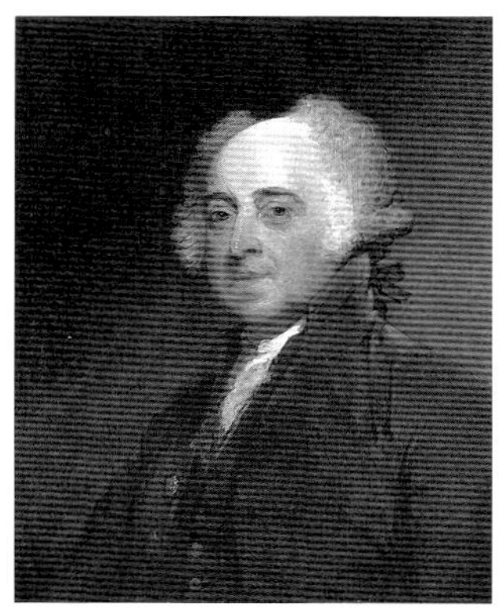

John Adams, c. 1825
Wood, 0.660 x 0.545 (26 x 21½)
Ailsa Mellon Bruce Fund
1979.4.1

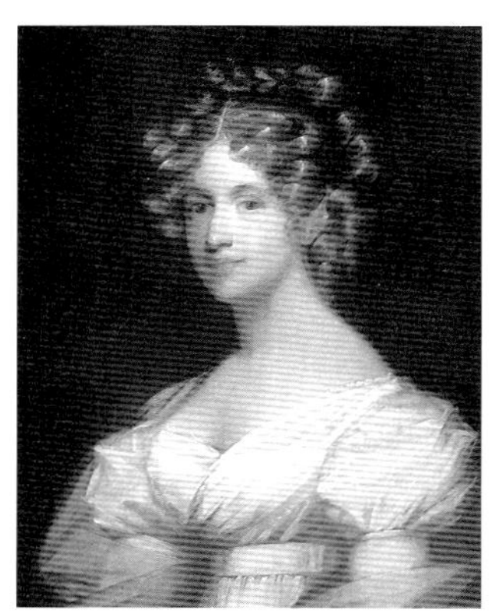

GILBERT STUART (?)
and UNKNOWN ARTIST

Mrs. Andrew Dexter (?), c. 1820
Wood, 0.740 x 0.600 (29⅛ x 23⅝)
Andrew W. Mellon Collection
1947.17.104

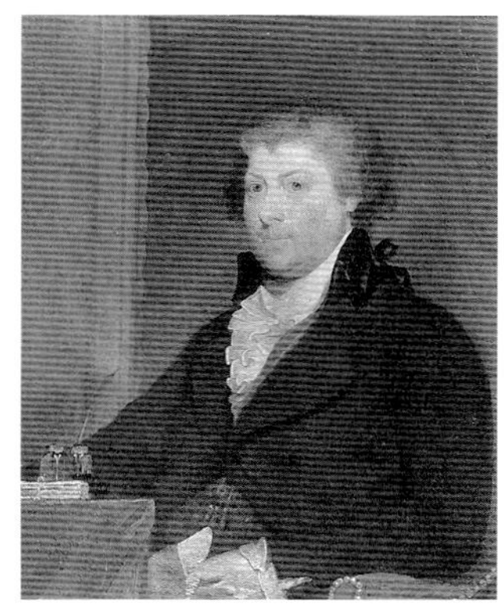

AFTER GILBERT STUART

William Seton, 1795 or after
Canvas, 0.435 x 0.359 (17⅛ x 14⅛)
Andrew W. Mellon Collection
1947.17.106

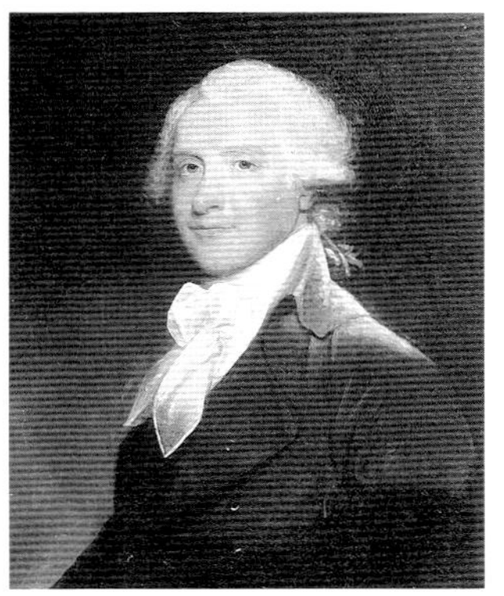

William Constable, 1796 or after
Canvas, 0.737 x 0.613 (29 x 24⅛)
Andrew W. Mellon Collection
1954.1.9

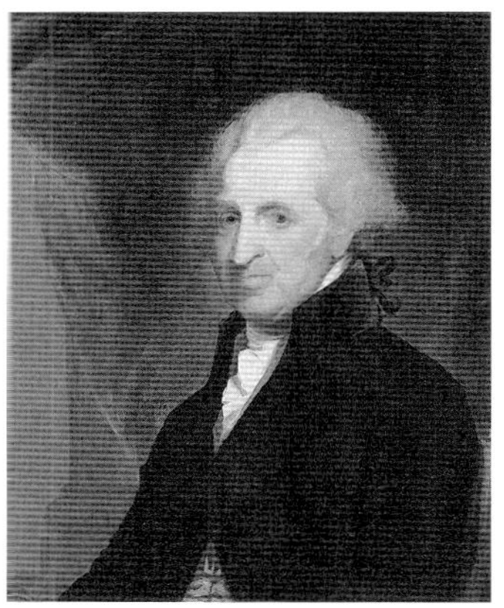

James Lloyd, 1808 or after
Canvas, 0.765 x 0.640 (30⅛ x 25⅛)
Andrew W. Mellon Collection
1947.17.107

THOMAS SULLY
1783–1872

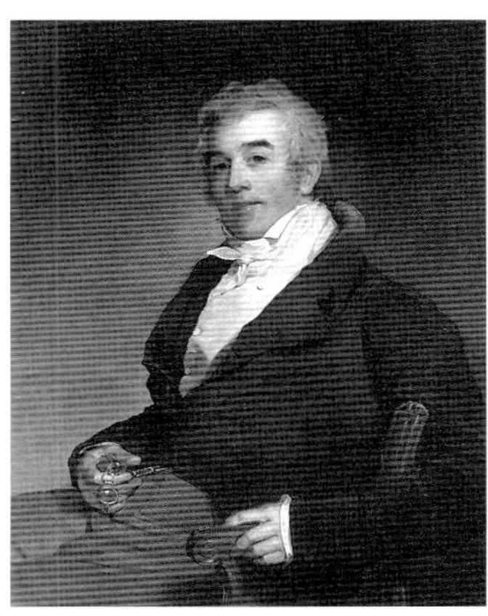

Joseph Dugan, 1810
Canvas, 0.918 x 0.735 (35⅛ x 29)
Gift of Herbert L. Pratt
1945.17.1

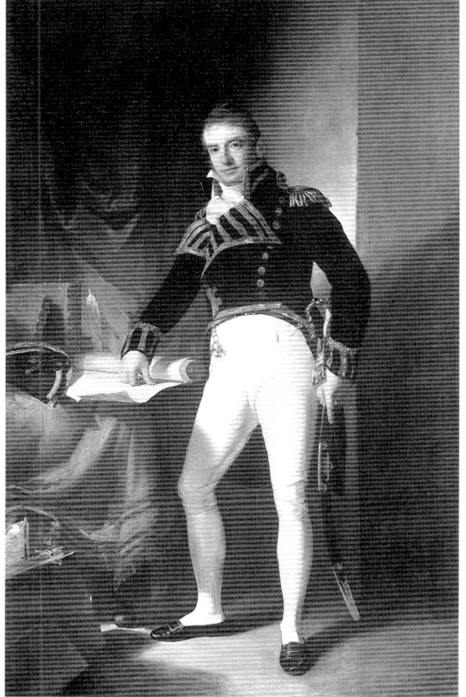

Captain Charles Stewart, 1811/1812
Canvas, 2.370 x 1.492 (93¼ x 58¾)
Gift of Maude Monell Vetlesen
1947.4.1

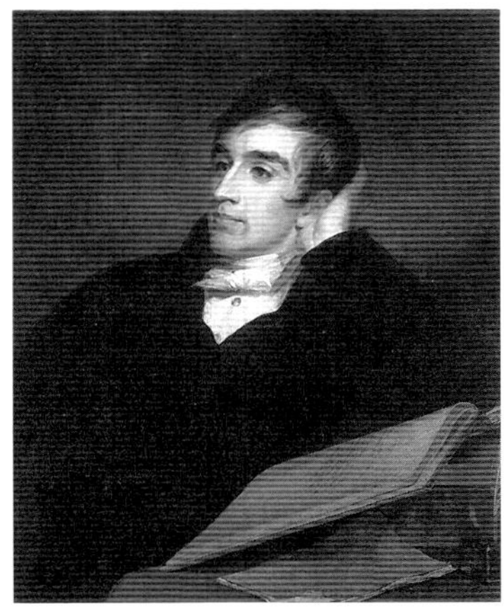

Robert Walsh, 1814
Canvas, 0.768 x 0.641 (30¼ x 25¼)
Andrew W. Mellon Collection
1947.17.11

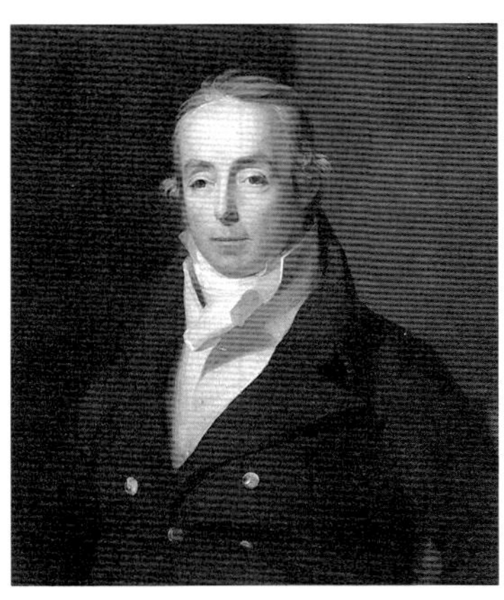

Abraham Kintzing, 1815
Canvas, 0.765 x 0.640 (30⅛ x 25¼)
Andrew W. Mellon Collection
1942.8.35

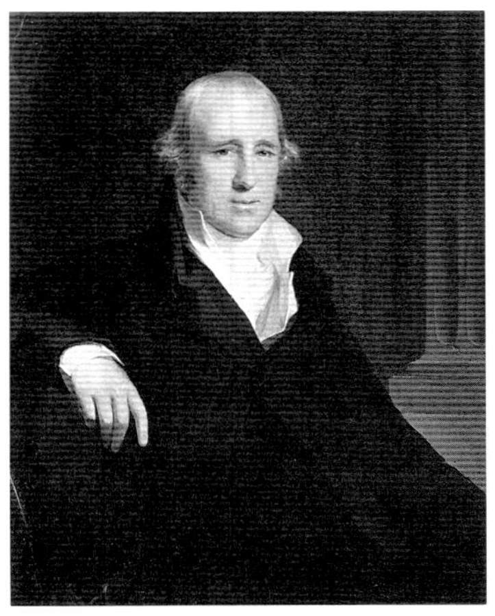

Henry Pratt, 1815
Canvas, 0.918 x 0.735 (36⅛ x 29)
Gift of Clarence Van Dyke Tiers
1942.13.1

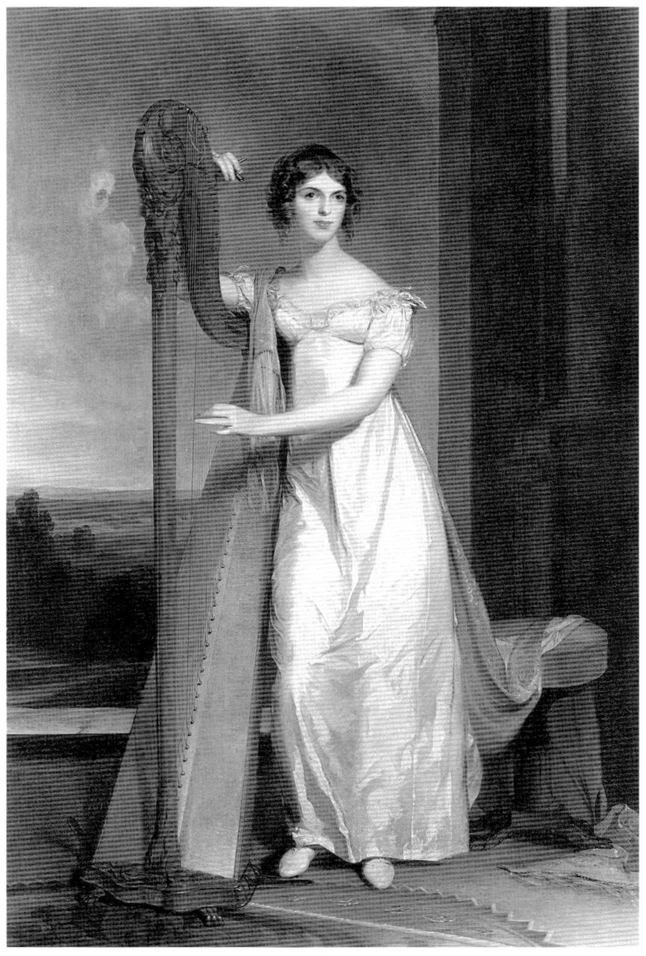

Lady with a Harp: Eliza Ridgely, 1818
Canvas, 2.145 x 1.425 (84⅜ x 56⅛)
Inscribed at lower left on harp pedestal: *TS* (in monogram) *1818*
Gift of Maude Monell Vetlesen
1945.9.1

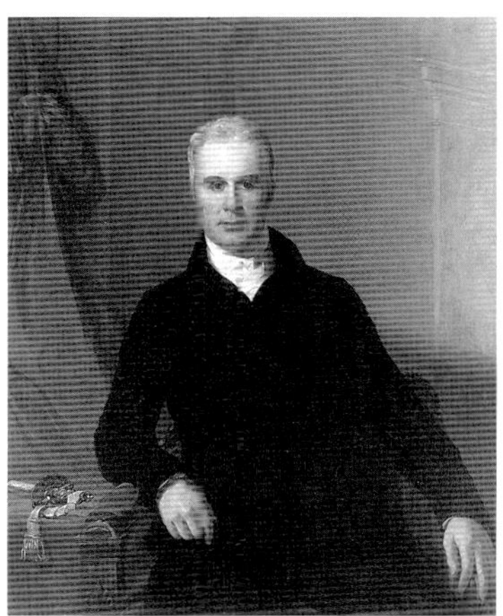

Governor Charles Ridgely of Maryland, 1820
Canvas, 1.270 x 1.015 (50 x 40)
Inscribed at lower left: *TS* (in monogram) *1820*
Gift of Mr. and Mrs. John Ridgely
1945.12.1

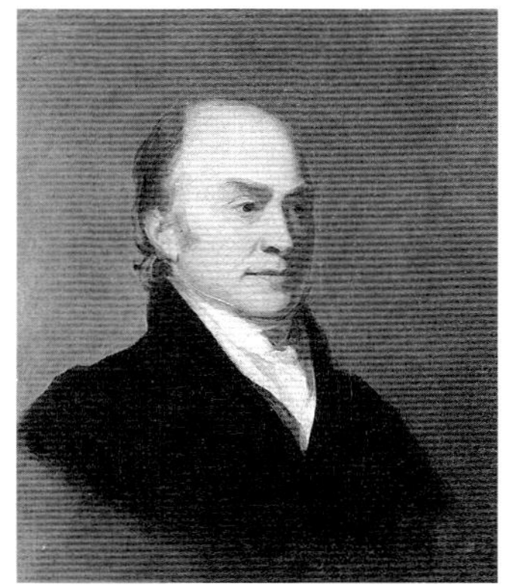

John Quincy Adams, 1824
Canvas, 0.610 x 0.510 (24⅛ x 20)
Andrew W. Mellon Collection
1942.8.30

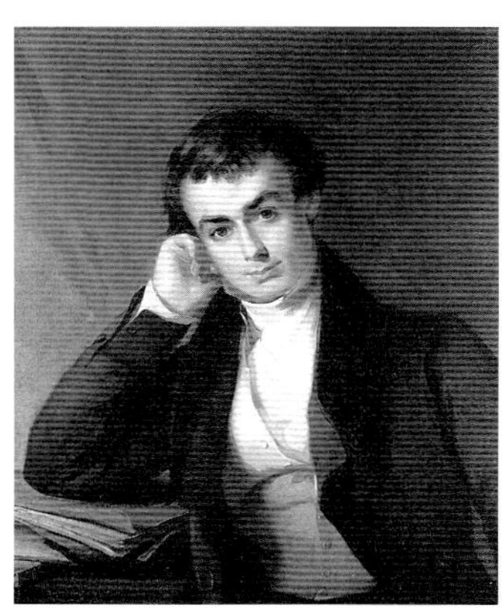

Thomas Alston, 1826
Canvas, 0.767 x 0.637 (30¼ x 25⅛)
Inscribed at lower left: *TS* (in monogram) *1826*
Andrew W. Mellon Collection
1947.17.108

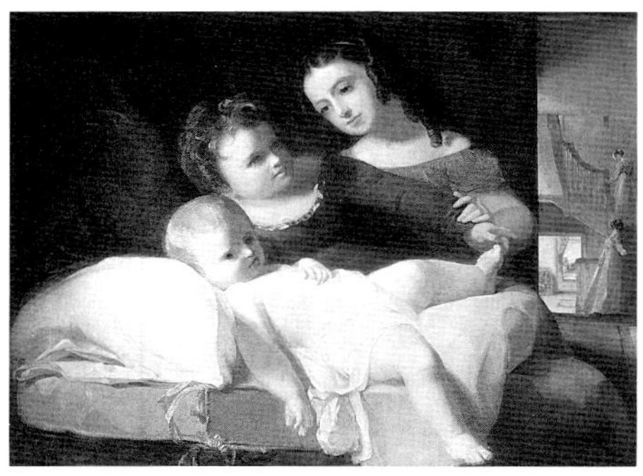

The Sicard–David Children, 1826
Canvas, 0.870 x 1.124 (34¼ x 44¼)
Inscribed at lower left: *TS* (in monogram) *18[. . .]*
Chester Dale Collection
1948.13.1

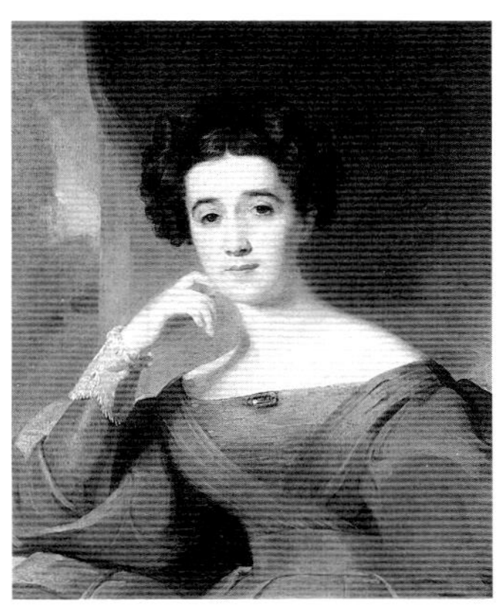

Mrs. William Griffin, 1830
Canvas, 0.765 x 0.640 (30⅛ x 25⅛)
Inscribed at lower left: *T S.* (in monogram) *1830*
Chester Dale Collection
1943.1.8

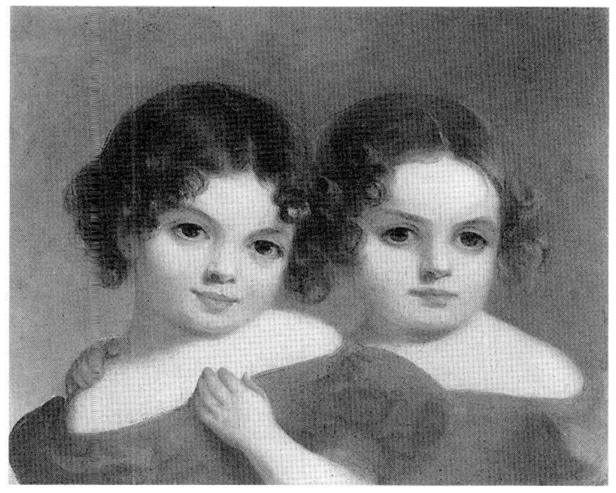

The Leland Sisters, c. 1830
Canvas, 0.412 x 0.507 (16¼ x 20)
Gift of Mrs. Philip Connors
1973.4.1

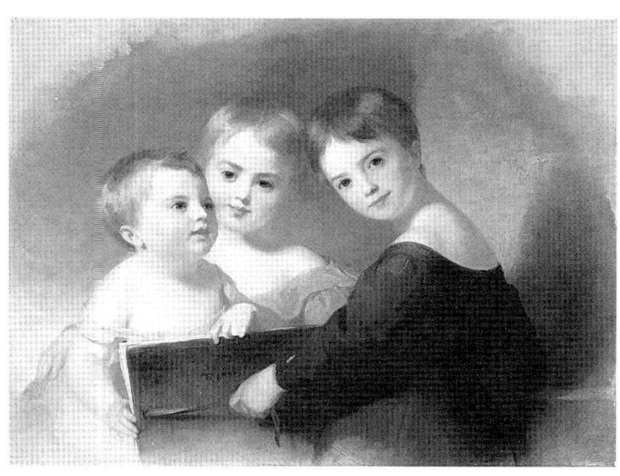

The Vanderkemp Children, 1832
Canvas, 0.708 x 0.913 (27⅞ x 36)
Inscribed at lower center on portfolio: *TS* (in monogram) *1832*
Gift of Countess Mona Bismarck
1966.11.1

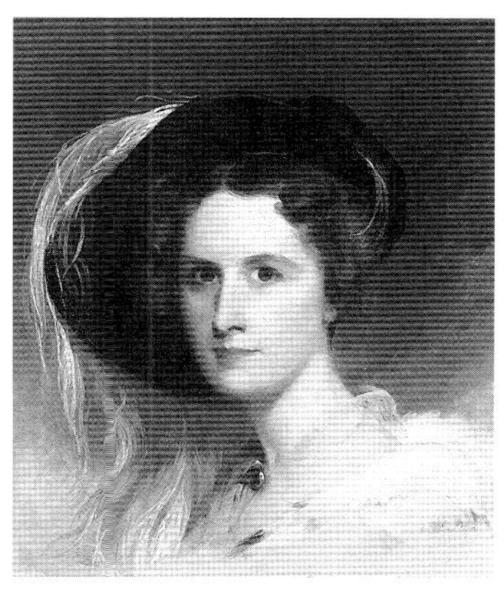

Ann Biddle Hopkinson, 1834
Canvas, 0.510 x 0.440 (20⅛ x 17¼)
Andrew W. Mellon Collection
1942.8.32

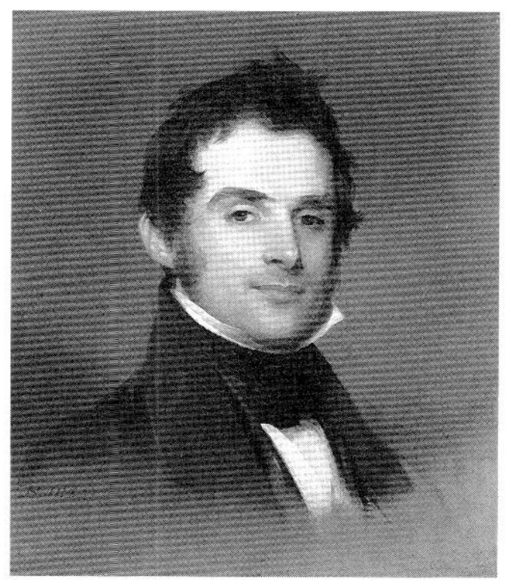

Francis Hopkinson, 1834
Canvas, 0.510 x 0.430 (20⅛ x 17⅛)
Inscribed at lower left: *TS.* (in monogram) *1834.*
Andrew W. Mellon Collection
1942.8.33

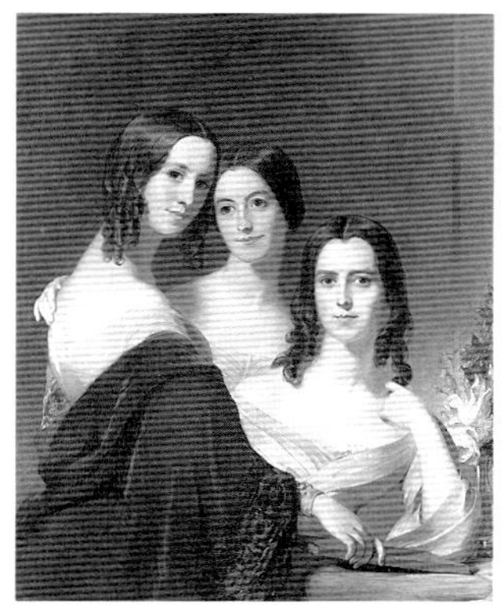

The Coleman Sisters, 1844
Canvas, 1.125 x 0.875 (44¼ x 34½)
Gift of William C. Freeman
1947.9.3

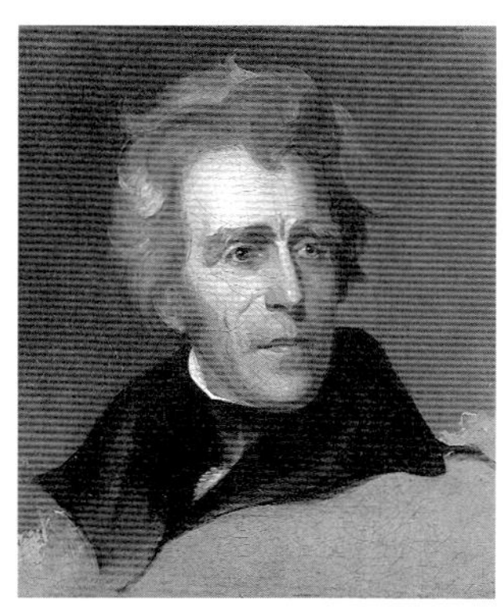

Andrew Jackson, 1845
Canvas, 0.518 x 0.438 (20⅜ x 17¼)
Andrew W. Mellon Collection
1942.8.34

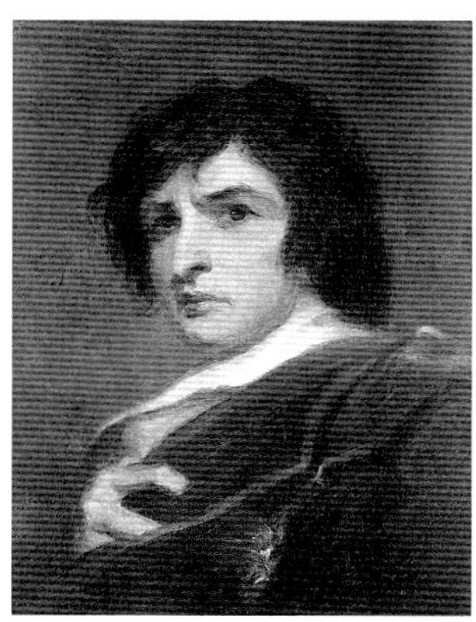

THOMAS SULLY
(1783–1872)
AFTER GILBERT STUART
(1755–1828)

John Philip Kemble, 1867
Canvas, 0.535 x 0.409 (21⅛ x 16⅛)
Andrew W. Mellon Collection
1947.17.111

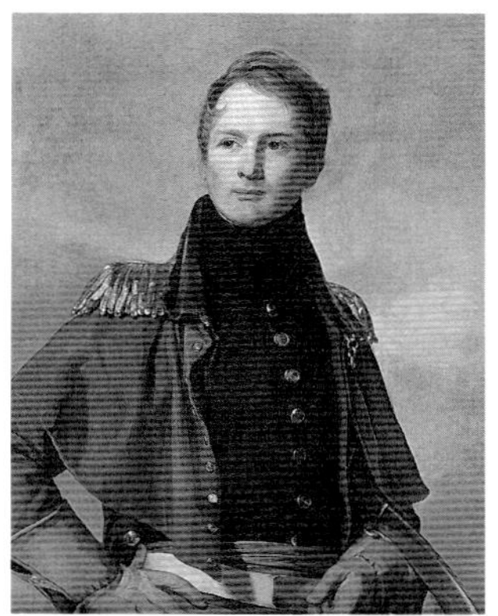

THOMAS WILCOCKS SULLY
(1811–1847)
and **THOMAS SULLY**
(1783–1872)

Major Thomas Biddle, 1832
Canvas, 0.905 x 0.695 (35⅝ x 27⅜)
Andrew W. Mellon Collection
1942.8.31

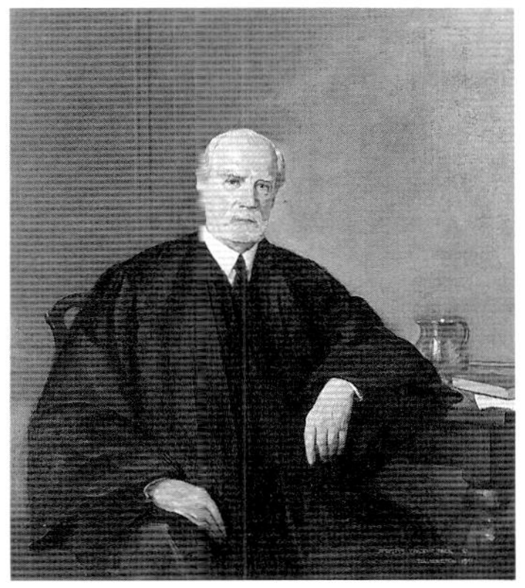

AUGUSTUS VINCENT TACK
1870–1949

Charles Evans Hughes, 1941
Canvas board, 1.296 x 1.146 (51 x 45⅛)
Inscribed at lower right: *AUGUSTUS VINCENT TACK c / WASHINGTON 1941*
Gift of Duncan Phillips
1942.1.1 Special Collection

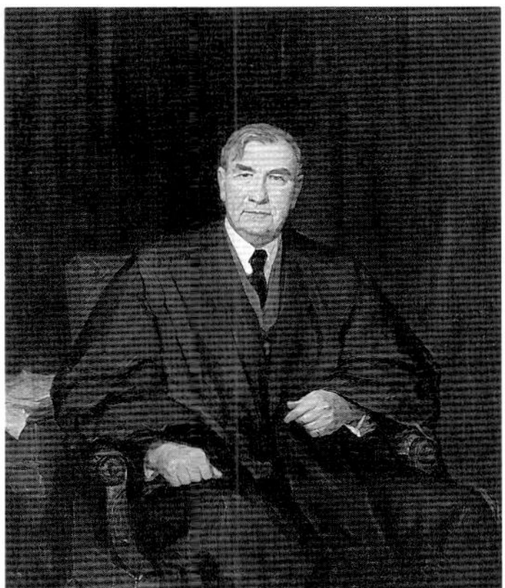

Harlan F. Stone, 1944
Canvas, 1.448 x 1.195 (57 x 47)
Inscribed at upper right: *AUGUSTUS VINCENT TACK*
Gift of Duncan Phillips
1944.4.1 Special Collection

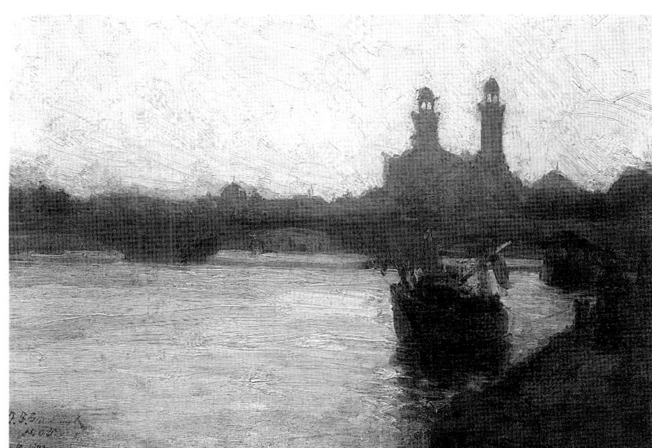

HENRY OSSAWA TANNER
1859–1937

The Seine, 1902
Canvas, 0.230 x 0.329 (9 x 13)
Inscribed at lower left: *F. F. Guterinsh / H.O. Ta[nner] / [. . .] 10, 1902*
Gift of the Avalon Foundation
1971.57.1

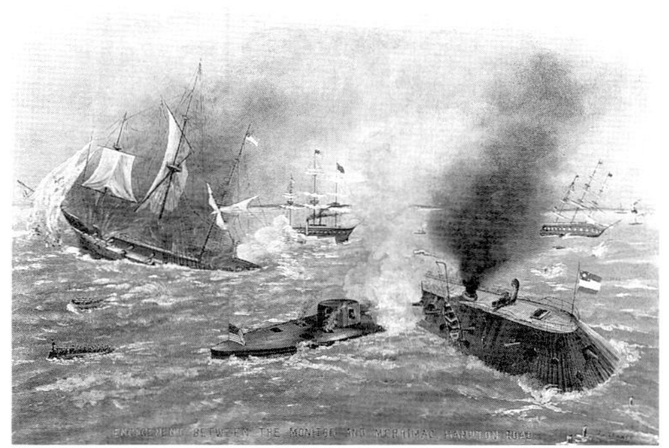

J. G. TANNER
active c. 1891

Engagement between the Monitor *and the* Merrimac, 1891 or after
Canvas, 0.661 x 0.915 (26 x 36)
Inscribed across bottom: *ENGAGEMENT BETWEEN THE MONITOR AND MERRIMAC, HAMPTON ROAD* [sic]; lower right: *J. G. TANNER*
Gift of Edgar William and Bernice Chrysler Garbisch
1953.5.36

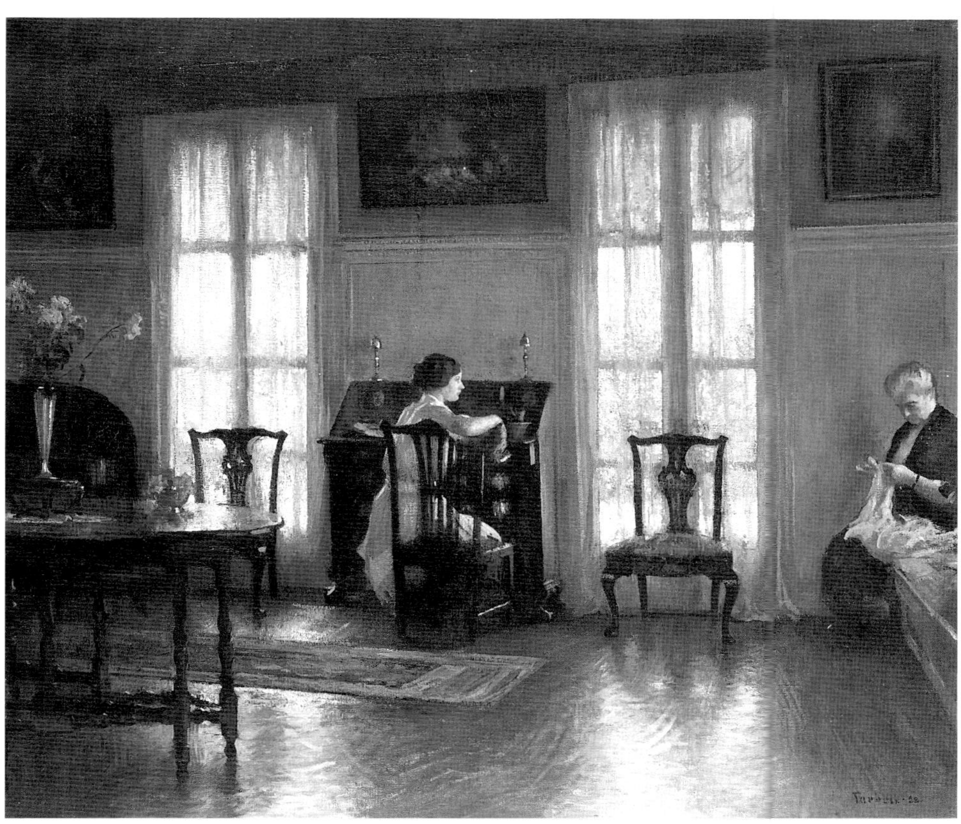

EDMUND CHARLES TARBELL
1862–1938

Mother and Mary, 1922
Canvas, 1.121 x 1.275 (44⅛ x 50¼)
Inscribed at lower right: *Tarbell.22.*
Gift of the Belcher Collection, Stoughton, Massachusetts
1967.1.1

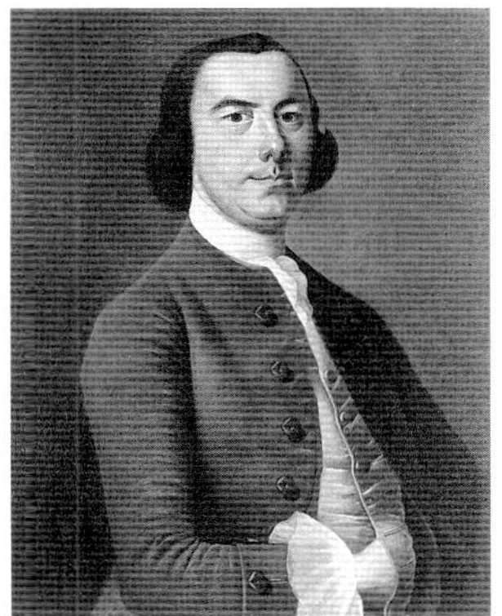

JEREMIAH THEUS
c. 1719–1774

Mr. Motte, c. 1760
Canvas, 0.762 x 0.635 (30 x 25 1/8)
Andrew W. Mellon Collection
1947.17.12

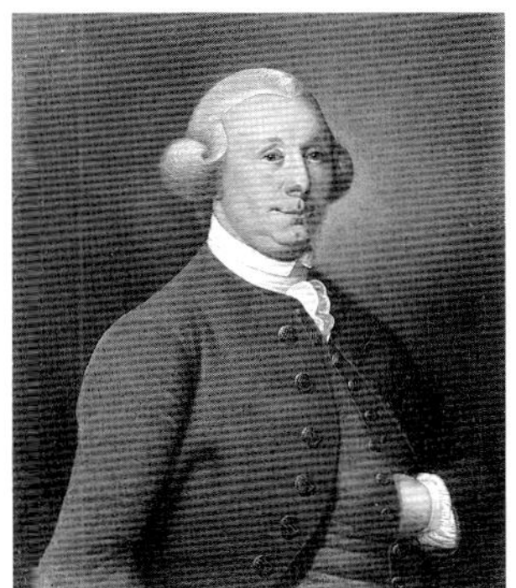

Mr. Cuthbert, c. 1765
Canvas, 0.753 x 0.623 (29 5/8 x 24 9/16)
Gift of Edgar William and Bernice Chrysler Garbisch
1965.15.6

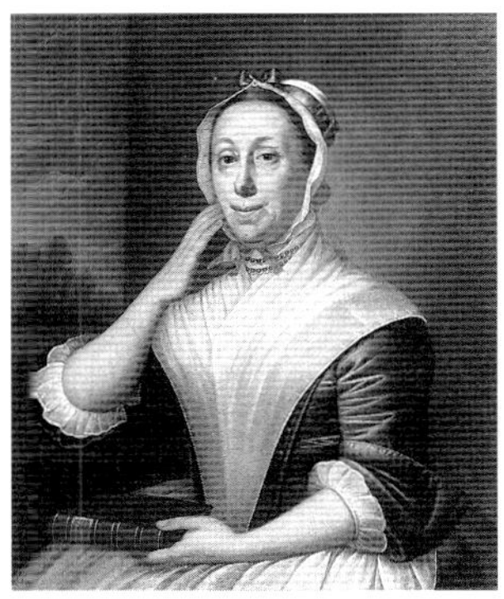

Mrs. Cuthbert, c. 1765
Canvas, 0.755 x 0.626 (29 11/16 x 24 5/8)
Gift of Edgar William and Bernice Chrysler Garbisch
1965.15.7

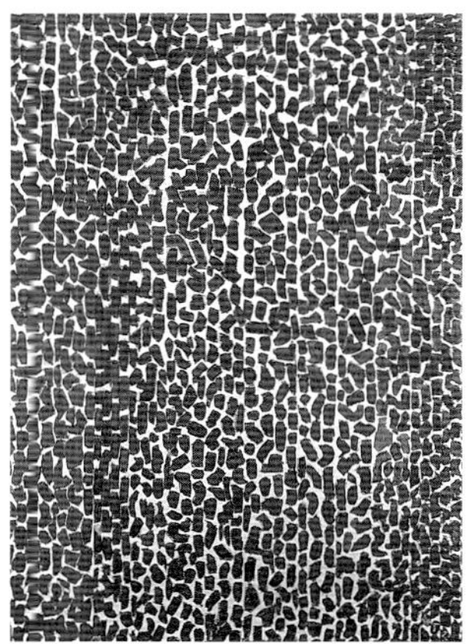

ALMA THOMAS
1891–1978

Red Rose Cantata, 1973
Canvas, 1.754 x 1.270 (69 x 50)
Inscribed at lower right: *A / W / T / 7 / 3*
Gift of Vincent Melzac
1976.6.1

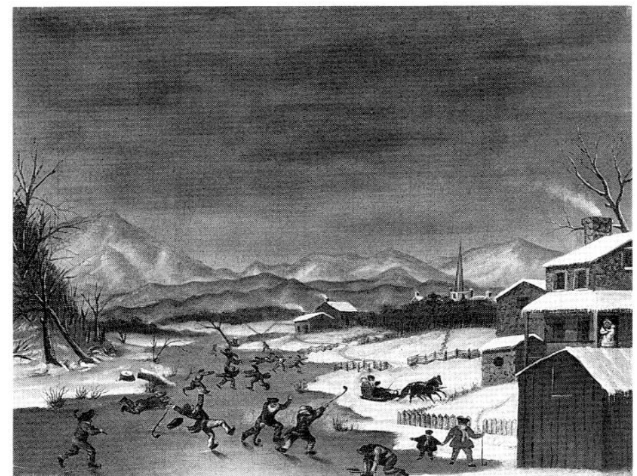

JOHN TOOLE
1815–1860

Skating Scene, c. 1835
Canvas, 0.369 x 0.462 (14 9/16 x 18 1/4)
Gift of Edgar William and Bernice Chrysler Garbisch
1958.9.6

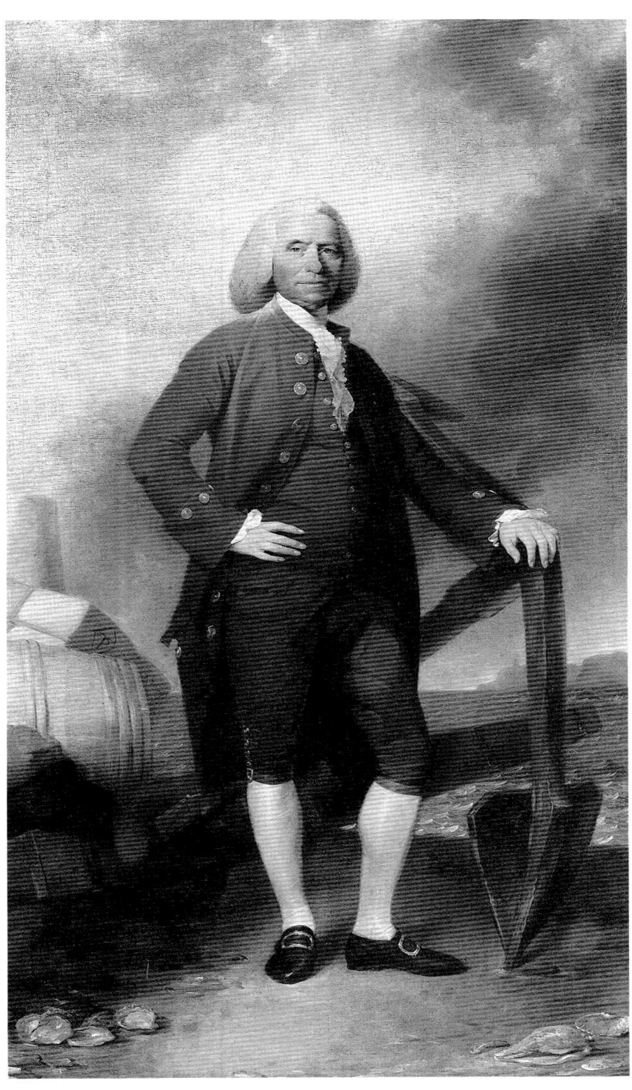

JOHN TRUMBULL
1756–1843

Patrick Tracy, 1784/1786
Canvas, 2.325 x 1.337 (91 1/2 x 52 5/8)
Gift of Patrick T. Jackson
1964.15.1

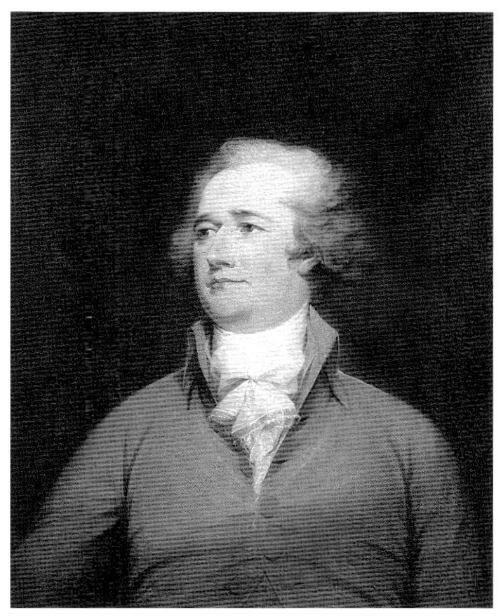

Alexander Hamilton, c. 1792
Canvas, 0.769 x 0.613 (30¼ x 24⅛)
Gift of the Avalon Foundation
1952.1.1

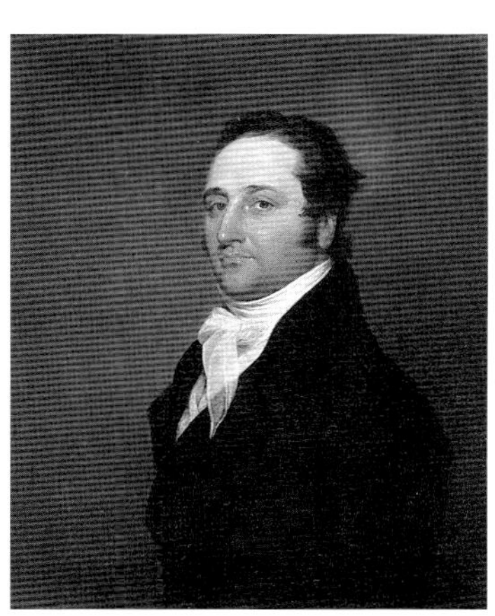

William Rogers, 1804/1808
Canvas, 0.775 x 0.635 (30½ x 25)
Andrew W. Mellon Collection
1947.17.13

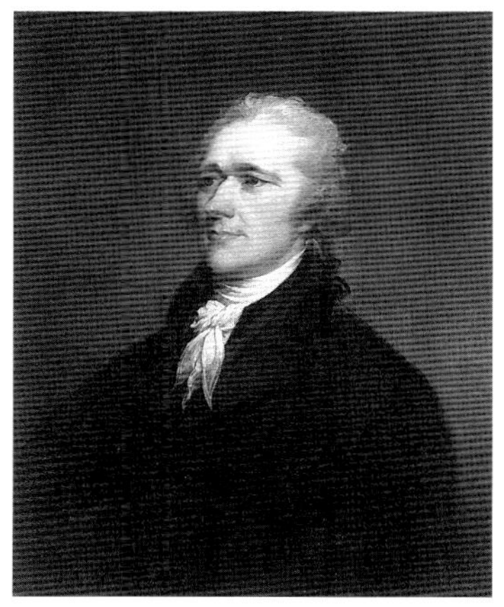

Alexander Hamilton, 1806
Canvas, 0.770 x 0.610 (30¼ x 24¼)
Andrew W. Mellon Collection
1940.1.8

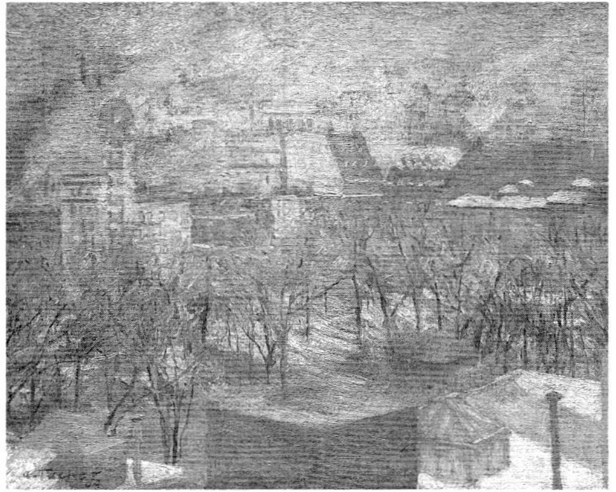

ALLEN TUCKER
1866–1939

Madison Square, Snow, 1904
Canvas, 0.508 x 0.609 (20 x 24)
Inscribed at lower left: *A. Tucker / 04*
Gift of the Allen Tucker Memorial
1971.13.2

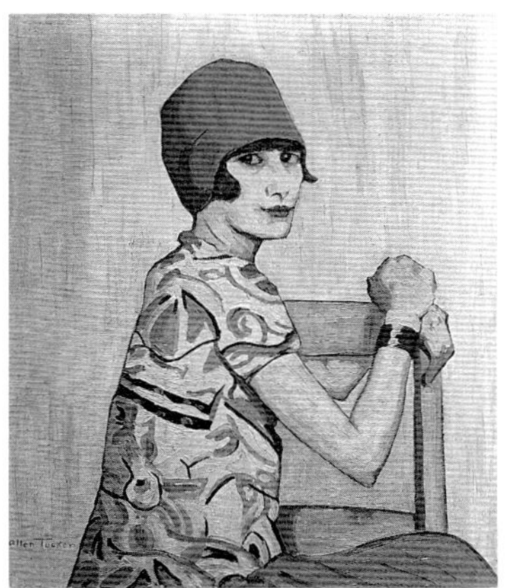

Bizarre, 1923
Canvas, 0.770 x 0.641 (30¼ x 25¼)
Inscribed at lower left: *Allen Tucker*
Gift of the Allen Tucker Memorial
1971.13.1

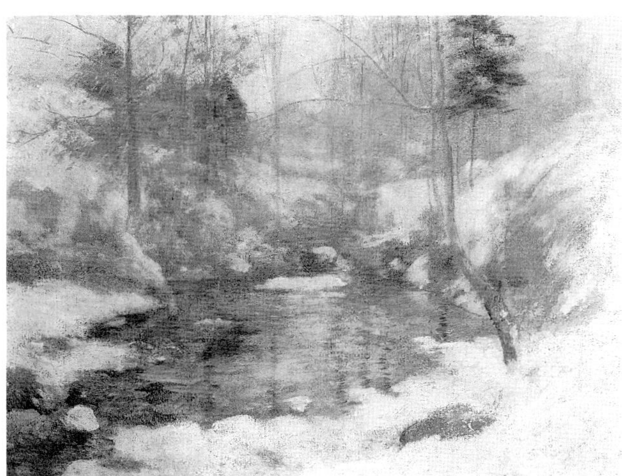

JOHN HENRY TWACHTMAN
1853–1902

Winter Harmony, c. 1890/1900
Canvas, 0.653 x 0.812 (25¾ x 32)
Inscribed at lower right: *J. H. Twachtman*
Gift of the Avalon Foundation
1964.22.1

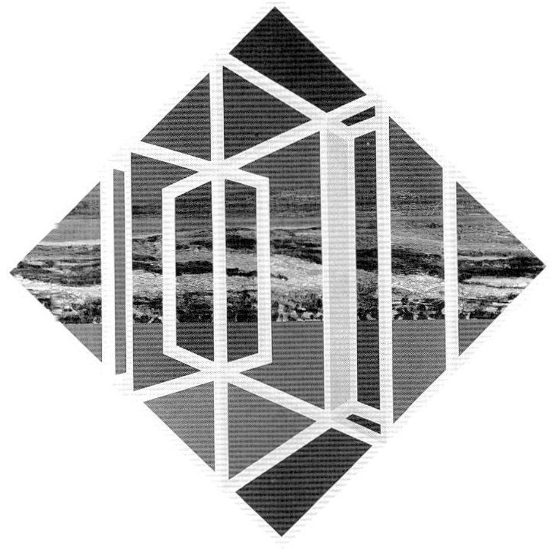

JAMES TWITTY
born 1916

Blue Water, 1974
Canvas, diamond: 2.583 x 2.593
(101 x 102⅛)
Inscribed at center right: *Twitty*
Gift of the artist in memory of Lester Cooke
1974.46.1

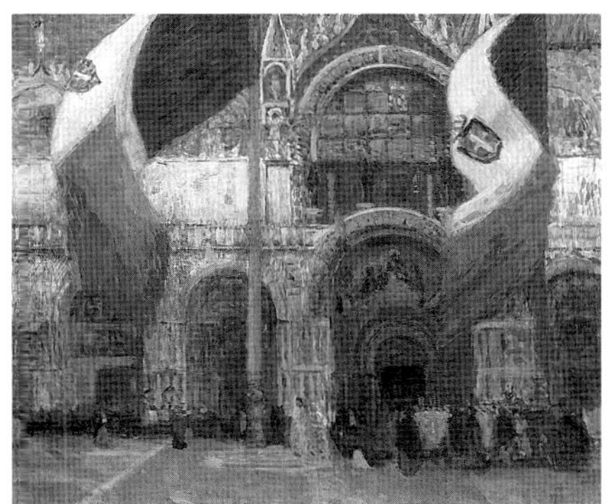

EUGENE LAWRENCE VAIL
1857–1934

The Flags, Saint Mark's, Venice—Fete Day, c. 1903
Canvas, 0.820 x 0.926 (32¼ x 36½)
Inscribed at lower right: *Eugene Vail*
Gift of Gertrude Mauran Vail
1973.1.1

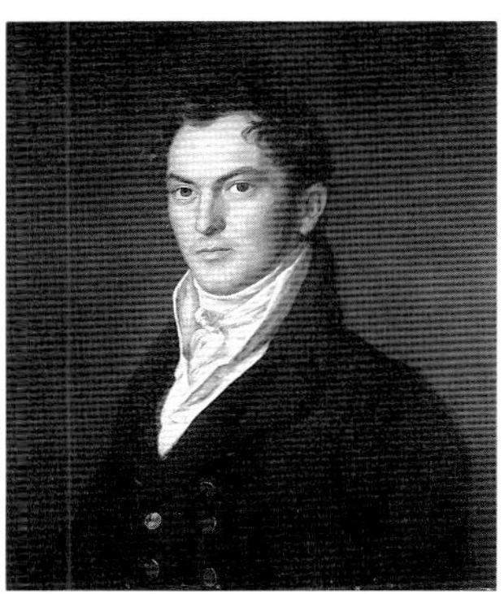

JOHN VANDERLYN
1775–1852

Zachariah Schoonmaker, 1815/1818
Canvas, 0.665 x 0.565 (26¼ x 22¼)
Andrew W. Mellon Collection
1942.8.36

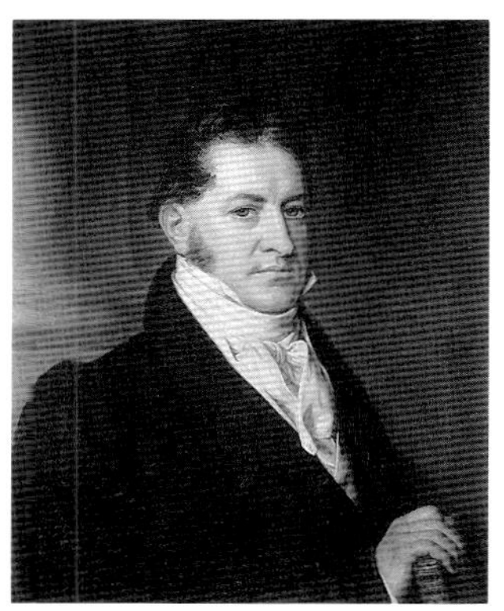

John Sudam, 1830
Canvas, 0.762 x 0.635 (30 x 25)
Andrew W. Mellon Collection
1947.17.14

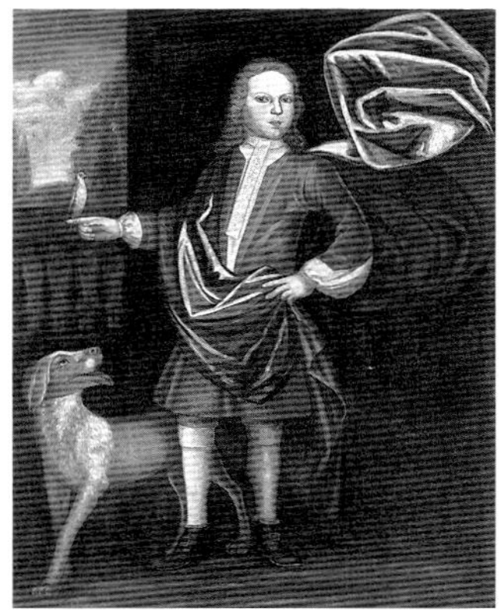

ATTRIBUTED TO
PIETER VANDERLYN
c. 1687–1778

Boy of the Beekman Family, c. 1720
Canvas, 1.308 x 1.037 (51½ x 40⅞)
Gift of Edgar William and Bernice Chrysler Garbisch
1978.80.11

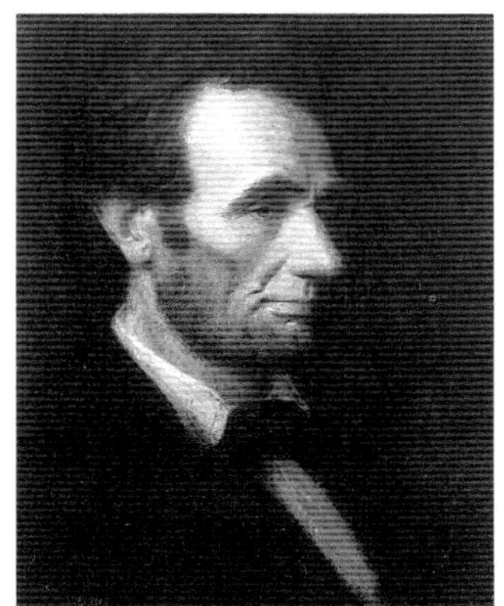

DOUGLAS VOLK
1856–1935

Abraham Lincoln, 1908 and 1917
Canvas, 0.514 x 0.410 (20¼ x 16⅛)
Inscribed at lower left: *c 1908 / Douglas Volk*
Andrew W. Mellon Collection
1947.17.17

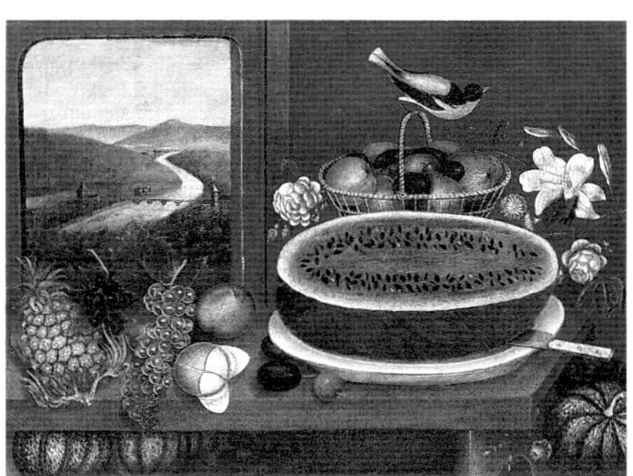

WAGGUNO
active 1858

Fruit and Baltimore Oriole, 1858
Canvas, 0.560 x 0.721 (22 x 28⅜)
Gift of Edgar William and Bernice Chrysler Garbisch
1980.62.47

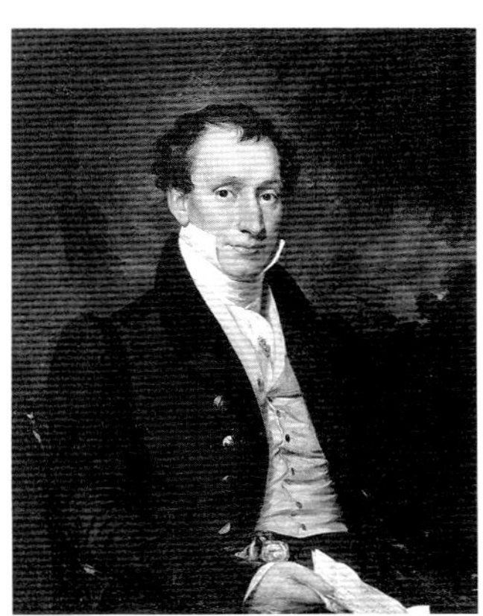

SAMUEL LOVETT WALDO
1783–1861

Robert G. L. De Peyster, 1828
Wood, 0.840 x 0.640 (33 x 25¼)
Inscribed at lower right on letter: *WALDO*; and: *New York July 1828 / Robt. G. L. Depeyster*
Andrew W. Mellon Collection
1942.8.38

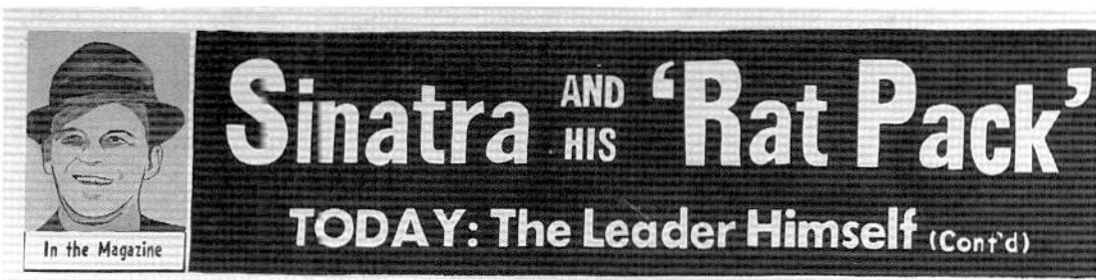

ANDY WARHOL
1928–1987

A Boy for Meg, 1962
Canvas, 1.829 x 1.321 (72 x 52)
Inscribed at upper left on stretcher: *Andy Warhol*
Gift of Mr. and Mrs. Burton Tremaine
1971.87.11

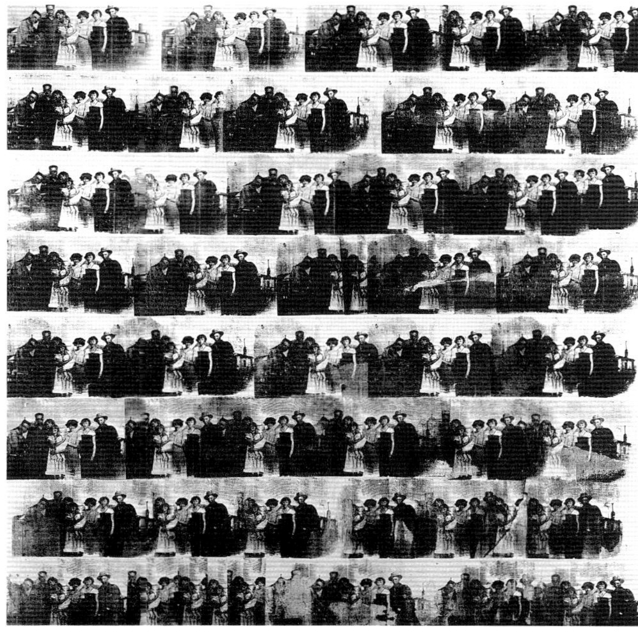

Let Us Now Praise Famous Men (Rauschenberg Family), 1963
Canvas, 2.082 x 2.082 (82 x 82)
Gift of Mr. and Mrs. William Howard Adams
1982.96.1

SUSAN C. WATERS
1823–1900

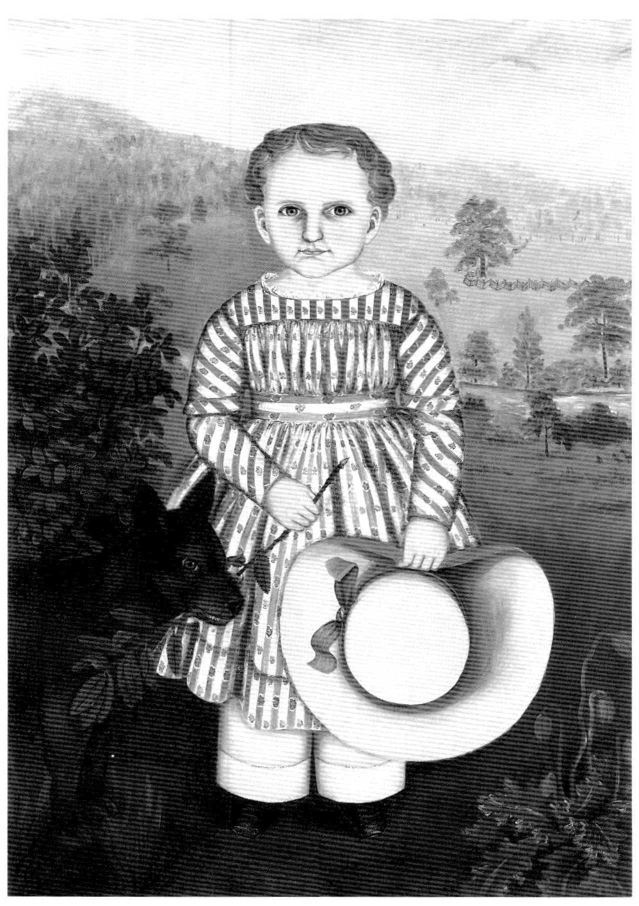

Henry L. Wells, 1845
Canvas, 1.016 x 0.715 (40 x 28⅛)
Gift of Edgar William and Bernice Chrysler Garbisch
1955.11.8

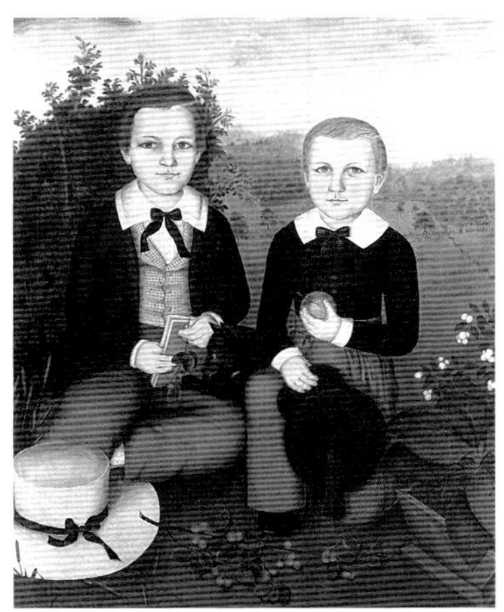

Brothers, c. 1845
Canvas, 1.117 x 0.888 (44 x 35)
Gift of Edgar William and Bernice Chrysler Garbisch
1956.13.8

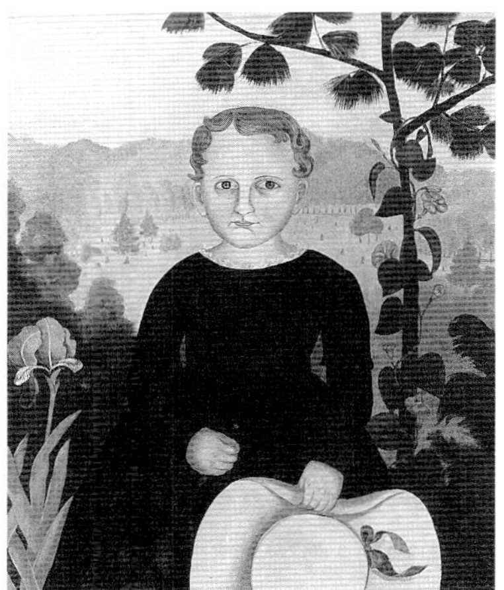

AFTER SUSAN C. WATERS

Henry L. Wells, 1845 or after
Canvas, 0.765 x 0.638 (30⅛ x 25⅛)
Gift of Edgar William and Bernice Chrysler Garbisch
1953.5.38

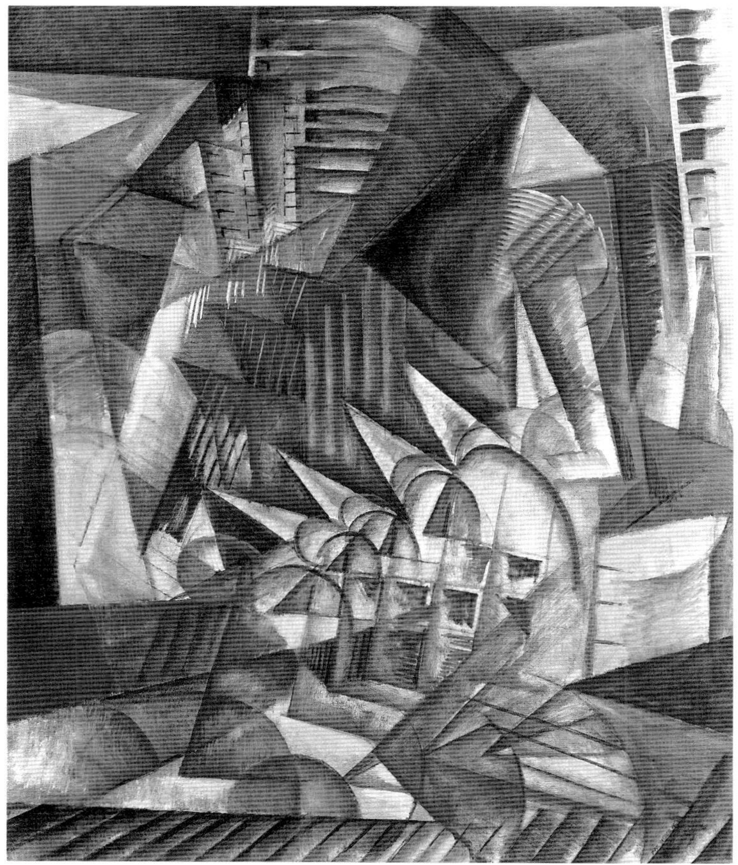

MAX WEBER
1881–1961

Rush Hour, New York, 1915
Canvas, 0.920 x 0.769 (36¼ x 30¼)
Inscribed at lower right: *MAX WEBER 1915*
Gift of the Avalon Foundation
1970.6.1

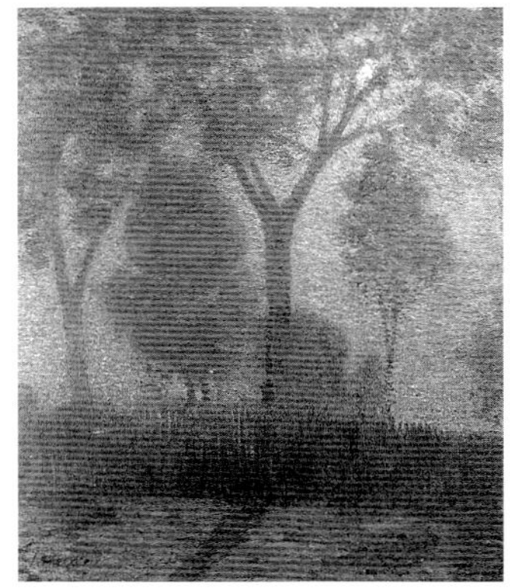

JULIAN ALDEN WEIR
1852–1919

Moonlight, c. 1905
Canvas, 0.610 x 0.508 (24 x 20)
Inscribed at lower left: *J Alden Weir*
Chester Dale Collection
1954.4.1

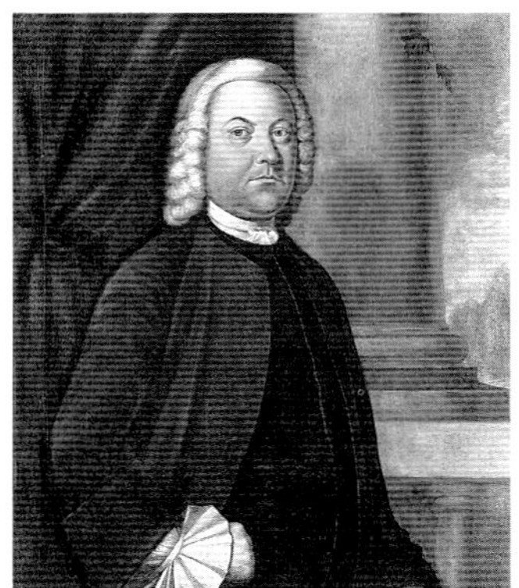

BENJAMIN WEST
1738–1820

Dr. Samuel Boude, 1755/1756
Canvas, 0.904 x 0.765 (35⅝ x 30⅛)
Gift of Edgar William and Bernice Chrysler Garbisch
1964.23.7

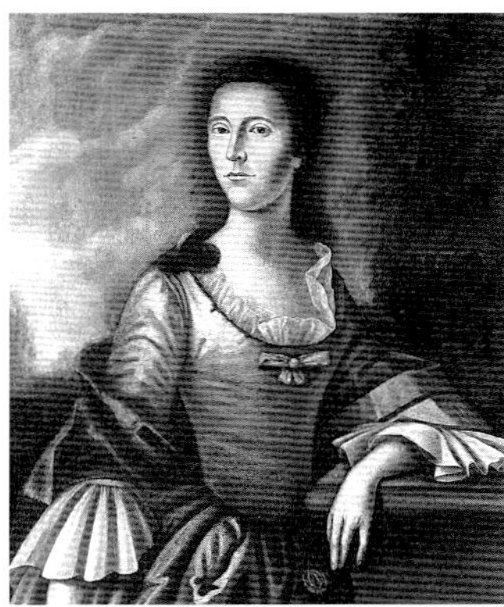

Mrs. Samuel Boude, 1755/1756
Canvas, 0.904 x 0.763 (35 9/16 x 30 1/16)
Gift of Edgar William and Bernice Chrysler Garbisch
1964.23.8

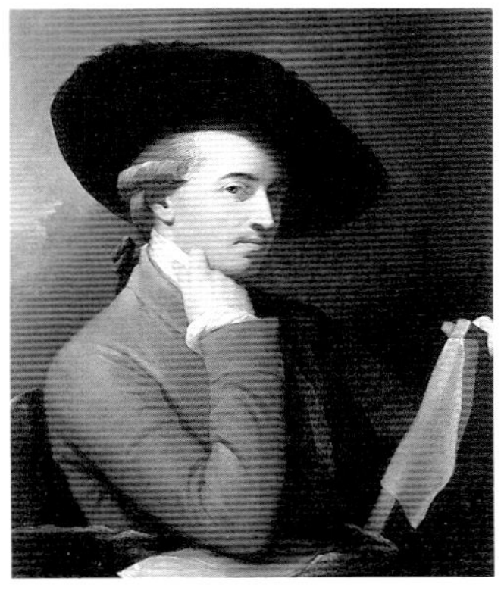

Self-Portrait, c. 1770
Canvas, 0.758 x 0.630 (29 13/16 x 24 13/16)
Andrew W. Mellon Collection
1942.8.39

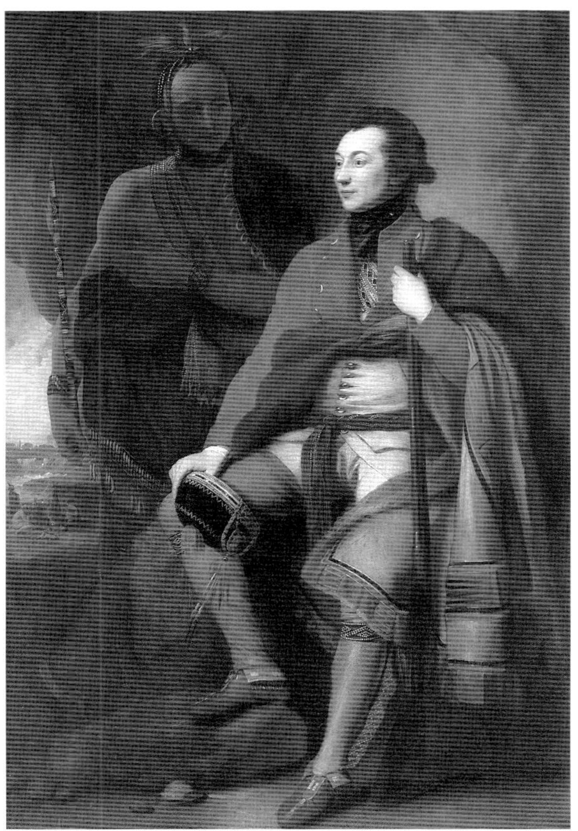

Colonel Guy Johnson, 1776
Canvas, 2.030 x 1.380 (79¾ x 54½)
Andrew W. Mellon Collection
1940.1.10

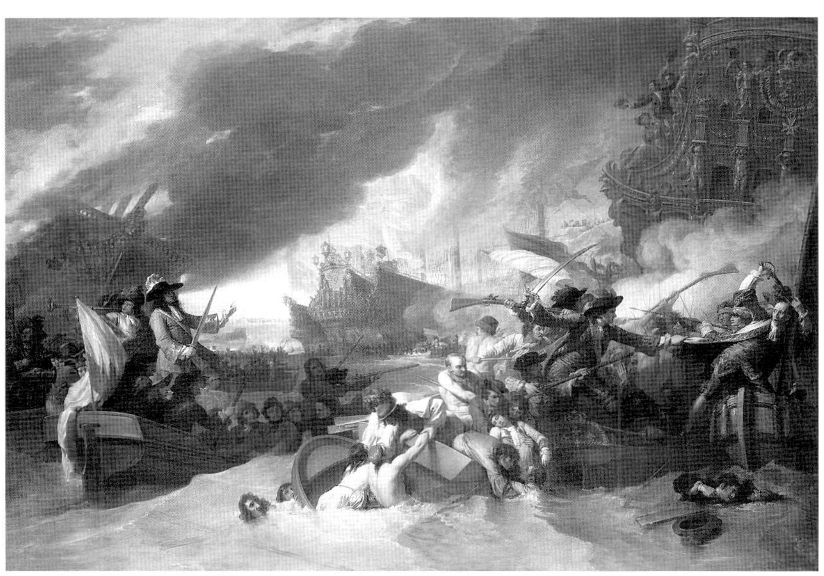

The Battle of La Hogue, 1778
Canvas, 1.527 x 2.140 (60⅛ x 84¼)
Andrew W. Mellon Fund
1959.8.1

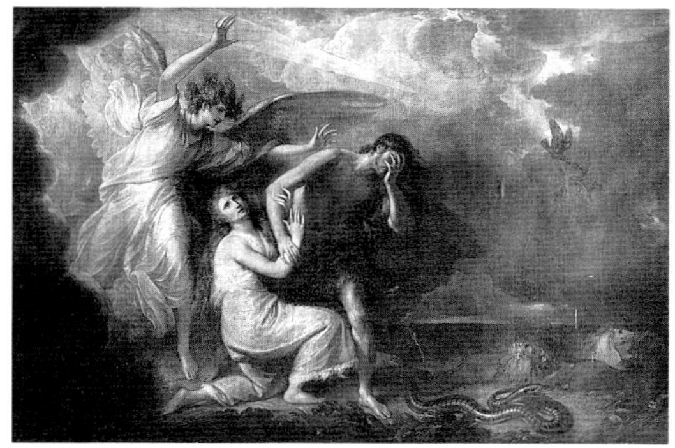

The Expulsion of Adam and Eve from Paradise, 1791
Canvas, 1.868 x 2.781 (73 9/16 x 109 1/2)
Inscribed at lower left: *B. West [. . .]*
Avalon Fund and Patrons' Permanent Fund
1989.12.1

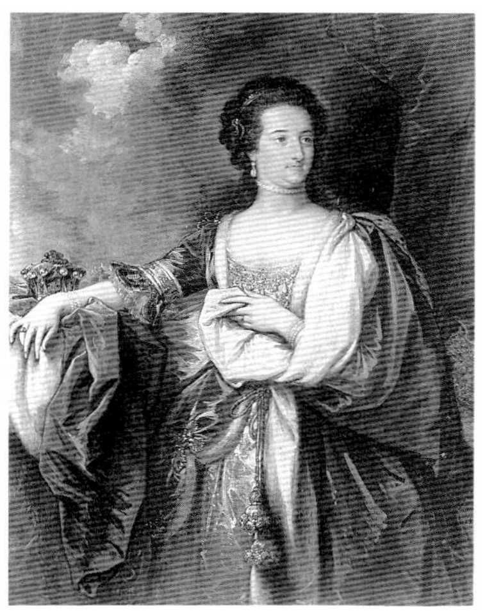

Elizabeth, Countess of Effingham, c. 1797
Canvas, 1.464 x 1.158 (57 5/8 x 45 5/8)
Inscribed at lower right: *B. West*
Andrew W. Mellon Collection
1947.17.101

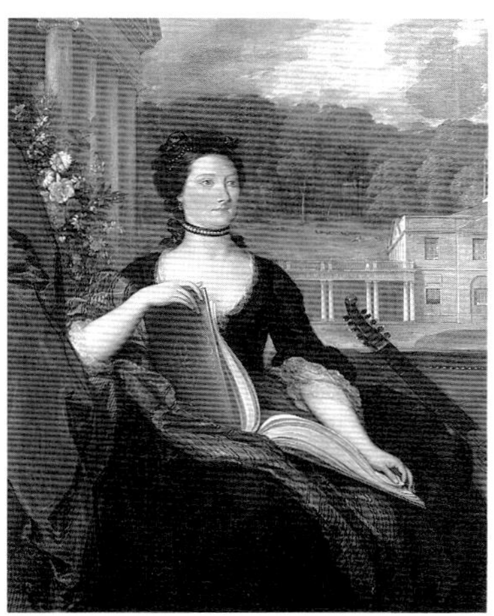

Mrs. William Beckford, c. 1799
Canvas, 1.460 x 1.150 (57 1/2 x 45 1/4)
Andrew W. Mellon Collection
1947.17.23

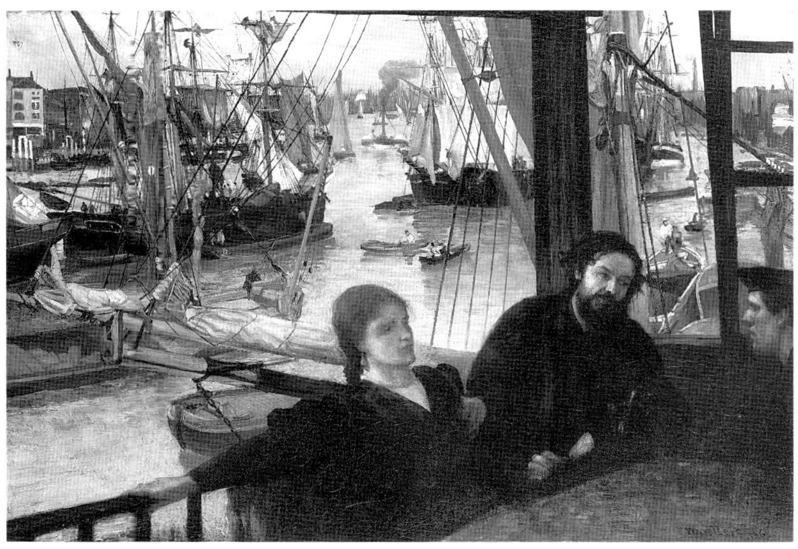

JAMES MCNEILL WHISTLER
1834–1903

Wapping on Thames, 1860/1864
Canvas, 0.720 x 1.018 (28⅜ x 40⅛)
Inscribed at lower right: *Whistler. 1861.*
John Hay Whitney Collection
1982.76.8

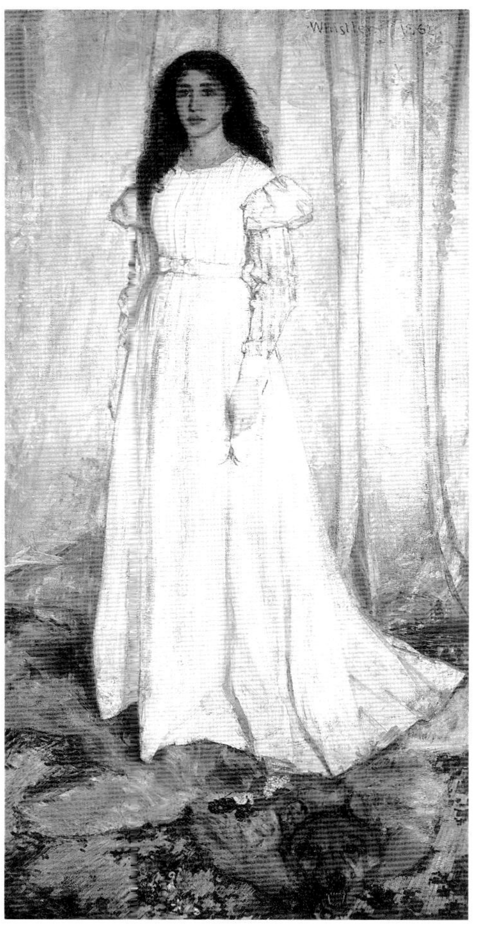

The White Girl (Symphony in White, No.1), 1862
Canvas, 2.147 x 1.080 (84½ x 42½)
Inscribed at upper right: *Whistler. 1862.*
Harris Whittemore Collection
1943.6.2

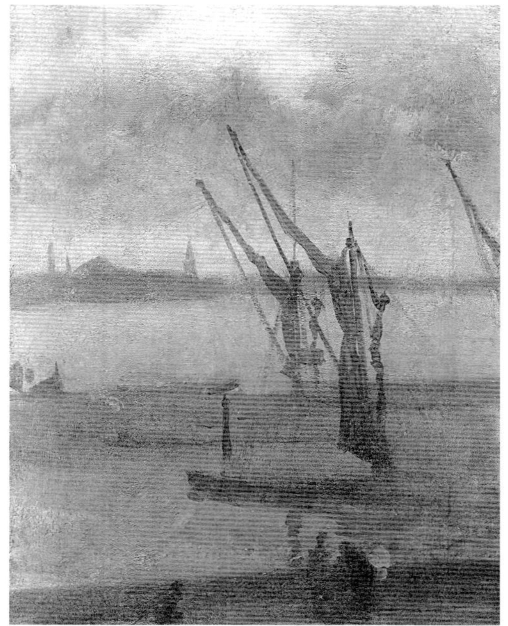

Chelsea Wharf: Grey and Silver, c. 1875
Canvas, 0.61[illegible] x 0.460 (24¼ x 18⅛)
Widener Collection
1942.9.99

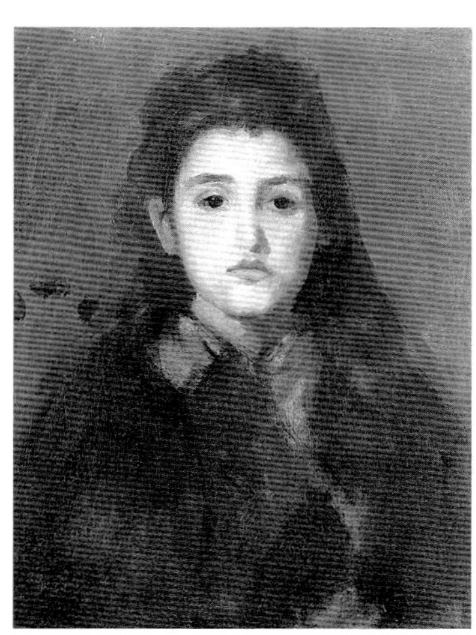

Head of a Girl, c. 1883
Canvas, 0.517 x 0.381 (20⅜ x 15)
Inscribed at center left with the artist's butterfly mark
Gift of Curt H. Reisinger
1948.16.2

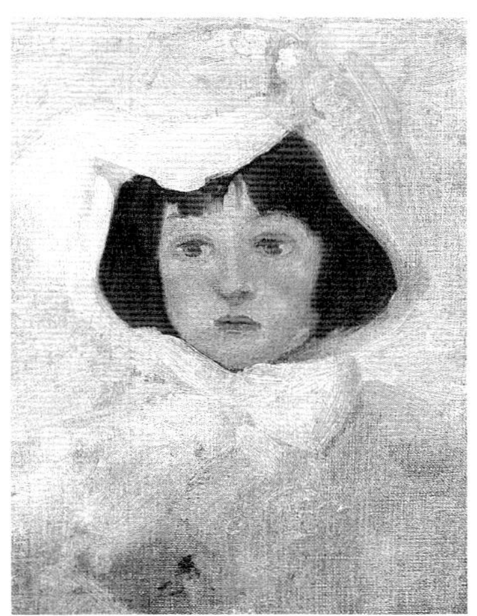

Little Girl in White, c. 1890/1900
Canvas, 0.359 x 0.261 (14⅛ x 10¼)
Inscribed at center left with the artist's butterfly mark
Chester Dale Collection
1963.10.71

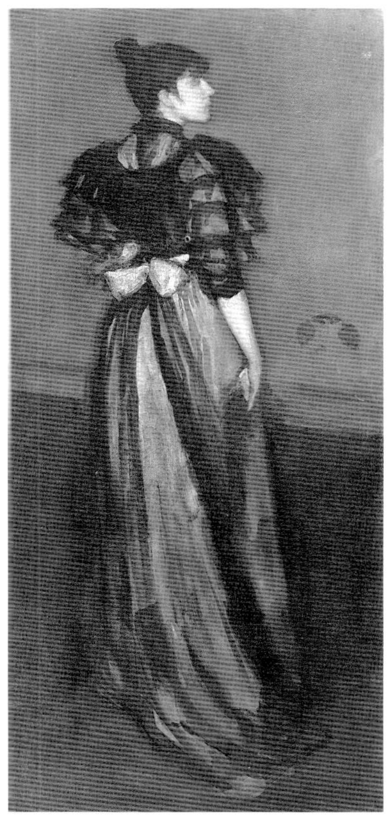

Mother of Pearl and Silver: The Andalusian, c. 1894
Canvas, 1.915 x 0.900 (75 3/8 x 35 3/8)
Inscribed at center right with the artist's butterfly mark
Harris Whittemore Collection
1943.6.1

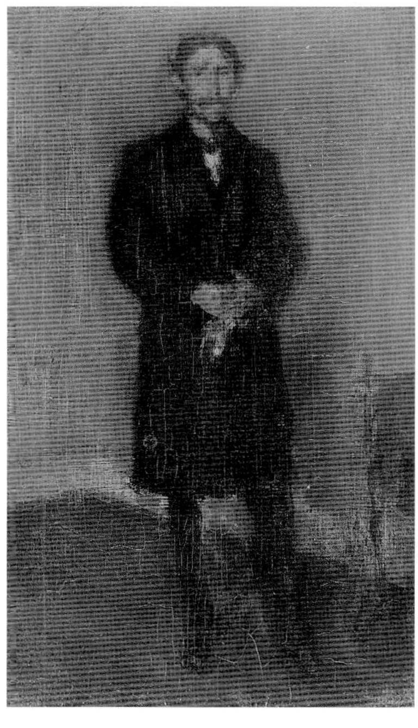

Alexander Arnold Hannay, c. 1896
Wood, 0.218 x 0.126 (8 5/8 x 5)
Inscribed at center left with the artist's butterfly mark
Rosenwald Collection
1943.11.7

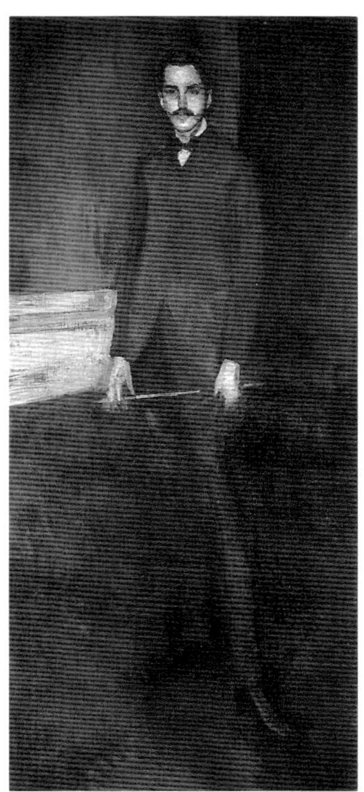

George W. Vanderbilt, 1897/1902
Canvas, 2.087 x 0.912 (82⅛ x 35⅞)
Gift of Edith Stuyvesant Gerry
1959.3.3

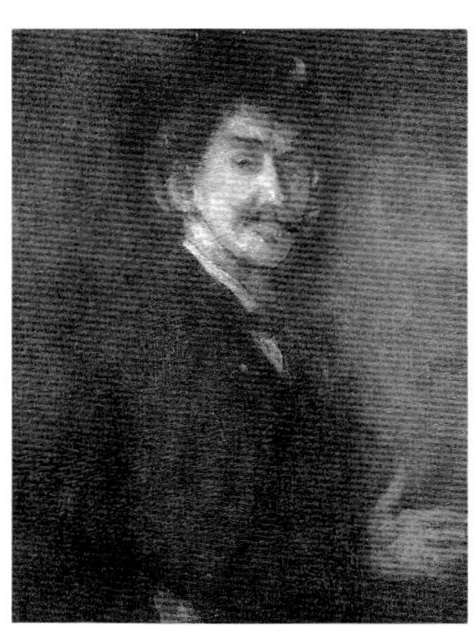

Brown and Gold: Self-Portrait, c. 1900
Canvas, 0.624 x 0.465 (24½ x 18¼)
Inscribed at center right with the artist's butterfly mark
Gift of Edith Stuyvesant Gerry
1959.3.2

IRVING R. WILES
1861–1948

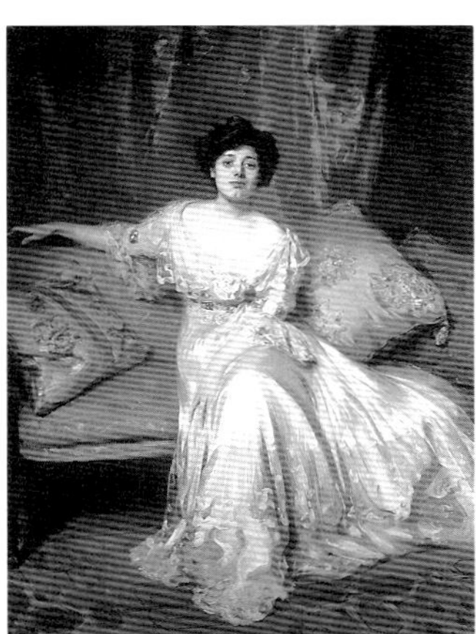

Miss Julia Marlowe, 1901
Canvas, 1.885 x 1.407 (74¼ x 55⅜)
Inscribed at upper left: *Miss Julia Marlowe / Irving R. Wiles 1901*; lower left: *copyright 1901 / by Irving Ramsay Wiles*
Gift of Julia Marlowe Sothern
1951.6.1

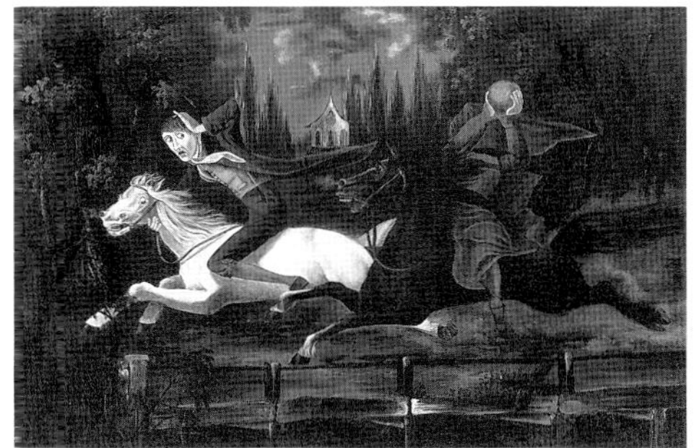

AFTER WILLIAM JOHN WILGUS

Ichabod Crane and the Headless Horseman, c. 1855
Canvas, 0.533 x 0.767 (21 x 30¼)
Gift of Edgar William and Bernice Chrysler Garbisch
1971.83.21

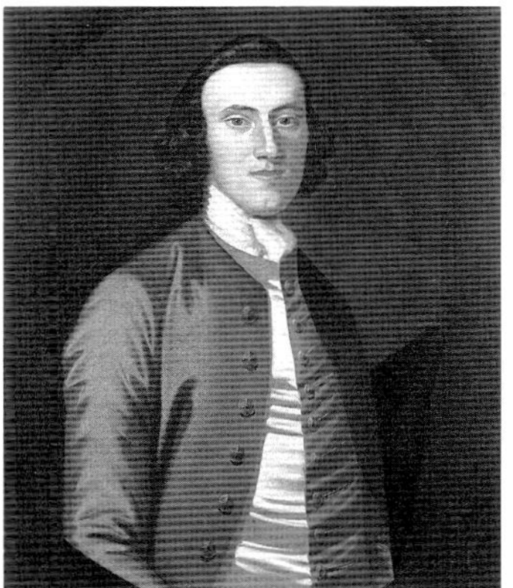

JOHN WOLLASTON
active 1742–1775

Lewis Morris (?), 1749/1752
Canvas, 0.764 x 0.634 (30 1/16 x 25)
Andrew W. Mellon Collection
1942.8.41

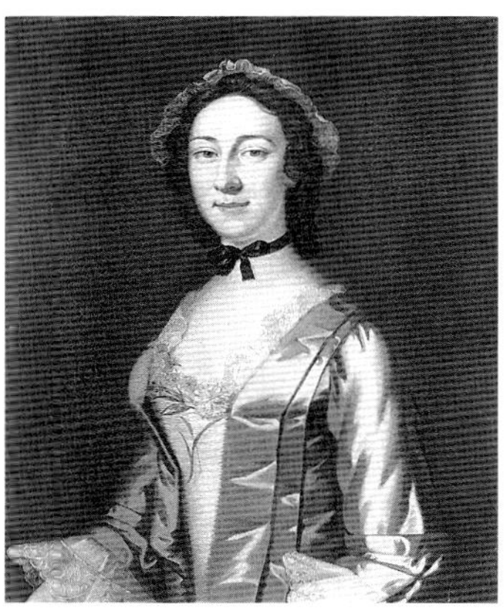

Mary Walton Morris, 1749/1752
Canvas, 0.763 x 0.635 (30 x 25)
Andrew W. Mellon Collection
1942.8.40

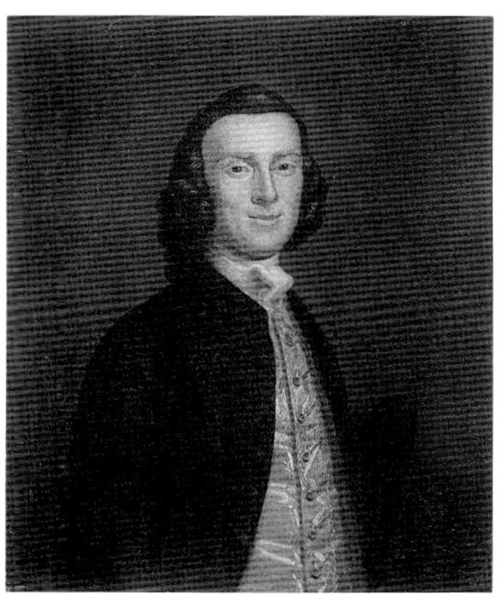

John Stevens, c. 1749/1752
Canvas, 0.765 x 0.636 (30⅛ x 25 1/16)
Andrew W. Mellon Collection
1947.17.103

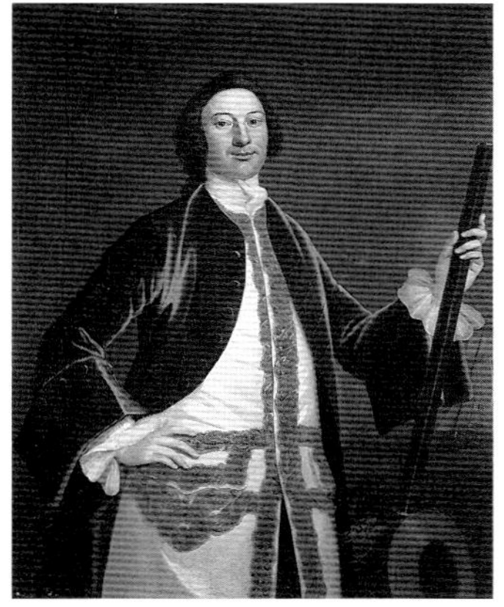

Lieutenant Archibald Kennedy (?), c. 1750
Canvas, 1.273 x 1.019 (50⅛ x 40⅛)
Andrew W. Mellon Collection
1947.17.105

GRANT WOOD
1892–1942

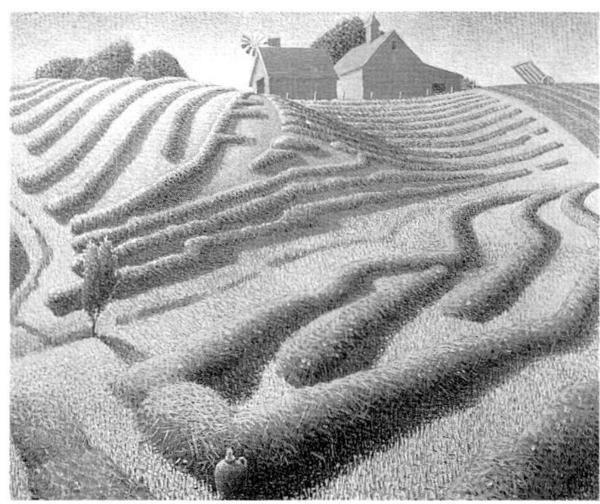

Haying, 1939
Canvas, 0.328 x 0.377 (12⅞ x 14⅞)
Inscribed at lower left: *c GRANT / WOOD / 1939*
Gift of Mr. and Mrs. Irwin Strasburger
1982.7.1

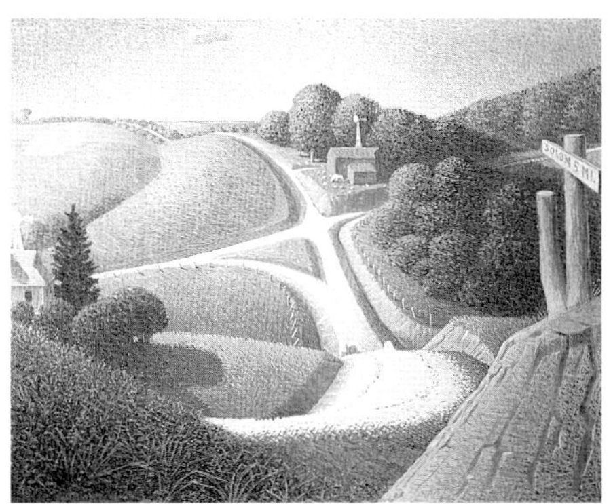

New Road, 1939
Canvas, 0.330 x 0.379 (13 x 14$^{15}/_{16}$)
Inscribed at lower left: *c GRANT WOOD 1939*
Gift of Mr. and Mrs. Irwin Strasburger
1982.7.2

ALEXANDER HELWIG WYANT
1836–1892

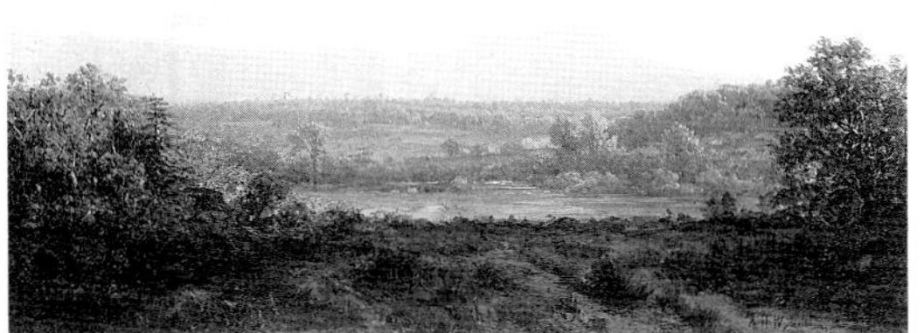

Peaceful Valley, c. 1860
Canvas, 0.177 x 0.310 (7 x 12¼)
Inscribed at lower right: *A H. Wyant*
Gift of James C. Stotlar
1965.10.1

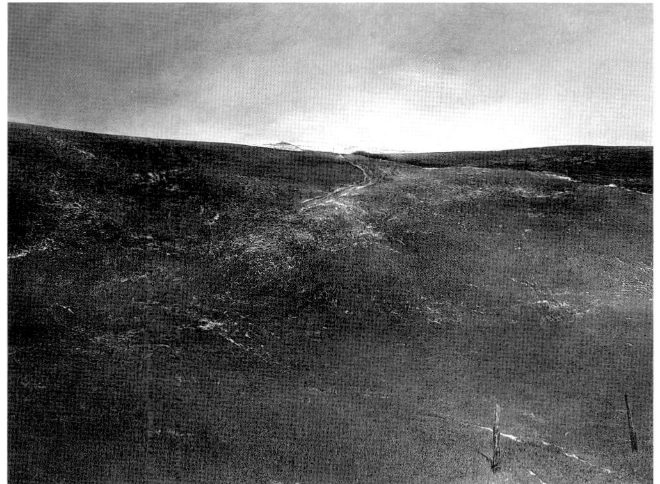

ANDREW WYETH
born 1917

Snow Flurries, 1953
Panel, 0.945 x 1.220 (37¼ x 48)
Gift of Dr. Margaret I. Handy
1977.57.1

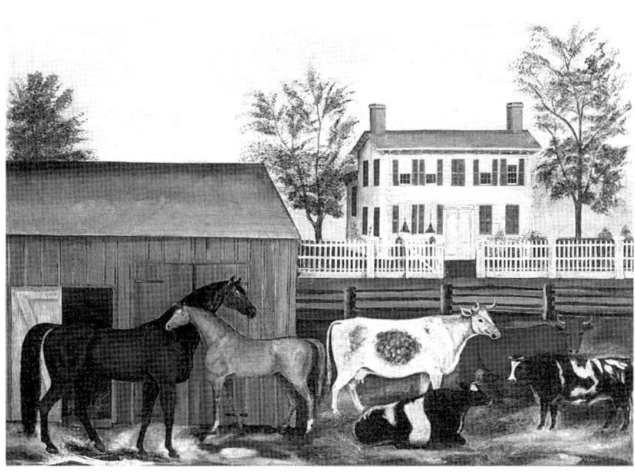

AMZI EMMONS ZELIFF
1831–1915

The Barnyard, late 19th century
Canvas, 0.616 x 0.825 (24¼ x 32½)
Inscribed at lower right: *A. E. ZELIFF*
Gift of Edgar William and Bernice Chrysler Garbisch
1955.11.1

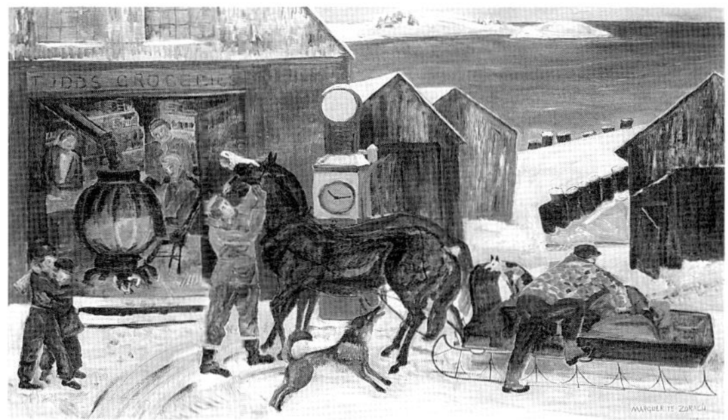

MARGUERITE ZORACH
1887–1968

Christmas Mail, 1930
Canvas, 0.633 x 1.080 (26⅛ x 42½)
Inscribed at lower right: *MARGUERITE ZORACH / 1936* [sic]
Collection of the Zorach Children
1974.13.1

Anonymous American

Works by unknown artists are arranged alphabetically by title. Entries of the same title are listed by accession number.

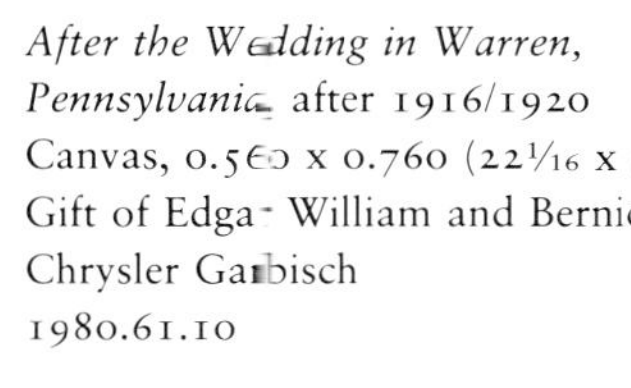

After the Wedding in Warren, Pennsylvania, after 1916/1920
Canvas, 0.560 x 0.760 (22 1/16 x 29 5/16)
Gift of Edgar William and Bernice Chrysler Garbisch
1980.61.10

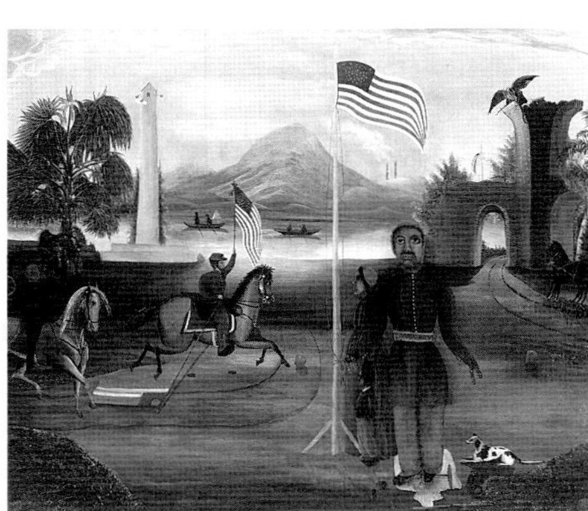

Allegory of Freedom, 1863 or after
Canvas, 0.943 x 1.092 (37 1/8 x 43)
Gift of Edgar William and Bernice Chrysler Garbisch
1955.11.4

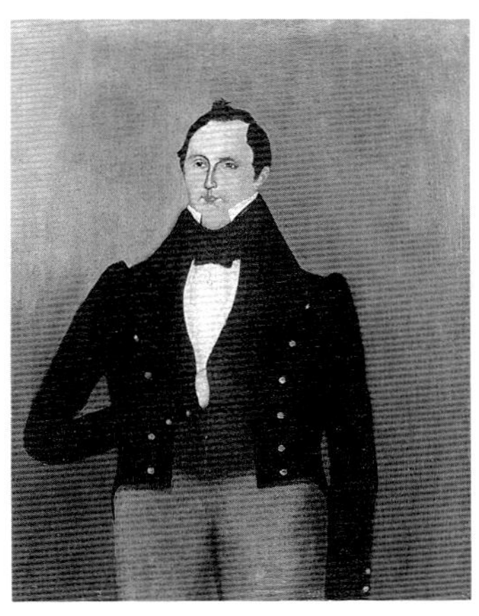

Anonymous Man, c. 1830
Wood, 0.467 x 0.360 (18 3/8 x 14 1/8)
Gift of Edgar William and Bernice Chrysler Garbisch
1953.5.84

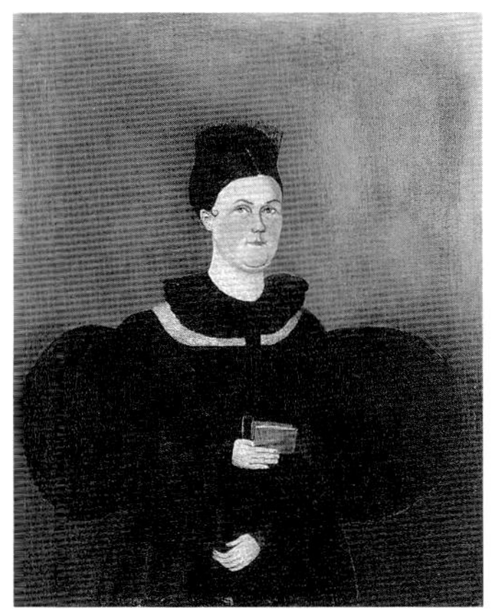

Anonymous Woman, c. 1830
Wood, 0.468 x 0.361 (18 7/16 x 14 1/2)
Gift of Edgar William and Bernice Chrysler Garbisch
1953.5.85

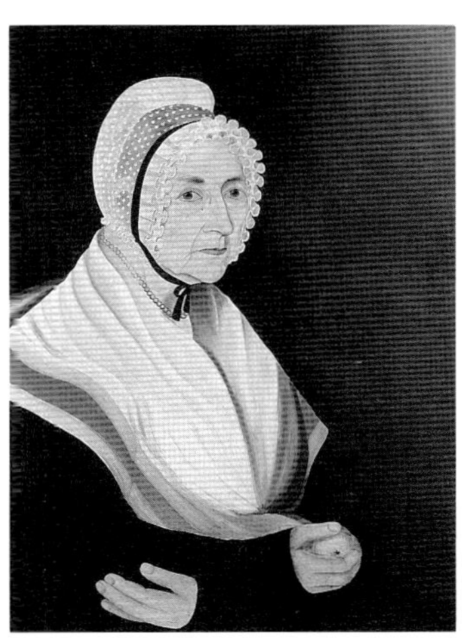

Annis Cook (?) Holding an Apple, c. 1830
Wood, 0.819 x 0.595 (32 1/4 x 23 7/16)
Gift of Edgar William and Bernice Chrysler Garbisch
1955.11.5

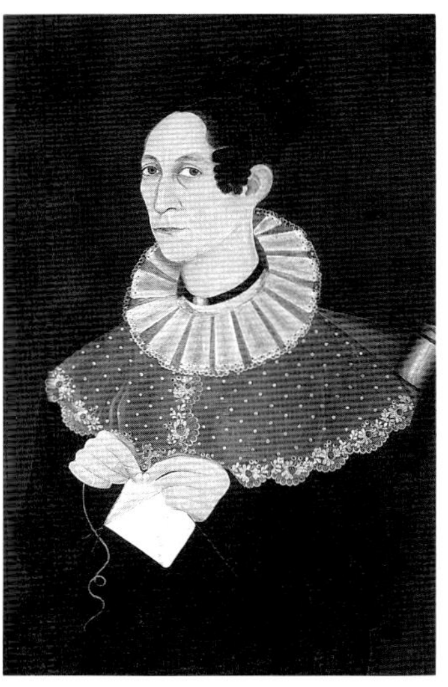

Sarah Cook Arnold (?) Knitting, c. 1830
Wood, 0.896 x 0.580 (35 5/16 x 22 13/16)
Gift of Edgar William and Bernice Chrysler Garbisch
1955.11.6

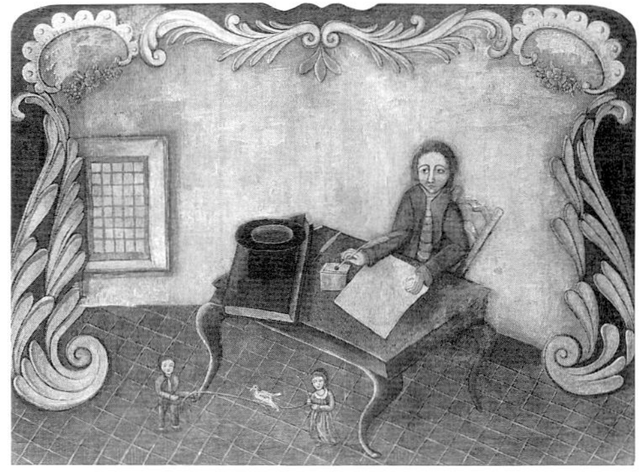

At the Writing Table, c. 1790
Canvas (fireboard), 1.013 x 1.270 (39⅞ x 50)
Gift of Edgar William and Bernice Chrysler Garbisch
1953.5.75

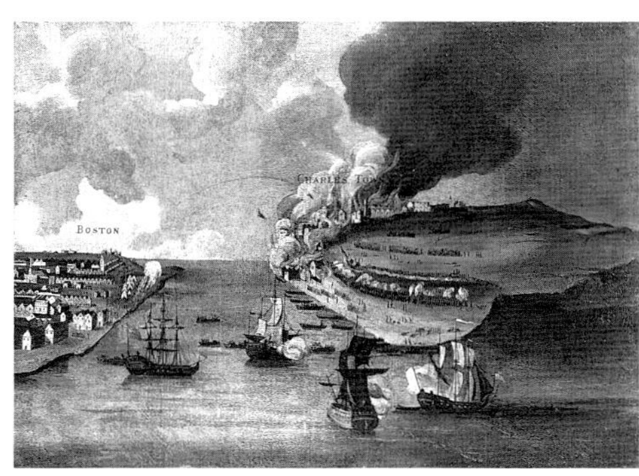

Attack on Bunker's Hill, with the Burning of Charles Town, 1783 or after
Canvas, 0.533 x 0.708 (21 x 27⅞)
Inscribed center left above horizon: *BOSTON*; upper right in flames: *CHARLES TOWN*
Gift of Edgar William and Bernice Chrysler Garbisch
1953.5.86

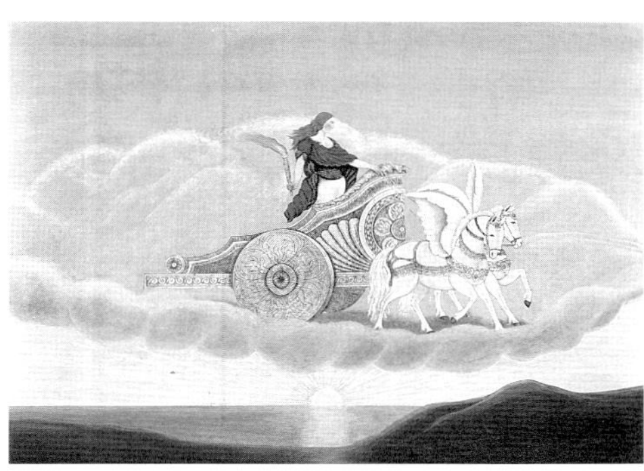

Aurora, mid-19th century
Wood, 0.610 x 0.819 (24 x 32¼)
Gift of Edgar William and Bernice Chrysler Garbisch
1957.11.7

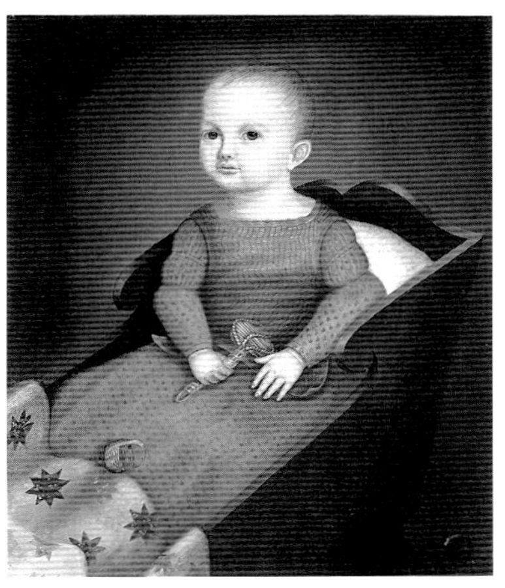

Baby in Blue Cradle, c. 1840
Canvas, 0.690 x 0.580 (27⅜ x 22 13/16)
Gift of Edgar William and Bernice Chrysler Garbisch
1959.11.3

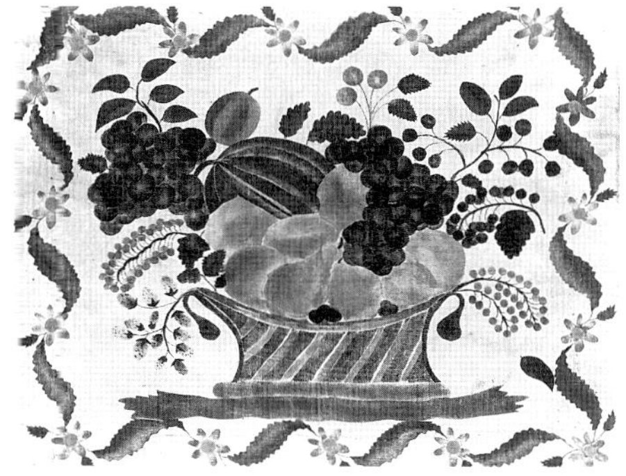

Basket of Fruit, c. 1830
Velvet, 0.400 x 0. 489 (15¾ x 19¼)
Gift of Edgar William and Bernice
Chrysler Garbisch
1953.5.103

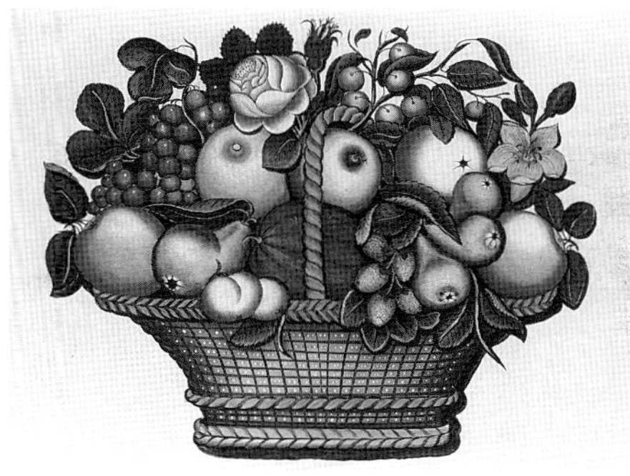

Basket of Fruit with Flowers, c. 1830
Wood, 0.351 x 0.455 (13¾ x 17⅞)
Gift of Edgar William and Bernice
Chrysler Garbisch
1980.62.43

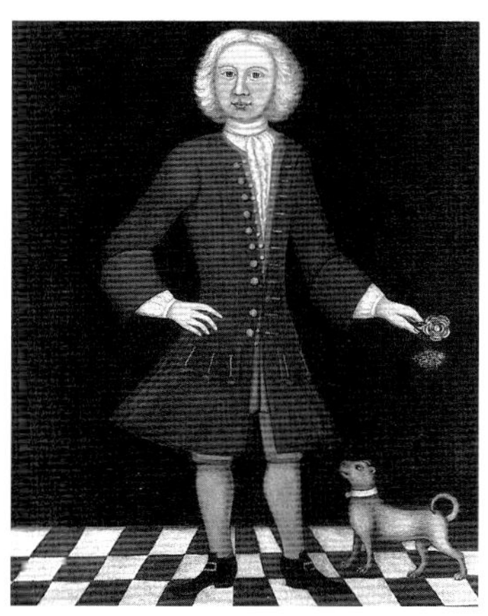

Jonathan Bentham, c. 1725
Canvas, 1.165 x 0.889 (45⅞ x 35)
Gift of Edgar William and Bernice
Chrysler Garbisch
1959.11.4

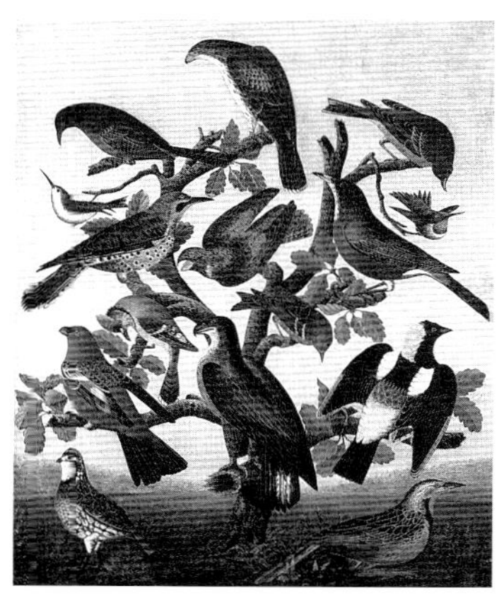

Birds, c. 1840
Canvas, 0.431 x 0.355 (17 x 14)
Gift of Edgar William and Bernice
Chrysler Garbisch
1978.80.12

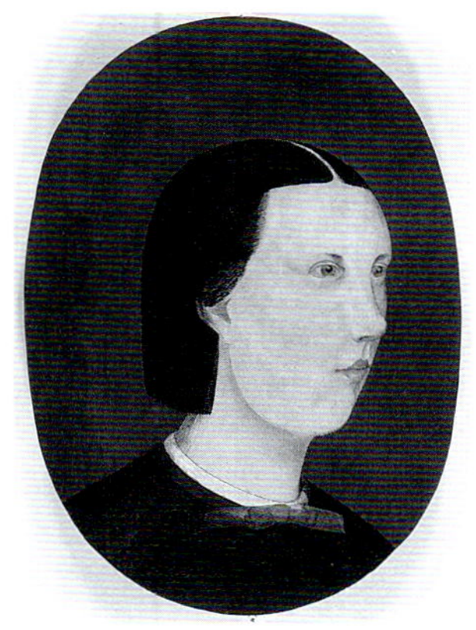

Blue Eyes, c. 1850
Wood, oval: 0.457 x 0.324 (18 x 12¾)
Gift of Edgar William and Bernice
Chrysler Garbisch
1953.5.68

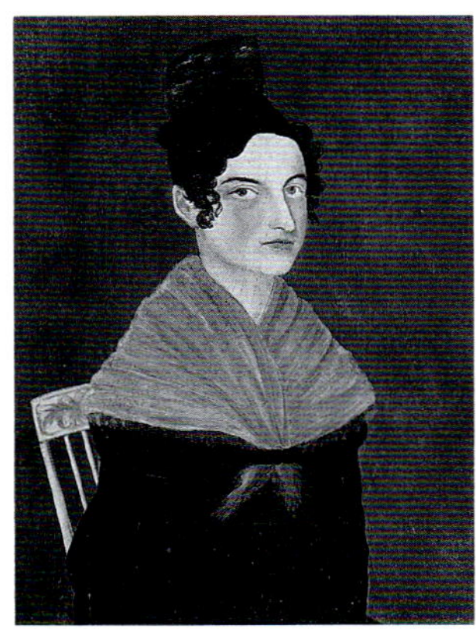

The Blue Shawl, c. 1820
Wood, 0.229 x 0.177 (9 x 6 15/16)
Gift of Edgar William and Bernice
Chrysler Garbisch
1953.5.74

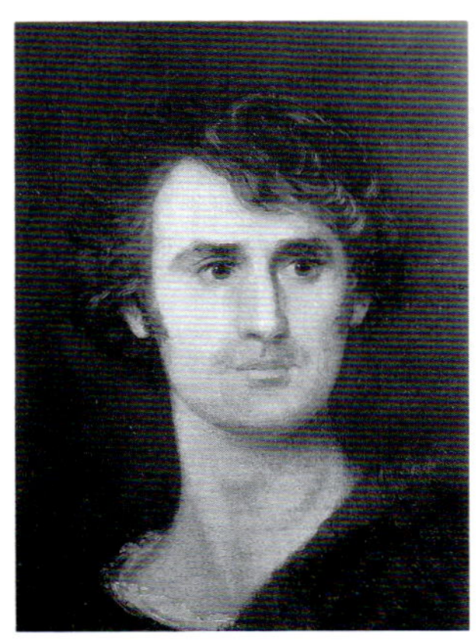

Junius Brutus Booth, c. 1830
Cardboard, 0.508 x 0.378 (20 x 14⅞)
Andrew W. Mellon Collection
1947.17.55

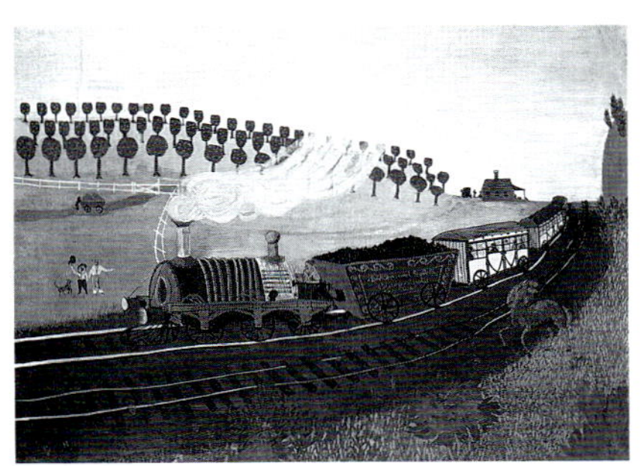

Boston and North Chungahochie Express,
after 1916/1919
Composition board, 0.472 x 0.624
(18 9/16 x 24 9/16)
Gift of Edgar William and Bernice
Chrysler Garbisch
1971.83.12

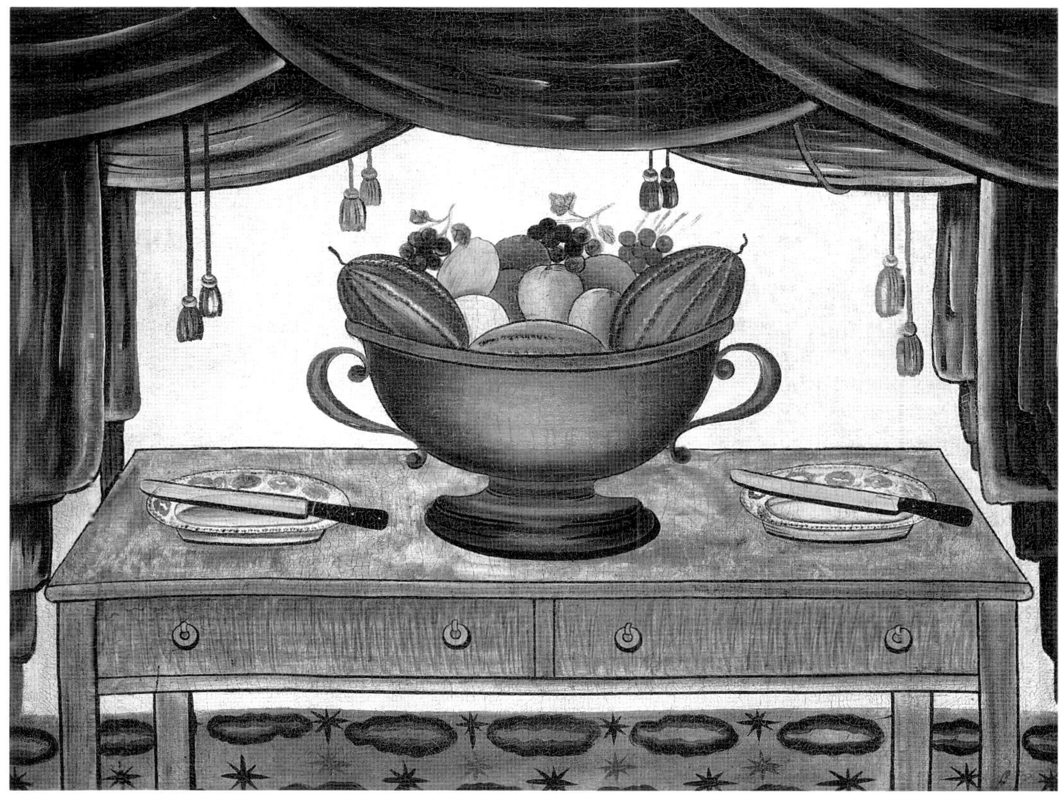

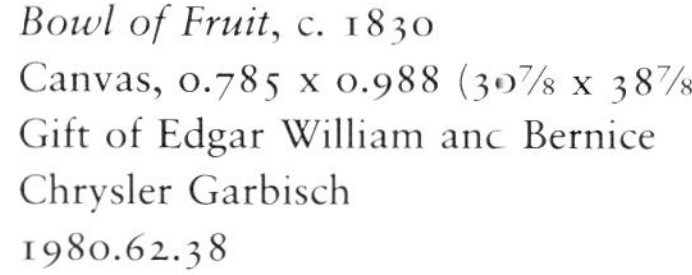

Bowl of Fruit, c. 1830
Canvas, 0.785 x 0.988 (30⅞ x 38⅞)
Gift of Edgar William and Bernice Chrysler Garbisch
1980.62.38

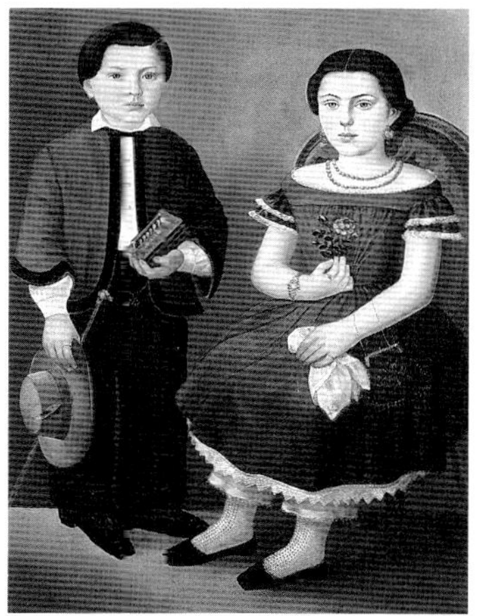

Boy and Girl, c. 1850
Canvas, 1.073 x 0.816 (42¼ x 32⅛)
Gift of Edgar William and Bernice Chrysler Garbisch
1956.13.7

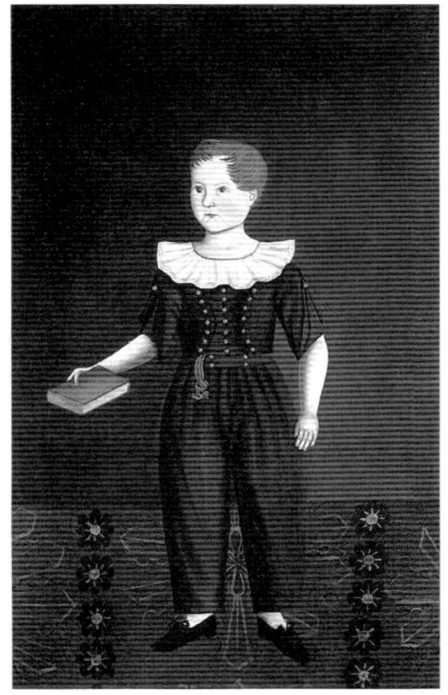

Boy in Blue, c. 1820/1830
Canvas, 1.114 x 0.705 (43⅞ x 27¾)
Gift of Edgar William and Bernice Chrysler Garbisch
1953.5.60

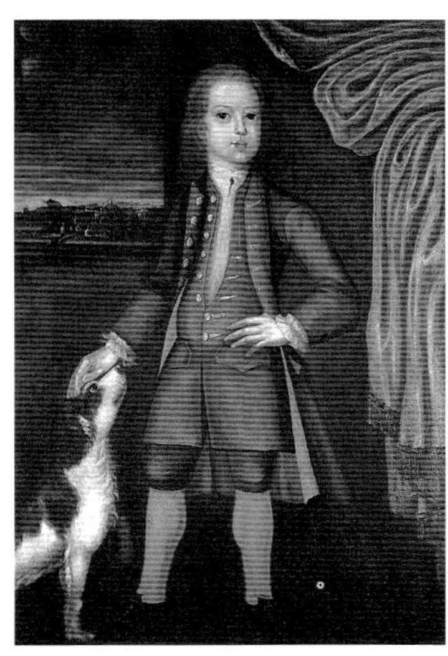

Boy in Blue Coat, c. 1730
Canvas, 1.215 x 0.835 (47¾ x 32¾)
Gift of Edgar William and Bernice Chrysler Garbisch
1959.11.5

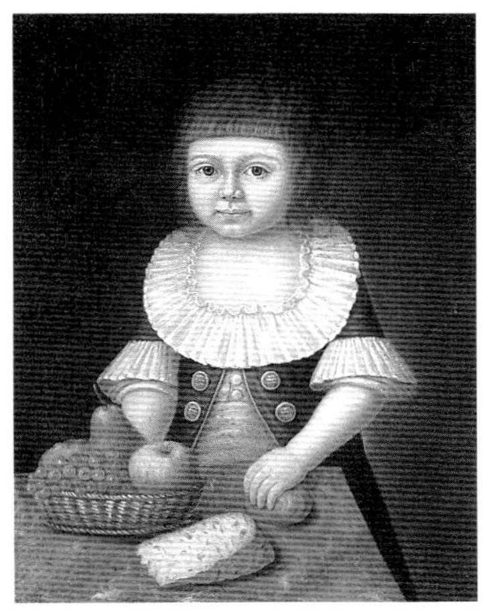

Boy with a Basket of Fruit, c. 1790
Canvas, 0.570 x 0.439 (22½ x 17¼)
Gift of Edgar William and Bernice Chrysler Garbisch
1971.83.13

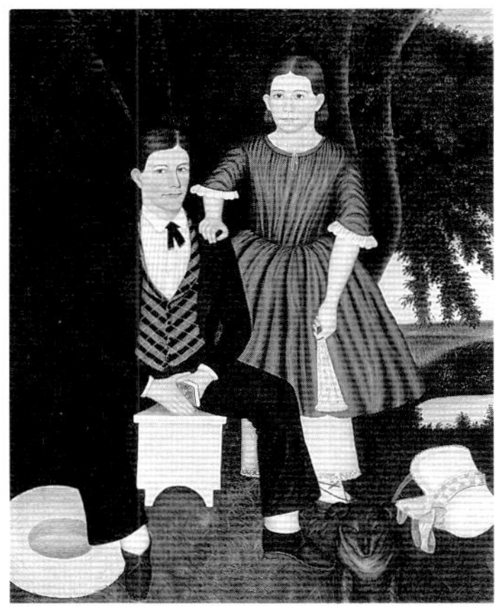

Brother and Sister, c. 1845
Canvas, 1.272 x 1.016 (50⅛ x 40)
Gift of Edgar William and Bernice Chrysler Garbisch
1953.5.61

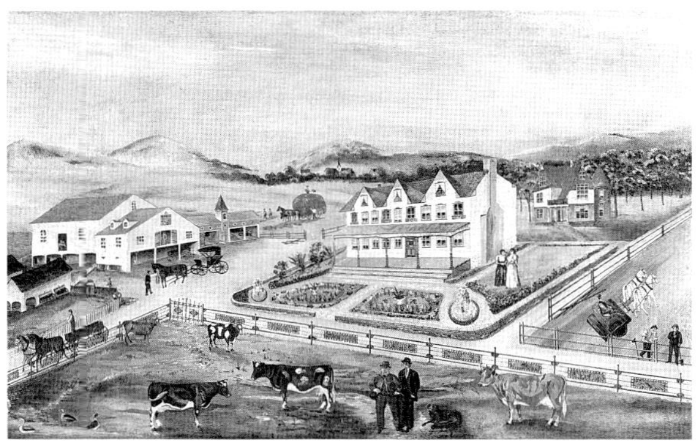

Bucks County Farm Outside Doylestown, Pennsylvania, c. 1890
Canvas, 0.670 x 0.932 (23⅞ x 36¹¹⁄₁₆)
Gift of Edgar William and Bernice Chrysler Garbisch
1980.61.6

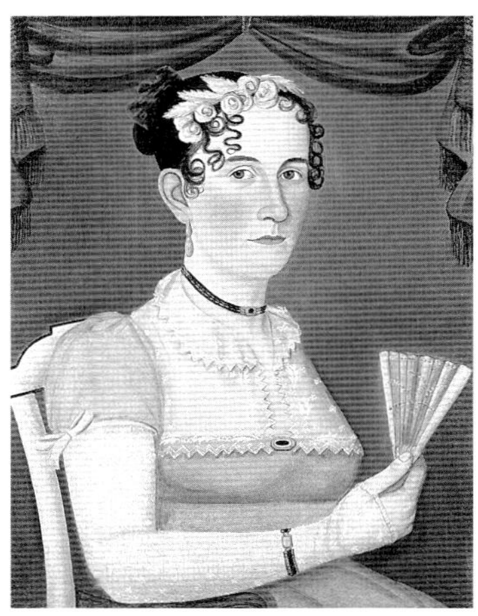

Sophia Burpee, c. 1813
Canvas, 0.562 x 0.432 (22⅛ x 17)
Gift of Edgar William and Bernice Chrysler Garbisch
1953.5.44

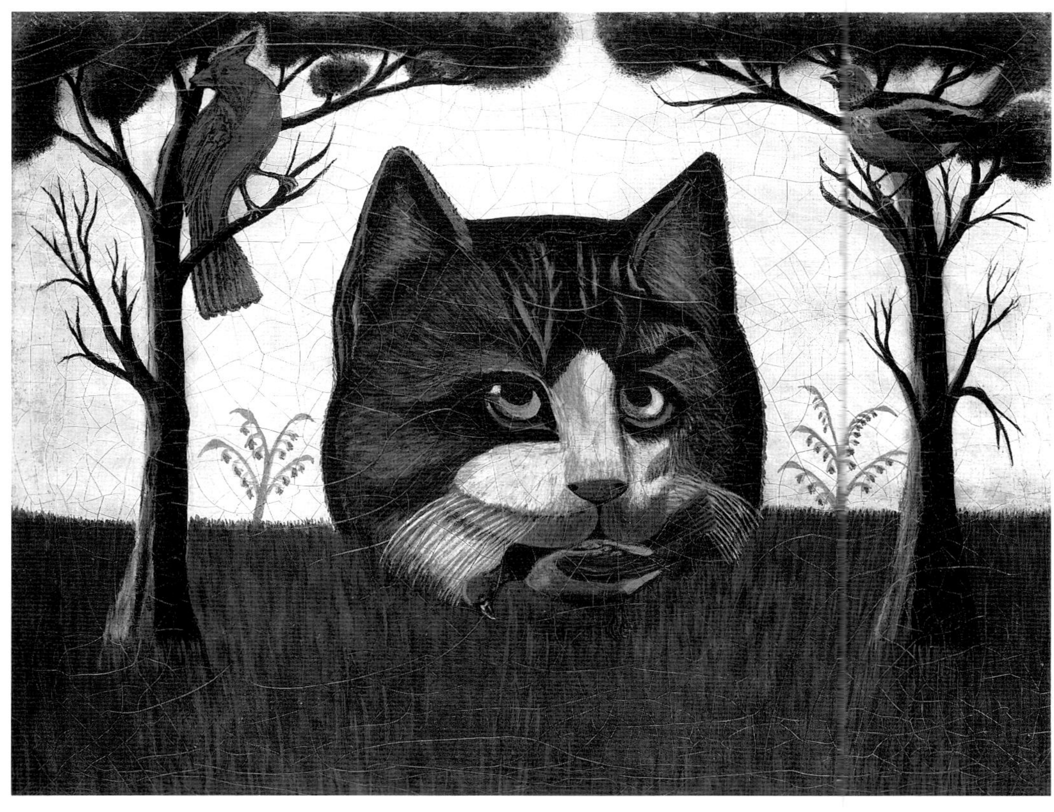

The Cat, probably second half 19th century
Canvas, 0.407 x 0.508 (16 x 20)
Gift of Edgar William and Bernice Chrysler Garbisch
1980.62.25

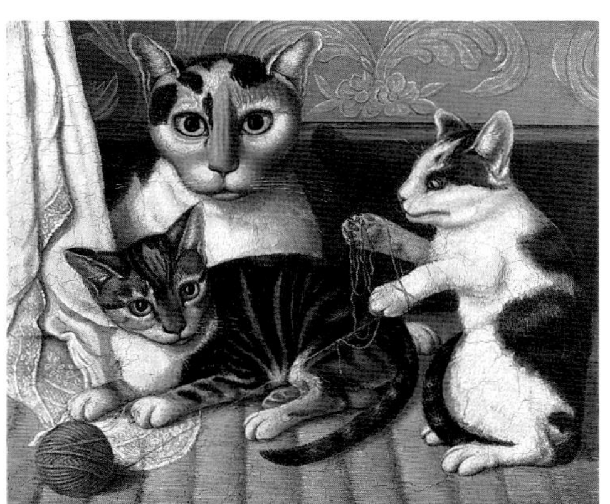

Cat and Kittens, c. 1872/1883
Millboard, 0.300 x 0.350 (11¾ x 13¾)
Gift of Edgar William and Bernice Chrysler Garbisch
1958.9.8

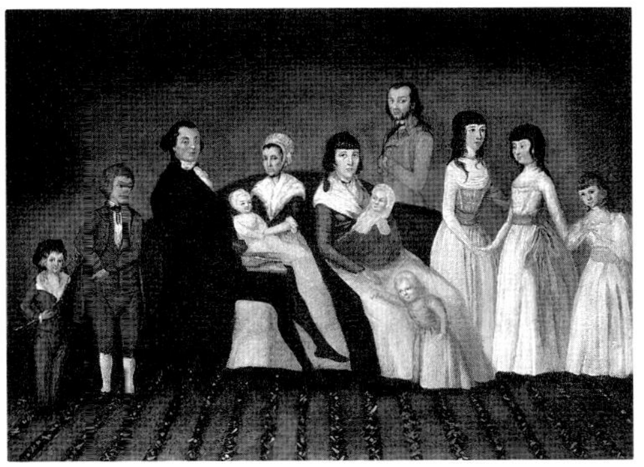

The Cheney Family, c. 1795
Canvas, 0.490 x 0.650 (19¼ x 25⅝)
Gift of Edgar William and Bernice
Chrysler Garbisch
1958.9.9

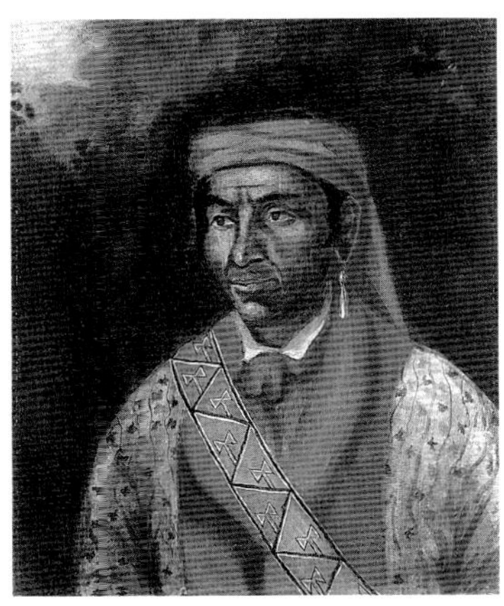

Chief Jumper of the Seminoles, possibly
1837/1838
Canvas, 0.762 x 0.629 (30 x 24¾)
Gift of Edgar William and Bernice
Chrysler Garbisch
1953.5.77

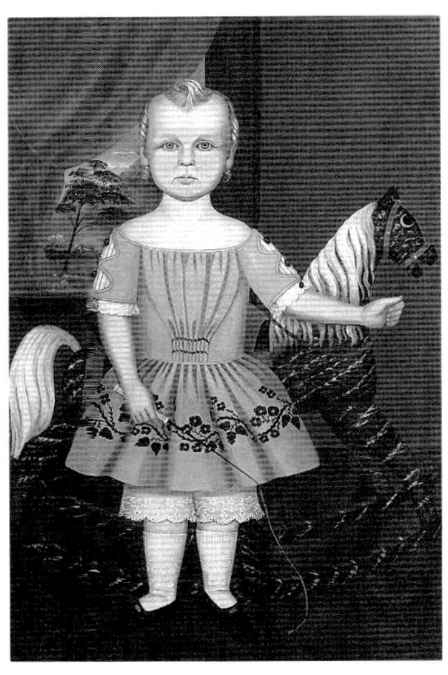

Child with Rocking Horse, c. 1850
Canvas, 1.032 x 0.686 (40⅝ x 27)
Gift of Edgar William and Bernice
Chrysler Garbisch
1959.11.6

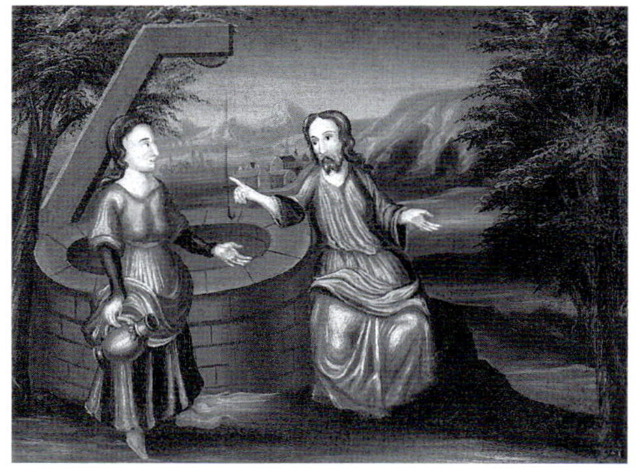

Christ and the Woman of Samaria, c. 1720/1740
Canvas, 0.515 x 0.662 (20¼ x 26⅛)
Gift of Edgar William and Bernice Chrysler Garbisch
1953.5.91

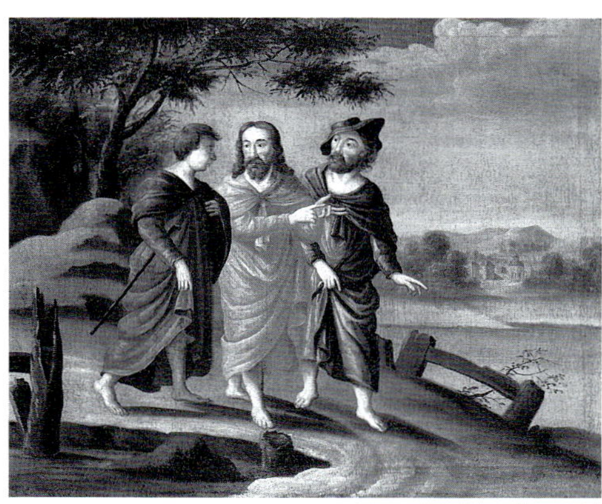

Christ on the Road to Emmaus, c. 1720/1740
Canvas, 0.642 x 0.771 (25¼ x 30⅜)
Gift of Edgar William and Bernice Chrysler Garbisch
1966.13.6

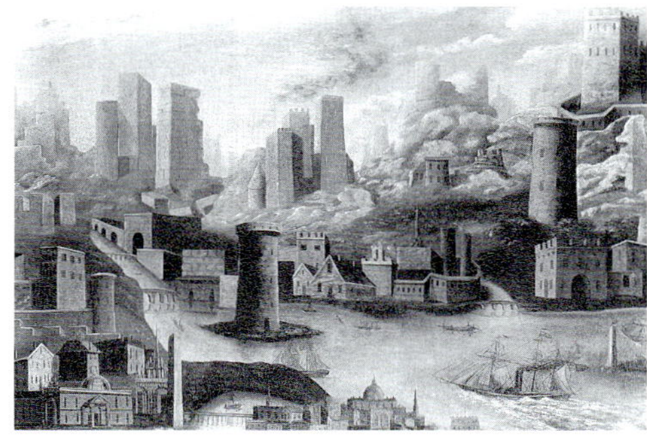

A City of Fantasy, mid-19th century
Canvas, 0.730 x 1.032 (28¾ x 40⅝)
Gift of Edgar William and Bernice Chrysler Garbisch
1967.20.3

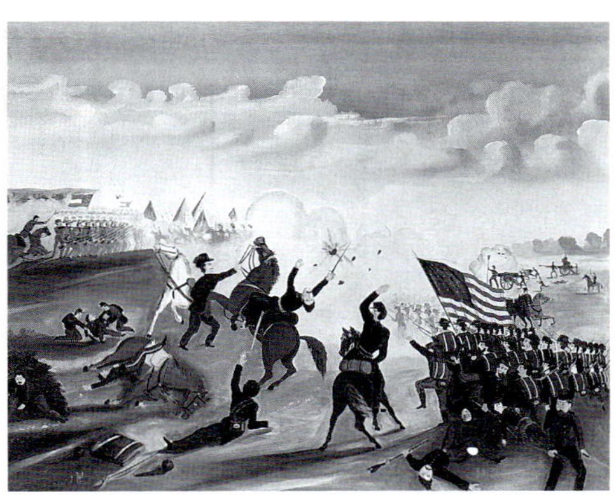

Civil War Battle, 1861 or after
Canvas, 0.917 x 1.025 (36⅛ x 44¼)
Gift of Edgar William and Bernice Chrysler Garbisch
1959.11.7

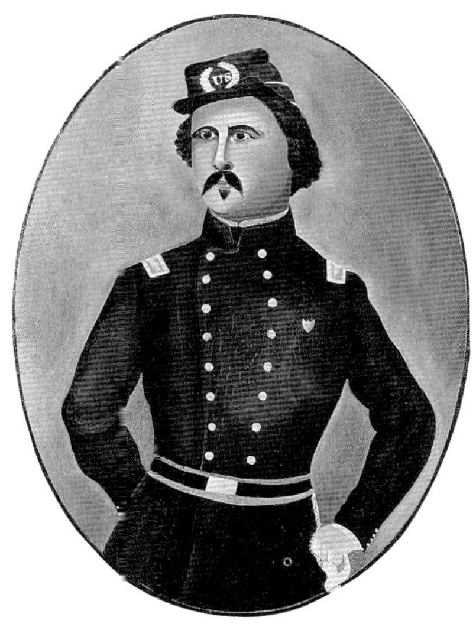

The Colonel, c. 1865
Wood, oval: 0.531 x 0.400 (20⅞ x 15¾)
Gift of Edgar William and Bernice Chrysler Garbisch
1953.5.78

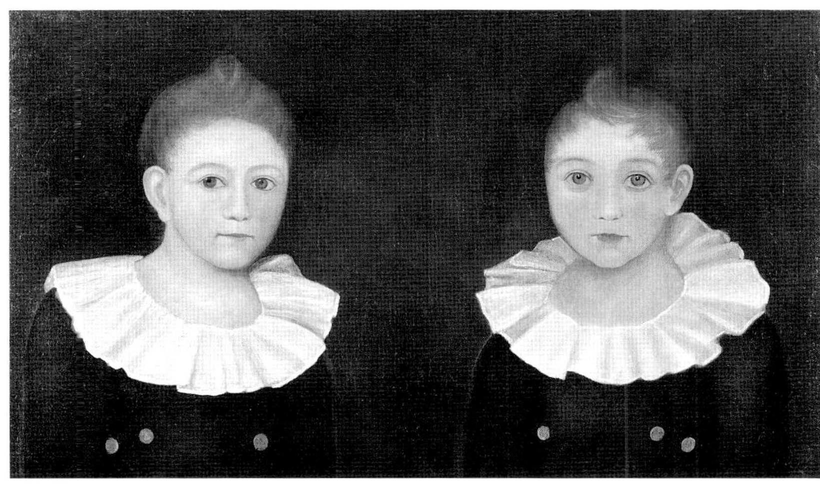

The Congdon Brothers, c. 1830
Canvas, 0.383 x 0.640 (15 x 25¼)
Gift of Edgar William and Bernice Chrysler Garbisch
1978.80.13

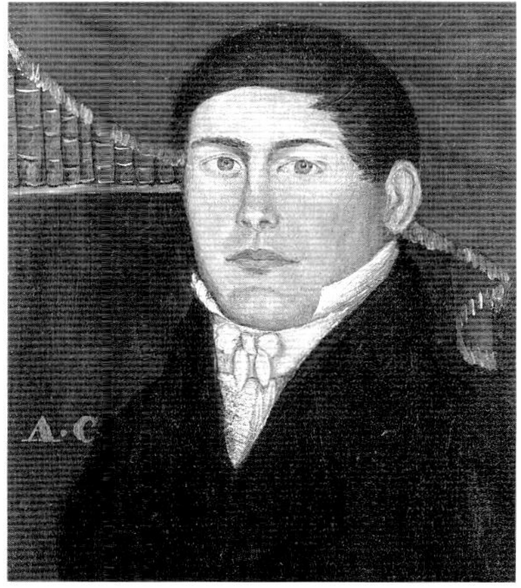

Dr. Alvah Cook, c. 1820
Wood, 0.187 x 0.157 (7 5/16 x 6 3/16)
Inscribed at lower left: *A.C*
Gift of Edgar William and Bernice Chrysler Garbisch
1955.11.21

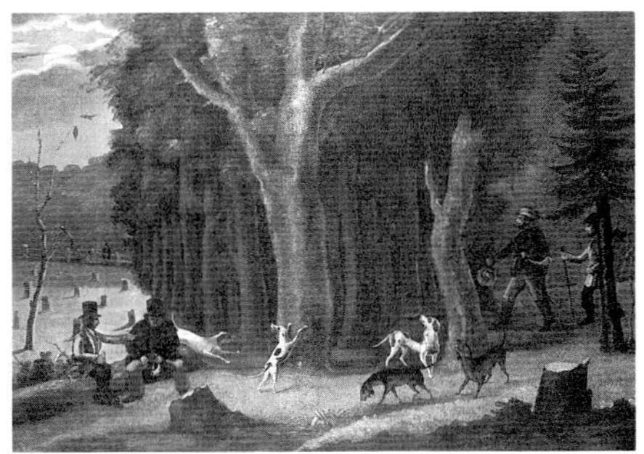

Coon Hunt, third quarter 19th century
Canvas, 0.756 x 1.007 (29 3/4 x 39 5/8)
Gift of Edgar William and Bernice Chrysler Garbisch
1953.5.97

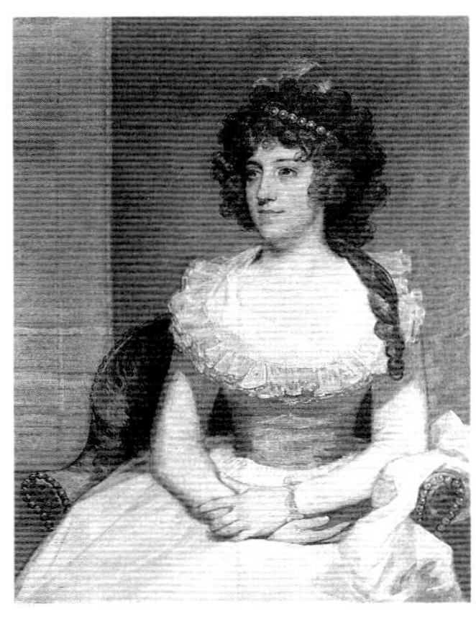

Matilda Caroline Cruger (?), late 18th or early 19th century
Canvas, 0.921 x 0.718 (36 1/4 x 28 1/4)
Andrew W. Mellon Collection
1942.8.13

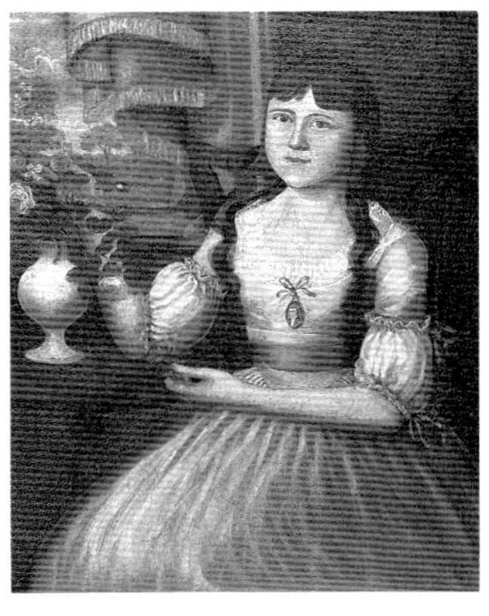

Miss Daggett of New Haven, Connecticut (possibly Amelia Martha), c. 1795
Canvas, 0.913 x 0.724 (36 1/8 x 28 1/2)
Gift of Edgar William and Bernice Chrysler Garbisch
1956.13.9

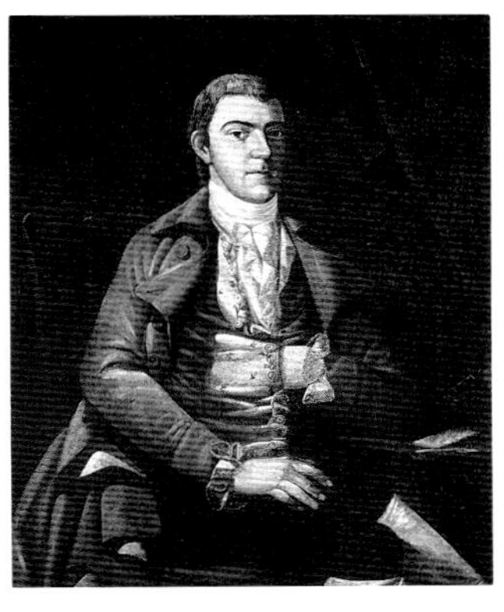

Elisha Doane, c. 1783
Canvas, 1.017 x 0.842 (40 1/16 x 33 1/8)
Chester Dale Collection
1943.1.3

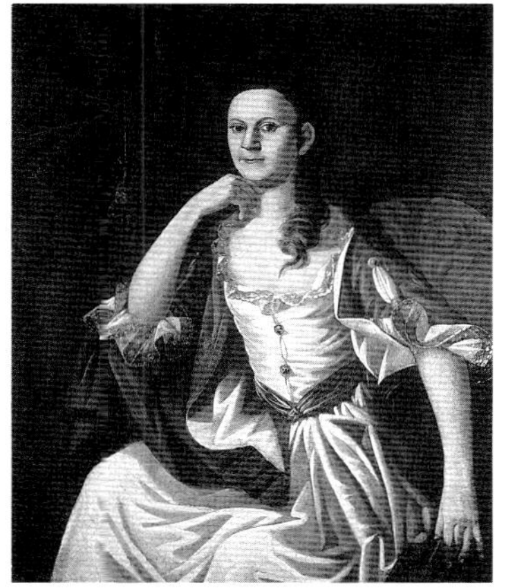

Jane Cutler Doane, c. 1783
Canvas, 1.022 x 0.835 (40¼ x 32⅞)
Chester Dale Collection
1943.1.4

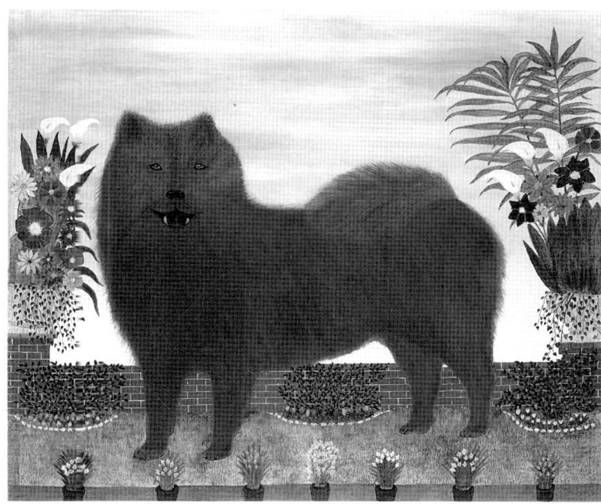

The Dog, early 20th century
Canvas, 0.895 x 1.054 (35¼ x 41½)
Gift of Edgar William and Bernice Chrysler Garbisch
1957.11.8

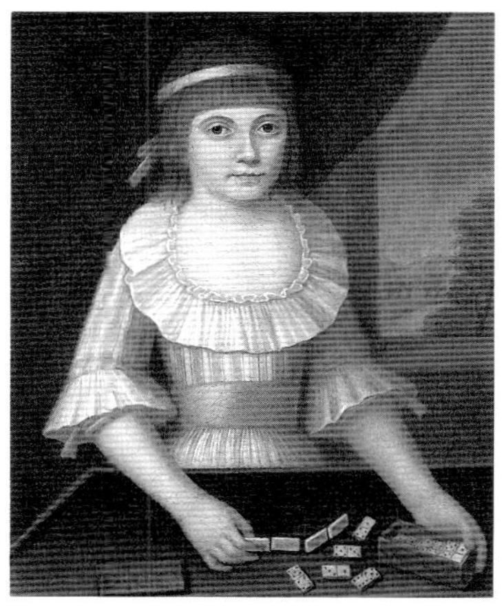

The Domino Girl, c. 1790
Canvas, 0.581 x 0.468 (22⅞ x 18⅜)
Gift of Edgar William and Bernice Chrysler Garbisch
1980.62.41

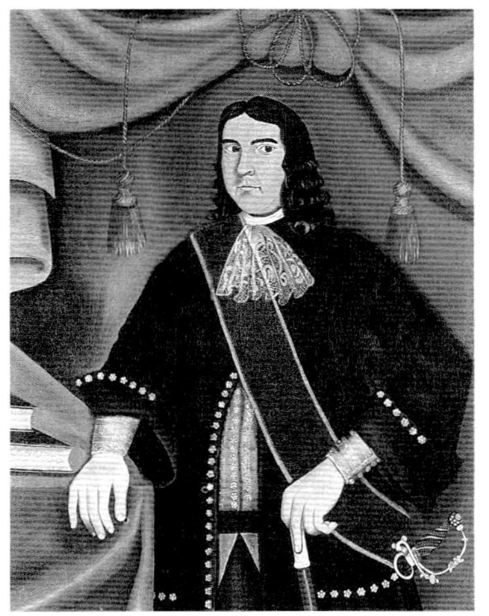

Samuel Eells, c. 1800
Canvas, 1.11[illegible] x 0.840 (43⅞ x 33⅛)
Gift of Edgar William and Bernice
Chrysler Garbisch
1971.83.15

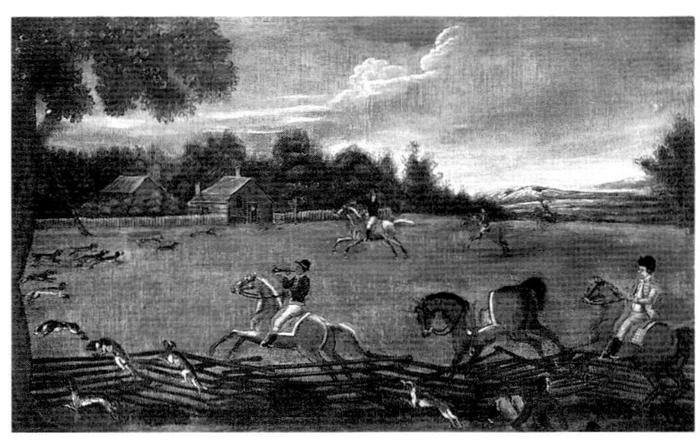

The End of the Hunt, c. 1800
Canvas, 0.876 x 1.368 (34½ x 53⅞)
Gift of Edgar William and Bernice
Chrysler Garbisch
1953.5.99

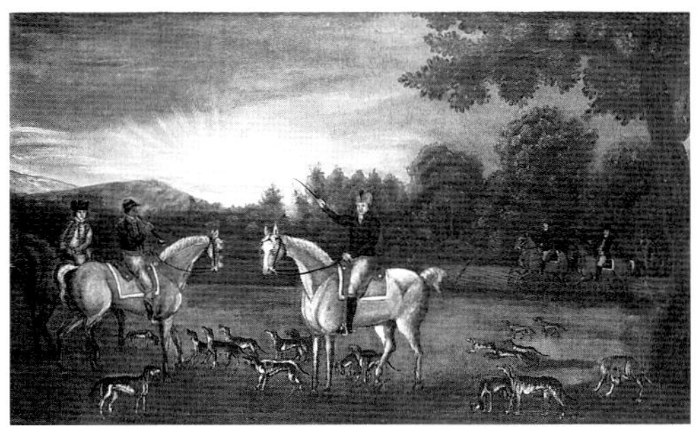

The Start of the Hunt, c. 1800
Canvas, 0.881 x 1.391 (34 11/16 x 54¾)
Gift of Edgar William and Bernice
Chrysler Garbisch
1953.5.98

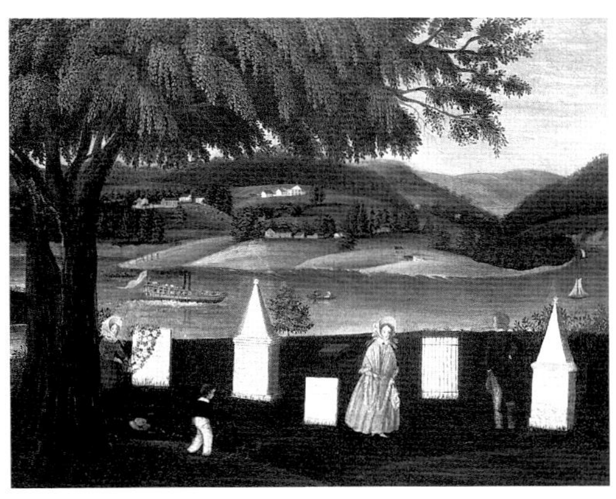

Family Burying Ground, c. 1835
Canvas, 0.5[illegible]0 x 0.610 (19¾ x 24)
Gift of Edgar William and Bernice
Chrysler Garbisch
1958.9.10

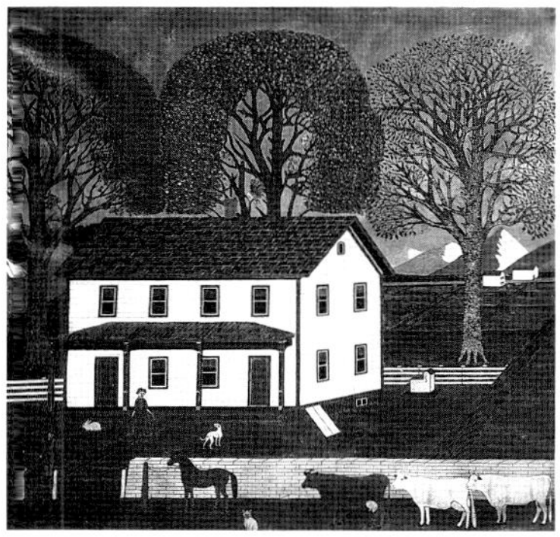

Farmhouse in Mahantango Valley, late 19th century
Canvas, 0.750 x 0.720 (29½ x 28¼)
Gift of Edgar William and Bernice Chrysler Garbisch
1953.5.94

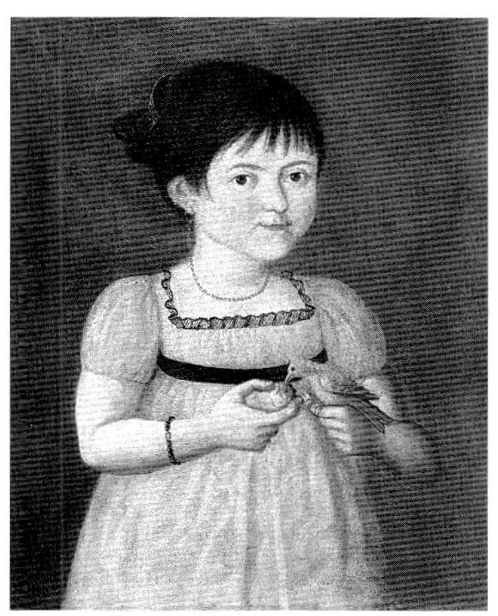

Feeding the Bird, c. 1800
Canvas, 0.560 x 0.432 (22$^{1}/_{16}$ x 17)
Gift of Edgar William and Bernice Chrysler Garbisch
1953.5.63

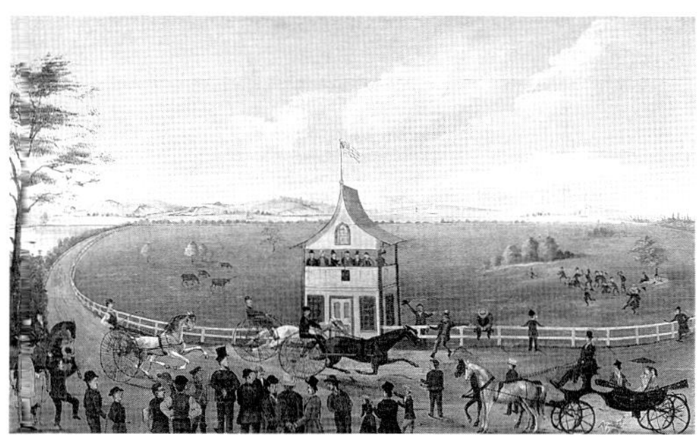

The Finish, c. 1860
Wood, support: 0.658 x 0 958 (25⅞ x 37⅝); painted surface: 0.587 x 0.952 (23⅛ x 37½)
Gift of Edgar William and Bernice Chrysler Garbisch
1980.61.9

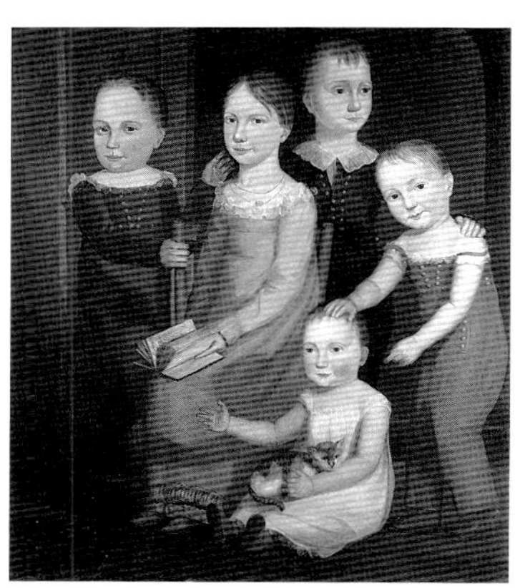

Five Children of the Budd Family, c. 1818
Canvas, 1.210 x 1.064 (47$^{11}/_{16}$ x 41⅞)
Gift of Edgar William and Bernice Chrysler Garbisch
1959.11.8

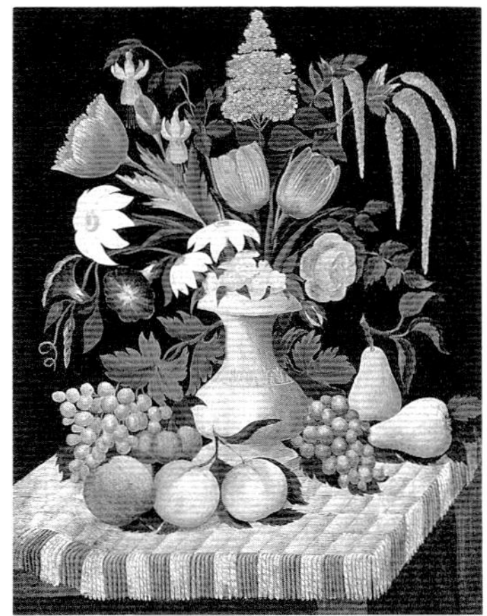

Flowers and Fruit, c. 1870
Canvas, picture surface: 0.755 x 0.560 (29 11/16 x 22
Gift of Edgar William and Bernice Chrysler Garbisch
1953.5.101

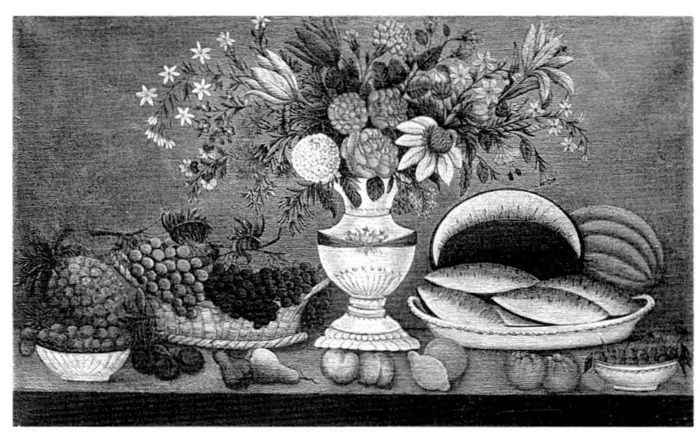

Fruit and Flowers, mid-19th century
Canvas, 0.670 x 1.050 (26 3/8 x 41 3/8)
Gift of Edgar William and Bernice Chrysler Garbisch
1966.13.7

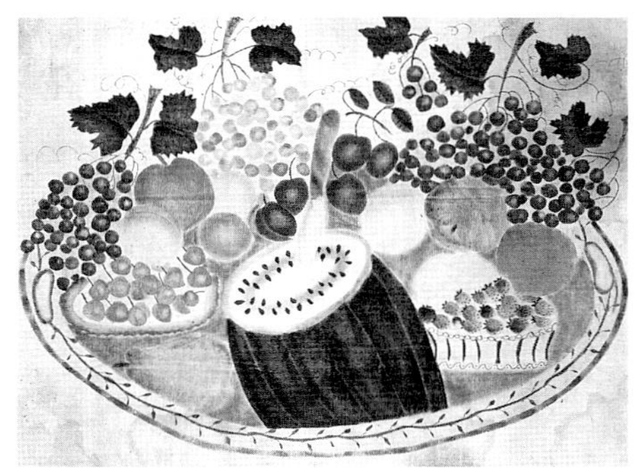

Fruit on a Tray, c. 1840
Velvet, 0.425 x 0.540 (16 3/4 x 21 1/4)
Gift of Edgar William and Bernice Chrysler Garbisch
1953.5.104

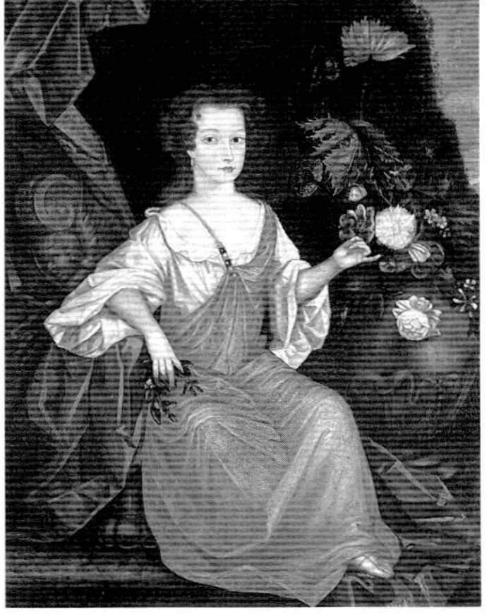

Full-length Portrait of Young Woman with Brown Hair—Bare Left Foot, c. 1710
Canvas, 1.373 x 1.046 (54 1/16 x 41 3/16)
Gift of Edgar William and Bernice Chrysler Garbisch
1980.62.40

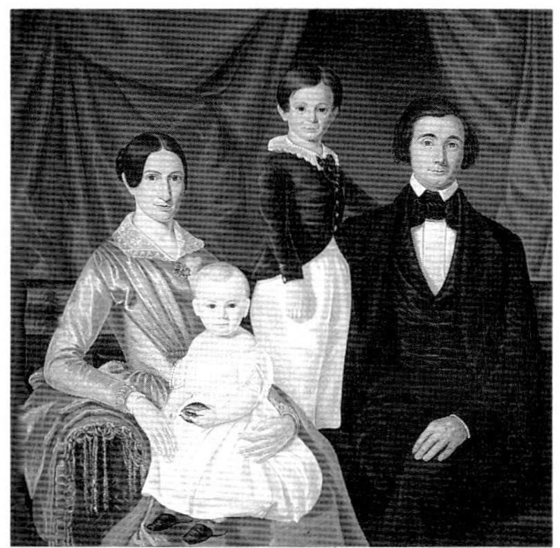

The Gage Family, 1846
Canvas, 1.370 x 1.374 (54 x 54⅛)
Gift of Edgar William and Bernice Chrysler Garbisch
1980.61.2

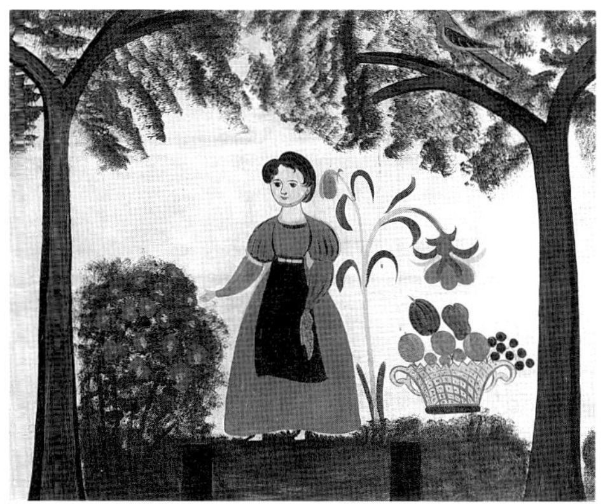

Girl in Red with Flowers and a Distelfink, c. 1830
Wood (fireboard), 0.930 x 1.080 (36⅝ x 42½)
Gift of Edgar William and Bernice Chrysler Garbisch
1978.80.14

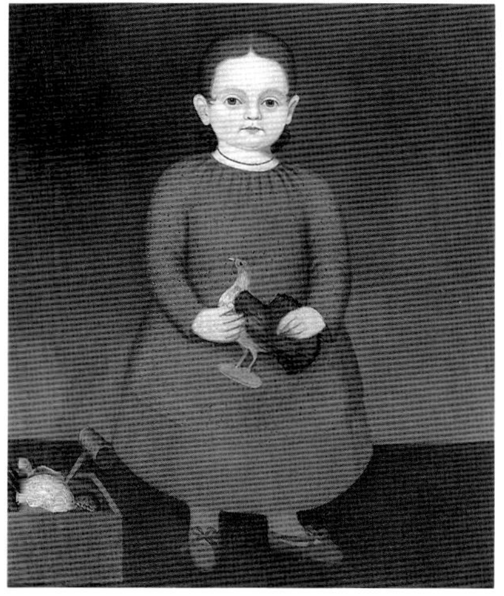

Girl with Toy Rooster, c. 1840
Canvas, 0.765 x 0.638 (30⅛ x 25⅛)
Gift of Edgar William and Bernice Chrysler Garbisch
1953.5.71

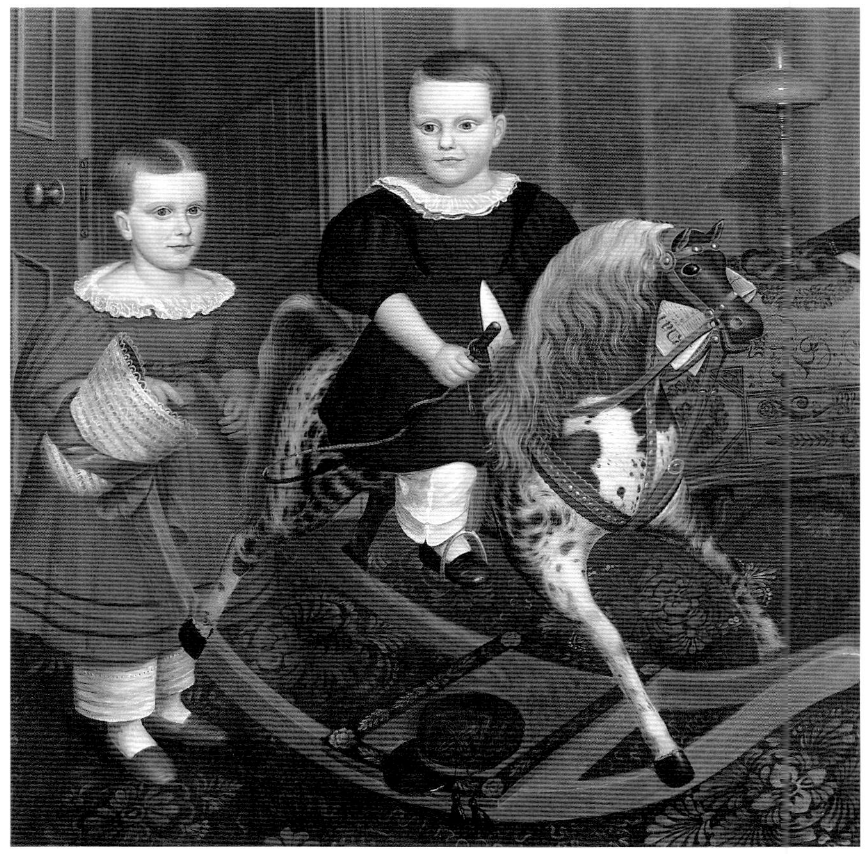

The Hobby Horse, c. 1850
Canvas, 1.035 x 1.016 (40¾ x 40)
Gift of Edgar William and Bernice Chrysler Garbisch
1955.11.23

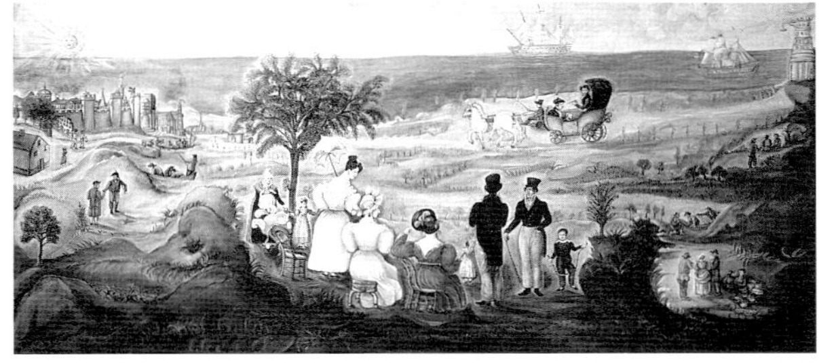

Horizon of the New World, c. 1830
Canvas, 0.775 x 1.676 (30½ x 66)
Gift of Edgar William and Bernice Chrysler Garbisch
1980.62.29

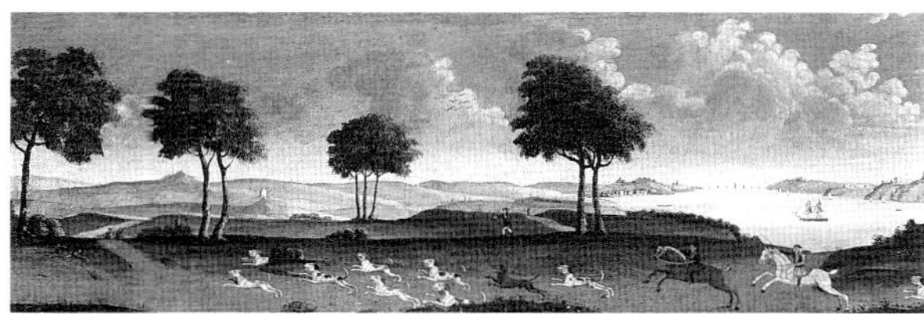

Hunting Scene with a Harbor, 18th century
Canvas, 0.490 x 1.408 (19 5/16 x 57 7/16)
Ailsa Mellon Bruce Collection
1970.17.103

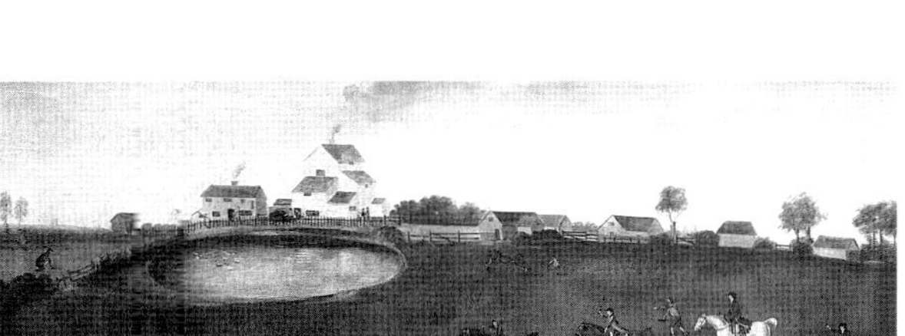

Hunting Scene with a Pond, 18th century
Canvas, 0.658 x 1.274 (25 7/8 x 50 1/8)
Ailsa Mellon Bruce Collection
1970.17.102

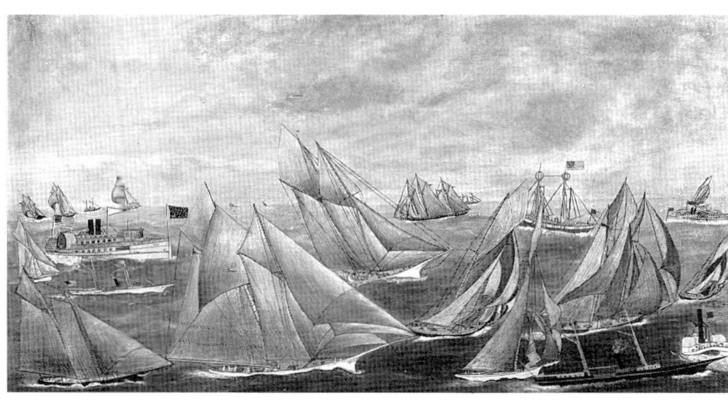

Imaginary Regatta of America's Cup Winners, 1889 or after
Canvas, 0.678 x 1.190 (26 5/8 x 46 7/8)
Gift of Edgar William and Bernice Chrysler Garbisch
1953.5.90

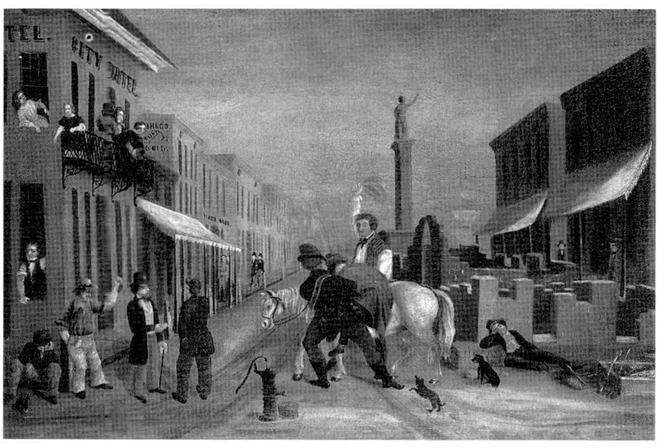

The Independent Voter, 1849 or after
Canvas, 0.904 x 1.315 (35 5/8 x 51 3/4)
Gift of Edgar William and Bernice Chrysler Garbisch
1980.61.8

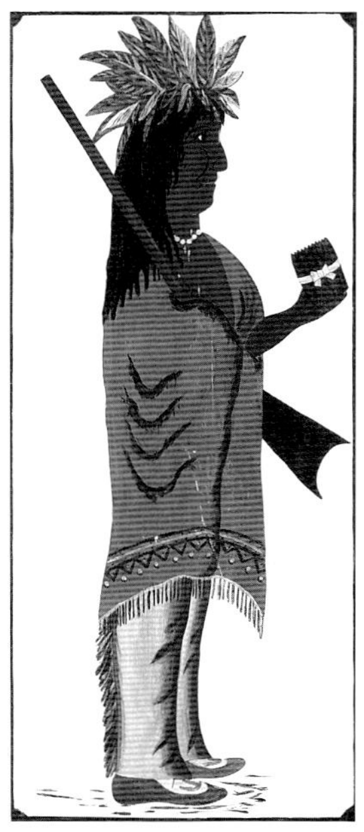

Indian Tobacco Shop Sign, second half 19th century
Wood, 1.364 x 0.578 (53 11/16 x 22 3/4)
Gift of Edgar William and Bernice Chrysler Garbisch
1980.62.33

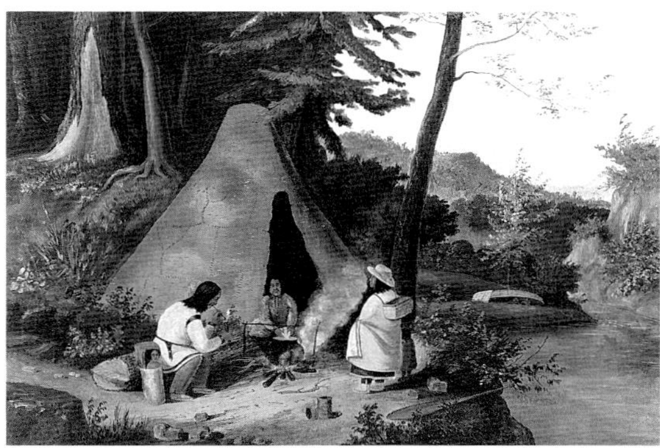

Indians Cooking Maize, second half 19th century
Canvas, 0.457 x 0.660 (18 x 26)
Gift of Edgar William and Bernice Chrysler Garbisch
1971.83.16

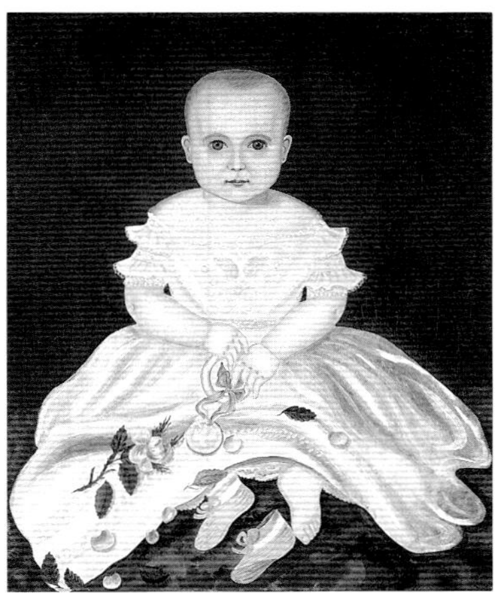

"*Innocence,*" c. 1830
Canvas, 0.690 x 0.566 (27 1/8 x 22 1/4)
Gift of Edgar William and Bernice Chrysler Garbisch
1980.62.30

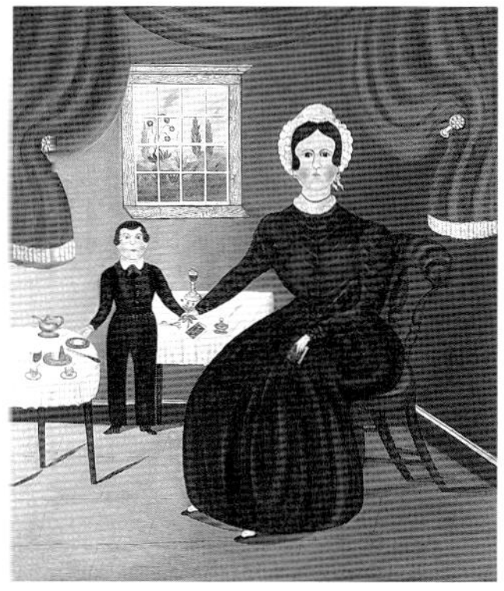

Interior Scene, c. 1840
Canvas, 0.711 x 0.600 (28 x 23⅝)
Gift of Edgar William and Bernice
Chrysler Garbisch
1980.61.12

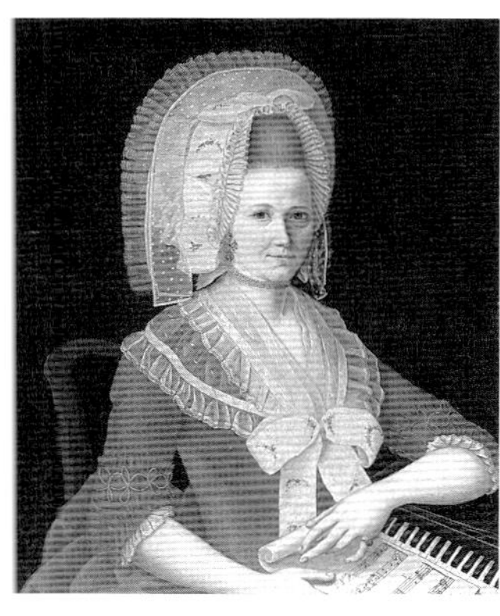

Lady Wearing Large White Cap, c. 1780
Canvas, 0.765 x 0.650 (30⅛ x 25⅝)
Gift of Edgar William and Bernice
Chrysler Garbisch
1980.62.45

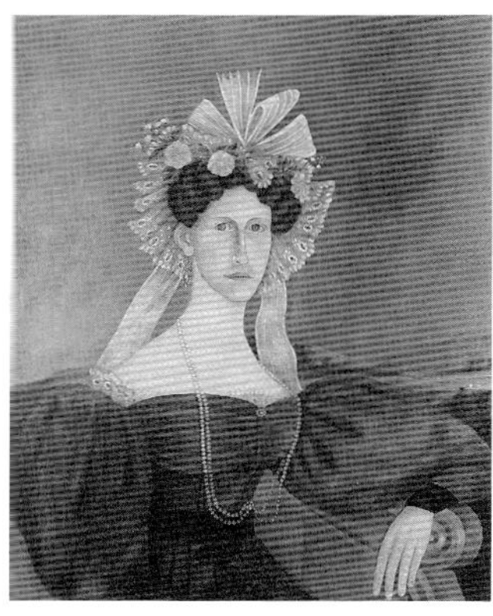

Lady Wearing Pearls, c. 1830
Canvas, 0.889 x 0.711 (35 x 28)
Gift of Edgar William and Bernice
Chrysler Garbisch
1953.5.73

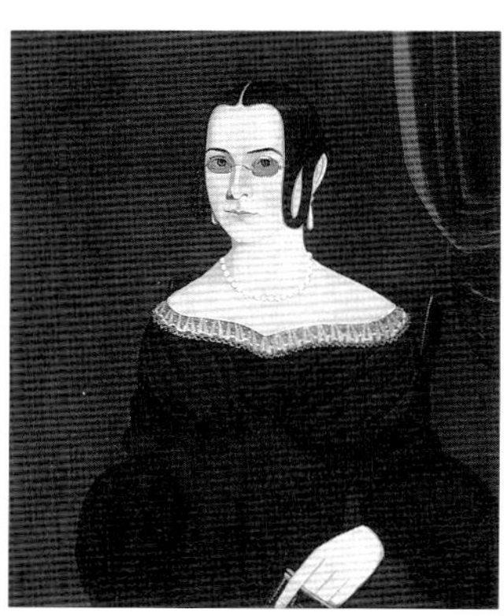

Lady Wearing Spectacles, c. 1840
Canvas, 0.769 x 0.639 (30¼ x 25¼)
Gift of Edgar William and Bernice
Chrysler Garbisch
1978.80.15

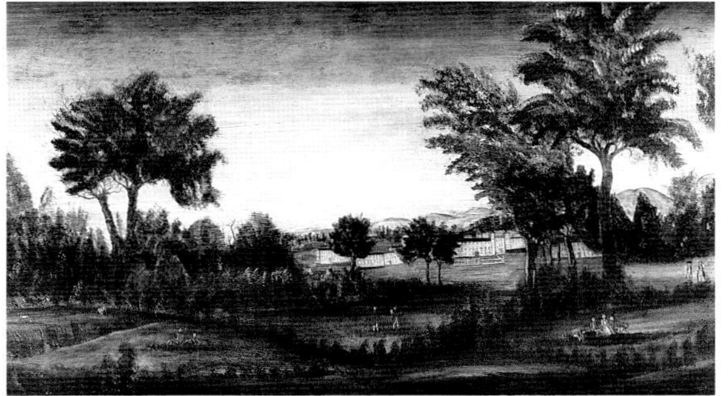

Landscape with Buildings, fourth quarter 18th century
Wood, 0.690 x 1.163 (27⅛ x 45¾)
Gift of Edgar William and Bernice Chrysler Garbisch
1956.13.10

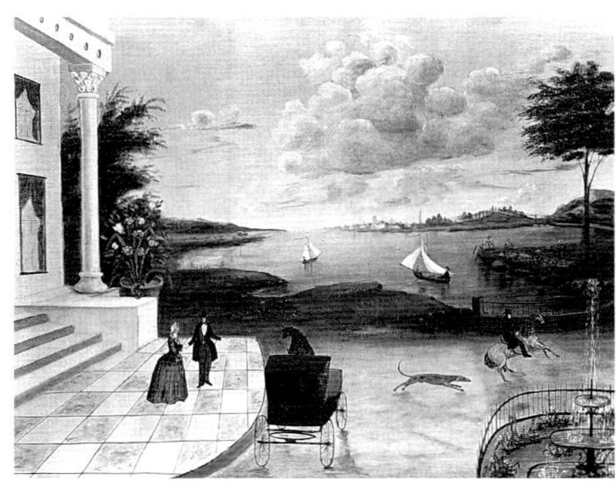

Leaving the Manor House, c. 1850/1855
Canvas, 0.68[illegible] x 0.867 (27 x 34⅛)
Gift of Edgar William and Bernice Chrysler Garbisch
1959.11.10

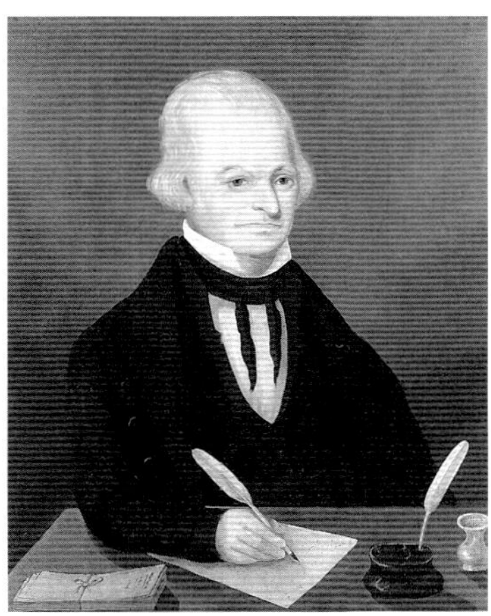

The Letter, c. 1825
Canvas, 0.920 x 0.735 (36¼ x 28⅞)
Gift of Edgar William and Bernice Chrysler Garbisch
1953.5.79

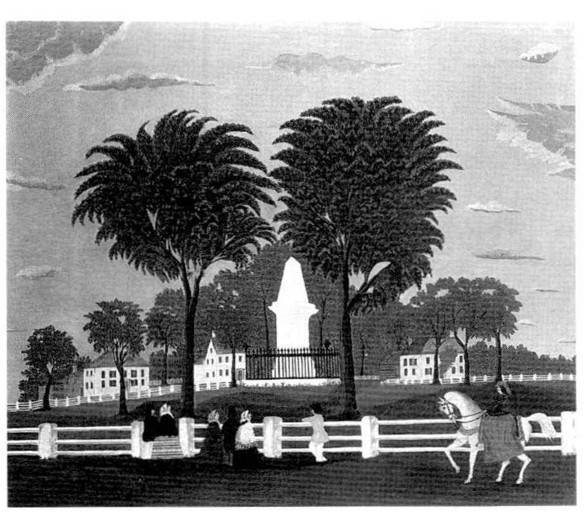

Lexington Battle Monument, 1853 or after
Canvas, 0.704 x 0.781 (27¾ x 30¾)
Gift of Edgar William and Bernice Chrysler Garbisch
1953.5.88

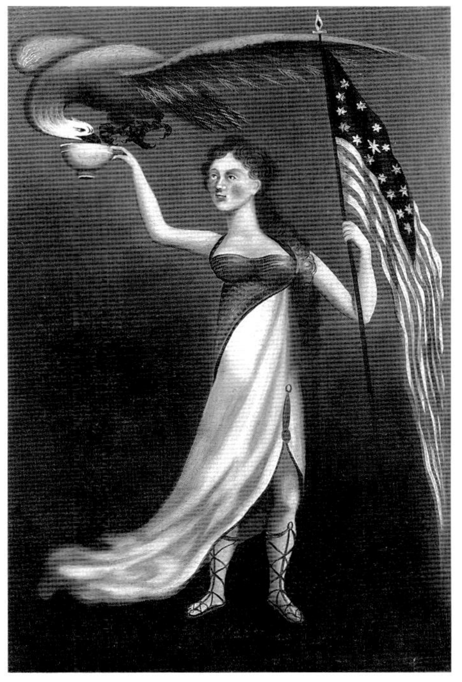

Liberty, c. 1800/1820
Canvas, 0.759 x 0.509 (29⅞ x 20$\frac{1}{16}$)
Gift of Edgar William and Bernice Chrysler Garbisch
1955.11.13

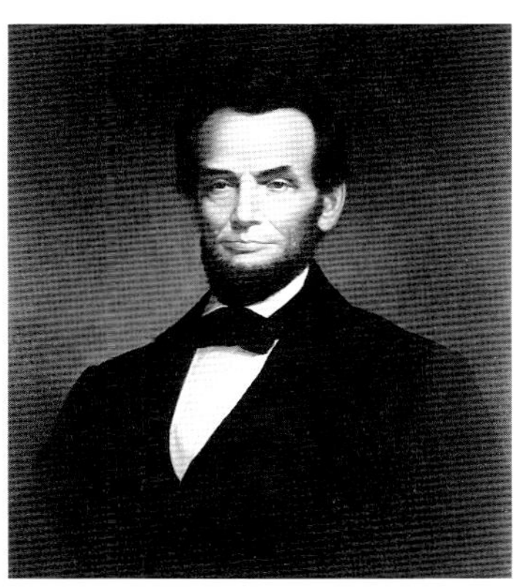

Abraham Lincoln, 1864 or after
Canvas, 0.762 x 0.636 (30 x 25)
Andrew W. Mellon Collection
1947.17.67

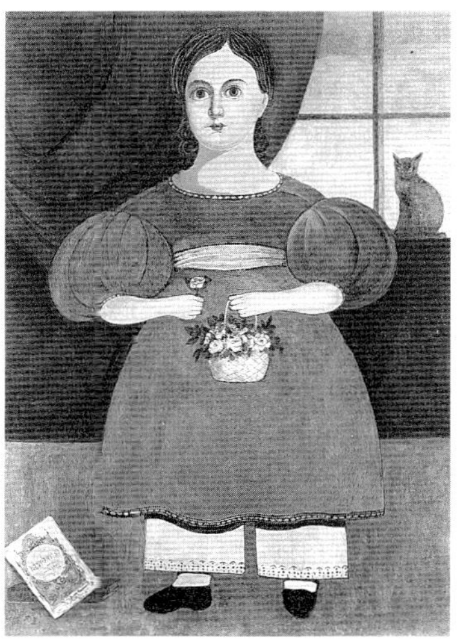

Little Girl and the Cat, after 1916/1919
Wood, 0.521 x 0.362 (20½ x 14$\frac{5}{16}$)
Gift of Edgar William and Bernice Chrysler Garbisch
1959.11.11

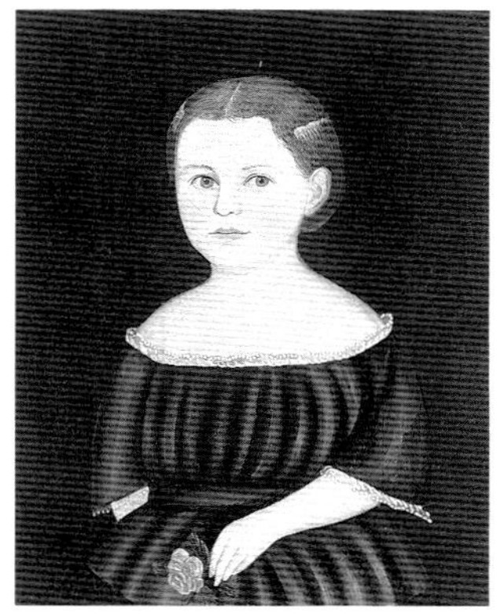

Little Girl in Blue Dress, c. 1840
Canvas, 0.262 x 0.210 (10 5/16 x 8 1/2)
Gift of Edgar William and Bernice Chrysler Garbisch
1953.5.72

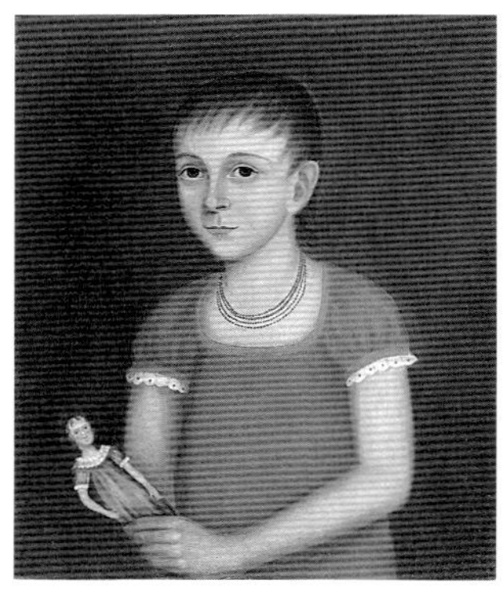

Little Girl with Doll, c. 1800/1820
Wood, 0.517 x 0.429 (20 3/4 x 16 7/8)
Gift of Edgar William and Bernice Chrysler Garbisch
1953.5.65

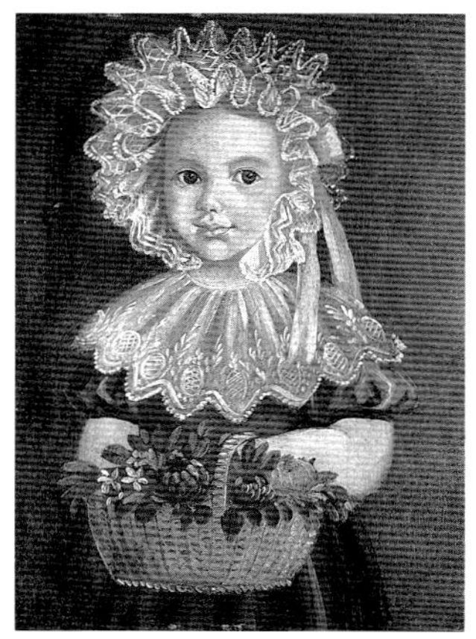

Little Girl with Flower Basket, c. 1830
Wood, 0.356 x 0.260 (14 x 10 1/4)
Gift of Edgar William and Bernice Chrysler Garbisch
1953.5.64

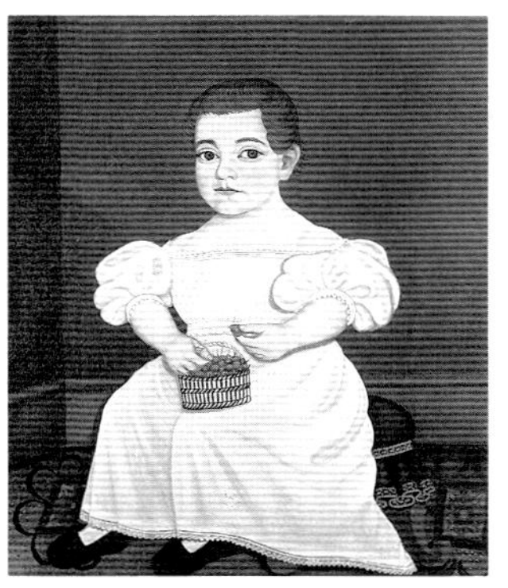

Little Miss Wyckoff, c. 1830
Canvas, 0.758 x 0.642 (29 3/4 x 25 5/16)
Gift of Edgar William and Bernice Chrysler Garbisch
1953.5.62

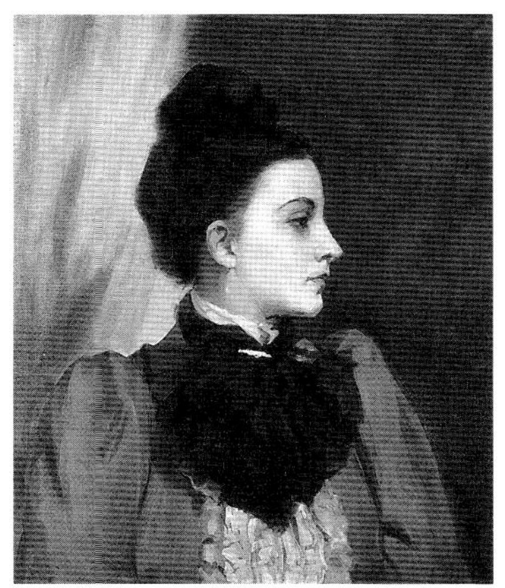

Madame G, c. 1910
Canvas, 0.613 x 0.508 (24⅛ x 20)
Chester Dale Collection
1963.10.64

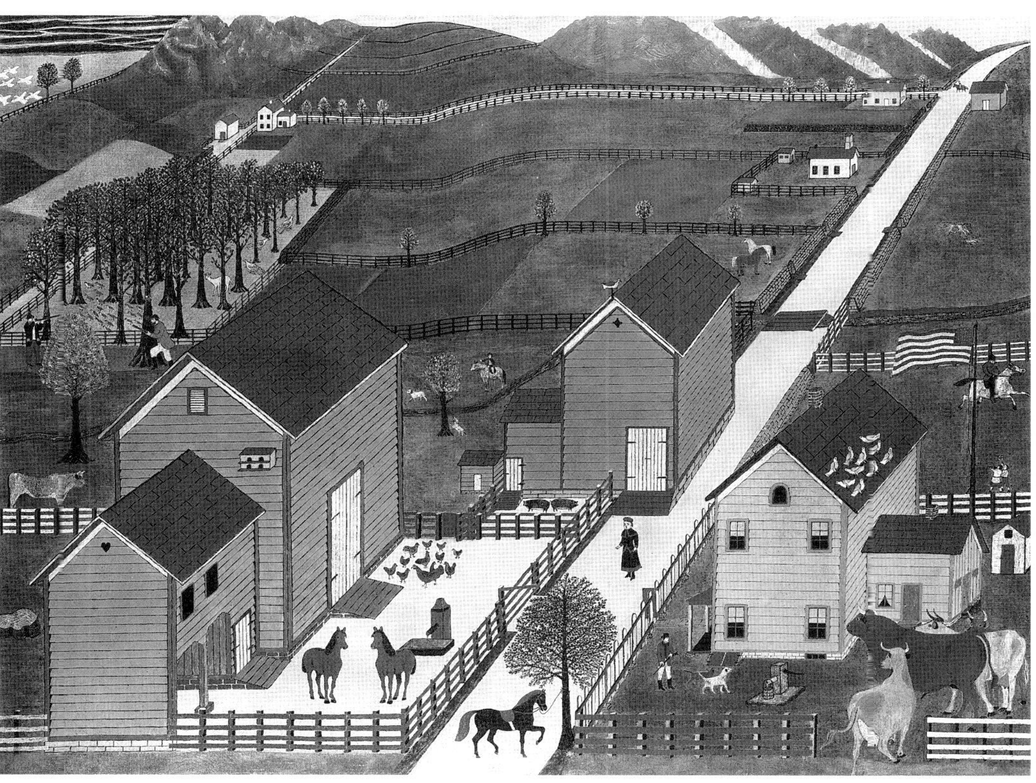

Mahantango Valley Farm, late 19th century
Canvas, 0.711 x 0.917 (28 x 36⅛)
Gift of Edgar William and Bernice
Chrysler Garbisch
1953.5.93

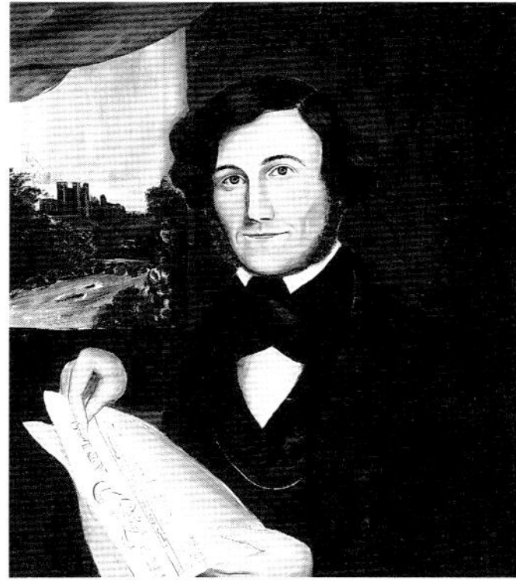

Man Named Hubbard Reading "Boston Atlas," 1843 or after
Canvas, 0.743 x 0.660 ($29\frac{1}{4}$ x 26)
Inscribed at lower left on newspaper: *THE E PLURIBUS UNIM ATLAS / [NO.] XVIII (?) Boston May 3, 184[3]./ WHIG PRINCIPAL / FOR PRESIDENT / HENRY CLAY*
Gift of Edgar William and Bernice Chrysler Garbisch
1978.80.2

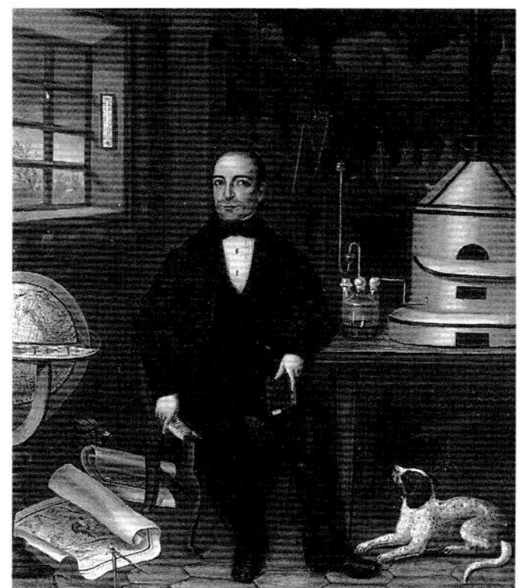

Man of Science, 1839 (?)
Canvas, 0.997 x 0.850 ($39\frac{1}{4}$ x $33\frac{1}{2}$)
Inscribed at lower left: *M[. . .]anz. fecit / [. . .]9*
Gift of Edgar William and Bernice Chrysler Garbisch
1971.83.8

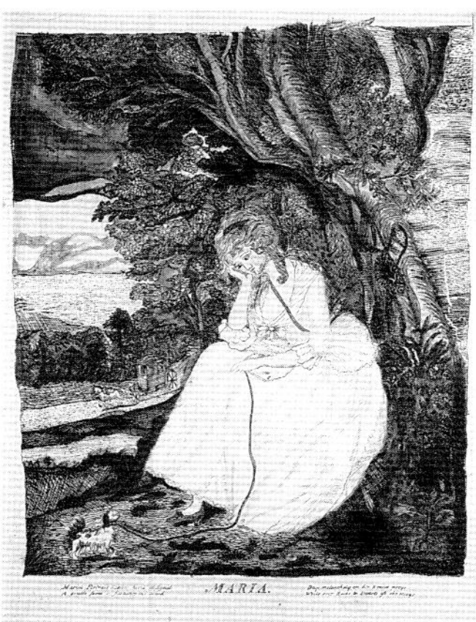

Maria, c. 1790
Silk, 0.384 x 0.292 ($15\frac{1}{8}$ x $11\frac{1}{2}$)
Inscribed at lower left: *Maria's Portrait Reader here's designed / a gentle form a sentimental mind*; lower center: *MARIA*; lower right: *Deep melancholy on her reason preys / While over Rocks & Deserts oft she strays*
Gift of Edgar William and Bernice Chrysler Garbisch
1953.5.46

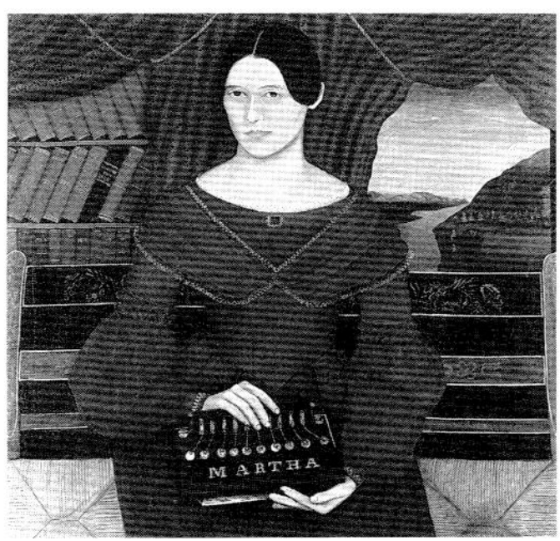

Martha, c. 1835
Canvas, 0.915 x 0.923 (36 x $36\frac{3}{8}$)
Inscribed on accordion: *MARTHA*
Gift of Edgar William and Bernice Chrysler Garbisch
1958.9.11

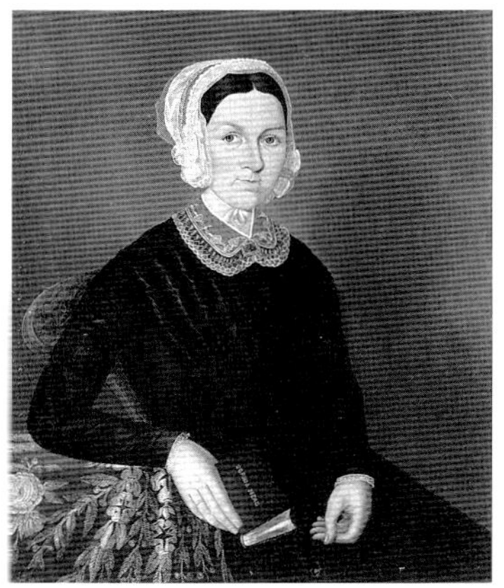

Sophia Mead, c. 1845
Canvas, 0.765 x 0.638 (30 1/8 x 25 1/8)
Inscribed at lower center on book:
SOPHIA MEAD
Gift of Edgar William and Bernice
Chrysler Garbisch
1953.5.47

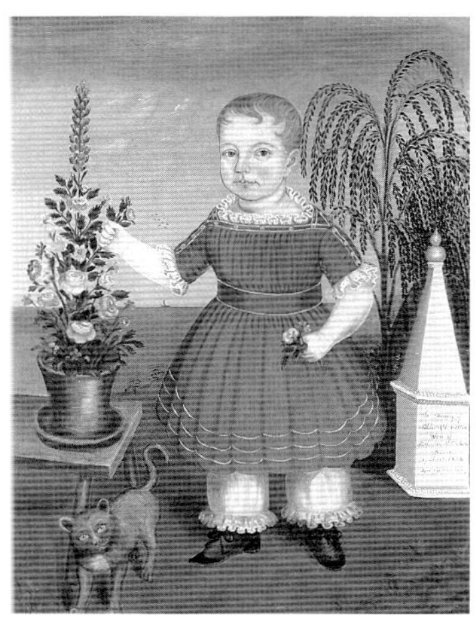

Memorial to Nicholas M S. Catlin,
c. 1852
Canvas, 0.984 x 0.732 (38 7/8 x 28 13/16)
Inscribed at center right on memorial: *In Memory of / Nicholas M S. Catlin / Son of / Nathan S. & Phebe C. Catlin / Died / April 19th 1852 / Age 1 yr 1 mo 15 days*
Gift of Edgar William and Bernice
Chrysler Garbisch
1955.11.7

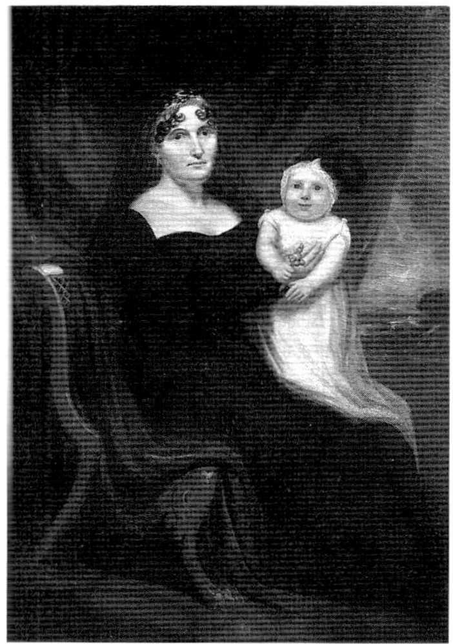

Mother and Child, c. 1810
Canvas, 1.537 x 1.054 (60 1/2 x 41 1/2)
Andrew W. Mellon Collection
1947.17.53

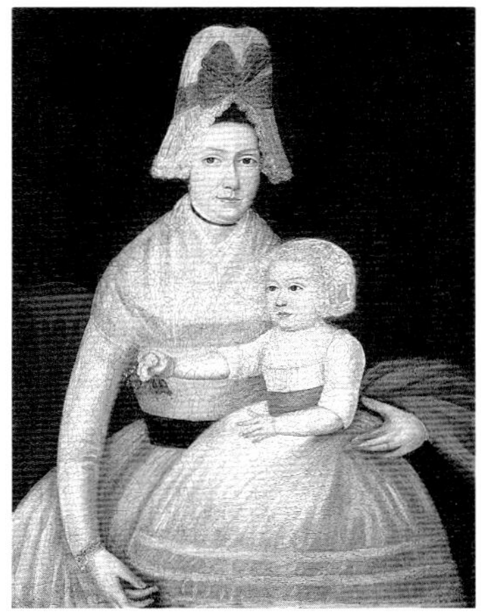

Mother and Child in White, c. 1790
Canvas, 0.895 x 0.687 ($35\frac{1}{4}$ x 27)
Gift of Edgar William and Bernice Chrysler Garbisch
1980.62.39

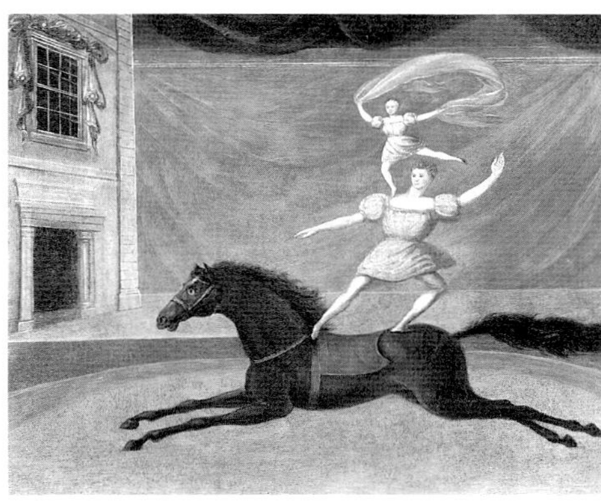

The Mounted Acrobats, 1825 or after
Wood, 0.403 x 0.476 ($15\frac{13}{16}$ x $18\frac{3}{4}$)
Gift of Edgar William and Bernice Chrysler Garbisch
1953.5.18

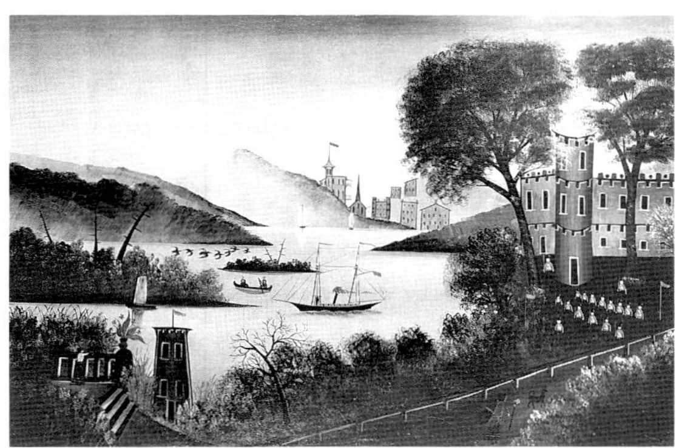

Mounting of the Guard, mid-19th century
Canvas, 0.675 x 1.000 ($26\frac{9}{16}$ x $39\frac{3}{8}$)
Gift of Edgar William and Bernice Chrysler Garbisch
1955.11.3

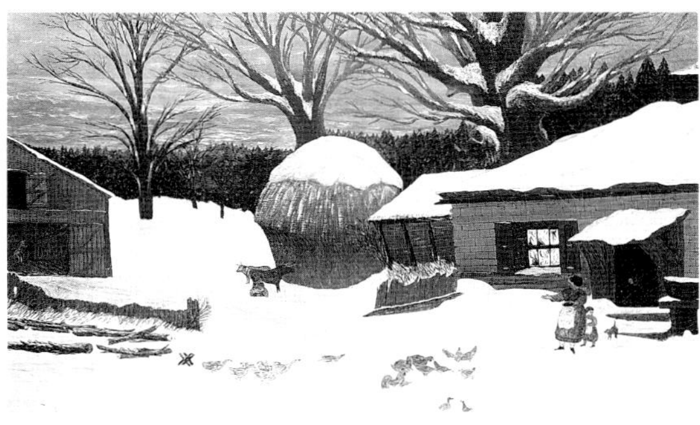

New England Farm in Winter, 1850 or after
Canvas, 0.597 x 0.978 ($23\frac{1}{2}$ x $38\frac{1}{2}$)
Gift of Edgar William and Bernice Chrysler Garbisch
1953.5.87

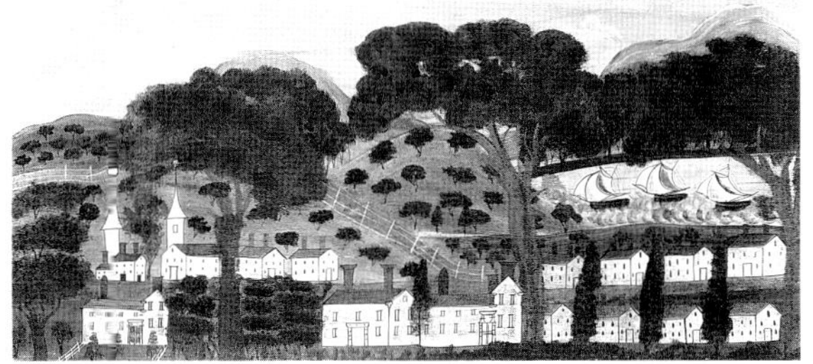

New England Village, early 19th century
Wood, 0.315 x 0.650 (12⅜ x 25 9/16)
Gift of Edgar William and Bernice Chrysler Garbisch
1955.11.12

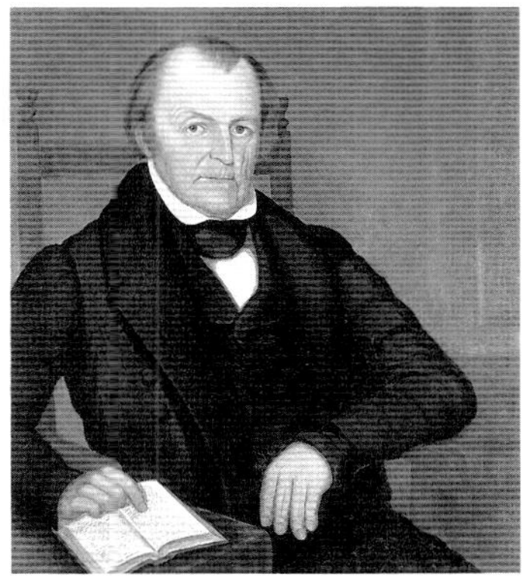

Old Man in Red Slat Back Chair, 1836/1840
Canvas, 0.800 x 0.705 (31½ x 27¾)
Gift of Edgar William and Bernice Chrysler Garbisch
1953.5.76

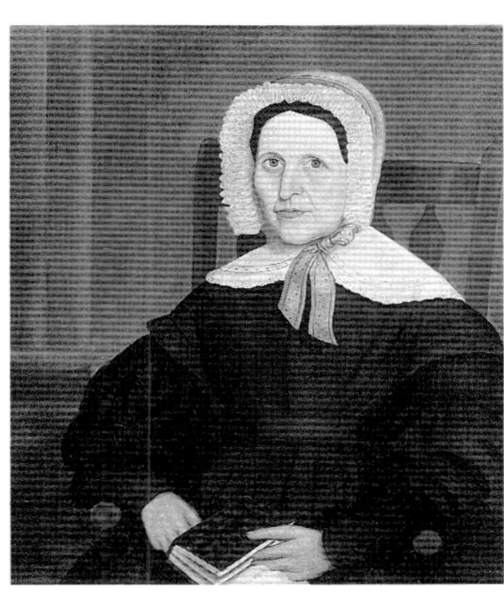

Woman in Red Arrowback Chair, 1836/1840
Canvas, 0.800 x 0.705 (31½ x 27¾)
Gift of Edgar William and Bernice Chrysler Garbisch
1953.5.37

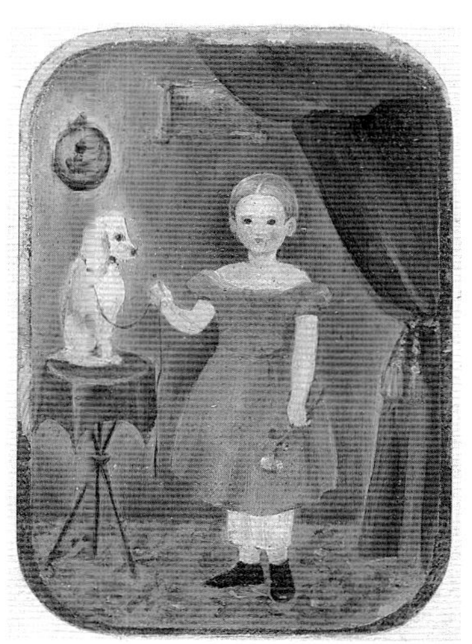

On Exhibition, probably fourth quarter 19th century
Tin mounted on fabric, 0.182 x 0.121 (7⅛ x 5)
Gift of Edgar William and Bernice Chrysler Garbisch
1953.5.69

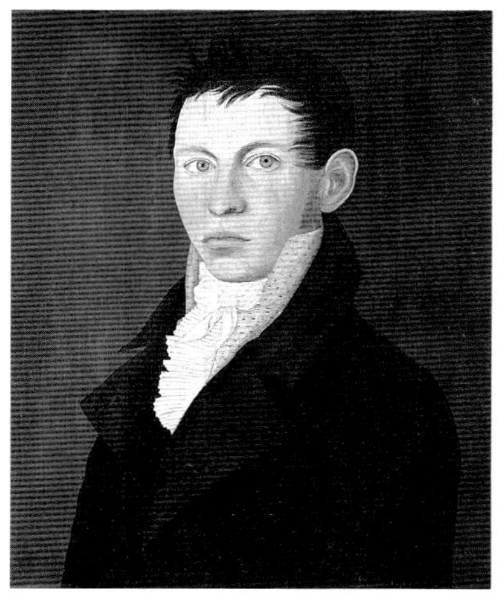

Harlan Page (?), 1815
Wood, 0.591 x 0.489 (23¼ x 19¼)
Incised in paint in upper left: *Aug 4 1815*
Gift of Edgar William and Bernice Chrysler Garbisch
1953.5.48

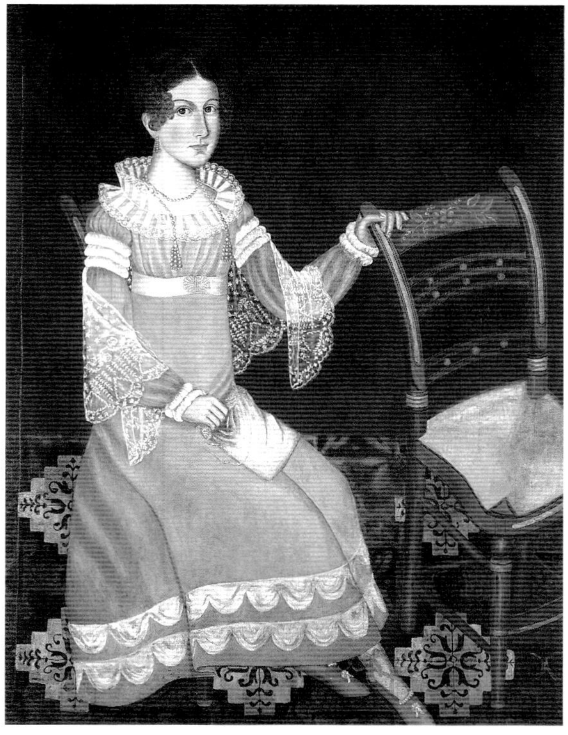

Martha Eliza Stevens Edgar Paschall, c. 1823
Canvas, 1.325 x 1.026 (52¼ x 40⅜)
Gift of Mary Paschall Young Doty and Katharine Campbell Young Keck
1983.95.1

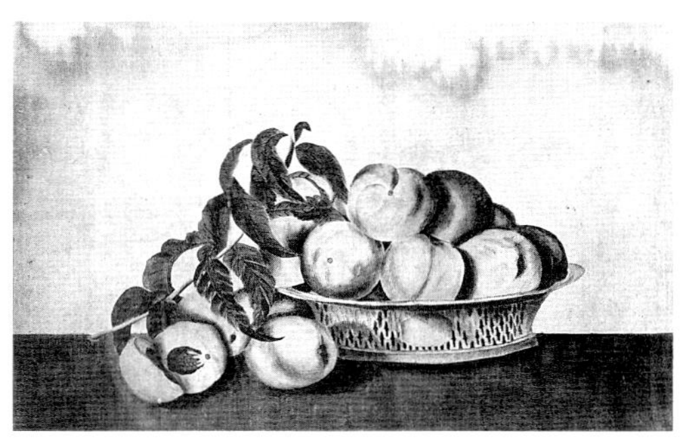

Peaches—Still Life, c. 1840
Velvet, 0.450 x 0.655 (17¾ x 25¾)
Gift of Edgar William and Bernice Chrysler Garbisch
1953.5.105

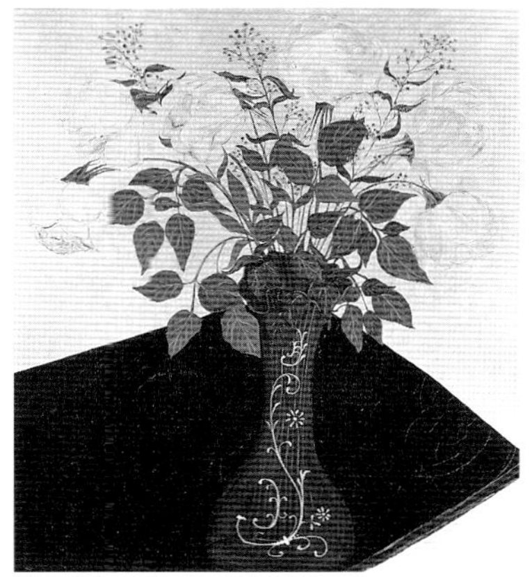

Pink Roses, fourth quarter 19th century
Canvas, 0.407 x 0.365 (16 x 14⅜)
Gift of Edgar William and Bernice
Chrysler Garbisch
1953.5.102

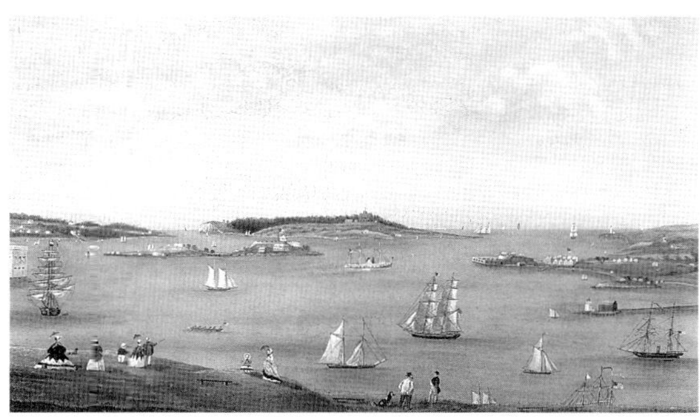

Portland Harbor, Maine, 1868/1871
Paperboard, 0.433 x 0.715 (17¹⁄₁₆ x 28⅛)
Gift of Edgar William and Bernice
Chrysler Garbisch
1971.83.17

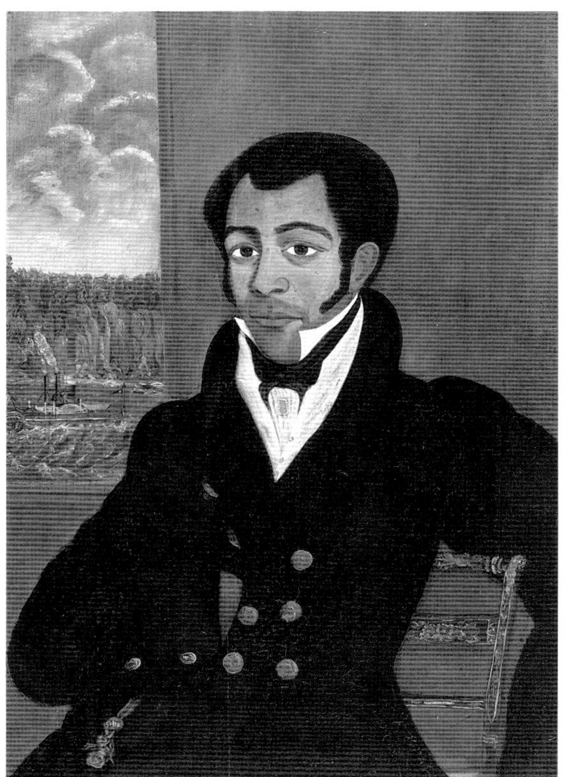

Portrait of a Black Man, probably 1829
Wood, 0.495 x 0.343 (19½ x 13½)
Gift of Edgar William and Bernice
Chrysler Garbisch
1953.5.22

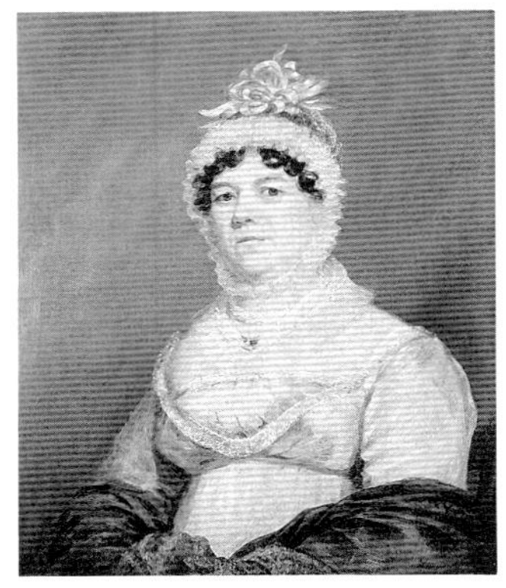

Portrait of a Lady, c. 1825
Canvas, 0.765 x 0.635 (30⅛ x 25)
Chester Dale Collection
1943.1.5

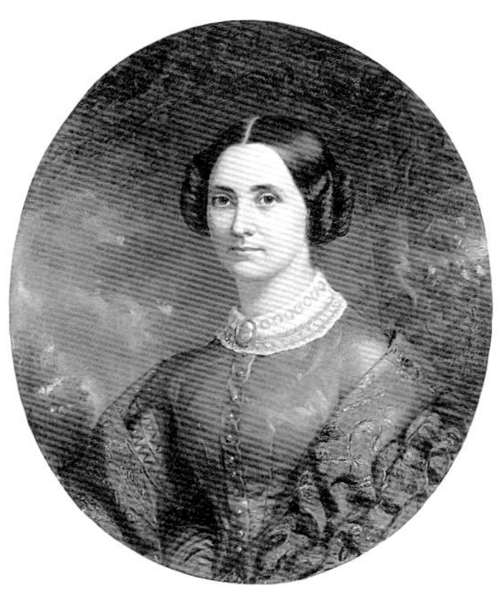

Portrait of a Lady, c. 1855
Canvas, oval: 0.762 x 0.638 (30 x 25⅛)
Falsely signed and dated, center right:
Henry Inman / 1844
Andrew W. Mellon Collection
1947.17.58

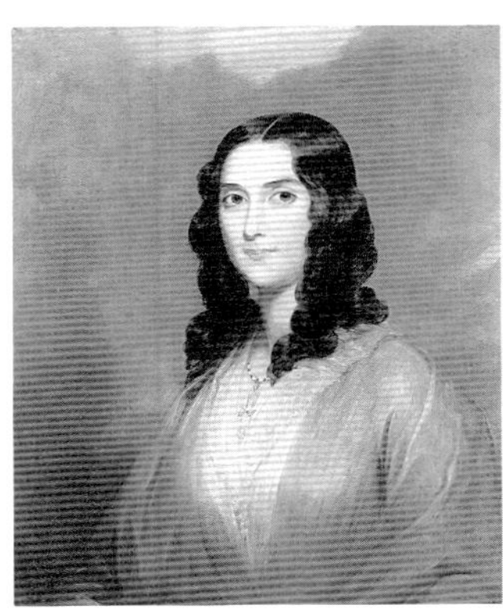

Portrait of a Lady, c. 1840
Canvas, 0.753 x 0.629 (29⅞ x 24¾)
Andrew W. Mellon Collection
1947.17.60

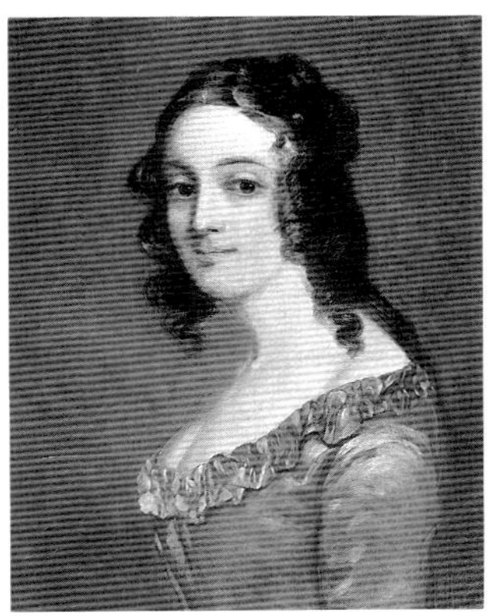

Portrait of a Lady, c. 1845
Canvas, 0.632 x 0.508 (24⅞ x 20)
Andrew W. Mellon Collection
1947.17.66

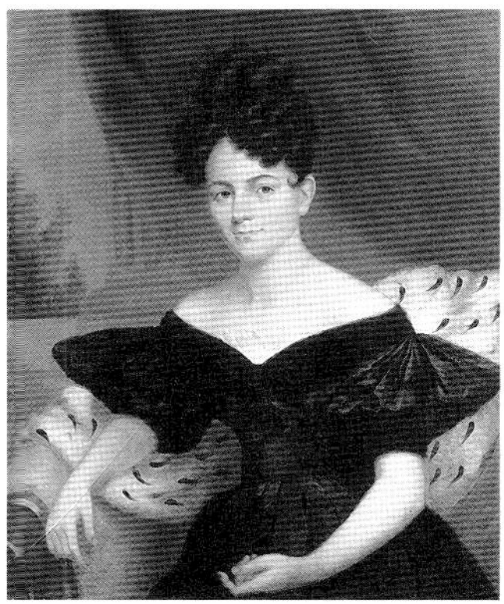

Portrait of a Lady, c. 1830
Canvas, 0.918 x 0.714 (36⅛ x 28⅛)
Andrew W. Mellon Collection
1947.17.75

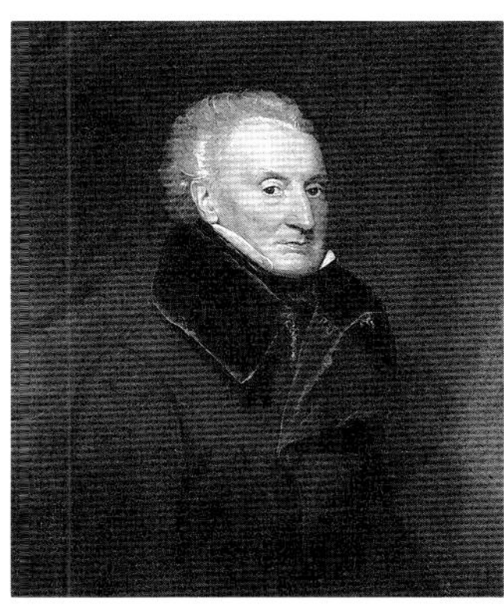

Portrait of a Man, c. 1835
Canvas, 0.770 x 0.635 (30¼ x 24⅞)
Andrew W. Mellon Collection
1942.8.8

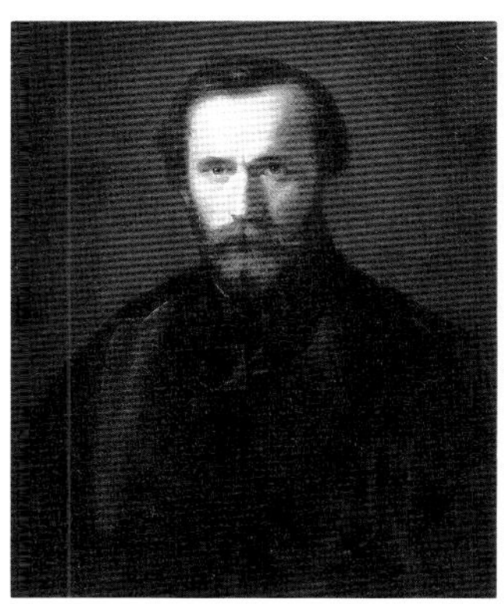

Portrait of a Man, c. 1865
Canvas, 0.648 x 0.543 (25½ x 21⅜)
Andrew W. Mellon Collection
1947.17.5

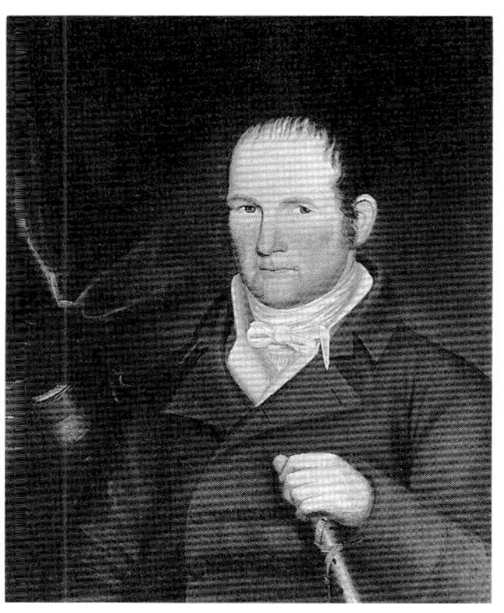

Portrait of a Man, c. 1810
Wood, 0.765 x 0.616 (30⅛ x 24¼)
Falsely signed and dated, lower left:
R Earl Pinx / 1798
Andrew W. Mellon Collection
1947.17.44

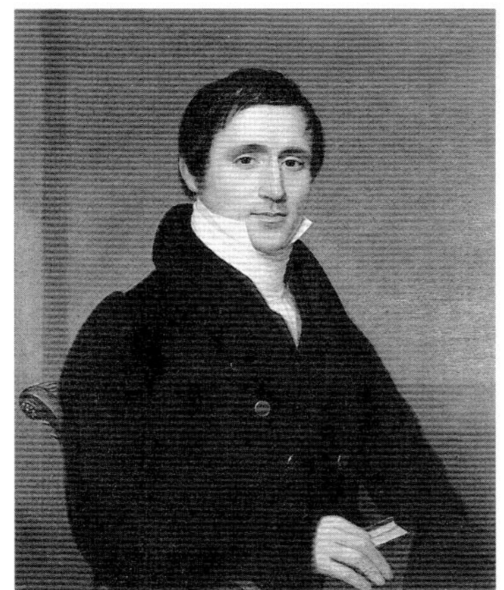

Portrait of a Man, c. 1830
Canvas, 0.762 x 0.613 (30 x 24⅛)
Andrew W. Mellon Collection
1947.17.51

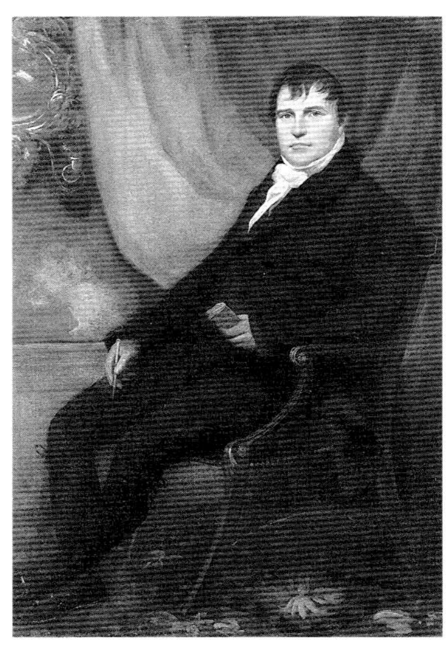

Portrait of a Man, c. 1810
Canvas, 1.540 x 1.057 (60⅝ x 41⅝)
Andrew W. Mellon Collection
1947.17.52

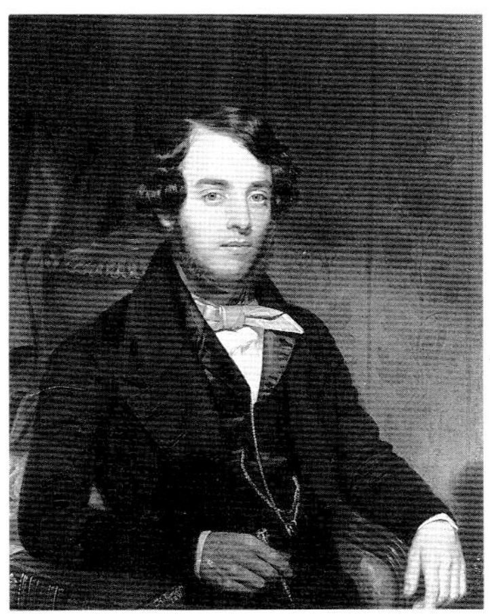

Portrait of a Man, c. 1845
Canvas, 0.864 x 0.686 (34 x 27)
Falsely signed and dated, lower left:
H. Inman / 1841
Andrew W. Mellon Collection
1947.17.59

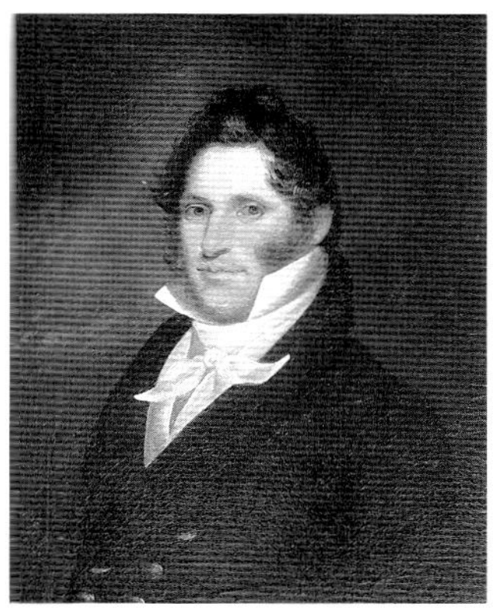

Portrait of a Man, c. 1825
Canvas, 0.768 x 0.638 (30¼ x 25⅛)
Andrew W. Mellon Collection
1947.17.61

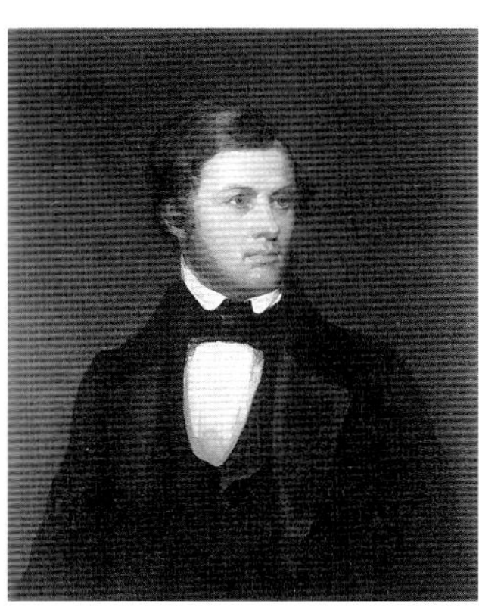

Portrait of a Man, c. 1845
Canvas, 0.762 x 0.635 (30 x 25)
Andrew W. Mellon Collection
1947.17.70

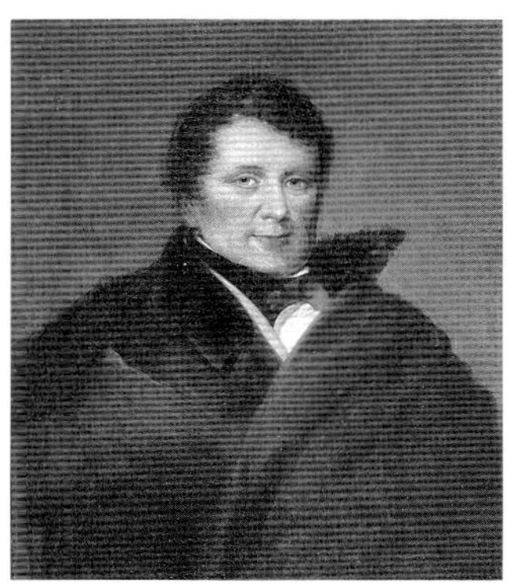

Portrait of a Man, c. 1830
Canvas, 0.762 x 0.635 (30 x 25)
Andrew W. Mellon Collection
1947.17.84

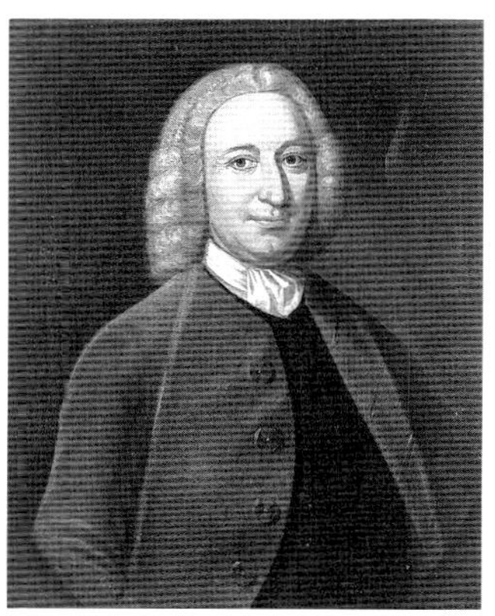

Portrait of a Man, mid-18th century
Canvas, 0.738 x 0.610 (29 x 24)
Falsely signed and dated, lower right: *JS 1734*
Andrew W. Mellon Collection
1947.17.93

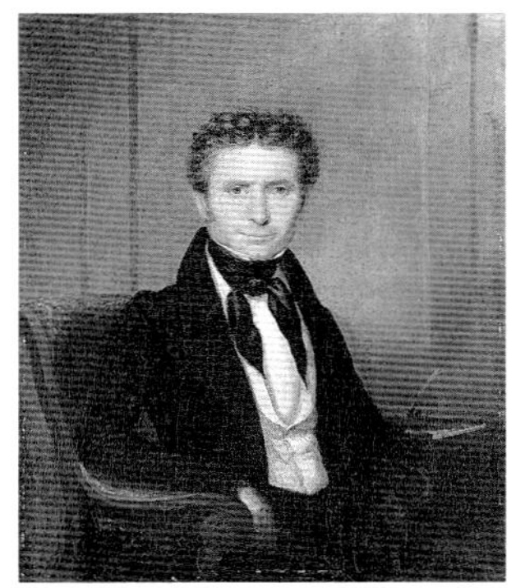

Portrait of a Man, c. 1845
Canvas, 0.362 x 0.305 (14¼ x 12)
Andrew W. Mellon Collection
1947.17.97

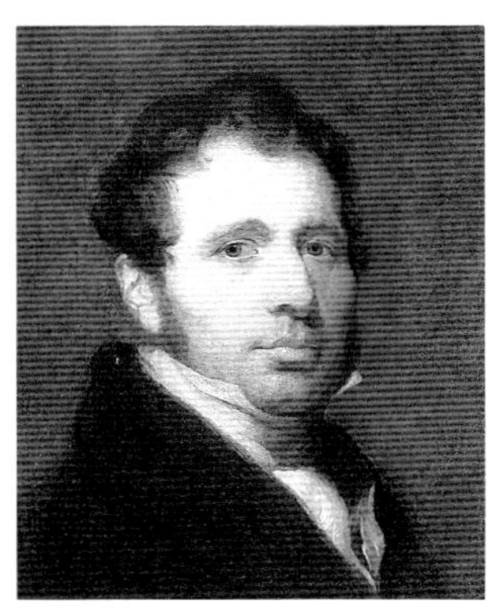

Portrait of a Man, c. 1820
Canvas, 0.445 x 0.356 (17½ x 14)
Andrew W. Mellon Collection
1947.17.109

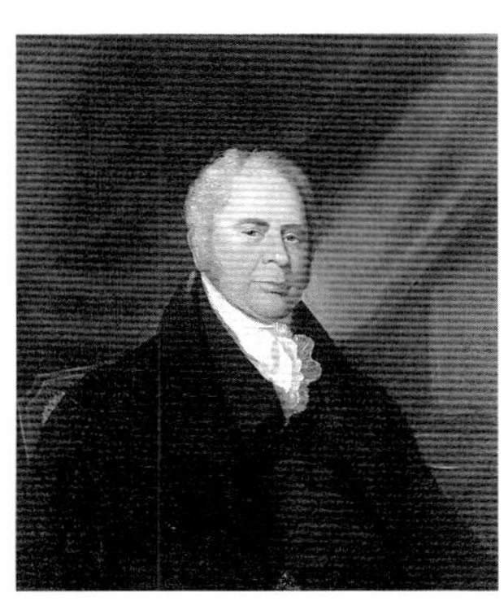

Portrait of a Man, c. 1825
Canvas, 0.762 x 0.635 (30 x 25)
Andrew W. Mellon Collection
1954.1.6

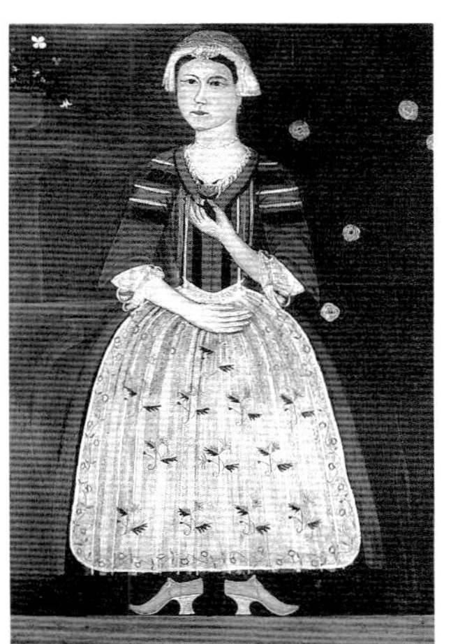

Catalyntje Post, c. 1747
Canvas, 1.336 x 0.904 (52⅝ x 35⅝)
Gift of Edgar William and Bernice Chrysler Garbisch
1980.62.34

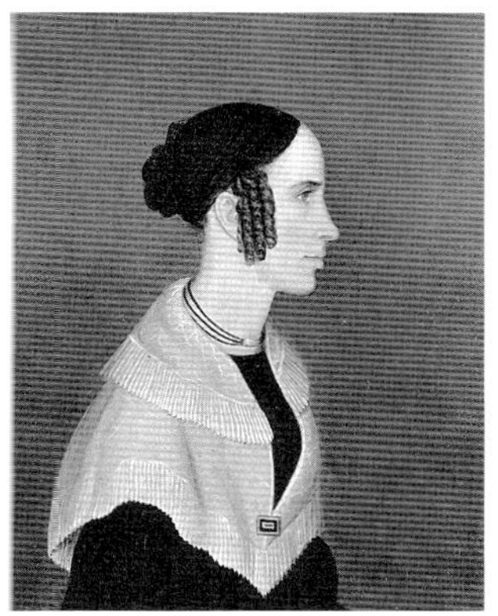

Profile Portrait of a Lady, c. 1835/1840
Wood, 0.229 x 0.175 (9 x 6 7/8)
Gift of Edgar William and Bernice Chrysler Garbisch
1953.5.83

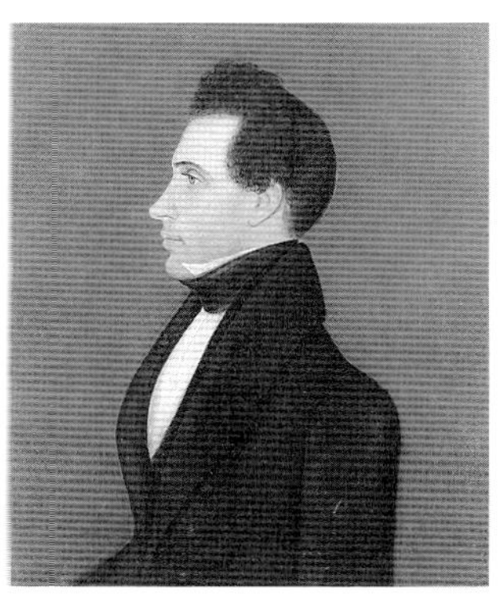

Profile Portrait of a Man, c. 1835/1840
Wood, 0.227 x 0.175 (8 5/16 x 6 13/15)
Gift of Edgar William and Bernice Chrysler Garbisch
1953.5.82

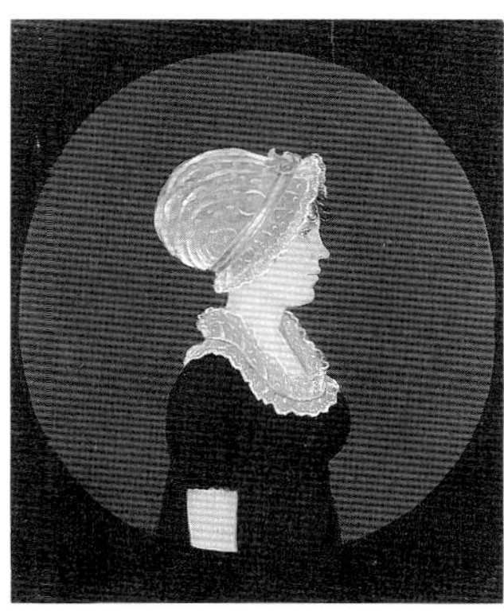

Profile Portrait of a Young Lady, c. 1810/1820
Wood, 0.304 x 0.250 (11 7/8 x 9 7/8)
Gift of Edgar William and Bernice Chrysler Garbisch
1953.5.10

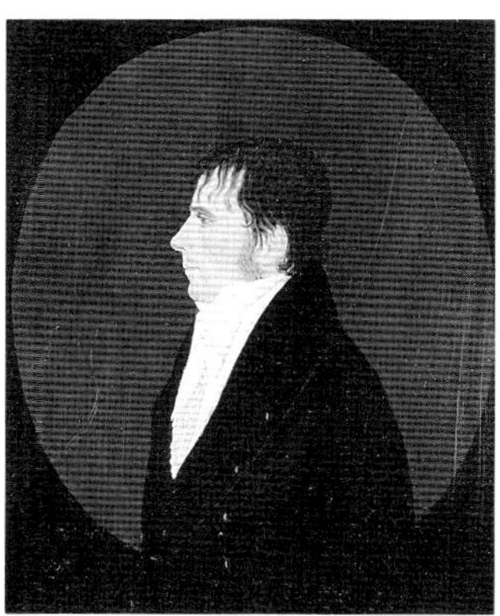

Profile Portrait of a Young Man, c. 1810/1820
Wood, 0.302 x 0.251 (11 7/8 x 9 7/8)
Gift of Edgar William and Bernice Chrysler Garbisch
1953.5.9

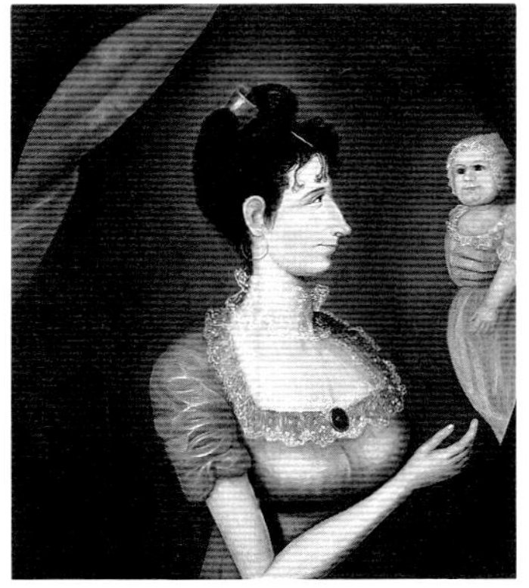

The Proud Mother, c. 1810
Canvas, 0.762 x 0.666 (30 x 26 3/16)
Gift of Edgar William and Bernice
Chrysler Garbisch
1971.83.18

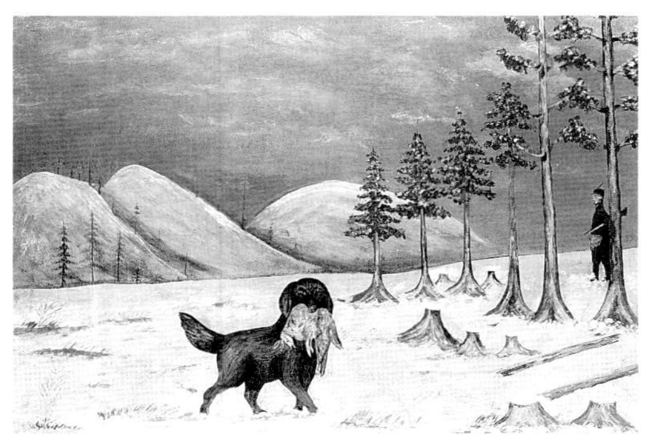

Retriever, second half 19th century
Canvas, 0.559 x 0.810 (22 x 31 7/8)
Gift of Edgar William and Bernice
Chrysler Garbisch
1953.5.96

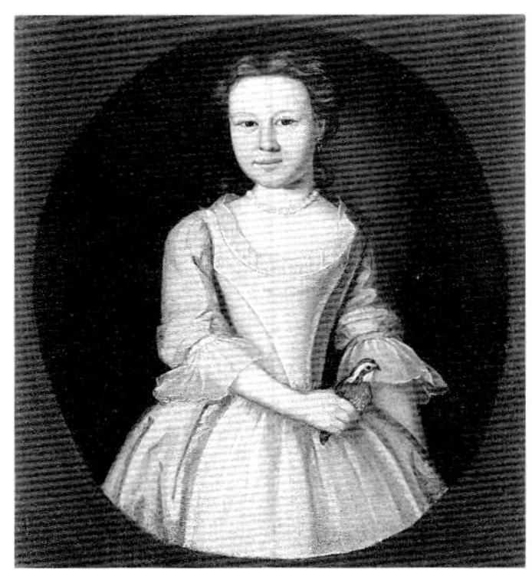

Margaret (?) Robins, c. 1745
Canvas, 0.670 x 0.607 (26 3/8 x 23 7/8)
Gift of Edgar William and Bernice
Chrysler Garbisch
1980.62.10

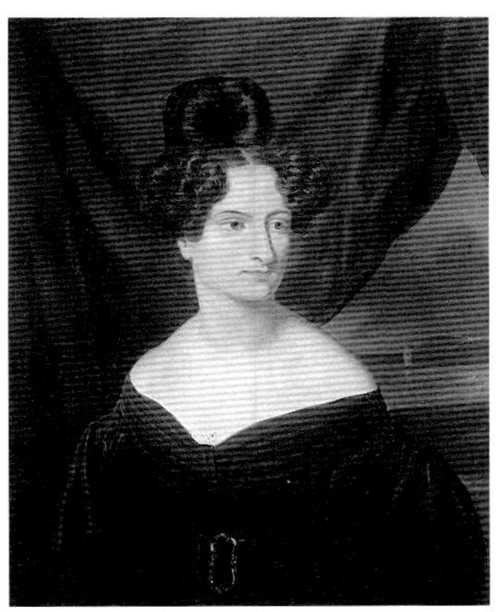

Miss Robinson, c. 1835
Canvas, 0.733 x 0.591 (28 7/8 x 23 1/4)
Andrew W. Mellon Collection
1947.17.46

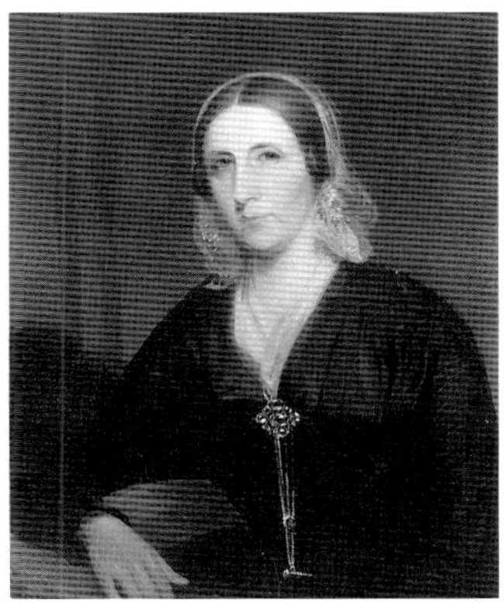

Ann C. Rudman, c. 1845
Canvas, 0.762 x 0.635 (30 x 25)
Andrew W. Mellon Collection
1947.17.79

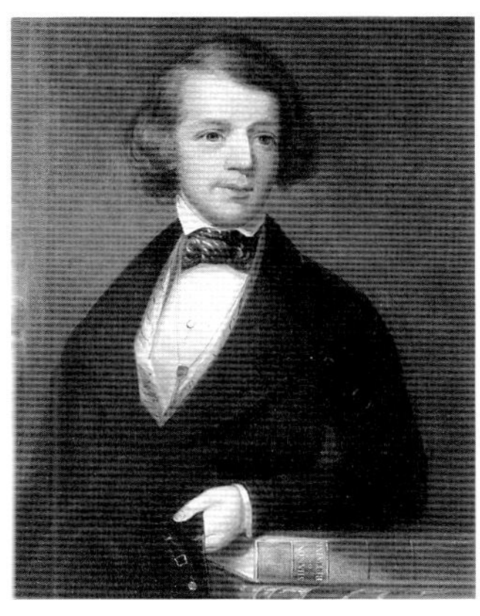

William C. Rudman, Jr., c. 1845
Canvas, 0.762 x 0.638 (30 x 25⅛)
Andrew W. Mellon Collection
1947.17.80

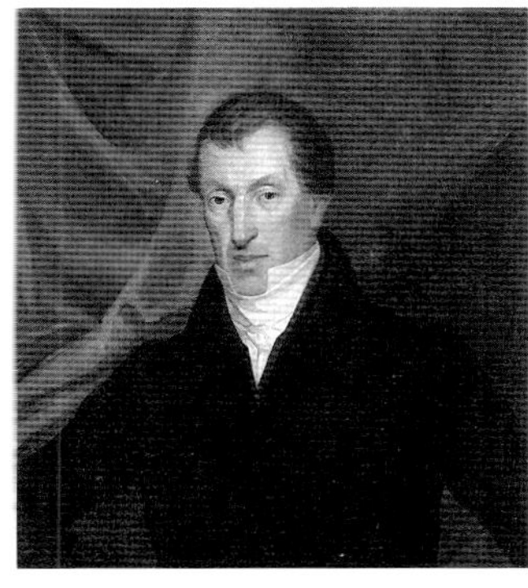

John Rush (?), c. 1830
Canvas, 0.765 x 0.660 (30⅛ x 26)
Chester Dale Collection
1943.1.7

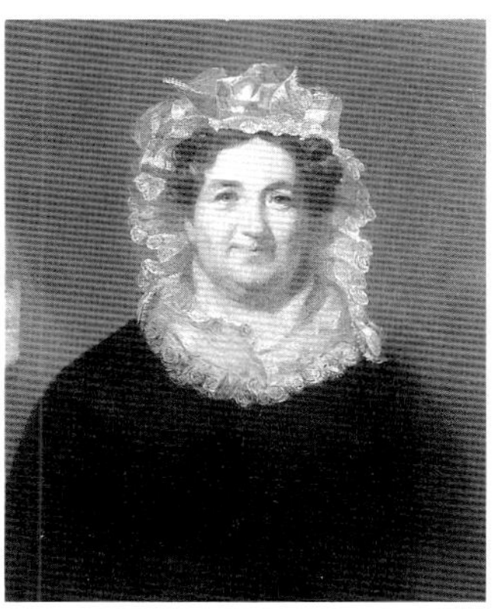

Miss Ryan (?), c. 1830
Canvas, 0.762 x 0.638 (30 x 25⅛)
Andrew W. Mellon Collection
1947.17.82

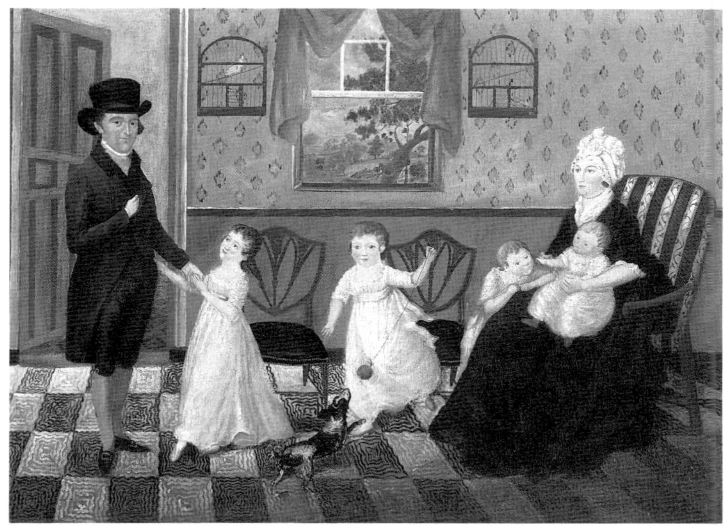

The Sargent Family, 1800
Canvas, 0.972 x 1.278 ($38\frac{5}{16}$ x $50\frac{9}{16}$)
Gift of Edgar William and Bernice Chrysler Garbisch
1953.5.49

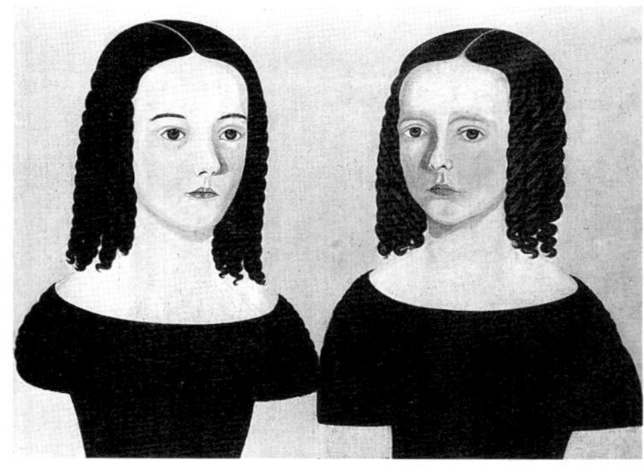

Sisters, c. 1840
Canvas, 0.460 x 0.608 ($18\frac{1}{8}$ x 24)
Gift of Edgar William and Bernice Chrysler Garbisch
1980.62.37

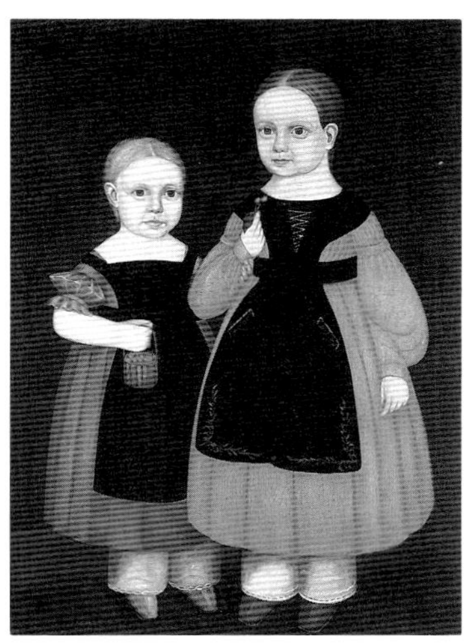

Sisters in Black Aprons, c. 1835/1840
Canvas, 0.943 x 0.672 ($37\frac{1}{8}$ x $26\frac{1}{2}$)
Gift of Edgar William and Bernice Chrysler Garbisch
1971.83.19

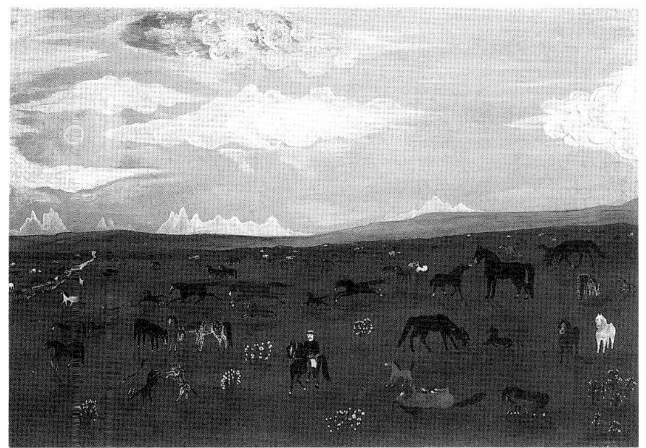

Spring on the Range, fourth quarter 19th century
Canvas, 0.537 x 0.745 (21 1/8 x 29 5/16)
Gift of Edgar William and Bernice Chrysler Garbisch
1971.83.14

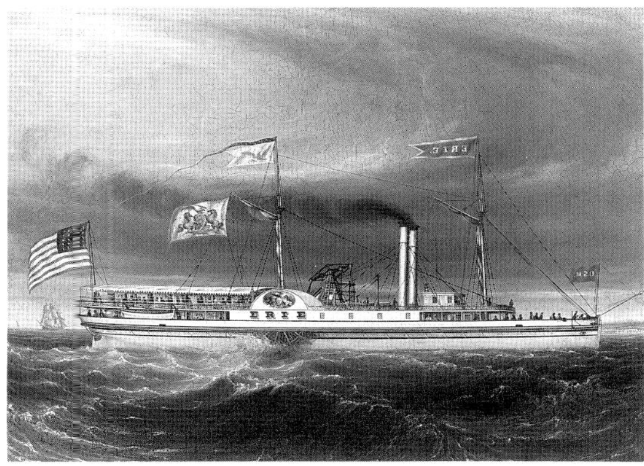

Steamship Erie, probably 1837
Canvas, 0.566 x 0.751 (22 1/4 x 29 9/16)
Inscribed on ship: *ERIE*
Gift of Edgar William and Bernice Chrysler Garbisch
1980.61.7

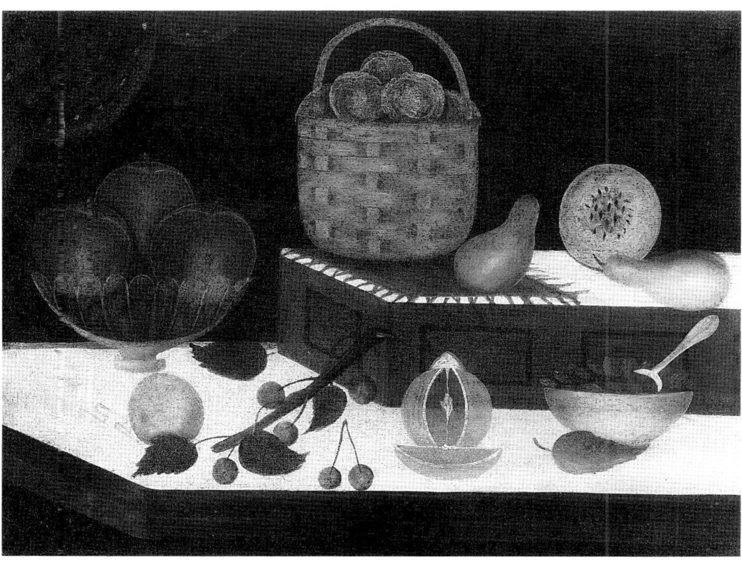

Still Life of Fruit, c. 1865/1880
Wood, 0.305 x 0.405 (12 x 15 15/16)
Gift of Edgar William and Bernice Chrysler Garbisch
1967.20.6

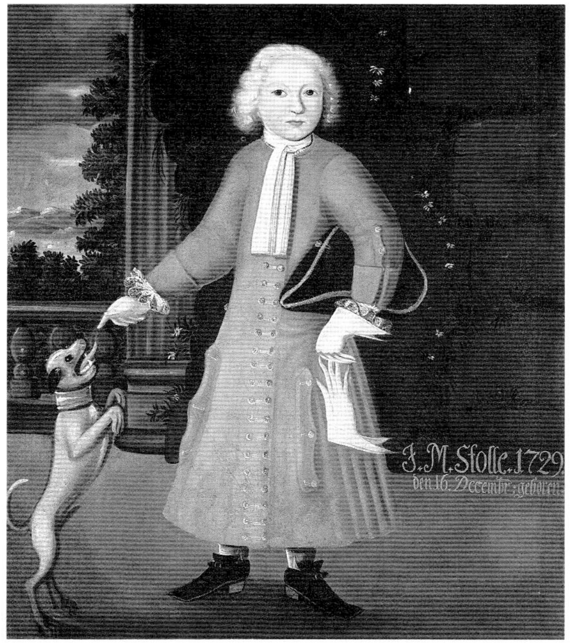

J. M. Stolle, c. 1734/1735
Canvas, 1.016 x 0.870 (40 x 34¼)
Inscribed at lower right: *J.M. Stolle.1729. / den 16.Decembr:geboren.*
Gift of Edgar William and Bernice Chrysler Garbisch
1980.62.24

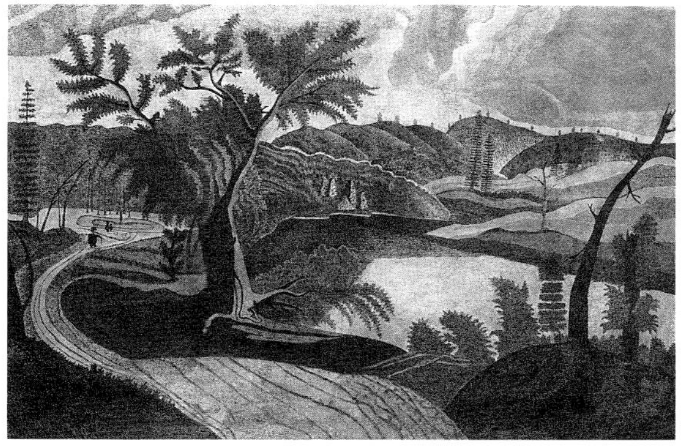

Stylized Landscape, second half 19th century
Canvas, 0.705 x 1.054 (27¾ x 41½)
Gift of Edgar William and Bernice Chrysler Garbisch
1967.20.7

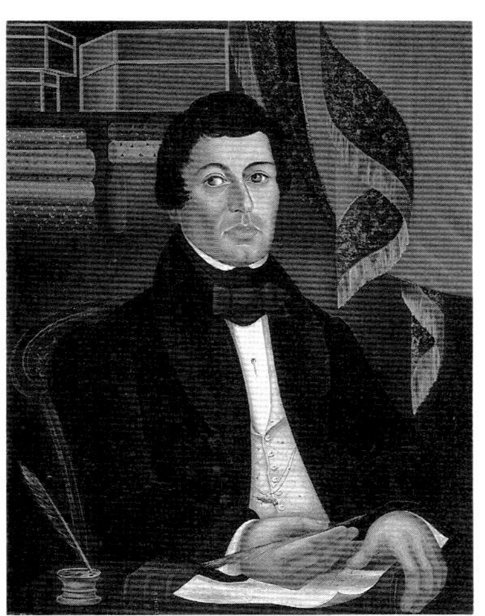

Textile Merchant, c. 1840
Canvas, 0.865 x 0.660 (34 x 26)
Gift of Edgar William and Bernice Chrysler Garbisch
1953.5.81

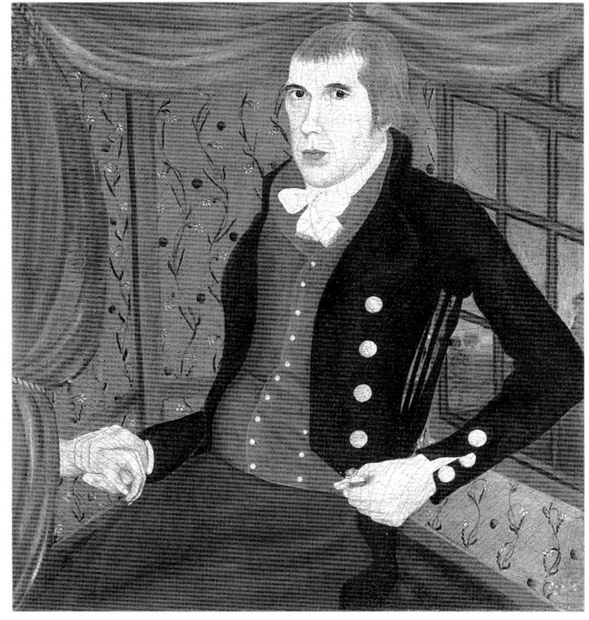

Dr. Philemon Tracy, c. 1790
Paper mounted on board, mounted on canvas, 0.791 x 0.734 (31 3/16 x 28 13/16)
Gift of Edgar William and Bernice Chrysler Garbisch
1980.62.44

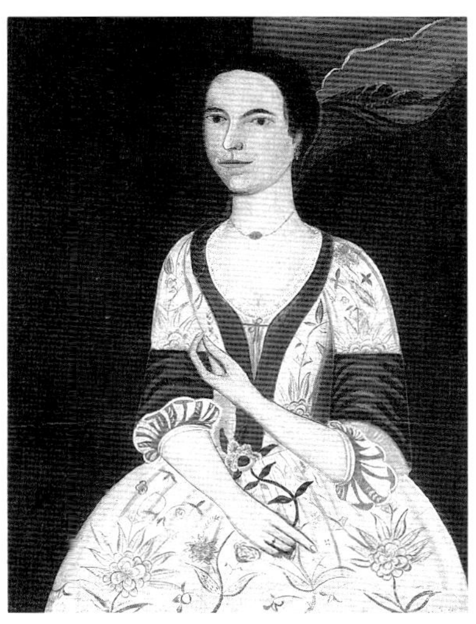

Susanna Truax, c. 1740
Canvas, 0.920 x 0.730 (36 1/4 x 27 3/4)
Gift of Edgar William and Bernice Chrysler Garbisch
1978.80.20

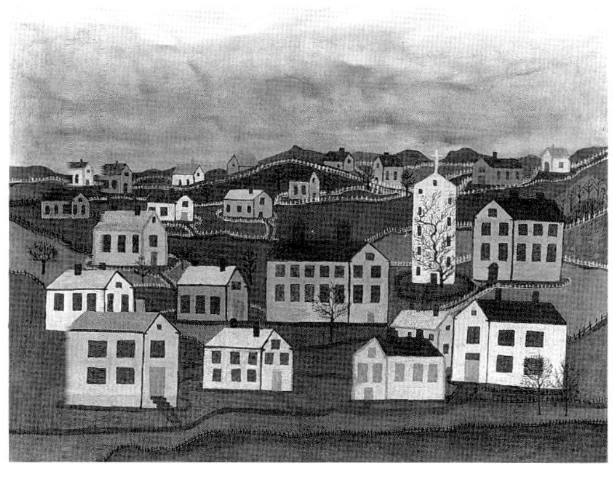

Twenty-two Houses and a Church, mid-19th century
Canvas, 0.612 x 0.765 (24 1/8 x 30 1/8)
Gift of Edgar William and Bernice Chrysler Garbisch
1958.9.13

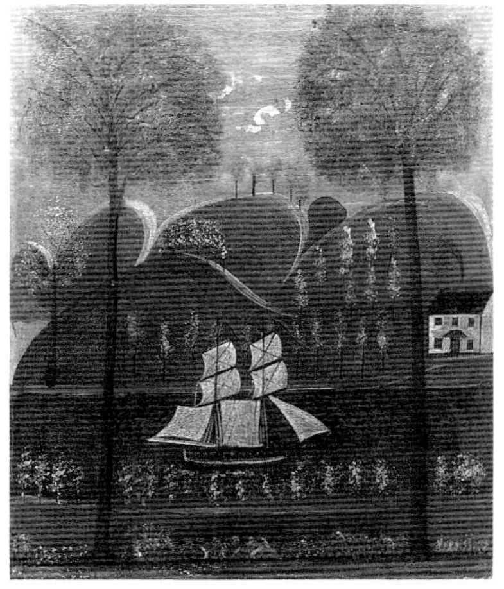

Under Full Sail, second quarter 19th century
Plaster, 0.657 x 0.527 (25 15/16 x 20 3/4); picture including engaged frame: 0.838 x 0.750 (33 x 29 1/2)
Gift of Edgar William and Bernice Chrysler Garbisch
1953.5.100

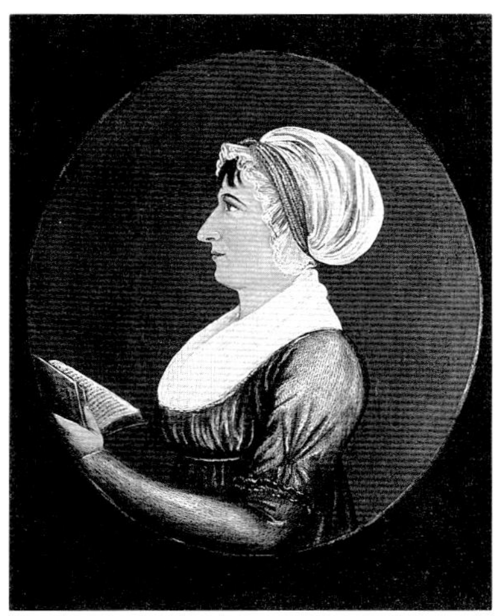

Jane L. Van Reid, c. 1810
Wood, 0.253 x 0.202 (10 x 8)
Gift of Edgar William and Bernice Chrysler Garbisch
1955.11.18

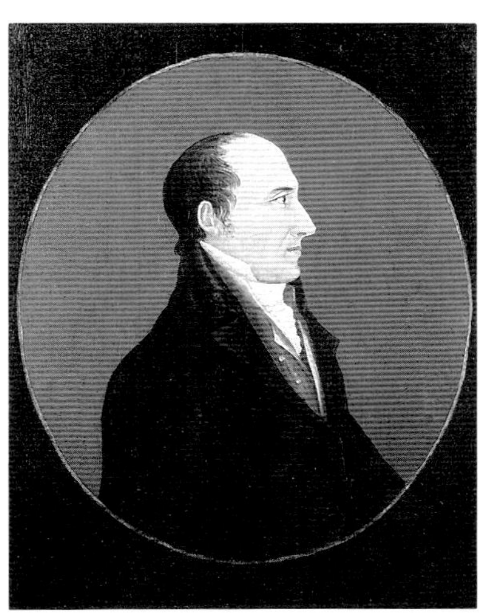

Wellington Van Reid, c. 1810
Wood, 0.253 x 0.200 (10 x 7 7/8)
Gift of Edgar William and Bernice Chrysler Garbisch
1955.11.17

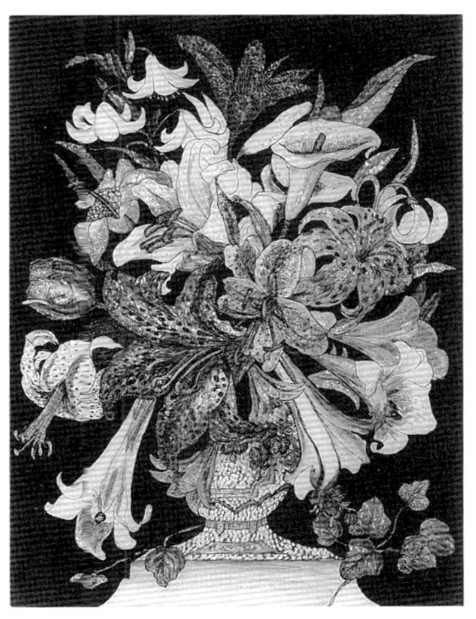

Vase of Lilies, probably 1930 or later
Reverse painting on glass with crumpled foil, 0.604 x 0.456 (23 3/4 x 18)
Gift of Edgar William and Bernice Chrysler Garbisch
1964.23.5

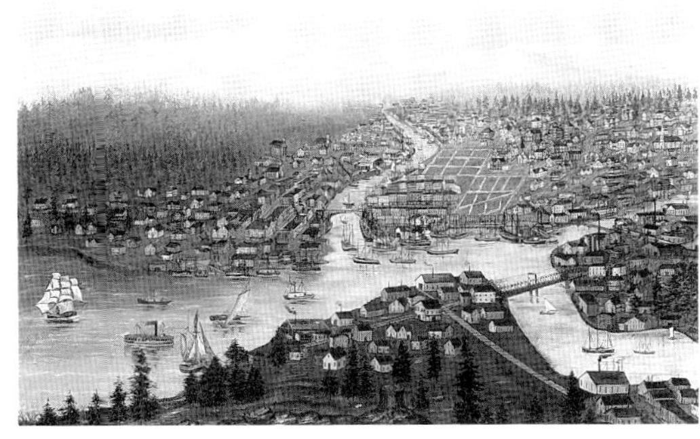

View of Aberdeen, Washington, probably 1903/1906
Canvas, 0.707 x 1.064 (27⅞ x 41⅞)
Gift of Edgar William and Bernice Chrysler Garbisch
1968.26.3

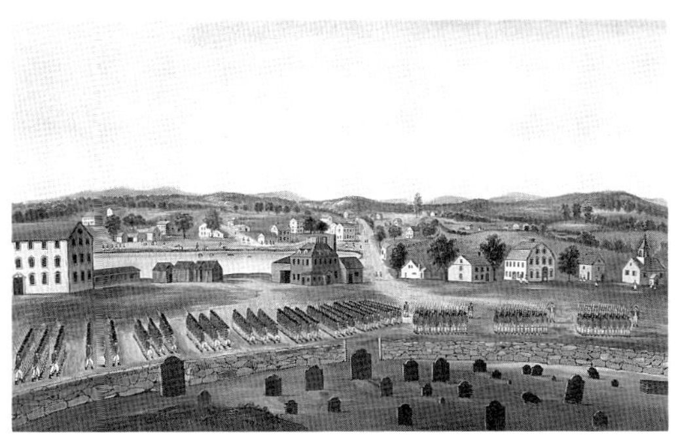

View of Concord, c. 1830
Canvas, 0.661 x 0.994 (26 x 39⅛)
Gift of Edgar William and Bernice Chrysler Garbisch
1978.80.21

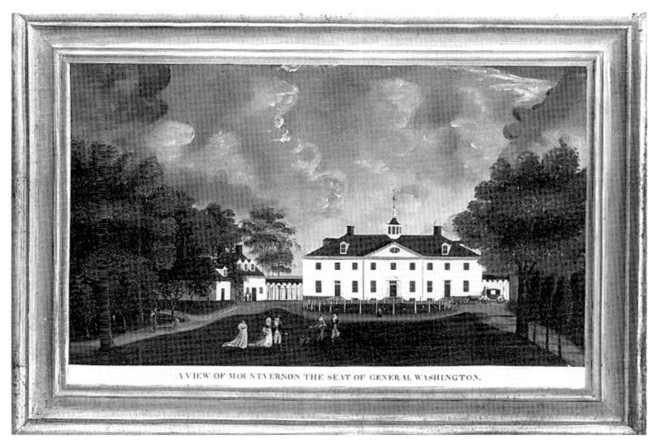

A View of Mount Vernon,
c. 1790 or after
Canvas (fireboard), 0.953 x 1.102 (37½ x 43⅜); picture without simulated frame, 0.584 x 0.892 (23 x 35⅛)
Inscribed across bottom: *A VIEW OF MOUNT.VERNON THE SEAT OF GENERAL WASHINGTON.*
Gift of Edgar William and Bernice Chrysler Garbisch
1953.5.89

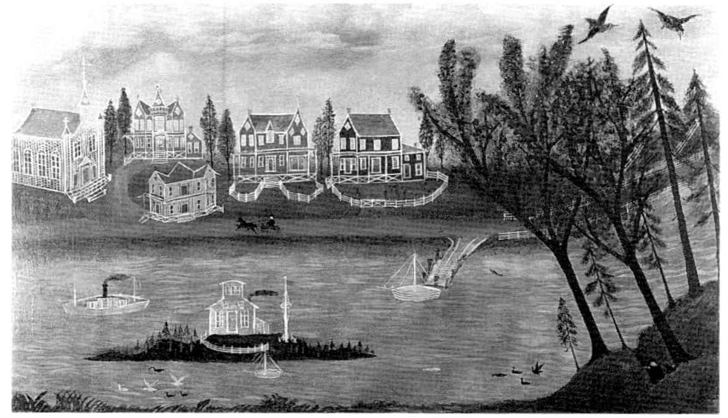

Village by the River, fourth quarter 19th century
Canvas, 0.510 x 0.851 (20 1/16 x 33 9/16)
Gift of Edgar William and Bernice Chrysler Garbisch
1958.9.14

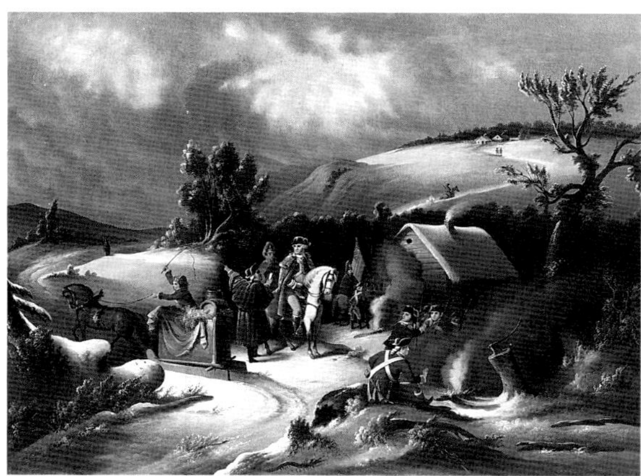

Washington at Valley Forge, mid-19th century
Canvas, 0.756 x 1.013 (29 3/4 x 39 7/8)
Gift of Edgar William and Bernice Chrysler Garbisch
1971.83.20

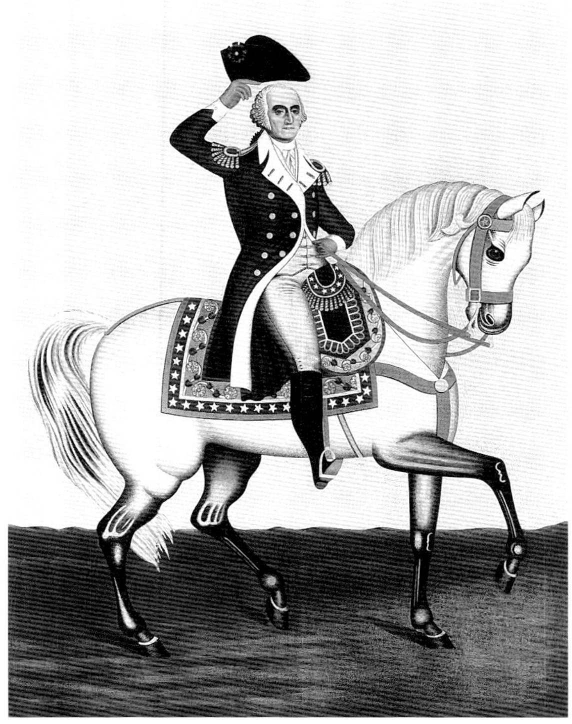

General Washington on a White Charger, first half 19th century
Wood, 0.965 x 0.749 (38 x 29 1/2)
Gift of Edgar William and Bernice Chrysler Garbisch
1955.11.22

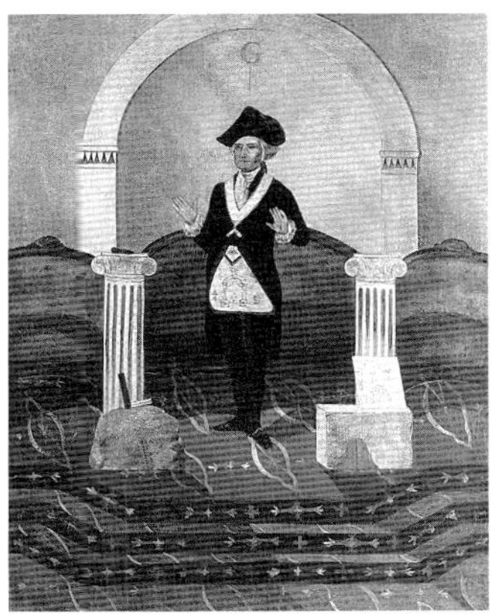

Washington, the Mason, c. 1868
Canvas, 0.384 x 0.305 (15⅛ x 12)
Gift of Edgar William and Bernice Chrysler Garbisch
1956.13.12

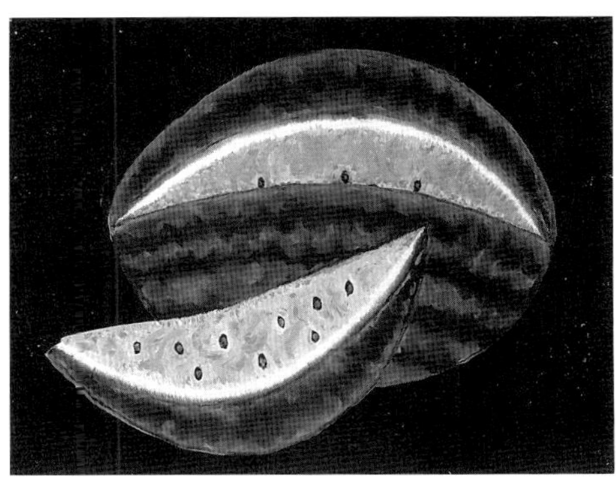

Watermelon, mid-19th century
Reverse painting on glass, 0.355 x 0.457 (14 x 18)
Gift of Edgar William and Bernice Chrysler Garbisch
1964.23.6

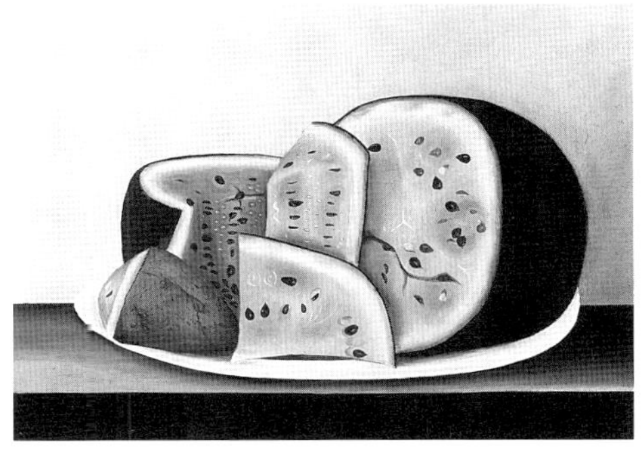

Watermelon on a Plate, mid-19th century
Canvas, 0.457 x 0.610 (18 x 24)
Gift of Edgar William and Bernice Chrysler Garbisch
1980.61.11

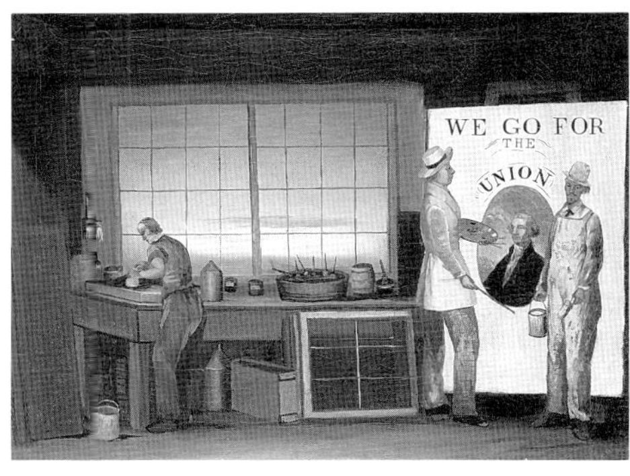

"We Go for the Union,' c. 1840/1850
Canvas, 0.462 x 0.615 (18 x 24)
Inscribed on sign: *WE GO FOR/THE/ UNION*
Gift of Edgar William and Bernice Chrysler Garbisch
1956.13.13

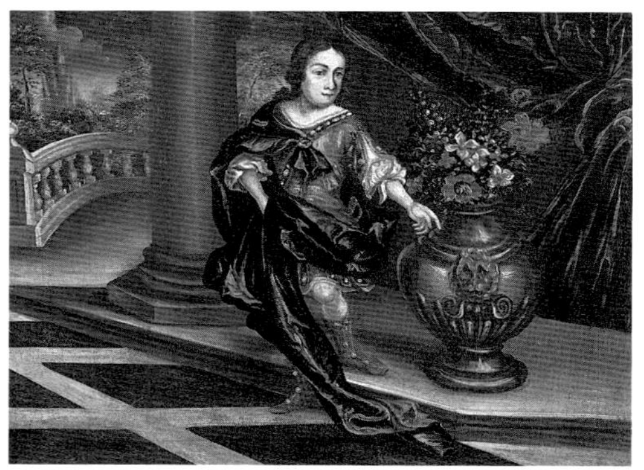

Young Man on Terrace, c. 1730
Canvas, 0.515 x 0.660 (20¼ x 26)
Gift of Edgar William and Bernice Chrysler Garbisch
1953.5.92

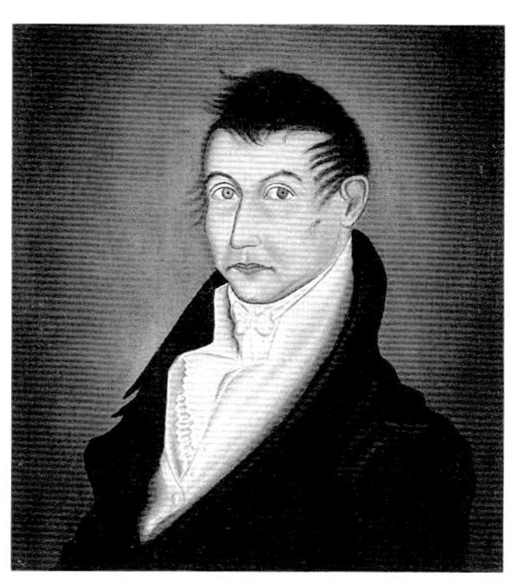

Young Man Wearing White Vest, c. 1810
Canvas, 0.642 x 0.571 (25¼ x 22½)
Gift of Edgar William and Bernice Chrysler Garbisch
1955.11.24

PAINTINGS TRANSFERRED IN 1962 TO THE NATIONAL PORTRAIT GALLERY

In addition to a National Gallery of Art, Andrew W. Mellon believed that this country should also have its own National Portrait Gallery. Among the American paintings in the Andrew W. Mellon Collection given to the National Gallery of Art were twenty portraits of important Americans. These the National Gallery held for a future National Portrait Gallery. Other collectors made donations for the same purpose.

While in the custody of the National Gallery these portraits were treated as part of its collection. Accordingly, whenever they were published during this period, they were identified as the property of the National Gallery of Art. It is because of this association that they are listed in this catalogue. They are given their traditional attributions and titles, which may not agree with the present designations of the National Portrait Gallery.

Artist and Title

John James Audubon, *Henry Clay*

John Woodhouse Audubon, *John James Audubon*

John Singleton Copley, *Henry Laurens*

Ralph E. W. Earl, *Andrew Jackson*

Jacob Eichholtz, *John Tyler*

George Fuller, *Self-Portrait*

George P. A. Healy, *James Buchanan*

George P. A. Healy, *Henry Clay*

George P. A. Healy, *Abraham Lincoln*

George P. A. Healy, *John Cardinal McCloskey*

George P. A. Healy, *Franklin Pierce*

George P. A. Healy, *Daniel Webster*

Thomas Hicks, *Stephen Foster*

John Wesley Jarvis, *De Witt Clinton*

James Reid Lambdin, *William Henry Harrison*

James Reid Lambdin, *John Marshall*

Emanuel Leutze, *Nathaniel Hawthorne*

Albert K. Murray, *James Vincent Forrestal*

Charles Willson Peale, *Benjamin Harrison*

Charles Willson Peale, *General William Moultrie*

Rembrandt Peale, *John Calhoun*

Rembrandt Peale, *George Washington*

Christian Schussele, *Men of Progress*

Thomas E. Stephens, *General Dwight D. Eisenhower*

Thomas E. Stephens, *General George C. Marshall*

Augustus Vincent Tack, *Harry S. Truman*

John Vanderlyn, *James Monroe*

PAINTINGS FORMERLY CONSIDERED AMERICAN

Changes adopted since the publication of *American Paintings: An Illustrated Catalogue* (1980)

Former Attribution	Current Attribution
1947.17.48 Anonymous American 18th Century *Portrait of a Lady* Third quarter 18th century	Anonymous British 18th Century *Portrait of a Lady* c. 1770/1775
1947.17.95 Anonymous American 18th Century *Portrait of a Lady* c. 1730	Maria Verelst (1680–1744) Dutch *Portrait of a Lady* c. 1715/1730, perhaps close to 1725
1980.61.13 Anonymous American 19th Century *Family Group in Interior with Seven People and a Dog* c. 1840	Anonymous British 19th Century *Portrait of an Unknown Family with a Terrier* c. 1825/1835
1947.17.29 Attributed to Mather Brown (1761–1831) *James, Fifth Duke of Hamilton* 1737/1740	Jeremiah Davison (c. 1695–1745) Scottish *James, Fifth Duke of Hamilton* 1737/1740
1942.8.15 Gilbert Stuart (1755–1828) *Mrs. William Hartigan* c. 1793	Carl Fredrik von Breda (1759–1818) Swedish *Mrs. William Hartigan* c. 1787/1796

CONCORDANCE OF OLD AND NEW ACCESSION NUMBERS

Old	New	Artist and Title
487	1940.1.1	Brown, Mather *William Vans Murray*
488	1940.1.2	Savage, Edward *The Washington Family*
489	1940.1.3	Stuart, Gilbert *Joseph Coolidge*
490	1940.1.4	Stuart, Gilbert *Mrs. Richard Yates*
491	1940.1.5	Stuart, Gilbert *Lawrence Reid Yates*
492	1940.1.6	Stuart, Gilbert *George Washington (Vaughan-Sinclair portrait)*
493	1940.1.7	Harding, Chester *John Randolph*
494	1940.1.8	Trumbull, John *Alexander Hamilton*
495	1940.1.9	Stuart, Gilbert *John Randolph*
496	1940.1.10	West, Benjamin *Colonel Guy Johnson*
550	1942.4.1	Copley, John Singleton *Baron Graham*
551	1942.4.2	Copley, John Singleton *The Red Cross Knight*
555	1942.8.2	Copley, John Singleton *Jane Browne*
556	1942.8.3	Duveneck, Frank *Leslie Pease Barnum*
557	1942.8.4	Duveneck, Frank *William Gedney Bunce*
559	1942.8.6	Jouett, Matthew Harris *Augustus Fielding Hawkins*
561	1942.8.8	Anonymous American 19th Century *Portrait of a Man*
562	1942.8.9	Peale, Charles Willson *John Philip de Haas*
563	1942.8.10	Quidor, John *The Return of Rip Van Winkle*
564	1942.8.11	Stuart, Gilbert *Captain Joseph Anthony*
565	1942.8.12	Stuart, Gilbert *Mr. Ashe*

Old	New	Artist and Title
566	1942.8.13	Anonymous American 19th Century *Matilda Caroline Cruger (?)*
567	1942.8.14	Stuart, Gilbert *Counsellor John Dunn*
569	1942.8.16	Stuart, Gilbert *Dr. William Hartigan (?)*
570	1942.8.17	Stuart, Gilbert *Commodore Thomas Macdonough*
571	1942.8.18	Stuart, Gilbert *George Pollock*
572	1942.8.19	Stuart, Gilbert *Mrs. George Pollock*
573	1942.8.20	Stuart, Gilbert *Stephen Van Rensselaer*
574	1942.8.21	Stuart, Gilbert *Sir Joshua Reynolds*
575	1942.8.22	Stuart, Gilbert *Mrs. William Robinson*
576	1942.8.23	Stuart, Gilbert *Edward Stow*
578	1942.8.25	Stuart, Gilbert *William Thornton*
579	1942.8.26	Stuart, Gilbert *Mrs. William Thornton*
580	1942.8.27	Stuart, Gilbert *George Washington (Vaughan portrait)*
581	1942.8.28	Stuart, Gilbert *Luke White*
582	1942.8.29	Stuart, Gilbert *Richard Yates*
583	1942.8.30	Sully, Thomas *John Quincy Adams*
584	1942.8.31	Sully, Thomas Wilcocks and Sully, Thomas *Major Thomas Biddle*
585	1942.8.32	Sully, Thomas *Ann Biddle Hopkinson*
586	1942.8.33	Sully, Thomas *Francis Hopkinson*
587	1942.8.34	Sully, Thomas *Andrew Jackson*
588	1942.8.35	Sully, Thomas *Abraham Kintzing*
589	1942.8.36	Vanderlyn, John *Zachariah Schoonmaker*
591	1942.8.38	Waldo, Samuel Lovett *Robert G. L. De Peyster*
592	1942.8.39	West, Benjamin *Self-Portrait*
593	1942.8.40	Wollaston, John *Mary Walton Morris*
594	1942.8.41	Wollaston, John *Lewis Morris (?)*
595	1942.10.1	Elliott, Charles Loring *Captain Warren Delano*
596	1942.7.1	Peale, Rembrandt *George Washington*
695	1942.9.99	Whistler, James McNeill *Chelsea Wharf: Grey and Silver*
696	1942.13.1	Sully, Thomas *Henry Pratt*
697	1942.13.2	Pratt, Matthew *The Duke of Portland*
701	1942.14.1	Stuart, Gilbert *John Bill Ricketts*
703	1943.1.2	Chase, William Merritt *A Friendly Call*
704	1943.1.3	Anonymous American 18th Century *Elisha Doane*
705	1943.1.4	Anonymous American 18th Century *Jane Cutler Doane*
706	1943.1.5	Anonymous American 19th Century *Portrait of a Lady*
707	1943.1.6	Morse, Samuel Finley Breese *Portrait of a Lady*
708	1943.1.7	Anonymous American 19th Century *John Rush (?)*
709	1943.1.8	Sully, Thomas *Mrs. William Griffin*

Old	New	Artist and Title
749	1943.6.1	Whistler, James McNeill *Mother of Pearl and Silver: The Andalusian*
750	1943.6.2	Whistler, James McNeill *The White Girl (Symphony in White, No.1)*
751	1943.9.1	Hassam, Childe *Allies Day, May 1917*
758	1943.11.7	Whistler, James McNeill *Alexander Arnold Hannay*
760	1943.13.1	Homer, Winslow *Breezing Up (A Fair Wind)*
764	1944.1.1	Harding, Chester *Amos Lawrence*
765	1944.3.1	Stuart, Gilbert *Horace Binney*
775	1944.13.1	Bellows, George *Both Members of This Club*
776	1944.15.1	Bellows, George *Maud Dale*
777	1944.17.1	Pratt, Matthew *Madonna of Saint Jerome*
778	1945.17.1	Sully, Thomas *Joseph Dugan*
779	1945.4.1	Inness, George *The Lackawanna Valley*
831	1945.9.1	Sully, Thomas *Lady with a Harp: Eliza Ridgely*
832	1945.12.1	Sully, Thomas *Governor Charles Ridgely of Maryland*
833	1945.11.1	Alexander, Francis *Aaron Baldwin*
886	1946.1.1	Ryder, Albert Pinkham *Siegfried and the Rhine Maidens*
889	1946.16.1	Eakins, Thomas *Archbishop Diomede Falconio*
893	1947.4.1	Sully, Thomas *Captain Charles Stewart*
903	1947.9.1	Eichholtz, Jacob *Mrs. Robert Coleman*
904	1947.9.2	Eichholtz, Jacob *Robert Coleman*
905	1947.9.3	Sully, Thomas *The Coleman Sisters*
906	1947.11.1	Homer, Winslow *Hound and Hunter*
907	1947.15.1	Copley, John Singleton *The Death of the Earl of Chatham*
910	1947.17.2	Durand, Asher Brown *Gouverneur Kemble*
911	1947.17.3	Eichholtz, Jacob *William Clark Frazer*
912	1947.17.4	Eichholtz, Jacob *James P. Smith*
913	1947.17.5	Anonymous American 19th Century *Portrait of a Man*
914	1947.17.6	Elliott, Charles Loring *William Sidney Mount*
915	1947.17.7	Huntington, Daniel *Henry Theodore Tuckerman*
916	1947.17.8	Inman, Henry *George Pope Morris*
917	1947.17.9	Mount, William Sidney *Charles Loring Elliott*
918	1947.17.10	Peale, Rembrandt, Attributed to *Timothy Matlack*
919	1947.17.11	Sully, Thomas *Robert Walsh*
920	1947.17.12	Theus, Jeremiah *Mr. Motte*
921	1947.17.13	Trumbull, John *William Rogers*
922	1947.17.14	Vanderlyn, John *John Sudam*
924	1947.17.16	Peale, Rembrandt *George Washington*
925	1947.17.17	Volk, Douglas *Abraham Lincoln*
926	1947.17.18	Alexander, Francis *Sarah Blake Sturgis (?)*
928	1947.17.20	Ames, Ezra *Maria Gansevoort Melville*

Old	New	Artist and Title
929	1947.17.21	Ames, Joseph Alexander *George Southward*
931	1947.17.23	West, Benjamin *Mrs. William Beckford*
932	1947.17.24	Benbridge, Henry *Portrait of a Man*
933	1947.17.25	Blackburn, Joseph *A Military Officer*
936	1947.17.28	Brown, Mather *Thomas Dawson, Viscount Cremorne*
938	1947.17.30	Clark, Alvan *Barnabus Clark*
945	1947.17.37	Durand, Asher Brown *Portrait of a Man*
950	1947.17.42	Earl, Ralph *Thomas Earle*
952	1947.17.44	Anonymous American 19th Century *Portrait of a Man*
953	1947.17.45	Eichholtz, Jacob *Phoebe Cassidy Freeman*
954	1947.17.46	Anonymous American 19th Century *Miss Robinson*
958	1947.17.50	Frothingham, James *Ebenezer Newhall*
959	1947.17.51	Anonymous American 19th Century *Portrait of a Man*
960	1947.17.52	Anonymous American 19th Century *Portrait of a Man*
961	1947.17.53	Anonymous American 19th Century *Mother and Child*
962	1947.17.54	Harding, Chester *Self-Portrait*
963	1947.17.55	Anonymous American 19th Century *Junius Brutus Booth*
964	1947.17.56	Huntington, Daniel *Dr. James Hall*
965	1947.17.57	Huntington, Daniel *Dr. John Edwards Holbrook*
966	1947.17.58	Anonymous American 19th Century *Portrait of a Lady*
967	1947.17.59	Anonymous American 19th Century *Portrait of a Man*
968	1947.17.60	Anonymous American 19th Century *Portrait of a Lady*
969	1947.17.61	Anonymous American 19th Century *Portrait of a Man*
970	1947.17.62	Johnson, David *Edwin Forrest*
971	1947.17.63	Johnson, Eastman *Joseph Wesley Harper, Jr.*
973	1947.17.65	Johnston, John *John Peck*
974	1947.17.66	Anonymous American 19th Century *Portrait of a Lady*
975	1947.17.67	Anonymous American 19th Century *Abraham Lincoln*
976	1947.17.68	Lawson, Thomas Bayley *William Morris Hunt*
978	1947.17.70	Anonymous American 19th Century *Portrait of a Man*
979	1947.17.71	Mare, John, Attributed to *Robert Monckton*
980	1947.17.72	Metcalf, Eliab *Self-Portrait*
981	1947.17.73	Ingham, Charles Cromwell *Coralie Livingston (?)*
982	1947.17.74	The Schuyler Limner (possibly Nehemiah Partridge) *Mr. Van Vechten*
983	1947.17.75	Anonymous American 19th Century *Portrait of a Lady*
985	1947.17.77	Neagle, John *Mrs. John Dickson*
986	1947.17.78	Neagle, John *Thomas W. Dyott*

Old	New	Artist and Title
987	1947.17.79	Anonymous American 19th Century *Ann C. Rudman*
988	1947.17.80	Anonymous American 19th Century *William C. Rudman, Jr.*
989	1947.17.81	Neagle, John *Reverend John Albert Ryan*
990	1947.17.82	Anonymous American 19th Century *Miss Ryan (?)*
992	1947.17.84	Anonymous American 19th Century *Portrait of a Man*
993	1947.17.85	Peale, Rembrandt *Richardson Stuart*
997	1947.17.89	Pine, Robert Edge *General William Smallwood*
1001	1947.17.93	Anonymous American 18th Century *Portrait of a Man*
1004	1947.17.96	Spencer, Frederick R. *Frances Ludlum Morris*
1005	1947.17.97	Anonymous American 19th Century *Portrait of a Man*
1009	1947.17.101	West, Benjamin *Elizabeth, Countess of Effingham*
1011	1947.17.103	Wollaston, John *John Stevens*
1012	1947.17.104	Stuart, Gilbert, Attributed to and Follower *Mrs. Andrew Dexter (?)*
1013	1947.17.105	Wollaston, John *Lieutenant Archibald Kennedy (?)*
1014	1947.17.106	Stuart, Gilbert, After *William Seton*
1015	1947.17.107	Stuart, Gilbert, After *James Lloyd*
1016	1947.17.108	Sully, Thomas *Thomas Alston*
1017	1947.17.109	Anonymous American 19th Century *Portrait of a Man*
1018	1947.17.110	Eichholtz, Jacob *Julianna Hazlehurst*
1019	1947.17.111	Sully, Thomas after Stuart, Gilbert *John Philip Kemble*
1022	1948.1.1	Fuller, George *Agnes Gordon Higginson, Wife of George Fuller*
1025	1948.7.1	Henri, Robert *Catharine*
1026	1948.8.1	Earl, Ralph *Daniel Boardman*
1029	1948.16.1	Sargent, John Singer *Repose*
1030	1948.16.2	Whistler, James McNeill *Head of a Girl*
1031	1948.13.1	Sully, Thomas *The Sicard-David Children*
1043	1949.2.1	Dove, Arthur *Moth Dance*
1044	1949.2.2	Hartley, Marsden *Landscape No. 5*
1046	1949.9.1	Henri, Robert *Young Woman in White*
1051	1950.18.1	Stuart, Gilbert *The Skater (Portrait of William Grant)*
1052	1950.5.1	Luks, George Benjamin *The Bersaglieri*
1054	1950.8.1	Clark, Alvan *Thomas Whittemore*
1055	1950.8.2	Clark, Alvan *Lovice Corbett Whittemore*
1058	1950.15.1	Jarvis, John Wesley *Thomas Paine*
1063	1951.5.3	Ryder, Albert Pinkham *Mending the Harness*
1064	1951.6.1	Wiles, Irving R. *Miss Julia Marlowe*
1066	1951.20.1	Sargent, John Singer *Mrs. William Crowninshield Endicott*
1067	1951.8.1	Homer, Winslow *Right and Left*

Old	New	Artist and Title
1068	1951.9.1	Audubon, John Woodhouse *Black-footed Ferret*
1069	1951.9.2	Audubon, John Woodhouse, Attributed to *A Young Bull*
1070	1951.9.3	Audubon, John James *Farmyard Fowls*
1072	1951.9.4	Audubon, John James, Studio of *Long-tailed Weasel*
1077	1951.9.9	Audubon, John Woodhouse *Long-tailed Red Fox*
1081	1952.1.1	Trumbull, John *Alexander Hamilton*
1108	1952.3.1	Sargent, John Singer *Mathilde Townsend*
1168	1952.12.1	Leonid *Faraduro, Portugal*
1172	1953.1.1	Kensett, John Frederick *Beacon Rock, Newport Harbor*
1180	1953.7.1	Eakins, Thomas *The Biglin Brothers Racing*
1181	1953.10.1	Haseltine, William Stanley *Marina Piccola, Capri*
1182	1953.9.1	Fuller, George *Violet*
1183	1953.9.2	Fuller, George *Mrs. Stephen Higginson*
1184	1953.11.1	Melchers, Gari *Andrew W. Mellon*
1185	1954.1.1	Lambdin, James Reid, Attributed to *Daniel Webster*
1186	1954.1.2	Courter, Franklin C. *Lincoln and His Son, Tad*
1189	1954.1.5	Eichholtz, Jacob *Henry Eichholtz Leman*
1190	1954.1.6	Anonymous American 19th Century *Portrait of a Man*
1193	1954.1.9	Stuart, Gilbert, After *William Constable*
1194	1954.1.10	Stuart, Gilbert *Sir John Dick*
1196	1954.2.1	Luks, George Benjamin *The Miner*
1197	1953.5.1	Allen, Luther *Lucia Leonard*
1198	1953.5.2	Bard, James *Steamer* St. Lawrence
1199	1953.5.3	Bonnell, William *Clement Bonnell*
1200	1953.5.4	Bundy, Horace *Vermont Lawyer*
1201	1953.5.5	Chandler, Joseph Goodhue *Charles H. Sisson*
1202	1953.5.6	Coe, Elias V. *Mrs. Phebe Houston*
1203	1953.5.7	Cooke, L. M. *Salute to General Washington in New York Harbor*
1204	1953.5.8	Earl, Ralph Eleaser Whiteside *Family Portrait*
1205	1953.5.9	Anonymous American 19th Century *Profile Portrait of a Young Man*
1206	1953.5.10	Anonymous American 19th Century *Profile Portrait of a Young Lady*
1207	1953.5.11	Eichholtz, Jacob *Mr. Kline*
1208	1953.5.12	Eichholtz, Jacob *Mr. Leman*
1209	1953.5.13	Eichholtz, Jacob *Joseph Leman*
1210	1953.5.14	Eichholtz, Jacob *Miss Leman*
1214	1953.5.17	Hofmann, Charles C. *Berks County Almshouse, 1878*
1215	1953.5.18	Anonymous American 19th Century *The Mounted Acrobats*
1216	1953.5.19	Jennys, William *Asa Benjamin*
1217	1953.5.20	Jennys, William *Mrs. Asa Benjamin*

Old	New	Artist and Title
1218	1953.5.21	Jennys, William *Everard Benjamin*
1219	1953.5.22	Anonymous American 19th Century *Portrait of a Black Man*
1221	1953.5.23	Lermond, Charles C. E. *Landscape with Churches*
1222	1953.5.24	The Beardsley Limner *Girl in a Pink Dress*
1223	1953.5.25	Mader, Louis *Berks County Almshouse, 1895*
1227	1953.5.26	Park, Linton *Flax Scutching Bee*
1228	1953.5.27	Park, Linton *The Burial*
1230	1953.5.28	Phillips, Ammi *Mr. Day*
1231	1953.5.29	Phillips, Ammi *Mrs. Day*
1232	1953.5.30	Phillips, Ammi *Henry Teller*
1233	1953.5.31	Phillips, Ammi *Jane Storm Teller*
1236	1953.5.32	Polk, Charles Peale *Anna Maria Cumpston*
1237	1953.5.33	Prior, William Matthew *Master Cleeves*
1240	1953.5.34	Stearns, William *Bowl of Fruit*
1241	1953.5.35	The Denison Limner *Elizabeth Denison*
1242	1953.5.36	Tanner, J. G. *Engagement between the* Monitor *and the* Merrimac
1243	1953.5.37	Anonymous American 19th Century *Woman in Red Arrowback Chair*
1244	1953.5.38	Waters, Susan C., After *Henry L. Wells*
1251	1953.5.40	H., J. *Abraham Clark and His Children*

Old	New	Artist and Title
1252	1953.5.41	Greenleaf, Benjamin *Portrait of J. L.*
1253	1953.5.42	Prior-Hamblin School *Husband*
1254	1953.5.43	Prior-Hamblin School *Daughter*
1255	1953.5.44	Anonymous American 19th Century *Sophia Burpee*
1259	1953.5.45	Hendrickson, Daniel, Attributed to *Catharine Hendrickson*
1262	1953.5.46	Anonymous American 18th Century *Maria*
1263	1953.5.47	Anonymous American 19th Century *Sophia Mead*
1264	1953.5.48	Anonymous American 19th Century *Harlan Page (?)*
1265	1953.5.49	Anonymous American 19th Century *The Sargent Family*
1266	1953.5.50	Powers, Asahel *William Sheldon (?)*
1267	1953.5.51	Powers, Asahel *Mrs. William Sheldon (?)*
1268	1953.5.52	Phillips, Ammi *Joseph Slade*
1269	1953.5.53	Phillips, Ammi *Alsa Slade*
1270	1953.5.54	Powers, Asahel *Hannah Fisher Stedman*
1272	1953.5.55	Skynner, Thomas *John Stone*
1273	1953.5.56	Skynner, Thomas *Eliza Welch Stone*
1274	1953.5.57	The Beardsley Limner *Charles Adams Wheeler*
1279	1953.5.58	Prior, William Matthew *Baby in Blue*
1282	1953.5.59	Phillips, Ammi *The Strawberry Girl*

Old	New	Artist and Title
1283	1953.5.60	Anonymous American 19th Century *Boy in Blue*
1284	1953.5.61	Anonymous American 19th Century *Brother and Sister*
1285	1953.5.62	Anonymous American 19th Century *Little Miss Wyckoff*
1286	1953.5.63	Anonymous American 18th Century *Feeding the Bird*
1287	1953.5.64	Anonymous American 19th Century *Little Girl with Flower Basket*
1288	1953.5.65	Anonymous American 19th Century *Little Girl with Doll*
1289	1953.5.66	Prior-Hamblin School *Little Girl with Slate*
1290	1953.5.67	Prior, William Matthew *Boy with Toy Horse and Wagon*
1291	1953.5.68	Anonymous American 19th Century *Blue Eyes*
1292	1953.5.69	Anonymous American 19th Century *On Exhibition*
1293	1953.5.70	Hamblin, Sturtevant J. *Little Girl with Pet Rabbit*
1294	1953.5.71	Anonymous American 19th Century *Girl with Toy Rooster*
1295	1953.5.72	Anonymous American 19th Century *Little Girl in Blue Dress*
1297	1953.5.73	Anonymous American 19th Century *Lady Wearing Pearls*
1299	1953.5.74	Anonymous American 19th Century *The Blue Shawl*
1300	1953.5.75	Anonymous American 18th Century *At the Writing Table*
1301	1953.5.76	Anonymous American 19th Century *Old Man in Red Slat Back Chair*
1302	1953.5.77	Anonymous American 19th Century *Chief Jumper of the Seminoles*
1303	1953.5.78	Anonymous American 19th Century *The Colonel*
1304	1953.5.79	Anonymous American 19th Century *The Letter*
1305	1953.5.80	Dunlap, William, Attributed to *Samuel Griffin*
1306	1953.5.81	Anonymous American 19th Century *Textile Merchant*
1307	1953.5.82	Anonymous American 19th Century *Profile Portrait of a Man*
1308	1953.5.83	Anonymous American 19th Century *Profile Portrait of a Lady*
1309	1953.5.84	Anonymous American 19th Century *Anonymous Man*
1310	1953.5.85	Anonymous American 19th Century *Anonymous Woman*
1313	1953.5.86	Anonymous American 18th Century *Attack on Bunker's Hill, with the Burning of Charles Town*
1314	1953.5.87	Anonymous American 19th Century *New England Farm in Winter*
1315	1953.5.88	Anonymous American 19th Century *Lexington Battle Monument*
1316	1953.5.89	Anonymous American 18th Century *A View of Mount Vernon*

Old	New	Artist and Title
1317	1953.5.90	Anonymous American 19th Century *Imaginary Regatta of America's Cup Winners*
1319	1953.5.91	Anonymous American 18th Century *Christ and the Woman of Samaria*
1321	1953.5.92	Anonymous American 18th Century *Young Man on Terrace*
1322	1953.5.93	Anonymous American 19th Century *Mahantango Valley Farm*
1323	1953.5.94	Anonymous American 19th Century *Farmhouse in Mahantango Valley*
1324	1953.5.95	Humphreys, Charles S. *The Trotter*
1326	1953.5.96	Anonymous American 19th Century *Retriever*
1327	1953.5.97	Anonymous American 19th Century *Coon Hunt*
1328	1953.5.98	Anonymous American 19th Century *The Start of the Hunt*
1329	1953.5.99	Anonymous American 19th Century *The End of the Hunt*
1331	1953.5.100	Anonymous American 19th Century *Under Full Sail*
1332	1953.5.101	Anonymous American 19th Century *Flowers and Fruit*
1333	1953.5.102	Anonymous American 19th Century *Pink Roses*
1334	1953.5.103	Anonymous American 19th Century *Basket of Fruit*
1335	1953.5.104	Anonymous American 19th Century *Fruit on a Tray*
1336	1953.5.105	Anonymous American 19th Century *Peaches—Still Life*
1340	1954.4.1	Weir, Julian Alden *Moonlight*
1341	1954.4.2	Blakelock, Ralph Albert *The Artist's Garden*
1342	1954.4.3	Henri, Robert *Snow in New York*
1347	1954.7.1	Stuart, Gilbert *John Adams*
1348	1954.7.2	Stuart, Gilbert *Mrs. John Adams*
1352	1954.9.2	Stuart, Gilbert *George Washington*
1353	1954.9.3	Stuart, Gilbert *Ann Barry*
1354	1954.9.4	Stuart, Gilbert *Mary Barry*
1360	1955.2.1	Peale, Rembrandt *Thomas Sully*
1419	1955.11.1	Zeliff, Amzi Emmons *The Barnyard*
1420	1955.11.2	Sachs, Lambert *The Herbert Children*
1421	1955.11.3	Anonymous American 19th Century *Mounting of the Guard*
1422	1955.11.4	Anonymous American 19th Century *Allegory of Freedom*
1423	1955.11.5	Anonymous American 19th Century *Annis Cook (?) Holding an Apple*
1424	1955.11.6	Anonymous American 19th Century *Sarah Cook Arnold (?) Knitting*
1425	1955.11.7	Anonymous American 19th Century *Memorial to Nicholas M. S. Catlin*
1426	1955.11.8	Waters, Susan C. *Henry L. Wells*

Old	New	Artist and Title
1427	1955.11.9	Jordan, Samuel *Eaton Family Memorial*
1428	1955.11.10	Lamb, A. A. *Emancipation Proclamation*
1429	1955.11.11	Stanley, Abram Ross *Eliza Wells*
1430	1955.11.12	Anonymous American 19th Century *New England Village*
1431	1955.11.13	Anonymous American 19th Century *Liberty*
1432	1955.11.14	Robinson, J. C. *Portrait of an Old Man*
1433	1955.11.15	Robinson, J. C. *Portrait of an Old Lady*
1434	1955.11.16	Hofmann, Charles C. *View of Benjamin Reber's Farm*
1435	1955.11.17	Anonymous American 19th Century *Wellington Van Reid*
1436	1955.11.18	Anonymous American 19th Century *Jane L. Van Reid*
1437	1955.11.19	Field, Erastus Salisbury *Man with Vial*
1438	1955.11.20	Field, Erastus Salisbury *Wife of Man with Vial*
1439	1955.11.21	Anonymous American 19th Century *Dr. Alvah Cook*
1440	1955.11.22	Anonymous American 19th Century *General Washington on a White Charger*
1441	1955.11.23	Anonymous American 19th Century *The Hobby Horse*
1442	1955.11.24	Anonymous American 19th Century *Young Man Wearing White Vest*
1453	1956.7.1	Henri, Robert *Edith Reynolds*
1456	1956.13.1	Budington, J. *Father and Son*
1457	1956.13.2	Chambers, Thomas *The Connecticut Valley*
1458	1956.13.3	Field, Erastus Salisbury *Ark of the Covenant*
1459	1956.13.4	Hashagen, A. *Ship* Arkansas *Leaving Havana*
1460	1956.13.5	MacKay *Catherine Brower*
1461	1956.13.6	Ropes, George *Mount Vernon*
1462	1956.13.7	Anonymous American 19th Century *Boy and Girl*
1463	1956.13.8	Waters, Susan C. *Brothers*
1464	1956.13.9	Anonymous American 18th Century *Miss Daggett of New Haven, Connecticut (possibly Amelia Martha)*
1465	1956.13.10	Anonymous American 18th Century *Landscape with Buildings*
1466	1956.13.11	Gerardus Duyckinck, Attributed to *Lady Undressing for a Bath*
1467	1956.13.12	Anonymous American 19th Century *Washington, the Mason*
1468	1956.13.13	Anonymous American 19th Century *"We Go for the Union"*
1469	1956.13.14	The Gansevoort Limner (possibly Pieter Vanderlyn) *Miss Van Alen*
1470	1956.15.1	Harding, Chester *Charles Carroll of Carrollton*
1473	1957.2.1	Eakins, Thomas *Louis Husson*
1474	1957.2.2	Eakins, Thomas *Mrs. Louis Husson*
1475	1957.3.1	Neagle, John *George Dodd*

Old	New	Artist and Title
1476	1957.3.2	Neagle, John *Mrs. George Dodd*
1477	1957.5.1	Harnett, William Michael *My Gems*
1479	1957.4.2	Melchers, Gari *The Sisters*
1486	1957.9.1	Neagle, John *Colonel Augustus James Pleasonton*
1487	1957.10.1	Stuart, Gilbert *Robert Liston*
1488	1957.11.1	Badger, Joseph *Captain Isaac Foster*
1489	1957.11.2	Badger, Joseph *Mrs. Isaac Foster*
1490	1957.11.3	Badger, Joseph *Isaac Foster, Jr.*
1491	1957.11.4	Badger, Joseph *Dr. William Foster*
1492	1957.11.5	Chipman *Melons and Grapes*
1493	1957.11.6	Coe, Elias V. *Henry W. Houston*
1494	1957.11.7	Anonymous American 19th Century *Aurora*
1495	1957.11.8	Anonymous American 20th Century *The Dog*
1496	1957.11.9	The Schuyler Limner (possibly Nehemiah Partridge) *Mr. Willson*
1498	1958.2.1	Sargent, John Singer *Mrs. Joseph Chamberlain*
1505	1958.5.1	Chambers, Thomas *Mount Auburn Cemetery*
1511	1958.9.1	Bauman, Leila T. *Geese in Flight*
1512	1958.9.2	Bauman, Leila T. *U.S. Mail Boat*
1513	1958.9.3	Bradley, John *Little Girl in Lavender*
1514	1958.9.4	Brown, W. H. *Bareback Riders*
1515	1958.9.5	Haddock, A. *Red Jacket*
1516	1958.9.6	Toole, John *Skating Scene*
1517	1958.9.7	Hilling, John *Burning of Old South Church, Bath, Maine*
1518	1958.9.8	Anonymous American 19th Century *Cat and Kittens*
1519	1958.9.9	Anonymous American 18th Century *The Cheney Family*
1520	1958.9.10	Anonymous American 19th Century *Family Burying Ground*
1521	1958.9.11	Anonymous American 19th Century *Martha*
1522	1958.9.12	Hopkins, Milton W. *Aphia Salisbury Rich and Baby Edward*
1523	1958.9.13	Anonymous American 19th Century *Twenty-two Houses and a Church*
1524	1958.9.14	Anonymous American 19th Century *Village by the River*
1531	1959.3.2	Whistler, James McNeill *Brown and Gold: Self-Portrait*
1532	1959.3.3	Whistler, James McNeill *George W. Vanderbilt*
1533	1959.4.1	Copley, John Singleton *Epes Sargent*
1534	1959.6.1	Eichholtz, Jacob *The Ragan Sisters*
1535	1959.8.1	West, Benjamin *The Battle of La Hogue*
1536	1959.11.1	Johnson, Joshua *The Westwood Children*
1537	1959.11.2	Stock, Joseph Whiting *Mary and Francis Wilcox*

Old	New	Artist and Title
1538	1959.11.3	Anonymous American 19th Century *Baby in Blue Cradle*
1539	1959.11.4	Anonymous American 18th Century *Jonathan Bentham*
1540	1959.11.5	Anonymous American 18th Century *Boy in Blue Coat*
1541	1959.11.6	Anonymous American 19th Century *Child with Rocking Horse*
1542	1959.11.7	Anonymous American 19th Century *Civil War Battle*
1543	1959.11.8	Anonymous American 19th Century *Five Children of the Budd Family*
1544	1959.11.9	Phillips, Ammi *Lady in White*
1545	1959.11.10	Anonymous American 19th Century *Leaving the Manor House*
1546	1959.11.11	Anonymous American 20th Century *Little Girl and the Cat*
1547	1959.11.12	Greenleaf, Benjamin *Lady in a White Mob Cap*
1550	1960.4.1	Copley, John Singleton *Colonel Fitch and His Sisters*
1552	1960.3.1	Savage, Edward *George Washington*
1599	1960.12.1	Stuart, Gilbert *Mrs. Robert Liston*
1600	1961.4.1	Greenwood, John *Mrs. Welshman*
1650	1961.7.1	Copley, John Singleton *The Copley Family*
1651	1961.8.1	Otis, Bass *John Smith Warner*
1652	1961.10.1	Carpenter, Francis Bicknell *Mrs. Henry C. Bowen*

Old	New	Artist and Title
1656	1961.15.1	Emmet, Lydia Field *Harriet Lancashire White and Her Children*
1658	1962.4.1	Sargent, John Singer *Street in Venice*
1659	1962.2.1	Inness, George *Lake Albano, Sunset*
1660	1962.6.1	Sargent, John Singer *Miss Grace Woodhouse*
1671	1963.10.7	Cassatt, Mary *Portrait of an Elderly Lady*
1728	1963.10.64	Anonymous American 20th Century *Madame G*
1731	1953.5.106	Miller, George M. *William Henry Vining*
1735	1963.10.71	Whistler, James McNeill *Little Girl in White*
1746	1963.10.82	Bellows, George *Blue Morning*
1747	1963.10.83	Bellows, George *The Lone Tenement*
1748	1963.10.84	Bellows, George *Nude with Red Hair*
1757	1963.10.93	Carlsen, Emil *Still Life with Fish*
1758	1963.10.94	Cassatt, Mary *The Boating Party*
1759	1963.10.95	Cassatt, Mary *Miss Mary Ellison*
1760	1963.10.96	Cassatt, Mary *The Loge*
1761	1963.10.97	Cassatt, Mary *Girl Arranging Her Hair*
1762	1963.10.98	Cassatt, Mary *Mother and Child*
1763	1963.10.99	Cassatt, Mary *Woman with a Red Zinnia*
1770	1963.10.106	Chase, William Merritt *Chrysanthemums*
1783	1963.10.119	Davies, Arthur B. *Sweet Tremulous Leaves*

Old	New	Artist and Title
1784	1963.10.120	Dearth, Henry Golden *Flecks of Foam*
1800	1963.10.136	Pène du Bois, Guy *Café du Dôme*
1801	1963.10.137	Pène du Bois, Guy *Hallway, Italian Restaurant*
1802	1963.10.138	Pène du Bois, Guy *The Politicians*
1803	1963.10.139	Pène du Bois, Guy *La Rue de la Santé*
1811	1963.10.147	Frieseke, Frederick Carl *The Basket of Flowers*
1820	1963.10.156	Hassam, Childe *Nude Seated*
1821	1963.10.157	Johnson, Eastman *The Early Scholar*
1852	1963.10.188	Paradise, John Wesley *Mrs. Elizabeth Oakes Smith*
1866	1963.10.202	Ranger, Henry Ward *Spring Woods*
1904	1963.6.1	Copley, John Singleton *Watson and the Shark*
1906	1963.9.1	Cropsey, Jasper Francis *Autumn—On the Hudson River*
1907	1963.9.2	Doughty, Thomas *Fanciful Landscape*
1913	1964.4.1	Homer, Winslow *Sunset*
1915	1964.19.1	Baer, George *Masouba*
1925	1964.13.1	Sargent, John Singer *Mrs. Adrian Iselin*
1926	1964.15.1	Trumbull, John *Patrick Tracy*
1927	1964.22.1	Twachtman, John Henry *Winter Harmony*
1933	1964.23.1	Chandler, Winthrop *Captain Samuel Chandler*
1934	1964.23.2	Chandler, Winthrop *Mrs. Samuel Chandler*
1935	1964.23.3	Field, Erastus Salisbury *"He Turned Their Waters into Blood"*

Old	New	Artist and Title
1936	1964.23.4	Hicks, Edward *The Cornell Farm*
1937	1964.23.5	Anonymous American 19th Century *Vase of Lilies*
1938	1964.23.6	Anonymous American 19th Century *Watermelon*
1939	1964.23.7	West, Benjamin *Dr. Samuel Boude*
1940	1964.23.8	West, Benjamin *Mrs. Samuel Boude*
1941	1965.2.1	Heade, Martin Johnson *Rio de Janeiro Bay*
1942	1943.14.1	Jarvis, John Wesley *Commodore John Rodgers*
1943	1947.13.1	Polk, Charles Peale *General Washington at Princeton*
1944	1965.6.1	Copley, John Singleton *Eleazer Tyng*
1946	1965.10.1	Wyant, Alexander Helwig *Peaceful Valley*
1949	1965.14.1	Church, Frederic Edwin *Morning in the Tropics*
1950	1965.15.1	Field, Erastus Salisbury *Mr. Pease*
1951	1965.15.2	Field, Erastus Salisbury *Mrs. Harlow A. Pease*
1952	1965.15.3	Alexander, Francis *Ralph Wheelock's Farm*
1953	1965.15.4	Sheffield, Isaac *Connecticut Sea Captain*
1954	1965.15.5	Sheffield, Isaac *Connecticut Sea Captain's Wife*
1955	1965.15.6	Theus, Jeremiah *Mr. Cuthbert*
1956	1965.15.7	Theus, Jeremiah *Mrs. Cuthbert*
1957	1965.15.8	Earl, Ralph *Dr. David Rogers*
1958	1965.15.9	Earl, Ralph *Martha Tennent Rogers and Daughter*

Old	New	Artist and Title
1959	1965.16.1	Catlin, George *Three Distinguished Warriors of the Sioux Tribe*
1960	1965.16.2	Catlin, George *A Sioux Chief, His Daughter, and a Warrior*
1961	1965.16.3	Catlin, George *The Sioux Chief with Several Indians*
1962	1965.16.4	Catlin, George *A Little Sioux Village*
1963	1965.16.5	Catlin, George *Scalp Dance—Sioux*
1964	1965.16.6	Catlin, George *Dog Dance—Sioux*
1965	1965.16.7	Catlin, George *Ball-Play of the Women—Sioux*
1966	1965.16.8	Catlin, George *A Dog Feast—Sioux*
1967	1965.16.9	Catlin, George *Facsimile of a Sioux Robe with Porcupine Quills*
1968	1965.16.10	Catlin, George *Buffalo Chase, Sioux Indians, Upper Missouri*
1969	1965.16.11	Catlin, George *After the Buffalo Chase—Sioux*
1970	1965.16.12	Catlin, George *A Sioux Village*
1971	1965.16.13	Catlin, George *Halsey's Bluff—Sioux Indians on the March*
1972	1965.16.14	Catlin, George *Sioux Village—Lac du Cygne*
1973	1965.16.15	Catlin, George *A Sioux War Party*
1974	1965.16.16	Catlin, George *Bivouac of a Sioux War Party*
1975	1965.16.17	Catlin, George *Amusing Dance—Sioux*
1976	1965.16.18	Catlin, George *Bivouac of a Sioux War Party at Sunrise*
1977	1965.16.19	Catlin, George *Crow Chief, His Wife, and a Warrior*
1978	1965.16.20	Catlin, George *Distinguished Crow Indians*
1979	1965.16.21	Catlin, George *A Crow Chief, a Warrior, and His Wife*
1980	1965.16.22	Catlin, George *A Crow Chief at His Toilette*
1981	1965.16.23	Catlin, George *Crow Warriors Bathing*
1982	1965.16.24	Catlin, George *A Crow Village on the Salmon River*
1983	1965.16.25	Catlin, George *A Crow Village and the Salmon River Mountains*
1984	1965.16.26	Catlin, George *A Small Crow Village*
1985	1965.16.27	Catlin, George *Two Blackfoot Warriors and a Woman*
1986	1965.16.28	Catlin, George *A Blackfoot Chief, His Wife, and a Medicine Man*
1987	1965.16.29	Catlin, George *Three Blackfoot Men*
1988	1965.16.30	Catlin, George *Arapaho Chief, His Wife, and a Warrior*
1989	1965.16.31	Catlin, George *Two Arapaho Warriors and a Woman*
1990	1965.16.32	Catlin, George *Assinneboine Warrior and His Family*
1991	1965.16.33	Catlin, George *Assinneboine Chief before and after Civilization*
1992	1965.16.34	Catlin, George *Two Nezperce Warriors and a Boy*

Old	New	Artist and Title
1993	1965.16 35	Catlin, George *Antelope Shooting—Assinneboine*
1994	1965.16 36	Catlin, George *A Cheyenne Chief, His Wife, and a Medicine Man*
1995	1965.16 37	Catlin, George *Three Cheyenne Warriors*
1996	1965.16 38	Catlin, George *Cheyenne Village*
1997	1965.16 39	Catlin, George *A Cheyenne Warrior Resting His Horse*
1998	1965.16.40	Catlin, George *Facsimile of a Cheyenne Robe*
1999	1965.16.41	Catlin, George *A Small Cheyenne Village*
2000	1965.16.42	Catlin, George *The Cheyenne Brothers Starting on Their Fall Hunt*
2001	1965.16.43	Catlin, George *The Cheyenne Brothers Returning from Their Fall Hunt*
2002	1965.16.44	Catlin, George *Four Kiowa Indians*
2003	1965.16.45	Catlin, George *Kiowa Chief, His Wife, and Two Warriors*
2004	1965.16.46	Catlin, George *Kiowa Indians Gathering Wild Grapes*
2005	1965.16.47	Catlin, George *Camanchee Chief, His Wife, and a Warrior*
2006	1965.16.48	Catlin, George *Camanchee Chief with Three Warriors*
2007	1965.16.49	Catlin, George *Camanchee Chief's Children and Wigwam*
2008	1965.16.50	Catlin, George *Sham Fight of the Camanchees*
2009	1965.16.51	Catlin, George *Camanchee Horsemanship*
2010	1965.16.52	Catlin, George *Battle between the Jicarilla Apachees and Camanchees*
2011	1965.16.53	Catlin, George *Camanchees Moving*
2012	1965.16.54	Catlin, George *Defile of a Camanchee War Party*
2013	1965.16.55	Catlin, George *Tawahquena Village*
2014	1965.16.56	Catlin, George *Pawneepict Chief, Two Daughters, and a Warrior*
2015	1965.16.57	Catlin, George *Three Shoshonee Warriors*
2016	1965.16.58	Catlin, George *Three Shoshonee Warriors Armed for War*
2017	1965.16.59	Catlin, George *Two Unidentified North American Indians*
2018	1965.16.60	Catlin, George *Pawnee Indians*
2019	1965.16.61	Catlin, George *A Pawnee Chief with Two Warriors*
2020	1965.16 62	Catlin, George *Facsimile of a Pawnee Doctor's Robe with Fantastic Professional Designs*
2021	1965.16 63	Catlin, George *Facsimile of a Pawnee Doctor's Robe*
2022	1965.16 64	Catlin, George *Pawnee Indians Approaching Buffalo*
2023	1965.16.65	Catlin, George *Encampment of Pawnee Indians at Sunset*
2024	1965.16.66	Catlin, George *Catching Wild Horses—Pawnee*
2025	1965.16.67	Catlin, George *A Pawnee Warrior Sacrificing His Favorite Horse*

Old	New	Artist and Title
2026	1965.16.68	Catlin, George *Osage Chief with Two Warriors*
2027	1965.16.69	Catlin, George *Osage Indians*
2028	1965.16.70	Catlin, George *Facsimile of an Omaha Robe*
2029	1965.16.71	Catlin, George *An Osage Indian Pursuing a Camanchee*
2030	1965.16.72	Catlin, George *Mandan War Chief with His Favorite Wife*
2031	1965.16.73	Catlin, George *Three Mandan Warriors Armed for War*
2032	1965.16.74	Catlin, George *Four Mandan Warriors, a Girl, and a Boy*
2033	1965.16.75	Catlin, George *Mandan Civil Chief, His Wife, and Child*
2034	1965.16.76	Catlin, George *An Aged Minatarree Chief and His Family*
2035	1965.16.77	Catlin, George *Three Minatarree Indians*
2036	1965.16.78	Catlin, George *Riccarree Chief and His Wife*
2037	1965.16.79	Catlin, George *Mandan Village—A Distant View*
2038	1965.16.80	Catlin, George *Catlin Feasted by the Mandan Chief*
2039	1965.16.81	Catlin, George *Green Corn Dance—Minatarrees*
2040	1965.16.82	Catlin, George *Buffalo Dance—Mandan*
2041	1965.16.83	Catlin, George *Game of the Arrow—Mandan*
2042	1965.16.84	Catlin, George *A Foot War Party in Council—Mandan*
2043	1965.16.85	Catlin, George *A Mandan Medicine Man*
2044	1965.16.86	Catlin, George *Facsimile of the Robe of Mah-to toh-pa—Mandan*
2045	1965.16.87	Catlin, George *Mandan Ceremony—The Water Sinks Down*
2046	1965.16.88	Catlin, George *Three Iowa Indians*
2047	1965.16.89	Catlin, George *Three Iroquois Indians*
2048	1965.16.90	Catlin, George *Three Riccarree Indians*
2049	1965.16.91	Catlin, George *An Aged Ojibbeway Chief and Three Warriors*
2050	1965.16.92	Catlin, George *Two Ojibbeway Warriors and a Woman*
2051	1965.16.93	Catlin, George *Ojibbeway Indians*
2052	1965.16.94	Catlin, George *Saukie Warrior, His Wife, and a Boy*
2053	1965.16.95	Catlin, George *Black Hawk and Five Other Saukie Prisoners*
2054	1965.16.96	Catlin, George *Two Saukie Chiefs and a Woman*
2055	1965.16.97	Catlin, George *The Running Fox on a Fine Horse—Saukie*
2056	1965.16.98	Catlin, George *Menomonie Chief, His Wife, and Son*
2057	1965.16.99	Catlin, George *Old Menomonie Chief with Two Young Beaux*
2058	1965.16.100	Catlin, George *Two Ottoe Chiefs and a Woman*
2059	1965.16.101	Catlin, George *Weeco Chief, His Wife, and a Warrior*

Old	New	Artist and Title
2060	1965.16.102	Catlin, George *Three Piankeshaw Indians*
2061	1965.16.103	Catlin, George *Kaskaskia Chief, His Mother, and Son*
2062	1965.16.104	Catlin, George *Seneca Chief, Red Jacket, with Two Warriors*
2063	1965.16.105	Catlin, George *Puncah Indians*
2064	1965.16.106	Catlin, George *The Puncah Chief Surrounded by His Family*
2065	1965.16.107	Catlin, George *Ottowa Chief, His Wife, and a Warrior*
2066	1965.16.108	Catlin, George *Mohigan Chief and a Missionary*
2067	1965.16.109	Catlin, George *Three Peoria Indians*
2068	1965.16.110	Catlin, George *Nine Ojibbeway Indians in London*
2069	1965.16.111	Catlin, George *Iowa Indians Who Visited London and Paris*
2070	1965.16.112	Catlin, George *Ojibbeway Indians in Paris*
2071	1965.16.113	Catlin, George *Oneida Chief, His Sister, and a Missionary*
2072	1965.16.114	Catlin, George *Three Delaware Indians*
2073	1965.16.115	Catlin, George *Three Creek Indians*
2074	1965.16.116	Catlin, George *Two Choctaw Indians*
2075	1965.16.117	Catlin, George *Two Weeah Warriors and a Woman*
2076	1965.16.118	Catlin, George *Seminolee Indians, Prisoners at Fort Moultrie*
2077	1965.16.119	Catlin, George *Osceola and Four Seminolee Indians*
2078	1965.16.120	Catlin, George *Two Cherokee Chiefs*
2079	1965.16.121	Catlin, George *Kickapoo Indians Preaching and Praying*
2080	1965.16.122	Catlin, George *Three Potowotomie Indians*
2081	1965.16.123	Catlin, George *Shawano Indians*
2082	1965.16.124	Catlin, George *A K'nisteneux Warrior and Family*
2083	1965.16.125	Catlin, George *Three Micmac Indians*
2084	1965.16.126	Catlin, George *Yntah Medicine Man, a Warrior, and a Woman*
2085	1965.16.127	Catlin, George *Three Celebrated Ball Players—Choctaw, Sioux, and Ojibbeway*
2086	1965.16.128	Catlin, George *An Ojibbeway Village of Skin Tents*
2087	1965.16.129	Catlin, George *Buffalo Chase in the Snow Drifts—Ojibbeway*
2088	1965.16.130	Catlin, George *Amusing Dance—Saukie*
2089	1965.16.131	Catlin, George *Slaves' Dance—Saukie*
2090	1965.16.132	Catlin, George *Eagle Dance—Choctaw*
2091	1965.16.133	Catlin, George *Dance to the Berdache—Saukie*
2092	1965.16.134	Catlin, George *Bear Dance—K'nisteneux*
2093	1965.16.135	Catlin, George *Discovery Dance—Saukie*
2094	1965.16.136	Catlin, George *Snow Shoe Dance—Ojibbeway*

Old	New	Artist and Title
2095	1965.16.137	Catlin, George *Ball-Play Dance—Choctaw*
2096	1965.16.138	Catlin, George *Gathering Wild Rice—Winnebago*
2097	1965.16.139	Catlin, George *Fort Pierre*
2098	1965.16.140	Catlin, George *Facsimile of an Ojibbeway Robe*
2099	1965.16.141	Catlin, George *Salmon Spearing—Ottowas*
2100	1965.16.142	Catlin, George *Funeral of Black Hawk—Saukie*
2101	1965.16.143	Catlin, George *War Dance of the Saukie*
2102	1965.16.144	Catlin, George *Three Navaho Indians*
2103	1965.16.145	Catlin, George *Apachee Chief and Three Warriors*
2104	1965.16.146	Catlin, George *Four Apachee Indians*
2105	1965.16.147	Catlin, George *Two Apachee Warriors and a Woman*
2106	1965.16.148	Catlin, George *Four Navajo Warriors*
2107	1965.16.149	Catlin, George *Flathead Indians*
2108	1965.16.150	Catlin, George *Four Flathead Indians*
2109	1965.16.151	Catlin, George *A Flathead Chief with His Family*
2110	1965.16.152	Catlin, George *Nayas Indian Chief, His Wife, and a Warrior*
2111	1965.16.153	Catlin, George *Nayas Indians*
2112	1965.16.154	Catlin, George *An Old Nayas Indian, His Granddaughter, and a Boy*
2113	1965.16.155	Catlin, George *Two Young Hyda Men*
2114	1965.16.156	Catlin, George *Three Young Chinook Men*
2115	1965.16.157	Catlin, George *Klahoquaht Chief, His Wife, and Son*
2116	1965.16.158	Catlin, George *Klatsop Indians*
2117	1965.16.159	Catlin, George *Three Walla Walla Indians*
2118	1965.16.160	Catlin, George *Facsimile of a Sioux Robe*
2119	1965.16.161	Catlin, George *A Stone Warrior, His Wife, and a Boy*
2120	1965.16.162	Catlin, George *Copper Chief, His Wife, and Children*
2121	1965.16.163	Catlin, George *Spokan Chief, Two Warriors, and a Boy*
2122	1965.16.164	Catlin, George *Athapasca Chief, His Wife, and a Warrior*
2123	1965.16.165	Catlin, George *Four Dogrib Indians*
2124	1965.16.166	Catlin, George *Three Se[illegible]sh Indians*
2125	1965.16.167	Catlin, George *Two Chippewyan Warriors and a Woman*
2126	1965.16.168	Catlin, George *Three Esquimaux*
2127	1965.16.169	Catlin, George *Aleutian Chief and Two Warriors*
2128	1965.16.170	Catlin, George *Cochimtee Chief, His Wife, and a Warrior*
2129	1965.16.171	Catlin, George *Mohave Chief, a Warrior, and His Wife*
2130	1965.16.172	Catlin, George *A Yuma Chief, His Daughter, and a Warrior*

Old	New	Artist and Title
2131	1965.16.173	Catlin, George *Three Yumaya Indians*
2132	1965.16.174	Catlin, George *Five Maya Indians*
2133	1965.16.175	Catlin, George *Buffalo Chase*
2134	1965.16.176	Catlin, George *Buffalo Chase, with Accidents*
2135	1965.16.177	Catlin, George *Catlin and Indian Attacking Buffalo*
2136	1965.16.178	Catlin, George *A Buffalo Wallow*
2137	1965.16.179	Catlin, George *Buffalo Chase—Bulls Protecting the Calves*
2138	1965.16.180	Catlin, George *Bulls Fighting*
2139	1965.16.181	Catlin, George *K'nisteneux Indians Attacking Two Grizzly Bears*
2140	1965.16.182	Catlin, George *Pipe Dance—Assinneboine*
2141	1965.16.183	Catlin, George *Horse Racing—Minatarrees*
2142	1965.16.184	Catlin, George *Catlin Painting the Portrait of Mah-to-toh-pa—Mandan*
2143	1965.16.185	Catlin, George *Prairie Dog Village*
2144	1965.16.186	Catlin, George *Fort Union*
2145	1965.16.187	Catlin, George *Making Flint Arrowheads—Apachees*
2146	1965.16 188	Catlin, George *Facsimile of Chief Four Men's Robe—Mandan*
2147	1965.16 189	Catlin, George *An Indian Encampment at Sunset*
2148	1965.16 190	Catlin, George *Curious Grassy Bluffs, St. Peter's River*
2149	1965.16.191	Catlin, George *View in the "Grand Detour," Upper Missouri*
2150	1965.16.192	Catlin, George *Falls of the Snake River*
2151	1965.16.193	Catlin, George *Grassy Bluffs, Upper Missouri*
2152	1965.16.194	Catlin, George *Prairie Meadows Burning*
2153	1965.16.195	Catlin, George *View of "Pike's Tent"*
2154	1965.16.196	Catlin, George *Scene from the Lower Mississippi*
2155	1965.16.197	Catlin, George *Catlin and Two Companions Shooting Buffalo*
2156	1965.16.198	Catlin, George *Nayas Village—Indians Bathing*
2157	1965.16.199	Catlin, George *The Scalper Scalped—Pawnees and Cheyennes*
2158	1965.16.200	Catlin, George *An Apachee Village*
2159	1965.16.201	Catlin, George *Salmon River Mountains*
2160	1965.16.202	Catlin, George *"Paint Me"—Apachee*
2161	1965.16.203	Catlin, George *Nishnabotana Bluffs, Upper Mississippi*
2162	1965.16.204	Catlin, George *Camanchees Lancing a Buffalo Bull*
2163	1965.16.205	Catlin, George *Wounded Buffalo Bull*
2164	1965.16.206	Catlin, George *Dying Buffalo Bull*
2165	1965.16.207	Catlin, George *View of Chicago in 1837*
2166	1965.16.208	Catlin, George *American Pasturage—Prairies of the Platte*
2167	1965.16.209	Catlin, George *View of the Lower Mississippi*

Old	New	Artist and Title
2168	1965.16.210	Catlin, George *Cedar Bluffs*
2169	1965.16.211	Catlin, George *Caddoe Indians Gathering Wild Strawberries*
2170	1965.16.212	Catlin, George *Indian File—Iowa*
2171	1965.16.213	Catlin, George *Mired Buffalo and Wolves*
2172	1965.16.214	Catlin, George *A Whale Ashore—Klahoquat*
2173	1965.16.215	Catlin, George *Excavating a Canoe—Nayas Indians*
2174	1965.16.216	Catlin, George *Launching a Canoe—Nayas Indians*
2175	1965.16.217	Catlin, George *An Indian Council—Sioux*
2176	1965.16.218	Catlin, George *Grizzly Bears Attacking Buffalo*
2177	1965.16.219	Catlin, George *Nayas Village at Sunset*
2178	1965.16.220	Catlin, George *Nayas Village at Night*
2179	1965.16.221	Catlin, George *An Indian Ladder—Nayas Indians*
2180	1965.16.222	Catlin, George *Five Caribbe Indians*
2181	1965.16.223	Catlin, George *Three Woyaway Indians*
2182	1965.16.224	Catlin, George *Three Taruma Indians*
2183	1965.16.225	Catlin, George *Four Goo-a-give Indians*
2184	1965.16.226	Catlin, George *Four Arawak Indians*
2185	1965.16.227	Catlin, George *Zurumati Indians*
2186	1965.16.228	Catlin, George *Three Zurumati Indians*
2187	1965.16.229	Catlin, George *Four Zurumati Children*

Old	New	Artist and Title
2188	1965.16.230	Catlin, George *Four Macouchi Indians*
2189	1965.16.231	Catlin, George *A Connibo Indian Family*
2190	1965.16.232	Catlin, George *Bride and Groom on Horseback—Connibo*
2191	1965.16.233	Catlin, George *A Chetibo Family*
2192	1965.16.234	Catlin, George *Four Sepibo Indians*
2193	1965.16.235	Catlin, George *Five Iquito Indians*
2194	1965.16.236	Catlin, George *Three Conagua Men*
2195	1965.16.237	Catlin, George *Four Xingu Indians*
2196	1965.16.238	Catlin, George *Four Angustura Indians*
2197	1965.16.239	Catlin, George *Four Mura Indians*
2198	1965.16.240	Catlin, George *Marahua Indians*
2199	1965.16.241	Catlin, George *Orejone Chief and Family*
2200	1965.16.242	Catlin, George *Orejone Indians*
2201	1965.16.243	Catlin, George *Three Chaymas Men*
2202	1965.16.244	Catlin, George *Chaco Chief, His Wife, and a Warrior*
2203	1965.16.245	Catlin, George *Members of the Payaguas Tribe*
2204	1965.16.246	Catlin, George *Lengua Chief, His Two Wives, and Four Children*
2205	1965.16.247	Catlin, George *Lengua Medicine Man with Two Warriors*
2206	1965.16.248	Catlin, George *Members of the Botocudo Tribe*
2207	1965.16.249	Catlin, George *Botocudo Chief, His Wife, and a Young Man*

Old	New	Artist and Title
2208	1965.16.250	Catlin, George *Three Auca Children*
2209	1965.16.251	Catlin, George *A Puelchee Chief and Two Young Warriors*
2210	1965.16.252	Catlin, George *Patagon Chief, His Brother, and Daughter*
2211	1965.16.253	Catlin, George *Three Young Tobos Men*
2212	1965.16.254	Catlin, George *Four Fuegian Indians*
2213	1965.16.255	Catlin, George *The Great Ant-Eater*
2214	1965.16.256	Catlin, George *The Handsome Dance—Goo-a-give*
2215	1965.16.257	Catlin, George *Ostrich Chase, Buenos Aires—Auca*
2216	1965.16.258	Catlin, George *Pont de Palmiers and Tiger Shooting*
2217	1965.16.259	Catlin, George *Turtle Hunt*
2218	1965.16.260	Catlin, George *A Fight with Peccaries—Caribbe*
2219	1965.16.261	Catlin, George *Ignis Fatuus—Zurumati*
2220	1965.16.262	Catlin, George *View of the Pampa del Sacramento*
2221	1965.16.263	Catlin, George *Shore of the Essequibo*
2222	1965.16.264	Catlin, George *Luxuriant Forest on the Bank of the Amazon*
2223	1965.16.265	Catlin, George *A Caribbe Village in Dutch Guiana*
2224	1965.16.266	Catlin, George *View in the Crystal Mountains*
2225	1965.16.267	Catlin, George *Arawak Village*
2226	1965.16.268	Catlin, George *The Beetle Crevice*
2227	1965.16.269	Catlin, George *Shore of the Trombetas*
2228	1965.16.270	Catlin, George *An Indian Village—Shore of the Amazon*
2229	1965.16.271	Catlin, George *Interior of an Amazon Forest—Zurumati*
2230	1965.16.272	Catlin, George *An Amazon Forest—Looking Ashore*
2231	1965.16.273	Catlin, George *Rhododendron Mountain*
2232	1965.16.274	Catlin, George *View of the Crystal Mountains, Brazil*
2233	1965.16.275	Catlin, George *Return from a Turtle Hunt—Connibo*
2234	1965.16.276	Catlin, George *Wild Cattle Grazing on the Pampa del Sacramento*
2235	1965.16.277	Catlin, George *Spearing by Moonlight—Chaco*
2236	1965.16.278	Catlin, George *Driving the Pampas for Wild Cattle—Connibo*
2237	1965.16.279	Catlin, George *A Small Orejona Village*
2238	1965.16.280	Catlin, George *An Omagua Village—Boat Sketch*
2239	1965.16.281	Catlin, George *A Mura Encampment—Boat Sketch*
2240	1965.16.282	Catlin, George *A Mayoruna Village*
2241	1965.16.283	Catlin, George *A Yahua Village—Boat Sketch*
2242	1965.16.284	Catlin, George *View of the Shore of the Amazon—Boat Sketch*

Old	New	Artist and Title
2243	1965.16.285	Catlin, George *Encampment of Cocomas—Looking Ashore*
2244	1965.16.286	Catlin, George *Tapuya Encampment*
2245	1965.16.287	Catlin, George *Mauhees Encampment*
2246	1965.16.288	Catlin, George *A Lagoon of the Upper Amazon*
2247	1965.16.289	Catlin, George *Indian Camp in the Forest*
2248	1965.16.290	Catlin, George *Painting the Tobos Chief*
2249	1965.16.291	Catlin, George *A Small Tobos Village*
2250	1965.16.292	Catlin, George *Ignis Fatuus, Rio Uruguay*
2251	1965.16.293	Catlin, George *An Alligator's Nest*
2252	1965.16.294	Catlin, George *Entrance to a Lagoon, Shore of the Amazon*
2253	1965.16.295	Catlin, George *A Connibo Village*
2254	1965.16.296	Catlin, George *Connibos Starting for Wild Horses*
2255	1965.16.297	Catlin, George *Grand Lavoir, Pampa del Sacramento*
2256	1965.16.298	Catlin, George *Painting the Lengua Chief*
2257	1965.16.299	Catlin, George *Shore of the Uruguay—Making a Sketch*
2258	1965.16.300	Catlin, George *Lengua Indians Ascending the Rapids of the Rio Uruguay*
2259	1965.16.301	Catlin, George *A Small Lengua Village*
2260	1965.16.302	Catlin, George *A Small Lengua Village, Uruguay*
2261	1965.16.303	Catlin, George *A Small Village—Payaguas Indians*
2262	1965.16.304	Catlin, George *A Small Village of Remos Indians*
2263	1965.16.305	Catlin, George *A Sepibo Village*
2264	1965.16.306	Catlin, George *Mouth of the Rio Purus*
2265	1965.16.307	Catlin, George *Halting to Make a Sketch*
2266	1965.16.308	Catlin, George *A Connibo Wigwam*
2267	1965.16.309	Catlin, George *Pacapacurus Village*
2268	1965.16.310	Catlin, George *Spearing by Torchlight*
2269	1965.16.311	Catlin, George *Chief and Members of the Konza Tribe*
2270	1965.16.312	Catlin, George *Indians and Horses in a Forest*
2271	1965.16.313	Catlin, George *Omaha Chief, His Wife, and a Warrior*
2272	1965.16.314	Catlin, George *Black Hawk and the Prophet—Saukie*
2273	1965.16.315	Catlin, George *War Dance of the Apachees*
2274	1965.16.316	Catlin, George *The Expedition Leaving Fort Frontenac on Lake Ontario. November 18, 1678*
2275	1965.16.317	Catlin, George *The Expedition Encamped below the Falls of Niagara. January 20, 1679*
2276	1965.16.318	Catlin, George *Portage Around the Falls of Niagara at Table Rock*
2277	1965.16.319	Catlin, George *La Salle Driving the First Bolt for the Griffin. January 26, 1679*

Old	New	Artist and Title
2278	1965.16.320	Catlin, George *Returning to Fort Frontenac by Sled. February 1679*
2279	1965.16.321	Catlin, George *Launching of the* Griffin. *July 1679*
2280	1965.16.322	Catlin, George *First Sailing of the* Griffin *on Lake Erie. August 7, 1679*
2281	1965.16.323	Catlin, George *The* Griffin *Entering the Harbor at MacKinaw. August 27, 1679*
2282	1965.16.324	Catlin, George *La Salle and Party Arrive at the Village of the Illinois. January 1, 1680*
2283	1965.16.325	Catlin, George *La Salle's Party Feasted in the Illinois Village. January 2, 1680*
2284	1965.16.326	Catlin, George *De Tonty Suing for Peace in the Iroquois Village. January 2, 1680*
2285	1965.16.327	Catlin, George *Father Hennepin and Two Companions Made Prisoners by the Sioux. April 1680*
2286	1965.16.328	Catlin, George *Father Hennepin and Companions Passing Lover's Leap. April 1680*
2287	1965.16.329	Catlin, George *Father Hennepin at the Falls of St. Anthony. May 1, 1680*
2288	1965.16.330	Catlin, George *Father Hennepin Leaving the Mississippi to Join La Salle. May 8, 1680*
2289	1965.16.331	Catlin, George *La Salle Crossing Lake Michigan on the Ice. December 8, 1681*
2290	1965.16.332	Catlin, George *La Salle's Party Entering the Mississippi in Canoes. February 6, 1682*
2291	1965.16.333	Catlin, George *La Salle Taking Possession of the Land at the Mouth of the Arkansas. March 10, 1682*
2292	1965.16.334	Catlin, George *Chief of the Taensa Indians Receiving La Salle. March 20, 1682*
2293	1965.16.335	Catlin, George *La Salle Erecting a Cross and Taking Possession of the Land. March 25, 1682*
2294	1965.16.336	Catlin, George *La Salle Claiming Louisiana for France. April 9, 1682*
2295	1965.16.337	Catlin, George *Wreck of the* Aimable *on the Coast of Texas. 1685*
2296	1965.16.338	Catlin, George *La Salle Meets a War Party of Cenis Indians on a Texas Prairie. April 25, 1686*
2297	1965.16.339	Catlin, George *Expedition Encamped on a Texas Prairie. April 1686*
2298	1965.16.340	Catlin, George *La Salle Received in the Village of the Cenis Indians. May 6, 1686*
2299	1965.16.341	Catlin, George *La Salle Assassinated by Duhaut. May 19, 1686*
2300	1965.16.342	Catlin, George *Vapor Bath—Minatarree*
2301	1965.16.343	Catlin, George *Two Sioux Chiefs, a Medicine Man, and a Woman with a Child*
2302	1965.16.344	Catlin, George *Facsimile of a Mandan Robe*
2303	1965.16.345	Catlin, George *Buffalo Lancing in the Snow Drifts—Sioux*
2304	1965.16.346	Catlin, George *See-non-ty-a, an Iowa Medicine Man*

Old	New	Artist and Title
2305	1965.16.347	Catlin, George *The White Cloud, Head Chief of the Iowas*
2306	1965.16.348	Catlin, George *The Female Eagle—Shawano*
2307	1965.16.349	Catlin, George *Boy Chief—Ojibbeway*
2308	1965.16.350	Catlin, George *A Village of Skin Tents*
2309	1965.16.351	Catlin, George *Spearing by Torchlight on the Amazon*
2311	1966.3.1	Feininger, Lyonel *Zirchow VII*
2312	1966.6.1	La Farge, John *The Entrance to the Tautira River, Tahiti Fisherman Spearing a Fish*
2313	1966.10.1	Peale, Charles Willson *Benjamin and Eleanor Ridgely Laming*
2314	1966.11.1	Sully, Thomas *The Vanderkemp Children*
2317	1966.13.1	Chambers, Thomas *The Hudson Valley, Sunset*
2318	1966.13.2	Feke, Robert *Captain Alexander Graydon*
2319	1966.13.3	Kemmelmeyer, Frederick *First Landing of Christopher Columbus*
2320	1966.13.4	Beckett, Francis A. *Blacksmith Shop*
2321	1966.13.5	Hamblin, Sturtevant J. *The Younger Generation*
2322	1966.13.6	Anonymous American 18th Century *Christ on the Road to Emmaus*
2323	1966.13.7	Anonymous American 19th Century *Fruit and Flowers*
2327	1967.1.1	Tarbell, Edmund Charles *Mother and Mary*
2328	1967.8.1	Cole, Thomas *The Notch of the White Mountains (Crawford Notch)*
2330	1967.9.1	Moran, Thomas *The Much Resounding Sea*
2333	1967.12.1	Feininger, Lyonel *Storm Brewing*
2334	1967.20.1	Mark, George Washington *Marion Feasting the British Officer on Sweet Potatoes*
2335	1967.20.2	Müller, Fritz *Capture of the* Savannah *by the* U.S.S. Perry
2336	1967.20.3	Anonymous American 19th Century *A City of Fantasy*
2337	1967.20.4	Skynner, Thomas *Portrait of a Man*
2338	1967.20.5	Skynner, Thomas *Portrait of a Woman*
2339	1967.20.6	Anonymous American 19th Century *Still Life of Fruit*
2340	1967.20.7	Anonymous American 19th Century *Stylized Landscape*
2341	1968.1.1	Copley, John Singleton *Mrs. Metcalf Bowler*
2345	1968.3.1	Kuhn, Walt *Pumpkins*
2346	1968.7.1	Kensett, John Frederick *Landing at Sabbath Day Point, Lake George*
2351	1968.26.1	Bradshaw, J. W. *Plains Indian*
2352	1968.26.2	Chambers, Thomas *Felucca off Gibraltar*
2353	1968.26.3	Anonymous American 20th Century *View of Aberdeen, Washington*
2354	1968.25.1	Kuhn, Walt *Wisconsin*
2357	1969.5.1	Frieseke, Frederick Carl *Memories*
2359	1970.1.1	Sloan, John *The City from Greenwich Village*
2360	1970.6.1	Weber, Max *Rush Hour, New York*

Old	New	Artist and Title
2361	1969.11.1	Chambers, Thomas *Storm-Tossed Frigate*
2362	1969.11.2	Huge, Jurgan Frederick *Composite Harbor Scene with Castle*
2365	1970.2 1	Calcagno, Lawrence *Black Light*
2366	1970.2 2	Calcagno, Lawrence *San Andreas III*
2370	1970.15.1	Jackson, Billy Morrow *Eve*
2391	1970.17.19	Cassatt, Mary *Children Playing on the Beach*
2472	1970.17.100	Hassam, Childe *Oyster Sloop, Cos Cob*
2474	1970.17.102	Anonymous American 18th Century *Hunting Scene with a Pond*
2475	1970.17.103	Anonymous American 18th Century *Hunting Scene with a Harbor*
2496	1970.17.124	Leonid *Derrynane Harbor, Ireland*
2534	1970.3[illegible].1	Hartley, Marsden *The Aero*
2536	1970.23.1	Nesbitt, Lowell *Stairway Landing*
2537	1970.28.1	Hultberg, John *The Island*
2538	1970.2[illegible].1	Louis, Morris *Beta Kappa*
2539	1970.34.1	Healy, George Peter Alexander *Roxanna Atwater Wentworth*
2540	1970.34.2	Stuart, Gilbert *Benjamin Tappan*
2541	1970.34.3	Stuart, Gilbert *Mrs. Benjamin Tappan*
2543	1970.27.1	Hartley, Marsden *Mount Katahdin, Maine*
2544	1971.3.1	Dodd, Lamar *Winter Valley*
2548	1970.37.1	Reinhardt, Ad *Black Painting No. 34*
2550	1971.16.1	Cole, Thomas *The Voyage of Life: Childhood*
2551	1971.16.2	Cole, Thomas *The Voyage of Life: Youth*
2552	1971.16.3	Cole, Thomas *The Voyage of Life: Manhood*
2553	1971.16.4	Cole, Thomas *The Voyage of Life: Old Age*
2554	1971.12.1	Glackens, William *Family Group*
2555	1971.13.1	Tucker, Allen *Bizarre*
2556	1971.13.2	Tucker, Allen *Madison Square, Snow*
2559	1971.52.1a-d	De Kooning, Willem *Legend and Fact*
2562	1971.57.1	Tanner, Henry Ossawa *The Seine*
2564	1971.83.1	Bard, James *Towboat* John Birkbeck
2565	1971.83.2	Ferrill, Martin Edgar *Country Dance*
2566	1971.83.3	Field, Erastus Salisbury *Biel Le Doyt*
2567	1971.83.4	Field, Erastus Salisbury *Paul Smith Palmer*
2568	1971.83.5	Field, Erastus Salisbury *Mrs. Paul Smith Palmer and Her Twins*
2569	1971.83.6	Humphreys, Charles S. *Budd Doble Driving Goldsmith Maid at Belmont Driving Park*
2570	1971.83.7	Johnson, Joshua *Sarah Ogden Gustin*
2571	1971.83.8	Anonymous American 19th Century *Man of Science*
2572	1971.83.9	Prior, William Matthew *Little Miss Fairfield*
2573	1971.83.10	Raleigh, Charles S. *Law of the Wild*
2574	1971.83.11	Smith, Dana *Southern Resort Town*
2575	1971.83.12	Anonymous American 20th Century *Boston and North Chungahochie Express*

Old	New	Artist and Title
2576	1971.83.13	Anonymous American 18th Century *Boy with a Basket of Fruit*
2577	1971.83.14	Anonymous American 19th Century *Spring on the Range*
2578	1971.83.15	Anonymous American 19th Century *Samuel Eells*
2579	1971.83.16	Anonymous American 19th Century *Indians Cooking Maize*
2580	1971.83.17	Anonymous American 19th Century *Portland Harbor, Maine*
2581	1971.83.18	Anonymous American 19th Century *The Proud Mother*
2582	1971.83.19	Anonymous American 19th Century *Sisters in Black Aprons*
2583	1971.83.20	Anonymous American 19th Century *Washington at Valley Forge*
2584	1971.83.21	Wilgus, William John, After *Ichabod Crane and the Headless Horseman*
2599	1972.9.13	Kuhn, Walt *Dryad*
2600	1972.9.14	Kuhn, Walt *Green Apples and Scoop*
2601	1972.9.15	Kuhn, Walt *Hare and Hunting Boots*
2602	1972.9.16	Kuhn, Walt *The White Clown*
2603	1972.9.17	Kuhn, Walt *Zinnias*
2611	1972.7.1	Albright, Ivan Le Lorraine *There Were No Flowers Tonight*
2613	1971.87.1	Crawford, Ralston *Lights in an Aircraft Plant*
2614	1971.88.2	Donati, Enrico *Cat's Eyes*
2617	1971.87.4	Kline, Franz *C & O*
2618	1971.87.5	Komodore, Bill *Vermont*
2622	1971.89.1	Smith, Leon Polk *Stretch of Black III*
2626	1971.87.11	Warhol, Andy *A Boy for Meg*
2627	1971.87.12	Kline, Franz *Four Square*
2630	1972.45.1	Jenkins, Paul *Phenomena Sound of Sundials*
2638	1973.1.1	Vail, Eugene Lawrence *The Flags, Saint Mark's, Venice—Fete Day*
2639	1973.3.1	Street, Robert *George Washington Deal*
2640	1973.3.2	Street, Robert *Elizabeth Price Thomas*
2641	1973.4.1	Sully, Thomas *The Leland Sisters*
2645	1973.8.1	Lawrence, Jacob *Daybreak—A Time to Rest*
2646	1973.19.1	Hendricks, Barkley Leonnard *Sir Charles, Alias Willy Harris*
2647	1973.19.2	Hendricks, Barkley Leonnard *George Jules Taylor*
2654	1973.16.1	Inness, George *View of the Tiber near Perugia*
2657	1974.19.1	Peto, John Frederick *The Old Violin*
2658	1974.15.1	Resnick, Milton *Mound*
2659	1973.67.1	Chambers, Thomas *Bay of New York, Sunset*
2660	1973.67.2	Chambers, Thomas *Threatening Sky, Bay of New York*
2661	1974.14.1	Corbett, Edward *Washington, D.C. November 1963 III*
2662	1974.16.1	Davis, Gene *Satan's Flag*
2663	1973.70.1	Henri, Robert *Volendam Street Scene*

Old	New	Artist and Title
2666	1973.72.1	Pereira, I. Rice *Green Mass*
2667	1973.72.2	Pereira, I. Rice *Zenith*
2668	1973.71.2	Pereira, I. Rice *Transfluent Lines*
2669	1974.13.1	Zorach, Marguerite *Christmas Mail*
2670	1974.45.1	Stanczak, Julian *Shimmer*
2671	1974.46.1	Twitty, James *Blue Water*
2675	1974.87.2	Lebrun, Rico *The Ragged One*
2677	1974.108.1	Stuart, Gilbert *Mrs. Lawrence Lewis*
2678	1975.42.1	Benton, Thomas Hart *Trail Riders*
2679	1985.20.1	Copley, John Singleton *Mrs. Adam Babcock*
2681	1975.78.1	Feitelson, Lorser *Untitled*
2685	1975.98.1	Noland, Kenneth *The Clown*
2687	1975.100.1	Smith, Tony *Untitled*
2690	1976.6.1	Thomas, Alma *Red Rose Cantata*
2691	1976.25.1	Copley, John Singleton *Harrison Gray*
2693	1976.27.1	Eakins, Thomas *Harriet Husson Carville*
2697	1976.37.1	Pollock, Jackson *Number 1, 1950 (Lavender Mist)*
2698	1976.50.1	Curry, John Steuart *Circus Elephants*
2699	1976.50.2	Metcalf, Willard Leroy *Midsummer Twilight*
2703	1976.64.1	Louis, Morris *133*
2707	1977.47.13	Rothko, Mark *Orange and Tan*
2708	1977.57.1	Wyeth, Andrew *Snow Flurries*
2710	1977.75.1	Corse, Mary Ann *Untitled*
2711	1977.75.2	Dutterer, William *Equal, No. 2*
2712	1977.75.3	Irwin, Robert *Untitled*
2713	1977.75.4	Liberman, Alexander *Omega IV*
2714	1977.75.5	Poons, Larry *Tristan da Cugna*
2715	1978.6.1	Casilear, John William *View on Lake George*
2716	1978.6.2	Durand, Asher Brown *Forest in the Morning Light*
2717	1978.6.3	Durand, Asher Brown *A Pastoral Scene*
2718	1978.6.4	Edmonds, Francis William *The Bashful Cousin*
2719	1978.6.5	Kensett, John Frederick *Beach at Beverly*
2721	1978.12.1	Cropsey, Jasper Francis *The Spirit of War*
2723	1978.20.1	Motherwell, Robert *Reconciliation Elegy*
2727	1978.40.1	Mehring, Howard *Sequence*
2728	1978.39.1	Olitski, Jules *Unlocked*
2731	1978.72.1	Johnson, Eastman *The Brown Family*
2733	1978.60.1	Dewing, Thomas Wilmer *Lady with a Lute*
2734	1977.4.1	Benson, Frank Weston *Portrait in White*
2735	1978.80.1	Chambers, Thomas *New York Harbor with Pilot Boat* George Washington
2736	1978.80.2	Anonymous American 19th Century *Man Named Hubbard Reading "Boston Atlas"*

Old	New	Artist and Title
2737	1978.80.3	Field, Erastus Salisbury *The Taj Mahal*
2738	1978.80.4	Field, Erastus Salisbury *Pharaoh's Army Marching*
2739	1978.80.5	Field, Erastus Salisbury *Leverett Pond*
2740	1978.80.6	Field, Erastus Salisbury *Man with a Tune Book: Mr. Cook (?)*
2741	1978.80.7	Goode, M. A. *Still Life*
2742	1978.80.8	Johnson, Joshua *Mr. Baylor*
2743	1978.80.9	Prior, William Matthew *Child with Straw Hat*
2744	1978.80.10	Hamblin, Sturtevant J. *Little Girl Holding Apple*
2745	1978.80.11	Vanderlyn, Pieter, Attributed to *Boy of the Beekman Family*
2746	1978.80.12	Anonymous American 19th Century *Birds*
2747	1978.80.13	Anonymous American 19th Century *The Congdon Brothers*
2748	1978.80.14	Anonymous American 19th Century *Girl in Red with Flowers and a Distelfink*
2749	1978.80.15	Anonymous American 19th Century *Lady Wearing Spectacles*
2750	1978.80.16	Phillips, Ammi *Catherine A. May*
2751	1978.80.17	Smith, Royall Brewster *Eliza R. Read*
2752	1978.80.18	Smith, Royall Brewster *John G. Read*
2753	1978.80.19	Hamblin, Sturtevant J. *Sisters in Blue*
2754	1978.80.20	Anonymous American 18th Century *Susanna Truax (?)*
2755	1978.80.21	Anonymous American 19th Century *View of Concord*
2756	1978.79.1	Copley, John Singleton *Adam Babcock*
2757	1979.5.1	Stuart, Gilbert *George Washington (Athenaeum portrait)*
2758	1979.4.1	Stuart, Gilbert *John Adams*
2759	1986.71.1	Stuart, Gilbert *Thomas Jefferson*
2760	1979.4.2	Stuart, Gilbert *James Madison*
2761	1979.4.3	Stuart, Gilbert *James Monroe*
2762	1979.13.1	Gorky, Arshile *The Artist and His Mother*
2763	1979.13.2	Gorky, Arshile *One Year the Milkweed*
2764	1979.13.3	Gorky, Arshile *Organization*
2766	1979.28.1	Noland, Kenneth *Another Time*
2767	1979.29.1	Stella, Frank *Chyrow II*
2769	1979.80.1	Bellows, George *Florence Davey*
2774	1980.11.1	Copley, John Singleton *Mrs. Samuel Alleyne Otis (Elizabeth Gray)*
2775	1980.11.2	Stuart, Gilbert *Samuel Alleyne Otis*
2776	1980.6.1	Davis, Gene *Narcissus III*
2777	1980.29.1	Lane, Fitz Hugh *Lumber Schooners at Evening on Penobscot Bay*
2782	1980.73.1	Noland, Kenneth *Sound*
2783	1980.62.1	Davies, T. *Ship in Full Sail*

Old	New	Artist and Title
2784	1980.62.2	Bond, Charles V. *Still Life: Fruit, Bird, and Dwarf Pear Tree*
2785	1980.61.1	The Pollard Limner, Attributed to *William Metcalf (?)*
2786	1980.62.3	Call, H. *Prize Bull*
2787	1980.62.4	Chambers, Thomas *Boston Harbor*
2788	1980.62.5	Chambers, Thomas *Packet Ship Passing Castle Williams, New York Harbor*
2789	1980.61.2	Anonymous American 19th Century *The Gage Family*
2790	1980.62.70	Durand, John *John Lothrop*
2791	1980.62.6	Durand, John *Mrs. John Lothrop*
2792	1980.62.7	Field, Erastus Salisbury *Woman Holding a Book*
2793	1980.62.8	Stock, Joseph Whiting *Girl with Reticule and Rose*
2794	1980.62.9	Hayes, George A. *Bare Knuckles*
2795	1980.62.10	Anonymous American 18th Century *Margaret Robins (?)*
2796	1980.62.11	Hicks, Edward *Penn's Treaty with the Indians*
2797	1980.62.12	Hicks, Edward *The Grave of William Penn*
2798	1980.62.13	Hicks, Edward *The Landing of Columbus*
2799	1980.62.14	Hicks, Edward, Attributed to *Portrait of a Child*
2800	1980.62.15	Hicks, Edward *Peaceable Kingdom*
2801	1980.61.3	Johnson, Joshua *Family Group*
2802	1980.61.4	Johnson, Joshua *Adelina Morton*
2803	1980.62.16	Mayhew, Frederick *John Harrisson*
2804	1980.62.17	Mayhew, Frederick *Mrs. John Harrisson and Daughter*
2805	1980.62.69	Faris, Joseph Anderson *The Neigh of an Iron Horse*
2806	1980.62.18	Prior, William Matthew *The Burnish Sisters*
2807	1980.62.19	Hamblin, Sturtevant J. *Sisters in Red*
2808	1980.62.20	Randall, A. M. *Basket of Fruit with Parrot*
2809	1980.62.21	Senior, C. F. *The Sportsman's Dream*
2810	1980.62.22	Stanley, Abram Ross *Joshua Lamb*
2811	1980.62.23	Stock, Joseph Whiting *Baby in Wicker Basket*
2812	1980.62.24	Anonymous American 18th Century *J. M. Stolle*
2813	1980.62.68	Stouter, D. G. *On Point*
2814	1980.62.25	Anonymous American 19th Century *The Cat*
2815	1980.62.26	The Denison Limner *Captain Elisha Denison*
2816	1980.62.27	The Denison Limner *Mrs. Elizabeth Noyes Denison*
2817	1980.62.28	The Denison Limner *Miss Denison of Stonington, Connecticut (possibly Matilda Denison)*
2818	1980.62.29	Anonymous American 19th Century *Horizon of the New World*
2819	1980.62.30	Anonymous American 19th Century *"Innocence"*
2820	1980.62.31	The Gansevoort Limner (possibly Pieter Vanderlyn) *Susanna Truax*

Old	New	Artist and Title
2821	1980.62.32	Granger, Charles Henry *Muster Day*
2822	1980.62.33	Anonymous American 19th Century *Indian Tobacco Shop Sign*
2823	1980.62.34	Anonymous American 18th Century *Catalyntje Post*
2824	1980.62.35	The Sherman Limner *Portrait of a Man in Red*
2825	1980.62.36	The Sherman Limner *Portrait of a Lady in Red*
2826	1980.62.37	Anonymous American 19th Century *Sisters*
2827	1980.62.38	Anonymous American 19th Century *Bowl of Fruit*
2828	1980.62.39	Anonymous American 18th Century *Mother and Child in White*
2829	1980.62.40	Anonymous American 18th Century *Full-length Portrait of Young Woman with Brown Hair—Bare Left Foot*
2830	1980.61.5	The Gansevoort Limner (possibly Pieter Vanderlyn) *Young Lady with a Fan*
2831	1980.62.41	Anonymous American 18th Century *The Domino Girl*
2832	1980.62.42	Chandler, Joseph Goodhue *Girl with Kitten*
2833	1980.61.6	Anonymous American 19th Century *Bucks County Farm Outside Doylestown, Pennsylvania*
2834	1980.62.43	Anonymous American 19th Century *Basket of Fruit with Flowers*
2835	1980.61.7	Anonymous American 19th Century *Steamship* Erie
2836	1980.62.44	Anonymous American 18th Century *Dr. Philemon Tracy*
2837	1980.61.8	Anonymous American 19th Century *The Independent Voter*
2838	1980.62.45	Anonymous American 18th Century *Lady Wearing Large White Cap*
2839	1980.61.9	Anonymous American 19th Century *The Finish*
2840	1980.61.10	Anonymous American 20th Century *After the Wedding in Warren, Pennsylvania*
2841	1980.61.11	Anonymous American 19th Century *Watermelon on a Plate*
2842	1980.62.46	Rowley, Reuben, Attributed to *Dr. John Safford and Family*
2843	1980.61.12	Anonymous American 19th Century *Interior Scene*
2845	1980.62.47	Waggunor *Fruit and Baltimore Oriole*
2848	1981.46.1	Morse, Samuel Finley Breese *Eliphalet Terry*
2849	1981.46.2	Morse, Samuel Finley Breese *Lydia Coit Terry*
2850	1981.54.1	Salmon, Robert *The Ship Favorite Maneuvering Off Greenock*
2851	1981.86.1	Frankenthaler, Helen *Wales*
2855	1982.7.1	Wood, Grant *Haying*
2856	1982.7.2	Wood, Grant *New Road*
2860	1982.33.1	Seitz, William Chapin *Millstone #1*
2861	1982.35.1	Stella, Frank *Jarama I[illegible]*

Old	New	Artist and Title
2862	1971.83.22	Hensel, Salome *To the Memory of the Benevolent Howard*
2864	1982.73.1	Heade, Martin Johnson *Cattleya Orchid and Three Brazilian Hummingbirds*
2866	1982.53.1	Stella, Frank *Sacramento Mall Proposal #4*
2867	1982.76.1	Bellows, George *Club Night*
2871	1982.76.5	Eakins, Thomas *Baby at Play*
2872	1982.76.6	Hopper, Edward *Cape Cod Evening*
2874	1982.76.8	Whistler, James McNeill *Wapping on Thames*
2875	1983.1.1	Bellows, George *Anne with a Japanese Parasol*
2876	1983.1.2	Bellows, George *Little Girl in White (Queenie Burnett)*
2877	1983.1.3	Bellows, George *My Family*
2878	1983.1.4	Bellows, George *Nude with Hexagonal Quilt*
2879	1983.1.5	Bellows, George *Tennis Tournament*
2880	1982.96.1	Warhol, Andy *Let Us Now Praise Famous Men (Rauschenberg Family)*
2892	1983.1.27	Cassatt, Mary *Child in a Straw Hat*
2893	1983.1.28	Cassatt, Mary *Little Girl in a Blue Armchair*
2905	1983.1.30	Okada, Kenzo *Blue*
2906	1983.1.31	Okada, Kenzo *Kasaner*

Special Collection

Old	New	Artist and Title
SP 2	1944.16.1	Bellows, George *Chester Dale*
SP 3	1942.1.1	Tack, Augustus Vincent *Charles Evans Hughes*
SP 5	1942.9.101	Sargent, John Singer *Peter A. B. Widener*
SP 6	1944.4.1	Tack, Augustus Vincent *Harlan F. Stone*
SP 8	1950.19.1	Stephens, Thomas E. *Fred M. Vinson*
SP 9	1953.2.3	Seyffert, Leopold *Samuel Henry Kress*
SP 10	1961.9.93	Seyffert, Leopold *Rush Harrison Kress*
SP 11	1955.8.1	Cox, Gardner *Lessing J. Rosenwald*
SP 16	1962.1.1	Cox, Gardner *Earl Warren*

ARTIST INDEX

TITLE INDEX

Title	Artist	Accession #	Page #
Benjamin Tappan	Stuart, Gilbert	1970.34.2	355
Mrs. Benjamin Tappan	Stuart, Gilbert	1970.34.3	356
Berkeley No. 52	Diebenkorn, Richard	1986.68.1	159
Berks County Almshouse, 1878	Hofmann, Charles C.	1953.5.17	203
Berks County Almshouse, 1895	Mader, Louis	1953.5.25	230
The Bersaglieri	Luks, George Benjamin	1950.5.1	229
Beta Kappa	Louis, Morris	1970.21.1	228
The Bicycle Race	Feininger, Lyonel	1985.64.17	176
Biel Le Doyt	Field, Erastus Salisbury	1971.83.3	178
The Biglin Brothers Racing	Eakins, Thomas	1953.7.1	165
Birds	Anonymous American 19th Century	1978.80.12	389
Birth of Cephalopods	Rothko, Mark	1986.43.22	296
Bivouac of a Sioux War Party	Catlin, George	1965.16.16	47
Bivouac of a Sioux War Party at Sunrise	Catlin, George	1965.16.18	48
Bizarre	Tucker, Allen	1971.13.1	370
Black Hawk and Five Other Saukie Prisoners	Catlin, George	1965.16.95	48
Black Hawk and the Prophet—Saukie	Catlin, George	1965.16.314	49
Black Light	Calcagno, Lawrence	1970.2.1	37
Black Painting No. 34	Reinhardt, Ad	1970.37.1	271
Black-footed Ferret	Audubon, John Woodhouse	1951.9.1	22
A Blackfoot Chief, His Wife, and a Medicine Man	Catlin, George	1965.16.28	48
Blacksmith Shop	Beckett, Francis A.	1966.13.4	27
Blond Figure	Soyer, Raphael	1989.25.1	339
Blue	Okada, Kenzo	1983.1.30	252
Blue Eyes	Anonymous American 19th Century	1953.5.68	390
Blue Morning	Bellows, George	1963.10.82	28
The Blue Shawl	Anonymous American 19th Century	1953.5.74	390
Blue Water	Twitty, James	1974.46.1	371
The Boating Party	Cassatt, Mary	1963.10.94	41
Boston and North Chungahochie Express	Anonymous American 20th Century	1971.83.12	390
Boston Harbor	Chambers, Thomas	1980.62.4	137
Both Members of This Club	Bellows, George	1944.13.1	29

Title	Artist	Accession #	Page #
Botocudo Chief, His Wife, and a Young Man	Catlin, George	1965.16.249	107
Bowl of Fruit	Anonymous American 19th Century	1980.62.38	391
Bowl of Fruit	Stearns, William	1953.5.34	341
Boy and Girl	Anonymous American 19th Century	1956.13.7	391
Boy Chief—Ojibbeway	Catlin, George	1965.16.349	49
A Boy for Meg	Warhol, Andy	1971.87.11	373
Boy in Blue	Anonymous American 19th Century	1953.5.60	392
Boy in Blue Coat	Anonymous American 18th Century	1959.11.5	392
Boy of the Beekman Family	Vanderlyn, Pieter, Attributed to	1978.80.11	372
Boy with a Basket of Fruit	Anonymous American 18th Century	1971.83.13	392
Boy with Toy Horse and Wagon	Prior, William Matthew	1953.5.67	266
Breezing Up (A Fair Wind)	Homer, Winslow	1943.13.1	204
Bride and Groom on Horseback—Connibo	Catlin, George	1965.16.232	108
Brother and Sister	Anonymous American 19th Century	1953.5.61	393
Brothers	Waters, Susan C.	1956.13.8	374
Brown and Gold: Self-Portrait	Whistler, James McNeill	1959.3.2	382
The Brown Family	Johnson, Eastman	1978.72.1	213
Bucks County Farm Outside Doylestown, Pennsylvania	Anonymous American 19th Century	1980.62.6	393
Budd Doble Driving Goldsmith Maid at Belmont Driving Park	Humphreys, Charles S.	1971.83.6	207
Buffalo Chase	Catlin, George	1965.16.175	49
Buffalo Chase—Bulls Protecting the Calves	Catlin, George	1965.16.179	50
Buffalo Chase in the Snow Drifts—Ojibbeway	Catlin, George	1965.16.129	50
Buffalo Chase, Sioux Indians, Upper Missouri	Catlin, George	1965.16.10	50
Buffalo Chase, with Accidents	Catlin, George	1965.16.176	50
Buffalo Dance—Mandan	Catlin, George	1965.16.82	51
Buffalo Lancing in the Snow Drifts—Sioux	Catlin, George	1965.16.345	51

Title	Artist	Accession #	Page #
A Buffalo Wallow	Catlin, George	1965.16.178	51
Buildings with Snowbank, Cliffside, New Jersey	Marin, John	1986.54.2	231
Bulls Fighting	Catlin, George	1965.16.180	52
The Burial	Park, Linton	1953.5.27	254
Burning of Old South Church, Bath, Maine	Hilling, John	1958.9.7	203
The Burnish Sisters	Prior, William Matthew	1980.62.18	267
C & O	Kline, Franz	1971.87.4	219
Caddoe Indians Gathering Wild Strawberries	Catlin, George	1965.16.211	52
Café du Dôme	Pène du Bois, Guy	1963.10.136	258
Camanchee Chief, His Wife, and a Warrior	Catlin, George	1965.16.47	52
Camanchee Chief with Three Warriors	Catlin, George	1965.16.48	52
Camanchee Chief's Children and Wigwam	Catlin, George	1965.16.49	53
Camanchee Horsemanship	Catlin, George	1965.16.51	53
Camanchees Lancing a Buffalo Bull	Catlin, George	1965.16.204	53
Camanchees Moving	Catlin, George	1965.16.53	53
Cape Cod Evening	Hopper, Edward	1982.76.6	206
Captain Alexander Graydon	Feke, Robert	1966.13.2	178
Captain Charles Stewart	Sully, Thomas	1947.4.1	359
Captain Elisha Denison	The Denison Limner	1980.62.26	157
Captain Isaac Foster	Badger, Joseph	1957.11.1	23
Captain Joseph Anthony	Stuart, Gilbert	1942.8.11	347
Captain Samuel Chandler	Chandler, Winthrop	1964.23.1	140
Captain Warren Delano	Elliott, Charles Loring	1942.10.1	175
Capture of the Savannah *by the* U.S.S. Perry	Müller, Fritz	1967.20.2	239
A Caribbe Village in Dutch Guiana	Catlin, George	1965.16.265	108
The Cat	Anonymous American 19th Century	1980.62.25	394
Cat and Kittens	Anonymous American 19th Century	1958.9.8	394
Cat's Eyes	Donati, Enrico	1971.88.2	160
Catalyntje Post	Anonymous American 18th Century	1980.62.34	422
Catching Wild Horses—Pawnee	Catlin, George	1965.16.66	54

Title	Artist	Accession #	Page #
Catharine	Henri, Robert	1948.7.1	200
Catharine Hendrickson	Hendrickson, Daniel, Attributed to	1953.5.45	198
Catherine A. May	Phillips, Ammi	1978.80.16	260
Catherine Brower	MacKay	1956.13.5	230
Catlin and Indian Attacking Buffalo	Catlin, George	1965.16.177	54
Catlin and Two Companions Shooting Buffalo	Catlin, George	1965.16.197	54
Catlin Feasted by the Mandan Chief	Catlin, George	1965.16.80	54
Catlin Painting the Portrait of Mah-to-toh-pa—Mandan	Catlin, George	1965.16.184	55
Cattleya Orchid and Three Brazilian Hummingbirds	Heade, Martin Johnson	1982.73.1	197
Cedar Bluffs	Catlin, George	1965.16.210	55
Ceremonial	Rothko, Mark	1986.43.7	301
Chaco Chief, His Wife, and a Warrior	Catlin, George	1965.16.244	108
Charles Adams Wheeler	The Beardsley Limner	1953.5.57	27
Charles Carroll of Carrollton	Harding, Chester	1956.15.1	192
Charles Evans Hughes	Tack, Augustus Vincent	1942.1.1	365
Charles H. Sisson	Chandler, Joseph Goodhue	1953.5.5	139
Charles Loring Elliott	Mount, William Sidney	1947.17.9	238
Chelsea Wharf: Grey and Silver	Whistler, James McNeill	1942.9.99	380
The Cheney Family	Anonymous American 18th Century	1958.9.9	395
Chester Dale	Bellows, George	1944.16.1	32
A Chetibo Family	Catlin, George	1965.16.233	108
The Cheyenne Brothers Returning from Their Fall Hunt	Catlin, George	1965.16.43	56
The Cheyenne Brothers Starting on Their Fall Hunt	Catlin, George	1965.16.42	56
A Cheyenne Chief, His Wife, and a Medicine Man	Catlin, George	1965.16.36	56
Cheyenne Village	Catlin, George	1965.16.38	56
A Cheyenne Warrior Resting His Horse	Catlin, George	1965.16.39	57
Chief and Members of the Konza Tribe	Catlin, George	1965.16.311	57

Title	Artist	Accession #	Page #
Chief Jumper of the Seminoles	Anonymous American 19th Century	1953.5.77	395
Chief of the Taensa Indians Receiving La Salle. March 20, 1682	Catlin, George	1965.16.334	134
Child in a Straw Hat	Cassatt, Mary	1983.1.17	40
Child with Rocking Horse	Anonymous American 19th Century	1959.11.6	395
Child with Straw Hat	Prior, William Matthew	1978.80.9	267
Children Playing on the Beach	Cassatt, Mary	1970.17.19	39
Christ and the Woman of Samaria	Anonymous American 18th Century	1953.5.91	396
Christ on the Road to Emmaus	Anonymous American 18th Century	1966.13.6	396
Christmas Mail	Zorach, Marguerite	1974.13.1	385
Chrysanthemums	Chase, William Merritt	1963.10.106	141
Chyrow II	Stella, Frank	1979.29.1	341
Circus Elephants	Curry, John Steuart	1976.50.1	155
The City from Greenwich Village	Sloan, John	1970.1.1	337
A City of Fantasy	Anonymous American 19th Century	1967.20.3	396
Civil War Battle	Anonymous American 19th Century	1959.11.7	396
Clement Bonnell	Bonnell, William	1953.5.3	34
The Clown	Noland, Kenneth	1975.98.1	248
Club Night	Bellows, George	1982.76.1	28
Cobalt Night	Krasner, Lee	1984.40.1	222
Cochimtee Chief, His Wife, and a Warrior	Catlin, George	1965.16.170	57
The Coleman Sisters	Sully, Thomas	1947.9.3	364
The Colonel	Anonymous American 19th Century	1953.5.78	397
Colonel Augustus James Pleasonton	Neagle, John	1957.9.1	240
Colonel Fitch and His Sisters	Copley, John Singleton	1960.4.1	151
Colonel Guy Johnson	West, Benjamin	1940.1.10	377
Commodore John Rodgers	Jarvis, John Wesley	1943.14.1	211
Commodore Thomas Macdonough	Stuart, Gilbert	1942.8.17	357
Composite Harbor Scene with Castle	Huge, Jurgan Frederick	1969.11.2	207
The Congdon Brothers	Anonymous American 19th Century	1978.80.13	397

Title	Artist	Accession #	Page #
Mr. Day	Phillips, Ammi	1953.5.28	261
Mrs. Day	Phillips, Ammi	1953.5.29	261
Daybreak—A Time to Rest	Lawrence, Jacob	1973.8.1	225
The Death of the Earl of Chatham	Copley, John Singleton	1947.15.1	151
Defile of a Camanchee War Party	Catlin, George	1965.16.54	60
Miss Denison of Stonington, Connecticut (possibly Matilda Denison)	The Denison Limner	1980.62.28	158
Derrynane Harbor, Ireland	Leonid	1970.17.124	226
Dionysius	Newman, Barnett	1988.57.2	241
Discovery Dance—Saukie	Catlin, George	1965.16.135	60
Distinguished Crow Indians	Catlin, George	1965.16.20	60
The Dog	Anonymous American 20th Century	1957.11.8	399
Dog Dance—Sioux	Catlin, George	1965.16.6	61
A Dog Feast—Sioux	Catlin, George	1965.16.8	61
The Domino Girl	Anonymous American 18th Century	1980.62.41	399
Doric Circus	Rauschenberg, Robert	1985.28.1	270
Driving the Pampas for Wild Cattle—Connibo	Catlin, George	1965.16.278	110
Dryad	Kuhn, Walt	1972.9.13	223
The Duke of Portland	Pratt, Matthew	1942.13.2	265
Dying Buffalo Bull	Catlin, George	1965.16.206	61
Eagle Dance—Choctaw	Catlin, George	1965.16.132	61
Earl Warren	Cox, Gardner	1962.1.1	153
The Early Scholar	Johnson, Eastman	1963.10.157	212
Eaton Family Memorial	Jordan, Samuel	1955.11.9	216
Ebenezer Newhall	Frothingham, James	1947.17.50	185
Edith Reynolds	Henri, Robert	1956.7.1	199
Edward Stow	Stuart, Gilbert	1942.8.23	351
Edwin Forrest	Johnson, David	1947.17.62	212
Eighth Station	Newman, Barnett	1986.65.8	246
Eleazer Tyng	Copley, John Singleton	1965.6.1	149
Eleventh Station	Newman, Barnett	1986.65.11	247
Eliphalet Terry	Morse, Samuel Finley Breese	1981.46.1	237
Elisha Doane	Anonymous American 18th Century	1943.1.3	398

Title	Artist	Access on #	Page #
Eliza R. Read	Smith, Royall Brewster	1978.80.17	338
Eliza Welch Stone	Skynner, Thomas	1953.5.56	337
Eliza Wells	Stanley, Abram Ross	1955.11.11	340
Elizabeth Denison	The Denison Limner	1953.5.35	157
Mrs. Elizabeth Noyes Denison	The Denison Limner	1980.62.27	157
Mrs. Elizabeth Oakes Smith	Paradise, John Wesley	1963.10.188	253
Elizabeth Price Thomas	Street, Robert	1973.3.2	345
Elizabeth, Countess of Effingham	West, Benjamin	1947.17.101	378
Emancipation Proclamation	Lamb, A. A.	1955.11.10	224
Encampment of Cocomas—Looking Ashore	Catlin, George	1965.16.285	110
Encampment of Pawnee Indians at Sunset	Catlin, George	1965.16.65	62
The End of the Hunt	Anonymous American 19th Century	1953.5.99	400
Engagement between the Monitor *and the* Merrimac	Tanner, J. G.	1953.5.36	366
Entrance to a Lagoon, Shore of the Amazon	Catlin, George	1965.16.294	110
The Entrance to the Tautira River, Tahiti Fisherman Spearing a Fish	La Farge, John	1966.6.1	224
Epes Sargent	Copley, John Singleton	1959.4.1	147
Equal, No. 2	Dutterer, William	1977.75.2	163
Eve	Jackson, Billy Morrow	1970.15.1	210
Everard Benjamin	Jennys, William	1953.5.21	212
Excavating a Canoe—Nayas Indians	Catlin, George	1965.16.215	62
The Expedition Encamped below the Falls of Niagara. January 20, 1679	Catlin, George	1965.16.317	130
Expedition Encamped on a Texas Prairie. April 1686	Catlin, George	1965.16.339	136
The Expedition Leaving Fort Frontenac on Lake Ontario. November 18, 1678	Catlin, George	1965.16.316	130
The Expulsion of Adam and Eve from Paradise	West, Benjamin	1989.12.1	378
Facsimile of a Cheyenne Robe	Catlin, George	1965.16.40	62
Facsimile of a Mandan Robe	Catlin, George	1965.16.344	62
Facsimile of a Pawnee Doctor's Robe	Catlin, George	1965.16.63	63
Facsimile of a Pawnee Doctor's Robe with Fantastic Professional Designs	Catlin, George	1965.16.62	63

Title	Artist	Accession #	Page #
Facsimile of a Sioux Robe	Catlin, George	1965.16.160	64
Facsimile of a Sioux Robe with Porcupine Quills	Catlin, George	1965.16.9	64
Facsimile of an Ojibbeway Robe	Catlin, George	1965.16.140	63
Facsimile of an Omaha Robe	Catlin, George	1965.16.70	63
Facsimile of Chief Four Men's Robe—Mandan	Catlin, George	1965.16.188	64
Facsimile of the Robe of Mah-to-toh-pa—Mandan	Catlin, George	1965.16.86	64
Falls of the Snake River	Catlin, George	1965.16.192	65
Family	Rothko, Mark	1986.43.97	280
Family Burying Ground	Anonymous American 19th Century	1958.9.10	400
Family Group	Glackens, William	1971.12.1	187
Family Group	Johnson, Joshua	1980.61.3	213
Family Portrait	Earl, Ralph Eleaser Whiteside	1953.5.8	170
Fanciful Landscape	Doughty, Thomas	1963.9.2	160
Fanny/Fingerpainting	Close, Chuck	1987.2.1	143
Fantasy at Dawn (recto)	Rothko, Mark	1986.43.5a	304
Fantasy at Dawn (verso)	Rothko, Mark	1986.43.5b	308
Faraduro, Portugal	Leonid	1952.12.1	226
Farmhouse in Mahantango Valley	Anonymous American 19th Century	1953.5.94	401
Farmyard Fowls	Audubon, John James	1951.9.3	22
Father and Son	Budington, Jonathan	1956.13.1	36
Father Hennepin and Companions Passing Lover's Leap. April 1680	Catlin, George	1965.16.328	133
Father Hennepin and Two Companions Made Prisoners by the Sioux. April 1680	Catlin, George	1965.16.327	133
Father Hennepin and Companions at the Falls of St. Anthony. May 1, 1680	Catlin, George	1965.16.329	133
Father Hennepin Leaving the Mississippi to Join La Salle. May 8, 1680	Catlin, George	1965.16.330	133
Feeding the Bird	Anonymous American 18th Century	1953.5.63	401
Felucca off Gibraltar	Chambers, Thomas	1968.26.2	137
The Female Eagle—Shawano	Catlin, George	1965.16.348	65

Title	Artist	Accession #	Page #
Four Mura Indians	Catlin, George	1965.16.239	113
Four Navajo Warriors	Catlin, George	1965.16.148	68
Four Sepibo Indians	Catlin, George	1965.16.234	113
Four Square	Kline, Franz	1971.87.12	218
Four Xingu Indians	Catlin, George	1965.16.237	113
Four Zurumati Children	Catlin, George	1965.16.229	113
Fourteenth Station	Newman, Barnett	1986.65.14	248
Fourth Station	Newman, Barnett	1986.65.4	244
Frances Ludlum Morris	Spencer, Frederick R.	1947.17.96	340
Francis Hopkinson	Sully, Thomas	1942.8.33	363
Fred M. Vinson	Stephens, Thomas E.	1950.19.1	343
A Friendly Call	Chase, William Merritt	1943.1.2	141
Fruit and Baltimore Oriole	Wagguno	1980.62.47	372
Fruit and Flowers	Anonymous American 19th Century	1966.13.7	402
Fruit on a Tray	Anonymous American 19th Century	1953.5.104	402
Full-length Portrait of Young Woman with Brown Hair—Bare Left Foot	Anonymous American 18th Century	1980.62.40	402
Funeral of Black Hawk—Saukie	Catlin, George	1965.16.142	68
The Gage Family	Anonymous American 19th Century	1980.61.2	403
Game of the Arrow—Mandan	Catlin, George	1965.16.83	69
Gathering Wild Rice—Winnebago	Catlin, George	1965.16.138	69
Geese in Flight	Bauman, Leila T.	1958.9.1	25
General Washington at Princeton	Polk, Charles Peale	1947.13.1	262
General Washington on a White Charger	Anonymous American 19th Century	1955.11.22	432
General William Smallwood	Pine, Robert Edge	1947.17.89	262
Mr. George Cotton Smith	Henri, Robert	1986.93.1	200
Mrs. George Cotton Smith	Henri, Robert	1986.93.2	200
George Dodd	Neagle, John	1957.3.1	240
Mrs. George Dodd	Neagle, John	1957.3.2	240
George Jules Taylor	Hendricks, Barkley Leonnard	1973.19.2	198
George Pollock	Stuart, Gilbert	1942.8.18	347
Mrs. George Pollock	Stuart, Gilbert	1942.8.19	347

Title	Artist	Accession #	Page #
George Pope Morris	Inman, Henry	1947.17.8	209
George Southward	Ames, Joseph Alexander	1947.17.21	21
George W. Vanderbilt	Whistler, James McNeill	1959.3.3	382
George Washington	Peale, Rembrandt	1942.7.1	256
George Washington	Peale, Rembrandt	1947.17.16	257
George Washington	Savage, Edward	1960.3.1	334
George Washington	Stuart, Gilbert	1954.9.2	352
George Washington (Athenaeum portrait)	Stuart, Gilbert	1979.5.1	355
George Washington (Vaughan portrait)	Stuart, Gilbert	1942.8.27	349
George Washington (Vaughan-Sinclair portrait)	Stuart, Gilbert	1940.1.6	350
George Washington Deal	Street, Robert	1973.3.1	344
Girl Arranging Her Hair	Cassatt, Mary	1963.10.97	40
Girl in a Pink Dress	The Beardsley Limner	1953.5.24	27
Girl in Red with Flowers and a Distelfink	Anonymous American 19th Century	1978.80.14	403
Girl with Kitten	Chandler, Joseph Goodhue	1980.62.42	139
Girl with Reticule and Rose	Stock, Joseph Whiting	1980.62.8	343
Girl with Toy Rooster	Anonymous American 19th Century	1953.5.71	403
Gouverneur Kemble	Durand, Asher Brown	1947.17.2	161
Governor Charles Ridgely of Maryland	Sully, Thomas	1945.12.1	361
Miss Grace Woodhouse	Sargent, John Singer	1962.6.1	331
Grand Lavoir, Pampa del Sacramento	Catlin, George	1965.16.297	114
Grassy Bluffs, Upper Missouri	Catlin, George	1965.16.193	69
The Grave of William Penn	Hicks, Edward	1980.62.12	202
The Great Ant-Eater	Catlin, George	1965.16.255	114
Green Apples and Scoop	Kuhn, Walt	1972.9.14	223
Green Corn Dance—Minatarrees	Catlin, George	1965.16.81	69
Green Mass	Pereira, I. Rice	1973.72.1	259
Grey Sea	Marin, John	1987.19.1	232
The Griffin *Entering the Harbor at MacKinaw. August 27, 1679*	Catlin, George	1965.16.323	132
Grizzly Bears Attacking Buffalo	Catlin, George	1965.16.218	70
Hallway, Italian Restaurant	Pène du Bois, Guy	1963.10.137	258
Halsey's Bluff—Sioux Indians on the March	Catlin, George	1965.16.13	70

Title	Artist	Accession #	Page #
Hunting Scene with a Pond	Anonymous American 18th Century	1970.17.102	405
Husband	Prior-Hamblin School	1953.5.42	268
Ichabod Crane and the Headless Horseman	Wilgus, William John, After	1971.83.21	383
Ignis Fatuus, Rio Uruguay	Catlin, George	1965.16.292	115
Ignis Fatuus—Zurumati	Catlin, George	1965.16.261	115
Imaginary Regatta of America's Cup Winners	Anonymous American 19th Century	1953.5.90	405
In the Shade	Rothko, Mark	1986.56.650	272
The Independent Voter	Anonymous American 19th Century	1980.61.8	405
Indian Camp in the Forest	Catlin, George	1965.16.289	115
An Indian Council—Sioux	Catlin, George	1965.16.217	71
An Indian Encampment at Sunset	Catlin, George	1965.16.189	71
Indian File—Iowa	Catlin, George	1965.16.212	71
An Indian Ladder—Nayas Indians	Catlin, George	1965.16.221	72
Indian Tobacco Shop Sign	Anonymous American 19th Century	1980.62.33	406
An Indian Village—Shore of the Amazon	Catlin, George	1965.16.270	115
Indians and Horses in a Forest	Catlin, George	1965.16.312	116
Indians Cooking Maize	Anonymous American 19th Century	1971.83.16	406
"Innocence"	Anonymous American 19th Century	1980.62.30	406
Interior	Rothko, Mark	1986.43.26	280
Interior of an Amazon Forest—Zurumati	Catlin, George	1965.16.271	116
Interior Scene	Anonymous American 19th Century	1980.61.12	407
Iowa Indians Who Visited London and Paris	Catlin, George	1965.16.111	72
Mrs. Isaac Foster	Badger, Joseph	1957.11.2	23
Isaac Foster, Jr.	Badger, Joseph	1957.11.3	23
The Island	Hultberg, John	1970.28.1	207
J. M. Stolle	Anonymous American 18th Century	1980.62.24	428
Jack-in-the-Pulpit No. II	O'Keeffe, Georgia	1987.58.1	250
Jack-in-the-Pulpit No. III	O'Keeffe, Georgia	1987.58.2	250

Title	Artist	Accession #	Page #
Jack-in-the-Pulpit No. IV	O'Keeffe, Georgia	1987.58.3	251
Jack-in-the-Pulpit No. V	O'Keeffe, Georgia	1987.58.4	251
Jack-in-the-Pulpit No. VI	O'Keeffe, Georgia	1987.58.5	252
Dr. James Hall	Huntington, Daniel	1947.17.56	208
James Lloyd	Stuart, Gilbert, After	1947.17.107	359
James Madison	Stuart, Gilbert	1979.4.2	354
James Monroe	Stuart, Gilbert	1979.4.3	357
James P. Smith	Eichholtz, Jacob	1947.17.4	174
Jane Browne	Copley, John Singleton	1942.8.2	147
Jane Cutler Doane	Anonymous American 18th Century	1943.1.4	399
Jane L. Van Reid	Anonymous American 19th Century	1955.11.18	430
Jane Storm Teller	Phillips, Ammi	1953.5.31	262
Jarama II	Stella, Frank	1982.35.1	342
John Adams	Stuart, Gilbert	1954.7.1	356
Mrs. John Adams	Stuart, Gilbert	1954.7.2	356
John Adams	Stuart, Gilbert	1979.4.1	358
John Beale Bordley	Peale, Charles Willson	1984.2.1	254
John Bill Ricketts	Stuart, Gilbert	1942.14.1	349
Mrs. John Dickson	Neagle, John	1947.17.77	239
Dr. John Edwards Holbrook	Huntington, Daniel	1947.17.57	208
John G. Read	Smith, Royall Brewster	1978.80.18	339
John Harrisson	Mayhew, Frederick	1980.62.16	234
Mrs. John Harrisson and Daughter	Mayhew, Frederick	1980.62.17	234
Mrs. John Lothrop	Durand, John	1980.62.6	163
John Lothrop	Durand, John	1980.62.70	162
Mrs. John Marin	Marin, John	1986.54.8	233
John Peck	Johnston, John	1947.17.65	215
John Philip de Haas	Peale, Charles Willson	1942.8.9	255
John Philip Kemble	Sully, Thomas, after Stuart, Gilbert	1947.17.111	364
John Quincy Adams	Sully, Thomas	1942.8.30	362
John Randolph	Harding, Chester	1940.1.7	193
John Randolph	Stuart, Gilbert	1940.1.9	353
John Rush (?)	Anonymous American 19th Century	1943.1.7	425

Title	Artist	Accession #	Page #
Dr. John Safford and Family	Rowley, Reuben, Attributed to	1980.62.46	329
John Smith Warner	Otis, Bass	1961.8.1	253
John Stevens	Wollaston, John	1947.17.103	383
John Stone	Skynner, Thomas	1953.5.55	337
John Sudam	Vanderlyn, John	1947.17.14	371
Jonathan Bentham	Anonymous American 18th Century	1959.11.4	389
Mrs. Joseph Chamberlain	Sargent, John Singer	1958.2.1	332
Joseph Coolidge	Stuart, Gilbert	1940.1.3	357
Joseph Dugan	Sully, Thomas	1945.17.1	359
Joseph Leman	Eichholtz, Jacob	1953.5.13	171
Joseph Slade	Phillips, Ammi	1953.5.52	260
Joseph Wesley Harper, Jr.	Johnson, Eastman	1947.17.63	213
Joshua Lamb	Stanley, Abram Ross	1980.62.22	340
Miss Julia Marlowe	Wiles, Irving R.	1951.6.1	382
Julianna Hazlehurst	Eichholtz, Jacob	1947.17.110	172
Junius Brutus Booth	Anonymous American 19th Century	1947.17.55	390
K'nisteneux Indians Attacking Two Grizzly Bears	Catlin, George	1965.16.181	72
A K'nisteneux Warrior and Family	Catlin, George	1965.16.124	73
Kasaner	Okada, Kenzo	1983.1.31	252
Kaskaskia Chief, His Mother, and Son	Catlin, George	1965.16.103	73
Kickapoo Indians Preaching and Praying	Catlin, George	1965.16.121	73
Kiowa Chief, His Wife, and Two Warriors	Catlin, George	1965.16.45	73
Kiowa Indians Gathering Wild Grapes	Catlin, George	1965.16.46	74
Klahoquaht Chief, His Wife, and Son	Catlin, George	1965.16.157	74
Klatsop Indians	Catlin, George	1965.16.158	74
Mr. Kline	Eichholtz, Jacob	1953.5.11	171
La Rue de la Santé	Pène du Bois, Guy	1963.10.139	258
La Salle and Party Arrive at the Village of the Illinois. January 1, 1680	Catlin, George	1965.16.324	132
La Salle Assassinated by Duhaut. May 19, 1686	Catlin, George	1965.16.341	136
La Salle Claiming Louisiana for France. April 9, 1682	Catlin, George	1965.16.336	135

Title	Artist	Accession #	Page #
La Salle Crossing Lake Michigan on the Ice. December 8, 1681	Catlin, George	1965.16.331	134
La Salle Driving the First Bolt for the Griffin. *January 26, 1679*	Catlin, George	1965.16.319	131
La Salle Erecting a Cross and Taking Possession of the Land. March 25, 1682	Catlin, George	1965.16.335	135
La Salle Meets a War Party of Cenis Indians on a Texas Prairie. April 25, 1686	Catlin, George	1965.16.338	135
La Salle Received in the Village of the Cenis Indians. May 6, 1686	Catlin, George	1965.16.340	136
La Salle Taking Possession of the Land at the Mouth of the Arkansas. March 10, 1682	Catlin, George	1965.16.333	134
La Salle's Party Entering the Mississippi in Canoes. February 6, 1682	Catlin, George	1965.16.332	134
La Salle's Party Feasted in the Illinois Village. January 2, 1680	Catlin, George	1965.16.325	132
The Lackawanna Valley	Inness, George	1945.4.1	209
Lady in a White Mob Cap	Greenleaf, Benjamin	1959.11.12	189
Lady in White	Phillips, Ammi	1959.11.9	260
Lady Undressing for a Bath	Duyckinck, Gerardus, Attributed to	1956.13.11	164
Lady Wearing Large White Cap	Anonymous American 18th Century	1980.62.45	407
Lady Wearing Pearls	Anonymous American 19th Century	1953.5.73	407
Lady Wearing Spectacles	Anonymous American 19th Century	1978.80.15	407
Lady with a Harp: Eliza Ridgely	Sully, Thomas	1945.9.1	361
Lady with a Lute	Dewing, Thomas Wilmer	1978.60.1	158
A Lagoon of the Upper Amazon	Catlin, George	1965.16.288	116
Lake Albano, Sunset	Inness, George	1962.2.1	209
Landing at Sabbath Day Point, Lake George	Kensett, John Frederick	1968.7.1	217
The Landing of Columbus	Hicks, Edward	1980.62.13	201
Landscape No. 5	Hartley, Marsden	1949.2.2	194
Landscape with Buildings	Anonymous American 18th Century	1956.13.10	408
Landscape with Churches	Lermond, Charles C. E.	1953.5.23	227

Title	Artist	Accession #	Page #
Landscape with Houses and Trees	Marin, John	1986.54.4	231
Launching a Canoe—Nayas Indians	Catlin, George	1965.16.216	74
Launching of the Griffin. *July 1679*	Catlin, George	1965.16.321	131
Law of the Wild	Raleigh, Charles S.	1971.83.10	269
Mrs. Lawrence Lewis	Stuart, Gilbert	1974.108.1	353
Lawrence Reid Yates	Stuart, Gilbert	1940.1.5	348
Leaving the Manor House	Anonymous American 19th Century	1959.11.10	408
Legend and Fact	Kooning, Willem De	1971.52.1a-d	220–221
The Leland Sisters	Sully, Thomas	1973.2.1	363
Mr. Leman	Eichholtz, Jacob	1953.5.12	171
Miss Leman	Eichholtz, Jacob	1953.5.14	171
Lengua Chief, His Two Wives, and Four Children	Catlin, George	1965.16.246	116
Lengua Indians Ascending the Rapids of the Rio Uruguay	Catlin, George	1965.16.300	117
Lengua Medicine Man with Two Warriors	Catlin, George	1965.16.247	117
Leslie Pease Barnum	Duveneck, Frank	1942.8.3	163
Lessing J. Rosenwald	Cox, Gardner	1955.8.1	153
Let Us Now Praise Famous Men (Rauschenberg Family)	Warhol, Andy	1982.96.1	373
The Letter	Anonymous American 19th Century	1953.5.79	408
Leverett Pond	Field, Erastus Salisbury	1978.80.5	181
Lewis Morris (?)	Wollaston, John	1942.8.41	383
Lexington Battle Monument	Anonymous American 19th Century	1953.5.88	408
Liberty	Anonymous American 19th Century	1955.11.13	409
Lieutenant Archibald Kennedy (?)	Wollaston, John	1947.17.105	384
Lights in an Aircraft Plant	Crawford, Ralston	1971.87.1	154
Lincoln and His Son, Tad	Courter, Franklin C.	1954.1.2	153
Line and Curve	O'Keeffe, Georgia	1987.58.6	249
Little Girl and the Cat	Anonymous American 20th Century	1959.11.11	409
Little Girl Holding Apple	Hamblin, Sturtevant J.	1978.80.10	191
Little Girl in a Blue Armchair	Cassatt, Mary	1983.1.18	38

Title	Artist	Accession #	Page #
Little Girl in Blue Dress	Anonymous American 19th Century	1953.5.72	410
Little Girl in Lavender	Bradley, John	1958.9.3	34
Little Girl in White	Whistler, James McNeill	1963.10.71	380
Little Girl in White (Queenie Burnett)	Bellows, George	1983.1.2	28
Little Girl with Doll	Anonymous American 19th Century	1953.5.65	410
Little Girl with Flower Basket	Anonymous American 19th Century	1953.5.64	410
Little Girl with Pet Rabbit	Hamblin, Sturtevant J.	1953.5.70	191
Little Girl with Slate	Prior-Hamblin School	1953.5.66	268
Little Miss Fairfield	Prior, William Matthew	1971.83.9	267
Little Miss Wyckoff	Anonymous American 19th Century	1953.5.62	410
A Little Sioux Village	Catlin, George	1965.16.4	75
The Loge	Cassatt, Mary	1963.10.96	39
The Lone Tenement	Bellows, George	1963.10.83	29
Long-tailed Red Fox	Audubon, John Woodhouse	1951.9.9	22
Long-tailed Weasel	Audubon, John James, Studio of	1951.9.4	22
Louis Husson	Eakins, Thomas	1957.2.1	166
Mrs. Louis Husson	Eakins, Thomas	1957.2.2	168
Lovice Corbett Whittemore	Clark, Alvan	1950.8.2	143
Lucia Leonard	Allen, Luther	1953.5.1	21
Luke White	Stuart, Gilbert	1942.8.28	346
Lumber Schooners at Evening on Penobscot Bay	Lane, Fitz Hugh	1980.29.1	225
Luxuriant Forest on the Bank of the Amazon	Catlin, George	1965.16.264	117
Lydia Coit Terry	Morse, Samuel Finley Breese	1981.46.2	237
Madame G	Anonymous American 20th Century	1963.10.64	411
Madison Square, Snow	Tucker, Allen	1971.13.2	370
Madonna of Saint Jerome	Pratt, Matthew	1944.17.1	265
Mahantango Valley Farm	Anonymous American 19th Century	1953.5.93	411
Major Thomas Biddle	Sully, Thomas Wilcocks and Sully, Thomas	1942.8.31	364
Making Flint Arrowheads—Apachees	Catlin, George	1965.16.187	75

Title	Artist	Accession #	Page #
Man Named Hubbard Reading "Boston Atlas"	Anonymous American 19th Century	1978.80.2	412
Man of Science	Anonymous American 19th Century	1971.83.8	412
Man with a Tune Book: Mr. Cook (?)	Field, Erastus Salisbury	1978.80.6	181
Man with Vial	Field, Erastus Salisbury	1955.11.19	179
Mandan Ceremony—The Water Sinks Down	Catlin, George	1965.16.87	75
Mandan Civil Chief, His Wife, and Child	Catlin, George	1965.16.75	75
A Mandan Medicine Man	Catlin, George	1965.16.85	76
Mandan Village—A Distant View	Catlin, George	1965.16.79	76
Mandan War Chief with His Favorite Wife	Catlin, George	1965.16.72	76
Marahua Indians	Catlin, George	1965.16.240	117
Marble Mantel	Knaths, Karl	1984.29.1	219
Margaret Robins (?)	Anonymous American 18th Century	1980.62.10	424
Maria	Anonymous American 18th Century	1953.5.46	412
Maria Gansevoort Melville	Ames, Ezra	1947.17.20	21
Marina Piccola, Capri	Haseltine, William Stanley	1953.10.1	195
Marion Feasting the British Officer on Sweet Potatoes	Mark, George Washington	1967.20.1	234
Martha	Anonymous American 19th Century	1958.9.11	412
Martha Eliza Stevens Edgar Paschall	Anonymous American 19th Century	1983.95.1	416
Martha Tennent Rogers and Daughter	Earl, Ralph	1965.15.9	168
Mary and Francis Wilcox	Stock, Joseph Whiting	1959.11.2	344
Mary Barry	Stuart, Gilbert	1954.9.4	352
Miss Mary Ellison	Cassatt, Mary	1963.10.95	39
Mary Walton Morris	Wollaston, John	1942.8.40	383
Masouba	Baer, George	1964.19.1	24
Master Cleeves	Prior, William Matthew	1953.5.33	267
Mathilde Townsend	Sargent, John Singer	1952.3.1	332
Matilda Caroline Cruger (?)	Anonymous American 18th/19th Century	1942.8.13	398
Maud Dale	Bellows, George	1944.15.1	31

Title	Artist	Accession #	Page #
Mauhees Encampment	Catlin, George	1965.16.287	118
A Mayoruna Village	Catlin, George	1965.16.282	118
Melons and Grapes	Chipman	1957.11.5	141
Members of the Botocudo Tribe	Catlin, George	1965.16.248	118
Members of the Payaguas Tribe	Catlin, George	1965.16.245	118
Memorial to Nicholas M. S. Catlin	Anonymous American 19th Century	1955.11.7	413
Memories	Frieseke, Frederick Carl	1969.5.1	185
Memory	Rothko, Mark	1986.43.65	302
Mending the Harness	Ryder, Albert Pinkham	1951.5.3	329
Menomonie Chief, His Wife, and Son	Catlin, George	1965.16.98	77
Mrs. Metcalf Bowler	Copley, John Singleton	1968.1.1	148
Midsummer Twilight	Metcalf, Willard Leroy	1976.50.2	236
A Military Officer	Blackburn, Joseph	1947.17.25	33
Millstone #1	Seitz, William Chapin	1982.33.1	334
The Miner	Luks, George Benjamin	1954.2.1	229
Minna	Rothko, Mark	1986.43.99	274
Mired Buffalo and Wolves	Catlin, George	1965.16.213	77
Mohave Chief, a Warrior, and His Wife	Catlin, George	1965.16.171	77
Mohigan Chief and a Missionary	Catlin, George	1965.16.108	77
Moonlight	Weir, Julian Alden	1954.4.1	376
Morning in the Tropics	Church, Frederic Edwin	1965.14.1	142
Moth Dance	Dove, Arthur	1949.2.1	160
Mother and Child	Anonymous American 19th Century	1947.17.53	413
Mother and Child	Cassatt, Mary	1963.10.98	41
Mother and Child in White	Anonymous American 18th Century	1980.62.39	414
Mother and Mary	Tarbell, Edmund Charles	1967.1.1	366
Mother of Pearl and Silver: The Andalusian	Whistler, James McNeill	1943.6.1	381
Mr. Motte	Theus, Jeremiah	1947.17.12	367
Mound	Resnick, Milton	1974.15.1	271
Mount Auburn Cemetery	Chambers, Thomas	1958.5.1	138
Mount Katahdin, Maine	Hartley, Marsden	1970.27.1	194
Mount Vernon	Ropes, George	1956.13.6	272

Title	Artist	Accession #	Page #
Nude with Hexagonal Quilt	Bellows, George	1983.1.4	32
Nude with Red Hair	Bellows, George	1963.10.84	31
Number 1, 1950 (Lavender Mist)	Pollock, Jackson	1976.37.1	263
Number 2	Rothko, Mark	1986.43.131	311
Number 3	Rothko, Mark	1986.43.3	309
Number 5	Rothko, Mark	1986.43.133	326
Number 7, 1951	Pollock, Jackson	1983.77.1	264
Number 7	Rothko, Mark	1986.43.120	312
Number 7	Rothko, Mark	1986.43.134	326
Number 8	Rothko, Mark	1986.43.139	326
Number 8	Rothko, Mark	1986.43.147	315
Number 9 or Number 22	Rothko, Mark	1986.43.2	309
Number 10	Rothko, Mark	1986.43.1	309
Number 10	Rothko, Mark	1986.43.145	313
Number 10, 1947 (Number 12, 1948)	Rothko, Mark	1986.43.136	312
Number 11	Rothko, Mark	1986.43.144	316
Number 11	Rothko, Mark	1986.43.154	320
Number 15	Rothko, Mark	1986.43.142	313
Number 18	Rothko, Mark	1986.43.132	314
Ojibbeway Indians	Catlin, George	1965.16.93	79
Ojibbeway Indians in Paris	Catlin, George	1965.16.112	80
An Ojibbeway Village of Skin Tents	Catlin, George	1965.16.128	80
Old Man in Red Slat Back Chair	Anonymous American 19th Century	1953.5.76	415
Old Menomonie Chief with Two Young Beaux	Catlin, George	1965.16.99	80
An Old Nayas Indian, His Granddaughter, and a Boy	Catlin, George	1965.16.154	81
Old Swedish Church, New Castle, Delaware: Close View	Marin, John	1986.54.6	232
Old Swedish Church, New Castle, Delaware: Distant View	Marin, John	1986.54.7	232
The Old Violin	Peto, John Frederick	1974.19.1	259
Olivia	Emmet, Lydia Field	1983.96.1	175
Olympian Play	Rothko, Mark	1986.43.72	296
An Omagua Village—Boat Sketch	Catlin, George	1965.16.280	119
Omaha Chief, His Wife, and a Warrior	Catlin, George	1965.16.313	81
Omega IV	Liberman, Alexander	1977.75.4	227

Title	Artist	Accession #	Page #
The Omen	Rothko, Mark	1986.43.128	293
The Omen of the Eagle	Rothko, Mark	1986.43.107	293
On Exhibition	Anonymous American 19th Century	1953.5.69	415
On Point	Stouter, D. G.	1980.62.68	344
133	Louis, Morris	1976.64.1	229
One Year the Milkweed	Gorky, Arshile	1979.13.2	189
Oneida Chief, His Sister, and a Missionary	Catlin, George	1965.16.113	81
Orange and Tan	Rothko, Mark	1977.27.13	318
Orejona Chief and Family	Catlin, George	1965.16.241	119
Orejona Indians	Catlin, George	1965.16.242	120
Organization	Gorky, Arshile	1979.13.3	188
Osage Chief with Two Warriors	Catlin, George	1965.16.68	81
An Osage Indian Pursuing a Camanchee	Catlin, George	1965.16.71	82
Osage Indians	Catlin, George	1965.16.69	82
Osceola and Four Seminolee Indians	Catlin, George	1965.16.119	82
Ostrich Chase, Buenos Aires—Auca	Catlin, George	1965.16.257	120
Ottowa Chief, His Wife, and a Warrior	Catlin, George	1965.16.107	82
Oyster Sloop, Cos Cob	Hassam, Childe	1970.17.100	196
Pacapacurus Village	Catlin, George	1965.16.309	120
Packet Ship Passing Castle Williams, New York Harbor	Chambers, Thomas	1980.62.5	138
Pagan Void	Newman, Barnett	1988.57.1	241
"Paint Me"—Apachee	Catlin, George	1965.16.202	83
Painting the Lengua Chief	Catlin, George	1965.16.298	121
Painting the Tobos Chief	Catlin, George	1965.16.290	121
A Pastoral Scene	Durand, Asher Brown	1978.6.3	162
Patagon Chief, His Brother, and Daughter	Catlin, George	1965.16.252	121
Patrick Tracy	Trumbull, John	1964.15.1	368
Paul Mellon	Draper, William Franklin	1983.75.1	161
Paul Smith Palmer	Field, Erastus Salisbury	1971.83.4	179
Mrs. Paul Smith Palmer and Her Twins	Field, Erastus Salisbury	1971.83.5	180
A Pawnee Chief with Two Warriors	Catlin, George	1965.16.61	83
Pawnee Indians	Catlin, George	1965.16.60	83

Title	Artist	Accession #	Page #
Portrait of a Lady	Anonymous American 19th Century	1947.17.58	418
Portrait of a Lady	Anonymous American 19th Century	1947.17.60	418
Portrait of a Lady	Anonymous American 19th Century	1947.17.66	418
Portrait of a Lady	Anonymous American 19th Century	1947.17.75	419
Portrait of a Lady	Morse, Samuel Finley Breese	1943.1.6	238
Portrait of a Lady in Red	The Sherman Limner	1980.62.36	336
Portrait of a Man	Anonymous American 18th Century	1947.17.93	421
Portrait of a Man	Anonymous American 19th Century	1942.8.8	419
Portrait of a Man	Anonymous American 19th Century	1947.17.5	419
Portrait of a Man	Anonymous American 19th Century	1947.17.44	419
Portrait of a Man	Anonymous American 19th Century	1947.17.51	420
Portrait of a Man	Anonymous American 19th Century	1947.17.52	420
Portrait of a Man	Anonymous American 19th Century	1947.17.59	420
Portrait of a Man	Anonymous American 19th Century	1947.17.61	421
Portrait of a Man	Anonymous American 19th Century	1947.17.70	421
Portrait of a Man	Anonymous American 19th Century	1947.17.84	421
Portrait of a Man	Anonymous American 19th Century	1947.17.93	421
Portrait of a Man	Anonymous American 19th Century	1947.17.97	422
Portrait of a Man	Anonymous American 19th Century	1947.17.109	422
Portrait of a Man	Anonymous American 19th Century	1954.1.6	422
Portrait of a Man	Benbridge, Henry	1947.17.24	32
Portrait of a Man	Durand, Asher Brown	1947.17.37	161
Portrait of a Man	Skynner, Thomas	1967.20.4	336
Portrait of a Man in Red	The Sherman Limner	1980.62.35	336

Title	Artist	Accession #	Page #
Portrait of a Woman	Skynner, Thomas	1967.20.5	337
Portrait of an Elderly Lady	Cassatt, Mary	1963.10.7	40
Portrait of an Old Lady	Robinson, J. C.	1955.11.15	271
Portrait of an Old Man	Robinson, J. C.	1955.11.14	272
Portrait of J. L.	Greenleaf, Benjamin	1953.5.41	190
Portrait of the Doyles	Beal, Jack	1984.86.1	26
Prairie Dog Village	Catlin, George	1965.16.185	85
Prairie Meadows Burning	Catlin, George	1965.16.194	85
Prize Bull	Call, H.	1980.62.3	37
Profile Portrait of a Lady	Anonymous American 19th Century	1953.5.83	423
Profile Portrait of a Man	Anonymous American 19th Century	1953.5.82	423
Profile Portrait of a Young Lady	Anonymous American 19th Century	1953.5.10	423
Profile Portrait of a Young Man	Anonymous American 19th Century	1953.5.9	423
The Proud Mother	Anonymous American 19th Century	1971.83.18	424
A Puelchee Chief and Two Young Warriors	Catlin, George	1965.16.251	122
The Pugilist	Rothko, Mark	1986.43.93	275
Pumpkins	Kuhn, Walt	1968.3.1	224
Puncah Chief Surrounded by His Family	Catlin, George	1965.16.106	85
Puncah Indians	Catlin, George	1965.16.105	86
The Ragan Sisters	Eichholtz, Jacob	1959.6.1	173
The Ragged One	Lebrun, Rico	1974.87.2	226
Ralph Wheelock's Farm	Alexander, Francis	1965.15.3	20
Reconciliation Elegy	Motherwell, Robert	1978.20.1	238
The Red Cross Knight	Copley, John Singleton	1942.4.2	151
Red Jacket	Haddock, A.	1958.9.5	190
Red Rose Cantata	Thomas, Alma	1976.6.1	367
The Red School House	Homer, Winslow	1985.64.21	203
Repose	Sargent, John Singer	1948.16.1	333
Retriever	Anonymous American 19th Century	1953.5.96	424
Return from a Turtle Hunt—Connibo	Catlin, George	1965.16.275	122
The Return of Rip Van Winkle	Quidor, John	1942.8.10	269

Title	Artist	Accession #	Page #
Dr. Samuel Boude	West, Benjamin	1964.23.7	376
Mrs. Samuel Boude	West, Benjamin	1964.23.8	376
Mrs. Samuel Chandler	Chandler, Winthrop	1964.23.2	140
Samuel Eells	Anonymous American 19th Century	1971.83.15	400
Samuel Griffin (?)	Dunlap, William, Attributed to	1953.5.80	161
Samuel Henry Kress	Seyffert, Leopold	1953.2.3	335
San Andreas III	Calcagno, Lawrence	1970.2.2	36
Sarah Blake Sturgis (?)	Alexander, Francis	1947.17.18	20
Sarah Cook Arnold (?) Knitting	Anonymous American 19th Century	1955.11.6	387
Sarah Ogden Gustin	Johnson, Joshua	1971.83.7	214
The Sargent Family	Anonymous American 19th Century	1953.5.49	426
Satan's Flag	Davis, Gene	1974.16.1	156
Saukie Warrior, His Wife, and a Boy	Catlin, George	1965.16.94	87
Scalp Dance—Sioux	Catlin, George	1965.16.5	87
The Scalper Scalped—Pawnees and Cheyennes	Catlin, George	1965.16.199	88
Scene from the Lower Mississippi	Catlin, George	1965.16.196	88
Sea Fantasy	Rothko, Mark	1986.43.8	305
Second Station	Newman, Barnett	1986.65.2	244
See-non-ty-a, an Iowa Medicine Man	Catlin, George	1965.16.346	88
The Seine	Tanner, Henry Ossawa	1971.57.1	365
Self-Portrait	Harding, Chester	1947.17.54	192
Self-Portrait	Metcalf, Eliab	1947.17.72	235
Self-Portrait	West, Benjamin	1942.8.39	376
Seminolee Indians, Prisoners at Fort Moultrie	Catlin, George	1965.16.118	89
Seneca Chief, Red Jacket, with Two Warriors	Catlin, George	1965.16.104	89
A Sepibo Village	Catlin, George	1965.16.305	122
Sequence	Mehring, Howard	1978.40.1	235
Seventh Station	Newman, Barnett	1986.65.7	245
Sham Fight of the Camanchees	Catlin, George	1965.16.50	89
Shawano Indians	Catlin, George	1965.16.123	89
Shell No. 1	O'Keeffe, Georgia	1987.58.7	250

Title	Artist	Accession #	Page #
Thomas W. Dyott	Neagle, John	1947.17.78	239
Thomas Whittemore	Clark, Alvan	1950.8.1	142
Threatening Sky, Bay of New York	Chambers, Thomas	1973.67.2	139
Three Auca Children	Catlin, George	1965.16.250	126
Three Blackfoot Men	Catlin, George	1965.16.29	93
Three Celebrated Ball Players—Choctaw, Sioux, and Ojibbeway	Catlin, George	1965.16.127	93
Three Chaymas Men	Catlin, George	1965.16.243	126
Three Cheyenne Warriors	Catlin, George	1965.16.37	94
Three Creek Indians	Catlin, George	1965.16.115	94
Three Delaware Indians	Catlin, George	1965.16.114	94
Three Distinguished Warriors of the Sioux Tribe	Catlin, George	1965.16.1	94
Three Esquimaux	Catlin, George	1965.16.168	95
Three Iowa Indians	Catlin, George	1965.16.88	95
Three Iroquois Indians	Catlin, George	1965.16.89	95
Three Mandan Warriors Armed for War	Catlin, George	1965.16.73	95
Three Micmac Indians	Catlin, George	1965.16.125	96
Three Minatarree Indians	Catlin, George	1965.16.77	96
Three Navaho Indians	Catlin, George	1965.16.144	96
Three Omagua Men	Catlin, George	1965.16.236	126
Three Peoria Indians	Catlin, George	1965.16.109	96
Three Piankeshaw Indians	Catlin, George	1965.16.102	97
Three Potowotomie Indians	Catlin, George	1965.16.122	97
Three Riccarree Indians	Catlin, George	1965.16.90	97
Three Selish Indians	Catlin, George	1965.16.166	98
Three Shoshonee Warriors	Catlin, George	1965.16.57	98
Three Shoshonee Warriors Armed for War	Catlin, George	1965.16.58	98
Three Taruma Indians	Catlin, George	1965.16.224	127
Three Walla Walla Indians	Catlin, George	1965.16.159	98
Three Woyaway Indians	Catlin, George	1965.16.223	127
Three Young Chinook Men	Catlin, George	1965.16.156	99
Three Young Tobos Men	Catlin, George	1965.16.253	127
Three Yumaya Indians	Catlin, George	1965.16.173	99
Three Zurumati Indians	Catlin, George	1965.16.228	127
Thru the Window	Rothko, Mark	1986.56.653	286

Title	Artist	Accession #	Page #
Timothy Matlack	Peale, Rembrandt, Attributed to	1947.17.10	257
To the Memory of the Benevolent Howard	Hensel, Salome	1971.83.22	201
De Tonty Suing for Peace in the Iroquois Village. January 2, 1680	Catlin, George	1965.16.326	132
Towboat John Birkbeck	Bard, James	1971.83.1	25
Trail Riders	Benton, Thomas Hart	1975.42.1	33
Transfluent Lines	Pereira, I. Rice	1973.71.2	258
Tristan da Cugna	Poons, Larry	1977.75.5	264
The Trotter	Humphreys, Charles S.	1953.5.95	207
Tunk Mountains, Maine	Marin, John	1986.54.9	233
Turtle Hunt	Catlin, George	1965.16.259	128
Twelfth Station	Newman, Barnett	1986.65.12	247
Twenty-two Houses and a Church	Anonymous American 19th Century	1958.9.13	429
Two Apachee Warriors and a Woman	Catlin, George	1965.16.147	99
Two Arapaho Warriors and a Woman	Catlin, George	1965.16.31	99
Two Blackfoot Warriors and a Woman	Catlin, George	1965.16.27	100
Two Cherokee Chiefs	Catlin, George	1965.16.120	100
Two Chippewyan Warriors and a Woman	Catlin, George	1965.16.167	100
Two Choctaw Indians	Catlin, George	1965.16.116	100
Two Nezperce Warriors and a Boy	Catlin, George	1965.16.34	101
Two Ojibbeway Warriors and a Woman	Catlin, George	1965.16.92	101
Two Ottoe Chiefs and a Woman	Catlin, George	1965.16.100	101
Two Saukie Chiefs and a Woman	Catlin, George	1965.16.96	101
Two Sioux Chiefs, a Medicine Man, and a Woman with a Child	Catlin, George	1965.16.343	102
Two Unidentified North American Indians	Catlin, George	1965.16.59	102
Two Weeah Warriors and a Woman	Catlin, George	1965.16.117	102
Two Young Hyda Men	Catlin, George	1965.16.155	102
U.S. Mail Boat	Bauman, Leila T.	1958.9.2	25
Under Full Sail	Anonymous American 19th Century	1953.5.100	430
Unlocked	Olitski, Jules	1978.39.1	253
Untitled	Corse, Mary Ann	1977.75.1	152
Untitled	Feitelson, Lorser	1975.78.1	178

Title	Artist	Accession #	Page #
Untitled	Irwin, Robert	1977.75.3	210
Untitled	Reinhardt, Ad	1988.60.1	271
Untitled	Rothko, Mark	1986.43.4	314
Untitled	Rothko, Mark	1986.43.14	312
Untitled	Rothko, Mark	1986.43.15	310
Untitled	Rothko, Mark	1986.43.16	310
Untitled	Rothko, Mark	1986.43.17	307
Untitled	Rothko, Mark	1986.43.18	310
Untitled	Rothko, Mark	1986.43.31	292
Untitled	Rothko, Mark	1986.43.32	292
Untitled	Rothko, Mark	1986.43.33	293
Untitled	Rothko, Mark	1986.43.34	295
Untitled	Rothko, Mark	1986.43.35	294
Untitled	Rothko, Mark	1986.43.36	292
Untitled	Rothko, Mark	1986.43.39	274
Untitled	Rothko, Mark	1986.43.58	297
Untitled	Rothko, Mark	1986.43.59	294
Untitled	Rothko, Mark	1986.43.60	296
Untitled	Rothko, Mark	1986.43.61	298
Untitled	Rothko, Mark	1986.43.62	297
Untitled	Rothko, Mark	1986.43.63	302
Untitled	Rothko, Mark	1986.43.64	308
Untitled	Rothko, Mark	1986.43.66	308
Untitled	Rothko, Mark	1986.43.67	308
Untitled	Rothko, Mark	1986.43.68	304
Untitled	Rothko, Mark	1986.43.70	300
Untitled	Rothko, Mark	1986.43.71	298
Untitled	Rothko, Mark	1986.43.73	298
Untitled	Rothko, Mark	1986.43.75	310
Untitled	Rothko, Mark	1986.43.76	314
Untitled	Rothko, Mark	1986.43.77	314
Untitled	Rothko, Mark	1986.43.78	315
Untitled	Rothko, Mark	1986.43.79	315
Untitled	Rothko, Mark	1986.43.80	306
Untitled	Rothko, Mark	1986.43.81	311
Untitled	Rothko, Mark	1986.43.82	311

Title	Artist	Accession #	Page #
Untitled	Rothko, Mark	1986.43.83	311
Untitled	Rothko, Mark	1986.43.84	312
Untitled	Rothko, Mark	1986.43.85	302
Untitled	Rothko, Mark	1986.43.86	299
Untitled	Rothko, Mark	1986.43.87	303
Untitled	Rothko, Mark	1986.43.88	302
Untitled	Rothko, Mark	1986.43.89	303
Untitled	Rothko, Mark	1986.43.102	306
Untitled	Rothko, Mark	1986.43.103	303
Untitled	Rothko, Mark	1986.43.104	295
Untitled	Rothko, Mark	1986.43.106	295
Untitled	Rothko, Mark	1986.43.108	299
Untitled	Rothko, Mark	1986.43.109	293
Untitled	Rothko, Mark	1986.43.112	284
Untitled	Rothko, Mark	1986.43.116	284
Untitled	Rothko, Mark	1986.43.123	295
Untitled	Rothko, Mark	1986.43.124	296
Untitled	Rothko, Mark	1986.43.125	299
Untitled	Rothko, Mark	1986.43.126	298
Untitled	Rothko, Mark	1986.43.127	300
Untitled	Rothko, Mark	1986.43.129	300
Untitled	Rothko, Mark	1986.43.135	318
Untitled	Rothko, Mark	1986.43.137	327
Untitled	Rothko, Mark	1986.43.138	316
Untitled	Rothko, Mark	1986.43.140	327
Untitled	Rothko, Mark	1986.43.141	320
Untitled	Rothko, Mark	1986.43.143	313
Untitled	Rothko, Mark	1986.43.146	320
Untitled	Rothko, Mark	1986.43.148	319
Untitled	Rothko, Mark	1986.43.150	321
Untitled	Rothko, Mark	1986.43.151	324
Untitled	Rothko, Mark	1986.43.152	327
Untitled	Rothko, Mark	1986.43.153	317
Untitled	Rothko, Mark	1986.43.155	319
Untitled	Rothko, Mark	1986.43.157	317
Untitled	Rothko, Mark	1986.43.158	316

Title	Artist	Accession #	Page #
Untitled	Rothko, Mark	1986.43.159	317
Untitled	Rothko, Mark	1986.43.160	319
Untitled	Rothko, Mark	1986.43.161	318
Untitled	Rothko, Mark	1986.43.162	321
Untitled	Rothko, Mark	1986.43.171	326
Untitled	Rothko, Mark	1986.43.173	329
Untitled	Rothko, Mark	1986.56.654	287
Untitled	Rothko, Mark	1986.56.661	276
Untitled	Smith, Tony	1975.100.1	339
Untitled (black and gray)	Rothko, Mark	1986.43.163	327
Untitled (black and gray)	Rothko, Mark	1986.43.164	328
Untitled (black and gray)	Rothko, Mark	1986.43.165	328
Untitled (black and gray)	Rothko, Mark	1986.43.166	328
Untitled: Circus	Marin, John	1986.54.12	234
Untitled (the eagle and the hare?)	Rothko, Mark	1986.43.105	294
Untitled (female portrait)	Rothko, Mark	1986.56.660	273
Untitled (figures and mannequins)	Rothko, Mark	1986.43.24	284
Untitled (figures around a piano)	Rothko, Mark	1986.43.54	286
Untitled (girl with pigtails)	Rothko, Mark	1986.43.90	276
Untitled (Harvard Mural)	Rothko, Mark	1986.43.168	325
Untitled (Harvard Mural)	Rothko, Mark	1986.43.169	325
Untitled (head)	Rothko, Mark	1986.43.110	290
Untitled (male portrait)	Rothko, Mark	1986.43.91	277
Untitled (man and globe at window)	Rothko, Mark	1986.43.38	289
Untitled (man and seated woman)	Rothko, Mark	1986.56.652	273
Untitled (man and woman holding hands)	Rothko, Mark	1986.43.42	281
Untitled (man lying on park bench)	Rothko, Mark	1986.43.49	283
Untitled (man with green face)	Rothko, Mark	1986.43.100	277
Untitled (man with paddle and ball)	Rothko, Mark	1986.56.658	287
Untitled (musicians)	Rothko, Mark	1986.43.121	278
Untitled (nude)	Rothko, Mark	1986.43.115	289
Untitled (nude)	Rothko, Mark	1986.56.662	281
Untitled (nude) (recto)	Rothko, Mark	1986.43.117a	285
Untitled (nude and mantel)	Rothko, Mark	1986.43.111	291
Untitled (portrait of Irene Goldin?)	Rothko, Mark	1986.43.43	280
Untitled (reclining nude)	Rothko, Mark	1986.43.50	282

Title	Artist	Accession #	Page #
Untitled (woman and child in interior)	Rothko, Mark	1986.43.95	278
Untitled (woman and girl in an interior)	Rothko, Mark	1986.43.48	283
Untitled (woman arranging flowers)	Rothko, Mark	1986.43.92	279
Untitled (woman at window)	Rothko, Mark	1986.43.118	287
Untitled (woman in a subway)	Rothko, Mark	1986.56.657	291
Untitled (woman sitting on a couch)	Rothko, Mark	1986.43.98	278
Untitled (woman under tree) (verso)	Rothko, Mark	1986.56.649b	286
Untitled (woman with sculpture)	Rothko, Mark	1986.43.57	282
Untitled (women in a hat shop)	Rothko, Mark	1986.43.55	283
Miss Van Alen	The Gansevoort Limner (possibly Pieter Vanderlyn)	1956.13.14	186
Mr. Van Vechten	The Schuyler Limner (possibly Nehemiah Partridge)	1947.17.74	334
The Vanderkemp Children	Sully, Thomas	1966.11.1	363
Vapor Bath—Minatarree	Catlin, George	1965.16.342	103
Variations on a Rhythm—U	Jonson, Raymond	1988.72.1	215
Vase of Lilies	Anonymous American 20th Century	1964.23.5	431
Vermont	Komodore, Bill	1971.87.5	219
Vermont Lawyer	Bundy, Horace	1953.5.4	36
View in the "Grand Detour," Upper Missouri	Catlin, George	1965.16.191	103
View in the Crystal Mountains	Catlin, George	1965.16.266	128
View of "Pike's Tent"	Catlin, George	1965.16.195	103
View of Aberdeen, Washington	Anonymous American 20th Century	1968.26.3	431
View of Benjamin Reber's Farm	Hofmann, Charles C.	1955.11.16	203
View of Chicago in 1834	Catlin, George	1965.16.207	103
View of Concord	Anonymous American 19th Century	1978.80.21	431
A View of Mount Vernon	Anonymous American 18th Century	1953.5.89	431
View of the Crystal Mountains, Brazil	Catlin, George	1965.16.274	128
View of the Lower Mississippi	Catlin, George	1965.16.209	104
View of the Pampa del Sacramento	Catlin, George	1965.16.262	128
View of the Shore of the Amazon—Boat Sketch	Catlin, George	1965.16.284	129
View of the Tiber near Perugia	Inness, George	1973.16.1	210

Title	Artist	Accession #	Page #
White Line	Francis, Sam	1985.56.1	183
Wife of Man with Vial	Field, Erastus Salisbury	1955.11.20	179
Wild Cattle Grazing on the Pampa del Sacramento	Catlin, George	1965.16.276	129
Mrs. William Beckford	West, Benjamin	1947.17.23	378
William C. Rudman, Jr.	Anonymous American 19th Century	1947.17.80	425
William Clark Frazer	Eichholtz, Jacob	1947.17.3	173
William Constable	Stuart, Gilbert, After	1954.1.9	358
Mrs. William Crowninshield Endicott	Sargent, John Singer	1951.20.1	331
Dr. William Foster	Badger, Joseph	1957.11.4	24
William Gedney Bunce	Duveneck, Frank	1942.8.4	164
Mrs. William Griffin	Sully, Thomas	1943.1.8	362
Dr. William Hartigan (?)	Stuart, Gilbert	1942.8.16	347
William Henry Vining	Miller, George M.	1953.5.106	236
William Metcalf (?)	The Pollard Limner, Attributed to	1980.61.1	263
William Morris Hunt	Lawson, Thomas Bayley	1947.17.68	226
Mrs. William Robinson	Stuart, Gilbert	1942.8.22	355
William Rogers	Trumbull, John	1947.17.13	369
William Seton	Stuart, Gilbert, After	1947.17.106	358
William Sheldon (?)	Powers, Asahel	1953.5.50	264
Mrs. William Sheldon (?)	Powers, Asahel	1953.5.51	265
William Sidney Mount	Elliott, Charles Loring	1947.17.6	174
William Thornton	Stuart, Gilbert	1942.8.25	352
Mrs. William Thornton	Stuart, Gilbert	1942.8.26	353
William Vans Murray	Brown, Mather	1940.1.1	35
Mr. Willson	The Schuyler Limner (possibly Nehemiah Partridge)	1957.11.9	334
Winter Harmony	Twachtman, John Henry	1964.22.1	370
Winter Landscape	Marin, John	1986.54.1	230
Winter Valley	Dodd, Lamar	1971.3.1	159
Wisconsin	Kuhn, Walt	1968.25.1	223
Woman Holding a Book	Field, Erastus Salisbury	1980.62.7	179
Woman in Red Arrowback Chair	Anonymous American 19th Century	1953.5.37	415
Woman Sewing	Rothko, Mark	1986.43.28	281

Title	Artist	Accession #	Page #
Woman with a Red Zinnia	Cassatt, Mary	1963.10.99	41
Wounded Buffalo Bull	Catlin, George	1965.16.205	106
Wreck of the Aimable, *on the Coast of Texas. 1685*	Catlin, George	1965.16.337	135
A Yahua Village	Catlin, George	1965.16.283	129
Yellow Painting	Newman, Barnett	1988.57.3	242
Yntah Medicine Man, a Warrior, and a Woman	Catlin, George	1965.16.126	106
A Young Bull	Audubon, John Woodhouse, Attributed to	1951.9.2	23
Young Lady with a Fan	The Gansevoort Limner (possibly Nehemiah Partridge)	1980.61.5	187
Young Man on Terrace	Anonymous American 18th Century	1953.5.92	434
Young Man Wearing White Vest	Anonymous American 19th Century	1955.11.24	434
Young Woman in White	Henri, Robert	1949.9.1	199
The Younger Generation	Hamblin, Sturtevant J.	1966.13.5	192
A Yuma Chief, His Daughter, and a Warrior	Catlin, George	1965.16.172	106
Zachariah Schoonmaker	Vanderlyn, John	1942.8.36	371
Zenith	Pereira, I. Rice	1973.72.2	259
Zinnias	Kuhn, Walt	1972.9.17	223
Zirchow VII	Feininger, Lyonel	1966.3.1	177
Zurumati Indians	Catlin, George	1965.16.227	129

TRIBAL INDEX: GEORGE CATLIN

North American Tribes

Tribe	Title	Accession #	Page #
	Camanchee Horsemanship	1965.16.51	53
	Camanchees Lancing a Buffalo Bull	1965.16.204	53
	Camanchees Moving	1965.16.53	53
	Defile of a Camanchee War Party	1965.16.54	60
	An Osage Indian Pursuing a Camanchee	1965.16.71	82
	Sham Fight of the Camanchees	1965.16.50	89
CENIS	*La Salle Meets a War Party of Cenis Indians on a Texas Prairie. April 25, 1686*	1965.16.338	135
	La Salle Received in the Village of the Cenis Indians. May 6, 1686	1965.16.340	136
CHEROKEE	*Two Cherokee Chiefs*	1965.16.120	100
CHEYENNE	*The Cheyenne Brothers Returning from Their Fall Hunt*	1965.16.43	56
	The Cheyenne Brothers Starting on Their Fall Hunt	1965.16.42	56
	A Cheyenne Chief, His Wife, and a Medicine Man	1965.16.36	56
	Cheyenne Village	1965.16.38	56
	A Cheyenne Warrior Resting His Horse	1965.16.39	57
	Facsimile of a Cheyenne Robe	1965.16.40	62
	The Scalper Scalped—Pawnees and Cheyennes	1965.16.199	88
	A Small Cheyenne Village	1965.16.41	91
	Three Cheyenne Warriors	1965.16.37	94
CHINOOK	*Three Young Chinook Men*	1965.16.156	99
CHIPPEWYAN	*Two Chippewyan Warriors and a Woman*	1965.16.167	100
CHOCTAW	*Ball-Play Dance—Choctaw*	1965.16.137	46
	Eagle Dance—Choctaw	1965.16.132	61
	Three Celebrated Ball Players—Choctaw, Sioux, and Ojibbeway	1965.16.127	93
	Two Choctaw Indians	1965.16.116	100
COCHIMTEE	*Cochimtee Chief, His Wife, and a Warrior*	1965.16.170	57
COPPER	*Copper Chief, His Wife, and Children*	1965.16.162	57
CREEK	*Three Creek Indians*	1965.16.115	94
CROW	*A Crow Chief at His Toilette*	1965.16.22	58
	A Crow Chief, a Warrior, and His Wife	1965.16.21	58

Tribe	Title	Accession #	Page #
	Crow Chief, His Wife, and a Warrior	1965.16.19	58
	A Crow Village and the Salmon River Mountains	1965.16.25	58
	A Crow Village of Skin Tents on the Salmon River	1965.16.350	59
	A Crow Village on the Salmon River	1965.16.24	59
	Crow Warriors Bathing	1965.16.23	59
	Distinguished Crow Indians	1965.16.20	60
	A Small Crow Village	1965.16.26	92
DELAWARE	*Three Delaware Indians*	1965.16.114	94
DOGRIB	*Four Dogrib Indians*	1965.16.165	67
ESQUIMAUX	*Three Esquimaux*	1965.16.168	95
FLATHEAD	*A Flathead Chief with His Family*	1965.16.151	66
	Flathead Indians	1965.16.149	66
	Four Flathead Indians	1965.16.150	67
HYDA	*Two Young Hyda Men*	1965.16.155	102
ILLINOIS	*La Salle and Party Arrive at the Village of the Illinois. January 1, 1680*	1965.16.324	132
	La Salle's Party Feasted in the Illinois Village. January 2, 1680	1965.16.325	132
IOWA	*Indian File—Iowa*	1965.16.212	71
	Iowa Indians Who Visited London and Paris	1965.16.111	72
	See-non-ty-a, an Iowa Medicine Man	1965.16.346	88
	Three Iowa Indians	1965.16.88	95
	The White Cloud, Head Chief of the Iowas	1965.16.347	105
IROQUOIS	*Three Iroquois Indians*	1965.16.89	95
	De Tonty Suing for Peace in the Iroquois Village. January 2, 1680	1965.16.326	132
K'NISTENEUX	*Bear Dance—K'nisteneux*	1965.16.134	47
	K'nisteneux Indians Attacking Two Grizzly Bears	1965.16.181	72
	A K'nisteneux Warrior and Family	1965.16.124	73
KASKASKIA	*Kaskaskia Chief, His Mother, and Son*	1965.16.103	73
KICKAPOO	*Kickapoo Indians Preaching and Praying*	1965.16.121	73

Tribe	Title	Accession #	Page #
KIOWA	*Four Kiowa Indians*	1965.16.44	68
	Kiowa Chief, His Wife, and Two Warriors	1965.16.45	73
	Kiowa Indians Gathering Wild Grapes	1965.16.46	74
KLAHOQUAHT	*Klahoquaht Chief, His Wife, and Son*	1965.16.157	74
	A Whale Ashore—Klahoquat	1965.16.214	105
KLATSOP	*Klatsop Indians*	1965.16.158	74
KONZA	*Chief and Members of the Konza Tribe*	1965.16.311	57
MANDAN	*Buffalo Dance—Mandan*	1965.16.82	51
	Catlin Feasted by the Mandan Chief	1965.16.80	54
	Catlin Painting the Portrait of Mah-to-toh-pa —Mandan	1965.16.184	55
	Facsimile of a Mandan Robe	1965.16.344	62
	Facsimile of Chief Four Men's Robe—Mandan	1965.16.188	64
	Facsimile of the Robe of Mah-to-toh-pa —Mandan	1965.16.86	64
	A Foot War Party in Council—Mandan	1965.16.84	66
	Four Mandan Warriors, a Girl, and a Boy	1965.16.74	68
	Game of the Arrow—Mandan	1965.16.83	69
	Mandan Ceremony—The Water Sinks Down	1965.16.87	75
	Mandan Civil Chief, His Wife, and Child	1965.16.75	75
	A Mandan Medicine Man	1965.16.85	76
	Mandan Village—A Distant View	1965.16.79	76
	Mandan War Chief with His Favorite Wife	1965.16.72	76
	Three Mandan Warriors Armed for War	1965.16.73	95
MENOMONIE	*Menomonie Chief, His Wife, and Son*	1965.16.98	77
	Old Menomonie Chief with Two Young Beaux	1965.16.99	80
MICMAC	*Three Micmac Indians*	1965.16.125	96
MINATARREE	*An Aged Minatarree Chief and His Family*	1965.16.76	42
	Green Corn Dance—Minatarrees	1965.16.81	69
	Horse Racing—Minatarrees	1965.16.183	71
	Three Minatarree Indians	1965.16.77	96
	Vapor Bath—Minatarree	1965.16.342	103
MOHAVE	*Mohave Chief, a Warrior, and His Wife*	1965.16.171	77
MOHIGAN	*Mohigan Chief and a Missionary*	1965.16.108	77

Tribe	Title	Accession #	Page #
NAVAHO	*Four Navaho Warriors*	1965.16.148	68
	Three Navaho Indians	1965.16.144	96
NAYAS	*Excavating a Canoe—Nayas Indians*	1965.16.215	62
	An Indian Ladder—Nayas Indians	1965.16.221	72
	Launching a Canoe—Nayas Indians	1965.16.216	74
	Nayas Indian Chief, His Wife, and a Warrior	1965.16.152	78
	Nayas Indians	1965.16.153	78
	Nayas Village—Indians Bathing	1965.16.198	79
	Nayas Village at Night	1965.16.220	78
	Nayas Village at Sunset	1965.16.219	78
	An Old Nayas Indian, His Granddaughter, and a Boy	1965.16.154	81
NEZPERCE	*Two Nezperce Warriors and a Boy*	1965.16.34	101
OJIBBEWAY	*An Aged Ojibbeway Chief and Three Warriors*	1965.16.91	42
	Boy Chief—Ojibbeway	1965.16.349	49
	Buffalo Chase in the Snow Drifts—Ojibbeway	1965.16.129	50
	Facsimile of an Ojibbeway Robe	1965.16.140	63
	Nine Ojibbeway Indians in London	1965.16.110	79
	Ojibbeway Indians	1965.16.93	79
	Ojibbeway Indians in Paris	1965.16.112	80
	An Ojibbeway Village of Skin Tents	1965.16.128	80
	Snow Shoe Dance—Ojibbeway	1965.16.136	92
	Three Celebrated Ball Players—Choctaw, Sioux, and Ojibbeway	1965.16.127	93
	Two Ojibbeway Warriors and a Woman	1965.16.92	101
OMAHA	*Facsimile of an Omaha Robe*	1965.16.70	63
	Omaha Chief, His Wife, and a Warrior	1965.16.313	81
ONEIDA	*Oneida Chief, His Sister, and a Missionary*	1965.16.113	81
OSAGE	*Osage Chief with Two Warriors*	1965.16.68	81
	An Osage Indian Pursuing a Camanchee	1965.16.71	82
	Osage Indians	1965.16.69	82
OTTOE	*Two Ottoe Chiefs and a Woman*	1965.16.100	101
OTTOWA	*Ottowa Chief, His Wife, and a Warrior*	1965.16.107	82
	Salmon Spearing—Ottowas	1965.16.141	87

Tribe	Title	Accession #	Page #
PAWNEE	*Catching Wild Horses—Pawnee*	1965.16.66	54
	Encampment of Pawnee Indians at Sunset	1965.16.65	62
	Facsimile of a Pawnee Doctor's Robe	1965.16.63	63
	Facsimile of a Pawnee Doctor's Robe with Fantastic Professional Designs	1965.16.62	63
	A Pawnee Chief with Two Warriors	1965.16.61	83
	Pawnee Indians	1965.16.60	83
	Pawnee Indians Approaching Buffalo	1965.16.64	84
	A Pawnee Warrior Sacrificing His Favorite Horse	1965.16.67	84
	The Scalper Scalped—Pawnees and Cheyennes	1965.16.199	88
PAWNEEPICT	*Pawneepict Chief, Two Daughters, and a Warrior*	1965.16.56	84
PEORIA	*Three Peoria Indians*	1965.16.109	96
PIANKESHAW	*Three Piankeshaw Indians*	1965.16.102	97
POTOWOTOMIE	*Three Potowotomie Indians*	1965.16.122	97
PUNCAH	*Puncah Chief Surrounded by His Family*	1965.16.106	85
	Puncah Indians	1965.16.105	86
RICCARREE	*Riccarree Chief and His Wife*	1965.16.78	86
	Three Riccarree Indians	1965.16.90	97
SAUKIE	*Amusing Dance—Saukie*	1965.16.130	43
	Black Hawk and Five Other Saukie Prisoners	1965.16.95	48
	Black Hawk and the Prophet—Saukie	1965.16.314	49
	Dance to the Berdache—Saukie	1965.16.133	60
	Discovery Dance—Saukie	1965.16.135	60
	Funeral of Black Hawk—Saukie	1965.16.142	68
	The Running Fox on a Fine Horse—Saukie	1965.16.97	86
	Saukie Warrior, His Wife, and a Boy	1965.16.94	87
	Slaves' Dance—Saukie	1965.16.131	91
	Two Saukie Chiefs and a Woman	1965.16.96	101
	War Dance of the Saukies	1965.16.143	104
SELISH	*Three Selish Indians*	1965.16.166	98
SEMINOLEE	*Osceola and Four Seminolee Indians*	1965.16.119	82
	Seminolee Indians, Prisoners at Fort Moultrie	1965.16.118	89

Tribe	Title	Accession #	Page #
SENECA	*Seneca Chief, Red Jacket, with Two Warriors*	1965.16.104	89
SHAWANO	*The Female Eagle—Shawano*	1965.16.348	65
	Shawano Indians	1965.16.123	89
SHOSHONEE	*Three Shoshonee Warriors*	1965.16.57	98
	Three Shoshonee Warriors Armed for War	1965.16.58	98
SIOUX	*After the Buffalo Chase—Sioux*	1965.16.11	42
	Amusing Dance—Sioux	1965.16.17	43
	Ball-Play of the Women—Sioux	1965.16.7	46
	Bivouac of a Sioux War Party	1965.16.16	47
	Bivouac of a Sioux War Party at Sunrise	1965.16.18	48
	Buffalo Chase, Sioux Indians, Upper Missouri	1965.16.10	50
	Buffalo Lancing in the Snow Drifts—Sioux	1965.16.345	51
	Dog Dance—Sioux	1965.16.6	61
	A Dog Feast—Sioux	1965.16.8	61
	Facsimile of a Sioux Robe	1965.16.160	64
	Facsimile of a Sioux Robe with Porcupine Quills	1965.16.9	64
	Father Hennepin and Two Companions Made Prisoners by the Sioux. April 1680	1965.16.327	133
	Halsey's Bluff—Sioux Indians on the March	1965.16.13	70
	An Indian Council—Sioux	1965.16.217	71
	A Little Sioux Village	1965.16.4	75
	Scalp Dance—Sioux	1965.16.5	87
	A Sioux Chief, His Daughter, and a Warrior	1965.16.2	90
	The Sioux Chief with Several Indians	1965.16.3	90
	A Sioux Village	1965.16.12	90
	Sioux Village—Lac du Cygne	1965.16.14	91
	A Sioux War Party	1965.16.15	91
	Three Celebrated Ball Players—Choctaw, Sioux, and Ojibbeway	1965.16.127	93
	Three Distinguished Warriors of the Sioux Tribe	1965.16.1	94
	Two Sioux Chiefs, a Medicine Man, and a Woman with a Child	1965.16.343	102
SPOKAN	*Spokan Chief, Two Warriors, and a Boy*	1965.16.163	92
STONE	*A Stone Warrior, His Wife, and a Boy*	1965.16.161	92

Tribe	Title	Accession #	Page #
TAENSA	*Chief of the Taensa Indians Receiving La Salle. March 20, 1682*	1965.16.334	134
TAWAHQUENA	*Tawahquena Village*	1965.16.55	93
WALLA WALLA	*Three Walla Walla Indians*	1965.16.159	98
WEEAH	*Two Weeah Warriors and a Woman*	1965.16.117	102
WEECO	*Weeco Chief, His Wife, and a Warrior*	1965.16.101	104
WINNEBAGO	*Gathering Wild Rice—Winnebago*	1965.16.138	69
YNTAH	*Yntah Medicine Man, a Warrior, and a Woman*	1965.16.126	106
YUMA	*Three Yumaya Indians*	1965.16.173	99
	A Yuma Chief, His Daughter, and a Warrior	1965.16.172	106

South American Tribes

Tribe	Title	Accession #	Page #
ANGUSTURA	*Four Angustura Indians*	1965.16.238	111
AROWAK	*Arowak Village*	1965.16.267	107
	Four Arowak Indians	1965.16.226	112
AUCA	*Ostrich Chase, Buenos Aires—Auca*	1965.16.257	120
	Three Auca Children	1965.16.250	126
BOTOCUDO	*Botocudo Chief, His Wife, and a Young Man*	1965.16.249	107
	Members of the Botocudo Tribe	1965.16.248	118
CARIBBE	*A Caribbe Village in Dutch Guiana*	1965.16.265	108
	A Fight with Peccaries—Caribbe	1965.16.260	110
	Five Caribbe Indians	1965.16.222	111
CHACO	*Chaco Chief, His Wife, and a Warrior*	1965.16.244	108
	Spearing by Moonlight—Chaco	1965.16.277	125
CHAYMAS	*Three Chaymas Men*	1965.16.243	126
CHETIBO	*A Chetibo Family*	1965.16.233	108
COCOMAS	*Encampment of Cocomas—Looking Ashore*	1965.16.285	110

Tribe	Title	Accession #	Page #
CONNIBO	*Bride and Groom on Horseback—Connibo*	1965.16.232	108
	A Connibo Indian Family	1965.16.231	109
	A Connibo Village	1965.16.295	109
	A Connibo Wigwam	1965.16.308	109
	Connibos Starting for Wild Horses	1965.16.296	109
	Driving the Pampas for Wild Cattle—Connibo	1965.16.278	110
	Return from a Turtle Hunt—Connibo	1965.16.275	122
FUEGIAN	*Four Fuegian Indians*	1965.16.254	112
GOO-A-GIVE	*Four Goo-a-give Indians*	1965.16.225	112
	The Handsome Dance—Goo-a-give	1965.16.256	114
IQUITO	*Five Iquito Indians*	1965.16.235	111
LENGUA	*Lengua Chief, His Two Wives, and Four Children*	1965.16.246	116
	Lengua Indians Ascending the Rapids of the Rio Uruguay	1965.16.300	117
	Lengua Medicine Man with Two Warriors	1965.16.247	117
	Painting the Lengua Chief	1965.16.298	121
	A Small Lengua Village	1965.16.301	123
	A Small Lengua Village, Uruguay	1965.16.302	124
MACOUCHI	*Four Macouchi Indians*	1965.16.230	112
MARAHUA	*Marahua Indians*	1965.16.240	117
MAUHEE	*Mauhees Encampment*	1965.16.287	118
MAYA	*Five Maya Indians*	1965.16.174	111
MAYORUNA	*A Mayoruna Village*	1965.16.282	118
MURA	*Four Mura Indians*	1965.16.239	113
	A Mura Encampment—Boat Sketch	1965.16.281	119
OMAGUA	*An Omagua Village—Boat Sketch*	1965.16.280	119
	Three Omagua Men	1965.16.236	126
OREJONA	*Orejona Chief and Family*	1965.16.241	119
	Orejona Indians	1965.16.242	120
	A Small Orejona Village	1965.16.279	124
PACAPACURUS	*Pacapacurus Village*	1965.16.309	120

Tribe	Title	Accession #	Page #
PATAGON	*Patagon Chief, His Brother, and Daughter*	1965.16.252	121
PAYAGUAS	*Members of the Payaguas Tribe*	1965.16.245	118
	A Small Village—Payaguas Indians	1965.16.303	125
PUELCHEE	*A Puelchee Chief and Two Young Warriors*	1965.16.251	122
REMOS	*A Small Village of Remos Indians*	1965.16.304	124
SEPIBO	*Four Sepibo Indians*	1965.16.234	113
	A Sepibo Village	1965.16.305	122
TAPUYA	*Tapuya Encampment*	1965.16.286	126
TARUMA	*Three Taruma Indians*	1965.16.224	127
TOBOS	*Painting the Tobos Chief*	1965.16.290	121
	A Small Tobos Village	1965.16.291	124
	Three Young Tobos Men	1965.16.253	127
WOYAWAY	*Three Woyaway Indians*	1965.16.223	127
XINGU	*Four Xingu Indians*	1965.16.237	113
YAHUA	*A Yahua Village*	1965.16.283	129
ZURUMATI	*Four Zurumati Children*	1965.16.229	113
	Ignis Fatuus—Zurumati	1965.16.261	115
	Interior of an Amazon Forest—Zurumati	1965.16.271	116
	Three Zurumati Indians	1965.16.228	127
	Zurumati Indians	1965.16.227	129

SUBJECT INDEX

Numbers not preceded by prefixes are page numbers.

CEREMONIES

HISTORICAL SUBJECTS

LITERARY SUBJECTS

MYTHOLOGICAL SUBJECTS

NONREPRESENTATIONAL

OBJECTS

RELIGIOUS SUBJECTS

SCENES FROM EVERYDAY LIFE

STILL LIFE

TIME OF DAY

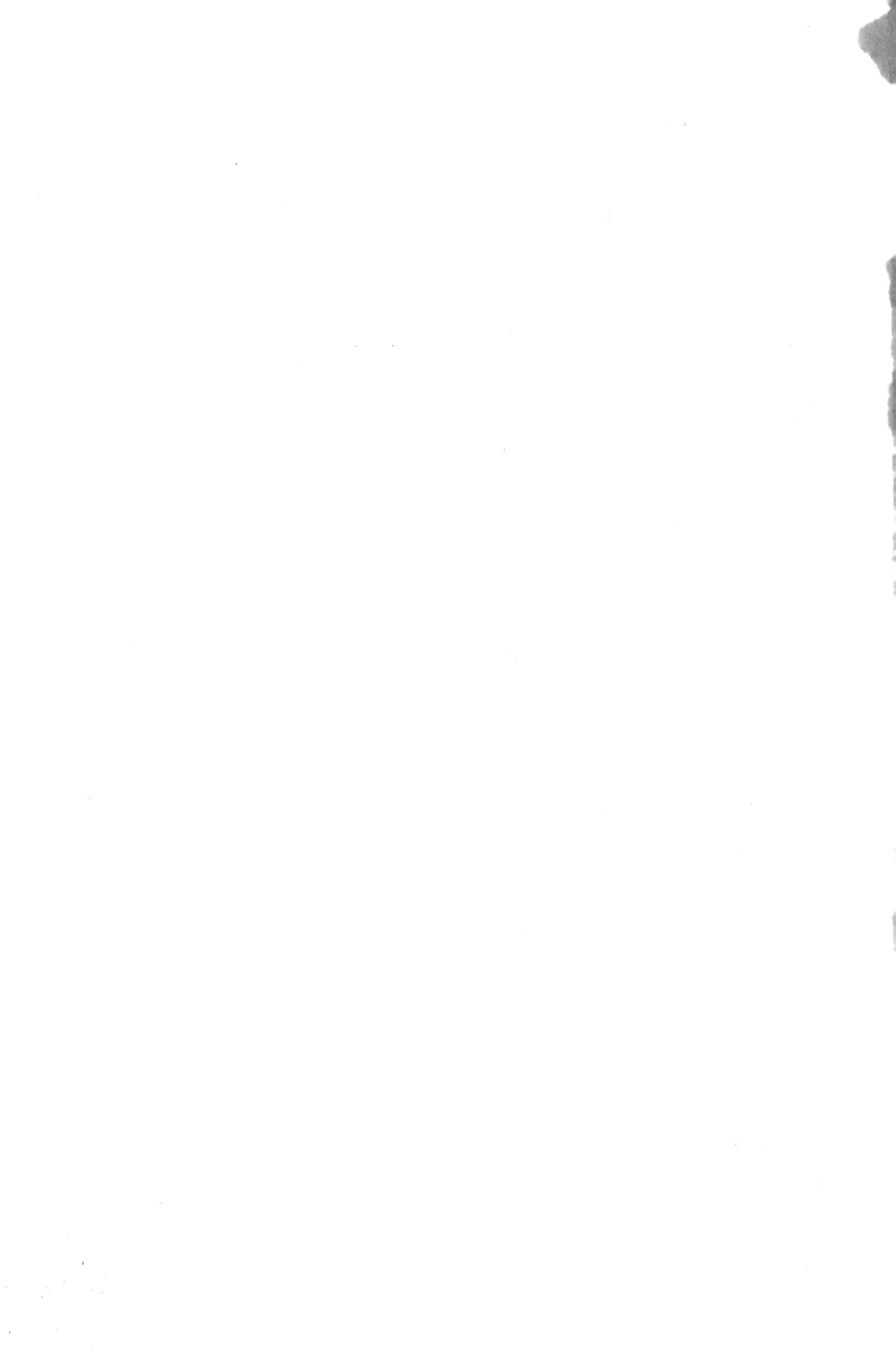